THE ATLAS OF WORLD GEOGRAPHY

THE ATLAS OF WORLD GEOGRAPHY

CONSULTANT EDITOR

PROFESSOR EMRYS JONES

INTRODUCTION BY

MAGNUS MAGNUSSON

PEERAGE BOOKS

Contents

THE PHYSICAL WORLD

8 **The Earth in Space** – The Universe; our Galaxy; the Solar System; the Earth's motion; seasons: the Moon's motion; eclipses; tides.

12 **Latitude, Longitude and Time** – Finding latitude and longitude; measurement of time; calendars; time zones.

14 **The Atmosphere** – Composition of the atmosphere; altitude, temperature and pressure; winds and wind belts.

16 **Weather** – Cloud types; rain; storms; meteorology; water cycle.

18 **Climate** – Factors influencing climate; types of climate; world climate zones.

20 **The Oceans** – Size of the Oceans; composition of seawater; ocean currents, the ocean floor.

22 **Formation of the Earth** – Solidification; changes in the atmosphere; Earth structure; continental drift; earthquakes; mountains and volcanoes; geysers.

28 **Shaping of the Land** – Erosion and deposition; limestone caves; stalactites and stalagmites; glaciers; deserts; coasts.

32 **Physical Statistics** – The Earth; oceans; rivers; lakes; mountains.

THE LIVING WORLD

34 **Vegetation** – Variation with soils, landform, climate and altitude; world vegetation zones.

36 **Evolution** – Fossils; Darwin's theory of evolution; geological eras, periods and epochs.

38 **Animal Life** – Animals of the polar regions, forests, mountains, grasslands, deserts, fresh waters, seashores and oceans; animal movements.

44 **Threats to Life** – Defenceless animals; conservation; pollution

Introduction

The world we live in is the most marvellous place imaginable. At one time, no one had any idea how the Earth had come about, or how large it was, or what shape it was, or how it fitted into the visible universe of Sun and Moon and planets and stars. They were all great marvels, the ultimate mystery for man's mind to grapple with.

We know that people have always been fascinated by this subject because, as soon as man developed the ability to express his thoughts in writing, some 5,000 years ago, just about the first thing he did was to try to answer some of the riddles of the Universe. Who created it? And why? And how?

Questions of that kind were answered in terms of mythology: the Universe was created by gods, for the enjoyment of mankind. These gods had different functions — a god of the storms, a god of the sea, a god of the plants, and so on. In this way, early man recognized that there were innumerable natural forces which he could observe, but not control; and he tried to come to terms with these natural

HUMAN GEOGRAPHY

46 **The Human Race** – Caucasoids, Mongoloids and Negroids; distinguishing features; world distribution.

48 **Languages and Religions** – Language families; writing; major religions; religions throughout the world.

50 **Population** – World population distribution, density and growth.

54 **The Growth of Towns** – Industrialization, overcrowding, the world's largest cities.

56 **Health, Wealth and Poverty** – Economics and life expectancy in developed and developing countries; diet and disease; food distribution; aid for developing countries.

THE ECONOMIC WORLD

58 **Vegetable Food Resources** – World crops and diet; cereals; potatoes; sugar; cocoa; coffee and tea.

61 **Animal Food Resources** – Cattle, pigs and sheep; butter, eggs, cheese and milk; world fisheries and whaling.

63 **Natural Products for Manufacturing** – Rubber; fibres; silk, wool and cotton; timber; tobacco.

65 **Mineral Resources** – Metals and ores, asbestos; diamonds; phosphates; potash; salt; sulphur.

69 **Fuel and Energy** – Oils; hydro-electric power; coal and lignite; gas; nuclear power.

72 **Occupations, Manufacturing and Production** – Agriculture, manufacturing and services; gross domestic product; food; vehicles; yarn; wood-pulp; steel.

76 **Transport** – Cars and commercial road-vehicles; merchant fleets; pipelines; railways; aviation.

78 **World Trade** – Imports and exports; invisible trade; international finance and reserve currencies.

phenomena by attributing them to personified gods with whom he could negotiate, or to whom he could pray.

Today we are still asking the same sort of questions: what *is* the Universe? How was it formed? When did it happen? How and when did our planet Earth come into being? What is it made of? What makes the weather happen? What made the mountains? And what is man's place on this great planet, which is such a tiny speck in the infinite vastness of the Universe?

Many of these questions can now be answered with some assurance — and the answers are to be found in this book. There are still marvels and mysteries that are beyond our understanding, of course (and I hope there always will be!); there are almost unimaginable stretches of time and space that are far beyond the reach of even our most powerful telescopes. But we know a great deal now about the world today — about our world, and our place in it.

Finding out about the world has been one of the great achievements of the human mind. The wonder of the world is by no means lessened by knowing more and more about it; on the contrary, it is greatly increased.

Knowledge about our world is not only useful; it is tremendous fun. When you travel from one part of the country to another, or from one part of the world to another, the journey becomes infinitely more exciting if you know why the landscapes are so different, why the people are so different, why customs and languages and styles of living are so different.

Knowing about the world — which means knowing about yourself and all the other people in it, whether they are black, white or yellow — is the beginning of all knowledge. Enjoy it!

Magnus Magnusson

Maps

1 THE WORLD-Physical
2-3 THE WORLD-Political
4-5 The Polar Regions
6-7 The Atlantic Ocean
Equatorial Scale

8-9 EUROPE-Physical
European Organizations
10 EUROPE-Political
11 THE BRITISH ISLES-Political
12-13 England and Wales
14 Scotland
15 Ireland
16 The Netherlands, Belgium and Luxembourg
17 France
18-19 Northern France
20-21 Southern France
22-23 Central Europe
24-25 Germany and Switzerland
26-27 Austria, Czechoslovakia and Hungary
28 Poland
29 Spain and Portugal
30-31 Western Spain and Portugal
32-33 Eastern Spain
34-35 The Mediterranean Lands
36-37 Northern Italy and Western Yugoslavia
38-39 Southern Italy
40-41 Yugoslavia and Bulgaria
42-43 Greece and Albania
44-45 Denmark and Southern Sweden
46-47 Scandinavia and the Baltic Lands
48-49 The USSR in Europe
50-51 The Union of Soviet Socialist Republics
52 ASIA-Physical
53 ASIA-Political
54 The Holy Land
55 Arabia and The Horn of Africa
56-57 The Near and Middle East
58-59 South Asia
60-61 The Indo-Gangetic Plain
South Asia-Political
62 Southern India and Sri Lanka
63 Mainland South-East Asia
Malaya and Singapore
64-65 The East Indies
Java and Madura
66 Japan
Southern Japan
67 China
68-69 Eastern China and Korea

70 AFRICA-Physical
71 AFRICA-Political
72-73 Northern Africa
74-75 Central and South Africa
76-77 The Pacific Ocean Equatorial Scale

78-79 AUSTRALASIA-Physical
AUSTRALIA-Political
80-81 Eastern Australia
82-83 Western Australia
84-85 South-East Australia
New Zealand
Samoa
Fiji and Tonga
New Zealand and Dependencies
86-87 NORTH AMERICA-Physical
NORTH AMERICA-Political
88-89 Canada
Alaska
90-91 Eastern Canada
92-93 Western Canada
94-95 The United States
Hawaii
96-97 North-Eastern United States
98-99 The Eastern United States
100-101 The Middle United States
102-103 The Western United States
104 Mexico
Panama Canal
105 The West Indies
Bermuda
Leeward Island
Windward Island
Trinidad and Tobago
Jamaica
106 SOUTH AMERICA-Physical
107 SOUTH AMERICA-Political
108-109 Central South America
110-111 South America North
112 South America South

Half title page **Tilling with a primitive plough and a donkey near Marrakech in Morocco.**

Title pages **Chapel Porth, Cornwall, England.**

Page 6 above left **A modern combine harvester is manoeuvred beside a loading wagon during the harvesting of green crops in Germany.**

Page 6 above right **Peasant farmers ploughing with oxen in the Benares region of Northern India.**

Page 6 below right **A lioness keeps a watchful eye on her cubs at play.**

Acknowledgments

The publishers would like to thank the following individuals and organizations for their kind permission to reproduce the photographs in this book:

Heather Angel 42 below right, 43 below; Aquila Photographics (W S Paton) 6 below right, (P D V Weaving) 40 above right; Ardea Photograhics (Ian Beames) 40 centre right, (M D England) 42 below left, (K W Fink) 40 above left, (Su Gooders) 35 below right, (P Green) 36, (Eric Lindgren) 40 below left, (R F Porter) 44, (Swedberg) 45 above, (R &V Taylor) 43 above left; Barnaby's Picture Library (H Kanus) 55 below; BBC 4-5; Almanna Bokenfeld, Iceland 23; Camera Press Ltd. 24; John Cleare, Mountain Camera 33; Bruce Coleman Ltd. 39, (J Burton) 11 above; Sonia Halliday 49 left; Robert Harding Associates 30 above right, 66, (J M Stewart). 51 Above; Angelo Hornak 49 right, 92; Alan Hutchison Library endpapers, 25 above, 68, 71, (S E Porlock) 57, 58; London Features International 86; Photri 87 above; National Coal Board 70; Photo Aquatics (Hermann Gruhl) 43 above right; Pic on Tour/Charlie 40-41 below, 55 above; Picturepoint Ltd. 7, 47 left, 77, 81, 82, 84-85, 85 above, below left and below right, 87 below left and below right, 89 above, 91 below, 94; R K Pilsbury 17, (2) (3) (5) (6) (7) (8) (9) (10); Popperfoto 21, 54, 75, 89 above centre and below centre, 93, (W M Simmons) 91 above; David Prout 12 below; Rex Features Ltd. 14; Spectrum Colour Library 8 below, 16-17, 26, 30-31 below, 31, 35 below left, 41 above, 51 below, 56 right; John Topham Picture Library (Dumas) 42 above, (L Garbison) 35 above, (Mousseau) 45 below left, (M Wilkins) 12 above, (Windridge) 17, (1) (4); A G Waltham 29; Keith Wicks 13 above, 73; ZEFA (R Everts) 27, 82-83, (R Halin) 17 centre below, 32, 62, 63, (H Helbing) 6 above left, 59, (H Hoffmann-Buchardi) 47 right, (Dr Hans Kramarz) 64, (E Landschak) 45 below right, (Photo Leidmann) 1, (Th Luttge) 56 left, (G Marche) 95, (Dr F Sauer) 37, (D H Teuffen) 30 left, (F Walther) 6 above right, 46.

Illustrations by: Diagram Ltd., Eric Jewell Associates, Illustra Design Ltd., Osborne/Marks

Front jacket photography: far left, Zefa Picture Library; left, NASA; right and far right, Alister Scott.
Back jacket photograph: Robert Estall.
Title pages photograph: Harry Williams.

First published in Great Britain in 1977 by
Octopus Books Ltd

This edition published in 1984 by
Peerage Books
59 Grosvenor Street
London W1

Reprinted 1985, 1986

ISBN 1 85052 002 X

Printed in Hong Kong

The Physical World

The Earth in Space

To most of us, the Earth seems to be a very big place. Our hands would have to be enlarged more than 100 million times to be able to grasp the Earth. Yet, in their journeys to the Moon, American astronauts saw the Earth appear to shrink until it seemed small enough to hold in their hands. With their own eyes, these men have been able to see just how tiny our world really is in comparison with the great depths of space.

But we, too, can get an idea of our place in the Universe just by looking up into the sky. Only two bodies in the heavens appear to be of any size — the Moon and the Sun. The Moon is a small world, its diameter being only a quarter of the Earth's diameter, whereas the Sun is huge — 109 times greater in diameter than the Earth. But the Sun and Moon look the same size from the Earth because, although the Sun is about 400 times bigger in diameter than the Moon, it is about 400 times farther from the Earth than the Moon is.

Nine main planets move in oval paths around the Sun. The Earth is one of these planets. All the planets are lit by the Sun and do not produce their own light. Some are smaller and some larger but, whatever their size, they are all so far away from the Earth that they appear merely as dots of light in the night sky. Like our world, most of them have one or more moons moving around them, but these are so small that they can be seen from Earth only with the aid of a telescope. The Sun's group of planets, together with their moons and other bodies, such as comets and asteroids (minor planets), is called the Solar System. The orbit of its outermost member, Pluto, averages nearly 6,000 million kilometres (3,750 million miles) from the Sun; your hand would have to be more than 100 million million times its actual size to hold the Solar System!

Almost all the asteroids orbit the Sun in a broad belt between the orbits of Mars and Jupiter. Thousands of asteroids have been discovered and all are extremely small compared with the main planets of the Solar System. Comets are bodies that come from the depths of space. As they approach the Sun, they become visible and usually display a glowing tail of charged particles. After passing close to the Sun, comets travel back to the outer edges of the Solar System. Some comets reappear at regular intervals.

Although the Solar System may seem enormous, in fact it is only a tiny corner of the Universe. A glance into the night sky reveals thousands of stars, many of them like our Sun, which is a common kind of star. The Sun is in fact a member of a vast group of stars called the Galaxy. With the naked eye, we can see only a small proportion of these — the ones that are relatively close or very bright. All together, the Galaxy contains 100,000 million stars, all so distant that they appear, even through the most powerful telescopes, as dots of light. Distances are so great in astronomy that they have to be measured in light-years. One light-year is the distance that light travels in a year, and it is equal to nearly 10 million million kilometres (6.2 million million miles). On this scale, the Galaxy is 100,000 light-years across, and the Universe does not stop there. Scattered throughout space are millions of other galaxies. No one knows how big the Universe really is because it extends beyond the reach of our telescopes. But these instruments have detected bodies that could be as much as 15,600 million light-years away. For comparison, the farthest distance that man has travelled into space — to the Moon — takes light a mere 1¼ seconds to cross.

The Motion of the Earth

Every day, the Sun crosses the sky, rising at dawn in the east and setting at dusk in the west. Night comes as the Sun moves beyond

1
2
3
4

Above: **The planets, to scale, with their moons (top), and the Solar System with distances to scale (bottom). The nine planets, with their average distances from the Sun, are:**

1. Mercury: 57,900,000 km
2. Venus: 108,210,000 km
3. Earth: 149,600,000 km
4. Mars: 227,930,000 km
5. Jupiter: 778,340,000 km
6. Saturn: 1,427,000,000 km
7. Uranus: 2,869,600,000 km
8. Neptune: 4,496,700,000 km
9. Pluto: 5,900,000,000 km

The asteroids, or minor planets, make up the belt between Mars and Jupiter.

Left: **The Earth, as seen from space by American Apollo astronauts.**

Right: **The Earth is in the Solar System, which is a small part of the Galaxy, one of millions of galaxies in the Universe.**

the horizon to the other side of the world and our side is shaded from its light. We say, for convenience, that the Sun crosses or moves in the sky, but it is, in fact, the Earth that is moving, and not the Sun. The Earth rotates once every 24 hours, spinning in a west-to-east direction but, to anyone on the Earth's surface, the Sun *appears* to move from east to west. With one rotation of the Earth, a day and night passes. However, the length of day and night vary throughout the year. In summer, the days are long and nights short, while winter is a time of short days and long nights. These changes happen because the Earth's axis is tilted. The Earth's axis is an imaginary line about which the Earth rotates; it runs through the middle of the Earth from the North Pole to the South Pole. If this line were exactly at right angles to the plane of the Earth's orbit around the Sun, then all days and nights would be exactly the same length — 12 hours each — and there would be no seasons. But the axis is tilted at an angle of 23½°. As the Earth moves around the Sun in its orbit, first one pole tilts towards the Sun and then the other pole does. The Earth's movement around the Sun thus causes seasonal changes in world climate.

When it is summer in the Northern Hemisphere, the North Pole is tilted towards the Sun, making the Sun appear to be high in the sky at midday. Days are long and it is warm, because the Sun's rays come straight down through the atmosphere and can heat the ground for a long time. At the same time, it is winter in the Southern Hemisphere. The South Pole is pointing away from the Sun, making the Sun appear to be low in the sky in the Southern Hemisphere. The days are short and nights long, and it is cold because the Sun's rays enter the atmosphere at a narrow angle and have little time to heat the ground. Six months later, the poles are pointing the other way and it is winter in the Northern Hemisphere and summer in the Southern Hemisphere. In between, spring and autumn occurs in each hemisphere. Then neither pole is tilted very much towards or away from the Sun. As a result, days and nights are about the same length during both the spring and autumn months.

The day on which the Sun appears to get to its highest point in the sky is the longest day of the year and is called the *summer solstice.* In the Northern Hemisphere, it is about June 21. The shortest day is called the *winter solstice* and is about December 22 in the Northern Hemisphere. In the Southern Hemisphere, these dates are reversed. On days called *equinoxes,* day and night last exactly the same time all over the world. The vernal (spring) equinox occurs on about March 21 and the autumnal equinox on about September 22. However, these days tend to mark the beginnings of the seasons rather than their midpoints. This is because it takes time for the ground to warm up after winter or cool down after summer.

The Motion of the Moon

The Moon moves around the Earth in an orbit, just as the Earth moves around the Sun, and takes nearly 27⅓ days to go once around the Earth. However, the Moon rotates very slowly, spinning only once in the time it takes to go around the Earth. This means that the Moon always keeps the same face towards the Earth and, from Earth, we can never see the other side.

But the Moon does appear to change. Sometimes, it looks like a crescent, then a semi-circle and a full circle. These changes are called *phases.* They happen because we do not always see all of the side of the Moon that is lit up by the Sun. At new moon, the dark

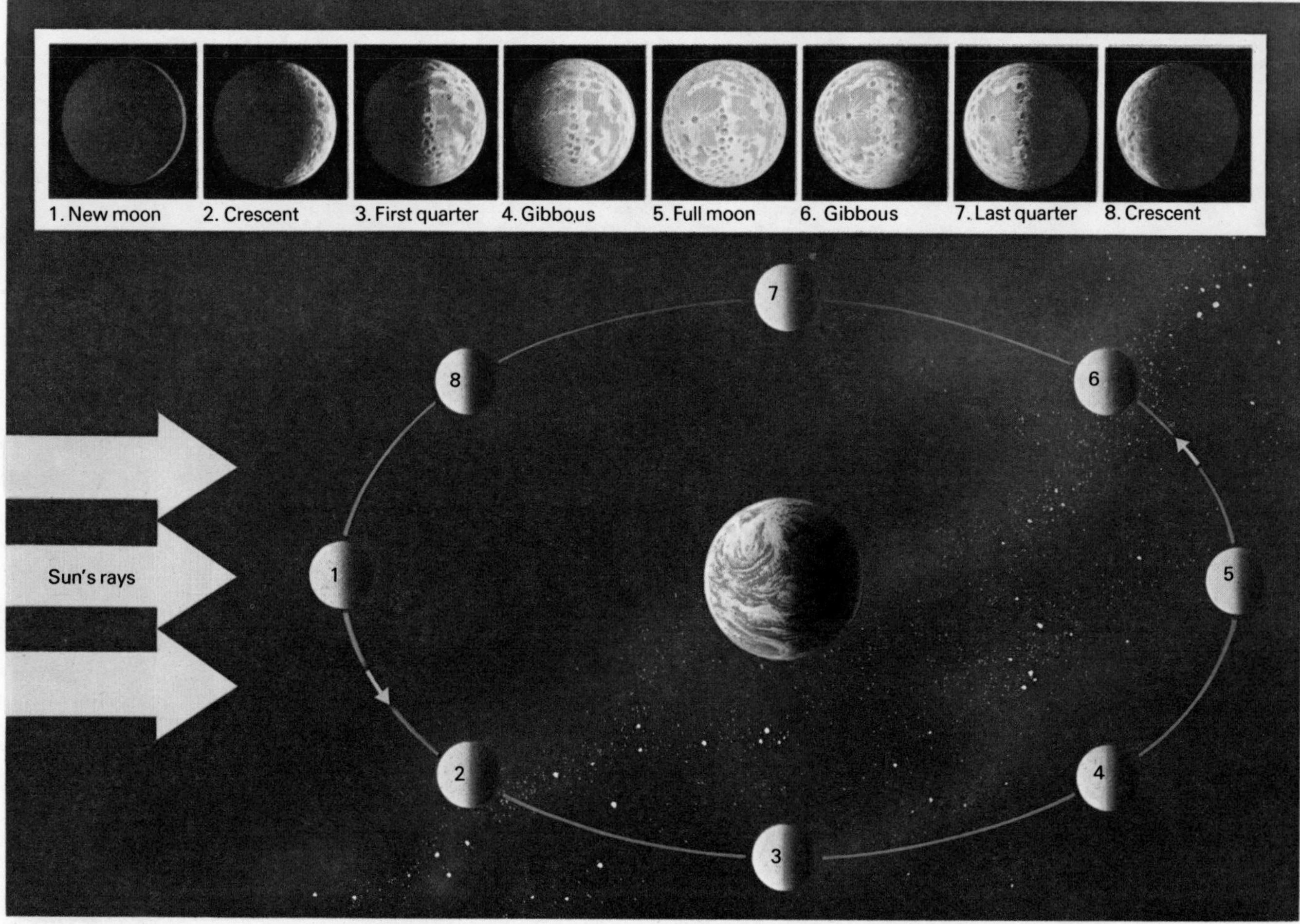
1. New moon
2. Crescent
3. First quarter
4. Gibbous
5. Full moon
6. Gibbous
7. Last quarter
8. Crescent
Sun's rays
1
2
3
4
5
6
7
8

side is towards us and we see nothing. Then, as the Moon moves around the Earth, a little of the lit-up side comes into view and we see a crescent. As more of the lit-up side comes round, the crescent grows into a semi-circle and then we have half moon. This grows into a full circle — full moon — when we can see all the lit-up side. Then the full moon shrinks to a half moon and then to a crescent again before we have another new moon. The time it takes for the Moon to go through one complete cycle of phases is just over 29½ days. This is also the length of one complete day and night at any point on the Moon.

The Moon's motion also causes *eclipses* to occur from time to time. When the Moon comes directly between the Earth and the Sun, its shadow sweeps across the Earth's surface. Anyone within the shadow will see the Sun's disc blocked out by the Moon, producing a total eclipse of the Sun, or total *solar eclipse.* Around the Moon's shadow or *umbra,* is a region of partial shadow called the *penumbra.* In places where only the penumbra falls, only part of the Sun's disc is hidden by the Moon. This kind of eclipse is called a partial eclipse. A total eclipse lasts only a few minutes, but a partial eclipse may last for an hour or so. A *lunar eclipse,* or eclipse of the Moon, happens when the Earth comes directly between the Moon and the Sun and the Earth's shadow falls across the Moon, hiding it from view for a short while. Because the orbit of the Moon is tilted, eclipses do not happen every month but usually only once or twice a year.

The Moon also causes tides to occur on the Earth. The gravitational attraction of the Moon slightly raises the level of the ocean beneath the Moon. At the same time, the motion of the Earth causes another rise in level to occur on the opposite side of the world. As the Earth rotates beneath these rises, they appear to move around the world, producing a high tide twice a day. In between, the level falls, giving low tides. The rises in level are also influenced by the Sun. When the Sun is in line with the Moon and the Earth — at new moon and full moon — the rise and fall of the tides is large, giving *spring tides.* Between new moon and full moon, when the Sun, Earth and Moon form a right angle, the rise and fall is small, giving *neap tides.*

Above: **An eclipse of the Moon occurs when the Earth's shadow passes over the Moon.**

Right: **A total eclipse of the Moon occurs when the Moon is completely within the Earth's shadow. Before and after, when it is partly in the Earth's shadow, a partial eclipse occurs.**

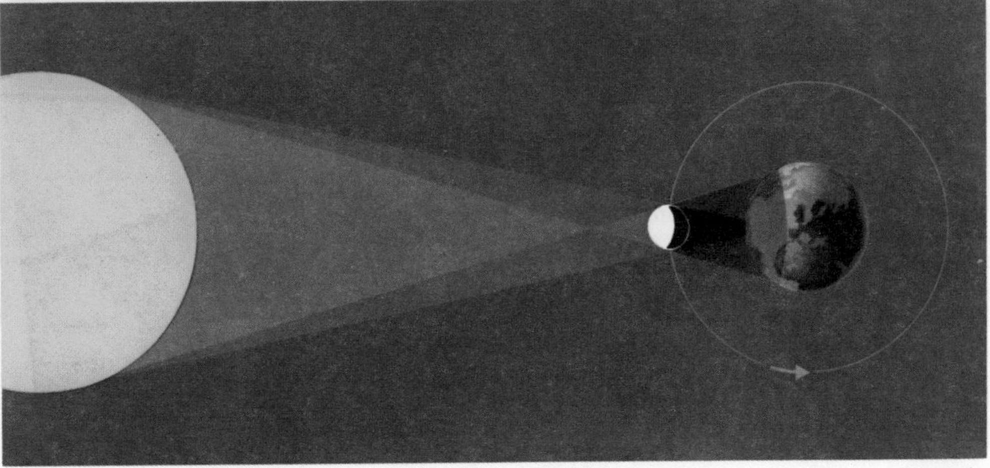

Below right: **An eclipse of the Sun occurs when the Moon's shadow falls on the Earth's surface. A total eclipse, in which the Sun is completely obscured by the Moon, occurs only in a small region. But, on either side of this region, the Moon partly shades the surface and a partial eclipse can be seen.**

Left: **The Moon goes through a cycle of phases as it revolves around the Earth. At new moon (1), the dark side is towards the Earth, and the Moon is almost invisible. Then, as the Moon moves in its orbit, the illuminated side comes into view. First we see a crescent moon (2) and this widens into a half moon (3). Then comes a gibbous moon (4) before a full moon is reached (5), when the Moon is halfway through its orbit and the illuminated side faces the Earth. Then the shape shrinks to become gibbous (6), half moon (7) and crescent (8), before we are back to new moon. The whole cycle takes just over 29½ days.**

Latitude, Longitude and Time

Latitude and Longitude

Imaginary lines of latitude and longitude divide up the Earth's surface. These lines enable us to locate any place with precision. Latitude shows that a place is on a line running east-west a certain distance north (N) or south (S) of the Equator. The Equator is at 0° latitude, the North Pole at 90°N and the South Pole at 90°S. All other places come somewhere in between. Longitude shows that the place is also on a particular line running north-south. The line of 0° longitude runs from the North Pole to the South Pole through Greenwich Observatory in Britain. All other lines of longitude are related to this line, being up to 180° west (W) or 180° east (E) of it. To find the position of any place on the Earth's surface, it is necessary to give its latitude and longitude. This defines a pair of lines, and the place is at their intersection.

Latitude can be found by observing the positions of certain stars or the Sun in relation to the horizon. Longitude is found by measuring the time at which the Sun or certain stars reach a particular height in the sky.

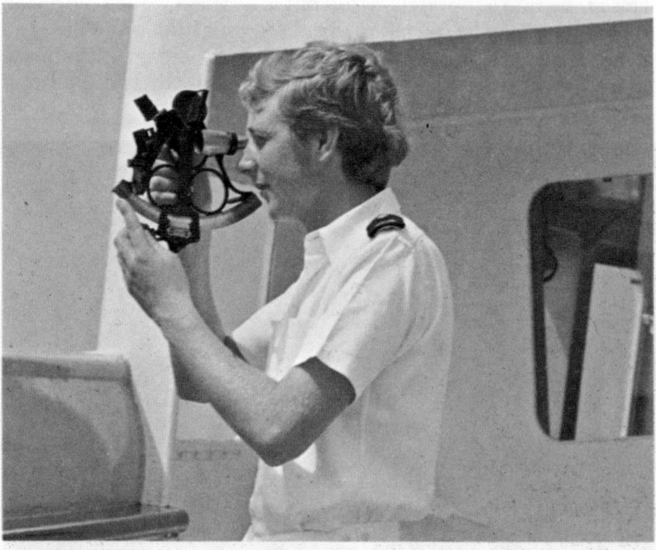

Time

Although we have many kinds of clocks and watches to tell the time, basically time is measured by the motion of the Earth. A day is the time it takes for the Earth to rotate once on its axis in relation to the Sun. This length of time is then divided into 24 hours, each consisting of 60 minutes, each of 60 seconds. This division into hours, minutes and seconds has no special meaning; it is simply convenient for our everyday lives. We also use months in measuring time, but this is a very approximate method as our months vary in length from 28 to 31 days. A year — the time it takes the Earth to go once around the Sun — is a good unit for measuring long periods of time, not only because it is long, but also because it can be measured very precisely. To the nearest second, a year is 365 days 5 hours 48 minutes and 46 seconds.

These odd hours, minutes and seconds have given people a lot of trouble in producing a calendar in which a particular date always occurs at the same time of the year. This is necessary to keep the months and days in step with the seasons. The ancient Egyptians thought that the year was exactly 365 days long, but every new year arrived one quarter of a day too early with such a calendar. After a time, the seasons began to get obviously later in the year. Julius Caesar realized what was wrong and, in 46 BC, produced a calendar in which most years still had 365 days, but every fourth year — a leap year — had 366 days. This made the average year longer by 6 hours, but this was now 11 minutes too much. By the 1500s, the calendar was several days out and, in 1582, Pope Gregory XIII changed the calendar again. He decreed that every century year (for example 1700, 1800) would not be a leap year unless it could be divided by 400 (for example 1600, 2000). This calendar reduced the error in the length of the year to an average of 26 seconds and it is the calendar that we now use.

However, for all this scientific accuracy, our calendar still has months of different lengths named by the ancient Romans, and the same date falls on a different day of the week from year to year. People have worked out a calendar in which every date always falls on the same day of the week. With this calendar, it would not be necessary to print new diaries and calendars every year, as each year would be exactly the same as the one before.

Another problem that occurs with telling the time is one's location on the Earth's surface. Because everyone expects it to be light at noon and dark at midnight (except in polar regions, where it may be light or dark for months at a time), the world is divided into several different time zones.

PRIME MERIDIAN
OF THE WORLD
EAST
LONGITUDE
WEST
LONGITUDE

Left: **A naval officer uses a sextant to find his position. The sextant measures the angle between the horizon and the Sun or a star. With this information and the exact time, he can work out his position.**

Right: **One kind of sundial, man's first reliable clock. The angle of the shadows changes as the Sun moves from east to west, and thus shows the time of day. The length of the shadows at any particular time varies according to the season.**

Below left: **The line of 0° longitude, which is called the prime meridian, passes through Greenwich Observatory in London. All positions of longitude are measured in degrees east or west of this line.**

Below: **The world is divided into several time zones. As people travel from one zone to another, they change their watches to match the local time.**

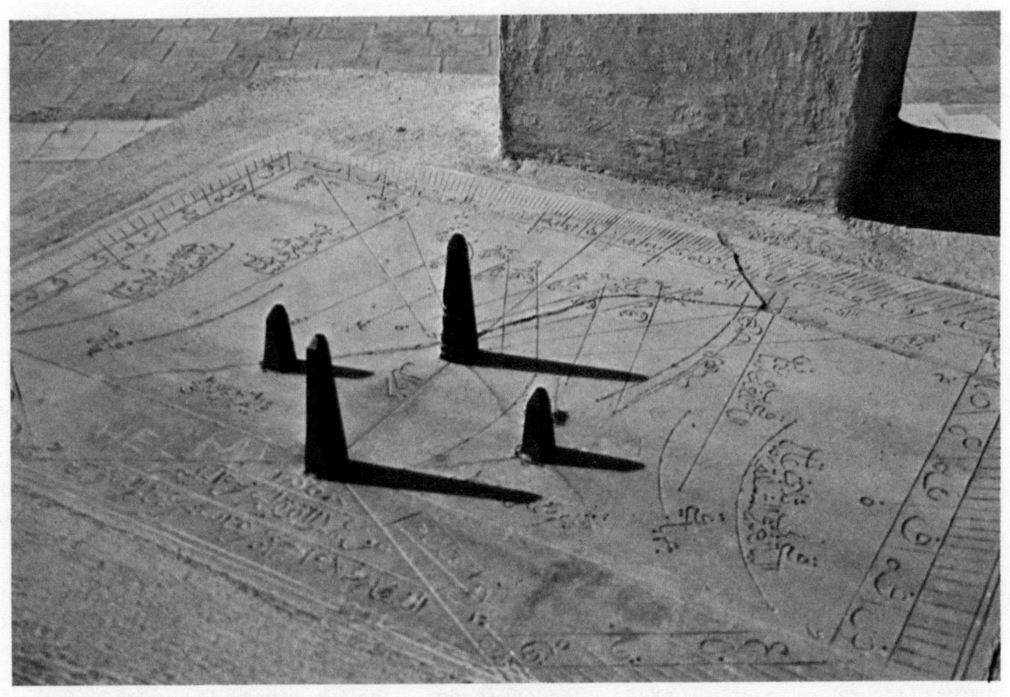

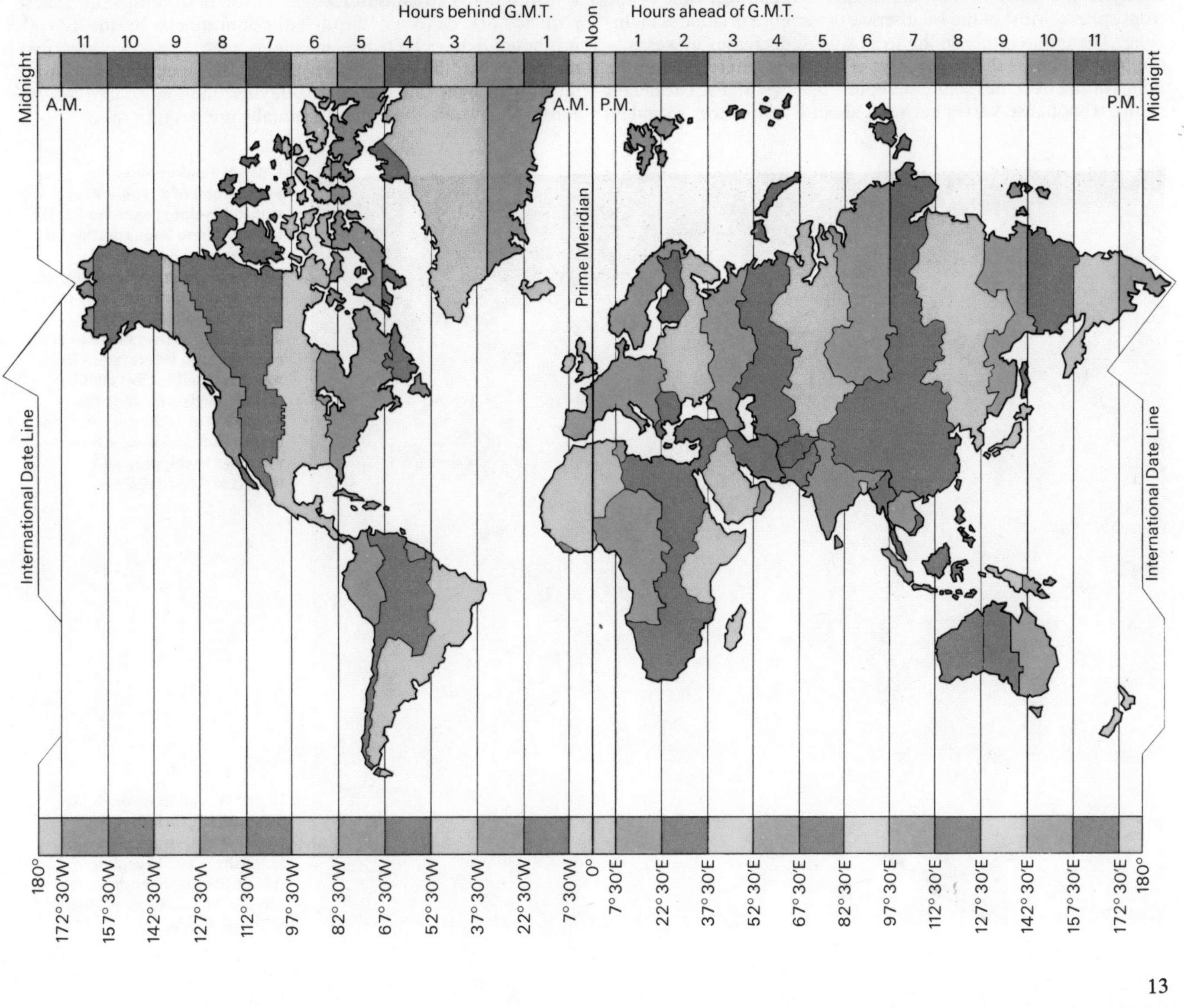

Hours behind G.M.T. Noon Hours ahead of G.M.T.

Midnight 11 10 9 8 7 6 5 4 3 2 1 Noon 1 2 3 4 5 6 7 8 9 10 11 Midnight

A.M. A.M. P.M. P.M.

Prime Meridian

International Date Line

International Date Line

180° 172° 30'W 157° 30'W 142° 30'W 127° 30'W 112° 30'W 97° 30'W 82° 30'W 67° 30'W 52° 30'W 37° 30'W 22° 30'W 7° 30'W 0° 7° 30'E 22° 30'E 37° 30'E 52° 30'E 67° 30'E 82° 30'E 97° 30'E 112° 30'E 127° 30'E 142° 30'E 157° 30'E 172° 30'E 180°

The Atmosphere

About 5,000 million million tonnes of gas make up the Earth's atmosphere. A column of air, weighing about one tonne, is pressing down on our shoulders. But we do not feel this pressure, because it is balanced by the same air pressure within our bodies.

The atmosphere is essential for life on Earth. It contains oxygen for animals and carbon dioxide for plants. The ozone layer in the stratosphere protects life on Earth by absorbing most of the Sun's harmful ultraviolet radiation. And the general circulation of the atmosphere redistributes heat around the globe, thus acting like a giant thermostat.

Dry air is composed of nitrogen (78.09% by volume), oxygen (20.95%) and argon (0.93%), together with minute proportions of other gases, including carbon dioxide, neon, helium, methane, krypton, nitrous oxide, hydrogen, ozone and xenon. The amount of carbon dioxide varies considerably from place to place, being greatest over cities and lowest over countryside. Air also contains tiny specks of dust and other substances, such as salt crystals (derived from ocean spray). There are also varying amounts of water vapour evaporated from the Earth's surface, especially from the oceans.

About five-sixths of the total mass of the atmosphere, including nearly all the water vapour, is confined to the lowest zone — the troposphere. Most of the weather we experience originates in this zone. The temperature in the troposphere decreases upwards to the tropopause — the upper limit of the troposphere. There, the temperature becomes stable at about −55°C (−67°F). The height of the tropopause varies between about 8 kilometres (5 miles) over the poles to about 11 kilometres (7 miles) over the middle latitudes and 18 kilometres (11 miles) over the Equator.

Above the tropopause is the lower stratosphere, where conditions are relatively calm and so jet aircraft often fly there. However, strong winds called jet streams blow through the upper troposphere and the lower stratosphere. Reaching speeds of 160 kilometres per hour (100 m.p.h.), these winds can be an obstacle or an aid to high-flying aircraft. Above the tropopause, temperatures remain stable at first but, eventually, they start to rise, reaching about 2°C (36°F) just above the ozone layer.

Beyond the stratosphere, from about 50 to 500 kilometres (30 to 300 miles) above sea level is the ionosphere. Here, temperatures decrease at first, reaching about −70°C (−94°F) at a height of 80 kilometres (50 miles) above sea level. Then temperatures start to rise steadily in the ionosphere, reaching more than 2,000°C (3,600°F) at 400 kilometres (250 miles). The ionosphere is so called because the thinly-distributed gas molecules are ionized (electrically charged) by solar radiation. These charged particles are important in radio communications because they reflect some radio waves. Radio communications are sometimes interrupted by occasional magnetic storms, when the ionosphere is disturbed by streams of charged particles from the Sun. These particles are deflected through the ionosphere by the Earth's magnetic field. Over the magnetic poles, they collide with molecules in the ionosphere and cause spectacular glowing displays of light called *aurorae.* Beyond the ionosphere lies the exosphere, where the thin air gradually merges into space.

Left: **A weather-satellite photograph of a typhoon, or tropical cyclone, over the Pacific Ocean. These large rotating air systems, which are called hurricanes in the Atlantic Ocean, bring fierce winds and may cause serious flooding and great devastation as they move over coastal areas. Information from weather satellites has enabled meteorologists to study the formation of typhoons, chart their movements and issue advance warnings to shipping and threatened coastal areas.**

Right: **A section through the atmosphere, including the troposphere, stratosphere, ionosphere and exosphere. Alongside the diagram are the temperatures and air pressures at different levels.**

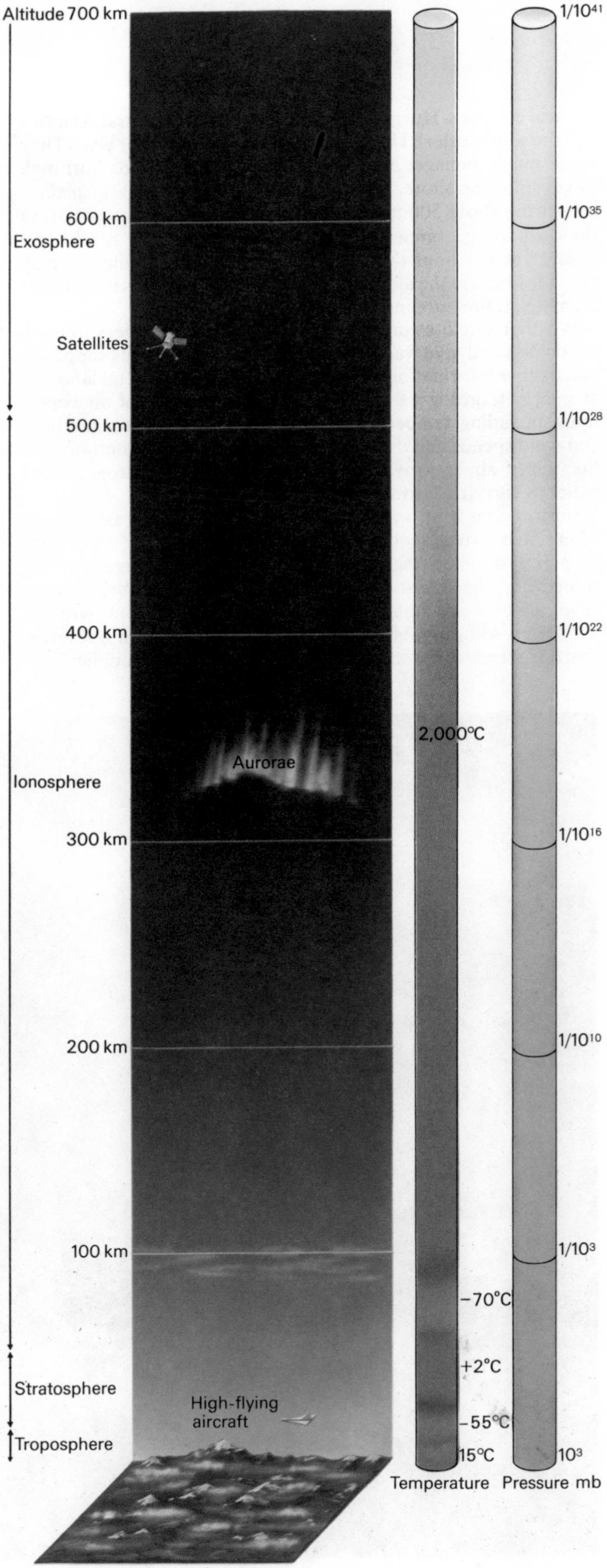

Altitude 700 km
600 km
Exosphere
Satellites
500 km
400 km
Aurorae
Ionosphere
300 km
200 km
100 km
Stratosphere
High-flying aircraft
Troposphere

2,000°C
−70°C
+2°C
−55°C
15°C
Temperature

$1/10^{41}$
$1/10^{35}$
$1/10^{28}$
$1/10^{22}$
$1/10^{16}$
$1/10^{10}$
$1/10^{3}$
10^{3}
Pressure mb

Winds

The air in the atmosphere is constantly circulating. It is like a vast machine powered by the Sun. But heat is unevenly distributed, the effect of the Sun being greatest at the Equator, where it passes directly overhead. As a result, there are great variations in air pressure, causing air currents (winds) to flow from high pressure areas towards low pressure areas.

At the Equator, air near the ground is heated, making it expand and rise. As a result, equatorial regions are characterized by a low-pressure air system, called the *doldrums.* On both sides of the Equator, air flows towards the doldrums in the trade-wind belts. The warm air rising above the equatorial zone cools as it ascends and spreads out north and south. Finally it sinks back to Earth around latitudes 30° North and 30° South, creating two high-pressure belts called the *horse latitudes.* At the surface, some of the descending air flows into the trade winds, and some flows polewards in the westerlies. The westerlies meet cold, dense air flowing from the poles along the polar front. The intermingling of warm, light, sub-tropical air with cold, dense polar air creates rotating low-pressure systems, called *depressions.* These bring changeable, stormy weather to middle latitudes.

This simple pattern of atmospheric circulation is complicated by several factors. First, because the Earth spins on its axis, winds do not flow north-south, but are deflected to the right in the northern hemisphere and to the left in the southern hemisphere. Winds are also deflected by mountain ranges. Another important factor is the seasonal development of large and fairly stable air masses. For example, the interiors of large mid-latitude continents heat up in summer. Large low-pressure air masses form, into which winds are drawn. But, in winter, these continental interiors are cold, and so high-pressure air masses form, from which icy winds blow outwards.

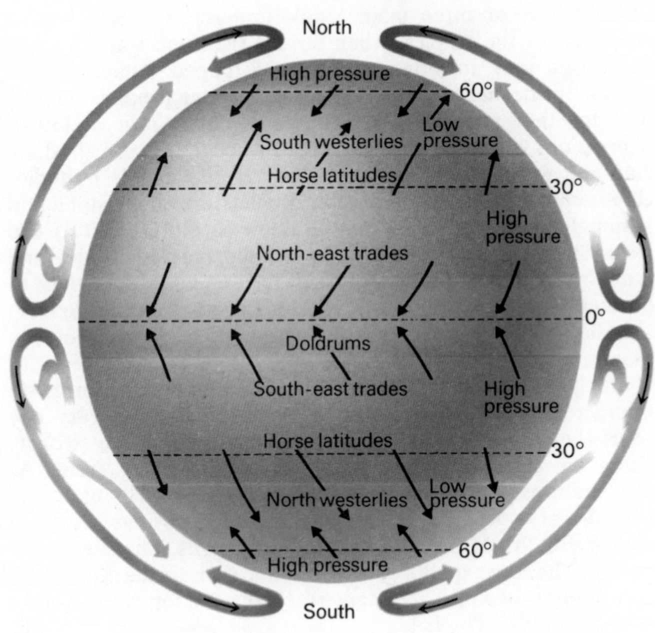
North
High pressure
60°
South westerlies
Low pressure
Horse latitudes
30°
High pressure
North-east trades
0°
Doldrums
South-east trades
High pressure
Horse latitudes
30°
North westerlies
Low pressure
60°
High pressure
South

Above: **The main wind belts on the Earth's surface, and the main air-circulation currents in the atmosphere. Air circulates because uneven heating of the Earth gives rise to air-pressure variations in the atmosphere. The air moves as winds, from high-pressure to low-pressure regions. The general pattern of prevailing winds shown here does not take account of local and seasonal variations.**

Weather

Weather is the day-to-day condition of the air. The chief elements of weather are the temperature and pressure of the air, wind speeds and directions, and the amount of moisture in the air — particularly if the moisture is being precipitated as rain, snow, hail, sleet, dew or frost.

All air contains moisture in the form of water vapour, which is water in gaseous form. Warm air can hold more water vapour than cold air. When warm air is cooled, usually by moving upwards in the troposphere, its capacity to hold water vapour decreases. Finally, *dew point* is reached — that is, the air is completely saturated, having a relative humidity of 100 per cent. Further cooling beyond dew point leads to water vapour condensing around nucleii, such as specks of dust or salt, to form water droplets or, in cold air, minute ice crystals. Large quantities of condensed water vapour form clouds.

There are two main kinds of clouds: cumuliform ('heap' clouds) and stratiform ('layer' clouds). Clouds are classified according to their height. Low clouds, within 2.5 kilometres (1.6 miles) of the surface, include: grey stratus; cumulus, a white heap cloud; cumulonimbus, a heap thundercloud; nimbostratus, a layer cloud often blurred by rain or snow; and stratocumulus, a greyish-white layer cloud. Medium-height clouds, from 2.5 to 6 kilometres (1.6 to 3.7 miles) are the greyish-white, rounded altocumulus, and the altostratus, which is a greyish layer cloud. Above 6 kilometres (3.7 miles) are the high clouds, including the feathery cirrus, cirrocumulus and cirrostratus.

Clouds form part of the water cycle, by which water is continually conveyed from the salty oceans to the land, where it is released from the air as precipitation. This provides the land with the fresh water needed by animal and plant life. Finally, the water completes the cycle by returning to the oceans.

Rainfall is of three main kinds. *Convectional rain* occurs, especially in the tropics, when hot air rises and water vapour condenses into towering, often anvil-topped cumulonimbus clouds. Inside the turbulent clouds, the water droplets collide, fuse together and fall as raindrops. *Cyclonic rain* occurs in depressions when warm air rises above wedges of cold air along cold and warm fronts and occlusions. In the middle latitudes, clouds contain super-cooled water droplets, which are still liquid although their temperature may be as low as −40°C (−40°F), and ice crystals. The ice crystals collide with supercooled droplets and grow in size. They then start to fall, melting near the surface to become raindrops or, if the air is cold, they join together to form snowflakes. *Orographic rain* is caused when air rises over a mountain range.

Precipitation is a feature of storms. The commonest storms are thunderstorms, about 45,000 of which break out every day somewhere in the world. Thunderstorms occur when strongly rising air currents cause cumulonimbus clouds to form. As temperatures within the clouds fall, the outer shells of super-cooled water droplets freeze and acquire a positive electrical charge. But, when the core subsequently freezes, it has a negative charge. The core expands as it freezes and shatters the outer shell, tiny splinters of which waft upwards, giving the top of the cloud a positive charge. The heavier cores remain lower down, building up a large negative charge. The air between the cloud and ground normally acts as an electrical insulator. But, when the charge on the cloud becomes great enough, the insulation breaks down and lightning — a gigantic spark — occurs. Along the lightning's path, heat causes a violent expansion of the air, and the resultant compression wave is heard as thunder.

Other storms include large, rotating hurricanes, also called tropical cyclones. Hurricanes strike the coasts of Central America and the southeastern United States about 11 times per year. They cause much damage, especially because strong winds hurl high waves onto the shore, causing flooding. Tornadoes are smaller, measuring about 500 metres (1,600 feet) across. Wind speeds in these rotating, funnel-like columns of air may reach 650 kilometres per hour (400 m.p.h.). In tornadoes, buildings may explode because the air pressure outside the buildings is far lower than the air pressure inside them.

Weather satellites orbiting the Earth help forecasters to track hurricanes and give warnings of their advance, besides supplying much other information. At surface weather stations, on land and at sea, meteorologists take regular measurements of air conditions, including temperature, pressure, humidity, precipitation, and wind speeds and directions. Information about conditions in the upper air is provided by radiosondes — hydrogen-filled balloons carrying instruments.

Information from weather stations is sent to forecast centres, where it is often analysed by computers. Synoptic charts are prepared, summarizing weather conditions over a large area. By comparing the latest synoptic chart with preceding charts, developments are noted. Meteorologists deduce how weather conditions will probably change and express them on a forecast chart, from which forecasts are made for the general public.

Grey stratus clouds

Cumulus clouds

Cumulonimbus clouds

Nimbostratus clouds

Stratocumulus clouds

Altocumulus clouds

Altostratus clouds

Cirrus clouds

Cirrocumulus clouds

Cirrostratus clouds

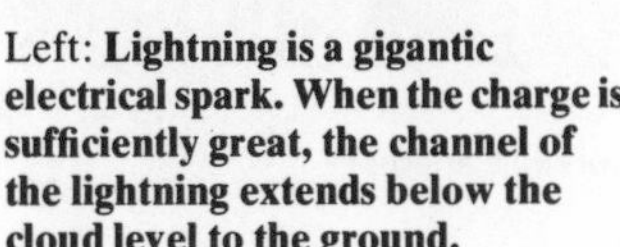

Above: **Weather stations use white shelters, called Stevenson screens, to enclose thermometers and, sometimes, other instruments used to measure air conditions. The air can circulate freely through the louvres, so that the instruments, protected from the Sun and the wind, make true readings.**

Left: **Lightning is a gigantic electrical spark. When the charge is sufficiently great, the channel of the lightning extends below the cloud level to the ground.**

Right: **The diagram shows how water continuously circulates from sea to land and back again in the water, or hydrologic cycle. Through this cycle, land areas obtain a regular supply of fresh water, which is essential to the Earth's plant and animal life.**

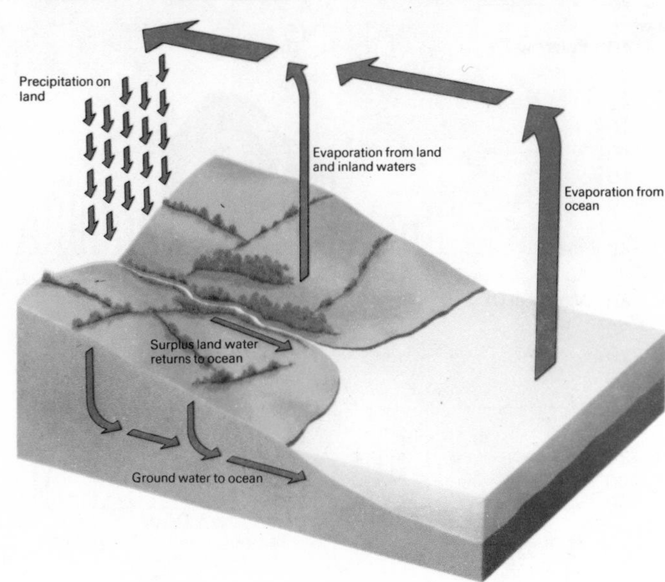
Precipitation on land
Evaporation from land and inland waters
Evaporation from ocean
Surplus land water returns to ocean
Ground water to ocean

Climate

Climate is the typical or average weather of a place based on records covering a period of years. The word climate comes from the Greek word *klima,* which means slope. The Greeks believed that the Earth 'sloped' from the Mediterranean southwards to the hot equatorial zone and northwards to the cold polar region. Hence, a Greek scholar Parmenides suggested in about 500 BC that there were five climatic zones. The central equatorial zone was hot all the year round. The middle latitudes in both hemispheres had summer and winter seasons. And the polar regions were cold all the year round.

But other factors, such as the terrain and the proximity to the sea, complicate this simple pattern. For example, mountains and plateaux have cooler climates than surrounding plains, because temperatures fall, on average, by about 6°C (11°F) for every kilometre (0.6 mile) of altitude. For example, in Kenya, which straddles the Equator, the coastal port of Mombasa has average temperatures of 27°C (81°F) all the year round. But, on the high southwestern plateau in the interior, average temperatures are 10°C to 20°C (50°F to 68°F), and so the plateau has proved more attractive to European settlers than the coast.

The terrain influences the rainfall too. For example, when winds from the oceans are forced to rise over coastal mountain ranges, they lose most of their moisture during their ascent. Beyond the crest of the mountains, the winds are dry and there is often a 'rain shadow' area.

The oceans have a considerable effect on climate. The Sun's rays heat the surfaces of land areas more intensely and faster than they heat the sea. But land areas cool extremely quickly, whereas bodies of water retain heat about two-and-a-half times as readily as land. Generally, in maritime areas, winds from the oceans warm the land in winter and cool it in summer. This moderating influence is particularly pronounced, for example, along the west coasts of land masses in the middle latitudes of the northern hemisphere, where the prevailing winds are southwesterlies. But, beyond the moderating influence of the oceans, the continental interiors have extreme climates. In southwestern Ireland, the

Left: **Climate around the world.**

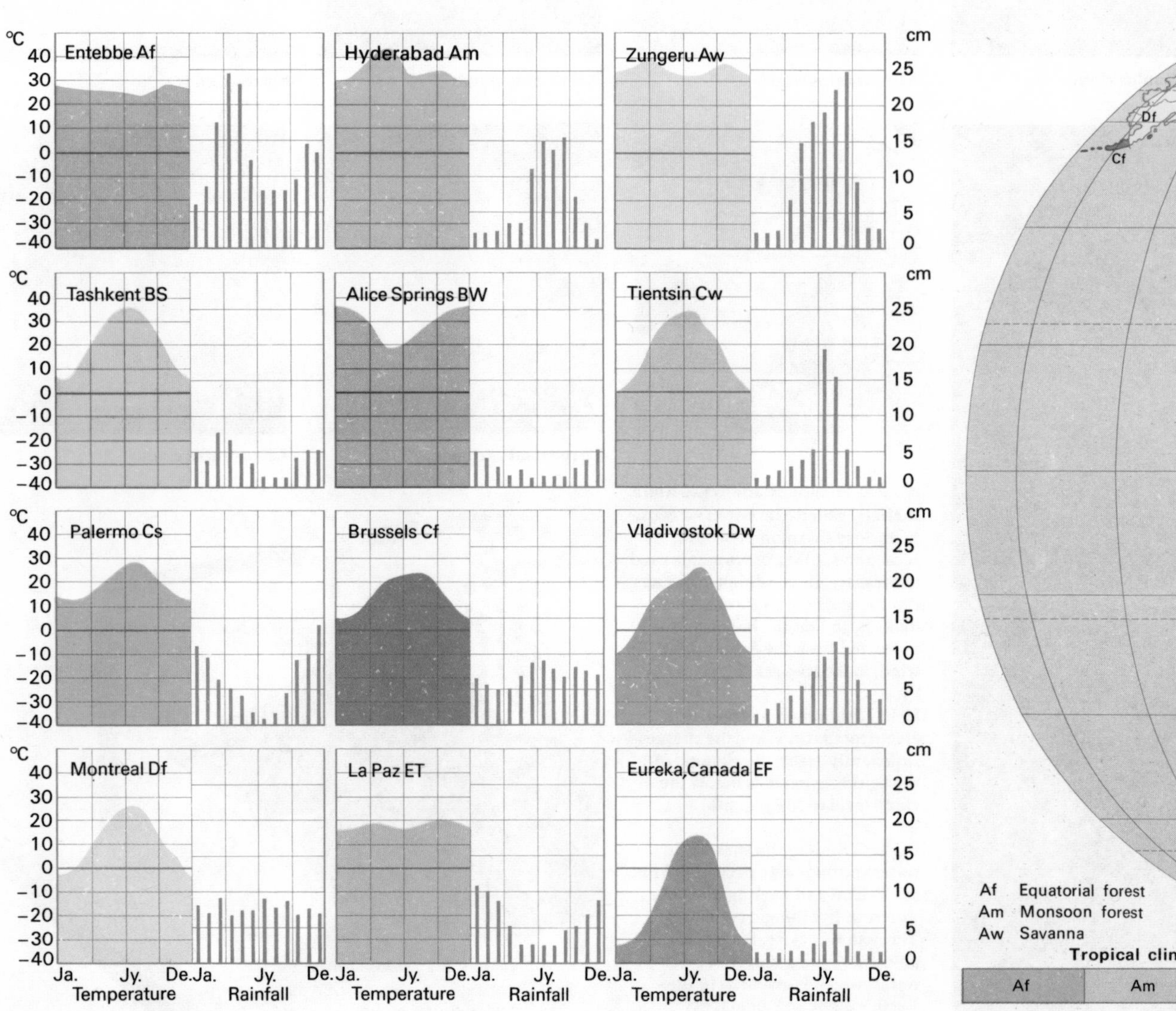

Entebbe Af
Hyderabad Am
Zungeru Aw
Tashkent BS
Alice Springs BW
Tientsin Cw
Palermo Cs
Brussels Cf
Vladivostok Dw
Montreal Df
La Paz ET
Eureka,Canada EF
°C
cm
Ja. Jy. De.
Temperature
Rainfall
Af Equatorial forest
Am Monsoon forest
Aw Savanna
Tropical climates

average temperature in the coldest month is 5°C (41°F) and the average in the warmest month is 16°C (61°F) — an average annual temperature range of only 11°C (20°F). But, in the same latitude, south of Moscow, the average temperature in the coldest month is −11°C (12°F) and, in the warmest month, it is 21°C (70°F) — an average annual temperature range of 32°C (58°F).

Ocean currents affect climate too. The icy Labrador current flows southwards down the eastern coast of Canada, and St. John's in Newfoundland, for example, has cold winters, with an average temperature in the coldest month of −5°C (23°F). St. John's lies in the same latitude as Brittany, which has mild winters. The coastlands of northwestern Europe are warmed in winter by onshore winds that pass over an extension of the warm Gulf Stream — an ocean current that originates in the Caribbean.

There are various ways of classifying climates, but most classifications used today are based on the work of Russian meteorologist Vladimir Köppen in the early 1900s. Köppen classified climates according to temperature and rainfall. He distinguished five main climatic types, coding them **A, B, C, D** and **E.** Type **A** is the tropical, rainy climate, with average temperatures of over 18°C (64°F) in every month of the year. Type **B** is a dry climate, with an average of less than 250 millimetres (10 inches) of rain per year and a high evaporation rate. Type **C** is the middle-latitude, warm temperate climate, with average temperatures in the coldest month from −3°C to 18°C (27°F to 64°F). Type **D** is a cold and snowy climate, with an average temperature of less than −3°C (27°F) in the coldest month, but the average temperature in the warmest month is more than 10°C (50°F). And type **E** is the polar climate, with an average temperature of less than 10°C (50°F) in the warmest month. Cold, mountain regions, once included in type **E**, are now usually classified **H**.

To distinguish between rainfall patterns, a second group of symbols has been added: **S** (dry steppelands), **W** (deserts), **f** (places with ample, well-distributed rainfall), **m** (monsoon, or seasonal rainfall), **s** (a dry summer) and **w** (a dry winter). To distinguish between polar climates, the code **T** represents tundra and **F** signifies ice-sheet climates. Hence, type **Af** is equatorial forest, which is hot and wet all the year round, whereas **Aw** is tropical savanna, with summer rains and a winter drought.

Other symbols are: **a** (hot summers), **b** (warm summers), **c** (cool summers), **d** (very cold winters), **h** (dry and hot) and **k** (dry and cold). Hence, the code **Cfb** means a middle-latitude, warm temperate climate, with ample, well-distributed rainfall and warm summers — the characteristic climate of northwestern Europe.

Below: **World climate zones.**

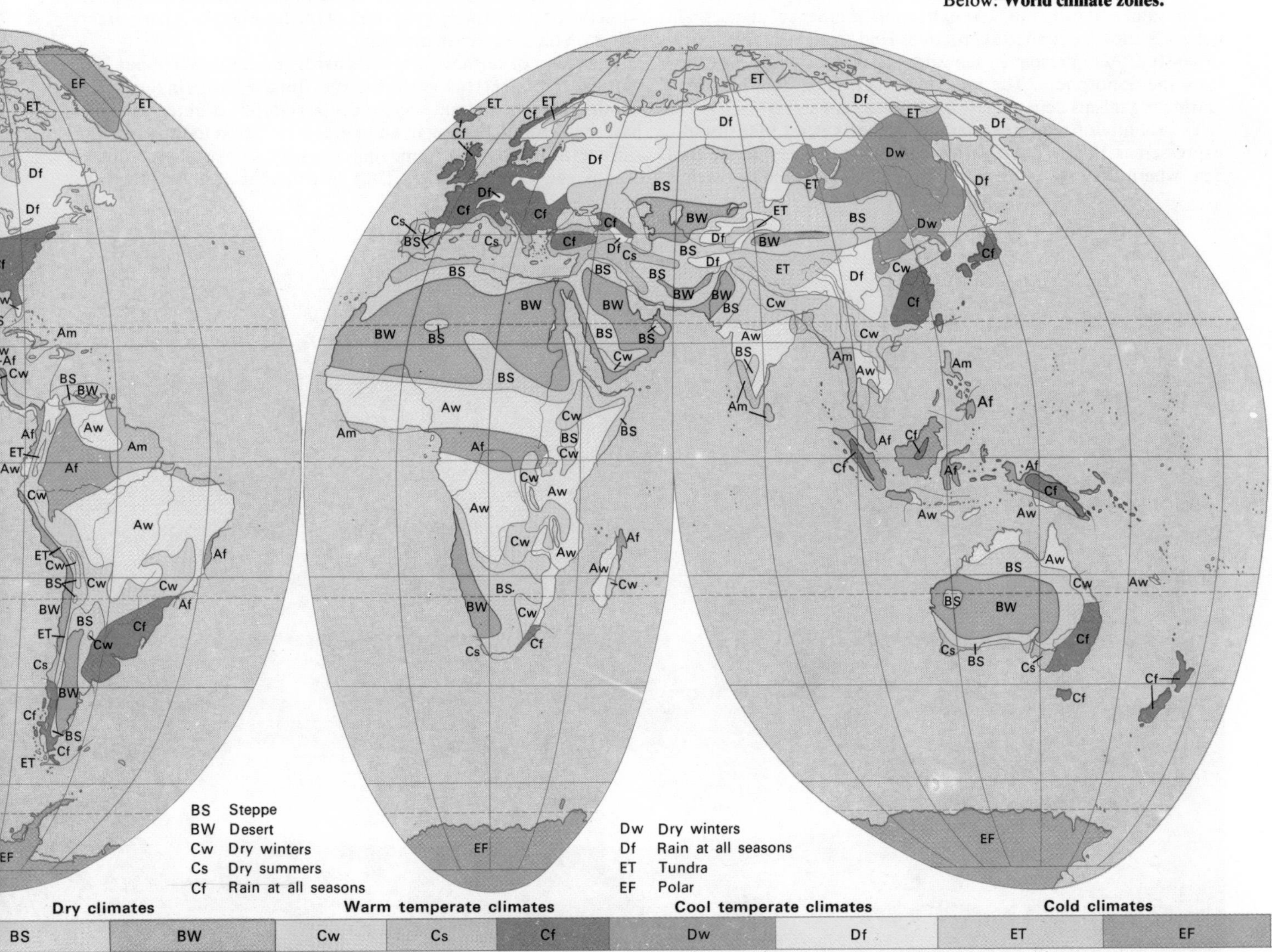
BS Steppe
BW Desert
Cw Dry winters
Cs Dry summers
Cf Rain at all seasons
Dw Dry winters
Df Rain at all seasons
ET Tundra
EF Polar
Dry climates
Warm temperate climates
Cool temperate climates
Cold climates
BS
BW
Cw
Cs
Cf
Dw
Df
ET
EF

The Oceans

The oceans, which are interconnected, cover 70.8 per cent of the Earth's surface. The largest ocean, the Pacific, sprawls over the vast area of 165,236,000 square kilometres (63,798,000 square miles) — more than the combined area of all the continents. The oceans have an average depth of about 3.5 kilometres (2.2 miles), but the deepest known point is in Challenger Deep, part of the Mariana Trench in the Pacific, which is 11.033 kilometres (6.855 miles) deep.

The water in the oceans totals about 1,300 million cubic kilometres (312 million cubic miles) — more than 97 per cent of the world's total water. On average, seawater contains about 3.5 per cent by weight of dissolved substances. Nearly 3 per cent is composed of chlorine and sodium, which together form sodium chloride (common salt). Other substances, such as sulphur, magnesium, potassium and calcium, are present in abundance in seawater, and there are minute proportions of many other elements. In fact, seawater is a great treasure trove of valuable and useful minerals, but the extraction of most of them is extremely costly and, therefore, uneconomic. The only important substances currently obtained from seawater are common salt, magnesium and bromine. The extraction of other substances will probably not be undertaken until land reserves are nearly exhausted. Also present in seawater are various gases dissolved from the atmosphere. The most important is oxygen, on which marine organisms depend.

The salinity of seawater averages 35 parts per 1,000 (usually expressed as 35‰), but it varies from place to place. In the Red Sea, where the rate of evaporation is high, the salinity reaches 41‰. But, in the Baltic Sea, rivers supply large amounts of fresh water and the salinity is lowered to 7.2‰. Salinity and temperature affect the density of seawater, high salinity and low temperatures both causing the water to have a relatively high density. The temperature of ocean water varies between −2°C (28°F) — its approximate freezing point — and 29°C (84°F).

Density differences contribute to the continuous circulation of ocean waters, because dense water sinks beneath less dense water. However, the chief movements of ocean water are: tides, caused by the gravitational pull of the Moon and, to a lesser extent, the Sun; waves, which move water particles in a circular orbit, but not horizontally, except on shores; and ocean currents.

Surface ocean currents generally follow prevailing winds although, because of the Earth's spin, they swing to the right of the wind direction in the Northern Hemisphere and to the left in the Southern Hemisphere. Generally, currents cause the surface waters of the Northern Hemisphere to circulate in a clockwise direction. In the Southern Hemisphere, the circulation is anti-clockwise. Surface currents are classed as *cold* if they flow from polar regions towards the tropics, and *warm* if they flow polewards from the tropics. The temperature of offshore currents has a great effect on the climates of coastlands.

The effect of surface currents is hardly noticeable at about 350 metres (1,150 feet) below the surface. But the waters in the ocean depths are not still, and several deep, vigorous counter-currents have been found flowing in an opposite direction to those on the surface. Scientists have found that, even in the deepest parts of the oceans, the water is moving. They base this conclusion on the fact

Sea level
Transform fault
Mohorovičić discontinuity

that fishes have been found at great depths. If the water were still, the oxygen dissolved from the air would have been used up long ago and no fishes could possibly survive.

The study of the ocean floor has been of tremendous importance in establishing how the oceans were formed and how the continents have drifted around the Earth's surface. The ocean floor consists of three main zones: the continental shelf, the continental slope and the abyss. The gently sloping continental shelves border the continents, extending outwards to a depth of about 180 metres (600 feet). They vary considerably in width. For example, the continental shelf off northwestern Europe extends about 300 kilometres (190 miles) west of Land's End. But, off the west coast of South America, there is practically no continental shelf. The shelves are, in fact, submerged parts of the continents. Islands that rise above water level are called continental islands to distinguish them from oceanic islands, which rise from the abyss.

The continental shelves end at the start of the continental slope, the true edge of the continents. The continental slope descends steeply down to the abyss.

The abyss contains large, sediment-covered plains, interrupted by lofty volcanic mountains, some of which surface as islands, and long, broad ridges, 2 to 4 kilometres (1.2 to 2.5 miles) high and up to 4,000 kilometres (2,500 miles) wide. One ridge runs the whole length of the Atlantic Ocean. These ridges, which surface in places such as Iceland, are centres of volcanic activity and earthquakes. Other important features of the abyss are yawning chasms called oceanic trenches.

Left: **Thor Heyerdahl's papyrus boat *Ra,* like those of ancient Egypt, was driven by winds and currents.**

Below: **A section through the Atlantic Ocean. In order to show the details clearly, the vertical scale has been exaggerated.**

rift
Crust (including sediments)

Formation of the Earth

The Restless Earth

The Earth was formed about 4,600 million years ago from a great cloud of gas, rock and dust that was orbiting around a new star, the Sun. Gradually, heavier materials, such as iron and nickel, sank towards the centre, while lighter materials rose to the surface. And parts of the molten surface hardened into a thin, solid crust of igneous rocks, probably consisting mostly of basalt.

But cracking and reheating often broke up the outer shell and, from remelting, even lighter granitic rocks separated out. When they hardened, these rocks formed the first parts of the continental crust. Gases and water vapour were released from the rocks by continuous volcanic eruptions. These gases formed the atmosphere. Great storms must have raged over the Earth and rains eroded the hardened igneous rock. Streams swept eroded fragments into primeval lakes and seas, where they accumulated to form the first sedimentary rocks.

The early atmosphere probably contained only a minute proportion of oxygen, because volcanic gases are deficient in this life-giving gas. But, after the evolution of oxygen-producing plants around 1,900 million years ago, the proportion of oxygen steadily increased.

The Earth today has an equatorial diameter of 12,756 kilometres (7,926 miles). Measured from pole to pole, however, the diameter is 43 kilometres (27 miles) less, because our planet is not a true sphere, being slightly flattened at the poles and bulging at the Equator. Our knowledge of the Earth's interior is based on the behaviour of seismic (earthquake) waves as they travel through the Earth. From a study of how these waves bend, scientists have concluded that the centre of the Earth's core is a solid sphere with a diameter of about 2,740 kilometres (1,700 miles). The rocks in the solid core are about three times as dense as those in the crust. Surrounding the inner core is a liquid outer core, which is about 2,100 kilometres (1,300 miles) thick. Temperatures in the outer core range from 2,000°C to 5,000°C (3,600°F to 9,000°F), and movements in this molten material probably generate the electricity that gives the Earth its magnetic properties. Between the outer core and the crust is the dense mantle, which is about 2,900 kilometres (1,800 miles) thick. The mantle is mostly solid but, at its top, some rocks are molten or semi-solid. Heating causes these rocks to rise and spread beneath the crust in convection currents.

The Earth's crust beneath the oceanic abyss is only about 6 kilometres (3.7 miles) thick. But the continental crust is mostly 35 to 50 kilometres (22 to 25 miles) in thickness, reaching 60 kilometres (37 miles) under high mountain ranges. There are other contrasts between oceanic and continental crust. First, the basaltic oceanic crust is 3.0 times as dense as water, whereas granitic continental crust is only 2.7 times as dense as water. And all oceanic crust has been formed within the last 200 million years, whereas the continents contain rocks that are more than 3,500 million years old.

The study of the oceanic crust has contributed to the generally accepted theory of *plate tectonics,* or *continental drift.* Scientists now believe that the crust is cracked into a series of 'plates' which are moving around the Earth's surface. The continents are composed of light materials and they rest upon the moving plates.

Plate edges occur along the mid-oceanic ridges. Along these ridges, new crustal rock is being added as molten material wells up from below. For example, in the Atlantic Ocean, studies of rock samples reveal that rocks become progressively older east and west of the mid-Atlantic ridge. These rock samples often contain magnetized particles, which were aligned towards the Earth's magnetic poles when the rock hardened. But these particles have been twisted out of alignment — further evidence of movement.

As a result of this movement, the oceans are widening, or spreading, at 1 to 10 centimetres (0.4 to 4 inches) per year. But the Earth is not expanding, for the crust is being destroyed at other plate edges. These are the oceanic trenches. Here, one plate is pushed beneath another to about 700 kilometres (430 miles) below the surface, before it is finally melted and destroyed. Some

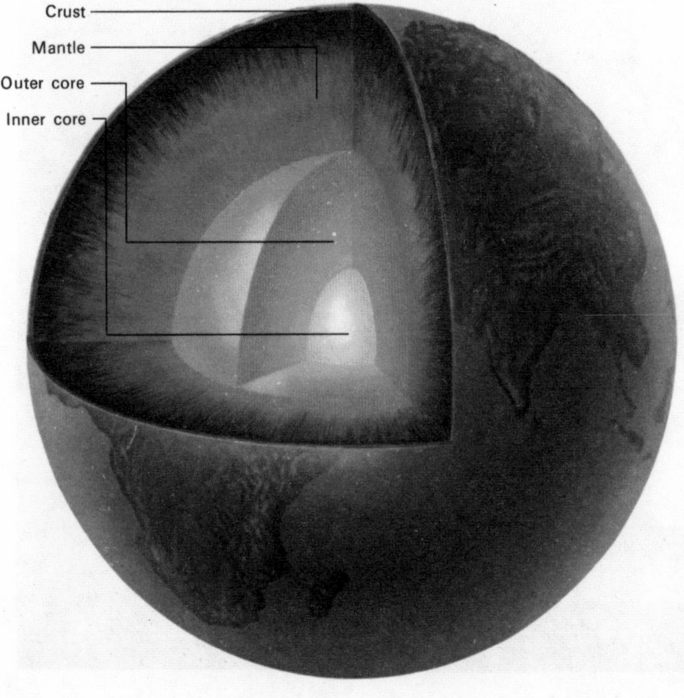
Crust
Mantle
Outer core
Inner core

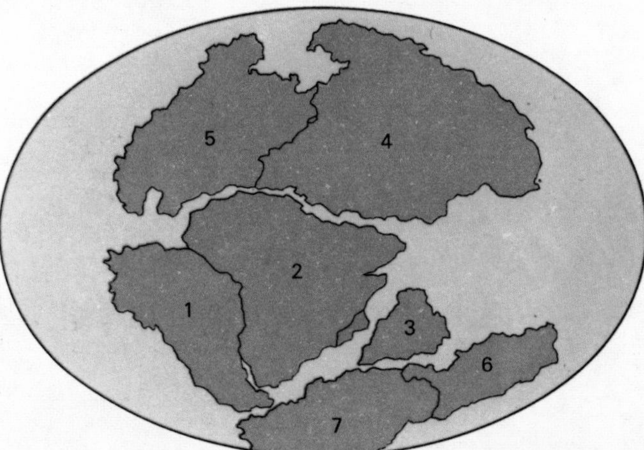
5
4
2
1
3
6
7

Left: **Zones within the Earth.**

Above: **A super-continent, called Pangaea, existed about 200 million years ago. Since then, the continents have broken away and drifted apart to their present positions.**

Right: **The volcanic island of Surtsey, on the mid-Atlantic ridge. This island appeared off the Icelandic coast in November, 1963 and grew rapidly. After three weeks, its crater had risen to 120 metres (390 feet) above sea level and was almost 1 kilometre (0.6 mile) across.**

of the melted rock may return to the surface through the overriding plate to form a chain of volcanic islands, roughly parallel to the trench. Another type of plate edge, a transform fault, occurs where plates move horizontally alongside each other.

Scientists now believe that, about 200 million years ago, all the continental land masses were grouped together in one super-continent, called Pangaea. The northern part of Pangaea, called Laurasia, consisted of North America and most of Eurasia. The southern part, Gondwanaland, consisted of South America, Africa, the Indian sub-continent, Australia and Antarctica. In the last 180 million years, Pangaea has split apart and the continents have drifted to their present positions. The Indian sub-continent, after separating from Gondwanaland, moved northward and eventually linked up with Asia.

Earthquakes

As plates drift apart, the movement occurs in sudden jerks, which cause earthquakes.

Earthquakes can occur anywhere. They are caused mostly by sudden movements along faults in rocks triggering off destructive vibrations. The most destructive earthquakes occur when the focus (point of origin) is within about 60 kilometres (37 miles) of the Earth's surface. The point on the Earth's surface directly above the focus is called the epicentre. About 10,000 earthquakes are recorded annually, although, on average, only 10 cause major destruction. By plotting the epicentres of all the earthquakes on a world map, it is evident that earthquakes predominate around the edges of the plates. They are much less common in areas away from plate edges.

The intensity of earthquakes is measured on a scale devised by C. F. Richter in 1935. An earthquake rated 2 on the Richter scale is hardly noticeable. But a magnitude of 5 causes some damage, and magnitude 7 is severe. One of the most intensive earthquakes in recent times had a magnitude of 8.9. It occurred in the Prince William Sound off Alaska on March 28, 1964.

This earthquake triggered off a so-called tidal wave — a misnomer because such waves have nothing to do with tides. Hence, scientists use the Japanese term *tsunami.* These fast waves travel through the water at speeds up to 800 kilometres per hour (500 m.p.h.). In the open sea, they may pass unnoticed, because the wave height (the vertical distance between the crest and the trough) is usually less than one metre (three feet). But the energy contained in a tsunami is tremendous, especially because, unlike a normal wave, it extends through the entire depth of the water. As tsunamis approach coasts, the wave height increases rapidly, and they batter the land with terrifying force. The Alaskan earthquake of March 1964 caused a tsunami that reached a height of 67 metres (220 feet).

In recent times, scientists have been trying to find ways of alleviating the tension along faults and producing methods of reliable forecasting. One area of research is California in the United States. A long plate edge in California, called the San Andreas fault, is a transform fault. The jagged plate edges become jammed together until the pressure becomes so intense that the plates suddenly lurch forward. In 1906, the plates along the San Andreas fault, which is 960 kilometres (600 miles) long, moved violently. The ground shook with tremendous force and buildings in San Francisco swayed and collapsed. The shift along the fault near San Francisco was about 4.6 metres (15 feet). Broken gas pipes and overturned stoves caused raging fires.

Since 1906, many minor earthquakes have occurred around the San Andreas fault, and scientists now fear that San Francisco may again be threatened. They have, however, made some interesting discoveries. They have found that waste water pumped down disused wells lubricates faults, causing minor tremors. But, if water is pumped out of a well, the dry rocks become firmly locked together. Scientists have, therefore, suggested that they should

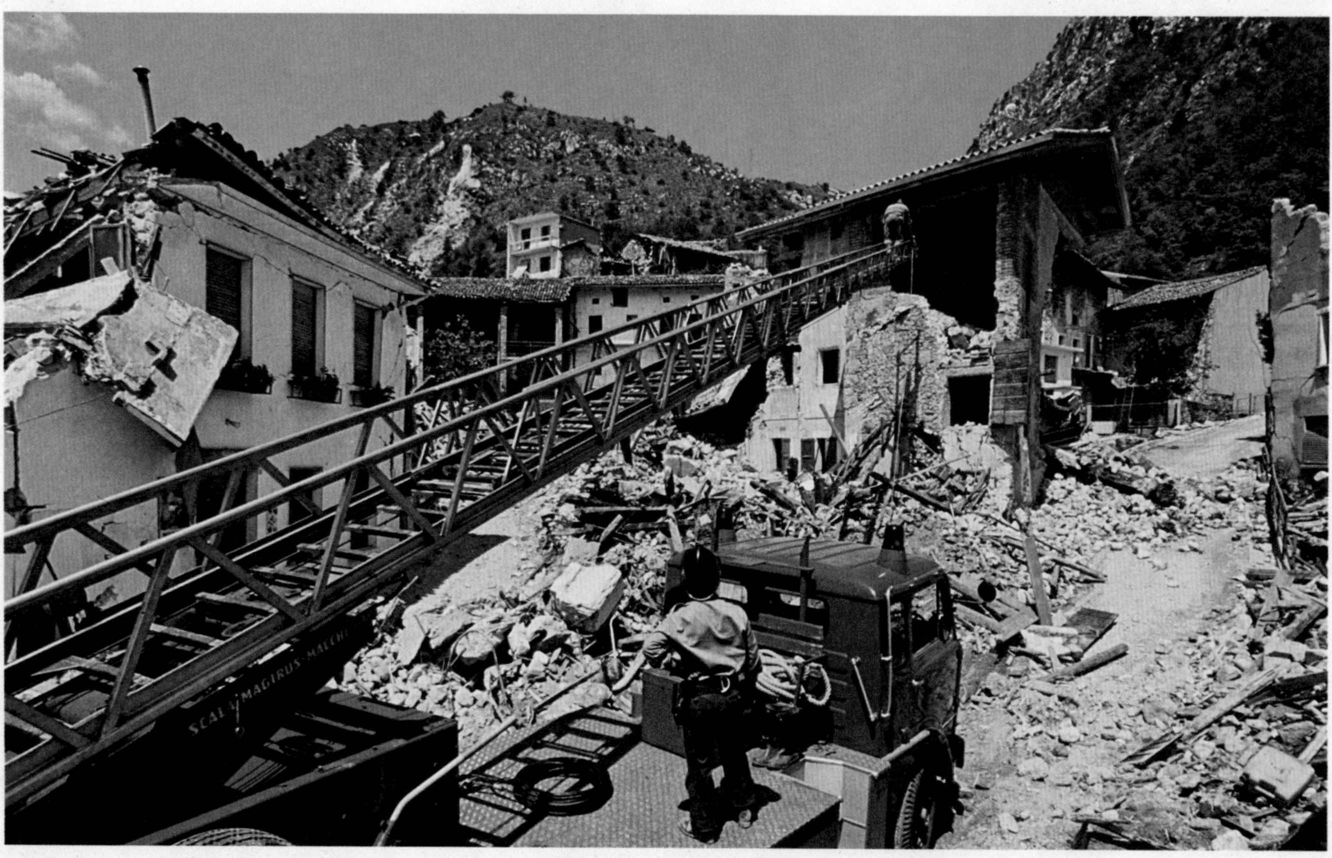
SCAI MAGIRUS MACCHI

EARTHQUAKES

The most destructive earthquake occurred in September 1923, in Japan. After the earthquake, fires, caused mainly by overturned stoves, raged through Tokyo and Yokohama, and about 143,000 people lost their lives. The highest death toll caused by a single earthquake was 830,000. This disaster occurred in Shensi province, China, in 1556.

Right: **This building in the Philippines collapsed during an earthquake in August 1976.**

Below left: **Earthquake damage in Osoppo, Italy: a fireman inspects a house which is in danger of collapsing.**

Below: **World map showing continental plate boundaries, volcanoes and earthquake zones.**

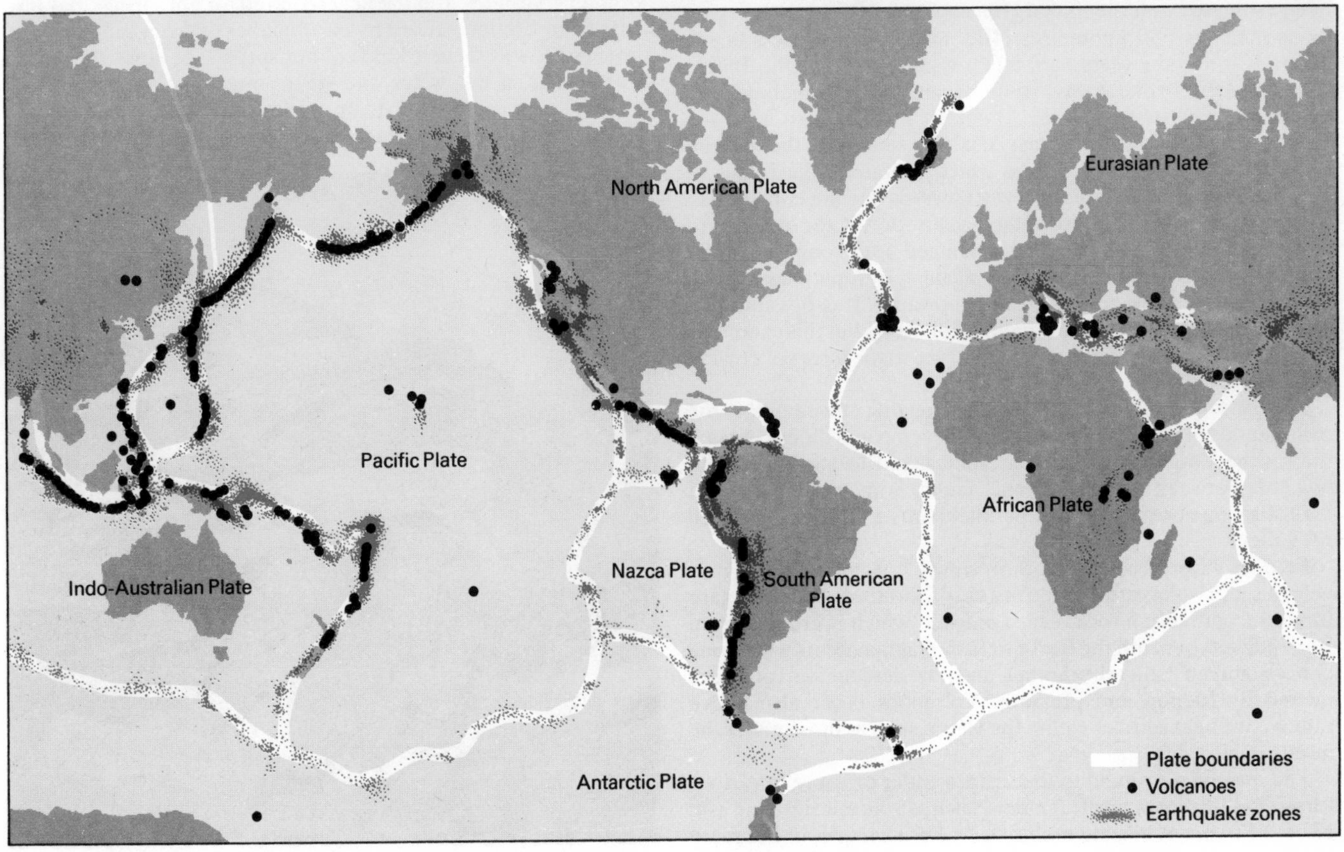

North American Plate
Eurasian Plate
Pacific Plate
African Plate
Nazca Plate
South American Plate
Indo-Australian Plate
Antarctic Plate
Plate boundaries
Volcanoes
Earthquake zones

drill a series of wells along the San Andreas fault. If they pumped all the ground water from two wells, they would lock the fault at those points. Then, if they pumped water into a third well, between the two dry wells, they might set off a minor earthquake, which would relieve the pressure at that point. By leap-frogging along the fault in this way, they might induce many small quakes and avert a major tragedy. This method would be costly, though not as costly as the destruction of San Francisco.

Attempts at earthquake forecasting have been developing recently, especially in China, a country which has had more than its share of earthquake tragedies. Several methods have been proposed. One involves recording any slight tilting of the ground. Such tilting was noticed in the city of Haicheng in early 1975. About 100,000 people were evacuated two hours before a severe earthquake. But, despite this and other claimed successes, a severe earthquake at Tangshan in July, 1976 was not predicted.

Another possible method of forecasting is to record variations in the amount of a radioactive gas, radon, in well water. Radon, which results from the decay of radium, is normally trapped in rocks. But, if the rocks crack and open, the gas escapes and is dissolved in ground water. The onset of earthquakes may also be indicated by changes in the elasticity and electrical resistance of rocks. And, the Chinese claim, odd animal behaviour often precedes earthquakes.

Mountains and Volcanoes

The study of plate tectonics has not only helped us to understand better the causes and nature of earthquakes, it has also provided us with a much deeper understanding of how mountains are formed. There are three main kinds of mountains: fold mountains, block mountains and volcanoes.

Fold mountains are raised up when level layers of rock are squeezed together by tremendous lateral force. The rock layers are buckled upwards into large, complex folds. For example, it has been estimated that the folded Himalayas have been compressed by as much as 650 kilometres (400 miles). This process began about 120 million years ago, when a plate bearing the Indian sub-continent broke away from ancient Gondwanaland and began to drift towards Asia. About 50 million years ago, the Indian plate was pushing against Asia. The sediments that floored the intervening Tethys Sea and which contained the fossils of ancient sea creatures were squeezed upwards into the Himalayas.

Similarly, in the last 30 million years or so, the northward movement of the African plate rammed intervening, smaller plates in the Mediterranean area against Europe, causing the folded Alpine range to rise steadily upwards. It is possible that both the Himalayas and the Alps are still rising, but this cannot be measured because, even as mountains rise, so the forces of erosion plane them down.

The drifting plates create tension and tugging movements in the continental rocks they contain. Faults develop and blocks of land, such as the Vosges and Black Forest areas of Europe, are pushed upwards between roughly parallel faults. Sometimes, blocks of land slip downwards between parallel faults to form steep-sided rift valleys.

Fold and block mountains form slowly but, periodically, new volcanic mountains are created in a very short time. Volcanoes are formed from molten rock, called *magma,* which is erupted from large pockets beneath the Earth's crust. Magma occurs where one plate is forced beneath another and the descending rocks are melted by friction and pressure. Volcanoes occur also above radioactive heat sources within the Earth, such as those under the mid-oceanic ridges.

The magma is erupted to the surface under pressure in various forms, ranging from tiny fragments, such as volcanic dust and ash, to broad rivers of blazing molten lava. For example, in February 1943, a small hole opened up in a cornfield in Mexico, near the village of Parícutin. Hot ash erupted from the hole and piled up in a small cone. One day later, lava began to flow from the vent, and layer upon layer covered the surrounding land, continuously raising the new mountain's level. Two years later, the volcano, which had been christened Parícutin, stood about 500 metres (1,640 feet) above the level of the former cornfield, the greatest height it has yet attained. Parícutin was the first mountain whose birth and growth were witnessed and studied by scientists.

There are about 535 active volcanoes in the world, including 80 under the oceans. They are classified according to the way in which they erupt. Broadly, there are explosive, quiet and intermediate volcanoes. Explosive volcanoes contain magma that is highly charged with explosive gases. These gases expand and explode in the hot magma, shattering it into fragments of dust, ash, cinders and larger lumps called volcanic bombs. Explosive volcanoes are usually cone-shaped with steep sides. The greatest volcanic explosion in recent times destroyed the volcanic island of Krakatoa in 1883. The explosion set off a terrible tsunami, which killed 36,000 people in the nearby islands of Java and Sumatra.

Quiet volcanoes contain magma with little gas. They erupt by discharging streams of bubbling lava, which flows swiftly from the vent, often covering great distances before solidifying. Quiet volcanoes are flattened and shield-like in shape.

Many volcanoes are intermediate and combine both explosive and quiet eruptions. For example, the famous eruption of Vesuvius in AD 79 was explosive. Clouds of hot ash were flung into the air, burying the prosperous town of Pompeii. The nearby town of Herculaneum was engulfed by a mud-flow, consisting of hot ash mixed with rainwater. No lava streams appeared in AD 79, but they have accompanied most later eruptions. Scientific observatories have been set up around many active volcanoes in order to give warning of possible eruptions.

Hot springs and emissions of gas and steam are associated with dormant volcanoes. But the heat required for hot springs may also come from friction caused by earthquakes or from radioactivity. Geysers are spectacular kinds of hot springs, because they erupt tall columns of hot water and steam into the air. Some geyser eruptions are caused by steam pushing the water upwards. In other cases, gases in the heated water force it up.

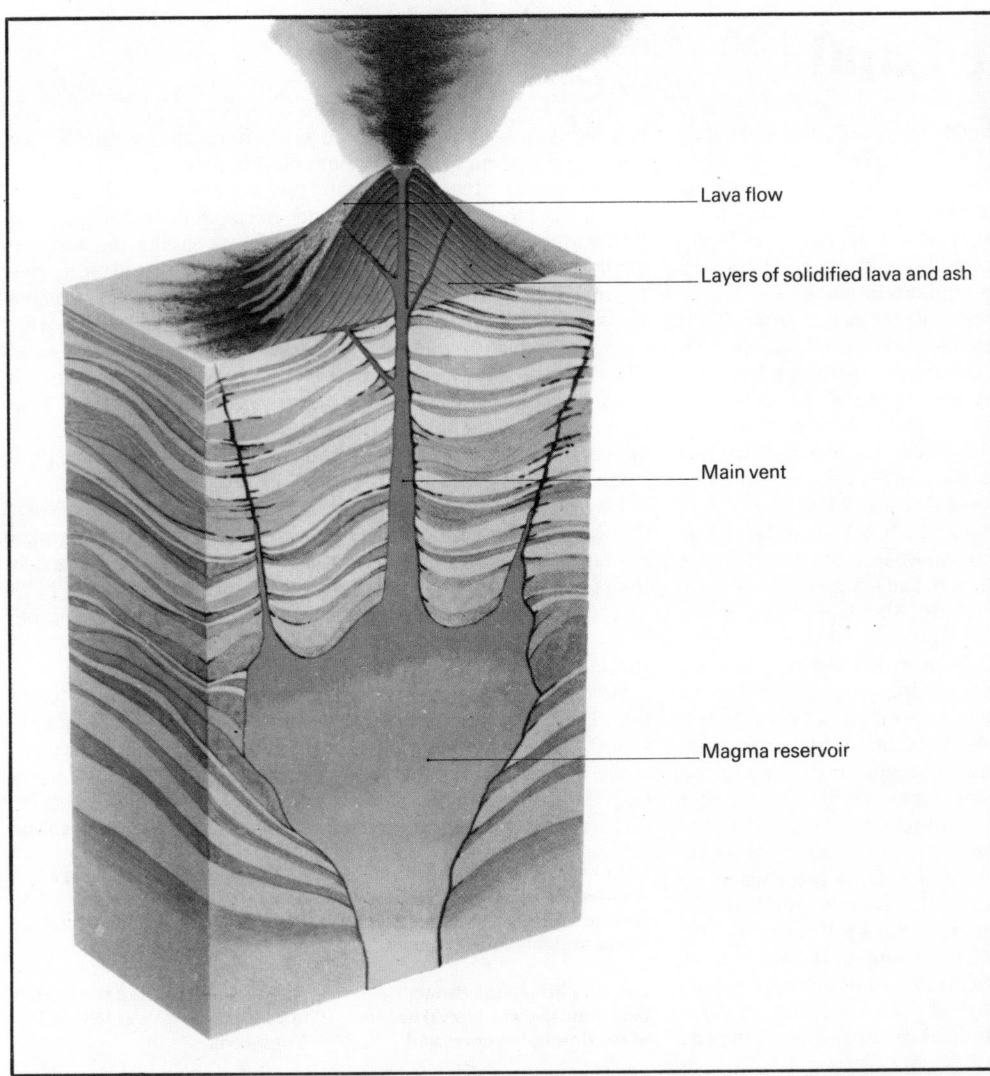
Lava flow
Layers of solidified lava and ash
Main vent
Magma reservoir

VOLCANIC ERUPTIONS

Scientists estimate that the greatest volcanic explosion in recorded history occurred in about 1470 BC, when the volcanic island of Santorini (now Thira), in the Aegean Sea, erupted with the power of 130 times the greatest H-bomb blast. The explosion removed about 62 square kilometres (15 cubic miles) of rock. Scientists also think that the eruption generated a tsunami, 50 metres (164 feet) high, which may have obliterated the Minoan civilization on Crete. The greatest eruption recently had only about one-fifth of the power of the Santorini eruption. It occurred in 1883 at Krakatoa, a volcanic island between Java and Sumatra. The sound of the explosion was heard more than 4,700 kilometres (2,900 miles) away.

Left: **Molten magma is forced upwards through the vent of a volcano, where it forms fine ash, rocky fragments or lava streams.**

Left: **The photograph of exposed rocks in Dyfed (formerly Pembrokeshire) in southwestern Wales shows how rock strata can be folded by Earth movements. In this case, the top part of the fold has been thrust over the bottom part along a fault in the rock.**

Right: **The Alps are a range of recently folded mountains. They were squeezed upwards as the Earth's plate bearing Africa moved towards the European plate. Smaller, intervening plates were rammed against the European mainland and the sedimentary rocks between were folded upwards. But, even as mountains rise, natural forces, such as weathering and valley glaciers, wear them down.**

Shaping of the Land

We tend to think of landscapes as unchanging and, in one person's lifetime, the land does not seem to alter, unless it is subject to human interference. But, in fact, the land is constantly changing, albeit slowly. Geologists estimate that, on average, about 3.4 centimetres (1.3 inches) of land is removed overall from North America every 1,000 years. Over millions of years, therefore, such erosion can remove the highest mountain ranges.

The rate of natural erosion varies considerably. It proceeds at its fastest rate in mountainous regions and is least effective on plains. Eroded material is broken down into smaller and smaller fragments during its transportation until it finally comes to rest, usually on the floors of seas or lakes. There, it accumulates in layers which become compacted together, possibly forming the building material for new mountain ranges which will arise millions of years later, only to be worn down in their turn.

A group of processes instrumental in the break up and decay of rocks are called weathering. Mechanical weathering occurs in hot deserts when rocks are rapidly heated and cooled. The widely alternating temperatures crack the outer shells of rocks, which peel away like layers of an onion — a process called *exfoliation.* And, in moist, temperate regions, water accumulates in rock crevices. But, when it freezes, the ice occupies nine per cent more space than the water. So it exerts such pressure on the rocks that it eventually prises them apart. Also included in mechanical weathering are the actions of plants and animals. For example, the downward-probing roots of trees can break boulders apart, and burrowing animals play a major role in the disintegration of rocks.

Chemical weathering involves the decay or dissolving of rocks. For example, *hydrolysis* is a process of rock decay caused by chemical reactions between water and minerals, such as the conversion of potash feldspar in granite into kaolin, a clay. The removal of rocks in solution results, for example, from a process called *carbonation.* Carbonation occurs in limestone rocks, which consist mostly of calcium carbonate and are insoluble in pure water. But rainwater, which contains carbon dioxide from the air, is a weak solution of carbonic acid. It reacts chemically with limestone to form soluble calcium bicarbonate.

Limestone plateaux are usually bleak areas. The exposed rocks are riven by vertical joints and horizontal bedding planes. Rainwater dissolves and widens the joints, giving the surface a paving-stone character. The surface is also pitted with deep fissures called swallow-holes, sink-holes or pot-holes. Some of these holes are dry, while others are entrances for streams, which plunge down into the subterranean world of limestone caves. These complex networks of passages and caverns were formed by water percolating through the joints and bedding planes. Many caves contain redeposited calcium carbonate in such features as hanging stalactites, pillar-like stalagmites and thin, wavy deposits resembling rock curtains.

One of the hazards of pot-holing (exploring limestone caves) is that heavy rainstorms can rapidly raise the level of subterranean rivers, trapping and drowning those within. These underground rivers usually return to the surface as a spring at the base of the limestone outcrop. Springs occur when any *aquifer* (water-bearing rock layer), such as limestone or sandstone, appears at the surface. Springs form the sources of streams and rivers.

Rivers are major agents of erosion, transportation and deposition. In their upper reaches, or youthful stage, they tumble down steep gradients, sweeping stones and, occasionally, boulders along their beds. As the loose fragments bump along the river beds they wear away more rock, causing downward erosion. This gives youthful rivers their characteristic steep-sided V-shaped

Below left: **Rivers are agents of erosion and deposition. Oxbow lakes are formed when meandering rivers straighten their courses.**

Below: **This section through limestone shows a typical network of swallow holes, caves and underground streams. Gorges occur when caves collapse. Stalactites and stalagmites are deposited in caves.**

Right: **Stalactites and stalagmites in a limestone cave at Divica, in Yugoslavia.**

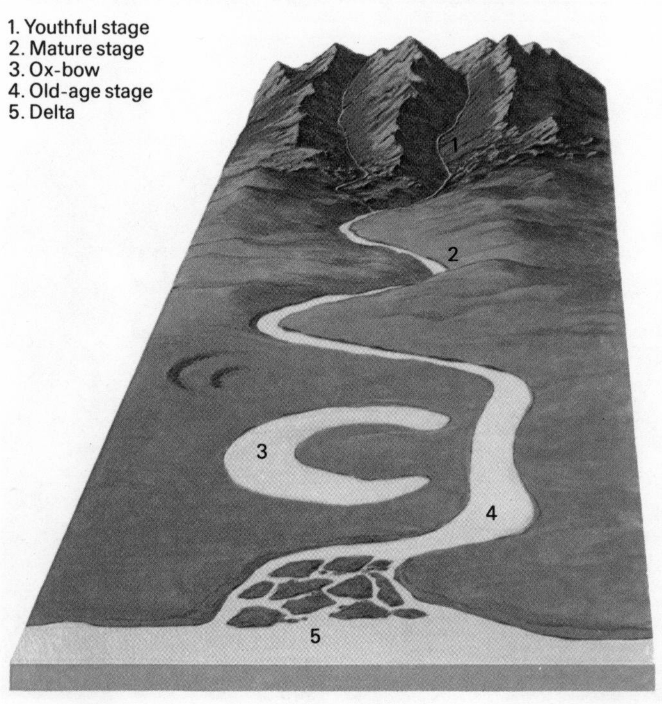
1. Youthful stage
2. Mature stage
3. Ox-bow
4. Old-age stage
5. Delta
1
2
3
4
5

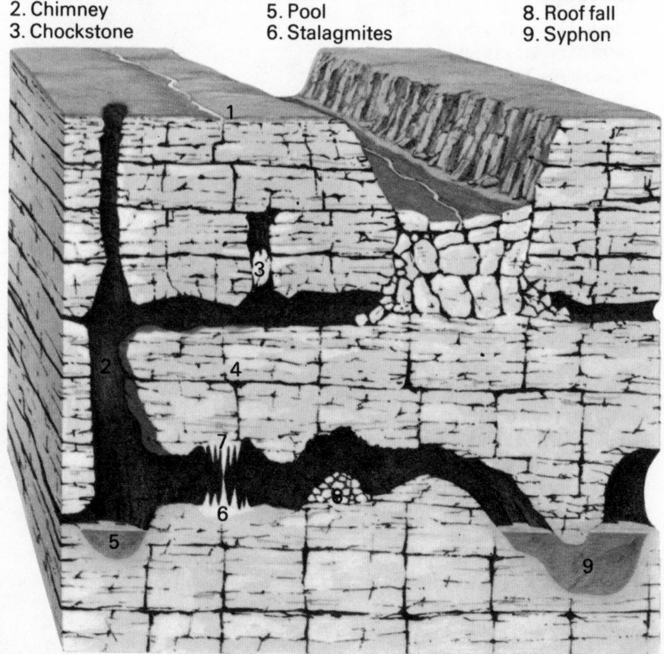
1. Swallow hole
2. Chimney
3. Chockstone
4. Joints
5. Pool
6. Stalagmites
7. Stalactites
8. Roof fall
9. Syphon
1
2
3
4
5
6
7
8
9

cross-section. But, when youthful rivers cross hard rocks, waterfalls and rapids occur.

In its mature stage, the river valley is broader, but erosion continues, especially as the outer bends are undercut. In old age, there is little river erosion, but sluggish, old-age rivers are major agents of transportation. The eroded material is mostly fine-grained silt or dissolved substances. When an old-age river floods, fertile silt is spread over the land. But most eroded material reaches the sea, at which point it may accumulate in deltas, if tides are weak, or be spread over the sea floor.

Occasionally, spectacular valleys result from the *rejuvenation* of old-age rivers. Rejuvenation occurred, for example, when a flat, coastal plain was uplifted to form the Colorado Plateau in the south-western United States. With a gradually increasing gradient, the Colorado River has etched the magnificent Grand Canyon into the plateau.

Ice sheets and glaciers in polar or mountain regions, the wind in arid and semi-arid areas, and the restless sea around coasts are other agents of erosion, transportation and deposition.

During the Pleistocene Ice Age, which began about 600,000 years ago and ended between 10,000 and 20,000 years ago, thick ice covered much of North America and northern Eurasia. The advance and retreat of the ice had a great effect on scenery.

In the world today, there are only two large ice sheets, one covering nearly all of Antarctica, and the other 85 per cent of Greenland. There are also smaller ice sheets in parts of northern Canada, Iceland, Norway and Spitzbergen. And valley glaciers occur above the permanent snowline in mountain regions in most parts of the world, even on the Equator. The total volume of land ice is the equivalent of 2.15 per cent of the world's total water supply. If all this ice were to melt, the sea level would rise by 60 to 90 metres (200 to 300 feet).

Large bodies of ice mould scenery as they slide downhill. Valley glaciers display the fastest movement, usually about one metre (three feet) per day, whereas the ice sheet of Antactica takes about a year to advance the same distance. Sometimes, the volume of a valley glacier is suddenly increased, for example, by an earthquake that dislodges snow and sends it crashing onto the glacier's source. This happened in 1936–7 on the Black Rapids glacier, Alaska, whose speed, as a result, reached a maximum of 60 metres (200 feet) in one day.

Glaciers transport weathered rock on their surfaces, within the ice or frozen in the base. Jagged rock fragments in the base of glaciers scrape over the land, eroding deep U-shaped valleys. Fiords are formerly glaciated valleys now filled by the sea. Near the source of valley glaciers, the ice freezes around projecting rocks and plucks them away. This action creates armchair-shaped basins called *cirques.* When two cirques are back to back, ice

erosion creates a knife-edge ridge, called an *arête,* between them. When three or more cirques occur back to back, a pyramidal peak, or *horn,* is formed.

Ice-eroded rock fragments, ranging in size from fine clay to boulders, are finally dumped as *moraine.* Around the snouts of glaciers, ridges of terminal moraine often accumulate. And streams issuing from glaciers transport the moraine for some distance. Large boulders composed of different rocks from the bedrock are sometimes dumped by the ice. Such boulders are called *erratics.*

Many land features in hot deserts were carved by water, either in the past, when the climate was different, or during occasional storms that occur every few years. But a major agent of desert erosion is wind-blown sand. Because sand particles are heavy, even the strongest winds cannot lift them much higher than an adult's shoulders. Erosion, therefore, occurs at low levels. But sandstorms can strip the paint off cars and frost their windscreens. Similarly, wind-blown sand can cut deeply into layers of softer rock or lines of weakness. And it can lead to the carving of mushroom rocks, which are supported by a narrow, precarious-looking pedestal. Wind-blown sand also scours rock surfaces, creating extensive depressions.

Sand covers only parts of the world's hot deserts. There are large areas of sandless *hammada* (bare rock) and *reg* (gravelly plains). Areas of sand are called *erg.* The sand accumulates in drifting dunes, some of which are crescent-shaped (*barchans*) and others are long ridges (*seif dunes*). Sand dunes are also features of some coasts.

Around coasts, the sea is constantly wearing away land, breaking up rocks into smaller particles and transporting debris out to sea or along the coast to create new land areas. Storm waves have great power. Hurled at cliffs, the waves trap and compress air in crevices. When the pressure is released, the air expands with explosive force, shattering the cliff rocks. Storm waves also lift up and bombard the shore with loose material, ranging from sand to boulders. The sea's weaponry undermines coastal rocks, cutting bays, caves, and natural arches through headlands. When natural arches collapse, rocky islets, or *stacks,* are left isolated in the sea.

Wave erosion is most effective on softer rocks. The Holderness coast of southeastern Yorkshire, England, is composed of glacial deposits. Since Roman times, the sea has removed a belt of around 4 to 5 kilometres (2.5 to 3 miles) of land from this coast.

Waves usually approach land at an oblique angle but, after the waves break, the water flows back at right angles to the shore. This means that the water and its load of sand and gravel move in a zig-zag path along the shore. When the direction of the coast changes, the loose material is dropped to form low ridges called *spits.* Some spits, called *tombolos,* link the mainland to an island.

Far left: **The Aletsch glacier in Switzerland is Europe's largest.**

Left: **Chesil Beach in Dorset, England has been formed by shingle deposited by the tides.**

Below: **This mushroom rock in Bahrain has been undercut by the abrasive action of wind-blown sand.**

Right: **This stretch of coastline in Northern Ireland is being steadily eroded by the sea. Wave action carves out bays. And caves, worn in headlands, meet to form natural arches. When the arches collapse, isolated stacks remain.**

Physical Statistics

The Earth

Dimensions: The Earth is flattened at the poles and bulges slightly at the Equator. Hence, the equatorial diameter and circumference are larger than the polar diameter and circumference.
Equatorial diameter: 12,756 kilometres (7,926 miles).
Equatorial circumference: 40,075 kilometres (24,901 miles).
Polar diameter: 12,713 kilometres (7,899 miles).
Polar circumference: 40,007 kilometres (24,859 miles).
Area: 510,061,938 square kilometres (196,936,480 square miles).
Land and water: Land covers 148,324,824 square kilometres (57,268,670 square miles) — about 29 per cent of the Earth's surface. Water covers 361,737,114 square kilometres (139,667,810 square miles) — about 71 per cent of the Earth's surface.
Mass: 5,976 million million metric tonnes (5,882 million million tons).

The Oceans

Size: Pacific Ocean 165,236,000 square kilometres (63,798,000 square miles); Atlantic Ocean 81,660,000 square kilometres (31,529,000 square miles); Indian Ocean 73,442,000 square kilometres (28,356,000 square miles); Arctic Ocean 14,351,000 square kilometres (5,541,000 square miles).
Volume of water: 1,300 million cubic kilometres (312 million cubic miles).
Deepest Point: 11.033 kilometres (6.856 miles), Challenger Deep in the Marianas Trench in the Pacific Ocean.
Highest wave in the open sea: 34 metres (112 feet) recorded in the Pacific by the U.S.S. *Ramapo* in 1933.
Largest islands: Greenland, 2,175,485 square kilometres (839,961 square miles); New Guinea 820,617 square kilometres (316,843 square miles); Borneo 743,211 square kilometres (286,956 square miles).
Highest oceanic mountain: Mauna Kea, Hawaii, rises 10,203 metres (33,474 feet) from the sea floor. (Mauna Kea is only 4,205 metres (13,796 feet) above sea level.)

Rivers

The World's Ten Largest Rivers

River	Continent	Length
Nile	Africa	6,670 km (4,145 miles)
Amazon	South America	6,448 km (4,007 miles)
Mississippi-Missouri	North America	6,270 km (3,896 miles)
Yangtze	Asia	4,990 km (3,101 miles)
Zaire	Africa	4,670 km (2,902 miles)
Amur	Asia	4,410 km (2,740 miles)
Hwang Ho	Asia	4,350 km (2,703 miles)
Lena	Asia	4,260 km (2,647 miles)
Mekong	Asia	4,180 km (2,597 miles)
Niger	Africa	4,180 km (2,597 miles)

The Amazon and its tributaries occupy the world's largest river basin, covering 7,045,000 square kilometres (2,720,000 square miles). One tributary, the Madeira, is the world's longest tributary. The Amazon also has the greatest flow of water, with an average discharge into the Atlantic of 120,000 cubic metres per second (4.2 million cubic feet per second).

Lakes

The largest lake, or inland sea, is the salty Caspian Sea, which is enclosed between Iran and the U.S.S.R. It covers 424,198 square kilometres (163,784 square miles). The largest freshwater lake, Lake Superior, lies between Canada and the United States. It has an area of 82,400 square kilometres (31,815 square miles). The highest large lake is Lake Titicaca, which is in the Andes range between Peru and Bolivia. Its surface is 3,812 metres (12,507 feet) above sea level. The lowest lake is the Dead Sea, whose shoreline is 395 metres (1,296 feet) below the mean sea level of the nearby Mediterranean Sea.

Mountains

World's highest mountains: Mount Everest 8,848 metres (29,029 feet) in the Himalayan range; K2 (Mount Godwin-Austen) 8,611 metres (28,251 feet) in the Karakoram range; Kanchenjunga 8,598 metres (28,209 feet) in the Himalayan range.
Highest in Africa: Mount Kilimanjaro 5,895 metres (19,341 feet).
Highest in North America: Mount McKinley 6,194 metres (20,320 feet)
Highest in South America: Mount Aconcagua 6,960 metres (22,835 feet).
Highest in Europe: Mount Elbrus 5,633 metres (18,481 feet).
Highest in Australia: Mount Kosciusko 2,230 metres (7,316 feet).
Highest in New Zealand: Mount Cook 3,764 metres (12,349 feet).

Above: **The River Amazon has a greater flow of water than any other river. It discolours the Atlantic Ocean for about 300 kilometres (190 miles) off the coast of Brazil.**

Right: **Mount Everest, in the Himalayas, is the world's highest peak. The first men to reach the summit were Sir Edmund Hillary and Tensing Norgay on May 29, 1953.**

The Living World

Vegetation

The natural vegetation of a place results from the interaction of soils, landforms and climate. Soils are complex substances, composed mostly of weathered particles, together with some humus (the decayed remains of plants and animals), water, air and countless micro-organisms. The nature of some soils depends on such factors as the bedrock or poor drainage. But the character of most soils is determined by climate. Such *zonal* soils are divided broadly into *pedalfers* in wet regions and *pedocals* in regions with much less rainfall.

For example, in rainy, tropical regions, soils are heavily leached — that is, soluble minerals are dissolved out of the top layer and removed completely or redeposited lower down. Characteristic wet tropical soils are the heavily-leached, reddish latosols, the top layer of which is laterite. This contains mostly insoluble substances, including iron, which colours the soil, bauxite and manganese. Other pedalfers include the greyish podzols of cold, snowy climates. Podzols are also heavily leached.

In regions with comparatively little rainfall, there is much less leaching and the top layers are coloured by humus. For example, the black chernozems of steppelands and the dark brown soils of prairies are pedocals coloured by decayed grass.

Soil and natural vegetation regions, therefore, follow a broadly similar pattern to climatic regions. When geographers talk of natural vegetation, they mean the climax vegetation — that is, the most flourishing vegetation that could occur in an area with particular soils and climate, providing it has not been altered by man. For example, the broadleaf forests of the eastern United States and western and central Europe have been mostly cut down. But, if man ceased to interfere with the natural plant life of these regions, broadleaf forests would probably reassert themselves before long.

Polar ice sheets, ice caps and adjacent areas that are permanently covered by snow are almost devoid of plant life. But the polar tundra has a short warm summer, when the top few centimetres of the soil thaw. Flat areas become marshes, and mosses, lichens and various flowering plants thrive. Beneath the surface layer, however, is permafrost — permanently frozen ground. This factor, together with the cold, prevents the growth of trees, other than dwarf shrubs.

Cold, snowy climates are characterized by vast forests of conifers. Conifers are especially well adapted to cold climates. Their narrow, conical shapes prevent over-loading by snow, their

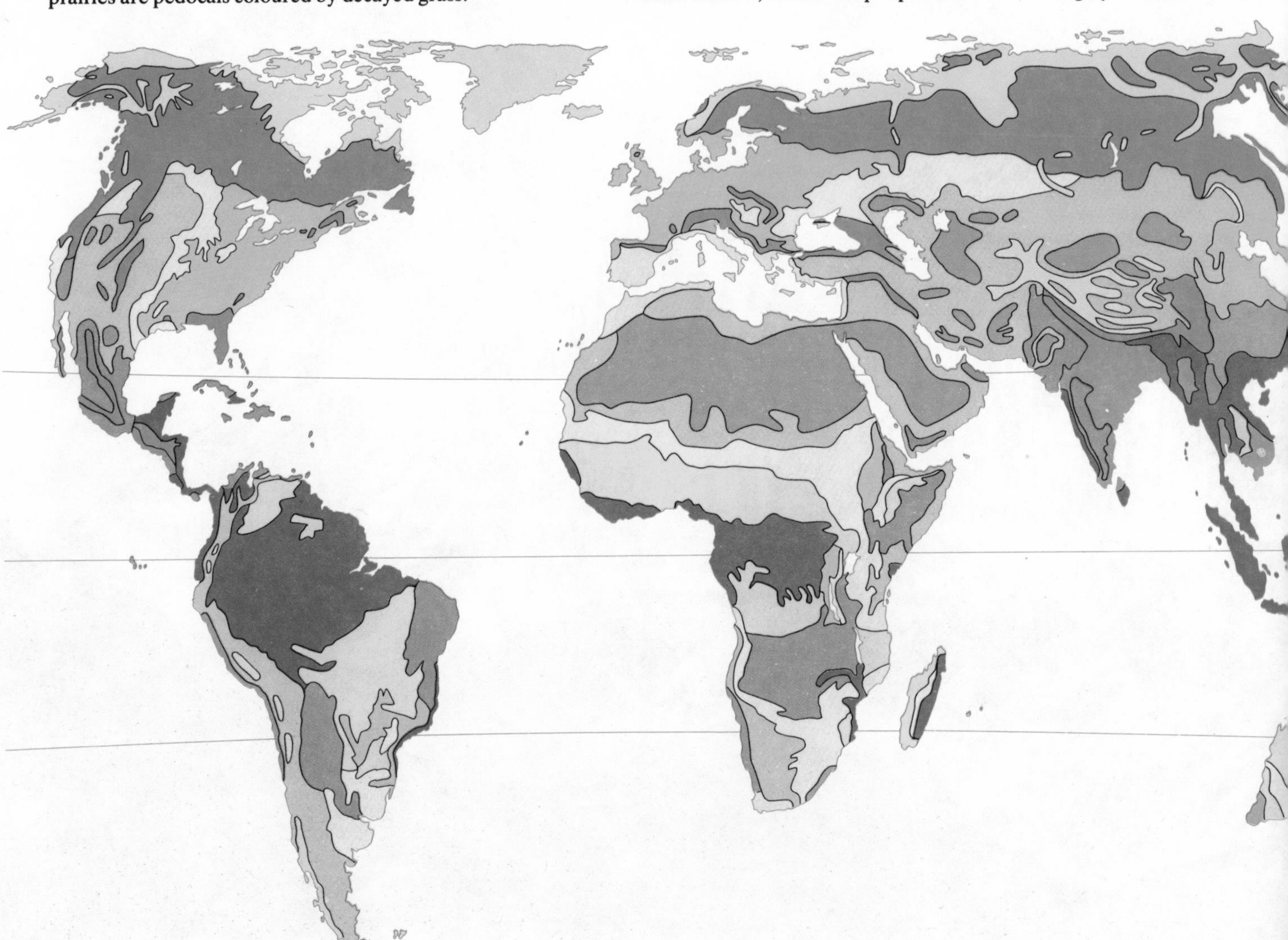

shallow roots absorb moisture, even when the subsoil freezes, and thick barks give protection against the cold. With the exception of larches, conifers are evergreens. Conifers also grow in Mediterranean regions, where their adaptations fit them to withstand the summer drought.

The boreal (northern) coniferous forests merge southwards into the broadleaf, or deciduous, forest belt. Deciduous trees are adapted to moist, temperate climates, with some rainfall throughout the year and temperatures above 6°C (43°F) for six months of the year. In autumn, deciduous trees shed their leaves, which form a thick carpet of humus on the forest floor. When the forests are cut down, their rich brown soils are very productive.

Grasslands are of two main kinds: the mid-latitude grasslands in continental interiors, including steppelands and prairies; and the tropical grasslands. In the mid-latitude grasslands, trees are rare, partly because of the aridity and partly because winters are extremely cold. Savanna is a term for tropical grassland, broken by scattered trees or patches of forest and merging into thorn forest and dry scrub. Tropical grasslands lie broadly between the equatorial forests and the sub-tropical deserts.

The world's hot deserts contain various xerophytes (drought-resistant plants). Adaptations include long, shallow roots, which absorb moisture from a large area; thick stems, which store water; and waxy coverings, which reduce loss of moisture by transpiration. Some plants spring to life after the rare, infrequent rainstorms, and they may seed within two weeks of sprouting. The seeds may lie dormant for several years until the next rainstorm starts a new growth cycle.

The tropical forests include rain forests, with rain all the year round, and monsoon forests, where the rainfall is markedly seasonal. With abundant rainfall and high temperatures, tropical forests are luxuriant, and hundreds of species may occur in a small area. Trees grow to 30 to 40 metres (100 to 130 feet), with some protruding to more than 50 metres (160 feet). The thick canopy of leaves in the tree tops blocks out light from the forest floor, so few plants grow on the ground. Most of the other forest plants are climbers, such as vines, or epiphytes (parasitical plants).

Mountain regions have varying vegetation according to the altitude. Ascending some high mountains around the Equator is like taking a short trip to the poles. One can start in tropical forest, then climb through changing belts of vegetation and finally encounter tundra and polar conditions around the peak.

Natural vegetation

- Tundra & ice
- Coniferous forest
- Broadleaf forest
- Mediterranean scrub
- Grassland
- Savanna
- Sub tropical forest
- Dry tropical scrub & thorn forest
- Monsoon forest
- Tropical rain forest
- Scrub, steppe and semidesert
- Desert

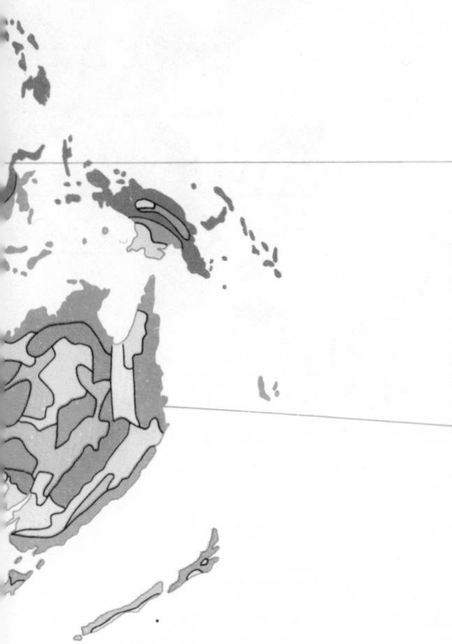

Right: **Parts of the world's hot deserts are covered by barren shifting sands. Permanent settlement is possible only at oases.**

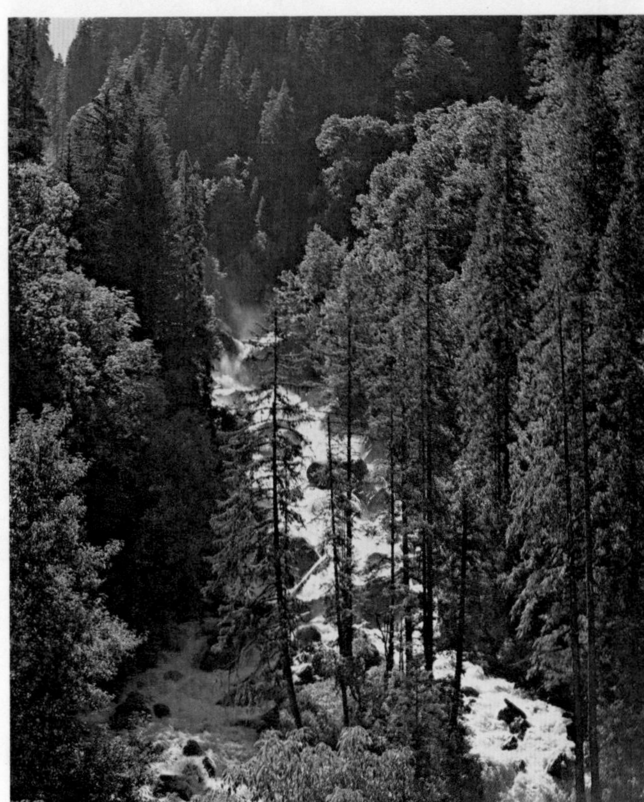

Below right: **The Himalayan foothills support luxuriant forests. But the vegetation gradually changes with altitude.**

Below: **The prairies of Alberta, in Canada, are part of the world's vast mid-latitude grasslands.**

Evolution

Fossils, found in sedimentary rocks, are evidence of ancient life. Fast burial is a prerequisite for fossilization because, otherwise, plants and animals decay quickly. But, once buried, teeth, bones and other hard parts, such as shells and woody tissue, may be preserved. Many remains are petrified (turned to stone) by the replacement of each molecule of the organism by a molecule of a mineral. Some fossils are casts or moulds of organisms, while plant leaves and soft-bodied creatures, such as jellyfish, can be preserved as smears of carbon. Other fossils include animal droppings, footprints and holes bored by worms.

Ancient Greek scholars realized that most fossils were the remains of sea creatures and concluded that the rocks in which they occurred were once under the sea. But, when ancient Greece declined, this understanding was lost. For about 2,000 years, many fanciful ideas were advanced to explain fossils. Some people thought that they were the work of the Devil, who had put them in rocks to confuse us. Fossil belemnites, extinct creatures similar to cuttlefishes, are still sometimes called 'Devil's thunderbolts.'

In the 1700s, the Scottish geologist James Hutton deduced that sedimentary rocks were formed mostly on the floors of seas and

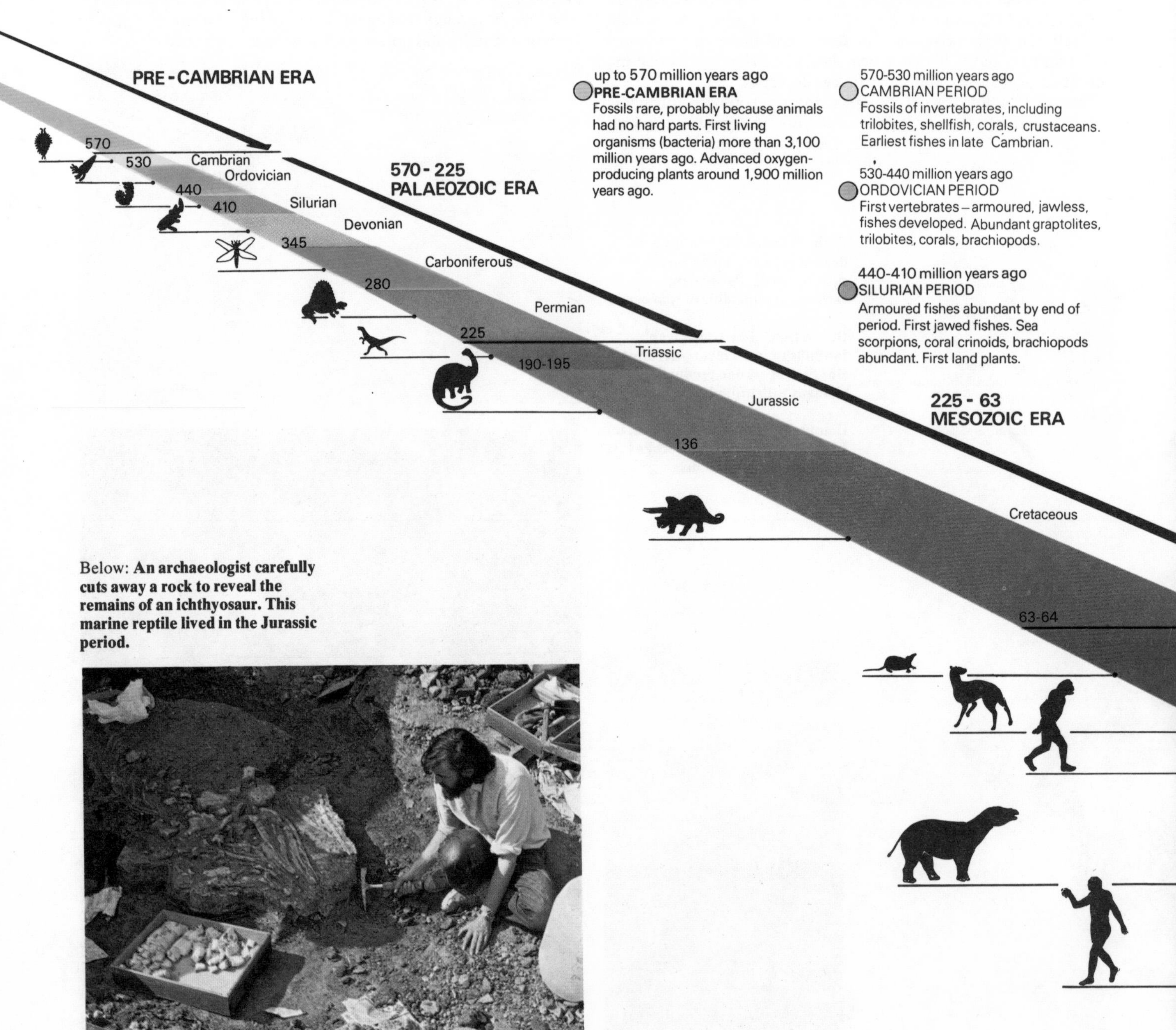

PRE-CAMBRIAN ERA
570
530
Cambrian
Ordovician
440
410
Silurian
Devonian
345
Carboniferous
280
Permian
225
190-195
Triassic
Jurassic
136
Cretaceous
63-64
570 - 225
PALAEOZOIC ERA
225 - 63
MESOZOIC ERA
up to 570 million years ago
PRE-CAMBRIAN ERA
Fossils rare, probably because animals had no hard parts. First living organisms (bacteria) more than 3,100 million years ago. Advanced oxygen-producing plants around 1,900 million years ago.
570-530 million years ago
CAMBRIAN PERIOD
Fossils of invertebrates, including trilobites, shellfish, corals, crustaceans. Earliest fishes in late Cambrian.
530-440 million years ago
ORDOVICIAN PERIOD
First vertebrates – armoured, jawless, fishes developed. Abundant graptolites, trilobites, corals, brachiopods.
440-410 million years ago
SILURIAN PERIOD
Armoured fishes abundant by end of period. First jawed fishes. Sea scorpions, coral crinoids, brachiopods abundant. First land plants.

Below: **An archaeologist carefully cuts away a rock to reveal the remains of an ichthyosaur. This marine reptile lived in the Jurassic period.**

lakes. Their formation was slow, but they accumulated in great thicknesses before, eventually, they were raised up to form new land. The slow rate of sedimentation made Hutton and others appreciate that the Earth must be extremely old.

In the early 1800s, a British canal engineer William Smith collected fossils and began to classify rocks according to the fossils in them. He understood that, if two rock layers, however far apart, contained the same kind of fossils, then they were of the same age. Geologists were then able to work out the sequence, or relative ages, of sedimentary rocks, grouping them into eras, periods and epochs. The meaning of fossils was further clarified by the work of Charles Darwin, who advanced the theory of evolution by natural selection in his *Origin of the Species* (1859). In the early 1900s, the discovery that radioactive elements decay at specific rates made it possible to provide absolute dates for rocks and their associated fossils.

Although many gaps occur in the fossil record, a clear pattern of evolutionary history has emerged. When a plant or animal group evolves from its ancestral form, such as the first reptiles from the amphibians in the Carboniferous period, the group first passes through a *divergence phase,* in which the group diverges from its ancestors by producing new features. *Improvement* follows as the group's new features are adapted by natural selection. Then, by a process called *adaptive radiation,* the group spreads to all available environments. For example, the reptiles evolved large and small species that lived on land, in the sea and in the air. Finally, however, comes *extinction.*

From a study of Earth history, extinction seems to be the fate of all species, even the most successful. Most large reptiles became extinct at the end of the Mesozoic era. Many theories have been advanced to explain what happened, including climatic changes, overpopulation, the bombardment of the Earth by cosmic rays, and the destruction of their eggs by mammals. But the extinction of species, whatever the reason, always seems to involve some change in the environment to which the group is unable to adapt.

410-345 million years ago
DEVONIAN PERIOD
Age of Fishes. Amphibians evolved near end of period. Plants spread on land. First insects. Graptolites died out.

345-280 million years ago
CARBONIFEROUS PERIOD
Amphibians increased. Reptiles evolved. Insects common. Many corals, brachiopods and fishes in seas.

280-225 million years ago
PERMIAN PERIOD
Reptiles spread on land. Ammonites in seas. But trilobites and many other sea creatures died out.

225-190 million years ago
TRIASSIC PERIOD
First dinosaurs and large sea reptiles. Ammonites abundant. First mammals evolved.

190-136 million years ago
JURASSIC PERIOD
Large reptiles, including dinosaurs and flying reptiles (pterosaurs) abundant. First bird (archaeopteryx) appeared. Ammonites and belemnites abundant in seas. Some mammals on land.

136-63 million years ago
CRETACEOUS PERIOD
Reptiles, including dinosaurs, dominated the land, but most died out at end of period, as did ammonites and many other sea creatures. Small mammals lived throughout period.

63-2 million years ago
TERTIARY
Palaeocene 63-44 million years ago
Rapid development of mammals.
Eocene 44-38 million years ago
First horses and elephants.
Oligocene 38-26 million years ago
Early apes; ancestors of many modern mammals.
Miocene 26-7 million years ago
Greatest variety of mammals.
Pliocene 7-2 million years ago
Man-apes in Africa. Many larger mammals died out.

2-0 million years ago
QUATERNARY PERIOD
Pleistocene 2-0.01 million years ago
Rise of man. Woolly mammoths and rhinos in cold northern hemisphere.
Recent 0.01-0 million years ago
Modern man.

Above: **The petrified remains of a pterosaur (flying reptile), which lived in the Jurassic period.**

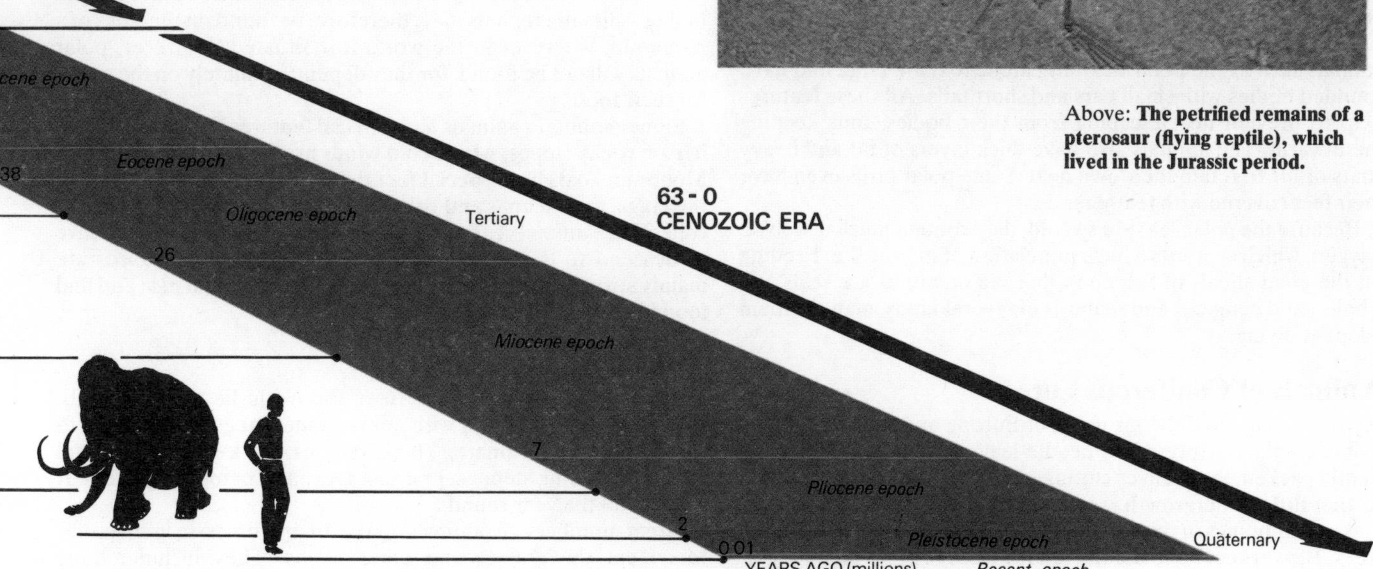
Palaeocene epoch
38
Eocene epoch
Oligocene epoch
Tertiary
63 - 0
CENOZOIC ERA
26
Miocene epoch
7
Pliocene epoch
2
0.01
Pleistocene epoch
Quaternary
YEARS AGO (millions)
Recent epoch

Animal Life

Virtually every part of our planet is inhabited by animals. Only the icy wastes at the poles, the chill summits of the highest mountains and the thin air of the upper atmosphere are devoid of life — apart from human visitors. Elsewhere, animals exist in profusion and in great diversity.

There are two main reasons why the Earth possesses a wide range of animals. Physical barriers — mountain chains, oceans and seas, and deserts — separate the land into six zoogeographic regions, each containing its own particular kinds of animals. The barriers prevent the animals from intermixing, and distinct populations have evolved in each one. For example, the Australian region has monotreme animals, such as the duck-billed platypus, and many marsupials, including kangaroos. And the neo-tropical region contains most of the hummingbirds. Because islands in the ocean are isolated from the rest of the world, they often contain special kinds of animals not found elsewhere. In the oceans, different kinds of animals live at different depths.

The second factor that determines the kind of animals that live in a particular region is climate. Each of the climatic zones of the world has its own kind of animal life, because the animals have evolved to suit the conditions there. Similar environments tend to produce similar animals, even though they may be in different parts of the world and of different animal families. Desert animals, for example, are often very alike wherever they are found, having been shaped by the same harsh conditions. In considering the kinds of animals that inhabit the Earth, it is, therefore, better to look at them in the various climatic zones rather than the zoogeographic regions.

Animals of the Polar Regions

The polar regions are basically different from each other: the Arctic consists of a frozen sea surrounded by cold coasts, while the Antarctic is an ice-covered continent surrounded by cold seas. However, both regions are white with snow and ice. In the Arctic, many of the animals are also white so that they cannot easily be seen against their surroundings. In this way, they escape the attentions of other animals that hunt them or, if they are themselves hunters, they cannot easily be spotted by their prey. These white animals include the polar bear, arctic fox, arctic hare and snowy owl. In the Antarctic, few animals live on the ice cap because it is so cold, but many are found on the surrounding islands. Many of them, such as seals and penguins, and Arctic animals such as the polar bear and arctic fox, are large and have rounded bodies with small ears and short tails. All these features help to prevent heat escaping from their bodies, thus keeping them warm. The animals also have thick layers of fat and heavy coats of fur to retain their own heat. Some polar birds even have their feet covered with feathers.

Because the polar seas are so cold, they contain much dissolved oxygen, which supports a huge population of marine life. Feeding on the great shoals of fish and other sea creatures are seals and whales, and penguins and seabirds of several kinds, many of them adept at diving.

Animals of Coniferous Forests

Across Canada and the far north of Europe and Asia stretches a belt of coniferous forest. The needle-leaved evergreen trees stand tightly packed, their leaves cutting out the light all the year round so that little undergrowth surrounds their trunks. Many animals make their homes in this cold, forbidding place. Some feed on the trees. Beavers eat the bark and fell the trees to build their lodges; grouse consume the leaves and buds, and crossbills can cut open the cones with their special crossing beaks to get at the seeds inside. Squirrels clamber about the trees, opening cones and storing the seeds for winter. Chipmunks also store seeds but hibernate for the winter, waking now and then when they get hungry. Insect-eating birds, such as woodpeckers and tits, work their way over the branches, pecking in crevices in the bark. Small mammals, such as voles and lemmings, wander over the ground eating plants and burrow beneath the snow in winter to find food. Other animals survive by preying on these creatures. Bears, lynxes and weasels hunt among the trees; hawks and falcons swoop from the air by day, and owls do so by night.

Animals of the Deciduous Forests

South of the coniferous forest, and also in the southernmost parts of the southern hemisphere, lies a broad belt of deciduous forest. Here the climate is mild and the trees shed their leaves in winter. Leaf mould builds up on the ground and light comes in, enabling a tangled undergrowth of shrubs and bushes to grow among the trees. Evergreen trees may be found too. Many different kinds of animals live in the forest. The leaves are easier to eat than the tough leaves of conifers, and caterpillars and aphids munch their way through plants, while deer browse among the trees. Birds, such as finches, and squirrels, mice and other small mammals take the seeds and buds. Other birds, including European warblers, and mammals, such as hedgehogs, seek insects in the forest. These insect eaters find food scarce in winter, so the birds migrate to warmer climes or rely on seeds, while the mammals may hibernate for the winter. Predators also hunt among the trees, as they do in coniferous forests. They include foxes, snakes, polecats, badgers, wild cats and birds of prey. However, their prey is not always defenceless — the skunk is famous for the way it squirts an evil-smelling liquid at predators, and many potential victims hide safely among the leaves and undergrowth.

Animals of Mountains

Because it gets colder as you go up a mountain, several different zones of life exist. There may be deciduous forest at the bottom, coniferous forest halfway up, and then a polar scene with scanty plants and snow at the top. Kinds of animals similar to those found in these climatic regions may, therefore, be found on the sides of a mountain, wherever in the world it is situated. However, polar animals will not be found, for they depend ultimately on the ocean for their food.

Some mountain animals have special features that help them to live on rocky slopes, where cold winds howl and few plants grow. Mountain goats have special feet that enable them to leap among the crags, and vicunas and yaks have woolly coats to keep out the cold. These animals can survive on poor plant food, but may have to descend to lower slopes for the winter. Mountain birds are mainly strong fliers, such as eagles, or small birds that nest and find food in rock crevices.

Animals of Grasslands

Between the forests and deserts of the world lie the grasslands, vast grassy plains dotted with a few stunted trees that manage to grow in the dry climate. These regions are known by several names, including steppes, prairies, savannas, pampas and veld. It is warm all the year round.

Great numbers of animals make their homes in grasslands. Many eat the grasses and other plants. They include: large mammals, such as antelopes, zebras, gazelles, bison, elephants, giraffes, rhinoceroses, wild horses and kangaroos; small mammals, such as hares and rodents; flightless birds, such as emus and ostriches; and flocks of weaver birds that raid crops in the grasslands, as do locusts and other insects. Living on these animals in turn are insect eaters, like anteaters and armadillos, and the much-feared flesh eaters, including rattlesnakes and cobras, vultures, hyenas, wild dogs, lions and cheetahs.

Being in the open, the victims of these hunting animals cannot hide from danger. Many roam the grasslands in herds, finding safety in numbers, and the elephant is just too big to be worth attacking. Smaller animals, which may have to run for their lives, possess powerful legs and feet that enable them to sprint for long periods. The smallest animals retreat into their burrows when danger threatens.

Animals of Deserts

Desert regions occur on each side of the Equator. Little, if any, rain falls throughout the year, and it is usually very hot by day, though often cold by night. The stony or sandy ground supports little plant growth. Some animals do manage to survive in these harsh conditions, but they are faced with two main problems — how to keep cool and how to save water.

Many desert animals are small — a feature that helps them to lose heat — and live in burrows. Some, such as scorpions, avoid the daytime heat by staying in their burrows, seeking food only at night. Others, such as lizards, may prefer to hunt by day, but retire into their burrows or into shade during the hottest hours. The desert fox is one of several desert animals with large ears, which help to radiate excess body heat. And some animals hop or scurry over the hot sand to escape its heat. These adaptations also help the animals to hear and escape their predators. Many desert animals, including camels, are able to withstand high body temperatures and lack of water without harm. Their bodies may even be able to produce water from a diet of seeds or plants, so that they never need to drink. Gerbils survive in this way. And because they do not sweat, they retain as much water as possible inside their bodies. Some water is inevitably lost with body wastes, but desert animals reduce this amount to the minimum possible.

Animals of Tropical Forests

Along the Equator lies a belt of tropical forest. It is always hot and has frequent rain. Trees crowd together and fight for the light, producing a thick tangle of leaves and branches.

Many animals live among the leaves and branches of the forest. They are either able to fly or are good climbers. Toucans, parrots and other birds take fruit, hummingbirds seek nectar in flowers, and butterflies and moths flutter here and there. Many of these animals are brightly coloured, though the colours do not show up so vividly among the leaves. Sloths clamber among the branches, and monkeys swing to and fro, feeding from the trees. Chameleons seek insects in the leaves, changing colour to match their surroundings, and bats hunt insects in the air. Some animals, including several lizards and squirrels, have developed ways of gliding from one tree to another. On the ground, compact animals, such as pigs and rodents, push through the undergrowth, often eating ants and other insects that abound. Pheasants scratch about the forest floor, and lizards and snakes burrow in the litter of dead leaves. Feeding on the plant-eating and insect-eating animals are the hunters, such as tigers, leopards and jaguars, civets and snakes. They seek their victims in the trees and on the ground, often hunting by night.

Below: **A king penguin colony on the island of South Georgia.**

Far top left: **The Rocky Mountain goat lives among the high peaks of the Rocky Mountains in North America, easily scaling the rocky crags.**

Above left: **The red squirrel brings colour and life to the gloom and quiet of the coniferous forest.**

Below left: **The scorpion lives in the desert. It uses its claws to dig a burrow to escape the heat, and stings with its tail.**

Far bottom left: **A tube-nosed bat hangs upside-down from a branch. Bats can fly in the dark, using sound to navigate.**

Right: **A jay feeds its young. Jays are birds of deciduous forests. They collect acorns and bury them to form a winter food reserve.**

Below: **A herd of elephants heads for a water hole. Many elephants live on the grasslands of Africa, mostly in reserves, where they are protected from hunters and ivory poachers.**

Animals of Fresh Water

Rivers, ponds and lakes are home to many different kinds of animals. Fish sweep up food particles from the water, eating water plants, insects and other small water creatures, or even hunting other fish. Birds are a common sight, finding food in the water in several ways. Grebes, for example, dive for their food, while many ducks dabble at the surface. Kingfishers plunge into the water from the air, but herons stand or wade patiently in the shallows, waiting to make a catch. Insects abound, dragonflies hovering in the air, and pond skaters rowing themselves across the water surface. Amphibians breed in water, and many frogs, toads and newts remain in or around water all their lives. Reptiles and mammals are less common, for they feed and breed mostly away from water. However, crocodiles and turtles live in warm inland waters, and some snakes can swim. Otters and water voles can dive for food, and hippos rest in water, but come ashore to feed.

Fish can survive beneath the ice through a freezing winter, though such conditions make life hard for water birds.

Animals of the Seashore

Animals that live permanently on seashores where tides come and go every day face great problems of survival. One moment they are living in cool water and the next they may find themselves in the open air, being scorched by the sun. Only special kinds of animals can live in these conditions. On rocky shores, barnacles, mussels and other shellfish close their shells tightly as the tide goes down. Sea anemones pull in their stinging tentacles and close up, while small mobile animals, such as shrimps and crabs, take refuge in rock pools. On sandy and muddy shores, shellfish and worms burrow into the damp mud or sand to prevent their bodies drying up. Some have tubes that lead to the surface to obtain food and oxygen. These small shore dwellers feed on seaweeds, on minute creatures in the water, sand or mud, or on food particles that they sift from the water or sand. The seashore is also the home of larger animals. Birds wade in the shallows, peck in the sand or mud, or fly out to sea to find food. Seals and turtles come ashore in large numbers to breed.

Above: **Crocodiles live mostly in inland waters, where they often lie with their nostrils just above the surface. They capture other animals in their powerful jaws and drag them beneath the surface, where they tear apart and devour their victims.**

Right: **The common hippopotamus is the largest freshwater mammal. Common hippos live in African rivers, sleeping and resting by day and emerging at night to feed on plants near the water.**

Far right: **A sea anemone lies ready for a small fish or other creature to approach its stinging tentacles. It will then pull in its paralyzed victim and slowly digest it.**

Animals of the Oceans

The world's oceans contain a vast range of animals, from microscopic protozoans to the blue whale, the largest animal that has ever lived. In the oceans' surface layers drift huge numbers of minute plants and animals known as *plankton.* All other sea creatures depend on plankton for food, either by eating it directly or by consuming other plankton-eating animals.

Marine animals are classed into two groups — those that swim in the sea and those that live at the bottom. In waters near the shore, where light penetrates to the sea bed, an interesting array of creatures may be found. Flatfish swim over the sea floor, changing their body patterns to match the background, wherever they settle. This enables them to escape the attention of hunting animals. Lobsters and crabs, armed with a heavy shell and threatening pincers, scuttle about, and octopuses and cuttlefish wander or hide, squirting out a cloud of ink to confuse any enemy that appears. Starfish and sea urchins, and corals and sponges are among the many other strange animals of the seabed.

Fish of all kinds swim out in the open sea. Some live in great shoals, finding safety in numbers, and they are often coloured silvery-white, which makes them almost invisible in the water. Other creatures of the open sea include turtles, squids and sea mammals, such as whales and dolphins, which must continually rise to the surface to breathe air. The depths of the open sea are completely dark as light cannot penetrate very far. There, many animals are luminous and produce their own light to hunt or find a mate. The sea floor is often covered with mud, on which long-legged creatures walk and others lie.

Animal Movements

Not all creatures are content to remain in one place all their lives. Locusts, for example, wander in search of food, settling wherever they find enough to eat, and leaving when they have stripped everything bare. But many animals make regular journeys called migrations to find food and to raise their young.

The best-known migrations are those of birds. In spring, many fly to their breeding grounds, where there will be enough food to feed their young when they are born. This food supply disappears as the winter comes, and so the birds fly back to their winter quarters to find food until the spring arrives again. In the tropics, where there may be no real summer or winter, birds may migrate in the wet and dry seasons instead. Some mammals migrate too. Caribou walk long distances between breeding grounds and winter quarters, and whales may swim from one ocean to another.

Several fishes make extraordinary migrations that take years. Eels are born in mid-ocean and migrate to the rivers of surrounding lands, where they grow up before returning to the ocean to breed. Salmon migrate in the opposite direction, being born inland and then swimming out to sea. After several years, the adult salmon swim back to their birthplace to breed.

Below left: **The shark is one of the most feared animals of the sea, though not all sharks attack man.**

Below right: **A ray, one of the flatfishes, is related to the sharks. Like sharks, rays have cartilage, not true bones. Most rays live on the sea bed, their colour matching their surroundings for camouflage.**

Bottom: **The lobster lives on the sea bed close to the shore, feeding on plants and animals.**

Threats to Life

Animals are shaped by evolution to fit their environment — unlike man, who can change his environment to suit himself. If an animal cannot change to meet man's demands on nature, then it may find itself in danger. In clearing forests to create fields for farming, or in making space for houses, man destroys the habitats of particular animals and takes away their sources of food. His domestic animals may kill them, or man himself may hunt them for their meat or for valuable products such as ivory and furs.

Animals that live on islands uninhabited by man are highly vulnerable, as they have evolved to suit a special environment. For example, birds may have lost the power to fly because there are no predatory animals with which to contend. The arrival of man changes things so abruptly that these overspecialized animals may not survive for long. The flightless dodo of Mauritius, for example, was extinct less than two centuries after the arrival of Portuguese sailors there in the early 1500s. However, not only rare, defenceless creatures are threatened. In less than a century, man succeeded in wiping out the passenger pigeon, millions of which once lived in North America. The demise of the passenger pigeon is a warning that one should never be complacent about the conservation of wildlife.

Measures are now being organized on a world-wide scale to help save animals in danger of extinction. International conferences limit the number of whales that may be captured, and a vast campaign is under way to raise money to save the tiger. Many governments ban hunting and create national parks and nature reserves to shelter rare animals. But these measures are not always very effective, or may be too late. Whalers are beginning to find that their limits have been too high and that some species of whales have nearly vanished. A hunting ban is difficult to enforce in some countries, and hunters may even enter parks and reserves. Accidents may happen: the use of DDT as a pesticide has done wonders to control insect pests but also nearly succeeded in wiping out several birds of prey. Conservationists are, therefore, also conducting projects to save threatened animals directly by removing them from their endangered habitats to zoos or breeding centres. There, efforts are made to get the animals to breed in captivity. When numbers have increased, the animals are returned to the wild. This has often been successful; the nene, or Hawaiian goose — down to about 30 birds in 1950 — is now up to about 1,000, and many birds have been repatriated.

Wherever man spreads, the waste he creates causes pollution, which threatens life on this planet, including his own existence. Instead of being treated in sewage farms, human wastes are sometimes dumped into rivers and seas. This may be hazardous to health,for example, shellfish caught in a bay near a town may be contaminated with sewage. In addition, particularly in rivers, decomposition of the sewage by bacteria uses up oxygen needed by fish and other animals. Detergents from kitchen sinks make matters worse, and the water may lose virtually all its oxygen, resulting in the loss of its animal life. Industrial wastes are also dumped into rivers and seas, sometimes with harmful effects. At Minamata in Japan, people died in the 1950s from eating fish contaminated with mercury compounds discharged into the sea from a local plastics factory. However, increasing awareness of these dangers has led to anti-pollution measures that are cleaning up many rivers. Less rosy is the outlook for oil pollution, as supertankers carry crude oil about the world in ever-larger quantities, and undersea oil drilling becomes more common. Huge leaks of oil into the sea may now occur with any accident involving a tanker or oil rig, threatening all marine life in the area.

The atmosphere is liable to pollution in several ways too. Burning fuel causes the release of gases into the air. Sulphur dioxide is among the most dangerous, for it dissolves in rain-water to produce a weak acid that can worsen breathing troubles and eat away the surfaces of buildings and statues. Furthermore, the pollutants may be blown long distances by winds and so affect places far away. In January 1974, all the winds in Europe converged on Norway for 12 days, depositing so much acid that fish were killed in lakes and rivers. Motor-cars emit lead compounds and oxides of nitrogen from their exhausts. Nitrogen oxides may contribute to breathing difficulties. In many places, air pollution has been reduced by banning the burning of coal and by treating fumes before they leave factory chimneys and the exhausts of motor-cars.

In the upper atmosphere, a layer of ozone gas prevents ultraviolet radiation from the Sun reaching the ground in harmful quantities. Scientists are worried that the ozone layer may be affected by pollution. Chemicals called fluorocarbons, released by aerosol sprays, and nitrogen oxides from jet aircraft (especially supersonic airliners, which fly very high) may be slowly destroying the ozone layer. Any resulting increase in ultraviolet rays reaching the ground could produce more skin cancer. So it may become necessary to ban aerosol sprays and there is a slight possibility that supersonic flight could be banned.

A third form of pollution, which may also affect future generations, is radioactivity. All waste from nuclear power stations produces harmful radiation, and some remains dangerous for centuries. At present, it is stored away so that no-one is harmed. But there is cause for alarm. A nuclear accident could release substantial amounts of radioactive material into the air. Nuclear installations have leaked to a small degree, and there are rumours that a nuclear accident killed many people in the U.S.S.R. several years ago. If governments build new 'fast' reactors to produce more energy, then there is a greater likelihood of a nuclear disaster because, unlike today's 'slow' reactors, fast reactors could possibly explode. Furthermore, there will be much greater amounts of long-lived radioactive waste to store, and the reactors will use plutonium, which is extremely poisonous as well as highly radioactive. For these reasons, many people are pressing governments to develop alternative energy supplies, such as wave power and solar energy, which are not polluting.

Left: **A seabird lies dead on the shore, smothered in oil.**

Above right: **In many parts of the world, waste products from factories are simply discharged into rivers and seas. As a result, fish may become contaminated with chemicals harmful to the fish or to anyone eating them.**

Right: **Oil pollution may threaten the livelihood of seaside resorts. Here a group of people clean up a beach in Brittany, France, after oil has been washed ashore.**

Far right: **A haze of pollution hangs over a town in Germany.**

Human Geography

The Human Race

Scientists consider that man and the apes are primates with a common, extinct ancestor. From fossil discoveries, we now know that various forms of man-like creatures evolved over the last 12 million years. The chief factors distinguishing man-like creatures from apes are man's larger brain and his ability to walk upright. Around 35,000 years ago, one species of man, *Homo sapiens,* became dominant, and all other forms, such as Neanderthal man, became extinct. *Homo sapiens* had been in existence for at least 70,000 years before that time.

All modern men and women, therefore, belong to the species *Homo sapiens.* And so, scientifically, all people belong to one race — the human race. But people display differing physical features, including skin colour, eye and hair colour, skull shapes, height and build. Anthropologists have devised various methods of classifying mankind, but it is generally accepted that there are three broad sub-groups. They are, in order of population size, the 'white-skinned' Caucasoids, the 'yellow-skinned' Mongoloids and the 'black-skinned' Negroids.

The term Caucasoid was first coined in the 1700s by the scientist J. F. Blumenbach, who used it to describe the people of the Caucasus mountain region between the Black Sea and the Caspian Sea — a region that was probably the original homeland of many of Europe's peoples. The term Caucasoid is now used to include a broad group of people who form the indigenous populations of Europe, southwestern Asia, India and northern and eastern Africa.

Caucasoids vary considerably. For example, skin colour ranges from white to dark brown, and eye colouring from light blue to dark brown. Hair varies from straight to curly, although body and facial hair is more abundant among Caucasoids than among other sub-groups. Caucasoids generally have narrow, prominent noses and thin lips, but all kinds of skull shapes occur, from long-headed to round-headed. The chief Caucasoid groups are the Mediterraneans, Alpines, Nordics, Lapps, East Baltics, Irano-Afghans, southern Indians, and northern and eastern Africans. However, intermixing has blurred the distinguishing features of these types in many areas.

Mediterraneans include the narrow-faced Basques of France and Spain, who are more properly called 'early Mediterraneans', because they are the purest descendants of the prehistoric inhabitants of Europe. The Mediterraneans proper are long-headed and dark-haired, with olive to light brown skins. They are found both north and south of the Mediterranean Sea and include Spaniards, Italians and Arabs. Alpine people are of medium height and they are sturdily built. Their round heads distinguish them from Mediterraneans and Nordics. The Nordics of Scandinavia are typically long-headed, tall people with blue eyes and blond hair.

The short Lapps have round heads, like the East Baltics of northeastern and eastern Europe and many Russians. On the otherhand, the Irano-Afghans of Afghanistan, Baluchistan, northwestern India and Iran are physically similar to Nordics, except for their darker hair and skin colouring. The Dinarics of southeastern Europe and the Armenians are similar to the Irano-Afghans.

The southern Indians are mostly of the Mediterranean type, except for their darker skins. African Caucasoids include the Berbers of northern Africa and some of the peoples of northeastern Africa, including some Ethiopians, Somalis and Sudanese. However, through intermixing, they have acquired some Negroid features. Mixed groups broadly included in the Caucasoid sub-group, include Polynesians, the Vedda of southern India and Australoids, including the Australian Aborigines. The Australoids, also called 'archaic whites', are sometimes considered to be a separate sub-group.

From the early 1500s, Europeans have spread around the world, exploring and colonizing the Americas, Africa and Australia. As a result, Caucasoids are the most widely spread of the three sub-groups.

Mongoloids are distinguished by their yellowish skin, straight black hair, flat faces and noses, high cheek bones and, in many cases, slanted eyes — caused by a skin fold of the upper eyelid. These features are displayed by the short-legged, thick-set Classic Mongoloids, including Eskimoes, Japanese, Koreans and northern Chinese.

The other Mongoloids do not have slanted eyes. They include: the broad-faced, rather thick-lipped Turkics of central Asia; the narrow-faced Tibetans, or Himalayans; the short and graceful Indonesian-Malays, including the Burmese, southern Chinese, Filipinos and Thais; and the American Indians, whose ancestors entered the Americas sometime between 20,000 and 10,000 years ago.

American Indians differ in various ways from typical Mongoloids. Their skin is often reddish or yellowish-brown, and their noses are prominent and seldom flat. But they have black hair, high cheek bones and little body hair.

The Negroids of Africa, south of the Sahara, mostly have very dark skins, thick, outward-turning lips, broad noses and narrow heads, with a protruding upper jaw. This sub-group includes some of the world's tallest people — the Nilotes — and the shortest — the Negrillos, or pygmies. Descendants of African slaves live in large numbers in the Americas, although they have intermixed considerably with Caucasoids. Asian Negroids include the Papuans of New Guinea and the Negritos, or pygmies, of Malaysia and many Pacific islands.

Left: **This woman from northern Thailand belongs to the Indonesian-Malay sub-group of the Mongoloid peoples. The Indonesian-Malays do not have the slanting eyes of the Classic Mongoloids.**

Above right: **Peoples of the world.**

Right: **This European mother and her children belong to the Caucasoid group of mankind. Within the Caucasoid group, there are many variations in the appearance of individuals.**

Far right: **The Hausa of northern Nigeria are essentially Negroid, although they speak a Hamitic tongue and they have intermixed to some extent with peoples from the north. As a result, they tend to be taller and often have narrower noses than the typical Negroes of the West African coastlands.**

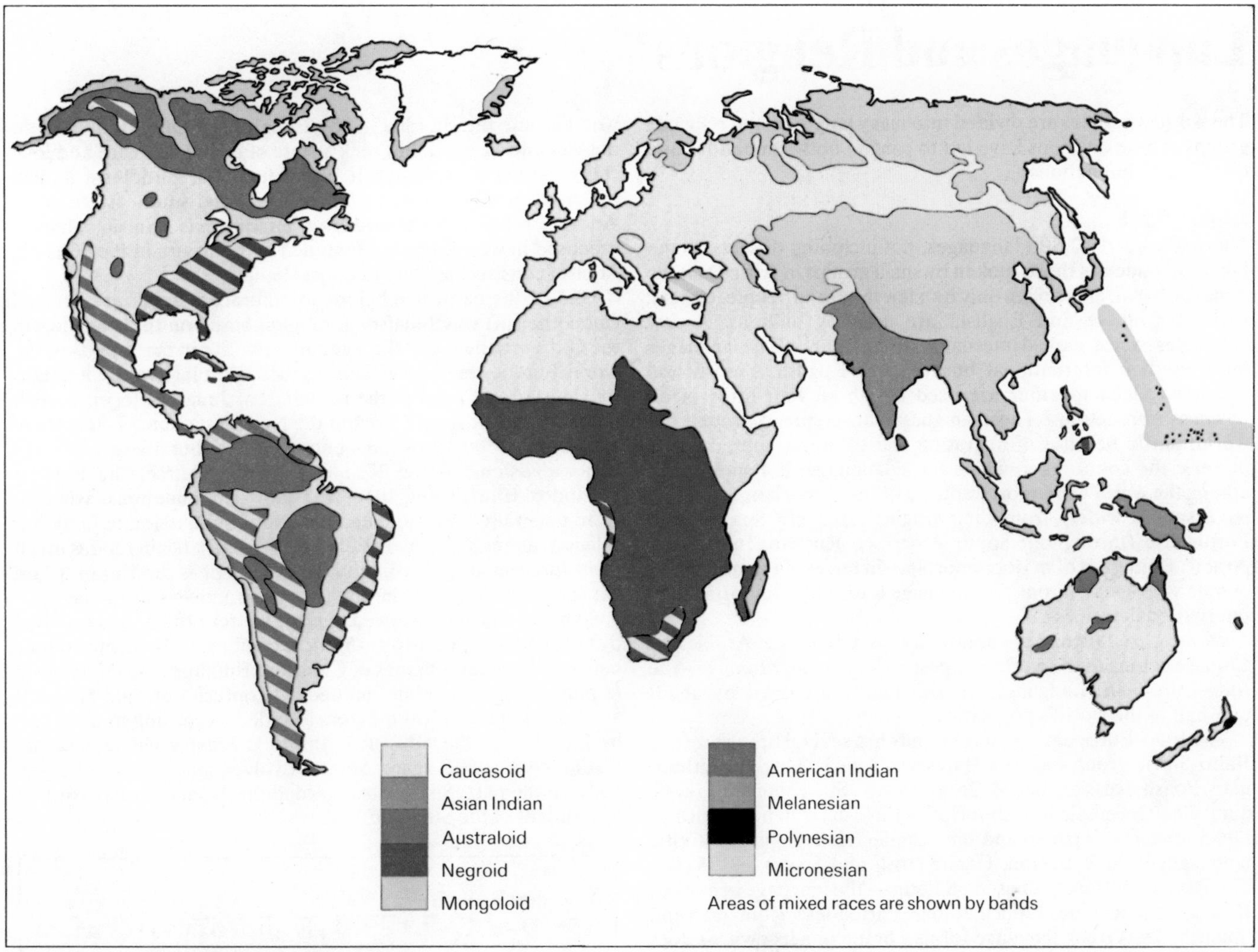

Caucasoid
Asian Indian
Australoid
Negroid
Mongoloid
American Indian
Melanesian
Polynesian
Micronesian
Areas of mixed races are shown by bands

Languages and Religions

The world's peoples are divided into many language and religious groups. These divisions have led to conflict between nations and divisions within nations.

Languages

There are nearly 2,800 languages, not including dialects. Some languages, such as those spoken by small groups in Africa and the Amazon basin, are spoken only by a few thousand people. Others, such as Chinese and English, are used by millions. A few languages have achieved international importance. The languages most used in international business are English, French and German, which together are used for about four-fifths of all business transactions. These languages have spread around the world, partly because of migration and colonization and partly because the countries in which these languages are spoken are among the world's foremost trading nations. Other languages that have spread widely from their original area are Spanish and Portuguese (throughout South America), Russian, Italian and Arabic. Chinese is of major importance in terms of the number of people who speak it, but this language is of minor importance in international business.

Of the great languages mentioned above, all except Arabic and Chinese belong to the world's largest single language family — the Indo-European. Languages of this family are used by about one-half of the world's population.

The Indo-European language family has several branches. The Balto-Slavic group includes Bulgarian, Czech, Latvian, Lithuanian, Polish, Russian, Serbo-Croat, Slovak, Slovenian and Ukrainian. The Germanic branch includes English, Dutch, Flemish (a Dutch dialect), German and the Scandinavian languages. Celtic languages include Breton, Gaelic (Irish and Scots) and Welsh. The Romance branch is based on Latin — the language of ancient Rome — and includes French, Italian, Portuguese, Romanian and Spanish. The Greek language forms a branch on its own, as does Albanian. The Iranian group includes Persian and Pushtu, the language of the Afghans. And the Indo-Aryan branch includes Bengali and Hindi.

The second largest language family is the Sino-Tibetan, which accounts for more than one-fifth of the world's population. It includes Burmese, Chinese (Sinitic), Thai and Tibetan. The other main language families are spoken by far fewer people. They include: the Semitic-Hamitic-Kushitic group, which includes Arabic and Hebrew; the Uralic and Altaic families, including Mongol, Finnish, and Turkish; the Japanese and Korean family; the Dravidian family of southern India; the Malayo-Polynesian family; the Mon-Khmer family of southeastern Asia; the languages of black Africa; and the American Indian languages.

Religions

Most religions combine the worship of one or several gods with ethical rules of conduct, although some are chiefly ethical and philosophical. There are 10 major religions: Christianity, Islam, Hinduism, Confucianism, Buddhism, Shinto, Taoism, Judaism, Sikhism and Jainism.

Hinduism is an ancient Indian religion, which is also followed by people in Malaysia, Mauritius, the Pacific islands and parts of eastern and southern Africa. Hinduism dates back to about 2500 BC. Hindus believe in one supreme power, Brahman, but they worship many gods, who are seen as reflections of Brahman. Incorporated in Hinduism are beliefs in reincarnation, the caste system and the sacredness of cattle. Buddhism developed from Hinduism. Its founder was Siddartha Gautama (560–480 BC), who became the Buddha — the Enlightened One. Buddhists do not worship any god, but seek a state of complete peace and love called Nirvana. Although it began in India, Buddhism is now practised mostly in China, Japan, Tibet and southeastern Asia. Another religion developed from Hinduism is Jainism, which is practised in western India. Founded by Mahavira in the 500s BC, Jainism consists basically of ethical beliefs.

One of the earliest religions to embrace a belief in one God (monotheism) was Judaism, a religion based on the teachings in the Old Testament and the Talmud. Jews live in many parts of the world, but they regard Palestine as their spiritual home. Christianity incorporates most of the teachings of Judaism, together with the teachings of Jesus Christ in the New Testament. Today there are about 3,000 Christian denominations, but there are three major divisions — the Roman Catholic Church, the Eastern Orthodox Church and the Protestant denominations. Islam, a word generally taken to mean peace and submission to God, is a religion taught by Muhammad (AD 570–632). Islam retains much from Judaism and Christianity. Its holy book is the Koran. Islam has spread through northern Africa and southwestern Asia.

Sikhism, which is followed in northwestern India, was founded by Guru Nanak (AD 1469–1538). It combines Hindu and Islamic beliefs. The great religions of China are Buddhism, Confucianism (a philosophical religion founded by Confucius around 500 BC), and Taoism (a mystical religion, founded, according to tradition, by Lao Tzu in the 500s BC). Shinto is Japan's native religion. Dating back 2,500 years, Shinto involves the worship of many gods. In the past, Shintoists regarded the Japanese emperor as a descendant of the Sun God.

Assyrian (carved)

Ancient Hebrew (painted)

Egyptian hieroglyphic (painted)

Some modern non-latin type faces

Greek
ΑΒΓΔΕΖΗΘΙΚΛΜΝΞΟΠΡΣΤΥΦΧΨΩϚ

Cyrillic
АБВГДЕЖЗИЙІКЛМНОПРСТУФХЦЧШ

Arabic
في عام ١٨٩٧ وصل إلى إنجلترا أ نموذج

Bengali
১৮৯৭ খ্রীস্টাব্দে আধুনিক মডেলের একটি

Telugu
నిన్న మాయింటికి వచ్చిన యతిథి యేమియు

Japanese
国土の位置と地形

Chinese
父獨子出有之限地位司，能
司在提印芬刷奥業司上有

Above: **The Sultan Ahmet Mosque in Istanbul, one of the finest of Islamic buildings.**

Below left: **Writing styles of ancient and modern times.**

Right: **A Christian church in Bavaria, in the southern part of West Germany.**

Below: **Distribution of religious groups around the world.**

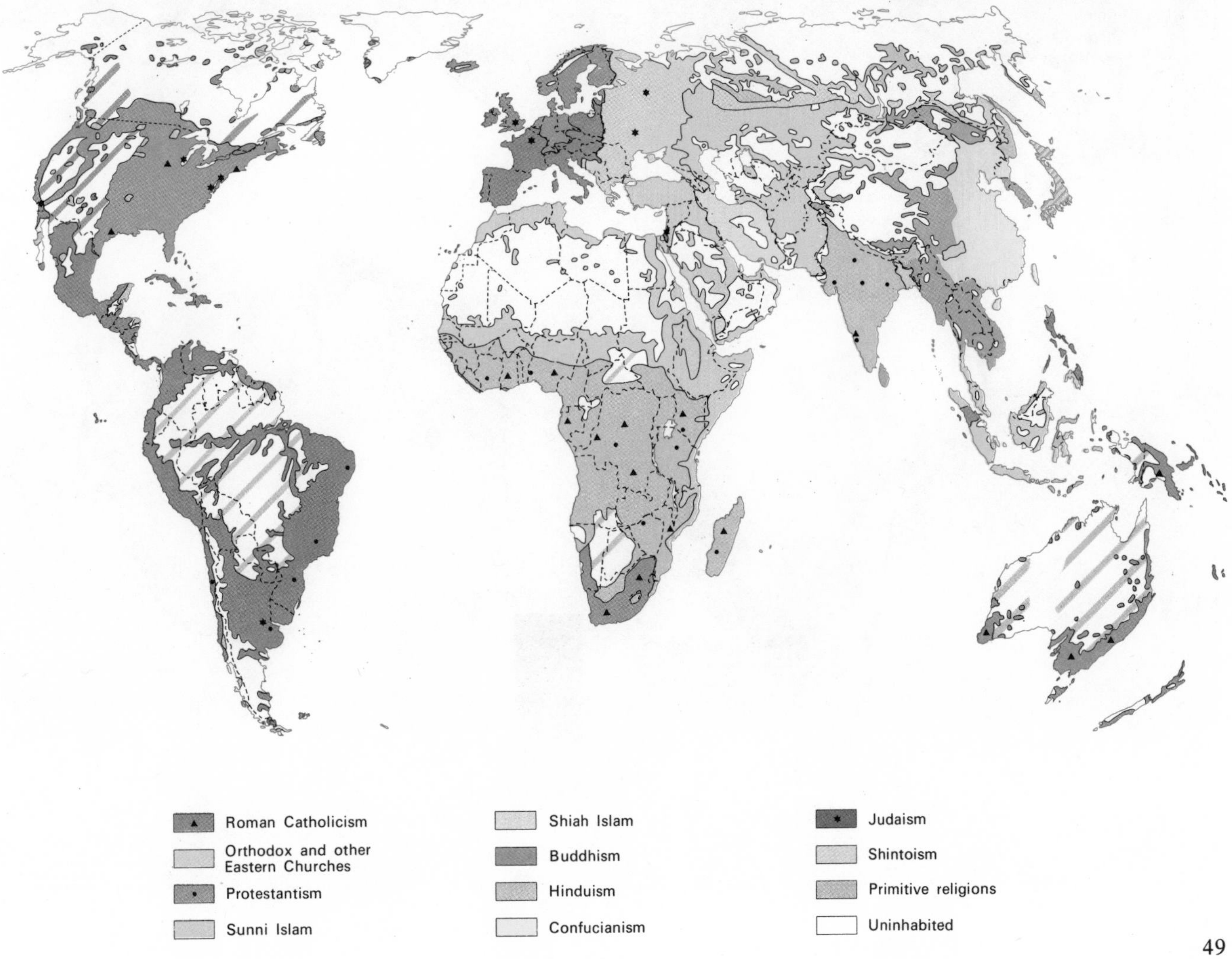

Roman Catholicism
Orthodox and other Eastern Churches
Protestantism
Sunni Islam
Shiah Islam
Buddhism
Hinduism
Confucianism
Judaism
Shintoism
Primitive religions
Uninhabited

Population

The world's population is very unevenly distributed. Vast tracts of land are too cold, too dry or too rugged and mountainous to support more than a few people. On the other hand, in parts of the farming belts, which total no more than 10 per cent of the Earth's land area, and in industrial zones, people are crowded together.

On average, in 1982, there were about 33 people to every square kilometre of land (86 per square mile), excluding the icy continent of Antarctica, which has no permanent population. But Europe had a population density of 100 per square kilometre (258 per square mile) and Asia was second with 95 per square kilometre (246 per square mile). By contrast, Oceania, which includes Australia — two-thirds of which is virtually empty because it is desert — had only 2.9 people per square kilometre (7.5 per square mile), while the U.S.S.R. and North America had about 12 per square kilometre (31 per square mile).

The world's ten largest countries, by area, are the U.S.S.R.,

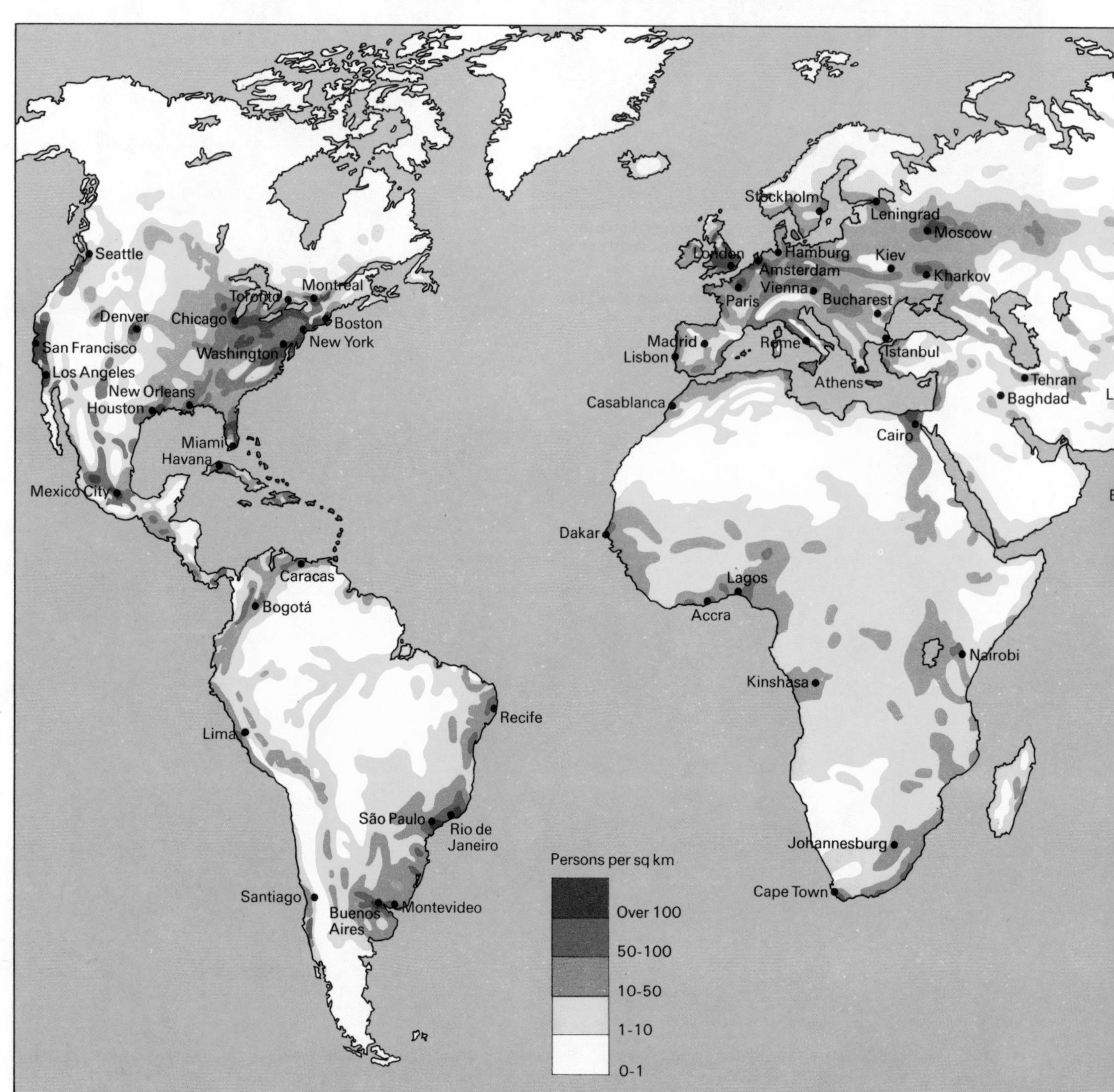
Seattle
Montreal
Toronto
Denver
Chicago
Boston
New York
San Francisco
Washington
Los Angeles
New Orleans
Houston
Miami
Havana
Mexico City
Caracas
Bogotá
Recife
Lima
São Paulo
Rio de Janeiro
Santiago
Buenos Aires
Montevideo
Stockholm
Leningrad
Moscow
London
Hamburg
Kiev
Amsterdam
Kharkov
Vienna
Paris
Bucharest
Madrid
Lisbon
Rome
Istanbul
Athens
Tehran
Baghdad
Casablanca
Cairo
Dakar
Lagos
Accra
Nairobi
Kinshasa
Johannesburg
Cape Town
Persons per sq km
Over 100
50-100
10-50
1-10
0-1

Canada, China, the United States, Brazil, Australia, India, Argentina, Sudan and Algeria. But the ten most populated countries in 1980 were China (964 million), India (650 million) the U.S.S.R. (264 million), the United States (226 million), Indonesia (148 million), Japan (118 million), Brazil (118 million), Bangladesh (86 million), Pakistan (79 million) and Nigeria (74 million).

In 1982, the world had an estimated population of 4,506 million, and it was increasing by about 1.6 million per week. This is the fastest and most massive population increase in history. Around 6000 BC, the world had an estimated population of about 200 million. It then increased steadily until, in AD 1000, it had reached just over 300 million. After that, the rate of increase

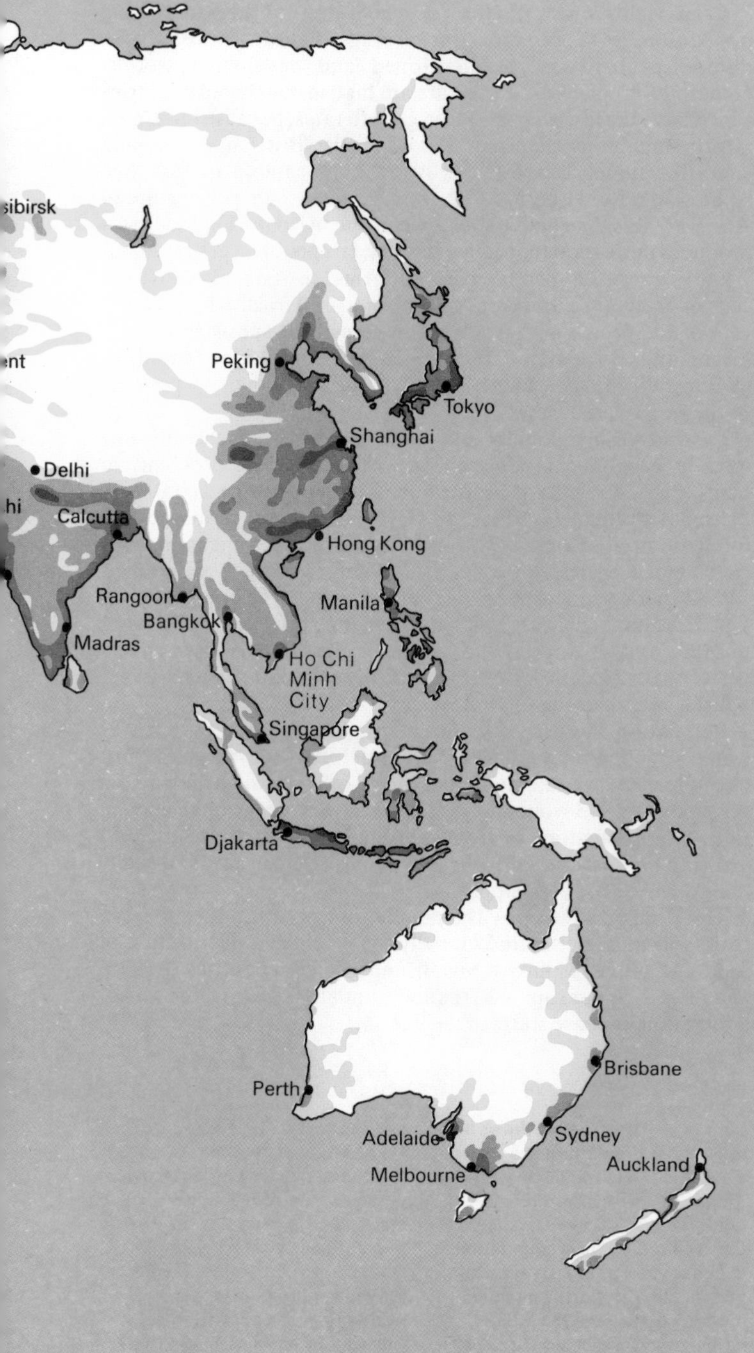
Peking
Tokyo
Shanghai
Delhi
Calcutta
Hong Kong
Rangoon
Bangkok
Manila
Madras
Ho Chi Minh City
Singapore
Djakarta
Perth
Brisbane
Adelaide
Sydney
Melbourne
Auckland

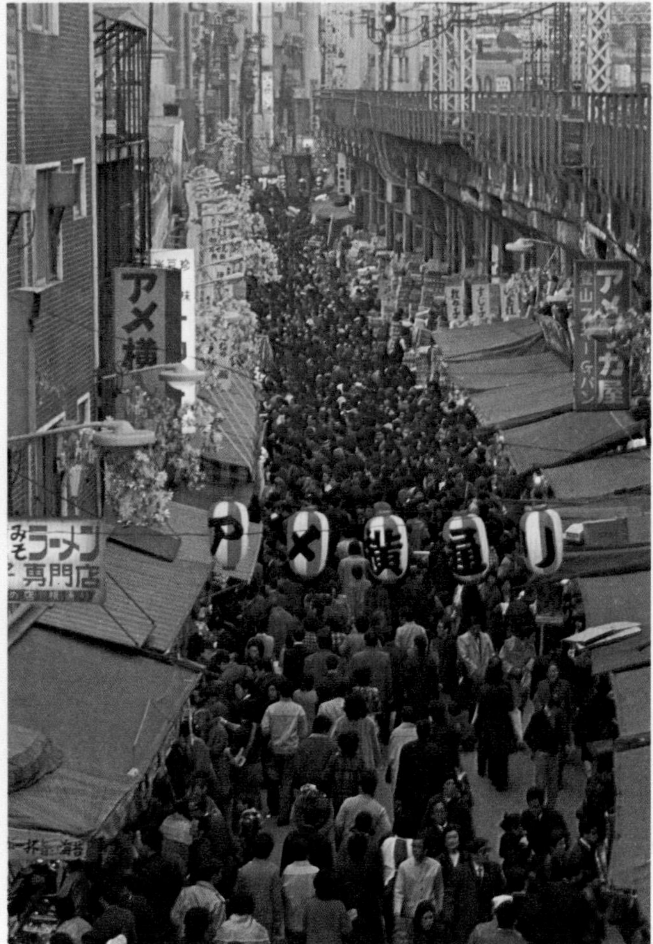
アメ横
アメ横通り
みそラーメン
専門店

Top: **Mongolia contains large areas of bleak plateaux and mountains. Because of the severe and extreme climate, Mongolia is thinly-populated and most of the people are nomadic pastoralists.**

Above: **A crowded street in Tokyo, Japan's capital. Japan is densely populated but, in recent years, its annual rate of population growth has been reduced to only 1.3 per cent.**

began to accelerate, and the 1,000 million mark was passed in the 1800s. By the mid-1920s, it was nearly 2,000 million, and it doubled again in the following 50 years.

The explosion in world populations results from a net increase of births over deaths, mainly caused by a gradual decrease in infant mortality and longer average life spans. In the world as a whole, the average birth rate for the years 1965–74 was 33 per 1,000 people and the average death rate for the same period was 13 per 1,000. And, in 1970–4, there was a net increase in world population of about 1.9 per cent per year. If this rate continues, the world's population will double in the next 37 years.

There are considerable variations in population increases from country to country and from continent to continent. For example, the population of Pakistan has been estimated to be increasing by 2.9 per cent per year — an extremely fast rate that would double Pakistan's population in only 25 years. But, in France, it would take more than 110 years for the population to double at the slow rate of 0.6 per cent per year.

Among the continents, the populations of Africa and Latin America (including Central America and Caribbean countries) are increasing at the fast rate of 2.7 per cent per year. This rate would double the population in only 26 years. Africa has the highest birth rate of all the continents — 46 per 1,000 people per year — but it also has the highest death rate — 20 per 1,000 people per year. Latin America has a lower birth rate at 37 per 1,000 per year, but its death rate is also much lower at 9 per 1,000 people. Asia's birth rate is almost as high as Latin America's at 34 per 1,000 people per year, but the death rate of 13 per 1,000 is considerably higher. Hence, the net average rate of population increase in Asia is lower at 2.2 per cent per year (1970–7 average) and it would take 33 years for the population to double at this rate.

By contrast, the populations of North America and the U.S.S.R. are increasing by 0.9 per cent per year, which means that it would take 78 years for their populations to double if this rate were maintained. And, in Europe, the average rate of increase is only 0.6 per cent per year. Europe and North America have the lowest birth rates at 17 per 1,000 people per year.

The highest population increases have thus been taking place in the developing world, and the lowest increases have occurred in the developed, industrialized world. In Asia, Japan is the only truly industrialized country and, significantly, its average rate of population increase is well below the average for Asia at 1.2 per cent per year. Part of the reason for this contrast is that, in developing countries, a high proportion of the people live at subsistence level. It is not surprising that many poor farmers may see their only hope for survival in old age as having enough sons to support them.

The average rate of population increase in the developed world is 1.1 per cent per year, whereas the rate in the developing world is more than twice as much, averaging 2.3 per cent. One of the most striking consequences of this difference is reflected in the age structures of the two worlds.

In Africa, Asia and Latin America, the populations are more youthful than in the developed world. On average, about 40 out of every 100 people are under 15 years of age; 56 are between 15 and 64; and only 4 out of every 100 are 65 or over. This contrasts with Europe, North America, Oceania and the U.S.S.R., where 27 out of every 100 people are under 15 years of age; 63 are between 15 and 64; and 10 are 65 or over.

The large and increasing school-age populations in developing countries already have too few educational facilities and teachers. Also, the developing world has a lower proportion of people of working age, and the average life expectation is much lower. The developed countries face different problems, such as the high and increasing proportion of older people, who do not contribute directly to the economy. For example, the average life expectation for Canadian men and women in 1931 was 60 years and 62.1 years respectively. But by 1978, it had risen to an average of 74 years for both sexes.

The population explosion poses a threat to the Earth's resources. One vital resource is farmland, which is limited in extent by climate and topography. Today the world has about 1,440 million hectares (3,558 million acres) of farmland — that is, land under the plough or under permanent crops. In 1982, when the world's population stood at about 4,506 million, the average amount of farmland per person was just under one-third of a hectre (nearly four-fifths of an acre). By the year 2000, the world's population will have increased to about 6.300 million at current rates of growth. The average amount of farmland per person will then be reduced to just over one-fifth of a hectare (slightly more than half an acre).

Crop yields must, therefore, rise if the world's increasing population is to be fed. But average figures conceal wide differences between the developed and developing worlds. Generally, crop yields per hectare are high in developed countries which have the lowest population growth rates, because farming is mostly highly mechanized and efficient. But, in developing countries, standards are generally low. For example, in Asia, rice is the staple food but, in 1970, average rice yields per hectare in Asia were less than half of those in Europe. Also the United States produces more food than it needs to feed its people, yet only about 2 out of every 100 people work on farms. In Asia, about 64 per cent of the people work on farms. And, in Africa, where 74 per cent of the people are farm workers, mostly at subsistence level, severe famines are all too frequent. In such poor African countries as Burundi, Malawi, Niger and Rwanda, more than 85 per cent of the people are farmers.

Fast-increasing populations, combined with a generally low level of economic production, are causing severe problems in many areas. A country's production is often expressed as its Gross National Product (GNP). The GNP is the total domestic and foreign output of a country. For example, in 1979, the industrialized United States had a total GNP of $2,337,090 million, or $10,820 per person, whereas one of the poorest developing nations. Upper Volta, had a GNP of $1,000 million and a per capita GNP of $180. And, in Upper Volta, the per capita GNP declined by one per cent per year in 1970–8 because the population increased at a faster rate than the GNP.

Population increase also threatens other resources, such as water supplies, mineral reserves and fossil fuel reserves. For example, it was estimated that the world's known petroleum resources in 1973 would be used up in only 27 years at the current rates of production. With increasing demand from an ever-growing population, oil wells will eventually run dry and many metals will be in short supply.

The problems posed by the population explosion are global in scale and must be treated globally, by a sensible distribution of food and other resources. Significantly, when countries develop and raise their per capita GDPs and standards of living, the rate of population increase starts to decline.

Opposite: **The diagram shows how the world's population has grown since 1650. At first, the increase was steady. But, after the 1,000 million mark had been passed in the 1800s, the rate of population increase accelerated. By the mid-1920s, the world had 2,000 million people, and the 4,000 million mark was passed in 1976—the population having doubled in just over 50 years. Today, the average rate of population increase is estimated to be 1.9 per cent per year — a rate which, if it is maintained, will double the world's population in only 37 years. The diagram also shows that the fastest growing populations are in the developing, or poorer countries. The slowest rates of population growth occur in developed nations.**

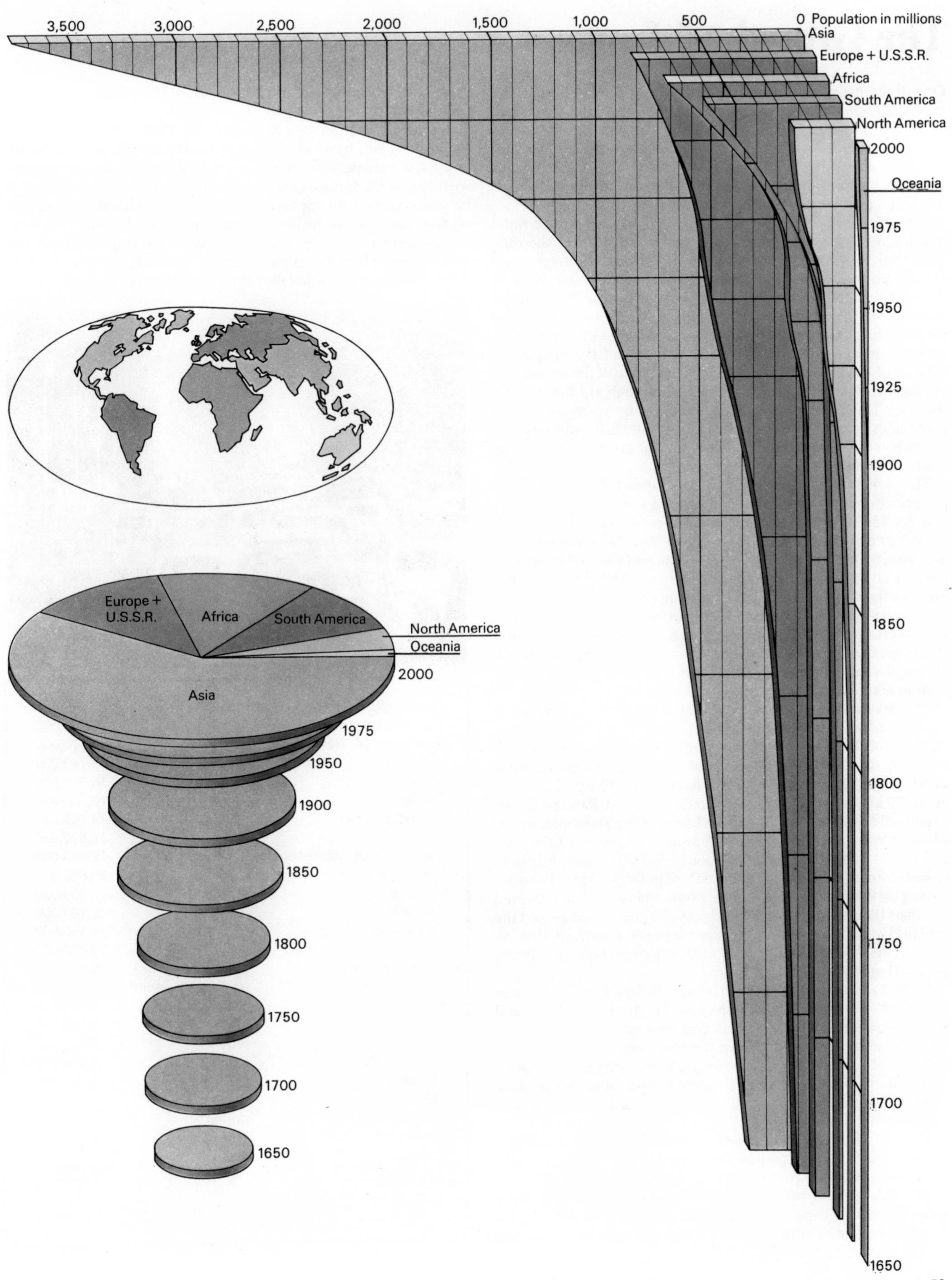
3,500
3,000
2,500
2,000
1,500
1,000
500
0 Population in millions
Asia
Europe + U.S.S.R.
Africa
South America
North America
2000
Oceania
1975
1950
1925
1900
1850
1800
1750
1700
1650
Europe + U.S.S.R.
Africa
South America
North America
Oceania
Asia
2000
1975
1950
1900
1850
1800
1750
1700
1650

The Growth of Towns

One of the main features that distinguishes developed countries from their less fortunate developing neighbours is that developed countries have large manufacturing industries. On the other hand, the economies of most developing countries are based mainly on the production of primary products — food and raw materials, although such developing countries as Brazil and China do have important pockets of manufacturing industries.

Industrialization is the chief factor that has led to the rapid development of cities and towns since the late 1700s, when the Industrial Revolution began, at first in Britain, although rural manufacturing remains important in Norway and Switzerland. In the world as a whole, about one-third of the people live in urban areas. But, in the developed world, between two-thirds and nine-tenths of the people live and work in cities and towns. By contrast, in parts of Africa, only 10 per cent of the people are urbanized. In Asia, an average of only one-third of the people live in urban areas and, in Latin America, about half are town or city dwellers. However, as developing countries try to diversify their economies by establishing manufacturing industries and services, so more and more people are leaving the countryside for the towns and cities.

The earliest towns grew up in Mesopotamia following the start of agriculture and the production of food surpluses 6,000 years ago. By 3500 BC, there were many well-established towns in the area. Towns were later set up in Egypt and the Mediterranean area and, to the east, in India, central Asia and China. These early towns were essentially centres of trade and craft industries, but many of the sites were chosen because they were easily defended. In the towns, people had time to develop the arts and sciences, and so it was the towns that provided the stimulus for the development of the great early civilizations. But most towns remained small, although some ancient Chinese cities may have had about one million inhabitants.

The development of Paris is typical of many cities. It was first established as a settlement on an island in the River Seine. Because of the island, the settlement provided an easy bridging point of the river, and Paris developed as a communications centre. When it was taken by the Romans in 52 BC, it covered about 40 hectares (100 acres). As trade increased, Paris gradually expanded onto the north and south banks of the Seine and, by the Middle Ages, it covered nearly 8 square kilometres (3 square miles) and had a population of about 150,000. France began to industrialize in the early 1800s, and Paris grew quickly as factories sprang up in and around it. By the 1840s, industrial Paris covered 10 times the area of medieval Paris, and its population passed the 900,000 mark. Today, with its large suburbs, it sprawls over an area of 480 square kilometres (185 square miles) and has a population of nearly 10,100,000.

In the early days of the Industrial Revolution, many new towns arose on coalfields, ironfields and other places where natural resources were to hand. But, as communications improved, so cities could be founded far from the resources they required for their people and industries. For example, ports handling imports and exports became industrial centres, and other cities were established on the expanding railway networks, especially at railway junctions.

Modern cities face many problems, including large-scale crime, noise, pollution, communications breakdowns, such as traffic jams, and a lack of community sense that may cause loneliness.

In the developing world, the lack of capital makes it difficult for governments to cope with the rapid expansion of their cities. Country people migrate to urban areas in search of better-paid jobs, higher standards of living and more amenities. The population of Brazil's cities, for example, will increase by an estimated 32 million people during the 1980s. This means that these cities will have to provide at least five million new family houses, otherwise ugly shanty towns with serious health hazards will arise. And, as most of the new arrivals are unskilled, there will be serious urban unemployment, unless the industrial expansion is fast enough to provide sufficient jobs. In one country, communist China, the government has been trying to reverse the world trend towards urbanization by diverting people back to rural communities, which they are trying to make self-sufficient.

TOTAL

The World's Largest 25 cities*		Population
Tokyo/Yokahama	(Japan)	21,700,000
New York/N.E. New Jersey	(United States)	20,800,000
Mexico City	(Mexico)	18,700,000
São Paulo	(Brazil)	16,600,000
Shanghai	(China)	16,300,000
Beijing (Peking)	(China)	13,700,000
Rio de Janeiro	(Brazil)	12,600,000
Los Angeles/Long Beach	(United States)	12,400,000
Greater Buenos Aires	(Argentina)	10,800,000
Calcutta	(India)	10,100,000
Paris	(France)	10,100,000
Ōsaka/Kobe	(Japan)	10,100,000
Seoul	(Korea)	10,000,000
Greater Bombay	(India)	10,000,000
London	(United Kingdom)	9,800,000
Rhein-iuhr	(West Germany)	9,100,000
Djakarta	(Indonesia)	8,900,000
Cairo/Geiza/Imbaba	(Egypt)	8,500,000
Chicago/N.W. Indiana	(United States)	8,500,000
Moscow	(USSR)	8,000,000
Milan	(Italy)	7,100,000
Madras	(India)	6,900,000
Manila	(Indonesia)	6,800,000
Tehran	(Iran)	6,700,000
Istanbul	(Turkey)	6,600,000

*Projected figures for 1985 from *World Population Trends and Policies*, 1981 Monitoring Report, VOL 1: United Nations, 1981.

Above left: **Italy, like most developed countries, suffers from traffic congestion in urban areas. The populations of urban areas in most parts of the world are increasing in size, partly as a result of natural population growth and partly because of rural depopulation.**

Above: **Land and housing are so limited in the crowded British colony of Hong Kong that many people have to live in boats.**

Right: **Many towns in Taiwan, like others in developing nations, are surrounded by shanty towns, where crime, disease and poverty are rife. Shanty towns develop when the urban building programmes cannot keep pace with the fast-increasing populations. Yet, in most countries, the exodus of people from the countryside continues, because the best-paid jobs are nearly all to be found in the towns.**

Health, Wealth and Poverty

Developed countries are distinguished from developing countries by their far higher per capita GNPs. For example, in 1979 France had a per capita GNP of US $9,940; West Germany, $11,730; the Netherlands, $10,240; the United Kingdom, $6,340; and the United States, $10,820. People who live in these, or other developed countries, can expect to live much longer, on average, than people in developing countries. For example, average life expectations in 1978 were as follows: France, 73 years (as opposed to 71 in 1960); West Germany, 72 years (69 in 1960); the Netherlands, 74 years (73 in 1960); the United Kingdom, 73 years (70 in 1960); and the United States, 73 years (70 in 1960).

Complete statistics are lacking in many developing countries. But the United Nations estimates for average life expectations in some of them were as follows: Ghana, 48 years; India, 51 years; Indonesia, 47 years; and Senegal, 42 years. The per capita GNPs in 1979 were: Ghana $400; India $190; Indonesia $380; and Senegal $430. Some African countries have even lower average life expectations and per capita GNPs.

Low economic production, poverty and short life expectations are all, therefore, inter-related. Experts estimate that 300 to 400 million people, mostly children in the developing world, are suffering from malnutrition. For good health, people need a balanced diet. They need carbohydrates and fats, which provide energy. They need proteins for the growth of bones, cells and muscles, and smaller amounts of mineral salts and vitamins, which enable the body to make use of foods consumed. But, in the developing world, many people suffer from deficiency diseases, caused by a lack of one or more of these essential elements.

Kwashiokor is a disorder caused by a lack of protein, although sufferers may be eating sufficient carbohydrates in the form of cereals. In fact, it is estimated that about half of the world's population obtain two-thirds or less of the proteins they require for good health. Survivors of deficiency diseases in childhood may be left with impaired mental powers and their bodies may be stunted. Yet these children are the adults of the future, on whose shoulders rests the responsibility for raising their countries' economic production.

In many developing countries, periodic droughts, attacks of pests, and various plant and animal diseases often cause terrible famines. For example, in the dry Sahelian savanna, south of the Sahara Desert, years of drought occurred in the late 1960s and early 1970s. Hundreds of thousands of cattle perished, crops failed and many people suffered great hardship and starvation.

The food that is available in many places is unevenly distributed. Even in developed countries, unequal distribution of wealth causes poverty and malnutrition in some areas. In some cases, in developing nations, the consumption of certain foods has been forbidden by ancient customs. In East Africa, in the early 1960s, many Masai people were starving as a result of drought, but they refused solid foods, such as maize meal, because their traditional diet consisted of milk and blood. Also, in developing countries, many people get poor-quality or inadequate food, which impairs their general health.

People whose general standard of health is low lack resistance to disease. Among such people, the infant mortality rate is also high, standards of hygiene are often low and medical facilities are extremely limited. In northern Nigeria, there was only one doctor for every 100,000 people in the mid-1960s, while the United States had about 150 per 100,000 people. In developing countries, money is lacking for medicines, hospitals and other health facilities. For example, in the mid-1960s, the United States had around 750 times as much money available to spend on health per person as Nigeria.

Much aid for developing countries is channelled through the U.N. For example, the World Health Organization has mounted a campaign in Africa to reduce the incidence of malaria by preventive medicine and the eradication of the mosquitoes' habitats. But new health hazards are sometimes created as developing countries progress. For example, hydro-electric stations at the Kariba Dam in southern Africa and the Aswan High Dam in Egypt provide cheap electricity for manufacturing industries. But, behind the dams, lakes Kariba and Nasser have provided vast breeding grounds for the parasite that communicates the dangerous disease bilharzia.

One interesting development in some countries has been the utilization of the limited cash available to train medical auxiliaries. These are not doctors, but they are given a short and, therefore, cheap training that enables them to diagnose illnesses, treat the simpler cases and educate people in hygiene and birth control. Patients they are unable to help are referred to the few hospitals, which are mostly in the towns. Medical auxiliaries have an especially important role in large developing countries, where the population is widely scattered.

A
MEHTA
கர்ப்ப நிலை
கருப்பையில் கரு வளர்தல்
பெண்ணின் எலும்பு
வாழ்க்கை ரகசியம

Left: **Many nations have promoted campaigns to educate people in birth control methods in an attempt to slow down fast rates of population increase. Such measures should eventually lead to economic stability and a higher standard of general health. But many people oppose most birth control methods for religious reasons.**

Right: **Victims of the severe drought and famine that occurred in the Sahel region of West Africa in 1972-4.**

The Economic World

Vegetable Food Resources

Vegetable foods — that is, plants of all kinds — are the basis of all animal life, including Man. Even carnivores — flesh-eaters — depend for their food on animals that feed on plants. Man is an omnivore, with teeth adapted to eating either meat or vegetable foods. There are about as many domestic animals as people in the world, and they have to share the vegetable crop. But meat is an extravagant way of using food resources. A given amount of cereal food might provide the nutritional needs of, say, twenty people when eaten as cereal. But it would suffice for only two to eight people when fed to animals and eaten in the form of meat or other animal products.

The world's greatest crop-growing regions are not always those with the highest populations. As a result, many areas of the world are not self-sufficient in food supplies, and have to import a great deal of their needs. For example, Western Europe has to import a large amount of cereals, particularly maize (corn) and hard wheat. Many countries, particularly the poorest of the developing countries, do produce all their own food, but only to a very poor standard of nutrition.

In such countries, farming plays a major part in the lives of the people. For example, over large areas of West Africa, nine workers out of ten are engaged in agriculture. In Bangladesh, eight out of ten are farmers, yet the country still does not produce enough food for its needs. Some difficulties are caused by unreliable climate, poor soil, or a population too large for the available farming land. But generally, the shortage of food is due to old-fashioned and inefficient methods of cultivation.

For these countries, there is hope for the future in what has come to be called the Green Revolution, which has been taking place over the past 20 years. The men behind this revolution are the plant breeders. They are continually raising new varieties of plants that produce heavier crops than those formerly grown. During the late 1960s and early 1970s, yields of rice and wheat in many Asian countries increased by amounts ranging from 20 per cent to 100 per cent. This Green Revolution has also changed trading patterns. For example, Japan and the Philippines, which were big importers of rice in the early 1960s, have now become exporters of this crop.

The most important vegetable crops are the cereals, which provide the bulk of the world's food and the feed for its animals. The two leading cereals are rice, which is the staple food of Asia, and so of about half the world's population, and wheat. Wheat is grown in all parts of the world, including Asia. In the forms of bread, pasta, and breakfast cereals, it forms an important part of the diet in the northern hemisphere. Maize (corn), the third-ranking cereal, is used largely as animal feed.

Root crops are widely cultivated for human and animal consumption. Potatoes are a leading crop in Europe, North America, and the U.S.S.R.; sweet potatoes and yams are grown in China, Japan, and Korea; and cassava is grown in Africa, Asia and parts of South America. Pulses — beans, peas, lentils and chickpeas — form a vital part of the diet in many poor countries. Sugar, from sugar-beet and sugar-cane, is important as a high-energy food. Edible oils, obtained from olives, oilpalms, soybeans and groundnuts, are used in cooking and as an alternative to butter.

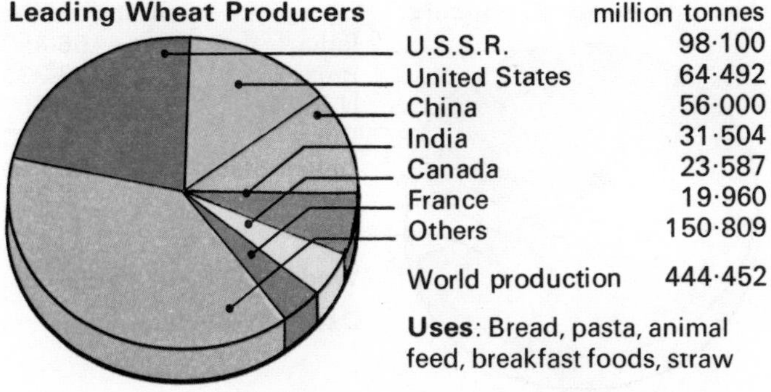
Leading Wheat Producers
million tonnes
U.S.S.R. 98·100
United States 64·492
China 56·000
India 31·504
Canada 23·587
France 19·960
Others 150·809
World production 444·452
Uses: Bread, pasta, animal feed, breakfast foods, straw

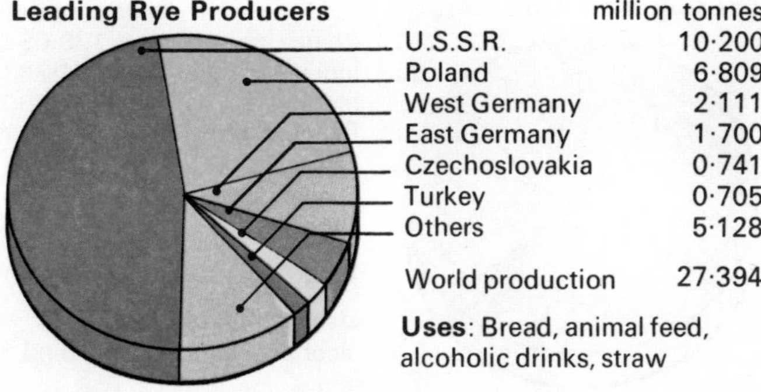
Leading Rye Producers
million tonnes
U.S.S.R. 10·200
Poland 6·809
West Germany 2·111
East Germany 1·700
Czechoslovakia 0·741
Turkey 0·705
Others 5·128
World production 27·394
Uses: Bread, animal feed, alcoholic drinks, straw

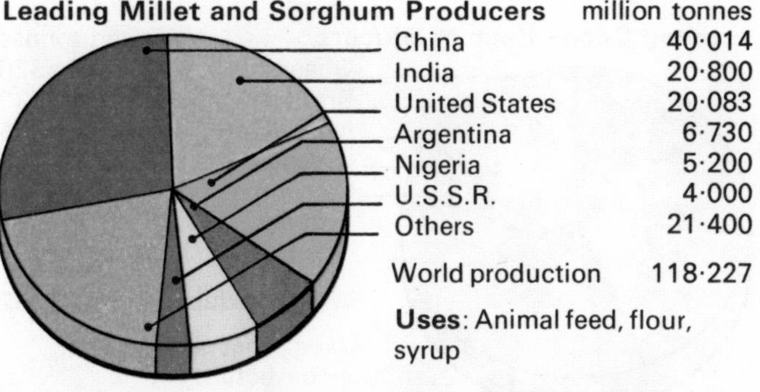
Leading Millet and Sorghum Producers
million tonnes
China 40·014
India 20·800
United States 20·083
Argentina 6·730
Nigeria 5·200
U.S.S.R. 4·000
Others 21·400
World production 118·227
Uses: Animal feed, flour, syrup

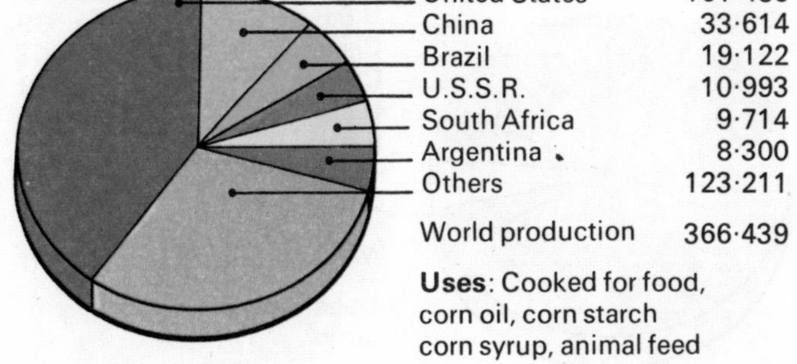
Leading Maize (Corn) Producers
million tonnes
United States 161·485
China 33·614
Brazil 19·122
U.S.S.R. 10·993
South Africa 9·714
Argentina 8·300
Others 123·211
World production 366·439
Uses: Cooked for food, corn oil, corn starch corn syrup, animal feed

Below left: **Much farm work in developing countries is done by hand, resulting in low production.**

Below: **Machinery like this combine harvester can greatly increase production.**

Vegetable Food Resources

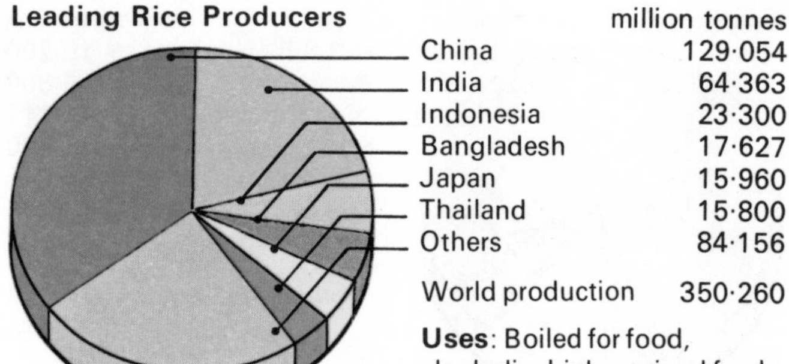

Leading Rice Producers
million tonnes
China 129·054
India 64·363
Indonesia 23·300
Bangladesh 17·627
Japan 15·960
Thailand 15·800
Others 84·156
World production 350·260
Uses: Boiled for food, alcoholic drinks, animal feed, straw

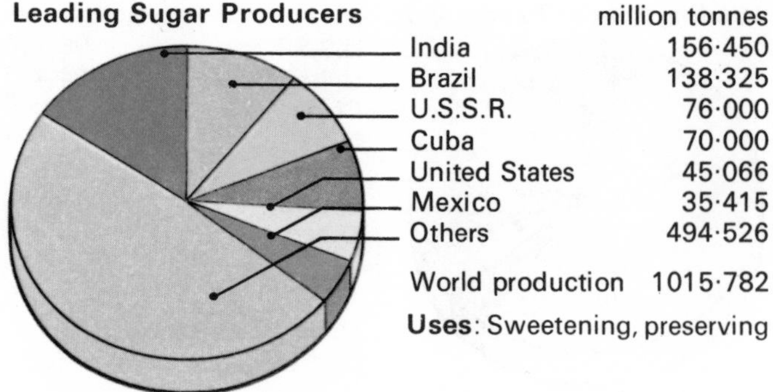

Leading Sugar Producers
million tonnes
India 156·450
Brazil 138·325
U.S.S.R. 76·000
Cuba 70·000
United States 45·066
Mexico 35·415
Others 494·526
World production 1015·782
Uses: Sweetening, preserving

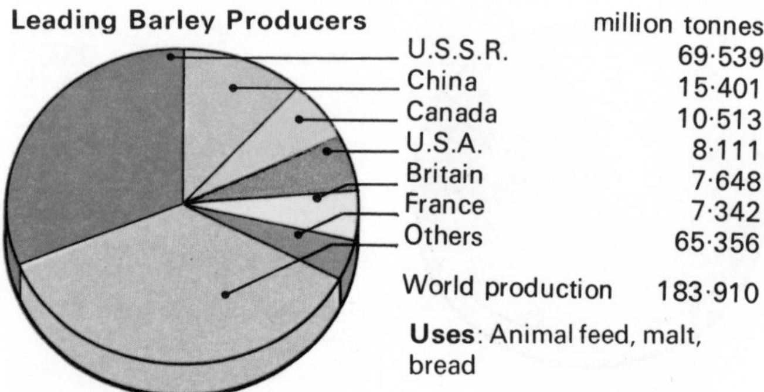

Leading Barley Producers
million tonnes
U.S.S.R. 69·539
China 15·401
Canada 10·513
U.S.A. 8·111
Britain 7·648
France 7·342
Others 65·356
World production 183·910
Uses: Animal feed, malt, bread

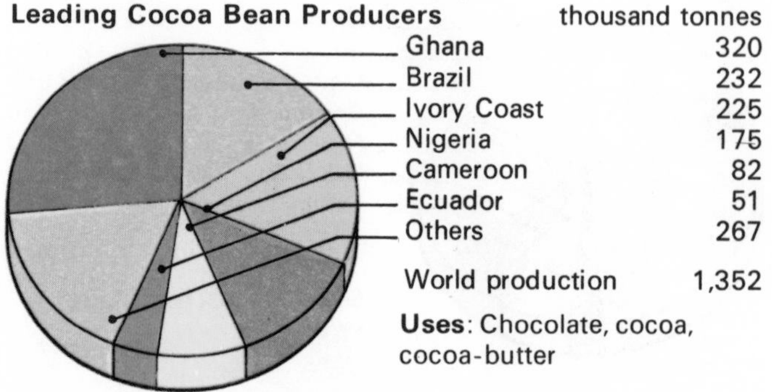

Leading Cocoa Bean Producers
thousand tonnes
Ghana 320
Brazil 232
Ivory Coast 225
Nigeria 175
Cameroon 82
Ecuador 51
Others 267
World production 1,352
Uses: Chocolate, cocoa, cocoa-butter

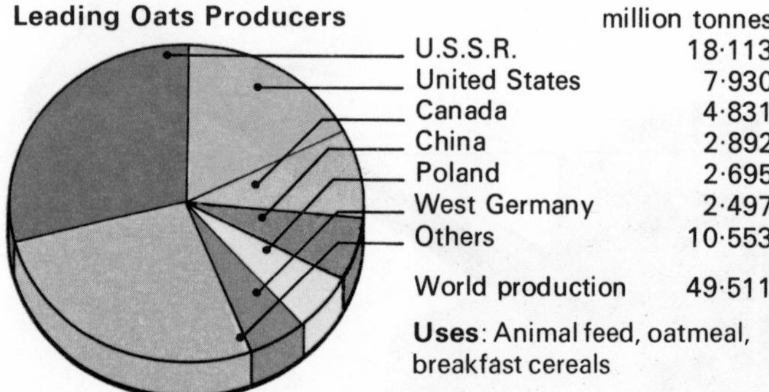

Leading Oats Producers
million tonnes
U.S.S.R. 18·113
United States 7·930
Canada 4·831
China 2·892
Poland 2·695
West Germany 2·497
Others 10·553
World production 49·511
Uses: Animal feed, oatmeal, breakfast cereals

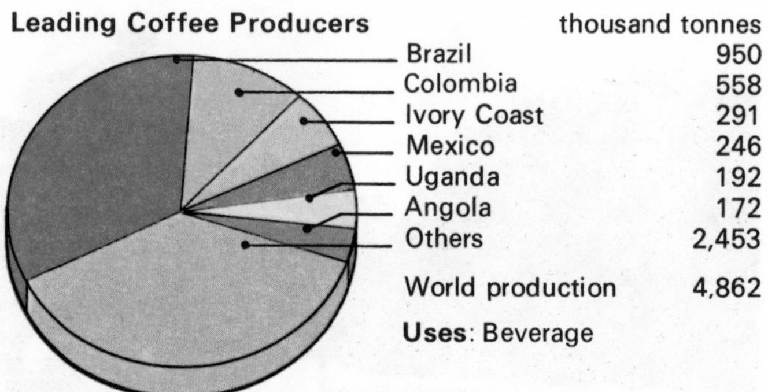

Leading Coffee Producers
thousand tonnes
Brazil 950
Colombia 558
Ivory Coast 291
Mexico 246
Uganda 192
Angola 172
Others 2,453
World production 4,862
Uses: Beverage

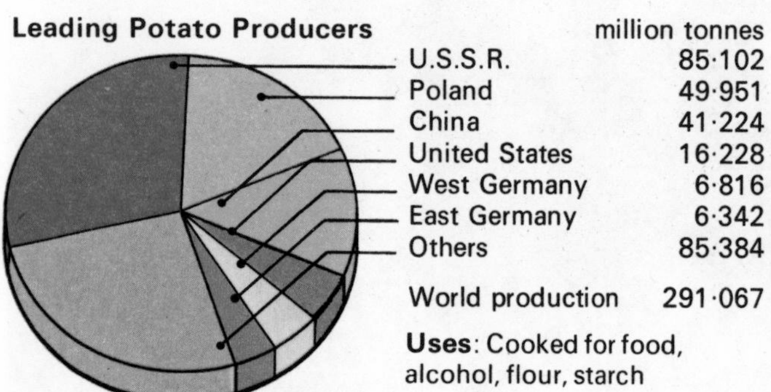

Leading Potato Producers
million tonnes
U.S.S.R. 85·102
Poland 49·951
China 41·224
United States 16·228
West Germany 6·816
East Germany 6·342
Others 85·384
World production 291·067
Uses: Cooked for food, alcohol, flour, starch

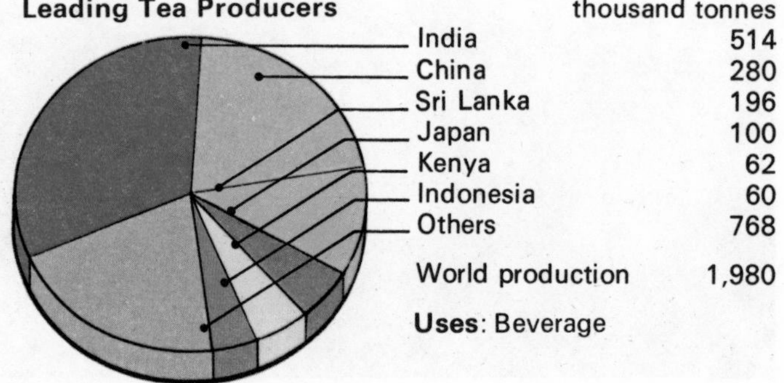

Leading Tea Producers
thousand tonnes
India 514
China 280
Sri Lanka 196
Japan 100
Kenya 62
Indonesia 60
Others 768
World production 1,980
Uses: Beverage

Animal Food Resources

Although Man is largely a vegetable eater, meat and animal products form a valuable part of his diet. Meat provides a ready source of protein and fat — two essentials for health — and contains many vitamins. It also contains minerals such as iron, copper and phosphorus. The smell of cooked meat has been found to stimulate the digestive juices.

The main meats are beef, mutton and lamb, and pork. In some countries, particularly around the Mediterranean Sea, the flesh of goats is regularly eaten. In all parts of the world, people also eat the flesh of poultry and some other birds, such as ducks and geese.

Another valuable animal product is milk, usually from cows, though goat's milk and ewe's milk are also drunk in small quantities. Milk contains much the same nutrients as meat. A great deal of it is consumed in the form of butter and cheese, which contain a greater concentration of fats than plain milk.

Meat is raised largely in the grassland areas of the world; dairy cattle are kept mostly in the temperate zone countries, particularly in Europe, the United States, New Zealand and Australia. Sheep can be grazed on hilly land with poorer grass than required by cattle.

INDIA'S 'SACRED COWS'
Although India leads the world in the number of cattle produced, this can be misleading unless all the factors are known.

The cow is sacred to the Hindus, who form 85 per cent of India's people, and so they eat no beef—and the slaughter of cows, as distinct from bulls, is banned by the country's constitution. Although bullocks are the principal draft animals, India's huge cattle population includes a large number of useless beasts, and the milk yield from cows is among the world's lowest.

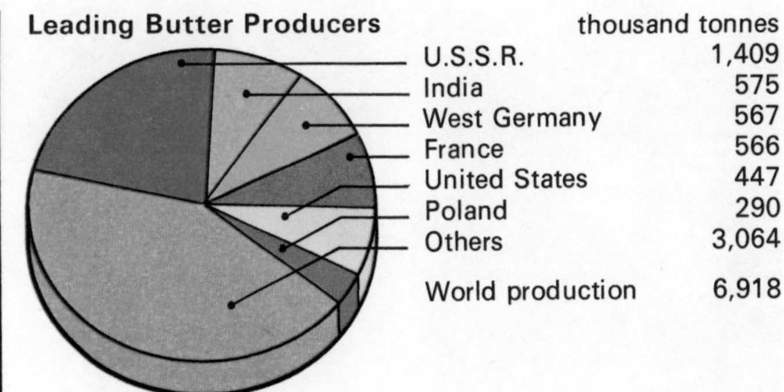

Leading Butter Producers
thousand tonnes
U.S.S.R. 1,409
India 575
West Germany 567
France 566
United States 447
Poland 290
Others 3,064
World production 6,918

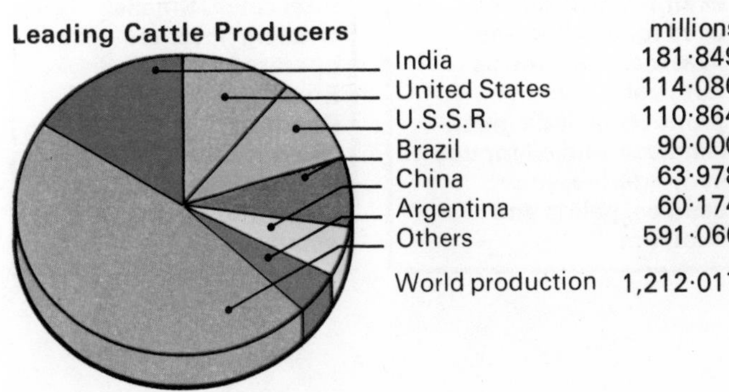

Leading Cattle Producers
millions
India 181·849
United States 114·086
U.S.S.R. 110·864
Brazil 90·000
China 63·978
Argentina 60·174
Others 591·066
World production 1,212·017

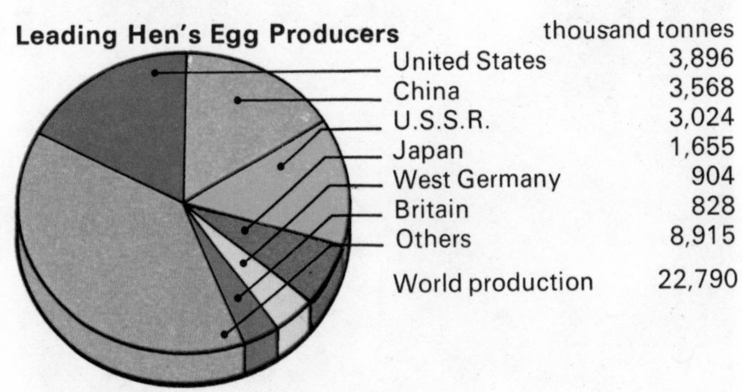

Leading Hen's Egg Producers
thousand tonnes
United States 3,896
China 3,568
U.S.S.R. 3,024
Japan 1,655
West Germany 904
Britain 828
Others 8,915
World production 22,790

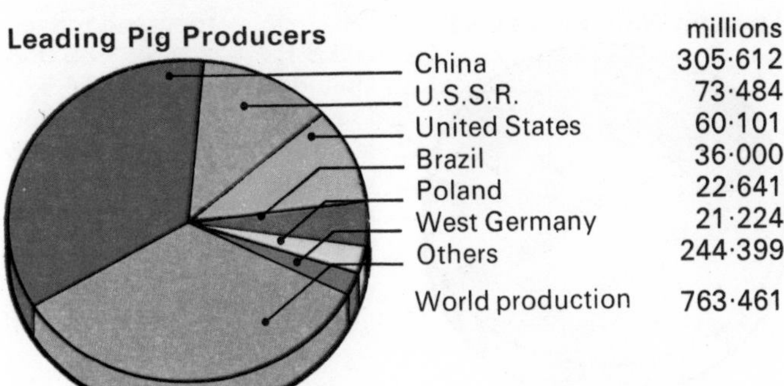

Leading Pig Producers
millions
China 305·612
U.S.S.R. 73·484
United States 60·101
Brazil 36·000
Poland 22·641
West Germany 21·224
Others 244·399
World production 763·461

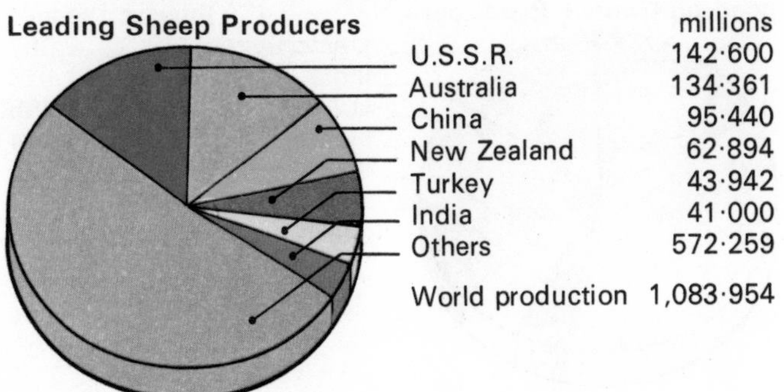

Leading Sheep Producers
millions
U.S.S.R. 142·600
Australia 134·361
China 95·440
New Zealand 62·894
Turkey 43·942
India 41·000
Others 572·259
World production 1,083·954

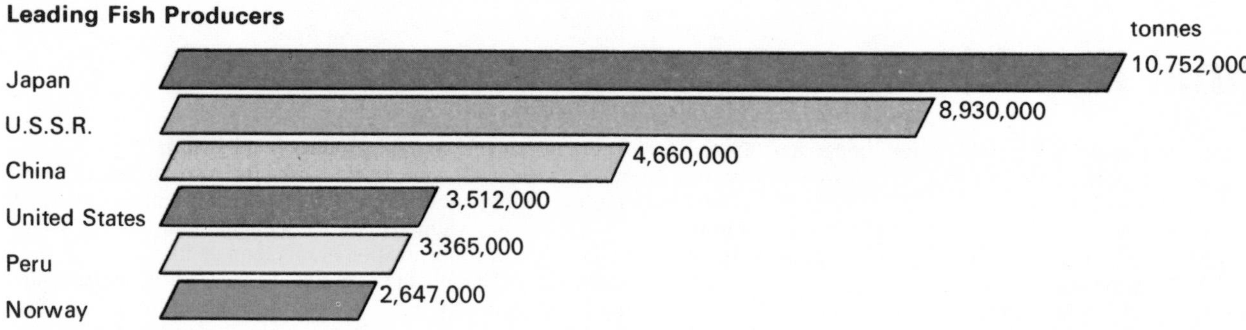
Leading Fish Producers
tonnes
Japan 10,752,000
U.S.S.R. 8,930,000
China 4,660,000
United States 3,512,000
Peru 3,365,000
Norway 2,647,000

WORLD FISHERIES

Fishing fleets of the world catch about 72 million tonnes of fish every year, and the total is constantly rising. There is a serious danger of over-fishing, and some traditional fishing grounds, such as those off Iceland, are already yielding significantly lower catches than they used to.

Fish are rich in protein and form an important part of the world diet. But some fish, and the waste of others, are used for other purposes. For example, fish-meal is used for chicken and livestock feed and as fertilizer. Other fish products include glue, isinglass, and oil for use in margarine, soap, candles, paints and linoleum.

WHALING

Whales are hunted largely for their oil, which is mostly made into margarine, but also for their flesh, which is esteemed in some countries, such as Japan. Overhunting has seriously reduced the world's whale population. Strenuous international efforts are now being made to limit whale catches.

The two main whaling countries are the U.S.S.R. and Japan, which take about 74 per cent of the total catch. Smaller whaling fleets are operated by Australia, Brazil, Canada, Chile, Denmark, Iceland, Norway, Peru, Portugal, South Africa and Spain. The world annual catch is about 15,000,000 tonnes.

Left: **Making cheese at Roquefort, France. The cheese, named after its place of origin, is made from the milk of goats and ewes.**

Right: **A worker tapping a rubber tree. Each tree yields about 18 litres (4 gallons) of latex a year, for up to 30 years.**

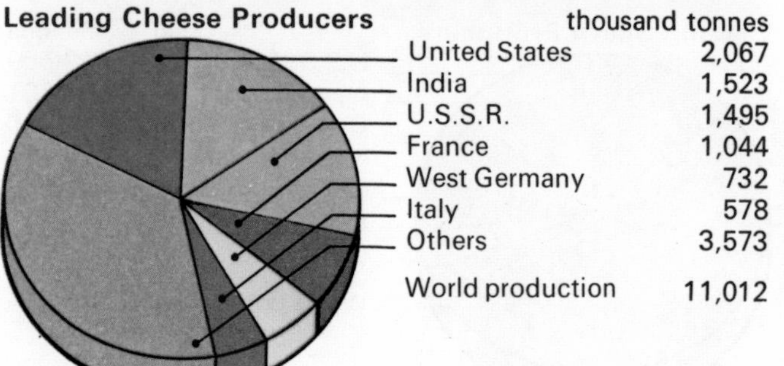
Leading Cheese Producers
thousand tonnes
United States 2,067
India 1,523
U.S.S.R. 1,495
France 1,044
West Germany 732
Italy 578
Others 3,573
World production 11,012

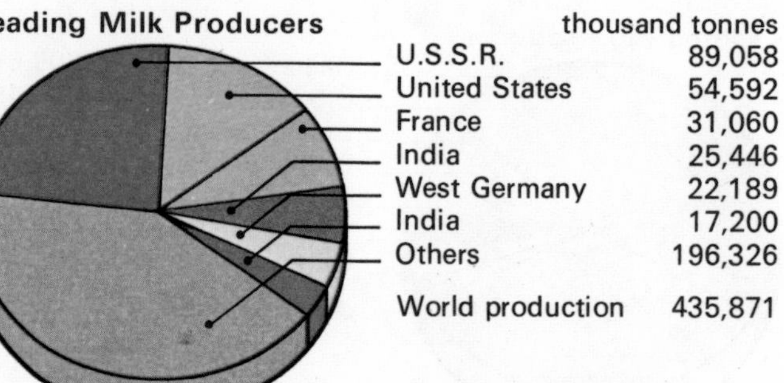
Leading Milk Producers
thousand tonnes
U.S.S.R. 89,058
United States 54,592
France 31,060
India 25,446
West Germany 22,189
India 17,200
Others 196,326
World production 435,871

Natural Products for Manufacturing

Vegetable and animal products are used not only for food, but also as raw materials for manufacturing. Unlike mineral resources, animal and vegetable resources can be continually replenished, though reliance on wild crops has greatly reduced the world's timber stocks.

Before the advent of man-made fibres, people had to rely entirely on natural products for making fabrics and ropes. The most important vegetable fibre is cotton, which is used mostly for cloth. Flax is used for making linen and cord, and the leading producers are the U.S.S.R., Poland, France and Czechoslovakia. Hemp, used for carpeting, ropes, sailcloth and other coarse fabrics, comes mostly from the U.S.S.R., India, Romania and China. Jute, mainly used for sacking and hessian, is produced mostly in India, Bangladesh, China and Burma. Sisal, from which twine is made, comes mostly from East Africa.

The two main animal fibres are wool, produced mostly from sheep — though goats and rabbits also produce limited amounts — and silk, made by the silkworm moth, *Bombyx mori.*

Natural rubber, in great demand for motor-car tyres, is produced largely in southeastern Asia, though synthetic rubber is now made in even larger quantities. Most tobacco is grown for smoking, but it is used for numerous other products, including insecticides and drugs.

The world's forests yield many products. Forest lands have been greatly reduced in the past 2,000 years — for example, in Roman times, a large part of Britain was under forest. But today, careful management is ensuring that new growth is largely keeping up with demand, especially in the quick-growing softwoods.

Timber in its various forms is the most important forest product. Some of it is used as logs for telegraph poles and other items, while a great deal is turned into squared timber of various sections. Some timber is made into veneers, most of which is laminated to form plywood. Wood that is not suitable for such uses can be turned into chips, which are bonded with plastic glues into chipboards, or shredded into fibres for making into hardboards and similar products.

Newsprint is made from woodpulp, which is wood ground up in water. The many substances derived from wood include chemicals, such as acetone, methanol and glycerine, and such products as explosives, plastics and rayon.

Leading Rubber Producers

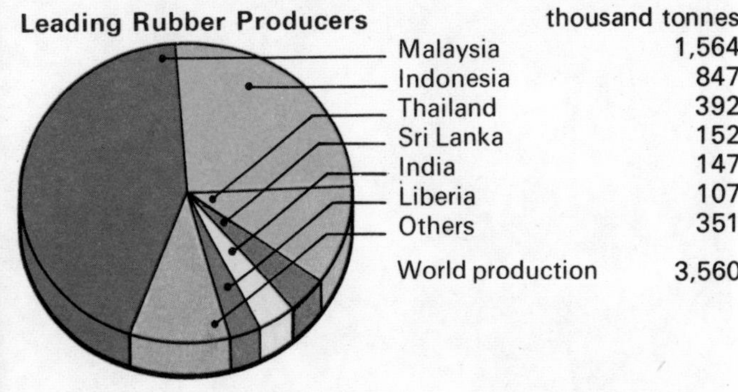
thousand tonnes
Malaysia 1,564
Indonesia 847
Thailand 392
Sri Lanka 152
India 147
Liberia 107
Others 351
World production 3,560

Leading Natural Fibre Producers

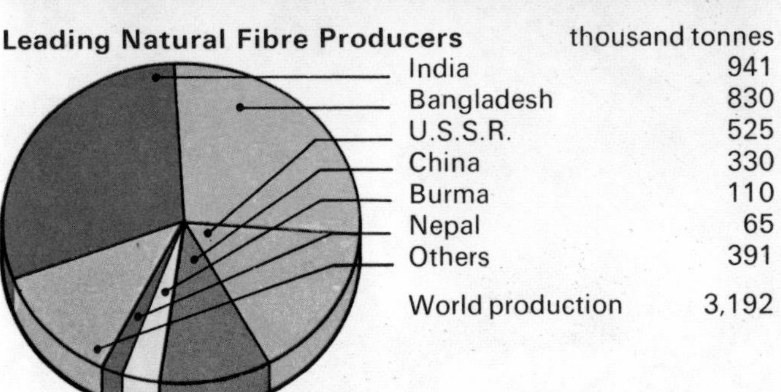
thousand tonnes
India 941
Bangladesh 830
U.S.S.R. 525
China 330
Burma 110
Nepal 65
Others 391
World production 3,192

Leading Raw Silk Producers

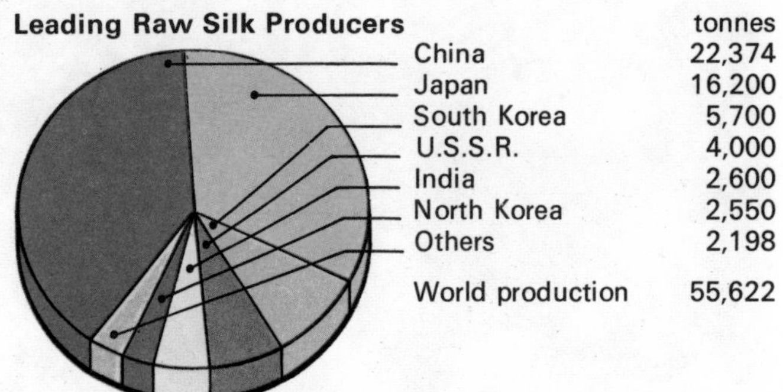
tonnes
China 22,374
Japan 16,200
South Korea 5,700
U.S.S.R. 4,000
India 2,600
North Korea 2,550
Others 2,198
World production 55,622

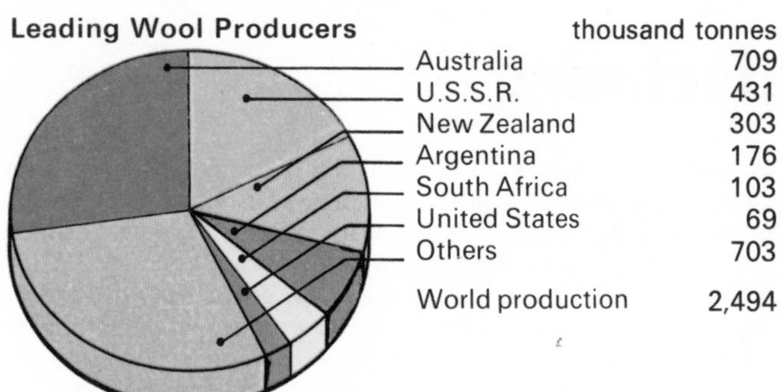
Leading Wool Producers
thousand tonnes
Australia 709
U.S.S.R. 431
New Zealand 303
Argentina 176
South Africa 103
United States 69
Others 703
World production 2,494

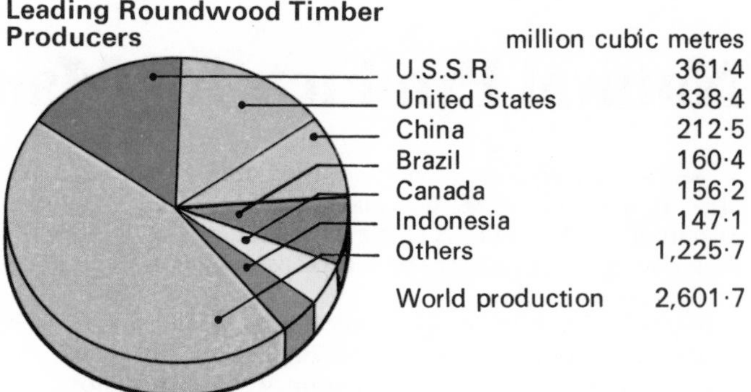
Leading Roundwood Timber Producers
million cubic metres
U.S.S.R. 361·4
United States 338·4
China 212·5
Brazil 160·4
Canada 156·2
Indonesia 147·1
Others 1,225·7
World production 2,601·7

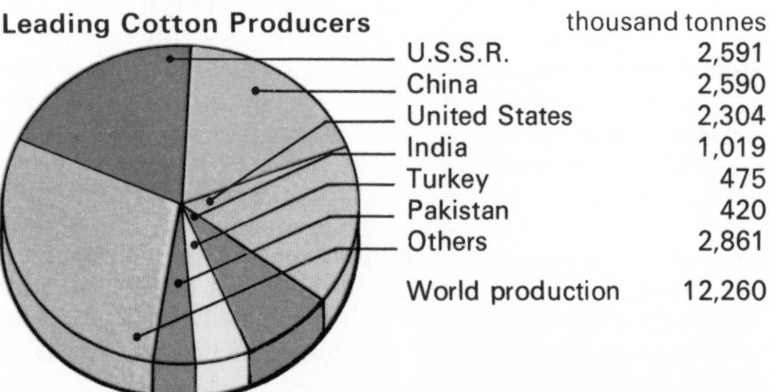
Leading Cotton Producers
thousand tonnes
U.S.S.R. 2,591
China 2,590
United States 2,304
India 1,019
Turkey 475
Pakistan 420
Others 2,861
World production 12,260

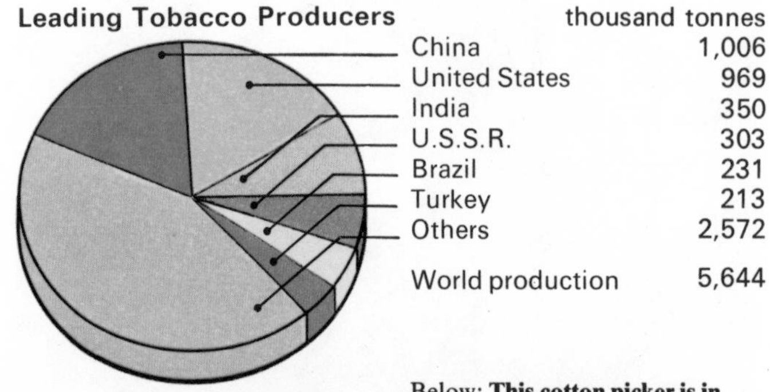
Leading Tobacco Producers
thousand tonnes
China 1,006
United States 969
India 350
U.S.S.R. 303
Brazil 231
Turkey 213
Others 2,572
World production 5,644

Below: **This cotton picker is in Uzbekistan, in the U.S.S.R.**

Mineral Resources

The wealth of the world's industrialized countries is based on supplies of minerals, particularly the metals. When the Industrial Revolution began in the 1750s, and for many years afterwards, processing plants and factories that used metals were built near their sources. Today the industrialized countries import large quantities of minerals, often from many thousands of miles away, while modern technology demands the use of a great variety of metals and other substances that are found in different locations.

Iron is the most important of all metals, and a United Nations survey in the 1950s showed that the world supply of iron ore would last at least 800 years. The ore is distributed all over the globe, but some deposits, particularly those of Africa and the Americas, are especially rich, and it is cheaper to produce iron from these sources. Of the world's leading iron producers, the U.S.S.R. has some of the richest deposits and has, therefore, no need to import iron ore.

Most iron is made into steel, an alloy that is harder and more useful than pure iron. All steel contains small quantities of carbon, a chemical element that is readily obtainable, but most steels have some other metal or metals mixed in to give them particular properties. For example, chromium, nickel and cobalt all help to make steel resistant to corrosion; tungsten and vanadium give it hardness; manganese gives it high tensile strength; and molybdenum gives it more elasticity.

These *ferro-alloys*, as they are called, come from much more limited sources than iron, so countries that have them possess a great strategic advantage in world politics. For example, the United States and Canada between them produce more than 75

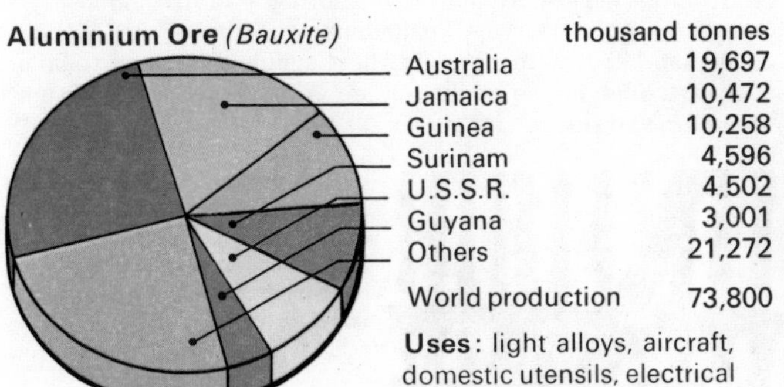

Aluminium Ore (Bauxite)
thousand tonnes
Australia 19,697
Jamaica 10,472
Guinea 10,258
Surinam 4,596
U.S.S.R. 4,502
Guyana 3,001
Others 21,272
World production 73,800
Uses: light alloys, aircraft, domestic utensils, electrical apparatus

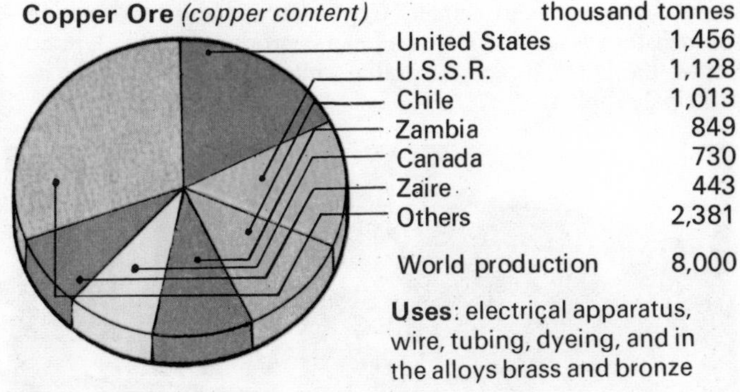

Copper Ore (copper content)
thousand tonnes
United States 1,456
U.S.S.R. 1,128
Chile 1,013
Zambia 849
Canada 730
Zaire 443
Others 2,381
World production 8,000
Uses: electrical apparatus, wire, tubing, dyeing, and in the alloys brass and bronze

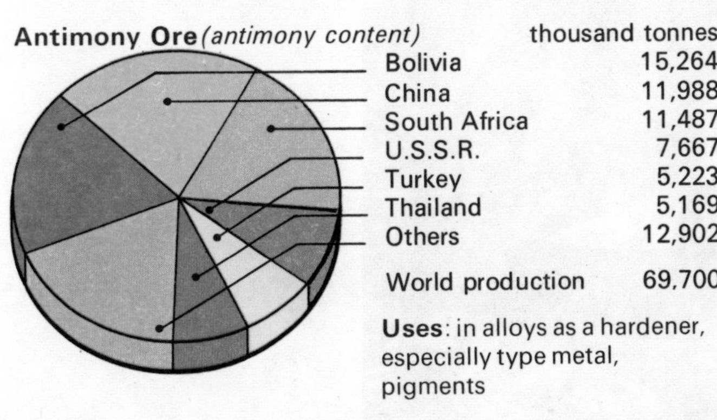

Antimony Ore (antimony content)
thousand tonnes
Bolivia 15,264
China 11,988
South Africa 11,487
U.S.S.R. 7,667
Turkey 5,223
Thailand 5,169
Others 12,902
World production 69,700
Uses: in alloys as a hardener, especially type metal, pigments

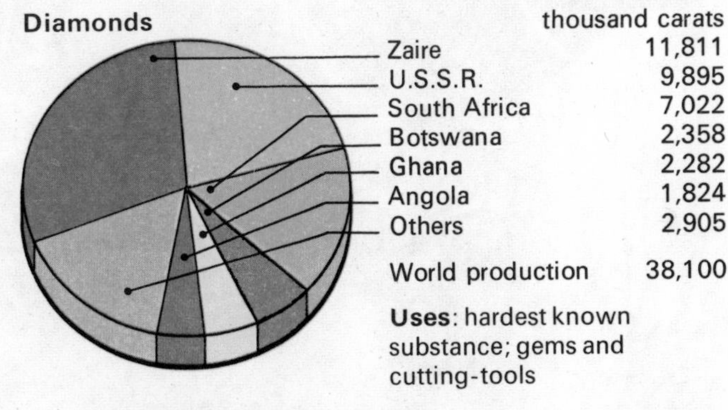

Diamonds
thousand carats
Zaire 11,811
U.S.S.R. 9,895
South Africa 7,022
Botswana 2,358
Ghana 2,282
Angola 1,824
Others 2,905
World production 38,100
Uses: hardest known substance; gems and cutting-tools

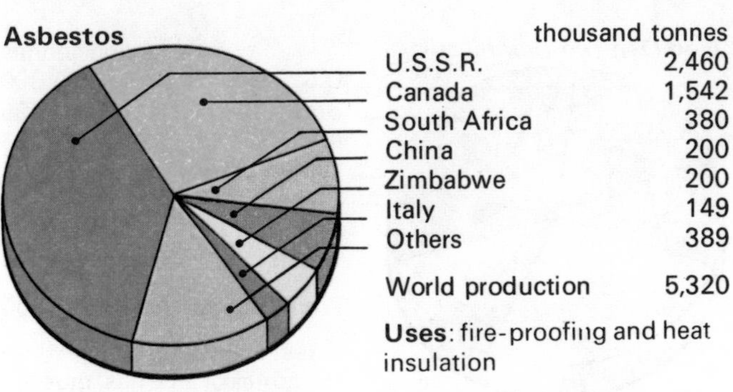

Asbestos
thousand tonnes
U.S.S.R. 2,460
Canada 1,542
South Africa 380
China 200
Zimbabwe 200
Italy 149
Others 389
World production 5,320
Uses: fire-proofing and heat insulation

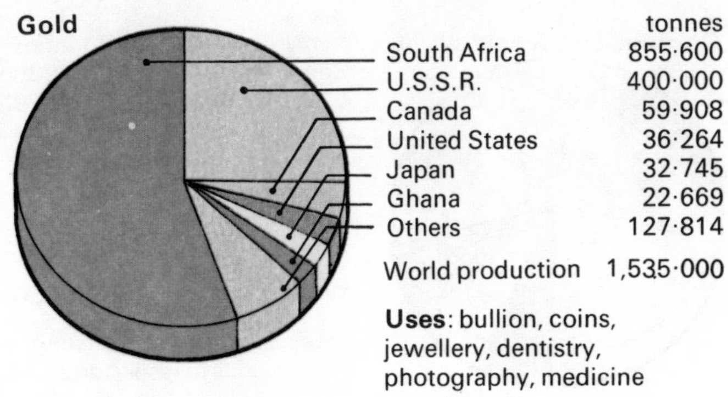

Gold
tonnes
South Africa 855·600
U.S.S.R. 400·000
Canada 59·908
United States 36·264
Japan 32·745
Ghana 22·669
Others 127·814
World production 1,535·000
Uses: bullion, coins, jewellery, dentistry, photography, medicine

per cent of the world's molybdenum; Canada, New Caledonia and the U.S.S.R. produce 71 per cent of the nickel; and Zaire produces 59 per cent of the cobalt.

Equally vital in modern industry are the non-ferrous metals — that is, those that are not used in alloys with iron. Among the most important of these metals is copper, which is widely used for electrical work and in plumbing. Outside North America and the U.S.S.R., main supplies occur in Zaire and Zambia in Africa, and in Chile and Peru in South America. A fall in the world price of copper caused these four countries to cut production in 1975. But their strategic importance remains, and they will have a considerable influence on world markets when prices are higher again.

Other important non-ferrous metals include aluminium, lead, zinc and tin. Aluminium is one of the most abundant chemical elements in the Earth's crust, and is certainly the most abundant of all metals. But it is difficult to extract, even from its best source, bauxite, which can be either a hard rock or soft mud. Australia and Jamaica head the world's sources of bauxite.

Tin, for which Cornwall in England was once famous as a source, now comes principally from Malaysia and Indonesia in southeastern Asia, and Bolivia. Lead is produced by the United States, the U.S.S.R. and Australia, while zinc has Canada as its principal supplier.

The precious metals — gold, silver and platinum and its related metals, such as palladium — are valued because of their natural beauty as much as for their industrial importance. Gold, of which South Africa has, by far, the largest supply, is used largely as a form of currency. Most of the gold mined goes straight into bank vaults or is used to make jewellery. Silver, less used today for money, has more industrial uses, and the U.S.S.R. and Canada lead in silver production. Platinum metals come from North America, South Africa, the U.S.S.R. and South America.

The world is using minerals, especially metals, at such a rate that scientists are forecasting serious shortages of some of them. Fortunately, pressure for supplies has stimulated research, so that known resources have actually increased. In 1965, for example, copper reserves were estimated at 140 million tonnes but, in 1973, nearly 300 million tonnes were known. But even with scrap copper providing half the world's needs, supplies are being used up at an alarming rate.

A report issued in 1975 by the United States National Academy of Sciences suggested that real shortages of five metals — chromium, gold, mercury, palladium, and tin — could occur during the 1980s. Other metals whose supply also seems to be in danger, though not so imminent, are antimony, silver, tungsten, vanadium and zinc.

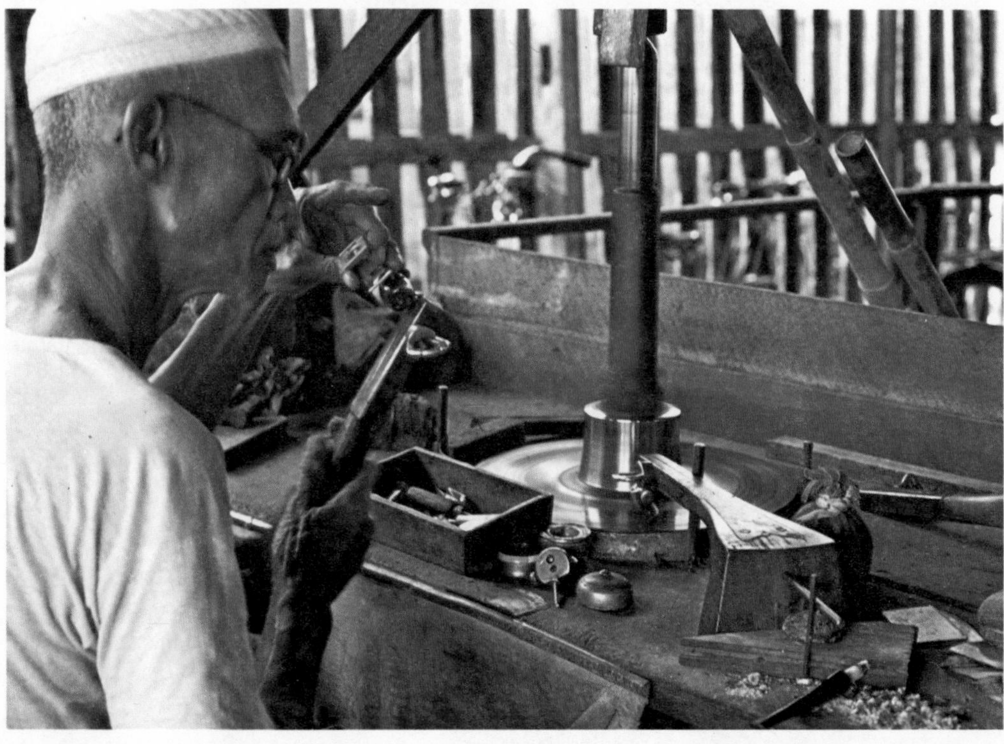

Left: **A worker cuts a diamond for use as a gem-stone. This operator is at Martapura, in Indonesian Borneo; major centres of the industry are in the Netherlands and Israel.**

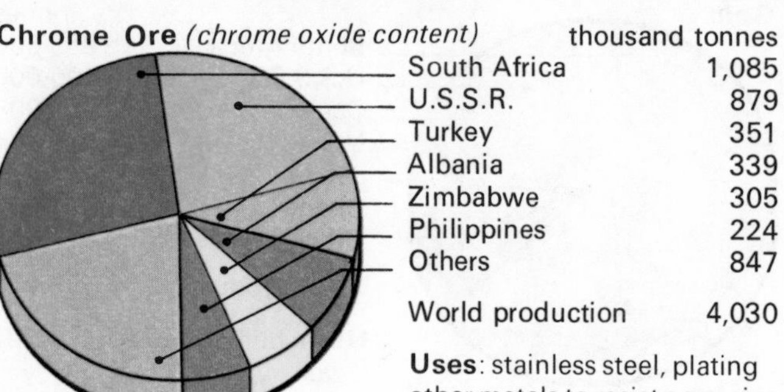
Chrome Ore *(chrome oxide content)*
thousand tonnes
South Africa 1,085
U.S.S.R. 879
Turkey 351
Albania 339
Zimbabwe 305
Philippines 224
Others 847
World production 4,030
Uses: stainless steel, plating other metals to resist corrosion

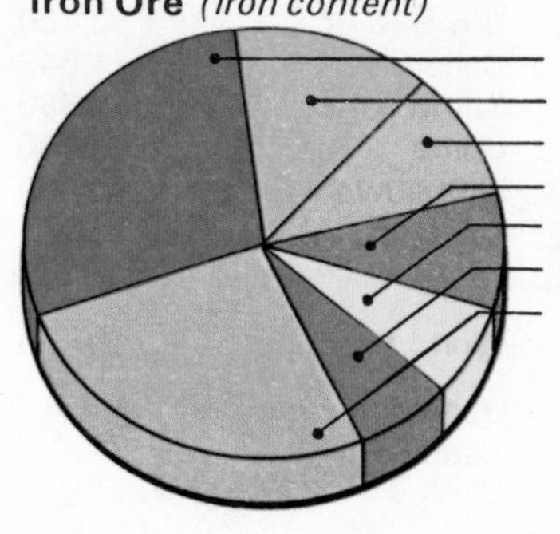
Iron Ore *(iron content)*
million tonnes
U.S.S.R. 130·890
Brazil 60·596
Australia 58·263
United States 50·152
China 43·230
Canada 34·992
Others 134·576
World production 512·700
Uses: machinery and structures of all kinds, mostly as steel

Lead Ore *(lead content)*

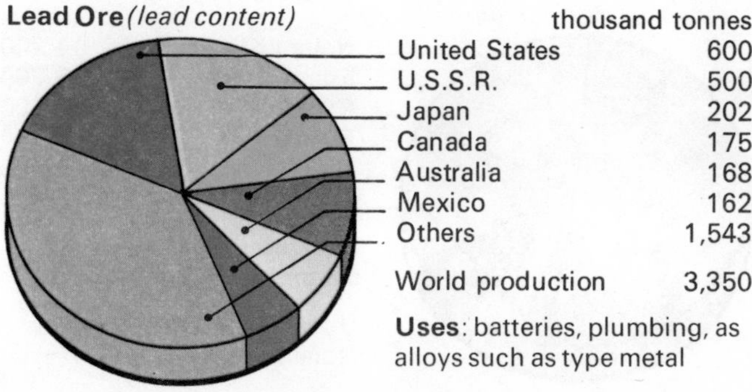

	thousand tonnes
United States	600
U.S.S.R.	500
Japan	202
Canada	175
Australia	168
Mexico	162
Others	1,543
World production	3,350

Uses: batteries, plumbing, as alloys such as type metal

Nickel Ore *(nickel content)*

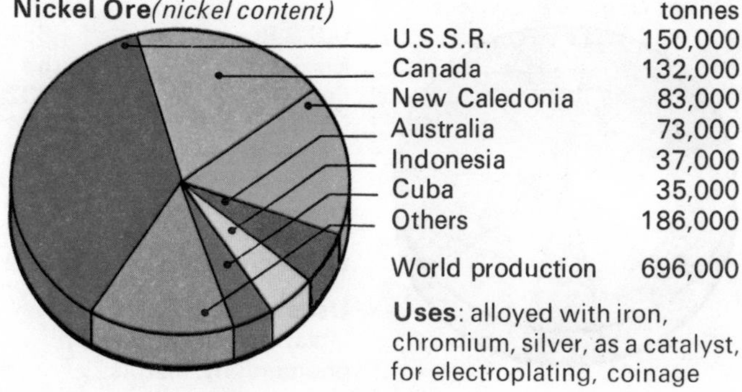

	tonnes
U.S.S.R.	150,000
Canada	132,000
New Caledonia	83,000
Australia	73,000
Indonesia	37,000
Cuba	35,000
Others	186,000
World production	696,000

Uses: alloyed with iron, chromium, silver, as a catalyst, for electroplating, coinage

Magnesium Ore *(crude magnesite)*

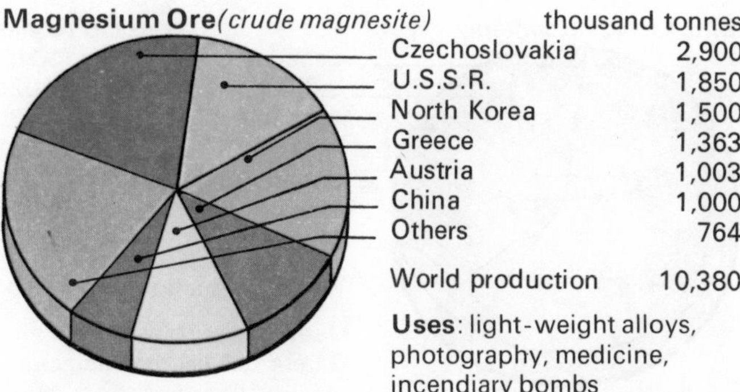

	thousand tonnes
Czechoslovakia	2,900
U.S.S.R.	1,850
North Korea	1,500
Greece	1,363
Austria	1,003
China	1,000
Others	764
World production	10,380

Uses: light-weight alloys, photography, medicine, incendiary bombs

Phosphate Rock *(Phosphorus pentoxide content)*

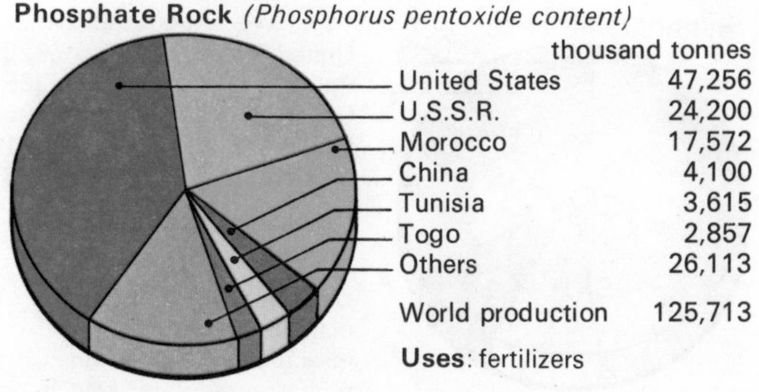

	thousand tonnes
United States	47,256
U.S.S.R.	24,200
Morocco	17,572
China	4,100
Tunisia	3,615
Togo	2,857
Others	26,113
World production	125,713

Uses: fertilizers

Manganese Ore *(manganese content)*

	thousand tonnes
U.S.S.R.	2,904
South Africa	2,338
Gabon	941
Brazil	900
Australia	811
India	655
Others	961
World production	9,510

Uses: steel, fertilizers, paints, photography

Potash *(Potassium monoxide content)*

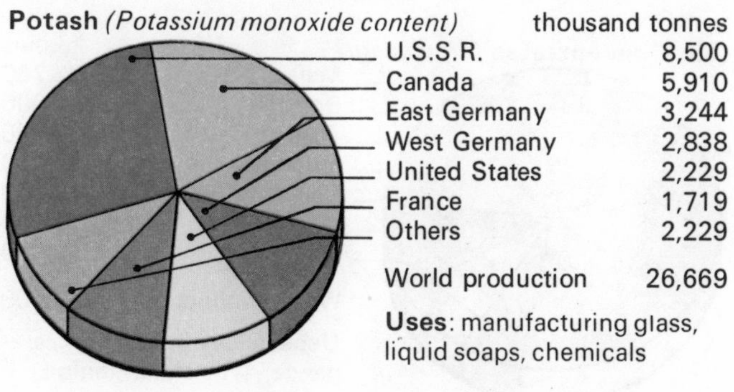

	thousand tonnes
U.S.S.R.	8,500
Canada	5,910
East Germany	3,244
West Germany	2,838
United States	2,229
France	1,719
Others	2,229
World production	26,669

Uses: manufacturing glass, liquid soaps, chemicals

Mercury

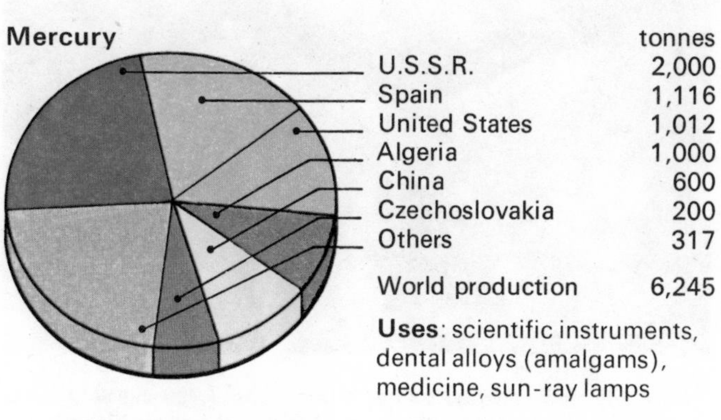

	tonnes
U.S.S.R.	2,000
Spain	1,116
United States	1,012
Algeria	1,000
China	600
Czechoslovakia	200
Others	317
World production	6,245

Uses: scientific instruments, dental alloys (amalgams), medicine, sun-ray lamps

Salt

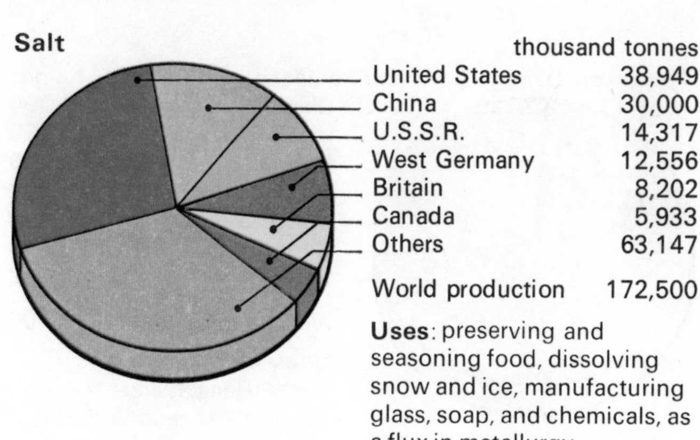

	thousand tonnes
United States	38,949
China	30,000
U.S.S.R.	14,317
West Germany	12,556
Britain	8,202
Canada	5,933
Others	63,147
World production	172,500

Uses: preserving and seasoning food, dissolving snow and ice, manufacturing glass, soap, and chemicals, as a flux in metallurgy

Silver Ore *(silver content)*

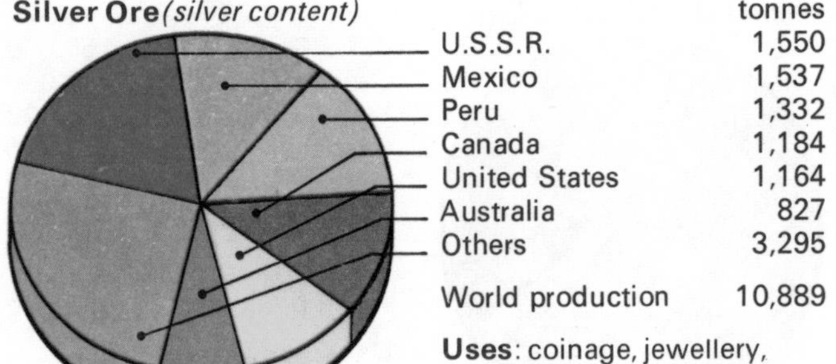

	tonnes
U.S.S.R.	1,550
Mexico	1,537
Peru	1,332
Canada	1,184
United States	1,164
Australia	827
Others	3,295
World production	10,889

Uses: coinage, jewellery, tablewear, electroplating, photography, mirrors

Uranium Ore *(uranium content)*

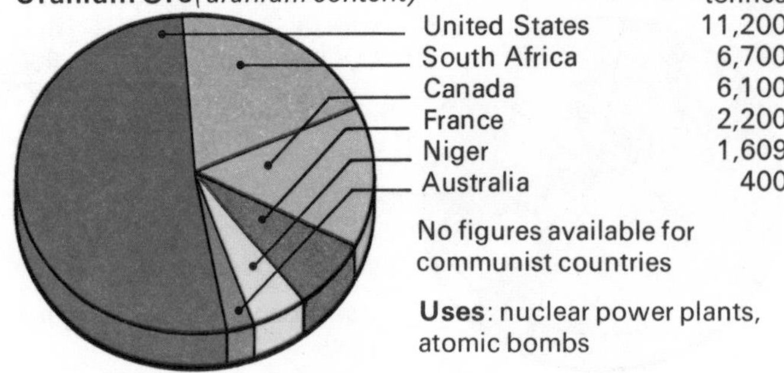

	tonnes
United States	11,200
South Africa	6,700
Canada	6,100
France	2,200
Niger	1,609
Australia	400

No figures available for communist countries

Uses: nuclear power plants, atomic bombs

Sulphur *(unrefined)*

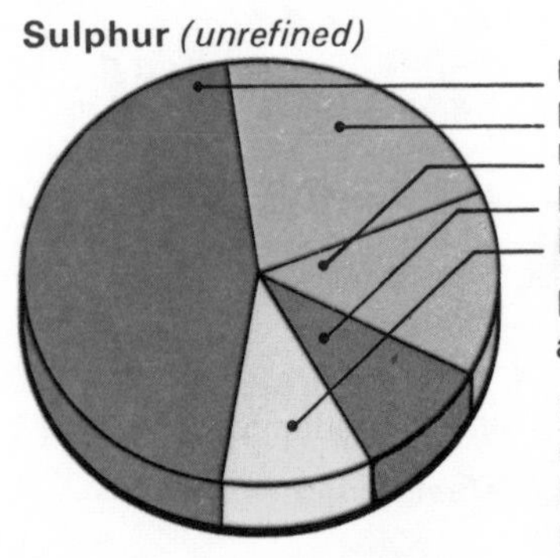

	thousand tonnes
United States	5,822
Poland	4,765
U.S.S.R.	2,500
France	1,841
Mexico	1,856

No reliable world total available.

Uses: making gunpowder, matches, fertilizers, insecticides, vulcanizing rubber; as sulphuric acid, in numerous manufacturing processes

Zinc Ore *(zinc content)*

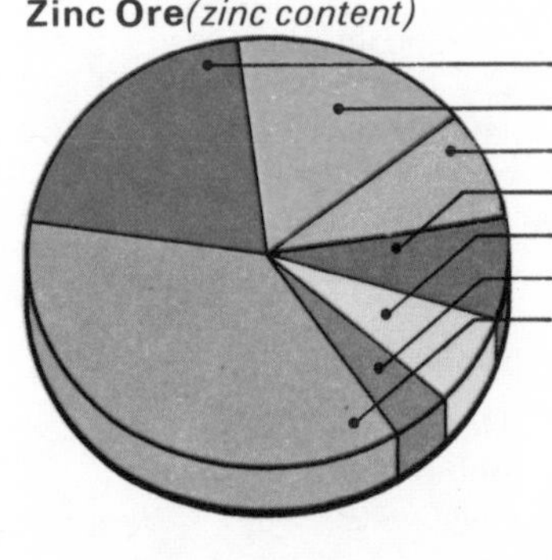

	thousand tonnes
Canada	1,203
U.S.S.R.	1,020
Australia	528
Peru	491
United States	294
Mexico	246
Others	2,542
World production	6,324

Uses: alloys (brass, bronze, German silver), galvanizing, manufacturing paint, cosmetics, rubber goods, and dental cements; in medicine

Tin Concentrates *(tin content)*

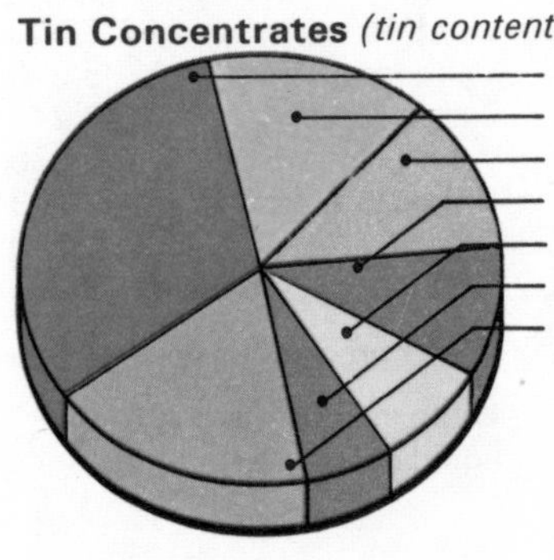

	tonnes
Malaysia	62,700
Bolivia	30,900
Thailand	30,200
Indonesia	27,400
China	18,000
U.S.S.R.	18,000
Others	49,000
World production	236,200

Uses: alloys (brass, bronze, pewter, type metal), tinfoil, tinplate, collapsible tubes, bearings, solder

Tungsten Ore *(tungstic acid content)*

	tonnes
China	11,300
U.S.S.R.	10,350
Bolivia	3,759
South Korea	3,513
United States	3,436
North Korea	2,700
Others	15,542
World production	50,600

Uses: very hard steel, electric-lamp filaments, electronic apparatus, X-ray apparatus

Above: **Mining for gold at Elsburg, in the Witwatersrand of South Africa. Mines here vary in depth from 900 to 3,700 metres (3,000 to 12,000 feet), and are highly mechanized.**

Fuel and Energy

Modern civilization depends largely on plentiful sources of fuel to provide heat and power. The principal sources of heat and power today are provided by the *fossil fuels,* which were formed by decaying plant and animal life millions of years ago. The main fossil fuels are coal, oil and natural gas. In developed countries, all industry has been founded on these three fuels. Most of our electricity is produced in power stations, where coal or oil are used to turn water to steam. The steam drives turbines, which turn huge electricity generators. Coal, the most important fuel of the 1800s, has now taken third place to oil and natural gas.

The principal sources of oil, the most important fossil fuel, are the Middle East, North America, the North Sea, the U.S.S.R., Venezuela, Argentina, Indonesia, Libya and Nigeria. In the mid-1970s, the United States, although itself a big producer, was consuming about 30 per cent more oil than it produced, and relied heavily on imports from Venezuela, Canada and the Middle East. Western Europe produced very little oil and relied almost entirely on imports from the Middle East, Libya and Nigeria. Japan, another major user, also had to import nearly all its oil.

But the discovery and exploitation of new resources means that the pattern of the world's fuel supplies and distribution is changing all the time. The development of North Sea natural gas fields made Britain independent of gas imports in the mid-1970s. And Britain, Norway and the Netherlands were set to be independent in oil from the same source by the early 1980s. The ever-increasing cost of fuel from the Middle East has stimulated research for new sources.

Although the world's stocks of fossil fuels are vast, and more remain to be found and developed, there is already a serious threat of shortages — and, once exhausted, fossil fuels cannot be replaced. World coal stocks may last for about 800 years, but oil and gas are likely to be used up early next century. However, alternative sources of power are being developed.

An extremely important alternative to fossil fuels is hydro-

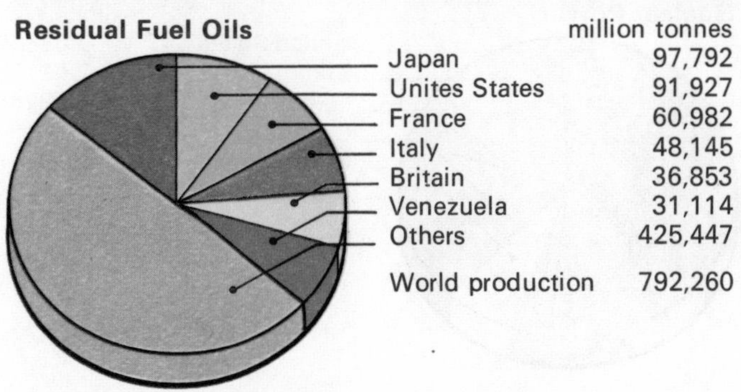

Residual Fuel Oils
million tonnes
Japan 97,792
Unites States 91,927
France 60,982
Italy 48,145
Britain 36,853
Venezuela 31,114
Others 425,447
World production 792,260

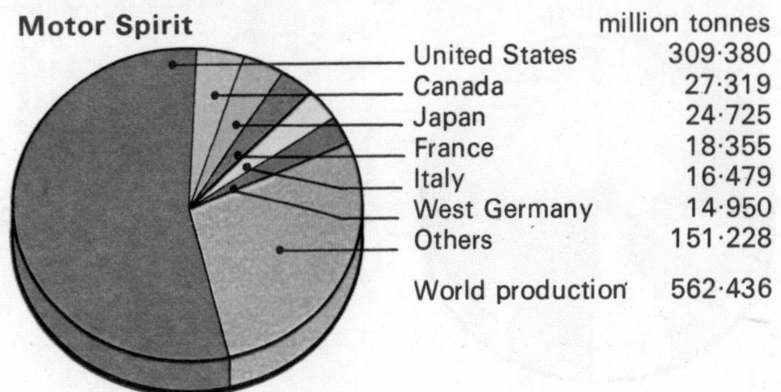

Motor Spirit
million tonnes
United States 309·380
Canada 27·319
Japan 24·725
France 18·355
Italy 16·479
West Germany 14·950
Others 151·228
World production 562·436

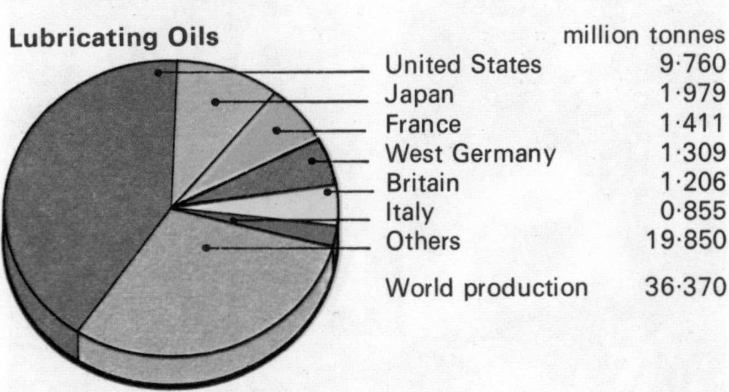

Lubricating Oils
million tonnes
United States 9·760
Japan 1·979
France 1·411
West Germany 1·309
Britain 1·206
Italy 0·855
Others 19·850
World production 36·370

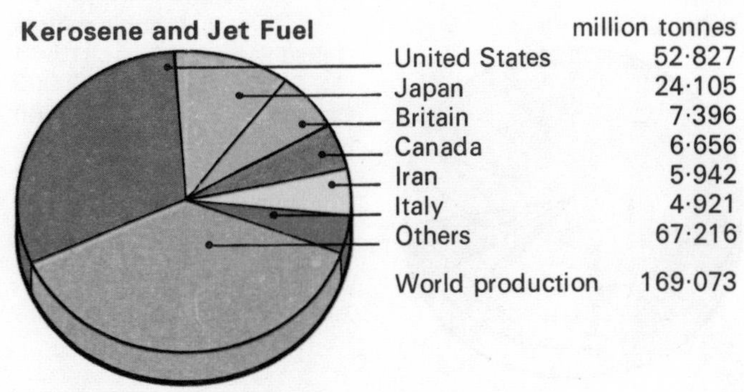

Kerosene and Jet Fuel
million tonnes
United States 52·827
Japan 24·105
Britain 7·396
Canada 6·656
Iran 5·942
Italy 4·921
Others 67·216
World production 169·073

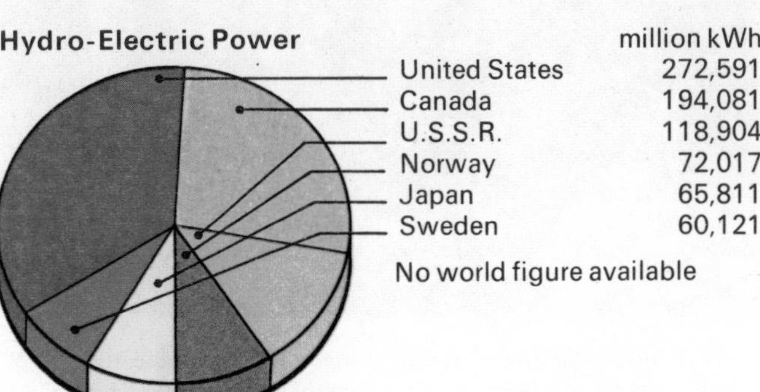

Hydro-Electric Power
million kWh
United States 272,591
Canada 194,081
U.S.S.R. 118,904
Norway 72,017
Japan 65,811
Sweden 60,121
No world figure available

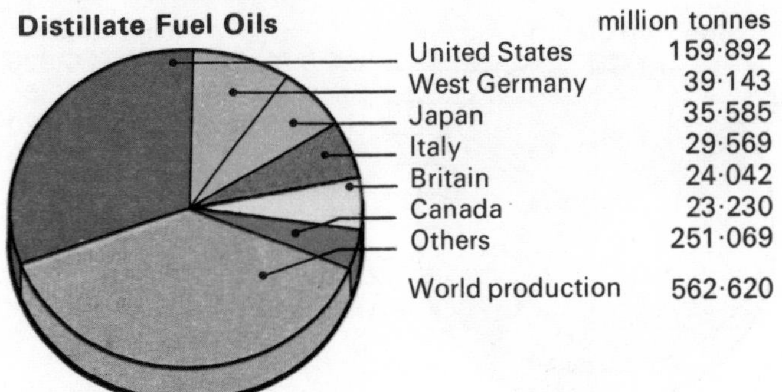

Distillate Fuel Oils
million tonnes
United States 159·892
West Germany 39·143
Japan 35·585
Italy 29·569
Britain 24·042
Canada 23·230
Others 251·069
World production 562·620

electric power, using the flow of rivers and the movement of the sea to drive generators. Many countries already make great use of hydro-electric power. Norway, for example, generates 99 per cent of its electricity this way.

Nuclear power, using the heat released by the fission (splitting up) of uranium atoms, is extremely important too. Britain is one of the leaders in this field, with about 10 per cent of its electricity coming from nuclear power stations. Uranium is, fortunately, in good supply, though high-grade ores — rocks from which the metal can easily be extracted — are less common. The main known reserves of uranium are in North America, Zaire, South Africa, Australia, France and Czechoslovakia. China and the U.S.S.R. have kept their resources of uranium secret, but it is thought they have substantial reserves. Modern breeder-reactors not only generate heat by nuclear fission, but also 'breed' more fuel at the same time.

A more useful long-term source of power is nuclear fusion. Fusion plants work on the same principle as the sun, fusing together atoms of hydrogen to form helium — a slightly heavier gas. In the process, great heat is released. Research on this process is likely to continue for several years, but success will solve fuel and energy problems for all time, because the hydrogen fuel can be readily extracted from water.

With the increasing use of nuclear power, conservationists are becoming more and more concerned about the possibility of pollution by waste products from nuclear power stations. Most of these products are radioactive and need to be stored extremely carefully in order to reduce the chance of pollution and the consequent endangering of life. Such waste products gradually decrease in radioactivity but, in some cases, it would take thousands of years for the radioactivity to decrease to a safe level.

Two other major sources of power are the heat of the Sun and the internal heat of the Earth. Various forms of solar cells have been devised to absorb the Sun's heat and convert it into electricity. But panels in which running water absorbs the Sun's heat are generally more successful. Even in climates where there is a fair amount of cloud, the use of heat collected by roof-mounted solar panels can considerably reduce fuel bills.

The Earth's heat is easiest to harness in places where there is volcanic activity, or where hot springs exist. Geothermal energy has been most successfully developed in Iceland, New Zealand and the southwestern part of the United States.

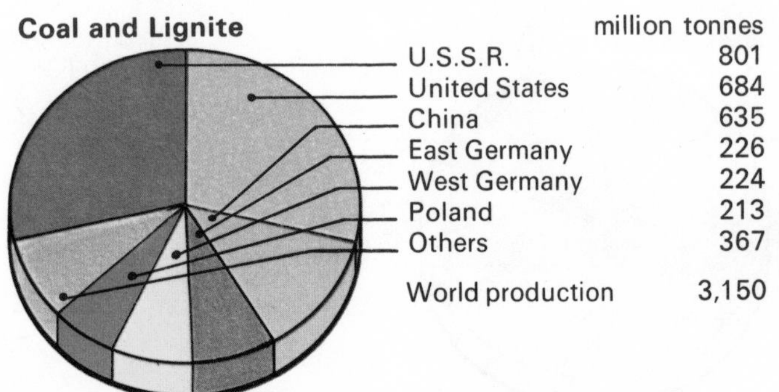
Coal and Lignite
million tonnes
U.S.S.R. 801
United States 684
China 635
East Germany 226
West Germany 224
Poland 213
Others 367
World production 3,150

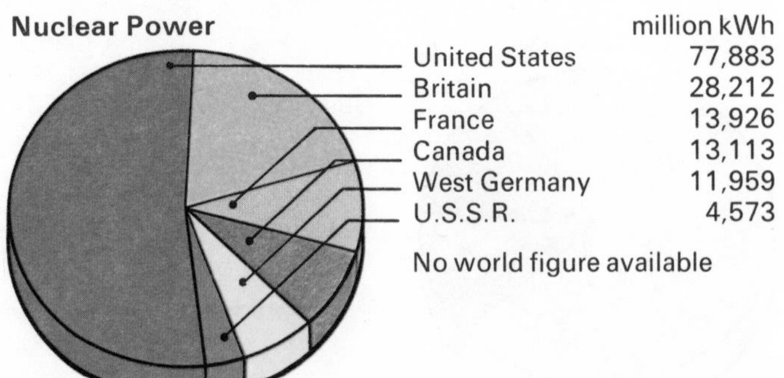
Nuclear Power
million kWh
United States 77,883
Britain 28,212
France 13,926
Canada 13,113
West Germany 11,959
U.S.S.R. 4,573
No world figure available

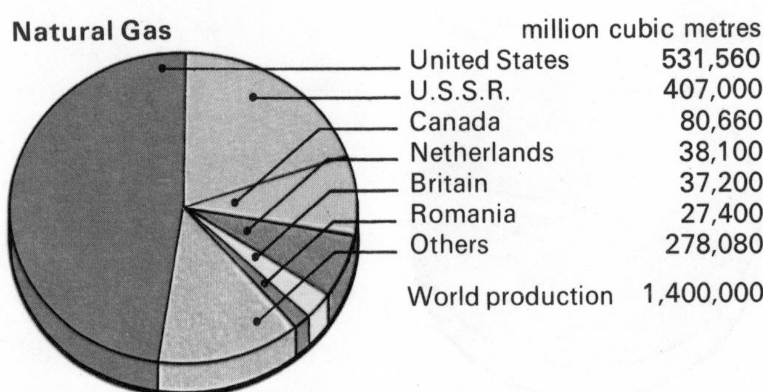
Natural Gas
million cubic metres
United States 531,560
U.S.S.R. 407,000
Canada 80,660
Netherlands 38,100
Britain 37,200
Romania 27,400
Others 278,080
World production 1,400,000

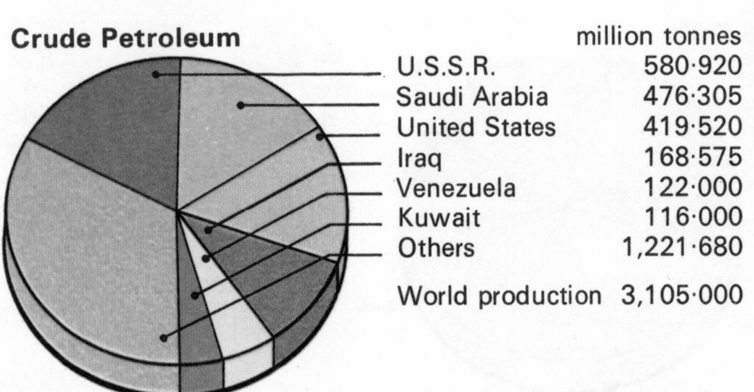
Crude Petroleum
million tonnes
U.S.S.R. 580·920
Saudi Arabia 476·305
United States 419·520
Iraq 168·575
Venezuela 122·000
Kuwait 116·000
Others 1,221·680
World production 3,105·000

Above: **Drilling for oil in Nigeria, which ranks seventh in world oil production.**

Right: **Modern coal-cutting machinery in a typical, highly mechanized British mine.**

Occupations, Manufacturing and Production

Basic requirements of all peoples are food and shelter, and for this reason the simplest economies are based on the provision of these two things. In parts of Africa and South America, primitive tribes practise subsistence farming, growing just enough food for themselves and their families. The production of a surplus, which can be sold to purchase other goods, is the first step towards development.

Subsistence farming is uneconomic because it requires enormous effort for comparatively little output. Even today, many important countries still have large parts of their working population engaged in agriculture, simply because they are using old-fashioned methods requiring a great deal of labour. For example, 74 per cent of India's workers are in agriculture, but India still has to import some food. In contrast, only 4.2 per cent of the workers are engaged in agriculture in the United States — a major food exporter. Other countries with high proportions of workers in agriculture are Bangladesh (74 per cent) and China (an estimated 62 per cent).

The major manufacturing countries are those of Western and Central Europe, where industrialization began, the United States, Canada and the U.S.S.R. The pattern is changing all the time. Many of the developing nations, particularly former colonies, are increasing their industries by leaps and bounds, although they still have a long way to go before they catch up with the economies of the European countries.

A measure of a country's industrialization and prosperity is the proportion of its working population engaged in 'services' — non-productive occupations. These include communications, such as transport, press and television, many professional services, such as medicine and law, and the work of civil servants, bankers, shopkeepers, and many more. The United States, for example, has over 60 per cent of workers in services.

Another way of looking at a country's way of working is to consider its Gross Domestic Product — that is, the total value of all the goods and services its people produce in a year. India's 74 per cent engaged in farming contribute 40 per cent of the country's annual wealth, while 48 per cent of West Germany's GDP is produced by the 48 per cent working in industry. It is notable that, in developed countries heavily orientated towards agricultural production — such as Australia, New Zealand and Argentina — the proportion of the GDP produced by it is small: 5 per cent, 10 per cent and 13 per cent respectively.

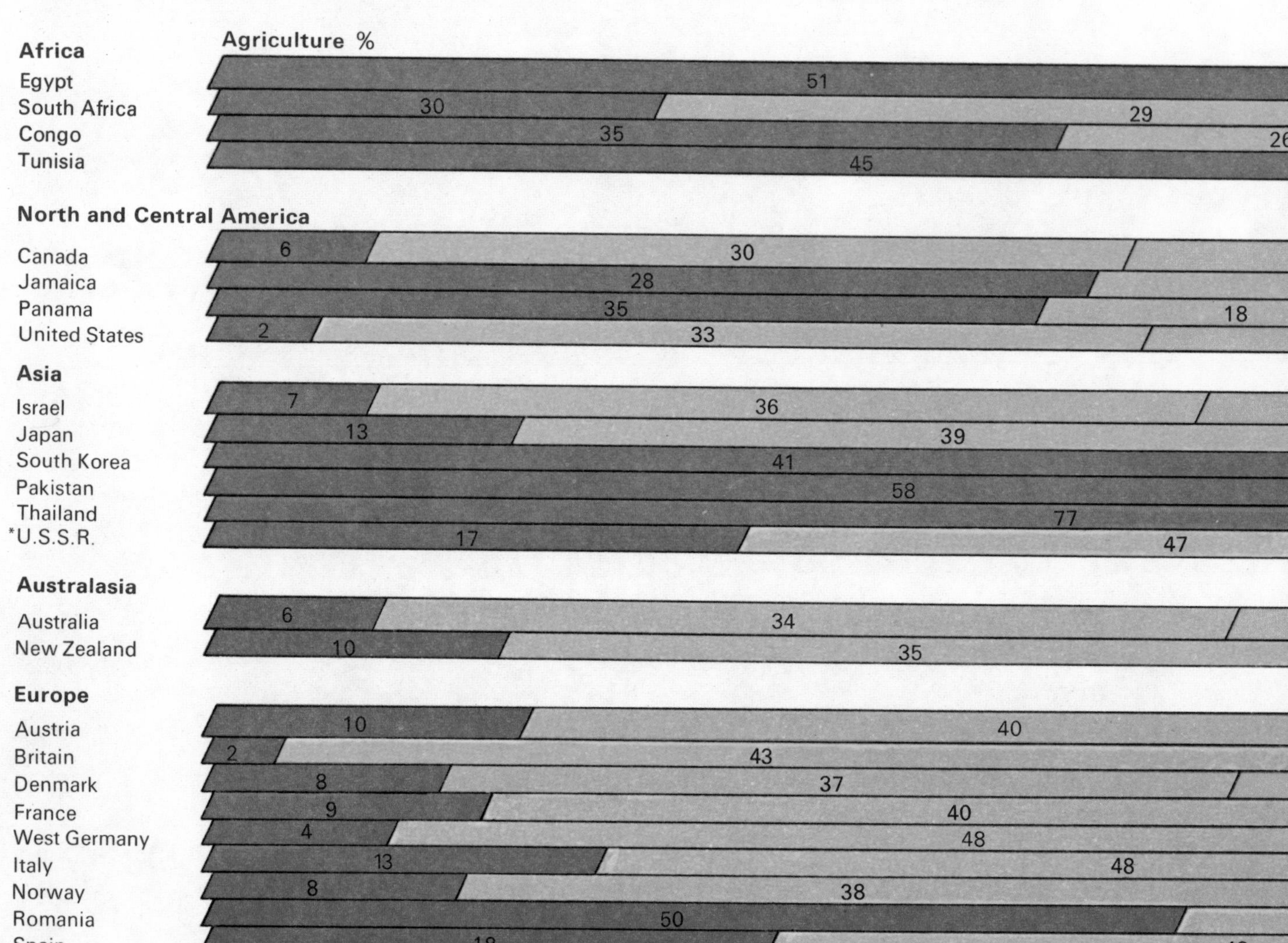

Agriculture %
Africa
Egypt 51
South Africa 30 29
Congo 35 26
Tunisia 45
North and Central America
Canada 6 30
Jamaica 28
Panama 35 18
United States 2 33
Asia
Israel 7 36
Japan 13 39
South Korea 41
Pakistan 58
Thailand 77
*U.S.S.R. 17 47
Australasia
Australia 6 34
New Zealand 10 35
Europe
Austria 10 40
Britain 2 43
Denmark 8 37
France 9 40
West Germany 4 48
Italy 13 48
Norway 8 38
Romania 50
Spain 18 43

* Includes European part of the U.S.S.R.

BBC tv
colour

Right: **A television cameraman at work during an outside broadcast. Most workers in radio and television are among those engaged in services – occupations that do not result in the production of goods.**

Below: **The chart shows the proportion of workers engaged in agriculture, industry and services in various countries.**

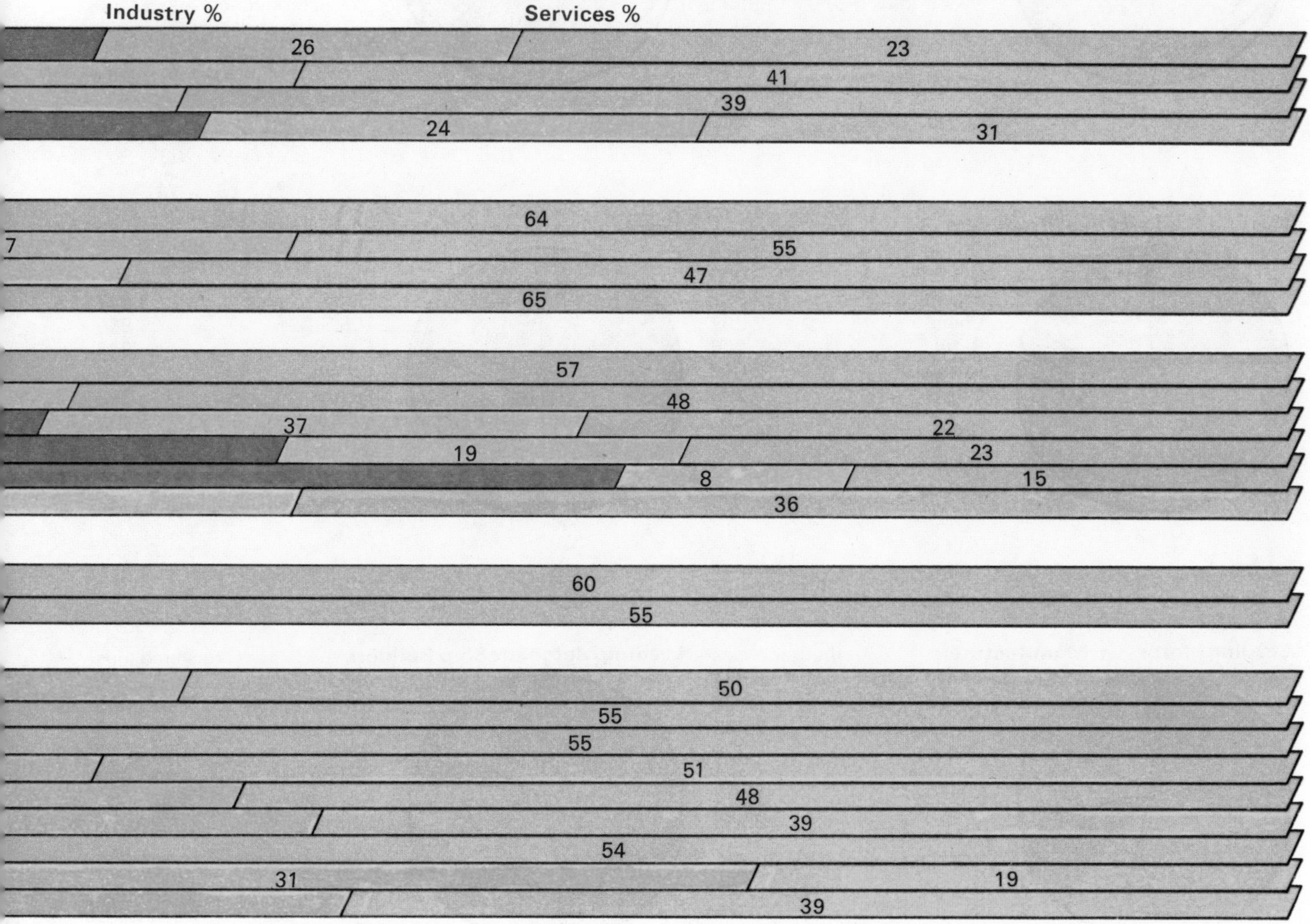

Industry % | Services %

26 | 23
41
39
24 | 31

64
7 | 55
47
65

57
48
37 | 22
19 | 23
8 | 15
36

60
55

50
55
55
51
48
39
54
31 | 19
39

Leading Wheat Flour Manufacturers

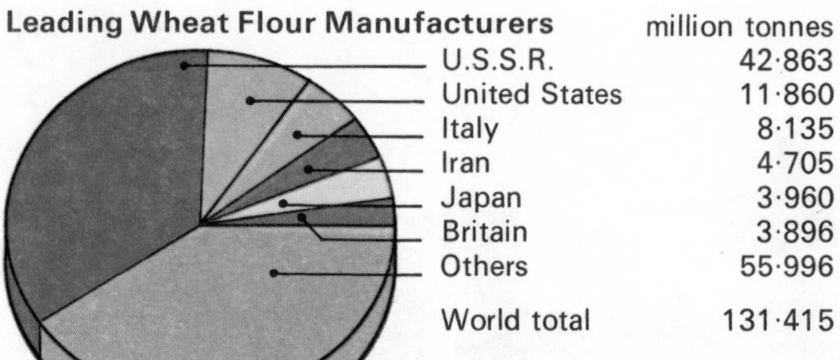

	million tonnes
U.S.S.R.	42·863
United States	11·860
Italy	8·135
Iran	4·705
Japan	3·960
Britain	3·896
Others	55·996
World total	131·415

Leading Mutton and Lamb Producers

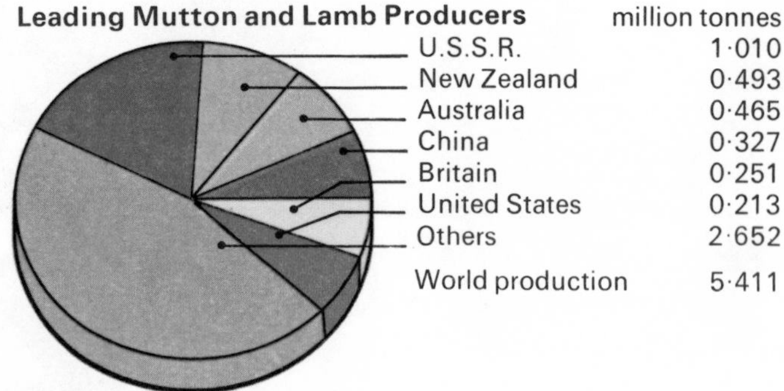

	million tonnes
U.S.S.R.	1·010
New Zealand	0·493
Australia	0·465
China	0·327
Britain	0·251
United States	0·213
Others	2·652
World production	5·411

Leading Raw Sugar Manufacturers

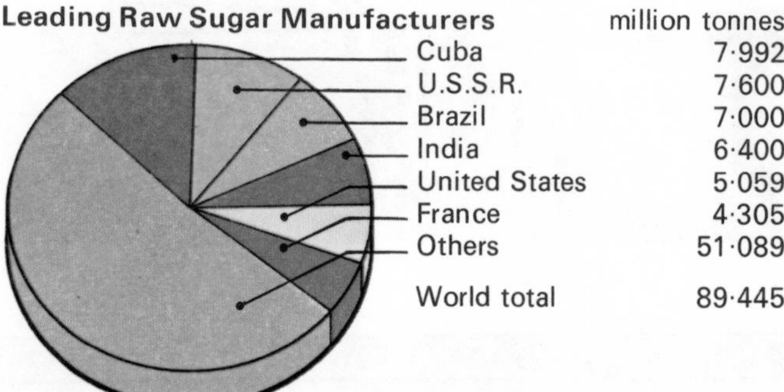

	million tonnes
Cuba	7·992
U.S.S.R.	7·600
Brazil	7·000
India	6·400
United States	5·059
France	4·305
Others	51·089
World total	89·445

Leading Pork Producers

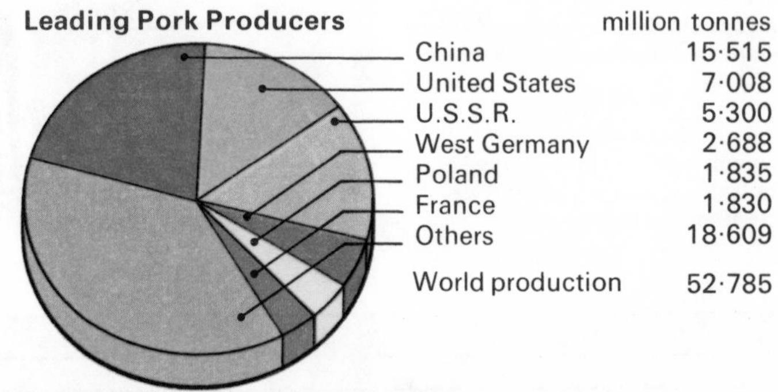

	million tonnes
China	15·515
United States	7·008
U.S.S.R.	5·300
West Germany	2·688
Poland	1·835
France	1·830
Others	18·609
World production	52·785

Leading Beef and Veal Producers

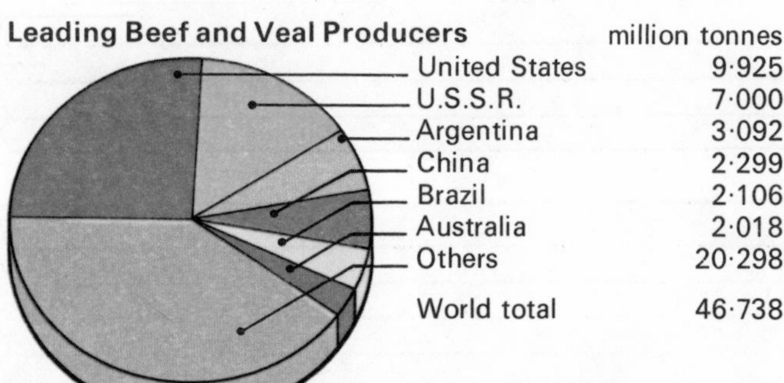

	million tonnes
United States	9·925
U.S.S.R.	7·000
Argentina	3·092
China	2·299
Brazil	2·106
Australia	2·018
Others	20·298
World total	46·738

Leading Commercial Vehicle Manufacturers

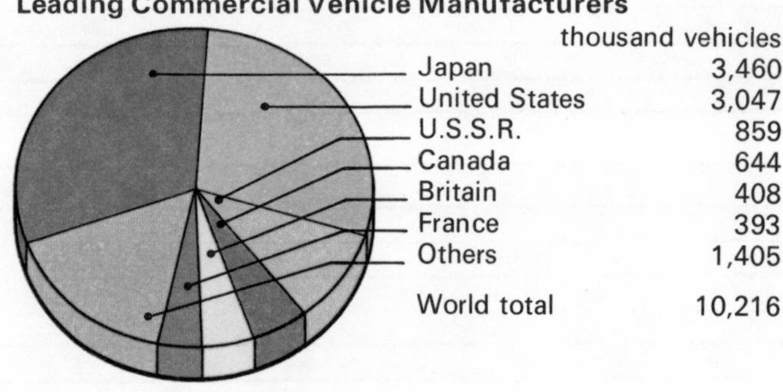

	thousand vehicles
Japan	3,460
United States	3,047
U.S.S.R.	859
Canada	644
Britain	408
France	393
Others	1,405
World total	10,216

Leading Motor-car Manufacturers

	thousand cars
United States	8,434
Japan	6,176
West Germany	3,933
France	3,220
Italy	1,481
U.S.S.R.	1,314
Others	6,253
World total	30,811

Leading Merchant Ship Builders

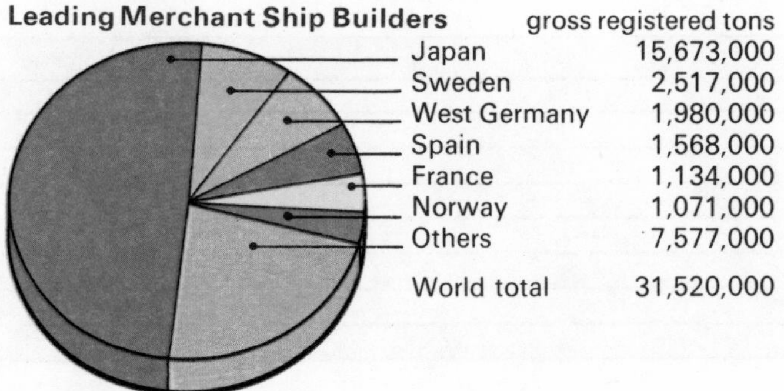

	gross registered tons
Japan	15,673,000
Sweden	2,517,000
West Germany	1,980,000
Spain	1,568,000
France	1,134,000
Norway	1,071,000
Others	7,577,000
World total	31,520,000

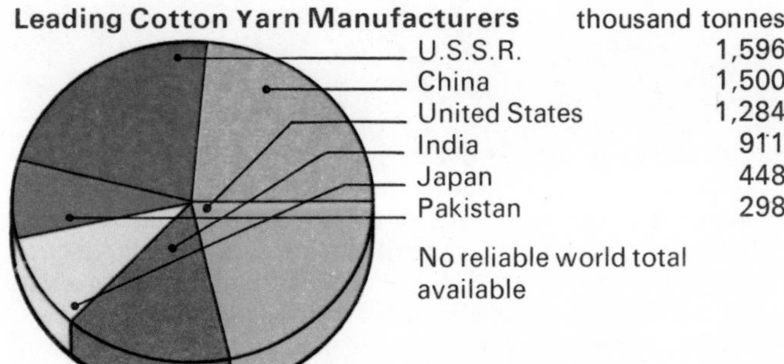
Leading Cotton Yarn Manufacturers
thousand tonnes
U.S.S.R. 1,596
China 1,500
United States 1,284
India 911
Japan 448
Pakistan 298
No reliable world total available

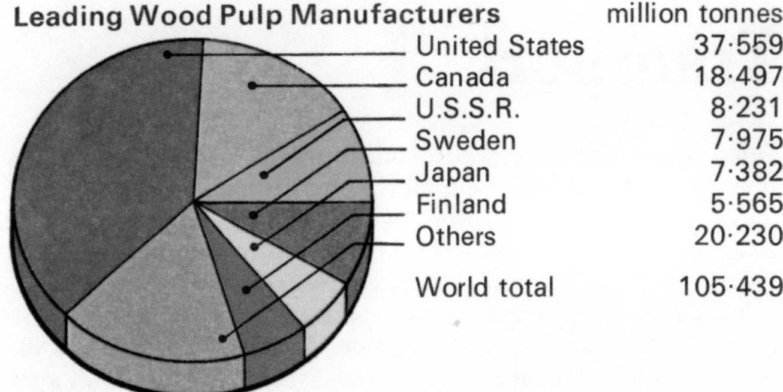
Leading Wood Pulp Manufacturers
million tonnes
United States 37·559
Canada 18·497
U.S.S.R. 8·231
Sweden 7·975
Japan 7·382
Finland 5·565
Others 20·230
World total 105·439

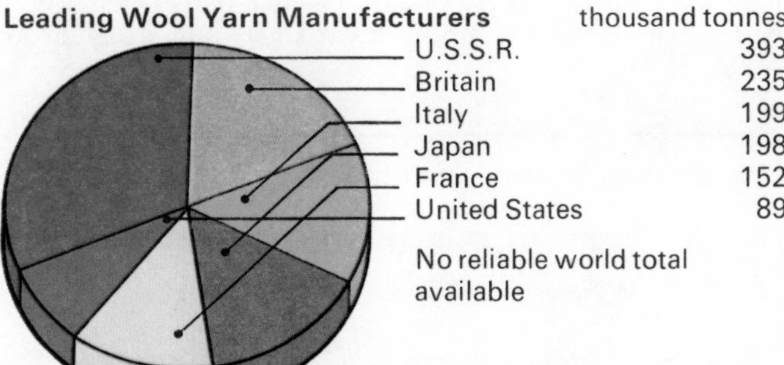
Leading Wool Yarn Manufacturers
thousand tonnes
U.S.S.R. 393
Britain 235
Italy 199
Japan 198
France 152
United States 89
No reliable world total available

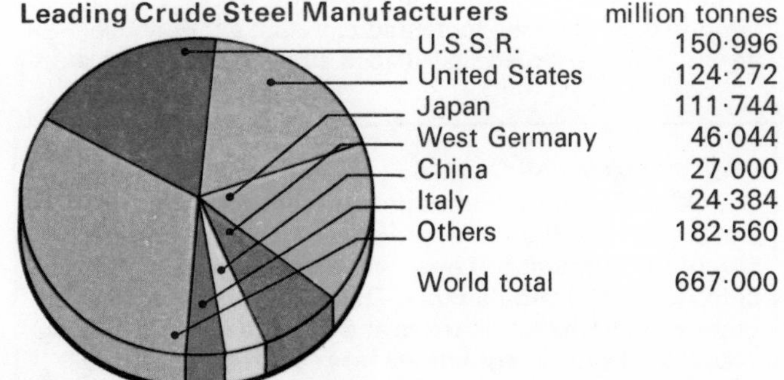
Leading Crude Steel Manufacturers
million tonnes
U.S.S.R. 150·996
United States 124·272
Japan 111·744
West Germany 46·044
China 27·000
Italy 24·384
Others 182·560
World total 667·000

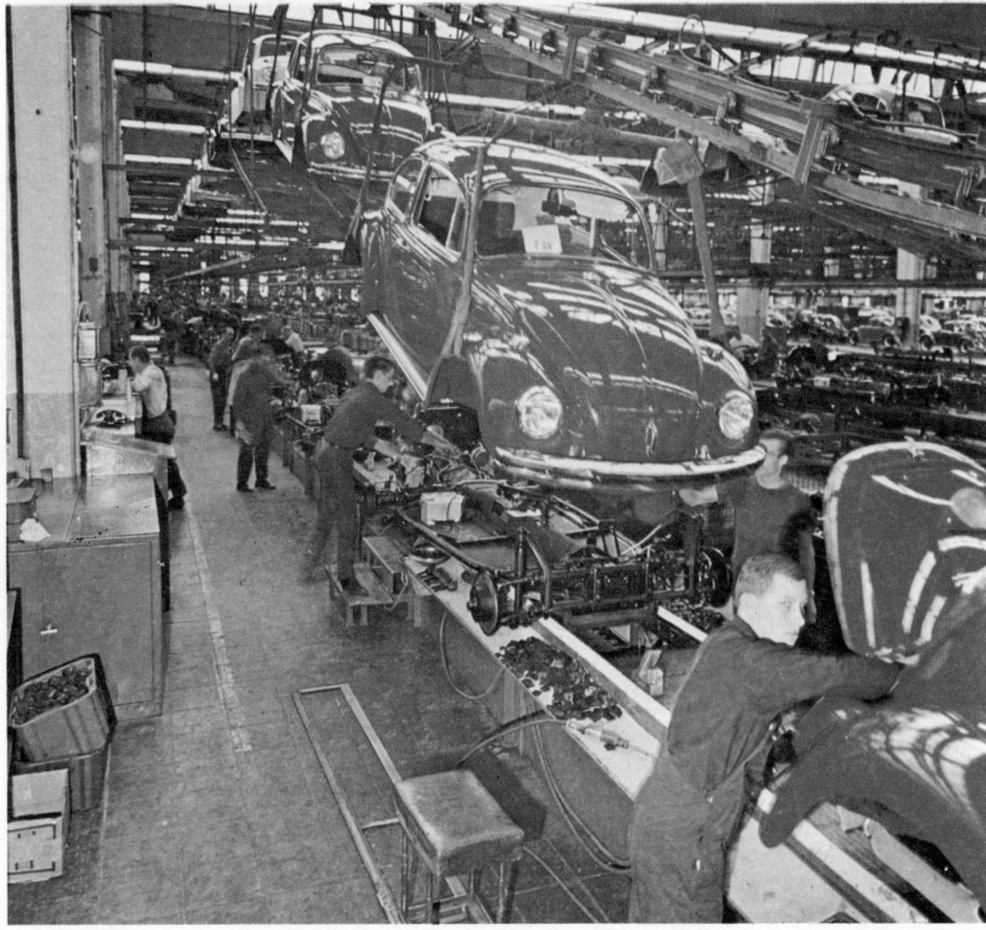

Left: **Car bodies meeting their chassis on an assembly line at the Volkswagen factory in West Germany. Mass production methods were first introduced into the car industry in the United States by Ransom E. Olds in 1901. They have become the pattern for much industrial production of today.**

Transport

Good transport is the key to all industrial development and trade. It is essential to carry raw materials from their sources to where they are processed and turned into manufactured products, and also to carry those products to people who want to buy them. Transport is also needed to carry people from place to place.

The three basic kinds of transport are by land, sea and air. Patterns of transport change with the demands of traffic and the development of technology. Before World War II, most passenger traffic across the Atlantic Ocean was by sea; but, with the development of aviation, most transatlantic travellers now fly. Ships are still the cheapest and most efficient way of moving bulk cargoes from one place to another over long distances and, with the growth of fast highways and powerful trucks, road and sea transport are becoming more and more linked. Containers that can be carried by road and loaded straight onto ships are an increasingly popular way of carrying all but the bulkiest goods.

Liquids such as petroleum and natural gas are carried by a combination of giant, ocean-going tankers and overland pipelines. Major pipeline systems extend across North America, Western Europe and the U.S.S.R. The Russian system links with pipelines from the Arab oil states of the Middle East and also with Western Europe. All these networks are being continually extended as new supplies of oil and gas are developed.

Railways, the backbone of land transport in the late 1800s and for the first half of this century, are giving way in many parts of the world to road traffic, which is more economical to run and delivers goods from door to door. Inland waterways — rivers and canals — have maintained their importance in some parts of the world, particularly Western Europe, where there are many major navigable rivers.

PRINCIPAL MERCHANT FLEETS

It is difficult to say which country in the world actually has the largest merchant shipping fleet, because many shipping companies of other countries register their ships in Liberia and Panama. This is because these two countries charge lower taxes and enforce rules governing wages and safety regulations less severely. The table which follows gives an indication, in gross tonnage rather than numbers of vessels, of ship registrations.

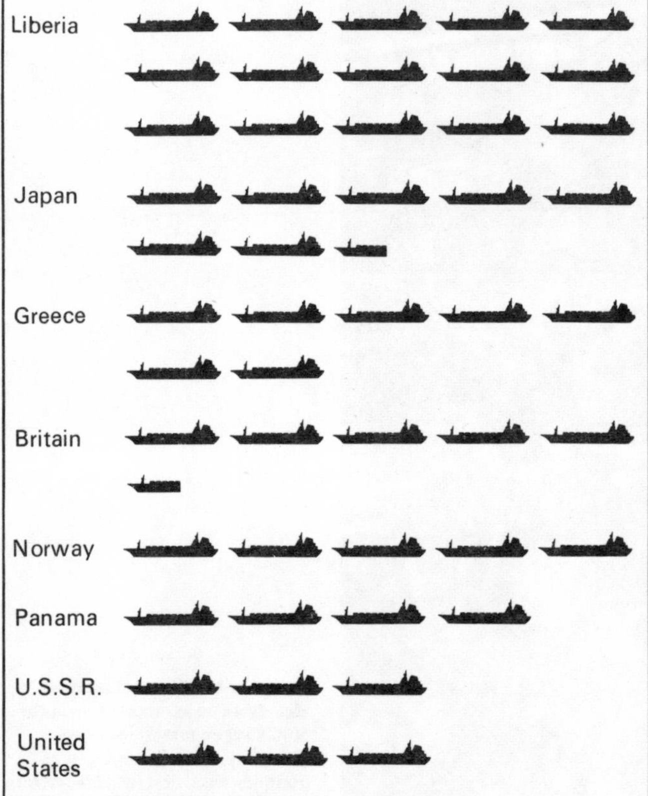
Liberia
Japan
Greece
Britain
Norway
Panama
U.S.S.R.
United States

Each symbol equals 5 million tons. Figures based on Lloyd's Register of Shipping.

Leading Car-owning Countries

United States

New Zealand

Canada

Australia

Sweden

West Germany

Each symbol equals 100 cars per 1000 people.

Leading Commercial-vehicle-owning Countries

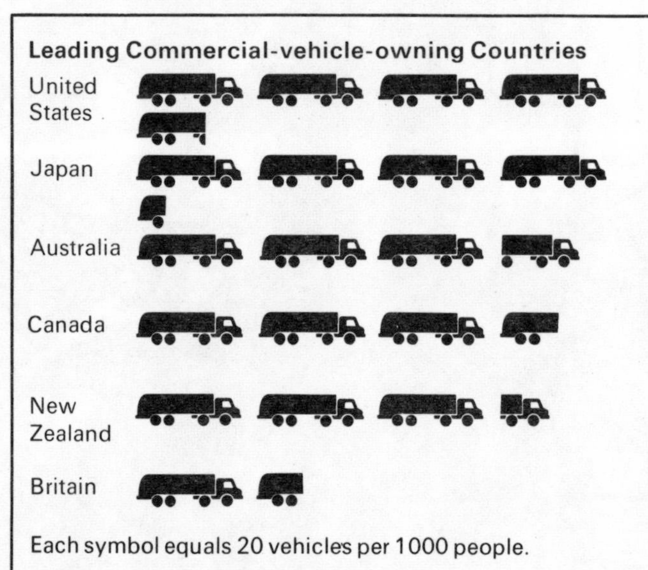
United States
Japan
Australia
Canada
New Zealand
Britain

Each symbol equals 20 vehicles per 1000 people.

Below: **Sea transport remains the best and most economical method of carrying bulky cargo over long distances. Here, a bus is being loaded onto a ship at Miami Harbor in Florida.**

The volume of sea and air traffic has meant a great deal of international co-operation to ensure speedy and safe communication. Countries co-operate in providing up-to-date charts for shipping and weather forecasting. Some particularly busy sea routes, such as the English Channel, are 'policed' by the countries bordering them to make sure ships keep to recognized channels and so avoid collisions. Air transport comes under the control of a United Nations agency, the International Civil Aviation Organization, which has its headquarters in Montreal, Canada.

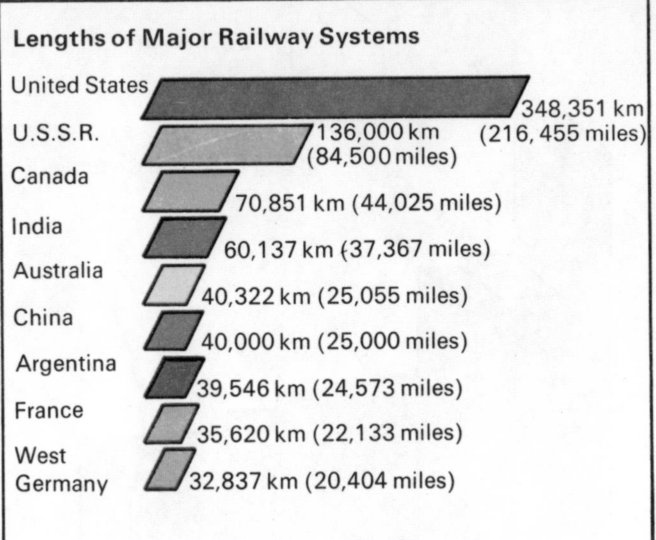
Lengths of Major Railway Systems
United States
348,351 km (216, 455 miles)
U.S.S.R.
136,000 km (84,500 miles)
Canada
70,851 km (44,025 miles)
India
60,137 km (37,367 miles)
Australia
40,322 km (25,055 miles)
China
40,000 km (25,000 miles)
Argentina
39,546 km (24,573 miles)
France
35,620 km (22,133 miles)
West Germany
32,837 km (20,404 miles)

AVIATION FLEETS AND CONSTRUCTION

The world's airlines have around 10,000 passenger aircraft in service, but the numbers are constantly fluctuating. This is because new developments, such as faster and larger aircraft, make it possible to operate services efficiently with fewer planes, while developing countries, such as those of Africa, are building up their airlines.

The aircraft industry is concentrated in the United States, which has more than half the market, the U.S.S.R. with one-third, and the countries of Western Europe, particularly Britain, France, West Germany, Italy and the Netherlands. Canada also has a thriving construction industry. The enormous cost of development of new aircraft is tending to concentrate the industry into fewer and larger units, with several countries sharing the development and construction of new kinds of aircraft.

World Trade

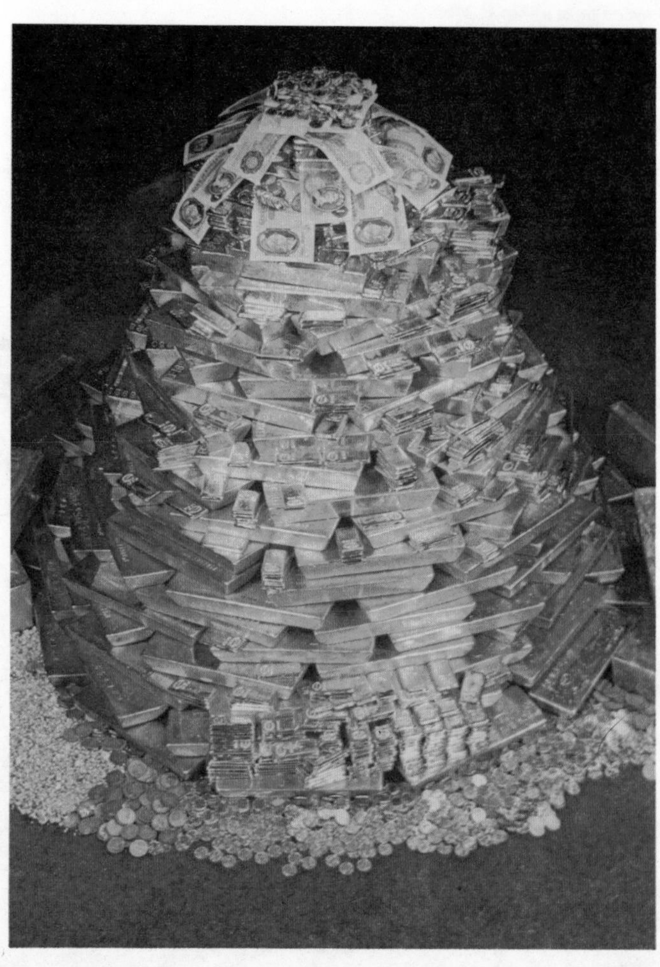

World trade has developed over hundreds of years. Even back in medieval times, European countries used to export goods made by their craftsmen to other parts of the globe to pay for raw materials not available at home. With the growth of the Industrial Revolution from the 1750s onwards, this pattern of trade became intensified. Today, the countries of Europe are highly industrialized. Together with the United States, Canada and Japan, which have developed along European lines, they export manufactured goods and import mostly raw materials and food.

The developing countries of the world rely for their trade on minerals they can mine and food they can grow. To an extent, this even applies to the Europeanized countries, such as Australia, New Zealand and South Africa, whose industries still do not play a dominant part in their economies, even though they may absorb the bulk of the workforce.

However, clear-cut trading patterns in the style of the 1800s, when the industrialized countries produced all the world's goods, no longer exist. Most countries now have some industry and are developing more rapidly, while the biggest of all industrialized countries, the United States, is a major exporter of foodstuffs such as cereals. There is a growing tendency for countries to specialize in goods and services. For example, the Netherlands and Israel lead in cutting diamonds; Britain is a centre for banking and insurance; Japan is outstanding for photographic equipment; and Denmark and New Zealand are major producers of butter.

Financing international trade is a complicated business. Banks and other finance organizations, including the International Monetary Fund, operate the international finance market, through which traders can obtain currency to pay for the goods they buy. For example, a merchant in Brazil (currency, cruzeiros) may buy goods from India (rupees), which are carried in an American ship (dollars) and insured in Britain (pounds). Through the international banking network, the merchant can get the money he needs — even though Brazil may not possess any rupees. The necessary currency may well come through New York or London, two of the world's leading financial centres.

The Principal Food Importing and Exporting Countries

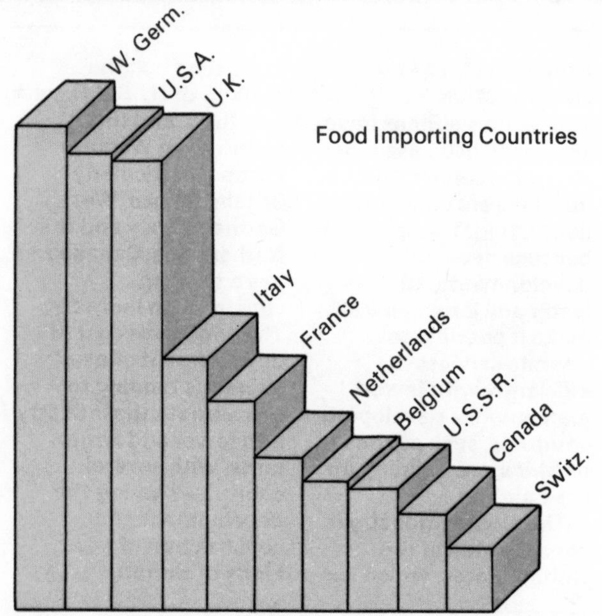
Food Importing Countries
W. Germ.
U.S.A.
U.K.
Italy
France
Netherlands
Belgium
U.S.S.R.
Canada
Switz.

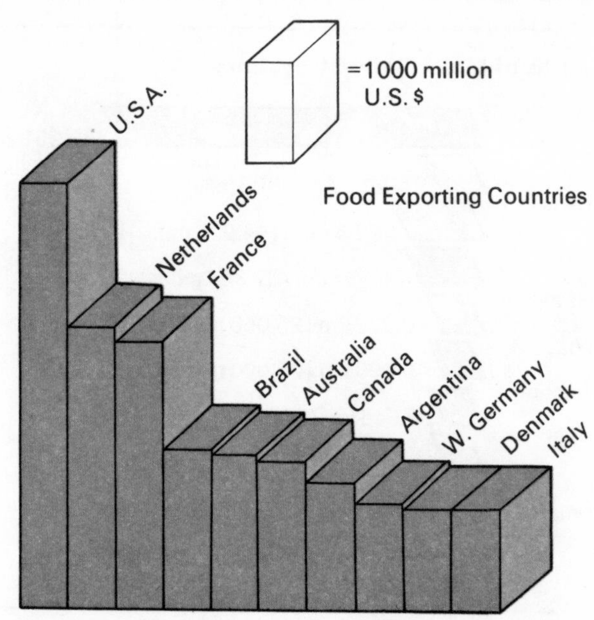
=1000 million U.S. $
Food Exporting Countries
U.S.A.
Netherlands
France
Brazil
Australia
Canada
Argentina
W. Germany
Denmark
Italy

INVISIBLE TRADE

Although most international trade consists of buying and selling goods, there is one form of trading that consists of selling and buying services. This is often called *invisible trade.* Some countries, particularly Britain, invariably import more goods than they export, but make up the difference in invisible exports.

Services under the heading of invisible exports include: freight charges by air and sea; banking; insurance; income from investments in other countries; spending by foreign visitors; and, to a lesser extent, payments of royalties or the transfer of money earned by citizens working abroad.

RESERVE CURRENCIES

Amounts of the world's currencies are held by other countries as part of their assets. Generally, only comparatively small sums of money are involved, but a number of currencies are held in great quantities; these are known as *reserve currencies.*

For many years, the two main reserve currencies have been the US $ and the £ sterling, though today West German Deutsche Marks are increasingly held as reserves. Other currencies play a lesser role.

Above left: **A million pounds in gold bullion, notes and coins photographed in the vaults of Hambros Bank in the City of London.**

Overleaf: **A busy dockyard scene at Dar-es-Salaam, Tanzania.**

Annual Imports and Exports of Leading Countries

Figures are in millions of US$.

Country	Imports	Exports	Country	Imports	Exports
Algeria	10,560	12,410	Iraq	12,936	26,352
Argentina	6,400	7,800	Ireland (Republic)	11,153	8,502
Australia	22,331	22,061	Israel	8,593	5,528
Austria	24,456	17,502	Italy	99,475	77,685
			Japan	141,289	130,469
Belgium with Luxembourg	71,612	64,499	Kuwait	7,285	20,332
Brazil	25,002	20,132	Malaysia	7,849	11,077
Britain	120,154	115,117	Mexico	19,460	15,348
Canada	62,566	67,529	Netherlands	78,073	73,826
Chile	5,821	4,818	New Zealand	5,473	5,421
Colombia	4,739	3,925	Nigeria	15,792	26,742
Cuba	5,100	5,300	Norway	16,956	18,299
Czechoslovakia	14,300	13,200	Philippines	8,182	5,704
Denmark	19,322	16,742	Poland	na	na
Finland	15,632	14,168	Portugal	6,534	3,480
France	134,874	116,016	Saudi Arabia	33,060	102,548
Germany (East)	17,600	16,200	Spain	34,078	26,720
Germany (West)	187,933	192,901	Sweden	33,438	30,912
Ghana	937	933	Switzerland	36,360	29,647
Greece	9,614	3,885	Turkey	5,070	2,261
Hungary	10,200	8,800	United States	252,997	220,706
India	12,600	5,906	Venezuela	11,390	23,000
Indonesia	7,202	15,590	Yugoslavia	15,076	8,989
Iran	17,700	21,700	Zaire	835	1,632

ATLAS OF THE WORLD

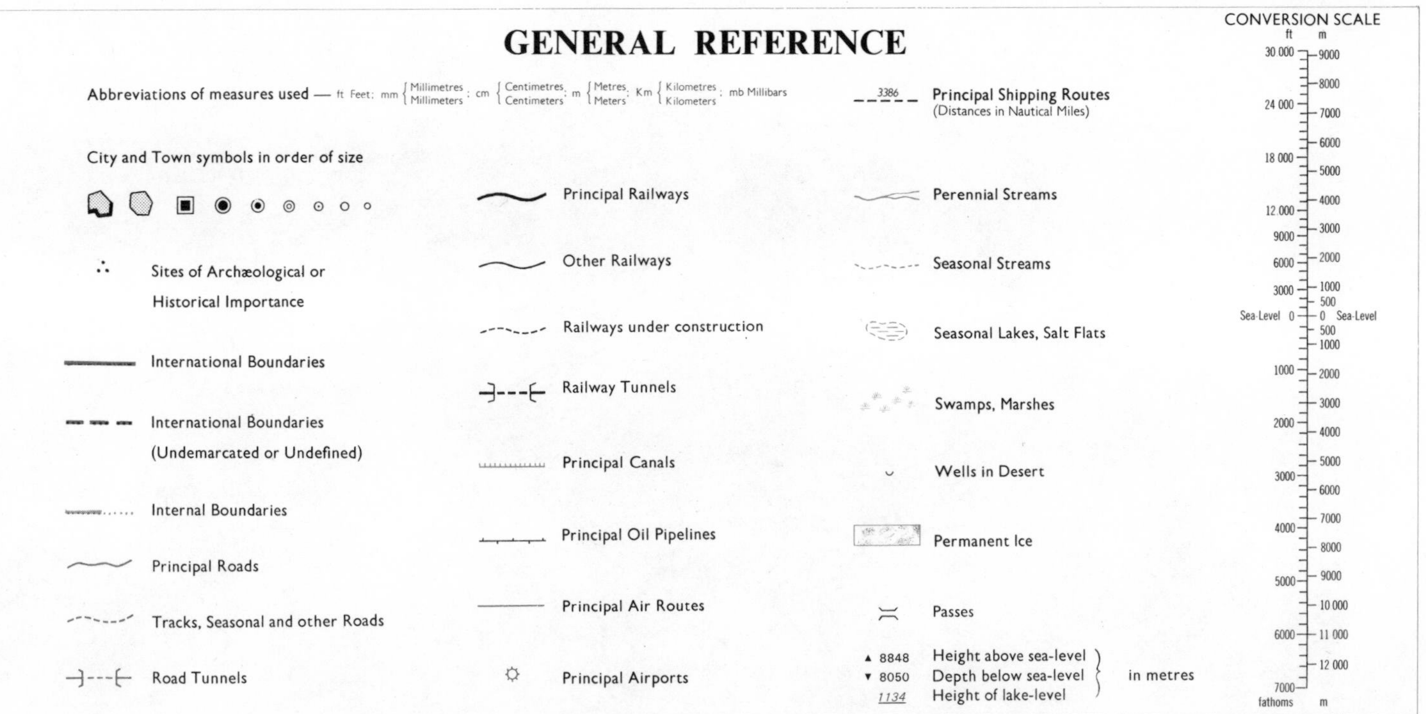
GENERAL REFERENCE
Abbreviations of measures used — ft Feet; mm Millimetres / Millimeters; cm Centimetres / Centimeters; m Metres / Meters; Km Kilometres / Kilometers; mb Millibars
City and Town symbols in order of size
Sites of Archæological or Historical Importance
International Boundaries
International Boundaries (Undemarcated or Undefined)
Internal Boundaries
Principal Roads
Tracks, Seasonal and other Roads
Road Tunnels
Principal Railways
Other Railways
Railways under construction
Railway Tunnels
Principal Canals
Principal Oil Pipelines
Principal Air Routes
Principal Airports
3386
Principal Shipping Routes (Distances in Nautical Miles)
Perennial Streams
Seasonal Streams
Seasonal Lakes, Salt Flats
Swamps, Marshes
Wells in Desert
Permanent Ice
Passes
▲ 8848 Height above sea-level
▼ 8050 Depth below sea-level
1134 Height of lake-level
in metres
CONVERSION SCALE
ft m
30 000 9000 8000 24 000 7000 6000 18 000 5000 4000 12 000 9000 3000 6000 2000 3000 1000 500
Sea-Level 0 0 Sea-Level
500 1000 1000 2000 3000 2000 4000 5000 3000 6000 7000 4000 8000 9000 5000 10 000 6000 11 000 12 000 7000
fathoms m

THE WORLD: Physical

1:150 000 000

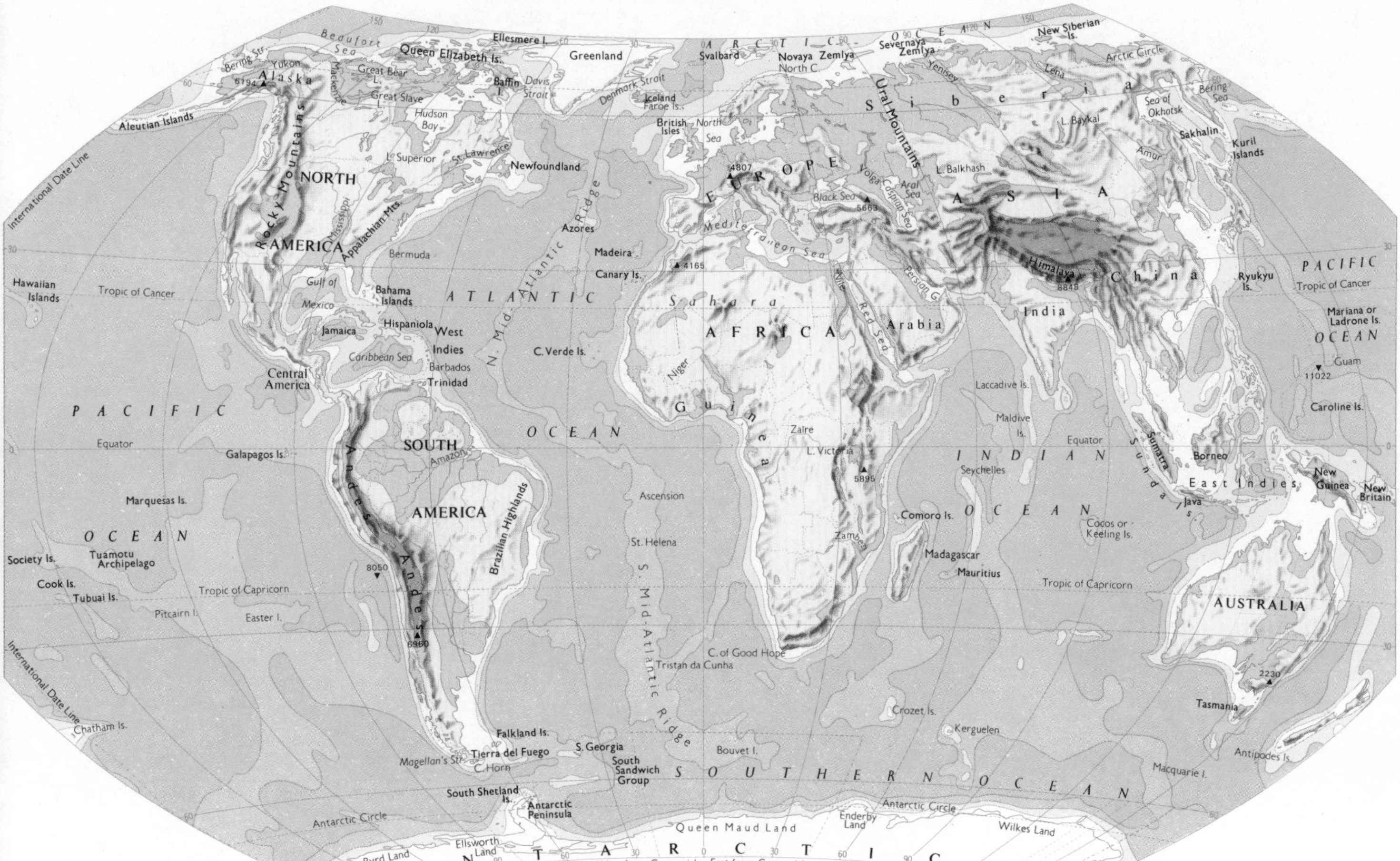

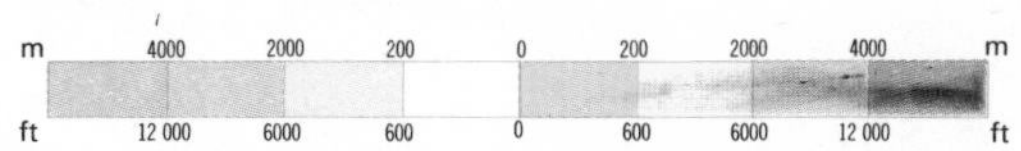

m	4000	2000	200	0	200	2000	4000	m
ft	12 000	6000	600	0	600	6000	12 000	ft

Projection: *Hammer Equal Area*

Projection: *Hammer Equal Area*

ARCTIC OCEAN
Franz Joseph Ld.
Severnaya Zemlya
New Siberian Is.
East Siberian Sea
Laptev Sea
Kara Sea
Barents Sea
Novaya Zemlya
Svalbard (Norway)
UNION OF SOVIET SOCIALIST REPUBLICS
RUSSIAN SOVIET FEDERAL SOCIALIST REPUBLIC
Siberia
Arctic Circle
Bering Sea
Sea of Okhotsk
Kamchatka
Sakhalin
Kuril Islands
Leningrad
Moskva
Gorkiy
Sverdlovsk
Novosibirsk
Omsk
Krasnoyarsk
Irkutsk
Chelyabinsk
Magnitogorsk
Karaganda
Tashkent
Alma Ata
Dushanbe
Volgograd
Kuybyshev
Saratov
Orenburg
Kharkov
Kiyev
Donetsk
Odessa
Rostov
Baku
Tbilisi
Yerevan
KAZAKHSTAN
UZBEKISTAN
TURKMENISTAN
KIRGIZIA
MONGOLIA
CHINA
Tibet
Ulaanbaatar
Harbin
Changchun
Shenyang
Peiping
Tientsin
Taiyuan
Tsinan
Tsingtao
Lanchow
Sian
Chengtu
Chungking
Wuhan
Nanking
Shanghai
Changsha
Kunming
Foochow
Taipei
Kwangchow
Hong Kong
Vladivostok
Sapporo
JAPAN
Tōkyō
Yokohama
Nagoya
Kyōto
Ōsaka
Kōbe
Sōul
Pusan
Sea of Japan
East China Sea
TAIWAN
PACIFIC OCEAN
Tropic of Cancer
Mariana or Ladrone Is.
Wake I. (U.S.)
Guam (U.S.)
Caroline Is.
(U.S. Trust Territory)
Marshall Is.
Gilbert Is. (Br.)
Nauru
Equator
Stockholm
Oslo
Helsinki
København
Hamburg
Berlin
Praha
Wien
Warszawa
Budapest
Bucuresti
Beograd
Paris
Milano
Roma
Napoli
Barcelona
Istanbul
Ankara
TURKEY
Black Sea
Caspian Sea
Mediterranean Sea
Athinai
Tunis
Tarābulus
LIBYA
EGYPT
El Qâhira
El Iskandarîya
Libyan Desert
Baghdād
Tehrān
IRAN (PERSIA)
Eşfahān
Shīrāz
Persian Gulf
Nejd
Ar Riyāḑ
SAUDI ARABIA
Makkah
Red Sea
U.A.E.
OMAN
SOUTH YEMEN
YEMEN
G. of Aden
AFGHANISTAN
Kabul
PAKISTAN
Karachi
Lahore
Rawalpindi
Srinagar
INDIA
Delhi
Agra
Kanpur
Lucknow
Varanasi
Calcutta
Dacca
Ahmadabad
Bombay
Pune
Nagpur
Hyderabad
Bangalore
Madras
Tiruchchirappalli
Colombo
SRI LANKA (CEYLON)
Arabian Sea
Bay of Bengal
BURMA
Rangoon
THAILAND (SIAM)
Bangkok
Hanoi
Hainan
VIETNAM
Ho Chi Minh City
CAMBODIA
G. of Siam
South China Sea
Manila
PHILIPPINES
Quezon City
Cebu
MALAYSIA
Kuala Lumpur
Singapore
Borneo
Sumatra
Sulawesi
INDONESIA
Jakarta
Bandung
Surabaya
Ujung Pandang
Sunda Islands
Timor
Timor Sea
Arafura Sea
PAPUA NEW GUINEA
New Britain
New Ireland
Solomon Is.
Tuvalu (Ellice Is.)
Vanuatu Republic
Fiji Is.
New Caledonia (Fr.)
AUSTRALIA
NORTHERN TERRITORY
QUEENSLAND
WESTERN AUSTRALIA
SOUTH AUSTRALIA
NEW SOUTH WALES
VICTORIA
TASMANIA
Darwin
Brisbane
Sydney
Canberra
Melbourne
Adelaide
Perth
Great Australian Bight
Tasman Sea
NEW ZEALAND
Auckland
Wellington
Christchurch
North I.
South I.
Tropic of Capricorn
SUDAN
Khartoum
ETHIOPIA
Addis Abeba
CHAD
NIGER
NIGERIA
Lagos
CENTRAL AFRICAN REPUBLIC
ZAÏRE (CONGO)
Kinshasa
KENYA
Nairobi
Mogadishu
SOMALI REP.
TANZANIA
ANGOLA
ZAMBIA
MOZAMBIQUE
ZIMBABWE
BOTSWANA
SOUTH WEST AFRICA (NAMIBIA)
SOUTH AFRICA
Johannesburg
Pretoria
Durban
Cape Town
Port Elizabeth
C. of Good Hope
MADAGASCAR
Tananarive
Mozambique Chan.
Seychelles
INDIAN OCEAN
Réunion (Fr.)
Amsterdam (Fr.)
St. Paul (Fr.)
Kerguelen (Fr.)
Crozet Is. (Fr.)
SOUTHERN OCEAN
Antarctic Circle
Enderby Land
Wilkes Land
AUSTRALIAN DEPENDENCY
TERRE ADÉLIE
S. Magnetic Pole 1965
Ross Sea
König Haakon VII Sea
East from Greenwich

4 POLAR REGIONS

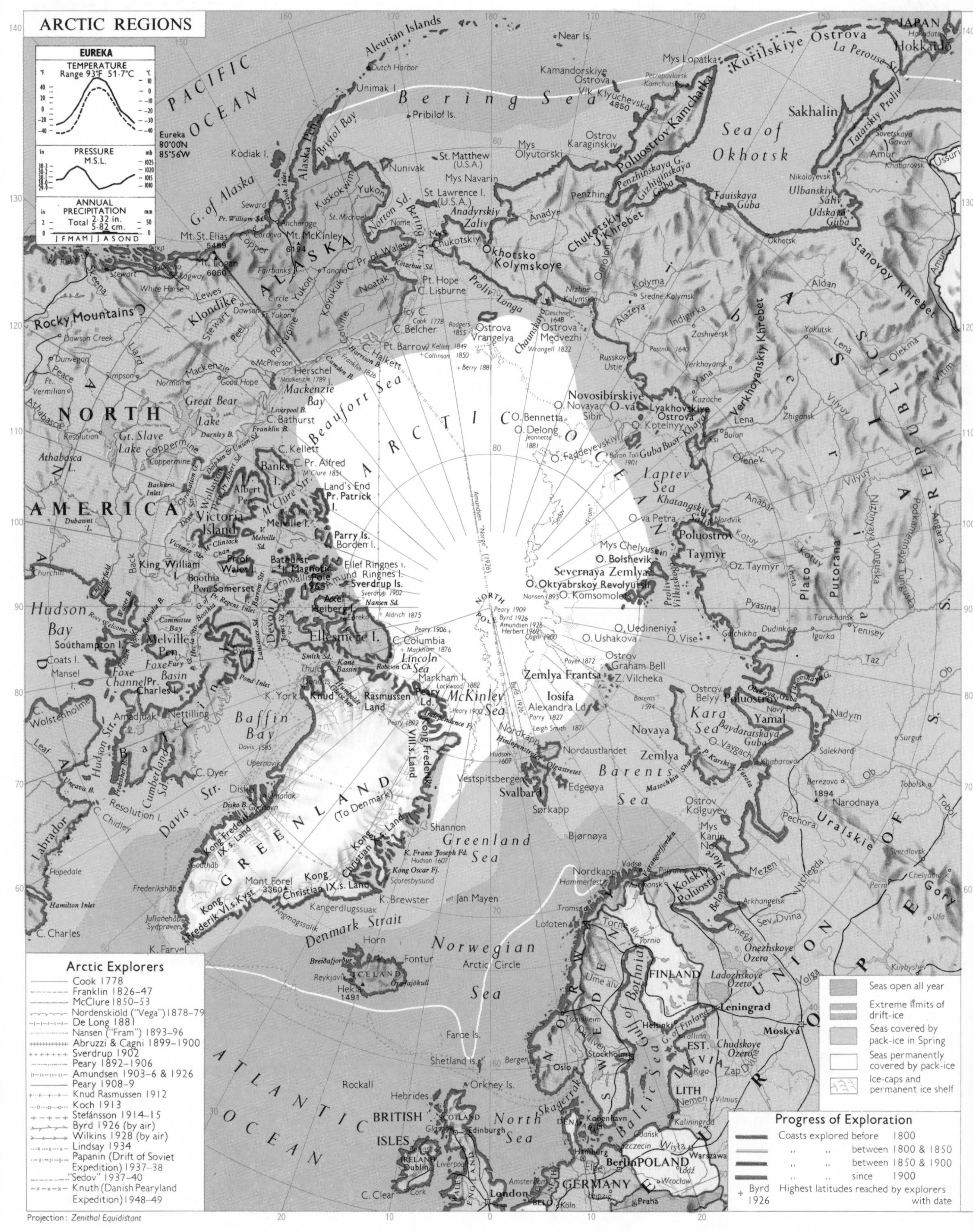

ARCTIC REGIONS
EUREKA
TEMPERATURE
Range 93°F 51·7°C
Eureka
80°00'N
85°56'W
PRESSURE
M.S.L.
ANNUAL
PRECIPITATION
Total 2·32 in.
5·82 cm.
J F M A M J J A S O N D
PACIFIC OCEAN
Aleutian Islands
Bering Sea
Sea of Okhotsk
G. of Alaska
ALASKA
NORTH AMERICA
CANADA
Rocky Mountains
Hudson Bay
Baffin Bay
Beaufort Sea
ARCTIC OCEAN
Laptev Sea
Kara Sea
Barents Sea
Greenland Sea
Norwegian Sea
North Sea
Baltic Sea
ATLANTIC OCEAN
Davis Str.
Denmark Strait
GREENLAND (To Denmark)
ICELAND
BRITISH ISLES
NORWAY
SWEDEN
FINLAND
POLAND
GERMANY
JAPAN
Hokkaido
Sakhalin
Kamchatka
Svalbard
Novaya Zemlya
Severnaya Zemlya
Zemlya Frantsa Iosifa
Novosibirskiye O-va
Ellesmere I.
Victoria Island
Banks I.
Baffin I.
NORTH POLE
Arctic Circle
Arctic Explorers
Cook 1778
Franklin 1826–47
McClure 1850–53
Nordenskiöld ("Vega") 1878–79
De Long 1881
Nansen ("Fram") 1893–96
Abruzzi & Cagni 1899–1900
Sverdrup 1902
Peary 1892–1906
Amundsen 1903–6 & 1926
Peary 1908–9
Knud Rasmussen 1912
Koch 1913
Stefánsson 1914–15
Byrd 1926 (by air)
Wilkins 1928 (by air)
Lindsay 1934
Papanin (Drift of Soviet Expedition) 1937–38
"Sedov" 1937–40
Knuth (Danish Pearyland Expedition) 1948–49
Seas open all year
Extreme limits of drift-ice
Seas covered by pack-ice in Spring
Seas permanently covered by pack-ice
Ice-caps and permanent ice shelf
Progress of Exploration
Coasts explored before 1800
" " between 1800 & 1850
" " between 1850 & 1900
" " since 1900
+ Byrd 1926 Highest latitudes reached by explorers with date
Projection: Zenithal Equidistant

1:35 000 000

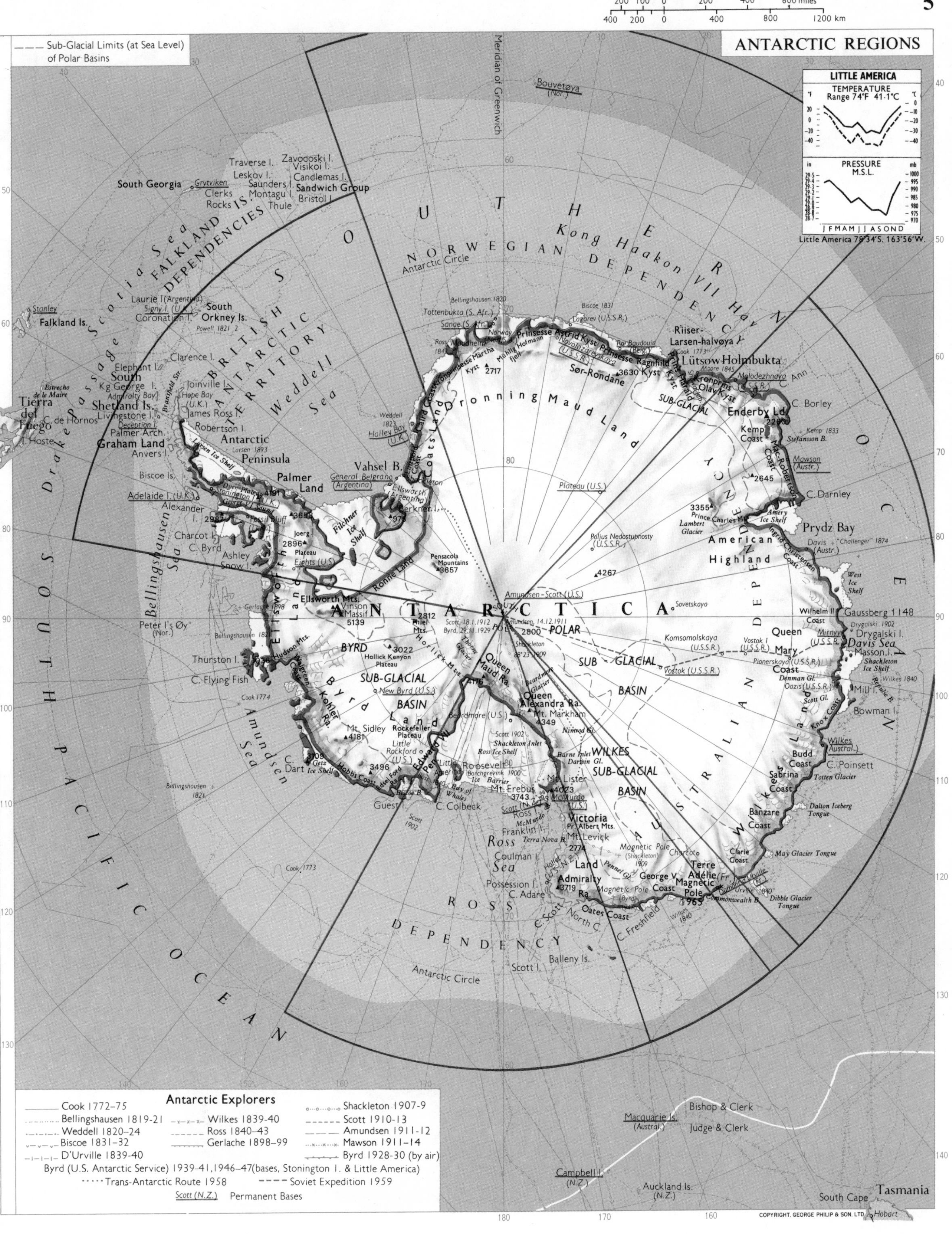
ANTARCTIC REGIONS
Sub-Glacial Limits (at Sea Level) of Polar Basins
LITTLE AMERICA
TEMPERATURE
Range 74°F 41·1°C
PRESSURE
M.S.L.
J F M A M J J A S O N D
Little America 78°34'S. 163°56'W.
ANTARCTICA
SOUTHERN OCEAN
SOUTH PACIFIC OCEAN
NORWEGIAN DEPENDENCY
FALKLAND IS. DEPENDENCIES
BRITISH ANTARCTIC TERRITORY
AUSTRALIAN DEPENDENCY
ROSS DEPENDENCY
Meridian of Greenwich
Antarctic Circle
Bouvetøya (Nor.)
South Georgia
Grytviken
Traverse I.
Leskov I.
Zavodoski I.
Visikoi I.
Candlemas I.
Saunders I.
Montagu I.
Bristol I.
Thule
Sandwich Group
Clerks Rocks
Scotia Sea
Stanley
Falkland Is.
Laurie I.(Argentina)
Signy I. (U.K.)
Coronation I.
South Orkney Is.
Drake Passage
Tierra del Fuego
Estrecho de le Maire
C. de Hornos
I. Hoste
Clarence I.
Elephant I.
South Shetland Is.
Kg.George I.
Livingstone I.
Deception I.
Joinville I.
Hope Bay (U.K.)
James Ross I.
Robertson I.
Palmer Arch.
Graham Land
Anvers I.
Antarctic Peninsula
Biscoe Is.
Adelaide I. (U.K.)
Alexander I.
Charcot I.
C. Byrd
Ashley Snow I.
Palmer Land
Weddell Sea
Vahsel B.
General Belgrano (Argentina)
Halley Bay (U.K.)
Filchner Ice Shelf
Ronne Land
Pensacola Mountains
Bellingshausen Sea
Peter I's Øy (Nor.)
Thurston I.
C. Flying Fish
Amundsen Sea
C. Dart
Guest I.
C. Colbeck
Ellsworth Land
Ellsworth Mts.
Vinson Massif 5139
BYRD SUB-GLACIAL BASIN
Byrd Land
Hollick Kenyon Plateau
New Byrd (U.S.)
Mt. Sidley 4181
Rockefeller Plateau
Little Rockford (U.S.)
Little America
Roosevelt I.
Ross Ice Shelf
Bay of Whales
Mt. Erebus 3743
Scott (N.Z.)
McMurdo (U.S.)
Ross I.
Franklin I.
Ross Sea
Coulman I.
Possession I.
C. Adare
Scott I.
Balleny Is.
Queen Maud Ra.
Queen Alexandra Ra.
Mt. Markham 4349
Amundsen-Scott (U.S.)
SOUTH POLE
POLAR SUB-GLACIAL BASIN
Plateau (U.S.)
Polius Nedostupnosty (U.S.S.R.)
Vostok (U.S.S.R.)
Komsomolskaya (U.S.S.R.)
Sovetskaya
WILKES SUB-GLACIAL BASIN
Victoria Land
Mt. Lister 4023
Mt. Levick
Admiralty Ra.
Magnetic Pole
Terre Adélie (Fr.)
George V Coast
Oates Coast
C. Freshfield
C. Scott
North C.
Dumont d'Urville (Fr.)
Commonwealth B.
Dibble Glacier Tongue
Clarie Coast
Banzare Coast
Sabrina Coast
Budd Coast
Wilkes (Austral.)
C. Poinsett
Totten Glacier
Dalton Iceberg Tongue
May Glacier Tongue
Wilkes Land
Knox Coast
Bowman I.
Mill I.
Queen Mary Coast
Mirnyy (U.S.S.R.)
Pionerskaya (U.S.S.R.)
Davis Sea
Drygalski I.
Gaussberg 1148
Wilhelm II Coast
Masson I.
Shackleton Ice Shelf
West Ice Shelf
Prydz Bay
Davis (Austr.)
American Highland
Lambert Glacier
Amery Ice Shelf
C. Darnley
Mawson (Austr.)
Mac.Robertson Coast
Kemp Coast
Enderby Ld.
C. Borley
C. Ann
Molodezhnaya (U.S.S.R.)
Lützow Holmbukta
Kronprins Olav Kyst
Riiser-Larsen-halvøya
Sør-Rondane
Prinsesse Ragnhild Kyst
Prinsesse Astrid Kyst
Roi Baudouin (Belg.)
Novolazarevskaya (U.S.S.R.)
Lazarev (U.S.S.R.)
Dronning Maud Land
Kong Haakon VII Hav
Sanae (S. Afr.)
Tottenbukta (S. Afr.)
Princesse Martha Kyst
Caird Coast
Coats Land
Macquarie Is. (Austral.)
Bishop & Clerk
Judge & Clerk
Campbell I. (N.Z.)
Auckland Is. (N.Z.)
South Cape
Tasmania
Hobart
Antarctic Explorers
Cook 1772–75
Bellingshausen 1819–21
Weddell 1820–24
Biscoe 1831–32
D'Urville 1839–40
Wilkes 1839–40
Ross 1840–43
Gerlache 1898–99
Shackleton 1907–9
Scott 1910–13
Amundsen 1911–12
Mawson 1911–14
Byrd 1928–30 (by air)
Byrd (U.S. Antarctic Service) 1939-41,1946–47(bases, Stonington I. & Little America)
Trans-Antarctic Route 1958
Soviet Expedition 1959
Scott (N.Z.) Permanent Bases

6 THE ATLANTIC OCEAN

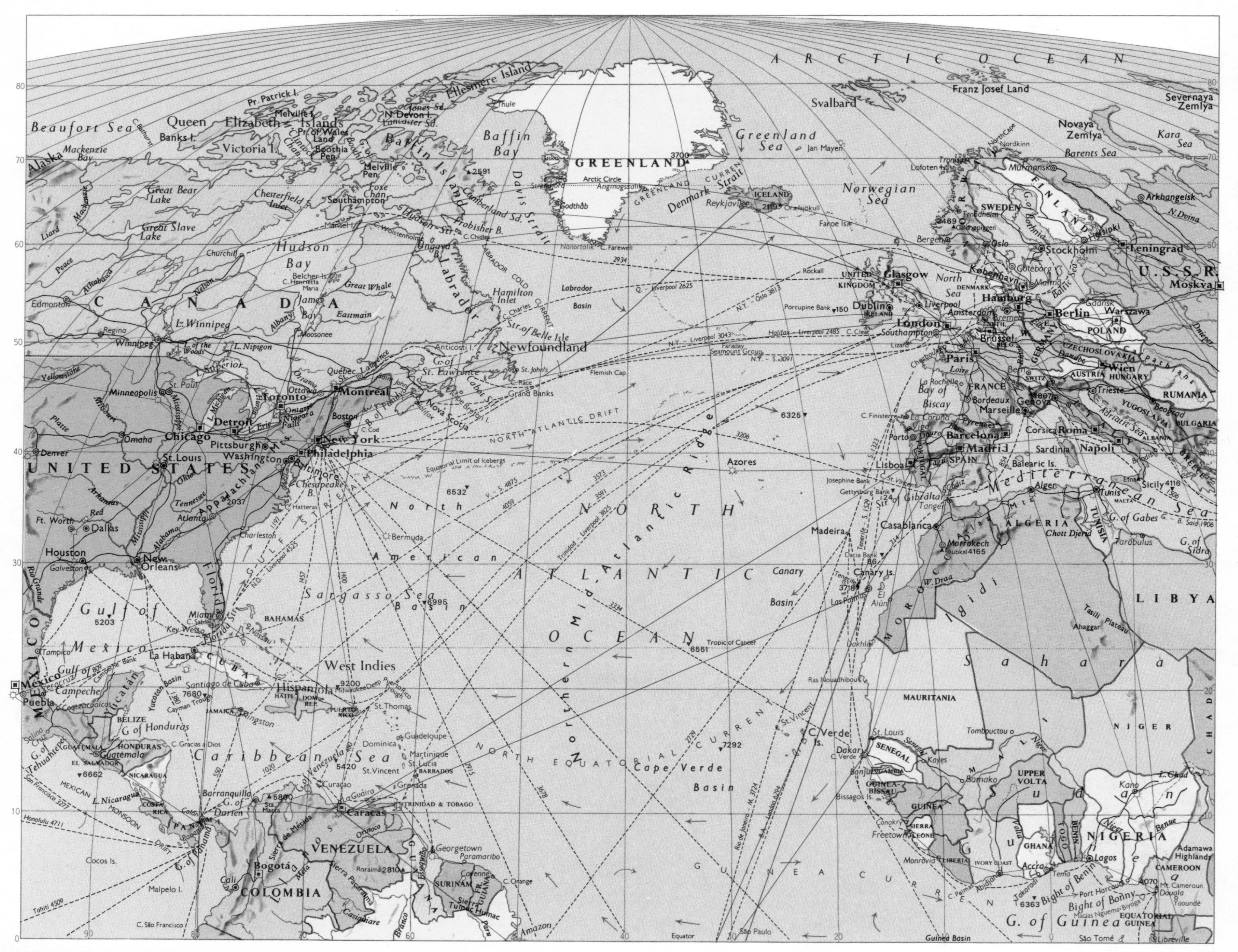

ARCTIC OCEAN
Franz Josef Land
Svalbard
Severnaya Zemlya
Novaya Zemlya
Kara Sea
Barents Sea
Greenland Sea
Norwegian Sea
GREENLAND
ICELAND
Reykjavik
Denmark Strait
Baffin Bay
Davis Strait
Baffin Island
Ellesmere Island
Queen Elizabeth Islands
Beaufort Sea
Hudson Bay
Labrador
Newfoundland
CANADA
UNITED STATES
Montreal
Toronto
New York
Philadelphia
Boston
Washington
Chicago
Detroit
New Orleans
Houston
Dallas
Miami
Gulf of Mexico
MEXICO
Caribbean Sea
West Indies
Sargasso Sea
Bermuda
NORTH ATLANTIC OCEAN
North American Basin
Northern Mid Atlantic Ridge
NORTH ATLANTIC DRIFT
NORTH EQUATORIAL CURRENT
GUINEA CURRENT
Azores
Canary Is.
Canary Basin
Madeira
C. Verde Is.
Cape Verde Basin
Tropic of Cancer
Equator
Bay of Biscay
North Sea
FINLAND
SWEDEN
U.S.S.R.
Moskva
Leningrad
Stockholm
London
Paris
Dublin
Glasgow
Berlin
Hamburg
Amsterdam
Madrid
Lisboa
Barcelona
Roma
Napoli
PORTUGAL
SPAIN
FRANCE
POLAND
RUMANIA
YUGOSLAVIA
BULGARIA
Mediterranean Sea
ALGERIA
TUNISIA
LIBYA
MOROCCO
Casablanca
Sahara
MAURITANIA
NIGER
NIGERIA
SENEGAL
GUINEA
UPPER VOLTA
GHANA
BENIN
TOGO
CAMEROON
Lagos
Dakar
G. of Guinea
Bight of Benin
Bight of Bonny
VENEZUELA
COLOMBIA
Caracas
Bogotá
SURINAM
Georgetown
Amazon

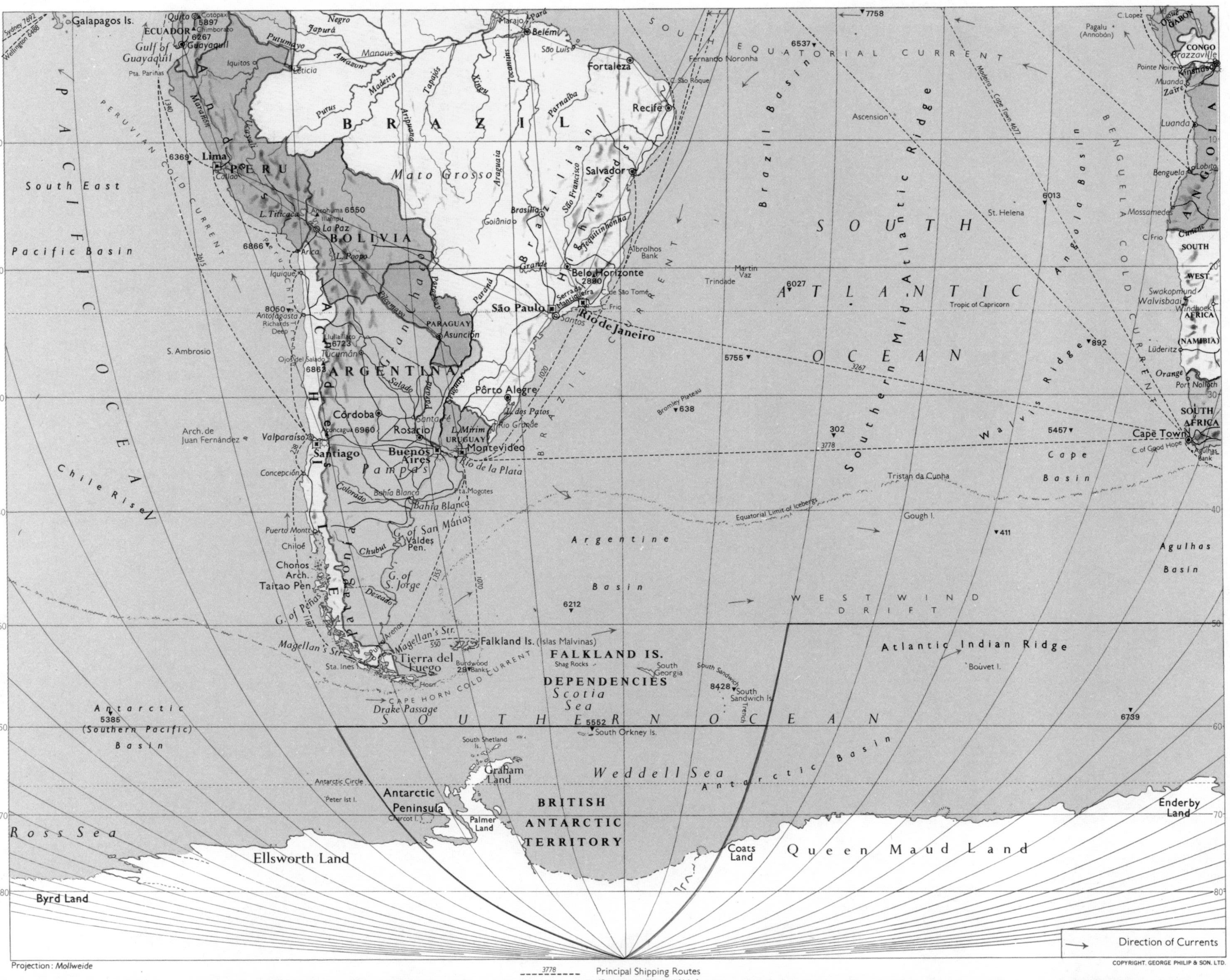
PACIFIC OCEAN
South East Pacific Basin
PERUVIAN COLD CURRENT
Chile Rise
Galapagos Is.
Gulf of Guayaquil
ECUADOR
Quito
Guayaquil
Lima
Callao
PERU
Iquitos
Ucayali
Marañon
Andes
L. Titicaca
La Paz
BOLIVIA
Arica
Iquique
Antofagasta
Valparaiso
Santiago
Concepción
Puerto Montt
Chiloé
Chonos Arch.
Taitao Pen.
G. of Penas
Magellan's Str.
Tierra del Fuego
Drake Passage
CAPE HORN COLD CURRENT
S. Ambrosio
Arch. de Juan Fernández
Córdoba
Rosario
Buenos Aires
ARGENTINA
Pampas
Colorado
Bahía Blanca
G. of San Matías
Valdes Pen.
G. of S. Jorge
Chubut
Deseado
Falkland Is. (Islas Malvinas)
FALKLAND IS. DEPENDENCIES
Scotia Sea
South Georgia
Shag Rocks
South Sandwich Is.
South Sandwich Trench
South Orkney Is.
South Shetland Is.
Graham Land
Palmer Land
Antarctic Peninsula
BRITISH ANTARCTIC TERRITORY
Weddell Sea
Ellsworth Land
Byrd Land
Ross Sea
Antarctic (Southern Pacific) Basin
Peter Ist I.
Antarctic Circle
Coats Land
Queen Maud Land
Enderby Land
Montevideo
URUGUAY
Pôrto Alegre
Rio de la Plata
PARAGUAY
Asunción
Paraguay
Pilcomayo
Gran Chaco
São Paulo
Santos
Rio de Janeiro
Belo Horizonte
Brasília
Goiânia
Salvador
Recife
Fortaleza
Belém
São Luís
BRAZIL
Mato Grosso
Amazon
Manaus
Madeira
Negro
Japurá
Purus
Tapajós
Xingu
Tocantins
Araguaia
São Francisco
Paraná
Parnaíba
Abrolhos Bank
Fernando Noronha
C. São Roque
Trindade
Martin Vaz
SOUTH ATLANTIC OCEAN
SOUTH EQUATORIAL CURRENT
BRAZIL CURRENT
Brazil Basin
Southern Mid-Atlantic Ridge
Ascension
St. Helena
Tropic of Capricorn
Walvis Ridge
Angola Basin
Cape Basin
Argentine Basin
Tristan da Cunha
Gough I.
Equatorial Limit of Icebergs
WEST WIND DRIFT
Atlantic Indian Ridge
Bouvet I.
Agulhas Basin
SOUTHERN OCEAN
Antarctic Basin
BENGUELA COLD CURRENT
Pagalu (Annobón)
C. Lopez
GABON
CONGO
Brazzaville
Kinshasa
Pointe Noire
Zaire
Luanda
ANGOLA
Lobito
Benguela
Mossamedes
Cunene
C. Frio
SOUTH WEST AFRICA (NAMIBIA)
Swakopmund
Walvisbaai
Windhoek
Lüderitz
Orange
Port Nolloth
SOUTH AFRICA
Cape Town
C. of Good Hope
Agulhas Bank
Madeira - Cape Town 4677
Direction of Currents
Principal Shipping Routes (Distances in Nautical Miles)
Projection: Mollweide
COPYRIGHT. GEORGE PHILIP & SON, LTD.

E.E.C. Members
E.F.T.A. Member
All E.F.T.A. and associated states have Free Trade Agreements with the E.E.C.
States with Association Agreement with E.E.C.
Associate Member of E.F.T.A.
States with Trading Agreement with E.E.C.
Warsaw Pact Countries
The E.E.C. has Trading Agreements with certain countries in the Mediterranean, Pacific and Latin American areas.
EUROPEAN ORGANIZATIONS
1:40 000 000
Arctic Circle
Iceland
Reykjavik
Hekla 1491
Öræfajökull 2119
NORWEGIAN SEA
Faroe Is.
Rockall
St. Kilda
Hebrides
Shetland Is.
Orkney Is.
British Isles
Ben Nevis 1343
Edinburgh
NORTH SEA
Lindesnes
Jutlan
Ireland
Belfast
Irish Sea
Dublin
St. George's Channel
Snowdon 1085
Great Britain
Cardiff
Thames
London
Lands End
Scilly Is.
English Channel
Channel Is.
Str. of Dover
Amsterdam
Netherlands
Frisian Is.
Weser
Brussel
Rhine
Westerwald
Ardennes
Eifel
Taunus
Meuse
Hunsrück
Brittany
Paris
Seine
Vosges
Black Forest
Loire
Saône
Jura
Zürich
Massif Central
Mt. Dore 1886
Cevennes
Rhône
Mt. Blanc 4807
ALPS
Po
Garonne
Gironde
Bay of Biscay
4861
3734
C. Clear
C. Finisterre
Cantabrian Mts.
Old Castile
Iberian Peninsula
Douro
Maladetta 3404
Pyrenees
Ebro
G. of Lion
Riviera
Ligurian Sea
Madrid
Lisboa
C. da Roca
Tagus
New Castile
Guadiana
Sierra Morena
Corsica
Sardinia
Str. of Bonifacio
C. St. Vincent
Balearic Is.
Guadalquivir
Andalusia
Mulhacen 3478
Sa. Nevada
C. Trafalgar
Str. of Gibraltar
Gibraltar
MEDITERR
Tyr
ATLANTIC OCEAN
Flores
Terceira
Pico
Azores
Sao Miguel
6293
Madeira
Casablanca
Er Rif
Alger
Maritime Atlas
Tunis
C. Bon
Plateau of the Shotts
Great Atlas
Saharan Atlas
Toubkal 4165
Gulf of Gabes
Sahara
Palma
Tenerife
Canary Is.
Gran Canaria
Fuerteventura
Tropic of Cancer
Projection: Bonne.
West from Greenwich
m
ft

Nordkapp
Nordkinn
Lofoten
Kebnekaise 2123
L. Inari
Torne älv
Lappland
Kola Peninsula
Kanin Peninsula
Tundra
Pechora
Narodnaya 1894
Telpos Iz. 1617
West Siberian Plain
Ob
Irtysh
White Sea
Mezen
Scandinavia
Umeälv
Indalsälven
Gulf of Bothnia
Finland
Onega
N. Dvina
L. Onega
Ural Mountains
Tobol
Lake Ladoga
Svir
Åland Is.
Helsinki
Oslo
Stockholm
Mälaren
Vänern
Vättern
Gulf of Finland
Neva
Leningrad
Rybinsk Res.
Kama
L. Chudskoye
Gorkiy
Volga
Skaw
Gotland
Valdai Hills
Kattegat
BALTIC SEA
København
Dvina
Moskva
Oka
Obshchi Syrt
Ural
Central Russian Uplands
Volga Heights
Kirgiz Steppe
North European Plain
Neman
Elbe
Berlin
Vistula
Oder
Warszawa
Pripet
Pripet Marshes
Ore Mts.
Praha
Sudetes
Bohemian Forest
Danube
Inn
Moravian Hts.
Tatra 2655
Carpathians
Kiyevo
Dnieper
Ukraine
Tsimlyansk Res.
Don
Ust Urt Plateau
Karagiye Depression -132
Caspian Sea
-28
Kara Bogaz
Wien
Bug
Dniester
Prut
Odessa
Sea of Azov
Kuban
Terek
Budapest
Bakony Forest
Plain of Hungary
Mureș
Tisza
Drava
Sava
Transylvanian Alps
Mouths of the Danube
Crimea
Strait of Kerch
Elbrus 5633
Caucasus
Transcaucasia
Kura
Baku
Dinaric Alps
Dalmatia
Adriatic Sea
București
Beograd
Wallachia
Morava
Black Sea
2211
Araks
Apennines
Tiber
Gran Sasso 2914
Roma
Sofiya
Balkans
Balkan Peninsula
Rhodope
İstanbul
Bosporus
Pontine Mts.
Ararat 5165
L. Van
L. Urmia
Elburz Mts.
Tehran
Sea of Marmara
Str. of Otranto
Pindus
Dardanelles
Ankara
Kizil
Anatolia
Kurdistan
Strait of Messina
Calabria
Ionian Is.
Aegean Sea
L. Tuz
Erciyas 3770
Taurus Mts.
Ionian Sea
Etna 3263
Sicily
C. Spartivento
Athinai
Morea
Halab
Euphrates
Tigris
Mesopotamia
Baghdad
Pantelleria
Malta
5121
C. Matapan
Rhodes
MEDITERRANEAN SEA
Crete
Cyprus
Bayrūt
Levant
Syrian Desert
Persian Gulf
Tripoli
Tel Aviv-Yafo
Dead Sea -395
Gulf of Sidra
Nile Delta
East from Greenwich

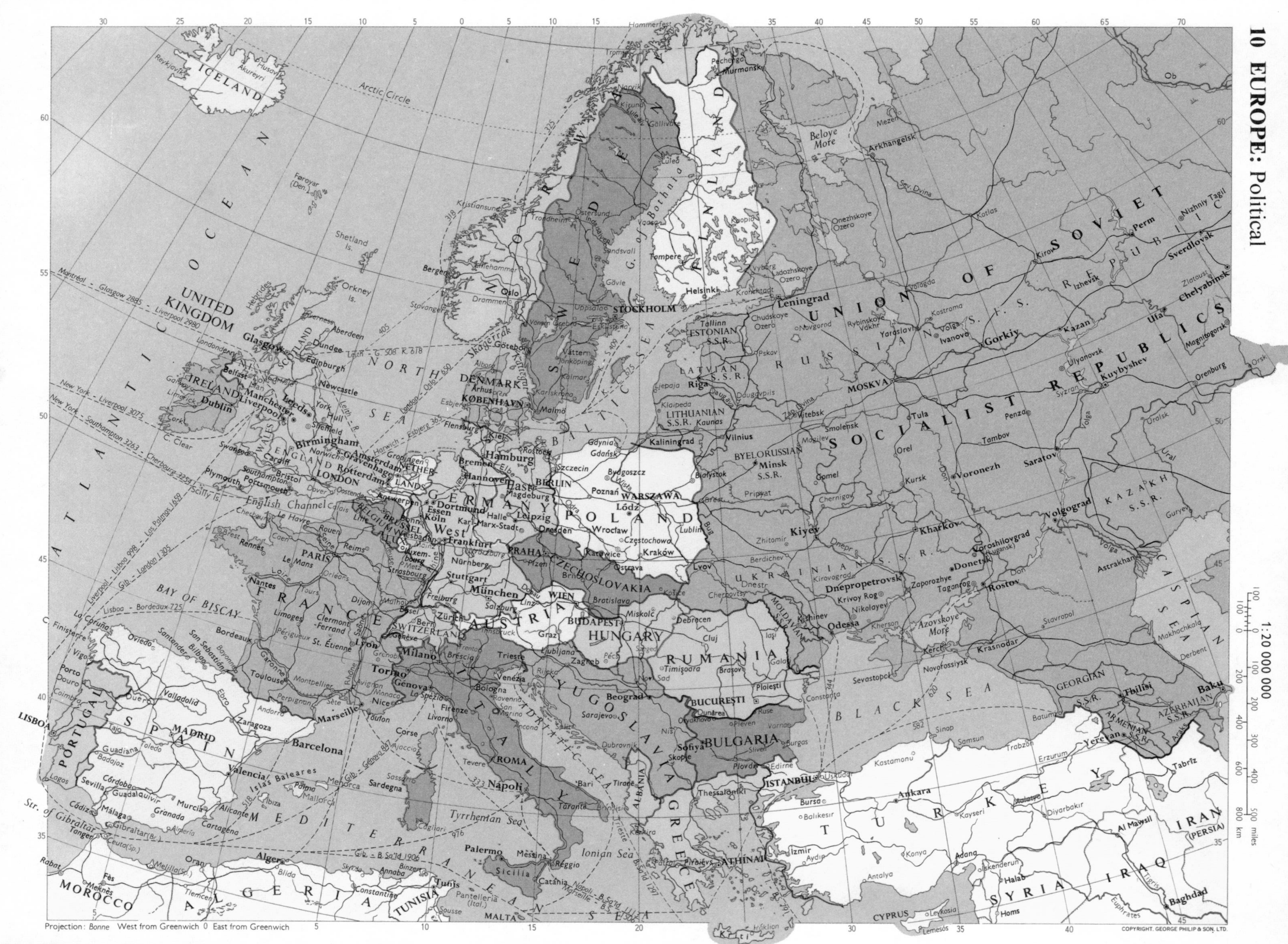
1:20 000 000
100 0 100 200 300 400 500 miles
100 0 200 400 600 800 km
UNION OF SOVIET SOCIALIST REPUBLICS
R. S. F. S. R.
UKRAINIAN S.S.R.
BYELORUSSIAN S.S.R.
KAZAKH S.S.R.
GEORGIAN S.S.R.
ARMENIAN S.S.R.
AZERBAIJAN S.S.R.
MOLDAVIAN S.S.R.
LITHUANIAN S.S.R.
LATVIAN S.S.R.
ESTONIAN S.S.R.
FINLAND
SWEDEN
NORWAY
DENMARK
POLAND
CZECHOSLOVAKIA
HUNGARY
RUMANIA
BULGARIA
YUGOSLAVIA
ALBANIA
GREECE
TURKEY
SYRIA
IRAQ
IRAN (PERSIA)
CYPRUS
AUSTRIA
SWITZERLAND
GERMANY
ITALY
FRANCE
BELGIUM
NETHERLANDS
LUX.
UNITED KINGDOM
IRELAND
ICELAND
SPAIN
PORTUGAL
MOROCCO
ALGERIA
TUNISIA
MALTA
ATLANTIC OCEAN
NORTH SEA
BALTIC SEA
BLACK SEA
CASPIAN SEA
MEDITERRANEAN SEA
ADRIATIC SEA
Tyrrhenian Sea
Ionian Sea
BAY OF BISCAY
English Channel
G. of Bothnia
Beloye More
Arctic Circle
MOSKVA
Leningrad
STOCKHOLM
Helsinki
Oslo
KØBENHAVN
WARSZAWA
BERLIN
PRAHA
WIEN
BUDAPEST
BUCUREŞTI
Sofiya
Beograd
ATHINAI
ISTANBUL
Ankara
ROMA
PARIS
LONDON
Dublin
MADRID
LISBOA
Reykjavik
Projection: Bonne   West from Greenwich 0 East from Greenwich
COPYRIGHT, GEORGE PHILIP & SON, LTD.

1:4 000 000

20 0 20 40 60 miles
20 0 20 40 60 80 km
The DISTRICTS of Northern Ireland have been numbered and can be identified by reference to this table.
1 Londonderry
2 Limavady
3 Coleraine
4 Ballymoney
5 Moyle
6 Larne
7 Ballymena
8 Magherafelt
9 Cookstown
10 Strabane
11 Omagh
12 Fermanagh
13 Dungannon
14 Craigavon
15 Armagh
16 Newry & Mourne
17 Banbridge
18 Down
19 Lisburn
20 Antrim
21 Newtownabbey
22 Carrickfergus
23 North Down
24 Ards
25 Castlereagh
26 Belfast
1 Merseyside
2 Greater Manchester
3 West Yorkshire
4 South Yorkshire
5 West Glamorgan
6 Mid Glamorgan
7 South Glamorgan
Orkney Is.
ORKNEY
Shetland Is.
SHETLAND
HIGHLAND
ATLANTIC OCEAN
NORTH SEA
IRISH SEA
ENGLISH CHANNEL
St. George's Channel
Bristol Channel
Cardigan Bay
SCOTLAND
IRELAND
NORTHERN IRELAND
WALES
ENGLAND
GRAMPIAN
TAYSIDE
CENTRAL
FIFE
LOTHIAN
STRATHCLYDE
BORDERS
DUMFRIES AND GALLOWAY
WESTERN ISLES
NORTHUMBERLAND
TYNE & WEAR
DURHAM
CLEVELAND
CUMBRIA
NORTH YORKSHIRE
HUMBERSIDE
LANCASHIRE
LINCOLN
NOTTS
DERBY
CHESHIRE
STAFFORD
LEICESTER
NORFOLK
SUFFOLK
CAMBRIDGE
NORTHAMPTON
WARWICK
SHROPSHIRE
HEREFORD AND WORCESTER
GLOUCESTER
OXFORD
BUCKS
BEDFORD
HERTFORD
ESSEX
LONDON
KENT
SURREY
BERKS
WILTS
HANTS
WEST SUSSEX
EAST SUSSEX
ISLE OF WIGHT
DORSET
SOMERSET
AVON
DEVON
CORNWALL
GWENT
POWYS
DYFED
GWYNEDD
CLWYD
ISLE OF MAN
DONEGAL
SLIGO
LEITRIM
MAYO
ROSCOMMON
LONGFORD
CAVAN
MONAGHAN
LOUTH
MEATH
WESTMEATH
CONNACHT
GALWAY
OFFALY
KILDARE
DUBLIN
WICKLOW
LAOIS
LEINSTER
CLARE
LIMERICK
TIPPERARY
KILKENNY
CARLOW
WEXFORD
WATERFORD
MUNSTER
KERRY
CORK
West from Greenwich
East from Greenwich

Projection: *Conical with two standard parallels*

12 ENGLAND AND WALES

NORTH SEA
IRISH SEA
North Channel
Firth of Clyde
Firth of Forth
Solway Firth
SCOTLAND
Southern Uplands
Cheviot Hills
Pennines
Cumbrian Mts.
N. York Moors
York Wolds
Lincoln Wolds
The Wash
The Fens
Holderness
NORTHUMBERLAND
TYNE & WEAR
DURHAM
CLEVELAND
CUMBRIA
NORTH YORKSHIRE
LANCASHIRE
W. YORKSHIRE
SOUTH YORKSHIRE
HUMBERSIDE
MERSEYSIDE
CHESHIRE
DERBY
NOTTS
LINCOLN
NORFOLK
STAFFORD
CLWYD
GWYNEDD
ISLE OF MAN
Anglesey
Arran
Kintyre
Galloway
Edinburgh
Glasgow
Stirling
Dumfries
Newcastle
Sunderland
Middlesbrough
Carlisle
Leeds
Bradford
Manchester
Liverpool
Sheffield
Hull
York
Nottingham
Derby
Lincoln
Preston
Blackpool
Lancaster
Douglas
Belfast

1:2 000 000
10 0 10 20 30 40 50 miles
10 0 10 20 30 40 50 60 70 80 km
ENGLISH CHANNEL
FRANCE
Bristol Channel
Cardigan Bay
Carmarthen Bay
Channel Islands
Alderney
Guernsey
Sark
St. Peter Port
Jersey
St. Helier
SCILLY ISLES
On same Scale
Isles of Scilly
St. Mary's
Penzance
Land's End
St. Ives
LONDON
Birmingham
Bristol
Cardiff
Swansea
Plymouth
Exeter
Southampton
Portsmouth
Bournemouth
Brighton
Oxford
Reading
Cambridge
Ipswich
Colchester
Southend
Leicester
Northampton
Coventry
Wolverhampton
Gloucester
Cheltenham
Swindon
Bath
Weymouth
Torquay
Truro
Falmouth
Lizard
Hastings
Eastbourne
Dover
Folkestone
Canterbury
Margate
Ramsgate
Lowestoft
Dieppe
Rouen
Le Havre
Cherbourg
Caen
C. de la Hague
SUFFOLK
ESSEX
KENT
EAST SUSSEX
WEST SUSSEX
SURREY
HANTS
BERKS
WILTS
DORSET
DEVON
CORNWALL
SOMERSET
AVON
GLOUCESTER
OXFORD
BUCKS
HERTFORD
BEDFORD
NORTHAMPTON
CAMBRIDGE
WARWICK
WORCESTER
HEREFORD & WORCESTER
SHROPSHIRE
POWYS
DYFED
GWENT
MID GLAMORGAN
WEST GLAMORGAN
SOUTH GLAMORGAN
ISLE OF WIGHT
Dartmoor
Exmoor
Lundy
West from Greenwich
East from Greenwich
COPYRIGHT, GEORGE PHILIP & SON, LTD.
Projection: Conical with two standard parallels.

14 SCOTLAND

1:2 000 000

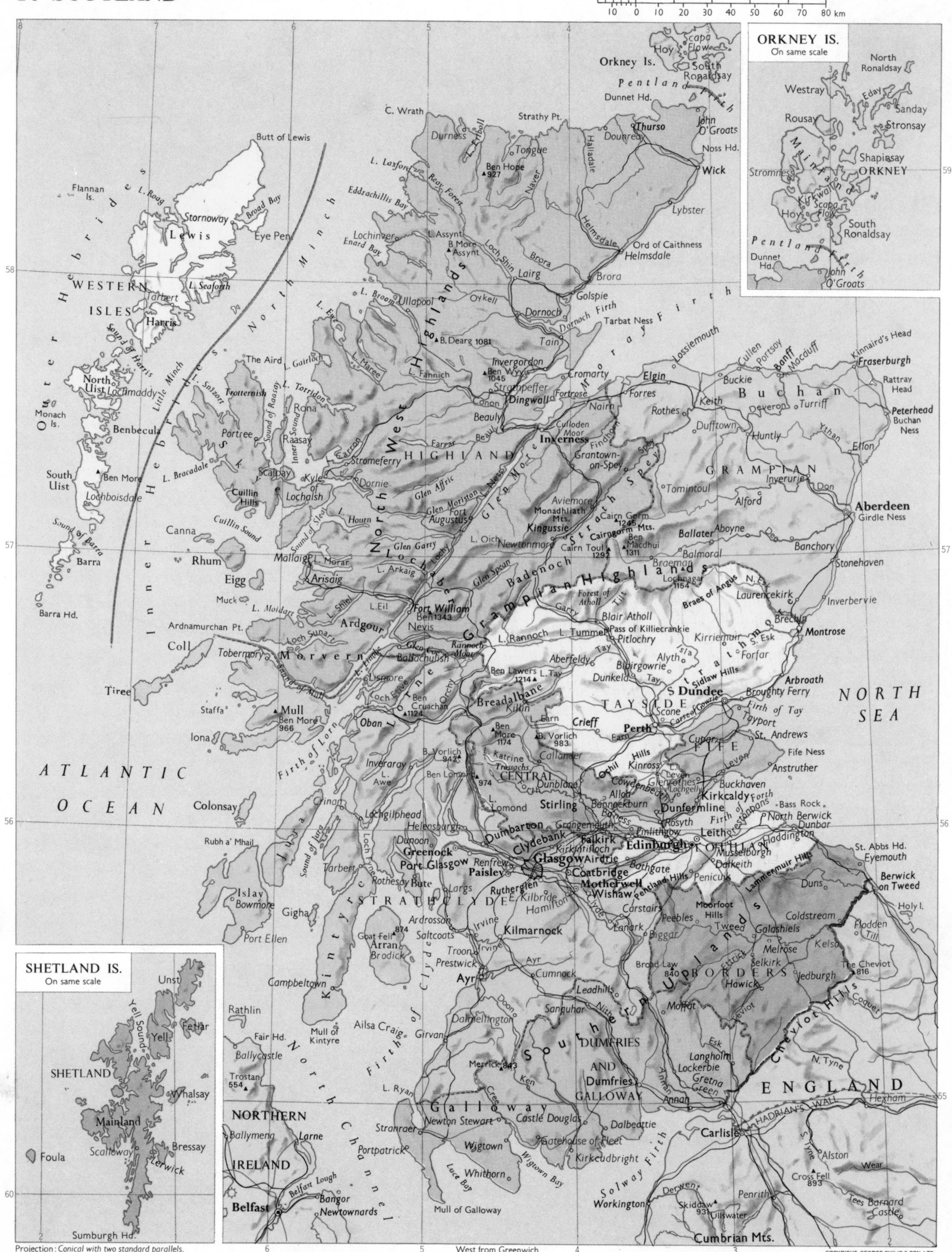

10 0 10 20 30 40 50 miles
10 0 10 20 30 40 50 60 70 80 km
ORKNEY IS.
On same scale
North Ronaldsay
Westray
Eday
Sanday
Rousay
Stronsay
Mainland
Shapinsay
ORKNEY
Stromness
Kirkwall
Scapa Flow
Hoy
South Ronaldsay
Pentland Firth
Dunnet Hd.
John O'Groats
SHETLAND IS.
On same scale
Unst
Yell Sound
Yell
Fetlar
SHETLAND
Whalsay
Mainland
Bressay
Foula
Scalloway
Lerwick
Sumburgh Hd.
Orkney Is.
Hoy
Scapa Flow
South Ronaldsay
Pentland Firth
Dunnet Hd.
John O'Groats
C. Wrath
Strathy Pt.
Thurso
Dounreay
Noss Hd.
Wick
Durness
Tongue
Ben Hope 927
Naver
Halladale
Lybster
Helmsdale
Ord of Caithness
Brora
Butt of Lewis
Flannan Is.
L. Roag
Stornoway
Broad Bay
Lewis
Eye Pen.
L. Seaforth
WESTERN ISLES
Tarbert
Harris
Sound of Harris
North Uist
Lochmaddy
Monach Is.
Benbecula
South Uist
Ben More
Lochboisdale
Sound of Barra
Barra
Barra Hd.
Outer Hebrides
Inner Hebrides
Little Minch
North Minch
L. Laxford
Reay Forest
Eddrachillis Bay
Lochinver
Enard Bay
L. Assynt
B. More Assynt
Loch Shin
Lairg
Oykell
Golspie
Dornoch
Dornoch Firth
Tarbat Ness
Tain
L. Broom
Ullapool
North West Highlands
B. Dearg 1081
Invergordon
Ben Wyvis 1045
Cromarty
Moray Firth
Lossiemouth
Elgin
Forres
Nairn
Fortrose
Dingwall
Strathpeffer
Beauly
Inverness
Culloden Moor
L. Gairloch
L. Maree
L. Fannich
The Aird
Trotternish
L. Torridon
Rona
Raasay
Portree
L. Snizort
L. Bracadale
Skye
Cuillin Hills
Scalpay
Kyle of Lochalsh
Stromeferry
L. Carron
HIGHLAND
Dornie
Glen Affric
Glen Moriston
Fort Augustus
Loch Ness
Glen More
L. Hourn
Sound of Sleat
Canna
Cuillin Sound
Rhum
Eigg
Muck
Mallaig
L. Morar
Arisaig
L. Moidart
L. Shiel
L. Arkaig
Glen Garry
L. Oich
Loch Lochy
Fort William
Ben Nevis 1343
L. Eil
Ardgour
Ardnamurchan Pt.
Coll
Tobermory
Morvern
Loch Sunart
Glen Coe
Ballachulish
Rannoch Moor
Tiree
Sound of Mull
Lismore
Loch Linnhe
Loch Etive
Ben Cruachan 1124
Staffa
Mull
Ben More 966
Iona
Oban
Firth of Lorn
Colonsay
Jura
Sound of Jura
Crinan
Lochgilphead
Inveraray
L. Awe
Loch Fyne
Rubh a' Mhail
Islay
Bowmore
Port Ellen
Gigha
Tarbert
Kintyre
Campbeltown
Rathlin
Fair Hd.
Ballycastle
Trostan 554
Mull of Kintyre
North Channel
Ailsa Craig
Arran
Goat Fell 874
Brodick
Firth of Clyde
Rothesay
Bute
Dunoon
Greenock
Port Glasgow
Helensburgh
Dumbarton
Largs
Ardrossan
Saltcoats
Irvine
Troon
Prestwick
Ayr
Girvan
Dalmellington
L. Ryan
Stranraer
Portpatrick
NORTHERN IRELAND
Ballymena
Larne
Belfast
Belfast Lough
Bangor
Newtownards
Mull of Galloway
Luce Bay
Wigtown
Wigtown Bay
Whithorn
Newton Stewart
Galloway
Merrick 843
Castle Douglas
Gatehouse of Fleet
Kirkcudbright
Dalbeattie
Solway Firth
Dumfries
DUMFRIES AND GALLOWAY
Annan
Gretna Green
Southern Uplands
Sanquhar
Leadhills
Cumnock
Kilmarnock
STRATHCLYDE
Paisley
Renfrew
Glasgow
Clydebank
Rutherglen
E. Kilbride
Hamilton
Motherwell
Wishaw
Coatbridge
Airdrie
Kirkintilloch
Lanark
Carstairs
Biggar
Peebles
Moffat
Broad Law 840
BORDERS
Galashiels
Melrose
Selkirk
Hawick
Jedburgh
Kelso
Coldstream
Duns
Berwick on Tweed
Eyemouth
St. Abbs Hd.
Lammermuir Hills
Moorfoot Hills
Pentland Hills
Penicuik
Dalkeith
Musselburgh
LOTHIAN
Haddington
Dunbar
North Berwick
Bass Rock
Edinburgh
Leith
Linlithgow
Bathgate
Falkirk
Grangemouth
Rosyth
Dunfermline
Firth of Forth
Kirkcaldy
Buckhaven
Leven
Glenrothes
Cowdenbeath
Alloa
Stirling
Bannockburn
Dunblane
Callander
L. Lomond
Ben Lomond 974
B. Vorlich 942
L. Katrine
Trossachs
CENTRAL
Ochil Hills
Kinross
FIFE
Cupar
St. Andrews
Fife Ness
Anstruther
Tayport
Firth of Tay
Dundee
Broughty Ferry
Arbroath
Carse of Gowrie
Perth
Scone
Crieff
B. Vorlich 983
Ben More 1174
Killin
L. Earn
Breadalbane
TAYSIDE
Ben Lawers 1214
L. Tay
Aberfeldy
Dunkeld
Blairgowrie
Alyth
Sidlaw Hills
Strathmore
Forfar
Kirriemuir
Pitlochry
Pass of Killiecrankie
Blair Atholl
L. Rannoch
L. Tummel
Forest of Atholl
Grampian Highlands
Braes of Angus
Lochnagar 1154
Brechin
Montrose
Laurencekirk
Inverbervie
Stonehaven
Badenoch
Glen Spean
Kingussie
Newtonmore
Monadhliath Mts.
Aviemore
Cairngorm Mts.
Cairn Gorm 1245
Ben Macdhui 1311
Cairn Toul 1292
Braemar
Balmoral
Ballater
Aboyne
Banchory
Dee
Aberdeen
Girdle Ness
Don
Inverurie
Alford
Tomintoul
GRAMPIAN
Grantown-on-Spey
Strath Spey
Findhorn
Dufftown
Huntly
Rothes
Keith
Buckie
Cullen
Portsoy
Banff
Macduff
Buchan
Deveron
Turriff
Ythan
Ellon
Fraserburgh
Kinnaird's Head
Rattray Head
Peterhead
Buchan Ness
NORTH SEA
ATLANTIC OCEAN
Cheviot Hills
The Cheviot 816
Tweed
Till
Flodden
Holy I.
Coquet
Esk
Langholm
Lockerbie
Liddel
N. Tyne
ENGLAND
HADRIAN'S WALL
Hexham
Carlisle
S. Tyne
Alston
Cross Fell 893
Wear
Tees
Barnard Castle
Penrith
Workington
Derwent
Skiddaw 931
Ullswater
Cumbrian Mts.
West from Greenwich

Projection: *Conical with two standard parallels.*

1:2 000 000

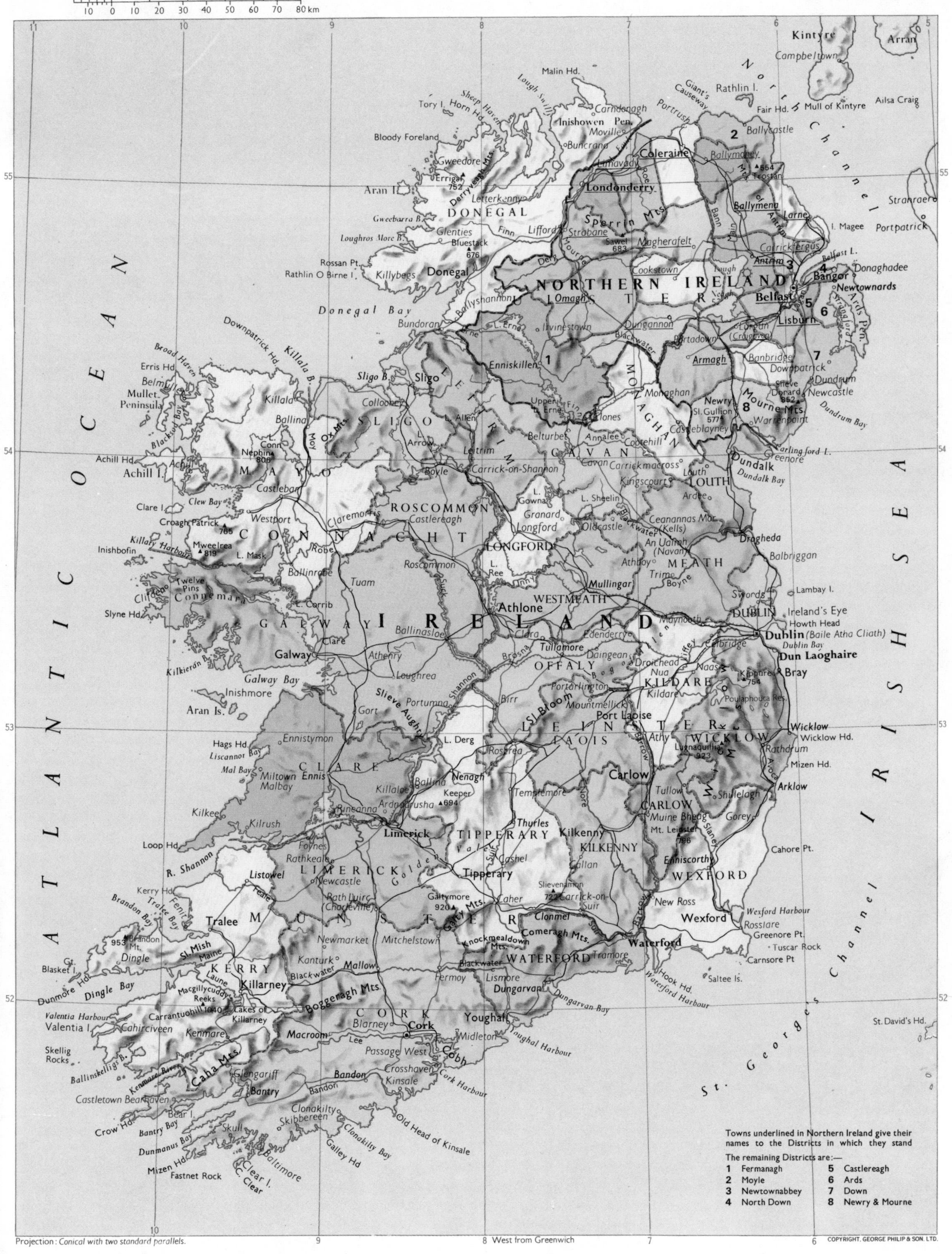

10 0 10 20 30 40 50 miles
10 0 10 20 30 40 50 60 70 80 km
ATLANTIC OCEAN
IRISH SEA
North Channel
St. Georges Channel
NORTHERN IRELAND
IRELAND
ULSTER
CONNACHT
LEINSTER
MUNSTER
DONEGAL
SLIGO
LEITRIM
MAYO
ROSCOMMON
LONGFORD
CAVAN
MONAGHAN
LOUTH
MEATH
WESTMEATH
GALWAY
OFFALY
KILDARE
LAOIS
WICKLOW
CARLOW
KILKENNY
WEXFORD
WATERFORD
TIPPERARY
CLARE
LIMERICK
CORK
KERRY
DUBLIN
Kintyre
Arran
Campbeltown
Rathlin I.
Giant's Causeway
Portrush
Fair Hd.
Mull of Kintyre
Ailsa Craig
Stranraer
Portpatrick
Malin Hd.
Lough Swilly
Sheep Haven
Tory I.
Horn Hd.
Carndonagh
Inishowen Pen.
Moville
Buncrana
Bloody Foreland
Gweedore
Errigal 752
Derryveagh Mts.
Aran I.
Letterkenny
Gweebarra B.
Loughros More B.
Glenties
Bluestack 676
Finn
Lifford
Strabane
Rossan Pt.
Rathlin O Birne I.
Killybegs
Donegal
Donegal Bay
Ballyshannon
Bundoran
Coleraine
Limavady
Londonderry
Sperrin Mts.
Sawel 683
Magherafelt
Ballycastle
Ballymoney
Ballymena
Larne
Trostan 554
Mts. of Antrim
I. Magee
Carrickfergus
Antrim
Belfast L.
Donaghadee
Bangor
Newtownards
Belfast
Lisburn
Ards Pen.
Cookstown
Lough Neagh
Omagh
Dungannon
Irvinestown
Blackwater
Portadown
Lurgan (Craigavon)
Banbridge
Armagh
Downpatrick
Dundrum
Newcastle
Slieve Donard 852
Dundrum Bay
Mourne Mts.
Warrenpoint
Newry
Sl. Gullion 577
Castleblayney
Enniskillen
L. Erne
Upper L. Erne
Clones
Monaghan
Carlingford L.
Greenore
Dundalk
Dundalk Bay
Downpatrick Hd.
Broad Haven
Killala B.
Erris Hd.
Belmullet
Mullet Peninsula
Killala
Ballina
L. Conn
Nephin 806
Achill Hd.
Achill I.
Blacksod Bay
Sligo B.
Sligo
Collooney
Ox Mts.
Moy
L. Allen
L. Arrow
Leitrim
Boyle
Carrick-on-Shannon
Belturbet
Annalee
Cootehill
Cavan
Carrickmacross
Kingscourt
Ardee
Castlebar
Clew Bay
Clare I.
Westport
Croagh Patrick 765
Killary Harbour
Mweelrea 819
L. Mask
Inishbofin
Claremorris
Castlereagh
L. Gowna
Granard
Longford
L. Sheelin
Oldcastle
Ceanannas Mor (Kells)
An Uaimh (Navan)
Drogheda
Balbriggan
Robe
Ballinrobe
Roscommon
L. Ree
Inny
Athboy
Trim
Boyne
Mullingar
Swords
Lambay I.
Tuam
Suck
Twelve Pins
Connemara
Clifden
L. Corrib
Slyne Hd.
Athlone
Ireland's Eye
Howth Head
Maynooth
Dublin (Baile Atha Cliath)
Dublin Bay
Dun Laoghaire
Ballinasloe
Clara
Edenderry
Tullamore
Daingean
Brosna
Bog of Allen
Liffey
Celbridge
Droichead Nua
Naas
Kippure 754
Bray
Galway
Clare
Athenry
Loughrea
Kilkieran B.
Galway Bay
Inishmore
Aran Is.
Slieve Aughty
Portumna
Shannon
Birr
Gort
Portarlington
Kildare
Mountmellick
Sl. Bloom
Port Laoise
Poulaphouca Res.
Wicklow
Wicklow Hd.
Wicklow Mts.
Hags Hd.
Ennistymon
Liscannor Bay
Mal Bay
Miltown Malbay
Ennis
L. Derg
Roscrea
Athy
Barrow
Lugnaquilla 923
Rathdrum
Mizen Hd.
Avoca
Arklow
Ballina
Killaloe
Nenagh
Keeper 694
Ardnacrusha
Templemore
Nore
Carlow
Tullow
Shillelagh
Gorey
Kilkee
Kilrush
Bunratty
Limerick
Thurles
Kilkenny
Muine Bheag
Mt. Leinster 796
Slaney
Loop Hd.
R. Shannon
Foynes
Rathkeale
Newcastle
Golden Vale
Cashel
Suir
Tipperary
Callan
Enniscorthy
Cahore Pt.
Listowel
Kerry Hd.
Tralee B.
Brandon Bay
Fenit
Feale
Rath Luirc (Charleville)
Galtymore 920
Galty Mts.
Caher
Slievenamon 721
Carrick-on-Suir
Clonmel
New Ross
Wexford
Wexford Harbour
Rosslare
Greenore Pt.
Tralee
Sl. Mish
Brandon Mt. 953
Dingle
Maine
Newmarket
Mitchelstown
Knockmealdown Mts.
Comeragh Mts.
Waterford
Tramore
Tuskar Rock
Carnsore Pt.
Gt. Blasket I.
Kanturk
Mallow
Blackwater
Fermoy
Lismore
Dungarvan
Saltee Is.
Hook Hd.
Waterford Harbour
Dunmore Hd.
Dingle Bay
Laune
Killarney
Macgillycuddy's Reeks
Carrantuohill 1040
Lakes of Killarney
Boggeragh Mts.
Dungarvan Bay
Valentia Harbour
Valentia I.
Cahirciveen
Kenmare
Macroom
Blarney
Cork
Lee
Youghal
Midleton
Youghal Harbour
St. David's Hd.
Skellig Rocks
Ballinskelligs B.
Kenmare River
Caha Mts.
Glengariff
Passage West
Cobh
Crosshaven
Cork Harbour
Bandon
Kinsale
Castletown Bearhaven
Bantry
Clonakilty
Bear I.
Skibbereen
Clonakilty Bay
Old Head of Kinsale
Crow Hd.
Bantry Bay
Skull
Dunmanus Bay
Baltimore
Galley Hd
Mizen Hd.
Fastnet Rock
Clear I.
C. Clear
Towns underlined in Northern Ireland give their names to the Districts in which they stand
The remaining Districts are:—
1 Fermanagh
2 Moyle
3 Newtownabbey
4 North Down
5 Castlereagh
6 Ards
7 Down
8 Newry & Mourne
Projection: Conical with two standard parallels.
West from Greenwich

NETHERLANDS, BELGIUM AND LUXEMBOURG

1:2 500 000

10 0 10 20 30 40 50 miles

10 0 10 20 30 40 50 60 70 80 km

NORTH SEA

ENGLAND

NETHERLANDS

BELGIUM

LUXEMBOURG

FRANCE

GERMANY

Projection: Conical with two standard parallels

East from Greenwich

1:5 000 000

0 20 40 60 80 100 Statute Miles

0 40 80 120 160 Km

FRENCH DEPARTMENTS

A.	01	Ain
Ai.	02	Aisne
Al.	03	Allier
A.H.P.	04	Alpes-de Haute-Provence
H.A.	05	Hautes-Alpes
A.M.	06	Alpes-Maritimes
Ar.	07	Ardèche
Ard.	08	Ardennes
Ari.	09	Ariège
Aub.	10	Aube
Aud.	11	Aude
Av.	12	Aveyron
B.R.	13	Bouches-du-Rhône
C.	14	Calvados
Ca.	15	Cantal
Ch.	16	Charente
Ch.M.	17	Charente-Maritime
Che.	18	Cher
Co.	19	Corrèze
	20	Corse a) Haute-Corse b) Corse du Sud
C.O.	21	Côte-d'Or
C.N.	22	Côtes-du-Nord
Cr.	23	Creuse
D.	24	Dordogne
Do.	25	Doubs
Dr.	26	Drôme
E.	27	Eure
E.L.	28	Eure-et-Loir
F.	29	Finistère (Nord et Sud)
G.	30	Gard
H.G.	31	Haute-Garonne
Ge.	32	Gers
Gi.	33	Gironde
H.	34	Hérault
I.V.	35	Ille-et-Vilaine
I.	36	Indre
I.L.	37	Indre-et-Loire
Is.	38	Isère
J.	39	Jura
L.	40	Landes
L.C.	41	Loir-et-Cher
Lo.	42	Loire
H.L.	43	Haute-Loire
L.A.	44	Loire-Atlantique
Loi.	45	Loiret
Lot	46	Lot
L.G.	47	Lot-et-Garonne
Loz.	48	Lozère
M.L.	49	Main-et-Loire
M.	50	Manche
Ma.	51	Marne
H.M.	52	Haut-Marne
May.	53	Mayenne
M.M.	54	Meurthe-et-Moselle
Me.	55	Meuse
Mo.	56	Morbihan
Mos.	57	Moselle
N.	58	Nièvre
No.	59	Nord
O.	60	Oise
Or.	61	Orne
P.C.	62	Pas-de-Calais
P.D.	63	Puy-de-Dôme
P.A.	64	Pyrénées Atlantiques
H.P.	65	Hautes Pyrénées
P.O.	66	Pyrénées (Orientales)
B.R.	67	Bas Rhin
H.R.	68	Haut Rhin
Rh.	69	Rhône
H.S.	70	Haute Saône
S.L.	71	Saône-et-Loire
S.	72	Sarthe
Sa.	73	Savoie
H.Sa.	74	Haute-Savoie
	75	Paris
S.Me.	76	Seine-Maritime
S.M.	77	Seine-et-Marne
Yv.	78	Yvelines
D.S.	79	Deux-Sèvres
So.	80	Somme
T.	81	Tarn
T.G.	82	Tarn-et-Garonne
V.	83	Var
Va.	84	Vaucluse
Ve.	85	Vendée
Vi.	86	Vienne
H.V.	87	Haute Vienne
Vo.	88	Vosges
Y.	89	Yonne
B.	90	Belfort
Es.	91	Essonne
H.Se.	92	Hauts-de-Seine
S.St.D.	93	Seine-St. Denis
V.M.	94	Val-de-Marne
V.O.	95	Val-d'Oise

CORSICA

On same scale

Projection: Conical with two standard parallels

West from Greenwich — East from Greenwich

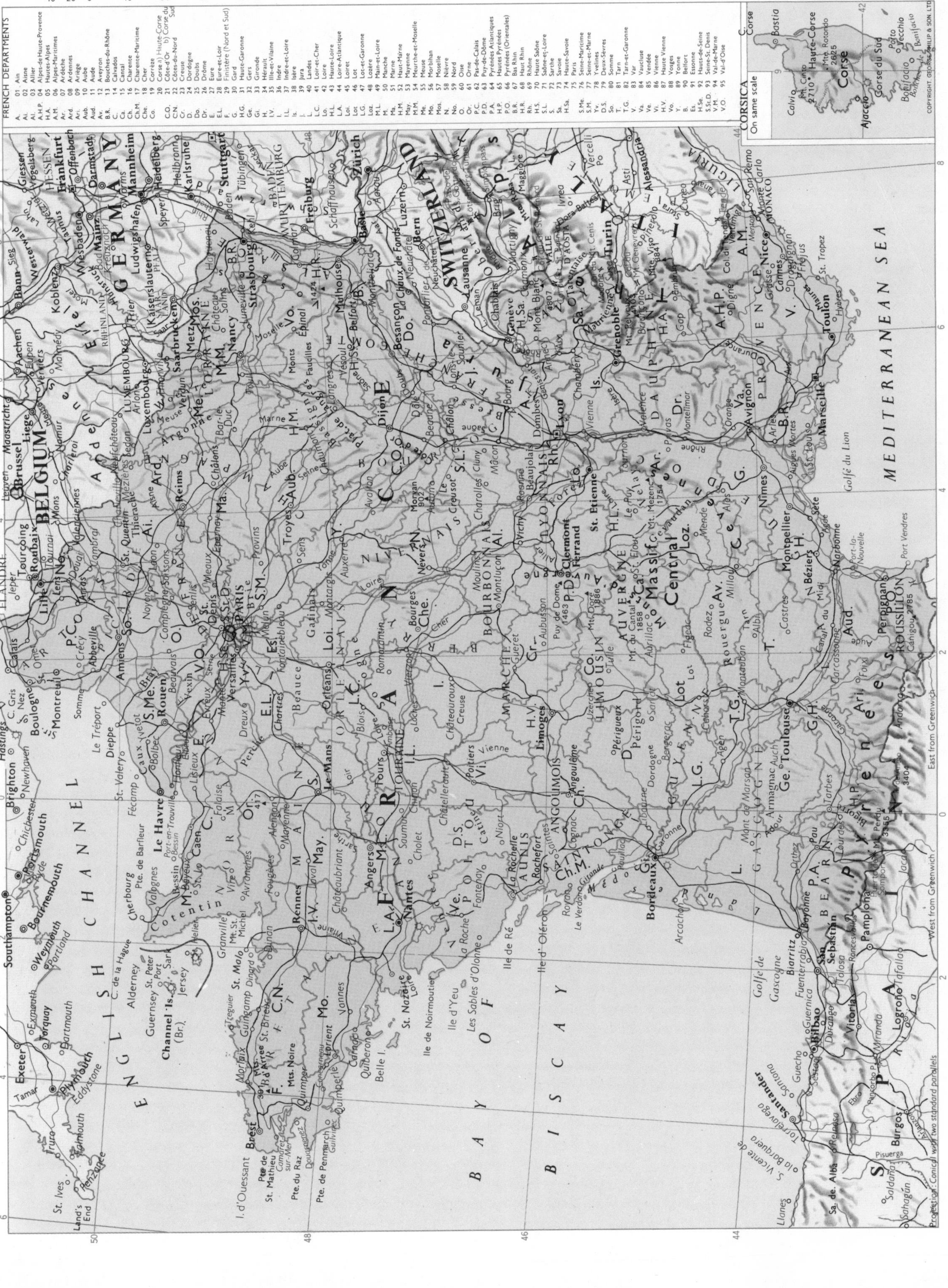

18 NORTHERN FRANCE

DÉPARTEMENTS IN THE PARIS AREA
1 Ville de Paris
2 Seine-St. Denis
3 Val-de-Marne
4 Hauts-de-Seine
Projection: Conical with two standard parallels
West from Greenwich
East from Greenwich
ENGLAND
English Channel
Lyme Bay
Baie de la Seine
CHANNEL ISLANDS
Guernsey
Jersey
Alderney
Sark
Golfe de St. Malo
BAY OF BISCAY
Baie de Bourgneuf
Pertuis Breton
Pertuis d'Antioche
Exeter
Plymouth
Southampton
Portsmouth
Bournemouth
Brighton
Hastings
Eastbourne
Weymouth
Dartmoor
South Downs
Cherbourg
Le Havre
Rouen
Caen
Brest
Quimper
Lorient
Vannes
St. Brieuc
Rennes
Nantes
St. Nazaire
Laval
Le Mans
Angers
Tours
Blois
Alençon
Cholet
La Roche-sur-Yon
La Rochelle
Niort
Poitiers
Rochefort
Saintes
Cognac
Angoulême
Châtellerault
Saumur
Morlaix
Fougères
Évreux
Dieppe
Lisieux
Bayeux
CALVADOS
BRETAGNE
NORMANDIE
MAINE
ANJOU
TOURAINE
POITOU
AUNIS
ANGOUMOIS
Collines de Normandie
Collines du Perche
Monts d'Arrée
Montagne Noire
Île d'Ouessant (Ushant)
Belle Île
Île de Groix
Île de Noirmoutier
Île d'Yeu
Île de Ré
Île d'Oléron
Loire
Vilaine
Sarthe
Vienne
Charente

1:2 500 000

10 0 10 20 30 40 50 miles

10 0 10 20 30 40 50 60 70 80 km

BELGIUM

GERMANY

LUXEMBOURG

FRANCE

SWITZERLAND

ITALY

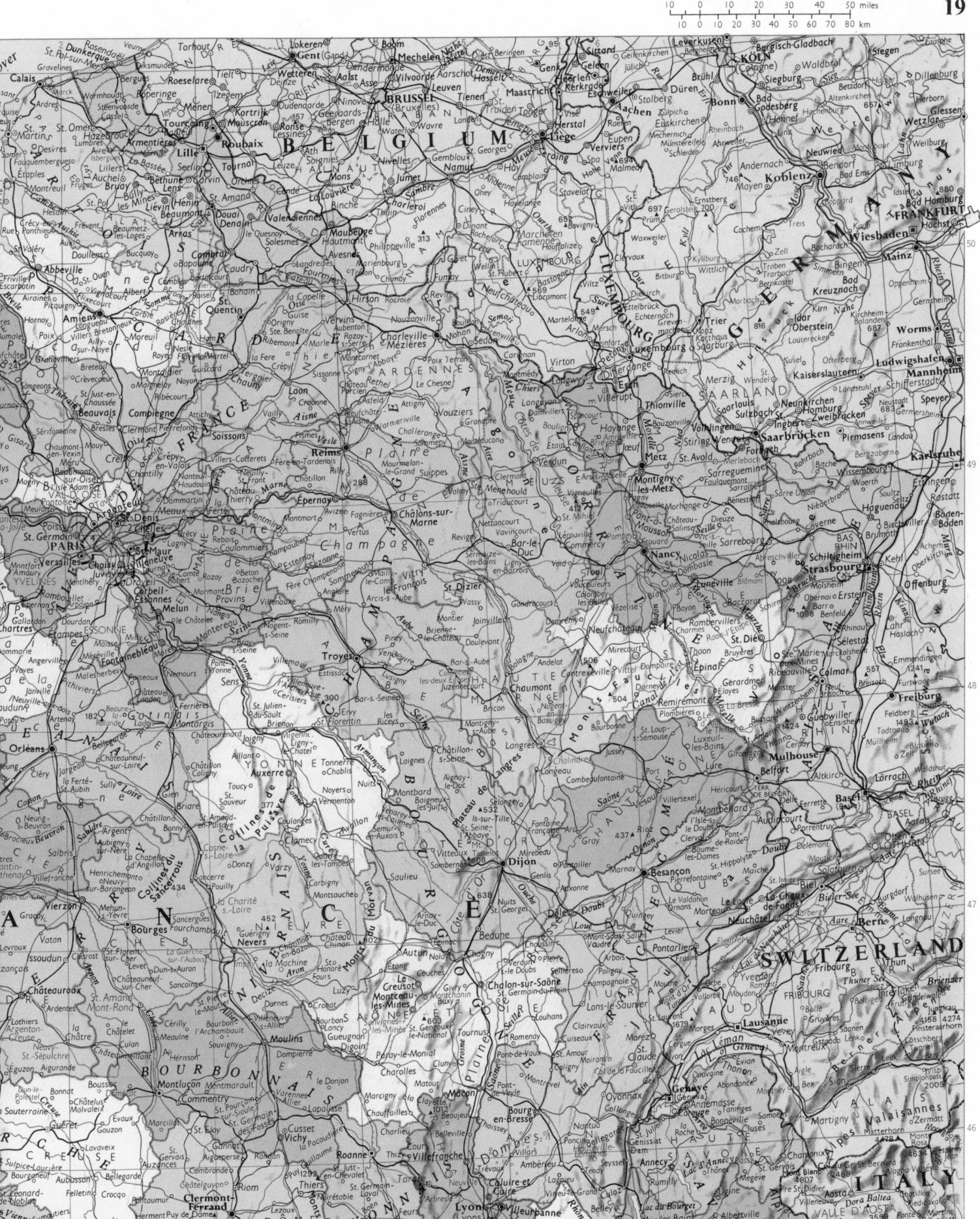

20 SOUTHERN FRANCE

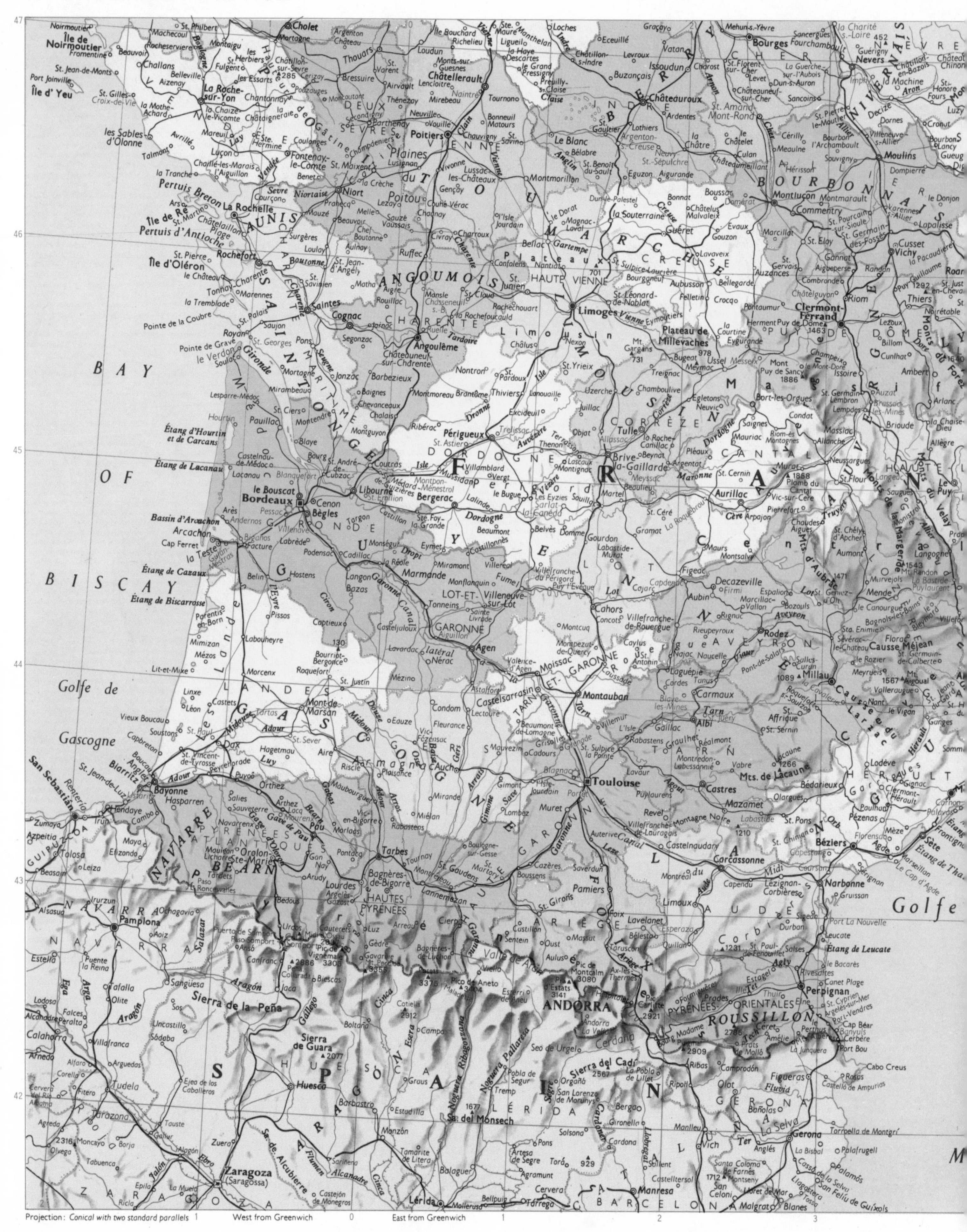
BAY OF BISCAY
Golfe de Gascogne
Golfe du Lion
Pertuis Breton
Pertuis d'Antioche
Île de Noirmoutier
Île d' Yeu
Île de Ré
Île d'Oléron
Bassin d'Arcachon
AUNIS
SAINTONGE
ANGOUMOIS
POITOU
LIMOUSIN
MARCHE
BERRY
BOURBONNAIS
NIVERNAIS
AUVERGNE
PERIGORD
GUYENNE
GASCOGNE
LANDES
BÉARN
NAVARRE
LANGUEDOC
ROUSSILLON
FRANCE
Massif Central
Causse Méjean
Plateau de Millevaches
Mts. de Lacaune
Montagne Noire
Canal du Midi
Corbières
PYRÉNÉES ATLANTIQUES
HAUTES PYRÉNÉES
PYRÉNÉES ORIENTALES
ANDORRA
SPAIN
ARAGON
CATALUÑA
NAVARRA
Sierra de la Peña
Sierra de Guara
Sierra del Cadí
Sa. del Monsech
Pic de Aneto 3404
Pic de Vignemale 3303
La Rochelle
Rochefort
Saintes
Cognac
Angoulême
Poitiers
Niort
Limoges
Périgueux
Bordeaux
Libourne
Bergerac
Agen
Montauban
Toulouse
Albi
Castres
Rodez
Millau
Carcassonne
Narbonne
Béziers
Perpignan
Bayonne
Biarritz
Pau
Tarbes
Lourdes
Mont-de-Marsan
Clermont-Ferrand
Vichy
Moulins
Montluçon
Châteauroux
Bourges
Nevers
Le Puy
Aurillac
Brive-la-Gaillarde
Tulle
Cahors
San Sebastián
Pamplona
Zaragoza
Huesca
Lérida
Gerona
Figueras

Projection: *Conical with two standard parallels* 1 West from Greenwich 0 East from Greenwich 1 2 3

1:2 500 000

10 0 10 20 30 40 50 miles
10 0 10 20 30 40 50 60 70 80 km
SWITZERLAND
ITALY
CORSICA
LIGURIAN SEA
EDITERRANEAN SEA
du Lion
Golfo di Génova
Luzern
Zuger See
Schwyz
Glarus
Bern
Neuchâtel
Biel
Bieler-See
La Chaux-de-Fonds
Le Locle
Pontarlier
Yverdon
Fribourg
Lausanne
Lac Léman
Lac de Genève
Genève
(Genova)
Montreux
Vevey
Thun
Thuner See
Interlaken
Brienzer See
Berner Alpen
Sion
Sierre
Martigny
Brig
Simplon Tunnel
Alpes Valaisannes
Zermatt
Matterhorn
Monte Rosa
Chur
Davos
Vierwaldstätter See
UNTERWALDEN
Altdorf
GRAUBÜNDEN
Landquart
Klosters
St. Moritz
Piz Bernina
4049
Tirano
Sondrio
Valtellina
Bormio
Ortles
3899
Locarno
Bellinzona
Lugano
Lago di Lugano
Como
Lago Maggiore
Varese
Domodóssola
Aosta
Mont Blanc
4807
Alpi Pennine
Chamonix
Annecy
Lac d'Annecy
Chambéry
Aix-les-Bains
Lac du Bourget
Albertville
Lyon
(Lyons)
Villeurbanne
Vénissieux
Caluire-et-Cuire
Villefranche
St. Étienne
Firminy
Vienne
Grenoble
Valence
Romans
Voiron
Bourg en Bresse
Mâcon
Chalon-sur-Saône
Beaune
Dôle
Le Creusot
Montceau-les-Mines
Autun
Paray-le-Monial
Charolles
Lons-le-Saunier
Oyonnax
Nantua
Bellegarde
Thonon
Évian
Annemasse
SAVOIE
HAUTE SAVOIE
VAUD
VALAIS
TICINO
JURA
Torino
(Turin)
Moncalieri
Pinerolo
Ivrea
Biella
Vercelli
Novara
Milano
(Milan)
Monza
Sesto
Legnano
Gallarate
Busto Arsizio
Saronno
Rho
Vigévano
Pavia
Lodi
Crema
Cremona
Bergamo
Lecco
Brescia
Piacenza
Parma
Alessandria
Asti
Casale Monferrato
Voghera
Tortona
Novi Ligure
Cuneo
Mondovì
Savona
Genova
(Genoa)
Rapallo
Chiávari
La Spezia
Carrara
Massa
Viareggio
Pietrasanta
Livorno
(Leghorn)
Arno
Gorgona
Capraia
Elba
Pianosa
Sanremo
Impéria
Ventimiglia
Monaco
Monte Carlo
Menton
Nice
Cannes
Antibes
Grasse
Fréjus
St. Raphaël
St. Tropez
Toulon
Hyères
Marseille
(Marseilles)
Aubagne
La Ciotat
Aix-en-Provence
Arles
Avignon
Nîmes
Orange
Carpentras
Cavaillon
Montélimar
Gap
Digne
Briançon
Embrun
Sisteron
Manosque
PROVENCE
ALPES-DE-HAUTE-PROVENCE
ALPES MARITIMES
HAUTES-ALPES
DRÔME
ISÈRE
DAUPHINÉ
VAUCLUSE
BOUCHES-DU-RHÔNE
VAR
Camargue
Étang de Berre
Îles d'Hyères
Côte d'Azur
Rhône
Durance
Isère
Po
Massif du Pelvoux
4103
Mont Viso
3841
Mont Cenis
Lanslebourg
Modane
Bastia
Calvi
L'Île Rousse
Corte
Ajaccio
Sartène
Porto-Vecchio
Bonifacio
Monte Cinto
2710
HAUTE-CORSE
CORSE-DU-SUD
Étang de Biguglia
G. de St. Florent
G. de Porto
G. de Sagone
G. d'Ajaccio
G. de Valinco
C. Corse
Îles Sanguinaires
Îles Cerbicales
Î. de Cavallo
2940

NORTH SEA
BALTIC
NETHERLANDS
BELGIUM
LUX.
GERMANY
WEST
EAST
CZECHOSLOVAKIA
AUSTRIA
SWITZERLAND
FRANCE
ITALY
ADRIATIC SEA
Golfo di Génova
Golfo di Venézia
Flensburg
Kiel
Lübeck
Hamburg
Bremen
Bremerhaven
Wilhelmshaven
Rostock
Stralsund
Schwerin
Szczecin (Stettin)
Hannover
Braunschweig
Magdeburg
BERLIN
Potsdam
Frankfurt
Poznań
Amsterdam
's-Gravenhage (The Hague)
Rotterdam
Utrecht
Antwerpen
Brussel (Bruxelles)
Liège
Lille
Düsseldorf
Köln (Cologne)
Dortmund
Essen
Bonn
Aachen
Kassel
Halle
Leipzig
Dresden
Karl-Marx-Stadt (Chemnitz)
Erfurt
Frankfurt
Wiesbaden
Mainz
Mannheim
Saarbrücken
Luxembourg
Reims
Metz
Nancy
Strasbourg
Stuttgart
Nürnberg
Würzburg
Regensburg
Augsburg
München (Munich)
Praha (Prague)
Plzeň (Pilsen)
Brno (Brünn)
Linz
Wien (Vienna)
Salzburg
Innsbruck
Graz
Klagenfurt
Basel
Zürich
Bern
Luzern
Lausanne
Genève
Dijon
Besançon
Lyon
Grenoble
St. Étienne
Avignon
Marseille
Nice
MONACO
Torino (Turin)
Milano (Milan)
Génova (Genoa)
Verona
Venézia (Venice)
Trieste
Bologna
Firenze (Florence)
Ljubljana
Zagreb
Rijeka
Projection: Conical with two standard parallels
East from Greenwich

1:5 000 000

24 GERMANY AND SWITZERLAND

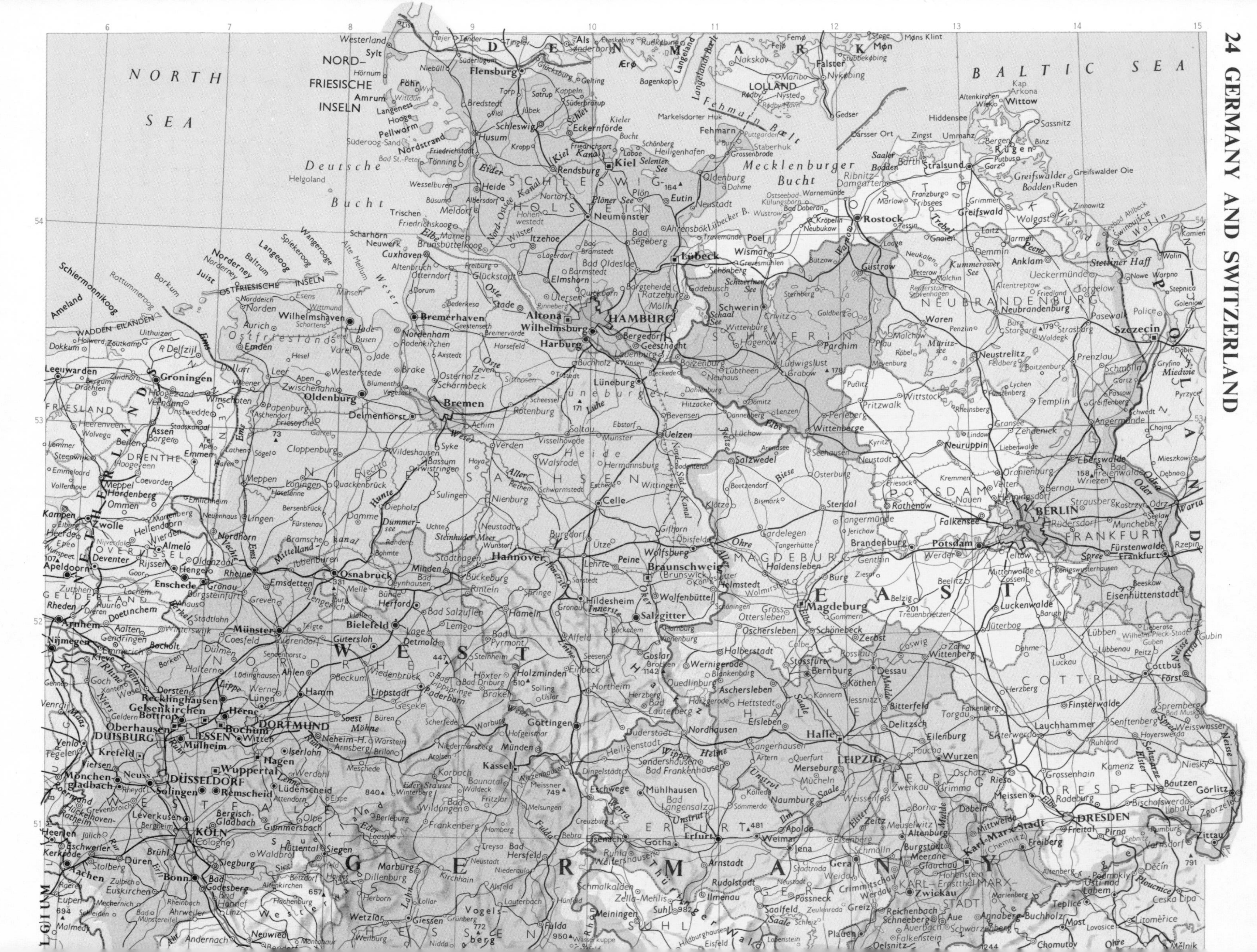

BALTIC SEA
NORTH SEA
POLAND
DENMARK
EAST GERMANY
WEST GERMANY
NETHERLANDS
BELGIUM
NORD-FRIESISCHE INSELN
OSTFRIESISCHE INSELN
WADDEN EILANDEN
Deutsche Bucht
Mecklenburger Bucht
Fehmarn Bælt
SCHLESWIG-HOLSTEIN
NIEDERSACHSEN
NORDRHEIN-WESTFALEN
HESSEN
ROSTOCK
SCHWERIN
NEUBRANDENBURG
POTSDAM
FRANKFURT
MAGDEBURG
COTTBUS
HALLE
LEIPZIG
DRESDEN
ERFURT
GERA
SUHL
KARL-MARX-STADT
BERLIN
HAMBURG
Bremen
Hannover
Magdeburg
Rostock
Lübeck
Kiel
Schwerin
Braunschweig
Halle
Erfurt
Kassel
Göttingen
Osnabrück
Münster
DORTMUND
ESSEN
DÜSSELDORF
KÖLN
Bonn
Aachen
Groningen
Flensburg
Szczecin
Potsdam
Cottbus
Oldenburg
Wilhelmshaven
Bremerhaven
Cuxhaven
Bielefeld
Gera
Jena
Weimar
Gotha
Zwickau
Karl-Marx-Stadt
Wuppertal
DUISBURG
Gelsenkirchen
Bochum
Hagen
Hamm
Nord-Ostsee Kanal
Mittelland-kanal
Nord-Süd Kanal

1:2 500 000

10 0 10 20 30 40 50 miles
10 0 10 20 30 40 50 60 70 80 km

CZECHOSLOVAKIA
SWITZERLAND
ITALY
YUGOSLAVIA
AUSTRIA
FRANCE
LUXEMBOURG
SAARLAND
RHEINLAND-PFALZ
BADEN WÜRTTEMBERG
BAYERN
OBERÖSTERREICH
PRAHA (PRAGUE)
Plzeň
České Budějovice
Karlovy Vary
Linz
Salzburg
Innsbruck
MÜNCHEN (Munich)
Augsburg
Regensburg
Ingolstadt
Nürnberg
Fürth
Erlangen
Bamberg
Bayreuth
Würzburg
Schweinfurt
FRANKFURT
Wiesbaden
Mainz
Offenbach
Darmstadt
Mannheim
Ludwigshafen
Heidelberg
Heilbronn
Karlsruhe
Pforzheim
STUTTGART
Esslingen
Ludwigsburg
Reutlingen
Tübingen
Ulm
Freiburg
Konstanz
Friedrichshafen
Basel
Zürich
Winterthur
Luzern
Bern
Biel
Lausanne
Genève
Strasbourg
Colmar
Mulhouse
Saarbrücken
Kaiserslautern
Koblenz
Trier
Luxembourg
Metz
Nancy
Bolzano
Trento
Merano
Udine
Como
Villach
Klagenfurt
Passau
Landshut
Straubing
Rosenheim
Kempten
Memmingen
Bodensee
Donau
Danube
Oberpfälzer Wald
Bayerischer Wald
Lac Léman (L. Geneva)
Lago Maggiore
Conical with two standard parallels
East from Greenwich

DRESDEN
Karl-Marx-Stadt
Erfurt
Gera
Zwickau
Plauen
Hof
Coburg
Bamberg
Bayreuth
Würzburg
Schweinfurt
Aschaffenburg
Erlangen
Fürth
Nürnberg
Heilbronn
Ludwigsburg
STUTTGART
Esslingen
Göppingen
BADEN-WÜRTTEMBERG
Ulm
Neu Ulm
Augsburg
Ingolstadt
Regensburg
Straubing
Landshut
Passau
MÜNCHEN
(Munich)
Rosenheim
Kempten
Memmingen
Friedrichshafen
Ravensburg
Garmisch-Partenkirchen
Salzburg
Innsbruck
Linz
Wels
Steyr
Graz
Leoben
Kapfenberg
Klagenfurt
Villach
Maribor
Celje
Ljubljana
Zagreb
Trieste
Udine
Gorizia
Monfalcone
Bolzano
Merano
Trento
Rovereto
Bergamo
Brescia
Vicenza
Treviso
Belluno
PRAHA
(PRAGUE)
Plzeň
Karlovy Vary
Kladno
Liberec
Jablonec
České Budějovice
Jihlava
Chomutov
Most
Teplice
Ústí nad Labem
Děčín
Kolín
Pardubice
Jindřichův Hradec
SWITZER-LAND
LIECHTENSTEIN
VORARLBERG
HESSEN
Thüringer Wald
Frankenwald
Fichtelgebirge
Böhmer Wald
Bayerischer Wald
Schwäbische Alb
Fränkische Alb
Lechtaler Alpen
Zillertaler Alpen
Hohe Tauern
Niedere Tauern
Karnische Alpen
Karawanken
Ötztaler Alpen
Donau
Danube
Inn
Main
Enns
Drau
Mur
Vltava
Labe (Elbe)
Chiemsee
Ammersee
SALZBURG
KÄRNTEN
STEIERMARK
OBERÖSTERREICH
NIEDERÖST
VENEZIA GIULIA
FRIULI
ALTO ADIGE
TRENTINO
LOMBARDIA
JIHOČESKÝ
ZÁPADOČESKÝ
STŘEDOČESKÝ
SEVEROČESKÝ
ČESKÁ SOCIALISTICKÁ
G E R M A N Y
A U S T R I A
I T A L Y
C Z E C
Y U G
9
10
11
12
13
14
15
16
50
49
48
47
46

1:2 500 000

10 0 10 20 30 40 50 miles

10 0 10 20 30 40 50 60 70 80 km

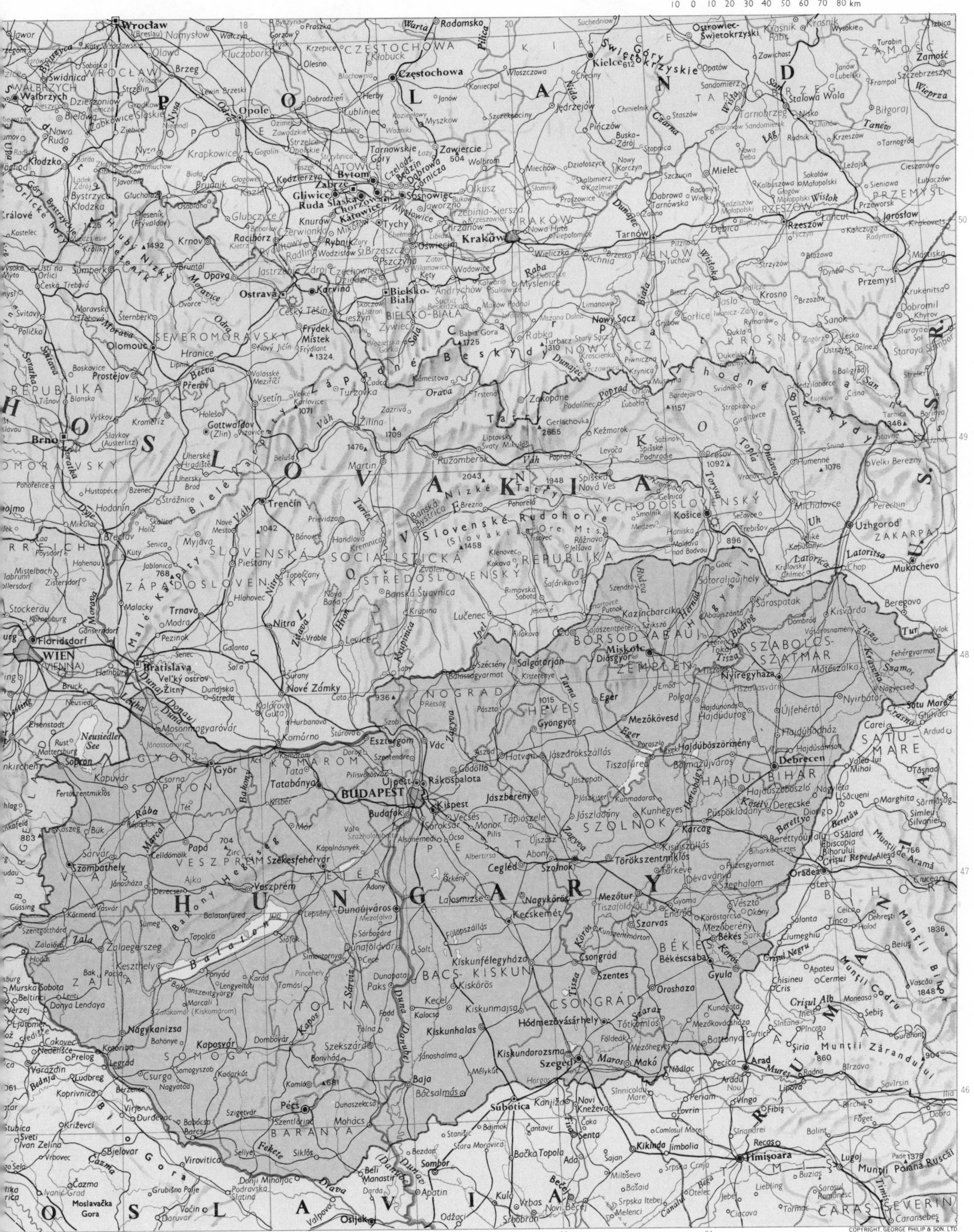

POLAND
SLOVAKIA
HUNGARY
RUMANIA
U.S.S.R.
Wrocław (Breslau)
Opole
Częstochowa
Kielce
Katowice
Gliwice
Zabrze
Bytom
Chorzów
Sosnowiec
Kraków
Tarnów
Rzeszów
Przemyśl
Jarosław
Nowy Sącz
Bielsko-Biała
Ostrava
Olomouc
Brno
Opava
Karviná
Žilina
Trenčín
Nitra
Trnava
Bratislava
WIEN (VIENNA)
Floridsdorf
Košice
Prešov
Uzhgorod
Mukachevo
Miskolc
Eger
Debrecen
Nyíregyháza
BUDAPEST
Győr
Sopron
Szombathely
Veszprém
Székesfehérvár
Kecskemét
Szolnok
Szeged
Pécs
Kaposvár
Nagykanizsa
Dunaújváros
Baja
Subotica
Arad
Timişoara
Oradea
Sombor
Osijek
Balaton
Neusiedler See
Tatry
Karpaty
Beskydy
Dunaj
Duna (Danube)
Tisza
Wisła
Odra
Váh
Orava
1:2 500 000
East from Greenwich

1:2 500 000
10 0 10 20 30 40 50 miles
10 0 10 20 30 40 50 60 70 80 km
COPYRIGHT GEORGE PHILIP & SON, LTD.
Projection: Conical with two standard parallels
East from Greenwich
U. S. S. R.
P O L A N D
CZECHOSLOVAKIA
VÝCHODOČESKÝ
BALTIC SEA
Zatoka Gdańska
Zalew Wiślany
Kaliningrad (Königsberg)
Baltiisk (Pillau)
WARSZAWA (WARSAW)
Łódź
Kraków
Wrocław (Breslau)
Poznań
Gdańsk (Danzig)
Gdynia
Sopot
Szczecin (Stettin)
Bydgoszcz
Toruń
Białystok
Lublin
Katowice
Częstochowa
Radom
Kielce
Olsztyn
Elbląg
Koszalin
Słupsk
Gorzów Wielkopolski
Zielona Góra
Legnica
Opole
Płock
Włocławek
Kalisz
Leszno
Konin
Sieradz
Piotrków Trybunalski
Skierniewice
Ciechanów
Ostrołęka
Łomża
Suwałki
Siedlce
Biała Podlaska
Chełm
Zamość
Tarnobrzeg
Piła
Wisła
Odra (Oder)
Warta
Noteć
Narew
Bug
Pilica
Nysa
Neisse
Bóbr
Kwisa
Brda
Drawa
Wieprz
Frankfurt
Forst
Görlitz
Zittau
Liberec
Jablonec
Mladá Boleslav
Trutnov
Náchod
Brest
Grodno
Orlické hory
Góry Świętokrzyskie

1:5,000,000

50 0 50 100 miles

50 0 50 100 150 km

F R A N C E

Montpellier
Béziers
Narbonne
Golfe du Lion
Toulouse
Bayonne
Biarritz
Perpignan
Pau
Lourdes

P y r é n é e s

ANDORRA

Gerona
Barcelona
Badalona
Hospitalet
Tarrasa
Sabadell
Lérida
Tarragona
Golfo de San Jorge

B a l e a r e s

Menorca
Mallorca
Palma
Ibiza
Formentera
Cabrera

NAVARRA
Pamplona
San Sebastián
Bilbao
Vitoria
Logroño
Zaragoza
Huesca

A R A G O N

VASCONGADAS
Sierra de la Demanda
Soria
Burgos
Palencia

C A S T I L L A L A V I E J A

Valladolid
Zamora
Salamanca
Segovia
Ávila
Sierra de Gredos

M A D R I D

Guadalajara
Cuenca
Serranía de Cuenca
Teruel
Castellón de la Plana
Sagunto
Valencia
Golfo de Valencia
Albufera de Valencia
Denia
Alicante
Elche
Murcia
Cartagena
Lorca
Almería

C A S T I L L A L A N U E V A

Toledo
Montes de Toledo
Ciudad Real
La Mancha
Albacete

E X T R E M A D U R A

Cáceres
Badajoz
Mérida

S I E R R A M O R E N A

Córdoba
Jaén
Sa. Nevada
Granada
Guadix
Málaga

Sevilla
Jerez
Cádiz
Huelva
Golfo de Cádiz
Strait of Gibraltar
La Línea de la Concepción
Gibraltar (Br.)
Ceuta (Sp.)
Tánger
Tetouan

M O R O C C O

A L G E R I A
Alger
Blida
Oran
Mostaganem

P O R T U G A L

GALICIA
La Coruña
El Ferrol
Santiago de Compostela
Pontevedra
Vigo
Orense
Lugo

ASTURIAS
Gijón
Oviedo
León

Cordillera Cantábrica

TRAS OS MONTES
Braga
Porto
DOURO LITORAL
BEIRA ALTA
BEIRA LITORAL
BEIRA BAIXA
Coimbra

ESTREMADURA
RIBATEJO
Santarém
Lisboa
Setúbal

ALTO ALENTEJO
Évora
BAIXO ALENTEJO

ALGARVE

A T L A N T I C O C E A N

M E D I T E R R A N E A N S E A

Bay of Biscay

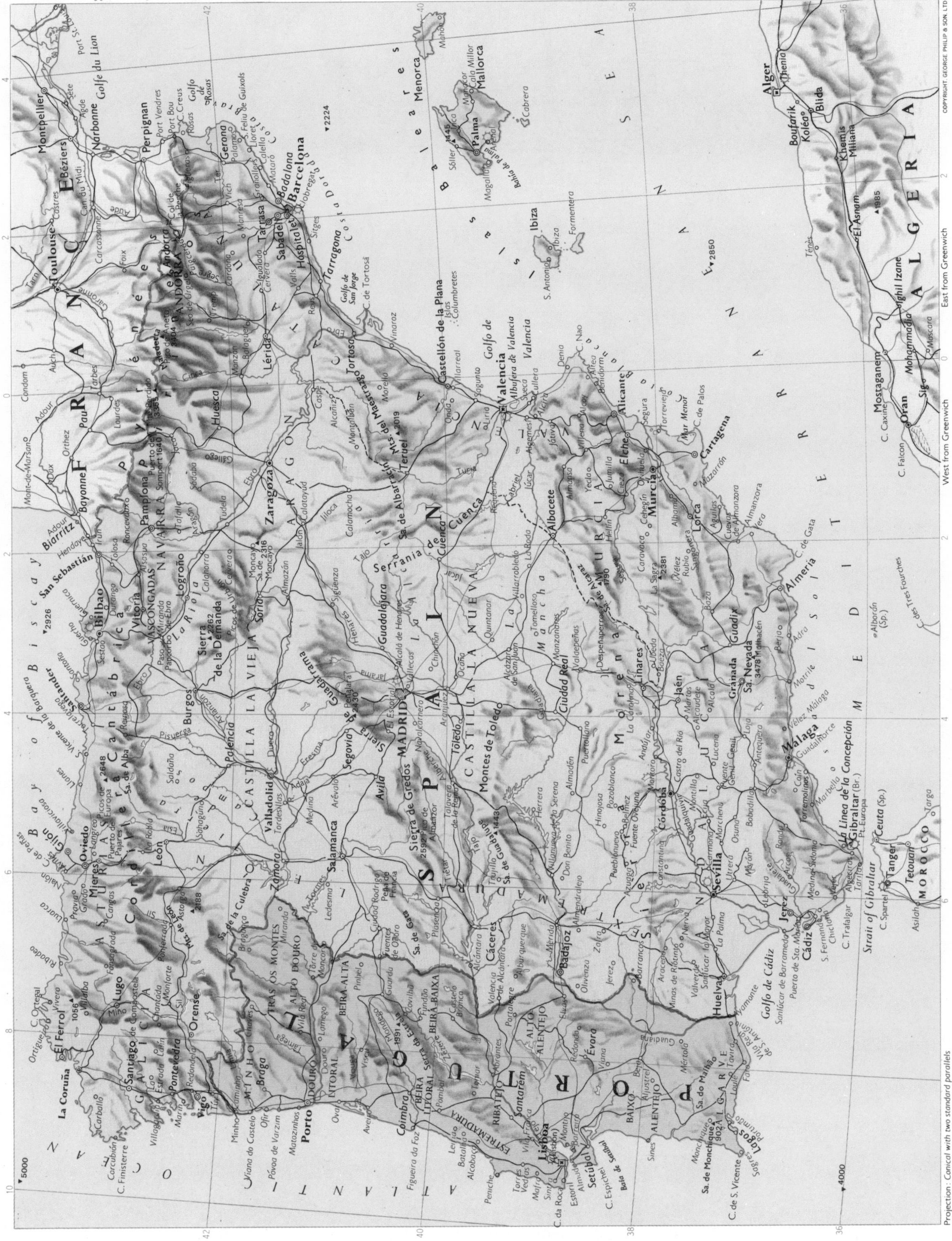

Projection: Conical with two standard parallels

West from Greenwich

East from Greenwich

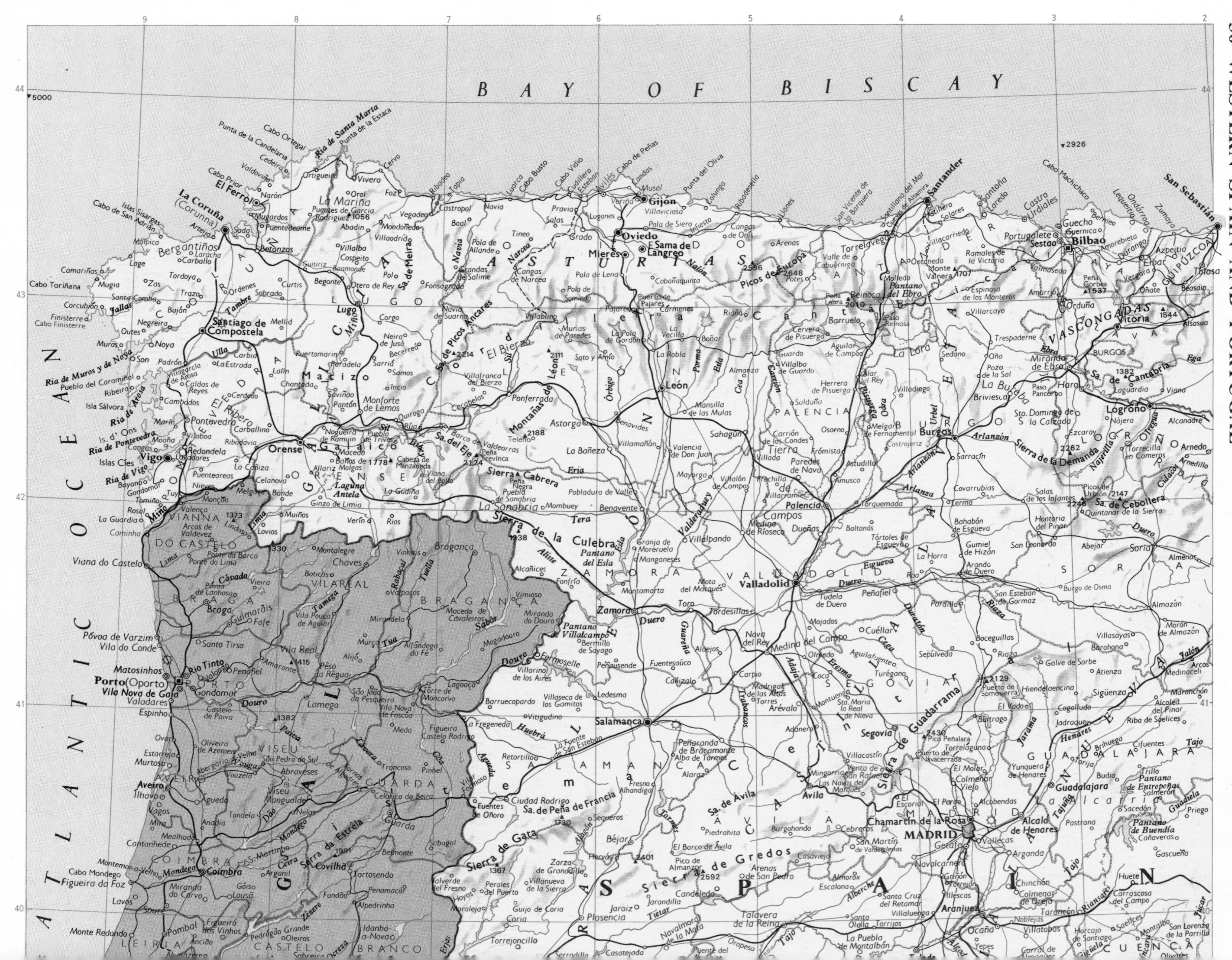
BAY OF BISCAY
ATLANTIC OCEAN
San Sebastián
Bilbao
Santander
Gijón
Oviedo
La Coruña (Corunna)
El Ferrol
Santiago de Compostela
Lugo
Orense
Vigo
León
Burgos
Logroño
Vitoria
Palencia
Valladolid
Zamora
Salamanca
Segovia
Avila
Guadalajara
MADRID
Porto (Oporto)
Vila Nova de Gaia
Braga
Coimbra
Aveiro
Sierra de Gredos
Sierra de Guadarrama
Sierra de la Culebra
Sierra de la Demanda
Duero
Douro
Miño
Tajo

MEDITERRANEAN SEA
MOROCCO
Golfo de Cádiz
Strait of Gibraltar
Golfo de Almería
Costa del Sol
Algarve
LISBOA (LISBON)
Sevilla (Seville)
Córdoba
Granada
Málaga
Cádiz
Huelva
Jaén
Almería
Badajoz
Cáceres
Mérida
Ciudad Real
Évora
Beja
Faro
Setúbal
Portalegre
Santarém
Gibraltar (Br.)
Ceuta (Sp.)
Melilla (Sp.)
Tanger (Tangier)
Tetouan
Larache
Algeciras
Jerez de la Frontera
Sierra Nevada
Montes de Toledo
Guadalquivir
Guadiana
Tejo
Cabo de São Vicente
Cabo de Sines
Baía de Setúbal
Playa de Castilla
West from Greenwich

Projection: Conical with two standard parallels

1:2 500 000

10 0 10 20 30 40 50 miles

10 0 10 20 30 40 50 60 70 80 km

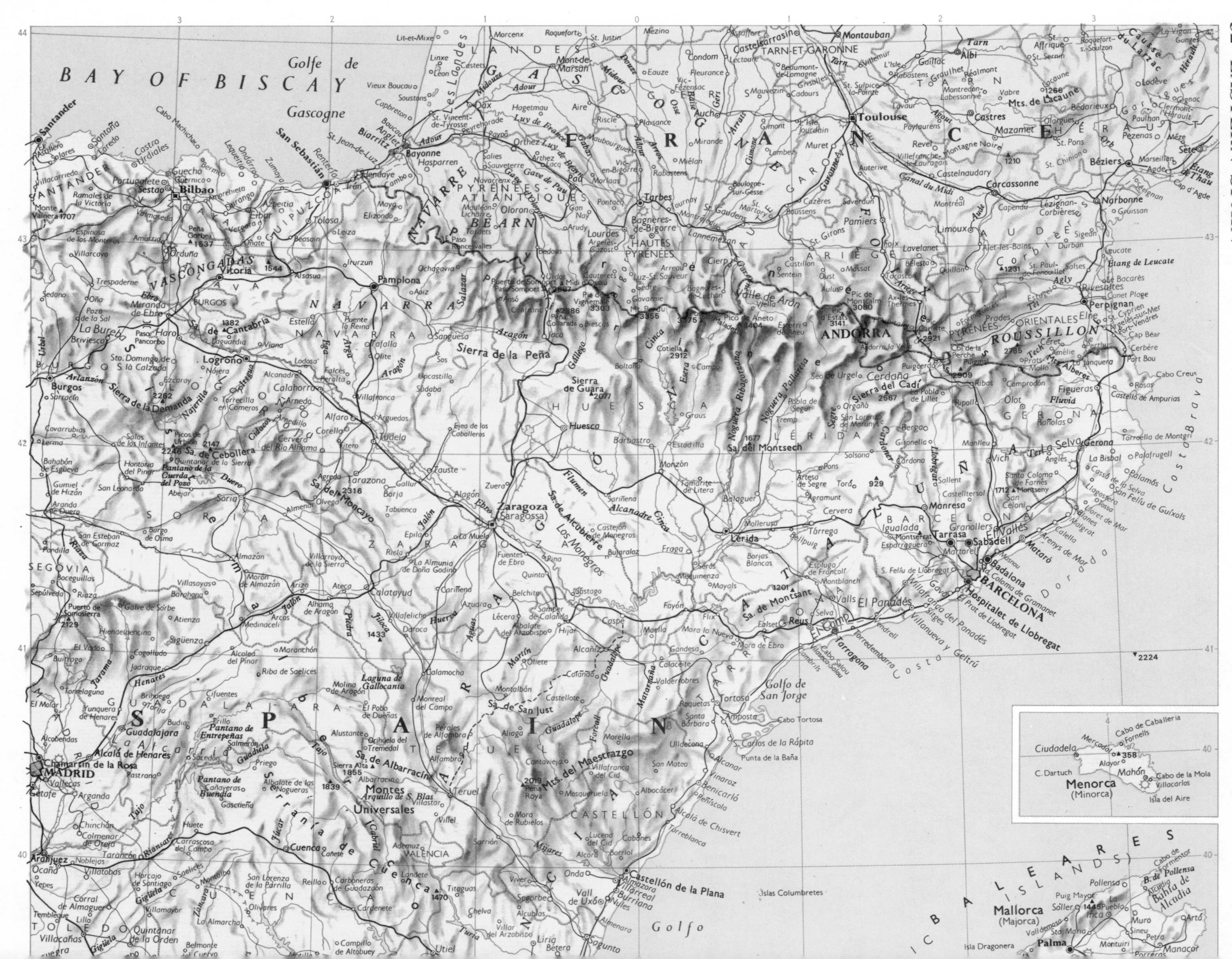
BAY OF BISCAY
Golfe de Gascogne
BARCELONA
MADRID
Zaragoza (Saragossa)
Toulouse
ANDORRA
ROUSSILLON
Menorca (Minorca)
Mallorca (Majorca)
Palma
Bilbao
San Sebastián
Pamplona
Logroño
Burgos
Tarragona
Lérida
Castellón de la Plana
Teruel
Cuenca
Guadalajara
Huesca
Perpignan
Carcassonne
Béziers
Narbonne
Bayonne
Biarritz
Santander
Vitoria
Soria
Tarbes
Pau
Sabadell
Tarrasa
Badalona
Hospitalet de Llobregat
Gerona
Manresa
Mataró
Reus
Tortosa
Calatayud
Alcalá de Henares
Aranjuez
Sierra de la Demanda
Sa. de Albarracín
Montes Universales
Sa. del Moncayo
Sierra de Guara
Los Monegros

1:2 500 000

miles
km
MEDITERRANEAN SEA
2850
ALGERIA
MOROCCO
ALGER (Algiers)
Boufarik
Koléa
Blida
El Arba
Bou Ismail
Cherchel
Gouraya
Ténès
C. Kramis
Médéa
Miliana
Khemis Miliana
Berrouaghia
Ksar el Boukhari
El Asnam
1985
Tissemsilt
Chabounia
Hamadia
Tiaret
Ksar-Chellala
Guelt es Stel
Bl. Taguine
Zemmora
Ighil Izane
Aïn Tédelès
Mostaganem
Mohammadia
Mascara
Sig
Arzew
C. Caxine
C. Falcon
Misserghin
ORAN
Aïn Témouchent
Beni Saf
Sidi-Bel-Abbès
Neftah Sidi Boubekeur
Ghazaouet
Nedroma
Berkane
Moulouya
C. Tres Forcas
Melilla (Sp.)
Nador
Selouane
C. del Agua
Alborán (Sp.)
Valencia
Albufera de Valencia
Sueca
Cullera
Alcira
Tabernes de Valldigna
Grao de Gandía
Gandía
Oliva
Játiva
Denia
Jávea
Cabo de San Antonio
Cabo de la Nao
Calpe
Punta Ifach
Altea
Benidorm
Islote de Benidorm
Villajoyosa
Costa Blanca
Alcoy
Sa. de Aitana
1558
Onteniente
Villena
Yecla
Almansa
Caudete
Elda
Petrel
Novelda
Aspe
Alicante
Cabo de las Huertas
Elche
Santa Pola
Isla de Tabarca
Torrevieja
Guardamar del Segura
Orihuela
Murcia
Alcantarilla
Cieza
Jumilla
Hellín
Tobarra
Albacete
Chinchilla de Monte Aragón
La Roda
Villarrobledo
Tomelloso
Socuéllamos
Manzanares
Daimiel
Valdepeñas
Alcázar de San Juan
CIUDAD REAL
ALBACETE
MURCIA
ALICANTE
Sierra Morena
Sierra de Alcaraz
1790
Sierra de Segura
Sa. de Cazorla
Cazorla
Linares
Úbeda
Baeza
Jódar
Guadalquivir
Guadiana Menor
Castril
Huéscar
Orce
La Sagra
2381
Caravaca
Cehegín
Moratalla
Calasparra
Mula
Bullas
Lorca
Totana
Sa. Espuña
1584
Sa. de Almenara
Mazarrón
Golfo de Mazarrón
Cartagena
Mar Menor
Cabo de Palos
San Javier
San Pedro del Pinatar
Cabo Tiñoso
Águilas
Cabo Cope
Huércal Overa
Cuevas del Almanzora
Vera
Garrucha
Mojácar
Carboneras
Punta de los Muertos
Níjar
Almería
Golfo de Almería
Cabo de Gata
Punta del Sabinal
Sierra de Gádor
Sa. de los Filabres
Almanzora
Albox
Baza
2269
Guadix
Granada
Sierra Nevada
Mulhacén
3478
La Veleta
3392
Las Alpujarras
Motril
Cabo Sacratif
GRANADA
Ibiza (Iviza)
Formentera
192
Isla del Espardell
I. Espalmador
San Francisco Javier
Cabo Berberia
Punta de Cala Codolar
Sta. Eulalia
San José
475
Isla del Vedra
Isla Cunillera
San Antonio Abad
San Miguel
San Juan Bautista
Punta Grosa
Isla de Tagomago
ISLAS BALEARES
Bahía de Palma
C. Blanco
Isla Conejera
Cabrera
Cabo de Salinas
Santany
Campos del Puerto
Projection: Conical with two standard parallels
West from Greenwich
East from Greenwich
COPYRIGHT, GEORGE PHILIP & SON, LTD.

FRANCE
SPAIN
PORTUGAL
SWITZERLAND
BELGIUM
NETH.
LUX.
GERMANY
MOROCCO
ALGERIA
TUNISIA
MALTA
MONACO
SAN MARINO
MEDITERRANEAN
Bay of Biscay
English Channel
Tyrrhenian Sea
Ligurian Sea
Golfe du Lion
Islas Baleares
LONDON
PARIS
MADRID
ROMA
Lisboa
Barcelona
Marseille
Alger
Tunis
Pyrenees
Cordillera Cantábrica
Sierra Morena
Haut Atlas
Plateaux
Corse
Sardegna
Sicilia
Projection: Conical with two standard parallels.
West from Greenwich 0 East from Greenwich

1:10 000 000
50 0 50 100 150 200 miles
50 0 100 200 300 km
POLAND
Poznań
Warszawa
Łódź
Radom
Lublin
Legnica
Wrocław
Kielce
Chorzów
Kraków
Tarnów
Przemyśl
Płock
Wisła (Vistula)
Brest
Pinsk
Polesye
Pripyat
Chernigov
Desna
Konotop
Sumy
Belgorod
Kharkov
Kazanskaya
Volgograd
Kiyev
Zhitomir
Lutsk
Rovno
Goryn
Styr
Bug
Dnepr
Pereyaslav-Khmelnitskiy
Belaya Tserkov
Poltava
Kremenchug
(Dnieper)
Slavyansk
Artemovsk
Donets
Voroshilovgrad (Lugansk)
Kamensk-Shakhtinskiy
Tsimlyanskoye Vdkhr.
Shakhty
Don
Novocherkassk
Rostov
Azov
Manych
Oz. Manych Gudilo
U. S. S. R.
UKRAINIAN S. S. R.
Berdichev
Vinnitsa
Cherkassy
Pavlograd
Gorlovka
Makeyevka
Donetsk
Dneprodzerzhinsk
Dnepropetrovsk
Zaporozhye
Taganrog
Lvov
Kamenets-Podol'skiy
Uman
Kirovograd
Krivoy Rog
Zhdanov (Mariupol)
Yeisk
Tikhoretsk
Stavropol
Armavir
Mogilev-Podolskiy
Pervomaysk
Voznesensk
Balta
Dnestr (Dniester)
MOLDAVIAN S.S.R.
Chernovtsy
Kolomyya
Prut
Nikolayev
Kherson
Melitopol
Berdyansk
Sea of Azov
Perekop
Kerch
Krasnodar
Kuban
Maykop
Ostrava
Jablunkovsky Pr.
Cieszyn
Tatry
2655
CZECHOSLOVAKIA
Brno
Slavkov
Váh
Hron
Banská Štiavnica
Košice
Miskolc
Tokaj
Tisza
Bratislava
Carpathians
Botoşani
Beltsy
Iaşi
Siret
Kishinev
Bendery
Tiraspol
Odessa
Belgorod Dnestrovskiy
Karkinitskiy Zaliv
Krymskaya (Crimea)
Feodosiya
Novorossiysk
Tuapse
Budapest
HUNGARY
Debrecen
Pietrosul 2305
Pietrosul 2102
Oradea
Kecskemét
Körös
Cluj
Raab
Graz
Mur
Balaton
Hódmezővásárhely
Szeged
Arad
RUMANIA
Mureş
Pécs
Subotica
Sibiu
Negoiu 2535
Braşov (Orasul Stalin)
Galaţi
Ismail
Brăila
Sulina
Carpaţii Meridionali
M. Tarkhankut
Yevpatoriya
Simferopol
1545
Sevastopol
Balaklava
Yalta
Sukhumi
Zagreb
Drava
Sombor
Timişoara
Novi Sad
Petrovaradin
Ploieşti
Piteşti
Constanţa
Brod
Sava
Beograd
Portile de Fier
Turnu-Severin
Bucureşti
Silistra
Dobrogea
BLACK SEA
YUGOSLAVIA
Banja Luka
Smederevo
Craiova
Dunărea (Danube)
Ruse
Tolbukhin
2211
BOSNA
Kragujevac
Vidin
Pleven
Varna
Ince Burnu
Sinop
Inebolu
Samsun
Giresun
Tirebolu
Trabzon
Rize
Sarajevo
Bosna
Drina
Morava
Niš
Stara Planina
Shipchenski
Tŭrnovo
Sliven
Burgas
Dalmacija
Split
Mostar
Durmitor 2522
Novi Pazar
SRBIJA
BULGARIA
Kuzey Anadolu Dağlari
Şebinl Karahisar
Vis
Lastovo
Dubrovnik (Ragusa)
CRNA GORA
Sofiya
Musala 2925
Maritsa
Plovdiv
Istanbul
Karadeniz Boğazi (Bosporus)
Zonguldak
Ereğli
Kastamonu
2565
Amasya
Tokat
Erzincan
Kotor
Cetinje
Skopje
Edirne
Rhodopi Planina
Üsküdar
İzmit
Bolu
Çankırı
Çorum
Sivas
Fırat
Shkodra
Šar Pl. 2764
Vardar
Strumica
Tekirdağ
Marmara Denizi
İznik Gölü
Beypazarı
Ankara
Kızıl Irmak
Yozgat
Mte. Gargano
Fóggia
Barletta
Bari
Tirana
Durrës
Elbasani
Bitola
Sérrai
Kaválla
Alexandroúpolis
Enez
Gelibolu (Gallipoli)
Bandırma
Bursa
Bilecik
Sakarya
Sivrihisar
Kırşehir
Kayseri
Erciyaş Dağı 3770
Gürün
Malatya
Keban
ALBANIA
Thessaloníki
Gökçeada
Çanakkale Boğazi
Çanakkale
Troy
Balıkesir
Eskişehir
TURKEY
Tuz Gölü
Brindisi
Táranto
Vlorë
Aliákmon
Óros Ólimbos 2917
Áthos 2033
Límnos
Kütahya
Afyon Karahisar
Bolvadin
Aksaray
Niğde
Seyhan
Maraş
Gaziantep
Golfo di Táranto
Str. of Otranto
Otranto
C. Sta. Maria di Leuca
Kérkira
Notia Pindhos
GREECE
Lárisa
Vólos
Vorίai Sporádhes
Aegean Sea
Lésvos
Ayvalık
Manisa
Turgutlu
Büyük Menderes
Eğridir Gölü
Eğridir
Beyşehir Gölü
Konya
Adana
Osmaniye
Iskenderun
Halab
La Sila 1929
Cosenza
Ionian Islands
Levkás
Návpaktos
Évvoia
Khíos
İzmir
Alaşehir
Isparta
Karaman
Tarsus
Mersin
Toros Dağları
Iskenderun Körfezi
Kefallinía
Korinthiakós Kólpos
Thívai
Athínai
Piraievs
Pátrai
Kórinthos
Ándros
Sámos
Ikaría
Aydın
Denizli
Burdur
Muğla
Antalya
Silifke
Antakya
SYRIA
Réggio
C. Spartivento
Stretto di Messina
Ionian Sea
Zákinthos
Olympia
Návplion
Pelopónnisos
Spárti
Kalamata
Pílos
Síros
Kikládhes
Náxos
Dhodhekánisos
Ródhos
Elmalı 3086
Antalya Körfezi
Megiste (Kastellorizon)
Al Ladhiqiyah
Baniyas
Hamā'
Homs
Siracusa
C. Passero
5121
Ákra Taínaron
Kíthira
Mílos
Thíra
Íos
Ródhos
4486
Morfou
Levkosia (Nicosia)
Ammókhostos (Famagusta)
Larnax
Lemesós
Troodhos 1951
CYPRUS
Tarabulus
3088
LEBANON
Kárpathos
Andikíthira
Khaniá
Ídhi Oros 2456
Iráklion
Kríti
Bayrût (Beirut)
Saydā
Dimashq (Damascus)
Jabal ash Sheikh 2814
Jabal ad Durūz
Boşra
4135
MEDITERRANEAN SEA
'Akko
Haifa
Jordan
Jerusalem
'Ammān
JORDAN
Tel Aviv-Yafo
ISRAEL
Gaza
Bahr el Miyet -395
Karak
Rashîd
Bahra el Burullus
Dumyât
Bûr Saîd
El 'Arîsh
Petra
Ma'ān
3174
Cyrene
Derna
Khalîj Bômba
Al Marj (Barce)
Tobruq
Banghāzī
Khalîg el Salûm
El Iskandarîya
El Mahalla el Kubra
Tanta
El Qantara
Ismâ'îlîya
Buheirat Murrat-el-Kubra
Suez Canal
Gebel el Tîh
Elat
Al 'Aqabah
Salûm
Matrûh
El 'Alamein
El Suweis
Khalîj Surt
Barqa
EL QÂHIRA
Khalîg el Suweis
Nile
Khalîj al 'Aqabah
LIBYA
EGYPT
El Faiyûm
Benî Suef
Es Sînâ' 2637
20
25
30
35
40
45

NORTHERN ITALY AND WESTERN YUGOSLAVIA

SWITZERLAND
FRANCE
ITALIA
LIGURIAN SEA
Golfo di Génova
CORSE
(CORSICA)
ILES D'HYERES
Arcipelago
Toscano
Elba
Capraia
Montecristo
Giglio
Pianosa
Gorgona
MILANO
(Milan)
TORINO
(Turin)
GÉNOVA
(Genoa)
MARSEILLE
(Marseilles)
Lyon
(Lyons)
Genève
(GENEVA)
Bern
Lausanne
Grenoble
Toulon
Nice
MONACO
Monte Carlo
Cannes
Bastia
Ajaccio
Livorno
(Leghorn)
La Spezia
Parma
Bérgamo
Brescia
Cremona
Pavia
Novara
Vercelli
Alessandria
Asti
Cúneo
Savona
San Remo
Impéria
Avignon
Aix-en-Provence
Arles
Chambéry
Annecy
Aosta
Fribourg
Luzern
Zug
Schwyz
Lugano
Como
Lecco
Varese
Sondrio
Trento
Mántova
Reggio
Módena
Massa
Carrara
Lucca
Pisa
Piombino
Valence
Villeurbanne
Vienne
SAVOIE
HAUTE-SAVOIE
VALAIS
TICINO
GRAUBÜNDEN
LOMBARDIA
PIEMONTE
LIGURIA
EMILIA
TOSCANA
PROVENCE
DAUPHINÉ
JURA
FRANCHE-COMTÉ
BOURGOGNE
VAUCLUSE
ALPES-MARITIMES
BOUCHES-DU-RHÔNE
ALPES-DE-HAUTE-PROVENCE
HAUTE-CORSE
CORSE-DU-SUD
VORARLBERG
LIECHTENSTEIN
ST. GALLEN
Lago Maggiore
L. di Como
Lago di Garda
Lac Léman
(L. Genéva)
Rhône
Po
Côte d'Azur
Riviera
Matterhorn
4478
Monte Rosa
4634
Mont Blanc
4807
Gran Paradiso
4061
Projection: Conical with two standard parallels
East from Greenwich

AUSTRIA
HUNGARY
YUGOSLAVIA
ITALIA
ADRIATIC SEA
SAN MARINO
Innsbruck
Graz
Klagenfurt
Villach
Maribor
Ljubljana
Zagreb
Karlovac
Rijeka (Fiume)
Trieste
Udine
Venézia (Venice)
Pádova
Vicenza
Treviso
Mestre
Bolzano (Bozen)
Merano
Belluno
Ferrara
Bologna
Ravenna
Rímini
Pésaro
Ancona
Firenze (Florence)
Arezzo
Perúgia
Assisi
Terni
Spoleto
Viterbo
Civitavécchia
ROMA (ROME)
Vatican City
Tívoli
L'Aquila
Pescara
Chieti
Téramo
Áscoli Piceno
S. Benedetto del Tronto
Vasto
Térmoli
Sulmona
Avezzano
Vieste
Monte Sant'Ángelo
Split
Šibenik
Zadar
Senj
Pula
Poreč
Rovinj
Banja Luka
Bihać
Gospić
Sisak
Nagykanizsa
Zalaegerszeg
Keszthely
Golfo di Venézia
Hohe Tauern
Niedere Tauern
Karnische Alpen
Karawanken
Zillertaler Alpen
Dinara Planina
Velebit Planina
Velika Kapela
Mala Kapela
Kvarner
Kvarnerić
Gran Sasso d'Italia
Dugi Otok
Lastovo
Vis
Hvar
Brač
Korčula
Mljet
Pelješac
Tremiti
Pianosa
Palagruža
Drava
Sava
Kupa
Una
Po
Reno
L. Trasimeno
L. di Bolsena
L. di Bracciano
Balaton

CORSE
CORSICA
CORSE-DU-SUD
Iles Sanguinaires
G. d'Ajaccio
Bouches de Bonifacio
Bonifacio
Porto-Vecchio
Sartène
Propriano
Iles Cerbicales
SARDEGNA
SARDINIA
Sássari
Alghero
Porto Tórres
Olbia
G. di Ólbia
Golfo dell' Asinara
Asinara
Nùoro
Oristano
Golfo di Oristano
Monti del Gennargentu
1834
Golfo di Orosei
Iglesias
Carbonia
San Pietro
Sant' Antíoco
Cágliari
Golfo di Cágliari
C. Spartivento
C. Carbonara
Serpentara
C. Teulada
G. di Palmas
TYRRHENIAN SEA
3719
3589
ROMA (Rome)
Vatican City
Tívoli
Latina
Frosinone
Terracina
Golfo di Gaeta
Ísole Ponziane
Ponza
Palmarola
Zannone
Ventotene
Íschia
(Naples)
Ustica
PALERMO
Trápani
Erice
Marsala
Mazara del Vallo
Ísole Égadi
Maréttimo
Favignana
Levanzo
Sciacca
Agrigento
Sicilian Channel
Iles de la Galite
Bizerte (Binzert)
Menzel-Bourguiba
Mateur
TUNIS
Halq el Oued (La Goulette)
Golfe de Tunis
C. Bon
Zembra
Nabeul
Hammamet
Zaghouan
Tébourba
Béja
Tabarka
El Kala
ALGERIA
TUNISIA
Pantelleria (It.)
836
1319
MEDITE
East from Greenwich

Projection: Conical with two standard parallels

1:2 500 000
miles
km
ADRIATIC SEA
IONIAN SEA
Strait of Otranto
G. di Manfredónia
Golfo di Táranto
G. di Salerno
G. di Policastro
Golfo di Sant'Eufémia
Golfo di Squillace
G. di Gióia
Isole Eólie o Lípari (Æolian Is.)
Strómboli
Panarea
Salina
Lípari
Vulcano
Filicudi
Alicudi
Str. di Messina
ABRUZZI
MOLISE
BASILICATA
CALABRIA
ALBANIA
L. di Lésina
Monte Sant'Ángelo
Manfredónia
S. Severo
Lucera
Fóggia
Campobasso
Benevento
Barletta
Trani
Bisceglie
Molfetta
Bari
Andria
Corato
Ruvo
Bitonto
Terlizzi
Cerignola
Canosa
Altamura
Gravina
Monopoli
Fasano
Martina Franca
Ostuni
Brindisi
Táranto
Grottáglie
Francavilla Fontana
Mesagne
Manduria
Lecce
Nardò
Galatina
Gallipoli
Otranto
C. d'Otranto
C. Santa Maria di Leuca
Matera
Potenza
Salerno
Nápoli
G. di Nápoli
Torre Annunziata
Castellammare di Stábia
Sorrento
Capri
Caserta
Avellino
Eboli
Sele
Agri
Sinni
Bradano
Basento
Ofanto
Crati
Neto
Tácina
Lauria
Castrovillari
Cosenza
Rossano
Crotone
C. delle Colonne
C. Rizzuto
Catanzaro
Nicastro
Vibo Valéntia
Tropea
Capo Vaticano
Palmi
Gióia Táuro
Scilla
Réggio di Calábria
Messina
Milazzo
Capo Peloro
C. Spartivento
Locri
Siderno
Catánia
Acireale
Etna 3340
Augusta
Siracusa
Ragusa
Módica
Noto
Pachino
C. Passero
Gela
Golfo di Gela
Caltagirone
Enna
Monti Nébrodi
Cefalù
Kérkira (Corfu)
Vlora
Durrësi (Durazzo)
Tirana
Berati
Laguna e Nartës
Gjiri i Vlorës
Karaburuni
Drini
Shkumbini
3065
4116
RANEAN SEA
Channel
15
16
17
18
19
41
40
39
38
37

HUNGARY
YUGOSLAVIA
ALBANIA
ADRIATIC SEA
TOLNA
SOMOGY
BARANYA
CSONGRÁD
BIHOR
ARAD
TIMIŞ
CARAŞ-SEVERIN
MEHEDINŢI
Autonomna Pokrajina Vojvodina
BOSNA I HERCEGOVINA
SRBIJA
CRNA GORA (MONTENEGRO)
Socijalisticka Autonomna Pokrajina Kosovo
MAKEDONIJA
DALMACIJA
SHKODRA
KUKËS
TIRANA-DURRËSI
Nagykanizsa
Kaposvár
Pécs
Mohács
Baja
Kiskunhalas
Szeged
Hódmezővásárhely
Makó
Orosháza
Gyula
Arad
Timişoara
Lugoj
Reşiţa
Hunedoara
Turnu-Severin
Subotica
Sombor
Kikinda
Zrenjanin
Novi Sad
Vršac
Pančevo
Zemun
Beograd (Belgrade)
Smederevo
Požarevac
Osijek
Vukovar
Vinkovci
Slavonski Brod
Banja Luka
Tuzla
Zenica
Sarajevo
Mostar
Dubrovnik
Kragujevac
Čačak
Kraljevo
Kruševac
Niš
Leskovac
Priština
Prizren
Skopje
Kumanovo
Titov Veles
Štip
Prilep
Bitola
Ohrid
Titograd
Shkodra (Shkoder)
Durrësi (Durazzo)
Tirana (Tiranë)
Elbasani
Vidin
Pernik
Kyustendil
Blagoevgrad
Dimitrovgrad (Caribrod)
Danube
Dunav
Drava
Sava
Tisa
Drina
Morava
Vardar
Neretva
Bosna
Ibar
Timok
Kopaonik
Fruška Gora
Ohridsko Jezero (L. Ohrid)
Prepansko Jezero (L. Prespa)
Skadarsko Jezero
Dojransko Jezero (L. Doiran)
Hvar
Korčula
Lastovo
Mljet
Projection: Conical with two standard parallels
East from Greenwich

1:2 500 000

10 0 10 20 30 40 50 miles

10 0 10 20 30 40 50 60 70 80 km

U. S. S. R.
UKRAINIAN S.S.R.
IZMAIL
R U M A N I A
TRANSILVANIA
WALACHIA
BULGARIA
TURKEY
GREECE
BLACK SEA
Muntii Făgăraş
Muntii Vrancei
Munţii Ciuc
Munţii Harghita
Stara Planina
Sredna Gora
Rodopi
Iztochni Rodopi
Srednî Rodopi
Zapadni Rodopi
Pirin Planina
Kotlenska Pl.
Preslavska Planina
Aytoska Pl.
Dunărea
Dunay
Danube
Braţul Chilia
Braţul Sulina
Braţul Sfintu Gheorghe
Lacul Razelm
Lacul Sinoe
Gura Portiţei
Ozero Yalpukh
Ozero Kitai
Ozero Sasyk
Karadeniz Boğazı (Bosporus)
Istranca Dağları
Burgaski Zaliv
Olt
Argeş
Prahova
Dîmboviţa
Ialomiţa
Iskŭr
Maritsa
Tundzha
Yantra
Kamchiya
Cluj
Turda
Tîrgu Mureş
Sighişoara
Mediaş
Alba-Iulia
Sibiu
Braşov
Bacău
Bîrlad
Tecuci
Focşani
Galaţi
Brăila
Tulcea
Constanţa
Mangalia
Ploieşti
Tîrgovişte
Piteşti
Rîmnicu Vîlcea
Craiova
Caracal
Alexandria
Giurgiu
BUCUREŞTI (Bucharest)
Călăraşi
Slobozia
Cernavodă
Ismail
Reni
Bolgrad
Kiliya
Vilkovo
Komrat
Chadyr-Lunga
Ruse (Ruschuk)
Silistra
Svishtov
Pleven
Vratsa
Lovech
Türnovo
Gabrovo
Kazanlŭk
Stara Zagora
Razgrad
Kolarovgrad (Shumen)
Tolbukhin (Dobrich Bazargic)
Varna
Burgas
Sliven
Yambol
Plovdiv (Philippopolis)
Pazardzhik
Sofiya (Sofia)
Khaskovo
Kŭrdzhali
Smolyan
Edirne (Adrianople)
Kırklareli
Lüleburgaz
Çorlu
İSTANBUL
Üsküdar
Beykoz
Drama
Xanthi
Komotini

42 GREECE AND ALBANIA

YUGOSLAVIA
ALBANIA
BULGARIA
MACEDONIA
THRAKIKÓN PÉLAGOS
Sofiya (Sofia)
Skopje
Tirana (Tiranë)
Thessaloníki (Salonica)
Plovdiv
Edirne
Stara Zagora
Pleven
Niš
Priština
Prizren
Titograd (Podgorica)
Shkodra (Shkodër)
Durrësi (Durazzo)
Vlorë (Valona)
Korça
Bitola
Ohrid
Kavalla
Xánthi
Sérrai
Kateríni
Lárisa
Vólos
Kérkira (Corfu)
Ioánnina
Thásos
Límnos
Samothráki
Ayios Evstrátios
Gökçeada
Çanakkale
Thermaikós Kólpos
Strimonikós Kólpos
Saros Körfezi

1:2 500 000

10 0 10 20 30 40 50 miles

10 0 10 20 30 40 50 60 70 80 km

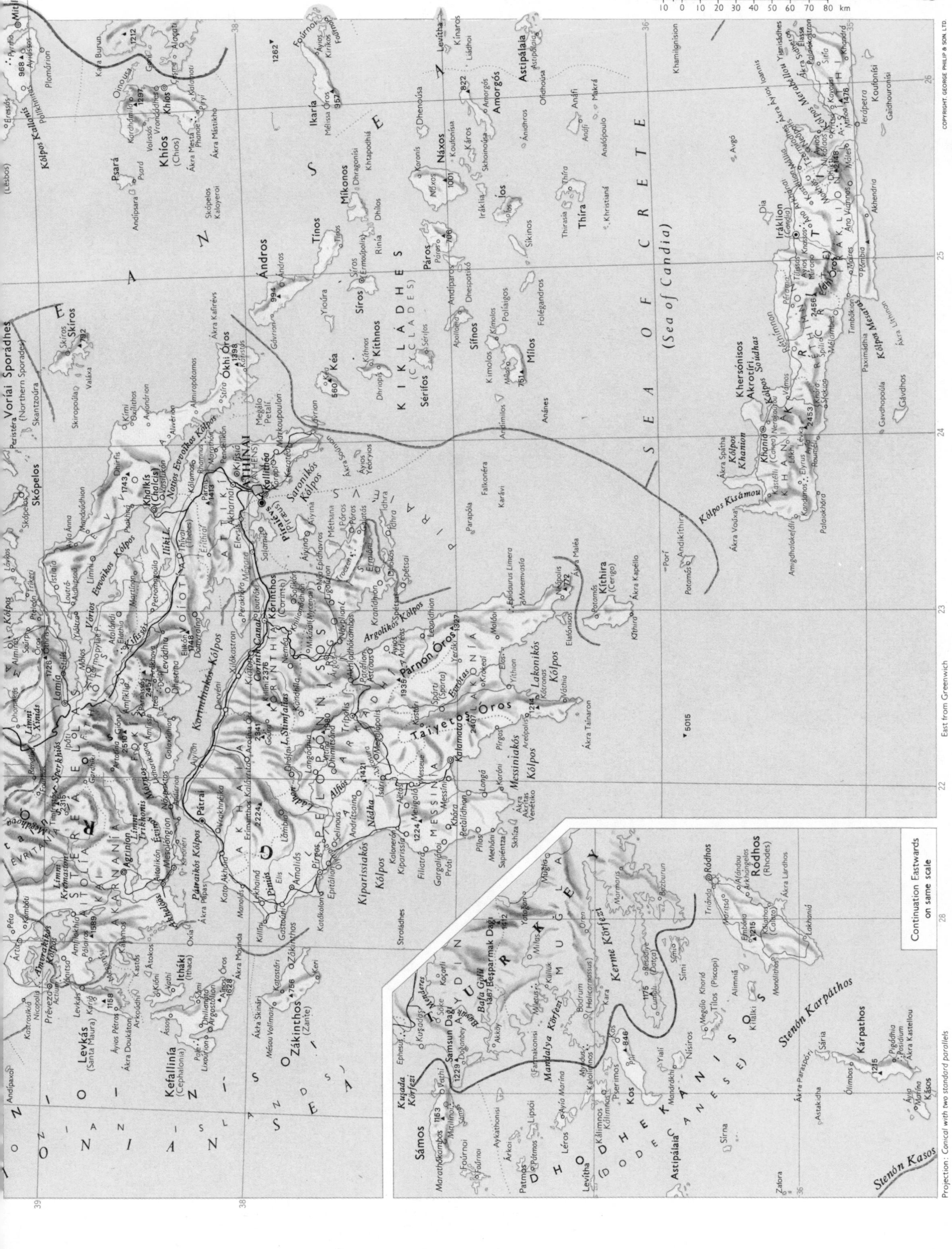

Continuation Eastwards on same scale

East from Greenwich

Projection: Conical with two standard parallels

Gulf of Bothnia
JÄMTLANDS LÄN
VÄSTERNORRLANDS LÄN
GÄVLEBORGS LÄN
KOPPARBERGS LÄN
UPPSALA LÄN
STOCKHOLMS LÄN
VÄSTMANLANDS LÄN
ÖREBRO LÄN
SÖDERMANLANDS LÄN
VÄRMLANDS LÄN
SØR-TRØNDELAG FYLKE
MØRE OG ROMSDAL FYLKE
HEDMARK FYLKE
OPPLAND FYLKE
BUSKERUD FYLKE
AKERSHUS FYLKE
ØSTFOLD F.
VESTFOLD
TELEMARK FYLKE
Trondheim
Östersund
Sundsvall
Härnösand
Örnsköldsvik
Hudiksvall
Söderhamn
Gävle
Falun
Borlänge
Mora
Uppsala
STOCKHOLM
Västerås
Örebro
Eskilstuna
Karlstad
OSLO
Hamar
Lillehammer
Drammen
Kongsberg
Skien
Porsgrunn
Kristiansund
Molde
Jotunheimen
Dovrefjell
Hardangervidda

1:2 500 000

10 0 10 20 30 40 50 miles

10 0 10 20 30 40 50 60 70 80 km

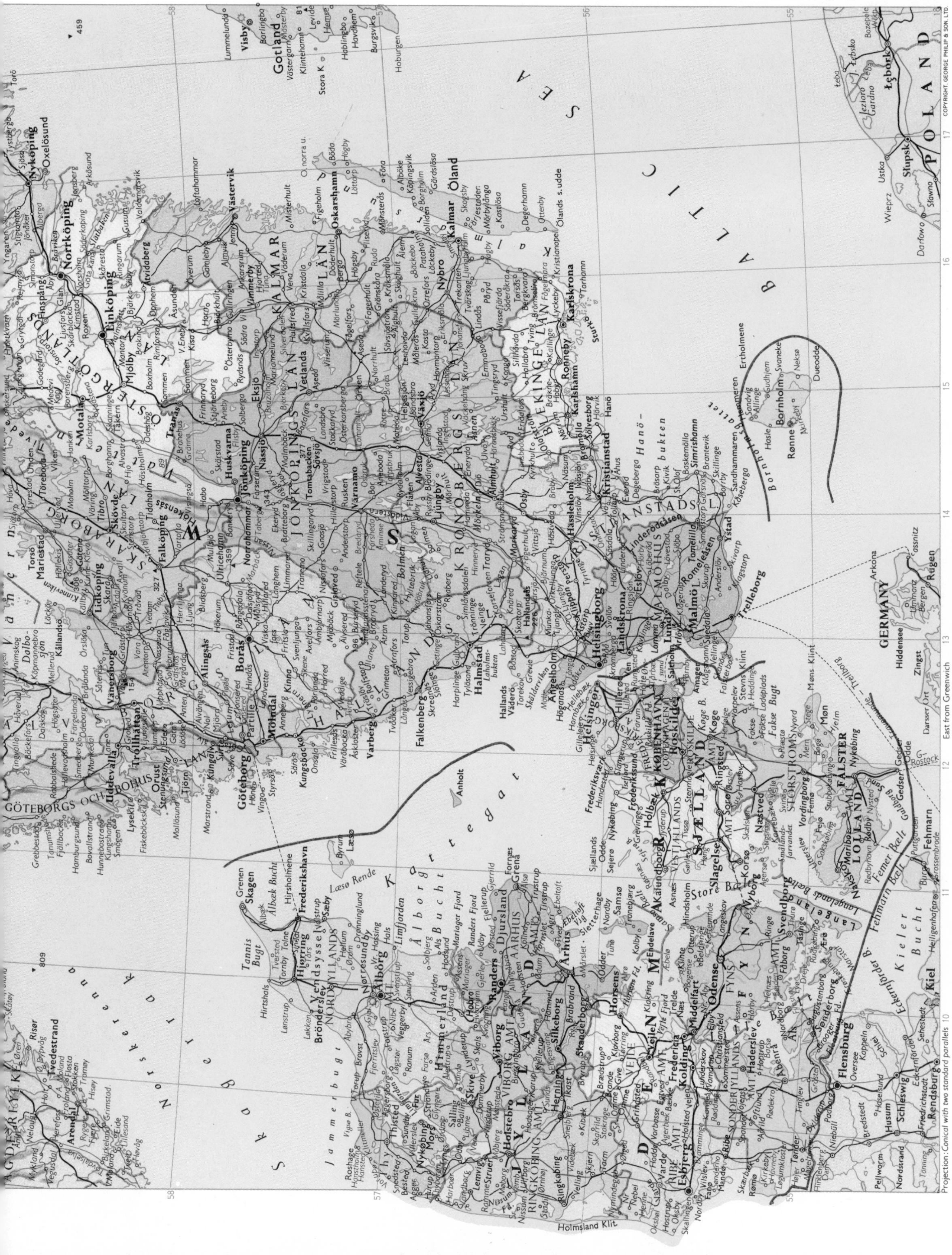

Projection: Conical with two standard parallels

East from Greenwich

ICELAND
on the same scale
as general map

1:5 000 000

20 10 0 20 40 60 80 100 miles
40 20 0 40 80 120 160 km

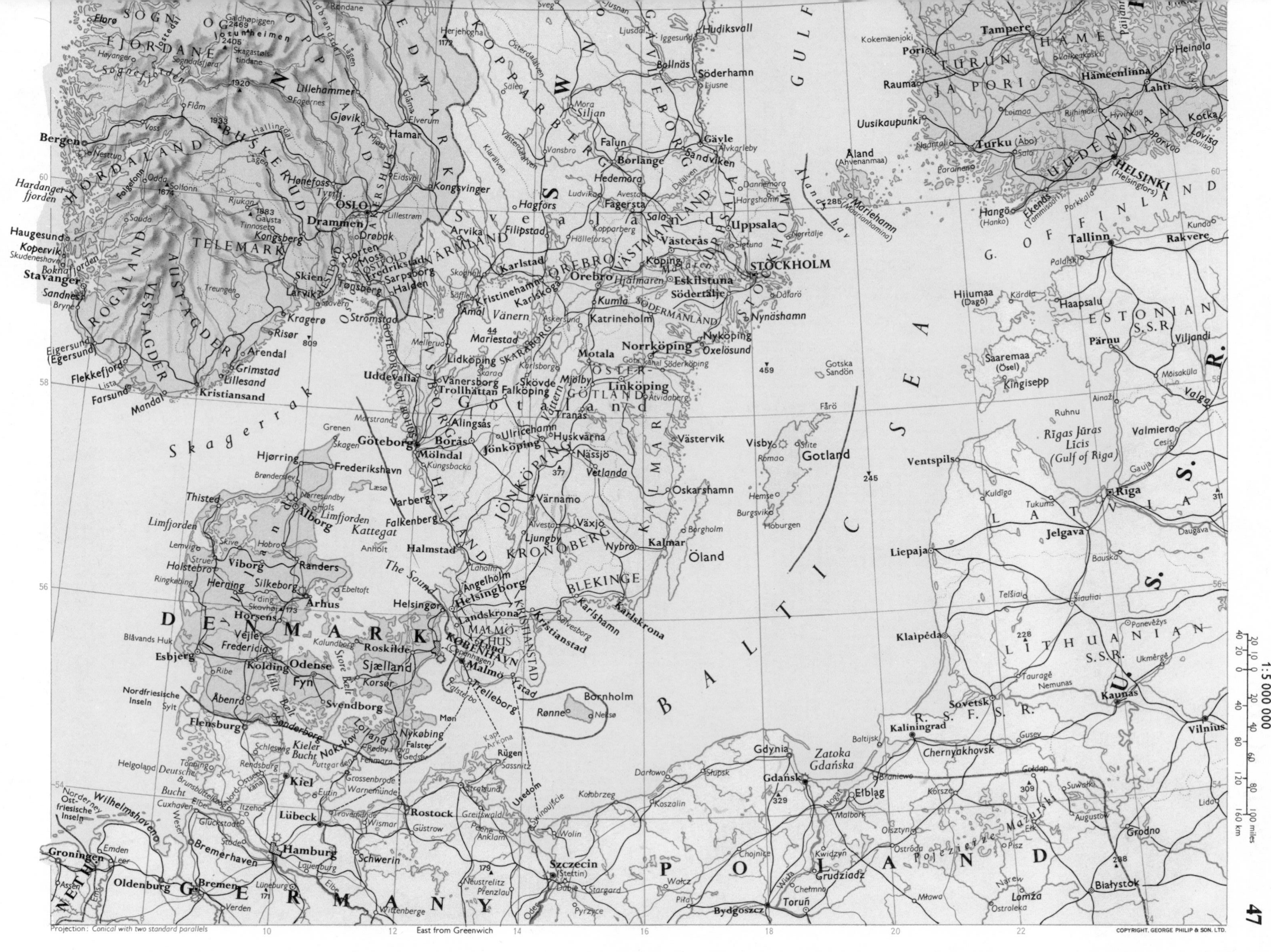

GULF OF FINLAND
BALTIC SEA
Skagerrak
Kattegat
The Sound
Ålands hav
Rīgas Jūras Līcis (Gulf of Riga)
Zatoka Gdańska
DENMARK
POLAND
GERMANY
LITHUANIAN S.S.R.
LATVIA
ESTONIAN S.S.R.
Svealand
Götaland
STOCKHOLM
HELSINKI (Helsingfors)
OSLO
KØBENHAVN (Copenhagen)
Tallinn
Riga
Gotland
Öland
Bornholm
Sjælland
Fyn
East from Greenwich
Projection: Conical with two standard parallels
COPYRIGHT, GEORGE PHILIP & SON, LTD.

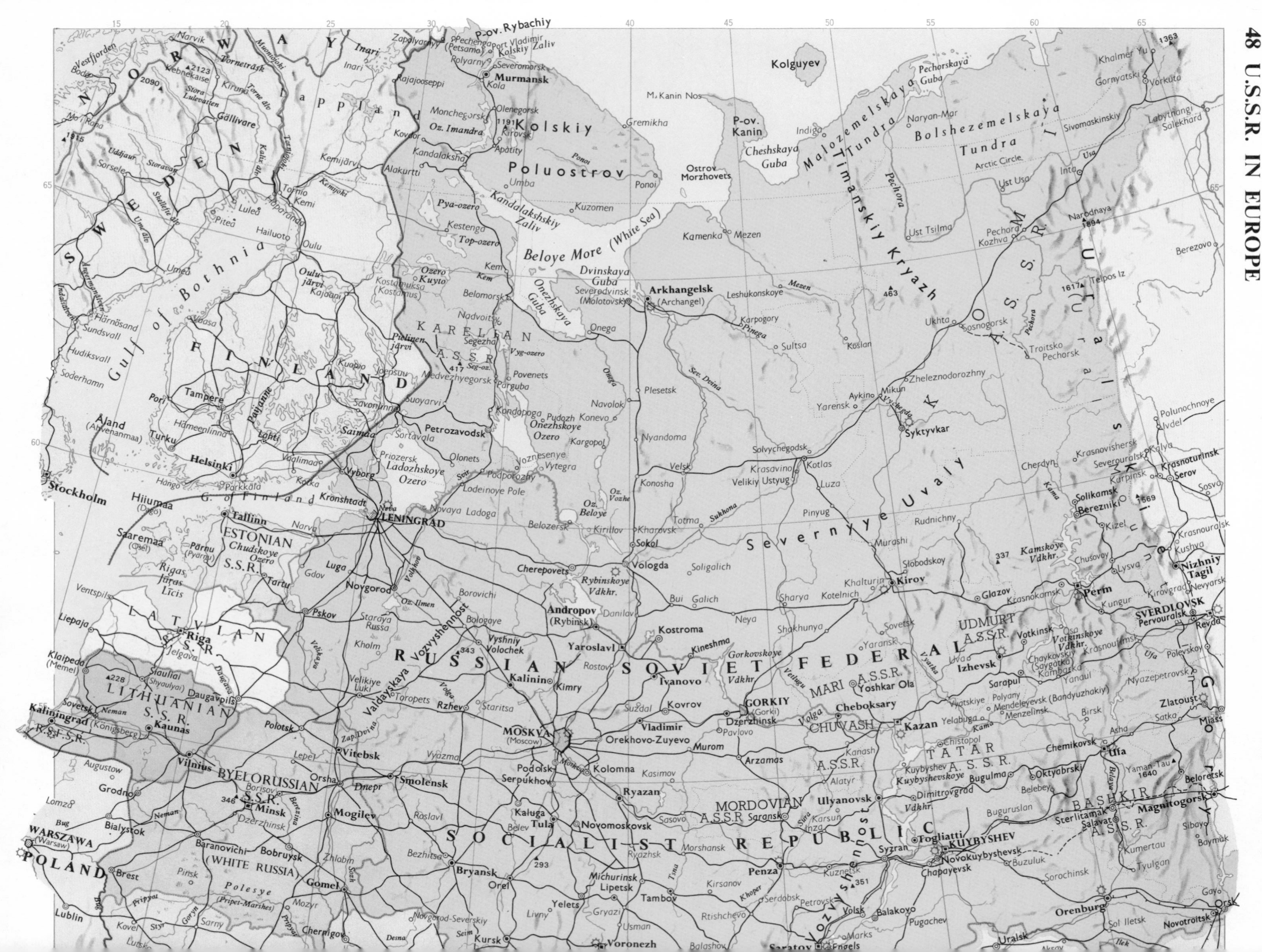

NORWAY
SWEDEN
FINLAND
Lappland
Gulf of Bothnia
G. of Finland
P-ov. Rybachiy
Murmansk
Kolskiy Poluostrov
Kandalakshskiy Zaliv
Beloye More (White Sea)
Dvinskaya Guba
Onezhskaya Guba
Kolguyev
M. Kanin Nos
P-ov. Kanin
Cheshskaya Guba
Ostrov Morzhovets
Malozemelskaya Tundra
Bolshezemelskaya Tundra
Pechorskaya Guba
Timanskiy Kryazh
Arctic Circle
Naryan-Mar
Vorkuta
Salekhard
Narodnaya 1894
Ural
Arkhangelsk (Archangel)
Severodvinsk (Molotovsk)
KARELIAN A.S.S.R.
Petrozavodsk
Ladozhskoye Ozero
Onezhskoye Ozero
Ukhta
Syktyvkar
Kotlas
Severnyye Uvaly
Kirov
Perm
Solikamsk
Berezniki
Nizhniy Tagil
SVERDLOVSK
Zlatoust
Magnitogorsk
Ufa
Orenburg
KUYBYSHEV
Togliatti
Syzran
Saratov
Engels
Penza
Ulyanovsk
Kazan
Izhevsk
UDMURT A.S.S.R.
MARI A.S.S.R.
Yoshkar Ola
Cheboksary
CHUVASH A.S.S.R.
TATAR A.S.S.R.
BASHKIR A.S.S.R.
MORDOVIAN A.S.S.R.
GORKIY (Gorki)
Dzerzhinsk
Ivanovo
Kostroma
Yaroslavl
Andropov (Rybinsk)
Vologda
Cherepovets
Rybinskoye Vdkhr.
LENINGRAD
Novgorod
Pskov
Kalinin
MOSKVA (Moscow)
Tula
Kaluga
Ryazan
Tambov
Voronezh
Lipetsk
Orel
Kursk
Bryansk
Smolensk
Vitebsk
Mogilev
Gomel
Minsk
Bobruysk
Brest
Grodno
Vilnius
Kaunas
Klaipeda (Memel)
Kaliningrad (Königsberg)
Riga
Tallinn
Tartu
Helsinki
Tampere
Turku
Oulu
Stockholm
RUSSIAN SOVIET FEDERAL SOCIALIST REPUBLIC
ESTONIAN S.S.R.
LATVIAN S.S.R.
LITHUANIAN S.S.R.
BYELORUSSIAN S.S.R. (WHITE RUSSIA)
Polesye (Pripet Marshes)
POLAND
WARSZAWA (Warsaw)
Lublin

1:10 000 000

100 50 0 50 100 150 200 miles

100 0 100 200 300 km

1 Kabardino-Balkar A.S.S.R.
2 North Ossetian A.S.S.R.
3 Nakhichevan A.S.S.R. (Azer.)
4 Checheno-Ingush A.S.S.R.

Projection: Conical with two standard parallels

East from Greenwich

UNION OF SOVIET SOCIALIST REPUBLICS

R.S.F.S.R.
1. Daghestan A.S.S.R.
2. Kabardino-Balkar A.S.S.R.
3. Mari A.S.S.R.
4. Mordovian A.S.S.R.
5. North Ossetian A.S.S.R.
6. Tatar A.S.S.R.
7. Udmurt A.S.S.R.
8. Chuvash A.S.S.R.
9. Checheno-Ingush A.S.S.R.
AZERBAIJAN
10. Nakhichevan A.S.S.R.
GEORGIA
11. Abkhaz A.S.S.R.
12. Adzhar A.S.S.R.
RUSSIAN SOVIET FEDE
KAZAKH S.S.R.
TURKMEN S.S.R.
UZBEK S.S.R.
KIRGIZ S.S.R.
TADZHIK S.S.R.
BYELORUSSIAN S.S.R.
UKRAINIAN S.S.R.
Barents Sea
Kara Sea
Black Sea
Caspian Sea
Moskva
Leningrad
Kiyev
Stalingrad (Volgograd)
Sverdlovsk
Novosibirsk
Tashkent
Alma Ata
Baku
Tbilisi
Yerevan
Minsk
Riga
Tallinn
Vilnius
Kishinev
Frunze
Dushanbe
Ashkhabad
East from Greenwich
Projection: Conical Orthomorphic with two standard parallels

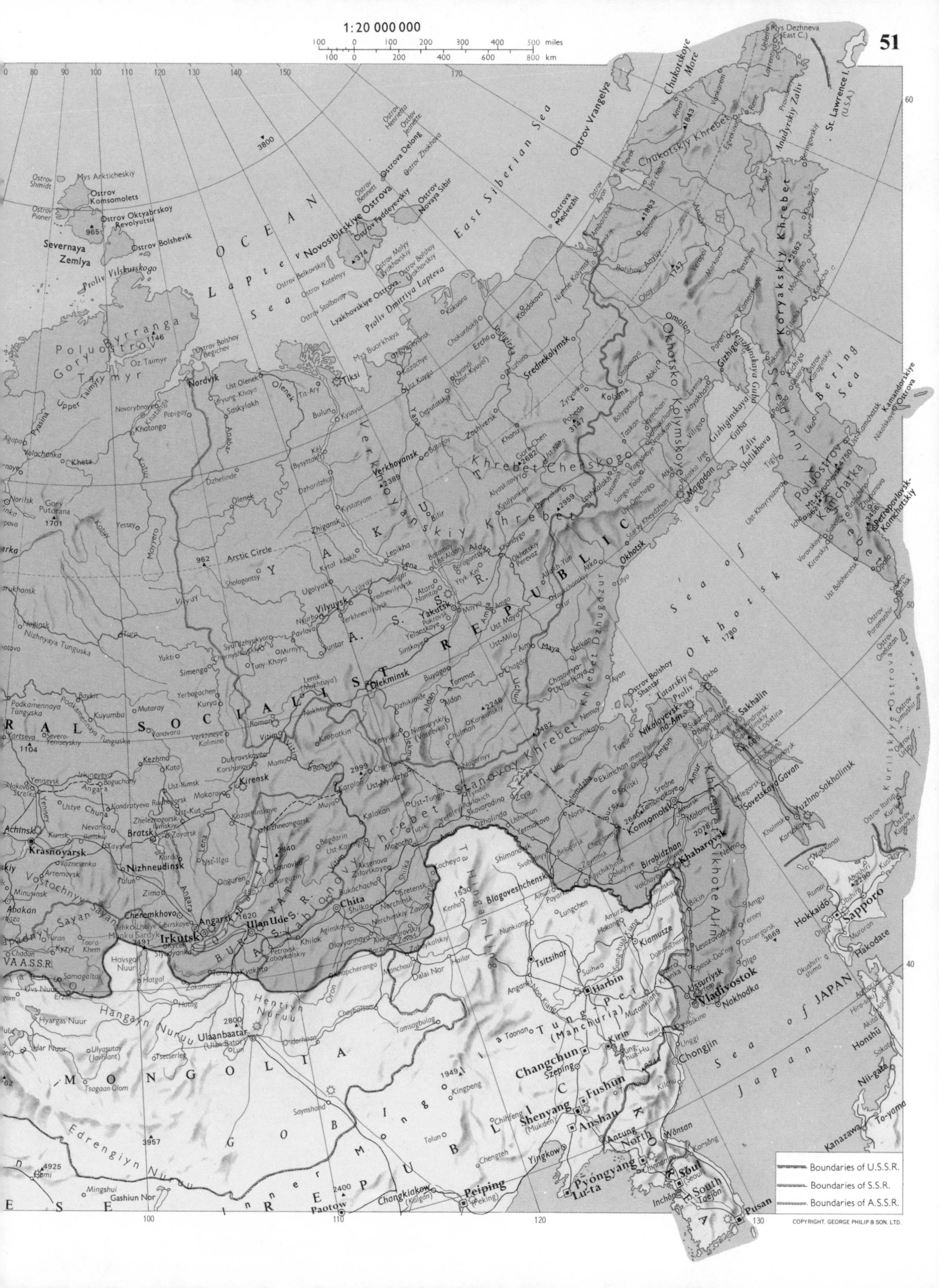
1:20 000 000
miles
km
Boundaries of U.S.S.R.
Boundaries of S.S.R.
Boundaries of A.S.S.R.
OCEAN
Laptev Sea
East Siberian Sea
Chukotskoye More
Bering Sea
Sea of Okhotsk
Sea of JAPAN
Japan
Ostrov Vrangelya
St. Lawrence I. (U.S.A.)
Mys Dezhneva (East C.)
Severnaya Zemlya
Ostrov Komsomolets
Ostrov Oktyabrskoy Revolyutsii
Ostrov Bolshevik
Proliv Vilkitskogo
Novosibirskiye Ostrova
Lyakhovskiye Ostrova
Proliv Dmitriya Lapteva
Ostrova Medvezhi
Poluostrov Taymyr
Gory Byrranga
Nordvik
Tiksi
Verkhoyansk
Verkhoyanskiy Khrebet
Khrebet Cherskogo
Chukotskiy Khrebet
Koryakskiy Khrebet
Sredinnyy Khrebet
Poluostrov Kamchatka
Petropavlovsk-Kamchatskiy
Magadan
Okhotsk
Srednekolymsk
Yakutsk
Vilyuysk
Olekminsk
Arctic Circle
YAKUT A.S.S. REPUBLIC
Stanovoy Khrebet
Yablonovyy Khrebet
Kirensk
Bratsk
Krasnoyarsk
Achinsk
Nizhneudinsk
Cheremkhovo
Angarsk
Irkutsk
Ulan Ude
Chita
BURYAT A.S.S.R.
Blagoveshchensk
Komsomolsk
Khabarovsk
Birobidzhan
Sikhote Alin
Nikolayevsk-na-Amure
Sakhalin
Sovetskaya Gavan
Yuzhno-Sakhalinsk
Kurilskiye Ostrova
Vladivostok
Ussuriysk
Nakhodka
Hokkaido
Sapporo
Hakodate
Honshū
Harbin
Tsitsihar
Kiamusze
Tung-Pei (Manchuria)
Kirin
Changchun
Shenyang (Mukden)
Fushun
Anshan
Chongjin
NORTH KOREA
SOUTH
Pyongyang
Soul (Seoul)
Pusan
Lu-ta
Peiping (Peking)
Changkiakow (Kalgan)
Paotow
MONGOLIA
Ulaanbaatar (Ulan Bator)
Hentiyn Nuruu
Hangayn Nuruu
Gobi
Inner Mongolia
Ta Hingan Ling
COPYRIGHT. GEORGE PHILIP & SON. LTD.

1:50 000 000

250 0 250 500 750 1000 miles

250 0 500 1000 1500 km

m: 6000, 4000, 2000, 1000, 400, 200, 0, 200–600, 2000–6000, 4000–12 000, 6000–18 000, 8000–24 000 m

ft: 18 000, 12 000, 6000, 3000, 1200, 600, 0, 600, 6000, 12 000, 18 000, 24 000 ft

East from Greenwich

Projection: Bonne

1:50 000 000

250 0 250 500 750 1000 miles

250 0 500 1000 1500 km

East from Greenwich

Projection: Bonne

54 THE HOLY LAND

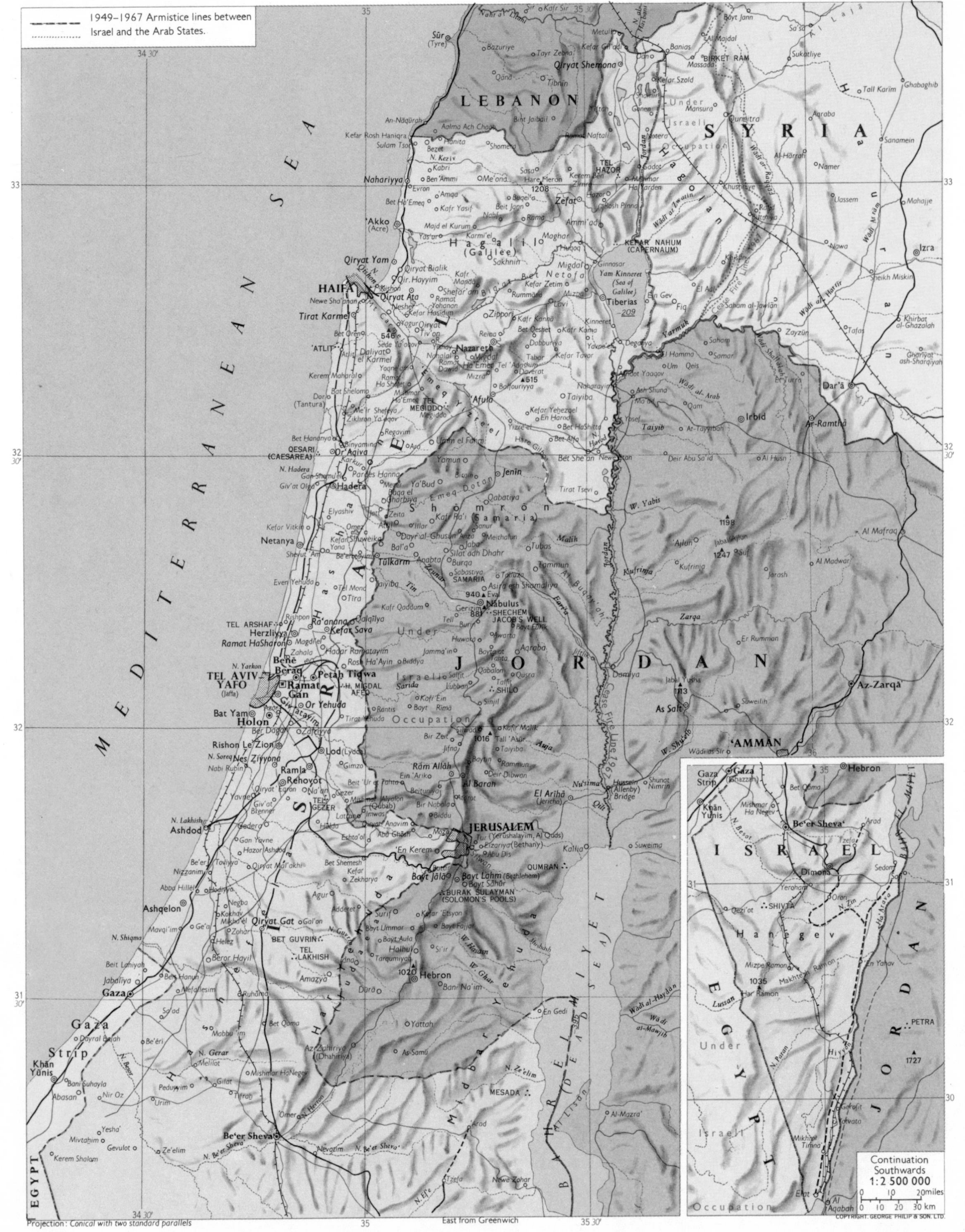

1:1 000 000
miles
km
1949–1967 Armistice lines between Israel and the Arab States.
MEDITERRANEAN SEA
LEBANON
SYRIA
JORDAN
ISRAEL
EGYPT
Under Israeli Occupation
Gaza Strip
Hagalil (Galilee)
Shomron (Samaria)
Hasharon
Hanegev
Yam Kinneret (Sea of Galilee)
BAHR EL LUT (DEAD SEA)
Cease Fire Line 1967
Jordan
Yarmuk
Haifa
Akko (Acre)
Nahariyya
Zefat
Tiberias
Nazareth
'Afula
Jenin
Tulkarm
Nabulus
Netanya
Herzliyya
TEL AVIV-YAFO (Jaffa)
Ramat Gan
Petah Tiqwa
Bat Yam
Holon
Rishon Le Zion
Lod (Lydda)
Ramla
Rehovot
Ashdod
Ashqelon
Gaza
Khan Yunis
Qiryat Gat
Be'er Sheva'
Hebron
Bayt Lahm (Bethlehem)
JERUSALEM
Ram Allah
El Ariha (Jericho)
QUMRAN
MESADA
En Gedi
Sûr (Tyre)
Qiryat Shemona
Irbid
Dar'a
Az-Zarqa'
'AMMAN
As Salt
Izra
Sheikh Miskin
Al Mafraq
Continuation Southwards
1:2 500 000
Dimona
Sedom
Mizpe Ramon
PETRA
Elat
Al 'Aqabah
Projection: Conical with two standard parallels
East from Greenwich

1:15 000 000

100 0 100 200 300 400 miles

100 0 100 200 300 400 500 600 km

Projection: Sanson-Flamsteed's Sinusoidal

East from Greenwich

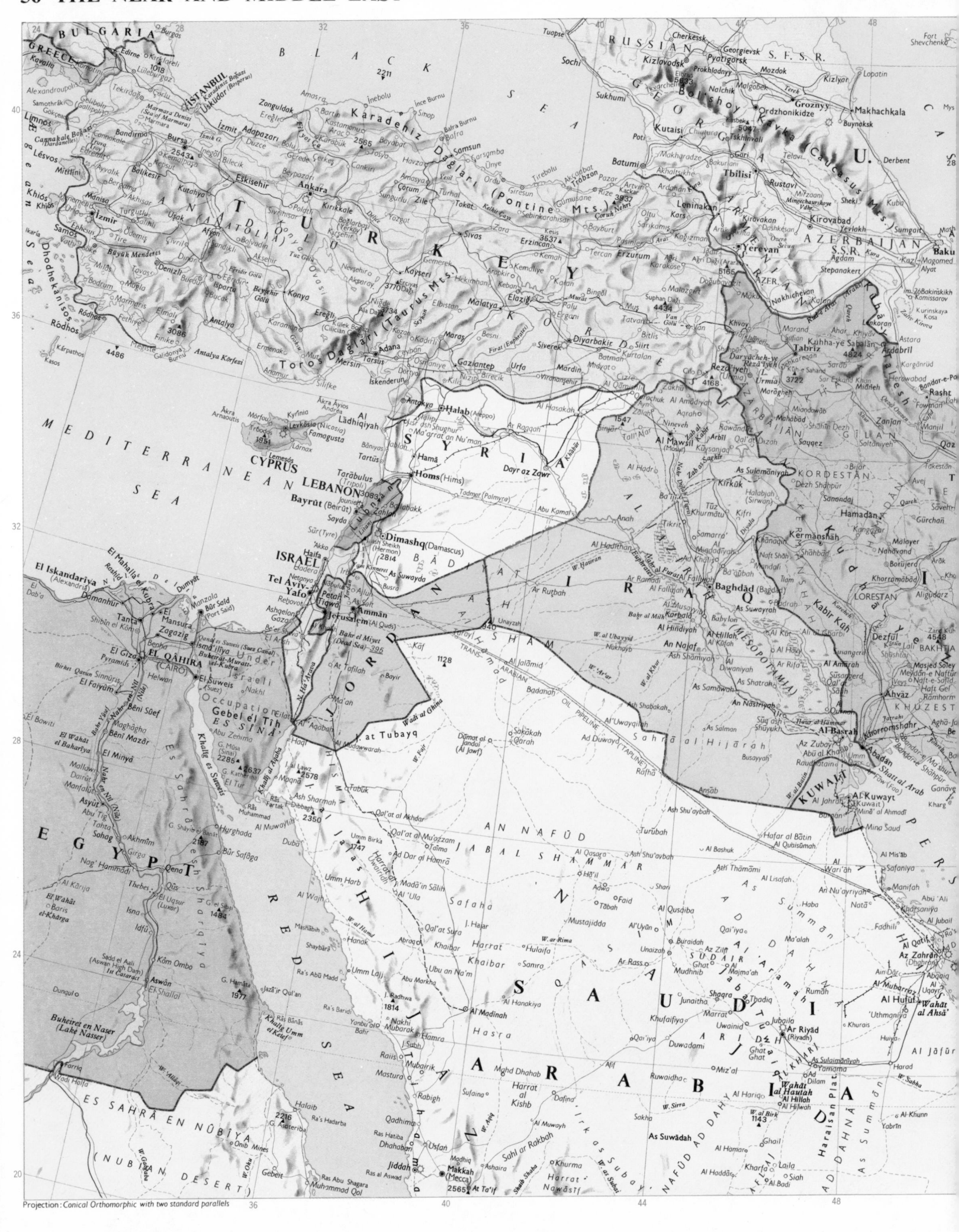
BULGARIA
GREECE
BLACK SEA
RUSSIAN S.F.S.R.
GEORGIA
ARMENIA
AZERBAIJAN S.S.R.
U.
TURKEY
ANATOLIA
Karadeniz Dağları (Pontine Mts.)
Toros Dağları (Taurus Mts.)
Bolshoy Kavkaz (Caucasus Mts.)
İSTANBUL
Ankara
İzmir
Bursa
Konya
Adana
Kayseri
Samsun
Trabzon
Erzurum
Tbilisi
Yerevan
Baku
Groznyy
Makhachkala
MEDITERRANEAN SEA
CYPRUS
Levkôsia (Nicosia)
LEBANON
Bayrût (Beirût)
SYRIA
Halab (Aleppo)
Homs (Hims)
Dimashq (Damascus)
Dayr az Zawr
ISRAEL
Tel Aviv-Yafo
Jerusalem (Al Quds)
JORDAN
Ammān
BĀDIYAT ASH SHAM
IRAQ
Baghdād (Baghdad)
Al Mawsil (Mosul)
Kirkūk
Al Basrah
MESOPOTAMIA
Tabrīz
Kermānshāh
Hamadān
KUWAIT
Al Kuwayt (Kuwait)
EGYPT
EL QÂHIRA (CAIRO)
El Iskandarîya (Alexandria)
Bûr Sa'îd (Port Said)
El Suweis (Suez)
Israeli Under Occupation
ES SINÂ
Aswân
Buheirat en Naser (Lake Nasser)
ES SAHRÂ EN NÛBÎYA
(NUBIAN DESERT)
RED SEA
SAUDI ARABIA
AN NAFŪD
JABAL SHAMMAR
HIJAZ
Al Madīnah
Makkah (Mecca)
Jiddah
Ar Riyād (Riyadh)
Al Hufūf
AD DAHNĀ
TRANS-ARABIAN OIL PIPELINE (TAPLINE)
PERSIAN GULF
Projection: Conical Orthomorphic with two standard parallels

1:10 000 000

100 0 100 200 300 miles
100 0 100 200 300 400 500 km

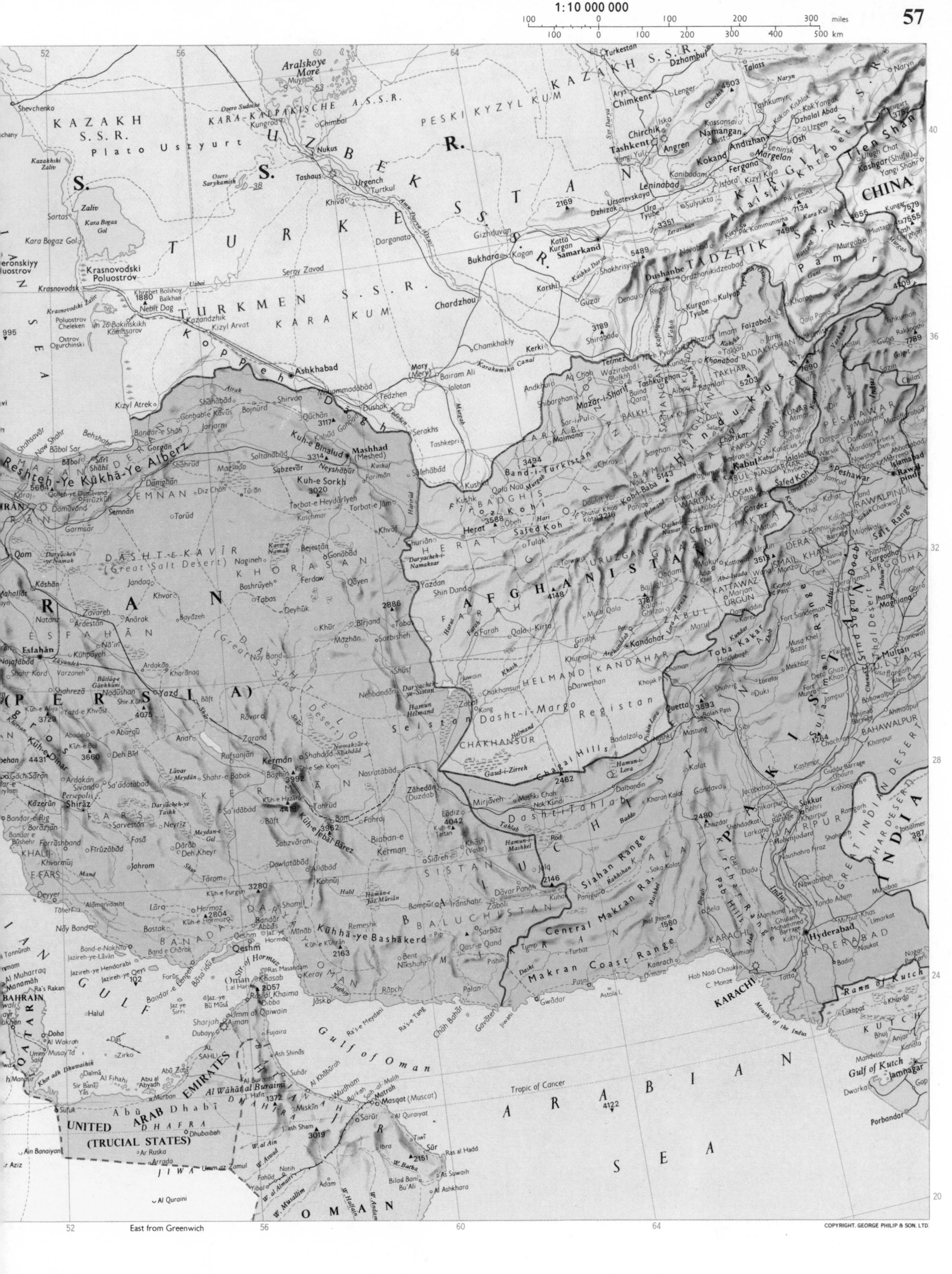
Aralskoye More
KAZAKH S.S.R.
Plato Ustyurt
KARA-KALPAKSKAYA A.S.S.R.
PESKI KYZYL KUM
UZBEK S.S.R.
TURKESTAN
TURKMEN S.S.R.
KARA KUM
Kopet Dagh
Kara Bogaz Gol
Krasnovodski Poluostrov
Krasnovodsk
Ashkhabad
Mary (Merv)
Chardzhou
Bukhara
Samarkand
Tashkent
Chimkent
Dzhambul
Namangan
Andizhan
Fergana
Margelan
Kokand
Osh
Leninabad
Dushanbe
TADZHIK S.S.R.
KIRGIZ S.S.R.
Tien Shan
Kashgar (Shufu)
CHINA
Pamir
Termez
Kerki
Nukus
Urgench
Tashauz
Khiva
Karshi
Mazar-i-Sharif
Kunduz
Faizabad
BADAKHSHAN
Hindu Kush
Kabul
Jalalabad
Peshawar
Islamabad
Rawalpindi
Salt Range
Herat
Band-i-Turkistan
Koh-i-Baba
Safed Koh
Ghazni
Gardez
AFGHANISTAN
Kandahar
Farah
Shin Dand
HELMAND
Registan
Dasht-i-Margo
CHAKHANSUR
Chagai Hills
Quetta
PAKISTAN
Sulaiman Range
Multan
Dera Ismail Khan
Sukkur
Jacobabad
Kirthar Range
Hyderabad
Karachi
Central Makran Ra.
Makran Coast Range
BALUCHISTAN
Gwadar
Pasni
Mouths of the Indus
Rann of Kutch
Gulf of Kutch
Jamnagar
Porbandar
INDIA
GREAT INDIAN DESERT
THAR DESERT
Bahawalpur
Indus
Reshteh-ye Kūhhā-ye Alberz
Tehran
Qom
Mashhad (Meshed)
Kuh-e Binalud
DASHT-E KAVĪR (Great Salt Desert)
KHORASAN
DASHT-E LUT (Great Sand Desert)
IRAN (PERSIA)
Esfahān
Yazd
Kermān
Shirāz
Zāhedān (Duzdab)
Seistan
Hamun Helmand
Kūh-e Jebāl Bārez
Kūhhā-ye Bashākerd
Bandar Abbās
Qeshm
Str. of Hormuz
GULF
BAHRAIN
Manamah
QATAR
Doha
UNITED ARAB EMIRATES (TRUCIAL STATES)
Abū Dhabī
Dubayy
Sharjah
Ras al Khaima
Al Buraimi
Masqat (Muscat)
Matrah
Sūr
Ras al Hadd
OMAN
Gulf of Oman
Tropic of Cancer
ARABIAN SEA
4122
East from Greenwich

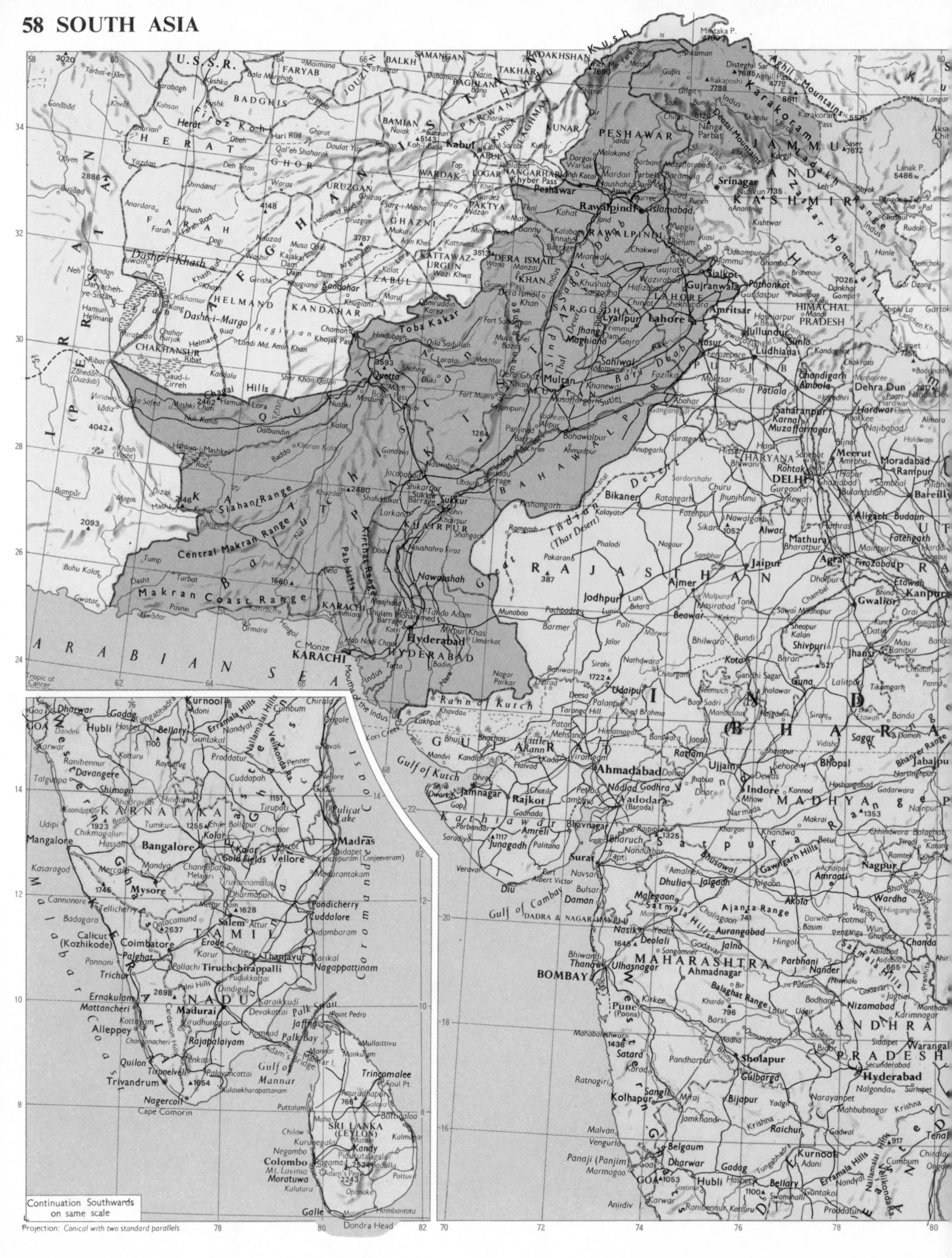
U.S.S.R.
BALKH
SAMANGAN
FARYAB
JOUZJAN
BADAKHSHAN
TAKHAR
BAGHLAN
BADGHIS
Herat
HERAT
BAMIAN
PARWAN
KAPISA
LAGHMAN
KUNAR
Kabul
KABUL
GHOR
WARDAK
LOGAR
NANGARHAR
Khyber Pass
Peshawar
PESHAWAR
URUZGAN
PAKTYA
GHAZNI
FARAH
Farah
AFGHANISTAN
Dasht-i-Khash
KATTAWAZ-URGUN
ZABUL
Kandahar
KANDAHAR
HELMAND
Dasht-i-Margo
Registan
CHAKHANSUR
Chagai Hills
Hamun-i-Lora
Nok Kundi
Dalbandin
Hamun-i-Mashkel
Quetta
Bolan Pass
Toba Kakar
QUETTA
KALAT
BALUCHISTAN
Siahan Range
Central Makran Range
Makran Coast Range
Kirthar Range
Pab Hills
Pasni
Gwadar
Ormara
Sonmiani
KARACHI
C. Monze
Mouths of the Indus
HYDERABAD
Hyderabad
Nawabshah
KHAIRPUR
Sukkur
Jacobabad
Larkana
DERA ISMAIL KHAN
Sulaiman Range
Fort Munro
Dera Ghazi Khan
Multan
MULTAN
BAHAWALPUR
Bahawalpur
Sahiwal
Lyallpur
Jhang Maghiana
SARGODHA
Sind Sagar Doab
Thal
Rawalpindi
Islamabad
RAWALPINDI
Gujranwala
Sialkot
Lahore
LAHORE
PAKISTAN
Indus
IRAN (PERSIA)
Ribat
Zahedan (Duzdab)
Hamun Helmand
Daryacheh-ye-Sistan
ARABIAN SEA
Tropic of Cancer
Hindu Kush
Tirich Mir 7690
Karakoram
Aghil Mountains
Gilgit
Rakaposhi 7788
Nanga Parbat 8126
Deosai Mountains
K2 8611
Kargil
Srinagar
JAMMU AND KASHMIR
Ladakh Range
Zaskar Mountains
Lanak P. 5486
Mintaka P.
Karakoram Pass
Pathankot
Amritsar
Jullundur
Ludhiana
Simla
HIMACHAL PRADESH
PUNJAB
Patiala
Chandigarh
Ambala
Dehra Dun
Nanda Devi 7817
Hardwar
Saharanpur
Muzaffarnagar
HARYANA
Meerut
Moradabad
Rampur
Bareilly
DELHI
Rohtak
Aligarh
Budaun
Bikaner
Great Indian Desert (Thar Desert)
RAJASTHAN
Jaipur
Ajmer
Jodhpur
Alwar
Mathura
Agra
Firozabad
Etawah
Kanpur
Gwalior
Jhansi
Shivpuri
Guna
Kota
Udaipur
Rann of Kutch
Gulf of Kutch
Bhuj
GUJARAT
Little Rann
Ahmadabad
Vadodara (Baroda)
Jamnagar
Rajkot
Kathiawar
Junagadh
Bhavnagar
Gulf of Cambay
Diu
Daman
Surat
DADRA & NAGAR HAVELI
INDIA (BHARAT)
Ujjain
Indore
Bhopal
Sagar
Jabalpur
MADHYA PRADESH
Satpura Range
Ajanta Range
Nagpur
Wardha
Amraoti
Akola
Malegaon
Dhulia
Jalgaon
Nasik
Aurangabad
Jalna
Deolali
MAHARASHTRA
BOMBAY
Thana
Ulhasnagar
Pune (Poona)
Ahmadnagar
Parbhani
Nander
Nizamabad
Balaghat Range
Satara
Sholapur
Gulbarga
Bijapur
ANDHRA PRADESH
Hyderabad
Secunderabad
Warangal
Ratnagiri
Kolhapur
Sangli
Belgaum
Dharwar
Hubli
Panaji (Panjim)
Marmagao
GOA
Raichur
Kurnool
Bellary
Erramala Hills
Western Ghats
KARNATAKA
Mangalore
Shimoga
Davangere
Bangalore
Kolar
Kolar Gold Fields
Mysore
Madras
Vellore
Pulicat Lake
Tirupati
Cuddapah
Nellore
Ongole
Pondicherry
Cuddalore
Salem
Coimbatore
Calicut (Kozhikode)
Cannanore
TAMIL NADU
Tiruchchirappalli
Thanjavur
Nagappattinam
Madurai
Dindigul
Palghat
Trichur
Ernakulam
Mattancheri
KERALA
Alleppey
Quilon
Trivandrum
Tirunelveli
Nagercoil
Cape Comorin
Malabar Coast
Coromandel Coast
Palk Strait
Palk Bay
Adam's Bridge
Gulf of Mannar
Jaffna
Point Pedro
Mannar I.
Trincomalee
Anuradhapura
Batticaloa
SRI LANKA (CEYLON)
Kandy
Colombo
Mt. Lavinia
Moratuwa
Negombo
Galle
Dondra Head
Continuation Southwards on same scale
Projection: Conical with two standard parallels

1:10 000 000

50 0 50 100 150 200 miles

50 0 50 100 150 200 250 300 km

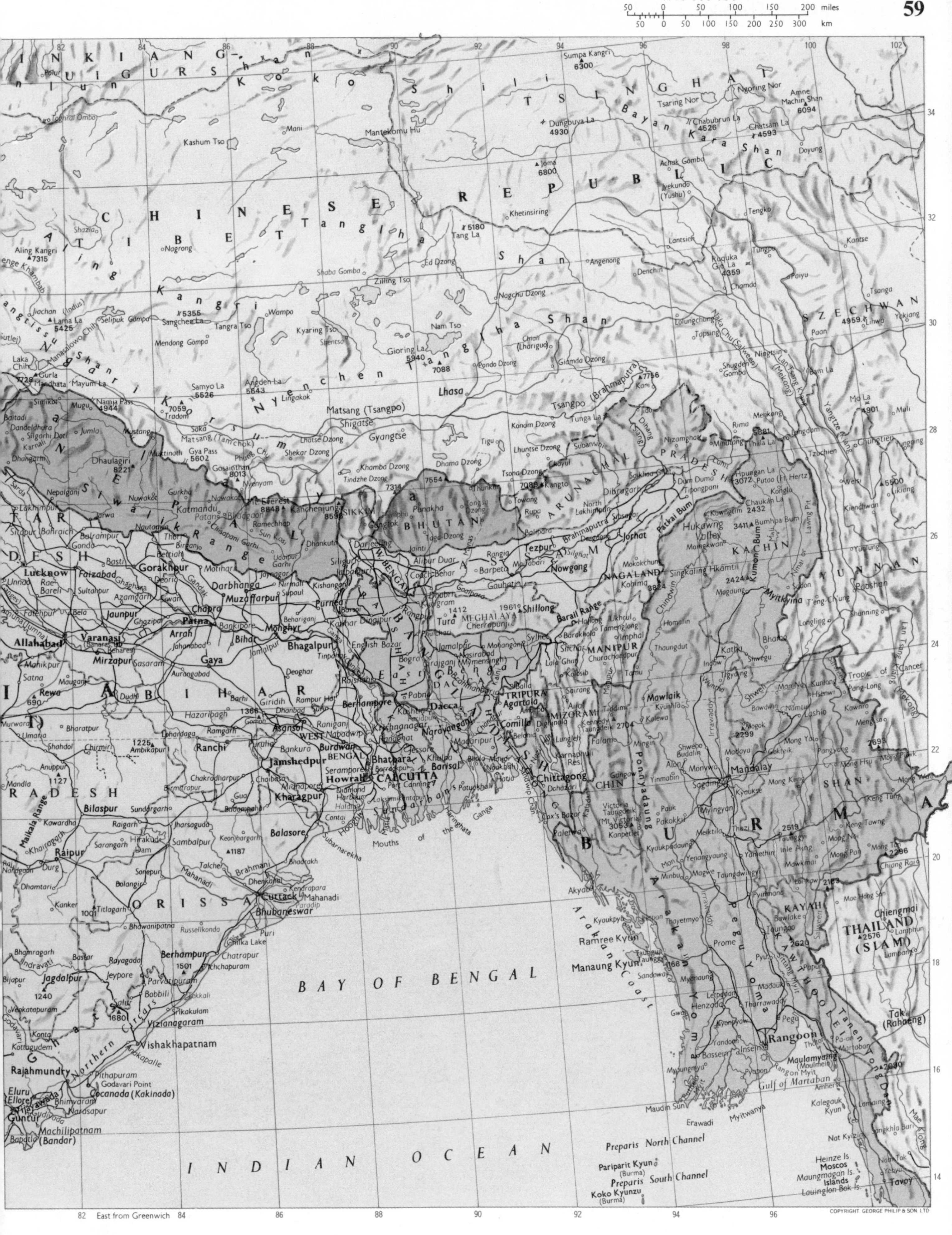
SINKIANG-UIGUR
Kunlun Shan
Koko Shili
TSINGHAI
Bayan Kara Shan
CHINESE PEOPLE'S REPUBLIC
TIBET
Tanglha Shan
Aling Kangri
Kangri
Nyenchen Tanglha Shan
Lhasa
Matsang (Tsangpo)
Shigatse
Gyangtse
Tsangpo (Brahmaputra)
NEPAL
Dhaulagiri 8221
Mt. Everest 8848
Kanchenjunga 8598
Katmandu
Siwalik Range
SIKKIM
BHUTAN
ARUNACHAL PRADESH
ASSAM
NAGALAND
MANIPUR
MEGHALAYA
Shillong
TRIPURA
MIZORAM
UTTAR PRADESH
Lucknow
Allahabad
Varanasi
Gorakhpur
Patna
BIHAR
Gaya
Ranchi
Jamshedpur
WEST BENGAL
CALCUTTA
Howrah
Bhagalpur
BANGLADESH
Dacca
Chittagong
Comilla
Mouths of the Ganga
ORISSA
Cuttack
Bhubaneswar
Berhampur
Sambalpur
Raipur
Bilaspur
MADHYA PRADESH
Vishakhapatnam
Vizianagaram
Rajahmundry
Cocanada (Kakinada)
Machilipatnam (Bandar)
Guntur
Northern Circars
BAY OF BENGAL
INDIAN OCEAN
Preparis North Channel
Preparis South Channel
Paripari Kyun (Burma)
Koko Kyunzu (Burma)
BURMA
KACHIN
Myitkyina
Mandalay
CHIN
SHAN
KAYAH
KAWTHOOLEI
Rangoon
Bassein
Henzada
Prome
Moulmein
Pegu Yoma
Arakan Yoma
Arakan Coast
Ramree Kyun
Manaung Kyun
Gulf of Martaban
Tavoy
Tenasserim
YUNNAN
SZECHWAN
THAILAND (SIAM)
Chiengmai
Tropic of Cancer
Irrawaddy
Salween
Chindwin
Lan Tsang Kiang (Mekong)

60 THE INDO-GANGETIC PLAIN

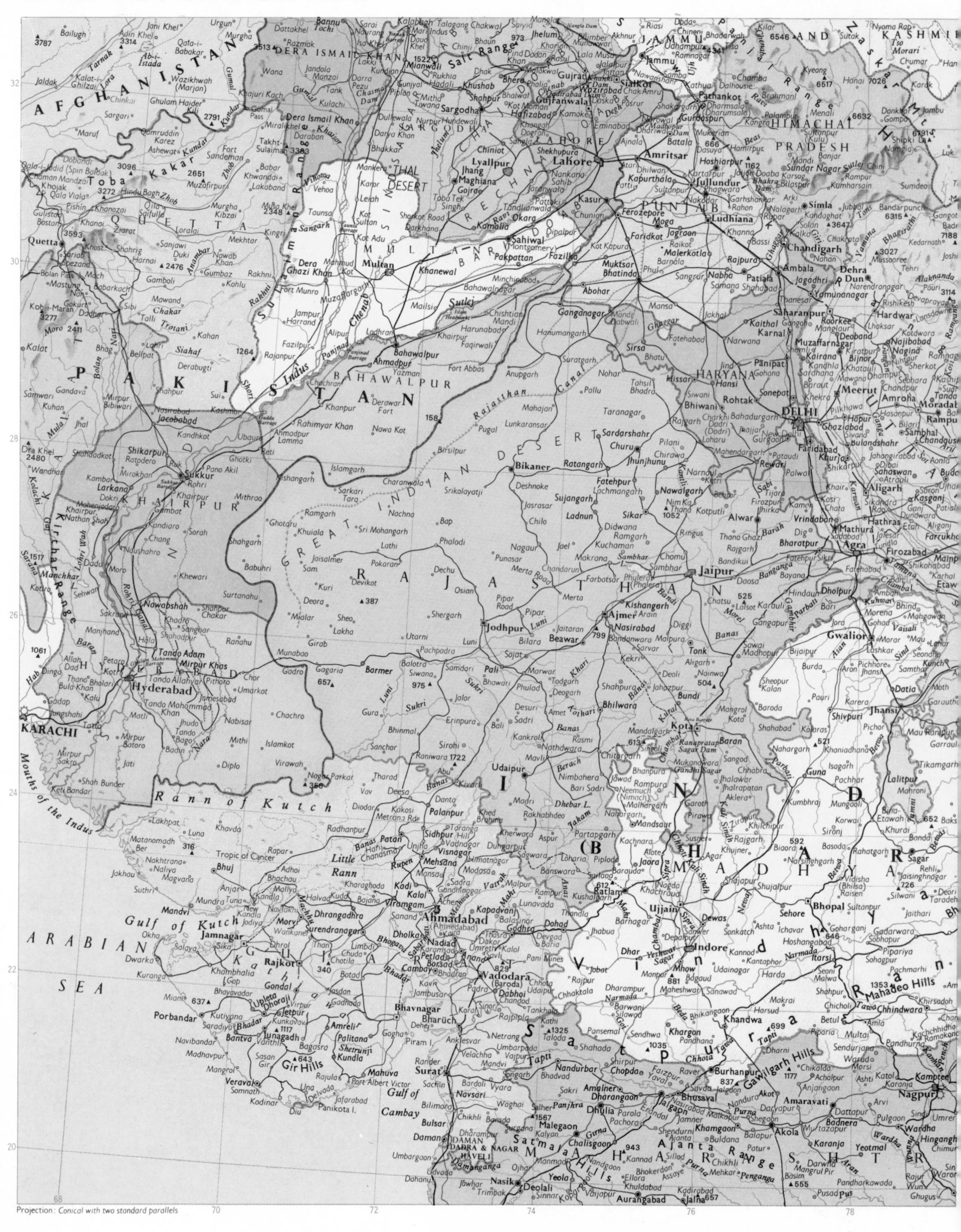
AFGHANISTAN
PAKISTAN
KASHMIR
JAMMU
HIMACHAL PRADESH
PUNJAB
HARYANA
DELHI
RAJASTHAN
GREAT INDIAN DESERT
THAL DESERT
BAHAWALPUR
KHAIRPUR
HYDERABAD
QUETTA
GUJARAT
MADHYA PRADESH
MAHARASHTRA
INDIA
ARABIAN SEA
Gulf of Kutch
Gulf of Cambay
Rann of Kutch
Little Rann
Mouths of the Indus
Tropic of Cancer
Salt Range
Sulaiman Range
Kirthar Range
Vindhya Range
Satpura Range
Ajanta Range
Satmala Hills
Gir Hills
Gawilgarh Hills
Mahadeo Hills
Indus
Sutlej
Chenab
Jhelum
Ravi
Beas
Narmada
Tapti
Chambal
Quetta
Karachi
Hyderabad
Sukkur
Larkana
Jacobabad
Shikarpur
Nawabshah
Multan
Bahawalpur
Dera Ghazi Khan
Dera Ismail Khan
Sargodha
Lyallpur
Lahore
Sahiwal
Amritsar
Jullundur
Ludhiana
Chandigarh
Simla
Ambala
Patiala
Bhatinda
Ferozepore
Jammu
Pathankot
Gurdaspur
Dehra Dun
Saharanpur
Meerut
Ghaziabad
Faridabad
Aligarh
Mathura
Agra
Hissar
Rohtak
Bikaner
Jodhpur
Jaipur
Ajmer
Udaipur
Kota
Alwar
Bharatpur
Gwalior
Jhansi
Bhopal
Indore
Ujjain
Dewas
Ratlam
Ahmadabad
Vadodara
Surat
Rajkot
Jamnagar
Bhavnagar
Junagadh
Porbandar
Bhuj
Nasik
Aurangabad
Akola
Amaravati
Nagpur
Burhanpur
Bhusaval
Jalgaon
Dhulia
Malegaon
Khandwa
Sagar
Daman
Diu
DAMAN
DADRA & NAGAR HAVELI
68
70
72
74
76
78
32
30
28
26
24
22
20
Projection: Conical with two standard parallels

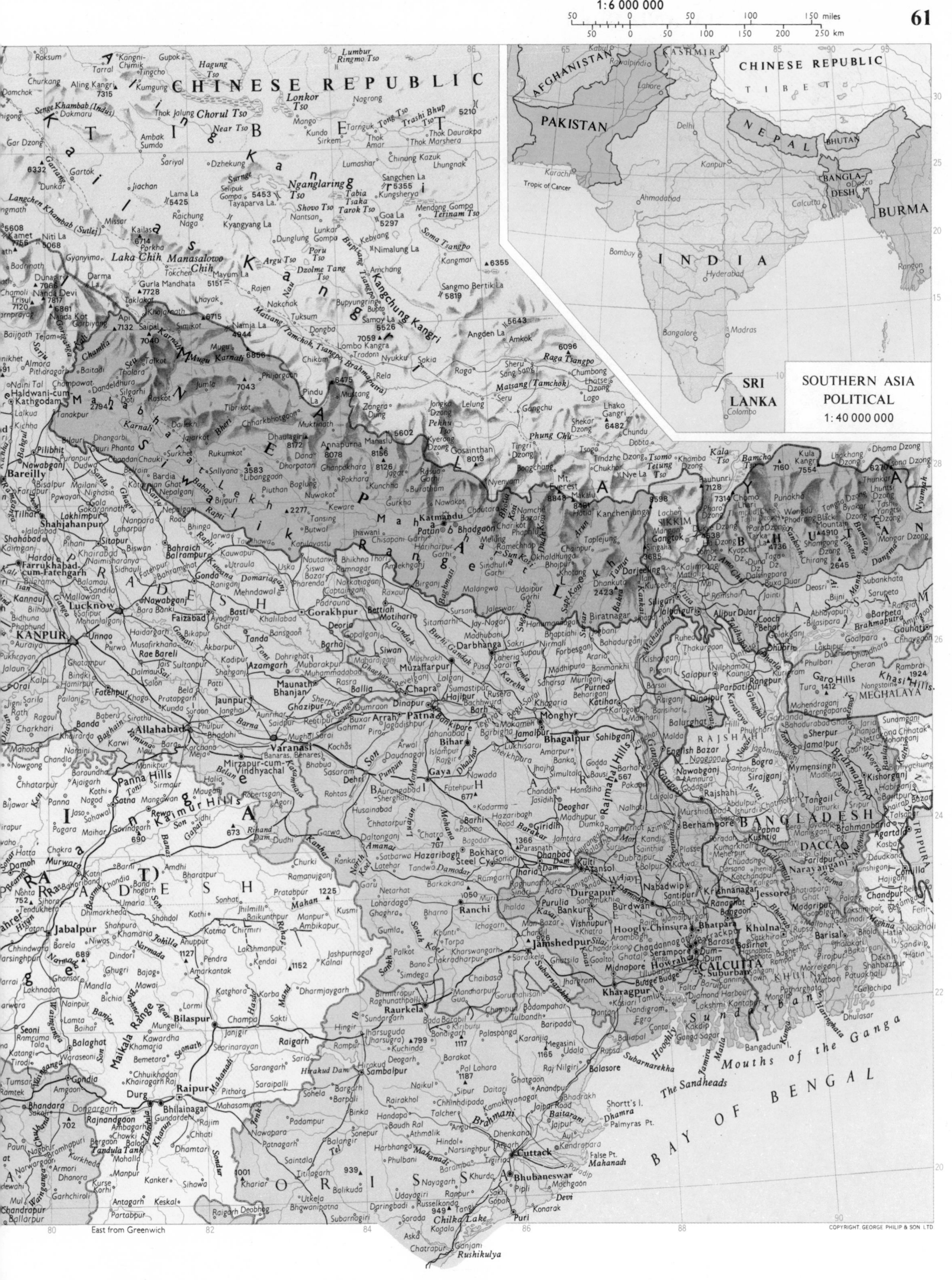
1:6 000 000
50 0 50 100 150 miles
50 0 50 100 150 200 250 km
CHINESE REPUBLIC
AFGHANISTAN
PAKISTAN
NEPAL
BHUTAN
BANGLADESH
BURMA
INDIA
SRI LANKA
SOUTHERN ASIA
POLITICAL
1:40 000 000
Tropic of Cancer
T I B E T
SIKKIM
BHUTAN
BAY OF BENGAL
Mouths of the Ganga
The Sandheads
Sunderbans
O R I S S A
MEGHALAYA
TRIPURA
CALCUTTA
DACCA
Katmandu
Allahabad
Varanasi
Patna
KANPUR
Lucknow
Jabalpur
Raipur
Cuttack
Bhubaneswar
Mt. Everest 8848
Annapurna 8078
Dhaulagiri 8172
Kanchenjunga
East from Greenwich

SOUTHERN INDIA AND SRI LANKA

1:6 000 000

50 0 50 100 150 miles

50 0 50 100 150 200 250 km

MAHARASHTRA

MADHYA PRADESH

ORISSA

ANDHRA PRADESH

KARNATAKA

TAMIL NADU

KERALA

GOA

BOMBAY

HYDERABAD

MADRAS

BANGALORE

BAY OF BENGAL

ARABIAN SEA

Gulf of Manaar (Mannar)

Coromandel Coast

Malabar Coast

Western Ghats

Eastern Ghats

SRI LANKA (CEYLON)

SRI LANKA
On same scale

Projection: Conical with two standard parallels

East from Greenwich

1:10 000 000
50 0 50 100 150 200 miles
50 0 100 200 300 km
CHINA
BURMA
SHAN
CHIN
KAYAH
KAWTHOOLEI
LAOS
THAILAND
(SIAM)
CAMBODIA
VIETNAM
WESTERN
MALAYSIA
MALAYA
INDONESIA
INDIA
BANGLADESH
Andaman
(India)
Islands
North
Andaman
Middle
Andaman
South
Andaman
Little
Andaman
ANDAMAN
SEA
Gulf of Martaban
Gulf of Siam
Gulf of
Tongking
SOUTH CHINA SEA
Arakan Coast
Preparis North Channel
Preparis South Channel
Coco Channel
Andaman Strait
Duncan Passage
Ritchies Archipelago
Myeik Kyunzu
(Mergui
Archipelago)
Isthmus of Kra
Phnom Dang Raek
Mandalay
Rangoon
Bassein
Akyab
Prome
Henzada
Maulamyaing
Tavoy
Mergui
Krung
Thep
(Bangkok)
Thonburi
Chiengmai
Nakhon
Ratchasima
(Khorat)
Luang Prabang
Vientiane
Phnom Penh
Kampot
Hanoi
Haiphong
Hue
Da Nang (Tourane)
Ho Chi Minh City
Vinh
Nanning
Hainan
Szemao
Pakhoi
Kota Baharu
Alor Setar
George Town
Pulau
Pinang
Kuala Lumpur
Ipoh
Kuantan
Melaka
Johor Baharu
SINGAPORE
Strait of Malacca
SUMATERA
Kepulauan
Natuna Besar
Kepulauan
Anambas
Kepulauan
Natuna Selatan
Kepulauan
Tambelan
Phu Quoc
Mui Ca Mau
Côn Dao
Kho Khot Kra
Chumphon
Surat Thani
Songkhla
Phuket
East from Greenwich
MALAYA AND SINGAPORE
1:6 000 000
50 0 50 miles
50 0 50 km
THAILAND
(SIAM)
PERLIS
KEDAH
PINANG
PERAK
KELANTAN
TERENGGANU
PAHANG
SELANGOR
NEGERI
SEMBILAN
MELAKA
JOHOR
MALAYA
Kuala
Terengganu
Taiping
Kelang
Seremban
Bandar Maharani
(Muar)
Bandar Penggaram
(Batu Pahat)
Keluang
Straits of Singapore
Projection: Conical with two standard parallels
COPYRIGHT. GEORGE PHILIP & SON LTD

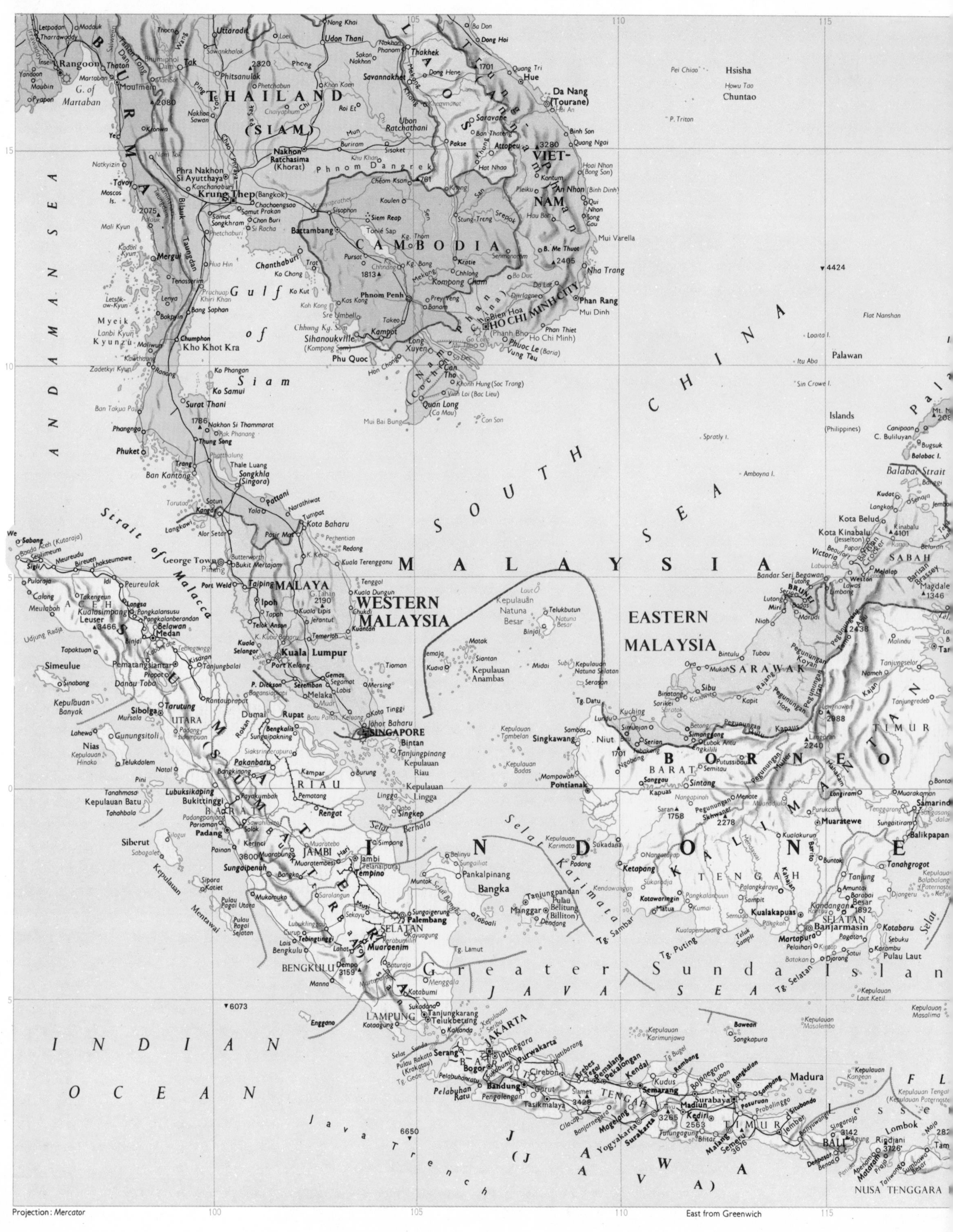
B U R M A
Rangoon
G. of Martaban
Moulmein
T H A I L A N D
(S I A M)
Uttaradit
Udon Thani
Phitsanulok
Nakhon Ratchasima (Khorat)
Ubon Ratchathani
Phnom Dangrek
Phra Nakhon Si Ayutthaya
Krung Thep (Bangkok)
L A O S
Thakhek
Savannakhet
Pakse
Attopeu
Hue
Da Nang (Tourane)
Quang Ngai
VIET-NAM
Kontum
An Nhon (Binh Dinh)
Qui Nhon
Mui Varella
B. Me Thuot
Nha Trang
Phan Rang
Mui Dinh
HO CHI MINH CITY
Phan Thiet
Vung Tau
C A M B O D I A
Siem Reap
Tonlé Sap
Battambang
Kompong Cham
Phnom Penh
Kampot
Sihanoukville (Kompong Som)
Phu Quoc
Long Xuyen
Can Tho
Quan Long (Ca Mau)
Con Son
Chanthaburi
Gulf of Siam
Mergui
Tavoy
Chumphon
Kho Khot Kra
Ranong
Ko Samui
Surat Thani
Nakhon Si Thammarat
Phuket
Trang
Songkhla (Singora)
Pattani
A N D A M A N   S E A
Hsisha
Chuntao
S O U T H   C H I N A   S E A
Spratly I.
Amboyna I.
Palawan
Islands (Philippines)
Balabac Strait
Kota Baharu
Alor Setar
George Town
Strait of Malacca
Taiping
Ipoh
MALAYA
WESTERN MALAYSIA
Kuala Lumpur
Port Kelang
Seremban
Melaka
Johor Baharu
SINGAPORE
M A L A Y S I A
EASTERN MALAYSIA
Kepulauan Natuna Besar
Kepulauan Anambas
Kota Kinabalu (Jesselton)
4101
SABAH
BRUNEI
Bandar Seri Begawan
S A R A W A K
Sibu
Kuching
Mukah
Bintulu
Miri
Sabang
Banda Aceh (Kutaraja)
ACEH
Medan
Belawan
Simeulue
Nias
Sibolga
Padang
Siberut
Pakanbaru
R I A U
Kepulauan Riau
Kepulauan Lingga
Jambi
JAMBI
Palembang
Bangka
Pangkalpinang
Belitung (Billiton)
Bengkulu
BENGKULU
LAMPUNG
Telukbetung
Tanjungkarang
Enggano
S U M A T E R A (SUMATRA)
B O R N E O
K A L I M A N T A N
BARAT
TENGAH
SELATAN
TIMUR
Pontianak
Singkawang
Ketapang
Banjarmasin
Balikpapan
Samarinda
Tarakan
I N D O N E S I A
Selat Karimata
Greater Sunda Islands
J A V A   S E A
JAKARTA
Bogor
Bandung
Cirebon
Semarang
Surabaya
Madura
Yogyakarta
Surakarta
Malang
J A W A (JAVA)
BALI
Lombok
NUSA TENGGARA
I N D I A N   O C E A N
Java Trench
6650
6073
4424

Projection: Mercator

East from Greenwich

1:12 500 000
100 0 100 200 300 miles
100 0 100 200 300 400 500 km
JAVA AND MADURA
1:7 500 000
50 0 50 100 150 miles
50 0 50 100 150 200 km
Jakarta
Bandung
Cirebon
Semarang
Surakarta
Yogyakarta
Surabaya
Malang
Madura
Bali
Kepulauan Karimunjawa
Bawean
LUZON
Manila
Quezon City
Polillo Islands
Catanduanes
Mindoro
Marinduque
Sibuyan Sea
San Bernardino Strait
Samar
Leyte
Tacloban
Panay
Iloilo
Negros
Cebu
Bohol
Mindanao Sea
Mindanao
Zamboanga
Davao
Dinagat
Siargao
Puerto Princesa
Basilan
Sulu Arch.
Tawitawi
Sibutu Passage
SULU SEA
CELEBES SEA
Kepulauan Talaud
Pulau Sangihe
Manado
Halmahera
Morotai
Ternate
MOLUCCA SEA
Kep. Bacan
Kepulauan Sula
Kepulauan Obi
Buru
Seram (Ceram)
Ambon
Misool
Waigeo
Jazirah Doberai (Vogelkop)
Manokwari
Kepulauan Schouten
Biak
Yapen
Teluk Cendrawasih
IRIAN JAYA
Pegunungan Van Rees
Pegunungan Maoke
Puncak Jaya 5029
Puncak Trikora 4760
Jayapura (Hollandia)
Merauke
P. Kolepom
Teluk Flamingo
PAPUA NEW GUINEA
SULAWESI (CELEBES)
Teluk Tomini
Gorontalo
Palu
Poso
Kendari
Ujung Pandang
Kabaena
Muna
Butung
Selayar
Teluk Bone
BANDA SEA
Kepulauan Kai
Kepulauan Aru
Kepulauan Tanimbar
Yamdena
Kepulauan Leti
Wetar
Timor
Dili
Kupang
Roti
Sawu Sea
Sumba
Flores
Sumbawa
Alor
FLORES SEA
Lesser Sunda Islands
NUSA TENGGARA TIMUR
ARAFURA SEA
PACIFIC OCEAN
Palau Islands
Babelthuap
Yap Islands
Ulithi Atoll
Ngulu Atoll
Sorol Atoll
Caroline Islands
(U.S. Trust Territory of the Pacific Islands)
Sonsorol Islands
Pulo-Anna
Merir
Tobi
Helen Atoll
Equator
Mindanao Trench
10,497
9540

SEA OF JAPAN

PACIFIC OCEAN

East from Greenwich

1:5 000 000

25 0 25 50 75 100 miles

25 0 50 100 150 km

Projection: *Conical with two standard parallels*

Continuation Southwards on same scale

East from Greenwich

1:10 000 000

100 50 0 50 100 150 200 miles

100 0 100 200 300 km

Projection: *Bonne*

REFERENCE TO PREFECTURES

HOKKAIDŌ DISTRICT	KINKI DISTRICT
1 Hokkaidō	24 Hyogo
TŌHOKU DISTRICT	25 Kyōto
2 Aomori	26 Shiga
3 Akita	27 Ōsaka
4 Iwate	28 Nara
5 Yamagata	29 Mie
6 Miyagi	30 Wakayama
7 Fukushima	CHŪGOKU DISTRICT
CHŪBU DISTRICT	31 Tottori
8 Niigata	32 Okayama
9 Ishikawa	33 Shimane
10 Toyama	34 Hiroshima
11 Fukui	35 Yamaguchi
12 Gifu	SHIKOKU DISTRICT
13 Nagano	36 Kagawa
14 Yamanashi	37 Tokushima
15 Aichi	38 Ehime
16 Shizuoka	39 Kōchi
KANTŌ DISTRICT	KYŪSHŪ DISTRICT
17 Gumma	40 Fukuoka
18 Tochigi	41 Saga
19 Saitama	42 Nagasaki
20 Ibaraki	43 Kumamoto
21 Tōkyō	44 Ōita
22 Chiba	45 Miyazaki
23 Kanagawa	46 Kagoshima

1:20 000 000

100 0 100 200 300 400 miles

100 0 100 200 300 400 500 600 km

UNION OF SOVIET SOCIALIST REPUBLICS
U. S. S. R.
KAZAKH S.S.R.
KIRGIZ S.S.R.
MONGOLIA
INNER MONGOLIA
CHINA
TIBET
TSINGHAI
SINKIANG-UIGUR
Takla Makan
NORTH KOREA
SOUTH KOREA
JAPAN
YELLOW SEA
EAST CHINA SEA
SOUTH CHINA SEA
BAY OF BENGAL
INDIA
NEPAL
BHUTAN
ASSAM
BURMA
LAOS
VIETNAM
THAILAND (SIAM)
PHILIPPINES
TAIWAN (Formosa)
JAMMU & KASHMIR
PEIPING
SHANGHAI
HONG KONG
Tropic of Cancer
Projection: Bonne
East from Greenwich
COPYRIGHT, GEORGE PHILIP & SON, LTD.

 EASTERN CHINA AND KOREA

U.S.S.R.

MONGOLIA

INNER MONGOLIAN AUTONOMOUS REGION

HEILUNG-KIANG

KIRIN

LIAONING

HOPEH

SHANTUNG

SHANSI

NINGSIA HUI A.R.

NORTH KOREA

SOUTH KOREA

SEA OF JAPAN

YELLOW SEA

Po Hai (Gulf of Chihli)

Korea Bay

THE GREAT WALL

HARBIN
Tsitsihar
Hailar
Ulanhot
Kirin
Changchun
SHENYANG (Mukden)
Fushun
Penki
Anshan
Liaoyang
Antung
Chinchow
Yingkow
LU-TA
Tairen (Dairen)
Lushun (Port Arthur)
Chengteh
BEIJING (Peking)
Changkiakow
Suanhwa
TIENTSIN
Tangku
Tangshan
Chinwangtao
Paoting
Shihkiachwang
TAIYUAN
Yangchuan
Fenyang
Tating
Paotow
Huhehot
Potow
Tsinan
Changchow
Tzepo
Tsingtao
Wells
Yehsien
Anyang
Changchih
Kiaohsien
Pyongyang
SOUL (Seoul)
Inchon
Taejon
Taegu
PUSAN
Kwangju
Hungnam
Wonsan
Chita
Irkutsk
Ulan Ude
Ulaanbaatar (Ulan Bator)
Khabarovsk
Blagoveshchensk
Vladivostok
Lanchow
Pingliang
Wuchung

1:10 000 000

50 0 50 100 150 200 250 miles

50 0 50 100 150 200 250 300 350 400 km

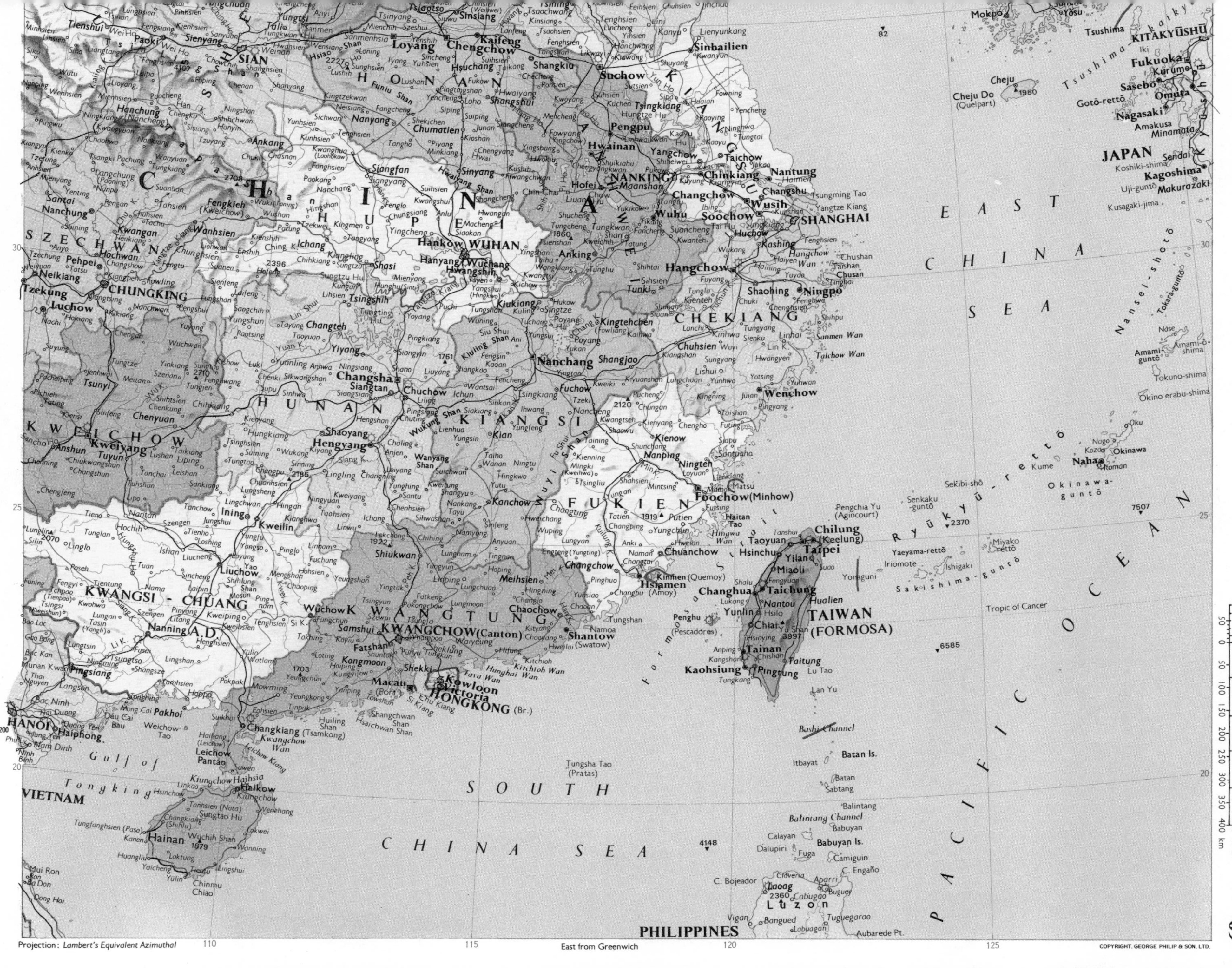

EAST CHINA SEA
SOUTH CHINA SEA
PACIFIC OCEAN
JAPAN
TAIWAN (FORMOSA)
PHILIPPINES
VIETNAM
CHINA
HUPEH
HUNAN
KIANGSI
FUKIEN
CHEKIANG
KIANGSU
ANHWEI
HONAN
KWANGTUNG
KWANGSI - CHUANG
KWEICHOW
SZECHWAN
SHANGHAI
NANKING
HANGCHOW
WUHAN
CHUNGKING
KWANGCHOW (Canton)
HONGKONG (Br.)
Nanchang
Changsha
Kaohsiung
Luzon
Hainan
Gulf of Tongking
Tropic of Cancer
Nansei-shotō
Ryūkyū-rettō
East from Greenwich
Projection: Lambert's Equivalent Azimuthal
COPYRIGHT, GEORGE PHILIP & SON, LTD.

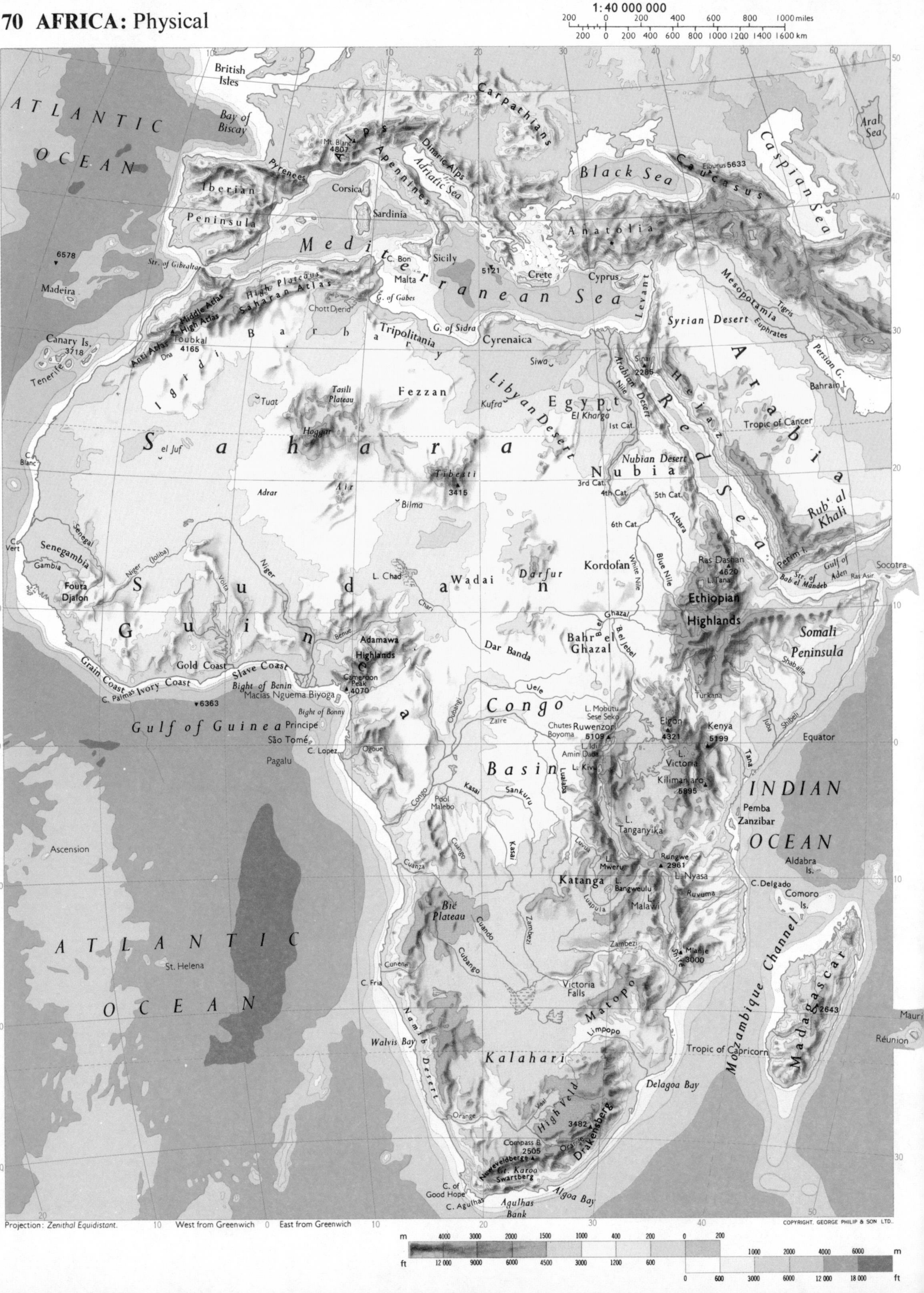

1:40 000 000
200 0 200 400 600 800 1000 miles
200 0 200 400 600 800 1000 1200 1400 1600 km
ATLANTIC OCEAN
British Isles
Bay of Biscay
Carpathians
Alps
Mt. Blanc 4807
Pyrenees
Iberian Peninsula
Corsica
Sardinia
Dinaric Alps
Apennines
Adriatic Sea
Black Sea
Caucasus
Elburus 5633
Caspian Sea
Aral Sea
Anatolia
Mediterranean Sea
C. Bon
Sicily
Malta
5121
Crete
Cyprus
Levant
6578
Madeira
Str. of Gibraltar
High Plateaus
Saharan Atlas
Middle Atlas
High Atlas
Anti Atlas
Toubkal 4165
Dra
G. of Gabes
Chott Djerid
G. of Sidra
Tripolitania
Cyrenaica
Barbary
Canary Is.
3718
Tenerife
Igidi
Siwa
Sinai 2285
Arabian Desert
Nile
Hejaz
Red Sea
Mesopotamia
Tigris
Euphrates
Syrian Desert
Persian G.
Bahrain
Arabia
Tropic of Cancer
Tuat
Tasili Plateau
Fezzan
Libyan Desert
Kufra
Egypt
El Kharga
1st Cat.
Hoggar
Sahara
el Juf
C. Blanc
Tibesti
3415
Nubian Desert
Nubia
3rd Cat.
4th Cat.
5th Cat.
Adrar
Air
Bilma
6th Cat.
Atbara
Rub' al Khali
C. Vert
Senegal
Senegambia
Gambia
Fouta Djalon
Niger (Joliba)
Volta
Niger
Sudan
L. Chad
Wadai
Darfur
Kordofan
White Nile
Blue Nile
Ras Dashan 4620
L. Tana
Perim I.
Gulf of Aden
Str. of Bab el Mandeb
Ras Asir
Socotra
Chari
Ethiopian Highlands
Guinea
Benue
Adamawa Highlands
Bahr el Ghazal
Bel Ghazal
Bel Jebel
Dar Banda
Somali Peninsula
Shaballe
Grain Coast
Gold Coast
Slave Coast
Ivory Coast
C. Palmas
Bight of Benin
Cameroon Peak 4070
Macias Nguema Biyoga
6363
Bight of Bonny
Uele
Turkana
Gulf of Guinea
Principe
São Tomé
C. Lopez
Pagalu
Ogooue
Oubangi
Zaire
Congo Basin
L. Mobutu Sese Seko
Chutes Boyoma
Ruwenzori 5109
Elgon 4321
Kenya 5199
Juba
Shibeli
Equator
L. Idi Amin Dada
L. Kivu
Lualaba
L. Victoria
Tana
Kasai
Sankuru
Congo
Pool Malebo
Kilimanjaro 5895
INDIAN OCEAN
Pemba
Zanzibar
Ascension
Cuango
Kasai
L. Tanganyika
Lovua
L. Mweru
Rungwe 2961
Aldabra Is.
Cuanza
Katanga
L. Bangweulu
L. Nyasa
Malawi
Ruvuma
C. Delgado
Comoro Is.
Bié Plateau
Luapula
Cuando
Zambezi
Mozambique Channel
ATLANTIC OCEAN
St. Helena
Cunene
Cubango
Mlanje 3000
Shire
C. Fria
Victoria Falls
Matopo
Madagascar
2643
Mauri
Réunion
Namib Desert
Walvis Bay
Limpopo
Kalahari
Tropic of Capricorn
Delagoa Bay
High Veld
Vaal
Orange
3482
Drakensberg
Compass B. 2505
Orange
Nuweveldberge
Gr. Karoo
Swartberg
C. of Good Hope
C. Agulhas
Agulhas Bank
Algoa Bay
Projection: Zenithal Equidistant.
West from Greenwich
East from Greenwich
m 4000 3000 2000 1500 1000 400 200 0 200
ft 12 000 9000 6000 4500 3000 1200 600
1000 2000 4000 6000 m
0 600 3000 6000 12 000 18 000 ft

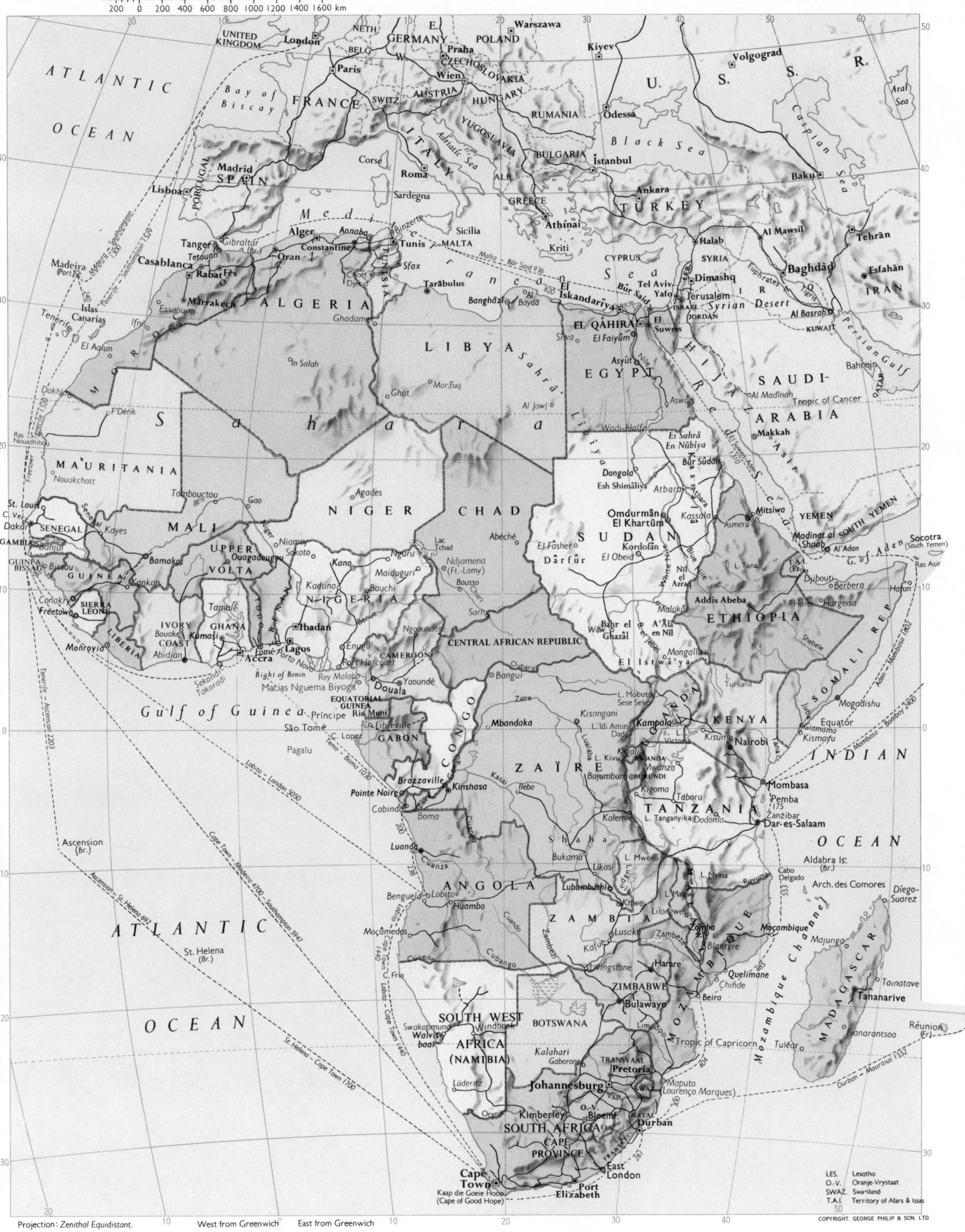
1:40 000 000
200 0 200 400 600 800 1000 miles
200 0 200 400 600 800 1000 1200 1400 1600 km
ATLANTIC OCEAN
UNITED KINGDOM
London
NETH.
E. GERMANY
W. GERMANY
BELG.
Paris
FRANCE
SWITZ.
AUSTRIA
Warszawa
POLAND
Praha
CZECHOSLOVAKIA
Wien
HUNGARY
Kiyev
Volgograd
U. S. S. R.
Aral Sea
Caspian Sea
RUMANIA
Odessa
YUGOSLAVIA
Bay of Biscay
Madrid
SPAIN
PORTUGAL
Lisboa
Corse
Roma
ITALY
Adriatic Sea
BULGARIA
Black Sea
İstanbul
ALB.
Sardegna
GREECE
Athínai
Ankara
TURKEY
Baku
Sicilia
MALTA
Kriti
CYPRUS
Halab
SYRIA
Al Mawsil
Tehrān
Baghdād
Esfahān
IRAN
Mediterranean Sea
Tanger
Gibraltar (Br.)
Tetouan
Alger
Annaba
Binzerte
Tunis
Oran
Constantine
Sfax
TUNISIA
Casablanca
Rabat
Fès
Madeira (Port.)
Marrakech
Essaouira
ALGERIA
Tarābulus
Banghāzī
Al Bayda
El Iskandarîya
Bûr Saîd
Tel Aviv-Yafo
Dimashq
Jerusalem
ISRAEL
JORDAN
Syrian Desert
Euphrates
Tigris
Al Basrah
KUWAIT
Persian Gulf
Islas Canarias
Tenerife
Ifni
Ghadamès
EL QÂHIRA
El Suweis
Siwa
El Faiyûm
El Aaiún
In Salah
LIBYA
Sahrâ' Libîya
Asyût
Nile
EGYPT
Bahrein
QATAR
SAUDI ARABIA
Al Madīnah
Tropic of Cancer
Dakhla
MOROCCO
Ghat
Marzūq
Al Jawf
Aswân
Red Sea
HIJĀZ
F'Dérik
Sahara
Wadi Halfa
Es Sahrâ En Nûbiya
Makkah
Asir
Ras Nouadhibou
MAURITANIA
Nouakchott
Dongola
Bûr Sûdân
Esh Shimâliya
Atbara
Tombouctou
Gao
Agadès
NIGER
CHAD
St. Louis
C. Vert
Dakar
SENEGAL
GAMBIA
Banjul
Kayes
MALI
Omdurmân
El Khartûm
Kassala
Mitsiwa
Asmera
YEMEN
SOUTH YEMEN
Madinat al Shaab
Al 'Adan
Socotra (South Yemen)
Gulf of Aden
Ras Asir
Niamey
Abéché
SUDAN
Kordofân
El Fâsher
Dârfûr
El Obeid
Blue Nile
White Nile
GUINEA-BISSAU
Bissau
UPPER VOLTA
Ouagadougou
Bamako
Sokoto
Kano
Ngurū
Lac Tchad
Ndjamena (Ft.-Lamy)
Maiduguri
L. Tana
T.A.I. (Fr.)
Djibouti
Berbera
Hargeisa
Hafun
GUINEA
Kankan
Kaduna
Bauchi
Bousso
Chari
Conakry
Freetown
SIERRA LEONE
NIGERIA
Tamale
Addis Abeba
ETHIOPIA
Harer
LIBERIA
Monrovia
IVORY COAST
Bouake
Abidjan
GHANA
Kumasi
TOGO
BENIN
Ibadan
Lagos
Accra
Lomé
Porto Novo
Enugu
Benue
Sarh
Ngaoundéré
CENTRAL AFRICAN REPUBLIC
Bahr el Ghazâl
Wâw
A'Âli en Nil
Malakâl
Bahr el Jebel
Mongalla
El Istwâ'ya
Shebele
SOMALI REP.
Sekondi-Takoradi
Bight of Benin
Port Harcourt
Rey Malabo
CAMEROON
Macías Nguema Biyogo
Douala
Yaoundé
Bangui
Ubangi
L. Turkana
EQUATORIAL GUINEA
Rio Muni
Gulf of Guinea
Príncipe
São Tomé
Libreville
GABON
C. Lopez
Pagalu
CONGO
Zaire
Mbandaka
L. Mobutu Sese Seko
Kisangani
UGANDA
Kampala
L. Idi Amin Dada
KENYA
Kisumu
Nairobi
Mogadishu
Juba
Giamama
Kismayu
Equator
INDIAN OCEAN
L. Victoria
Lualaba
L. Kivu
RWANDA
Kigali
BURUNDI
Bujumbura
Mwanza
ZAÏRE
Kasai
Ilebo
Brazzaville
Kinshasa
Pointe Noire
Cabinda
Boma
Kigoma
Tabora
TANZANIA
Dodoma
Mombasa
Pemba
Zanzibar
Dar-es-Salaam
Kalemie
L. Tanganyika
Kwango
Ascension (Br.)
Luanda
Shaba
Bukama
Likasi
L. Mweru
Cuanza
ANGOLA
Lubumbashi
L. Nyasa
Cabo Delgado
Aldabra Is. (Br.)
Arch. des Comores
Diégo-Suarez
Ruvuma
Benguela
Lobito
Huambo
Kitwe
ZAMBIA
L. Malawi
MALAWI
Lilongwe
Zomba
Blantyre
Moçambique
MOZAMBIQUE
Mozambique Channel
Majunga
MADAGASCAR
Lusaka
Kafue
Zambezi
Moçâmedes
Cuando
Cubango
Cunene
Livingstone
Harare
Quelimane
Chinde
Beira
Tamatave
Tananarive
Fianarantsoa
Tuléar
Réunion (Fr.)
St. Helena (Br.)
ZIMBABWE
Bulawayo
Frio
SOUTH WEST AFRICA (NAMIBIA)
Swakopmund
Walvis baai
Windhoek
BOTSWANA
Kalahari
Gaborone
Limpopo
Tropic of Capricorn
TRANSVAAL
Pretoria
Johannesburg
Lüderitz
SWAZ.
Maputo (Lourenço Marques)
Vaal
O.-V.
Orange
Kimberley
Bloemf.
LES.
NATAL
Durban
SOUTH AFRICA
CAPE PROVINCE
TRANSKEI
East London
Cape Town
Kaap die Goeie Hoop (Cape of Good Hope)
Port Elizabeth
Madeira – Southampton 1300
Tenerife – Southampton 1529
Malta – Bûr Said 936
Lobito – London 5050
Tenerife – Ascension 2203
Ascension – St. Helena 692
Cape Town – Madeira 4700 – Southampton 5947
St. Helena – Cape Town 1700
Lobito – Cape Town 1440
Aden – Mombasa 1602
Mombasa – Bombay 2400
Durban – Mauritius 1552
El Suweis – Aden 1310
LES. Lesotho
O.-V. Oranje-Vrystaat
SWAZ. Swaziland
T.A.I. Territory of Afars & Issas

Projection: Zenithal Equidistant. West from Greenwich East from Greenwich

NORTH ATLANTIC OCEAN

ALGERIA
MOROCCO
MAURITANIA
MALI
NIGER
SENEGAL
GAMBIA
GUINEA-BISSAU
GUINEA
SIERRA LEONE
LIBERIA
IVORY COAST
GHANA
TOGO
BENIN
BURKINA FASO (Upper Volta)
NIGERIA
TUNISIA
SPAIN

Sahara
Ahaggar
Tanezrouft
Plateau du Tademait
Erg Chech
El Djouf
Adrar des Iforas
Aïr (Azbine)
Haut Atlas
Moyen Atlas
Anti Atlas
Er Rif
Hauts Plateaux
Atlas Saharien
Fouta Djalon
Islas Canarias
Madeira (Port.)
Arquipélago dos Bijagós
Bight of Benin
Lake Volta

Projection: Sanson Flamsteed's Sinusoidal
West from Greenwich
East from Greenwich

1:15 000 000

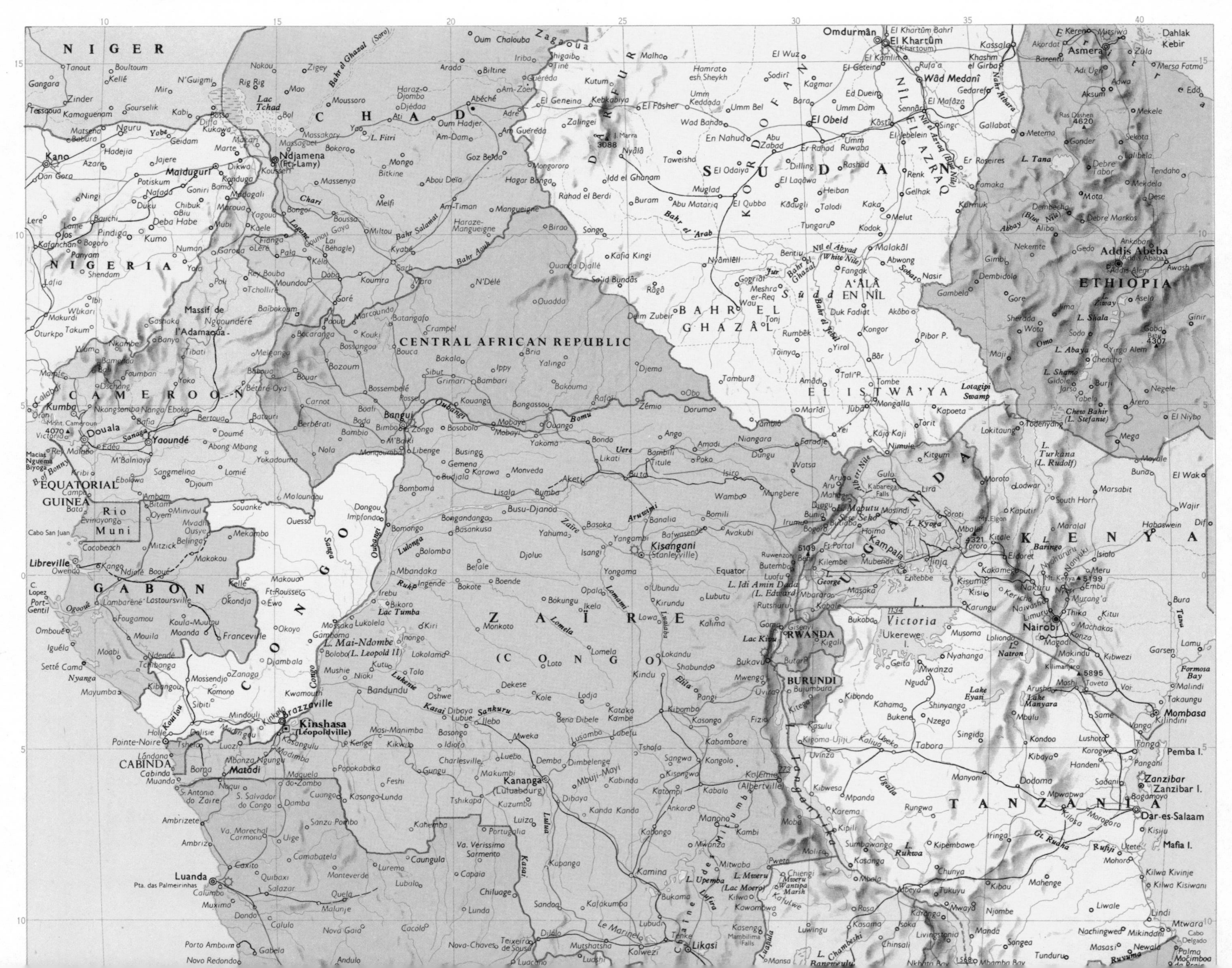
NIGER
NIGERIA
CHAD
SUDAN
ETHIOPIA
KENYA
UGANDA
TANZANIA
RWANDA
BURUNDI
CENTRAL AFRICAN REPUBLIC
CAMEROON
GABON
CONGO
ZAÏRE (CONGO)
EQUATORIAL GUINEA
Rio Muni
CABINDA
Addis Abeba
El Khartûm
Omdurmân
Nairobi
Mombasa
Dar-es-Salaam
Zanzibar
Kampala
Kinshasa (Léopoldville)
Brazzaville
Luanda
Libreville
Yaoundé
Douala
Bangui
Ndjamena (Ft.-Lamy)
Kisangani (Stanleyville)
Kananga (Luluabourg)
Likasi
Kano
Maiduguri
Asmera
Victoria
L. Tanganyika
L. Turkana (L. Rudolf)
Lac Tchad
Massif de l'Adamaoua

ATLANTIC OCEAN
INDIAN OCEAN
ANGOLA
ZAMBIA
MOZAMBIQUE
ZIMBABWE
BOTSWANA
Kalahari
SOUTH WEST AFRICA (NAMIBIA)
Damaraland
Namaland
SOUTH AFRICA
CAPE PROVINCE
TRANSVAAL
ORANJE-VRYSTAAT (O.F.S.)
NATAL
LESOTHO
SWAZILAND
TRANSKEI
Windhoek
Harare
Bulawayo
Lusaka
Pretoria
Johannesburg
Maputo (Lourenço Marques)
Bloemfontein
Kimberley
Pietermaritzburg
Durban
East London
Port Elizabeth
Cape Town (Kaapstad)
Tropic of Capricorn
Mozambique Channel
MADAGASCAR
On same scale as General Map
Antananarivo (Tananarive)
1:15 000 000
100 0 100 200 300 400 miles
100 0 100 200 300 400 500 600 km
Projection: Sanson Flamsteed's Sinusoidal
East from Greenwich
COPYRIGHT, GEORGE PHILIP & SON, LTD.

EUROPE
Leningrad
Moskva
Sverdlovsk
Omsk
Novosibirsk
Tomsk
U. S. S. R.
Barnaul
Irkutsk
Ozero Baykal
Chita
Ulan Ude
Semipalatinsk
Karaganda
L. Balkhash
Aral Sea
Alma Ata
Tashkent
Samarkand
Hovd
Ulyasutay
Ulaanbaatar
MONGOLIA
Altai
ASIA
Wulumuchi
SINKIANG-UIGUR
Lop Nor
Manchuria
Harbin
Changchun
Shenyang
Blagoveshchensk
Amur
Khabarovsk
Vladivostok
Sea of Okhotsk
Okhotsk
Sakhalin
Kamchatka
Petropavlovsk
Komandorskie Is. (U.S.S.R.)
Near I.
Kiska I.
Andreanov Is.
Aleutian Is.
Aleutian Trench
Bering Sea
Kuril Is.
Kuril Trench
10,542
La Perouse Strait
Hakodate
Sea of Japan
Sendai
JAPAN
TOKYO
Yokohama
Kyoto
Osaka
Nagoya
Shikoku
Kyūshū
Kitakyūshū
Nagasaki
Fuji-san 3776
Japan Trench
10,554
8412
Peiping
Tientsin
Tsinan
N. KOREA
KOREA
Sŏul
Pusan
Lu-ta
Tsingtao
Lanchow
Sian
Hwang Ho
CHINA
Kunlun
TIBET
Lhasa
Mt. Everest 8848
Himalaya
Chungking
Wuhan
Nanking
SHANGHAI
Hangchow
Yellow Sea
Changsha
Wenchow
Foochow
Hsiamen
East China Sea
Taipei
Taiwan (Formosa)
Ryūkyū Is.
Kunming
Kwangchow
MACAU (Port.)
HONG KONG
Hanoi
Hainan
AFGHANISTAN
Kabul
Srinagar
Lahore
PAKISTAN
Delhi
Agra
Kanpur
Varanasi
NEPAL
Brahmaputra
BANGLADESH
Calcutta
Chittagong
INDIA
Hyderabad
Madras
Bay of Bengal
BURMA
Rangoon
Mandalay
THAILAND (SIAM)
Bangkok
CAMBODIA
VIETNAM
LAOS
Phnom Penh
Ho Chi Minh City
Gulf of Siam
Andaman Is.
Mergui Arch.
Isthmus of Kra
Nicobar Is.
SRI LANKA
Colombo
C. Camau
George Town
MALAYA
Kuala Lumpur
Melaka
MALAYSIA
SINGAPORE
Sumatra
Nias
Natuna
SARAWAK
BRUNEI
Labuan
SABAH
Kinabalu 4101
South China Sea
Palawan
Mindoro
Manila
PHILIPPINES
Samar
10,497
Mindanao
Mindanao Trench
Sulu Sea
Celebes Sea
C. Engano
Borneo
Celebes
Halmahera
Moluccas
INDONESIA
Bangka
Palembang
Java Sea
Jakarta
Sunda Strait
Semarang
Surabaya
Java
Bali
Lombok
Sumbawa
Flores Sea
Flores
Sumba
Timor
Banda Sea
Buru
Ceram
Amboina
Irian Jaya
Dampier Strait
5029
7440
Aru Is.
Tanimbar Is.
Java Trench
7450
Sunda Islands
Christmas I. (Austral.)
Cocos (Keeling) Is. (Austral.)
INDIAN OCEAN
Arafura Sea
Torres Strait
Thursday I.
C. York
C. Arnhem
Darwin
G. of Carpentaria
Ashmore Is.
Wyndham
Cairns
Newcastle Waters
NORTHERN TERRITORY
Townsville
Mt. Isa
N.W. Cape
Onslow
AUSTRALIA
Great Dividing Range
Rockhampton
Alice Springs
Longreach
QUEENSLAND
Shark Bay
WESTERN AUSTRALIA
Maryborough
Oodnadatta
L. Eyre
Brisbane
Ipswich
Geraldton
SOUTH AUSTRALIA
Darling
Kalgoorlie
NEW SOUTH WALES
Perth
Fremantle
Geographe Bay
Albany
Great Australian Bight
Adelaide
Murray
Sydney
Newcastle
Katoomba
Wollongong
Canberra
Mt. Kosciusko 2230
VICTORIA
Ballarat
Melbourne
Geelong
Encounter Bay
K. George Sd.
Bass Strait
Launceston
TASMANIA
Hobart
Tasman Sea
East Australian Current
Coral Sea
Mariana Is. U.S. Trust Terr.
Mariana Trench
Guam (U.S.)
11,022
Micronesia
Yap
Palau Is.
Truk
Ponape
Caroline Islands
U.S. Trust Territory of the Pacific Islands
Melanesia
Admiralty Is.
Bismarck Arch.
New Ireland
Rabaul
New Britain
9103
PAPUA NEW GUINEA
Port Moresby
Solomon Islands (U.K.)
Guadalcanal
Honiara
Louisiade Arch. (Austral.)
Sta. Cruz I. (U.K.)
9165
New Hebrides (U.K. & Fr.)
Chesterfield Is. (Fr.)
New Caledonia (Fr.)
Noumea
Loyalty Is. (Fr.)
7570
Norfolk I. (Aust.)
Lord Howe I. (Aust.)
Lord Howe Rise
Bonin Is.
Volcano Is.
Marcus I.
Marcus Necker Ridge
Wake I. (U.S.)
South Honshu Ridge
Emperor Seamount Chain
Midway Is. (U.S.)
Lisianski I. (U.S.)
Hawaiian Ridge
6603
7188
KURO SIWO
OYA SIWO
Marshall Is. U.S. Trust Terr.
Bikini Atoll
Eniwetok Atoll
Jaluit
Makin
Gilbert Is. (U.K.)
Nauru Is.
Nauru
Ocean I. (U.K.)
Baker I. (U.S.)
Canton I.
TUVALU (Ellice Is.)
Funafuti
Tokelau Is.
Rotuma
Wallis Arch.
Futuna (Fr.)
SAMOA
Apia
FIJI
Vanua Levu
Viti Levu
Suva
Tonga Trench
Niue (Savage I.) (N.Z.)
TONGA Friendly Is.
10,822
Kermadec Is. (N.Z.)
Kermadec Trench
10,047
NORTH EQUATORIAL CURRENT
EQUATORIAL COUNTER CURRENT
SOUTH EQUATORIAL
International Date Line
PACIFIC OCEAN
Auckland
Hamilton
NEW ZEALAND
Palmerston N.
Wellington
Cook Strait
Nelson
Mt. Cook 3764
Christchurch
Oamaru
Dunedin
Invercargill
Stewart I.
Chatham Is. (N.Z.)
Bounty Is. (N.Z.)
Antipodes Is. (N.Z.)
Auckland Is. (N.Z.)
Macquarie Is. (Austral.)
Campbell I. (N.Z.)
Amsterdam I. (Fr.)
St. Paul I. (Fr.)
Mid-Oceanic Ridge
South-East Indian Ridge
Mid-Indian Ridge
Indian Rise
Indian-Antarctic Ridge
Crozet Is. (Fr.)
Kerguelen (Fr.)
Heard Is. (Aust.)
Cape Town - Fremantle 5615
Cape Town - Melbourne 5814
Cape Town - Hobart 5838
Al 'Adan - Melbourne 6445
Colombo - Fremantle 3120
Singapore - Brisbane 3772
Yokohama - Vancouver 4280
S. - A. 1274
W. 1293
F. - A. 1353
Projection: Mollweide's Homolographic
East from Greenwich
5615 Principal Shipping Routes
(Distances in Nautical Miles)

ALASKA
Bristol Bay
Gulf of Alaska
Juneau
Sitka
Prince of Wales I.
Prince Rupert
Kitimat
Queen Charlotte Is.
Unimak
L. Athabaska
Churchill
Hudson Bay
Dawson Creek
Lynn Lake
Belcher Is.
CANADA
Edmonton
Prince Albert
Saskatoon
L. Winnipeg
James Bay
Schefferville
Hamilton Inlet
Labrador
Strait of Belle Isle
GREENLAND
C. Farewell
BRITISH ISLES
NORTH AMERICA
Rocky Mountains
Vancouver
Vancouver I.
Victoria
Calgary
Medicine Hat
Regina
Winnipeg
L. Superior
Duluth
Sault Ste Marie
Montréal
Québec
G. of St. Lawrence
Anticosti
Newfoundland
Fredericton
Pr. Edward I.
C. Breton I.
C. Race
Saint John
Sable I.
C. Sable
Seattle
Tacoma
Portland
Spokane
Helena
Bismarck
Missouri
Butte
Boise
Snake
St. Paul
Minneapolis
Milwaukee
Michigan
Huron
Ottawa
Toronto
L. Ontario
Erie
Buffalo
Boston
C. Blanco
Mendocino Seascarp
C. Mendocino
Cheyenne
Des Moines
CHICAGO
Detroit
Pittsburgh
NEW YORK
Philadelphia
Baltimore
Washington
Richmond
Norfolk
Sacramento
Oakland
San Francisco
Salt Lake City
Denver
Kansas
St. Louis
Indianapolis
Cincinnati
Colorado
UNITED STATES
Memphis
Appalachian Mts.
C. Hatteras
4418
Oklahoma
Little Rock
Mississippi
Santa Fé
Los Angeles
San Diego
Dallas
Atlanta
Savannah
Jacksonville
El Paso
Ciudad Juárez
Austin
Houston
Galveston
San Antonio
New Orleans
Mobile
Tampa
Miami
Bermuda (U.K.)
ATLANTIC
OCEAN
NORTH
New York - Southampton 3091
New York - Recife 3678
N.Y. - C. 1972
Panama - Liverpool 4530
6741
2419
2091
822
Murray Seascarp
CALIFORNIAN CURRENT
Guadalupe
6225
Pto. Eugenia
Gulf of California
Sierra Madre
MEXICO
Torreón
Monterrey
Gulf of Mexico
Florida Strait
BAHAMAS
Tropic of Cancer
Laysan I. (U.S.)
Hawaiian Is. (U.S.A.)
Oahu
Honolulu
Hawaii
C. S. Lucas
Tampico
San Luis Potosí
Aguascalientes
Guadalajara
México
Puebla
5700
Veracruz
Mérida
Yucatan Channel
La Habana
CUBA
West Indies
Hispaniola
9200
DOM. REP.
HAITI
PUERTO RICO
St. Thomas (U.S.)
Virgin Is.
Leeward Is.
7680
JAMAICA
Kingston
Santo Domingo
Guadeloupe (Fr.)
Martinique (Fr.)
BARBADOS
Clarion Fracture Zone
Revilla Gigedo Is. (Mexico)
Johnston I. (U.S.)
PACIFIC
CURRENT
3277
Acapulco
BELIZE
HONDURAS
Caribbean Sea
GUATEMALA
Guatemala
Tegucigalpa
SALVADOR
Salvador
NICARAGUA
Managua
4711
S.E. MONSOON DRIFT
CENTRAL AMERICA
COSTA RICA
San José
Barranquilla
Curaçao (Ne.)
Windward Is.
TRINIDAD & TOBAGO
Maracaibo
Caracas
Orinoco
VENEZUELA
Clipperton Fracture Zone
Clipperton I. (Fr.)
Colón
Panamá
PANAMA
Canal
3666
Christmas Island Ridge
CURRENT
Palmyra Is. (U.S.)
Washington I. (U.K.)
Fanning I. (U.K.)
Christmas I.
OCEAN
Cocos I.
Medellín
Bogotá
Cali
COLOMBIA
835
Equator
Jarvis I. (U.S.)
C. S. Francisco
Quito
ECUADOR
Chimborazo 6267
Cuenca
Iquitos
Guayaquil
Galápagos (Ecuador)
Manaus
Amazon
Canterbury I.
Phœnix Is. (U.K. & U.S.)
Malden I.
Starbuck I.
EQUATORIAL CURRENT
Tahiti - Panamá 4570
C. Pariñas
BRAZIL
SOUTH
Lobos I.
Chiclayo
Trujillo
706
Marquesas Is. (Fr.)
Tongareva
Penrhyn Is.
Manihiki
Danger Is.
Suwarrow Is. (Suvorov)
Tutuila (U.S.)
Caroline I.
Vostok I.
Flint I.
PERU
6369
Lima
Callao
AMERICA
PERUVIAN CURRENT
Cuzco
L. Titicaca
Illampu & Ancohuma 6550
La Paz
BOLIVIA
Arequipa
Arica
6866
Peru-Chile Trench
Cook Islands
Society Is. (Fr.)
Leeward Is.
Windward Is.
Tahiti (Fr.)
Tuamotu Archipelago (Fr.)
Tuamotu Ridge
Auckland - Panamá 6510
East Pacific Ridge
Southeast Pacific Basin
Austral Seamount Chain
Hervey Is.
Rarotonga
Tropic of Capricorn
Iquique
Chile
8050
Antofagasta
PARAGUAY
Asunción
Salta
Tucumán
Corrientes
Pto. Alegre
Tubuai Is. (Austral Is.) (Fr.)
Rapa Iti (Fr.)
Pitcairn I. (U.K.)
Ducie I. (U.K.)
Sala-y-Gomez (Chile)
Easter Is. (Chile)
San Félix (Chile)
San Ambrosio (Chile)
ANDES
Córdoba
Santa Fé
Paysandú
Rosario
URUGUAY
Montevideo
Arch. de Juan Fernández (Chile)
Alejandro Selkirk
Robinson Crusoe
Aconcagua 6960
Valparaíso
Santiago
Buenos Aires
La Plata
Río de la Plata
Concepción
ARGENTINA
Mar del Plata
Neuquen
Pacific-Antarctic Ridge
Chile Rise
West Wind Drift
SOUTH
G. of San Matias
ATLANTIC
Chonos Arch.
P.A. - Valparaiso 1414
1355
1295
Buenos Aires - Montevideo
Patagonia
G. of San Jorge
P. Deseado
Argentine Basin
6212
OCEAN
c Basin
Pacific-Antarctic Basin
G. of Penas
Wellington I.
CAPE HORN CURRENT
Sta. Cruz
Punta Arenas
P.A.
Falkland Is. (U.K.)
Stanley
Str. of Magellan
Tierra del Fuego
C. Horn
South Georgia
160
140
120
100
West from Greenwich
80
60
40
20
60
50
40
30
20
10
0
10
20
30
40
50

TIMOR SEA
INDIAN OCEAN
WESTERN AUSTRALIA
NORTHERN TERRITORY
SOUTH AUST
Kimberley
Canning Basin
Great Sandy Desert
Gibson Desert
Great Victoria Desert
Tanami Desert
Eucla Basin
Nullarbor Plain
Great Australian Bight
Perth
Darwin
Alice Springs
Kalgoorlie
Geraldton
Broome
Ayers Rock
Macdonnell Ras.
Musgrave Ranges
Projection: Bonne
East from Greenwich
Boundaries of the artesian basins

1:12 000 000
miles
km
AUSTRALASIA
PHYSICAL
1:80 000 000
AUSTRALIA
PACIFIC OCEAN
SOUTHERN OCEAN
INDIAN OCEAN
New Guinea
New Britain
New Ireland
Bismarck Arch.
Solomon Is.
Guadalcanal
Celebes
Ceram
Banda Sea
Timor
Sumbawa
Flores
Java Trench
Timor Sea
Arafura Sea
Thursday I.
Torres Strait
Arnhem Land
Gulf of Carpentaria
C. York Pen.
Louisiade Arch.
Coral Sea
Santa Cruz Is.
New Hebrides
Îles Chesterfield (Fr.)
Nouvelle Calédonie
Nouméa
Îles Loyauté
Fiji Is.
Viti Levu
Suva
Samoa Is.
Tutuila
Tropic of Capricorn
Great Divide
Darling
Murray
Australian Alps
Bass Strait
TASMANIA
South Australian Basin
Norfolk I.
Lord Howe I.
Lord Howe Ridge
Kermadec Is.
Tasman Sea
NEW ZEALAND
Chatham Is.
ft
m
12000
6000
600
200
2000
4000
QUEENSLAND
NEW SOUTH WALES
VICTORIA
CORAL SEA ISLANDS TERRITORY
PACIFIC OCEAN
Tasman Sea
Gulf of Carpentaria
Great Barrier Reef
Great Dividing Range
Great Artesian Basin
Cape York Peninsula
Thursday I.
Banks I.
Prince of Wales I.
C. York
Newcastle B.
Endeavour Str.
Wessel Is.
Melville B.
C. Arnhem & Gove Pen.
Nhulunbuy
P. Bradshaw
Caledon B.
C. Grey
Blue Mud B.
Alyangula
Groote Eylandt
C. Beatrice
Sir Edward Pellew Group
Vanderlin I.
Borroloola
Mornington I.
C. van Diemen
Wellesley Is.
Bentinck I.
P. Musgrave
Shelburne B.
C. Grenville
Temple B.
C. Weymouth
C. Direction
Duifken Pt.
Albatross B.
Weipa
Wenlock
McIlwraith Ra.
Archer
C. Keer-Weer
Holroyd
Coen
Princess Charlotte B.
Bathurst B.
C. Melville
Osprey Rf.
Coleman
Normanby
C. Flattery
C. Bedford
Laura
Cooktown
Mitchell
C. Tribulation
Trinity Bay
Mossman
C. Grafton
Chillagoe
Mareeba
Cairns
Atherton
Bartle Frere
1611
Innisfail
Gilbert
Normanton
Burketown
Georgetown
Croydon
Newcastle Ra.
Ravenshoe
Einasleigh
Forsayth
Gregory Ra.
Norman
Seaview Ra.
Hinchinbrook I.
Ingham
Palm Is.
Halifax B.
Townsville
C. Cleveland
C. Bowling Green
Home Hill
Ayr
Bowen
Proserpine
Collinsville
Whitsunday I.
Cumberland Is.
Leichhardt
Dobbyn
Camooweal
Kajabbi
Flinders
Mount Isa
Mary Kathleen
Cloncurry
Julia Cr.
Richmond
Pentland
Charters Towers
Hughenden
Mt. Dalrymple
1277
Netherdale
Repulse B.
Mackay
Sarina
C. Palmerston
Broad Sd.
Broadsound Ra.
Denham Ra.
Isaac
Selwyn Range
Selwyn
Duchess
Urandangi
Dajarra
Georgina
LANDSBOROUGH
FLINDERS
BARKLY
Winton
Muttaburra
Boulia
Diamantina
Belyando
Blair Athol
Clermont
Peak Ra.
Drummond Ra.
Aramac
Longreach
Ilfracombe
Barcaldine
Alpha
CAPRICORN
Emerald
Nogoa
Mackenzie
C. Townshend
Townshend I.
Yeppoon
Rockhampton
Keppel B.
Thomson
Bedourie
Eyre Cr.
L. Machattie
Jundah
Barcoo
Blackall
Yaraka
Warrego Ra.
Springsure
Mt. Morgan
C. Capricorn
Curtis I.
Gladstone
P. Curtis
Biloela
Dawson
Bustard Head
Windorah
Mt. Acland
975
Expedition Ra.
Monto
Burnett
Bundaberg
Hervey Bay
Sandy C.
Fraser I.
Birdsville
Adavale
Augathella
Theodore
Childers
Injune
Taroom
Gayndah
Wandoan
Maryborough
Gympie
L. Yamma Yamma
Charleville
Quilpie
Bulloo
Grey Range
Mitchell
Roma
Miles
WARREGO
Condamine
Murgon
Wondai
Kingaroy
Nanango
Nambour
Bribie I.
Moreton B.
Cooper Creek
Wyandra
Maranoa
Balonne
Dalby
Moreton I.
Thargomindah
Cunnamulla
BALONNE
St. George
Moonie
Toowoomba
Ipswich
Brisbane
N. Stradbroke I.
Southport
Warrego
Dirranbandi
Goondiwindi
Warwick
Stanthorpe
Murwillumbah
Mt. Barney
1356
Sutherland Pt.
C. Byron
Mungindi
Macintyre
Lismore
Ballina
Casino
Gwydir
Moree
Warialda
Inverell
Glen Innes
Clarence
Grafton
Maclean
New England Range
The Round Mountain
1615
Coffs Harbour
Armidale
Tamworth
Liverpool Plains
Liverpool Ra.
Macleay
Kempsey
Port Macquarie
Taree
1585
Barrington Tops
Muswellbrook
Singleton
Maitland
Cessnock
Sugarloaf Pt.
P. Stephens
5944
Newcastle
Hawkesbury R.
SYDNEY & Port Jackson
Wollongong
Shellharbour
Nowra
Jervis B.
Batemans B.
Twofold B.
Disaster B.
Howe
Mallacoota Inlet
C. Everard
Lihou Reef & Cays
Mellish Reef
Marion Reef
Îles Avon
Îles Chesterfield
Frederick Reef
Kenn Reef
Swain Rfs.
Saumarez Rf.
Bellona Rfs.
Wreck Reef
Bird I.
Cato I.
Tropic of Capricorn
Tibooburra
Paroo
L. Callabonna
L. Frome
Paroo Chan.
Bourke
Walgett
Barwon
Bogan
Narrabri
Coonamble
Gunnedah
Castlereagh
Macquarie
Cobar
Nyngan
Gilgandra
Wilcannia
Darling
Broken Hill
Barrier Ra.
Radium Hill
Menindee
Narromine
Dubbo
Wellington
Mudgee
Orange
Bathurst
Lithgow
Katoomba
Penrith
Ivanhoe
Roto
Condobolin
Parkes
L. Cargelligo
Forbes
Cowal
Hillston
Lachlan
Cowra
Murray River
Wentworth
Mildura
Renmark
Loxton
Murrumbidgee Irrigation Area
Griffith
Hay
Leeton
Narrandera
Cootamundra
Young
Yass
Canberra
Goulburn
Bowral
Balranald
Murrumbidgee
STURT
Junee
Wagga Wagga
Tumut
Queanbeyan
Riverina
Deniliquin
Swan Hill
Kerang
Pinnaroo
Ouyen
Wimmera
Echuca
Shepparton
Wangaratta
Albury
L. Hume
Mt. Bogong
1986
Mt. Kosciusko
2230
Cooma
Bega
Bombala
Bendigo
Maryborough
Castlemaine
Stawell
Horsham
Bordertown
Ararat
Ballarat
Hamilton
Geelong
MELBOURNE
Australian Alps
Gippsland
Bairnsdale
Orbost
Snowy
Yallourn
Moe
Sale
Morwell
Traralgon
Ninety Mile Beach
Corner Inlet
Wonthaggi
Phillip I.
Port Phillip B.
C. Otway
Colac
Warrnambool
Port Fairy
Portland
C. Bridgewater
Discovery B.
C. Northumberland
Mt. Gambier
Millicent
Penola
Naracoorte
Kingston S.E.
Coorong
The Coorong
Encounter B.
Victor Harbor
Backstairs Pass.
Kangaroo I.
Alexandrina
Murray Bridge
Mt. Lofty Ra.
Adelaide
Gawler
Elizabeth
G. St. Vincent
Yorke Penin.
Spencer Gulf
Wallaroo
Kadina
Burra
Jamestown
P. Pirie
Whyalla
Peterborough
Port Augusta
Quorn
Hawker
St. Mary's Pk.
1165
Flinders Ranges
L. Torrens
Leigh Creek
Copley
Woomera
Pimba
L. Macfarlane
L. Eyre (North)
L. Eyre (South)
L. Gregory
L. Blanche
Strzelecki Cr.
Warburton
Macumba
AUSTRALIA
Hay
Mount Isa
Avon Downs
Austral Downs
Tableland
Simpson Desert
Australian Alps
MELBOURNE
Ballarat
Geelong
Castlemaine
Gippsland
Bairnsdale
Orbost
Snowy
Moe
Sale
Yallourn
Morwell
Traralgon
Ninety Mile Beach
Corner Inlet
Wilsons Promontory
Bass Strait
King I.
Flinders I.
Furneaux Group
Cape Barren I.
C. Portland
Clarke I.
Hunter I.
C. Grim
Devonport
Burnie
Ulverstone
Beaconsfield
Scottsdale
Launceston
Ben Lomond
1573
Sandy C.
Zeehan
1617
Mt. Ossa
St. Marys
Strahan
Queenstown
Great L.
Freycinet Penin.
Macquarie Harb.
TASMANIA
New Norfolk
Low Rocky Pt.
Hobart
Tasman Penin.
P. Arthur
Storm B.
P. Davey
Huonville
Bruny I.
S.E. Cape
on same scale
COPYRIGHT, GEORGE PHILIP & SON, LTD.

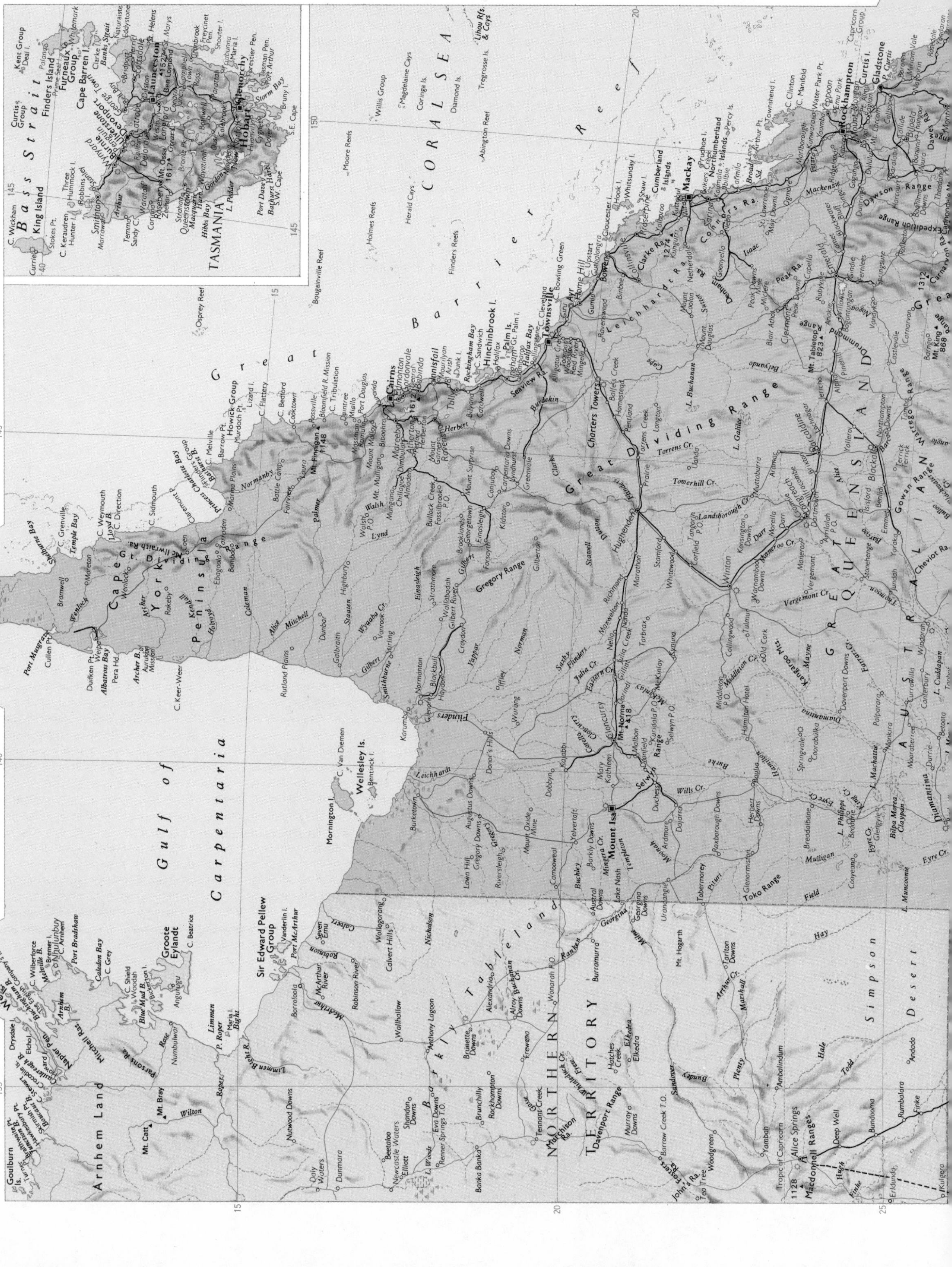

Bass Strait

TASMANIA

CORAL SEA

Great Barrier Reef

Gulf of Carpentaria

Cape York Peninsula

Great Dividing Range

QUEENSLAND

GREAT AUSTRALIAN

NORTHERN TERRITORY

Barkly Tableland

Arnhem Land

Simpson Desert

1:8 000 000

50 0 50 100 150 200 miles
50 0 100 200 300 km

Projection: Bonne

East from Greenwich

INDONESIA
TIMOR SEA
INDIAN OCEAN
NORTHERN TERRITORY
Timor
Sumba
Sumbawa
Sawa
Roti
Melville I.
Bathurst I.
Darwin
Joseph Bonaparte Gulf
Bonaparte Archipelago
King Leopold Ranges
Great Sandy Desert
Gibson Desert
Tanami Desert
Hamersley Range
Eighty Mile Beach
Port Hedland
Broome
Derby
Wyndham
Kununurra
Dampier
Onslow
Exmouth
Lake Mackay
Lake Disappointment
Rowley Shoals
Tropic of Capricorn
Mt. Ord 1007
Mt. Hann 776
Mt. Bruce 1226
Mt. Newman 1128
Mt. Zeil 1510
Mt. Liebig 1524
Mt. Singleton 808
Mt. Greenwood 152
Macdonnell Ranges
Durack Range
Fitzroy
Ord
Ashburton
Gregory Ra.
Chichester Ra.
Ophthalmia Ra.
Stuart Bluff Ra.
Reynolds Ra.
10
15
20
120
125
130

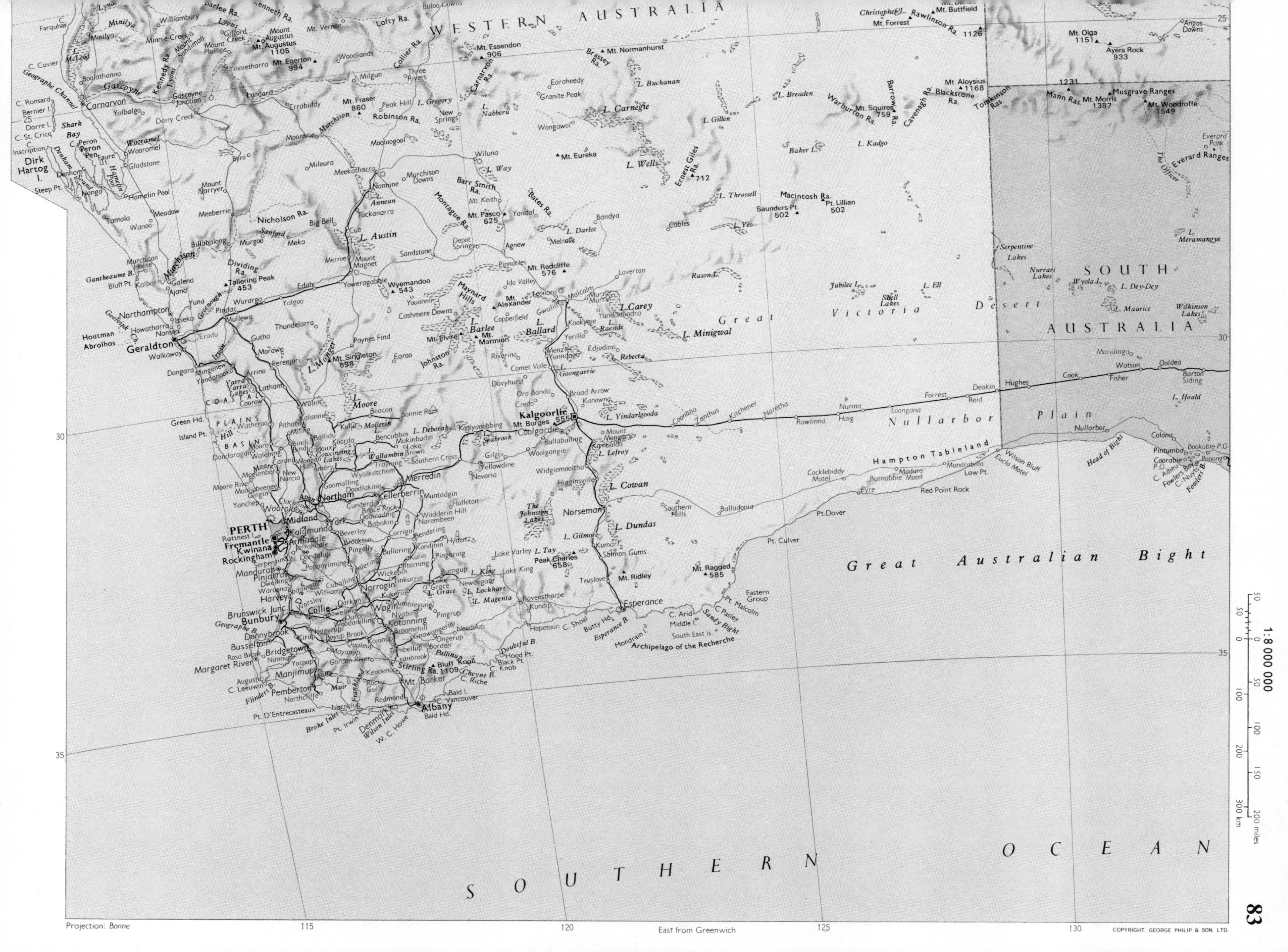
1:8 000 000
50 0 50 100 150 200 miles
50 0 100 200 300 km
WESTERN AUSTRALIA
SOUTH AUSTRALIA
SOUTHERN OCEAN
Great Australian Bight
Nullarbor Plain
Great Victoria Desert
Hampton Tableland
PERTH
Fremantle
Kwinana
Rockingham
Mandurah
Bunbury
Busselton
Margaret River
Albany
Geraldton
Carnarvon
Kalgoorlie
Coolgardie
Esperance
Norseman
Northam
Merredin
Shark Bay
Dirk Hartog I.
Houtman Abrolhos
Archipelago of the Recherche
Ayers Rock 933
Mt. Olga 1151
Musgrave Ranges
Mt. Woodroffe 1549
Everard Ranges
Head of Bight
Eucla Motel
Cook
Hughes
Deakin
Ooldea
C. Leeuwin
Pt. D'Entrecasteaux
Projection: Bonne
East from Greenwich
COPYRIGHT, GEORGE PHILIP & SON. LTD.

1: 4 500 000

20 0 20 40 60 80 100 miles

20 0 40 80 120 160 km

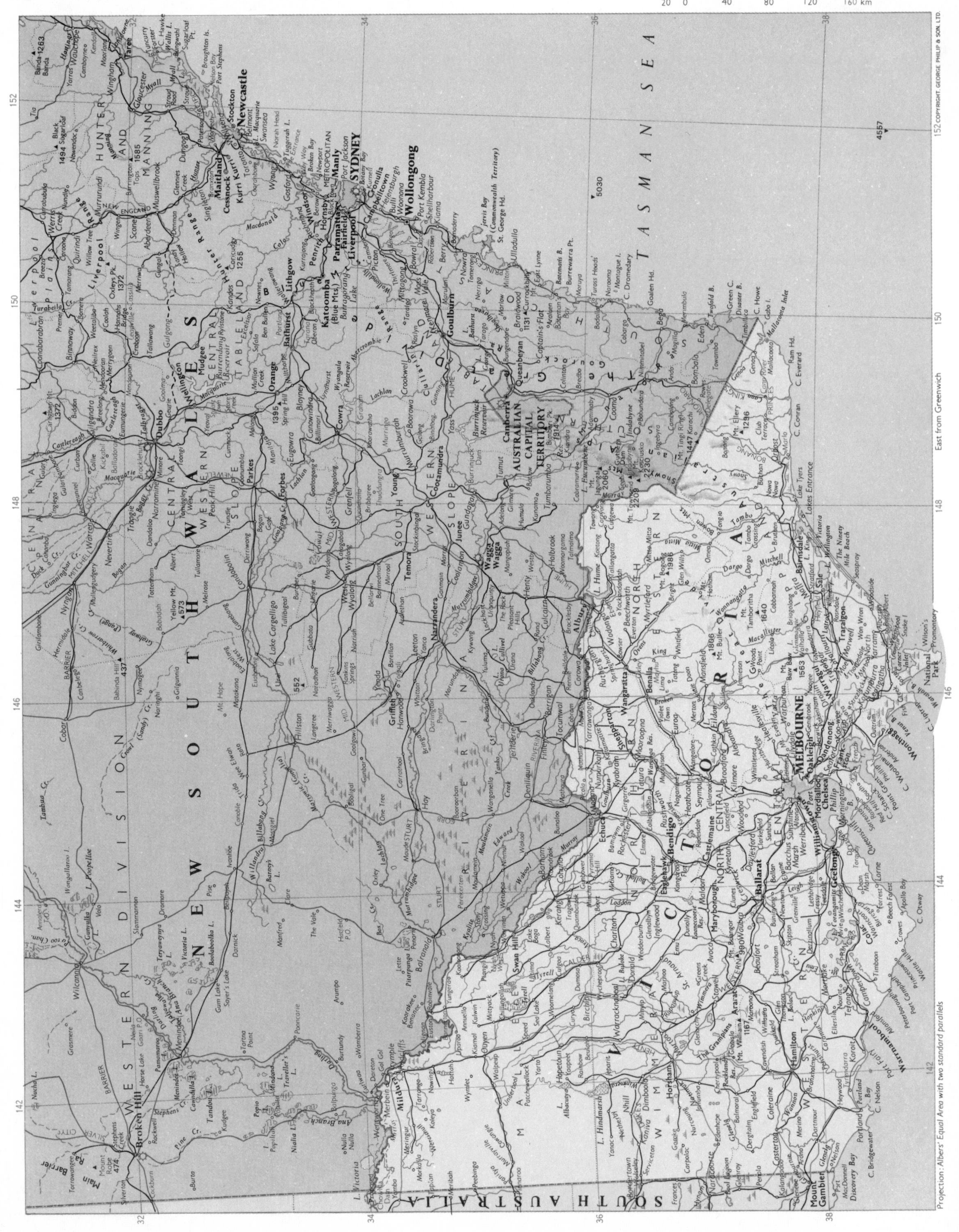
NEW SOUTH WALES
VICTORIA
TASMAN SEA
SOUTH AUSTRALIA
AUSTRALIAN CAPITAL TERRITORY
WESTERN DIVISION
SYDNEY
MELBOURNE
Canberra
Newcastle
Wollongong
Broken Hill
Wilcannia
Mildura
Albury
Wagga Wagga
Ballarat
Geelong
Bendigo
Dubbo
Orange
Bathurst
Goulburn
Warrnambool
Hamilton
Horsham
Swan Hill
Echuca
East from Greenwich
Projection: Albers' Equal Area with two standard parallels
COPYRIGHT. GEORGE PHILIP & SON, LTD.

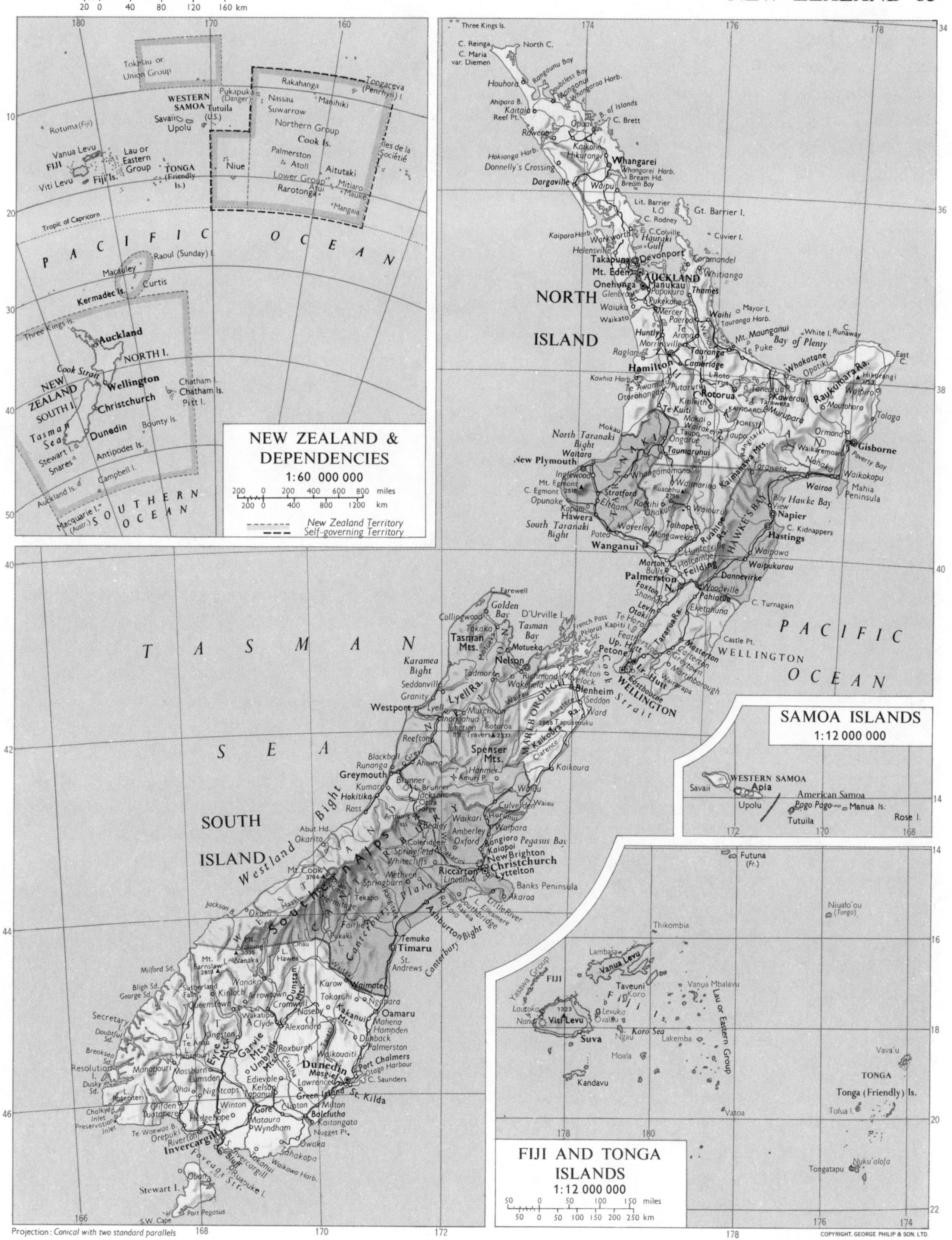
1:6 000 000
20 0 20 40 60 80 100 miles
20 0 40 80 120 160 km
NEW ZEALAND & DEPENDENCIES
1:60 000 000
200 0 200 400 600 800 miles
200 0 400 800 1200 km
New Zealand Territory
Self-governing Territory
Tokelau or Union Group
WESTERN SAMOA
Savaii
Upolu
Tutuila (U.S.)
Pukapuka (Danger)
Rakahanga
Tongareva (Penrhyn) I.
Nassau
Manihiki
Suwarrow
Northern Group
Cook Is.
Îles de la Société
Palmerston Atoll
Niue
Aitutaki
Lower Group
Rarotonga
Mangaia
Rotuma (Fiji)
Vanua Levu
FIJI
Viti Levu
Fiji Is.
Lau or Eastern Group
TONGA (Friendly Is.)
Tropic of Capricorn
PACIFIC OCEAN
Raoul (Sunday) I.
Macauley
Curtis
Kermadec Is.
Three Kings Is.
Auckland
NORTH I.
Cook Strait
NEW ZEALAND
Wellington
SOUTH I.
Christchurch
Chatham I.
Chatham Is.
Pitt I.
Tasman Sea
Dunedin
Bounty Is.
Stewart I.
Snares
Antipodes Is.
Campbell I.
Auckland Is.
Macquarie I. (Austr.)
SOUTHERN OCEAN
NORTH ISLAND
Three Kings Is.
C. Reinga
C. Maria var. Diemen
North C.
Houhora
Kaitaia
Whangarei
Dargaville
Gt. Barrier I.
Takapuna
Devonport
AUCKLAND
Manukau
Onehunga
Thames
Hamilton
Tauranga
Bay of Plenty
Whakatane
Rotorua
Te Kuiti
Taumarunui
Gisborne
North Taranaki Bight
New Plymouth
Mt. Egmont 2518
C. Egmont
Stratford
Hawera
South Taranaki Bight
Wanganui
Napier
Hastings
HAWKE'S BAY
Bay Hawke Bay
Mahia Peninsula
C. Kidnappers
Palmerston N.
Dannevirke
C. Turnagain
Masterton
Petone
WELLINGTON
Cook Strait
PACIFIC OCEAN
TASMAN SEA
SOUTH ISLAND
C. Farewell
Golden Bay
D'Urville I.
Tasman Bay
Tasman Mts.
Nelson
Motueka
Blenheim
Westport
Greymouth
Hokitika
Kaikoura
Spenser Mts.
Westland Bight
Southern Alps
Mt. Cook 3764
Christchurch
Lyttelton
Banks Peninsula
Canterbury Plains
Canterbury Bight
Ashburton
Timaru
Oamaru
Dunedin
Port Chalmers
Invercargill
Bluff
Foveaux Str.
Stewart I.
S.W. Cape
Milford Sd.
Queenstown
L. Wakatipu
L. Te Anau
L. Manapouri
Resolution I.
SAMOA ISLANDS
1:12 000 000
WESTERN SAMOA
Savaii
Apia
Upolu
American Samoa
Pago Pago
Tutuila
Manua Is.
Rose I.
Futuna (Fr.)
Niuafo'ou (Tonga)
Thikombia
Vanua Levu
Taveuni
FIJI
Yasawa Group
Fiji Is.
Lautoka
Nandi
Viti Levu 1323
Levuka
Ovalau
Suva
Koro Sea
Lakemba
Lau or Eastern Group
Kandavu
Vatoa
Vava'u
TONGA
Tonga (Friendly) Is.
Tofua I.
Nuku'alofa
Tongatapu
FIJI AND TONGA ISLANDS
1:12 000 000
50 0 50 100 150 miles
50 0 50 100 150 200 250 km
Projection: Conical with two standard parallels
COPYRIGHT, GEORGE PHILIP & SON, LTD.

ARCTIC OCEAN
ATLANTIC OCEAN
PACIFIC
Greenland
Iceland
Greenland Sea
Denmark Strait
Davis Strait
Baffin Bay
Baffin Island
Ellesmere I.
Devon I.
Axel Heiberg
Sverdrup Land
Queen Elizabeth Islands
Melville I.
Prince of Wales I.
Victoria I.
Banks I.
Beaufort Sea
Hudson Bay
James Bay
Hudson Strait
Ungava Peninsula
Southampton I.
Melville Pen.
Foxe Basin
Foxe Channel
Boothia Pen.
Gulf of Boothia
Cumberland Sound
Frobisher Bay
Labrador
Newfoundland
Gulf of St. Lawrence
Nova Scotia
Bay of Fundy
Laurentian Plateau
Appalachian Mts.
Allegheny Mts.
Blue Ridge
Cumberland Plateau
Ozark Plateau
Chesapeake Bay
New York
Philadelphia
Washington
Montreal
Quebec
Ottawa
Toronto
Hamilton
Detroit
Chicago
St. Louis
Memphis
Atlanta
Minneapolis
Kansas City
Dallas
Denver
Winnipeg
Regina
Edmonton
Calgary
Vancouver
Seattle
Portland
San Francisco
Los Angeles
L. Michigan
L. Superior
Lake Winnipeg
Great Slave L.
Great Bear L.
Mississippi
Missouri
Great Plains
Llano Estacado
Rocky Mountains
Wasatch Mountains
Colorado Plateau
Great Basin
Sierra Nevada
Cascade Range
Coast Mountains
Selkirk Mts.
Mackenzie Mts.
Brooks Range
Alaska Range
Alaska Pen.
Gulf of Alaska
Alexander Archipelago
Queen Charlotte Islands
Queen Charlotte Sound
Juan de Fuca Strait
Vancouver I.
Bering Strait
Bering Sea
Aleutian Islands
Wrangel I.
St. Lawrence I.
Nunivak I.
Kodiak I.
Asia
Mendocino Seascarp
Murray Seascarp
Tropic of Cancer
Bermuda
C. Barrow
C. Hatteras
Mt. McKinley 6194
Mt. Logan 6050
Mt. Elbert 4399
Blanca Pk. 4364
Mt. Robson 3954
Mt. Rainier 4392
Death Valley
Yukon
Mackenzie
Fraser
Columbia
Snake
Sacramento
Peace
Athabasca
Churchill
Nelson
N. Saskatchewan
S. Saskatchewan
Hudson
Ohio
Red
Arkansas
Gila
Finlay
Back
Dubawnt
Chesterfield Inlet
Lower
50
40
30
20
60
70
80
100
120
140

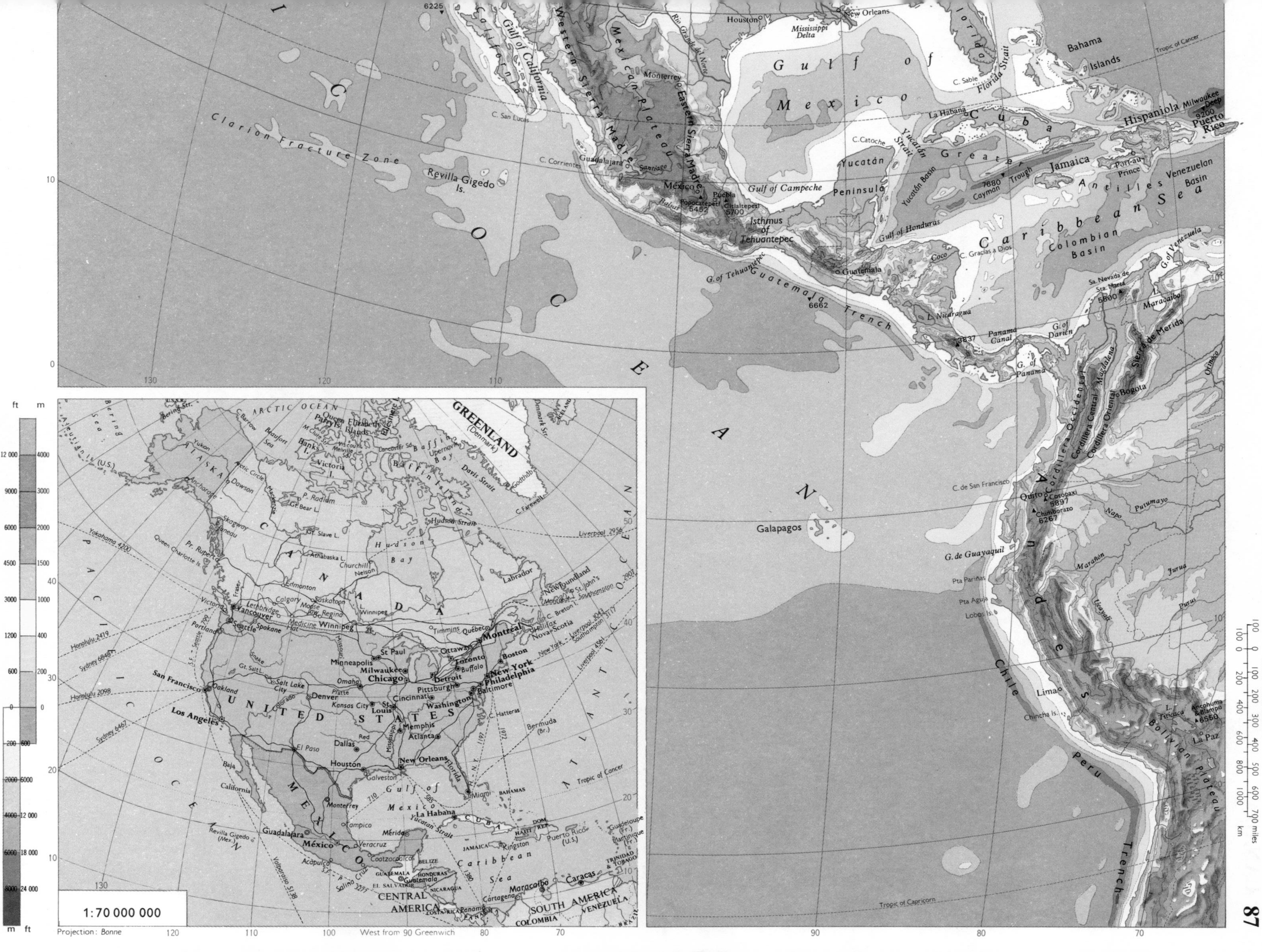
Gulf of Mexico
Mississippi Delta
New Orleans
Houston
Florida
Florida Strait
C. Sable
Bahama Islands
Tropic of Cancer
Cuba
La Habana
Jamaica
Hispaniola
Puerto Rico
Milwaukee Deep
9200
Port-au-Prince
Venezuelan Basin
Caribbean Sea
Greater Antilles
Colombian Basin
Cayman Trough
7680
Yucatán Strait
Yucatán Basin
Yucatán Peninsula
C. Catoche
Gulf of Campeche
Gulf of Honduras
Coco
C. Gracias a Dios
Isthmus of Tehuantepec
G. of Tehuantepec
Guatemala
Guatemala Trench
6662
L. Nicaragua
3837
Panama Canal
G. of Panamá
G. of Darién
Sa. Nevada de Sta. Marta
5800
G. of Venezuela
Maracaibo
Sierra de Mérida
Cordillera Oriental
Cordillera Central
Cordillera Occidental
Magdalena
Bogotá
Orinoco
C. de San Francisco
Quito
Cotopaxi
5897
Chimborazo
6267
Putumayo
Napo
Marañón
Juruá
Purus
Ucayali
Andes
G. de Guayaquil
Pta Pariñas
Pta Aguja
Lobos Is.
Lima
Chincha Is.
Chile Peru Trench
L. Titicaca
Ancohuma
6550
La Paz
Bolivian Plateau
Tropic of Capricorn
Galapagos
Pacific Ocean
Mexican Plateau
Eastern Sierra Madre
Western Sierra Madre
Rio Grande del Norte
Monterrey
México
Puebla
Popocatepetl
5452
Citlaltepetl
5700
Balsas
Santiago
Guadalajara
C. Corrientes
Gulf of California
California
C. San Lucas
6225
Revilla Gigedo Is.
Clarion Fracture Zone
1:30 000 000
100 0 100 200 300 400 500 600 700 miles
100 0 200 400 600 800 1000 km
ARCTIC OCEAN
Bering Sea
Bering Str.
Aleutian Is. (U.S.)
ALASKA
Yukon
Barrow
Beaufort Sea
Anchorage
Dawson
Arctic Circle
Mackenzie
Skagway
Juneau
Queen Elizabeth Islands
Parry Is.
Banks I.
Victoria I.
Baffin Island
Baffin Bay
Davis Strait
GREENLAND (Denmark)
Godthåb
C. Farewell
Denmark Str.
Hudson Strait
Hudson Bay
Churchill
Nelson
Gt. Bear L.
Gt. Slave L.
Athabaska L.
Labrador
Newfoundland
St. John's
CANADA
Edmonton
Calgary
Saskatoon
Regina
Winnipeg
Lethbridge
Vancouver
Victoria
Seattle
Spokane
Portland
Pr. Rupert
Queen Charlotte Is.
Yokohama 4200
Liverpool 2956
Timmins
Québec
Montreal
Ottawa
Toronto
Buffalo
Detroit
Boston
New York
Philadelphia
Baltimore
Washington
Pittsburgh
Cincinnati
Halifax
Nova Scotia
C. Breton I.
C. Hatteras
Bermuda (Br.)
St Paul
Minneapolis
Milwaukee
Chicago
Omaha
Denver
Kansas City
St Louis
Memphis
Atlanta
Salt Lake City
Gt. Salt L.
San Francisco
Oakland
Los Angeles
Honolulu 2419
Honolulu 2098
Sydney 6848
Sydney 6467
UNITED STATES
El Paso
Dallas
Houston
Galveston
New Orleans
Florida
Miami
BAHAMAS
Gulf of Mexico
MEXICO
Monterrey
Tampico
Mérida
Guadalajara
México
Veracruz
Acapulco
Coatzacoalcos
Baja California
Revilla Gigedo (Mex.)
Valparaiso 5138
La Habana
Yucatán Strait
CUBA
JAMAICA
Kingston
HAITI
DOM. REP.
Puerto Rico (U.S.)
Guadeloupe (Fr.)
Martinique (Fr.)
TRINIDAD & TOBAGO
Caribbean Sea
BELIZE
GUATEMALA
HONDURAS
EL SALVADOR
NICARAGUA
COSTA RICA
Panamá
CENTRAL AMERICA
Cartagena
Maracaibo
Caracas
SOUTH AMERICA
VENEZUELA
COLOMBIA
Tropic of Cancer
PACIFIC OCEAN
ATLANTIC OCEAN
1:70 000 000
Projection: Bonne
West from 90 Greenwich
ft m
12 000 4000
9000 3000
6000 2000
4500 1500
3000 1000
1200 400
600 200
0 0
200 600
2000 6000
4000 12 000
6000 18 000
8000 24 000
m ft

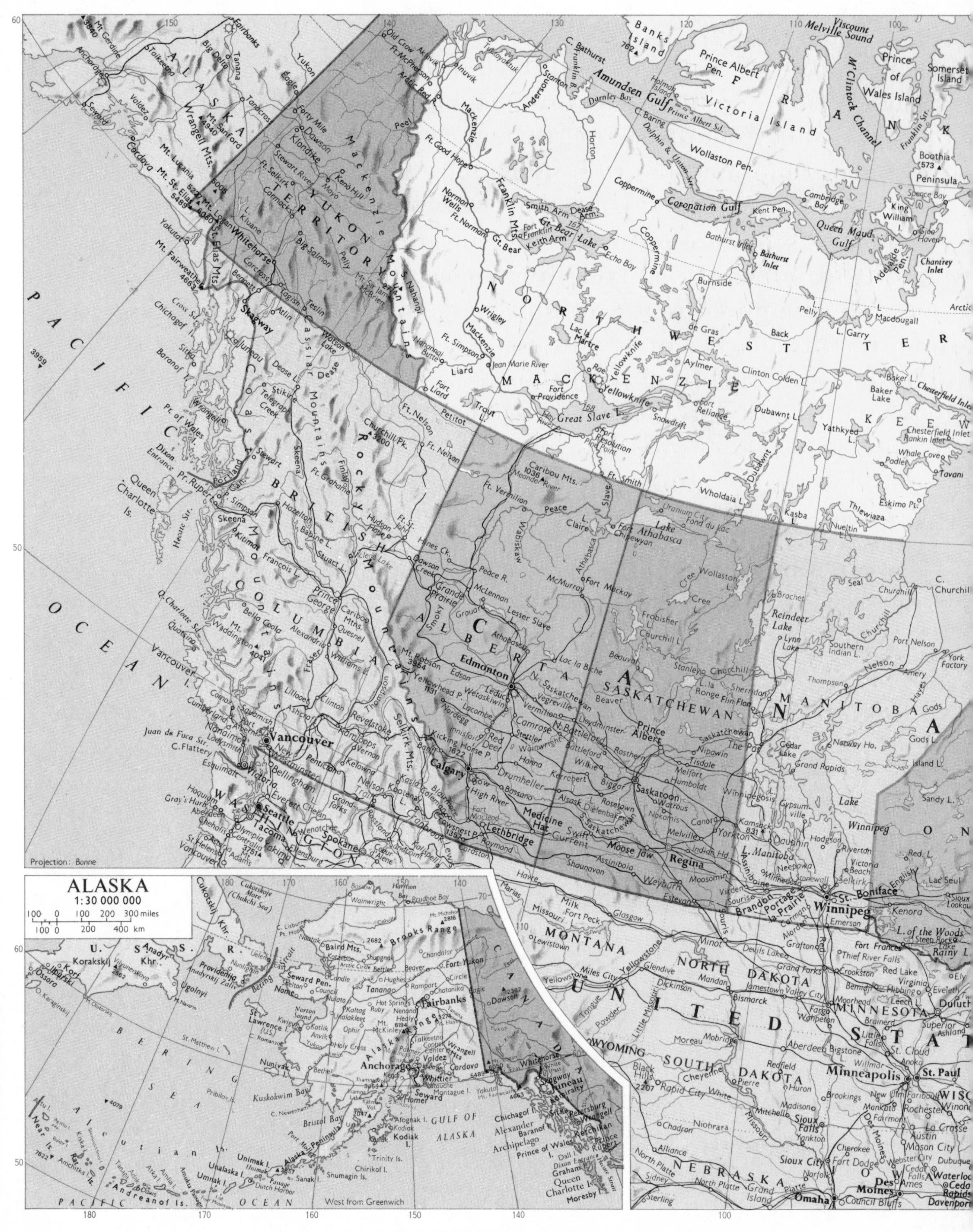
PACIFIC OCEAN
YUKON TERRITORY
BRITISH COLUMBIA
ALBERTA
SASKATCHEWAN
MANITOBA
NORTHWEST TERRITORIES
MACKENZIE
KEEWATIN
FRANKLIN
ALASKA
WASHINGTON
MONTANA
NORTH DAKOTA
SOUTH DAKOTA
MINNESOTA
WYOMING
NEBRASKA
UNITED STATES
Vancouver
Victoria
Edmonton
Calgary
Saskatoon
Regina
Winnipeg
Whitehorse
Dawson
Yellowknife
Seattle
Tacoma
Spokane
Minneapolis
St. Paul
Great Slave L.
Gt. Bear Lake
Lake Athabasca
Amundsen Gulf
Victoria Island
Banks Island
Coronation Gulf
Queen Maud Gulf
Mackenzie Mountains
Rocky Mountains
Coast Mts.
Queen Charlotte Is.
Vancouver I.
Projection: Bonne
ALASKA
1:30 000 000
100 0 100 200 300 miles
100 0 200 400 km
U.S.S.R.
BERING SEA
Aleutian Is.
Brooks Range
Alaska Range
Fairbanks
Anchorage
Juneau
Kodiak I.
GULF OF ALASKA
PACIFIC OCEAN
CANADA
West from Greenwich

1:15 000 000

100 50 0 100 200 300 400 miles
100 0 100 200 300 400 500 600 km

G R E E N L A N D

•Angmagssalik

Kong Frederik VI's Kyst

2850

Sondre Stromfjord
Holsteinsborg
Christianshåb
Disko Godthåb

Davis Strait
Frederikshåb
Ivigtut
Julianehåb Nanortalik

Kap Farvel

Baffin Bay

Devon Island
Lancaster Sound
Arctic Bay Bylot I. Pond Inlet
Brodeur Milne Pond Inlet
Peninsula Inlet
Gulf of
Boothia

Melville
Peninsula

Foxe Prince
Basin Charles
 I.

Southampton
I.

Hudson Strait

C. Chidley

Ungava Bay

L A B R A D O R

Q U E B E C

N E W F O U N D L A N D

St. John's

Hudson

Bay

James Bay

O N T A R I O

Lake Superior

Thunder Bay

Gulf of
St. Lawrence

PR. EDWARD I.
Charlottetown

NOVA SCOTIA
Halifax
Dartmouth

NEW
BRUNSWICK
Moncton
Saint
John

MAINE

QUÉBEC
Trois Rivières
MONTRÉAL
Ottawa

NEW
HAMPSHIRE
VERMONT

Boston
MASS.

TORONTO
Hamilton Buffalo
London NEW YORK
 Rochester Syracuse Utica
 Albany
 Providence
 New Haven
 New York
 NEW JERSEY
CHICAGO DETROIT Cleveland
ILLINOIS INDIANA OHIO PENNSYLVANIA
Milwaukee

ATLANTIC OCEAN

West from Greenwich COPYRIGHT. GEORGE PHILIP & SON. LTD.

N W T E R R I T O R I E S
MANITOBA
H U D S O N B A Y
North Belcher Is.
Baker's Dozen Is.
Belcher Islands
Nastapoka Is.
Richmond Gulf
L. Minto
Clearwater L.
Little Whale
Great Whale
Lac Bienville
Poste de la Baleine (Great Whale River)
C. Henrietta Maria
J A M E S B A Y
Akimiski I.
Fort George
Fort Albany
Moosonee
Moose Factory
Eastmain
Fort Rupert (Rupert House)
L. Mistassini
O N T A R I O
Q
L. Nipigon
Thunder Bay
Isle Royale
L A K E S U P E R I O R
Sault Ste. Marie
Timmins
Kirkland Lake
Rouyn
Val d'Or
Kapuskasing
Cochrane
Sudbury
North Bay
Elliot Lake
Manitoulin I.
Georgian Bay
L A K E H U R O N
Parry Sound
Pembroke
OTTAWA
MONTREAL
Trois Rivières
Shawinigan
Kingston
TORONTO
HAMILTON
L A K E O N T A R I O
ROCHESTER
BUFFALO
SYRACUSE
Utica
Albany
Binghamton
Adirondack Mountains
Catskill Mts.
L A K E E R I E
Erie
CLEVELAND
TOLEDO
DETROIT
Windsor
London
Sarnia
Flint
Grand Rapids
Lansing
Saginaw
Bay City
M I C H I G A N
MILWAUKEE
CHICAGO
Madison
Green Bay
Rockford
W I S C O N S I N
I L L I N O I S
Lambert's Equivalent Azimuthal
I N D I A N A
O H I O
P E N N S Y L V A N I A
N E W Y O R K

1:7 000 000
50 0 50 100 150 200 miles
50 0 50 100 150 200 250 300 km
NEWFOUNDLAND
COAST OF LABRADOR
LABRADOR
QUEBEC
NEWFOUNDLAND
NEW BRUNSWICK
NOVA SCOTIA
PRINCE EDWARD ISLAND
MAINE
GULF OF ST. LAWRENCE
ATLANTIC OCEAN
St. Lawrence
Gaspé Peninsula
Shickshock Mts.
Anticosti I.
Jacques Cartier Passage
Gaspé Passage
Cabot Strait
Str. of Belle Isle
Belle I.
Long Range Mts.
Mealy Mts.
Cape Breton Island
Magdalen Is. (Quebec)
SAINT-PIERRE ET MIQUELON (Fr.)
Miquelon
Langlade
St. Pierre
Avalon Peninsula
St. John's
Corner Brook
Gander
Bay of Fundy
Sable I. (Nova Scotia)
Halifax
Dartmouth
Saint John
Fredericton
Moncton
Charlottetown
Summerside
Sydney
Glace Bay
New Waterford
Sydney Mines
Truro
New Glasgow
Stellarton
Yarmouth
Campbellton
Dalhousie
Bathurst
Chatham
Edmundston
Rimouski
Rivière du Loup
Quebec
Lauzon
Lévis
Sherbrooke
Chicoutimi
Arvida
Alma
Port Alfred
Sept Îles
Schefferville
Happy Valley
Goose Bay
Churchill Falls
Labrador City
Wabush City
Manicouagan
Lac Melville
Michikamau L.
Bangor
Portland
Augusta
BOSTON
Lowell
Lynn
Quincy
Brockton
Manchester
Nashua
Concord
Portsmouth
Gloucester
West from Greenwich
70
65
60
55
50
45

YUKON TERRITORY
NORTH WEST
BRITISH COLUMBIA
ALBERTA
ALASKA
WASHINGTON
IDAHO
PACIFIC OCEAN
QUEEN CHARLOTTE ISLANDS
VANCOUVER ISLAND
ALEXANDER ARCH.
GREAT SLAVE LAKE
WOOD BUFFALO NATIONAL PARK
Cassiar Mountains
Rocky Mountains
Skeena Mountains
Coast Mountains
Cariboo Mountains
Selkirk Mountains
Birch Mountains
Caribou Mts.
Horn Mts.
Buffalo Head Hills
Whitehorse
Yellowknife
Fort Simpson
Fort Nelson
Fort St. John
Dawson Creek
Grande Prairie
Peace River
Prince Rupert
Prince George
Kitimat
Edmonton
Red Deer
Calgary
Lethbridge
Medicine Hat
Kamloops
Kelowna
Vernon
Penticton
Nelson
Vancouver
North Vancouver
New Westminster
Victoria
Nanaimo
Port Alberni
Bellingham
Seattle
Everett
Jasper
Banff
Juneau
Ketchikan
Dixon Entrance
Hecate Strait
Queen Charlotte Str.
Mackenzie
Liard
Peace
Athabasca
Fraser
Thompson
Columbia
Projection: Lambert's Equivalent Azimuthal
West from Greenwich
130
125
120
115
55
50

1:7 000 000

50 0 50 100 150 200 miles

50 0 50 100 150 200 250 300 km

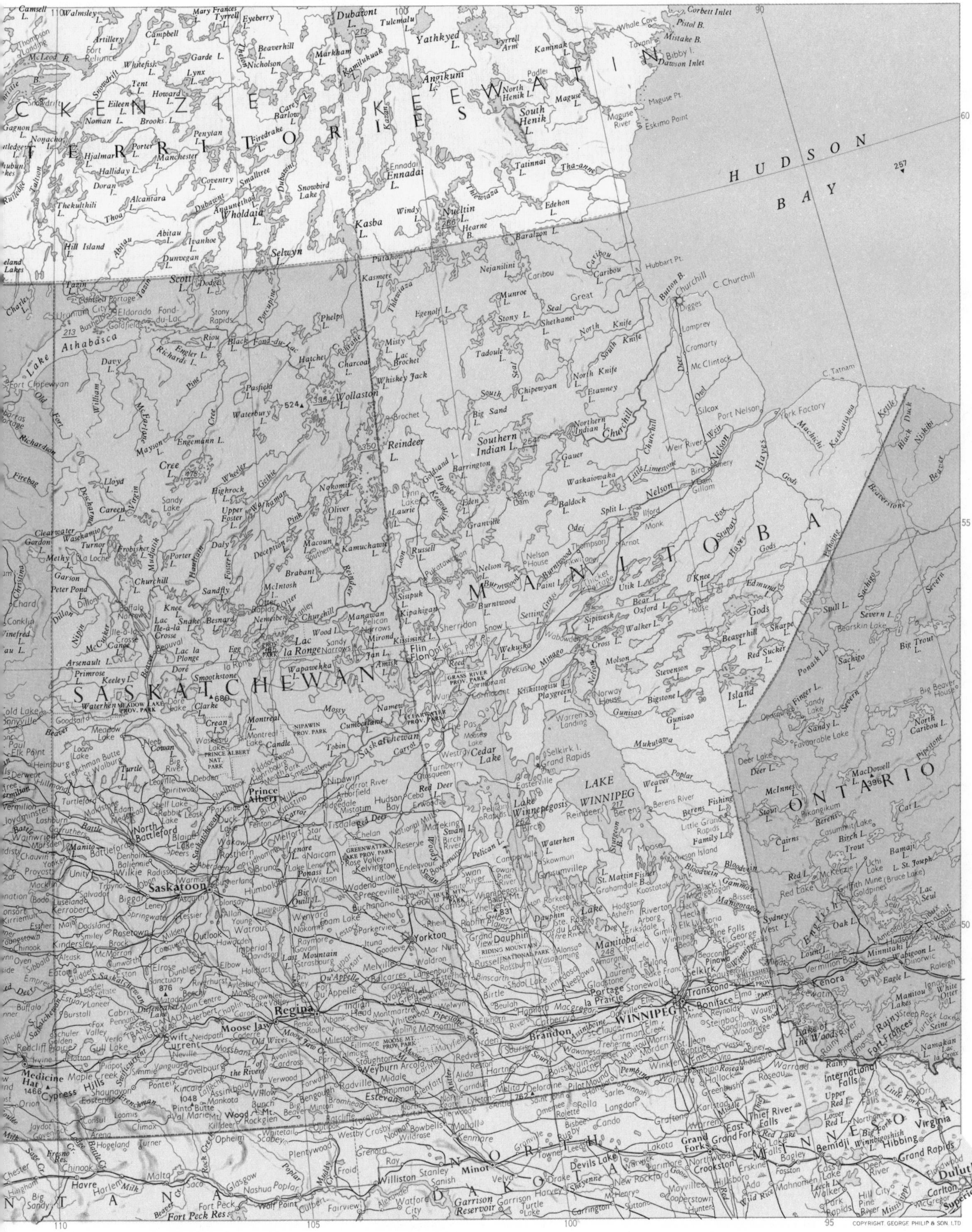

KEEWATIN

MACKENZIE

TERRITORIES

HUDSON BAY

SASKATCHEWAN

MANITOBA

ONTARIO

NORTH DAKOTA

MINNESOTA

MONTANA

LAKE WINNIPEG

Lake Winnipegosis

Lake Manitoba

Lake Athabasca

Reindeer L.

Wollaston L.

Southern Indian L.

Lake of the Woods

Regina

Saskatoon

Winnipeg

Prince Albert

Brandon

Moose Jaw

Yorkton

Churchill

Flin Flon

The Pas

Kenora

Minot

Duluth

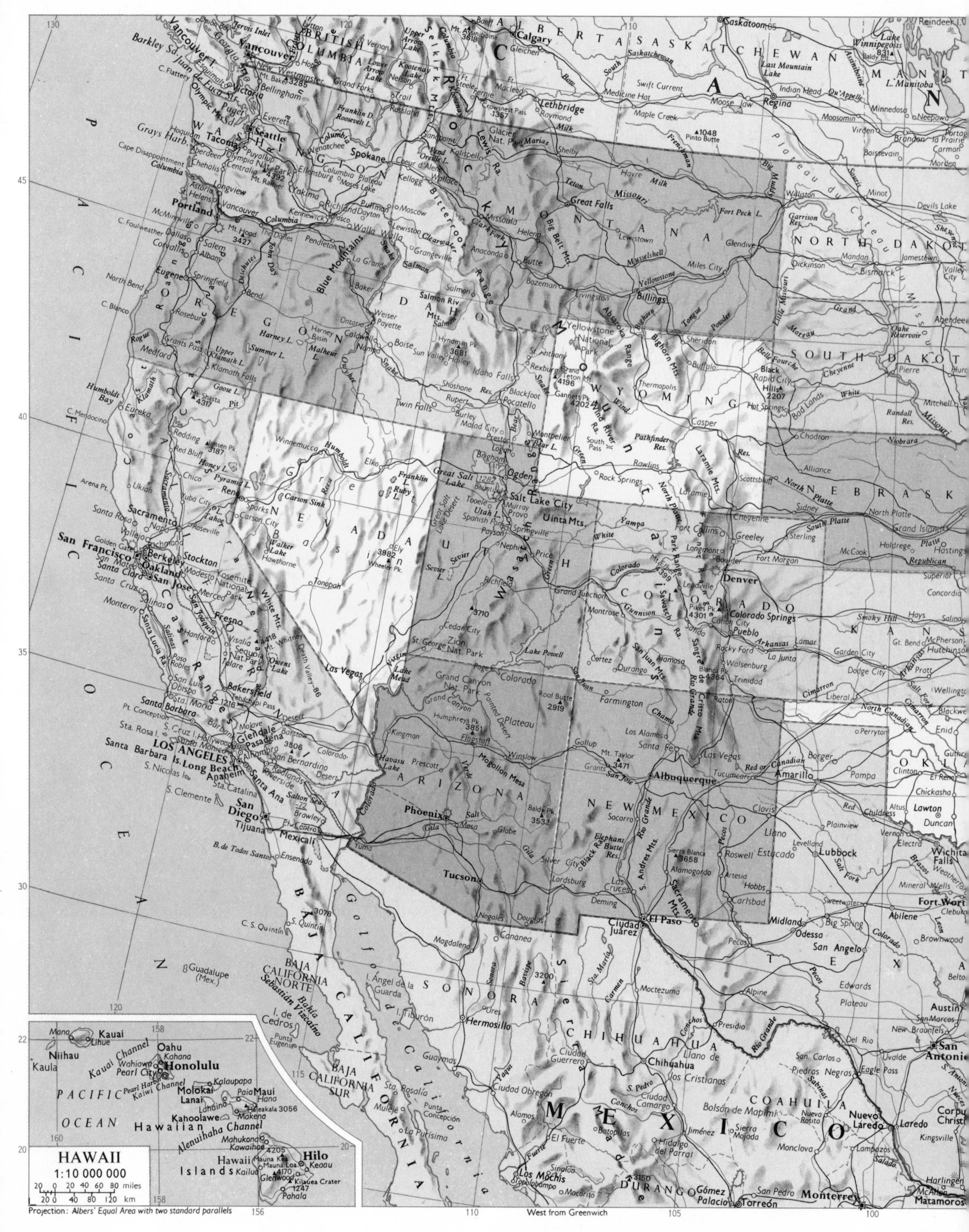

BRITISH COLUMBIA
ALBERTA
SASKATCHEWAN
CANADA
MANITOBA
PACIFIC OCEAN
ROCKY MTS.
WASHINGTON
OREGON
CALIFORNIA
IDAHO
MONTANA
WYOMING
NEVADA
UTAH
ARIZONA
COLORADO
NEW MEXICO
NORTH DAKOTA
SOUTH DAKOTA
NEBRASKA
KANSAS
OKLAHOMA
TEXAS
MEXICO
BAJA CALIFORNIA NORTE
BAJA CALIFORNIA SUR
SONORA
CHIHUAHUA
COAHUILA
DURANGO
Golfo de California
Great Basin
Coast Ranges
Sierra Nevada
Cascade Range
Blue Mountains
Bitterroot Range
Wasatch Range
Uinta Mts.
Wind River Ra.
Bighorn Mts.
Laramie Mts.
Sangre de Cristo Mts.
Sierra Madre
Great Salt Lake
Great Salt Lake Desert
Yellowstone National Park
Grand Canyon Nat. Park
Zion Nat. Park
Yosemite National Park
Sequoia Nat. Park
Death Valley -86
Mojave Desert
Colorado Desert
Painted Desert
Colorado Plateau
Mogollon Mesa
Edwards Plateau
Llano Estacado
Bolsón de Mapimí
Vancouver
Victoria
Seattle
Tacoma
Olympia
Spokane
Portland
Salem
Eugene
Medford
Boise
Pocatello
Idaho Falls
Great Falls
Helena
Butte
Billings
Missoula
Calgary
Lethbridge
Regina
Saskatoon
Medicine Hat
Reno
Carson City
Sacramento
San Francisco
Oakland
Berkeley
San Jose
Stockton
Fresno
Bakersfield
Santa Barbara
LOS ANGELES
Pasadena
Glendale
Long Beach
Anaheim
Santa Ana
San Diego
Tijuana
Mexicali
Las Vegas
Phoenix
Tucson
Yuma
Flagstaff
Salt Lake City
Ogden
Provo
Cheyenne
Casper
Denver
Colorado Springs
Pueblo
Albuquerque
Santa Fe
Roswell
El Paso
Ciudad Juárez
Lubbock
Amarillo
Midland
Odessa
San Angelo
Abilene
Austin
San Antonio
Laredo
Nuevo Laredo
Monterrey
Chihuahua
Hermosillo
Torreón
Gómez Palacio
Los Mochis
Ciudad Obregón
Bismarck
Pierre
Rapid City
Wichita Falls
Lawton
HAWAII
1:10 000 000
Kauai
Niihau
Oahu
Honolulu
Pearl City
Molokai
Lanai
Maui
Kahoolawe
Hawaiian Islands
Hawaii
Hilo
Mauna Kea 4205
Mauna Loa 4170
PACIFIC OCEAN
Kauai Channel
Kaiwi Channel
Alenuihaha Channel

Projection: Albers' Equal Area with two standard parallels

West from Greenwich

1:12 000 000

50 0 50 100 150 200 250 300 miles

50 0 50 100 150 200 250 300 350 400 450 km

CANADA
ONTARIO
QUEBEC
NEW BRUNSWICK
Lake Winnipeg
Winnipeg
Lake of the Woods
Thunder Bay
Lake Superior
Sault Ste. Marie
Lake Michigan
Lake Huron
Georgian Bay
Lake Erie
Lake Ontario
L. Nipissing
L. Champlain
Ottawa
MONTREAL
Québec
TORONTO
Hamilton
Niagara Falls
Sherbrooke
St. Lawrence
MINNESOTA
Minneapolis
St. Paul
Duluth
WISCONSIN
Milwaukee
Madison
MICHIGAN
DETROIT
Lansing
Grand Rapids
IOWA
Des Moines
ILLINOIS
CHICAGO
Peoria
Springfield
INDIANA
Indianapolis
OHIO
Cleveland
Columbus
Cincinnati
Dayton
Toledo
PENNSYLVANIA
PHILADELPHIA
Pittsburgh
NEW YORK
Buffalo
Rochester
Syracuse
Albany
VERMONT
NEW HAMPSHIRE
MAINE
MASS.
Boston
Providence
CONN.
Hartford
NEW JERSEY
Baltimore
Washington D.C.
WEST VIRGINIA
Charleston
VIRGINIA
Richmond
Norfolk
KENTUCKY
Louisville
Lexington
MISSOURI
St. Louis
Kansas City
TENNESSEE
Nashville
Memphis
Knoxville
Chattanooga
NORTH CAROLINA
Charlotte
Raleigh
SOUTH CAROLINA
Columbia
Charleston
GEORGIA
Atlanta
Savannah
ALABAMA
Birmingham
Montgomery
Mobile
MISSISSIPPI
Jackson
ARKANSAS
Little Rock
LOUISIANA
Baton Rouge
New Orleans
Shreveport
Dallas
Houston
Galveston
Tulsa
Wichita
Omaha
FLORIDA
Jacksonville
Tampa
Orlando
Miami
Key West
Appalachian Mts.
Delta of the Mississippi
GULF OF MEXICO
ATLANTIC OCEAN
Atlantic City
Delaware Bay
Albemarle Sd.
Pamlico Sd.
C. Hatteras
Raleigh Bay
Onslow Bay
Long Bay
Charleston Harb.
Florida Bay
Florida Keys
BAHAMAS
Grand Bahama I.
Gt. Abaco
Eleuthera I.
Andros I.
Cat I.
Exuma Sound
Long I.
N.W. Providence Chan.
N.E. Providence Channel
Penobscot Bay
Martha's Vineyard
Nantucket

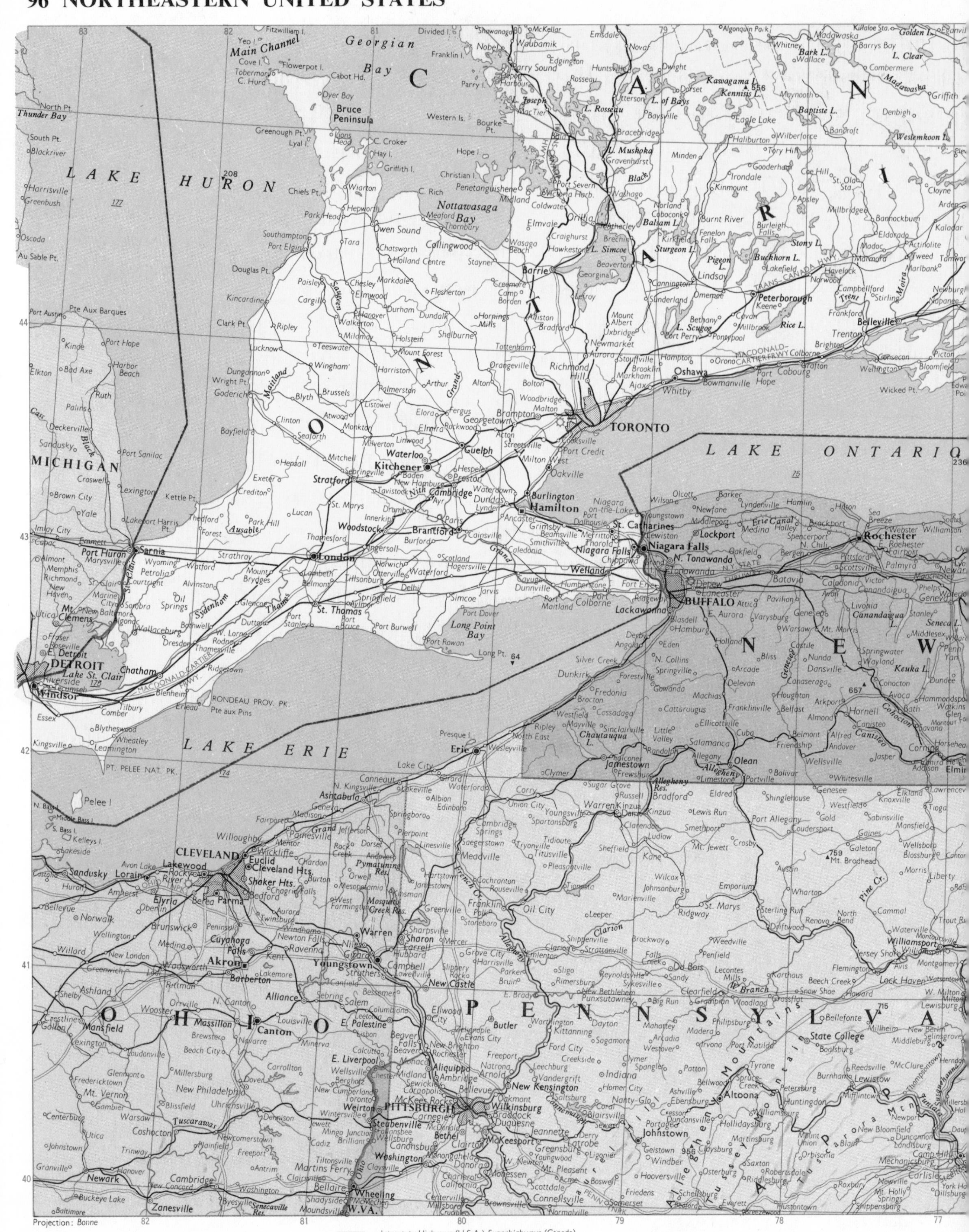

LAKE HURON
Georgian Bay
CANADA
ONTARIO
MICHIGAN
LAKE ONTARIO
LAKE ERIE
NEW YORK
OHIO
PENNSYLVANIA
TORONTO
BUFFALO
DETROIT
CLEVELAND
PITTSBURGH
Hamilton
Niagara Falls
Rochester
London
Kitchener
Guelph
Waterloo
Brantford
Windsor
Sarnia
Port Huron
Erie
Akron
Canton
Youngstown
Peterborough
Belleville
Oshawa
Barrie
Lockport
Welland
St. Catharines
Jamestown
Olean
Johnstown
Altoona
Williamsport
State College
Wheeling
Bruce Peninsula
Nottawasaga Bay
Long Point Bay
Projection: Bonne

Interstate Highways (U.S.A.), Superhighways (Canada)

Interstate Highways and Superhighways under Construction

1:2 500 000

10 0 10 20 30 40 50 60 miles

10 0 10 20 30 40 50 60 70 80 90 km

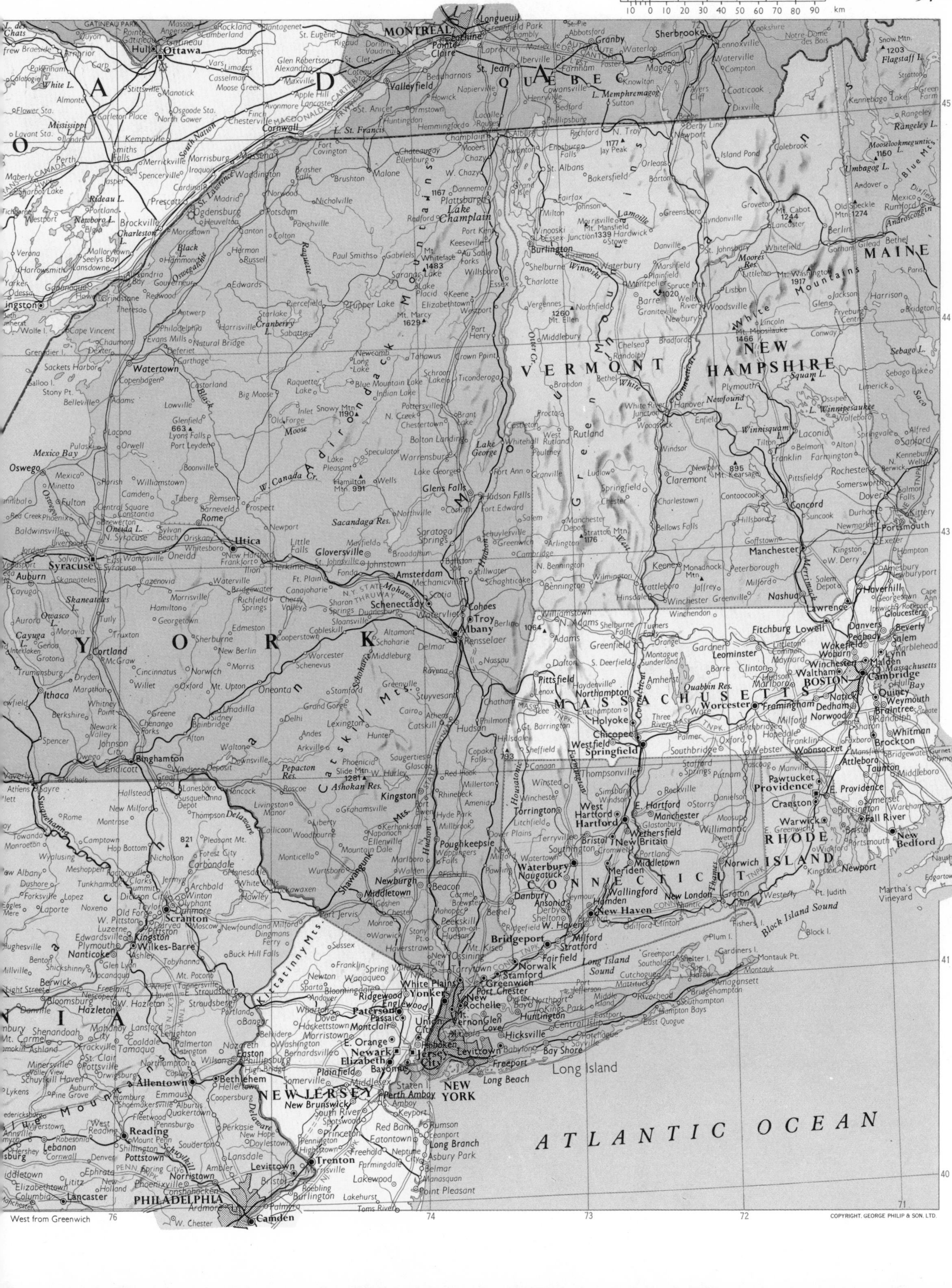

West from Greenwich

QUEBEC

ONTARIO

LAKE SUPERIOR

LAKE HURON

LAKE ONTARIO

LAKE ERIE

Georgian Bay

NEW HAMPSHIRE

VERMONT

NEW YORK

MAINE

MASSACHUSETTS

PENNSYLVANIA

NEW JERSEY

DELAWARE

MARYLAND

WEST VIRGINIA

VIRGINIA

OHIO

INDIANA

KENTUCKY

MICHIGAN

WISCONSIN

MONTREAL

BOSTON

NEW YORK CITY

PHILADELPHIA

BALTIMORE

WASHINGTON

PITTSBURGH

CLEVELAND

BUFFALO

TORONTO

Ottawa

DETROIT

CHICAGO

MILWAUKEE

CINCINNATI

Columbus

Indianapolis

Richmond

Norfolk

Albany

Syracuse

Rochester

Sault Ste. Marie

Isle Royale

1:6 000 000

50 0 50 100 miles
50 0 50 100 150 km
Continuation Eastwards On same scale
MAINE
NEW HAMPSHIRE
Bangor
Portland
Augusta
Lewiston
Houlton
Presque Isle
Old Town
Portsmouth
TENNESSEE
NORTH CAROLINA
SOUTH CAROLINA
GEORGIA
ALABAMA
FLORIDA
ATLANTIC OCEAN
GULF OF MEXICO
BAHAMAS
Great Abaco I.
Grand Bahama I.
Nashville
Knoxville
Chattanooga
Raleigh
Durham
Greensboro
Charlotte
Wilmington
Columbia
Charleston
Savannah
Atlanta
Augusta
Macon
Columbus
Albany
Birmingham
Montgomery
Mobile
Pensacola
Tallahassee
Jacksonville
Orlando
Tampa
St. Petersburg
Ft. Lauderdale
Miami
West Palm Beach
Pamlico Sound
C. Hatteras
West from Greenwich
Projection: Alber's Equal Area with two standard parallels
COPYRIGHT GEORGE PHILIP & SON LTD

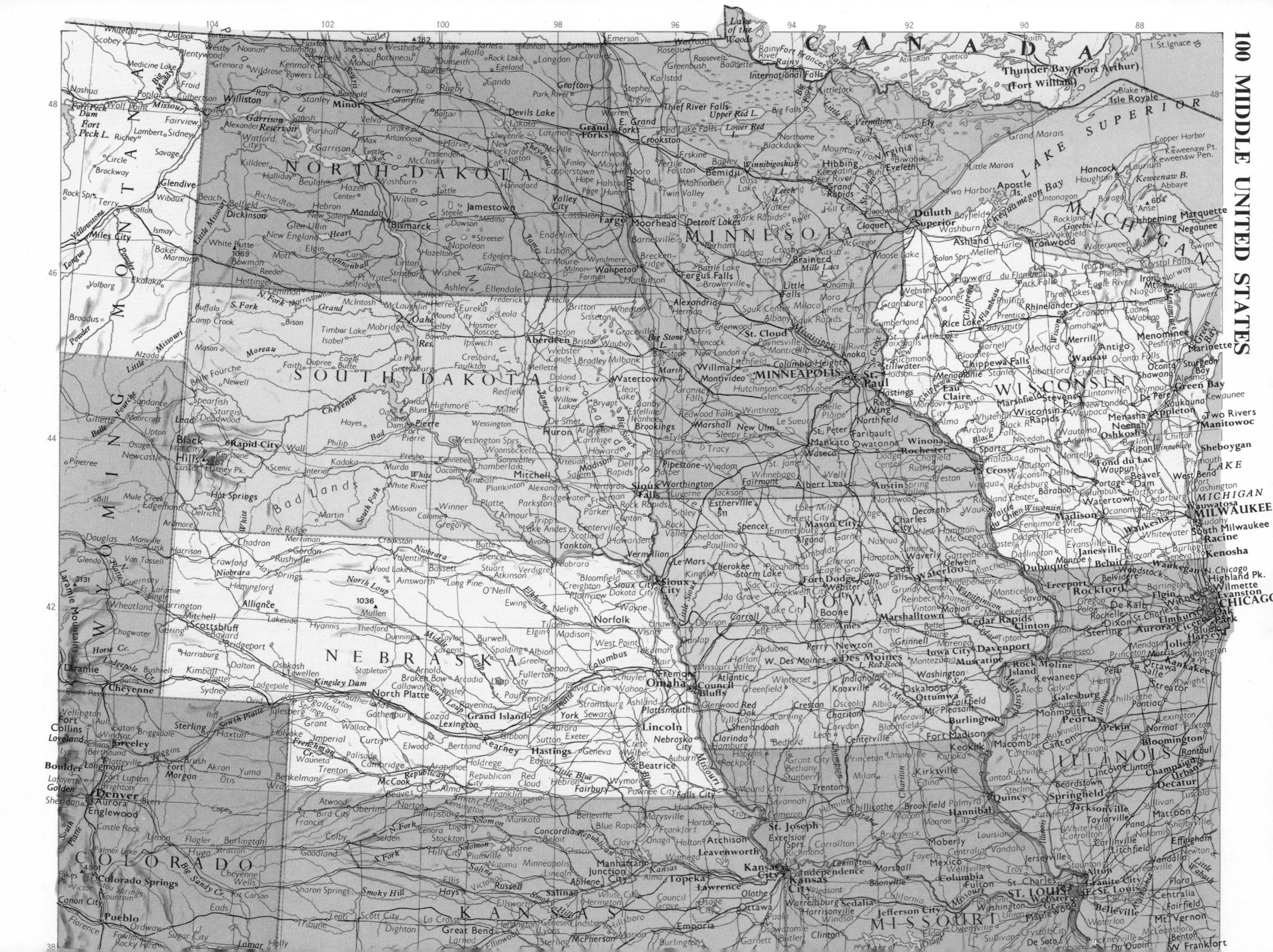
CANADA
LAKE SUPERIOR
LAKE MICHIGAN
MICHIGAN
MINNESOTA
WISCONSIN
IOWA
ILLINOIS
MISSOURI
NORTH DAKOTA
SOUTH DAKOTA
NEBRASKA
KANSAS
MONTANA
WYOMING
COLORADO
MINNEAPOLIS
St. Paul
MILWAUKEE
CHICAGO
ST. LOUIS
Kansas City
Omaha
Des Moines
Denver
Duluth
Bismarck
Lincoln
Topeka
Cheyenne
Laramie Mountains
Black Hills
Bad Lands

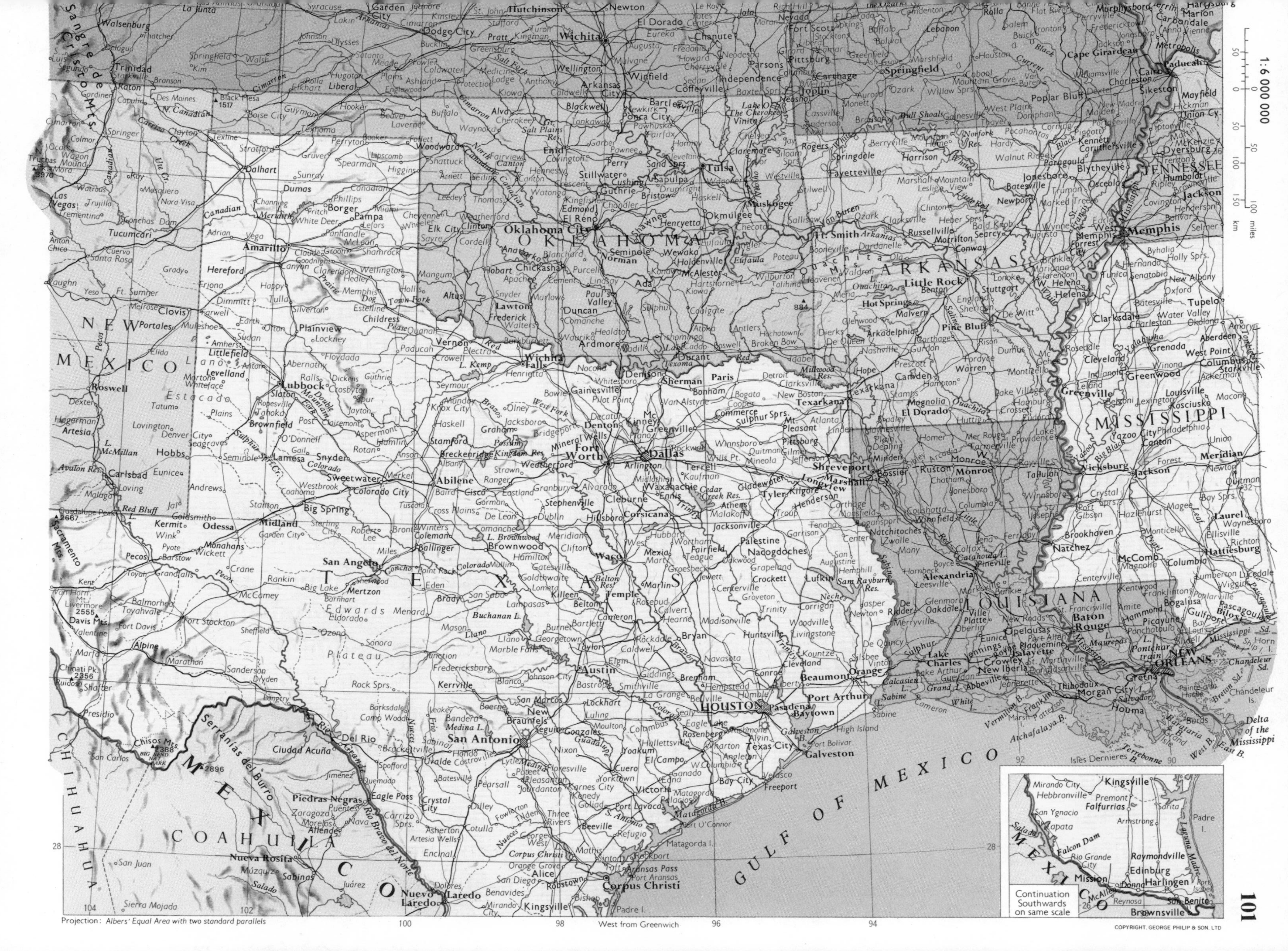
1:6 000 000
0 50 100 miles
50 0 50 100 150 km
OKLAHOMA
ARKANSAS
MISSISSIPPI
TENNESSEE
LOUISIANA
TEXAS
NEW MEXICO
MEXICO
COAHUILA
CHIHUAHUA
GULF OF MEXICO
Edwards Plateau
Llano Estacado
Serranías del Burro
Sangre de Cristo Mts.
Sacramento Mts.
Oklahoma City
Tulsa
Wichita
Little Rock
Memphis
Dallas
Fort Worth
Houston
San Antonio
Austin
New Orleans
Baton Rouge
Jackson
Shreveport
Amarillo
Lubbock
Corpus Christi
Galveston
Delta of the Mississippi
Continuation Southwards on same scale
West from Greenwich
Projection: Albers' Equal Area with two standard parallels
COPYRIGHT, GEORGE PHILIP & SON, LTD

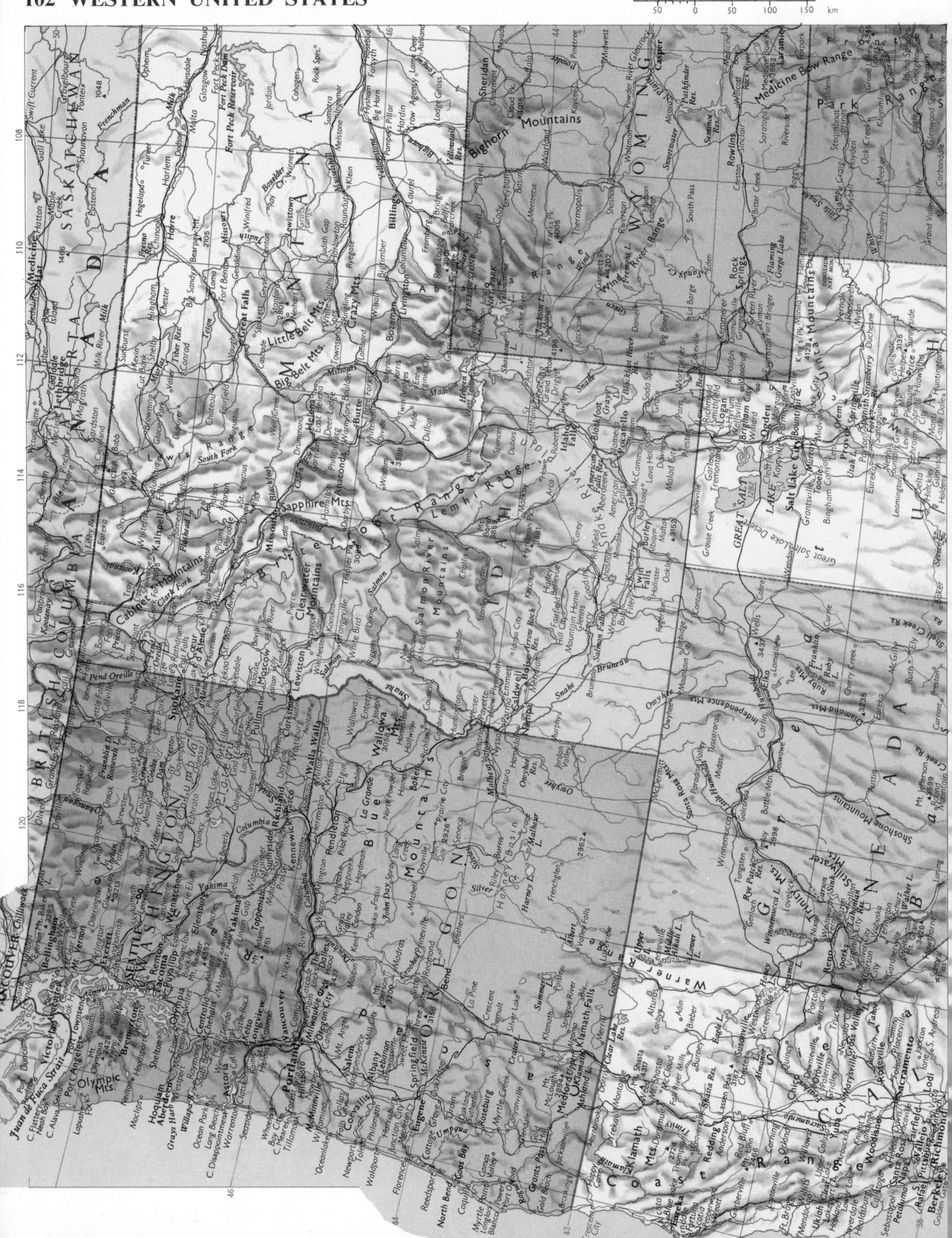
1:6 000 000
50 0 50 100 miles
50 0 50 100 150 km

COLORADO
San Juan Mts.
Sangre de Cristo Mts.
NEW MEXICO
Santa Fe
Albuquerque
Rio Grande
Las Cruces
El Paso
Ciudad Juárez
TEXAS
Sacramento Mts.
ARIZONA
Colorado Plateau
Grand Canyon
Flagstaff
Phoenix
Mesa
Tucson
Nogales
Yuma
Gila Bend Mts.
CALIFORNIA
Sierra Nevada
LOS ANGELES
San Diego
SAN FRANCISCO
Oakland
San Jose
Fresno
Bakersfield
Santa Barbara
Las Vegas
Death Valley
Mojave Desert
Salton Sea
Mexicali
Tijuana
Ensenada
Sierra de Juarez
Golfo de California
MEXICO
SONORA
Hermosillo
CHIHUAHUA
Chihuahua
Santa Lucia Range
Channel Is.
Pt. Concepcion
Cedros I.
Tiburón
West from Greenwich
COPYRIGHT, GEORGE PHILIP & SON, LTD.

1:12 000 000

100 0 100 200 miles

100 0 100 200 300 km

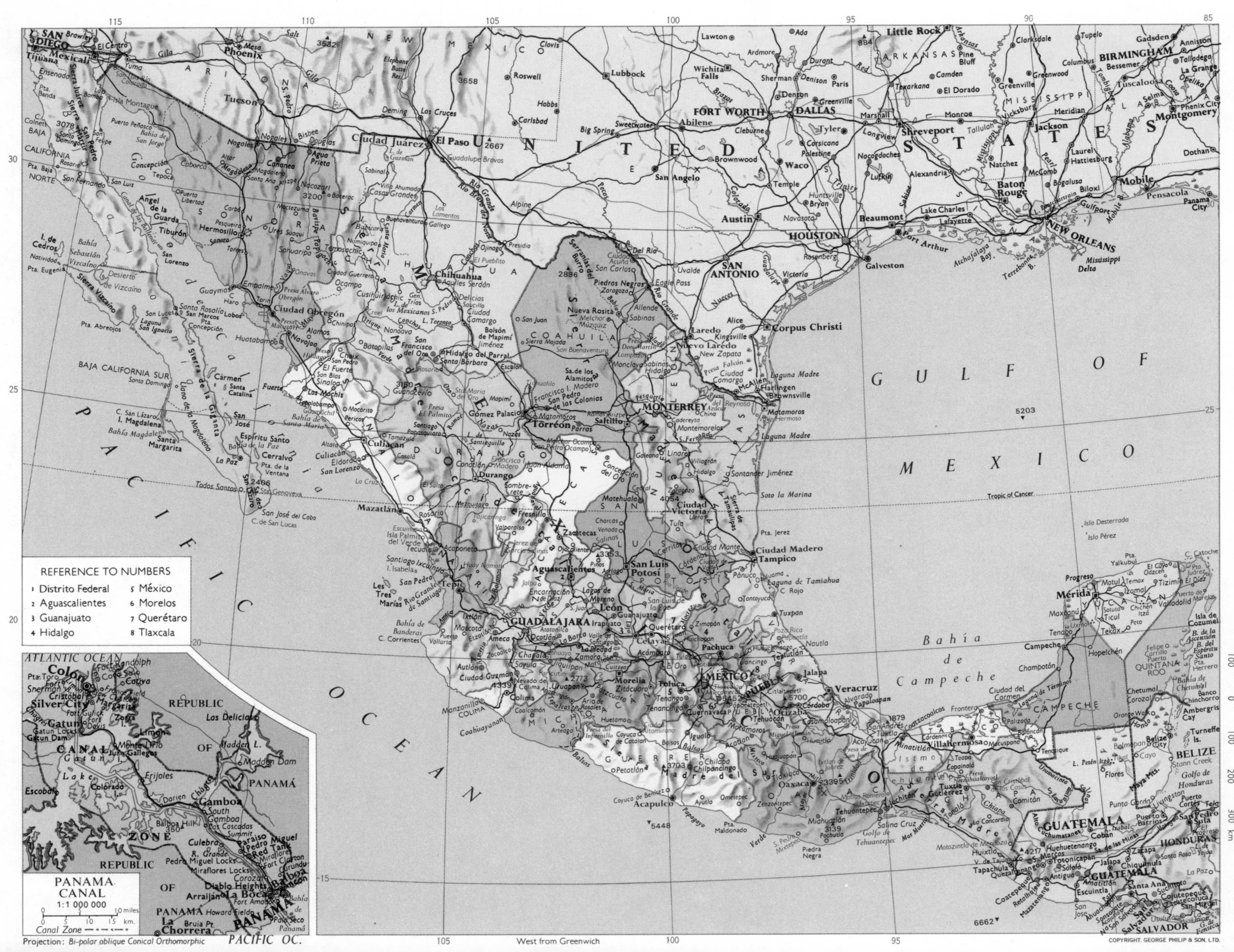
GULF OF MEXICO
PACIFIC OCEAN
Bahía de Campeche
UNITED STATES
MEXICO
GUADALAJARA
MONTERREY
HOUSTON
NEW ORLEANS
SAN ANTONIO
DALLAS
FORT WORTH
GUATEMALA
BELIZE
HONDURAS
SALVADOR
Tropic of Cancer
REFERENCE TO NUMBERS
1 Distrito Federal
2 Aguascalientes
3 Guanajuato
4 Hidalgo
5 México
6 Morelos
7 Querétaro
8 Tlaxcala
ATLANTIC OCEAN
PANAMA CANAL
1:1 000 000
Canal Zone
PACIFIC OC.
West from Greenwich
Projection: Bi-polar oblique Conical Orthomorphic

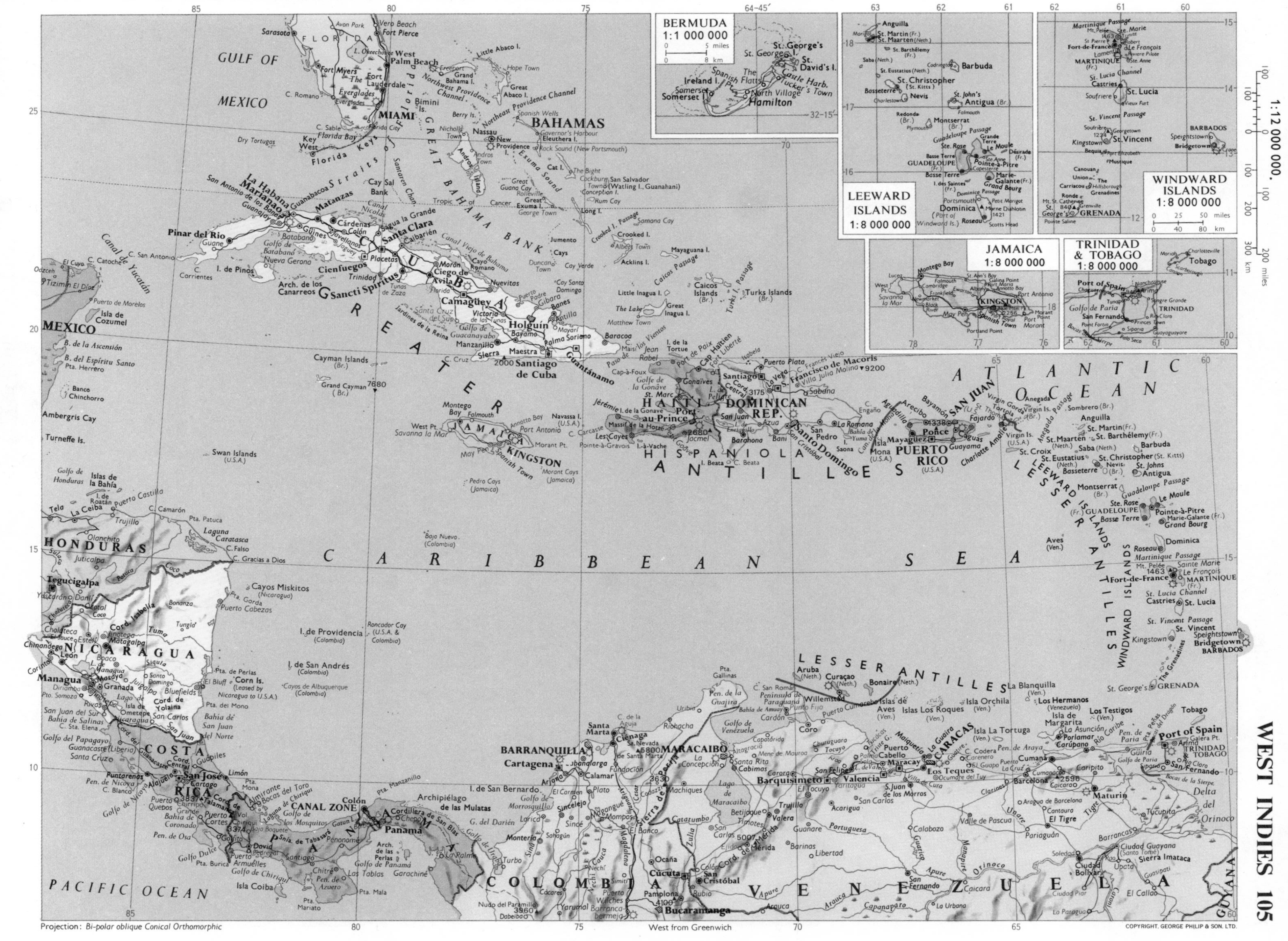
1:12 000 000
100 0 100 200 miles
100 0 100 200 300 km
GULF OF MEXICO
BAHAMAS
GREAT BAHAMA BANK
BERMUDA
1:1 000 000
Hamilton
LEEWARD ISLANDS
1:8 000 000
WINDWARD ISLANDS
1:8 000 000
JAMAICA
1:8 000 000
TRINIDAD & TOBAGO
1:8 000 000
ATLANTIC OCEAN
CARIBBEAN SEA
GREATER ANTILLES
LESSER ANTILLES
LEEWARD ISLANDS
WINDWARD ISLANDS
HISPANIOLA
CUBA
JAMAICA
HAITI
DOMINICAN REP.
PUERTO RICO
SAN JUAN
KINGSTON
Port-au-Prince
Santo Domingo
La Habana
MIAMI
Nassau
Santiago de Cuba
Camagüey
Holguín
Guantánamo
Port of Spain
TRINIDAD & TOBAGO
BARBADOS
Bridgetown
GRENADA
MARTINIQUE
Dominica
GUADELOUPE
St. Lucia
St. Vincent
Antigua
Barbuda
VENEZUELA
CARACAS
MARACAIBO
Maracay
Valencia
Barquisimeto
COLOMBIA
BARRANQUILLA
Cartagena
Santa Marta
Bucaramanga
Cúcuta
PANAMA
Panamá
CANAL ZONE
Colón
COSTA RICA
San José
NICARAGUA
Managua
HONDURAS
Tegucigalpa
MEXICO
Isla de Cozumel
Canal de Yucatán
Cayman Islands
Swan Islands
PACIFIC OCEAN
West from Greenwich
Projection: Bi-polar oblique Conical Orthomorphic
COPYRIGHT, GEORGE PHILIP & SON, LTD.

1:30 000 000

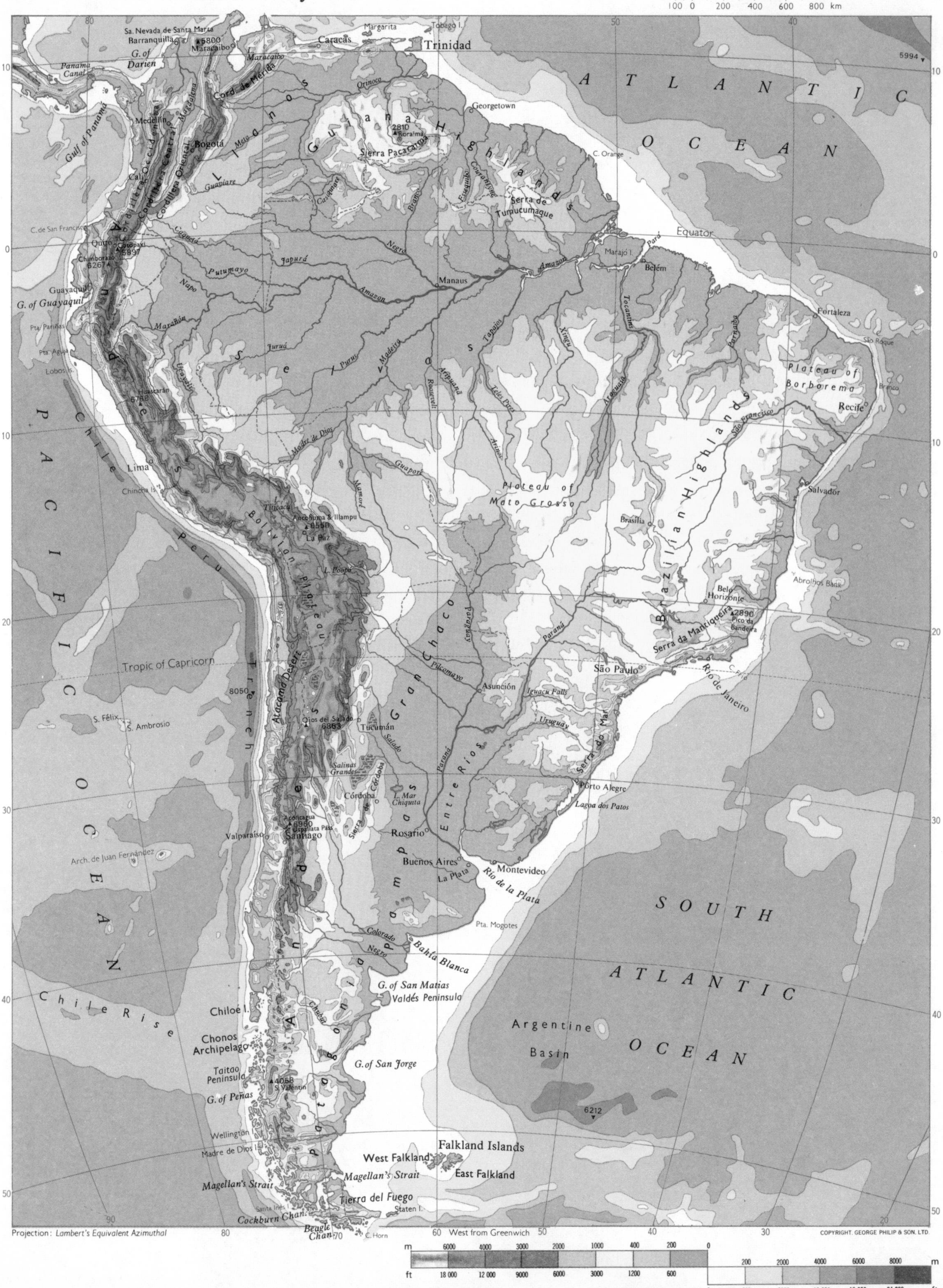

Projection: Lambert's Equivalent Azimuthal

1:30 000 000

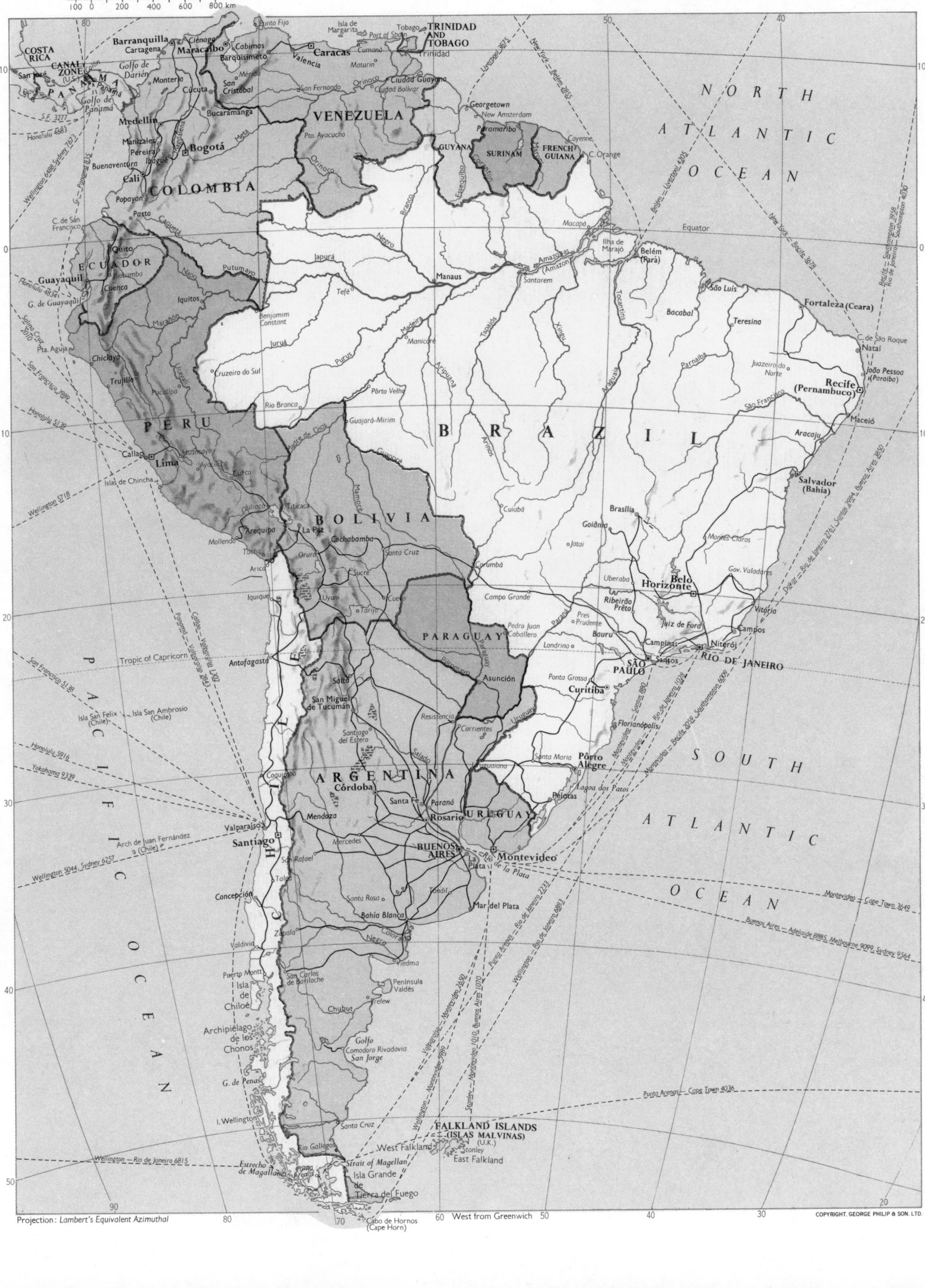

100 0 100 200 300 400 500 miles

100 0 200 400 600 800 km

NORTH ATLANTIC OCEAN

SOUTH ATLANTIC OCEAN

PACIFIC OCEAN

BRAZIL

VENEZUELA

COLOMBIA

ECUADOR

PERU

BOLIVIA

PARAGUAY

ARGENTINA

URUGUAY

CHILE

GUYANA

SURINAM

FRENCH GUIANA

TRINIDAD AND TOBAGO

FALKLAND ISLANDS (ISLAS MALVINAS) (U.K.)

COSTA RICA

CANAL ZONE (U.S.A.)

PANAMA

Tropic of Capricorn

Equator

Projection: *Lambert's Equivalent Azimuthal*

West from Greenwich

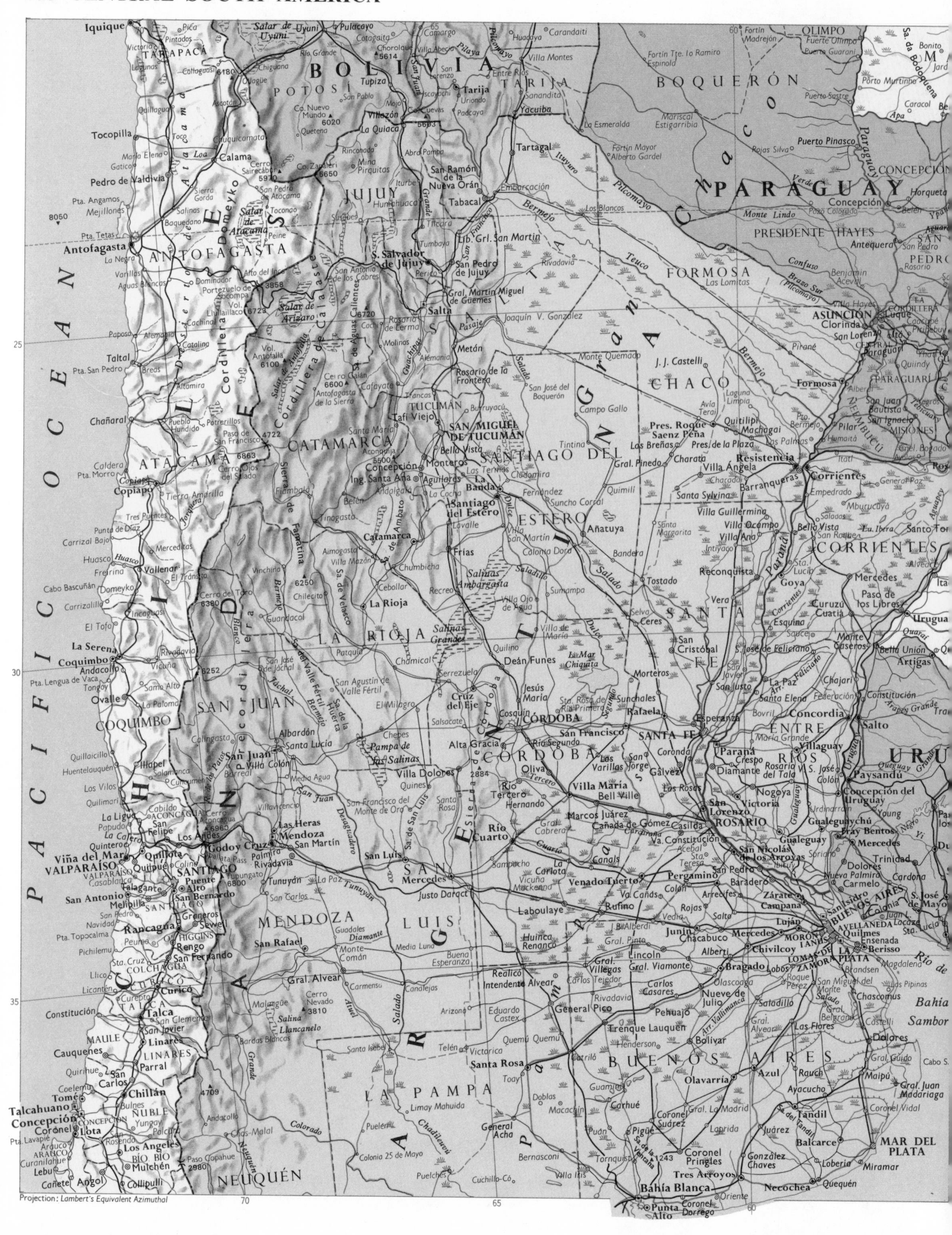

PACIFIC OCEAN
CHILE
BOLIVIA
PARAGUAY
ARGENTINA
ANDES
Gran Chaco
BOQUERÓN
OLIMPO
PRESIDENTE HAYES
FORMOSA
CHACO
SALTA
JUJUY
TUCUMÁN
CATAMARCA
SANTIAGO DEL ESTERO
LA RIOJA
SAN JUAN
CÓRDOBA
SANTA FE
CORRIENTES
ENTRE RÍOS
MENDOZA
SAN LUIS
LA PAMPA
BUENOS AIRES
NEUQUÉN
TARAPACÁ
ANTOFAGASTA
ATACAMA
COQUIMBO
SANTIAGO
COLCHAGUA
CURICÓ
TALCA
MAULE
LINARES
ÑUBLE
CONCEPCIÓN
ARAUCO
BÍO BÍO
POTOSÍ
TARIJA
CONCEPCIÓN
SAN PEDRO
CORDILLERA
PARAGUARÍ
ÑEEMBUCÚ
MISIONES
Iquique
Tocopilla
Calama
Antofagasta
Taltal
Chañaral
Copiapó
Vallenar
La Serena
Coquimbo
Ovalle
Viña del Mar
VALPARAÍSO
SANTIAGO
San Antonio
Rancagua
San Fernando
Curicó
Talca
Linares
Parral
Chillán
Talcahuano
Concepción
Los Angeles
Angol
Uyuni
Tupiza
Villazón
La Quiaca
Tarija
Yacuiba
Tartagal
Salta
S. Salvador de Jujuy
SAN MIGUEL DE TUCUMÁN
Santiago del Estero
Catamarca
La Rioja
San Juan
Mendoza
San Luis
San Rafael
CÓRDOBA
Río Cuarto
Villa María
SANTA FE
ROSARIO
Paraná
Resistencia
Corrientes
Formosa
ASUNCIÓN
Concepción
Puerto Pinasco
Concordia
Paysandú
Salto
BUENOS AIRES
LA PLATA
MAR DEL PLATA
Bahía Blanca
Santa Rosa
Tandil
Olavarría
Azul
Junín
Pergamino
Venado Tuerto
General Pico
Necochea
Tres Arroyos
Salado
Bermejo
Pilcomayo
Paraná
Uruguay
Colorado
Río de la Plata
Salar de Uyuni
Salar de Atacama
Salinas Grandes
Mar Chiquita
Aconcagua 6960
Cerro Ojos del Salado 6863
25
30
35
70
65
60

Projection: Lambert's Equivalent Azimuthal

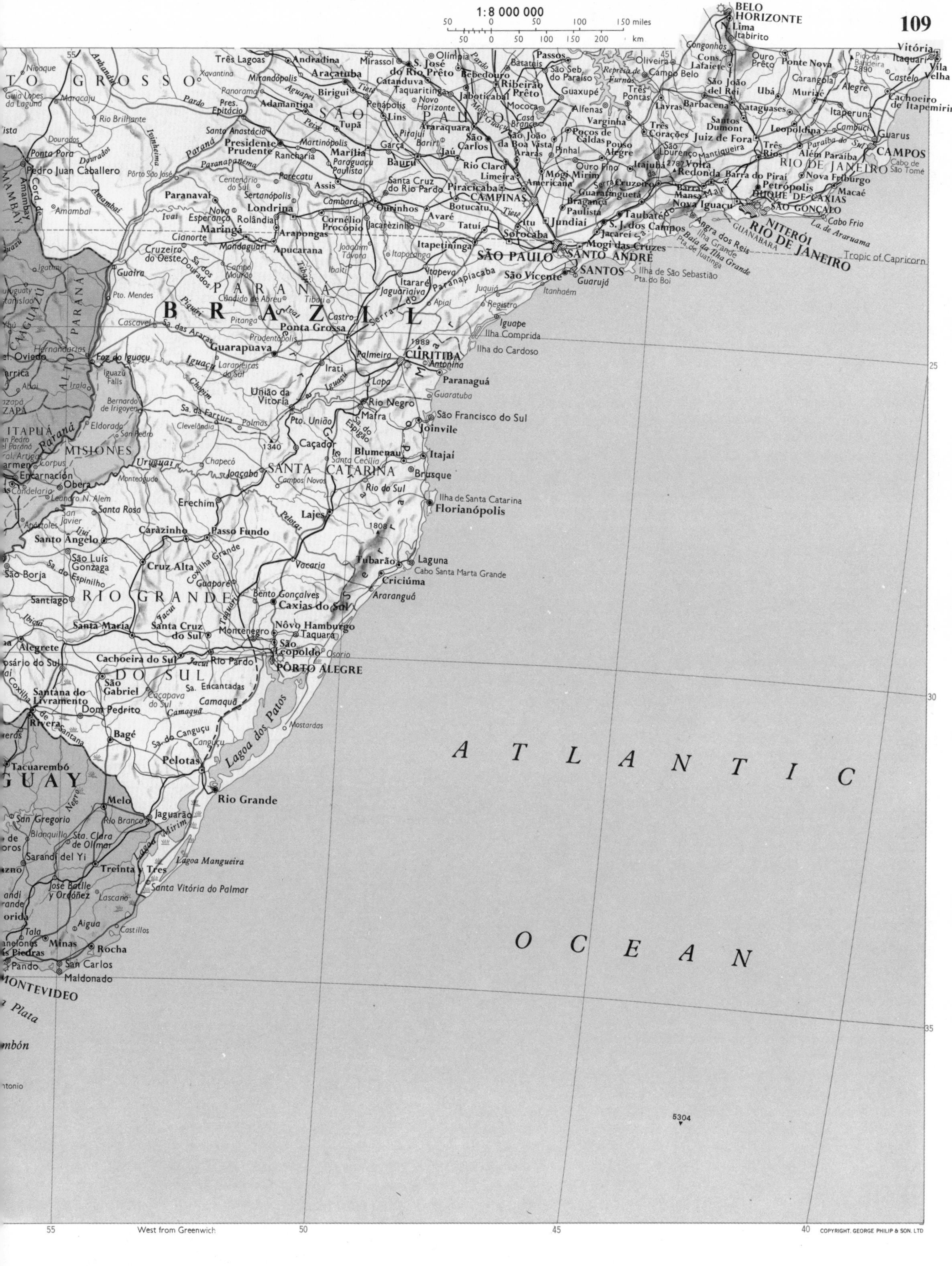
1:8 000 000
50 0 50 100 150 miles
50 0 50 100 150 200 km
BELO HORIZONTE
N. Lima
Itabirito
Vitória
Itaquari
Vila Velha
Castelo
Cachoeiro de Itapemirim
Três Lagoas
Andradina
Mirassol
Olímpia
S. José do Rio Prêto
Bebedouro
Batatais
Passos
Oliveira
Congonhas
Cons. Lafaiete
Ouro Prêto
Ponte Nova
Carangola
Alegre
Araçatuba
Birigui
Catanduva
Taquaritinga
Jaboticabal
Ribeirão Prêto
São Seb. do Paraíso
Guaxupé
Campo Belo
São João del Rei
Ubá
Muriaé
Itaperuna
Mirandópolis
Xavantina
Panorama
Adamantina
Penápolis
Novo Horizonte
Mococa
Alfenas
Varginha
Três Pontas
Lavras
Barbacena
Cataguases
Santos Dumont
Juiz de Fora
Leopoldina
Cambuci
Guarus
CAMPOS
Pres. Epitácio
SÃO PAULO
Tupã
Lins
Araraquara
São Carlos
Casa Branca
São João da Boa Vista
Poços de Caldas
Pouso Alegre
Três Corações
São Lourenço
Itajubá
Mantiqueira
Três Rios
Além Paraíba
RIO DE JANEIRO
Cabo de São Tomé
Santo Anastácio
Presidente Prudente
Martinópolis
Marília
Garça
Bariri
Jaú
Bauru
Rancharia
Paraguaçu Paulista
Rio Claro
Limeira
Araras
Pinhal
Mogi Mirim
Ouro Fino
Volta Redonda
Barra do Piraí
Nova Friburgo
Petrópolis
Macaé
Duque de Caxias
São Gonçalo
Niterói
RIO DE JANEIRO
Cabo Frio
La. de Araruama
Tropic of Capricorn
Guanabara
Angra dos Reis
Ilha Grande
Baía da Ilha Grande
Pta. de Juatinga
Paranapanema
Porecatu
Assis
Santa Cruz do Rio Pardo
Piracicaba
Americana
CAMPINAS
Guaratinguetá
Cruzeiro
Barra Mansa
Nova Iguaçu
Paranavaí
Nova Esperança
Londrina
Rolândia
Cambará
Ourinhos
Botucatu
Bragança Paulista
Jundiaí
Taubaté
S. J. dos Campos
Jacareí
Mogi das Cruzes
Maringá
Cianorte
Arapongas
Cornélio Procópio
Jacarèzinho
Avaré
Tatuí
Itu
Sorocaba
Cruzeiro do Oeste
Mandaguari
Apucarana
Itapetininga
SÃO PAULO
SANTO ANDRÉ
SANTOS
Guarujá
São Vicente
Ilha de São Sebastião
Pta. do Boi
Itanhaém
Guaíra
Pto. Mendes
PARANÁ
BRAZIL
Itararé
Jaguariaíva
Itapeva
Paranapiacaba
Juquiá
Registro
Iguape
Ilha Comprida
Ilha do Cardoso
Cascavel
Sa. das Araras
Pitanga
Castro
Ponta Grossa
Guarapuava
Foz do Iguaçu
Iguaçu Falls
Palmeira
CURITIBA
1889
Antonina
Paranaguá
Irati
Lapa
Guaratuba
União da Vitória
Rio Negro
Mafra
São Francisco do Sul
Joinvile
Pto. União
Caçador
Blumenau
Itajaí
Brusque
SANTA CATARINA
Chapecó
Joaçaba
Campos Novos
Rio do Sul
Ilha de Santa Catarina
Florianópolis
Erechim
Lajes
1808
Carazinho
Passo Fundo
Santo Ângelo
São Luís Gonzaga
Cruz Alta
Vacaria
Tubarão
Laguna
Cabo Santa Marta Grande
Criciúma
Araranguá
São Borja
Santiago
RIO GRANDE
Guaporé
Bento Gonçalves
Caxias do Sul
Santa Maria
Santa Cruz do Sul
Montenegro
Nôvo Hamburgo
Taquara
São Leopoldo
Osório
PÔRTO ALEGRE
Alegrete
Cachoeira do Sul
Rio Pardo
DO SUL
São Gabriel
Sa. Encantadas
Caçapava do Sul
Camaquã
Santana do Livramento
Rivera
Dom Pedrito
Bagé
Sa. do Canguçu
Canguçu
Lagoa dos Patos
Mostardas
Pelotas
Rio Grande
Tacuarembó
URUGUAY
Melo
Jaguarão
Rio Branco
Lagoa Mirim
Lagoa Mangueira
San Gregorio
Sta. Clara de Olimar
Sarandí del Yi
Treinta y Tres
Santa Vitória do Palmar
José Batlle y Ordóñez
Lascano
Aiguá
Castillos
Minas
Rocha
Pando
San Carlos
Maldonado
MONTEVIDEO
Pedro Juan Caballero
Ponta Porã
Dourados
Amambaí
Maracaju
Rio Brilhante
MATO GROSSO
Encarnación
Oberá
Leandro N. Alem
Santa Rosa
Posadas
MISIONES
Eldorado
Corpus
Apóstoles
ALTO PARANÁ
ATLANTIC OCEAN
5304
West from Greenwich
55
50
45
40
25
30
35

NICARAGUA
COSTA RICA
PANAMA
CANAL ZONE
COLOMBIA
VENEZUELA
ECUADOR
PERU
BOLIVIA
CHILE
ARGENTINA
PARAGUAY
TRINIDAD & TOBAGO
GRENADA
RORAIMA
AMAZONAS
ACRE
RONDÔNIA
PACIFIC OCEAN
Equator
Cocos Ridge
Milne Edwards Trench
Peru - Chile Trench
Krümmel Trench
Malpelo (Colombia)
Islas del Maíz (Nic., U.S.)
San Andrés (Colombia)
Cayos de Albuquerque (Colombia)
Managua
Granada
Masaya
Bluefields
L. de Nicaragua
San Juan de Norte
Puerto Limón
Puntarenas
San José
Colón
Panamá
David
Golfo de Panamá
Barranquilla
Cartagena
Santa Marta
Riohacha
Maracaibo
Cabimas
Coro
Curaçao
Aruba
Bonaire (Neth.)
Caracas
La Guaira
Valencia
Barquisimeto
Puerto Cabello
Maracay
Cumaná
Barcelona
Port of Spain
Ciudad Bolívar
Ciudad Guayana
Maturín
Orinoco
San Cristóbal
Cúcuta
Mérida
Bucaramanga
Medellín
Manizales
Pereira
Armenia
Ibagué
BOGOTÁ
Cali
Buenaventura
Popayán
Neiva
Pasto
Tumaco
Esmeraldas
Quito
Cotopaxi 5896
Chimborazo 6267
Riobamba
Guayaquil
Cuenca
Machala
Loja
G. de Guayaquil
Talara
Paita
Piura
Desierto de Sechura
Chiclayo
Cajamarca
Trujillo
Chimbote
Huascarán 6768
Huaraz
Huánuco
Callao
LIMA
Huancayo
Huancavelica
Ayacucho
Cuzco
Pisco
Ica
Arequipa
Mollendo
Tacna
Arica
Iquique
Tocopilla
Lago Titicaca
Puno
La Paz
Illimani 6462
Oruro
Cochabamba
Santa Cruz
Sucre
Potosí
Tarija
Uyuni
Trinidad
Iquitos
Amazonas
Marañón
Ucayali
Putumayo
Caquetá
Japurá
Solimões (Amazonas)
Negro
Manaus
Purus
Juruá
Madeira
Porto Velho
Rio Branco
Cruzeiro do Sul
Serra Pacaraima
Sierra Parima
Mt. Roraima 2810
Chaco Boreal
Projection: Sanson-Flamsteed's Sinusoidal

80 75 70 65 60 West from

1:16 000 000

100 0 100 200 300 400 500 miles

100 0 100 200 300 400 500 600 700 800 km

ATLANTIC OCEAN
Equator
SURINAM
FR. GUIANA
Paramaribo
Cayenne
C. Orange
AMAPÁ
Macapá
C. do Norte
Estuario do Rio Amazonas
Ilha Caviana
Ilha de Marajó
Belém (Pará)
Amazonas (Amazon)
Santarém
PARÁ
Tocantins
MARANHÃO
São Luís (Maranhão)
Bacabal
Caxias
Teresina
Parnaíba
Fortaleza (Ceará)
CEARÁ
Rocas
Fernando de Noronha (Braz.)
Aracati
Mossoró
RIO GRANDE DO NORTE
Natal
C. de São Roque
PARAÍBA
João Pessoa (Paraíba)
Campina Grande
PIAUÍ
Floriano
PERNAMBUCO
Caruaru
RECIFE (Pernambuco)
Juàzeiro
Paulo Afonso
ALAGOAS
Maceió
SERGIPE
Aracajú
BAHIA
Feira de Santana
Alagoinhas
Salvador (Bahia)
Vitória da Conquista
Ilhéus
BRAZIL
GOIÁS
MATO GROSSO
Planalto do Mato Grosso
DIST. FED.
Brasília
Anápolis
Goiânia
Montes Claros
Teófilo Otoni
Diamantina
Gov. Valadares
MINAS GERAIS
Uberlândia
Uberaba
Belo Horizonte
ESPÍRITO SANTO
Vitória
Campo Grande
Ribeirão Prêto
Araçatuba
Marília
Bauru
SÃO PAULO
Juiz de Fora
Campos
Petrópolis
Campinas
RIO DE JANEIRO
Niterói
GUANABARA
Trindade (Braz.)
6059
1850
1678
1340
Greenwich
55
50
45
40
35
30
10
5
0
15
20

1:16 000 000

100 50 0 100 200 300 miles

100 0 100 200 300 400 km

PARAGUAY
URUGUAY
BRAZIL
PARANÁ
SANTA CATARINA
RIO GRANDE DO SUL
ARGENTINA
CHILE
PATAGONIA
SOUTH ATLANTIC OCEAN
Peru—Chile Trench
Richard's Trench
Tropic of Capricorn
Gran Chaco
Chaco Boreal
Chaco Central
Chaco Austral
Desierto de Atacama
Puna de Atacama
Asunción
Concepción
Encarnación
Villarrica
SÃO PAULO
RIO DE JANEIRO
GUANABARA
Santos
Campinas
Curitiba
Paranaguá
Ponta Grossa
Londrina
Maringá
Florianópolis
Blumenau
Joinvile
Pôrto Alegre
Pelotas
Rio Grande
Santa Maria
Passo Fundo
Lagoa dos Patos
MONTEVIDEO
Paysandú
Salto
Rivera
Melo
Maldonado
Rocha
BUENOS AIRES
La Plata
Avellaneda
Rosario
Santa Fe
Paraná
Córdoba
Río Cuarto
Mendoza
San Juan
La Rioja
Catamarca
San Miguel de Tucumán
Santiago del Estero
Salta
S. Salvador de Jujuy
Resistencia
Corrientes
Posadas
Formosa
Mar del Plata
Bahía Blanca
Necochea
Tandil
Azul
Olavarría
Santa Rosa
Neuquén
Viedma
Carmen de Patagones
Golfo San Matías
Puerto Madryn
Trelew
Rawson
Península Valdés
Golfo Nuevo
Comodoro Rivadavia
Golfo San Jorge
Pto. Deseado
San Julián
Santa Cruz
Bahía Grande
Río Gallegos
Estrecho de Magallanes (Magellan's Str.)
Punta Arenas
Tierra del Fuego
Ushuaia
Canal Beagle
I. de los Estados (Staten I.)
Estrecho de Le Maire
Cabo de Hornos (C. Horn)
Islas Diego Ramírez
I. Hoste
I. Navarino
Islas Wollaston
I. Santa Inés
Arch. Reina Adelaida
Canal Concepción
I. Wellington
Archipiélago de los Chonos
I. de Chiloé
Puerto Montt
Osorno
Valdivia
Temuco
Concepción
Talcahuano
Chillán
Talca
Curicó
Rancagua
SANTIAGO
Valparaíso
Viña del Mar
Coquimbo
La Serena
Ovalle
Copiapó
Antofagasta
Tocopilla
Calama
Carlos de Bariloche
FALKLAND ISLANDS (ISLAS MALVINAS) (Br.)
West Falkland
East Falkland
Stanley
Falkland Sound
Jason Is
South Georgia (Br.)
5830
6960
6863
6800

Projection: Sanson-Flamsteed's Sinusoidal

60 West from Greenwich 55

INDEX

The number in bold type which precedes each name in the index refers to the number of the page where that feature or place will be found.

The geographical co-ordinates which follow the place name are sometimes only approximate but are close enough for the place name to be located.

An open square □ signifies that the name refers to an administrative division of a country while a solid square ■ follows the name of a country.

Rivers have been indexed to their mouth or to their confluence.

The alphabetical order of names composed of two or more words is governed primarily by the first word and then by the second. This is an example of the rule:

West Wyalong
West Yorkshire
Westbrook
Westbury
Westerland
Western Australia

Names composed of a proper name (Gibraltar) and a description (Strait of) are positioned alphabetically by the proper name. All river names are followed by R. If the same word occurs in the name of a town and a geographical feature, the town name is listed first followed by the name or names of the geographical features.

Names beginning with M', Mc are all indexed as if they were spelled Mac.

If the same place name occurs two or more times in the index and all are in the same country, each is followed by the name of the administrative subdivision in which it is located. The names are placed in the alphabetical order of the subdivisions. For example:

Stour, R., Dorset
Stour, R., Hereford and Worcester
Stour, R., Kent
Stour, R., Suffolk

If the same place name occurs twice or more in the index and the places are in different countries they will be followed by the country names and the latter in alphabetical order.

Sheffield, U.K.
Sheffield, U.S.A.

If there is a mixture of these situations, the primary order is fixed by the alphabetical sequence of the countries and the secondary order by that of the country subdivisions. In the latter case the country names are omitted.

Rochester, U.K.
Rochester, Minn. (U.S.A.) are omitted from
Rochester, N.H. (U.S.A.) the index
Rochester, N.Y. (U.S.A.)
Rochester, Pa. (U.S.A.)

The following is a list of abbreviations used in the index

A.S.S.R. – *Autonomous Soviet Socialist Republic*
Ala. – *Alabama*
Alas. – *Alaska*
Ang. – *Angola*
Arch. – *Archipelago*
Arg. – *Argentina*
Ariz. – *Arizona*
Ark. – *Arkansas*
B. – *Baie, Bahîa, Bay, Boca, Bucht, Bugt*
B.C. – *British Columbia*
Br. – *British*
C. – *Cabo, Cap, Cape*
C.A.R. – *Central African Republic*
C. Prov. – *Cape Province*
Calif. – *California*
Chan. – *Channel*
Col. – *Colombia*
Colo. – *Colorado*
Conn. – *Connecticut*
Cord. – *Cordillera*
D.C. – *District of Columbia*
Del. – *Delaware*
Dep. – *Dependency*
Des. – *Desert*
Dist. – *District*
Dom. Rep. – *Dominican Republic*
E. – *East*
Eng. – *England*
Fd. – *Fjord*
Fed. – *Federal, Federation*
Fla. – *Florida*
Fr. – *France, French*
G. – *Golfe, Golfo, Gulf, Guba*
Ga. – *Georgia*
Gt. – *Great*
Hants. – *Hampshire*
Hd. – *Head*
Hts. – *Heights*
I.(s) – *Ile, Ilha, Insel, Isla, Island (s)*
Id. – *Idaho*
Ill. – *Illinois*
Ind. – *Indiana*
J. – *Jezero (L.)*
K. – *Kap, Kapp*
Kans. – *Kansas*
Kep. – *Kepulauan (I.)*
Kól. – *Kólpos (B.)*
Ky. – *Kentucky*
L. – *Lac, Lacul, Lago, Lagoa, Lake, Limni, Loch, Lough*
La. – *Louisana*
Ld. – *Land*
Mad. P. – *Madhýa Pradesh*
Man. – *Manitoba*
Mass. – *Massachusetts*
Md. – *Maryland*
Me. – *Maine*
Mich. – *Michigan*
Minn. – *Minnesota*
Miss. – *Mississippi*
Mo. – *Missouri*
Mont. – *Montana*
Mt.(s) – *Mont, Monte, Monti, Muntii, Montaña, Mountain (s)*
Mys. – *Mysore*
N. – *North, Northern*
N.B. – *New Brunswick*
N.C. – *North Carolina*
N.D. – *North Dakota*
N.H. – *New Hampshire*
N. Ire. – *Northern Ireland*
N.J. – *New Jersey*
N. Mex. – *New Mexico*
N.S.W. – *New South Wales*
N.Y. – *New York*
N.Z. – *New Zealand*
Nat. Park – *National Park*
Nebr. – *Nebraska*
Neth. – *Netherlands*
Nev. – *Nevada*
Newf. – *Newfoundland*
Nic. – *Nicaragua*
Nig. – *Nigeria*
O.F.S. – *Orange Free State*
Okla. – *Oklahoma*
Ont. – *Ontario*
Oreg. – *Oregon*
Os. – *Ostrov (I.)*
Oz – *Ozero (L.)*
P. – *Pass, Passo, Pasul*
P.N.G. – *Papua New Guinea*
Pa. – *Pennsylvania*
Pak. – *Pakistan*
Pass. – *Passage*
Pen. – *Peninsula*
Pk. – *Peak*
Plat. – *Plateau*
Pol. – *Poluostrov*
Port. – *Portugal, Portuguese*
Prov. – *Province, Provincial*
Pt. – *Point*
Pta. – *Ponta, Punta*
Pte. – *Pointe*
Que. – *Quebec*
Queens. – *Queensland*
R. – *Rio, River*
R.S.F.S.R. – *Russian Soviet Federal Socialist Republic*
Ra.(s) – *Range(s)*
Reg. – *Region*
Rep. – *Republic*
Res. – *Reserve, Reservoir*
S. – *South*
S. Africa – *South Africa*
S.C. – *S. Carolina*
S.D. – *South Dakota*
S. Leone – *Sierra Leone*
S.S.R. – *Soviet Socialist Republic*
Sa. – *Serra, Sierra*
Sask. – *Saskatchewan*
Scot. – *Scotland*
Sd. – *Sound*
Sp. – *Spain, Spanish*
St. – *Saint*
Str. – *Strait, Stretto*
Switz. – *Switzerland*
Tanz. – *Tanzania*
Tas. – *Tasmania*
Tenn. – *Tennessee*
Terr. – *Territory*
Tex. – *Texas*
U.K. – *United Kingdom*
U.S.A. – *United States of America*
U.S.S.R. – *Union of Soviet Socialist Republics*
Ut. P. – *Uttar Pradesh*
Va. – *Virginia*
Vdkhr. – *Vodokhranilishche (Res.)*
Ven. – *Venezuela*
Vic. – *Victoria*
Vt. – *Vermont*
W. – *West*
W. Va. – *West Virginia*
Wis. – *Wisconsin*
Wyo. – *Wyoming*
Yorks. – *Yorkshire*
Yug. – *Yugoslavia*

A

24 Aachen 50 47N 6 4E
73 A'Âlâ en Nîl □ 8 50N 29 55E
25 Aalen 48 49N 10 6E
16 Aalsmeer 52 17N 4 43E
16 Aalst 50 56N 4 2E
16 Aalten 51 56N 6 35E
25 Aarau 47 23N 8 4E
25 Aare, R. 47 37N 8 13E
25 Aargau □ 47 26N 8 10E
45 Aarhus □ 56 15N 10 15E
16 Aarschot 50 59N 4 49E
72 Aba 5 10N 7 19E
55 Abā Saud 17 15N 43 55E
56 Abadan 30 22N 48 20E
30 Abadin 43 21N 7 29W
109 Abai 25 58S 55 54W
51 Abakan 53 40N 91 10E
32 Abanilla 38 12N 1 3W
57 Abarqu 31 10N 53 20E
54 Abasan 31 19N 34 21E
66 Abashiri 44 0N 144 15E
66 Abashiri-Wan, G. 44 0N 144 30E
50 Abay 49 38N 72 53E
74 Abaya, L. 6 30N 37 50E
50 Abaza 52 39N 90 6E
54 Abba Hillēl 31 42N 34 38E
19 Abbeville, Fr. 50 6N 1 49E
99 Abbeville, U.S.A. 30 0N 92 7W
36 Abbiategrasso 45 23N 8 55E
58 Abbottabad 34 10N 73 15E
73 Abéché 13 50N 20 35E
30 Abejar 41 48N 2 47W
45 Åbenrå 55 3N 9 25E
72 Abeokuta 7 3N 3 19E
13 Aberayron 52 15N 4 16W
13 Aberdare 51 43N 3 27W
84 Aberdeen, Australia 32 9S 150 56E
14 Aberdeen, U.K. 57 9N 2 6W
102 Aberdeen, Id. 42 57N 112 50W
99 Aberdeen, Miss. 33 49N 88 13W
100 Aberdeen, S.D. 45 28N 98 29W
102 Aberdeen, Wash. 46 59N 123 50W
13 Aberdovey 52 33N 4 3W
14 Aberfeldy 56 37N 3 50W
30 Abergaria-a-Velha 40 41N 8 32W
13 Abergavenny 51 49N 3 1W
13 Aberystwyth 52 25N 4 6W
55 Abhā 18 0N 42 34E
72 Abidjan 5 26N 3 58W
100 Abilene, Kans. 39 0N 97 16W
101 Abilene, Tex. 32 22N 99 40W
13 Abingdon 51 40N 1 17W
49 Abkhaz A.S.S.R. 43 0N 41 0E
51 Abkit 64 10N 157 10E
60 Abohar 30 10N 74 10E
72 Abomey 7 10N 2 5E
74 Abong Mbang 4 0N 13 8E
27 Abony 47 12N 20 3E
73 Abou Deïa 11 20N 19 20E
14 Aboyne 57 4N 2 48W
56 Abqaiq 26 0N 49 45E
31 Abrantes 39 24N 8 7W
30 Abraveses 40 41N 7 55E
19 Abreschviller 48 39N 7 6E
37 Abruzzi □ 42 15N 14 0E
102 Absaroka Ra. 44 40N 110 0W
56 Abū al Khasib 30 25N 48 0E
55 Abu Arish 16 53N 42 48E
73 Abu Dis 19 12N 33 38E
54 Abū Ghōsh 31 48N 35 6E
73 Abu Hamed 19 32N 33 13E
73 Abu Tig 27 4N 31 15E
73 Abū Zabad 12 25N 29 10E
57 Abū Zabī 24 28N 54 36E
73 Abyad, Gebel Reg. 17 30N 28 0E
104 Acajutla 13 36N 89 50W
104 Acámbaro 20 0N 100 40W
104 Acaponeta 22 30N 105 20W
104 Acapulco 16 51N 99 56W
111 Acará 1 57S 48 11W
104 Acatlan 18 10N 98 3W
104 Acayucan 17 59N 94 58W
36 Accéglio 44 28N 6 59E
72 Accra 5 35N 0 6W
12 Accrington 53 46N 2 22W
64 Aceh □ 4 50N 96 0E
39 Acerra 40 57N 14 22E
31 Aceuchal 38 39N 6 30W
60 Achalpur 21 22N 77 32E
26 Achenkirch 47 32N 11 45E
26 Achensee, L. 47 26N 11 45E
60 Acher 23 10N 72 32E
15 Achill 53 56N 9 55W
15 Achill, I. 53 58N 10 5W
51 Achinsk 56 20N 90 20E
39 Acireale 37 37N 15 9E
105 Acklins I. 22 30N 74 0W
92 Acme 51 33N 113 30W
108 Aconcagua, Cerro, Mt. 32 39S 70 0W
108 Aconcagua □ 32 15S 70 30W
39 Acquaviva delle Fonti 40 53N 16 50E
36 Acqui 44 40N 8 28E
110 Acre □ 9 1S 71 0W
39 Acri 39 29N 16 23E
27 Acs 47 42N 18 0E
55 Ad Dam 20 33N 44 45E
56 Ad Dammam 26 20N 50 5E
56 Ad Khālis 33 40N 44 55E
101 Ada, U.S.A. 34 50N 96 45W
40 Ada, Yug. 45 49N 20 9E
30 Adaja, R. 41 32N 4 52W
55 Adale 2 58N 46 27E
109 Adamantina 21 42S 51 4W
73 Adamaoua, Massif de l' 7 20N 12 20E
36 Adamello, Mt. 46 10N 10 34E
97 Adams, Mass. 42 38N 73 8W
100 Adams, Wis. 43 59N 89 50W
102 Adams, Mt. 46 10N 121 28W
62 Adam's Bridge 9 15N 79 40E
62 Adam's Pk. 6 55N 80 45E
31 Adamuz 38 2N 4 32W
56 Adana 37 0N 35 16E
30 Adanero 40 56N 4 36W
65 Adaut 8 8S 131 7E
36 Adda, R. 45 8N 9 53E
73 Addis Ababa= Addis Abeba 9 2N 38 42E
73 Addis Abeba 9 2N 38 42E
81 Adelaide 34 52S 138 30E
5 Adelaide I. 67 15S 68 30W
88 Adelaide Pen. 67 40N 98 0W
82 Adelaide River 13 15S 131 7E
32 Ademuz 40 5N 1 13W
55 Aden= Al 'Adan 12 50N 45 0E
55 Aden, G. of 13 0N 50 0E
36 Adige, R. 45 10N 12 20E
62 Adilabad 19 33N 78 35E
62 Adirampattinam 10 28N 79 20E
97 Adirondack Mts. 44 0N 74 15W
41 Adjud 46 7N 27 10E
82 Admiralty, G. 14 20S 125 55E
102 Admiralty Inlet 48 0N 122 40W
92 Admiralty I. 57 50N 134 30W
76 Admiralty Is. 2 0S 147 0E
62 Adoni 15 33N 77 18E
27 Adony 47 6N 18 52E
20 Adour, R. 43 32N 1 32W
61 Adra, India 23 30N 86 42E
33 Adra, Sp. 36 43N 3 3W
39 Adrano 37 40N 14 19E
72 Adrar des Iforas, Mts. 19 40N 1 40E
37 Ádria 45 4N 12 3E
98 Adrian 41 55N 84 0W
62 Adur 9 8N 76 40E
49 Adzhar A.S.S.R. 42 0N 42 0E
43 Ægean Sea 37 0N 25 0E
67 Aerhtai Shan, Mts. 48 0N 90 0E
45 Ærø, I. 54 53N 10 20E
45 Ærøskøbing 54 53N 10 20E
57 Afghanistan ■ 33 0N 65 0E
55 Afgoi 2 7N 44 59E
39 Afragola 40 54N 14 15E
71 Africa 5 0N 20 0E
111 Afuá 0 15S 50 10W
54 Afula 32 37N 35 17E
56 Afyon 38 20N 30 15E
72 Agadez 16 58N 7 59E
72 Agadir 30 28N 9 25W
51 Agapa 71 27N 89 15E
61 Agartala 23 50N 91 23E
41 Agăş 46 28N 26 15E
62 Agashi 19 32N 72 47E
65 Agats 5 34S 138 5E
72 Agboville 5 55N 4 15W
20 Agde 43 19N 3 28E
20 Agen 44 12N 0 38E
45 Agger 56 47N 8 13E
39 Agira 37 40N 14 30E
20 Agly, R. 42 47N 3 2E
83 Agnew 28 1S 120 30E
20 Agout, R. 43 47N 1 41E
60 Agra 27 17N 77 58E
32 Agreda 41 51N 1 55W
38 Agrigento 37 19N 13 33E
43 Agrinion 38 37N 21 27E
39 Agrópoli 40 23N 14 59E
111 Agua Clara 20 25S 52 45W
104 Agua Prieta 31 20N 109 32W
110 Aguadas 5 40N 75 38W
105 Aguadilla 18 27N 67 10W
91 Aguanish 50 14N 62 2W
104 Aguascalientes 22 0N 102 12W
104 Aguascalientes □ 22 0N 102 20W
30 Agueda 40 34N 8 27W
31 Aguilar 37 31N 4 40W
30 Aguilar de Campóo 42 47N 4 15W
108 Aguilares 27 26S 65 35W
33 Aguilas 37 23N 1 35W
75 Agulhas, K. 34 52S 20 0E
54 Agur 31 42N 34 55E
72 Ahaggar, Reg. 23 0N 6 30E
85 Ahaura 42 20S 171 32E
24 Ahaus 52 4N 7 1E
24 Ahlen 51 45N 7 52E
60 Ahmadabad 23 0N 72 40E
62 Ahmadnagar 19 7N 74 46E
60 Ahmadpur 29 12N 71 10E
24 Ahrensbök 54 0N 10 34E
104 Ahuachapán 13 54N 89 52W
56 Ahvāz 31 20N 48 40E
47 Ahvenanmaa= Åland, I. 60 15N 20 0E
55 Ahwar 13 31N 46 42E
57 Aibaq 36 15N 68 5E
66 Aichi □ 35 0N 137 15E
39 Aidone 37 26N 14 26E
19 Aignay-le-Duc 47 40N 4 43E
109 Aigua 34 12S 54 45W
20 Aigueperse 46 3N 3 13E
21 Aigues-Mortes 43 35N 4 2E
21 Aigues-Mortes, G. d' 43 31N 4 3E
20 Aiguillon 44 18N 0 21E
68 Aihun 49 55N 127 30E
59 Aijal 23 40N 92 44E
99 Aiken 33 44N 81 50W
14 Ailsa Craig, I. 55 15N 5 7W
51 Aim 59 0N 133 55E
111 Aimorés 19 30S 41 4W
21 Ain □ 46 5N 5 20E
72 Aïn Beida 35 50N 7 35E
56 Ain Dār 25 55N 49 10E
55 Ainabo 9 0N 46 25E
43 Aínos Óros 38 10N 20 35E
72 Aïr 18 0N 8 0E
14 Airdrie 55 53N 3 57W
20 Aire, Landes 43 40N 0 20W
19 Aire, Pas-de-Calais 50 37N 2 22E
19 Aire, R., Fr. 49 19N 4 49E
12 Aire, R., U.K. 53 44N 0 44W
20 Airvault 46 50N 0 8W
19 Aisne, R. 49 26N 2 50E
19 Aisne □ 49 42N 3 40E
33 Aitana, Sa. de 38 35N 0 24W
43 Aitolía kai Akarnanía □ 38 45N 21 18E
43 Aitolikón 38 26N 21 21E
67 Aitush 39 54N 75 40E
41 Aiud 46 19N 23 44E
21 Aix-en-Provence 43 32N 5 27E
21 Aix-les-Bains 45 41N 5 53E
20 Aix-les-Thermes 42 43N 1 51E
43 Aíyina, I. 37 45N 23 26E
42 Aiyínion 40 28N 22 28E
43 Aiyion 38 15N 22 5E
18 Aizenay 46 44N 1 38W
21 Ajaccio 41 55N 8 40E
21 Ajaccio, G. d' 41 52N 8 40E
83 Ajana 27 56S 114 35E
96 Ajax 43 50N 79 1W
73 Ajdabiyah 30 54N 20 4E
54 'Ajlun 32 18N 35 47E
57 Ajman 25 25N 55 30E
60 Ajmer 26 28N 74 37E
103 Ajo 32 18N 112 54W
62 Akalkot 17 32N 76 12E
85 Akaroa 43 49S 172 59E
66 Akashi 34 45N 135 0E
44 Akershus □ 60 10N 11 15E
74 Aketi 2 38N 23 47E
43 Akhaía □ 38 5N 21 45E
43 Akharnaí 38 5N 23 44E
56 Akhisar 38 56N 27 48E
43 Akhladhókambos 37 31N 22 35E
73 Akhmîm 26 31N 31 47E
90 Akimiski I. 52 50N 81 30W
66 Akita 39 45N 140 0E
66 Akita □ 39 40N 140 30E
72 Akjoujt 19 45N 14 15W
54 Akko 32 35N 35 4E
50 Akkol 43 36N 70 45E
88 Aklavik 68 25N 135 0W
66 Akō 34 45N 134 24E
60 Akola 20 42N 77 2E
73 Akordat 15 30N 37 40E
60 Akot 21 10N 77 10E
89 Akpatok I. 60 30N 68 0W
46 Akranes 64 19N 22 6W
96 Akron 41 7N 81 31W
50 Aksarka 66 31N 67 50E
56 Aksehir 38 18N 31 30E
51 Aksenovo Zilovskoye 53 20N 117 40E
67 Aksu 41 4N 80 5E
73 Aksum 14 5N 38 40E
50 Aktogay 44 25N 76 44E
50 Aktyubinsk 50 10N 57 3E
72 Aku 6 40N 7 18E
72 Akure 7 15N 5 5E
46 Akureyri 65 40N 18 5W
59 Akyab 20 15N 92 45E
55 Al 'Adan 12 50N 45 0E
56 Al Amārah 31 55N 47 15E
56 Al 'Aqabah 29 37N 35 0E
54 Al Barah 31 55N 35 12E
56 Al Basrah 30 30N 47 55E
73 Al Bayḍā 32 30N 21 40E
57 Al Buraimi 24 15N 55 53E
56 Al Hadithan 34 0N 41 13E
56 Al Hadr 35 35N 42 44E
56 Al Hasa, Reg. 25 40N 50 0E
56 Al Hasakah 36 35N 40 45E
55 Al Hauta 16 5N 48 20E
55 Al Hawra 13 49N 47 37E
56 Al Hillah, Iraq 32 30N 44 25E
56 Al Hillah, Saudi Arabia 23 35N 46 50E
23 Al Hilwah 23 24N 46 48E
56 Al Hindiyah 32 30N 44 10E
72 Al-Hoceïma 35 15N 3 58W
56 Al Hufūf 25 25N 49 45E
56 Al Jahrah 29 25N 47 40E
56 Al Jalāmid 31 20N 39 45E
55 Al Jazir 18 30N 56 31N
56 Al Jazirah, Reg. 26 10N 21 20E
56 Al Jubail 27 0N 49 50E
55 Al Juwara 19 0N 57 13E
57 Al Khābūrah 23 57N 57 5E
55 Al Khalaf 20 30N 57 56E
73 Al Khums 32 40N 14 17E
56 Al Kūt 32 30N 46 0E
56 Al Kuwayt 29 20N 48 0E
56 Al Ladhiqiyah 35 30N 35 45E
55 Al Līth 20 9N 40 15E
56 Al Madīnah 24 35N 39 52E
54 Al Mafraq 32 17N 36 14E
57 Al Manamāh 26 10N 50 30E
73 Al Marj 32 25N 20 30E
55 Al Masīrah 20 25N 58 50E
55 Al Matamma 16 43N 33 22E
56 Al Mawsil 36 15N 43 5E
54 Al Mazra' 31 18N 35 32E
56 Al Miqdadıyah 34 0N 45 0E
56 Al Mubarraz 25 30N 49 40E
57 Al Muharraq 26 15N 50 40E
55 Al Mukha 13 18N 43 15E
56 Al Qamishli 37 10N 41 10E
56 Al Qatif 26 35N 50 0E
73 Al-Qatṛūn 24 56N 15 3E
55 Al Qunfidha 19 3N 41 4E
55 Al Ubailah 21 59N 50 57E
73 Al 'Ugaylah 30 12N 19 10E
57 Al Wakrah 25 10N 51 40E
56 Al Wari 'ah 27 50N 47 30E
36 Ala 45 46N 11 0E
68 Ala Shan, Reg. 40 0N 104 0E
99 Alabama, R. 31 8N 87 57W
99 Alabama □ 31 0N 87 0W
111 Alagôa Grande 7 3S 35 35W
111 Alagôas □ 9 0S 36 0W
111 Alagoinhas 12 0S 38 20W
32 Alagón 41 46N 1 12W
30 Alagón, R. 39 44N 6 53W
105 Alajuela 10 2N 84 8W
48 Alakurtti 67 0N 30 30E
103 Alameda 35 10N 106 43W
103 Alamogordo 32 59N 106 0W
103 Alamosa 37 30N 106 0W
62 Aland 17 36N 76 35E
47 Åland, I. 60 15N 20 0E
31 Alandroal 38 41N 7 24W
31 Alanis 38 3N 5 43W
50 Alapayevsk 57 52N 61 42E
30 Alar del Rey 42 38N 4 20W
32 Alaraz 40 45N 5 17W
68 Alashanchih 38 58N 105 14E
88 Alaska □ 65 0N 150 0W
88 Alaska, G. of 58 0N 145 0W
88 Alaska Pen. 56 0N 160 0W
88 Alaska Ra. 62 50N 151 0W
38 Alatri 41 44N 13 21E
48 Alatyr 54 45N 46 35E
110 Alausi 2 0S 78 50W
30 Álava □ 42 48N 2 28W
81 Alawoona 34 45S 140 30E
36 Alba 44 41N 8 1E
30 Alba de Tormes 40 50N 5 30W
40 Albac 46 28N 23 1E
33 Albacete 39 0N 1 50W
33 Albacete □ 38 50N 2 0W
45 Ålbæk 57 14N 10 26E
33 Albaida 38 51N 0 31W
32 Albalate del Arzobispo 41 6N 0 31W
41 Alba-Iulia 46 4N 23 35E
42 Albania ■ 41 0N 20 0E
38 Albano Laziale 41 44N 12 40E
83 Albany, Australia 35 1S 117 58E
99 Albany, Ga. 31 40N 84 10W
97 Albany, N.Y. 42 40N 73 47W
102 Albany, Oreg. 44 41N 123 0W
90 Albany, R. 52 17N 81 31W

108 Albardón 31 20s 68 30w
32 Albarracin 40 25N 1 26w
32 Albarracin, Sa. de 40 30N 1 30w
99 Albemarle 35 27N 80 15w
36 Albenga 44 3N 8 12 E
30 Alberche, R. 39 58N 4 46w
33 Alberique 39 7N 0 31w
32 Alberes, Mts. 42 28N 2 56w
92 Alberni 49 20N 124 50w
24 Albersdorf 54 8N 9 19 E
91 Albert, Canada 45 51N 64 38w
19 Albert, Fr. 50 0N 2 38 E
74 Albert, L.= Mobutu Sese Seko, L. 1 30N 31 0 E
100 Albert Lea 43 32N 93 20w
74 Albert Nile, R. 3 36N 32 2 E
105 Albert Town 18 17N 77 33w
92 Alberta □ 54 40N 115 0w
84 Alberton 38 35s 146 40 E
21 Albertville 45 40N 6 22 E
74 Albertville= Kalemie 5 55s 29 9 E
57 Alberz, Reshteh-Ye-Kūkhā-Ye, Mts. 36 0N 52 0 E
20 Albi 43 56N 2 9 E
111 Albina, 5 37N 54 15w
36 Albino 45 46N 9 17 E
98 Albion 42 15N 84 45w
33 Alboran, I. 35 57N 3 0w
33 Alborea 39 17N 1 24w
45 Ålbôrg 57 2N 9 54 E
33 Albox 37 23N 2 8w
31 Albufeira 37 5N 8 15w
33 Albuñol 36 48N 3 11w
103 Albuquerque 35 5N 106 47w
39 Alburno, Mt. 40 32N 15 20 E
31 Alburquerque 39 15N 6 59w
84 Albury 36 3s 146 56 E
31 Alcácer do Sol 38 22N 8 33w
31 Alcáçovas 38 23N 8 9w
32 Alcalá de Chisvert 40 19N 0 13 E
31 Alcalá de Guadaira 37 20N 5 50w
31 Alcalá de los Gazules 36 29N 5 43w
30 Alcalá de Henares 40 28N 3 22w
31 Alcalá la Real 32 27N 3 57w
38 Alcamo 37 59N 12 55 E
32 Alcanadre 42 24N 2 7w
32 Alcanadre, R. 41 37N 0 12w
32 Alcanar 40 33N 0 28 E
31 Alcanede 39 25N 8 49w
31 Alcanena 39 27N 8 40w
32 Alcaníz 41 2N 0 8w
111 Alcántara, Brazil 2 20s 44 30w
31 Alcântara, Sp. 39 41N 6 57w
33 Alcantarilla 37 59N 1 12w
33 Alcaracejos 38 24N 4 58w
33 Alcaraz 38 40N 2 29w
33 Alcaraz, Sa. de 38 40N 2 20w
31 Alcaudete 37 35N 4 5w
31 Alcazar de San Juan 39 24N 3 12w
33 Alcira 39 9N 0 30w
30 Alcobaça 39 32N 9 0w
30 Alcobendas 40 32N 3 38w
32 Alcolea del Pinar 41 2N 2 28w
31 Alcora 40 5N 0 14w
31 Alcoutim 37 25N 7 28w
33 Alcoy 38 43N 0 30w
32 Alcubierre, Sa. de 41 45N 0 22w
32 Alcublas 39 48N 0 43w
32 Alcudia 39 51N 3 9 E
32 Alcudia, B. de 39 45N 3 14 E
31 Alcudia, Sa. de la 38 34N 4 30w
71 Aldabra Is. 9 22s 46 28 E
51 Aldan, R. 63 28N 129 35 E
13 Aldeburgh 52 9N 1 35 E
31 Aldeia Nova 37 55N 7 24w
18 Alderney, I. 49 42N 2 12w
13 Aldershot 51 15N 0 43w
72 Aleg 17 3N 13 55w
109 Alegre 20 50s 41 40w
109 Alegrete 29 40s 56 0w
50 Aleisk 52 40N 83 0 E
77 Alejandro Selkirk, I. 33 50s 80 15w
49 Aleksandrov Gai 50 15N 48 35 E
51 Aleksandrovsk-Sakhalinskiy 50 50N 142 20 E
51 Aleksandrovskiy Zavod 50 40N 117 50 E
50 Aleksandrovskoye 60 35N 77 50 E
28 Aleksandrów Kujawski 52 53N 18 43 E
28 Aleksandrów Łódzki 51 49N 19 17 E
40 Aleksinac 43 31N 21 12 E
109 Além Paraíba 21 52s 42 41w
45 Ålen 62 49N 11 17 E
18 Alençon 48 27N 0 4 E
94 Alenuihaha Chan. 20 25N 156 0w
56 Aleppo=Ḥalab 36 10N 37 15 E
21 Aléria 42 5N 9 30 E
92 Alert Bay 50 30N 127 35w
21 Alès 44 9N 4 5 E
36 Alessandria 44 54N 8 37 E
76 Aleutian Is. 52 0N 175 0w
92 Alexander Arch. 57 0N 135 0w
75 Alexander Bay 28 36s 16 33 E
99 Alexander City 32 56N 85 57w
5 Alexander I. 69 0s 70 0w
85 Alexandra 45 14s 169 25 E
73 Alexandria=El Iskandarîya 31 0N 30 0 E
90 Alexandria, Canada 45 19N 74 38w
41 Alexandria, Rumania 43 57N 25 24 E
75 Alexandria, S. Africa 33 38s 26 28 E
101 Alexandria, La. 31 20N 92 30w
100 Alexandria, Minn. 45 50N 95 20w
98 Alexandria, Va. 38 47N 77 1w
97 Alexandria Bay 44 20N 75 52w
42 Alexandroúpolis 40 50N 25 24 E
32 Alfambra 40 33N 1 5w
32 Alfaro 42 10N 1 50w
41 Alfatar 43 59N 27 13 E
24 Alfeld 52 0N 9 49 E
109 Alfenas 21 25s 45 57w
37 Alfonsine 44 30N 12 1 E
14 Alford 53 16N 0 10 E
12 Alfreton 53 6N 1 22w
50 Alga 49 46N 57 20 E
31 Algar 36 40N 5 39w
29 Algarve, Reg. 37 15N 8 10w
31 Algeciras 36 9N 5 28w
33 Algemesí 39 11N 0 27w
72 Alger 36 42N 3 8 E
72 Algeria ■ 35 10N 3 0 E
38 Alghero 40 34N 8 20 E
72 Algiers=Alger 36 42N 3 8 E
75 Algoabaai 33 50s 25 45 E
31 Algodanales 36 54N 3 48w
90 Algonquin Prov. Park 45 35N 78 35w
33 Alhama de Almería 36 57N 2 34w
32 Alhama de Aragón 41 18N 1 54w
33 Alhama de Murcia 37 51N 1 25w
33 Alhambra, Sp. 38 54N 3 4w
103 Alhambra, U.S.A. 34 0N 118 10w
31 Alhaurín el Grande 36 39N 4 41w
32 Aliaga 40 40N 0 42w
42 Aliákmon, R. 40 30N 22 36 E
40 Alibunar 45 5N 20 57 E
33 Alicante 38 23N 0 30w
33 Alicante □ 38 30N 0 37w
101 Alice 27 47N 98 1w
92 Alice Arm 55 29N 129 23w
82 Alice Downs 17 45s 127 56 E
80 Alice Springs 23 40s 135 50 E
75 Alicedale 33 15s 26 4 E
60 Aligarh 27 55N 78 10 E
56 Aligudarz 33 25N 49 45 E
30 Alijó 41 16N 7 27w
45 Alingsås 57 56N 12 31 E
61 Alipore 22 32N 88 24 E
61 Alipur Duar 26 30N 89 35 E
96 Aliquippa 40 38N 80 18w
75 Aliwal Nord 30 45s 26 45 E
30 Aljezur 37 18N 8 49w
31 Aljustrel 37 55N 8 10w
16 Alkmaar 52 37N 4 45 E
103 All American Canal 32 45N 115 0w
61 Allahabad 25 25N 81 58 E
93 Allan 51 53N 106 4w
91 Allard Lake 50 40N 63 10w
30 Allariz 42 11N 7 50w
20 Allassac 45 15N 1 29 E
86 Allegheny Mts. 38 0N 80 0w
96 Allegheny, R. 40 27N 80 0w
20 Allègre 45 12N 3 41 E
104 Allende 28 20N 100 50w
97 Allentown 40 36N 75 30w
26 Allentsteig 48 31N 15 20 E
62 Alleppey 9 30N 76 28 E
24 Aller, R. 52 57N 9 11 E
21 Allevard 45 24N 6 5 E
100 Alliance, Nebr. 42 10N 102 50w
96 Alliance, Ohio 40 53N 81 7w
20 Allier, R. 46 58N 3 4 E
20 Allier □ 46 25N 3 0 E
80 Alligator Creek 19 23s 146 58 E
90 Alliston 44 15N 79 55w
14 Alloa 56 7N 3 49w
21 Allos 44 15N 6 38 E
62 Alluru Kottapatnam 15 30N 80 10 E
90 Alma, Canada 48 35N 71 40w
91 Alma, U.S.A. 43 25N 84 40w
50 Alma Ata 43 15N 76 57 E
31 Almada 38 40N 9 9w
80 Almaden 17 22s 144 40 E
31 Almadén 38 49N 4 52w
31 Almagro 38 50N 3 45w
33 Almansa 38 51N 1 5w
30 Almanza 42 39N 5 3w
30 Almanzor, P. de 40 15N 5 18w
33 Almanzora, R. 37 14N 1 46w
40 Almaş, Mt. 44 49N 22 12 E
32 Almazán 41 30N 2 30w
32 Almazora 39 57N 0 3w
111 Almeirim, Brazil 1 30s 52 0w
31 Almeirim, Port. 39 12N 8 37w
32 Almenara 39 46N 0 14w
16 Almelo 52 22N 6 42 E
32 Almenar 41 43N 2 12w
33 Almenara, Sa. de 37 34N 1 32w
31 Almendralejo 38 41N 6 26w
33 Almería 36 52N 2 32w
33 Almería, G. de 36 40N 2 30w
33 Almería □ 37 20N 2 20w
45 Älmhult 56 32N 14 10 E
105 Almirante 9 10N 82 30w
43 Almirós 39 11N 22 45 E
31 Almodóvar 37 11N 8 2w
31 Almodóvar del Campo 38 43N 4 10w
31 Almogia 36 50N 4 32w
61 Almora 29 38N 79 4 E
33 Almoradi 38 7N 0 46w
30 Almorox 40 14N 4 24w
31 Almuñécar 36 43N 3 41w
45 Almvik 57 49N 16 30 E
12 Alnwick 55 25N 1 42w
59 Alon 22 12N 95 5 E
93 Alonsa 50 50N 99 0w
65 Alor, I. 8 15s 124 30 E
63 Alor Setar 6 7N 100 22 E
31 Alora 36 49N 4 46w
31 Alosno 37 33N 7 7w
83 Aloysius, Mt. 26 0s 128 38 E
30 Alpedrinha 40 6N 7 27w
98 Alpena 45 6N 83 24w
21 Alpes-Maritimes □ 43 55N 7 10 E
21 Alpes-de-Haute-Provence □ 44 8N 6 10 E
80 Alpha 24 8s 146 39 E
36 Alpi Apuane, Mts. 44 7N 10 14 E
36 Alpi Atesine, Mts. 46 55N 11 30 E
25 Alpi Lepontine, Mts. 46 22N 8 27 E
36 Alpi Orobie, Mts. 46 7N 10 0 E
25 Alpi Pennine, Mts. 46 0N 7 30 E
25 Alpi Retiche, Mts. 46 45N 10 0 E
31 Alpiarça 39 15N 8 35w
101 Alpine 30 35N 103 35w
8 Alps, Mts. 47 0N 8 0 E
80 Alroy Downs 19 20s 136 5 E
45 Als, I. 54 59N 9 55 E
19 Alsace, Reg. 48 15N 7 25 E
32 Alsasua 42 54N 2 10w
24 Alsfeld 50 44N 9 19 E
12 Alston 54 48N 2 26w
46 Alta 69 55N 23 12 E
108 Alta Gracia 31 40s 64 30w
92 Alta Lake 50 10N 123 0w
46 Altaelv, R. 69 57N 23 17 E
110 Altagracia 10 45N 71 30w
52 Altai, Mts. 48 0N 90 0 E
67 Altai, Mts.= Aerhtai Shan, Mts. 48 0N 90 0 E
111 Altamira 3 0s 52 10w
39 Altamura 40 50N 16 33 E
68 Altanbulag 50 19N 106 30 E
25 Altdorf 46 52N 8 36 E
33 Altea 38 38N 0 2w
24 Altenberg 50 46N 13 47 E
24 Altenburg 50 59N 12 28 E
26 Altenmarkt 47 43N 14 39 E
31 Alter do Chão 39 12N 7 40w
19 Altkirch 47 37N 7 15 E
25 Altmühl, R. 48 55N 11 52 E
29 Alto-Alentejo, Reg. 38 50N 7 40w
111 Alto Araguaia 17 15s 53 20w
109 Alto Paraná □ 25 0s 54 50w
13 Alton, U.K. 51 8N 0 59w
100 Alton, U.S.A. 38 55N 90 5w
24 Altona 53 32N 9 56 E
96 Altoona 40 32N 78 24w
25 Altstätten 47 22N 9 33 E
101 Altus 34 30N 99 25w
67 Altyn Tagh, Mts. 39 0N 89 0 E
55 Alula 11 50N 50 45 E
65 Alusi 7 35s 131 40 E
32 Alustante 40 36N 1 40w
101 Alva 36 50N 98 50w
30 Alvaiázere 39 49N 8 23w
104 Alvarado 18 40N 95 50w
44 Alvdalen, R. 59 23N 13 30 E
31 Alverca 38 56N 9 1w
45 Alvesta 56 54N 14 35 E
84 Alvie 38 15s 143 30 E
31 Alvito 38 15N 8 0w
45 Alvsborgs □ 58 30N 12 30 E
46 Älvsbyn 65 39N 20 59 E
60 Alwar 27 38N 76 34 E
62 Alwaye 10 8N 76 24 E
49 Alyat Pristan 39 59N 49 28 E
14 Alyth 56 38N 3 15w
73 Am-Timan 11 0N 20 10 E
89 Amadjuak 64 0N 72 50w
89 Amadjuak L. 65 0N 71 0w
31 Amadora 38 45N 9 13w
97 Amagansett 40 58N 72 8w
66 Amagasaki 34 42N 135 20 E
45 Amager, I. 55 37N 12 37 E
66 Amakusa-Shotō, Is. 32 15N 130 10 E
44 Åmål 59 2N 12 40 E
62 Amalapuram 16 35N 81 55 E
43 Amaliás 37 47N 21 22 E
60 Amalner 21 5N 75 5 E
109 Amambaí 20 30s 56 0w
109 Amambay □ 23 0s 56 0w
50 Amangeldy 50 10N 65 10 E
39 Amantea 39 8N 16 3 E
111 Amapá 2 5N 50 50w
111 Amapá □ 1 40N 52 0w
111 Amarante, Brazil 6 14s 42 50w
30 Amarante, Port. 41 16N 8 5w
60 Amaravati= Amraoti 20 55N 77 45 E
62 Amaravati, R. 10 58N 78 12 E
31 Amaraleja 38 12N 7 13w
111 Amargosa 13 2s 39 36w
101 Amarillo 35 14N 101 46w
37 Amaro, Mt. 42 5N 14 6 E
56 Amasya 40 40N 35 50 E
104 Amatitlán 14 29N 90 38w
111 Amazon= Amazonas, R. 2 0s 53 30w
111 Amazonas, R. 2 0s 53 30w
110 Amazonas □ 4 20s 64 0w
60 Ambala 30 23N 76 56 E
62 Ambalangoda 6 15N 80 5 E
62 Ambalapuzha 9 25N 76 25 E
75 Ambanja 13 40s 48 27 E
51 Ambarchik 69 40N 162 20 E
108 Ambargasta, Salinas, Reg. 29 0s 64 30w
62 Ambarnath 19 12N 73 22 E
62 Ambasamudram 8 43N 77 25 E
110 Ambato 1 5s 78 42w
75 Ambatolampy 19 20s 47 35 E
25 Amberg 49 25N 11 52 E
104 Ambergris Cay 18 0N 88 0w
21 Ambérieu 45 57N 5 20 E
85 Amberley 43 9s 172 44 E
20 Ambert 45 33N 3 44 E
12 Ambleside 54 26N 2 58w
65 Ambon 3 35s 128 20 E
75 Ambositra 20 31s 47 25 E
103 Amboy 34 33N 115 51w
75 Ambre, C. d' 12 40s 49 10 E
96 Ambridge 40 36N 80 15w
62 Ambur 12 47N 78 43 E
81 Amby 26 30s 148 11 E
50 Amderma 69 45N 61 30 E
104 Ameca 20 30N 104 0w
16 Ameland, I. 53 27N 5 45 E
37 Amélia 42 34N 12 25 E
20 Amèlie-les-Bains-Palalda 42 29N 2 41 E
51 Amen 68 45N 180 0 E
102 American Falls 42 46N 112 56 E
5 American Highland 73 0s 75 0 E
85 American Samoa, I. 14 20s 170 0w
109 Americana 22 45s 47 20w
99 Americus 32 0N 84 10w
16 Amersfoort 52 9N 5 23 E
83 Amery, Australia 31 9s 117 5 E
93 Amery, Canada 56 45N 94 0w
100 Ames 42 0N 93 40w
97 Amesbury 42 50N 70 52w
43 Amfiklia 38 38N 22 35 E
42 Amfípolis 40 48N 23 52 E
43 Amfissa 38 32N 22 22 E
43 Amflokhía 38 52N 21 9 E
51 Amga, R. 62 38N 134 32 E
51 Amgu 45 45N 137 15 E
59 Amherst, Burma 16 0N 97 40 E
91 Amherst, Canada 45 48N 64 8w
97 Amherst, Mass. 42 21N 72 30w
96 Amherst, Ohio 41 23N 82 15w
90 Amherstburg 42 6N 83 6w
37 Amiata, Mte. 42 54N 11 40 E
19 Amiens 49 54N 2 16 E
42 Amindaion 40 42N 21 42 E

53 Amirantes, Is. 6 0s 53 0E
12 Amlwch 53 24N 4 21w
54 'Ammān 32 0N 35 52E
25 Ammersee, L. 48 0N 11 7E
54 Ammi'ad 32 55N 35 32E
19 Amnéville 49 16N 6 9E
30 Amorebieta 43 13N 2 44w
43 Amorgós, I. 36 50N 25 59E
90 Amos 48 35N 78 5w
69 Amoy=Hsiamen 24 25N 118 4E
32 Amposta 40 43N 0 34E
91 Amqui 48 28N 67 27w
60 Amroati 20 55N 77 45E
60 Amreli 21 35N 71 17E
60 Amritsar 31 35N 74 57E
60 Amroha 28 53N 78 30E
24 Amrum, I. 54 37N 8 21E
16 Amsterdam, Neth. 52 23N 4 54E
97 Amsterdam, U.S.A. 42 58N 74 10w
3 Amsterdam, I. 37 30s 77 30E
26 Amstetten 48 7N 14 51E
50 Amu Darya, R. 43 40N 59 1E
88 Amukta Pass. 52 25N 172 0w
88 Amundsen G. 70 30N 123 0w
5 Amundsen Sea 72 0s 115 0w
51 Amur, R. 52 56N 141 10E
30 Amurrio 43 3N 3 0w
30 Amusco 42 10N 4 28w
43 Amvrakíkós Kól. 39 0N 20 55E
56 An Najaf 32 3N 44 15E
56 An Nasiriyah 31 0N 46 15E
63 An Nhon 13 53N 109 6E
56 An Nu'ayriyah 27 30N 48 30E
15 An Uaimh 53 39N 6 40w
54 Anabta 32 19N 35 7E
102 Anaconda 46 7N 113 0w
102 Anacortes 48 30N 122 40w
101 Anadarko 35 4N 98 15w
30 Anadia 40 26N 8 27w
56 Anadolu, Reg. 38 0w 39 0E
51 Anadyr 64 35N 177 20E
51 Anadyr, R. 64 55N 176 5E
38 Anagni 41 44N 13 8E
92 Anahim Lake 52 28N 125 18w
62 Anai Mudi, Mt. 10 12N 77 20E
62 Anaimalai Hills 10 20N 76 40E
62 Anakapalle 17 42N 83 6E
80 Anakie 23 32s 147 45E
64 Anambas, Kep. 3 20N 106 30E
66 Anan 33 54N 134 40E
60 Anand 22 32N 72 59E
62 Anantapur 14 39N 77 42E
58 Anantnag 33 45N 75 10E
111 Anápolis 16 15s 48 50w
57 Anar 30 55N 55 13E
56 Anatolia, Reg.= Anadolu, Reg. 38 0N 39 0E
108 Añatuya 28 20s 62 50w
18 Ancenis 47 21N 1 10w
88 Anchorage 61 10N 149 50w
30 Anciāo 39 56N 8 27w
110 Ancohuma, Mt. 16 0s 68 50w
37 Ancona 43 37N 13 30E
112 Ancud 42 0s 73 50w
112 Ancud, G. de 42 0s 73 0w
108 Andacollo 13 14s 71 6w
44 Andalsnes 62 35N 7 43E
31 Andalucía, Reg. 37 35N 5 0w
99 Andalusia 31 51N 86 30w
63 Andaman Is. 12 30N 92 30E
63 Andaman Sea 13 0N 96 0E
16 Andenne 50 30N 5 5E
25 Andermatt 46 38N 8 35E
24 Andernach 50 24N 7 25E
20 Andernos 44 44N 1 6w
102 Anderson, Calif. 40 30N 122 19w
98 Anderson, Ind. 40 5N 85 40w
99 Anderson, S.C. 34 32N 82 40w
88 Anderson, R. 69 43N 128 58w
106 Andes, Mts. 20 0s 68 0w
62 Andhra Pradesh □ 15 0N 80 0E
43 Andikíthira, I. 35 52N 23 15E
43 Andíparos, I. 37 0N 25 3E
50 Andizhan 41 10N 72 0E
57 Andkhui 36 52N 65 8E
32 Andorra ■ 42 30N 1 30E
13 Andover 51 13N 1 29w
32 Andraitx 39 35N 2 25E
88 Andreanof Is. 51 0N 178 0w
28 Andrespol 51 45N 19 34E
39 Ándria 41 13N 16 17E
40 Andrijevica 42 45N 19 48E
48 Andropov 58 3N 38 52E
105 Andros, I. 24 30N 78 0w
43 Ándros I. 37 50N 24 50E
105 Andros Town 24 43N 77 47w
27 Andrychów 49 51N 19 18E
31 Andújar 38 3N 4 5w
72 Anécho 6 12N 1 34E
105 Anegada I. 18 45N 64 20w
105 Anegada Pass. 18 15N 63 45w
32 Aneto, Pico de 42 37N 0 40E
68 Anganki 47 9N 123 48E
51 Angara, R. 58 6N 93 0E
51 Angarsk 52 30N 104 0E
81 Angaston 34 30s 139 8E
44 Ånge 62 31N 15 35E
104 Angel de la Guarda, I. 29 30N 113 30w
65 Angeles 15 9N 120 35E
45 Ängelholm 56 15N 12 58E
103 Angels Camp 38 8N 120 30w
46 Ångermanälven, R. 62 48N 17 56E
21 Angermünde 53 1N 14 0E
18 Angers 47 30N 0 35E
19 Angerville 48 19N 2 0E
32 Anglés 41 57N 2 38E
12 Anglesey, I. 53 17N 4 20w
20 Anglet 43 29N 1 21w
19 Anglure 48 35N 3 50E
4 Angmagssalik 65 40N 37 20w
74 Ango 4 10N 26 5E
75 Angoche 16 8s 40 0E
108 Angol 37 48s 72 43w
75 Angola ■ 12 0s 18 0E
96 Angola 42 38N 79 2w
20 Angoulême 45 39N 0 10E
20 Angoumois, Reg. 45 30N 0 25E
109 Angra dos Reis 23 0s 44 10w
50 Angren 41 1N 69 45E
105 Anguilla, I. 18 14N 63 5w
80 Angurugu 14 0s 136 25E
14 Angus, Braes of 56 51N 3 0w
45 Anholt, I. 56 42N 11 33E
69 Anhsien 31 30N 104 35E
69 Anhwei □ 33 15N 116 50E
40 Anina 45 5N 21 51E
60 Anjangaon 21 10N 77 20E
60 Anjar 23 6⅛ 70 10E
18 Anjou, Reg. 47 20N 0 15w
68 Anju 39 36N 125 40E
69 Ankang 32 38N 109 5E
56 Ankara 40 0N 32 54E
69 Anking 30 31N 117 2E
24 Anklam 53 51N 13 41E
60 Anklesvar 21 38N 73 3E
98 Ann Arbor 42 17N 83 45w
82 Anna Plains 19 17s 121 37E
72 Annaba 36 50N 7 46E
24 Annaberg-Buchholz 50 34N 12 58E
63 Annam, Reg.= Trung-Phan, Reg. 16 30N 107 30E
63 Annamitique, Chaîne, Mts. 17 0N 106 0E
14 Annan 54 59N 3 16w
14 Annan, R. 54 59N 3 16w
98 Annapolis 38 59N 76 30w
91 Annapolis Royal 44 44N 65 32w
61 Annapurna, Mt. 28 34N 84 50E
21 Annecy 45 55N 6 8E
21 Annecy, L. d' 45 52N 6 10E
21 Annemasse 46 12N 6 16E
67 Anning 24 58N 102 30E
99 Anniston 33 45N 85 50w
21 Annonay 45 15N 4 40E
21 Annot 43 58N 6 38E
43 Ano Viánnos 35 2N 25 21E
100 Anoka 45 10N 93 26w
69 Anping 23 0N 120 6E
25 Ansbach 49 17N 10 34E
68 Anshan 41 3N 122 58E
69 Anshun 26 2N 105 57E
67 Ansi 40 21N 96 10E
32 Ansó 42 51N 0 48w
82 Anson, B. 13 20s 130 6E
97 Ansonia 41 21N 73 6w
90 Ansonville 48 46N 80 43w
14 Anstruther 56 14N 2 40w
65 Ansuda 2 11s 139 22E
68 Anta 46 18N 125 34E
56 Antakya 36 14N 36 10E
75 Antalaha 14 57s 50 20E
56 Antalya 36 52N 30 45E
56 Antalya Körfezi 36 15N 31 30E
75 Antananarivo 18 55s 47 35E
5 Antarctica 90 0s 0 0
5 Antarctic Pen. 67 0s 60 0w
30 Antela, L. de 42 7N 7 40w
108 Antequera, Paraguay 24 8s 57 7w
31 Antequera, Sp. 37 5N 4 33w
103 Anthony 32 1N 106 37w
80 Anthony Lagoon 18 0s 135 30E
21 Antibes 43 34N 7 6E
21 Antibes, C. d' 43 31N 7 7E
91 Anticosti I. 49 20N 62 40w
18 Antifer, C. d' 49 41N 0 10E
100 Antigo 45 8N 89 5w
91 Antigonish 45 38N 61 58w
104 Antigua 14 34N 90 41w
105 Antigua, I. 17 0N 61 50w
105 Antilla 20 40N 75 50w
103 Antimony 38 7N 112 0w
20 Antioche, Pertuis d' 46 5N 1 30w
110 Antioquia 6 40N 75 55w
76 Antipodes Is. 49 45s 178 40E
108 Antofagasta 23 50s 70 30w
108 Antofagasta □ 23 30s 69 0w
108 Antofalla, Mt. 25 33s 67 56w
75 Antongil, B. d' 15 30s 49 50E
109 Antonina 25 26s 48 42w
75 António Enes= Angoche 16 8s 40 0E
18 Antrain 48 28N 1 30w
15 Antrim 54 43N 6 13w
15 Antrim □ 54 55N 6 10w
75 Antsirabe 19 55s 47 2E
68 Antung 40 10N 124 18E
16 Antwerp= Antwerpen 51 13N 4 25E
16 Antwerpen 51 13N 4 25E
16 Antwerpen □ 51 15N 4 40E
62 Anuradhapura 8 22N 80 28E
16 Anvers= Antwerpen 51 13N 4 25E
88 Anvik 62 40N 160 12w
68 Anyang 36 7N 114 26E
65 Anyer-Lor 6 6s 105 56E
69 Anyi 28 50N 115 31E
50 Anzhero Sudzhensk 56 10N 83 40E
38 Ánzio 41 28N 12 37E
32 Aoiz 42 46N 1 22w
66 Aomori 40 45N 140 45E
66 Aomori □ 40 45N 140 40E
60 Aonla 28 16N 79 11E
36 Aosta 45 43N 7 20E
73 Aozou 21 49N 17 25E
65 Aparri 18 22N 121 38E
40 Apatin 45 40N 19 0E
104 Apatzingán 19 0N 102 20w
16 Apeldoorn 52 13N 5 57E
24 Apen 53 12N 7 47E
64 Apenam 8 35s 116 13E
9 Apennines, Mts.= Appennini, Mts. 41 0N 15 0E
104 Apizaco 19 26N 98 9w
24 Apolda 51 1N 11 30E
73 Apollonia= Marsa Susa 32 52N 21 59E
100 Apostle Is. 47 0N 90 30w
109 Apóstoles 27 55s 55 45w
110 Apoteri 4 2N 58 32w
86 Appalachian Mts. 38 0N 80 0w
37 Appennini, Mts. 41 0N 15 0E
36 Appenino Ligure, Mts. 44 30N 9 0E
25 Appenzell □ 47 23N 9 23E
37 Appiano 46 27N 11 27E
12 Appleby 54 35N 2 29w
98 Appleton 44 17N 88 25w
111 Approuagne 4 20N 52 0w
39 Apricena 41 47N 15 25E
21 Apt 43 53N 5 24E
109 Apucarana 23 55s 51 33w
40 Apuseni, Mts. 46 30N 22 45E
57 Aq Chah 37 0N 66 5E
56 'Aqaba 29 31N 35 0E
56 'Aqaba, Khalīj al 28 15N 33 20E
73 Aqiq 18 14N 38 12E
54 Aqraba 32 9N 35 20E
111 Aquidauana 20 30s 55 50w
55 Ar Rab' al Khālī 21 0N 51 0E
54 Ar Ramthā 32 34N 36 0E
56 Ar Raqqah 35 56N 39 1E
56 Ar Riyāḍ 24 41N 46 42E
57 Ar Ruska 23 35N 53 30E
56 Ar Ruṭbah 33 0N 40 15E
73 Arab, Bahr el, R. 9 2N 29 28E
52 Arabia, Reg. 25 0N 45 0E
70 Arabian Des. 28 0N 32 30E
111 Aracajú 10 55s 37 4w
110 Aracataca 10 38N 74 9w
111 Aracati 4 30s 37 44w
109 Araçatuba 21 10s 50 30w
31 Aracena 37 53N 6 58w
31 Aracena, Sa. de 37 48N 6 40w
111 Araçuai 16 52s 42 4w
54 'Arad 31 17N 35 12E
27 Arad 46 10N 21 20E
27 Arad □ 46 20N 21 45E
32 Aragón, R. 42 13N 1 44w
32 Aragon, Reg. 41 0N 1 0w
38 Aragona 37 24N 13 36E
111 Araguacema 8 50s 49 20w
111 Araguaia, R. 5 21s 48 41w
111 Araguari 18 38s 48 11w
56 Arāk 34 0N 49 40E
61 Arakan Coast 19 0N 94 0E
59 Arakan Yoma, Mts. 20 0N 94 30E
49 Araks, R. 40 1N 48 28E
50 Aral Sea= Aralskoye More 44 30N 66 0E
50 Aralsk 46 50N 61 20E
50 Aralskoye More 44 30N 60 0E
61 Arambagh 22 53N 87 48E
15 Aran, I. 55 0N 8 30w
15 Aran Is. 53 5N 9 42w
32 Arán, Valle de 42 45N 1 0E
30 Aranda de Duero 41 39N 3 42w
30 Aranjuez 40 1N 3 40w
101 Aransas P. 28 0N 97 9w
109 Arapongas 23 29s 51 28w
109 Araranguá 29 0s 49 30w
109 Araraquara 21 50s 48 0w
109 Araras 22 22s 47 23w
84 Ararat 37 16s 143 0E
109 Araruama, L. de 23 0s 42 20w
110 Arauca 7 0N 70 40w
108 Arauco □ 37 50s 73 15w
111 Araxá 19 35s 46 55w
110 Araya, Pen. de 10 40N 64 0w
38 Arbatax 39 57N 9 42E
56 Arbīl 36 15N 44 5E
44 Arboga 59 24N 15 52E
21 Arbois 46 55N 5 46E
14 Arbroath 56 34N 2 35w
38 Arborea 39 46N 8 34E
19 Arc 47 28N 5 34E
20 Arcachon 44 40N 1 10w
20 Arcachon, Bassin d' 44 42N 1 10w
100 Arcadia 44 13N 91 29w
102 Arcata 40 55N 124 4w
37 Arcévia 43 29N 12 58E
48 Archangel= Arkhangelsk 64 40N 41 0E
97 Archbald 41 30N 75 31w
33 Archena 38 9N 1 16w
38 Arci, Mte. 39 47N 8 44E
19 Arcis-sur-Aube 48 32N 4 10E
36 Arco 45 55N 10 54E
93 Arcola 49 40N 102 30w
32 Arcos 41 12N 2 16w
31 Arcos de los Frontera 36 45N 5 49w
62 Arcot 12 53N 79 20E
111 Arcoverde 8 25s 37 4w
89 Arctic Bay 73 2N 85 11w
4 Arctic Ocean 78 0N 160 0w
88 Arctic Red River 67 15N 134 0w
56 Ardabīl 38 15N 48 18E
31 Ardales 36 53N 4 51w
44 Årdalstangen 61 15N 7 45E
21 Ardèche, R. 44 16N 4 39E
21 Ardèche □ 44 42N 4 16E
15 Ardee 53 51N 6 32w
16 Ardennes, Reg. 49 30N 5 10E
19 Ardennes □ 49 35N 4 40E
19 Ardentes 46 45N 1 50E
57 Ardestan 33 20N 52 25E
14 Ardgour, Reg. 56 45N 5 25w
41 Ardino 41 34N 25 9E
84 Ardlethan 34 22s 146 53E
101 Ardmore, Australia 21 39s 139 11E
101 Ardmore, U.S.A. 34 10N 97 5w
15 Ardnacrusha 52 43N 8 38w
14 Ardnamurchan Pt. 56 44N 6 14w
19 Ardres 50 50N 2 0E
14 Ardrossan 55 39N 4 50w
15 Ards □ 54 35N 5 30w
15 Ards Pen. 54 30N 5 25w
105 Arecibo 18 29N 66 42w
111 Areia Branca 5 0s 37 0w
30 Arenas 40 17N 5 6w
45 Arendal 58 28N 8 46E
32 Arenys de Mar 41 35N 2 33E
36 Arenzano 44 24N 8 40E
110 Arequipa 16 20s 71 30w
74 Arero 4 41N 38 50E
21 Arès 44 47N 1 8E
30 Arévalo 41 3N 4 43w
37 Arezzo 43 28N 11 50E
32 Arga, R. 42 18N 1 47w
31 Argamasilla de Alba 39 8N 3 5w
30 Arganda 40 19N 3 26w
20 Argelès-Gazost 43 0N 0 6w
20 Argelès-sur-Mer 42 34N 3 1E
19 Argent 47 33N 2 25E
37 Argenta 44 37N 11 50E
18 Argentan 48 45N 0 1w
37 Argentário, Mte. 42 23N 11 11E
21 Argentera, Mt. de l' 44 10N 7 18E
36 Argentera, P. 44 11N 7 17E
19 Argenteuil 48 57N 2 14E
91 Argentia 47 18N 53 58w
38 Argentiera, C. dell' 40 44N 8 8E
106 Argentine Basin, Reg. 44 0s 51 0E
112 Argentina ■ 35 0s 66 0w
112 Argentino, L. 50 10s 73 0w
20 Argenton Château 46 59N 0 27w
20 Argenton-sur-Creuse 46 36N 1 30E
18 Argentré 48 5N 0 40w
41 Arges, R. 44 10N 26 45E
73 Argo 19 28N 30 30E
43 Argolikós Kól. 37 20N 22 52E
43 Argolis □ 37 38N 22 50E
19 Argonne, Mts. 49 0N 5 20E

43 Árgos 37 40N 22 43 E
43 Argostólion 38 12N 20 33 E
103 Arguello, Pt. 34 34N 120 40W
51 Argun, R. 43 22N 45 55 E
82 Argyle, L. 16 20S 128 40 E
45 Århus 56 8N 10 11 E
39 Ariano Irpino 41 10N 15 4 E
110 Arica, Chile 18 32S 70 20W
110 Arica, Col. 1 30S 75 30W
83 Arid, C. 34 1S 123 10 E
66 Arida 33 29N 135 44 E
20 Ariège, R. 43 31N 1 32 E
20 Ariège □ 42 56N 1 30 E
105 Arima 10 38N 61 17W
14 Arisaig 56 50N 5 40W
62 Ariyalur 11 8N 79 8 E
32 Ariza 41 19N 2 3W
103 Arizona □ 34 20N 111 30W
110 Arjona 10 14N 75 22W
51 Arka 60 15N 142 0 E
67 Arka Tagh, Mts. 36 30N 90 0 E
101 Arkadelphia 34 5N 93 0W
43 Arkadhía □ 38 48N 21 3 E
14 Arkaig, L. 56 58N 5 10W
101 Arkansas, R. 33 48N 91 4W
101 Arkansas □ 35 0N 92 30W
101 Arkansas City 37 4N 97 3W
48 Arkhangelsk 64 40N 41 0 E
15 Arklow 52 48N 6 10W
24 Arkona, C. 54 41N 13 26 E
62 Arkonam 13 7N 79 43 E
20 Arlanc 45 25N 3 42 E
30 Arlanza, R. 42 6N 4 9W
30 Arlanzón, R. 42 3N 4 17W
26 Arlberg P. 49 9N 10 12 E
21 Arles 43 41N 4 40 E
101 Arlington 44 25N 97 4W
16 Arlon 49 42N 5 49 E
45 Arlöy 55 38N 13 5 E
83 Armadale 32 12S 116 0 E
15 Armagh 54 22N 6 40W
15 Armagh □ 54 16N 6 35W
20 Armagnac, Reg. 43 44N 0 10 E
19 Armançon, R. 47 57N 3 30 E
49 Armavir 45 2N 41 7 E
110 Armenia 4 35N 75 45W
49 Armenian S.S.R. □ 40 0N 41 10 E
40 Armeniş 45 13N 22 17 E
19 Armentières 50 40N 2 50 E
81 Armidale 30 30S 151 40 E
92 Armstrong, B.C. 50 25N 119 10W
90 Armstrong, Ont. 50 20N 89 0W
62 Armur 18 48N 78 16 E
19 Arnay-le-Duc 47 10N 4 27 E
32 Arnedo 42 12N 2 5W
16 Arnhem 51 58N 5 55 E
80 Arnhem, B. 12 20S 136 10 E
62 Arni 12 43N 79 19 E
36 Arno, R. 43 31N 10 17 E
96 Arnold 40 36N 79 44W
26 Arnoldstein 46 33N 13 43 E
90 Arnprior 45 23N 76 25W
24 Arnsberg 51 25N 8 10 E
24 Arnstadt 50 50N 10 56 E
31 Aroche 37 56N 6 57 E
30 Arosa, Ria de 42 28N 8 57W
41 Arpaşu de Jos 45 45N 24 38 E
38 Arpino 41 40N 13 35 E
81 Arrabury 26 45S 141 0 E
61 Arrah 25 35N 84 32 E
31 Arraiolos 38 44N 7 59W
14 Arran, I. 55 34N 5 12W
19 Arras 50 17N 2 46 E
20 Arreau 42 54N 0 22 E
20 Arrats, R. 44 6N 0 52 E
72 Arrecife 28 59N 13 40W
108 Arrecifes 34 5S 60 5N
18 Arrée, Mts. d' 48 26N 3 55W
83 Arrino 29 30S 115 40 E
18 Arromanches 49 20N 0 38W
31 Arronches 39 8N 7 16W
20 Arros, R. 43 30N 0 2W
18 Arrou 48 6N 1 8 E
92 Arrowhead 50 40N 117 55W
85 Arrowtown 44 57S 168 50 E
31 Arroyo de la Luz 39 30N 6 38W
20 Ars 46 13N 1 30W
41 Arsache 43 47N 25 45 E
68 Arshan 46 59N 120 0 E
37 Arsiero 45 49N 11 22 E
62 Arsikere 13 15N 76 15 E
19 Ars-sur-Moselle 49 5N 6 4 E
32 Artá 39 40N 3 20 E
43 Árta 39 8N 21 2 E
89 Artemovsk 48 35N 37 55 E
19 Artenay 48 5N 1 50 E
32 Artesa de Segre 41 54N 1 3 E
101 Artesia 32 55N 104 25W
80 Arthur, Pt. 22 7S 150 3 E
108 Artigas 30 20S 56 30W
19 Artois, Reg. 50 20N 2 30 E
56 Artvin 41 14N 41 44 E
65 Aru, Kep. 6 0S 134 30 E
74 Arua 3 1N 30 58 E
111 Aruanã 15 0S 51 10W
105 Aruba, I. 12 30N 70 0W
59 Arunachal Pradesh □ 28 0N 95 0 E
62 Aruppukottai 9 31N 78 8 E
74 Arusha 3 20S 36 40 E
102 Arvada 44 43N 106 6W
68 Arvayheer 46 15N 102 48 E
21 Arve, R. 46 12N 6 8 E
60 Arvi 20 59N 78 16 E
91 Arvida 48 16N 71 14W
46 Arvidsjaur 65 35N 19 10 E
44 Arvika 59 40N 12 36 E
50 Arys 42 26N 68 48 E
48 Arzamas 55 27N 43 55 E
72 Arzew 35 50N 0 23W
37 Arzignano 45 30N 11 20 E
26 Aš 50 13N 12 12 E
54 As Salt 32 2N 35 43 E
56 As Samāwah 31 15N 45 15 E
56 As Sulaimānīyah 24 8N 47 10 E
56 As Sulamāniyah 35 35N 45 29 E
57 As Suwaih 22 10N 59 33 E
56 As Suwayda 32 40N 36 30 E
56 As Suwayrah 32 55N 45 0 E
66 Asahikawa 43 45N 142 30 E
61 Asansol 23 40N 87 1 E
91 Asbestos 45 47N 71 58W
97 Asbury Park 40 15N 74 1W
104 Ascensión, B. de la 19 50N 87 20W
71 Ascension, I. 8 0S 14 15W
26 Aschach 48 23N 14 0 E
25 Aschaffenburg 49 58N 9 8 E
24 Aschersleben 51 45N 11 28 E
37 Ascoli Piceno 42 51N 13 34 E
39 Áscoli Satriano 41 11N 15 32 E
75 Aseb 13 0N 42 40 E
45 Aseda 57 10N 15 20 E
41 Asenovgrad 42 1N 24 51 E
103 Ash Fork 35 14N 112 32W
56 Ash Shāmiyah 31 55N 44 35 E
56 Ash Sharma 28 1N 35 18 E
54 Ash Shuna 32 32N 35 34 E
48 Asha 35 10N 33 38 E
85 Ashburton 43 53S 171 48 E
82 Ashburton, R. 37 52S 145 5 E
82 Ashburton Downs 23 25S 117 4 E
12 Ashby-de-la-Zouch 52 45N 1 29W
54 Ashdod 31 39N 34 35 E
54 Ashdot Yaaqov 32 39N 35 35 E
99 Asheboro 35 43N 79 46W
99 Asheville 35 39N 82 30W
13 Ashford 51 8N 0 53 E
66 Ashikaga 36 28N 139 29 E
12 Ashington 55 12N 1 35W
50 Ashkhabad 38 0N 57 50 E
98 Ashland, Ky. 38 25N 82 40W
96 Ashland, Ohio 40 52N 82 20W
102 Ashland, Oreg. 42 10N 122 38W
97 Ashland, Pa. 40 45N 76 22W
100 Ashland, Wis. 46 40N 90 52W
97 Ashley 41 12N 75 55W
54 Ashquelon 31 42N 34 55 E
96 Ashtabula 41 52N 80 50W
102 Ashton 44 6N 111 30W
12 Ashton-under-Lyne 53 30N 2 8W
1 Asia 45 0N 75 0 E
72 Asilah 35 29N 6 0W
38 Asinara, G. dell' 41 0N 8 30 E
38 Asinara, I. 41 5N 8 15 E
50 Asino 57 0N 86 0 E
55 Asir, Ras 11 55N 51 0 E
55 Asir, Reg. 18 40N 42 30 E
54 Asira esh Shamaliya 32 16N 35 16 E
44 Askim 59 35N 11 10 E
57 Asmar 35 10N 71 27 E
73 Asmera 15 19N 38 55 E
45 Asnen, L. 56 35N 15 45 E
36 Ásola 45 12N 10 25 E
33 Aspe 38 20N 0 40W
85 Aspiring, Mt. 44 23S 168 46W
21 Aspres 44 32N 5 44 E
59 Assam □ 25 45N 92 30 E
16 Asse 50 54N 4 6 E
16 Assen 53 0N 6 35 E
93 Assiniboia 49 40N 106 0W
92 Assiniboine, Mt. 50 52N 115 39W
93 Assiniboine, R. 49 53N 97 8W
109 Assis 22 40S 50 20W
37 Assisi 43 4N 12 36 E
14 Assynt, L. 58 25N 5 10W
49 Astara 38 30N 48 50 E
36 Asti 44 54N 8 11 E
43 Astipálaia, I. 36 32N 26 22 E
30 Astorga 42 29N 6 8W
102 Astoria 46 16N 123 50W
45 Astorp 56 6N 12 55 E
49 Astrakhan 46 25N 48 5 E
30 Asturias, Reg. 43 15N 6 0W
108 Asunción 25 21S 57 30W
73 Aswân 24 4N 32 57 E
73 Aswân High Dam 24 5N 32 54 E
73 Asyût 27 11N 31 4 E
56 At Ta'if 21 5N 40 27 E
106 Atacama Des. 24 0S 69 20W
108 Atacama, Salar de 24 0S 68 20W
108 Atacama □ 27 30S 70 0W
72 Atakpamé 7 31N 1 13 E
43 Atalándi 38 39N 22 58 E
66 Atami 35 0N 139 55 E
72 Atar 20 30N 13 5W
51 Atara 63 10N 129 10 E
31 Atarfe 37 13N 3 40W
50 Atasu 48 30N 71 0 E
73 Atbara 17 42N 33 59 E
73 'Atbara, Nahr, R 17 40N 33 56 E
50 Atbasar 51 48N 68 20 E
100 Atchison 39 40N 95 0W
32 Ateca 41 20N 1 49W
37 Atessa 42 5N 14 27 E
16 Ath 50 38N 3 47 E
92 Athabasca 54 45N 113 20W
93 Athabasca, L. 59 10N 109 30W
93 Athabasca, R. 58 40N 110 50W
15 Athboy 53 37N 6 55W
15 Athenry 53 18N 8 45W
99 Athens, Ala. 34 49N 86 58W
99 Athens, Ga. 33 56N 83 24W
98 Athens, Ohio 39 52N 82 64W
101 Athens, Tex. 32 11N 95 48W
43 Athens=Athínai 37 58N 23 46 E
80 Atherton 17 17S 145 30 E
43 Athínai 37 58N 23 46 E
15 Athlone 53 26N 7 57W
62 Athni 16 44N 75 6 E
14 Atholl, Forest of 56 51N 3 50W
91 Atholville 48 5N 67 5W
42 Athos, Mt. 40 9N 24 22 E
15 Athy 53 0N 7 0W
51 Atka 60 50N 151 48 E
88 Atka I. 52 15N 174 30W
99 Atlanta 33 50N 84 24W
100 Atlantic 41 25N 95 0W
98 Atlantic City 39 25N 74 25W
1 Atlantic Ocean 0 0 30 0W
72 Atlas, Anti, Mts. 30 0N 8 0W
72 Atlas, Moyen, Mts. 37 0N 5 0W
72 Atlas Saharien, Mts. 34 10N 3 30 E
92 Atlin 59 31N 133 41W
54 Atlit 32 42N 34 56 E
62 Atmakur 14 37N 79 40 E
99 Atmore 31 2N 87 30W
104 Atotonilco 20 20N 98 40W
31 Atouguia 39 20N 9 20W
37 Atri 42 35N 14 0 E
90 Attawapiskat 53 0N 82 30W
90 Attawapiskat L. 52 20N 88 0W
90 Attawapiskat, R. 52 57N 82 18W
26 Attersee 47 55N 13 31 E
26 Attersee, L. 47 52N 13 33 E
19 Attigny 49 28N 4 35 E
43 Attikí □ 38 10N 23 40 E
54 Attil 32 23N 35 4 E
97 Attleboro 41 56N 71 18W
58 Attock 33 52N 72 20 E
88 Attu I. 52 55N 173 0 E
62 Attur 11 35N 78 30 E
45 Atvidaberg 58 12N 16 0 E
100 Atwood 39 52N 101 3W
21 Aubagne 43 17N 5 37 E
19 Aube, R. 48 34N 3 43 E
19 Aube □ 48 15N 4 0 E
21 Aubenas 44 37N 4 24 E
19 Aubigny-sur-Nère 47 30N 2 24 E
20 Aubrac, Mts. d' 44 38N 2 58 E
99 Auburn, Ala. 32 57N 85 30W
102 Auburn, Calif. 38 50N 121 10W
99 Auburn, Me. 44 6N 70 14W
97 Auburn, N.Y. 42 57N 76 39W
20 Aubusson 45 57N 2 11 E
20 Auch 43 39N 0 36 E
19 Auchel 50 30N 2 39 E
85 Auckland 36 52S 174 46 E
76 Auckland Is. 51 0S 166 0 E
20 Aude □ 44 13N 3 15 E
90 Auden 50 17N 87 54W
18 Auderville 49 43N 1 57W
18 Audierne 48 1N 4 34W
19 Audincourt 47 30N 6 50 E
24 Aue 50 34N 12 43 E
24 Auerbach 50 30N 12 25 E
18 Auffay 49 43N 1 7 E
81 Augathella 25 48S 146 35 E
25 Augsburg 48 22N 10 54 E
83 Augusta, Australia 34 22S 115 10 E
39 Augusta, Italy 37 14N 15 12 E
99 Augusta, U.S.A. 33 29N 81 59W
99 Augusta 44 20N 69 46W
75 Augusto Cardoso 12 44S 34 50 E
28 Augustów 53 51N 23 0 E
83 Augustus, Mt. 24 20S 116 50 E
80 Augustus Downs 18 35S 139 55 E
18 Aulne, R. 48 17N 4 16W
19 Aulnoye 46 2N 0 22W
20 Aunis, Reg. 46 0N 0 50W
61 Aurangabad, Bihar 24 25N 84 18 E
60 Aurangabad, Maharashtra 19 50N 75 23 E
18 Auray 47 40N 3 0W
24 Aurich 53 28N 7 30 E
20 Aurillac 44 55N 2 26 E
100 Aurora, Colo. 39 44N 104 55W
98 Aurora, Ill. 41 42N 88 20W
96 Aurora, Ohio 41 21N 81 20W
47 Aust-Agde □ 58 55N 7 40 E
100 Austin, Minn. 43 37N 92 59W
102 Austin, Nev. 39 30N 117 1W
101 Austin, Tex. 30 20N 97 45W
78 Australia ■ 23 0S 135 0 E
84 Australian Alps, Mts. 36 30S 148 8 E
84 Australian Capital Terr. □ 35 15S 149 8 E
5 Australian Dependency □ 73 0S 90 0 E
26 Austria ■ 47 0N 14 0 E
19 Authie, R. 50 21N 1 38 E
104 Autlán 19 40N 104 30W
21 Autun 46 58N 4 17 E
82 Auvergne 15 39S 130 1 E
20 Auvergne, Mts. 45 20N 2 45 E
20 Auvergne, Reg. 45 30N 3 20 E
20 Auvézère, R. 45 12N 0 51 E
19 Auxerre 47 48N 3 32 E
21 Auxonne 47 10N 5 20 E
20 Auzances 46 2N 2 30 E
20 Auzat 45 27N 3 19 E
19 Avallon 47 30N 3 53 E
91 Avalon Pen. 47 0N 53 20W
62 Avanigadda 16 0N 80 56 E
109 Avaré 23 5S 48 55W
42 Ávas 40 57N 25 56 E
111 Aveiro, Brazil 3 10S 55 5W
30 Aveiro, Port. 40 37N 8 38W
30 Aveiro □ 40 40N 8 35W
108 Avellaneda 34 50S 58 10W
39 Avellino 40 54N 14 46 E
44 Averøya, I. 63 0N 7 35 E
39 Aversa 40 58N 14 11 E
110 Aves, Is. de 12 0N 67 40W
19 Avesnes 50 8N 3 55 E
44 Avesta 60 9N 16 10 E
20 Aveyron, R. 44 5N 1 16 E
20 Aveyron □ 44 22N 2 45 E
37 Avezzano 42 2N 13 24 E
14 Aviemore 57 11N 3 50W
39 Avigliano 40 44N 15 41 E
21 Avignon 43 57N 4 50 E
30 Ávila 40 39N 4 43W
30 Ávila, Sa. de 40 40N 5 0W
30 Ávila □ 40 30N 5 0W
30 Avilés 43 35N 5 57W
84 Avoca 37 5S 143 28 E
15 Avoca, R. 52 48N 6 10W
92 Avola, Canada 51 45N 119 30W
39 Avola, Italy 36 56N 15 7 E
39 Avola 36 56N 15 7 E
83 Avon, R, Australia 31 40S 116 7 E
13 Avon, R., Avon 51 30N 2 43W
13 Avon, R., Dorset 50 43N 1 46W
13 Avon, R., Gloucester 51 59N 2 10W
13 Avon □ 51 30N 2 40W
97 Avonmore 45 11N 74 57W
13 Avonmouth 51 30N 2 42W
18 Avranches 48 40N 1 20W
41 Avrig 45 43N 24 21 E
66 Awaji-Shima, I. 34 30N 134 50 E
57 Awali 26 0N 50 30 E
74 Awash 9 1N 40 10 E
85 Awatere, R. 41 37S 174 10 E
14 Awe, L. 56 15N 5 15W
73 Awjilah 29 8N 21 7 E
86 Axel Heiberg Ld. 80 0N 90 0W
20 Ax-les-Thermes 42 44N 1 50 E
13 Axminster 50 47N 3 1W
19 Ay 49 3N 4 0 E
66 Ayabe 35 20N 135 20 E
110 Ayacucho, Arg. 37 5S 58 20W
108 Ayacucho, Peru 13 0S 74 0W
50 Ayaguz 48 10N 80 0 E
31 Ayamonte 37 12N 7 24W
51 Ayan 56 30N 138 16 E
63 Ayer Itam 1 55N 103 11 E
42 Ayía Paraskevi 39 14N 26 16 E
42 Ayíos Evstrátios 39 34N 24 58 E
48 Aykin 62 20N 49 56 E
93 Aylesbury, Canada 50 55N 105 53W
13 Aylesbury, U.K. 51 48N 0 49W
88 Aylmer, L. 64 0N 109 0W
80 Ayr, Australia 19 35S 147 25 E
14 Ayr, U.K. 55 28N 4 37W
14 Ayr, R. 55 29N 4 28W
12 Ayre, Pt. of 54 27N 4 21W

41 Aytos 42 47N 27 16 E
56 Ayvalik 39 20N 26 46 E
54 Az Zahiriya 31 25N 34 58 E
56 Az Zahrān 26 10N 50 7 E
54 Az-Zarqā' 32 5N 36 4 E
56 Az Zilfi 26 12N 44 52 E
56 Az Zubayr 30 20N 47 50 E
31 Azambuja 39 4N 8 51W
61 Azamgarh 26 35N 83 13 E
56 Āzārbāijān □ 37 0N 44 30 E
72 Azare 11 55N 10 10 E
72 Azbine=Aïr 18 0N 8 0 E
49 Azerbaijan S.S.R. □ 40 20N 48 0 E
31 Aznalcóllar 37 32N 6 17W
54 Azor 32 2N 34 40 E
8 Azores, Is. 38 44N 29 0W
49 Azov 47 3N 39 25 E
49 Azov Sea= Azovskoye More 46 0N 36 30 E
49 Azovskoye More 46 0N 36 30 E
50 Azovy 64 55N 64 35 E
103 Aztec 36 54N 108 0W
105 Azua 18 25N 70 44W
31 Azuaga 38 16N 5 39W
31 Azuer, R. 39 8N 3 36W
105 Azuero, Pen. de 7 40N 80 30W
108 Azul 36 42S 59 43W

B

63 Ba Don 17 45N 106 26 E
30 Baamonde 43 7N 7 44W
57 Baba, Koh-i-, Mts. 34 40N 67 20 E
62 Baba Budan Hills 13 30N 75 40 E
41 Babadag 44 53N 28 48 E
110 Babahoyo 1 40S 79 30W
83 Babakin 32 11S 117 52 E
65 Babelthuap, I. 7 30N 134 36 E
80 Babinda 17 27S 146 0 E
65 Babo 2 30S 133 30 E
57 Bābol 36 40N 52 50 E
57 Babol Sar 36 45N 52 45 E
65 Babuyan Chan. 18 58N 122 0 E
69 Babuyan Is. 19 0N 122 0 E
56 Babylon, Iraq 32 40N 44 30 E
97 Babylon, U.S.A. 40 42N 73 20W
63 Bac Ninh 21 13N 106 4 E
63 Bac-Phan, Reg. 22 0N 105 0 E
63 Bac Quang 22 30N 104 48 E
111 Bacabal 5 20S 56 45W
65 Bacan, I. 1 0S 127 30 E
41 Bacău 46 35N 26 55 E
19 Baccarat 48 28N 6 42 E
25 Bacharach 50 3N 7 46 E
25 Bachelina 57 45N 67 20 E
88 Back, R. 67 15N 95 15W
40 Bačka Palanka 45 17N 19 27 E
40 Bačka Topola 45 48N 19 37 E
25 Backnang 48 57N 9 26 E
65 Bacolod 10 50N 123 0 E
27 Bacs-Kiskun □ 46 43N 19 30 E
27 Bácsalmás 46 8N 19 17 E
26 Bad Aussee 47 43N 13 45 E
24 Bad Driburg 51 44N 9 0 E
25 Bad Ems 51 22N 7 44 E
25 Bad Frankenhausen 51 21N 11 3 E
24 Bad Freienwalde 52 46N 14 2 E
24 Bad Godesberg 50 41N 7 4 E
24 Bad Hersfeld 50 52N 9 42 E
26 Bad Hofgastein 47 17N 13 6 E
25 Bad Homburg 50 17N 8 33 E
24 Bad Honnef 50 39N 7 13 E
26 Bad Ischl 47 44 13 38 E
25 Bad Kissingen 50 11N 10 5 E
25 Bad Kreuznach 49 47N 7 47 E
24 Bad Lauterberg 51 38N 10 29 E
26 Bad Leonfelden 48 31N 14 18 E
25 Bad Mergentheim 49 29N 9 47 E
25 Bad Nauheim 50 24N 8 45 E
24 Bad Oldesloe 53 56N 10 17 E
24 Bad Pyrmont 51 59N 9 5 E
24 Bad Salzuflen 52 8N 8 44 E
24 Bad Segeberg 53 58N 10 16 E
25 Bad Tölz 47 43N 11 34 E
24 Bad Wildungen 51 7N 9 10 E
62 Badagara 11 35N 75 40 E
31 Badajoz 38 50N 6 59W
31 Badajoz □ 38 40N 6 30W
57 Badakhshan □ 36 30N 71 0 E
32 Badalona 41 26N 2 15 E
57 Badalzal 29 50N 65 35 E
56 Badanah 30 58N 41 30 E
64 Badas 4 20N 114 37 E
27 Baden, Austria 48 1N 16 13 E
25 Baden, Switz. 47 28N 8 18 E
25 Baden-Baden 48 45N 8 14 E
25 Baden Württemberg □ 48 40N 9 0 E
14 Badenoch, Reg. 57 0N 4 0W
26 Badgastein 47 7N 13 9 E
57 Badghis □ 35 0N 63 0 E
37 Badia Polèsine 45 6N 11 30 E
60 Badnera 20 48N 77 44 E
62 Badulla 7 1N 81 7 E
31 Baena 37 37N 4 20W
31 Baeza 37 57N 3 25W
89 Baffin B. 72 0N 65 0W
89 Baffin I. 68 0N 77 0W
56 Bafra 41 34N 35 54W
57 Bāft 29 15N 56 38W
62 Bagalkot 16 10N 75 40W
74 Bagamoyo 6 28S 38 55 E
60 Bagasra 21 2N 70 57 E
51 Bagdarin 54 26N 113 36 E
109 Bagé 31 20S 54 15W
56 Baghdād 32 20N 44 30 E
61 Bagherhat 22 40N 89 47 E
38 Bagheira 38 5N 13 30 E
57 Baghīn 30 12N 56 45 E
57 Baghlan 36 12N 69 0 E
57 Baghlan □ 36 0N 68 30 E
37 Bagnacavallo 44 25N 11 58 E
39 Bagnara Cálabria 38 16N 15 49 E
20 Bagnères-de-Bigorre 43 5N 0 9 E
20 Bagnères-de-Luchon 42 47N 0 38 E
36 Bagni di Lucca 41 1N 10 37 E
37 Bagno di Romagna 43 50N 11 59 E
21 Bagnols-sur-Cèze 44 10N 4 36 E
91 Bagotville 48 22N 70 54W
67 Bagrash Kol, L. 42 0N 87 0 E
40 Bagrdan 44 5N 21 11 E
65 Baguio 16 26N 120 34 E
30 Bahabòn de Esgueva 41 52N 3 43W
60 Bahadurgarh 28 40N 76 57 E
105 Bahamas ■ 24 0N 74 0W
63 Bahau 2 48N 102 26 E
60 Bahawalnagar 30 0N 73 15 E
60 Bahawalpur 29 37N 71 40 E
60 Bahawalpur □ 29 5N 71 3 E
61 Baheri 28 45N 79 34 E
111 Bahia= Salvador 13 0S 38 30W
105 Bahia, Is. de la 16 45N 86 15W
111 Bahia □ 12 0N 42 0 E
108 Bahia Blanca 38 35S 62 13W
110 Bahia de Caráquez 0 40S 80 27W
112 Bahia Laura 48 10S 66 30W
110 Bahia Negra 20 5S 58 5W
73 Bahr el Ghazâl □ 7 0N 28 0 E
61 Bahraich 27 38N 81 50 E
57 Bahrain ■ 26 0N 50 35 E
111 Baião 2 50S 49 15W
41 Baicoi 45 3N 25 52 E
91 Baie Comeau 49 12N 68 10W
91 Baie T. Paul 47 28N 70 32W
56 Ba'iji 35 0N 43 30 E
15 Baile Atha Cliath=Dublin 53 20N 6 18W
31 Bailén 38 8N 3 48W
41 Bailești 44 1N 23 20 E
62 Bailhongal 15 55N 74 53 E
99 Bainbridge, Ga. 30 53N 84 34W
97 Bainbridge, N.Y. 42 17N 75 29W
88 Baird Mts. 67 10N 160 15W
84 Bairnsdale 37 48S 147 36 E
29 Baixo-Alentejo, Reg. 38 0N 8 40W
27 Baja 46 12N 18 59 E
104 Baja California Norte □ 30 0N 116 0W
104 Baja California Sur □ 26 0N 112 0W
81 Bajimba, Mt. 29 17S 152 6 E
61 Bajitpur 24 13N 91 0 E
80 Bajool 24 30S 150 35 E
50 Bakchar 57 0N 82 5 E
102 Baker, Calif. 36 16N 116 2W
100 Baker, Mont. 46 22N 104 12W
76 Baker I. 0 10N 176 35 E
88 Baker L. 64 0N 97 0W
102 Baker, Mt. 48 50N 121 49W
88 Baker Lake 64 20N 96 10W
90 Baker's Dozen Is. 57 30N 79 0W
103 Bakersfield 35 25N 119 0W
56 Bakhtiari □ 32 0N 49 0 E
49 Bakinskikh Komissarov 39 20N 49 15 E
27 Bakony Forest= Bakony Hegyseg, Reg. 47 10N 17 30 E
27 Bakony Hegyseg, Reg. 47 10N 17 30 E
49 Baku 40 25N 49 45 E
96 Bala 45 2N 79 38 E
54 Bal'a 32 20N 35 6 E
12 Bala, L. 52 53N 3 38W
64 Balabac I. 8 0N 117 0 E
64 Balabac Str. 7 53N 117 5 E
61 Balaghat 21 49N 80 12 E
62 Balaghat Ra. 18 50N 76 30 E
32 Balaguer 41 50N 0 50 E
81 Balaklava, Australia 34 7S 138 22 E
49 Balaklava, U.S.S.R. 44 30N 33 30 E
48 Balakovo 52 4N 47 55 E
61 Balangir 20 43N 83 35 E
60 Balapur 21 22N 76 45 E
48 Balashov 51 30N 43 10 E
61 Balasore 21 35N 87 3 E
27 Balassaguarmat 48 4N 19 15 E
27 Balaton, L. 46 50N 17 40 E
33 Balazote 38 54N 2 9W
104 Balboa 9 0N 79 30W
15 Balbriggan 53 35N 6 10W
108 Balcarce 38 0S 58 10W
41 Balchik 43 28N 28 11 E
85 Balclutha 46 15S 169 45 E
83 Bald, Hd. 35 6S 118 1 E
97 Baldwinsville 43 10N 76 19W
103 Baldy Pk. 33 55N 109 35W
32 Baleares, Is. 39 30N 3 0 E
80 Balfe's Creek 20 12S 145 55 E
64 Bali, I. 8 20S 115 0 E
56 Balikesir 39 35S 27 58 E
64 Balikpapan 1 10S 116 55 E
63 Baling 5 41N 100 55 E
69 Balintang Chan. 19 50N 122 0 E
59 Balipara 26 50N 92 45 E
111 Baliza 16 0S 52 20W
41 Balkan, Mts.= Stara Planina 43 15N 23 0 E
9 Balkan Pen. 42 0N 22 0 E
57 Balkh □ 36 30N 67 0 E
50 Balkhash 46 50N 74 50 E
50 Balkhash, Oz. 46 0N 74 50 E
14 Ballachulish 56 40N 5 10W
83 Balladonia 32 27S 123 51 E
84 Ballarat 37 33S 143 50 E
83 Ballard, L. 29 20S 120 10 E
61 Ballarpur 19 50N 79 23 E
14 Ballater 57 2N 3 2W
61 Ballia 25 46N 84 12 E
83 Ballidu 30 35S 116 45 E
81 Ballina, Australia 28 50S 153 31 E
15 Ballina, Mayo 54 7N 9 10W
15 Ballina, Tipperary 52 49N 8 27W
15 Ballinasloe 53 20N 8 12W
101 Ballinger 31 45N 99 58W
15 Ballinrobe 53 36N 9 13W
15 Ballycastle 55 12N 6 15W
15 Ballymena 54 53N 6 18W
15 Ballymena □ 54 53N 6 18W
15 Ballymoney 55 5N 6 30W
15 Ballymoney □ 55 5N 6 30W
15 Ballyshannon 54 30N 8 10W
112 Balmaceda 46 0S 71 50W
27 Balmazújváros 47 37N 21 21 E
14 Balmoral 57 3N 3 13W
75 Balovale 13 30S 23 15 E
61 Balrampur 27 30N 82 20 E
84 Balranald 34 38S 143 33 E
41 Bals 44 22N 24 5 E
104 Balsas, R. 17 55N 102 10W
49 Balta 48 2N 29 45 E
9 Baltic Sea 56 0N 20 0 E
28 Baltiisk 54 38N 19 55 E
15 Baltimore, Eire 51 29N 9 22W
98 Baltimore, U.S.A. 39 18N 76 37W
58 Baluchistan, Reg. 27 30N 65 0 E
57 Bam 29 7N 58 14 E
72 Bamako 12 34N 7 55W
74 Bambari 5 40N 20 35 E
80 Bambaroo 18 50S 146 10 E
25 Bamberg 49 54N 10 53 E
72 Bamenda 5 57N 10 11 E
57 Bamian □ 35 0N 67 0 E
57 Bampur 27 15N 60 21 E
63 Ban Aranyaprathet 13 41N 102 30 E
63 Ban Bua Yai 15 33N 102 26 E
63 Ban Houei Sai 20 22N 100 32 E
63 Ban Mae Sot 16 40N 98 30 E
63 Ban Nong Pling 15 40N 100 10 E
63 Ban Phai 16 4N 102 44 E
63 Ban Takua Pa 8 55N 98 25 E
57 Banadar Daryay Oman □ 25 30N 56 0 E
74 Banalia 1 32N 25 5 E
72 Banamba 13 29N 7 22W
80 Banana 24 32S 150 12 E
111 Bananal, I. de 11 30S 50 30W
73 Bânâs, Ras 23 57N 35 50 E
60 Banas, R. 25 55N 76 45 E
15 Banbridge 54 26N 6 16W
15 Banbridge □ 54 21N 6 16W
13 Banbury 52 4N 1 21W
14 Banchory 57 3N 2 30W
90 Bancroft 45 3N 77 51W
57 Band-e Charak 26 45N 54 20 E
57 Band-e Nakhīlu 26 58N 53 30 E
61 Banda 25 30N 80 26 E
64 Banda Aceh 5 35N 95 20 E
81 Banda Banda, Mt. 31 10S 152 28 E
65 Banda Sea 6 0S 130 0 E
57 Bandar Abbas 27 15N 56 15 E
63 Bandar Maharani 2 2N 102 34 E
63 Bandar Penggaram 1 50N 102 56 E
64 Bandar Seri Begawan 4 52N 115 0 E
57 Bandar-e Bushetir 28 55N 50 55 E
57 Bandar-e Lengeh 26 35N 54 58 E
56 Bandar-e Ma'shur 30 35N 49 10 E
56 Bandar-e-Pahlavi 37 30N 49 30 E
57 Bandar-e Rig 29 30N 50 45 E
57 Bandar-e Sháh 37 0N 54 10 E
56 Bandar-e Shahpur 30 30N 49 5 E
75 Bandawe 11 58S 34 5 E
109 Bandeira, Pico da 20 26S 41 47W
56 Bandirma 40 20N 28 0 E
15 Bandon 51 44N 8 45W
15 Bandon, R. 51 40N 8 35W
74 Bandundu 3 15S 17 22 E
65 Bandung 6 36S 107 48 E
33 Bañeres 38 44N 0 38W
105 Banes 20 58N 75 43W
92 Banff, Canada 51 20N 115 40W
14 Banff, U.K. 57 40N 2 32W
92 Banff Nat. Park 51 38N 116 22W
63 Bang Saphan 11 14N 99 28 E
75 Bangala Dam 21 7S 31 25 E
62 Bangalore 12 59N 77 40 E
61 Bangaon 23 0N 88 47 E
74 Bangassou 4 55N 23 55 E
73 Banghazı 32 11N 20 3 E
65 Bangil 7 36S 112 50 E
64 Bangka, I., Selatan 3 30S 105 30 E
65 Bangka, I., Utara 7 2S 112 46 E
65 Bangkalan 7 2S 112 46 E
63 Bangkok=Krung Thep 13 45N 100 31 E
59 Bangladesh ■ 24 0N 90 0 E
12 Bangor, Gwynedd 53 13N 4 9W
15 Bangor, N. Down 54 40N 5 40W
97 Bangor, Pa. 40 51N 75 13W
99 Bangor, Me. 44 48N 68 42W
65 Bangued 17 40N 120 37 E
74 Bangui 4 23N 18 35 E
74 Bangweulu, L. 11 0S 30 0 E
105 Bani 18 16N 70 22W
54 Bani Na'im 31 31N 35 10 E
73 Banınah 32 0N 20 12 E
40 Banja Luka 44 49N 17 26 E
65 Banjar 7 24S 108 30 E
64 Banjarmasin 3 20S 114 35 E
65 Banjarnegara 7 24S 109 42 E
72 Banjul 13 28N 16 40W
80 Banka Banka 18 50S 134 0 E
61 Bankipore 25 35N 85 10 E
86 Banks I. 73 30N 120 0W
85 Banks, Pen. 43 45S 173 15 E
61 Bankura 23 11N 87 18 E
15 Bann, R. 55 2N 6 35W
18 Bannalec 47 57N 3 42W
103 Banning 48 44N 91 56W
60 Bannu 33 0N 70 18S
14 Bannockburn 56 5N 3 55W
60 Bañolas 42 16N 2 44 E
30 Baños de Molgas 42 15N 7 40W
27 Banská Bystrica 48 46N 19 14 E
27 Banská Stiavnica 48 25N 18 55 E
60 Banswara 23 32N 74 24 E
65 Banten 6 5S 106 8 E
15 Bantry 51 40N 9 28W
15 Bantry, B. 51 35N 9 50W
65 Bantul 7 55S 110 19 E
60 Bantva 21 29N 70 12 E
62 Bantval 12 55N 75 0 E
41 Banya 42 33N 24 50 E
20 Banyuls 42 29N 3 8 E
62 Bapatla 15 55N 80 30 E
54 Baqa el Gharbiya 32 25N 35 2 E
40 Bar 42 8N 19 8 E
64 Barabai 2 32S 115 34 E
50 Barabinsk 55 20N 78 20 E
100 Baraboo 43 28N 89 46W
105 Baracoa 20 20N 74 30W
108 Baradero 33 52S 59 29S
105 Barahona, Dom. Rep. 18 13N 71 7W
30 Barahona, Sp. 41 17N 2 39W
59 Barail Ra. 25 15N 93 20 E
66 Barak □ 38 20N 140 0 E
59 Barakhola 25 0N 92 45 E
62 Baramati 18 11N 74 33 E
58 Baramula 34 15N 74 20 E
60 Baran 25 9N 76 40 E
92 Baranof 57 0N 135 10W
92 Baranof I. 57 0N 135 10W
48 Baranovichi 53 10N 26 0 E
27 Baranya □ 46 0N 18 15 E
65 Barat □, Java 7 0S 107 0 E

64 Barat, □ Kalimantan 0 0 S 111 0 E
64 Barat, Sumatera 1 0 S 101 0 E
Sumatera 1 0 S 101 0 E
65 Barat Daja, Kep. 7 30 S 128 0 E
109 Barbacena 21 15 S 43 56 W
110 Barbacoas 1 45 N 78 0 W
105 Barbados ■ 13 0 N 59 30 W
32 Barbastro 42 2 N 0 5 E
31 Barbate 36 13 N 5 56 W
75 Barberton, S. Africa 25 42 S 31 2 E
96 Barberton, U.S.A. 41 0 N 81 40 W
105 Barbuda, I. 17 30 N 61 40 W
80 Barcaldine 23 33 S 145 13 E
73 Barce=Al Marj 32 25 N 20 40 E
32 Barcelona, Sp. 41 21 N 2 10 E
110 Barcelona, Ven. 10 10 N 64 40 W
32 Barcelona □ 41 30 N 2 0 E
39 Barcellona Pozzo di Gotto 38 8 N 15 15 E
21 Barcelonnette 44 23 N 6 40 E
110 Barcelos 1 0 S 63 0 W
73 Bardaî 21 25 N 17 0 E
55 Bardera 2 20 N 42 0 S
73 Bardiyah 31 45 N 25 0 E
12 Bardsey I. 52 46 N 4 47 W
61 Bareilly 28 22 N 79 27 E
18 Barentin 49 33 N 0 58 E
4 Barents Sea 73 0 N 39 0 E
18 Barfleur 49 40 N 1 17 W
18 Barfleur, Pte. de 49 42 N 1 17 W
36 Barga 44 5 N 10 30 E
55 Bargal 11 25 N 51 0 E
80 Bargara 24 50 S 152 25 E
51 Barguzin 53 37 N 109 37 E
61 Barh 25 29 N 85 46 E
61 Barhaj 26 18 N 83 44 E
61 Barhi 24 15 N 85 25 E
60 Bari, India 26 39 N 77 39 E
39 Bari, Italy 41 6 N 16 52 E
60 Bari Doab, Reg. 30 20 N 73 0 E
110 Barinas 8 36 N 70 15 W
88 Baring, C. 70 0 N 116 30 W
73 Bâris 24 42 N 30 31 E
61 Barisal 22 30 N 90 20 E
64 Barisan, Bukit, Mts. 3 30 S 102 15 E
64 Barito, R. 4 0 S 114 50 E
57 Barkah 24 30 N 58 0 E
67 Barkha 31 0 N 81 45 E
80 Barkly Tableland 19 50 S 138 40 E
19 Bar-le-Duc 48 47 N 5 10 E
83 Barlee, L. 29 15 S 119 30 E
39 Barletta 41 20 N 16 17 E
84 Barmedman 34 9 S 147 21 E
60 Barmer 25 45 N 71 20 E
81 Barmera 34 15 S 140 28 E
12 Barmouth 52 44 N 4 3 W
60 Barnagar 23 7 N 75 19 E
12 Barnard Castle 54 33 N 1 55 W
50 Barnaul 53 20 N 83 40 E
100 Barnesville 33 6 N 84 9 W
13 Barnet 51 37 N 0 15 W
16 Barneveld 52 7 N 5 36 E
18 Barneville 49 23 N 1 46 W
12 Barnsley 53 33 N 1 29 W
13 Barnstaple 51 5 N 4 3 W
60 Baroda= Vadodara 22 20 N 73 10 E
73 Barqa 27 0 N 20 0 E
31 Barquinha 39 28 N 8 25 W
110 Barquisimeto 9 58 N 69 13 W
111 Barra 11 5 S 43 10 W
14 Barra, I. 57 0 N 7 30 W
111 Barra de Corda 5 30 S 45 10 W
109 Barra do Piraí 22 30 S 43 50 W
109 Barra Mansa 22 35 S 44 12 W
81 Barraba 30 21 S 150 35 E
61 Barrackpur 22 44 N 88 30 E
39 Barrafranca 37 22 N 14 10 E
110 Barranca 10 45 S 77 50 W
110 Barrancabermeja 7 0 N 73 50 W
110 Barrancas 8 55 N 62 5 W
31 Barrancos 38 10 N 6 58 W
108 Barranqueras 27 30 S 59 0 W
110 Barranquilla 11 0 N 74 50 W
111 Barras 1 45 S 73 13 W
90 Barraute 47 30 N 76 50 W
97 Barre 44 15 N 73 30 W
111 Barreiras 12 8 S 45 0 W
111 Barreirinhas 2 30 S 42 50 W
31 Barreiro 38 40 N 9 6 W
111 Barreiros 8 49 S 35 12 W
111 Barretos 20 30 S 48 35 W
92 Barrhead 54 10 N 114 30 W
90 Barrie 44 25 N 79 45 W
97 Barrington 41 43 N 71 20 W
12 Barrow, U.K. 54 8 N 3 15 W
88 Barrow, U.S.A. 71 16 N 156 50 W
82 Barrow, I. 20 45 S 115 20 E
15 Barrow, R. 52 46 N 7 0 W
80 Barrow Creek 21 30 S 133 55 E
30 Barruecopardo 41 4 N 6 40 W
30 Barruelo 42 54 N 4 17 W
13 Barry 51 23 N 3 19 W
90 Barry's Bay 45 30 N 77 40 W
62 Barsi 18 10 N 75 50 E
103 Barstow 34 58 N 117 2 W
19 Bar-sur-Aube 48 14 N 4 40 E
110 Bartica 6 25 N 58 40 W
101 Bartlesville 36 50 N 95 58 W
83 Barton Siding 30 31 S 132 39 E
12 Barton-upon-Humber 53 41 N 0 27 W
28 Bartoszyce 54 15 N 20 55 E
99 Bartow 27 53 N 81 49 W
68 Baruun Urt 46 46 N 113 15 E
60 Barwani 22 2 N 74 57 E
19 Bas Rhin □ 48 40 N 7 30 E
41 Basarabi 44 10 N 28 26 E
108 Bascuñan, C. 28 52 S 71 35 W
25 Basel 47 35 N 7 35 E
25 Basel Landschaft □ 47 26 N 7 45 E
39 Basento, R. 40 25 N 16 40 E
48 Bashkir A.S.S.R. □ 54 0 N 57 0 E
65 Basilan, I. 6 35 N 122 0 E
65 Basilan City= Lamitan 6 37 N 122 0 E
65 Basilan Str. 13 10 S 122 0 E
13 Basildon 51 34 N 0 29 E
39 Basilicata □ 40 30 N 16 0 E
13 Basingstoke 51 15 N 1 5 W
61 Basirhat 22 40 N 88 54 E
90 Baskatong Res. 46 46 N 75 50 W
25 Basle=Basel 47 35 N 7 35 E
62 Basmat 19 15 N 77 12 E
74 Basoka 1 16 N 23 40 E
14 Bass Rock 56 5 N 2 40 W
80 Bass, Str. 39 15 S 146 30 E
37 Bassano del Grappa 45 45 N 11 45 E
75 Bassas da India, I. 22 0 S 39 0 E
105 Basse Terre 16 0 N 61 40 W
59 Bassein, Burma 16 45 N 94 30 E
62 Bassein, India 19 26 N 72 48 E
105 Basseterre 17 17 N 62 43 W
100 Bassett 42 37 N 99 30 W
60 Bassi 30 44 N 76 21 E
19 Bassigny, Reg. 48 0 N 5 10 E
57 Bastak 27 15 N 54 25 E
61 Basti 26 52 N 82 55 E
21 Bastia 42 40 N 9 30 E
16 Bastogne 50 1 N 5 43 E
54 Bat Yam 32 2 N 34 44 E
74 Bata 1 57 N 9 50 E
65 Bataan, Pen. 14 38 N 120 30 E
105 Barabanó, G. de 22 30 N 82 30 W
51 Batagoy 67 38 N 134 38 E
51 Batamay 63 30 N 129 15 E
69 Batan Is. 20 25 N 121 59 E
65 Batang 6 55 S 109 40 E
65 Batangas 13 35 N 121 10 E
109 Batatais 20 54 S 47 37 W
96 Batavia 43 0 N 78 10 W
82 Batchelor 13 4 S 131 1 E
101 Batesville 35 48 N 91 40 W
13 Bath, U.K. 51 22 N 2 22 W
96 Bath, Me. 43 50 N 69 49 W
99 Bath, N.Y. 42 20 N 77 17 W
14 Bathgate 55 54 N 3 38 W
72 Bathurst=Banjul 13 28 N 16 40 W
84 Bathurst, Australia 33 25 S 149 31 E
91 Bathurst, Canada 47 37 N 65 43 W
88 Bathurst, C. 70 30 N 128 30 W
82 Bathurst, I., Australia 11 30 S 130 10 E
86 Bathurst I., Canada 76 30 N 130 10 W
88 Bathurst Inlet 67 15 N 108 30 W
91 Bathurst Mines 47 30 N 65 47 W
57 Batinah, Reg. 24 0 N 57 0 E
72 Batna 35 34 N 6 15 E
101 Baton Rouge 30 30 N 91 5 W
74 Batouri 4 30 N 14 25 E
63 Battambang 13 7 N 103 12 E
62 Batticaloa 7 43 N 81 45 E
39 Battipáglia 40 38 N 15 0 E
54 Battir 31 44 N 35 8 E
13 Battle 50 55 N 0 30 E
93 Battle, R. 52 45 N 108 15 W
98 Battle Creek 42 20 N 85 10 W
91 Battle Harbour 52 13 N 55 42 W
102 Battle Mountain 40 45 N 117 0 W
93 Battleford 52 45 N 108 15 W
27 Battonya 46 16 N 21 03 E
64 Batu, Kep. 0 30 S 98 25 E
63 Batu Gajah 4 28 N 101 3 E
63 Batu Pahat= Bandar Penggaram 1 50 N 102 56 E
49 Batumi 41 30 N 41 30 E
64 Baturadja 4 11 S 104 15 E
111 Baturité 4 28 S 38 45 W
65 Baubau 5 25 S 123 50 E
72 Bauchi 10 22 N 9 48 E
18 Baud 47 52 N 3 1 W
31 Bauer, C. 32 44 N 134 4 E
18 Baugé 47 31 N 0 8 W
80 Bauhinia Downs 24 35 S 149 18 E
24 Baunatal 51 19 N 9 15 E
109 Bauru 22 10 S 49 0 W
111 Baus 18 22 S 52 47½
24 Bautzen 51 11 N 14 25 W
59 Bawdwin 23 5 N 97 50 E
64 Bawean, I. 5 46 S 112 35 E
59 Bawlake 19 11 N 97 21 E
98 Bay City, Mich. 43 35 N 83 51 W
101 Bay City, Tex. 28 59 N 95 55 W
97 Bay Shore 40 44 N 73 15 W
85 Bay View 39 25 S 176 50 E
105 Bayamón 18 24 N 66 10 W
68 Bayan 47 20 N 107 55 E
67 Bayan Kara Shan, Mts. 34 0 N 98 0 E
68 Bayan-Uul 49 6 N 112 12 E
50 Bayanaul 50 45 N 75 45 E
68 Bayantsogt 47 58 N 105 1 E
25 Bayerischer Wald, Reg. 49 0 N 13 0 E
25 Bayern □ 49 7 N 11 30 E
18 Bayeux 49 17 N 0 42 W
51 Baykal, Oz. 53 0 N 108 0 E
51 Baykal, L.= Baykal, Oz. 53 0 N 108 0 S
51 Baykir 61 50 N 95 50 E
50 Baykonur 47 48 N 65 50 E
19 Bayon 48 30 N 6 20 E
20 Bayonne, Fr. 43 30 N 1 28 E
97 Bayonne, U.S.A. 40 40 N 74 5 W
25 Bayreuth 49 56 N 11 35 E
56 Bayrūt 33 53 N 35 31 E
54 Bayt Aula 31 37 N 35 2 E
54 Bayt Jālā 31 43 N 35 11 E
54 Bayt Lahm 31 43 N 35 12 E
54 Bayt Sāhūr 31 42 N 35 13 E
54 Baytin 31 56 N 35 14 E
101 Baytown 29 42 N 94 57 W
33 Baza 37 30 N 2 47 W
75 Bazaruto, I. do 21 40 S 35 28 E
20 Bazas 44 27 N 0 13 W
93 Beach 46 57 N 104 0 W
13 Beachy Hd. 50 44 N 0 16 E
83 Beacon, Australia 30 20 S 117 55 E
97 Beacon, U.S.A. 41 32 N 73 58 W
112 Beagle, Can. 55 0 S 68 30 W
85 Bealey 43 2 S 171 36 E
90 Beardmore 49 36 N 87 59 W
100 Beardstown 40 0 N 90 25 W
20 Béarn, Reg 43 28 N 0 36 W
20 Béarn, R. 43 40 N 0 47 W
33 Beas de Segura 38 15 N 2 53 W
32 Beasain 43 3 N 2 11 W
100 Beatrice 40 20 N 96 40 W
21 Beaucaire 43 48 N 4 39 E
91 Beauceville 46 13 N 70 46 W
81 Beaudesert 27 59 S 153 0 E
64 Beaufort, Malaysia 5 30 N 115 40 E
84 Beaufort, Australia 37 25 S 143 25 E
99 Beaufort, U.S.A. 34 45 N 76 40 W
86 Beaufort Sea 70 30 N 146 0 W
75 Beaufort West 32 18 S 22 36 E
90 Beauharnois 45 20 N 73 20 W
20 Beaujolais, Reg. 46 0 N 4 25 E
21 Beaulieu 43 45 N 7 20 E
14 Beauly 57 29 N 4 27 W
12 Beaumaris 53 16 N 4 7 W
18 Beaumont, Fr. 44 45 N 0 46 E
101 Beaumont, U.S.A. 30 5 N 94 8 W
19 Beaumont-sur-Oise 49 9 N 2 17 E
21 Beaune 47 2 N 4 50 E
93 Beausejour 50 5 N 96 35 E
19 Beauvais 49 25 N 2 8 E
93 Beauval 55 9 N 107 35 W
20 Beauvoir 46 12 N 0 30 W
20 Beauvoir-sur-Mer 46 55 N 2 1 W
96 Beaver, Canada 40 40 N 80 18 W
88 Beaver, U.S.A. 66 40 N 147 50 W
100 Beaver Dam 43 28 N 88 50 W
96 Beaver Falls 40 44 N 80 20 W
62 Beawar 26 3 N 74 18 E
109 Bebedouro 21 0 S 48 25 W
13 Beccles 52 27 N 1 33 E
40 Bečej 45 36 N 20 3 E
30 Becerreá 42 51 N 7 10 W
72 Béchar 31 38 N 2 18 E
98 Beckley 37 50 N 81 8 W
24 Beckum 51 47 N 8 5 E
18 Bécon 47 30 N 0 50 W
33 Bédar 37 11 N 1 59 W
20 Bédarieux 43 37 N 3 10 E
90 Bedford, Canada 45 10 N 73 0 W
75 Bedford, S. Africa 32 40 S 26 10 E
13 Bedford, U.K. 52 8 N 0 29 W
96 Bedford, Pa. 40 1 N 78 30 W
98 Bedford, Ind. 38 50 N 86 30 W
13 Bedford □ 52 4 N 0 28 W
92 Bednesti 53 50 N 123 10 W
80 Bedourie 24 30 S 139 30 E
27 Bedzin 50 19 N 19 7 E
24 Beelitz 52 14 N 12 58 E
81 Beenleigh 27 43 S 153 10 E
54 Be'er Sheva 31 15 N 34 48 E
54 Be'erotayim 32 19 N 34 59 E
12 Beeston 52 55 N 1 11 W
24 Beetzendorf 52 42 N 11 6 E
101 Beeville 28 27 N 97 44 W
84 Bega 36 41 S 149 51 E
40 Bega, Canalul 45 37 N 20 46 E
18 Bégard 48 38 N 3 18 W
30 Begonte 43 10 N 7 40 W
61 Begu-Sarai 25 24 N 86 9 E
56 Behbehan 30 30 N 50 15 E
57 Behshahr 36 45 N 53 35 E
68 Beijing 39 45 N 116 25 E
16 Beilen 52 52 N 6 27 E
25 Beilngries 49 1 N 11 27 E
75 Beira 19 50 S 34 52 E
29 Beira-Alta, Reg. 41 0 N 7 20 W
29 Beira-Baixa, Reg. 40 0 N 7 30 W
29 Beira Litoral, Reg. 40 0 N 7 30 W
56 Beirut=Bayrut 33 53 N 35 31 E
54 Beit Hanun 31 32 N 34 32 E
54 Beit'Ur et Tahta 31 54 N 35 5 E
75 Beitbridge 22 12 S 30 0 E
54 Beituniya 31 54 N 35 10 E
31 Beja, Port. 38 2 N 7 53 W
72 Béja, Tunisia 36 10 N 9 0 E
31 Beja □ 37 55 N 7 55 W
72 Béjaîa 36 42 N 5 2 E
30 Béjar 40 23 N 5 46 W
27 Békés 46 47 N 21 9 E
27 Békés □ 46 45 N 21 0 E
27 Békéscsaba 46 40 N 21 10 E
63 Bekok 2 20 N 103 7 E
61 Bela, India 25 50 N 82 0 E
58 Bela, Pak. 26 12 N 66 20 E
40 Bela Crkva 44 55 N 21 27 E
40 Bela Palanka 43 13 N 22 17 E
64 Belawan 3 33 N 98 32 E
49 Belaya Tserkov 49 45 N 30 10 E
90 Belcher Is. 56 20 N 79 20 W
32 Belchite 41 18 N 0 43 W
48 Belebey 54 72 N 54 7 E
111 Belém 1 20 S 48 30 W
108 Belén 27 40 S 67 5 W
103 Belen 34 40 N 106 50 W
41 Belene 43 39 N 25 10 E
55 Belet Uen 4 30 N 45 5 E
15 Belfast, U.K. 54 35 N 5 56 W
99 Belfast, U.S.A. 44 30 N 69 0 W
15 Belfast, L. 54 40 N 5 50 W
15 Belfast □ 54 35 N 5 56 W
19 Belfort 47 38 N 6 50 E
19 Belfort, Terr. de □ 47 38 N 6 52 E
62 Belgaum 15 55 N 74 35 E
16 Belgium ■ 51 30 N 5 0 E
15 Belgooly 51 44 N 8 30 W
49 Belgorod 50 35 N 36 35 E
49 Belgorod-Dnestrovskiy 46 11 N 30 23 E
40 Belgrade= Beograd 44 50 N 20 37 E
64 Belitung, Pulau, I. 3 10 S 107 50 E
104 Belize ■ 17 0 N 88 30 W
104 Belize City 17 25 N 88 0 W
108 Bell Ville 32 40 S 62 40 W
92 Bella Coola 52 25 N 126 40 W
108 Bella Unión 30 15 S 57 40 W
108 Bella Vista 28 33 S 59 0 W
36 Bellágio 45 59 N 9 15 E
96 Bellaire 40 1 N 80 46 W
62 Bellary 15 10 N 76 56 E
81 Bellata 29 53 S 149 46 E
18 Belle I. 47 20 N 3 10 W
91 Belle I, Str. of 51 30 N 56 30 W
100 Belle Fourche 44 43 N 103 52 W
99 Belle Glade 26 43 N 80 38 W
21 Belledonne, Mts. 45 11 N 6 0 E
98 Bellefontaine 40 20 N 83 45 E
21 Bellegarde 46 4 N 3 49 E
21 Belleville, Fr. 46 7 N 4 45 E
100 Belleville, Ill. 38 30 N 90 0 W
96 Belleville, N.Y. 43 46 N 76 10 W
92 Bellevue, Can. 46 35 N 84 10 W
96 Bellevue, U.S.A. 40 29 N 80 3 W
21 Belley 45 46 N 5 41 E
89 Bellin 60 0 N 70 0 W
81 Bellingen 30 25 S 152 50 E
102 Bellingham 48 45 N 122 27 W
5 Bellingshausen Sea 66 0 S 80 0 W
25 Bellinzona 46 11 N 9 1 E
97 Bellows Falls 43 10 N 72 30 W
32 Bellpuig 41 37 N 1 1 E
37 Belluno 46 8 N 12 6 E
97 Belmar 40 10 N 74 2 W
31 Bélmez 38 17 N 5 17 W
84 Belmont 33 4 S 151 42 E
111 Belmonte, Brazil 16 0 S 39 0 W
30 Belmonte, Port. 40 21 N 7 20 W

104 Belmopan 17 18N 88 30W
15 Belmullet 54 13N 9 58W
109 Belo Horizonte 19 55S 43 56W
51 Belogorsk 51 0N 128 20E
40 Belogradchik 43 37N 22 40E
100 Beloit 42 35N 89 0W
48 Belomorsk 64 35N 34 30E
48 Beloretsk 53 58N 58 24E
50 Belovo 54 30N 86 0E
48 Beloye, Oz. 60 10N 37 35E
48 Beloye More 66 0N 38 0E
48 Belozersk 60 0N 37 30E
39 Belpasso 37 37N 15 0E
38 Belsito 37 50N 13 47E
49 Belsty 47 48N 28 0E
81 Beltana 30 48S 138 25E
111 Belterra 2 45S 55 0W
101 Belton 31 4N 97 30W
15 Belturbet 54 6N 7 28W
39 Belvedere Marittimo 39 37N 15 52E
100 Belvidere 42 15N 88 55W
50 Belyy Os. 73 30N 71 0E
50 Belyy Yar 58 26N 84 30E
24 Belzig 52 8N 12 36E
31 Bembézar, R. 38 0N 5 20W
100 Bemidji 47 30N 94 50W
14 Ben Cruachan, Mt. 56 26N 5 8W
73 Ben Gardane 33 11N 11 11E
14 Ben Hope, Mt. 58 24N 4 36W
14 Ben Lawers, Mt. 56 33N 4 13W
81 Ben Lomond, Mt., Australia 30 1S 151 43E
14 Ben Lomond, Mt., U.K. 56 12N 4 39W
14 Ben Macdhui, Mt. 57 4N 3 40W
14 Ben More, Mt. 56 26N 6 2W
14 Ben More Assynt, Mt. 58 7N 4 51W
14 Ben Nevis, Mt. 56 48N 5 0W
14 Ben Wyvis, Mt. 57 40N 4 35W
74 Bena Dibele 4 4S 22 50E
31 Benagalbón 36 45N 4 15W
84 Benalla 36 30S 146 0E
61 Benares=Varanasi 25 22N 83 8E
30 Benavente 38 59N 8 49W
30 Benavides 42 30N 5 54W
14 Benbecula, I. 57 26N 7 20W
81 Benbonyathe Hill 30 25S 139 11E
83 Bencubbin 30 48S 117 52E
102 Bend 44 2N 121 15W
55 Bender Beila 9 30N 50 48E
83 Bendering 32 23S 118 18E
49 Bendery 46 50N 29 50E
84 Bendigo 36 40S 144 15E
54 Bene Beraq 32 5N 34 50E
26 Benešöv 49 46N 14 41E
19 Bénestroff 48 54N 6 45E
39 Benevento 41 7N 14 45E
19 Benfeld 48 22N 7 34E
73 Benghazi= Banghazī 32 11N 20 3E
64 Bengkalis 1 30N 102 10E
64 Bengkulu 3 50S 102 12E
64 Bengkulu □ 3 50S 102 10E
93 Bengough 49 25N 105 10W
75 Benguela 12 37S 13 25E
74 Beni 32 11S 148 43E
73 Beni Mazar 28 32N 30 44E
72 Beni Mellal 32 21N 6 21W
73 Benî Suêf 29 5N 31 6E
32 Benicarló 40 23N 0 23E
33 Benidorm 38 33N 0 9W
72 Benin, B. of 5 0N 3 0E
72 Benin City 6 20N 5 31E
33 Benisa 38 43N 0 3E
108 Benjamin Aceval 24 58S 57 34W
110 Benjamin Constant 4 40S 70 15W
80 Benlidi 24 35S 144 50E
99 Bennettsville 34 38N 79 39W
97 Bennington 42 52N 73 12W
18 Bénodet 47 53N 4 7W
75 Benoni 26 11S 28 18E
25 Bensheim 49 40N 8 38E
103 Benson 31 59N 110 19W
65 Benteng 6 10S 120 30E
101 Benton, Ark. 34 30N 92 35W
100 Benton, Ill. 38 0N 88 55W
98 Benton Harbor 42 10N 86 28W
63 Bentong 3 31N 101 55S
72 Benue, R. 7 47N 6 45E
40 Beograd 44 50N 20 37E
66 Beppu 33 15N 131 30E
54 Ber Dagan 32 1N 34 49E
42 Berati 40 43N 19 59E
73 Berber 18 0N 34 0E
55 Berbera 10 30N 45 2E
74 Berbérati 4 15N 15 40E
33 Berberia, C. 38 39N 1 24E
36 Berceto 44 30N 10 0E
25 Berchtesgaden 47 37N 13 1E
19 Berck 50 25N 1 36E
49 Berdicher 49 57N 28 30E
50 Berdsk 54 47N 83 2E
49 Berdyansk 46 45N 36 50E
55 Bereda 11 45N 51 0E
72 Berekum 7 29N 2 34W
93 Berens River 52 25N 97 0W
27 Berettyóújfalu 47 13N 21 33E
48 Berezniki 59 24N 56 46E
50 Berezovo 64 0N 65 0E
32 Berga 42 6N 1 48E
36 Bergamo 45 42N 9 40E
30 Bergantiños 43 20N 8 40W
24 Bergedorf 53 28N 10 12E
24 Bergen, E. Germany 50 24N 13 26E
16 Bergen, Neth. 52 40N 4 42E
47 Bergen, Norway 60 23N 5 27E
16 Bergen-op-Zoom 51 30N 4 18E
20 Bergerac 44 51N 0 30E
24 Bergheim 50 57N 6 38E
24 Bergisch-Gladbach 50 59N 7 9E
19 Bergues 50 58N 2 24E
16 Bergum 53 13N 5 59E
61 Berhampore 24 2N 88 27E
62 Berhampur 19 15N 84 54E
88 Bering Sea 66 0N 170 0W
4 Bering Str. 65 0N 168 0W
16 Beringen 51 3N 5 14E
51 Beringovskiy 63 3N 179 19E
108 Berisso 34 40S 58 0W
33 Berja 36 50N 2 56W
102 Berkeley 38 0N 122 20W
5 Berkner I. 79 30S 50 0W
41 Berkovitsa 43 16N 23 8E
13 Berkshire □ 51 30N 1 20W
31 Berlanga 38 17N 5 50W
24 Berleburg 51 3N 8 22E
31 Berlenga, I. 39 25N 9 30W
24 Berlin, Germany 52 32N 13 24W
97 Berlin, U.S.A. 44 29N 71 10W
31 Bermeja, Sa. 36 45N 5 11W
32 Bermeo 43 25N 2 47W
105 Bermuda, I. 32 45N 65 0W
25 Bern 46 57N 7 28E
25 Bern □ 46 45N 7 40E
39 Bernalda 40 24N 16 44E
103 Bernalillo 35 17N 106 37W
109 Bernardo de Irigoyen 26 15S 53 40W
24 Bernau 47 53N 12 20E
18 Bernay 49 5N 0 35E
26 Berndorf 47 59N 16 1E
25 Berne=Bern 46 57N 7 28E
25 Berner Alpen, Mts. 46 27N 7 35E
83 Bernier, I. 24 50S 113 12E
25 Bernina, Piz 46 20N 9 54E
26 Beroun 49 57N 14 5E
26 Berounka, R. 50 0N 13 47E
84 Berowra 33 35S 151 12E
21 Berre 43 28N 5 11E
21 Berre, Étang de 43 27N 5 5E
72 Berrechid 33 18N 7 36W
81 Berri 34 14S 140 35E
84 Berrigan 35 38S 145 49E
19 Berry, Reg. 47 0N 2 0E
24 Bersenbrück 52 33N 7 56E
19 Bertincourt 50 5N 2 58E
74 Bertoua 4 30N 13 45E
97 Berwick 41 4N 76 17W
12 Berwick-upon-Tweed 55 47N 2 0W
12 Berwyn Mts. 52 54N 3 26W
27 Berzence 46 12N 17 11E
19 Besançon 47 9N 6 0E
21 Bessèges 44 18N 4 8E
99 Bessemer 46 27N 90 0W
18 Bessin, Reg. 49 21N 1 0W
18 Bessines-sur-Gartempe 46 6N 1 22E
54 Bet Ha 'Emeq 32 58N 35 8E
54 Bet Ha Shitta 32 31N 35 27E
54 Bet Ha'tmeq 32 58N 35 8E
54 Bet Oren 32 43N 34 59E
54 Bet Qeshet 32 41N 35 21E
54 Be't She'an 32 30N 35 30E
54 Bet Shemesh 31 45N 35 0E
54 Bet Yosef 32 34N 35 33E
30 Betanzos 43 15N 8 12W
74 Bétaré-Oya 5 40N 14 5E
32 Betera 39 35N 0 28W
75 Bethanien 26 31S 17 8E
54 Bethany= Eizariya 31 47N 35 15E
97 Bethel, Conn. 41 22N 73 25W
96 Bethel, Pa. 40 20N 80 2W
97 Bethel, Vt. 43 50N 72 37W
54 Bethlehem, Jordan= Bayt Lahm 31 43N 35 12E
75 Bethlehem, S. Africa 28 14S 28 18E
97 Bethlehem, U.S.A. 40 39N 75 24W
75 Bethulie 30 30S 25 29E
19 Béthune 50 30N 2 38E
18 Béthune, R. 49 56N 1 5E
19 Betan Bazoches 48 42N 3 15E
80 Betoota 25 40S 140 42E
61 Bettiah 26 48N 84 33E
36 Bèttola 44 46N 9 35E
65 Betung 2 0S 103 10E
41 Beuca 44 14N 24 56E
21 Beuil 44 6N 7 0E
84 Beulah, Australia 35 58S 142 29E
93 Beulah, Canada 50 16N 101 2W
24 Bevensen 53 5N 10 34E
83 Beverley, Australia 32 9S 116 56E
12 Beverley, U.K. 53 52N 0 26W
92 Beverly, Canada 53 36N 113 21W
97 Beverly, U.S.A. 42 32N 70 50W
103 Beverly Hills 34 4N 118 29W
16 Beverwijk 52 28N 4 38E
25 Bex 46 15N 7 0E
72 Beyla 8 30N 8 38W
13 Bexhill 50 51N 0 29E
50 Beyneu 45 10N 55 3E
56 Beypazari 40 10N 31 48E
56 Beyşehir Gölü, L. 37 40N 31 45E
62 Bezawada= Vijayawada 16 31N 80 39E
40 Bezdan 45 28N 18 57E
54 Bezet 33 4N 35 8E
48 Bezhitsa 53 19N 34 17E
20 Béziers 43 20N 3 12E
61 Bhadrakh 21 10N 86 30E
62 Bhadravati 13 49N 76 15E
61 Bhagalpur 25 10N 87 0E
62 Bhaisa 19 10N 77 58E
60 Bhakkar 31 40N 71 5E
61 Bhakra Dam 31 30N 76 45E
59 Bhamo 24 15N 97 15E
62 Bhamragarh 19 30N 80 40E
61 Bhandara 21 5N 79 42E
61 Bhanrer Ra. 23 40N 79 45E
58 Bharūch 21 47N 73 0E
60 Bharatpur 27 15N 77 30E
60 Bhatinda 30 15N 74 57E
62 Bhatkal 13 58N 74 35E
61 Bhatpara 22 50N 88 25E
62 Bhattiprolu 16 7N 80 45E
60 Bhaun 32 55N 72 40E
62 Bhavani 11 27N 77 43E
60 Bhavnagar 21 45N 72 10E
60 Bhera 32 29N 72 57E
60 Bhilwara 25 25N 74 38E
62 Bhima, R. 17 20N 76 30E
62 Bhimavaram 16 30N 81 30E
60 Bhind 26 30N 78 46E
62 Bhiwandi 19 15N 73 0E
60 Bhiwani 28 50N 76 9E
62 Bhiwndi 19 15N 73 0E
62 Bhongir 17 30N 78 56E
60 Bhopal 23 20N 77 53E
62 Bhor 18 12N 73 53E
61 Bhubaneswar 20 15N 85 50E
60 Bhuj 23 15N 69 49E
60 Bhusaval 21 15N 69 49E
61 Bhutan ■ 27 25N 89 50E
27 Biała, R 49 46N 17 40E
28 Biała Piska 53 37N 22 5E
28 Biała Podlaska 52 4N 23 6E
28 Biała Podlaska □ 52 0N 23 0S
28 Białogard 54 2N 15 58E
28 Białystok 53 10N 23 10E
28 Białystok □ 52 50N 23 10E
39 Biancaville 37 39N 14 50E
20 Biarritz 43 29N 1 33W
25 Biasca 46 22N 18 58E
25 Biberach 48 5N 9 49E
25 Bibey, R. 42 24N 7 13W
72 Bibiani 6 30N 2 8W
91 Bic 48 20N 68 41W
39 Biccari 41 23N 15 12E
72 Bida 9 3N 5 58E
13 Bicester 51 53N 1 9W
62 Bidar 17 55N 77 35E
99 Biddeford 43 30N 70 28E
13 Bideford 51 1N 4 13W
63 Bidor 4 6N 101 15E
75 Bié 12 22S 16 55E
75 Bié Plat. 12 0S 16 0E
102 Bieber 41 4N 121 6W
25 Biel 47 8N 7 14E
28 Bielawa 50 43N 16 37E
27 Bielé Karpaty, Mts. 49 5N 18 0E
24 Bielefeld 52 2N 8 31E
36 Biella 45 33N 8 3E
28 Bielsk Podlaski 52 47N 23 12E
27 Bielsko-Biała 49 50N 19 8E
27 Bielsko Biała 49 45N 19 10E
63 Biên Hoa 10 57N 106 49E
25 Bienne=Biel 47 8N 7 14E
31 Bienvenida 38 18N 6 12W
32 Biescas 42 37N 0 20W
39 Biferno, R. 41 40N 14 38E
90 Big Beaver House 52 59N 89 50W
101 Big Bend Nat. Park 29 15N 103 15W
88 Big Delta 64 15N 145 0W
97 Big Moose 43 49N 74 58W
98 Big Rapids 43 42N 85 27W
93 Big River 53 50N 107 0W
88 Big Salmon 61 50N 136 0W
101 Big Spring 32 10N 101 25W
99 Big Stone Gap 36 52N 82 45W
90 Big Trout L. 53 40N 90 0W
20 Biganos 44 39N 0 59W
93 Biggar, Canada 52 10N 108 0W
14 Biggar, U.K. 55 38N 3 31W
82 Bigge, I. 14 35S 125 10E
81 Biggenden 25 31S 152 4E
102 Bighorn Mts. 44 30N 107 20W
20 Bigorre, Reg. 43 5N 0 2E
102 Bigtimber 45 33N 110 0W
37 Bihaí 44 49N 15 57E
61 Bihar 25 5N 85 40E
61 Bihar □ 25 0N 86 0E
27 Bihor □ 47 0N 22 10E
72 Bijagos, Arquipélago dos 11 15N 16 10W
62 Bijapur 26 2N 77 36E
40 Bijeljina 44 46N 19 17E
60 Bijnor 29 27N 78 11E
60 Bikaner 28 2N 73 18E
51 Bikin 46 50N 134 20E
76 Bikini Atoll, I. 12 0N 167 30E
60 Bilara 26 14N 73 53E
61 Bilaspur, Mad. P. 22 2N 82 15E
60 Bilaspur, Punjab 31 19N 76 50E
63 Bilauk Taungdan, Ra. 13 0N 99 0E
30 Bilbao 43 16N 2 56W
40 Bileća 42 53N 18 27E
56 Bilecik 40 5N 30 5E
51 Bilibino 68 3N 166 20E
51 Bilir 65 40N 131 20E
42 Bilishti 40 37N 20 59E
83 Billabalong 27 25S 115 49E
82 Billiluna 19 37S 127 41E
12 Billingham 54 36N 1 18W
102 Billings 45 43N 108 29W
44 Billingsfors 58 59N 12 15E
20 Billom 45 43N 3 20E
73 Bilma 18 50N 13 30E
40 Bilo Gora 45 53N 17 15E
80 Biloela 24 34S 150 31E
101 Biloxi 30 30N 89 0W
73 Biltine 14 40N 20 50E
80 Bilyana 18 5S 145 50E
65 Bima 8 22S 118 49E
60 Bina-Etawah 24 13N 78 14E
65 Binalbagan 10 12N 122 50E
64 Binatang 2 10N 111 40E
80 Binbee 20 19S 147 56E
16 Binche 50 26N 4 10E
83 Bindi Bindi 30 37S 116 22E
75 Bindura 17 18S 31 18E
81 Bingara, N.S.W. 29 40S 150 40E
81 Bingara, Queens. 28 10S 144 37E
25 Bingen 49 57N 7 53E
102 Bingham Canyon 40 31N 112 10W
97 Binghamton 42 9N 75 54W
63 Binh Dinh= An Nhon 13 55N 109 7E
63 Binh Son 15 20N 104 40E
64 Binjai 3 50N 98 30E
54 Binyamina 32 32N 34 56E
72 Binzerte 37 15N 9 50E
108 Bío Bío □ 37 35S 72 0W
37 Biograd 43 56N 15 29E
40 Biokovo 43 23N 17 0E
62 Bir 19 0N 75 54E
73 Bir Atrun 18 15N 26 40E
54 Bir Nabala 31 52N 35 12E
73 Bîr Shalatein 23 5N 35 25E
54 Bir Zeit 31 59N 35 11E
61 Biratnagar 26 18N 87 17E
93 Birch Hills 53 10N 105 10W
84 Birchip 35 52S 143 0E
79 Bird, I. 22 20S 155 20E
80 Birdsville 25 51S 139 20E
82 Birdum 15 50S 133 0E
64 Bireuen 5 14N 96 39E
109 Birigui 21 18S 50 16W
57 Birjand 32 57N 59 10E
12 Birkenhead 53 24N 3 1W
26 Birkfeld 47 21N 15 45E
41 Bîrlad 46 15N 27 38E
13 Birmingham, U.K. 52 30N 1 55W
99 Birmingham, U.S.A. 33 31N 86 50W
72 Birnin-Kebbi 12 32N 4 12E
51 Birobidzhan 48 50N 132 50E
15 Birr 53 7N 7 55W
93 Birtle 50 30N 101 5W
61 Bisalpur 28 14N 79 48E
103 Bisbee 31 30N 110 0W
20 Biscarrosse, Étang de 44 22N 1 10W
29 Biscay, B. of 45 0N 2 0W
39 Biscéglie 41 14N 16 30E
26 Bischofshofen 47 26N 13 14E

24 Bischofswerda 51 8N 14 11E
19 Bischwiller 48 47N 7 50E
103 Bishop 37 20N 118 26W
12 Bishop Auckland 54 40N 1 40W
91 Bishop's Falls 49 2N 55 24W
13 Bishop's Stortford 51 52 0 11E
72 Biskra 34 50N 5 52E
28 Biskupiec 53 53N 20 58E
100 Bismarck 46 49N 100 49W
76 Bismark Arch. 3 30S 148 30E
72 Bissau 11 45N 15 45W
93 Bissett 46 14N 78 4W
61 Biswan 27 29N 81 2E
40 Bitola 41 5N 21 21E
39 Bitonto 41 7N 16 40E
24 Bitterfeld 51 36N 12 20E
75 Bitterfontein 31 0S 18 32E
102 Bitterroot Ra. 46 0N 114 20W
38 Bitti 40 29N 9 20E
66 Biwa-Ko, L. 35 15N 135 45E
50 Biysk 52 40N 85 0E
66 Bizen 34 44N 134 9E
72 Bizerte=Binzerte 37 15N 9 50E
45 Bjärka 58 16N 15 44E
40 Bjelašnica, Mt. 43 11N 18 21E
37 Bjelovar 45 56N 16 49E
4 Bjørnøya, I 74 25N 19 0E
45 Bjuv 56 7N 12 56E
40 Blace 43 18N 21 17E
97 Black, R. 43 59N 76 4W
100 Black Hills, Mts 44 0N 103 50W
13 Black Mts. 51 52N 3 50W
9 Black Sea 43 30N 35 0E
72 Black Volta, R. 8 41N 1 33W
80 Blackall 24 26S 145 27E
80 Blackbull 18 0S 141 7E
12 Blackburn 53 44N 2 30W
102 Blackfoot 43 13N 112 12W
84 Blackheath 33 39S 150 17E
12 Blackpool 53 48N 3 3W
91 Blacks Harbour 45 3N 66 49W
91 Blackville 47 5N 65 58W
80 Blackwater 23 35S 149 0E
15 Blackwater, R., Cork 51 51N 7 50W
15 Blackwater, R., Dungannon 54 31N 6 34W
15 Blackwater, R., Meath 53 39N 6 43W
101 Blackwell 36 55N 97 20W
12 Blaenau Ffestiniog 53 0N 3 57W
20 Blagnac 43 38N 1 24E
49 Blagodarnoye 45 7N 43 37E
40 Blagoevgrad 42 2N 23 5E
51 Blagoveshchensk 50 20N 127 30E
93 Blaine Lake 52 51N 106 52W
80 Blair Atholl, Australia 22 42S 147 31E
14 Blair Atholl, U.K. 56 46N 3 50W
14 Blairgowrie 56 36N 3 20W
92 Blairmore 49 40N 114 25W
41 Blaj 46 10N 23 57E
19 Blamont 48 35N 6 50E
72 Blanc, C.= Ras Nouadhibou 37 15N 9 56E
21 Blanc, Mt. 45 50N 6 52E
112 Blanca, B. 39 10S 61 30W
103 Blanca Pk. 37 35N 105 29W
33 Blanco, C. 39 21N 2 51E
13 Blandford 50 52N 2 10W
103 Blanding 37 35N 109 30W
32 Blanes 41 40N 2 48E
19 Blangy 49 14N 0 17E
26 Blanice 49 10N 14 5E
109 Blanquillo 32 53S 55 37W
27 Blansko 49 22N 16 40E
75 Blantyre 15 45S 35 0E
15 Blarney 51 57N 8 35W
12 Blaydon 54 56N 1 47W
20 Blaye 45 8N 0 40W
84 Blayney 33 32S 149 14E
24 Bleckede 53 18N 10 43E
37 Bled 46 27N 14 7E
26 Bleiburg 46 35N 14 49E
45 Blekinge □ 56 15N 15 15E
85 Blenheim 41 38S 174 5E
13 Bletchley 51 59N 0 54W
72 Blida 36 30N 2 49E
90 Blind River 46 15N 83 0W
65 Blitar 8 5S 112 11E
97 Block I. 41 13N 71 35W
97 Block Island Sd. 41 10N 71 45W
75 Bloemfontein 29 6S 26 14E
18 Blois 47 35N 1 20E
28 Błonie 52 12N 20 37E
97 Bloomingdale 41 0N 74 20W
100 Bloomington, Ill. 40 25N 89 0W
98 Bloomington, Ind. 39 10N 86 30W
97 Bloomsburg 41 0N 76 30W
26 Bludenz 47 10N 9 50E
98 Blue Island 41 40N 87 41W
80 Blue Mud, B. 13 30S 136 0E
97 Blue Mts. 45 15N 119 0W
73 Blue Nile, R.= Nîl el Azraq, R. 10 30N 35 0E
86 Blue Ridge, Mts 36 30N 80 15W
98 Bluefield 37 18N 81 14W
105 Bluefields 12 0N 83 50W
80 Bluff, Australia 23 40S 149 0E
85 Bluff, N.Z. 46 36S 168 21E
83 Bluff Knoll, Mt. 34 23S 118 20E
98 Bluffton 40 43N 85 9W
109 Blumenau 27 0S 49 0W
12 Blyth 55 8N 1 32W
103 Blythe 33 40N 114 33W
101 Blytheville 35 56N 89 55W
72 Bo 7 55N 11 50W
110 Boa Vista 2 48N 60 30W
105 Boaco 12 29N 85 35W
74 Boali 4 48N 18 7E
31 Boatman 27 16S 146 55E
62 Bobbili 18 35N 83 30E
90 Bobcaygeon 44 33N 78 35W
72 Bobo-Dioulasso 11 8N 4 13W
41 Boboc 45 13N 26 59E
28 Bobr R. 52 4N 15 4E
48 Bobruysk 53 10N 29 15E
111 Bocaiuva 17 7S 43 49W
105 Bocas del Toro 9 15N 82 20W
30 Boceguillas 41 20N 3 39W
27 Bochnia 49 58N 29 27E
24 Bocholt 51 50N 6 35E
24 Bochum 51 28N 7 12E
21 Bocognano 42 5N 9 3E
40 Boçsa 45 21N 21 47E
74 Boda 4 19N 17 26E
51 Bodaybo 57 50N 114 0E
83 Boddington 32 50S 116 30E
46 Boden 65 50N 21 42E
25 Bodensee, L. 47 35N 9 25N
62 Bodhan 18 40N 77 55E
62 Bodinayakkanur 10 2N 77 10E
13 Bodmin 50 28N 4 44W
13 Bodmin Moor, Reg. 50 33N 4 36W
46 Bodø 67 17N 14 27E
27 Bodrog, R. 48 15N 21 35E
27 Bodva, R. 48 19N 20 45E
101 Bogalusa 30 50N 89 55W
84 Bogan Gate 33 6S 147 44E
80 Bogantungan 23 41S 147 17E
75 Bogenfels 27 25S 15 25E
81 Boggabri 30 45S 150 0E
13 Bognor Regis 50 47N 0 40W
65 Bogor 6 36S 106 48E
51 Bogorodskoye 52 22N 140 30E
110 Bogota 4 34N 74 0W
50 Bogotal 56 15N 89 50E
61 Bogra 24 26N 89 22E
51 Boguchany 58 40N 97 30E
19 Bohain 49 59N 3 28E
25 Böhmerwald, Mts. 49 30N 12 40E
65 Bohol, I. 9 58N 124 20E
55 Bohotleh 8 20N 46 25E
109 Boi, Pta. do 23 55S 45 15W
91 Boiestown 46 27N 66 26W
102 Boise 43 43N 116 9W
93 Boissevain 49 15N 100 0W
24 Boizenburg 55 16N 13 36E
65 Bojonegoro 7 9S 111 52E
72 Boké 10 56N 14 17W
47 Bokna, Fd. 59 12N 5 30E
74 Bokote 0 12S 21 8E
57 Bol, Kuh-e 30 40N 52 45E
72 Bolama 11 30N 15 30W
18 Bolbec 49 30N 0 30E
41 Boldeşti 45 3N 26 2E
28 Bolesławiec 51 17N 15 37E
110 Bolívar, Arg. 36 2S 60 53W
102 Bolívar, Col. 2 0N 77 0W
110 Bolivia ■ 17 6S 64 0W
106 Bolivian Plat. 19 0S 69 0W
40 Boljevac 43 31N 21 58E
21 Bollène 44 18N 4 45E
44 Bollnäs 61 22N 16 28E
31 Bollullos 37 19N 6 32W
45 Bolmen, L. 56 57N 13 45E
37 Bologna 44 30N 11 20E
19 Bologne 48 10N 5 8E
48 Bologoye 57 55N 34 0E
63 Boloven, Cao Nguyen, Mts. 15 10N 106 30E
61 Bolpur 23 40N 87 45E
37 Bolsena, L. di 42 35N 11 55E
51 Bolshevik, Os. 78 30N 102 0E
49 Bolshoi Kavkaz 42 50N 44 0E
50 Bolshoy Atlym 62 25N 66 50E
51 Bolshoy Shantar, Os. 55 0N 137 42E
12 Bolton 53 35N 2 26W
37 Bolzana 46 30N 11 20E
111 Bom Despacho 19 46S 45 15W
111 Bom Jesus da Lapa 13 10S 43 30W
74 Boma 5 50S 13 4E
84 Bomaderry 34 52S 150 37E
84 Bombala 36 56S 149 15E
62 Bombay 18 55N 72 50E
74 Bomboma 2 25N 18 55E
67 Bomda 29 59N 96 25E
73 Bon, C. 37 1N 11 2E
105 Bonaire, I. 12 10N 68 15W
82 Bonaparte Arch. 15 0S 124 30E
91 Bonaventure 48 5N 63 32W
91 Bonavista 48 40N 53 5W
91 Bonavista B. 48 58N 53 25W
37 Bondeno 44 53N 11 22E
72 Bondoukoro 9 51N 4 25W
72 Bondoukou 8 2N 2 47W
65 Bondowoso 7 56S 113 49E
65 Bone, Teluk, G. 4 10S 120 50E
14 Bo'ness 56 0N 3 38W
73 Bongor 10 35N 15 20E
101 Bonham 33 30N 96 10W
21 Bonifacio 41 24N 9 10E
38 Bonifacio, Bouches de 41 23N 9 10E
76 Bonin Is. 27 0N 142 0E
108 Bonito 21 8S 56 28W
24 Bonn 50 43N 7 6E
102 Bonners Ferry 48 38N 116 21W
18 Bonneval 48 11N 1 24E
21 Bonneville 46 5N 6 24E
83 Bonnie Rock 30 29S 118 22E
70 Bonny, B. of 4 0N 8 0E
93 Bonnyville 54 20N 110 45W
38 Bonorva 40 25N 8 47E
64 Bontang 0 10N 117 30E
65 Bonthain 5 34S 119 56E
16 Boom 51 6N 4 20E
81 Boonah 28 0S 152 35E
100 Boone 42 5N 93 46W
98 Boonville, Ind 38 3N 87 13W
100 Boonville, Mo. 38 57N 92 45W
97 Boonville, N.Y. 43 31N 75 20W
89 Boothia, G. of 70 0N 90 0W
88 Boothia Pen. 70 30N 95 0W
12 Bootle 53 28N 3 1W
74 Booué 0 5S 11 55E
81 Bopeechee 29 35S 137 30E
108 Boquerón 21 30S 60 0W
40 Bor 44 5N 22 7E
45 Borås 57 42N 13 1E
110 Borba 4 12S 59 34W
20 Bordeaux 44 50N 0 36W
83 Borden, Australia 34 3S 118 12E
91 Borden, Canada 46 18N 63 47W
14 Borders □ 55 30N 3 0W
84 Bordertown 36 14S 140 58E
36 Bordighera 43 47N 7 40E
16 Borger, Neth. 52 54N 7 33E
101 Borger, U.S.A. 35 40N 101 20W
36 Borgo 46 3N 11 27E
36 Borgomanera 45 41N 8 28E
36 Borgosésia 45 43N 8 9E
49 Borisoglebsk 51 27N 42 5E
48 Borisov 54 17N 28 28E
110 Borja 4 20S 77 40W
32 Borjas Blancas 41 31N 0 52E
24 Borken 51 3N 9 21E
73 Borkou 18 15N 18 50E
24 Borkum, I. 53 35N 6 41E
44 Borlänge 60 28N 14 33E
5 Borley, C. 66 15S 52 30E
25 Borna 51 8N 12 31E
64 Borneo, I. 1 0N 115 0E
45 Bornholm, I. 55 8N 14 55E
31 Bornos 36 48N 5 42W
51 Borogontsy 62 42N 131 8E
48 Borovichi 58 25N 35 55E
45 Borrby 55 27N 14 10E
32 Borriol 40 4N 0 4W
80 Borroloola 16 4S 136 17E
60 Borsad 22 24N 72 56E
48 Borsod-Abaüj-Zemplén □ 48 20N 21 0E
20 Bort-les-Orgues 45 24N 2 29E
56 Borujerd 33 55N 48 50E
51 Borzya 50 24N 116 31E
40 Bosanska Gradiška 45 9N 17 15E
37 Bosanska Kostajnica 45 11N 16 33E
37 Bosanska Krupa 44 53N 16 10E
37 Bosanski Novi 45 2N 16 22E
55 Bosaso 11 13N 49 8E
13 Boscasble 50 42N 4 42W
39 Boscotrecase 40 46N 14 28E
40 Bosna, R. 45 4N 18 29E
37 Bosna i Hercegovina □ 44 0N 18 0E
41 Bosporus, Str.= Karadeniz Boğazi, Str. 41 10N 29 10E
74 Bossangoa 6 35N 17 30E
101 Bossier City 32 28N 93 38W
12 Boston, U.K. 52 59N 0 2W
97 Boston, U.S.A. 42 20N 71 0W
60 Botad 22 15N 71 40E
84 Botany B. 34 2S 151 6E
41 Botevgrad 42 55N 23 47E
46 Bothnia, G. 63 0N 21 0E
80 Bothwell 42 37N 81 54W
75 Botletle, R. 20 10S 24 10E
41 Botoroaga 44 8N 25 32E
75 Botswana ■ 23 0S 24 0E
109 Botucatu 22 55S 48 30W
91 Botwood 49 6N 55 23W
72 Bou Saâda 35 11N 4 9E
72 Bouaké 7 40N 5 2W
74 Bouar 6 0N 15 40E
72 Bouârfa 32 32N 1 58E
21 Bouches-du-Rhône 43 37N 5 2E
82 Bougainville, C. 13 57S 126 4E
72 Bougouni 11 30N 7 20W
100 Boulder 40 3N 105 10W
103 Boulder City 36 0N 114 58W
80 Boulia 22 52S 139 51E
19 Bouligny 49 17N 5 45E
19 Boulogne-sur-Mer 50 42N 1 36E
102 Bountiful 40 57N 111 58W
20 Bourbon-Lancy 46 37N 3 45E
20 Bourbonnais, Reg. 46 28N 3 0E
45 Bourg 45 3N 0 34W
21 Bourg en Bresse 46 13N 5 12E
20 Bourg Madame 42 29N 1 58E
21 Bourg-de-Péage 45 2N 5 3E
20 Bourges 47 5N 2 22E
45 Bourget, L. du 45 44N 5 52E
18 Bourgneuf 47 2N 1 58W
18 Bourgneuf, B. de 47 3N 2 10W
19 Bourgogne, Reg. 47 0N 4 30E
21 Bourgoin-Jallieu 45 36N 5 17E
81 Bourke 30 8S 145 55E
90 Bourlamaque 48 5N 77 56W
13 Bournemouth 50 43N 1 53W
20 Boussac 46 22N 2 13E
20 Boussens 43 12N 1 2E
7 Bouvet, I. 55 0S 3 30E
92 Bow Island 49 50N 111 23W
83 Bowelling 33 25S 116 30E
80 Bowen 20 0S 148 16E
103 Bowie 32 15N 109 30W
12 Bowland Forest 54 0N 2 30W
98 Bowling Green, Ky. 37 0N 86 25W
98 Bowling Green, Ohio 41 22N 83 40W
80 Bowling Green, C. 19 19S 147 25E
100 Bowman 46 12N 103 21W
90 Bowmanville 43 55N 78 40W
14 Bowmore 55 45N 6 18W
92 Bowness 50 55N 114 25W
84 Bowser 36 19S 146 23E
93 Bowsman 52 15N 101 12W
16 Boxtel 51 36N 5 9E
15 Boyle 53 58N 8 19W
15 Boyne, R. 53 40N 6 34W
70 Boyoma, Chutes 0 12N 25 25E
83 Boyup Brook 33 47S 116 40E
102 Bozeman 45 40N 111 0W
74 Bozoum 6 25N 16 35E
36 Bra 44 41N 7 50E
16 Brabant □ 49 15N 5 20E
37 Brac, I. 43 20N 16 40E
37 Bracciano, L. di 42 6N 12 10E
90 Bracebridge 45 5N 79 20W
44 Bräcke 62 42N 15 32E
40 Brad 46 10N 22 50E
39 Brádano, R. 40 41N 16 20E
96 Braddock 40 24N 79 51W
99 Bradenton 27 25N 82 35W
12 Bradford, U.K. 53 47N 1 45W
96 Bradford, U.S.A. 41 58N 78 41W
91 Bradore Bay 51 27N 57 18W
101 Brady 31 8N 99 25W
14 Braemar 57 2N 3 20W
30 Braga 41 35N 8 32W
30 Braga □ 41 30N 8 30W
108 Bragado 35 2S 60 27W
111 Bragança 1 0S 47 2W
30 Bragança □ 41 30N 6 45W
109 Bragança Paulista 22 55S 46 52W
61 Brahmanbaria 23 50N 91 15E
61 Brahmani, R. 21 0N 85 15E
61 Brahmaputra, R. 26 30N 93 30E
12 Braich-y-Pwll, Pt. 52 47N 4 46W
41 Brăila 45 19N 27 59E
100 Brainerd 46 20N 94 10W
13 Braintree, U.K. 51 53N 0 34E
97 Braintree, U.S.A. 42 11N 71 0W
24 Brake 53 19N 8 30E
24 Brakel 51 43N 9 10E
92 Bralorne 50 50N 123 15W
90 Brampton, Canada 43 42N 79 46W
96 Brampton, U.S.A. 46 0N 97 46W
110 Branco, R. 1 30N 61 15W
45 Brande 55 47N 9 7E
24 Brandenburg 52 24N 12 33E
93 Brandon 49 50N 100 0W
26 Brandýs 50 10N 14 40E
28 Braniewo 54 25N 19 50E
96 Brantford 43 15N 80 15W
20 Brantôme 45 22N 0 39E
84 Branxholme 37 52S 141 49E
111 Brasília 15 55S 47 40W
111 Brasilia Legal 3 45S 55 40W

41 Braşov 45 7N 25 39 E
16 Brasschaat 51 19N 4 27 E
27 Bratislava 48 10N 17 7 E
51 Bratsk 56 10N 101 3 E
97 Brattleboro 42 53N 72 37W
41 Braţul Chilia, R. 45 25N 29 20 E
41 Braţul Sfîntu Gheorghe 45 0N 29 20 E
41 Braţul Sulina, R. 45 10N 29 20 E
26 Braunau 48 15N 13 3 E
24 Braunschweig 52 17N 10 28 E
13 Braunton 51 6N 4 9W
55 Brava 1 20N 44 8 E
103 Brawley 32 58N 115 30W
15 Bray 53 12N 6 6W
19 Bray, Reg. 49 40N 1 40 E
19 Bray-sur-Seine 48 25N 3 14 E
107 Brazil ■ 10 0S 50 0W
98 Brazil 39 30N 87 8W
106 Brazilian Highlands, Mts. 18 0S 46 30W
101 Brazol, R. 30 30N 96 20W
74 Brazzaville 4 9S 15 12 E
40 Brčko 44 54N 18 46 E
80 Breadalbane 23 48S 139 33 E
14 Breadalbane, Reg. 56 30N 4 15W
85 Bream, B. 35 56S 174 35 E
85 Bream Head 35 51S 174 36 E
65 Brebes 6 52S 109 3 E
14 Brechin 56 44N 2 40W
101 Breckenridge 32 48N 98 55W
13 Breckland, Reg. 52 30N 0 40 E
27 Breclav 48 46N 16 53 E
13 Brecon 51 57N 3 23W
13 Brecon Beacons, Mts. 51 53N 3 27W
16 Breda 51 35N 4 45 E
75 Bredasdorp 34 33S 20 2 E
84 Bredbo 35 38S 149 10 E
26 Bregenz 47 30N 9 45 E
46 Breidafjördur 65 20N 23 0W
21 Breil 43 56N 7 31 E
111 Brejo 3 41S 42 50W
24 Bremen 53 4N 8 47 E
24 Bremerhaven 53 34N 8 35 E
102 Bremerton 47 30N 122 48W
31 Brenes 37 32N 5 54W
101 Brenham 30 5N 96 27W
26 Brenner P. 47 0N 11 30 E
90 Brent, Canada 46 0N 78 30W
13 Brent, U.K. 51 33N 0 18W
13 Brentwood 51 37N 0 19W
36 Bréscia 45 33N 10 13 E
28 Breslau=Wrocław 51 5N 17 5 E
19 Bresles 49 25N 2 13 E
37 Bressanone 46 43N 11 40 E
14 Bressay, I. 60 10N 1 5W
21 Bresse, Plaine de 46 20N 5 10 E
20 Bressuire 46 51N 0 30W
18 Brest, Fr. 48 24N 4 31W
48 Brest, U.S.S.R. 52 10N 23 40 E
18 Bretagne, Reg. 48 0N 3 0W
41 Bretçu 46 7N 26 18 E
19 Breteuil 49 38N 2 18 E
20 Breton, Pertuis 46 16N 1 22W
85 Brett, C. 35 10S 174 20 E
111 Breves 1 38S 50 25W
81 Brewarrina 30 0S 146 51 E
99 Brewer 44 43N 68 50W
97 Brewster 41 23N 73 37W
99 Brewton 31 9N 87 2W
27 Brezno 48 50N 19 40 E
74 Bria 6 30N 21 58 E
21 Briançon 44 54N 6 39 E
19 Briare 47 38N 2 45 E
19 Bricon 48 5N 5 0 E
18 Bricquebec 49 29N 1 39W
13 Bridgend 51 30N 3 35W
97 Bridgeport 41 12N 73 12W
98 Bridgeton 39 29N 75 10W
83 Bridgetown, Australia 33 58S 116 7 E
105 Bridgetown, Barbados 13 0N 59 30W
91 Bridgetown, Canada 44 55N 65 12W
84 Bridgewater, Australia 36 36S 143 59 E
91 Bridgewater, Canada 44 25N 64 31W
13 Bridgnorth 52 33N 2 25W
13 Bridgwater 51 7N 3 0W
12 Bridlington 54 4N 0 10W
13 Bridport 50 43N 2 45W
19 Brie, Plaine de la 48 35N 3 10 E
19 Brie-Comte Robert 48 40N 2 35 E
19 Brienon 48 0N 3 35 E
25 Brienzersee, L. 46 44N 7 53 E
25 Brig 46 18N 7 59 E
12 Brigg 53 33N 0 30W
102 Brigham City 41 30N 112 1W
81 Brighton, Australia 35 1S 138 30 E
90 Brighton, Canada 44 3N 77 44W
13 Brighton, U.K. 50 50N 0 9W
18 Brignogan-Plages 48 40N 4 20W
21 Brignoles 43 25N 6 5 E
39 Bríndisi 40 39N 17 55 E
20 Brioude 45 18N 3 23 E
81 Brisbane 27 25S 152 54 E
37 Brisighella 44 13N 11 46 E
13 Bristol, U.K. 51 26N 2 35W
97 Bristol, Conn. 41 44N 72 37W
97 Bristol, Mass. 41 40N 71 15W
97 Bristol, Pa. 40 7N 74 52W
88 Bristol B. 58 0N 159 0W
13 Bristol Chan. 51 18N 3 30W
101 Bristow 35 5N 96 28W
5 British Antarctic Terr. 66 0S 45 0W
92 British Columbia □ 55 0N 125 15W
11 British Is. 55 0N 4 0W
75 Britstown 30 37S 23 30 E
90 Britt 45 46N 80 35W
100 Britton 45 50N 97 47W
20 Brive-la-Gaillarde 45 10N 1 32 E
30 Briviesca 42 32N 3 19W
80 Brixton 23 32S 144 52 E
27 Brno 49 10N 16 35 E
60 Broach 21 47N 73 0 E
83 Broad Arrow 30 23S 121 15 E
14 Broad Law, Mt. 55 30N 3 22W
84 Broadford 37 14S 145 4 E
12 Broads, The 52 30N 1 15 E
93 Brock 51 27N 108 42W
96 Brockport 43 12N 77 56W
97 Brockton 42 8N 71 2W
90 Brockville 44 37N 75 38W
89 Brodeur Pen. 72 0N 88 0W
14 Brodick 55 34N 5 9W
28 Brodnica 53 15N 19 25 E
100 Broken Bow 41 25N 99 35W
84 Broken Hill 31 58S 141 29 E
13 Bromley 51 20N 0 5 E
45 Bromölla 56 5N 14 25 E
45 Brönderslev 57 17N 9 55 E
39 Bronte 37 48N 14 49 E
80 Bronte Pk. 42 8S 146 30 E
100 Brookfield 39 50N 92 50W
101 Brookhaven 31 40N 90 25W
100 Brookings 44 19N 96 48W
88 Brooks Ra. 68 40N 147 0W
83 Brookton 32 22N 116 57 E
14 Broom, L. 57 55N 5 15W
82 Broome 18 0S 122 15W
83 Broomehill 33 40S 117 36 E
14 Brora 58 0N 3 50W
45 Brösarp 55 44N 14 8 E
15 Brosna, R. 53 8N 8 0W
40 Broşteni 47 14N 25 43 E
89 Broughton I. 67 35N 63 50W
14 Broughty Ferry 56 29N 2 50W
13 Brown Willy, Mt. 50 35N 4 34W
101 Brownfield 33 10N 102 15W
102 Browning 48 35N 113 10W
93 Brownlee 50 43N 105 59N
101 Brownsville 25 54N 97 30W
101 Brownwood 31 45N 99 0W
19 Bruay 50 29N 2 33 E
82 Bruce, Mt. 22 31S 118 6 E
90 Bruce Mines 46 20N 83 45W
96 Bruce Pen. 45 0N 81 15W
83 Bruce Rock 31 51S 118 2 E
25 Bruchsal 49 9N 8 39 E
26 Bruck 47 24N 15 16 E
13 Brue, R. 51 10N 2 50W
25 Brugg 47 29N 8 11 E
16 Brugge 51 13N 3 13 E
92 Brule 53 15N 117 38W
111 Brumado 14 13S 41 40W
19 Brumath 48 43N 7 40 E
64 Brunei ■ 4 52N 115 0 E
80 Brunette Downs 18 38S 135 57 E
44 Brunflo 63 4N 14 50 E
37 Brunico 46 48N 11 56 E
44 Brunkeberg 59 25N 8 30 E
85 Brunner 42 27S 171 20 E
93 Bruno 52 20N 105 30W
24 Brunsbüttelkoog 53 52N 9 13 E
16 Brunssum 50 57N 5 59 E
24 Brunswick, W. Germany= Braunschweig 52 17N 10 28 E
99 Brunswick, Ga. 31 10N 81 30W
99 Brunswick, Me. 43 53N 69 50W
96 Brunswick, Ohio 41 15N 81 50W
112 Brunswick, Pen. 53 30S 71 30W
83 Brunswick Junction 33 15S 115 50 E
40 Brusartsi 43 40N 23 5 E
109 Brusque 27 5S 49 0W
16 Brussel 50 51N 4 21 E
84 Bruthen 37 43S 147 48 E
16 Bruxelles= Brussel 50 51N 4 21 E
19 Bruyères 48 10N 6 40 E
28 Brwinow 52 9N 20 40 E
98 Bryan, Ohio 41 30N 84 30W
101 Bryan, Tex. 30 40N 96 27W
48 Bryansk 53 13N 34 25 E
47 Bryne 58 45N 5 36 E
40 Brzava, R. 45 21N 20 45 E
27 Brzeg 50 52N 17 30 E
28 Brzeg Din 51 16N 16 41 E
56 Bucak 37 28N 30 36 E
110 Bucaramanga 7 0N 73 0W
14 Buchan, Reg. 57 32N 2 8W
14 Buchan Ness, Pt. 57 29N 1 48W
93 Buchanan, Canada 51 40N 102 45W
72 Buchanan, Liberia 5 57N 10 2W
91 Buchans 49 0N 57 2W
24 Buchholz 53 19N 9 51 E
24 Bückeburg 52 16N 9 2 E
103 Buckeye 33 28N 112 40W
98 Buckhannon 39 2N 80 10W
14 Buckie 57 40N 2 58W
13 Buckingham, U.K. 52 0N 0 59W
90 Buckingham, U.S.A. 45 37N 75 24W
62 Buckingham Canal 14 0N 80 5 E
13 Buckinghamshire □ 51 50N 0 55W
91 Buctouche 46 30N 64 45W
41 Bucureşti 44 27N 26 10 E
98 Bucyrus 40 48N 83 0W
27 Budafok 47 26N 19 2 E
59 Budalin 22 20N 95 10 E
27 Budapest 47 29N 19 5 E
60 Budaun 28 5N 79 10 E
13 Bude 50 49N 4 33W
41 Budeşti 44 13N 26 30 E
61 Budge Budge 22 30N 88 25 E
37 Búdrio 44 31N 11 31 E
40 Budva 42 17N 18 50 E
110 Buenaventura 29 15S 69 40W
32 Buendia, Pantano de 40 25N 2 43W
108 Buenos Aires 34 30S 58 20W
112 Buenos Aires, L. 46 35S 72 30W
108 Buenos Aires □ 34 30 58 20W
93 Buffalo, Canada 50 49N 110 42W
96 Buffalo, U.S.A. 42 55N 78 50W
93 Buffalo Narrows 55 52N 108 28W
28 Bug, R. 51 20N 23 40 E
110 Buga 4 0N 77 0W
40 Bugojno 44 2N 17 25 E
48 Bugulma 54 38N 52 40 E
68 Bugun Shara, Mts. 48 30N 102 0 E
48 Buturuslan 53 39N 52 26 E
48 Bui 58 23N 41 27 E
13 Builth Wells 52 10N 3 26W
30 Buitrago 41 0N 3 38W
31 Bujalance 37 54N 4 23W
40 Bujanovac 42 27N 21 46 E
32 Bujaraloz 41 29N 0 10W
74 Bujumbura 3 16S 29 18 E
51 Bukachacha 52 55N 116 50 E
74 Bukavu 2 20S 28 52 E
74 Bukene 4 15S 32 48 E
50 Bukhara 39 50N 64 10 E
63 Bukit Mertajam 5 22N 100 28 E
64 Bukittinggi 0 20S 100 20 E
62 Bukkapatnam 14 14N 77 46 E
74 Bukoba 1 20S 31 49 E
67 Bulak 45 2N 82 5 E
60 Bulandshahr 28 28N 77 58 E
75 Bulawayo 20 7S 28 32 E
41 Bulgaria ■ 42 35N 25 30 E
55 Bulhar 10 25N 44 30 E
83 Bullabulling 31 0S 120 55 E
31 Bullaque, R. 39 20N 4 13W
82 Bullara 22 30S 114 2 E
83 Bullaring 32 28S 117 40 E
33 Bullas 38 2N 1 40W
80 Bullock Creek 17 40S 144 30 E
85 Bulls 40 10S 175 24 E
19 Bully-les-Mines 50 27N 2 44 E
55 Bulo Burti 3 50N 45 33 E
60 Bulsar 20 40N 72 58 E
51 Bulun 70 37N 127 30 E
74 Bumba 2 13N 22 30 E
41 Bumbeşti Jiu 45 10N 23 22 E
59 Bumhpa Bum, Mt. 26 40N 97 20 E
83 Bunbury 33 20S 115 35 E
15 Buncrana 55 8N 7 28W
81 Bundaberg 24 54S 152 22 E
60 Bundi 25 30N 75 35 E
80 Bundooma 24 54S 134 16 E
12 Bure, R. 52 38N 1 38 E
24 Burg 54 25N 11 10 E
41 Burgas 42 33N 27 29 E
41 Burgaski Zaliv, B. 42 30N 27 39 E
25 Burgdorf, Switz. 47 3N 7 37 E
24 Burgdorf, W. Germany 52 27N 10 0 E
27 Burgenland □ 47 20N 16 20 E
91 Burgeo 47 36N 57 34W
75 Burgersdorp 31 0S 26 20 E
30 Burgo de Osma 41 35N 3 4W
30 Burgos 42 21N 3 41W
30 Burgos □ 42 21N 3 41W
24 Burgstädt 50 55N 12 49 E
24 Burgsteinfurt 52 9N 7 23 E
31 Burguillos del Cerro 38 23N 6 35W
60 Burhanpur 21 18N 76 20 E
65 Burias, I. 13 5N 122 55 E
105 Burica, Pta 8 3N 82 51W
54 Burin 32 11N 35 15 E
63 Buriram 15 0N 103 0 E
80 Burketown 17 45S 139 33 E
72 Burkina Faso ■ 12 0N 0 30W
90 Burks Falls 45 37N 79 10W
102 Burley 42 37N 113 55W
96 Burlington, Canada 43 25N 79 45W
100 Burlington, Colo. 39 21N 102 18W
100 Burlington, Iowa 40 50N 91 5W
100 Burlington, Kans. 38 15N 95 47W
99 Burlington, N.C. 36 7N 79 27W
97 Burlington, N.J. 40 5N 74 50W
102 Burlington, Wash. 48 29N 122 19W
50 Burlyu-Tyube 46 30N 79 10 E
59 Burma ■ 21 0N 96 30 E
83 Burngup 33 0S 118 35 E
80 Burnie 41 4S 145 56 E
12 Burnley 53 47N 2 15W
102 Burns 43 40N 119 4W
92 Burns Lake 54 20N 125 45W
96 Burnt River 44 40N 78 42 E
93 Burntwood, L. 55 35N 99 40W
54 Burqa 32 18N 35 11 E
81 Burra 33 40S 138 55 E
84 Burrendong Res. 32 45S 149 10 E
32 Burriana 39 50N 0 4W
13 Burry Port 51 41N 4 17W
56 Bursa 40 15N 29 5 E
12 Burton-on-Trent 52 48N 1 39W
65 Buru, I. 3 30S 126 30 E
74 Burundi ■ 3 15S 30 0 E
64 Burung 0 21N 108 25 E
72 Burutu 5 20N 5 29 E
12 Bury 53 36N 2 19W
13 Bury St. Edmunds 52 15N 0 42 E
51 Buryat A.S.S.R. □ 53 0N 110 0 E
44 Buskerud □ 60 20N 9 0 E
40 Busovača 44 6N 17 53 E
19 Bussang 47 50N 6 50 E
83 Busselton 33 42S 115 15 E
16 Bussum 52 16N 5 10 E
30 Busto, C. 43 34N 6 28W
36 Busto Arsizio 45 38N 8 50 E
74 Busu-Djanoa 1 50N 21 5 E
65 Busuanga, I. 12 10N 120 12 E
24 Büsum 54 7N 8 50 E
74 Buta 2 50N 24 53 E
74 Butare 2 31S 29 52 E
14 Bute, I. 55 48N 5 2W
74 Butembo 0 9N 29 18 E
39 Butera 37 10N 14 10 E
74 Butiaba 1 50N 31 20 E
96 Butler 40 52N 79 52W
14 Butt of Lewis, Pt. 58 30N 6 20W
102 Butte, Mont. 46 0N 112 31W
100 Butte, Neb. 42 56N 98 54W
63 Butterworth 5 24N 100 23 E
65 Butuan 8 52N 125 36 E
65 Butung, I. 5 0S 122 45 E
49 Buturlinovka 50 50N 40 35 E
24 Butzbach 50 24N 8 40 E
61 Buxar 25 34N 83 58 E
12 Buxton 53 16N 1 54W
51 Buyaga 59 50N 127 0 E
68 Buyr Nuur, L. 47 50N 117 35 E
41 Buzău 45 10N 26 50 E
41 Buzău, R. 45 10N 27 20 E
66 Buzen 33 35N 131 5 E
37 Buzet 45 24N 13 58 E
48 Buzuluk 52 48N 52 12 E
97 Buzzards Bay 41 45N 70 38W
41 Byala, Bulgaria 42 53N 27 55 E
41 Byala, Bulgaria 43 28N 25 44 E
41 Byala Slatina 43 26N 23 55 E
28 Bydgoszcz 53 10N 18 0 E
28 Bydgoszcz □ 53 16N 18 0 E
48 Byelorussian S.S.R. □ 53 30N 27 0 E
103 Bylas 33 11N 110 9W
45 Bylderup 54 58N 9 8 E
89 Bylot I. 73 0N 78 0W
75 Byrd Ld. 79 30S 125 0W
5 Byrd Sub-Glacial Basin 82 0S 120 0W
81 Byrock 30 40S 146 27 E
81 Byron Bay 28 30S 153 30 E
46 Byske 64 59N 21 17 E
51 Byrranga, Gory 75 0N 100 0 E
27 Bystrzyca Kłodzka 50 19N 16 39 E
27 Bytom 50 25N 19 0 E
28 Bytów 54 10N 17 30 E
27 Bzenec 48 58N 17 18 E

C

63 Ca Mau, Mui, Pt. . . 8 35N 104 42E
108 Caacupé 25 23N 57 5W
109 Caaguazú □ 25 0N 55 45W
109 Caazapá □ 26 10S 56 0W
108 Caazapá 26 9S 56 24W
32 Caballeria, C. 40 5N 4 5E
91 Cabana 8 25S 78 5W
65 Cabanatuan 15 30N 121 5E
32 Cabanes 40 9N 0 2E
111 Cabedelo 7 0S 34 50W
31 Cabeza del Buey 38 38N 3 12W
110 Cabimas 10 30N 71 25W
74 Cabinda 5 40S 12 11E
102 Cabinet Mts. 48 8N 115 46W
112 Cabo Blanco 47 56S 65 47W
109 Cabo Frio 22 51S 42 3W
90 Cabonga Res. 47 35N 76 40W
81 Caboolture 27 5S 152 47E
75 Cabora Bassa Dam 15 30S 32 40E
104 Caborca 30 40N 112 10W
91 Cabot Str. 47 15N 59 40W
31 Cabra 37 30N 4 28W
33 Cabra del Santó. Cristo 37 42N 3 16W
33 Cabrera, I. 39 6N 2 59E
30 Cabrera, Sa. 42 12N 6 40W
93 Cabri 50 35N 108 25W
33 Cabriel, R. 39 14N 1 3W
110 Cabruta 7 50N 66 10W
109 Caçador 26 47S 51 0W
40 Čačak 43 54N 20 20E
109 Caçapava do Sul 30 30S 53 30W
31 Cáceres □ 39 45N 6 0W
31 Cáceres 39 26N 6 23W
90 Cache Bay 46 26N 80 0W
90 Cache Lake 49 55N 74 35W
111 Cachoeira 12 30S 39 0W
109 Cachoeira do Sul 30 3S 52 53W
109 Cachoeiro de Itapemirim 20 51S 41 7W
75 Caconda 13 48S 15 8E
27 Čadca 49 26N 18 45E
32 Cadí, Sa. del 42 17N 1 42E
90 Cadillac, Canada 49 45N 108 0W
98 Cadillac, U.S.A. 44 16N 85 25W
65 Cadiz, Philippines 11 30N 123 15E
31 Cádiz, Sp. 36 30N 6 20W
31 Cádiz □ 36 35N 5 50W
31 Cádiz, G. of 36 35N 6 20W
92 Cadomin 52 59N 117 28W
83 Cadoux 30 47S 117 8E
18 Caen 49 10N 0 22W
12 Caernarfon 53 8N 4 17W
12 Caernarfon B. 53 4N 4 40W
13 Caerphilly 51 34N 3 13W
54 Caesarea=Qesari 32 30N 34 53E
111 Caetité 13 50S 42 50W
65 Cagayan de Oro 8 30N 124 40E
37 Cagli 43 32N 12 38E
38 Cágliari 39 15N 9 6E
38 Cágliari, G. di 39 8N 9 10E
21 Cagnes-sur-Mer 43 40N 7 9E
105 Caguas 18 14N 66 4W
15 Caher 52 23N 7 56W
15 Cahirciveen 51 57N 10 13W
15 Cahore Pt. 52 34N 6 11W
20 Cahors 44 27N 1 27E
105 Caibarién 22 30N 79 30W
110 Caicara 7 50N 66 10W
111 Caicó 6 20S 37 0W
105 Caicos Is. 21 40N 71 40W
5 Caird Coast 75 0S 25 0W
14 Cairn Gorm, Mt. 57 7N 3 40W
14 Cairngorm Mts. 57 6N 3 42W
80 Cairns 16 55S 145 51E
73 Cairo, Egypt= El Qâhira 30 1N 31 14E
99 Cairo, Ga. 30 52N 84 12W
101 Cairo, Mo. 37 0N 89 10W
36 Cairo Montenotte 44 23N 8 16E
110 Cajamarca 7 5S 78 28W
111 Cajazeiras 7 0S 38 30W
72 Calabar 4 57N 8 20E
110 Calaboza 9 0N 67 20W
39 Calabria □ 39 4N 16 30E
31 Calaburras, Pta. de 36 31N 4 38W
112 Calafate 50 25S 72 25W
32 Calahorra 42 18N 1 59W
19 Calais 50 57N 1 56E
108 Calalaste, Cord. de 25 0S 67 0W
108 Calama 22 30S 68 55W
110 Calamar 10 15N 74 55W
65 Calamian Group, Is. 11 50N 119 55E
32 Calamocha 40 50N 1 17W
31 Calañas 37 40N 6 53W
32 Calanda 40 56N 0 15W
41 Călăraşi 44 14N 27 23E
33 Calasparra 38 14N 1 41W
38 Calatafimi 37 56N 12 50E
32 Calatayud 41 20N 1 40W
65 Calauag 13 55N 122 15E
31 Caldas da Rainha 39 24N 9 8W
30 Caldas de Reyes 42 36N 8 39W
12 Calder R. 53 44N 1 21W
102 Caldwell 43 45N 116 42W
75 Caledon 34 14S 19 26E
75 Caledon, R. 30 31S 26 5E
12 Calf of Man, I. 54 4N 4 48W
92 Calgary 51 0N 114 10W
110 Cali 3 25N 76 35W
62 Calicut 11 15N 75 43E
103 Caliente 37 43N 114 34W
96 California 40 4N 79 55W
103 California □ 37 25N 120 0W
104 California, G. de 27 0N 111 0W
104 California, Baja, Reg. 30 0N 115 0W
41 Călineşti 45 21N 24 18E
103 Calipatria 33 8N 115 30W
18 Callac 48 25N 3 27W
15 Callan 52 33N 7 25W
110 Callao 12 0S 77 0W
80 Callide 24 23S 150 33E
80 Calliope 24 0S 151 16E
33 Callosa de Ensarriá 38 40N 0 8W
33 Callosa de Segura 38 1N 0 53W
81 Caloundra 26 45S 153 10E
33 Calpe 38 39N 0 3E
39 Calatagirone 37 13N 14 30E
39 Caltanissetta 37 30N 14 3E
21 Caluire-et-Cuire 45 49N 4 51E
18 Calvados □ 49 5N 0 15W
21 Calvi 42 34N 8 45E
75 Calvinia 31 28S 19 45E
13 Cam, R. 52 21N 0 15E
63 Cam Lam 5 0N 109 10E
63 Cam Rhan 11 54N 109 12E
105 Camagüey 21 20N 78 0W
36 Camaiore 43 57N 10 18E
21 Camarat, C. 43 12N 6 41E
21 Camargue, Reg. 43 20N 4 38E
112 Camarones 44 50S 66 0W
30 Cambados 42 31N 8 49W
109 Cambará 23 2S 53 5W
60 Cambay 22 23N 72 33E
60 Cambay, G. of 20 45N 72 30E
63 Cambodia ■ 12 15N 105 0E
13 Camborne 50 13N 5 18W
19 Cambrai 50 11N 3 14E
13 Cambrian Mts. 52 10N 3 52W
96 Cambridge, Canada 43 20N 80 20W
85 Cambridge, N.Z. 37 54S 175 29E
13 Cambridge, U.K. 52 13N 0 8E
97 Cambridge, Mass. 42 20N 71 8W
97 Cambridge, N.Y. 43 2N 73 22W
96 Cambridge, Ohio 40 1N 81 22W
13 Cambridge □ 52 21N 0 5E
88 Cambridge B. 69 10N 105 0W
82 Cambridge, G. 14 45S 128 0E
32 Cambrils 41 8N 1 3E
109 Cambuci 21 34S 41 55W
84 Camden, Australia 34 5S 150 38E
99 Camden, Ala. 31 59N 87 15W
101 Camden, Ark. 33 30N 92 50W
97 Camden, N.J. 39 57N 75 1W
99 Camden, S.C. 34 17N 80 34W
37 Camerino 43 10N 13 4E
101 Cameron 30 53N 97 0W
63 Cameron Highlands, Mts. 4 27N 101 22E
73 Cameroon ■ 3 30N 12 30E
72 Cameroun, Mt. 4 45N 8 55E
111 Cametá 2 0S 49 30W
81 Camira Creek 29 15S 153 10E
111 Camocim 2 55S 40 50W
80 Camooweal 19 56S 138 7E
111 Camopi 3 45N 52 50W
39 Campagna 40 40N 15 5E
31 Campahario 38 52N 5 36W
108 Campana 34 10S 58 55W
39 Campania □ 40 50N 14 45E
112 Campana, I. 48 20S 75 10W
96 Campbell 41 5N 80 36W
76 Campbell I. 52 30S 169 0E
92 Campbell River 50 1N 125 15W
80 Campbell Town 41 52S 147 30E
84 Campbelltown, Australia 34 5S 150 48E
91 Campbellton, N.B. 47 57N 66 43W
92 Campbellton, Alta. 53 32N 113 15W
14 Campbeltown 55 25N 5 36W
104 Campeche 19 50N 90 32W
104 Campeche □ 19 50N 90 32W
104 Campeche, B. de 19 30N 93 0W
84 Camperdown 38 4S 143 12E
38 Campidano 39 30N 8 40E
32 Campillo de Altobuey 39 36N 1 49W
111 Campino Grande 7 20S 35 47W
109 Campinas 22 50S 47 0W
37 Campli 42 44N 13 40E
109 Campo Belo 21 0S 45 30W
33 Campo de Criptana 39 25N 3 7W
31 Campo de Gibraltar 36 15N 5 25W
111 Campo Formoso 10 30S 40 20W
111 Campo Grande 20 25S 54 40W
111 Campo Maior, Brazil 4 50S 42 12W
31 Campo Maior, Port. 38 59N 7 7W
109 Campo Mourão 24 3S 52 22W
110 Campalegre 2 48N 75 20W
39 Campobasso 41 34N 14 40E
38 Campobello di Licata 37 16N 13 55E
38 Campobello di Mazara 37 38N 12 45E
109 Campos 21 50S 41 20W
111 Campos Belos 13 10S 46 45W
33 Campos del Puerto 39 26N 3 1E
92 Camrose 53 0N 112 50W
63 Can Tho 10 2N 105 46E
88 Canada ■ 60 0N 100 0W
108 Cañada de Gómez 32 55S 61 30W
101 Canadian, R. 35 27N 95 3W
104 Canal Zone 9 10N 79 48W
33 Canáls, Sp. 38 58N 0 35W
108 Canáls, Arg. 33 35S 62 40W
96 Canandaigua 42 55N 77 18W
104 Cananea 31 0N 110 20W
72 Canarias, Is. 29 30N 17 0W
105 Canarreos, Arch. de los 21 35N 81 40W
72 Canary Is.= Canarias, Is. 29 30N 17 0W
99 Canaveral, C. 28 28N 80 31W
111 Canavieiras 15 45S 39 0W
84 Canberra 35 15S 149 8E
18 Cancale 48 40N 1 50W
19 Canche, R. 50 31N 1 39E
30 Candas 43 35N 5 45W
109 Candelaria 27 29S 55 44W
30 Candelaria, Pta. de la 43 45N 8 0W
30 Candeleda 40 10N 5 14W
109 Cândido de Abreu 24 35S 51 20W
88 Candle 65 55N 161 56W
108 Canelones 34 32S 56 10W
108 Cañete 37 50S 73 10W
20 Canet Plage 42 42N 3 3E
32 Canfranc 42 42N 0 31W
75 Cangamba 13 40S 19 54W
30 Cangas de Narcea 43 10N 6 32W
111 Canguaretama 6 20S 35 5W
109 Canguçu 31 22S 52 43W
38 Canicatti 37 21N 13 50E
64 Canipaan 8 33N 117 15E
30 Cañizal 41 20N 5 22W
33 Canjáyar 37 1N 2 44W
92 Canmore 51 7N 115 18W
84 Cann River 37 35S 149 6E
14 Canna, I. 57 3N 6 33W
56 Cannakale 40 5N 27 20E
56 Cannakale Boğazi= Dardenelles, Str. 40 10N 27 20E
62 Cannanore 11 53N 75 27E
21 Cannes 43 32N 7 0E
12 Cannock 52 42N 2 2W
100 Canon City 39 30N 105 20W
96 Canonsburg 40 15N 80 11W
93 Canora 51 40N 102 30W
39 Canosa di Púglia 41 13N 16 4E
91 Canso 45 20N 61 0W
32 Cantabria, Sa. 42 40N 2 30W
29 Cantábrica Cord. 43 0N 5 10W
20 Cantal □ 45 4N 2 45E
30 Cantanhede 40 20N 8 36W
85 Canterbury □ 43 45S 117 19E
80 Canterbury, Australia 33 55S 151 7E
13 Canterbury, U.K. 51 17N 1 5E
85 Canterbury Bight 44 16S 171 55E
85 Canterbury Plain 43 55S 171 22E
69 Canton, China= Kwangchow 23 10N 133 10E
100 Canton, Mo. 40 10N 91 33W
97 Canton, N.Y. 44 32N 75 3W
96 Canton, Ohio 40 47N 81 22W
76 Canton I. 36 12N 98 40W
36 Cantù 45 44N 9 8E
103 Canutillo 31 55N 106 36W
102 Canyon 44 43N 110 36W
103 Canyonlands Nat. Park 38 25N 109 30W
37 Cáorle 45 36N 12 51E
91 Cap Breton, I. 46 0N 61 0W
91 Cap Chat 49 6N 66 40W
105 Cap Haïtien 19 40N 72 20W
6 Cap Verde Is. 16 0N 24 0W
20 Capbreton 43 39N 1 26W
80 Cape Barren, I. 40 25S 184 15E
72 Cape Coast 5 5N 1 15W
89 Cape Dorset 64 30N 77 0W
89 Cape Dyer 66 30N 61 0W
101 Cape Girardeau 37 20N 89 30W
75 Cape Province □ 32 0S 23 0E
75 Cape Town 33 55S 18 22E
80 Cape York Pen. 13 30S 142 30E
111 Capela 10 15S 37 0W
80 Capella 23 2S 148 1E
20 Capendu 43 11N 2 31E
40 Čapljina 43 35N 17 43E
36 Capraia, I. 43 2N 9 50E
90 Capreol 46 40N 80 50W
39 Capri, I. 40 34N 14 15E
75 Caprivi Strip, Reg. 18 0S 23 0E
39 Capua 41 7N 14 5E
110 Caquetá, R. 3 8S 64 46W
41 Caracal 44 8N 24 22E
110 Caracas 10 30N 66 50W
111 Caracol 9 15S 64 20W
84 Caragabal 33 54S 147 50E
109 Carangola 20 50S 42 5W
83 Carani 30 57S 116 28E
40 Caransebeş 45 28N 22 18E
18 Carantec 48 40N 3 55W
105 Caratasca, L. 15 30N 83 40W
111 Caratinga 19 50S 42 10W
111 Caraúbas 5 50S 37 25W
33 Caravaca 38 8N 1 52W
36 Caravaggio 45 30N 9 39E
111 Caravelas 17 50S 39 20W
109 Caràzinho 28 0S 53 0W
30 Carballino 42 26N 8 5W
30 Carballo 43 13N 8 41W
93 Carberry 49 50N 99 25W
30 Carbia 42 48N 8 14W
38 Carbonara, C. 39 8N 9 30E
102 Carbondale, Colo. 39 30N 107 10W
101 Carbondale, Ill. 37 45N 89 10W
97 Carbondale, Pa. 41 37N 75 30W
91 Carbonear 47 42N 53 13W
33 Carboneras 37 0N 1 53W
32 Carboneras de Guadazaón 39 54N 1 50E
38 Carbonia 39 10N 8 30E
33 Carcagente 39 8N 0 28W
20 Carcans, Étang de, L. 45 8N 1 8E
20 Carcassonne 43 13N 2 20E
92 Carcross 60 20N 134 40W
82 Cardabia 23 2S 113 55E
62 Cardamon Hills 9 30N 77 15E
105 Cárdenas, Cuba 23 0N 81 30W
104 Cárdenas, Mexico 22 0N 99 41W
32 Cardenete 39 42N 1 41W
13 Cardiff 51 28N 3 11W
13 Cardigan 52 6N 4 41W
13 Cardigan Bay 52 30N 4 30W
108 Cardona 33 53S 57 18W
32 Cardoner, R. 41 41N 1 51E
109 Cardoso, I. do 25 5S 48 0W
93 Cardross 49 50N 105 40W
92 Cardston 49 15N 113 20W
80 Cardwell 18 14S 146 2E
27 Carei 47 40N 22 29E
18 Carentan 49 19N 1 15W
83 Carey, L. 29 0S 122 15E
20 Carnon 43 32N 3 59E
3 Cargados Garajos, Is. 17 0S 59 0E
21 Cargèse 42 7N 8 35E
108 Carhué 37 10S 62 50W
105 Caribbean Sea 15 0N 75 0W
92 Cariboo Mts. 53 0N 121 0W
19 Carignan 49 38N 5 10E
32 Cariñena 41 20N 1 13W
111 Carinhanha 14 15S 44 0W
38 Carinola 41 11N 13 58E
110 Caripito 10 2N 63 0W
39 Carlentini 37 15N 15 2E
90 Carleton Place 45 8N 76 11W
102 Carlin 40 50N 116 5W
15 Carlingford L. 54 0N 6 5W
100 Carlinville 39 20N 89 55W
12 Carlisle, U.K. 54 54N 2 55W
96 Carlisle, U.S.A. 40 12N 77 10W
20 Carlitte, Pic. 42 35N 1 54E
108 Carlos Casares 35 53S 61 20W
15 Carlow 52 50N 6 58W
15 Carlow □ 52 43N 6 50W
101 Carlsbad 32 20N 104 7W
88 Carmacks 62 0N 136 0W
36 Carmagnola 44 50N 7 42E
93 Carman 49 30N 98 0W
13 Carmarthen 51 52N 4 20W
20 Carmaux 44 3N 2 10E
54 Carmel, Mt. 32 45N 35 3E
108 Carmelo 34 0S 58 10W
110 Carmen, Col. 9 43N 75 6W
109 Carmen, Paraguay 27 13S 56 12W

112 Carmen de Patagones 40 50s 63 0w
80 Carmila 21 53s 149 5e
31 Carmona 37 28n 5 42w
83 Carnarvon, Australia 24 51s 113 42e
75 Carnarvon, S. Africa 30 56s 22 8e
62 Carnatic, Reg. 12 0n 79 0e
31 Carnaxide 38 43n 9 14w
15 Carndonagh 55 15n 7 16w
96 Carnegie 40 24n 80 4w
83 Carnegie, L. 26 5s 122 30e
15 Carnsore Pt. 52 10n 6 20w
111 Carolina 7 10s 47 30w
77 Caroline I. 9 15s 150 3w
65 Caroline Is. 8 0n 150 0e
93 Caron 50 30n 105 50w
39 Carovigno 40 42n 17 40w
27 Carpathians, Mts. 46 20n 26 0e
41 Carpatii Meridionali, Mts. 45 30n 25 0e
80 Carpentaria, G. of 14 0s 139 0e
80 Carpentaria Downs 18 44s 144 20e
21 Carpentras 44 3n 5 2e
36 Carpi 44 47n 10 52e
30 Carpio 41 13n 5 7w
36 Carrara 44 5n 10 7e
32 Carrascosa del Campo 40 2n 2 45w
15 Carrick-on-Shannon 53 57n 8 7w
15 Carrick-on-Suir 52 22n 7 30w
15 Carrickfergus 54 43n 5 50w
15 Carrickfergus □ 54 43n 5 50w
15 Carrickmacross 54 0n 6 43w
81 Carrieton 32 27s 138 27e
30 Carrión, R. 41 53n 4 32w
103 Carrizozo 33 40n 105 57w
100 Carroll 42 2n 94 55w
99 Carrollton 33 36n 85 5w
93 Carrot River 53 50n 101 17w
102 Carson City 39 12n 119 52w
102 Carson Sink 39 50n 118 40w
14 Carstairs 55 42n 3 41w
110 Cartagena, Col. 10 25n 75 33w
33 Cartagena, Sp. 37 38n 0 59w
110 Cartago, Col. 4 45n 75 55w
105 Cartago, Costa Rica 9 50n 84 0w
31 Cartaxo 39 10n 8 47w
31 Cartaya 37 16n 7 9w
18 Carteret 49 23n 1 47w
99 Cartersville 34 11n 84 48w
85 Carterton 41 2s 175 31e
101 Carthage, Mo. 37 10n 94 20w
97 Carthage, N.Y. 43 59n 75 37w
91 Cartwright 53 41n 56 58w
111 Caruaru 8 15s 35 55w
110 Carúpano 10 45n 63 15w
101 Caruthersville 36 10n 89 40w
19 Carvin 50 30n 2 57e
31 Carvoeira, C. 39 21n 9 24w
109 Casa Branca, Chile 33 20s 71 25w
31 Casa Branca, Port. 38 29n 8 12w
103 Casa Grande 32 53n 111 51w
111 Casa Nova 9 10s 41 5w
72 Casablanca 33 43n 7 24w
36 Casale Monferrato 45 8n 8 28e
36 Casalmaggiore 44 59n 10 25e
36 Casalpusterlengo 45 10n 9 40e
39 Casamássima 40 58n 16 55e
39 Casarano 40 0n 18 10e
104 Casas Grandes 30 22n 108 0w
30 Casatejada 39 54n 5 40w
102 Cascade Ra. 44 0n 122 10w
31 Cascais 38 41n 9 25w
36 Cáscina 43 40n 10 32e
39 Caserta 41 5n 14 20e
15 Cashel 52 31n 7 53w
108 Casilda 33 10s 61 10w
81 Casino 28 52s 153 3e
110 Casiquiare, R. 2 1n 67 7w
26 Cáslav 49 54n 15 22e
32 Caspe 41 14n 0 1w
112 Casper 42 52n 106 27w
9 Caspian Sea 43 0n 50 0e
32 Cassá de la Selva 41 53n 2 52e
39 Cassano Iónio 39 47n 16 20e
92 Cassiar Mts. 39 30n 130 30w
75 Cassinga 15 5s 16 23e
38 Cassino 41 30n 13 50e
21 Cassis 43 14n 5 32e
36 Castéggio 45 1n 9 8e
36 Castel San Giovanni 43 4n 9 25e
37 Castel San Pietro 44 23n 11 30e
39 Castelbuono 37 56n 14 4e
36 Castelfranco Emilia 44 37n 11 2e
37 Castelfranco Véneto 45 40n 11 56e
38 Castellammare, G. di 35 5n 12 55e
38 Castellammare del Golfo 38 2n 12 53e
39 Castellammare di Stábia 40 47n 14 29e
39 Castellana Grotte 40 53n 17 10e
21 Castellane 43 50n 6 31e
39 Castellaneta 40 40n 16 57e
32 Castello de Ampurias 42 15n 3 4e
32 Castellón □ 40 15n 0 5w
32 Castellón de la Plana 39 58n 0 3w
32 Castellote 40 48n 0 15w
109 Castelo 20 36s 41 12w
30 Castelo Branco 39 50n 7 31w
30 Castelo Branco □ 39 52n 7 54w
20 Castelnaudary 43 20n 1 58e
20 Castelsarrasin 44 2n 1 3e
32 Castelltersol 41 45n 2 8e
38 Casteltérmini 37 32n 13 38e
38 Castelvetrano 37 40n 12 46e
84 Casterton 37 30s 141 30e
20 Castets 43 52n 1 6w
37 Castiglione del Lago 43 7n 12 3e
36 Castiglione della Pescáia 42 46n 10 53e
37 Castiglione Fiorentina 43 20n 11 55e
31 Castilblanco 39 17n 5 5w
31 Castilla la Nueva, Reg. 39 45n 3 20w
31 Castilla, Playa de 37 0n 6 33w
30 Castilla la Vieja, Reg. 41 55n 4 0w
14 Castle Douglas 54 57n 3 57w
105 Castle Harbour 32 17n 64 44w
102 Castle Rock 46 20n 122 58w
15 Castlebar 53 52n 9 17w
15 Castleblayney 54 7n 6 44w
12 Castleford 53 43n 1 21w
92 Castlegar 49 20n 117 40w
84 Castlemaine 37 2s 144 12e
15 Castlereagh 53 47n 8 30w
15 Castlereagh □ 53 47n 8 30w
12 Castletown 54 4n 4 40w
15 Castletown Bearhaven 51 40n 9 54w
80 Castlevale 24 30s 146 48e
92 Castor 52 15n 111 50w
20 Castres 43 37n 2 13e
105 Castries 14 0n 60 50w
109 Castro, Brazil 24 45s 50 0w
112 Castro, Chile 42 30s 73 50w
111 Castro Alves 12 46s 39 33w
31 Castro del Rio 37 41n 4 29w
30 Castro Urdiales 43 23n 3 19w
31 Castro Verde 37 41n 8 4w
30 Castropol 43 32n 7 0w
39 Castrovillari 39 49n 16 11e
31 Castuera 38 43n 5 37w
105 Cat I. 24 30n 75 30w
109 Cataguases 21 23s 42 39w
111 Catalão 18 5s 47 52w
32 Cataluña, Reg. 41 40n 1 15e
108 Catamarca 28 30s 65 50w
108 Catamarca □ 28 30s 65 50w
109 Catanduva 21 5s 48 58w
39 Catánia 37 31n 15 4e
39 Catanzaro 38 54n 16 38e
65 Catarman 12 28n 124 1e
20 Catine, Reg. 46 30n 0 15w
79 Cato, I. 23 15s 155 32e
104 Catoche, C. 21 40n 87 0w
33 Catral 38 10n 0 47w
110 Catrimani 0 27n 61 41w
97 Catskill 42 14n 73 52w
97 Catskill Mts. 42 15n 74 15w
96 Cattaraugus 42 22n 78 52w
39 Cattólica 43 58n 12 43e
38 Cattólica Eraclea 37 27n 13 24e
49 Caucasus Mts.= Bolshoi Kavkaz 42 50n 44 0e
111 Caucia 3 40s 38 55w
18 Caudebec 49 30n 0 42e
33 Caudete 38 42n 1 2w
19 Caudry 50 7n 3 22e
18 Caulnes 48 18n 2 10w
39 Caulónia 38 23n 16 25e
108 Cauquenes 36 0s 72 30w
91 Causapscal 48 19n 67 12w
62 Cauvery, R. 11 10n 79 51e
39 Cava dei Tirreni 40 42n 14 42e
30 Cávado, R. 41 32n 8 48w
21 Cavaillon 43 50n 5 2e
21 Cavalaire 43 10n 6 33e
15 Cavan □ 53 58n 7 10w
15 Cavan 54 0n 7 22w
84 Cavendish 37 31s 142 2e
111 Caviana, I. 0 15n 50 0w
65 Cavite 14 20n 120 55e
40 Cavtat 42 35n 18 13e
111 Caxias 5 0s 43 27w
109 Caxias do Sul 29 10s 51 10w
74 Caxito 8 30s 13 30e
110 Cayambe 0 3n 78 22w
111 Cayenne 5 0n 52 18w
19 Cayeux-sur-Mer 50 10n 1 30e
105 Cayman Is. 19 40n 79 50w
104 Cayo 17 10n 89 0w
97 Cayuga L. 42 45n 76 45w
33 Cazorla, Sa. de 38 5n 2 55w
41 Căzăneşti 44 36n 27 3e
20 Cazaux, Étang de 44 30n 1 10e
20 Cazères 43 13n 1 5e
37 Čazma 45 45n 16 39e
75 Cazombo 12 0s 22 48e
33 Cazorla 37 55n 3 2w
30 Cea, R. 42 0n 5 36w
15 Ceanannas Mor 53 42n 6 53w
111 Ceara □ 5 0s 40 0w
111 Ceará=Fortaleza 3 35s 38 35w
30 Cebollera, Sa. de 42 0n 2 30w
30 Cebreros 40 27n 4 28w
65 Cebu 10 30n 124 0e
65 Cebu, I. 10 23n 123 58e
38 Ceccano 41 34n 13 18e
36 Cécina 43 19n 10 33e
30 Ceclavin 39 50n 6 45w
103 Cedar City 37 41n 113 3w
101 Cedar Creek Res. 32 15n 96 0w
100 Cedar Falls 42 39n 92 29w
93 Cedar L. 53 30n 100 30w
100 Cedar Rapids 42 0n 91 38w
99 Cedartown 34 1n 85 15w
92 Cedarvale 55 1n 128 22w
102 Cedarville 41 37n 120 13w
30 Cedeira 43 39n 8 2w
111 Cedro 6 34s 39 3w
104 Cedros, I. de 28 10n 115 20w
81 Ceduna 32 7s 133 46e
39 Cefalù 38 3n 14 1e
30 Cega, R. 41 33n 4 46w
27 Cegléd 47 11n 19 47e
39 Céglie Messápico 40 39n 17 31e
104 Celaya 20 31n 100 37w
15 Celbridge 53 20n 6 33w
65 Celebes, I.= Sulawesi, I. 2 0s 120 0e
65 Celebes Sea 3 0n 123 0e
37 Celje 46 16n 15 18e
24 Celle 52 37n 10 4e
30 Celorico da Beira 40 38n 7 24w
20 Cenon 44 50n 0 33w
109 Centenario do Sul 22 48s 51 37w
96 Centerville 40 3n 79 59w
100 Centerville 31 15n 95 56w
37 Cento 44 43n 11 16e
103 Central 32 46n 108 9w
14 Central □ 56 12n 4 25w
20 Central, Massif 45 0n 3 10e
74 Central African Republic ■ 7 0n 20 0e
97 Central Islip 40 49n 73 13w
58 Central Makan Ra. 26 30n 64 15e
100 Centralia, Ill. 38 32n 89 5w
102 Centralia, Wash. 46 46n 122 59w
39 Centúripe 37 37n 14 41e
40 Čepin 45 32n 18 34e
38 Ceprano 41 33n 13 30e
41 Ceptura 45 1n 26 21e
65 Ceram, I.= Seram, I. 3 10s 129 0e
20 Cerbère 42 26n 3 10e
41 Cerbu 44 46n 24 46e
31 Cercal 37 48n 08 40w
32 Cerdaña 42 22n 1 35e
20 Cère, R. 44 55n 1 53e
108 Ceres, Arg. 29 55s 61 55w
75 Ceres, S. Africa 33 21s 19 18e
20 Céret 42 30n 2 42e
39 Cerignola 41 17n 15 53e
56 Çerkeş 40 40n 32 58e
37 Cerknico 45 48n 14 21e
41 Cernavodă 44 22n 28 3e
19 Cernay 47 48n 7 10e
104 Cerralvo, I. 24 20n 109 45e
104 Cerritos 22 20n 100 20w
32 Cervera 41 40n 1 16e
30 Cervera de Pisuerga 42 51n 4 30w
37 Cérvia 44 15n 12 20e
39 Cervinara 41 2n 14 36e
21 Cervione 42 20n 9 29e
30 Cervo 43 40n 7 24w
37 Cesena 44 9n 12 14e
37 Cesenático 44 12n 12 22e
26 Česká Lípa 50 43n 14 35e
26 Česká Socialistická □ 49 30n 15 0e
27 Česká Třebová 49 54n 16 27e
26 Česke Budějovice 48 55n 14 25e
26 České Velenice 48 45n 15 1e
26 Český Brod 50 4n 14 52e
26 Český Krumlov 48 43n 14 21e
27 Český Těšín 49 45n 18 39e
84 Cessnock 33 0s 151 15e
37 Cetina, R. 43 26n 16 42e
40 Cetinje 42 23n 18 59e
72 Ceuta 35 52n 5 26w
20 Cevennes, Mts. 44 10n 3 50e
56 Ceyhan 37 4n 35 47e
62 Ceylon= Sri Lanka ■ 7 30n 80 50e
21 Chablais, Reg. 46 20n 6 45e
19 Chablis 47 47n 3 48e
108 Chacabuco 34 40s 60 27w
63 Chachoengsao 13 45n 101 12e
108 Chaco □ 25 0s 61 0w
73 Chad ■ 12 30n 17 15e
73 Chad, L. 13 30n 14 30w
100 Chadron 42 50n 103 0w
57 Chagai Hills 29 30n 63 0e
21 Chagny 46 57n 4 45e
3 Chagos Arch. 6 0s 72 0e
57 Chāh Bahār 25 20n 60 40e
61 Chaibasa 22 33n 85 49e
60 Chaj Doab, Reg. 32 0n 73 0e
108 Chajari 30 42n 58 0w
57 Chakhansur 31 10n 62 0e
57 Chakhansur □ 30 25n 62 0e
60 Chaklashi 22 40n 72 52e
61 Chakradharpur 22 45n 85 40e
60 Chakwal 32 50n 72 45e
20 Chalais 45 16n 0 3e
62 Chalakudi 10 18n 76 20e
19 Chalindrey 47 48n 5 26e
69 Chaling 26 55n 113 30e
60 Chalisgaon 20 30n 75 10e
20 Challans 46 50n 2 0w
110 Challapata 19 0s 66 50w
19 Challerange 49 18n 4 46e
21 Chalon-sur-Saône 46 48n 4 50e
19 Châlons-sur-Marne 48 58n 4 20e
30 Chamartín de la Rosa 40 28n 3 40w
60 Chamba 32 35n 76 10e
60 Chambal, R. 26 30n 79 15e
98 Chambersburg 39 53n 77 41w
21 Chambéry 45 34n 5 55e
75 Chambeshi 10 58s 31 5e
97 Chambly 45 27n 73 17w
91 Chambord 48 25n 72 6w
67 Chamdo 31 21n 97 2e
21 Chamonix 45 55n 6 51e
61 Champa 22 2n 82 43e
19 Champagne, Reg. 49 0n 4 40e
19 Champagne, Plaine de 49 0n 4 0e
21 Champagnole 46 45n 5 55e
100 Champaign 40 8n 88 14w
19 Champaubert 48 50n 3 45e
97 Champlain 46 27n 72 24w
97 Champlain, L. 44 30n 73 20w
104 Champotón 19 20n 90 50w
108 Chañaral 26 15s 70 50w
60 Chanasma 23 44n 72 5e
61 Chanda 19 57n 79 25e
88 Chandalar 67 30n 148 30w
60 Chandausi 28 27n 78 49e
101 Chandeleur Sd. 29 58n 88 40w
61 Chandernagore 22 52n 88 24e
91 Chandler, Canada 48 18n 64 46w
103 Chandler, U.S.A. 33 20n 111 56w
61 Chandpur, India 23 8n 90 42e
60 Chandpur, Pak. 29 8n 78 19e
62 Changanacheri 9 25n 76 31e
68 Changchih 36 7n 113 0e
69 Changchow, Fukien 24 32n 117 44e
69 Changchow, Kiangsu 31 45n 120 0e
68 Changchow, Shantung 36 55n 118 3e
68 Changchun 43 58n 125 9e
69 Changhua 24 2n 120 30e
68 Changkiakow 40 52n 114 45e
69 Changkiang 21 7n 110 21e
68 Changli 39 40n 119 19e
68 Changpai 41 26n 128 0e
68 Changpai Shan, Mts. 42 0n 128 0e
69 Changping, Fukien 25 30n 117 33e
68 Changping, Peiping 40 15n 116 15e
69 Changpu 24 2n 117 31e
69 Changsha 28 5n 113 1e
69 Changshu 31 33n 120 45e
69 Changtai 24 34n 117 50e
69 Changtieh 29 12n 111 43e
69 Changting 25 46n 116 30e
68 Changwu 42 21n 122 45e
67 Changyeh 39 0n 100 59e
62 Channaptna 12 40n 77 15e
13 Channel Is. 49 30n 2 40w
63 Chanthaburi 12 38n 102 12e
19 Chantilly 49 12n 2 38e
20 Chantonnay 46 40n 1 3w
101 Chanute 37 45n 95 25w
67 Chanyi 25 56n 104 1e

63 Chao Phraya, R. 13 32N 100 36 E
69 Chaoan 23 45N 117 11 E
69 Chaochow 23 45N 116 32 E
69 Chaohwa 32 16N 105 41 E
67 Chaotung 27 30N 103 40 E
68 Chaoyang 41 46N 120 16 E
104 Chapata, L. 20 10N 103 20W
50 Chapayevo 50 25N 51 10 E
48 Chapayevsk 53 0N 49 40 E
109 Chapecó 27 14S 52 41W
99 Chapel Hill 35 53N 79 3W
90 Chapleau 47 45N 83 30W
61 Chapra 25 48N 84 50 E
110 Charagua 19 45S 63 10W
110 Charambira, Pta. 4 20N 77 30W
110 Charaña 17 30S 69 35W
108 Charata 27 13S 61 14W
67 Charchan 38 4N 85 16 E
67 Charchan, R. 39 0N 86 0 E
13 Chard, U.K. 50 52N 2 59W
93 Chard, U.S.A. 55 55N 111 10W
50 Chardara 41 16N 67 59 E
50 Chardzhou 39 0N 63 20 E
20 Charente □ 45 50N 0 36W
20 Charente, R. 45 57N 1 5W
20 Charente-Maritime □ 45 50N 0 35W
73 Chari, R. 12 58N 14 31 E
57 Charikar 35 0N 69 10 E
67 Charkhlikh 39 16N 88 17 E
16 Charleroi 50 24N 4 27 E
98 Charles, C. 37 10N 75 52W
100 Charles City 43 2N 92 41W
101 Charleston, Mass. 34 2N 90 3W
99 Charleston, S.C. 32 47N 79 56W
98 Charleston, W. Va. 38 24N 81 36W
105 Charlestown, Nevis 17 8N 62 37W
97 Charlestown, U.S.A. 38 29N 85 40W
81 Charleville, Australia 26 24S 146 15 E
15 Charleville, Eire= Rath Luire 52 21N 8 40W
19 Charleville-Mézières 49 44N 4 40 E
99 Charlotte 35 16N 80 46W
105 Charlotte Amalie 18 22N 64 56W
98 Charlottesville 38 1N 78 30W
91 Charlottetown 46 19N 63 3W
84 Charlton 36 16S 143 24 E
100 Charlton 40 59N 93 20W
90 Charlton I. 52 0N 79 20W
91 Charny 46 43N 71 15W
21 Charolles 46 27N 4 16 E
20 Charroux 46 9N 0 25 E
80 Charters Towers 20 5S 146 13 E
18 Chartres 48 29N 1 30 E
108 Chascomús 35 30S 58 0W
41 Chatal Balkan= Udvoy, Mts. 42 50N 26 50 E
88 Chatanika 65 7N 147 31W
20 Château Chinon 47 4N 3 56 E
18 Château-du-Loir 47 40N 0 25 E
18 Château Gontier 47 50N 0 42W
19 Château Porcien 49 31N 4 13 E
18 Château Renault 47 36N 0 56 E
19 Château Thierry 49 3N 3 20 E
18 Château-la-Vallière 47 30N 0 20 E
18 Châteaubourg 48 7N 1 25W
18 Châteaubriant 47 43N 1 23W
18 Châteaudun 48 3N 1 20 E
18 Châteaulin 48 11N 4 8W
20 Châteaumeillant 46 35N 2 12 E
20 Châteauneuf-sur-Charente 45 36N 0 3W
19 Châteauneuf-sur-Loire 47 52N 2 13 E
20 Châteauroux 46 50N 1 40 E
20 Châtelaillon Plage 46 5N 1 5W
20 Châtelguyon 45 55N 3 4 E
20 Châtellerault 46 50N 0 30 E
13 Chatham, U.K. 51 22N 0 32 E
91 Chatham, N.B. 47 2N 65 28W
96 Chatham, Ont. 42 23N 82 15W
98 Chatham, Alas. 57 30N 135 0W
97 Chatham, N.Y. 42 21N 73 32W
76 Chatham Is. 44 0S 176 40W
92 Chatham Str. 57 0N 134 40W
20 Châtillon-en-Bazois 47 3N 3 39 E
21 Châtillon-en-Diois 44 41N 5 29 E
20 Châtillon-sur-Indre 46 48N 1 10 E
19 Châtillon-sur-Seine 47 50N 4 33 E
20 Châtillon-sur-Sèvre 46 56N 0 45W
99 Chattahoochee 30 43N 84 51W
99 Chattanooga 35 2N 85 17W
19 Chaulnes 49 48N 2 47 E
19 Chaumont 48 7N 5 8 E
19 Chauny 49 37N 3 12 E
21 Chaussin 46 59N 5 22 E
20 Chauvigny 46 34N 0 39 E
111 Chaves, Brazil 0 15S 49 55W
30 Chaves, Port. 41 45N 7 32W
26 Cheb 50 9N 12 20 E
48 Cheboksary 56 8N 47 30 E
98 Cheboygan 45 38N 84 29W
68 Chefoo=Yentai 37 30N 121 21 E
51 Chegdomyn 51 7N 132 52 E
102 Chehallis 46 44N 122 59W
69 Cheju 33 28N 126 30 E
69 Cheju Do, I. 33 29N 126 34 E
69 Chekiang □ 29 30N 120 0 E
112 Chelforó 39 0S 66 40W
50 Chelkar 47 40N 59 32 E
50 Chelkar Tengiz Solonchak 48 0N 62 30 E
19 Chelles 48 52N 2 33 E
28 Chełm 51 8N 23 30 E
28 Chełm □ 51 20N 23 20 E
28 Chełmno 53 20N 18 30 E
13 Chelmsford 51 44N 0 29 E
28 Chełmno 53 20N 18 30 E
84 Chelsea 38 5S 145 8 E
13 Cheltenham 51 55N 2 5W
50 Chelyabinsk 55 10N 61 35 E
92 Chemainus 48 54N 123 41W
75 Chemba 17 11S 34 53 E
48 Chemikovsk 54 58N 56 0W
18 Chemillé 47 14N 0 45W
63 Chemor 4 44N 101 6 E
102 Chemult 43 14N 121 54W
60 Chenab, R. 29 23N 71 2 E
69 Chengchow 34 47N 113 46 E
67 Chengkiang 24 58N 102 59 E
68 Chengteh 41 0N 117 55 E
68 Chengting 38 8N 114 37 E
67 Chengtu 30 45N 104 0 E
68 Chengyang 36 20N 120 16 E
69 Chenhsien 25 45N 112 37 E
69 Chenning 25 57N 105 51 E
68 Chentung 46 2N 123 1 E
69 Chenyuan 27 0N 108 20 E
41 Chepelare 41 44N 24 40 E
105 Chepo 9 10N 79 6W
13 Chepstow 51 39N 2 41W
100 Chequamegon B. 46 40N 90 30W
19 Cher □ 47 10N 2 30 E
18 Cherbourg 49 39N 1 40W
72 Cherchell 36 35N 21 63 E
48 Cherdyn 60 20N 56 20 E
51 Cheremkhovo 53 32N 102 40 E
50 Cherepanovo 54 15N 83 30 E
49 Cherkassy 49 30N 32 0 E
41 Cherni, Mt. 42 35N 23 28 E
48 Chernigov 51 28N 31 20 E
49 Chernovtsy 48 0N 26 0 E
51 Chernoye 70 30N 89 10 E
100 Cherokee 42 40N 95 30W
48 Cheropovets 59 5N 37 55 E
112 Cherquenco 38 35S 72 0W
51 Cherskogo Khrebet 65 0N 143 0 E
41 Cherven-Bryag 43 17N 24 7 E
13 Cherwell, R. 51 44N 1 15W
98 Chesapeake B. 38 0N 76 12W
12 Cheshire □ 53 14N 2 30W
33 Cheste 39 30N 0 41W
12 Chester, U.K. 53 12N 2 53W
98 Chester, Pa. 39 54N 75 20W
99 Chester, S.C. 34 44N 81 13W
12 Chesterfield 53 14N 1 26W
88 Chesterfield Inlet 63 30N 91 0W
76 Chesterfield Is. 19 52S 158 15 E
104 Chetumal 18 30N 88 20W
104 Chetumal, B. de 18 40N 88 10W
20 Chevanceaux 45 18N 0 14W
12 Cheviot, The, Mt. 55 28N 2 8W
12 Cheviot Hills 55 20N 2 30W
74 Chew Bahir, L. 4 40N 30 50 E
102 Chewelah 48 25N 117 56W
100 Cheyenne 41 9N 104 49W
100 Cheyenne, R. 44 40N 101 15W
60 Chhindwara 22 2N 78 59 E
63 Chi, R. 15 13N 104 45 E
69 Chiai 23 29N 120 25 E
75 Chianje 15 35S 13 40 E
104 Chiapas □ 17 0N 92 45W
39 Chiaramonte Gulfi 37 1N 14 41 E
36 Chiari 45 31N 9 55 E
36 Chiávari 44 20N 9 20 E
36 Chiavenna 46 18N 9 23 E
66 Chiba 35 30N 140 7 E
66 Chiba □ 35 30N 140 20 E
75 Chibemba 15 48S 14 8 E
90 Chibougamau 49 56N 74 24W
98 Chicago 41 45N 87 40W
98 Chicago Heights 41 29N 87 37W
92 Chichagof I. 58 0N 136 0W
13 Chichester 50 50N 0 47W
104 Chichén Itzá 20 40N 88 34W
66 Chichibu 36 5N 139 10 E
68 Chichirin 50 35N 123 45 E
101 Chickasha 35 0N 98 0W
31 Chiclana de la Frontera 36 26N 6 9W
110 Chiclayo 6 42S 79 50W
102 Chico 39 45N 121 54W
112 Chico, R. 43 50S 66 25W
97 Chicopee 42 6N 72 37W
91 Chicoutimi 48 28N 71 5W
62 Chidambaram 11 20N 79 45 E
89 Chidley, C. 60 30N 64 15W
25 Chiemsee, L. 47 53N 12 27 E
74 Chiengi 8 38S 29 10 E
63 Chiengmai 18 55N 98 55 E
37 Chienti, R. 43 18N 13 45 E
36 Chieri 45 0N 7 50 E
19 Chiers, R. 49 39N 5 0 E
37 Chieti 42 22N 14 10 E
68 Chihfeng 42 10N 118 56 E
69 Chihing 25 2N 113 45 E
69 Chihkiang 27 21N 109 45 E
68 Chihli, G. of= Po Hai, G. 38 30N 119 0 E
69 Chihsien 35 29N 114 1 E
104 Chihuahua 28 40N 106 3W
104 Chihuahua □ 28 40N 106 3W
50 Chiilí 44 10N 66 55 E
62 Chik Ballapur 13 25N 77 45 E
62 Chikmagalur 13 15N 75 45 E
62 Chikodi 16 26N 74 38 E
58 Chilas 35 25N 74 5 E
81 Childers 25 15S 152 17 E
101 Childress 34 30N 100 50W
107 Chile ■ 35 0S 71 15W
110 Chilete 7 10S 78 50W
75 Chililabombwe 12 18S 27 43 E
61 Chilka L. 19 40N 85 25 E
108 Chillán 36 40S 72 10W
100 Chillicothe, Mo. 39 45N 93 30W
98 Chillicothe, Ohio. 39 53N 82 58W
92 Chilliwack 49 10N 122 0W
112 Chiloé, I. de 42 50S 73 45W
104 Chilpancingo 17 30N 99 40W
84 Chiltern 36 10S 146 36 E
13 Chiltern Hills 51 44N 0 42W
69 Chilung 25 3N 121 45 E
75 Chilwa, L. 15 15S 35 40 E
67 Chimai 34 0N 101 39 E
110 Chimborazo, Mt. 1 20S 78 55W
110 Chimbote 9 0S 78 35W
50 Chimkent 42 40N 69 25 E
59 Chin □ 22 0N 93 0 E
67 China ■ 35 0N 100 0 E
105 Chinandega 12 30N 87 0W
110 Chincha Alta 13 20S 76 0W
81 Chinchilla 26 45S 150 38 E
33 Chinchilla de Monte Aragón 38 53N 1 40W
68 Chinchow 41 10N 121 2 E
75 Chinde 18 45S 36 30 E
59 Chindwin, R. 21 26N 95 15 E
69 Ching Ho, R. 34 20N 109 0 E
62 Chingleput 12 42N 79 58 E
75 Chingola 12 31S 27 53 E
75 Chingole 13 4S 34 17 E
68 Chinhae 35 9N 128 58 E
60 Chiniot 31 45N 73 0 E
68 Chinju 35 12N 128 2 E
69 Chinkiang 32 2N 119 29 E
103 Chino Valley 34 54N 112 28W
18 Chinon 47 10N 0 15 E
93 Chinook, Canada 51 28N 110 59W
102 Chinook, U.S.A. 48 35N 109 19W
61 Chinsura 22 53N 88 27 E
62 Chintamani 13 26N 78 3 E
68 Chinwangtao 40 0N 119 31 E
37 Chióggia 45 13N 12 15 E
92 Chip Lake 53 35N 115 35W
75 Chipata 13 38S 32 28 E
31 Chipiona 36 44N 6 26W
62 Chiplun 17 31N 73 34 E
96 Chippawa 43 5N 79 10W
13 Chippenham 51 27N 2 7W
100 Chippewa, R. 44 25N 92 10W
100 Chippewa Falls 44 56N 91 24W
104 Chiquimula 14 51N 89 37W
110 Chiquinquira 5 37N 73 50W
62 Chirala 15 50N 80 20 E
60 Chirawa 28 14N 75 42 E
62 Chirayinkil 8 41N 76 49 E
50 Chirchik 41 58N 69 15 E
88 Chirikof I. 55 50N 155 35W
105 Chiriquí, G. de 8 0N 82 10W
105 Chiriquí, L. de 9 10N 82 0W
105 Chiriqui, Mt. 8 55N 82 35W
75 Chiromo 16 30S 35 7 E
41 Chirpan 42 10N 25 19 E
75 Chisamba 14 55S 28 20 E
60 Christian Mandi 29 50N 72 55 E
51 Chita 52 0N 113 25 E
62 Chitapur 17 10N 76 50 E
75 Chitembo 13 30S 16 50 E
60 Chitorgarh 24 52N 74 43 E
62 Chitradurga 14 15N 76 28 E
105 Chitré 7 59N 80 27W
59 Chittagong 22 19N 91 55 E
61 Chittagong □ 24 5N 91 25 E
62 Chittoor 13 15N 79 5 E
62 Chittur 10 40N 76 45 E
33 Chiva 39 27N 0 41W
36 Chivasso 45 10N 7 52 E
108 Chivilcoy 35 0S 60 0W
26 Chlumec 50 9N 15 29 E
28 Chodziez 52 58N 17 0 E
62 Chodavaram 17 40N 82 50 E
112 Choele Choel 39 11S 65 40W
19 Choisy 48 45N 2 24 E
28 Choinice 53 42N 17 40 E
20 Cholet 47 4N 0 52W
105 Choluteca 13 20N 87 14W
75 Choma 16 48S 26 59 E
60 Chomu 27 15N 75 40 E
26 Chomutov 50 28N 13 23 E
63 Chon Buri 13 21N 101 1 E
68 Chonan 36 56N 127 3 E
110 Chone 0 40S 80 0W
68 Chongjin 41 51N 129 58 E
68 Chŏngju, N. Korea 39 41N 125 13 E
68 Chŏngju, S. Korea 36 39N 127 27 E
68 Chŏnju 35 50N 127 4 E
112 Chonos, Arch. de los 45 0S 75 0W
60 Chopda 21 20N 75 15 E
12 Chorley 53 39N 2 39W
27 Chorzow 50 18N 19 0 E
66 Chóshi 35 45N 140 45 E
28 Choszczno 53 7N 15 25 E
102 Choteau 47 50N 112 10W
68 Choybalsan 48 3N 114 28 E
85 Christchurch, N.Z. 43 33S 172 47W
13 Christchurch, U.K. 50 44N 1 47W
75 Christiana 27 52S 25 8 E
82 Christmas Creek 18 29S 125 23 E
77 Christmas I. 1 58N 157 27W
26 Chrudim 49 58N 15 43 E
27 Chrzanów 50 10N 19 21 E
50 Chu 43 36N 73 42 E
69 Chu Kiang, R. 24 50N 113 37 E
69 Chuanchow 24 57N 118 31 E
69 Chuanhsien 25 50N 111 12 E
66 Chūbu □ 36 45N 137 0 E
112 Chubut, R. 43 20S 65 5W
68 Chucheng 36 0N 119 16 E
69 Chuchow 27 56N 113 3 E
48 Chudskoye, Oz. 58 13N 27 30 E
88 Chugiak 61 25N 149 30W
66 Chūgoku □ 35 0N 133 0 E
66 Chūgoku-Sanchi, Mts. 35 0N 133 0 E
69 Chuhsien 30 51N 107 1 E
63 Chukai 4 13N 103 25 E
51 Chukotskiy Khrebet 68 0N 175 0 E
51 Chukotskoye More 68 0N 175 0W
103 Chula Vista 33 44N 117 8W
69 Chumatien 33 0N 114 4 E
51 Chumikan 54 40N 135 10 E
63 Chumphon 10 35N 99 14 E
68 Chuncho E9n 37 58N 127 44 E
69 Chunghsien 30 17N 108 4 E
69 Chungking 29 30N 106 30 E
67 Chungtien 28 0N 99 30 E
68 Chungwei 37 35N 105 10 E
60 Chunian 31 10N 74 0 E
74 Chunya 8 30S 33 27 E
25 Chur 46 52N 9 32 E
93 Churchill 58 45N 94 5W
93 Churchill, R., Man. 58 47N 94 12W
91 Churchill, R., Newf. 53 30N 60 10W
92 Churchill Pk. 58 10N 125 10W
60 Churu 28 20N 75 0 E
69 Chusan, I. 30 0N 122 20 E
48 Chuvash A.S.S.R. □ 53 30N 48 0 E
48 Chuvovoy 58 15N 57 40 E
65 Cianjur 6 81S 107 7 E
109 Cianorte 23 37S 52 37W
65 Cibatu 7 8S 107 59 E
98 Cicero 41 48N 87 48W
28 Ciechanów 52 52N 20 38 E
28 Ciechanów □ 53 0N 20 0 E
105 Ciego de Avila 21 50N 78 50W
110 Ciénaga 11 0N 74 10W
105 Cienfuegos 22 10N 80 30W
26 Cieplice Ślaskie Zdrój 50 50N 15 40 E
20 Cierp 42 55N 0 40 E
27 Cieszyn 49 45N 18 35 E
33 Cieza 38 17N 1 23W
32 Cifuentes 40 47N 2 37W
31 Cijara, Pantano, Res. 39 18N 4 52W
65 Cilacap 7 43S 109 0 E
101 Cimarron, R. 36 10N 96 17W
65 Cimahi 6 53S 107 33 E
36 Cimone, Mte. 44 12N 10 42 E
41 Cîmpina 45 10N 25 45 E
41 Cîmpulung 45 17N 25 3 E
32 Cinca, R. 41 26N 0 21 E
98 Cincinnati 39 10N 84 26W
37 Cíngoli 43 23N 13 10 E
21 Cinto, Mt. 42 24N 8 54 E
38 Circéo, Mte. 41 14N 13 3 E
88 Circle 47 26N 105 35W

98 Circleville, Ohio 39 35N 82 57W
103 Circleville, Utah 38 12N 112 24W
65 Cirebon 6 45S 108 32E
13 Cirencester 51 43N 1 59W
101 Cisco 32 25N 99 0W
41 Cislău 45 14N 26 33E
39 Cisternino 40 45N 17 26E
38 Cisterna di Latina 41 35N 12 50E
104 Citlaltepetl, Mt. 19 0N 97 20W
37 Città di Castello 43 27N 12 14E
37 Città Sant 'Angelo 42 32N 14 5E
37 Cittadella 45 39N 11 48E
39 Cittanova 38 22N 16 0E
41 Ciuc, Mt. 45 31N 25 55E
104 Ciudad Acuña 29 20N 101 10W
110 Ciudad Bolívar 8 5N 63 30W
104 Ciudad Camargo 27 41N 105 10W
104 Ciudad de Valles 22 0N 98 30W
104 Ciudad del Carmen 18 20N 97 50W
110 Ciudad Guayana 8 20N 62 35W
104 Ciudad Guzmán 19 40N 103 30W
104 Ciudad, Juárez 31 40N 106 28W
104 Ciudad Madero 22 19N 97 50W
104 Ciudad Mante 22 50N 99 0W
104 Ciudad Obregón 27 28N 109 59W
110 Ciudad Piar 7 27N 63 19W
31 Ciudad Real 38 59N 3 55W
31 Ciudad Real □ 38 50N 4 0W
30 Ciudad Rodrigo 40 35N 6 32W
104 Ciudad Victoria 23 41N 99 9W
32 Ciudadela 40 0N 3 50E
41 Ciulniţa 44 26N 27 22E
37 Cividale del Friuli 46 6N 13 25E
37 Civita Castellana 42 18N 12 24E
37 Civitanova Marche 43 18N 13 41E
37 Civitavécchia 42 6N 11 46E
56 Çivril 38 20N 29 55E
83 Clackline 31 40S 116 32E
13 Clacton 51 47N 1 10E
20 Clain, R. 46 47N 0 32E
96 Clairton 40 18N 79 54W
19 Clamecy 47 28N 3 30E
15 Clara 53 20N 7 38W
81 Clare 33 20S 143 50E
15 Clare □ 52 52N 8 55W
15 Clare, R. 53 20N 9 3W
97 Claremont 43 23N 72 20W
101 Claremore 36 20N 95 20W
15 Claremorris 53 45N 9 0W
112 Clarence, I. 54 0S 72 0W
82 Clarence, Str. 12 0S 131 0E
85 Clarence, R. 42 10S 173 56E
101 Clarendon 34 41N 91 20W
91 Clarenville 48 10N 54 1W
92 Claresholm 50 0N 113 45W
100 Clarinda 40 45N 95 0W
102 Clark Fork, R. 48 9N 116 15W
103 Clarkdale 34 53N 112 3W
91 Clarke City 50 12N 66 38W
91 Clarkes Harbour 43 25N 65 38W
98 Clarksburg 39 18N 80 21W
101 Clarksdale 34 12N 90 33W
102 Clarkston 46 28N 117 2W
99 Clarksville 36 32N 87 20W
15 Clear, I. 51 26N 9 30W
96 Clearfield 41 0N 78 27W
92 Clearwater, Canada 51 38N 120 2W
99 Clearwater, U.S.A. 27 58N 82 45W
90 Clearwater L. 56 10N 75 0W
101 Cleburne 32 18N 97 25W
13 Clee Hills 55 25N 2 35W
12 Cleethorpes 53 33N 0 2W
21 Clelles 44 50N 5 38E
80 Clermont, Australia 22 46S 147 38E
19 Clermont, Meuse 49 5N 5 4E
19 Clermont, Oise 49 22N 2 24E
20 Clermont-Ferrand 45 46N 3 4E
20 Clermont-l'Hérault 43 38N 3 26E
19 Clerval 47 25N 6 30E
19 Cléry 47 50N 1 46E
13 Clevedon 51 27N 2 51W
81 Cleveland, Australia 27 31S 153 3E
101 Cleveland, Miss. 33 34N 90 43W
96 Cleveland, Ohio. 41 28N 81 43W
99 Cleveland, Tenn. 35 9N 84 52W
101 Cleveland, Tex. 30 18N 95 0W
12 Cleveland □ 54 30N 1 12W
102 Cleveland, Mt. 48 56N 113 51W
96 Cleveland Hts. 41 32N 81 30W
12 Cleveleys 53 53N 3 3W
15 Clew B. 53 54N 9 50W
15 Clifden, Eire 53 30N 10 2W
85 Clifden, N.Z. 46 1S 167 42E
103 Clifton 33 8N 109 23W
98 Clifton Forge 37 49N 79 51W
99 Clingmans Dome, Mt. 35 35N 83 30W
92 Clinton, B.C. 51 0N 121 40W
90 Clinton, Ont. 43 38N 81 33W
85 Clinton, N.Z. 46 12S 169 23E
100 Clinton, Ark. 35 37N 92 30W
99 Clinton, Ill. 40 8N 89 0W
100 Clinton, Iowa 41 50N 90 18W
97 Clinton, Mass. 42 26N 71 40W
100 Clinton, Mo. 38 20N 93 40W
101 Clinton, N.C. 35 5N 78 15W
88 Clinton Colden L. 64 0N 107 0W
77 Clipperton I. 10 18N 109 13W
15 Clonakilty 51 37N 8 53W
80 Cloncurry 20 40S 140 28E
105 Clones 54 10N 7 13W
15 Clonmel 52 22N 7 42W
24 Cloppenburg 52 50N 8 3E
100 Cloquet 46 40N 92 30W
108 Clorinda 25 16S 57 45W
101 Clovis, Calif. 36 54N 119 45W
103 Clovis, N.Mex 34 20N 103 10W
21 Cluses 46 5N 6 35E
85 Clutha, R. 46 20S 169 49E
12 Clwyd □ 53 0N 3 15W
12 Clwyd, R. 53 20N 3 30W
89 Clyde, Canada 70 30N 68 30W
85 Clyde, N.Z. 45 12S 169 20E
14 Clyde, R. 55 56N 4 29W
14 Clyde, Firth of 55 42N 5 0W
14 Clydebank 55 54N 4 25W
30 Côa, R. 41 5N 7 6W
103 Coachella 33 44N 116 13W
91 Coachman's Cove 50 6N 56 20W
104 Coahuila □ 27 0N 112 30W
92 Coaldale, Canada 49 45N 112 35W
97 Coaldale, U.S.A. 40 50N 75 54W
103 Coalinga 36 10N 120 21W
12 Coalville 52 43N 1 21W
92 Coast Mts. 52 0N 126 0W
102 Coast Ra. 40 0N 124 0W
83 Coastal Plains Basin 30 10S 115 30E
14 Coatbridge 55 52N 4 2W
104 Coatepeque 14 46N 91 55W
91 Coaticook 45 10N 71 46W
89 Coats I. 62 30N 82 0W
5 Coats Ld. 77 0S 25 0W
104 Coatzalcoalcos 18 7N 94 35W
41 Cobadin 44 5N 28 13E
90 Cobalt 47 25N 79 42W
104 Coban 15 30N 90 21W
84 Cobar 31 27S 145 48E
15 Cobh 51 50N 8 18W
81 Cobham 30 10S 142 0E
90 Cobourg 44 0N 78 20W
25 Coburg 50 15N 10 58E
30 Coca 41 13N 4 32W
62 Cocanada= Kakinada 16 55N 82 20E
33 Cocentaina 38 45N 0 27W
110 Cochabamba 17 15S 66 20W
62 Cochin 9 55N 76 22E
63 Cochin-China, Reg.=Nam-Phan, Reg. 10 30N 106 0E
92 Cochrane, Alta. 51 20N 114 30W
90 Cochrane, Ont. 49 0N 81 0W
112 Cochrane, L. 47 10S 72 0W
84 Cockburn, Australia 32 5S 141 2E
112 Cockburn, Canada 54 30S 72 0W
105 Coco, R. 15 0N 83 8W
63 Coco Chan. 13 45N 93 0E
77 Cocos I. 5 25N 87 55W
3 Cocos Is. 12 12S 96 54E
86 Cod, C. 42 8N 70 10W
110 Codajás 3 40S 62 0W
37 Codigoro 44 50N 12 5E
111 Codó 4 30S 43 55W
36 Codogno 45 10N 9 42E
37 Codróipo 45 57N 13 0E
105 Codrington 17 43N 61 49W
102 Cody 44 35N 109 0W
80 Coen 13 52S 143 12E
24 Coesfeld 51 56N 7 10E
102 Coeur d'Alene 47 45N 116 51W
101 Coffeyville 37 0N 95 40W
31 Coffin, B. 34 20S 135 10E
81 Coffs Harbour 30 16S 153 5E
41 Cogealac 44 36N 28 36E
38 Coghinas, L. di 40 35S 9 2E
20 Cognac 45 41N 0 20W
97 Cohoes 42 47N 73 42W
84 Cohuna 35 45S 144 15E
105 Coiba, I. 7 30N 81 40W
112 Coig, R. 51 0S 69 10W
112 Coihaique 45 35S 72 8W
62 Coimbatore 11 2N 76 59E
30 Coimbra 40 15N 8 27W
30 Coimbra □ 40 15N 8 27W
31 Coín 36 40N 4 48W
110 Cojimies 0 20N 80 0W
104 Cojutepeque 13 41N 88 54W
84 Colac 38 10S 143 30E
62 Colachel 8 10N 77 15E
31 Colares 38 48N 9 30W
100 Colby 39 27N 101 2W
108 Colchagua □ 34 30S 71 0W
13 Colchester 51 54N 0 55E
93 Cold Lake 54 27N 110 10W
14 Coldstream 55 39N 2 14W
90 Coldwell 48 45N 86 30W
101 Coleman 31 52N 99 30W
84 Coleraine, Australia 37 36S 141 40E
15 Coleraine, U.K. 55 8N 6 40W
15 Coleraine □ 55 8N 6 40W
62 Coleroon, R. 11 22N 79 51E
75 Colesburg 30 45S 25 5E
112 Colhué Huapí, L. 45 30S 69 0W
104 Colima 19 10N 103 50W
104 Colima □ 19 10N 103 40W
111 Colinas 6 0S 44 10W
84 Colinton 35 50S 149 10E
14 Coll, I. 56 40N 6 35W
31 Collarenebri 29 33S 148 35E
36 Colle Salvetti 43 34N 10 27E
99 College Park 33 42N 84 27W
83 Collie 33 25S 116 30E
82 Collier, B. 16 0S 124 0E
36 Colline Metallifere, Mts. 43 10N 11 0E
80 Collingwood, Australia 22 20S 142 31E
90 Collingwood, Canada 44 30N 80 20W
85 Collingwood, N.Z. 40 42S 172 40E
80 Collinsville 20 30S 147 56E
108 Collipulli 37 55S 72 30W
15 Collooney 54 11N 8 28W
19 Colmar 48 5N 7 20E
31 Colmenar 36 54N 4 20W
30 Colmenar de Oreja 40 6N 3 25W
30 Colmenar Viejo 40 39N 3 47W
12 Colne 53 51N 2 11W
84 Colo, R. 33 20S 150 40E
37 Cologna Veneta 45 19N 11 21E
24 Cologne=Köln 50 56N 9 58E
19 Colombey-les-deux Églises 48 20N 4 50E
110 Colombia ■ 3 45N 73 0W
111 Colombia 3 24N 79 49W
62 Colombo 6 56N 79 58E
108 Colón, Buenos Aires 32 55S 61 5W
108 Colón, Entre Ríos 32 12S 58 30W
104 Colón, Panama 9 20N 80 0W
83 Colona 31 38S 132 5E
37 Colonèlla 42 52N 13 50E
108 Colonia 34 25S 57 50W
14 Colonsay, I. 56 4N 6 12W
103 Colorado □ 37 40N 106 0W
112 Colorado, R., Arg. 39 50S 62 8W
103 Colorado, R. Mex.–U.S.A. 31 45N 114 40W
101 Colorado, R., U.S.A. 28 36N 95 58W
103 Colorado Aqueduct 34 0N 115 20W
101 Colorado City 32 25N 100 50W
103 Colorado Plat. 36 40N 110 30W
100 Colorado Springs 38 55N 104 50W
101 Columbia, La. 32 7N 92 5W
100 Columbia, Mo. 38 58N 92 20W
97 Columbia, Pa. 40 2N 76 30W
99 Columbia, S.C. 34 0N 81 0W
99 Columbia, Tenn. 35 40N 87 0W
98 Columbia, District of □ 38 55N 77 0W
92 Columbia, Mt. 52 20N 117 30W
102 Columbia, R. 45 49N 120 0W
102 Columbia Falls 48 25N 114 16W
100 Columbia Heights 45 5N 93 10W
102 Columbia Plat. 47 30N 118 30W
32 Columbretes, I. 39 50N 0 50E
99 Columbus, Ga. 32 30N 84 58W
98 Columbus, Ind. 39 14N 85 55W
99 Columbus, Miss. 33 30N 88 26W
100 Columbus, N.D. 48 52N 102 48W
98 Columbus, Ohio 39 57N 83 1W
30 Colunga 43 29N 5 16W
85 Colville, C. 36 29S 175 21E
88 Colville, R. 70 25N 150 30W
12 Colwyn Bay 53 17N 3 44W
37 Comácchio 44 41N 12 10E
37 Comácchio, Valli di, L. 44 40N 12 10E
112 Comallo 41 0S 70 5W
41 Comana 44 10N 26 10E
19 Combeaufontaine 47 43N 5 45E
19 Combles 50 0N 2 50E
80 Comet 23 36S 148 38E
61 Comilla 23 22N 91 18E
38 Comino, C. 40 28N 9 47E
39 Cómiso 36 57N 14 35E
104 Comitán 16 18N 92 9W
89 Committee B. 68 0N 87 0W
20 Commentry 46 20N 2 46E
101 Commerce 33 15N 95 50W
19 Commercy 48 46N 5 34E
36 Como 45 48N 9 5E
36 Como, L. di 46 5N 9 17E
112 Comodoro Rivadavia 45 50S 67 40W
62 Comorin, C. 8 3N 77 40E
40 Comorişte 45 10N 21 35E
70 Comoro Is. 12 10S 44 15E
92 Comox 49 42N 125 0W
19 Compiègne 49 24N 2 50E
109 Comprida, I. 25 0S 80 50W
72 Conakry 9 29N 13 49W
80 Conard Junction 41 48S 143 70E
18 Concarneau 47 52N 3 56W
111 Conceição do Araguaia 8 0S 49 2W
111 Conceiçao do Barra 18 50S 39 50W
108 Concepción, Arg. 27 20S 65 35W
108 Concepción, Chile 36 50S 73 0W
108 Concepción, Paraguay 23 30S 57 20W
108 Concepción □ 37 0S 72 30W
112 Concepción, Canal. 50 50S 75 0W
103 Concepcion, Pt. 34 30N 120 34W
104 Concepción del Oro 24 40N 101 30W
108 Concepción del Uruguay 32 35S 58 20W
18 Conches 48 58N 0 58E
99 Concord, N.C. 35 28N 80 35W
97 Concord, N.H. 43 5N 71 30W
108 Concordia, Arg. 31 20S 58 2W
100 Concordia, U.S.A. 39 35N 97 40W
81 Condamine 26 55S 150 3E
19 Condé 50 26N 3 34E
84 Condobolin 33 4S 147 6E
20 Condom 43 57N 0 22E
37 Conegliano 45 53N 12 18E
19 Conflans 49 10N 5 52E
20 Confolens 46 2N 0 40E
12 Congleton 53 10N 2 12W
74 Congo ■ 1 0S 16 0E
74 Congo (Kinshasa)■ =Zaïre ■ 3 0S 22 0E
74 Congo, R.= Zaïre, R. 6 4S 12 24E
103 Congress 34 11N 112 56W
31 Conil 36 17N 6 10W
90 Coniston 46 32N 80 51W
62 Conjeeveram= Kanchipuram 12 52N 79 45E
80 Conjuboy 18 35S 144 45E
15 Connaucht □ 53 23N 8 40W
96 Conneaut 41 55N 80 32W
97 Connecticut □ 41 40N 72 40W
97 Connecticut, R. 41 17N 72 21W
96 Connellsville 40 5N 79 32W
15 Connemara 53 29N 9 45W
98 Connersville 39 40N 85 10W
93 Conquest 53 35N 107 0W
101 Conroe 30 15N 95 28W
12 Consett 54 51N 1 49W
97 Conshohocken 40 5N 75 18W
93 Consort 52 1N 110 46W
41 Constanţa 44 14N 28 38E
31 Constantina 37 51N 5 40W
72 Constantine 36 25N 6 42E
108 Constitución, Chile 35 20S 72 30W
108 Constitución, Uruguay 31 0S 58 10W
31 Consuegra 39 28N 3 43W
37 Contarina 45 2N 12 13E
19 Contrexéville 48 10N 5 53E
39 Conversano 40 57N 17 8E
101 Conway, Ark. 35 5N 92 30W
97 Conway, N.H. 43 58N 71 8W
99 Conway, S.C. 33 49N 79 2W
12 Conwy 53 17N 3 50W
12 Conwy R. 53 17N 3 50W
31 Coober Pedy 28 56S 134 45E
61 Cooch Behar 26 22N 89 29E
83 Cook 30 42S 130 48E
112 Cook, B. 55 10S 70 0W
88 Cook Inlet 59 0N 151 0W
77 Cook Is. 22 0S 157 0W
85 Cook, Mt. 43 36S 170 9E
85 Cook, Str. 41 15S 174 29E
99 Cookeville 36 12N 85 30W
80 Cooktown 15 30S 145 16E
15 Cookstown □ 54 40N 6 43W
81 Coolabah 31 0S 146 15E
81 Coolangatta 28 11S 153 29E
83 Coolgardie 30 55S 121 8E
103 Coolidge 33 1N 111 35W
103 Coolidge Dam 33 10N 110 30W
84 Cooma 36 12S 149 8E
84 Coonabarabran 31 14S 149 18E
81 Coonamble 30 56S 148 27E

83 Coonana ... 31 0s 123 0e
62 Coondapoor ... 13 42n 74 40e
81 Coongoola ... 27 43s 145 47e
62 Coonoor ... 11 10n 76 45e
99 Cooper ... 39 57n 75 7w
81 Cooper Creek, R., L. ... 28 0s 139 0e
81 Coorong, The ... 35 50s 139 20e
83 Coorow ... 29 50s 115 59e
81 Cooroy ... 26 22s 152 54e
102 Coos Bay ... 43 26n 124 7w
84 Cootamundra ... 34 36s 148 1e
15 Cootehill ... 54 5n 7 5w
33 Cope, C. ... 37 26n 1 28w
45 Copenhagen= København ... 55 41n 12 34e
39 Copertino ... 40 17n 18 2w
108 Copiapó ... 27 15s 70 20e
37 Copparo ... 44 52n 11 49e
88 Copper Center ... 62 10n 145 25w
90 Copper Cliff ... 46 30n 81 4w
92 Copper Mountain ... 49 20n 120 30w
88 Coppermine ... 68 0n 116 0w
41 Copşa Mică ... 46 6n 24 15e
12 Coquet, R. ... 55 22n 1 37w
74 Coquilhatville= Mbandaka ... 0 1n 18 18e
108 Coquimbo ... 30 0s 71 20w
108 Coquimbo □ ... 30 0s 71 0w
41 Corabia ... 43 48n 24 30e
110 Coracora ... 15 5s 73 45w
89 Coral Harbour ... 64 0n 83 0w
90 Coral Rapids ... 50 20n 81 40w
76 Coral Sea ... 15 0s 150 0e
96 Coraopolis ... 40 30n 80 10w
39 Corato ... 41 12n 16 22e
19 Corbeil-Essonnes ... 48 36n 2 25e
20 Corbières, Mts. ... 42 55n 2 35e
98 Corbin ... 37 0n 84 3w
31 Corbones, R. ... 37 36n 5 39w
13 Corby ... 52 29n 0 41w
33 Corcoles, R. ... 39 12n 2 40w
103 Corcoran ... 36 6n 119 35w
30 Corcubión ... 42 56n 9 12w
99 Cordele ... 31 55n 83 49w
108 Córdoba, Arg. ... 31 20s 64 10w
108 Córdoba, Arg. □ ... 31 22s 64 15w
104 Córdoba, Mexico ... 26 20n 103 20w
31 Córdoba, Sp. ... 37 50n 4 50w
108 Córdoba □, Arg. ... 31 22s 64 15w
31 Córdoba □, Sp. ... 38 5n 5 0w
65 Cordon ... 16 42n 121 32e
88 Cordova ... 60 36n 145 45w
80 Corfield ... 21 40s 143 21e
42 Corfu, I.= Kérkira, I. ... 39 38n 19 50e
30 Corgo ... 42 56n 7 25w
30 Coria ... 40 0n 6 33w
39 Corigliano Cálabro ... 39 36n 16 31e
43 Corinth, Greece= Kórinthos ... 37 56n 22 55e
99 Corinth, U.S.A. ... 34 54n 88 30w
43 Corinth Canal ... 37 48n 23 0e
111 Corinto, Brazil ... 18 20s 44 30w
105 Corinto, Nic. ... 12 30n 87 10w
15 Cork ... 51 54n 8 30w
15 Cork □ ... 51 54n 8 30w
38 Corleone ... 37 48n 13 16e
56 Çorlu ... 41 11n 27 49e
93 Cormorant ... 54 5n 100 45w
105 Corn Is. ... 12 0n 83 0w
109 Cornélio Procópio ... 23 7s 50 40w
91 Corner Brook ... 49 0n 58 0w
102 Corning, Calif. ... 39 56n 122 9w
96 Corning, N.Y. ... 42 10n 77 3w
90 Cornwall ... 45 5n 74 45w
13 Cornwall □ ... 50 26n 4 40w
110 Coro ... 11 30n 69 45w
111 Coroatá ... 4 20s 44 0w
110 Corocoro ... 17 15s 69 19w
85 Coromandel ... 36 45s 175 31e
62 Coromandel Coast Reg. ... 12 30n 81 0e
103 Corona ... 33 49n 117 36w
103 Coronado ... 32 45n 117 9w
105 Coronado, B. de ... 9 0n 83 40w
88 Coronation G. ... 68 0n 114 0w
108 Coronda ... 31 58s 60 56w
108 Coronel ... 37 0s 73 10w
108 Coronel Bogado ... 27 11s 56 18w
108 Coronel Dorrego ... 38 40s 61 10w
108 Coronel Oviedo ... 25 24s 56 30w
108 Coronel Pringles ... 38 0s 61 30w
108 Coronel Suárez ... 37 30s 62 0w
109 Corpus ... 27 10s 55 30w
101 Corpus Christi ... 27 50n 97 28w
30 Corral de Almaguer ... 39 45n 3 10w
36 Corréggio ... 44 46n 10 47e
20 Corrèze □ ... 45 20n 1 50e
15 Corrib, L. ... 53 25n 9 10w
108 Corrientes ... 27 30s 58 45w
108 Corrientes □ ... 28 0s 57 0w
105 Corrientes, C., Cuba ... 21 43n 84 30w
110 Corrientes, C., Col. ... 5 30n 77 34w
83 Corrigin ... 32 18s 117 45e
96 Corry ... 41 55n 79 39w
21 Corse, C. ... 43 1n 9 25e
21 Corse, I. ... 42 0n 9 0e
21 Corsica, I.= Corse, I. ... 42 0n 9 0e
101 Corsicana ... 32 5n 96 30w
21 Corte ... 42 19n 9 11e
31 Cortegana ... 37 52n 6 49w
103 Cortez ... 37 24n 108 35w
37 Cortina d'Ampezzo ... 46 32n 12 9e
97 Cortland ... 42 35n 76 11w
37 Cortona ... 43 16n 12 0e
31 Coruche ... 38 57n 8 30w
56 Çorum ... 40 30n 35 5e
110 Corumbá ... 19 0s 57 30w
102 Corvallis ... 44 36n 123 15w
104 Cosamalopan ... 18 23n 95 50w
39 Cosenza ... 39 17n 16 14e
41 Coşereni ... 44 38n 26 35e
96 Coshocton ... 40 17n 81 51w
19 Cosne-sur-Loire ... 47 24n 2 54e
108 Cosquín ... 31 15s 64 30w
36 Cossato ... 45 34n 8 10e
33 Costa Blanca, Reg. ... 38 25n 0 10w
32 Costa Brava, Reg. ... 41 30n 3 0e
31 Costa del Sol, Reg. ... 36 30n 4 30w
32 Costa Dorada, Reg. ... 40 45n 1 15e
105 Costa Rica ■ ... 10 0n 84 0w
41 Costeşti ... 44 40n 24 53e
38 Cost Smeralda ... 41 5n 9 35e
25 Coswig ... 51 52n 12 31e
65 Cotabato ... 7 8n 124 13e
21 Côte d'Azur, Reg. ... 43 25n 6 50e
19 Côte d'Or □ ... 47 30n 4 50e
21 Côte d'Or, Reg. ... 47 10n 4 50e
18 Cotentin, Reg. ... 49 30n 1 30w
19 Côtes de Meuse, Reg. ... 49 15n 5 22e
18 Côtes-du-Nord □ ... 48 28n 2 50w
72 Cotonou ... 6 20n 2 25e
110 Cotopaxi, Mt. ... 0 30s 78 30w
13 Cotswold Hills ... 51 42n 2 10w
102 Cottage Grove ... 43 48n 123 2w
24 Cottbus ... 51 44n 14 20e
24 Cottbus □ ... 51 43n 13 30e
103 Cottonwood ... 34 48n 112 1w
31 Couço ... 38 59n 8 17w
102 Coulee City ... 47 44n 119 12w
19 Coulommiers ... 48 50n 3 3e
21 Coulon, R. ... 43 51n 5 0e
88 Council, Alas. ... 64 55n 163 45w
102 Council, Id. ... 44 45n 116 30w
100 Council Bluffs ... 41 20n 95 50w
21 Couronne, C. ... 43 19n 5 3e
18 Courseulles ... 49 20n 0 29w
21 Cours ... 46 7n 4 19e
92 Courtenay ... 49 45n 125 0w
18 Courville ... 48 28n 1 15e
18 Coutances ... 49 3n 1 28w
20 Coutras ... 45 3n 0 8w
30 Covilhã ... 40 17n 7 31w
99 Covington, Ga. ... 33 36n 83 50w
98 Covington, Ky. ... 39 5n 84 30w
93 Cowan ... 52 5n 100 45w
83 Cowan, L. ... 31 45s 121 45e
84 Cowangie ... 35 12s 141 26e
90 Cowansville ... 45 14n 72 46w
14 Cowdenbeath ... 56 7n 3 20w
81 Cowell ... 33 38s 136 40e
13 Cowes ... 50 45n 1 18w
84 Cowra ... 33 49s 148 42e
111 Coxim ... 18 30s 54 55w
59 Cox's Bazar ... 21 25n 92 3e
104 Cozumel, I. de ... 20 30n 86 40w
75 Cradock ... 32 8s 25 36e
102 Craig ... 40 32n 107 44w
15 Craigavon □ ... 54 27n 6 26w
41 Craiova ... 44 21n 23 48e
74 Crampel ... 7 8n 19 8e
93 Cranberry Portage ... 54 36n 101 22w
80 Cranbrook, Tas. ... 42 0s 148 5e
83 Cranbrook, W. Australia ... 34 20s 117 35e
92 Cranbrook Canada ... 49 30n 115 55w
97 Cranston ... 41 47n 71 27w
41 Crasna ... 46 32n 27 51e
111 Crateús ... 5 10s 40 50w
111 Crato, Brazil ... 7 10s 39 25w
31 Crato, Port. ... 39 16n 7 39w
21 Crau, Reg. ... 43 32n 4 40e
98 Crawfordsville ... 40 2n 86 51w
13 Crawley ... 51 7n 0 10w
19 Crécy ... 48 50n 2 53e
93 Cree L. ... 57 30n 107 0w
19 Creil ... 49 15n 2 34e
36 Crema ... 45 21n 9 40e
36 Cremona ... 45 8n 10 2e
19 Crépy ... 49 37n 3 32e
19 Crépy-en-Valois ... 49 14n 2 54e
37 Cres, I. ... 44 58n 14 25e
102 Crescent City ... 41 45n 124 12w
108 Crespo ... 32 2s 60 20w
90 Cressman ... 47 40n 72 55w
21 Crest ... 44 44n 5 2e
92 Creston, Canada ... 49 10n 116 40w
100 Creston, U.S.A. ... 41 0n 94 20w
99 Crestview ... 30 45n 86 35w
43 Crete=Kriti, I. ... 35 10n 25 0e
43 Crete, Sea of ... 26 0n 25 0e
32 Creus, C. ... 42 20n 3 19e
20 Creuse □ ... 46 0n 2 0e
20 Creuse, R. ... 47 0n 0 34e
37 Crevalcore ... 44 41n 11 10e
33 Crevillente ... 38 12n 0 48w
12 Crewe ... 53 6n 2 28w
109 Criciúma ... 28 40s 49 23w
14 Crieff ... 56 22n 3 50w
37 Crikvenica ... 45 11n 14 40e
49 Crimea= Krymskaya, Reg. ... 45 0n 34 0e
24 Crimmitschau ... 50 48n 12 23e
14 Crinan ... 56 4n 5 30w
104 Cristóbal ... 9 10n 80 0w
101 Crockett ... 31 20n 95 30w
21 Croisette, C. ... 43 13n 5 20e
82 Croker, I. ... 11 12s 132 32e
14 Cromarty ... 57 40n 4 2w
12 Cromer ... 52 56n 1 18e
85 Cromwell ... 45 3s 169 14e
84 Cronulla ... 34 3s 151 8e
105 Crooked I. ... 22 50n 74 10w
100 Crookston ... 47 50n 96 40w
12 Cross Fell, Mt. ... 54 44n 2 29w
15 Crosshaven ... 51 48n 8 19w
97 Croton-on-Hudson ... 41 19n 73 55w
39 Crotone ... 39 5n 17 6e
102 Crow Agency ... 45 40n 107 30w
15 Crow Hd. ... 51 34n 10 9w
101 Crowley ... 30 15n 92 20w
97 Crown Point ... 41 24n 87 23w
92 Crowsnest P. ... 49 40n 114 40w
80 Croydon, Australia ... 18 15s 142 14e
13 Croydon, U.K. ... 51 18n 0 5w
18 Crozon ... 48 15n 4 30w
109 Cruz Alta ... 28 40s 53 32w
108 Cruz del Eje ... 30 45s 64 50w
109 Cruzeiro ... 22 50s 45 0w
109 Cruzeiro do Oeste ... 23 46s 53 4w
110 Cruzeiro do Sul ... 7 35s 72 35w
81 Crystal Brook ... 33 21s 138 13e
101 Crystal City ... 38 15n 90 23w
27 Csongrád ... 46 43n 20 12e
27 Csongrád □ ... 46 32n 20 15e
27 Csurgo ... 46 16n 17 9e
75 Cuamba ... 14 45s 36 22e
75 Cuando, R. ... 14 0s 19 30e
31 Cuba ... 38 10n 7 54w
105 Cuba ■ ... 22 0n 79 0w
83 Cuballing ... 32 50s 117 15e
110 Cucui ... 1 10n 66 50w
110 Cúcuta ... 7 54n 72 31w
62 Cuddalore ... 11 46n 79 45e
62 Cuddapah ... 14 30n 78 47e
30 Cudillero ... 43 33n 6 9w
83 Cue ... 27 20s 117 55e
30 Cuéllar ... 41 23n 4 21e
32 Cuenca, Sp. ... 40 5n 2 10w
110 Cuenca, Ecuador ... 2 50s 79 9w
32 Cuenca, Sp. □ ... 40 0n 2 0w
32 Cuenca, Sa. de ... 39 55n 1 50w
104 Cuernavaca ... 18 50n 99 20w
101 Cuero ... 29 5n 97 17w
111 Cuiabá ... 15 30s 56 0w
14 Cuillin Hills ... 57 14n 6 15w
21 Cuiseaux ... 46 30n 5 22e
104 Cuitzeo, L. ... 19 55n 101 5w
20 Culan ... 46 34n 2 20e
84 Culcairn ... 35 41s 147 3e
30 Culebra, Sa. de la ... 41 55n 6 20w
104 Culiacán ... 24 50n 107 40w
33 Cúllar de Baza ... 37 35n 2 34w
14 Cullen ... 57 45n 2 50w
82 Cullen, Pt. ... 11 50s 141 47e
33 Cullera ... 39 9n 0 17w
14 Culloden Moor ... 57 29n 4 7w
21 Culoz ... 45 47n 5 46e
85 Culverden ... 42 47s 172 49e
110 Cumaná ... 10 30n 64 5w
92 Cumberland, Canada ... 49 40n 125 0w
98 Cumberland, U.S.A. ... 39 40n 78 43w
89 Cumberland Pen. ... 67 0n 65 0w
86 Cumberland Plat. ... 36 0n 84 30w
89 Cumberland Sd. ... 65 30n 66 0w
31 Cumbres Mayores ... 38 4n 6 39w
12 Cumbria □ ... 54 44n 2 55w
12 Cumbrian, Mts. ... 54 30n 3 0w
31 Cummins ... 34 16s 135 44e
83 Cunderdin ... 31 39s 117 15e
75 Cunene, R. ... 17 20s 11 50e
36 Cúneo ... 44 23n 7 32e
81 Cunnamulla ... 28 4s 145 41e
93 Cupar, Canada ... 51 0n 104 10w
14 Cupar, U.K. ... 56 20n 3 0w
110 Cupica, G. de ... 6 25n 77 30w
40 Ćuprija ... 34 57n 21 26e
105 Curaçao ... 12 10n 69 0w
19 Cure, R. ... 47 40n 3 41e
110 Curiapo ... 8 33n 61 5w
108 Curicó ... 34 55s 71 20w
108 Curicó □ ... 34 50s 71 15w
109 Curitiba ... 25 20s 49 10w
111 Currais Novos ... 6 13s 36 30w
111 Curralinho ... 1 35s 49 30w
80 Currawilla ... 25 10s 141 20e
102 Currie ... 40 16n 114 45w
80 Curtis, I. ... 23 40s 151 15e
111 Curuçá ... 0 35s 47 50w
111 Cururupu ... 1 50s 44 50w
108 Curuzú Cuatiá ... 29 50s 58 5w
111 Curvelo ... 18 45s 44 27w
84 Curya ... 35 53s 142 54e
101 Cushing ... 31 43n 94 50w
36 Cusna, Mte. ... 44 17n 10 23e
20 Cusset ... 46 8n 3 28e
100 Custer ... 43 45n 103 38w
102 Cut Bank ... 48 40n 112 15w
39 Cutro ... 39 1n 16 58e
61 Cuttack ... 20 25n 85 57e
83 Cuvier, C. ... 23 14s 113 22e
24 Cuxhaven ... 53 51n 8 41e
96 Cuyahoga Falls ... 41 8n 81 30w
110 Cuzco, Mt. ... 20 0s 66 50w
110 Cuzco ... 13 32s 72 0w
80 Cygnet ... 43 8s 147 1e
56 Cyprus ■ ... 35 0n 33 0e
73 Cyrenaica=Barqa Reg. ... 27 0n 20 0e
73 Cyrene=Shahhat ... 32 39n 21 18e
27 Czechoslovakia ■ ... 49 0n 17 0e
27 Czechowice Dziedzice ... 49 54n 18 59e
27 Czeladz ... 50 16n 19 2e
28 Czempiń ... 52 9n 16 33e
27 Czerwionka ... 50 7n 18 37e
27 Częstochowa ... 50 49n 19 7e
28 Czestichowa □ ... 50 50n 19 0e
28 Człuchów ... 53 41n 17 22e

D

63 Da, R. ... 16 0n 107 0e
63 Da Lat ... 12 3n 108 32e
63 Da Nang ... 16 10n 108 7e
72 Dabakala ... 8 15n 4 20w
60 Dabhoi ... 22 10n 73 20e
28 Dąbie ... 53 27n 14 45e
72 Dabola ... 10 50n 11 5w
27 Dabrowa Gornieza ... 50 15n 19 10e
27 Dabrowa Tarnówska ... 50 10n 21 0e
61 Dacca ... 23 43n 90 26e
61 Dacca □ ... 24 0n 90 0e
25 Dachau ... 48 16n 11 27e
110 Dadanawa ... 3 0n 59 30w
60 Dadau ... 26 45n 67 45e
49 Dagesta A.S.S.R. □ ... 42 30n 47 0e
65 Dagupan ... 16 3n 120 33e
72 Dahomey ■= Benin ■ ... 8 0n 2 0e
31 Daimiel ... 39 5n 3 35w
15 Daingean ... 53 18n 7 15w
68 Dairen=Talien ... 39 0n 121 31e
73 Dairût ... 27 34n 30 43e
83 Dairy Creek ... 25 12s 115 48e
66 Daisetsu-Zan, Mt. ... 43 30n 142 57e
80 Dajarra ... 21 42s 139 30e
72 Dakar ... 14 34n 17 29w
72 Dakhla ... 23 50n 15 53w
49 Dakhovskaya ... 44 13n 40 13e
60 Dakor ... 22 45n 73 11e
40 Dakovica ... 42 22n 20 26e
40 Dakovo ... 45 19n 18 24e
68 Dalai Nor, L. ... 49 0n 117 50e
44 Dalälven, R. ... 60 38n 17 27e
68 Dalandzadgad ... 43 35n 104 30e
58 Dalbandin ... 28 53n 64 25e
14 Dalbeattie ... 54 56n 3 49w
81 Dalby ... 27 11s 151 16e
101 Dalhart ... 36 4n 102 31w
91 Dalhousie ... 48 0n 66 26w
54 Daliyat el Karmel ... 32 41n 35 3e
40 Dalj ... 45 29n 18 59e
14 Dalkeith ... 55 54n 3 4w

101 Dallas 32 47N 96 48W
57 Dalmā, I. 24 30N 52 20E
37 Dalmacija, Reg. 43 0N 17 0E
14 Dalmellington 55 20N 4 25W
51 Dalnerechensk 45 50N 133 40E
72 Daloa 6 53N 6 27W
90 Dalton, Canada 60 10N 137 0N
97 Dalton, Mass. 42 28N 73 11W
99 Dalton, Neb. 41 27N 103 0W
61 Daltonganj 24 3N 84 4E
82 Daly, R. 13 20S 130 19E
80 Daly Waters 16 15S 133 22E
60 Daman 20 25N 72 57E
60 Daman, Dadra & Nagar Haveli □ 20 25N 72 58E
73 Damanhûr 31 2N 30 28E
75 Damaraland, Reg. 22 33S 17 6E
56 Damascus= Dimashq 33 30N 36 18E
57 Damāvand 35 45N 52 10E
57 Damāvand, Qolleh-ye, Mt. 35 56N 52 8E
41 Dâmboviţa, R. 44 40N 26 0E
57 Dāmghan 36 10N 54 17E
73 Damietta= Dumyât 31 24N 31 48E
54 Damiya 32 6N 35 34E
24 Damme 52 32N 8 12E
61 Damodar, R. 23 17N 87 35E
61 Damoh 23 50N 79 28E
82 Dampier 20 39S 116 45E
65 Dampier, Selat 0 40S 130 40E
54 Dan 33 13N 35 39E
72 Danané 7 16N 8 9W
97 Danbury 41 23N 73 29W
84 Dandenong 37 52S 145 12E
77 Danger Is. 10 53S 165 49W
91 Daniel's Harbour 50 13N 57 35W
48 Danilov 58 16N 40 13E
40 Danilovgrad 42 38N 19 9E
24 Dannenberg 53 7N 11 4E
85 Dannevirke 40 12S 176 8E
96 Dannsville 42 32N 77 41W
9 Danube, R.= Donau, R. 45 20N 29 40E
97 Danvers 42 34N 70 55E
98 Danville, Ill. 40 10N 87 45W
98 Danville, Ky. 37 40N 84 45W
97 Danville, Vt. 44 24N 72 12W
99 Danville, Va. 36 40N 79 20W
28 Danzig= Gdánsk 54 22N 18 40E
84 Dapto 34 30S 150 47E
54 Dar'a 32 37N 36 6E
74 Dar-es-Salaam 6 50S 39 12E
57 Dārāb 28 50N 54 30E
58 Darband 34 30N 72 50E
61 Darbhanga 26 15N 86 3E
92 D'Arcy 50 35N 122 30W
56 Dardanelles= Cannakale Boğazi, Str. 40 0N 26 20E
36 Darfo 45 43N 10 11E
73 Dârfûr □ 15 35N 25 0E
73 Dârfûr, Reg. 12 35N 25 0E
58 Dargai 34 25N 71 45E
50 Dargan Ata 40 40N 62 20E
85 Dargaville 35 57S 173 52E
68 Darhan 49 27N 105 57E
110 Darién, G. del 9 0N 77 0W
61 Darjeeling 27 3N 88 18E
91 Dark Cove 49 54N 54 5W
83 Darkan 33 19S 116 37E
84 Darling, R. 34 4S 141 54E
81 Darling Downs 27 30S 150 30E
83 Darling Ra. 32 0S 116 30E
12 Darlington 54 33N 1 33W
28 Darłowo 54 26N 16 23E
41 Dármănesti 46 21N 26 33E
25 Darmstadt 49 51N 8 40E
88 Darnley, B. 69 30N 124 30W
32 Daroca 41 9N 1 25W
80 Darr 24 34S 144 52E
25 Darsser Ort, C. 44 27N 12 30E
13 Dart, R. 50 34N 3 56W
84 Dartmoor 37 56S 141 19E
13 Dartmoor, Reg. 50 36N 4 0W
80 Dartmouth, Australia 23 30S 144 40E
91 Dartmouth Canada 44 40N 63 30W
13 Dartmouth, U.K. 50 21N 3 35W
32 Dartuch, C. 39 55N 3 49E
40 Daruvar 45 36N 17 13E
50 Darvaza 40 12N 58 24E
60 Darwha 20 15N 77 45E
82 Darwin 12 20S 130 50E
82 Darwin River 12 49S 130 58E
56 Daryācheh-ye Reza'iyeh, L. 37 30N 45 30E
60 Daryapur 23 19N 71 50E
57 Das 35 5N 75 4E
73 Dashen, Ras, Mt. 13 10N 38 26E
68 Dashinchilen 47 50N 103 60E
58 Dasht, R. 25 10N 61 40E
57 Dasht-e Kavir, Des. 34 30N 55 0E
57 Dasht-e Lút, Des. 31 30N 58 0E
60 Daska 32 20N 74 21E
60 Datia 25 39N 78 27E
60 Dattapur 20 45N 78 15E
60 Daud Khel 32 53N 71 34E
48 Daugavpils 55 53N 26 32E
57 Daulat Yar 34 33N 65 46E
93 Dauphin 51 15N 100 5W
21 Daupniné, Reg. 45 15N 5 25E
62 Davangere 14 25N 75 50E
65 Davao 7 0N 125 40E
65 Davao G. 6 30N 125 48E
100 Davenport, Iowa 41 30N 90 40W
102 Davenport, Wash. 47 40N 118 5W
13 Daventry 52 16N 1 10W
105 David 8 30N 82 30W
88 Davis, Alas. 51 52N 176 39W
102 Davis, Calif. 38 39N 121 45W
91 Davis Inlet 55 50N 60 45W
5 Davis Sea 66 0S 92 0E
89 Davis Str. 68 0N 58 0W
25 Davos 46 48N 9 50E
88 Dawson 64 4N 139 25W
92 Dawson Creek 55 46N 120 14W
112 Dawson, I. 53 50S 70 50W
20 Dax 43 43N 1 3W
54 Dayr al-Ghusūn 32 21N 35 5E
56 Dayr az Zawr 35 20N 40 9E
54 Dayral Balah 31 25N 34 21E
98 Dayton, Ohio 39 45N 84 10W
102 Dayton, Wash. 46 20N 118 0W
99 Daytona Beach 29 14N 81 0W
83 D'Entrecasteaux, Pt. 34 50S 116 0E
75 De Aar 30 39S 24 0E
82 De Grey 20 30S 120 0E
82 De Grey, R. 20 12S 119 11E
100 De Kalb 41 55N 88 45W
99 De Land 29 1N 81 19W
101 De Ridder 30 48N 93 15W
100 De Soto 38 8N 90 34W
54 Dead Sea= Miyet, Bahr el 31 30N 35 30E
100 Deadwood 44 25N 103 43W
83 Deakin 30 46S 129 0E
13 Deal 51 13N 1 25E
13 Dean, Forest of 51 50N 2 35W
108 Deán Funes 30 20S 64 20W
88 Dease Arm, B. 66 45N 120 6W
92 Dease Lake 58 40N 130 5W
103 Death Valley 36 0N 116 40W
103 Death Valley Nat. Mon. 36 30N 117 0W
103 Death Valley Junction .15N 11630W
18 Deauville 49 23N 0 2E
40 Debar 41 21N 20 37E
27 Dębica 50 2N 21 25E
28 Dęblin 51 34N 21 50E
28 Dębno 52 45N 14 40E
73 Debre Markos 10 20N 37 40E
73 Debre Tabor 11 50N 38 5E
27 Debrecen 47 33N 21 42E
40 Dečani 42 30N 29 10E
99 Decatur, Ala. 34 35N 87 0W
99 Decatur, Ga. 33 47N 84 17W
100 Decatur, Ill. 39 50N 89 0W
98 Decatur, Ind. 40 52N 85 28W
20 Decazeville 44 34N 2 15E
62 Deccan, Reg. 14 0N 77 0E
26 Děčín 50 47N 14 12E
20 Decize 46 50N 3 28E
100 Decorah 43 20N 91 50W
97 Dedham 42 14N 71 10W
14 Dee, R. Scot. 57 4N 3 7W
12 Dee, R., Wales 53 15N 3 7W
80 Deep Well 24 25S 134 5E
81 Deepwater 29 25S 151 51E
91 Deer Lake 49 11N 57 27W
102 Deer Lodge 46 25N 112 40W
60 Deesa 24 18N 72 10E
98 Defiance 41 20N 84 20W
54 Deganya 32 43N 35 34E
31 Degebe, R. 38 21N 7 37W
55 Degeh Bur 8 14N 43 35E
44 Degerfors 64 16N 19 46E
25 Deggendorf 48 49N 12 59E
62 Degloor 18 34N 77 33E
57 Deh Bīd 30 39N 53 11E
62 Dehiwala 6 50N 79 57E
60 Dehra Dun 30 20N 78 4E
61 Dehri 24 50N 84 15E
54 Deir Dibwan 31 55N 35 15E
44 Deje 59 35N 13 29E
103 Del Norte 37 47N 106 27W
101 Del Rio 29 15N 100 50W
70 Delagoa B. 25 50S 32 45E
103 Delano 35 48N 119 13W
98 Delaware 40 20N 83 0W
98 Delaware □ 39 0N 75 40W
98 Delaware, R. 41 50N 75 15W
25 Delémont 47 22N 7 20E
96 Delevan 42 27N 78 28W
16 Delft 52 1N 4 22E
62 Delft I. 9 30N 79 40E
16 Delfzijl 53 20N 6 55E
74 Delgado, C. 10 45S 40 40E
73 Delgo 20 6N 30 40E
60 Delhi 28 38N 77 17E
104 Delicias 28 10N 105 30W
24 Delitzsch 51 32N 12 22E
19 Delle 47 30N 7 2E
97 Delmar 42 37N 73 47W
24 Delmenhorst 53 3N 8 37E
111 Delmiro Gonveia 9 24S 38 6W
37 Delnice 45 23N 14 50E
51 Delong, Os. 76 30N 153 0E
80 Deloraine 41 30S 146 40E
43 Delphi 38 28N 22 30E
98 Delphos 40 51N 84 17W
99 Delray Beach 26 27N 80 4W
103 Delta 38 44N 108 5W
81 Delungra 29 40S 150 45E
42 Delvinë 39 59N 20 4E
30 Demanda, Sa. de 42 15N 3 0W
103 Deming 48 49N 122 13W
24 Demmin 53 54N 13 2E
92 Demmit 55 26N 119 54W
99 Demopolis 32 31N 87 50W
64 Dempo, Mt. 4 2S 103 9E
16 Den Helder 52 54N 4 45E
19 Denain 50 20N 3 23E
50 Denau 38 16N 67 54E
12 Denbigh 53 11N 3 25W
64 Dendang 3 5S 107 54E
16 Dendermonde 51 2N 4 7E
83 Denham 25 55S 113 32E
93 Denholm 52 40N 108 0W
84 Deniliquin 35 32S 144 58E
101 Denison 33 45N 96 33W
56 Denizli 37 46N 29 6E
83 Denmark 34 57S 117 21E
45 Denmark ■ 56 0N 10 0E
4 Denmark Str. 67 0N 25 0W
64 Denpasar 8 39S 115 13E
101 Denton 33 13N 97 8W
100 Denver 39 43N 105 1W
60 Deoband 29 41N 77 41E
61 Deoghar 24 30N 86 59E
61 Deoha, R. 27 0N 79 90E
60 Deolali 19 56N 73 50E
61 Deoria 26 30N 83 47E
58 Deosai Mts. 35 10N 75 20E
96 Depew 42 55N 78 43W
83 Depot Springs 27 55S 120 3E
51 Deputatskiy 69 18N 139 54E
60 Dera Ghazi Khan 30 3N 70 38E
60 Dera Ismail Khan □ 31 50N 70 54E
49 Derbent 42 3N 48 18E
82 Derby, Australia 17 18S 123 38E
12 Derby, U.K. 52 55N 1 29W
97 Derby, U.S.A. 41 19N 73 5N
12 Derby □ 52 55N 1 29W
27 Derecske 47 21N 21 34E
15 Derg, L. 53 0N 8 20W
73 Derna 32 40N 22 35E
84 Derrinallum 37 57S 143 13E
84 Derriwong 33 6S 147 21E
15 Derryveagh Mts. 55 0N 8 40W
73 Derudub 17 31N 36 7E
43 Dervéni 38 8N 22 25E
12 Derwent R. Cumbria 54 42N 3 22W
12 Derwent, R. Derby 53 26N 1 44W
12 Derwent, R. Yorks 54 13N 0 35W
12 Derwentwater, L. 53 34N 3 9W
100 Des Moines 41 35N 93 37W
100 Des Moines, R. 41 15N 93 0W
112 Deseado, R. 40 0S 69 0W
36 Desenzano del Garda 45 28N 10 32E
103 Desert Center 33 45N 115 27W
48 Desna, R. 52 0N 33 15E
112 Desolación, I. 53 0S 74 10W
24 Dessau 51 50N 12 14E
19 Dèsvres 50 40N 1 50E
40 Deta 45 24N 21 13E
24 Detmold 51 56N 8 52E
98 Detroit 42 20N 83 3W
100 Detroit Lakes 46 49N 95 57W
16 Deurne, Belgium 51 13N 4 28E
16 Deurne, Neth. 51 28N 5 47E
24 Deutsche, B. 54 30N 7 30E
26 Deutschlandsberg 46 49N 15 13E
20 Deux-Sèvres □ 46 30N 0 20W
40 Deva 45 53N 22 55E
62 Devakottai 9 57N 78 49E
27 Dévaványa 47 2N 20 58E
16 Deventer 52 15N 6 10E
14 Deveron, R. 57 22N 3 0W
60 Devgad Baria 22 42N 73 54E
100 Devils Lake 48 7N 98 59W
13 Devizes 51 22N 1 59W
41 Devnya 43 13N 27 33E
92 Devon 53 22N 113 44W
13 Devon □ 50 45N 3 50W
86 Devon I. 75 0N 87 0W
80 Devonport, Australia 41 11S 146 21E
85 Devonport, N.Z. 36 49S 174 48E
13 Devonport, U.K. 50 22N 4 10W
60 Dewas 22 57N 76 4E
12 Dewsbury 53 42N 1 37W
57 Deyhūk 33 17N 57 30E
57 Deyyer 27 50N 51 55E
56 Dezfūl 32 23N 48 24E
56 Dezh Shāhpūr 35 31N 46 10E
56 Dhahaban 21 58N 39 3E
56 Dhahran= Az Zahrān 26 10N 50 7E
55 Dhamar 14 46N 44 23E
60 Dhampur 29 19N 78 31E
61 Dhamtari 20 42N 81 33E
61 Dhanbad 23 47N 86 26E
60 Dhar 22 36N 75 18E
60 Dharangaon 21 1N 75 16E
62 Dharapuram 10 44N 77 32E
62 Dharmapuri 12 8N 78 10E
62 Dharmavaram 14 25N 77 44E
60 Dharmsala 32 23N 76 19E
62 Dharwar 15 28N 75 1E
61 Dhaulagiri, Mt. 28 42N 83 31E
61 Dhenkanal 20 45N 85 35E
43 Dhenoúsa, I. 37 8N 25 48E
43 Dhesfina 38 25N 22 31E
42 Dhidhimotikhon 41 21N 26 30E
43 Dhimitsána 37 37N 22 3E
43 Dhodhekánisos, Is. 36 35N 27 10E
60 Dholka 22 44N 72 27E
60 Dholpur 26 42N 77 54E
62 Dhond 18 26N 74 40E
60 Dhrangadhra 23 0N 71 30E
60 Dhrol 22 34N 70 25E
61 Dhubri 26 1N 89 59E
55 Dhula 15 5N 48 5E
60 Dhulia 20 54N 74 47E
108 Diamante 32 5S 60 35W
111 Diamantina 18 5S 43 40W
80 Diamantina, R. 26 45S 139 10E
111 Diamantino 14 25S 56 27W
60 Dibai 28 13N 78 15E
74 Dibaya Lubue 4 12S 19 54E
57 Dibba 25 45N 56 16E
55 Dibi 4 12N 41 58E
59 Dibrugarh 27 29N 94 55E
100 Dickinson 46 53N 102 47W
97 Dickson City 41 27N 75 37W
92 Didsbury 51 40N 114 8W
60 Didwana 27 24N 74 34E
21 Die 44 45N 5 22E
93 Diefenbaker L. 51 0N 106 55W
3 Diego Garcia, I. 7 20S 72 25E
112 Diego Ramirez, Is. 56 30S 68 44W
75 Diégo-Suarez 12 16S 49 17E
63 Dien Bien Phu 21 23N 103 1E
24 Diepholz 52 35N 8 21E
18 Dieppe 49 56N 1 5E
16 Differdange 49 32N 5 32E
91 Digby 44 41N 65 50W
59 Dighinala 23 15N 92 5E
21 Digne 44 6N 6 14E
20 Digoin 46 29N 3 59E
59 Dihang, R. 27 30N 96 30E
56 Dijlah, Nahr 30 90N 47 50E
19 Dijon 47 19N 5 1E
50 Dikson 73 30N 80 35E
73 Dikwa 12 2N 13 56E
63 Di Linh, Cao Nguyen 11 35N 108 4E
65 Dili 8 33S 125 35E
24 Dillenburg 50 44N 8 17E
102 Dillon, Mont. 45 13N 112 38W
99 Dillon, S.C. 34 25N 79 22W
56 Dimashq 33 30N 36 18E
72 Dimbokro 6 39N 4 42W
84 Dimboola 36 27S 142 2E
41 Dîmbovnic, R. 44 28N 25 18E
41 Dimitrovgrad, Bulgaria 42 3N 25 36E
48 Dimitrovgrad, U.S.S.R. 54 25N 49 33E
40 Dimitrovgrad, Yug. 43 1N 22 47E
40 Dimovo 43 43N 22 50E
65 Dinagat, I. 10 10N 125 35E
61 Dinajpur 35 38N 88 38E
18 Dinan 48 27N 2 2W
16 Dinant 50 16N 4 55E
61 Dinapore 25 38N 85 5E
56 Dinar 38 4N 30 10E
57 Dinar, Kuh-e, Mt. 30 48N 51 40E
37 Dinara Planina, Mts. 43 50N 16 35E

18 Dinard 48 38N 2 4W
9 Dinaric Alps, Mts. 43 50N 16 35W
62 Dindigul 10 21N 77 58 E
15 Dingle 52 8N 10 15W
15 Dingle, B. 52 5N 10 15W
80 Dingo 23 39S 149 20 E
72 Dinguiraye 11 18N 10 43W
14 Dingwall 57 35N 4 29W
102 Dinosaur Nat. Mon. 40 32N 108 58W
103 Dinuba 36 32N 119 23W
27 Diósgyör 48 7N 20 43 E
72 Diourbel 14 40N 16 15W
65 Dipolog 8 36N 123 20 E
55 Dire Dawa 9 37N 41 52 E
105 Diriamba 11 53N 86 15W
83 Dirk Hartog, I. 25 48S 113 0 E
81 Dirranbandi 28 35S 148 14 E
102 Disappointment.C. 46 18N 124 3W
82 Disappointment, L. 23 30S 122 50 E
88 Discovery 63 0N 115 0W
84 Discovery, B. 38 12S 141 7 E
4 Disko, I. 69 50N 53 30W
13 Diss 52 23N 1 6 E
58 Disteghil Sar, Mt. 36 22N 75 12 E
111 Districto Federal □ 15 45S 47 45W
104 Distrito Federal □ 19 15N 99 10W
60 Diu 20 43N 70 69 E
18 Dives 49 18N 0 8W
18 Dives, R. 48 55N 0 5W
49 Divnoye 45 55N 43 27 E
100 Dixon 41 50N 89 29W
92 Dixon Entrance 54 25N 132 30W
56 Diyarbakir 37 55N 40 14 E
74 Djambala 2 33S 14 45 E
64 Djangeru 2 20S 116 29 E
72 Djelfa 34 30N 3 20 E
74 Djema 6 3N 25 19 E
73 Djerba, I. de 33 56N 11 0 E
72 Djerid, Chott el, Reg. 35 50N 8 30 E
55 Djibouti 11 36N 43 9 E
72 Djidjelli 36 52N 5 50 E
74 Djolu 0 37N 22 21 E
72 Djougou 9 42N 1 40 E
73 Djourab, Erg du 16 40N 18 50 E
74 Djugu 1 55N 30 30 E
46 Djúpivogur 64 40N 14 10W
44 Djursholm 59 24N 18 5 E
45 Djursland, Reg. 56 27N 10 40 E
49 Dnepr, R. 46 30N 32 18 E
49 Dneprodzerzhinsk 48 30N 34 37 E
49 Dnepropetrovsk 48 30N 35 0 E
49 Dnestr, R. 46 18N 30 17 E
49 Dnieper, R.= Dnepr, R. 46 30N 32 18 E
49 Dniester, R.= Dnestr, R. 46 18N 30 17 E
73 Doba 8 39N 16 51 E
24 Döbeln 51 7N 13 7 E
65 Dobo 5 46S 134 13 E
40 Doboj 44 44N 18 6 E
40 Dobra 45 54N 22 36 E
41 Dobruja, Reg. 44 30N 28 30 E
44 Döda Fallet. 63 4N 16 35 E
62 Dodballapur 13 18N 77 32 E
101 Dodge City 37 45N 100 1W
74 Dodoma 6 11S 35 45 E
93 Dodsland 51 48N 108 49W
16 Doetinchem 51 58N 6 17 E
41 Doftana 45 17N 25 45 E
92 Dog Creek 51 35N 122 18W
57 Doha 25 15N 51 36 E
60 Dohad 22 50N 74 15 E
59 Dohazari 22 10N 92 5 E
63 Doi Luang, Ra. 18 20N 101 30 E
40 Dojransko, J. 41 11N 22 44 E
18 Dol 48 34N 1 47W
91 Dolbeau 48 53N 72 14W
21 Dôle 47 6N 5 30 E
12 Dolgellau 52 44N 3 53W
38 Dolianova 39 23N 9 11 E
74 Dolisie 4 12S 12 41 E
41 Dolni Dŭbnik 43 24N 24 26 E
37 Dolo, Italy 45 25N 12 5 E
55 Dolo, Somali Rep. 4 13N 42 8 E
37 Dolomiti, Mts. 46 25N 11 50 E
108 Dolores, Arg. 36 19S 57 40W
108 Dolores, Uruguay 33 33S 58 13W
112 Dolphin, C. 51 15S 58 58W
88 Dolphin & Union Str. 69 5N 114 45W
109 Dom Pedrito 31 0S 54 40W
50 Dombarovskiy 50 46N 59 39 E
44 Dombås 62 5N 9 8 E
19 Dombasle 48 38N 6 21 E
21 Dombes, Reg. 46 0N 5 3 E
108 Domeyko, Cord. 24 30S 69 0W
18 Domfront 48 37N 0 4W
105 Dominica, I. 15 30N 61 20W
105 Dominica Pass 15 10N 61 20W
105 Dominican Rep. ■ 19 0N 70 40W
36 Domodossola 46 7N 8 17 E
19 Dompaire 48 13N 6 13 E
12 Don, R., Eng. 53 39N 0 59W
14 Don, R., Scot. 57 10N 2 4W
49 Don, R., U.S.S.R. 47 4N 39 18 E
31 Don Benito 38 57N 5 52W
15 Donaghadee 54 39N 5 33W
8 Donald 36 22S 143 0 E
92 Donalda 52 35N 112 34W
25 Donauwörth 48 43N 10 46 E
26 Donawitz 47 22N 15 4 E
12 Doncaster 53 32N 1 7W
62 Dondra Hd. 5 55N 80 35 E
15 Donegal 54 39N 8 7W
15 Donegal □ 54 50N 0 8W
15 Donegal, B. 54 30N 8 30W
49 Donetsk 48 0N 37 48 E
63 Dong Hoi 17 18N 106 36 E
83 Dongara 29 15S 114 56 E
61 Dongargarh 21 11N 80 45 E
18 Donges 47 18N 2 4W
73 Dongola 19 9N 30 22 E
40 Donji Vakuf 44 8N 17 25 E
91 Donnacona 46 40N 71 47W
85 Donnelly's Crossing 35 43S 173 33 E
83 Donnybrook 33 35S 115 48 E
96 Donora 40 11N 79 52W
80 Donor's Hills 18 42S 140 33 E
83 Doodlakine 31 35S 117 28 E
14 Doon, R. 55 26N 4 38W
54 Dor 32 37N 34 55 E
13 Dorchester 50 43N 2 26W
89 Dorchester, C. 65 29N 77 30W
20 Dordogne □ 45 10N 0 45 E
20 Dordogne, R. 45 2N 0 35W
16 Dordrecht 51 49N 107 45W
93 Dore Lake 54 56N 107 45W
90 Dorion 45 23N 74 3W
37 Dornberg 45 45N 13 50 E
26 Dornbirn 47 25N 9 44 E
14 Dornie 57 17N 5 30W
14 Dornoch 57 52N 4 2W
14 Dornoch Firth 57 52N 4 2W
67 Döröö Nuur, L. 47 40N 93 30 E
83 Dorre, I. 25 9S 113 7 E
81 Dorrigo 30 21S 152 43 E
13 Dorset □ 50 47N 2 20W
24 Dorsten 51 39N 6 58 E
24 Dortmund 51 31N 7 28 E
112 Dos Bahias, C. 44 55S 65 32W
31 Dos Hermanas 37 17N 5 55W
57 Doshi 35 37N 68 41 E
72 Dosso 13 3N 3 12 E
92 Dot 50 12N 121 25W
99 Dothan 31 13N 85 24W
19 Douai 50 22N 3 4 E
72 Douala 4 3N 9 42 E
18 Douarnenez 48 6N 4 20W
26 Doubrava, R. 49 40N 15 30 E
19 Doubs □ 47 10N 6 25 E
85 Doubtless, B. 34 55S 173 27 E
90 Doucet 48 15N 76 35W
12 Douglas, U.K. 54 9N 4 25W
103 Douglas, Ariz 31 21N 109 33W
99 Douglas, Ga. 31 31N 82 51W
100 Douglas, Wyo. 42 45N 105 24W
43 Doukáton, Ákra, Pt. 38 34N 20 30 E
19 Doulevant 48 22N 4 53 E
19 Doullens 50 9N 2 21 E
14 Dounreay 58 40N 3 28W
111 Dourada, Sa. 13 10S 48 45W
30 Douro, R. 41 8N 8 40W
29 Douro Litoral, Reg. 41 5N 8 20W
20 Douze, R. 43 54N 0 30W
12 Dove, R. 54 20N 0 55W
80 Dover, Australia 43 19S 147 1 E
13 Dover, U.K. 51 8N 1 19 E
98 Dover, Del. 39 10N 75 32W
97 Dover, N.H. 43 12N 70 56W
97 Dover, N.J. 40 53N 74 34W
97 Dover Plains 41 44N 73 35W
13 Dovey, R. 52 32N 4 0W
44 Dovrefjell, Mts. 62 6N 9 25 E
98 Dowagiac 41 59N 86 6W
57 Dowlātābad 28 18N 56 40 E
15 Down □ 54 24N 5 55W
13 Downham Market 52 36N 0 23 E
15 Downpatrick 54 20N 5 43W
97 Doylestown 40 19N 75 8W
21 Drac, R. 45 13N 5 41 E
41 Drăgăneşti Olt. 44 10N 24 32 E
41 Drăgănesti Vlaşca 44 6N 25 36 E
41 Drăgăşani 44 40N 24 16 E
40 Dragina 44 30N 19 25 E
40 Dragocvet 44 0N 21 15 E
21 Draguignan 43 32N 6 28 E
5 Drake Pass. 58 0S 70 0W
75 Drakensberg, Mts. 27 0S 30 0 E
42 Dráma 41 9N 24 8 E
42 Dráma □ 41 9N 24 8 E
44 Drammen 59 44N 10 15 E
26 Drau, R.= Drava R. 45 33N 18 55 E
37 Drava, R. 45 33N 18 55 E
19 Draveil 48 41N 2 25 E
92 Drayton Valley 53 13N 114 59W
16 Drenthe □ 52 45N 6 30 E
24 Dresden 51 3N 13 44 E
24 Dresden □ 51 10N 14 0 E
18 Dreux 48 44N 1 22 E
12 Driffield 54 0N 0 27W
40 Drin, R. 41 60N 19 32 E
42 Drin-i-zi 41 37N 20 28 E
37 Drniš 43 51N 16 10 E
15 Drogheda 53 43N 6 21W
49 Drogobych 49 20N 23 30 E
13 Droitwich 52 16N 2 9W
21 Drôme □ 44 35N 5 10 E
21 Drôme, R. 44 46N 4 46 E
84 Dromedary, C. 36 17S 150 10 E
80 Dronfield 53 19S 1 27W
20 Dronne, R. 45 2N 0 9W
5 Dronning Maud Ld. 75 0S 10 0 E
26 Drosendorf 48 52N 15 37 E
84 Drouin 38 8S 145 51 E
92 Drumheller 51 28N 112 42W
90 Drummondville 45 53N 72 30W
51 Druzhina 68 11N 14S 19 E
28 Drwęca R. 53 0N 18 42 E
41 Dryanovo 42 59N 25 28 E
93 Dryden 49 47N 92 50W
82 Drysdale, R. 13 59S 126 51 E
96 Du Bois 41 7N 78 46W
100 Du Quoin 38 0N 89 10W
80 Duaringa 23 42S 149 42 E
56 Dubā 27 10N 35 40 E
88 Dubawnt L. 63 0N 102 0W
57 Dubayy 25 18N 55 18 E
84 Dubbo 32 15S 148 36 E
15 Dublin, Eire 53 20N 6 15W
99 Dublin, U.S.A. 32 32N 82 54W
15 Dublin □ 53 20N 6 15W
102 Dubois 44 10N 112 14W
49 Dubovka 49 5N 44 50 E
61 Dubrajpur 23 48N 87 23 E
72 Dubreka 9 48N 13 31W
40 Dubrovnik 42 38N 18 7 E
51 Dubrovskoye 47 28N 42 40 E
100 Dubuque 42 30N 90 41W
102 Duchesne 40 10N 110 24W
80 Duchess 21 22S 139 52 E
77 Ducie I. 24 47S 124 50W
93 Duck Lake 52 47N 106 13W
93 Duck Mt. Prov. Park 51 36N 100 55W
24 Duderstadt 51 31N 10 16 E
51 Dudinka 69 25N 86 15 E
13 Dudley 52 30N 2 5W
62 Dudna, R. 19 17N 76 54 E
30 Dueñas 41 52N 4 33W
30 Duero, R. 41 37N 4 25W
14 Dufftown 57 26N 3 9W
37 Dugi Otok, I. 44 0N 15 0 E
37 Dugo Selo 45 51N 16 18 E
24 Duisburg 51 27N 6 42 E
57 Dukhan 25 25N 50 50 E
72 Duku 10 43N 10 43 E
105 Dulce, G. 8 40N 83 20W
41 Dulgopol 43 3N 27 22 E
24 Dülmen 51 49N 7 18 E
41 Dulovo 43 48N 27 9 E
80 Dululu 23 48S 150 15 E
100 Duluth 46 48N 92 10W
61 Dum-Dum 22 39N 88 26 E
59 Dum Duma 27 40N 95 40 E
64 Dumai 1 35N 101 20 E
101 Dumas 35 50N 101 58W
14 Dumbarton 55 58N 4 35W
83 Dumbleyung 33 17S 117 42 E
41 Dumbrăveni 46 14N 24 34 E
14 Dumfries 55 4N 3 37W
14 Dumfries-Galloway □ 55 12N 3 30W
84 Dumosa 35 52S 143 6 E
73 Dumyāt 31 25N 31 48 E
15 Dun Laoghaire 53 17N 6 9W
27 Dunaföldvár 46 50N 18 57 E
41 Dunarea= Donau, R. 45 20N 29 40 E
27 Dunaújváros 47 0N 18 57 E
40 Dunav 45 0N 20 21 E
40 Dunavtsi 42 57N 22 53 E
85 Dunback 42 23S 170 36 E
14 Dunbar 56 0N 2 32W
93 Dunblane, Canada 51 11N 106 52W
14 Dunblane, U.K. 56 10N 3 58W
92 Duncan, Canada 48 45N 123 40W
101 Duncan, U.S.A. 34 25N 98 0W
63 Duncan Pass. 11 0N 92 30 E
105 Duncan Town 22 20N 75 80W
96 Dundalk, Canada 44 10N 80 24W
15 Dundalk, U.K. 53 55N 6 45W
90 Dundas 43 17N 79 59W
83 Dundas, L. 32 35S 121 50 E
82 Dundas, Str. 11 15S 131 35 E
75 Dundee, S. Africa 28 11S 30 15 E
14 Dundee, U.K. 56 29N 3 0W
15 Dundrum 54 17N 5 50W
15 Dundrum, B. 54 12N 5 40W
60 Dundwara 27 48N 79 9 E
85 Dunedin 45 50S 170 33 E
14 Dunfermline 56 5N 3 28W
15 Dungannon 54 30N 6 47W
15 Dungannon □ 54 30N 6 47W
60 Dungarpur 23 52N 73 45 E
15 Dungarvan 52 6N 7 40W
67 Dunbure Shan, Mts. 35 0N 90 0 E
13 Dungeness, Pt. 50 54N 0 59 E
74 Dungu 3 42N 28 32 E
84 Dunkeld, Australia 37 40S 142 22 E
14 Dunkeld, U.K. 56 34N 3 36W
19 Dunkerque 51 2N 2 20 E
13 Dunkery Beacon 51 15N 3 37W
96 Dunkirk 42 30N 79 18W
72 Dunkwa 6 0N 1 47W
80 Dunmara 16 42S 133 25 E
97 Dunmore 41 27N 75 38W
15 Dunmore Hd. 53 37N 8 44W
99 Dunn 35 18N 78 36W
14 Dunnet Hd. 58 38N 3 22W
96 Dunnville 42 57N 79 37W
14 Dunoon 55 57N 4 56W
14 Duns 55 47N 2 20W
102 Dunsmuir 41 0N 122 10W
13 Dunstable 51 53N 0 31W
109 Duque de Caxias 22 45S 43 19W
96 Duquesne 40 22N 79 55W
85 D'Urville, I. 40 50S 173 55 E
54 Dūrā 31 30N 35 2 E
82 Durack, R. 15 33S 127 52 E
21 Durance, R. 43 55N 4 44 E
104 Durango, Mexico 24 3N 104 39W
30 Durango, Sp. 43 13N 2 40W
103 Durango, U.S.A. 37 10N 107 50W
104 Durango □ 25 0N 105 0W
83 Duranillin 33 30S 116 45 E
101 Durant 34 0N 96 25W
30 Duratón, R. 41 37N 4 7W
108 Durazno 33 25S 56 38W
75 Durban 29 49S 31 1 E
31 Durcal 37 0N 3 34W
40 Durdevac 46 2N 17 3 E
24 Düren 50 48N 6 30 E
61 Durg 21 15N 81 22 E
90 Durham, Canada 44 10N 80 48W
12 Durham, U.K. 54 47N 1 34W
99 Durham, U.S.A. 36 0N 78 55W
12 Durham □ 54 42N 1 45W
40 Durmitor, Mt. 43 18N 19 0 E
42 Durrësi 41 19N 19 28 E
18 Durtal 47 40N 0 18W
97 Duryea 41 20N 75 45W
50 Dushak 37 20N 60 10 E
50 Dushanbe 38 40N 68 50 E
85 Dusky, Sd. 45 47S 166 29 E
24 Düsseldorf 51 15N 6 46 E
88 Dutch Harbor 53 54N 166 35W
56 Duzce 40 50N 31 10 E
41 Dve Mogili 43 47N 25 55 E
48 Drinskaya Guba 65 0N 39 45 E
26 Dvur Králové 50 27N 15 50 E
60 Dwarka 22 18N 69 8 E
83 Dwellingup 32 38S 115 58 E
5 Dyer Plat. 70 0S 65 0W
101 Dyersburg 36 2N 89 20W
13 Dyfed □ 52 0N 4 30W
48 Dzerzhinsk 56 15N 43 15 E
50 Dzhalal Abad 41 0N 73 0 E
51 Dzhalinda 53 50N 124 0 E
50 Dzhambul 43 10N 71 0 E
49 Dzhankoi 45 40N 34 30 E
51 Dzhardzhan 68 43N 124 2 E
51 Dzhelinde 70 0N 114 20 E
50 Dzhezkazgan 47 10N 67 40 E
50 Dzhizak 40 20N 68 0 E
51 Dzhugdzur Khrebet, Ra. 57 30N 138 0 E
28 Działdowo 53 15N 20 15 E
27 Dzierżoniow 50 45N 16 39 E
67 Dzungaria, Reg. 44 10N 88 0 E
67 Dzungarian Gate= Dzungarskiye Vorota 45 25N 82 25 E
67 Dzungarskiye Vorota 45 25N 82 25 E
68 Dzuunbulag 46 58N 115 30 E
68 Dzuunmod 47 45N 106 58 E

E

88 Eagle 64 44N 141 29W
101 Eagle Pass 28 45N 100 35W

84 Eaglehawk 36 43S 144 16E
13 Ealing 51 30N 0 19W
103 Earlimart 35 57N 119 14W
14 Earn, L. 56 23N 4 14W
85 Earnslaw, Mt. 44 32S 168 27E
99 Easley 34 52N 82 35W
85 East, C. 37 42S 178 35E
91 East Angus 45 30N 71 40W
96 East Aurora 42 46N 78 38W
88 East C. 65 50N 168 0W
98 East Chicago 41 40N 87 30W
112 East Falkland 51 30S 58 30W
24 East Germany ■ 52 0N 12 30E
100 East Grand Forks 47 55N 97 5W
97 East Hartford 41 45N 72 39W
52 East Indies, Is. 0 0 120 0E
14 East Kilbride 55 48N 4 12W
98 East Lansing 42 44N 84 37W
96 East Liverpool 40 39N 80 35W
75 East London 33 0S 27 55E
90 East Main 52 20N 78 30W
97 East Orange 40 45N 74 15W
96 East Palestine 40 50N 80 32W
92 East Pine 55 48N 120 5W
99 East Point 33 40N 84 28W
97 East Providence 41 48N 71 22W
12 East Retford 53 19N 0 55W
100 East St. Lovis 38 36N 90 10W
51 East Siberian Sea 73 0N 160 0E
13 East Sussex □ 50 55N 0 20E
85 Eastbourne, N.Z. 41 19S 174 55E
13 Eastbourne, U.K. 50 46N 0 18E
93 Eastend 49 32N 108 50W
77 Easter Is. 27 0S 109 0W
62 Eastern Ghats, Mts. 15 0N 80 0E
64 Eastern Malaysia □ 3 0N 112 30E
13 Eastleigh 50 58N 1 21W
90 Eastmain, R. 52 20N 78 30W
97 Easton 40 41N 75 15W
91 Eastport 44 57N 67 0W
90 Eastview 45 27N 75 40W
93 Eatonia 51 20N 109 25W
97 Eatontown 40 18N 74 7W
100 Eau Claire 44 46N 91 30W
13 Ebbw Vale 51 47N 3 12W
84 Ebden 36 10S 147 1E
26 Ebensee 47 48N 13 46E
25 Eberbach 49 27N 8 59E
24 Eberswalde 52 49N 13 50E
25 Ebingen 48 13N 9 1E
39 Eboli 40 39N 15 2E
30 Ebro, Pantano del, L. 43 0N 3 58W
29 Ebro, R. 40 43N 0 54E
84 Echuca 36 3S 144 46E
31 Ecija 37 30N 5 10W
24 Eckernförde 54 26N 9 50E
18 Écommoy 47 50N 0 16E
110 Ecuador ■ 2 0S 78 0W
73 Ed Dâmer 17 27N 34 0E
73 Ed Debba 18 0N 30 51E
73 Ed Dueim 10 10N 28 20E
83 Edah 28 16S 117 10E
16 Edam 52 31N 5 3E
62 Edapally 11 19N 78 3E
14 Eday, I. 59 11N 2 47W
13 Eddystone Rock 50 11N 4 16W
16 Ede 52 4N 5 40E
12 Eden, R. 54 57N 3 1W
15 Edenderry 53 21N 7 3W
24 Eder, R. 51 13N 9 27E
13 Edge Hill 52 7N 1 28W
100 Edgeley 46 27N 98 41W
100 Edgemont 43 15N 103 53W
42 Edhessa 40 48N 22 5E
85 Edievale 45 49S 169 22E
101 Edinburg 26 22N 98 10W
14 Edinburgh 55 57N 3 12W
56 Edirne 41 40N 26 45E
82 Edith River 14 12S 132 2E
101 Edmond 35 37N 97 30W
80 Edmonton, Australia 17 2S 145 45E
92 Edmonton, Canada 53 30N 113 30W
91 Edmundston 47 23N 68 20W
56 Edremit 39 40N 27 0E
92 Edson 53 40N 116 28W
74 Edward, L.=Idi Amin Dada, L. 0 25S 29 40E
5 Edward VII Pen. 80 0S 160 0W
101 Edwards Plat. 30 30N 101 5W
97 Edwardsville 41 15N 75 56W
16 Eekloo 51 11N 3 33E
26 Eferding 48 18N 14 1E
98 Effingham 39 8N 88 30W
41 Eforie Sud 44 1N 28 37E
38 Égadi, Is. 37 55N 12 10E
90 Eganville 45 32N 77 5W
27 Eger 47 53N 20 27E
26 Eger=Cheb 50 1N 12 25E
26 Eggenburg 48 38N 15 50E
82 Eginbah 20 53S 119 47E
85 Egmont, Mt. 39 17S 174 5E
51 Egvekind 66 19N 179 10W
73 Egypt ■ 28 0N 31 0E
26 Ehrwald 47 24N 10 56E
66 Ehime □ 33 30N 132 40E
25 Eichstatt 48 53N 11 12E
81 Eidsvold 25 25S 151 12E
25 Eifel, Mts. 50 10N 6 45E
47 Eigersund 58 2N 66 1E
14 Eigg, I. 56 54N 6 10W
82 Eighty Mile Beach 19 30S 120 40E
14 Eil, L. 56 50N 5 15E
84 Eildon, L. 37 10S 146 0E
24 Eilenburg 51 28N 12 38E
80 Einasleigh 18 32S 144 5E
24 Einbeck 51 48N 9 50E
16 Eindhoven 51 26N 5 30E
15 Eire ■ 53 0N 8 0E
24 Eisenach 50 58N 10 18E
25 Eisenberg 50 59N 11 50E
26 Eisenerz 47 32N 15 54E
24 Eisenhüttenstadt 52 9N 14 41E
26 Eisenkappel 46 29N 14 36E
24 Eisleben 51 31N 11 31E
54 Eizariya 31 47N 35 15E
30 Eje, Sa. del 42 24N 6 54W
32 Ejea de los Caballeros 42 7N 1 9W
47 Ekenäs 59 58N 23 26E
85 Eketahuna 40 38S 175 43E
50 Ekibastuz 51 40N 75 22E
51 Ekimchan 53 0N 133 0W
45 Eksjö 57 40N 14 58W
72 El Aaiun 27 0N 12 0W
73 El Alamein 30 48N 28 58E
31 El Arahal 37 15N 5 33W
72 El Aricha 34 13N 1 16W
54 El Ariha 31 52N 35 27E
80 El Arish 17 49S 146 1E
73 El'Arîsh 31 8N 33 50E
72 El Asnam 36 10N 1 20E
30 El Astillero 43 24N 3 49W
30 El Barco de Avila 40 21N 5 31W
30 El Barco de Valdeorras 42 23N 7 0W
73 El Bawiti 28 25N 28 45E
72 El Bayadh 33 40N 1 1E
33 El Bonillo 38 57N 2 35W
103 El Cajon 32 49N 117 0W
101 El Campo 29 10N 96 20W
103 El Centro 32 50N 115 40W
112 El Cuy 39 55S 68 25W
55 El Dere 3 50N 47 8E
110 El Diviso 1 22N 78 14W
72 El Djouf 20 0N 11 30E
101 El Dorado, Ark. 33 10N 92 40W
101 El Dorado, Kans. 37 55N 96 56W
110 El Dorado, Venezuela 6 55N 61 30W
30 El Escorial 40 35N 4 7W
73 El Faiyûm 29 19N 30 50E
73 El Fâsher 13 33N 25 26E
30 El Ferrol 43 29N 3 14W
73 El Geneina 13 27N 22 45E
73 El Geteina 14 50N 32 27E
73 El Gezira 14 0N 33 0E
73 El Gîza 30 0N 31 10E
72 El Goléa 30 30N 2 50E
72 El Harrach 36 45N 3 5E
73 El Iskandarîya 31 0N 30 0E
73 El Istwâ'ya □ 5 0N 32 0E
72 El Jadida 33 16N 9 31W
73 El Jebelein 12 30N 32 45E
72 El Kef 36 12N 8 47E
73 El Khandaq 18 30N 30 30E
73 El Khârga 25 30N 30 33E
73 El Khartûm 15 31N 32 35E
73 El Khartum Bahrî 15 40N 32 31E
73 El Mafâza 13 38N 34 30E
73 El Mahalla el Kubra 31 0N 31 0E
73 El Mansura 31 0N 31 19E
73 El Minyâ 28 7N 30 33E
30 El Molar 40 42N 3 45W
74 El Niybo 4 32N 39 59E
73 El Obeid 13 8N 30 18E
104 El Oro 3 30S 79 50W
72 El Oued 33 20N 6 58E
32 El Panadés 41 10N 1 30E
103 El Paso 31 50N 106 30W
31 El Pedroso 37 51N 5 45W
32 El Prat de Llobregat 41 18N 2 3E
104 El Progreso 15 26N 87 51W
73 El Qâhira 30 1N 31 14E
73 El Qantara 30 51N 32 20E
73 El Qasr 25 44N 28 42E
73 El Qubba 11 10N 27 5E
101 El Reno 35 30N 98 0W
30 El Ribero 42 30N 8 30W
73 El Suweis 29 58N 32 31E
110 El Tigre 8 55N 64 15W
110 El Tocuyo 9 47N 69 48W
112 El Turbio 51 30S 72 40W
73 El Uqsur 25 41N 32 38E
32 El Vallés 41 35N 2 20E
110 El Vigia 8 38N 71 39W
73 El Wâhat el-Dakhla 26 0N 27 50E
73 El Wâhât el Khârga 24 0N 23 0E
84 Elaine 37 44S 144 2E
54 Elat 5 40S 133 5E
56 Elazig 38 37N 39 22E
36 Elba, I. 42 48N 10 15E
42 Elbasani 41 9N 20 9E
42 Elbasani-Berati □ 40 58N 20 0E
24 Elbe, R. 53 50N 9 0E
103 Elbert, Mt. 39 12N 106 36W
99 Elberton 34 7N 82 51W
18 Elbeuf 49 17N 1 2E
28 Elbląg 54 10N 19 25E
28 Elbląg □ 54 20N 19 30E
49 Elbrus, Mt. 43 30N 42 30E
52 Elburz Mts.= Alberz, Reshteh-Ye-Kakha-Ye 36 0N 52 0E
33 Elche 38 15N 0 42W
33 Elche de la Sierra 38 27N 2 3W
33 Elda 38 29N 0 47W
109 Eldorado, Arg. 26 28S 54 43W
93 Eldorado, Canada 59 35N 108 30W
74 Eldoret 0 30N 35 25E
103 Elephant Butte Res. 33 45N 107 30W
5 Elephant I. 61 0S 55 0W
105 Eleuthera I. 25 0N 76 20W
43 Elevsis 38 4N 23 26E
42 Elevtheroúpolis 40 52N 24 20E
14 Elgin, U.K. 57 39N 3 20W
98 Elgin, Ill. 42 0N 88 20W
102 Elgin, Ore. 45 37N 118 0W
100 Elgin, Tex. 30 21N 97 22W
74 Elgon, Mt. 1 10N 34 30E
65 Eliase 8 10S 130 55E
49 Elista 46 16N 44 14E
81 Elizabeth, Australia 34 45S 138 39E
97 Elizabeth, U.S.A. 40 37N 74 12W
99 Elizabeth City 36 18N 76 16W
99 Elizabethton 36 20N 82 13W
98 Elizabethtown, Ky. 37 40N 85 54W
97 Elizabethtown, Pa. 40 8N 76 36W
75 Elizabethville= Lubumbashi 11 32S 27 38E
32 Elizondo 43 12N 1 30W
28 Ełk 53 50N 22 22E
101 Elk City 35 25N 99 25W
90 Elk Lake 47 40N 80 25W
93 Elk Point 54 10N 110 55W
98 Elkhart 41 42N 85 55W
93 Elkhorn 50 0N 101 11W
41 Elkhovo 42 10N 26 40E
98 Elkins 38 53N 79 53W
92 Elko, Canada 49 20N 115 10W
102 Elko, U.S.A. 40 40N 115 50W
103 Ellen Mt. 38 4N 110 56W
82 Ellendale, Australia 17 56S 124 48E
100 Ellendale, U.S.A. 46 3N 98 30W
102 Ellensburg 47 0N 120 30W
97 Ellenville 41 42N 74 23W
86 Ellesmere I. 79 30N 80 0W
12 Ellesmere Port 53 17N 2 55W
76 Ellice Is= Tuvalu ■ 8 0S 176 0E
90 Elliot Lake 46 35N 82 35W
80 Elliott 41 5S 145 38E
81 Elliston 33 39S 134 55E
14 Ellon 57 21N 2 5W
62 Ellore=Eluru 16 48N 81 8E
100 Ellsworth 38 47N 98 15W
5 Ellsworth Ld. 75 30S 80 0W
5 Ellsworth Mts. 79 0S 85 0W
25 Ellwangen 48 57N 10 9E
96 Ellwood City 40 52N 80 19W
102 Elma 47 0N 123 30E
56 Elmali 36 44N 29 56E
98 Elmhurst 41 52N 87 58W
96 Elmira 42 8N 76 49W
84 Elmore 36 30S 144 37E
24 Elmshorn 53 44N 9 40E
20 Elne 42 36N 2 58E
19 Éloyes 48 6N 6 36E
93 Elrose 51 20N 108 0W
103 Elsinore 33 40N 117 15W
24 Elsterwerda 51 27N 13 32E
85 Eltham 39 26S 174 19E
62 Eluru 16 48N 81 8E
31 Elvas 38 50N 7 17W
98 Elwood 40 20N 85 50W
100 Ely 47 54N 91 52W
54 Elyashiv 32 23N 34 55E
96 Elyria 41 22N 82 8W
50 Emba 48 50N 58 8E
21 Embrun 44 34N 6 30E
74 Embu 0 32S 37 38E
24 Emden 53 22N 7 12E
80 Emerald 23 30S 148 11E
93 Emerson 49 0N 97 10W
36 Emilia Romagna □ 44 33N 10 40E
24 Emlichheim 52 37N 6 51E
45 Emmaboda 56 37N 15 32E
97 Emmaus 40 32N 75 30W
16 Emmen 52 48N 6 57E
24 Emmerich 51 50N 6 12E
102 Emmett 24 45S 144 30W
62 Emmiganuru 15 45N 77 30E
104 Empalme 28 1N 110 49W
75 Empangeni 28 50S 31 52E
36 Empoli 43 43N 10 57E
100 Emporia, Kans. 38 25N 96 16W
99 Emporia, Va. 36 41N 77 32W
96 Emporium 41 30N 78 17W
24 Ems, R. 51 9N 9 26E
24 Emsdetten 52 11N 7 31E
54 'En Kerem 31 47N 35 6E
73 En Nahud 12 45N 28 25E
54 'En Yahav 30 37N 35 11E
66 Ena 35 25N 137 25E
109 Encarnación 27 15S 56 0W
104 Encarnación de Diaz 21 30N 102 20W
110 Encontrados 9 3N 72 14W
63 Endau 2 40N 103 38E
65 Ende 8 45S 121 30E
80 Endeavour, Str. 10 45S 142 0E
92 Enderby 50 35N 119 10W
82 Enderby, I. 20 35S 116 30E
5 Enderby Ld. 66 0S 53 0E
97 Endicott 42 6N 76 2W
27 Endröd 46 55N 20 47E
13 Enfield 51 38N 0 4W
25 Engadin 46 30N 9 55E
105 Engaño, C., Dom. Rep. 18 30N 68 20W
65 Engaño, C., Philippines 18 35N 122 23E
48 Engels 51 28N 46 6E
64 Enggano 5 20S 102 40E
11 England ■ 53 0N 2 0W
91 Englee 50 45N 56 5W
90 Englehart 47 49N 79 52W
100 Englewood, Colo. 39 39N 104 59W
97 Englewood, N.J. 40 54N 73 59W
93 English, R. 50 12N 95 0W
61 English Bazar 24 58N 88 21E
8 English Chan. 50 0N 2 0W
101 Enid 36 26N 97 52W
16 Enkhuizen 52 42N 5 17E
44 Enköping 59 37N 17 4E
39 Enna 37 34N 14 15E
73 Ennedi 17 15N 22 0E
15 Ennis, Eire 52 51N 8 59W
101 Ennis, U.S.A. 32 15N 96 40W
15 Enniscorthy 52 30N 6 35W
15 Enniskillen 54 20N 7 40W
15 Ennistymon 52 56N 9 18W
26 Enns 48 12N 14 28E
26 Enns, R. 48 14N 14 32E
46 Enontekio 68 23N 23 38E
16 Enschede 52 13N 6 53E
108 Ensenada 31 50N 116 50W
74 Entebbe 0 4N 32 28E
102 Enterprise 45 25N 117 17W
75 Entre Rios 14 57S 37 20E
108 Entre Ríos □ 30 30S 58 30E
32 Entrepeñas, Pantano de, L. 40 34N 2 42W
72 Enugu 6 30N 7 30E
72 Enugu Ezike 7 0N 7 29E
39 Eólie o Lípari, I. 38 30N 14 50E
42 Epanomí 40 25N 22 59E
16 Epe 52 21N 5 59E
19 Épernay 49 3N 3 56E
19 Épernon 48 35N 1 40E
102 Ephraim 39 30N 111 37W
97 Ephrata 47 28N 119 32W
32 Epila 41 36N 1 17W
19 Épinal 48 19N 6 27E
43 Epitálion 37 37N 21 30E
13 Epping 51 42N 0 8E
74 Equatorial Guinea ■ 2 0N 8 0E
18 Équerdreville 49 40N 1 40W
73 Er Rahad 12 45N 30 32E
72 Er Rif 35 1N 4 1W
73 Er Roseires 11 55N 34 30E
83 Eradu 28 40S 115 2E
60 Erandol 20 56N 75 20E
36 Erba 45 49N 9 12E
51 Ercha 69 45N 147 20E
68 Erdene 44 30N 111 10E
68 Erdenedalay 46 3N 105 1E
5 Erebus, Mt. 77 35S 167 0E

109 Erechim 27 35s 52 15w
56 Ereğli 41 15N 31 30E
30 Eresma, R. 41 26N 4 45w
24 Erfurt 50 58N 11 2E
24 Erfurt □ 51 10N 10 30E
56 Ergani 38 26N 39 49E
49 Ergeni Vozvyshennost 47 0N 44 0E
68 Erhlien 43 42N 112 2E
30 Eria, R. 42 3N 5 44w
14 Eriboll, L. 58 28N 4 41w
38 Érice 38 4N 12 34E
96 Erie 42 10N 80 7w
98 Erie, L. 42 30N 82 0w
96 Erie Canal 43 15N 78 0w
55 Erigavo 10 35N 47 35E
93 Eriksdale 50 52N 98 5w
92 Erith 53 25N 116 46w
73 Eritrea □ 14 0N 41 0E
25 Erlangen 49 35N 11 0E
80 Erldunda 25 14s 133 12E
16 Ermelo 52 35N 5 35E
43 Ermióni 37 23N 23 15E
62 Ernakulam 9 59N 76 19E
15 Erne, L. 54 14N 7 30w
15 Erne, R. 54 30N 8 16w
62 Erode 11 24N 77 45E
62 Erramala Hills 15 30N 78 15E
19 Erstein 48 25N 7 38E
24 Erzgebirge Mts. 50 25N 13 0E
56 Erzurum 39 57N 41 15E
73 Es Sider 30 50N 18 21E
45 Esbjerg 55 29N 8 29E
30 Escalona 40 9N 4 29w
98 Escanaba 45 44N 87 5w
16 Esch 49 32N 6 0E
24 Eschwege 51 10N 10 3E
103 Escondido 33 9N 117 4w
104 Escuintla 14 20N 90 48w
32 Esera, R. 42 6N 0 15E
57 Esfahan 32 40N 51 38E
57 Esfahan □ 33 0N 53 0E
30 Esgueva, R. 41 40N 4 43w
73 Esh Shimâliya □ 20 0N 31 0E
54 Eshta'ol 31 47N 35 0E
12 Esk, R., Eng. 54 29N 0 37w
14 Esk, R., Scot. 54 58N 3 2w
14 Esk, North, R. 56 54N 2 38w
14 Esk, South, R. 56 40N 2 40w
44 Eskilstuna 59 22N 16 32E
93 Eskimo Point 61 10N 94 15w
56 Eskisehir 39 50N 30 35E
30 Esla, Pantano del, L. 41 45N 5 50w
30 Esla, R. 41 29N 6 3w
45 Eslöv 55 50N 13 20E
110 Esmeraldas 1 0N 79 40w
20 Espalion 44 32N 2 47E
90 Espanola 46 15N 81 46w
50 Espe 44 0N 74 5E
31 Espejo 37 40N 4 34w
83 Esperance 33 51s 121 53E
83 Esperance, B. 33 48s 121 55E
108 Esperanza 31 29s 61 3w
31 Espichel, C. 38 22N 9 16w
110 Espinal 4 9N 74 53w
111 Espinhaço, Sa. do 17 30s 43 30w
30 Espinho 41 1N 8 38w
104 Espíritu Santo, B. del 19 15N 79 40w
111 Espírito Santo □ 19 30s 40 30w
32 Espluga de Francolí 41 24N 1 7E
33 Espuña, Sa. 37 51N 1 35w
112 Esquel 42 40s 71 20w
108 Esquina 30 0s 59 30w
72 Essaouira 31 32N 9 42w
16 Essen, Belgium 51 28N 4 28E
24 Essen, W. Germany 51 28N 6 59E
13 Essex □ 51 48N 0 30E
25 Esslingen 48 43N 9 19E
19 Essonne □ 48 30N 2 20E
30 Estaca, Pta de la 43 46N 7 42w
32 Estadilla 42 4N 0 16E
112 Estados, I. de los 54 40s 64 30w
111 Estância, Brazil 11 15s 37 30w
103 Estancia, U.S.A. 34 50N 106 1w
37 Este 45 12N 11 40E
30 Esteban 43 33N 6 5w
105 Estelí 13 9N 86 22w
32 Estella 42 40N 2 0w
31 Estepa 37 17N 4 52w
31 Estepona 36 24N 5 7w
93 Esterhazy 50 37N 102 5w
19 Esternay 48 44N 3 33E
93 Estevan 49 10N 103 0w
100 Estheville 43 25N 94 50w
48 Estonian S.S.R. □ 48 30N 25 30E
31 Estoril 38 42N 9 23w
30 Estrêla, Sa. da 40 10N 7 45w
31 Estrella, Mt. 38 25N 3 35w
29 Estremadura, Reg. 39 0N 9 0w
31 Estremoz 38 51N 7 39w
111 Estrondo, Sa. de 7 20s 48 0w
27 Esztergom 47 47N 18 44E
18 Étables 48 38N 2 51w
60 Etah 27 35N 78 40E
19 Étain 49 13N 5 38E
19 Étampes 48 26N 2 10E
21 Étang 46 52N 4 10E
19 Étaples 50 30N 1 39E
60 Etawah 26 48N 79 6E
82 Ethel Creek 22 55s 120 11E
93 Ethelbert 51 32N 100 25w
55 Ethiopia ■ 8 0N 40 0E
70 Ethiopian Highlands, Mts. 10 0N 37 0E
14 Etive, L. 56 30N 5 12w
39 Etna, Mt. 37 45N 15 0E
75 Etoshapan 18 40s 16 30E
18 Étretat 49 42N 0 12E
25 Ettlingen 48 58N 8 25E
14 Ettrick, R. 55 31N 2 55w
104 Etzatlán 20 48N 104 5w
18 Eu 50 3N 1 26E
96 Euclid 41 32N 81 31w
84 Eucumbene, L. 36 2s 148 40E
99 Eufaula 31 55N 85 11w
102 Eugene 44 0N 123 8w
101 Eunice 30 35N 92 28w
16 Eupen 50 37N 6 3E
56 Euphrates, R.= Furat, Nahr al 33 30N 43 0E
18 Eure, R. 49 18N 1 12E
18 Eure □ 49 6N 1 0E
102 Eureka, Calif. 40 50N 124 0w
102 Eureka, Nev. 39 32N 116 2w
102 Eureka, Utah 40 0N 112 0w
84 Euroa 36 44s 145 35E
75 Europa, Île 22 20s 40 22E
30 Europa, Picos de 43 10N 5 0w
31 Europa, Pta. de 36 3N 5 21w
10 Europe 50 0N 20 0E
16 Europoort 51 57N 4 10E
24 Euskirchen 50 40N 6 45E
24 Eutin 54 7N 10 38E
81 Evans Head 29 7s 153 27E
97 Evans Mills 44 6N 75 48w
98 Evanston, Ill. 42 0N 87 40w
102 Evanston, Wyo. 41 10N 111 0w
98 Evansville 38 0N 87 35w
20 Evaux 46 12N 2 29E
100 Eveleth 47 35N 92 40w
54 Even Yehuda 32 16N 34 53E
61 Everest, Mt. 28 5N 86 58E
102 Everett 48 0N 122 10w
99 Everglades Nat. Park 25 50N 80 40w
13 Evesham 52 6N 1 57w
21 Evian 46 24N 6 35w
31 Évora □ 38 33N 7 50w
18 Évreux 49 0N 1 8E
43 Evritanía □ 39 5N 21 30E
54 Evron 32 59N 35 6E
18 Évron 48 23N 1 58w
42 Évros □ 41 10N 26 0E
43 Evvoia □ 38 40N 23 40E
14 Ewe, L. 57 49N 5 38w
100 Excellsior Springs 39 20N 94 10w
13 Exe, R. 50 37N 3 25w
13 Exeter, U.K. 50 43N 3 31w
97 Exeter, U.S.A. 42 59N 70 57w
13 Exmoor, Reg. 51 10N 3 55w
82 Exmouth, Australia 22 6s 114 0E
13 Exmouth, U.K. 50 37N 3 24w
82 Exmouth, G. 22 15s 114 15E
31 Extremadura, Reg. 39 30N 6 5w
105 Exuma Sd. 24 30N 76 20w
74 Eyasi, L. 3 30s 35 0E
14 Eye Pen. 58 20N 0 51E
14 Eyemouth 55 53N 2 5w
20 Eymoutiers 45 45N 1 45E
81 Eyre, L. 28 30s 136 45E
81 Eyre, Pen. 33 30s 137 17E

F

103 Fabens 31 30N 106 8w
45 Fåborg 55 6N 10 15E
37 Fabriano 43 20N 12 52E
110 Facatativa 4 49N 74 22w
20 Fracture 44 39N 0 58w
72 Fada N'Gourma 12 10N 0 30E
27 Fadd 46 28N 18 49E
37 Faenza 44 17N 11 53E
30 Fafe 41 27N 8 11w
41 Fagaraş 45 48N 24 58E
41 Făgăraş, Mt. 45 40N 24 40E
44 Fagernes 61 0N 9 16E
44 Fagersta 61 1N 15 46E
112 Fagnano, L. 54 30s 68 0w
57 Fahraj 29 0N 59 0E
69 Fahsien 21 19N 110 33E
57 Fahud 22 18N 56 28E
103 Fairbank 31 44N 110 12w
88 Fairbanks 64 59N 147 40w
100 Fairbury 40 5N 97 5w
84 Fairfield, Australia 37 45s 175 17E
99 Fairfield, Ala. 33 30N 87 0w
102 Fairfield, Calif. 38 14N 122 1w
97 Fairfield, Conn. 41 8N 73 16w
100 Fairfield, Ill. 38 20N 88 20w
100 Fairfield, Iowa 41 0N 91 58w
101 Fairfield, Tex. 31 40N 96 0w
85 Fairlie 44 5s 170 49E
100 Fairmont, Minn. 43 37N 94 30w
98 Fairmont, W. Va. 39 29N 80 10w
96 Fairport 43 8N 77 29w
80 Fairview, Australia 15 31s 144 17E
92 Fairview, Canada 56 5N 118 25w
88 Fairweather, Mt. 58 55N 137 45w
57 Faizabad, Afghanistan 37 7N 70 33E
61 Faizabad, India 26 45N 82 10E
60 Faizpur 21 14N 75 49E
105 Fajardo 18 20N 65 39w
12 Fakenham 52 50N 0 51E
65 Fakfak 3 0s 132 15E
45 Fakse, B. 55 11N 12 15E
68 Faku 42 31N 123 26E
18 Falaise 48 54N 0 12w
42 Falakrón Óros, Mt. 41 15N 23 58E
59 Falam 23 0N 93 45E
37 Falconara Marittima 43 37N 13 23E
101 Falfurrias 27 8N 98 8E
45 Falkenberg 56 54N 12 30E
24 Falkensee 52 35N 13 6E
24 Falkenstein 50 27N 12 24E
14 Falkirk 56 0N 3 47w
112 Falkland, Sd. 52 0s 60 0w
112 Falkland Is. □ 51 30s 59 0w
45 Falköping 58 12N 13 33E
97 Fall River 41 45N 71 5w
102 Fallon 39 31N 118 51w
100 Falls City 40 0N 95 40w
105 Falmouth, Jamaica 18 30N 77 40w
13 Falmouth, U.K. 50 9N 5 5w
97 Falmouth, U.S.A. 38 40N 84 20w
32 Falset 41 7N 0 50E
105 Falso, C. 17 45N 71 40w
45 Falster, I. 54 48N 11 58E
45 Falsterbo 55 23N 12 50E
44 Falun 60 37N 15 37E
56 Famagusta 35 8N 33 55E
69 Fangcheng 31 2N 118 13E
77 Fanning I. 3 51N 159 22w
37 Fano 43 50N 13 0E
45 Fanø, I. 55 25N 8 25E
92 Fanshaw 57 11N 133 30w
74 Faradje 3 50N 29 45E
72 Faranah 10 2N 10 45w
57 Farar 32 30N 62 17E
57 Farar □ 32 25N 62 10E
55 Farasán, Jazá'ir, I. 16 45N 41 55E
13 Fareham 50 52N 1 11w
85 Farewell, C. 39 36s 143 55E
100 Fargo 47 0N 97 0w
100 Faribault 44 15N 93 19w
60 Faridkot 30 44N 74 45E
61 Faridpur, Bangladesh 23 36N 89 53E
61 Faridpur, India 18 14N 79 34E
81 Farina 30 3s 138 15E
103 Farmington, N. Mex. 36 45N 108 28w
102 Farmington, Utah 41 0N 111 58w
13 Farnborough 51 17N 0 46w
12 Farne Is. 55 38N 1 37w
97 Farnham 45 20N 72 55w
111 Faro, Brazil 2 0s 56 45w
31 Faro, Port. 37 2N 7 55w
31 Faro □ 37 12N 8 10w
8 Faroe Is. 62 0N 7 0w
83 Farquhar, C. 23 38s 113 36E
57 Farráshband 28 57N 52 5E
96 Farrell 41 13N 80 29w
81 Farrell Flat 33 48s 138 48E
61 Farrukhabad 27 30N 79 32E
57 Fars □ 29 30N 55 0E
47 Farsund 58 5N 6 55E
4 Farvel, R. 59 48N 43 55w
57 Faryab □ 36 0N 65 0E
39 Fasano 40 50N 17 20E
15 Fastnet Rock 51 22N 9 27w
61 Fatehgarh 27 25N 79 35E
60 Fatehpur, Rajasthan 28 0N 75 4E
61 Fatehpur, Ut.P. 27 8N 81 7E
31 Fátima 39 37N 8 39w
69 Fatshan 23 0N 113 4E
19 Faucilles, Mts. 48 5N 5 50E
100 Faulkton 45 4N 99 8w
19 Faulquemont 49 3N 6 36E
83 Faure, I. 25 52s 113 50E
41 Faurei 45 6N 27 19E
75 Fauresmith 29 44s 25 17E
46 Fauske 67 17N 15 25E
38 Favara 37 19N 13 39E
21 Favone 41 47N 9 26E
46 Faxaflói, B. 64 29N 23 0w
101 Fayetteville, Ark. 36 0N 94 5w
99 Fayetteville, N.C. 35 0N 78 58w
32 Fayón 41 15N 0 20E
60 Fazilka 30 27N 74 2E
72 F'Dérik 22 40N 12 45E
15 Feale, R. 52 26N 9 28w
99 Fear, C. 33 45N 78 0w
85 Featherston 41 6s 175 20E
18 Fécamp 49 45N 0 22E
24 Fehmarn, I. 54 26N 11 10E
85 Feilding 40 13s 175 35E
111 Feira de Santana 12 15s 38 57w
27 Fejér □ 47 9N 18 30E
33 Felanitx 39 27N 3 7E
26 Feldbach 46 57N 15 52E
26 Feldkirch 47 15N 9 37E
26 Feldkirchen 46 44N 14 6E
104 Felipe Carillo Puerto 19 38N 88 3w
13 Felixstowe 51 58N 1 22w
37 Feltre 46 1N 11 55E
68 Fen Ho, R. 35 36N 110 42E
69 Fencheng 28 2N 115 46E
68 Fengcheng, Heilungkiang 45 41N 128 54E
68 Fengcheng, Liaoning 40 28N 124 4E
69 Fenghsien 33 56N 106 41E
69 Fengkieh 31 0N 109 33E
68 Fengtai 39 57N 116 21E
69 Fengyuan 24 10N 120 45E
12 Fens, Reg. 52 45N 0 2E
68 Fenyang 37 19N 111 46E
49 Feodosiya 45 2N 35 28E
19 Fère Champenoise 48 45N 4 0E
19 Fère-en-Tardenois 49 10N 3 30E
38 Ferentino 41 42N 13 14E
50 Fergana 40 23N 71 46E
90 Fergus 43 43N 80 24w
100 Fergus Falls 46 25N 96 0w
40 Feričanci 45 32N 18 0E
26 Ferlach 46 32N 14 18E
90 Ferland 50 19N 88 27w
15 Fermanagh □ 54 21N 7 40w
37 Fermo 43 10N 13 42E
30 Fermoselle 41 19N 6 27w
15 Fermoy 52 4N 8 18w
111 Fernando de Noronha, Is. 4 0s 33 10w
92 Fernie 49 30N 115 5w
80 Fernlees 23 51s 148 7E
62 Feroke 11 9N 75 46E
60 Ferozepore 30 55N 74 40E
42 Férrai 40 53N 26 10E
37 Ferrara 44 50N 11 36E
38 Ferrato, C. 39 18N 9 39E
31 Ferreira do Alentejo 38 4N 8 6w
20 Ferret, C. 44 38N 1 15w
72 Fès 34 0N 5 0w
41 Feteşti 44 22N 27 51E
14 Fetlar, I. 60 36N 0 52w
21 Feurs 45 45N 4 13E
73 Fezzan 27 0N 15 0E
75 Fianarantsoa 21 26s 47 5E
25 Fichtelgebirge, Mts. 50 10N 12 0E
75 Ficksburg 28 51s 27 53E
36 Fidenza 44 51N 10 3E
14 Fife □ 56 13N 3 2w
20 Figeac 44 37N 2 2E
30 Figueira Castelo Rodrigo 40 54N 6 58w
30 Figueira da Foz 40 7N 8 54w
30 Figueiro dos Vinhos 39 55N 8 16w
32 Figueras 42 18N 2 58E
72 Figuig 32 5N 1 11w
42 Fieri 40 43N 19 33E
85 Fiji ■ 17 20s 179 0E
33 Filabres, Sa. de los 37 13N 2 20w
5 Filchner Ice Shelf 78 0s 60 0w
12 Filey 54 13N 0 10w
41 Filiaşi 44 32N 23 31E
44 Filipstad 59 43N 14 9E
44 Fillefjell, Mts. 61 8N 8 10E
103 Fillmore 34 23N 118 58w
36 Finale Lígure 44 10N 8 21E
37 Finale nell 'Emília 44 50N 11 18E

33 Fiñana 37 10N 2 50W
14 Findhorn 57 30N 3 45W
98 Findlay 41 0N 83 41W
18 Finistère □ 48 20N 4 20W
30 Finisterre 42 54N 9 16W
30 Finisterre, C. 42 50N 9 19W
80 Finke 25 34S 134 35E
46 Finland ■ 70 0N 27 0E
48 Finland, G. of 60 0N 26 0E
84 Finley 35 38S 145 35E
92 Finnegan 51 7N 112 5W
80 Finnigan, Mt. 15 49S 145 17E
81 Finniss, C. 33 38S 134 51E
46 Finnmark □ 69 30N 25 0E
45 Finspång 58 45N 15 43E
25 Finsteraarhorn, Mt. 46 31N 8 10E
24 Finsterwalde 51 37N 13 42E
36 Fiorenzuola 44 56N 9 54E
37 Firenze 43 47N 11 15E
21 Firminy 45 23N 4 18E
60 Firozabad 27 10N 78 25E
41 Fîrţaneşti 45 48N 27 59E
57 Fīrūzābād 28 52N 52 35E
57 Fīrūzkūh 35 50N 52 40E
83 Fisher 30 30S 131 0E
97 Fishers I. 41 16N 72 2W
13 Fishguard 51 59N 4 59W
97 Fitchburg 42 35N 71 47W
32 Fitero 42 4N 1 52W
112 Fitz Roy 47 10S 67 0W
99 Fitzgerald 31 45N 83 10W
80 Fitzroy, R., Queens. 23 32S 150 52E
82 Fitzroy, R., W. Australia 17 31S 138 35E
82 Fitzroy Crossing 18 9S 125 38E
36 Fivizzana 44 14N 10 8E
74 Fizi 4 17S 28 55E
45 Fjellerup 56 29N 10 34E
44 Fla 60 25N 9 26E
103 Flagstaff 35 10N 111 40W
47 Flåm 60 52N 7 14E
12 Flamborough Hd. 54 8N 0 4W
102 Flaming Gorge L. 41 15N 109 30W
16 Flandre Occidentale □ 51 0N 3 0E
16 Flandre Orientale □ 51 0N 4 0E
16 Flandres, Plaines des 51 10N 3 15E
14 Flannan Is. 58 9N 7 52W
102 Flathead L. 47 50N 114 0W
80 Flattery, C., Australia 14 58S 145 21E
102 Flattery, C., U.S.A. 48 21N 124 31W
12 Fleetwood 53 55N 3 1W
47 Flekkefjord 58 18N 6 39E
44 Flen 59 4N 16 35E
24 Flensburg 54 46N 9 28E
18 Flers 48 47N 0 33W
13 Fletton 52 34N 0 13W
93 Flin Flon 54 46N 101 53W
83 Flinders, B. 34 19S 114 9E
80 Flinders, I. 40 0S 148 0E
81 Flinders, Ras. 31 30S 138 30E
12 Flint, U.K. 53 15N 3 7W
98 Flint, U.S.A. 43 0N 83 40W
77 Flint I. 11 26S 151 48W
32 Flix 41 14N 0 32E
19 Flixecourt 50 0N 2 5E
12 Flodden 55 37N 2 8W
100 Flora 38 40N 88 30W
37 Florence, Italy= Firenze 43 47N 11 15E
99 Florence, Ala. 34 50N 87 50W
103 Florence, Ariz. 33 0N 111 25W
102 Florence, Oreg. 44 0N 124 3W
99 Florence, S.C. 34 5N 79 50W
110 Florencia 1 36N 75 36W
104 Flores 16 50N 89 40W
65 Flores, I. 8 35S 121 0E
65 Flores Sea 6 30S 124 0E
111 Floriano 6 50S 43 0W
109 Florianópolis 27 30S 48 30W
108 Florida 34 7S 56 10W
99 Florida □ 28 30N 82 0W
87 Florida Str. 25 0N 80 0W
27 Floridsdorf 48 15N 16 25E
42 Flórina 40 48N 21 26E
42 Flórina □ 40 45N 21 20E
47 Florø 61 35N 5 1E
32 Flumen, R. 41 50N 0 25W
38 Flumendosa, R. 39 30N 9 25E
16 Flushing= Vlissingen 51 26N 3 34E
5 Flying Fish, C. 72 30S 103 0W
93 Foam Lake 51 40N 103 15W
40 Foča 43 31N 18 47E
41 Focşani 45 41N 27 15E
39 Fóggia 41 28N 15 31E
91 Fogo 49 43N 54 17W
26 Fohnsdorf 47 12N 14 40E
24 Föhr, I. 54 40N 8 30E
20 Foix 42 58N 1 38E
20 Foix, Reg. 43 0N 1 30E
43 Fokís □ 38 30N 22 15E
43 Folégandros, I. 36 37N 24 55E
90 Foleyet 48 15N 82 25W
37 Foligno 42 58N 12 40E
13 Folkestone 51 5N 1 11E
36 Follónica, G. di 42 54N 10 53E
93 Fond du Lac, Canada 59 20N 107 10W
100 Fond-du-Lac, U.S.A. 43 46N 88 26W
38 Fondi 41 21N 13 25E
30 Fonfría 41 37N 6 9W
104 Fonseca, G. de 13 10N 87 40W
19 Fontainebleau 48 24N 2 40E
110 Fonte Boa 2 25S 66 0W
20 Fontenay-le-Comte 46 28N 0 48W
69 Foochow 26 5N 119 18E
19 Forbach 49 10N 6 52E
84 Forbes 33 22S 148 0E
61 Forbesganj 26 17N 87 18E
32 Forcall, R. 40 40N 0 12W
25 Forchheim 49 42N 11 4E
96 Ford City 40 47N 79 11W
4 Forel, Mt. 66 52N 36 55W
92 Forest Lawn 51 4N 114 0W
92 Forestburg 52 35N 112 1W
91 Forestville 48 48N 69 20W
20 Forez, Mts. du 45 40N 3 50E
14 Forfar 56 40N 2 53W
19 Forges-les-Eaux 49 37N 1 30E
37 Forlí 44 14N 12 2E
12 Formby Pt. 53 33N 3 7W
33 Formentera, I. 38 40N 1 30E
32 Formentor, C. 39 58N 3 13E
38 Fórmia 41 15N 13 34E
111 Formiga 20 27S 45 25W
36 Formigine 44 37N 10 51E
108 Formosa, Arg. 26 15S 58 10W
111 Formosa, Brazil 15 32S 47 20W
108 Formosa □ 25 0S 60 0W
69 Formosa= Taiwan ■ 24 0N 121 0E
111 Formosa, Sa. 12 0S 55 0W
69 Formosa Str. 24 40N 124 0E
30 Fornos de Algodres 40 48N 7 32W
36 Fornovo di Taro 44 42N 10 7E
14 Forres 57 37N 3 38W
83 Forrest 38 22S 143 40E
101 Forrest City 35 1N 90 47W
44 Fors 60 14N 16 20E
80 Forsayth 18 33S 143 34E
44 Forsmo 63 16N 17 11E
24 Forst 51 43N 15 37E
102 Forsyth 46 14N 106 37W
90 Fort Albany 52 15N 81 35W
73 Fort-Archambault =Sarh 9 5N 18 23E
92 Fort Assinboine 54 20N 114 45W
14 Fort Augustus 57 9N 4 40W
102 Fort Benton 47 50N 110 40W
102 Fort Bragg 39 28N 123 50W
102 Fort Bridger 41 22N 110 20W
89 Fort Chimo 58 9N 68 12W
93 Fort Chipewyan 58 46N 111 9W
100 Fort Collins 40 30N 105 4W
90 Fort Coulonge 45 50N 76 45W
75 Fort-Dauphin 25 2S 47 0E
100 Fort Dodge 42 29N 94 10W
93 Fort Frances 48 35N 93 25W
88 Fort Franklin 65 30N 123 45W
90 Fort George 53 40N 79 0W
90 Fort George, R. 53 50N 77 0W
88 Fort Good Hope 66 14N 128 40W
92 Fort Graham 56 38N 124 35W
103 Fort Hancock 31 19N 105 56W
90 Fort Hope 51 30N 88 10W
91 Fort Kent 47 12N 68 30W
73 Fort-Lamy= Ndjamena 12 4N 15 8E
100 Fort Laramie 42 15W 104 30W
99 Fort Lauderdale 26 10N 80 5W
92 Fort Liard 60 20N 123 30W
92 Fort Mackay 57 12N 111 41W
91 Fort McKenzie 56 50N 69 0W
92 Fort Macleod 49 45N 113 30W
72 Fort MacMahon 29 51N 1 45E
88 Fort McPherson 67 30N 134 55W
100 Fort Madison 40 39N 91 20W
72 Fort Mirabel 29 31N 2 55E
100 Fort Morgan 40 10N 103 50W
99 Fort Myers 26 30N 82 0W
92 Fort Nelson 58 50N 122 30W
88 Fort Norman 64 57N 125 30W
99 Fort Payne 34 25N 85 44W
102 Fort Peck 47 1N 105 30W
102 Fort Peck Res. 47 40N 107 0W
99 Fort Pierce 27 29N 80 19W
74 Fort Portal 0 40N 30 20E
92 Fort Providence 61 20N 117 30W
93 Fort Qu'Appelle 50 45N 103 50W
92 Fort Resolution 61 10N 114 40W
74 Fort-Rousset 0 29S 15 55E
90 Fort Rupert 51 30N 78 40W
92 Fort St. James 54 30N 124 10W
92 Fort St. John 56 15N 120 50W
60 Fort Sandeman 31 20N 69 25E
92 Fort Saskatchewan 53 40N 113 15W
101 Fort Scott 38 0N 94 40W
88 Fort Selkirk 62 43N 137 22W
90 Fort Severn 56 0N 87 40W
92 Fort Simpson 61 45N 121 30W
50 Fort Slevchenko 44 30N 50 10E
101 Fort Smith 35 25N 94 25W
101 Fort Stockton 30 48N 103 2W
101 Fort Sumner 34 24N 104 8W
99 Fort Valley 32 33N 83 52W
92 Fort Vermilion 58 30N 115 57W
75 Fort Victoria 20 8S 30 55E
98 Fort Wayne 41 5N 85 10W
90 Fort William, Canada= Thunder Bay 48 20N 89 10W
14 Fort William, U.K. 56 48N 5 8W
101 Fort Worth 32 45N 97 25W
88 Fort Yukon 66 35N 145 12W
111 Fortaleza 3 35S 38 35W
105 Fort-de-France 14 36N 61 5W
82 Fortescue, R. 21 20S 116 5E
14 Forth, Firth of 56 5N 2 55W
14 Fortrose 57 35N 4 10W
102 Fortuna 48 38N 124 8W
88 Forty Mile 64 20N 140 30W
21 Fos 43 20N 4 57E
37 Fossacesia 42 15N 14 30E
36 Fossano 44 39N 7 40E
5 Fossil Bluff 71 15S 69 0W
37 Fossombrone 43 41N 12 49E
98 Fostoria 41 8N 83 25W
18 Fougères 48 21N 1 14W
14 Foula, I. 60 10N 2 5W
13 Foulness, I. 51 26N 0 55E
72 Foumban 5 45N 10 50E
20 Fourchambault 47 0N 3 3E
82 Fourcroy, C. 11 45S 130 2E
19 Fourmies 50 1N 4 2E
43 Foúrnoi, I. 37 36N 26 32E
72 Fouta Djalon, Mts. 11 20N 12 10W
85 Foveaux, Str. 46 42S 168 10E
13 Fowey 50 20N 4 39W
83 Fowlers, B. 31 59S 132 34E
69 Fowning 33 30N 119 40E
93 Fox Valley 50 30N 109 25W
89 Foxe Basin 68 30N 77 0W
89 Foxe Chan. 66 0N 80 0W
89 Foxe Pen. 65 0N 76 0W
85 Foxton 40 29S 175 18E
15 Foyle, L. 55 6N 7 18W
15 Foynes 52 37N 9 6W
30 Foz 43 33N 7 20W
109 Foz do Iguaçu 25 30S 54 30W
97 Frackville 40 46N 76 15W
32 Fraga 41 32N 0 21E
97 Framingham 42 17N 71 25W
111 Franca 20 25S 47 30W
37 Francavilla al Mare 42 25N 14 16E
39 Francavilla Fontana 40 32N 17 35E
17 France ■ 47 0N 3 0E
74 Franceville 1 38S 13 35E
19 Franche Comté, Reg. 46 30N 5 50E
91 Francis Harbour 52 34N 55 44W
75 Francistown 21 11S 27 32E
39 Francofonte 37 13N 14 50E
91 François 47 34N 56 44W
24 Frankenberg 51 3N 8 47E
25 Frankenwald, Mts. 50 18N 11 36E
98 Frankfort, Ind. 40 20N 86 33W
98 Frankfort, Ky. 38 12N 85 44W
24 Frankfurt □ 52 30N 14 0E
25 Frankfurt am Main 50 7N 8 40E
24 Frankfurt an der Oder 52 50N 14 31E
25 Fränkishe Alb. 49 20N 11 30E
100 Franklin, Nebr. 40 9N 98 55W
97 Franklin, N.H. 43 28N 71 39W
97 Franklin, N.J. 41 9N 74 38W
96 Franklin, Pa. 41 22N 79 45W
99 Franklin, Tenn. 35 54N 86 53W
98 Franklin, W. Va. 38 38N 79 21W
88 Franklin, Reg. 71 0N 99 0W
102 Franklin D. Roosevelt L. 48 30N 118 16W
88 Franklin Mts. 66 0N 125 0W
88 Franklin Str. 72 0N 96 0W
84 Frankston 38 8S 145 8E
50 Frantsa Iosifa, Zemlya, Is. 76 0N 62 0E
90 Franz 48 25N 85 30W
38 Frascati 41 48N 12 41E
96 Fraser 42 32N 82 57W
81 Fraser, I. 25 15S 153 10E
92 Fraser, R. 49 9N 123 12W
92 Fraser Lake 54 0N 124 50W
14 Fraserburgh 47 41N 2 0W
63 Fraser's Hill 3 43N 101 43E
41 Frăteşti 43 59N 25 59E
25 Frauenfeld 47 34N 8 54E
108 Fray Bentos 33 10S 58 15W
82 Frazier Downs 18 48S 121 42E
45 Fredericia 55 34N 9 45E
98 Frederick, Md. 39 25N 77 23W
101 Frederick, Okla. 34 22N 99 0W
98 Fredericksburg 38 16N 77 29W
91 Fredericton 45 57N 66 40W
45 Frederiksborg □ 55 50N 12 10E
4 Frederikshåb 62 0N 49 30W
45 Frederikshavn 57 28N 10 31E
45 Frederikssund 55 50N 12 3E
45 Frederiksvaerk 55 58N 12 2E
96 Fredonia 42 26N 79 20W
44 Fredrikstad 59 13N 10 57E
97 Freehold 40 15N 74 18W
97 Freeland 41 3N 75 48W
105 Freeport, Bahamas 26 30N 78 35W
100 Freeport, Ill. 42 18N 89 40W
97 Freeport, N.Y. 40 39N 73 35W
101 Freeport, Tex. 28 55N 95 22W
72 Freetown 8 30N 13 10W
31 Fregenal de la Sierra 38 10N 6 39W
24 Freiberg 50 55N 13 20E
25 Freiburg 48 0N 7 50E
112 Freire 39 0S 72 50W
25 Freising 48 24N 11 27E
26 Freistadt 48 30N 14 30E
24 Freital 51 0N 13 40E
21 Fréjus 43 25N 6 44E
83 Fremantle 32 1S 115 47E
100 Fremont, Nebr. 41 30N 96 30W
98 Fremont, Ohio 41 20N 83 5W
84 French, I. 38 20S 145 22E
111 French Guiana ■ 4 0N 53 0W
55 French Terr. of the Afars & Issas ■ 11 30N 42 15E
111 Fresco, R. 6 39S 51 59W
104 Fresnillo 23 10N 103 0W
103 Fresno 36 47N 119 50W
30 Fresno Alhandigo 40 42N 5 37W
25 Freudenstadt 48 27N 8 25E
80 Frewena 19 50S 135 50E
108 Frías 28 40S 65 5W
25 Fribourg 46 49N 7 9E
25 Fribourg □ 45 40N 7 0E
25 Friedberg 50 19N 8 45E
25 Friedrichshafen 47 39N 9 29E
26 Friesach 46 57N 14 24E
16 Friesland □ 53 5N 5 50E
75 Frio, C. 18 0S 12 0E
24 Fritzlar 51 8N 9 19E
37 Friuli Venezia Giulia □ 46 0N 13 0E
89 Frobisher B. 63 0N 67 0W
13 Frome 51 16N 2 17W
98 Front Royal 38 55N 78 10W
31 Fronteira 39 3N 7 39W
104 Frontera 18 30N 92 40W
20 Frontignan 43 27N 3 45E
38 Frosinone 41 38N 13 20E
44 Frösö 63 11N 14 35E
98 Frostburg 39 43N 78 57W
44 Frövi 59 28N 15 24E
41 Frumoasa 46 28N 25 48E
50 Frunze 42 54N 74 36E
111 Frutal 20 0S 49 0W
27 Frýdek Místek 49 40N 18 20E
43 Fthiótis □ 38 50N 22 25E
68 Fuchin 47 10N 132 0E
69 Fuchow 27 50N 116 14E
66 Fuchu 34 34N 133 14E
69 Fuchun Kiang, R. 30 10N 120 9E
31 Fuengirola 36 32N 4 41W
31 Fuente de Cantos 38 15N 6 18W
31 Fuente el Fresno 39 14N 3 46W
31 Fuente Ovejuna 38 15N 5 25W
31 Fuentes de Andalucia 37 28N 5 20W
32 Fuentes de Ebro 31 31N 0 38W
31 Fuentes de León 38 5N 6 32W
30 Fuentes de Oñoro 40 33N 6 52W
108 Fuerte Olimpo 21 0S 58 0W
72 Fuerteventura, I. 28 30N 14 0W
57 Fujaira 25 7N 56 18E
66 Fuji 35 9N 138 39E
66 Fuji-san, Mt. 35 22N 138 44E
66 Fuji-no-miya 35 20N 138 40E
66 Fujisawa 35 22N 139 29E
69 Fukien □ 26 0N 117 30E
66 Fukuchiyama 35 25N 135 9E
66 Fukui 36 0N 136 10E
66 Fukui □ 36 0N 136 12E
66 Fukuoka 33 30N 130 30E
66 Fukuoka □ 33 30N 131 0E
66 Fukushima 37 30N 140 15E
66 Fukushima □ 37 30N 140 15E
66 Fukuyama 34 35N 133 20E

24 Fulda 50 32N 9 41E
24 Fulda, R. 51 25N 9 39E
103 Fullerton 33 52N 117 58W
100 Fulton, Mo. 38 50N 91 55W
97 Fulton, N.Y. 43 20N 76 22W
19 Fumay 50 0N 4 40E
20 Fumel 44 30N 0 58E
66 Funabashi 35 45N 140 0E
76 Funafuti, I. 8 30S 179 0E
72 Funchal 32 45N 16 55W
110 Fundación 10 31N 74 11W
30 Fundão 40 8N 7 30W
91 Fundy, B. of 45 0N 66 0W
72 Funtua 11 31N 7 17E
56 Furat, Nahr al, R. 33 30N 43 0E
109 Furnas, Reprêsa de, L. 20 45S 46 0W
12 Furness 54 14N 3 8W
26 Fürstenfeld 47 3N 16 3E
25 Furstenfeldbruck 48 10N 11 15E
24 Furstenwalde 52 20N 14 3E
25 Fürth 49 29N 11 0E
89 Fury & Hecla Str. 69 40N 81 0W
110 Fusagasugá 4 21N 74 22W
68 Fushan 37 30N 121 5E
68 Fushun 42 0N 123 59E
68 Fusin 42 12N 121 33E
25 Füssen 47 12N 121 33E
69 Futing 27 15N 120 10E
69 Futsing 25 46N 119 29E
76 Futuna, I. 14 25S 178 20E
69 Fuyang 30 5N 119 56E
68 Fuyu 45 10N 124 50E
12 Fylde, R. 53 47N 2 56W
45 Fyn, I. 55 20N 10 30E
14 Fyne, L. 56 0N 5 20W
45 Fyns □ 55 15N 10 30E

G

72 Gabès 33 53N 10 2E
73 Gabès, G. de 34 0N 10 30E
74 Gabon ■ 0 10S 10 0E
75 Gaborone 24 37S 25 57E
97 Gabriels 44 26N 74 12W
41 Gabrovo 42 52N 25 27E
57 Gach-Sārān 30 15N 50 45E
40 Gacko 43 10N 18 33E
62 Gadag 15 30N 75 45E
60 Gadarwara 22 50N 78 50E
33 Gádor, Sa. de 36 57N 2 45W
99 Gadsden, Ala. 34 1N 86 0W
103 Gadsden, Ariz. 32 35N 114 47W
62 Gadwal 16 10N 77 50E
41 Găesti 44 48N 25 14E
38 Gaeta 41 12N 13 35E
38 Gaeta, G. di 41 0N 13 25E
99 Gaffney 35 10N 81 31W
72 Gafsa 34 24N 8 51E
91 Gagetown 45 46N 66 29W
72 Gagnoa 6 4N 5 55W
91 Gagnon 51 50N 68 5W
20 Gah 43 12N 0 27W
61 Gahmar 25 27N 83 55E
61 Gaibandha 25 20N 89 36E
26 Gail, R. 46 36N 13 53E
20 Gaillac 43 54N 1 54E
18 Gaillon 49 10N 1 20E
96 Gaines 41 45N 77 35W
99 Gainesville, Fla. 29 38N 82 20W
99 Gainesville, Ga. 34 17N 83 47W
101 Gainesville, Tex. 33 40N 97 10W
12 Gainsborough 53 23N 0 46W
81 Gairdner, L. 32 0S 136 0E
14 Gairloch, L. 57 43N 5 45W
75 Galangue 13 48S 16 3E
77 Galápagos, Is. 0 0N 89 0W
14 Galashiels 55 37N 2 50W
41 Galaţi 45 27N 28 2E
39 Galatina 40 10N 18 10E
39 Galátone 40 8N 18 3E
99 Galax 36 42N 80 57W
43 Galaxídhion 38 22N 22 23E
83 Galena 27 50S 114 41E
33 Galera 37 45N 2 33W
100 Galesburg 40 57N 90 23W
48 Galich 58 23N 42 18E
30 Galicia, Reg. 42 43N 8 0W
54 Galilee= Hagalil, Reg. 32 53N 35 18E
54 Galilee, Sea of= Kinneret, Yam 32 49N 35 36E
36 Gallarte 45 40N 8 48E
99 Gallatin 36 24N 86 27W
62 Galle 6 5N 80 10E
32 Gállego, R. 41 39N 0 51W
112 Gallegos, R. 51 35S 69 0W
110 Gallinas, Pta. 12 28N 71 40W
39 Gallipoli 40 8N 18 0E
98 Gallipolis 38 50N 82 10W
46 Gällivare 67 7N 20 32E
32 Gallocanta, L. de 40 58N 1 30W
14 Galloway, Reg. 55 0N 4 25W
14 Galloway, Mull of 54 38N 4 50W
103 Gallup 35 30N 108 54W
96 Galt= Cambridge 43 21N 80 19W
26 Galtür 46 58N 10 11E
30 Galve de Sorbe 41 13N 3 10W
101 Galveston 29 15N 94 48W
101 Galveston B. 29 30N 94 50W
108 Gálvez 32 0S 61 20W
15 Galway 53 16N 9 4W
15 Galway, B. 53 10N 9 20W
15 Galway □ 53 16N 9 3W
66 Gamagori 34 50N 137 14E
72 Gambaga 10 30N 0 28W
72 Gambia ■ 13 20N 15 45W
72 Gambia, R. 13 28N 16 34W
82 Gambier, C. 11 56S 130 57E
104 Gamboa 9 8N 79 42W
103 Gamerco 35 33N 108 56W
20 Gan 0 10S 71 10E
54 Gan Shamu'el 32 28N 34 56E
54 Gan Yavne 31 48N 34 42E
90 Gananoque 44 20N 76 10W
61 Gandak, R. 25 32N 85 5E
91 Gander 49 1N 54 33W
32 Gandesa 41 3N 0 26E
72 Gandi 12 55N 5 49E
33 Gandía 38 58N 0 9W
61 Ganga, Mouths of the 21 30N 90 0E
61 Ganga, R. 23 22N 90 32E
60 Ganganagar 29 56N 73 56E
60 Gangapur 26 32N 76 37E
62 Gangavati 15 30N 76 36E
59 Gangaw 22 5N 94 15E
61 Ganges, R.= Ganga, R. 23 22N 90 32E
61 Gangtok 27 20N 88 40E
60 Ganj 27 45N 78 47E
20 Gannat 46 7N 3 11E
27 Ganserdorf 48 20N 16 43E
72 Gao 18 0N 1 0E
72 Gaoual 11 45N 13 25W
21 Gap 44 33N 6 5E
111 Garanhuns 8 50S 36 30W
102 Garberville 40 11N 123 50W
109 Garça 22 14S 49 37W
21 Gard □ 44 2N 4 10E
36 Garda, L. di 45 40N 10 40E
24 Gardelegen 52 32N 11 21E
101 Garden City 38 0N 100 45W
57 Gardez 33 31N 68 59E
102 Gardiner 45 3N 110 53W
97 Gardner 42 35N 72 0W
55 Gardo 9 18N 49 20E
102 Garfield 47 3N 117 8W
43 Gargaliánoi 37 4N 21 38E
39 Gargano, Testa del, Pt. 41 49N 16 12E
38 Garigliano, R. 41 13N 13 45E
102 Garland 41 47N 112 10W
50 Garm 39 0N 70 20E
25 Garmisch-Partenkirchen 47 30N 11 5E
57 Garmsār 35 20N 52 25E
61 Garo Hills 25 30N 90 30E
55 Garoe 8 35N 48 40E
20 Garonne, R. 45 2N 0 36W
20 Garrigues, Reg. 43 40N 3 30E
102 Garrison 46 37N 112 56W
100 Garrison Res. 47 30N 102 0W
88 Garry, L. 65 40N 100 0W
90 Garson 50 5N 96 50W
20 Gartempe, R. 46 48N 0 50E
67 Gartok 31 59N 80 30E
24 Gartz 54 17N 13 21E
65 Garut 7 14S 107 53E
31 Garvão 37 42N 8 21W
85 Garvie, Mts. 45 27S 169 59E
98 Gary 41 35N 87 20W
110 Garzón 2 10N 75 40W
17 Gascogne, G. de 44 0N 2 0W
20 Gascogne, Reg. 43 45N 0 20E
83 Gascoyne, R. 24 52S 113 37E
83 Gascoyne Junction 25 3S 115 12E
72 Gashaka 7 20N 11 29E
91 Gaspé 48 52N 64 30W
91 Gaspé, C. 48 48N 64 7W
91 Gaspé Pass. 49 10N 64 0W
91 Gaspé Pen. 48 45N 65 40W
91 Gaspesian Prov. Park 49 0N 66 45W
99 Gastonia 35 17N 81 10W
43 Gastoúni 37 51N 21 15E
42 Gastoúri 39 34N 19 54E
112 Gastre 42 10S 69 15W
33 Gata, C. de 36 41N 2 13W
30 Gata, Sa. de 40 20N 6 20W
40 Gătaia 45 26N 21 30E
14 Gatehouse of Fleet 54 53N 4 10W
12 Gateshead 54 57N 1 37W
19 Gatinais, Reg. 48 5N 2 40E
20 Gâtine, Hauteurs de 46 40N 0 50W
97 Gatineau 45 28N 75 40W
90 Gatineau Nat. Park 45 30N 75 52W
75 Gatooma 18 21S 29 55E
104 Gatun 9 16N 79 55W
104 Gatun L. 9 7N 79 56W
31 Gaucín 36 31N 5 19W
61 Gauhati 26 5N 91 55E
5 Gaussberg, Mt. 66 45S 89 0E
32 Gavá 41 18N 2 0E
20 Gavarnie 42 44N 0 3W
57 Gavater 25 10N 61 23E
43 Gávdhos, I. 34 50N 24 6E
31 Gavião 39 28N 7 50W
44 Gavle 60 41N 17 13E
44 Gävleborgs □ 61 20N 16 15E
36 Gavorrano 42 55N 10 55E
18 Gavray 49 55N 1 20W
60 Gawilgarh Hills 21 15N 76 45E
81 Gawler 34 30S 138 42E
61 Gaya 24 47N 85 4E
81 Gayndah 25 35S 151 39E
54 Gaza 31 30N 34 28E
54 Gaza Strip 31 29N 34 25E
56 Gaziantep 37 6N 37 23E
28 Gdańsk 54 22N 18 40E
28 Gdansk □ 54 10N 18 30E
28 Gdynia 54 35N 18 33E
73 Gebeit Mine 21 3N 36 29E
73 Gedaref 14 2N 35 28E
54 Gedera 31 49N 34 46E
20 Gèdre 42 47N 0 2E
45 Gedser 54 35N 11 55E
84 Geelong 38 2S 144 20E
83 Geelvink, Chan. 28 30S 114 10E
16 Geeraadsbergen 50 45N 3 53E
24 Geesthacht 53 25N 10 20E
73 Geili 16 1N 32 37E
44 Geilo 60 32N 8 14E
25 Geislingen 47 55N 8 37E
74 Geita 2 48S 32 12E
39 Gela 37 3N 14 15E
39 Gela, G. di 37 0N 14 8E
16 Gelderland □ 52 5N 6 10E
16 Geldrop 51 25N 5 32E
16 Geleen 50 57N 5 49E
56 Gelibolu 40 28N 26 43E
25 Gelnhausen 50 12N 9 12E
24 Gelsenkirchen 51 30N 7 5E
24 Gelting 54 43N 9 53E
63 Gemas 2 37N 102 36E
16 Gembloux 50 34N 4 43E
74 Gemena 3 20N 19 40E
37 Gemona del Fruiuli 46 16N 13 7E
25 Gemünden 50 3N 9 43E
20 Gençay 46 23N 0 23E
108 General Acha 37 20S 64 38W
108 General Alvear 36 0S 60 0W
108 General Artigas 26 52S 56 16W
108 General Juan Madariaga 37 0S 57 0W
108 General Martin Miguel de Güemes 24 50S 65 0W
108 General Pico 35 45S 63 50W
108 General Pinedo 27 15S 61 30W
112 General Roca 30 0S 67 40W
41 General Toshevo 43 42N 28 6E
108 General Viamonte 35 1S 61 3W
108 General Villegas 35 0S 63 0W
96 Genesee, R. 43 16N 77 36W
25 Geneva= Genève, Switz. 46 12N 6 9E
96 Geneva, U.S.A. 42 53N 77 0W
25 Geneva, L.= Léman, L. 46 26N 6 30E
25 Genève 46 12N 6 9E
31 Genil, R. 37 42N 5 19W
21 Génissiat, Barrage de 46 1N 5 48E
16 Genk 50 58N 5 32E
38 Gennargentu, Mt. del 39 59N 9 19E
36 Genova 44 24N 8 56E
36 Génova, G. di 44 0N 9 0E
16 Gent 51 2N 3 37E
24 Genthin 52 24N 12 10E
83 Geographe, B. 33 30S 115 15E
83 Geographe, Chan. 24 30S 113 0E
75 George 33 58S 22 29E
97 George, L. 43 30N 73 30W
89 George R.=Port Nouveau-Quebec 58 30N 65 50W
80 George Town Australia 41 5S 148 55E
63 George Town, W. Malaysia 5 25N 100 19E
80 Georgetown, Australia 18 17S 143 33E
90 Georgetown, Ont. 43 40N 80 0W
91 Georgetown, P.E.I. 46 13N 62 24W
72 Georgetown, Gambia 13 30N 14 47W
110 Georgetown, Guyana 6 50N 58 12W
99 Georgetown, U.S.A. 33 22N 79 15W
99 Georgia □ 32 0N 82 0W
92 Georgia Str. 49 20N 124 0W
90 Georgian B. 45 15N 81 0W
49 Georgian S.S.R. □ 41 0N 45 0E
49 Georgiu-Dezh 51 3N 39 20E
49 Georgiyevsk 44 12N 43 28E
24 Gera 50 53N 12 5E
24 Gera □ 50 45N 11 30E
83 Geraldton, Australia 28 48S 114 32E
90 Geraldton, Canada 49 44N 86 59W
19 Gérardmer 48 3N 6 50E
88 Gerdine, Mt. 61 32N 152 50W
56 Gerede 40 45N 32 10E
33 Gérgal 37 7N 2 31W
25 Gerlafingen 47 10N 7 34E
55 Gerlogubi 6 53N 45 3E
92 Germansen Landing 55 43N 124 40W
75 Germiston 26 15S 28 5E
66 Gero 35 48N 137 14E
27 Gerlachovka, Mt. 49 11N 20 7E
32 Gerona 41 58N 2 46E
32 Gerona □ 42 11N 2 30E
20 Gers □ 43 35N 0 38E
20 Gers, R. 44 9N 0 39E
24 Geseke 51 38N 8 29E
30 Getafe 40 18N 3 44W
20 Gevaudan, Reg. 44 40N 3 40E
40 Gevgelija 41 9N 22 30E
21 Gex 46 21N 6 3E
102 Geyser 47 17N 110 30W
46 Geysir 64 19N 20 18W
54 Gezer 31 52N 34 55E
61 Ghaghara, R. 25 45N 84 40E
72 Ghana ■ 6 0N 1 0W
72 Ghardaîa 32 31N 3 37E
56 Ghat 24 59N 10 19E
61 Ghatal 22 40N 87 46E
62 Ghatprabha, R. 16 21N 75 51E
73 Ghazal, Bahr el, R. 9 31N 30 25E
72 Ghazaouet 35 8N 1 50W
60 Ghaziabad 28 42N 77 35E
61 Ghazipur 25 38N 83 35E
57 Ghazni 33 30N 68 17E
57 Ghazni □ 33 0N 68 0E
36 Ghedi 45 24N 10 16E
41 Gheorghe Gheorghiu-Dej 46 17N 26 47E
21 Ghisonaccia 42 1N 9 26E
57 Ghor □ 34 0N 64 20E
90 Ghost River 51 25N 83 20W
72 Ghudāmes 30 11N 9 29E
57 Ghuriān 34 17N 61 25E
15 Giant's Causeway 55 15N 6 30W
36 Giaveno 45 3N 7 20E
105 Gibara 21 0N 76 20W
38 Gibellina 37 48N 13 0E
75 Gibeon 25 7S 17 45E
31 Gibraléon 37 23N 6 58W
31 Gibraltar ■ 36 7N 5 22W
31 Gibraltar, Str. of 35 55N 5 40W
82 Gibson, Des. 24 0S 126 0E
19 Gien 47 40N 2 36E
24 Giessen 50 34N 8 40E
24 Gifhorn 52 29N 10 32E
66 Gifu 35 30N 136 45E
66 Gifu □ 36 0N 137 0E
104 Giganta, Sa. de la 25 30N 111 30W
14 Gigha, I. 55 42N 5 45W
36 Giglio, I. 42 20N 10 52E
20 Gignac 43 39N 3 32E
30 Gijón 43 32N 5 42W
103 Gila, R. 32 43N 114 33W
103 Gila Bend 32 57N 112 43W
56 Gilan □ 37 0N 49 0E
76 Gilbert Is. 1 0N 176 0E
93 Gilbert Plains 51 9N 100 28W
80 Gilbert River 18 9S 142 50E
83 Gilgai 31 15S 119 56E
84 Gilgandra 31 42S 148 39E
58 Gilgit 35 50N 74 15E
93 Gillam 56 20N 94 40W
80 Gilliat 20 40S 141 28E
13 Gillingham 51 23N 0 34E
90 Gilmour 44 48N 77 37W
103 Gilroy 37 10N 121 37W
80 Gindie 23 45S 148 10E
83 Gingin 31 22S 115 37E
54 Ginnosar 32 51N 35 32E
39 Ginosa 40 35N 16 45E
39 Gióia, G. di 38 30N 15 50E
39 Gióia del Colle 40 49N 16 55E
39 Gióia Táuro 38 26N 15 53E
43 Gióna, Mt. 38 38N 22 14E
65 Giong, Teluk, B. 4 50N 118 20E

21 Giovi, P. del 44 30N 8 55 E
39 Giovinazzo 41 10N 16 40 E
60 Gir Hills 21 0N 71 0 E
27 Giraltovce 49 7N 21 32 E
96 Girard 41 10N 80 42W
110 Girardot 4 18N 74 48W
14 Girdle Ness 57 9N 2 2W
56 Giresun 40 45N 38 30 E
73 Girga 26 17N 31 55 E
61 Giridih 24 10N 86 21 E
57 Girishk 31 47N 64 24 E
20 Gironde, R. 45 30N 1 0W
20 Gironde □ 44 45N 0 30W
32 Gironella 42 2N 1 53 E
14 Girvan 55 15N 4 50W
85 Gisborne 38 39S 178 5 E
45 Gislaved 57 18N 13 32 E
19 Gisors 49 15N 1 40 E
39 Giugliano in Campania 40 55N 14 12 E
37 Giulianova 42 45N 13 58 E
41 Giurgiu 43 52N 25 57 E
54 Giv'at Olga 32 28N 34 53 E
54 Giv'atayim 32 4N 34 49 E
19 Givet 50 8N 4 49 E
21 Givors 45 35N 4 45 E
57 Gizhiga 62 0N 150 27 E
51 Gizhiginskaya Guba 61 0N 158 0 E
28 Giżycko 54 2N 21 48 E
42 Gjirokastra 40 7N 20 16 E
88 Gjoa Haven 68 20N 96 0W
44 Gjøvik 60 47N 10 43 E
91 Glace Bay 46 11N 59 58W
92 Glacier B. Nat. Monument 58 45N 136 30W
102 Glacier Nat. Park 48 40N 114 0W
101 Gladewater 32 30N 94 58W
80 Gladstone, Queens. 23 52S 151 16 E
81 Gladstone, S. Australia 33 17S 138 22 E
93 Gladstone, Canada 50 20N 99 0W
44 Glåma, R. 59 12N 10 57 E
25 Glarus 47 3N 9 4 E
14 Glasgow, U.K. 55 52N 4 14W
98 Glasgow, U.S.A. 37 2N 85 55W
13 Glastonbury 51 9N 2 42W
24 Glauchau 50 50N 12 33 E
48 Glazov 58 0N 52 30 E
92 Gleichen 50 50N 113 0W
26 Gleisdorf 47 6N 15 44 E
14 Glen Affric 57 15N 5 0W
103 Glen Canyon Dam 37 0N 111 25W
103 Glen Canyon Nat. Recreation Area 37 30N 111 0W
14 Glen Coe 56 40N 5 0W
97 Glen Cove 40 51N 73 37W
14 Glen Garry 57 3N 5 7W
14 Glen More 57 12N 4 30 E
84 Glen Thompson 37 38S 142 35 E
84 Glenalbyn 36 30S 143 48 E
18 Glénans, Is. de 47 42N 4 0W
85 Glenbrook 33 46S 150 37 E
103 Glendale, Ariz. 33 40N 112 8W
103 Glendale, Calif. 34 7N 118 18W
102 Glendale, Oreg. 42 44N 123 29W
100 Glendive 47 7N 104 40W
81 Glenelg 34 58S 138 30 E
84 Glenelg, R. 38 3S 141 9 E
15 Glengariff 51 45N 9 33W
80 Glengyle 24 48S 139 37 E
81 Glenn Innes 29 44S 151 44 E
84 Glennies Creek 32 30S 151 8 E
80 Glenorchy 36 55S 142 41 E
80 Glenore 17 50S 141 12 E
80 Glenormiston 22 55S 138 50 E
102 Glenrock 42 53N 105 55W
14 Glenrothes 56 12N 3 11W
97 Glens Falls 43 20N 73 40W
15 Glenties 54 48N 8 18W
92 Glenwood, Canada 49 21N 113 24W
100 Glenwood, U.S.A. 45 38N 95 21W
102 Glenwood Springs 39 39N 107 15W
27 Gliwice 50 22N 18 41 E
103 Globe 33 25N 110 53W
26 Glödnitz 46 53N 14 7 E
26 Gloggnitz 47 41N 15 56 E
28 Głogów 51 37N 16 5 E
75 Glorieuses, Is. 11 30S 47 20 E
12 Glossop 53 27N 1 56W
84 Gloucester, Australia 32 0S 151 59 E
13 Gloucester, U.K. 51 52N 2 15W
97 Gloucester, U.S.A. 42 38N 70 39W
13 Gloucestershire □ 51 44N 2 10W
97 Gloversville 43 5N 74 18W
28 Głowno 51 59N 19 42 E
27 Glubczyce 50 13N 17 52 E
24 Glücksburg 54 48N 9 34 E
24 Glückstadt 53 46N 9 28 E
26 Gmünd, Kärnten 46 54N 13 31 E
26 Gmünd, Niederösterreich 48 45N 15 0 E
26 Gmunden 47 55N 13 48 E
28 Gniezno 52 30N 17 35 E
83 Gnowangerup 33 58S 117 59 E
63 Gô Công 10 12N 107 0 E
62 Goa 15 33N 73 59 E
62 Goa □ 15 33N 73 59 E
61 Goalpara 26 10N 90 40 E
14 Goat Fell, Mt. 55 37N 5 11W
74 Goba 7 1N 39 59 E
75 Gobabis 22 16S 19 0 E
68 Gobi, Des. 44 0N 111 0 E
62 Gobichettipalayam 11 31N 77 21 E
24 Goch 51 40N 6 9 E
62 Godavari, R. 16 37N 82 18 E
62 Godavari Pt. 17 0N 82 20 E
91 Godbout 49 20N 67 38W
90 Goderich 43 45N 81 41W
105 Golfito 8 41N 83 5W
4 Godhavn 69 15N 53 38W
60 Godhra 22 49N 73 40 E
27 Gödöllö 47 38N 19 25 E
108 Godoy Cruz 32 56S 68 52W
93 Gods L. 54 40N 94 10W
4 Godthåb 64 10N 51 46W
75 Goei Hoop, K.die =Good Hope, C. of 34 24S 18 30 E
16 Goeree 51 50N 4 0 E
16 Goes 51 30N 3 55 E
90 Gogama 47 35N 81 35W
80 Gogango 23 40S 150 2 E
28 Gogolin 50 30N 18 0 E
73 Gogriâl 8 30N 28 0 E
111 Goiânia 16 35S 49 20W
111 Goias □ 12 10S 48 0W
26 Goisern 47 38N 13 38 E
66 Gojo 34 21N 135 42 E
60 Gojra 31 10N 72 40 E
62 Gokak 16 11N 74 52 E
62 Gokarn 14 33N 74 17 E
59 Gokteik 22 26N 97 0 E
44 Göl 57 4N 9 42 E
61 Gola Gokarannath 28 4N 80 28 E
70 Gold Coast 4 0N 1 40W
28 Goldap 54 19N 22 19 E
92 Golden, Canada 51 20N 117 0W
100 Golden, U.S.A. 39 42N 105 30W
85 Golden B. 40 40S 172 50 E
62 Golden Rock 10 45N 78 48 E
93 Goldfields 37 45N 117 13W
99 Goldsboro 35 24N 77 59W
82 Goldsworthy 20 21S 119 30 E
31 Golega 39 24N 8 29W
28 Goleniów 53 35N 14 50 E
105 Golfito 8 41N 83 5W
21 Golo, R. 42 31N 9 32 E
14 Golspie 57 58N 3 58W
28 Golub Dobrzyń 53 7N 19 2 E
74 Goma 1 37S 29 10 E
61 Gomati, R. 25 32N 83 11 E
48 Gomel 52 28N 31 0 E
72 Gomera, I. 28 10N 17 5W
104 Gómez Palacio 25 40N 104 40W
24 Gommern 52 54N 11 47 E
57 Gonābād 34 15N 58 45 E
105 Gonaïves 19 20N 72 50W
61 Gonda 27 9N 81 58 E
60 Gondal 21 58N 70 52 E
73 Gonder 12 23N 37 30 E
61 Gondia 21 30N 80 10 E
30 Gondomar, Port 41 10N 8 35W
30 Gondomar, Sp. 42 7N 8 45W
19 Gondrecourt 48 26N 5 30 E
54 Gonen 33 7N 35 39 E
101 Gonzales 29 30N 97 30W
108 González Chaves 38 2S 60 5W
75 Good Hope, C. of 34 24S 18 30 E
12 Goole 53 42N 0 52W
84 Goolgowi 33 58S 154 39 E
83 Goomalling 31 19S 116 49 E
81 Goondiwindi 28 30S 150 21 E
16 Goor 52 13N 6 33 E
91 Goose Bay 53 15N 60 20W
62 Gooty 15 7N 77 41 E
61 Gopalganj 23 1N 89 55 E
25 Göppingen 48 42N 9 40 E
33 Gor 37 23N 2 58W
28 Gora R. 52 7N 17 28 E
61 Gorakhpur 26 47N 83 32 E
40 Goražde 43 40N 18 56 E
30 Gorbea, Peña 43 1N 2 50W
105 Gorda, Pta. 14 10N 83 10W
100 Gordon 42 49N 102 6W
83 Gordon River 34 10S 117 15 E
80 Gordonvale 17 5S 145 50 E
81 Gore, Australia 28 17S 151 29 E
74 Gore, Ethiopia 8 12N 35 32 E
85 Gore, N.Z. 46 5S 168 58 E
15 Gorey 52 41N 6 18W
110 Gorgona, I. 3 0N 78 10W
49 Goris 39 31N 46 23 E
37 Gorízia 45 56N 13 37 E
28 Gorka 51 39N 16 58 E
48 Gorki=Gorkiy 56 20N 44 0 E
48 Gorkiy 56 20N 44 0 E
48 Gorkovskoye Vdkhr 57 2N 43 4 E
27 Gorlice 49 35N 21 11 E
24 Görlitz 51 10N 14 59 E
49 Gorlovka 48 25N 37 58 E
41 Gorna Oryakhovitsa 43 7N 25 40 E
40 Gornja Tuzla 44 35N 18 46 E
40 Gornji Milanovac 44 0N 20 29 E
40 Gornji Vakuf 43 57N 17 34 E
50 Gorno Filinskoye 60 5N 70 0 E
48 Gornyatski 67 49N 64 20 E
65 Gorontalo 0 35N 123 13 E
15 Gort 53 4N 8 50W
48 Goryn, R. 52 8N 27 17 E
28 Gorzów Wielkopolski 52 43N 15 15 E
28 Gorzów Wielkopolski □ 52 40N 15 20 E
84 Gosford 33 23S 151 18 E
98 Goshen 41 36N 85 46W
24 Goslar 51 55N 10 23 E
37 Gospič 44 35N 15 23 E
13 Gosport 50 48N 1 8W
40 Gostiva 41 48N 20 57 E
28 Gostyń 51 50N 17 3 E
28 Gostynin 52 26N 19 29 E
45 Göteborg 57 43N 11 59 E
45 Göteborgs och Bohus □ 58 30N 11 30 E
45 Götene 58 33N 13 30 E
24 Gotha 50 56N 10 42 E
47 Gotland, I. 57 30N 18 30 E
41 Gotse Delchev 41 43N 23 46 E
66 Gōtsu 35 0N 132 14 E
24 Göttingen 51 31N 9 55 E
27 Gottwaldov 49 14N 17 40 E
16 Gouda 52 1N 4 42 E
7 Gough, I. 40 10S 9 45W
90 Govin Res. 48 35N 74 40W
84 Goulburn 32 22S 149 31 E
73 Gounou-Gaya 9 38N 15 31 E
20 Gourdon 44 44N 1 23 E
19 Gournay 49 29N 1 44 E
97 Gouverneur 44 18N 75 30W
20 Gouzon 46 12N 2 14 E
105 Governor's Harbour 25 10N 76 14W
13 Gower, Pen. 51 35N 5 10W
108 Goya 29 10S 59 10W
75 Graaff-Reinet 32 13S 24 32 E
24 Grabow 53 17N 11 31 E
37 Gračac 44 18N 15 57 E
105 Gracias a Dios, C. 15 0N 83 20W
37 Grado, Italy 45 40N 13 20 E
30 Grado, Sp. 43 23N 6 4W
41 Graeca, L. 44 5N 26 10 E
81 Grafton, Australia 29 35S 152 0 E
100 Grafton, U.S.A. 48 30N 97 25W
39 Gragnano 40 42N 14 30 E
90 Graham, Canada 49 20N 90 30W
99 Graham, N.C. 36 5N 79 22W
101 Graham, Tex. 33 7N 98 38W
92 Graham I. 53 40N 132 30W
5 Graham Ld. 65 0S 64 0W
93 Grahamdale 51 30N 98 34W
75 Grahamstown 33 19S 26 31 E
21 Graie, Alpi, Mts. 45 30N 7 10 E
70 Grain Coast, Reg. 4 20N 10 0W
111 Grajaú 5 50S 46 30W
28 Grajewo 53 39N 22 30 E
20 Gramat 44 48N 1 43 E
14 Grampian □ 57 20N 2 45W
14 Grampian Highlands, Mts. 56 50N 4 0W
42 Gramshi 40 52N 20 12 E
72 Gran Canaria, I. 27 55N 15 35W
106 Gran Chaco, Reg. 25 0S 61 0W
36 Gran Paradiso, Mt. 49 33N 7 17 E
37 Gran Sasso d'Italia, Mts. 42 25N 13 30 E
105 Granada, Nic. 11 58N 86 0W
31 Granada, Sp. 37 10N 3 35W
31 Granada □ 37 5N 4 30W
15 Granard 53 47N 7 30W
90 Granby 45 25N 72 45W
105 Grand Bahama I. 26 40N 78 30W
91 Grand Bank 47 6N 55 48W
72 Grand Bassam 5 10N 3 49W
105 Grand Bourg 15 53N 61 19W
103 Grand Canyon 36 10N 112 45W
103 Grand Canyon Nat. Park 36 15N 112 20W
105 Grand Cayman, I. 19 20N 81 20W
102 Grand Coulee Dam 48 0N 118 50W
91 Grand Falls 47 2N 67 46W
92 Grand Forks, Canada 49 0N 118 30W
100 Grand Forks, U.S.A. 48 0N 97 3W
98 Grand Haven 43 3N 86 13W
100 Grand Island 40 59N 98 25W
103 Grand Junction 39 0N 108 30W
72 Grand Lahou 5 10N 5 0W
18 Grand Lieu, L. de 47 6N 1 40W
100 Grand Marais 47 45N 90 25W
90 Grand' Mère 46 36N 72 40W
93 Grand Rapids, Canada 53 12N 99 19W
98 Grand Rapids, Mich. 42 57N 85 40W
100 Grand Rapids, Minn. 47 19N 93 29W
25 Grand St-Bernard, Col. du 45 53N 7 11 E
102 Grand Teton, Mt. 43 45N 110 57W
30 Grandas de Salime 43 13N 6 53W
112 Grande, B. 50 30S 68 20W
109 Grande, I. 23 9S 44 14W
94 Grande, R. 25 57N 97 9W
91 Grande Baie 48 19N 70 52W
91 Grande-Entrée 47 30N 61 40W
92 Grande Prairie 55 15N 118 50W
91 Grande Rivière 48 26N 64 30W
108 Grandes, Salinas, Reg. 29 37S 64 56W
31 Grândola 38 12N 8 35W
19 Grandvillers 49 40N 1 57 E
108 Graneros 34 5S 70 45W
14 Grangemouth 56 1N 3 43W
44 Grängesberg 60 6N 15 1 E
102 Grangeville 45 57N 116 4W
100 Granite City 38 45N 90 3W
85 Granity 41 39S 171 51 E
111 Granja 3 17S 40 50W
30 Granja de Moreruela 41 48N 5 44W
31 Granja de Torrehermosa 38 19N 5 35W
32 Granollers 41 39N 2 18 E
24 Gransee 53 0N 13 10 E
12 Grantham 52 55N 0 39W
14 Grantown-on-Spey 57 19N 3 36W
103 Grants 35 14N 107 57W
102 Grants Pass 42 30N 123 22W
102 Grantsville 40 35N 112 32W
18 Granville 48 50N 1 35W
33 Grao de Gandía 39 0N 0 27W
102 Grass Valley 39 18N 121 0W
21 Grasse 43 38N 6 56 E
25 Graubünden □ 46 45N 9 30 E
20 Graulhet 43 45N 1 58 E
32 Graus 42 11N 0 20 E
20 Grave, Pte. de 45 34N 1 4W
93 Gravelbourg 49 50N 105 35W
19 Gravelines 51 0N 2 10 E
90 Gravenhurst 44 52N 79 20W
81 Gravesend, Australia 29 35S 150 20 E
13 Gravesend, U.K. 51 25N 0 22 E
39 Gravina di Púglia 40 48N 16 25 E
19 Gray 47 27N 5 35 E
13 Grays 51 28N 0 23 E
93 Grayson 50 45N 102 40W
26 Graz 47 4N 15 27 E
31 Grazalema 36 46N 5 23W
40 Grdelica 42 55N 22 3 E
105 Great Abaco I. 26 15N 77 10W
80 Great Australian Basin 24 30S 143 0 E
83 Great Australian Bight 33 30S 130 0 E
105 Great Bahama Bank 23 15N 78 0W
85 Great Barrier I. 37 12S 175 25 E
80 Great Barrier Reef 19 0S 149 0 E
102 Great Basin 40 0N 116 30W
88 Great Bear L. 65 0N 120 0W
100 Great Bend 38 25N 98 55W
73 Great Bitter Lake 30 15N 32 40 E
15 Great Blasket, I. 52 5N 10 30W
8 Great Britain, I. 54 0N 2 15W
84 Great Divide, Mts. 23 0S 146 0 E
80 Great Dividing Range 25 0S 147 0 E
105 Great Exuma I. 23 30N 75 50W
102 Great Falls 47 27N 111 12W
105 Great Inagua I. 21 0N 73 20W
60 Great Indian Des. 28 0N 72 0 E
12 Great Orme's Hd. 53 20N 3 52W
12 Great Ouse, R. 52 47N 0 22 E
86 Great Plains 42 0N 100 0W
74 Great Ruaha, R. 7 56S 37 52 E
102 Great Salt L. 41 0N 112 30W
102 Great Salt Lake Des. 40 20N 113 50W
82 Great Sandy Des. 21 0S 124 0 E
92 Great Slave L. 61 30N 114 20W
99 Great Smoky Mt. Nat. Park 35 39N 83 30W
83 Great Victoria Des. 29 30S 126 30 E

90 Great Whale, R. 55 20N 77 45 E
90 Great Whale River=Poste de la Baleine 55 20N 77 40 E
12 Great Whernside, Mt. 54 9N 1 59W
12 Great Yarmouth 52 40N 1 45 E
105 Greater Antilles 20 0N 74 0W
12 Greater Manchester □ 53 35N 2 15W
64 Greater Sunda Is. 4 30S 113 0 E
30 Gredos, Sa. de 40 20N 5 0W
43 Greece ■ 40 0N 23 0 E
100 Greeley 40 30N 104 40W
98 Green Bay 44 30N 88 0W
98 Green B. 45 0N 87 30W
85 Green Island 45 54S 170 27 E
97 Green Mts. 44 0N 72 45W
103 Green River, Utah 39 0N 110 10W
102 Green River, Wyo. 41 32N 109 28W
98 Greencastle 39 40N 86 48W
99 Greeneville 31 50N 86 38W
98 Greenfield, Ind. 39 47N 85 51W
97 Greenfield, Mass. 42 38N 72 38W
97 Greenfield Park 45 26N 73 28W
4 Greenland ■ 66 0N 45 0W
4 Greenland Sea 73 0N 10 0W
14 Greenock 55 57N 4 45W
15 Greenore 54 2N 6 8W
83 Greenough, R. 28 51S 114 38 E
97 Greenport 41 5N 72 23W
99 Greensboro 36 7N 79 46W
98 Greensburg, Ind. 39 20N 85 30W
96 Greensburg, Pa. 40 18N 79 31W
72 Greenville, Liberia 5 7N 9 6W
96 Greenville, Ala. 31 50N 86 37 E
98 Greenville, Mich. 43 12N 85 14W
101 Greenville, Miss. 33 25N 91 0W
99 Greenville, N.C. 35 37N 77 26W
99 Greenville, Pa. 41 23N 80 22W
99 Greenville, S.C. 34 54N 82 24W
101 Greenville, Tex. 33 5N 96 5W
13 Greenwich, U.K. 51 28N 0 0
97 Greenwich, N.Y. 43 2N 73 36W
96 Greenwich, Ohio 41 1N 82 32W
101 Greenwood, Miss. 33 30N 90 4W
99 Greenwood, S.C. 34 13N 82 13W
80 Gregory Downs 18 35S 138 45 E
82 Gregory L. 20 10S 127 30 E
24 Greiffenberg 53 6N 13 57 E
24 Greifswald 54 6N 13 23 E
24 Greifswalder Bodden 54 12N 13 35 E
26 Grein 48 14N 14 51 E
24 Greiz 50 39N 12 12 E
48 Gremikha 67 50N 39 40 E
45 Grenå 56 26N 10 53 E
101 Grenada 33 45N 89 50W
105 Grenada, I. 12 10N 61 40W
84 Grenfell 33 52S 148 8 E
21 Grenoble 45 12N 5 42 E
65 Gresik 9 13S 112 38 E
101 Gretna 30 0N 90 2W
14 Gretna Green 55 0N 3 3W
24 Greven 52 7N 7 36 E
42 Grevená □ 40 2N 21 25 E
24 Grevenbroich 51 6N 6 32 E
16 Grevenmacher 49 41N 6 26 E
45 Grevie 56 22N 12 46 E
85 Grey, R. 42 27S 171 12 E
91 Grey Res. 48 20N 56 30W
102 Greybull 44 30N 108 3W
85 Greymouth 42 29S 171 13 E
85 Greytown, N.Z. 41 5S 175 29 E
75 Greytown, S. Africa 29 1S 30 36 E
102 Gridley 39 27N 121 47W
99 Griffin 33 15N 84 16W
84 Griffith 34 14S 145 46 E
93 Griffith Mine 50 47N 93 25W
96 Grimsby, Canada 43 12N 79 33W
12 Grimsby, U.K. 53 35N 0 5W
46 Grimsey, I. 66 33N 18 0W
92 Grimshaw 56 10N 117 40W
47 Grimstad 58 22N 8 35 E
25 Grindelwald 46 38N 8 2 E
45 Grindsted 55 46N 8 55 E
100 Grinnell 41 45N 92 50W
30 Griñon 40 13N 3 51W
37 Grintavec, Mt. 46 21N 14 32 E
19 Gris Nez, C. 50 50N 1 35 E
20 Grisolles 43 49N 1 19 E
37 Grmeč Planina 44 43N 16 16 E
48 Grodno 53 42N 23 52 E
28 Grodzisk Mãzowiecki 52 7N 20 37 E
28 Grodzisk Wlkp. 52 15N 16 22 E
18 Groix, I. de 47 38N 3 28W
24 Gronau 52 13N 7 2 E
46 Grong 64 25N 12 8 E
16 Groningen 53 15N 6 35 E
16 Groningen □ 53 16N 6 40 E
75 Groot-Brakrivier 34 2S 22 18 E
75 Groot Karoo, Reg. 32 35S 23 0 E
75 Groot Namakwaland=Namaland, Reg. 26 0S 18 0 E
80 Groote Eylandt, I. 14 0S 136 50 E
75 Grootfontein 19 31S 18 6 E
33 Grosa, Pta. 39 6N 1 36 E
26 Gross Glockner, Mt. 47 5N 12 40 E
24 Gross Ottersleben 52 5N 11 33 E
24 Grossenbrode 54 21N 11 4 E
24 Grossenhain 51 17N 13 32 E
37 Grosseto 42 45N 11 7 E
26 Grossgerungs 48 34N 14 57 E
97 Groton 41 22N 75 5W
39 Grottáglie 40 32N 17 25 E
96 Grove City 41 10N 80 5W
97 Groveton 44 34N 71 30W
37 Grožnjan 45 22N 13 43 E
49 Groznyy 43 20N 45 45 E
40 Grubišno Polje 45 44N 17 12 E
41 Grudovo 42 21N 27 10 E
28 Grudziądz 53 30N 18 47 E
39 Grumo Appula 41 2N 16 43 E
44 Grums 59 22N 13 5 E
25 Gruyères 46 35N 7 4 E
48 Gryazi 52 30N 39 58 E
5 Grytviken 53 50S 37 10W
25 Gstaad 46 28N 7 18 E
105 Guacanayabo, G. de 20 40N 77 20W
104 Guadalajara, Mexico 20 40N 103 20W
30 Guadalajara, Sp. 40 37N 3 12W
32 Guadalajara □ 40 47N 3 0W
31 Guadalcanal 38 5N 5 52W
76 Guadalcanal, I. 9 32S 160 12 E
31 Guadalén, R. 38 5N 3 32W
31 Guadalete, R. 36 35N 6 13W
31 Guadalimar, R. 37 58W 3 45W
31 Guadalmez, R. 38 46N 5 4W
32 Guadalope, R. 41 15N 0 3W
29 Guadalquivir, R. 36 47N 6 22W
31 Guadalupe, Sp. 39 27N 5 17W
103 Guadalupe, U.S.A. 34 59N 120 33W
31 Guadalupe, Sa. de 39 26N 5 25W
101 Guadalupe Pk. 31 50N 105 30W
30 Guadarrama, Sa. de 41 0N 4 0W
105 Guadeloupe, I. 16 20N 61 40W
105 Guadeloupe Pass. 16 50N 68 15W
31 Guadiana, R. 37 14N 7 22W
33 Guadiana Menor, R. 37 56N 3 15W
31 Guadiaro, R. 36 17N 5 17W
32 Guadiela, R. 40 22N 2 49W
33 Guadix 37 18N 3 11W
112 Guafo, B. del 43 35S 74 0W
109 Guaíra 24 5S 54 10W
112 Guaitecas, Is. 44 0S 74 30W
110 Guajira, Pen. de la 12 0N 72 0W
37 Gualdo Tadino 43 14N 12 46 E
108 Gualeguay 33 10S 59 20W
108 Gualeguaychú 33 3S 58 31W
76 Guam, I. 13 27N 144 45 E
105 Guanabacoa 23 8N 82 18W
109 Guanabara □ 23 0S 43 25W
105 Guanacaste 10 40N 85 30W
105 Guanajay 22 56N 82 42W
104 Guanajuato 21 0N 101 20W
104 Guanajuato □ 20 40N 101 20W
110 Guanare 8 42N 69 12W
105 Guantánamo 20 10N 75 20W
109 Guaporé 12 0S 64 0W
110 Guaporé, R. 29 10S 51 54W
110 Guaqui 16 41S 68 54W
32 Guara, Sa. de 42 19N 0 15W
109 Guarapari 20 40S 40 30W
109 Guarapuava 25 20S 51 30W
109 Guaratinguetá 22 49S 45 9W
109 Guaratuba 25 53S 48 38W
30 Guarda 40 32N 7 20W
30 Guarda □ 40 40N 7 20W
33 Guardamar del Segura 38 5N 0 39W
37 Guardiagrele 42 11N 14 11 E
30 Guardo 42 47N 4 50W
31 Guareña 38 51N 6 6W
30 Guareña, R. 41 29N 5 23W
109 Guaria □ 26 0S 56 30W
109 Guarujá 24 2S 46 25W
109 Guarus 21 30S 41 20W
110 Guasaualito 7 15N 70 44W
110 Guasipati 7 28N 61 54W
36 Guastalla 44 55N 10 40 E
104 Guatemala 14 38N 90 31W
104 Guatemala ■ 15 40N 90 30W
110 Guaviare, R. 4 3N 67 44W
109 Guaxupé 21 10S 47 5W
105 Guayama 17 59N 66 7W
110 Guayaquil 2 15S 79 52W
110 Guayaquil, G. de 3 10S 81 0W
37 Gúbbio 43 20N 12 34 E
28 Gubin 51 58N 14 45 E
63 Guchil 5 35N 102 10 E
68 Guchin-Us 45 28N 102 10 E
62 Gudalur 11 30N 76 29 E
44 Gudbrandsdalen 62 0N 9 14 E
62 Gudivada 16 30N 81 15 E
62 Gudiyatam 12 57N 78 55 E
62 Gudur 14 12N 79 55 E
19 Guebwiller 47 55N 7 12 E
30 Guecho 43 21N 2 59W
72 Guéckédou 8 40N 10 5W
72 Guelma 36 25N 7 29 E
96 Guelph 43 35N 80 20W
18 Guémené-sur-Scorff 48 4N 3 13W
18 Guer 47 54N 2 8W
18 Guérande 47 20N 2 26W
20 Guéret 46 11N 1 51 E
18 Guérigny 47 6N 3 10 E
30 Guernica 43 19N 2 40W
13 Guernsey, I. 49 30N 2 35W
104 Guerrero □ 17 30N 100 0W
21 Gueugnon 45 36N 4 3 E
37 Guglionesi 51 55N 14 54 E
109 Guia Lopes da Laguna 21 26S 56 7W
106 Guiana Highlands, Mts. 5 0N 60 0W
75 Guibes 26 41S 16 49 E
30 Guijo de Coria 40 6N 6 28W
13 Guildford 51 14N 0 34W
21 Guillaumes 44 5N 6 52 E
18 Guilvinec 47 48N 4 17W
111 Guimarães 2 9S 44 35W
30 Guimarãis 41 28N 8 24W
65 Guimaras, I. 10 35N 122 37 E
70 Guinea, Reg. 9 0N 3 0 E
72 Guinea ■ 10 20N 10 0W
70 Guinea, G. of 3 0N 2 30 E
72 Guinea-Bissau ■ 12 0N 15 0W
105 Güines 22 50N 82 0W
18 Guingamp 48 34N 3 10W
18 Guipavas 48 26N 4 29W
32 Guipuzcoa □ 43 12N 2 15W
110 Guiria 10 32N 62 1iw
19 Guiscard 49 40N 3 0 E
19 Guise 49 52N 3 35 E
30 Guitiriz 43 11N 7 50W
65 Guiuan 11 2N 125 44 E
20 Gujan-Mestres 44 38N 1 4W
60 Gujarat □ 23 20N 71 0 E
60 Gujranwala 32 10N 74 12 E
60 Gujrat 32 40N 74 2 E
62 Gulbarga 17 20N 76 50 E
62 Guledgud 16 3N 75 48 E
101 Gulfport 30 28N 89 3W
93 Gull Lake 50 10N 108 55W
50 Gulshad 46 45N 74 25 E
44 Gulsvik 60 24N 9 38 E
74 Gulu 2 48N 32 17 E
84 Gum Lake 32 42S 143 9 E
67 Guma 37 37N 78 18 E
60 Gumal, R. 31 56N 70 22 E
30 Gumiel de Hizán 41 46N 3 41W
80 Gumla 23 2N 84 32 E
66 Gumma □ 36 30N 138 20 E
24 Gummersbach 51 2N 7 32 E
72 Gummi 12 4N 5 9 E
60 Guna 24 40N 77 19 E
84 Gundagai 35 3S 148 6 E
81 Gunnedah 30 59S 150 15 E
84 Gunning 34 47S 149 14 E
103 Gunnison, Colo. 38 32N 106 56W
102 Gunnison, Utah 39 11N 111 48W
62 Guntakal 15 11N 77 27 E
99 Guntersville 34 18N 86 16W
62 Guntur 16 23N 80 30 E
64 Gunungsitoli 1 15N 97 30 E
93 Gunworth 51 20N 108 10W
25 Gunzenhausen 49 6N 10 45 E
56 Gürchān 34 55N 49 25 E
60 Gurdaspur 32 5N 75 25 E
60 Gurgaon 28 33N 77 10 E
81 Gurley 29 45S 149 48 E
63 Gurun 5 49N 100 27 E
111 Gurupá 1 20S 51 45W
50 Guryer 47 5N 52 0 E
72 Gusau 12 18N 6 31 E
38 Gúspini 39 32N 8 38 E
27 Güssing 47 3N 16 20 E
24 Güstrow 53 47N 12 12 E
27 Guta=Kalárovo 47 54N 18 0 E
24 Gütersloh 51 54N 8 25 E
83 Gutha 28 58S 115 55 E
101 Guthrie 35 55N 97 30W
110 Guyana ■ 5 0N 59 0W
20 Guyenne, Reg. 44 30N 0 40 E
81 Guyra 30 15S 151 40 E
59 Gwa 17 30N 94 40 E
58 Gwādar 25 10N 62 18 E
83 Gwalia 28 55S 121 20 E
60 Gwalior 26 12N 78 10 E
75 Gwanda 20 55S 29 0 E
28 Gwda, R. 53 4N 16 44 E
15 Gweedore 55 4N 8 15W
75 Gwelo 19 27S 29 49 E
13 Gwent □ 51 45N 3 0W
12 Gwynedd □ 53 0N 4 0W
50 Gydanskiy Pol. 70 0N 78 0 E
81 Gympie 26 11S 152 38 E
27 Gyoma 46 56N 20 58 E
27 Gyöngyös 47 48N 20 15 E
27 Györ 47 41N 17 40 E
27 Györ Sopron □ 47 40N 17 20 E
93 Gypsumville 51 45N 98 40W
27 Gyula 46 38N 21 17 E

H

63 Ha Dong 20 58N 105 46 E
63 Ha Giang 22 46N 104 56 E
63 Ha Tinh 18 20N 105 54 E
25 Haag 48 11N 12 12 E
16 Haarlem 52 23N 4 39 E
85 Haast, R. 43 50S 169 2 E
58 Hab Nadi Chauki 25 0N 66 50 E
61 Habiganj 24 24N 91 30 E
66 Hachinohe 40 30N 141 29 E
66 Hachiōji 33 3N 139 55 E
92 Hackett 52 9N 112 28 E
97 Hackettstown 40 51N 74 50W
60 Hadali 32 16N 72 11 E
54 Hadar Ramatayim 52 8N 34 45 E
57 Hadd, Ras al 22 35N 59 50 E
14 Haddington 55 57N 2 48W
72 Hadejia 12 30N 9 59 E
54 Hadera 32 27N 34 55 E
45 Haderslev 55 17N 9 30 E
55 Hadhramawt, Reg. 15 30N 49 30 E
12 Hadrian's Wall 55 0N 2 30 E
68 Haeju 38 12N 125 41 E
56 Hafar al Bátin 28 25N 46 50 E
60 Hafizabad 32 5N 73 40 E
59 Haflong 25 10N 93 5 E
46 Hafnarfjördur 64 3N 21 55W
54 Hagalil, Reg. 32 53N 35 18 E
62 Hagari, R. 15 44N 76 56 E
24 Hagen 51 21N 7 29 E
98 Hagerstown 39 39N 77 46W
20 Hagetmau 43 39N 0 37W
44 Hagfors 60 3N 13 45 E
46 Hagi, Iceland 65 28N 23 25W
66 Hagi, Japan 34 30N 131 30 E
18 Hague, C. de la 49 43N 1 57W
19 Haguenau 48 49N 7 47 E
54 Haifa 32 46N 35 0 E
83 Haig 30 55S 126 10 E
69 Haikow 20 0N 110 20 E
68 Hailar 49 12N 119 37 E
68 Hailar, R. 49 35N 117 55 E
102 Hailey 43 30N 114 15W
90 Haileybury 47 30N 79 38W
68 Hailun 47 24N 127 0 E
68 Hailung 42 46N 125 57 E
69 Haimen 31 48N 121 8 E
69 Hainan, I. 19 0N 110 0 E
16 Hainaut □ 50 30N 4 0 E
27 Hainburg 48 9N 16 56 E
92 Haines Junction 60 45N 137 30W
26 Hainfeld 48 3N 15 48 E
69 Haining 30 16N 120 47 E
63 Haiphong 20 55N 105 42 E
69 Haitan Tao, I. 25 30N 119 45 E
105 Haiti ■ 19 0N 72 30W
69 Haiyen 30 28N 120 57 E
27 Hajdu-Bihar □ 47 30N 21 30 E
27 Hajdúböszörmény 47 40N 21 30 E
27 Hajdúdurog 47 48N 21 30 E
27 Hajdúhadház 47 40N 21 40 E
27 Hajdúnánás 47 50N 21 26 E
27 Hajdúszoboszló 47 27N 21 22 E
61 Hajipur 25 45N 85 20 E
28 Hajnówka 52 45N 23 36 E
57 Hajr, Reg. 24 0N 56 34 E
45 Håkantorp 58 18N 12 55 E
66 Hakodate 41 45N 140 44 E
66 Haku-San, Mt. 36 9N 136 46 E
66 Hakui 36 53N 136 47 E
56 Ḥalab 36 10N 37 15 E
73 Halaib 22 5N 36 30 E
24 Halberstadt 51 53N 11 2 E
85 Halcombe 40 8S 175 30 E
44 Halden 59 7N 11 30 E
24 Haldensleben 52 17N 11 30 E
61 Haldwani 29 25N 79 30 E
94 Haleakala, Mt. 20 42N 156 15W
54 Halhul 31 35N 35 7 E
55 Hali 18 40N 41 15 E
90 Haliburton 45 3N 78 30W
91 Halifax, Canada 44 38N 63 35W
12 Halifax, U.K. 53 43N 1 51W
26 Hall 47 17N 11 30 E
89 Hall Lake 68 30N 81 0W
45 Hallands □ 57 0N 12 37 E

45 Hallandsås Mt. 56 23N 13 0 E
16 Halle, Belgium 50 44N 4 13W
24 Halle, E. Germany 51 29N 12 0 E
24 Halle □ 51 28N 11 58 E
44 Hällefors 59 46N 14 30 E
26 Hallein 47 40N 13 5 E
81 Hallett 33 25S 138 55 E
5 Halley Bay 76 30S 27 0W
44 Hallingdalselv, R. 60 24N 9 35 E
46 Hällnäs 64 18N 19 40 E
82 Halls Creek 18 20S 128 0 E
44 Hallsberg 59 5N 15 7 E
44 Hallstahammar 59 38N 16 15 E
26 Hallstatt 47 33N 13 38 E
97 Hallstead 41 56N 75 45W
65 Halmahera, I. 0 40N 128 0 E
45 Halmstad 56 37N 12 56 E
73 Halq el Oued 36 53N 10 10 E
24 Haltern 51 44N 7 10 E
56 Hamā 35 5N 36 40 E
66 Hamada 34 50N 132 10 E
56 Hamadān 34 52N 48 32 E
56 Hamadān □ 35 0N 48 40 E
66 Hamamatsu 34 45N 137 45 E
44 Hamar 60 48N 11 7 E
24 Hamburg, Germany 53 32N 9 59 E
96 Hamburg, U.S.A. 40 37N 95 38W
97 Hamden 41 21N 72 56W
47 Häme □ 61 30N 24 30 E
47 Hämeenlinna 61 3N 24 26 E
83 Hamelin Pool 26 22S 114 20 E
24 Hameln 52 7N 9 24 E
82 Hamersley Ra. 22 0S 117 45 E
68 Hamhung 40 0N 127 30 E
67 Hami 42 54N 93 28 E
84 Hamilton, Aus. 37 37S 142 0 E
105 Hamilton, Bermuda 32 15N 64 45W
96 Hamilton, Canada 43 20N 79 50W
85 Hamilton, N.Z. 37 47S 175 19 E
14 Hamilton, U.K. 55 47N 4 2W
102 Hamilton, Mont. 46 20N 114 6W
98 Hamilton, Ohio 39 20N 84 35W
80 Hamilton Hotel 22 45S 140 40 E
97 Hamilton Mt. 43 25N 74 22W
93 Hamiota 50 11N 100 38W
99 Hamlet 34 56N 79 40W
24 Hamm 51 40N 7 58 E
44 Hammarö, I. 59 20N 13 30 E
46 Hammerfest 70 33N 23 50 E
98 Hammond, Ind. 41 40N 87 30W
101 Hammond, La. 30 30N 90 28W
85 Hampden 45 18S 170 50 E
13 Hampshire □ 51 3N 1 20W
98 Hampton 37 4N 76 8W
56 Hamra 24 2N 38 55 E
44 Hamrånge 60 59N 17 5 E
69 Han Kiang, R. 30 32N 114 22 E
69 Hanchung 33 10N 107 2 E
100 Hancock 47 10N 88 35W
55 Handa, Japan 34 53N 137 0 E
66 Handa, Somalia 10 37N 51 2 E
74 Handeni 5 25S 38 2 E
27 Handlová 48 45N 18 35 E
54 Hanegev, Reg. 30 50N 35 0 E
92 Haney 49 12N 122 40W
103 Hanford 36 25N 119 45W
69 Hangchow 30 12N 120 1 E
69 Hangchow Wan, G. 30 30N 121 30 E
47 Hangö 59 59N 22 57 E
68 Hanh 51 32N 100 35 E
54 Hanita 33 5N 35 10 E
69 Hankow 30 32N 114 20 E
68 Hanku 39 16N 117 50 E
85 Hanmer 42 32S 172 50 E
92 Hanna 51 40N 112 0W
100 Hannibal 39 42N 91 22W
24 Hannover 52 23N 9 43 E
45 Hanö, B. 55 45N 14 60 E
45 Hanö, I. 56 0N 14 50 E
63 Hanoi 21 5N 150 40 E
90 Hanover, Canada 44 9N 81 2W
97 Hanover, N.H. 43 43N 72 17W
98 Hanover, Pa. 39 46N 76 59W
112 Hanover, I. 50 58S 74 40W
60 Hansi 29 10N 75 57 E
68 Hantan 36 42N 114 30 E
69 Hanyang 30 30N 114 19 E
46 Haparanda 65 52N 24 8 E
91 Happy Valley 155 53N 60 10W
60 Hapur 28 45N 77 45 E
68 Har-Ayrag 45 50N 109 30 E
67 Har Us Nuur, L. 48 0N 92 0 E
54 Har Yehuda, Reg. 31 40N 35 0 E
56 Harad 24 15N 49 0 E
55 Haradera 4 33N 47 38 E
75 Harare 17 50S 31 2 E
68 Harbin 45 46N 126 51 E
91 Harbour Breton 47 29N 55 50W
91 Harbour Deep 50 25N 56 30W
91 Harbour Grace 47 40N 53 22W
24 Harburg 53 27N 9 58 E
60 Harda 22 27N 77 5 E
47 Hardanger Fd. 60 15N 6 0 E
75 Hardap Dam 24 28S 17 48 E
16 Harderwijk 52 21N 5 36 E
75 Harding 30 22S 29 55 E
60 Hardwar 29 58N 78 16 E
112 Hardy, Pen. 55 30S 68 20W
55 Harer 9 20N 42 8 E
18 Harfleur 49 30N 0 10 E
55 Hargeisa 9 30N 44 2 E
62 Harihar 14 32N 75 44 E
62 Haripad 9 14N 76 28 E
12 Harlech 52 52N 4 7W
102 Harlem 48 29N 108 39W
16 Harlingen, Neth. 53 11N 5 25 E
101 Harlingen, U.S.A. 26 30N 97 50W
13 Harlow 51 47N 0 9 E
102 Harlowton 46 30N 109 54W
102 Harney L. 43 0N 119 0W
102 Harney Basin 43 30N 119 0W
100 Harney Pk. 43 52N 103 33W
44 Härnösand 62 38N 18 5 E
30 Haro 42 35N 2 55W
62 Harpanahalli 14 47N 75 59 E
99 Harriman 36 0N 84 35W
91 Harrington
Harbour 50 31N 59 30W
14 Harris, I. 57 50N 6 55W
98 Harrisburg, Ill. 37 42N 88 30W
97 Harrison, N.Y. 40 58N 73 43W
101 Harrison, Ohio 36 10N 93 4W
96 Harrisburg, Pa. 40 18N 76 52W
88 Harrison B. 70 25N 151 0W
98 Harrisonburg 38 28N 78 52W
100 Harrisonville 38 45N 93 45W
90 Harriston 43 57N 80 53W
12 Harrogate 53 59N 1 32W
13 Harrow 51 35N 0 15W
97 Hartford 41 47N 72 41W
91 Hartland 46 20N 67 32W
13 Hartland Pt. 51 2N 4 32W
12 Hartlepool 54 42N 1 11W
75 Hartley 18 10S 30 7 E
92 Hartley Bay 46 4N 80 45W
93 Hartney 49 30N 100 35W
99 Hartsville 34 23N 80 2W
60 Harunabad 29 35N 73 2 E
83 Harvey, Australia 33 4S 115 48 E
98 Harvey, U.S.A. 41 40N 87 40W
13 Harwich 51 56N 1 18 E
60 Haryana 29 0N 76 10 E
24 Harz, Mts. 51 40N 10 40 E
13 Haslemere 51 5N 0 41W
20 Hasparren 43 24N 1 18W
62 Hassan 13 0N 76 5 E
16 Hasselt 50 56N 5 21 E
72 Hassi Messaoud 31 15N 6 35 E
72 Hassi R'Mel 32 35N 3 24 E
45 Hässleholm 56 9N 13 46 E
85 Hastings, N.Z. 39 39S 176 52 E
13 Hastings, U.K. 50 51N 0 36 E
98 Hastings, Mich. 42 40N 85 20 E
100 Hastings, Neb. 40 34N 98 22W
103 Hatch 32 45N 107 8W
40 Hateg 45 36N 22 55 E
67 Hatgal 50 40N 100 0 E
60 Hathras 27 36N 78 6 E
61 Hatia I. 22 50N 91 20 E
99 Hatteras, C. 35 10N 75 30W
101 Hattiesburg 31 20N 89 20W
27 Hatvan 47 40N 19 45 E
47 Haugesund 59 23N 5 13 E
41 Haunţii
Sebeşului, Mt. 45 30N 23 30 E
55 Haura 13 50N 47 35 E
85 Hauraki, G. 36 35S 175 5 E
26 Hausruck, Mts. 48 6N 13 30 E
19 Haut-Rhin □ 48 0N 7 15 E
21 Haute-Corse □ 42 30N 9 20 E
20 Haute-Garonne □ 43 28N 1 30 E
20 Haute-Loire □ 45 5N 3 50 E
19 Haute-Marne □ 48 10N 5 20 E
91 Hauterive 49 10N 68 25W
19 Hautmont 50 15N 3 55 E
19 Haute-Saône □ 47 45N 6 10 E
21 Haute-Savoie □ 46 0N 6 20 E
20 Haute-Vienne □ 45 50N 1 10 E
21 Hautes-Alpes □ 44 40N 6 30 E
20 Hautes-Pyrénées □ 43 0N 0 10 E
13 Havant 50 51N 0 59W
90 Havelock 44 26N 77 53W
85 Havelock North 39 42S 176 53 E
13 Haverfordwest 51 48N 4 59W
97 Haverhill 42 50N 71 2W
62 Haveri 14 53N 75 24 E
13 Havering 51 33N 0 20 E
97 Haverstraw 41 12N 73 58W
26 Havlíckuv Brod 49 36N 15 33 E
102 Havre 48 40N 109 34W
91 Havre St. Pierre 50 18N 63 33W
56 Havza 41 0N 35 35 E
94 Hawaii □ 20 0N 155 0W
94 Hawaii, I. 20 0N 155 0W
85 Hawea, L. 44 28S 169 19 E
85 Hawera 39 35S 174 19 E
14 Hawick 55 25N 2 48W
90 Hawk Junction 48 5N 84 35W
85 Hawke, B. 39 25S 177 20 E
81 Hawker 31 59S 138 22 E
85 Hawke's Bay □ 39 45S 176 35 E
91 Hawke's Harbour 53 2N 55 50W
91 Hawkesbury,
Nova Scotia 45 40N 61 10W
90 Hawkesbury, Ont. 45 35N 74 40W
102 Hawthorne 38 37N 118 47W
84 Hay, Australia 34 30S 144 51 E
13 Hay, U.K. 52 4N 3 9W
92 Hay River 60 50N 115 50W
19 Hayange 49 20N 6 2 E
103 Hayden 40 30N 107 22W
80 Haydon 18 0S 141 30 E
88 Hayes, Mt. 63 37N 146 43W
93 Hayes, R. 57 3N 92 9W
13 Hayling I. 50 40N 1 0W
100 Hays 38 55N 99 25W
13 Haywards Heath 51 0N 0 5W
57 Hazārān,
Kūh-e, Mt. 29 35N 57 20 E
98 Hazard 37 18N 83 10W
61 Hazaribagh 23 58N 85 26 E
19 Hazebrouck 50 42N 2 31 E
92 Hazelton 55 20N 127 42W
97 Hazleton 40 58N 76 0W
54 Hazor 33 2N 35 2 E
57 Hazrat Imam 37 15N 68 50 E
102 Healdsburg 38 33N 122 51W
12 Heanor 53 1N 1 20W
3 Heard I. 53 0S 74 0 E
90 Hearst 49 40N 83 41W
91 Heart's Content 47 54N 53 27W
91 Heath Steele 48 30N 66 20W
81 Hebel 28 59S 147 48 E
91 Hebertville 47 0N 71 30W
14 Hebrides, Inner, Is. 57 20N 6 40W
14 Hebrides, Outer, Is. 57 50N 7 25W
89 Hebron, Canada 58 10N 62 50W
54 Hebron, Jordan 31 32N 35 6 E
92 Hecate Str. 53 10N 130 30W
44 Hedemora 60 18N 15 58 E
44 Hedmark □ 61 45N 11 0 E
16 Heemstede 52 19N 4 37 E
16 Heerde 52 24N 6 2 E
16 Heerenveen 52 57N 5 55 E
16 Heerlen 50 55N 6 0 E
24 Heide 54 10N 9 7 E
25 Heidelberg 49 23N 8 41 E
25 Heidenheim 48 40N 10 10 E
75 Heilbron 27 16S 27 59 E
25 Heilbronn 49 8N 9 13 E
24 Heiligenstadt 51 22N 10 9 E
68 Heilungkiang □ 47 30N 129 0 E
47 Heinola 61 13N 26 10 E
93 Heinsburg 53 50N 110 30W
59 Heinze Is. 14 25N 97 45 E
46 Hekla, Mt. 63 56N 19 35W
101 Helena, Ark. 34 30N 90 35W
102 Helena, Mont. 46 40N 112 0W
14 Helensburgh 56 0N 4 44W
85 Helensville 36 41S 174 29 E
54 Helez 31 36N 34 39 E
45 Helgasjön, L. 57 0N 14 54 E
24 Heligoland, I. 54 10N 7 51 E
75 Hell-Ville 13 25S 48 16 E
16 Hellendoorn 52 24N 6 27 E
33 Hellín 38 31N 1 40W
57 Helmand, Hamun 31 0N 61 0 E
57 Helmand □ 31 0N 64 0 E
57 Helmand, R. 31 12N 61 34 E
16 Helmond 51 29N 5 41 E
14 Helmsdale 58 7N 3 40W
24 Helmstedt 52 16N 11 0 E
45 Helsingborg 56 3N 12 42 E
47 Helsingfors=
Helsinki 60 15N 25 3 E
45 Helsingør 56 2N 12 35 E
47 Helsinki 60 15N 25 3 E
13 Helston 50 7N 5 17W
12 Helvellyn, Mt. 54 31N 3 1W
73 Helwân 29 50N 31 20 E
13 Hemel
Hempstead 51 45N 0 28W
32 Henares, R. 40 24N 3 30W
20 Hendaye 43 23N 1 47W
98 Henderson, Ky. 37 50N 87 38W
99 Henderson, N.C. 36 18N 78 23W
101 Henderson, Tex. 32 5N 94 49W
99 Hendersonville 35 21N 82 28W
81 Hendon 28 5S 151 50 E
16 Hengelo 52 15N 6 48 E
69 Hengyang 26 57N 112 28 E
19 Hénin Beaumont 50 25N 2 58 E
18 Hennebont 47 49N 3 19W
24 Henningsdorf 52 38N 13 13 E
90 Henrietta Maria, C. 55 10N 82 30W
74 Henrique de
Carvalho 9 39S 20 24 E
101 Henryetta 35 2N 96 0W
84 Henty 35 30N 147 0 E
59 Henzada 17 38N 95 35 E
102 Heppner 45 27N 119 34W
57 Herat 34 20N 62 7 E
57 Herat □ 34 20N 62 7 E
20 Hérault □ 43 34N 3 15 E
20 Hérault, R. 43 17N 3 26 E
93 Herbert 50 30N 107 10W
80 Herbert Downs 23 0S 139 11 E
40 Hercegnavi 42 30N 18 33 E
13 Hereford, U.K. 52 4N 2 42W
101 Hereford, U.S.A. 34 50N 102 28W
13 Hereford and
Worcester □ 52 14N 1 42W
16 Herentals 51 12N 4 51 E
24 Herford 52 7N 8 40 E
19 Héricourt 47 32N 6 55 E
25 Herisau 47 22N 9 17 E
97 Herkimer 43 0N 74 59W
18 Herm, I. 49 30N 2 28W
26 Hermagor-
Pressegger See, L. 46 38N 13 23 E
84 Hermidale 31 30S 146 42 E
102 Hermiston 45 50N 119 16W
85 Hermitage 43 44S 170 5 E
112 Hermite, I. 55 50S 68 0W
56 Hermon, Mt.=
Sheikh, Jabal ash 33 20N 26 0 E
104 Hermosillo 29 10N 111 0W
27 Hernad R. 47 56N 21 8 E
109 Hernandarias 25 20S 54 50W
108 Hernando 32 28S 64 50W
24 Herne 51 33N 7 12 E
13 Herne Bay 51 22N 1 8 E
45 Herning 56 8N 9 0 E
90 Heron Bay 48 40N 85 25W
56 Herowabad 37 37N 48 32 E
30 Herrera de
Pisuerga 42 35N 4 20W
31 Herrera del
Duque 39 10N 5 3W
101 Herrin 37 50N 89 0W
45 Herrljunga 58 5N 13 5 E
16 Herstal 50 40N 5 38 E
13 Hertford 51 47N 0 4W
13 Hertford □ 51 51N 0 5W
30 Hervás 40 16N 5 52W
77 Hervey Is. 19 30S 159 0W
24 Herzberg 51 38N 10 20 E
54 Herzliyya 32 10N 34 50 E
26 Herzogenburg 48 17N 15 41 E
24 Hessen □ 50 57N 9 20 E
24 Hettstedt 51 39N 11 30 E
18 Heve, C. de la 49 30N 0 5 E
27 Heves □ 47 50N 20 0 E
89 Hewett, C. 70 30N 68 0W
12 Hexham 54 58N 2 7W
12 Heysham 54 5N 2 53W
84 Heywood 38 8S 141 37 E
100 Hibbing 47 30N 93 0W
99 Hickory 35 46N 81 17W
97 Hicksville 40 46N 73 30W
66 Hida Sammyaku,
Mts. 36 0N 137 10 E
104 Hidalgo □ 20 30N 99 10W
104 Hidalgo del Parral 26 10N 104 50W
26 Hieflau 47 36N 14 46 E
72 Hierro, I. 27 57N 17 56W
69 Hifung 22 59N 115 17 E
66 Higashiósaka 34 39N 135 35 E
83 Higginsville 31 42S 121 38 E
99 High Point 35 57N 79 58W
92 High Prairie 55 30N 116 30W
92 High River 50 30N 113 50W
13 High Wycombe 51 37N 0 45W
70 High Veld 26 30S 30 0 E
14 Highland □ 57 30N 4 50W
98 Highland Park, Ill. 42 10N 87 50W
98 Highland Park,
Mich. 42 25N 83 6W
32 Hijar 41 10N 0 27W
56 Hijāz, Reg. 26 0N 37 30 E
66 Hikari 33 58N 131 56 E
66 Hikone 35 15N 136 10 E
85 Hikurangi 37 54S 178 5 E
24 Hildersheim 52 9N 9 55 E
16 Hillegom 52 18N 4 35 E
45 Hillerød 55 56N 12 19 E
13 Hillingdon 51 33N 0 29W
100 Hillsboro, Kan. 38 28N 97 10W
102 Hillsboro, Oreg. 45 31N 123 0W
101 Hillsboro, Tex. 32 0N 97 10W
90 Hillsport 49 27N 85 34W
84 Hillston 33 30S 145 31 E
94 Hilo 19 44N 155 5W
16 Hilversum 52 14N 5 10 E
60 Himachal
Pradesh □ 31 30N 77 0 E
52 Himalaya, Mts. 29 0N 84 0 E
66 Himeji 34 50N 134 40 E
66 Himi 36 50N 137 0 E
45 Himmerland, Reg. 56 50N 9 38 E
56 Hims=Homs 34 40N 36 45 E
80 Hinchinbrook, I. 18 20S 146 15 E
13 Hinckley 52 33N 1 21W
60 Hindaun 26 44N 77 5 E
84 Hindmarsh, L. 35 50S 141 55 E
57 Hindukush, Mts. 36 0N 71 0 E

62 Hindupur 13 49N 77 32 E
92 Hines Creek 56 20N 118 40W
69 Hingan 25 39N 110 43 E
60 Hinganghat 20 30N 78 59 E
68 Hingcheng 40 21N 120 10 E
102 Hingham 48 40N 110 29W
67 Hingi 25 4N 105 2 E
69 Hingning 24 2N 115 55 E
62 Hingoli 19 41N 77 15 E
69 Hingwa Wan, G. 25 0N 120 0 E
46 Hinnøy, I. 68 40N 16 28 E
31 Hinojosa del Duque 38 30N 5 17W
92 Hinton, Canada 53 26N 117 28W
98 Hinton, U.S.A. 37 40N 80 51W
61 Hirakud Dam 21 32N 83 45 E
66 Hiratsuka 35 40N 139 36 E
66 Hirosaki 40 35N 140 25 E
66 Hiroshima 34 30N 132 30 E
66 Hiroshima □ 34 30N 133 0 E
19 Hirson 49 55N 4 4 E
41 Hîrsova 44 41N 27 57 E
45 Hirtshals 57 36N 9 55 E
105 Hispaniola, I. 19 0N 71 0W
60 Hissar 29 12N 75 45 E
66 Hita 33 42N 130 52 E
66 Hitachi 36 40N 140 35 E
13 Hitchin 51 57N 0 16W
66 Hitoyoshi 32 13N 130 45 E
46 Hitra, I. 63 30N 8 45 E
44 Hjälmaren, L. 59 18N 15 40 E
45 Hjørring 57 29N 9 59 E
72 Ho 6 37N 0 27 E
63 Hoa Binh 20 52N 105 12 E
63 Hoa Da 11 16N 108 40 E
92 Hoadley 52 45N 114 30W
63 Hoai Nhon 14 28N 103 37 E
80 Hobart, Australia 42 50S 147 21 E
101 Hobart, U.S.A. 35 0N 99 5W
101 Hobbs 32 40N 103 3W
16 Hoboken, Belgium 51 11N 4 21 E
97 Hoboken, U.S.A. 40 45N 74 4W
45 Hobro 56 39N 9 46 E
69 Hichih 24 43N 107 43 E
63 Ho Chi Minh City 10 58N 106 40 E
26 Hochschwab, Mts. 47 36N 15 5 E
25 Höchst 50 6N 8 33 E
69 Hochwan 30 0N 106 15 E
25 Hockenheim 49 18N 8 33 E
66 Hodaka-Dake, Mt. 36 20N 137 30 E
55 Hodeida 14 50N 43 0 E
93 Hodgson 51 20N 97 40W
27 Hódmezövásárhely 46 28N 20 22 E
72 Hodna, Chott el 35 30N 5 0 E
27 Hodonin 48 50N 17 0 E
16 Hoek van Holland 52 0N 4 7 E
25 Hof 50 18N 11 55 E
69 Hofei 31 45N 116 36 E
44 Hofors 60 35N 16 15 E
66 Hōfu 34 0N 130 30 E
45 Höganas 56 12N 12 33 E
72 Hoggar= Ahaggar, Mts. 23 0N 6 30 E
45 Högsby 57 10N 16 3 E
24 Hohe Rhön, Mts. 50 24N 9 58 E
26 Hohe Tauern, Mts. 47 10N 12 30 E
26 Hohenems 47 22N 9 42 E
24 Hohenstein Ernsttahl 50 48N 12 43 E
68 Hohpi 35 59N 114 13 E
63 Hoi An 15 52N 108 19 E
74 Hoima 1 26N 31 21 E
68 Hokang 47 36N 130 28 E
45 Hökensås, Reg. 58 6N 14 2 E
68 Hokien 38 30N 116 2 E
85 Hokitika 42 42S 171 0 E
66 Hokkaidō □ 43 30N 143 0 E
66 Hokkaido, I. 43 30N 143 0 E
67 Hokow 22 39N 103 57 E
68 Holan Shan 38 40N 105 50 E
45 Holbæk 55 42N 11 40 E
84 Holbrook, Australia 35 42S 147 18 E
103 Holbrook, U.S.A. 35 0N 110 0W
101 Holdenville 35 5N 96 25W
12 Holderness, Pen. 53 45N 0 5W
62 Hole-Narsipur 12 48N 76 16 E
105 Holguín 20 50N 76 20W
26 Hollabrunn 48 34N 16 5 E
75 Hollams Bird I. 24 40S 14 30 E
98 Holland 42 47N 86 0W
65 Hollandia= Jayapura 2 28N 140 38 E
96 Hollidaysburg 40 26N 78 25W
103 Hollywood, Calif. 34 0N 118 10W
98 Hollywood, Fla. 26 0N 80 9W
88 Holman Island 70 43N 117 43W
44 Holmestrand 59 31N 10 14 E
44 Holmsjön, L. 62 26N 15 20 E
45 Holmsland Klit 56 0N 8 9 E
46 Holmsund 63 41N 20 20 E
54 Holon 32 2N 34 47 E
45 Holstebro 56 22N 8 33 E
88 Holy Cross 62 12N 159 47W
12 Holy, I., Eng. 55 42N 1 48W
12 Holy, I., Wales 53 17N 4 37W
12 Holyhead 53 18N 4 38W
97 Holyoke 42 14N 72 37W
24 Holzminden 51 49N 9 31 E
59 Homalin 24 55N 95 0 E
25 Homburg 49 19N 7 21 E
80 Home Hill 19 43S 147 25 E
102 Homedale 43 42N 116 59W
88 Homer 59 40N 151 35W
80 Homestead 20 20S 145 40 E
62 Homnabad 17 45N 77 5 E
40 Homoljske, Planina 44 15N 21 45 E
41 Homorod 46 5N 25 15 E
56 Homs 34 40N 36 45 E
69 Honan □ 33 50N 113 15 E
110 Honda 5 12N 74 45W
75 Hondeklipbaai 30 19S 17 17 E
104 Hondo, R. 19 26N 99 13W
105 Honduras ■ 14 40N 86 30W
104 Honduras, G. de 16 50N 87 0W
44 Hønefoss 60 10N 10 12 E
97 Honesdale 41 34N 75 17W
18 Honfleur 49 25N 0 10 E
45 Høng 55 30N 11 14 E
63 Hong Ha, R. 22 0N 104 0 E
69 Hong Kong ■ 22 11N 114 14 E
13 Honiton 50 48N 3 11W
94 Honolulu 21 19N 157 52W
66 Honshū, I. 36 0N 138 0 E
30 Hontoria del Pinar 41 50N 3 10W
83 Hood, Pt. 34 23S 119 34 E
16 Hoogeveen 52 44N 6 30 E
16 Hoogezand 53 11N 6 45 E
61 Hooghly, R. 21 56N 88 4 E
15 Hook Hd. 52 8N 6 57W
92 Hoonah 58 15N 135 30W
98 Hoopeston 40 30N 87 40W
16 Hoorn 52 38N 5 4 E
103 Hoover Dam 36 0N 114 45W
92 Hope, Canada 49 25N 121 25 E
101 Hope, U.S.A. 33 40N 93 30W
88 Hope, Pt. 68 20N 166 40W
5 Hope Bay 65 0S 55 0W
105 Hope Town 26 30N 76 30W
97 Hopedale 42 8N 71 33W
68 Hopei □ 39 25N 116 45 E
75 Hopetown 29 34S 24 3 E
84 Hopetoun, Vic. 35 48S 142 25 E
83 Hopetoun, W. Australia 33 54S 120 6 E
98 Hopkinsville 36 52N 87 26W
69 Hoppo 21 32N 109 6 E
102 Hoquiam 47 0N 123 55W
47 Hordaland □ 60 25N 6 45 E
41 Horezu 45 6N 24 0 E
25 Horgeh 47 15N 8 35 E
40 Horgos 46 10N 20 0 E
5 Horlick Mts. 84 0S 102 0W
57 Hormoz 27 35N 55 0 E
57 Hormoz, Jazireh-ye 27 4N 56 28 E
57 Hormoz, Kūh-e 27 40N 55 30 E
57 Hormuz, Str. of 26 30N 56 30 E
26 Horn 48 39N 15 40 E
112 Horn, C.= Hornos, C. de 55 50S 67 30W
12 Horncastle 53 13N 0 8W
96 Hornell 42 23N 77 41W
90 Hornepayne 49 14N 84 48W
112 Hornos, C. de 55 50S 67 30W
84 Hornsby 33 42S 151 2 E
12 Hornsea 53 55N 0 10W
45 Hornslet 56 18N 10 19 E
26 Hořovice 49 48N 13 53 E
108 Horqueta 23 15S 56 55W
45 Horsens 55 52N 9 51 E
84 Horsham, Australia 36 44S 142 13 E
13 Horsham, U.K. 51 4N 0 20W
44 Horten 59 25N 10 32 E
27 Hortobágy, R. 46 50N 20 32 E
60 Hoshiarpur 31 30N 75 58 E
62 Hospet 15 15N 76 20 E
32 Hospitalet de Llobregat 41 21N 2 6 E
112 Hoste, I. 55 0S 69 0W
88 Hot Springs, Alas. 64 55N 150 10W
101 Hot Springs, Ark. 34 30N 93 0W
100 Hot Springs, S.D. 43 25N 103 30W
67 Hotien 37 6N 79 59 E
46 Hoting 64 8N 16 15 E
12 Houghton-le-Spring 54 51N 1 28W
85 Houhora 34 49S 173 9 E
99 Houlton 46 5N 68 0W
101 Houma 29 35N 90 50W
20 Hourtin, Étang d' 45 10N 1 8W
14 Hourne, L. 57 7N 5 35W
101 Houston 29 50N 5 20W
13 Hove 50 50N 0 10W
68 Hövsgöl Nuur, L. 51 0N 100 30 E
81 Howard 25 16S 152 32 E
83 Howatharra 28 29S 114 33 E
84 Howe, C. 37 30S 150 0 E
97 Howe I. 44 17N 76 15W
61 Howrah 22 37N 88 27 E
15 Howth Hd. 53 21N 6 0W
14 Hoy, I. 58 50N 3 15W
47 Høyanger 61 25N 6 50 E
24 Hoyerswerda 51 26N 14 14 E
24 Höxter 51 46N 9 23 E
26 Hradec Králové 50 15N 15 50 E
27 Hranice 49 34N 17 45 E
27 Hron, R. 47 49N 18 45 E
28 Hrubieszów 50 49N 23 51 E
37 Hrvatska □ 45 20N 16 0 E
59 Hsenwi 23 22N 97 55 E
69 Hsiamen 24 28N 118 7 E
69 Hsiao Shan 34 0N 111 30 E
69 Hsinchow 19 37N 109 17 E
69 Hsinchu 24 55N 121 0 E
69 Hsuchang 34 2N 114 0 E
110 Huacho 11 10S 77 35W
69 Hualien 24 0N 121 30 E
110 Huancane 15 10S 69 50W
110 Huancavelica 12 50S 75 5W
110 Huancayo 12 5S 75 0W
69 Huangliu 18 30N 108 46 E
110 Huánuco 9 55S 76 15W
110 Huaraz 9 30S 77 32W
110 Huascarán, Mt. 9 0S 77 30W
108 Huasco, R. 28 27S 71 13W
104 Huatabampo 26 50N 109 50W
62 Hubli 15 22N 75 15 E
69 Huchow 30 57N 120 1 E
104 Huchuetenango 15 25N 91 30W
24 Hückelhoven Ratheim 51 5N 6 14W
12 Huddersfield 53 38N 1 49W
44 Hudiksvall 61 43N 17 10 E
97 Hudson, Mass. 42 23N 71 35W
97 Hudson, N.Y. 42 15N 73 46W
97 Hudson, R. 40 42N 74 2W
89 Hudson B. 60 0N 86 0W
97 Hudson Falls 43 18N 73 34W
92 Hudson Hope 56 0N 121 54W
89 Hudson Str. 62 0N 70 0W
63 Hué 16 30N 107 35 E
30 Huebrà, R. 41 2N 6 48W
31 Huelma 37 39N 3 28W
31 Huelva 37 18N 6 57W
31 Huelva □ 37 38N 7 0N
31 Huelva, R. 37 27N 6 0W
33 Huércal Overa 37 23N 2 3W
32 Huerva, R. 41 39N 0 52W
32 Huesca 42 8N 0 25W
32 Huesca, □ 42 20N 0 1 E
33 Huéscar 37 44N 2 35W
32 Huete 40 10N 2 43W
80 Hughenden 20 52S 144 10 E
83 Hughes, Australia 30 40S 129 30 E
88 Hughes, U.S.A. 66 3N 154 16W
68 Huhehot 40 52N 111 36 E
110 Huila, Mt. 3 0N 76 0W
69 Huiling Shan, I. 21 35N 111 57 E
108 Huinca Renancó 34 51S 64 22W
18 Huisne, R. 47 59N 0 11 E
104 Huixtla 15 9N 92 28W
59 Hukawng Valley 26 30N 96 30 E
69 Hukow 29 38N 116 25 E
68 Hulan 46 0N 126 44 E
54 Hūlda 31 50N 34 51 E
68 Hulin 45 45N 133 0 E
90 Hull, Canada 45 20N 75 40W
12 Hull, U.K. 53 45N 0 20W
12 Hull, R. 53 44N 0 19W
45 Hultsfred 57 30N 15 50 E
68 Huma 51 44N 126 42 E
68 Huma, R. 51 40N 126 44 E
110 Humaitá 7 35S 62 40W
12 Humber, R. 53 32N 0 8 E
12 Humberside □ 53 45N 0 20W
93 Humboldt, Canada 52 15N 105 9W
101 Humboldt, U.S.A. 35 50N 88 55W
102 Humboldt, R. 40 2N 118 31W
27 Humenné 48 55N 21 50 E
73 Hūn 29 2N 16 0 E
46 Hunaflói, B. 65 50N 21 0W
69 Hunan □ 27 30N 111 30 E
68 Hunchun 42 49N 130 31 E
40 Hunedoara 45 40N 22 50 E
69 Hung Ho, R. 33 0N 117 0 E
27 Hungary ■ 47 20N 19 20 E
69 Hunghai Wan, G. 20 30N 115 0 E
69 Hungshui Ho, R. 23 70N 110 30 E
69 Hunghu 29 49N 113 30 E
69 Hungkiang 27 0N 109 49 E
68 Hungnam 39 59N 127 40 E
69 Hungtze Hu, L. 33 20N 118 35 E
25 Hunsruck, Mts. 50 0N 7 30 E
12 Hunstanton 52 57N 0 30 E
62 Hunsur 12 16N 76 16 E
24 Hunte, R. 52 30N 8 19 E
84 Hunter, R. 32 50S 151 40 E
85 Hunterville 39 56S 175 35 E
90 Huntingdon, Canada 45 10N 74 10W
13 Huntingdon, U.K. 52 20N 0 11W
96 Huntingdon, U.S.A. 40 28N 78 1W
98 Huntington, Ind. 40 52N 85 30W
97 Huntington, N.Y. 40 52N 73 25W
98 Huntington, W. Va. 38 20N 82 30W
103 Huntington Beach 34 40N 118 0W
103 Huntington Park 33 58N 118 15W
85 Huntly, N.Z. 37 34S 175 11 E
14 Huntly, U.K. 57 27N 2 48W
90 Huntsville, Canada 45 20N 79 14W
99 Huntsville, Ala. 34 45N 86 35W
101 Huntsville, Tex. 30 50N 95 35W
80 Huonville 43 0S 147 5 E
69 Hupei □ 31 5N 113 5 E
41 Hurezani 44 49N 23 40 E
100 Huron 44 30N 98 20W
98 Huron, L. 45 0N 83 0W
103 Hurricane 37 10N 113 12W
85 Hurunui, R. 42 54S 173 18 E
46 Húsavik 66 3N 17 13W
45 Huskvarna 57 47N 14 15 E
54 Hussein Bridge 31 53N 35 33 E
24 Husum 54 27N 9 3 E
68 Hutag 49 25N 102 34 E
101 Hutchinson 38 3N 97 59W
26 Hüttenberg 46 56N 14 33 E
24 Hüttental 50 53N 8 1 E
54 Huwarā 32 9N 35 15 E
16 Huy 50 31N 5 15 E
40 Hvar, I. 43 11N 16 28 E
37 Hvarski Kan. 43 15N 16 35 E
46 Hvítá, R., Iceland 63 50N 21 0W
46 Hvítá, R., Iceland 64 40N 22 0W
69 Hwainan 32 44N 117 1 E
68 Hwang Ho, R. 37 32N 118 19 E
69 Hwangshih 30 27N 115 0 E
69 Hweian 25 2N 118 56 E
67 Hweitseh 26 32N 103 6 E
68 Hwo Shan, Mts. 37 0N 112 30 E
68 Hwohsien 36 30N 111 42 E
98 Hyannis 42 3N 101 45W
67 Hyargas Nuur, L. 49 0N 92 30 E
92 Hydaburg 55 15N 132 45W
97 Hyde Park 41 47N 73 56W
83 Hyden 32 24S 118 46 E
62 Hyderabad, India 17 10N 78 29 E
60 Hyderabad, Pak. 25 23N 68 36 E
60 Hyderabad □ 25 3N 68 24 E
21 Hyères 43 8N 6 9 E
21 Hyères, Îs. d' 43 0N 6 28 E
102 Hyndman Pk. 44 4N 114 0W
66 Hyōgo □ 35 15N 135 0 E
102 Hyrum 41 35N 111 56W
13 Hythe 51 4N 1 5 E
47 Hyvinkää 60 38N 25 0 E

I

41 Ianca 45 6N 27 29 E
49 Iaşi 47 10N 27 40 E
110 Iaurête 0 30N 69 5W
72 Ibadan 7 22N 3 58 E
110 Ibagué 4 27N 73 14W
109 Ibaiti 23 50S 50 10W
110 Ibarra 0 21N 78 7W
55 Ibb 14 1N 44 10 E
24 Ibbenbüren 52 16N 7 41 E
8 Iberian Pen. 40 0N 5 0W
90 Iberville 5 19N 73 17W
33 Ibiza 38 54N 1 26 E
33 Ibiza, I. 39 0N 1 30 E
65 Ibonma 3 22S 133 31 E
66 Ibusuki 31 16N 130 39 E
110 Icá 14 0S 75 30W
110 Içana 0 21N 67 19W
46 Iceland ■ 65 0N 19 0W
51 Icha 55 30N 156 0 E
69 Ichang 30 48N 111 29 E
66 Ichihara 35 35N 140 6 E
66 Ichinomiya 35 20N 136 50 E
68 Ichun 47 42N 129 8 E
102 Idaho □ 44 10N 114 0W
102 Idaho Falls 43 30N 112 10W
102 Idaho Springs 39 49N 105 30W
30 Idanha-a-Nova 39 50N 7 15W
25 Idar-Oberstein 49 43N 7 19 E
73 Idd el Ghanam 11 30N 24 25 E
73 Idehan Marzúq 24 50N 13 51 E
73 Idfû 25 0N 32 49 E
43 Idhi Óros, Mts. 35 15N 24 45 E
43 Ídhra 37 20N 23 28 E
64 Idi 4 55N 97 45 E
74 Idi Amin Dada, L. 0 25S 29 40 E
56 Idlip 35 55N 36 38 E
54 Idna 31 34N 34 58 E
75 Idutywa 32 8S 28 18 E
16 Ieper 50 51N 2 53 E
43 Ierápetra 35 0N 25 44 E
42 Ierissós 40 22N 23 52 E

37 Iesi 43 32N 13 12E
72 Ife 7 30N 4 31E
111 Igarapava 20 3S 47 47W
111 Igarapé Açu 1 4S 47 33W
51 Igarka 67 30N 87 20E
62 Igatpuri 19 40N 73 35E
38 Iglésias 39 19N 8 27E
89 Igloolik Island 69 20N 81 30W
93 Ignace 49 30N 91 40W
42 Igoumenítsa 39 32N 20 18E
109 Iguaçu, R. 25 30S 53 10W
104 Iguala 18 20N 99 40W
32 Igualada 41 37N 1 37E
109 Iguape 24 43S 47 33W
111 Iguatu 6 20S 39 18W
109 Iguazú Falls 25 2S 54 26W
68 Ihsien 41 45N 121 3E
66 Iida 35 35N 138 0E
46 Iisalmi 63 32N 27 10E
66 Iizuka 33 38N 130 42E
72 Ijebu Ode 6 47N 3 52E
16 Ijmuiden 52 28N 4 35E
16 Ijsel, R. 52 30N 6 0E
16 Ijsselmeer, L. 52 45N 5 20E
43 Ikaría, I. 37 35N 26 10E
45 Ikast 56 8N 9 10E
66 Ikeda 34 1N 133 48E
41 Ikhtiman 42 27N 23 48E
66 Iki, I. 33 45N 129 42E
65 Ilagan 17 9N 121 53E
68 Ilan 46 14N 129 33E
51 Ilanskiy 56 14N 96 3E
28 Iława 53 37N 19 33E
80 Ilbilbie 21 45S 149 20E
19 Île de France, Reg. 49 0N 2 20E
74 Ilebo 4 17S 20 47E
80 Ilfracombe, Australia 23 30S 144 30E
13 Ilfracombe, U.K. 51 13N 4 8W
109 Ilha Grande, B. de 23 9S 44 30W
111 Ilhéus 15 0S 39 10W
30 Ilhavo 40 33N 8 43W
40 Ilia 45 57N 22 40E
43 Ilia □ 37 45N 21 35E
88 Iliamna L. 59 30N 155 0W
88 Iliamna, Mt. 60 5N 153 9W
50 Ilich 41 0N 68 10E
43 Iliki, L. 38 24N 23 15E
42 Iliodhrómia, I. 39 12N 23 50E
37 Ilirska Bistrica 45 34N 14 14E
50 Iliysk=Kapchagai 44 10N 77 20E
62 Ilkal 15 57N 76 8E
12 Ilkeston 52 59N 1 19W
68 Ilkhuri Shan, Mts. 51 30N 124 0E
108 Illapel 32 0S 71 10W
18 Ille-et-Vilaine □ 48 10 1 30W
25 Iller, R. 48 23N 9 58E
30 Illescás 40 8N 3 51W
110 Illimani, Mt. 16 30S 67 50W
100 Illinois, R. 38 58N 90 27W
100 Illinois □ 40 15N 89 30W
72 Illizi 26 31N 8 32E
31 Illora 37 17N 3 53W
48 Ilmen, Oz. 5 15N 31 10E
24 Ilmenau 50 41N 10 55E
110 Ilo 17 40S 71 20W
65 Iloilo 10 45N 122 33E
72 Ilorin 8 30N 4 35E
65 Ilwaki 7 55S 126 30E
28 Iłżanka, R. 51 11N 21 14E
66 Imabari 34 4N 133 0E
51 Iman 45 50N 133 40E
48 Imandra, Oz. 67 45N 33 0E
66 Imari 33 15N 129 52E
42 Imathía □ 40 30N 22 15E
12 Immingham 53 37N 0 12W
37 Imola 44 20N 11 42E
111 Imperatriz 5 30S 47 20W
36 Impéria 43 52N 8 0E
93 Imperial, Canada 51 21N 105 28W
103 Imperial, U.S.A. 32 52N 115 34W
103 Imperial Dam 32 50N 114 30W
74 Impfondo 1 40N 18 0E
59 Imphal 24 15N 94 0E
26 Imst 47 15N 10 44E
54 Imwas 31 51N 34 59E
72 In Salah 27 10N 2 32E
85 Inangahua Junction 41 52S 171 59E
46 Inari 68 54N 27 5E
46 Inari, L. 69 0N 28 0E
32 Inca 39 43N 2 54E
68 Inchŏn 37 32N 126 45E
44 Indalsälven, R. 62 31N 17 27E
59 Indaw 24 15N 96 5E
101 Independence, Kans. 37 10N 95 50W
100 Independence, Mo. 39 3N 94 25W
102 Independence, Oreg. 44 53N 123 6W
41 Independenţa 45 25N 27 42E
58 India ■ 23 0N 77 30E
92 Indian Cabin 59 50N 117 12W
93 Indian Head 50 30N 103 35W
1 Indian Ocean 5 0S 75 0E
96 Indiana 40 38N 79 9W
98 Indiana □ 40 0N 86 0W
98 Indianapolis 39 42N 86 10W
100 Indianola 41 20N 93 38W
48 Indiga 67 50N 48 50E
40 Indija 45 6N 20 7E
64 Indonesia ■ 5 0S 115 0E
65 Indramaju 6 21S 108 20E
62 Indravati, R. 18 43N 80 17E
18 Indre, R. 47 16N 0 19E
19 Indre □ 46 45N 1 30E
18 Indre-et-Loire □ 47 12N 0 40E
60 Indus, Mouths of the 24 20N 67 50E
60 Indus, R. 24 20N 67 47E
56 Inebolu 41 55N 33 40E
56 Inegöl 40 5N 29 31E
33 Infantes 38 43N 3 1W
30 Infiesto 43 21N 5 21W
108 Ingenio Santa Ana 27 25S 65 40W
90 Ingersoll 43 4N 80 55W
80 Ingham 18 43S 146 10E
12 Ingleborough, Mt. 54 11N 2 23W
81 Inglewood, N.S.W. 28 25S 151 8E
84 Inglewood, Vic. 36 29S 143 53E
85 Inglewood, N.Z. 39 9S 174 14E
103 Inglewood 33 58N 118 27W
25 Intolstadt 48 45N 11 26W
49 Ingulec 47 42N 33 4E
75 Inhambane 23 54S 35 30E
75 Inharrime 24 30S 35 0E
69 Ining, Kwangsi-Chuang 25 8N 109 57E
67 Ining Sinkiang-Uigur 43 57N 81 20E
15 Inishmore, I. 53 8N 9 45W
15 Inishowen, Pen. 55 14N 7 15W
25 Inn, R. 48 35N 13 28E
26 Inn, R. 48 35N 13 28E
68 Inner Mongolian Autonomous Rep. □ 44 50N 117 40E
24 Innerste, R. 52 15N 9 50E
80 Innisfail, Australia 17 33S 146 5E
92 Innisfail, Canada 52 0N 114 0W
26 Innsbruck 47 16N 11 23E
28 Inowrocław 52 50N 18 20E
83 Inscription, C. 25 29S 112 59E
59 Insein 16 46N 96 18E
41 Însurăţei 44 50N 27 40E
48 Inta 66 2N 60 8E
108 Intendente Alvear 35 12S 63 32W
25 Interlaken 46 41N 7 50E
100 International Falls 48 30N 93 25W
112 Inútil, B. 53 30S 70 15W
88 Inuvik 68 25N 133 30W
14 Inverary 56 13N 5 5W
14 Inverbervie 56 50N 2 17W
85 Invercargill 46 24S 168 24E
81 Inverell 29 48S 151 36E
14 Invergordon 57 41N 4 10W
92 Invermere 50 51N 116 9W
91 Inverness, Canada 46 15N 61 19W
14 Inverness, U.K. 57 29N 4 12W
14 Inverurie 57 15N 2 21W
82 Inverway 17 50S 129 38E
81 Investigator, Str. 35 30S 137 0E
103 Inyokern 35 37N 117 54W
48 Inza 53 55N 46 25E
42 Ioánnina 39 42N 20 55E
42 Ioánnina □ 39 50N 20 57E
101 Iola 38 0N 95 20W
41 Ion Corvin 44 7N 27 50E
14 Iona, I. 56 20N 6 25W
98 Ionia 42 59N 85 7W
43 Ionian Is.= Iónioi Nísoi 38 40N 20 8E
43 Ionian Sea 37 30N 17 30E
43 Iónioi Nísoi 38 40N 20 8E
43 Íos, I. 36 41N 25 20E
100 Iowa □ 42 18N 93 30W
100 Iowa City 41 40N 91 35W
100 Iowa Falls 42 30N 93 15W
111 Ipameri 17 44S 48 9W
27 Ipel, R. 47 49N 18 52E
110 Ipiales 1 0N 77 45W
67 Ipin 28 58N 104 45E
42 Ipiros □ 39 30N 20 30E
63 Ipoh 4 36N 101 4E
81 Ipswich, Australia 27 38S 152 37E
13 Ipswich, U.K. 52 4N 1 9E
111 Ipu 4 23S 40 44W
108 Iquique 20 19S 70 5W
110 Iquitos 3 45S 73 10W
111 Iracoubo 5 30N 53 10W
43 Iráklion 35 20N 25 12E
43 Iráklion □ 35 10N 25 10E
57 Iran ■ 33 0N 53 0E
57 Iranshahr 27 75N 60 40E
104 Irapuato 20 40N 101 40W
56 Iraq ■ 33 0N 44 0E
109 Irati 25 25S 50 38W
54 Irbid 32 35N 35 48E
32 Iregua, R. 42 27N 2 24W
15 Ireland 53 0N 8 0W
105 Ireland I. 32 19N 64 50W
51 Iret 60 10N 154 5E
68 Iri 35 59N 127 0E
65 Irian Jaya □ 5 0S 140 0E
73 Iriba 15 7N 22 15E
74 Iringa 7 48S 33 43E
111 Iriri, R. 3 52S 52 37W
15 Irish Republic ■ 53 0N 8 0E
11 Irish Sea 54 0N 145 12E
51 Irkineyeva 58 30N 96 49E
51 Irkutsk 52 10N 104 20E
18 Iroise, B. 48 15N 4 45W
100 Iron Mountain 45 49N 88 4W
13 Ironbridge 52 38N 2 29W
98 Ironton 38 35N 82 40W
100 Ironwood 46 30N 90 10W
90 Iroquois Falls 48 40N 80 40W
59 Irrawaddy, R. 15 50N 95 6E
68 Irshih 47 8N 119 57E
39 Irsina 40 45N 16 15E
50 Irtysh, R. 61 4N 68 52E
74 Irumu 1 32N 29 53E
32 Irún 43 20N 1 52W
32 Irurzun 42 55N 1 50W
14 Irvine 55 37N 4 40W
15 Irvinestown 54 28N 7 38W
83 Irwin, Pt. 35 4S 116 56E
84 Irymple 34 14S 142 8E
60 Isa Khel 32 42N 71 16E
46 Ísafjördur 66 5N 23 9W
66 Isahaya 32 50N 130 3E
41 Işalnita 44 24N 23 44E
74 Isangi 0 52N 24 10E
25 Isar, R. 48 49N 12 58E
37 Isarco, R. 46 27N 11 18E
43 Isari 37 22N 22 0E
19 Isbergues 50 36N 2 24E
38 Íschia, I. 40 45N 13 51E
55 Iscia Baidoa 3 40N 43 0E
66 Ise 34 29N 136 42E
66 Ise-Wan, G. 34 45N 136 45E
45 Isefjord 55 53N 11 50E
36 Iseo, L. d' 45 43N 10 4E
21 Isère, R. 44 59N 4 51E
21 Isère □ 45 10N 5 50E
24 Iserlohn 51 22N 7 40E
39 Isérnia 41 35N 14 12E
69 Ishan 24 30N 108 41E
66 Ishikari-Wan 43 20N 141 20E
66 Ishikawa □ 36 30N 136 30E
50 Ishim, R. 57 45N 71 10E
66 Ishinomaki 38 32N 141 20E
58 Ishkuman 36 40N 73 50E
100 Ishpeming 46 30N 87 40W
74 Isiro 2 53N 27 58E
80 Isisford 24 15S 144 21E
56 Iskenderun 36 32N 36 10E
41 Iskŭr, R. 43 44N 24 27E
41 Iskŭr, Yazovir 42 30N 23 29E
14 Isla, R. 56 30N 3 25W
31 Isla Cristina 37 13N 7 17W
58 Islamabad 33 40N 73 0E
62 Islampur 17 2N 72 9E
83 Island, Pt. 30 20S 115 2E
93 Island L. 53 40N 94 30W
90 Island Falls 49 35N 81 20W
91 Islands, B. of 49 11N 58 15W
112 Islas Malvinas= Falkland Is. 51 30S 59 0W
14 Islay, I. 55 46N 6 10W
20 Isle, R. 44 55N 0 15W
12 Isle of Man □ 54 15N 4 30W
13 Isle of Wight □ 36 54N 76 43W
73 Ismâ'ilîya 30 37N 32 18E
73 Isna 25 17N 32 30E
38 Isola del Liri 41 39N 13 32E
56 Isparta 37 47N 30 30E
41 Isperikh 43 43N 26 50E
39 Ispica 36 47N 14 53E
54 Israel ■ 32 0N 34 50E
83 Isseka 28 22S 114 35E
20 Issoire 45 32N 3 15E
20 Issoudun 46 57N 2 0E
19 Is-sur-Tille 47 30N 5 10E
50 Issyk Kul, L. 42 30N 77 30E
56 Istanbul 41 0N 29 0E
43 Istiáia 38 57N 23 10E
37 Istra, Pen. 45 10N 14 0E
108 Itá 25 29S 57 21W
111 Itabira 19 29S 43 23W
111 Itabuna 14 48S 39 16W
111 Itacaré 14 18S 39 0W
111 Itaeté 13 0S 41 5W
111 Itaituba 4 10S 55 50W
109 Itajaí 27 0S 48 45W
109 Itajubá 22 24S 45 30W
37 Italy ■ 42 0N 13 0E
111 Itapecuru-Mirim 3 20S 44 15W
111 Itaperaba 12 32S 40 18W
109 Itaperuna 21 10S 42 0W
109 Itapetininga 23 36S 48 7W
109 Itapeva 23 59S 48 59W
109 Itaporanga 23 42S 49 29W
109 Itapuá □ 26 40S 55 40W
109 Itaquari 20 12S 40 25W
110 Itaquatiana 2 58S 58 30W
108 Itaqúi 29 0S 56 30W
109 Itararé 24 6S 49 23W
60 Itarsi 22 36N 77 51E
97 Ithaca 42 25N 76 30W
43 Itháki, I. 38 25N 20 40E
66 Ito 34 58N 139 5E
18 Iton, R. 49 9N 1 12E
109 Itu 23 10S 47 15W
111 Ituiutaba 19 0S 49 25W
68 Ituliho 50 40N 121 30E
111 Itumbiara 18 20S 49 10W
93 Ituna 51 10N 103 30W
24 Itzehoe 53 56N 9 31E
46 Ivalo 68 38N 27 35E
40 Ivangrad 42 51N 19 50E
84 Ivanhoe 32 56S 144 20E
49 Ivano-Frankovsk 49 0N 24 40E
48 Ivanovo 49 0N 24 40E
41 Ivaylovgrad 41 32N 26 8E
72 Ivory Coast ■ 7 30N 5 0E
45 Ivösjön, L. 56 8N 14 25E
36 Ivrea 45 30N 7 52E
89 Ivugivik 62 18N 77 50W
66 Iwaki 37 3N 140 55E
66 Iwakuni 34 15N 132 8E
66 Iwata 34 49N 137 59E
66 Iwate □ 39 30N 141 30E
72 Iwo 7 39N 4 9E
104 Ixtepec 16 40N 95 10W
104 Ixtlán 21 5N 104 28W
104 Izamal 20 56N 89 1W
28 Izbica Kujawski 52 25N 18 30E
16 Izegem 50 55N 3 12E
48 Izhevsk 56 50N 53 0E
56 Izmir 38 25N 27 8E
56 Izmit 40 45N 29 50E
31 Iznalloz 37 24N 3 30W
54 Izra 32 51N 36 15E
41 Iztochni Rodopi 41 40N 25 30E
66 Izumi-sano 34 40N 135 43E
66 Izumo 35 20N 132 55E

J

54 Jaba 32 20N 35 13E
54 Jabalíya 31 32N 34 27E
31 Jabalón, R. 38 53N 3 35W
61 Jabalpur 23 9N 79 58E
56 Jablah 35 20N 36 0E
26 Jablonec 50 43N 15 10E
28 Jabłonowo 53 23N 19 10E
109 Jaboticabal 21 15S 48 17W
32 Jaca 42 35N 0 33W
109 Jacareí 23 20S 46 0W
109 Jacarèzinho 23 5S 50 0W
81 Jackson, Australia 26 40S 149 30E
98 Jackson, Ky. 37 35N 83 22W
98 Jackson, Mich. 42 18N 84 25W
101 Jackson, Minn. 43 35N 95 30W
99 Jackson, Tenn. 35 40N 88 50W
92 Jackson Bay 50 32N 125 57W
85 Jacksons 42 46N 171 32E
99 Jacksonville, Fla. 30 15N 81 38W
100 Jacksonville, Ill. 39 42N 90 15W
99 Jacksonville, N.C. 34 50N 77 29W
101 Jacksonville, Tex. 31 58N 95 12W
99 Jacksonville Beach 30 19N 81 26W
105 Jacmel 18 20N 72 40W
60 Jacobabad 28 20N 68 29E
111 Jacobina 11 11S 40 30W
54 Jacob's Well 32 13N 35 13E
91 Jacques Cartier, Mt. 48 57N 66 0W
91 Jacques Cartier Pass. 49 50N 62 30W
25 Jade-Busen 53 30N 8 15E
30 Jadraque 40 55N 2 55W
31 Jaén 37 44N 3 43W
33 Jaén □ 37 50N 3 30W
54 Jaffa=Tel Aviv-Yafo 32 4N 34 48E
62 Jaffna 9 45N 80 2E
62 Jaffna Lagoon 9 35N 80 15E
60 Jagadhri 30 10N 77 20E
62 Jagdalpur 19 3N 82 6E
75 Jagersfontein 29 44S 25 27E
73 Jaghbub 29 42N 24 38E
60 Jagraon 30 50N 75 25E
62 Jagtial 18 50N 79 0E
109 Jaguarão 32 30S 53 30W

109 Jaguariaíva 24 10S 49 50W
105 Jaguey 22 35N 81 7W
84 Jagungal, Mt. 36 12S 148 28W
57 Jahrom 28 30N 53 31E
60 Jaipur 26 54N 72 52E
60 Jaisalmer 26 55N 70 55E
40 Jajce 44 19N 17 17E
61 Jajpur 20 53N 86 22E
65 Jakarta 6 9S 106 49E
46 Jakobstad 63 40N 22 43E
57 Jalalabad 34 30N 70 29E
60 Jalapur Jattan 32 38N 74 19E
104 Jalapa, Guatemala 14 45N 89 59W
104 Jalapa, Mexico 19 30N 96 50W
60 Jalgaon 21 0N 75 42E
104 Jalisco □ 20 0N 104 0W
60 Jalna 19 48N 75 57E
32 Jalón, R. 41 47N 1 4W
61 Jalpaiguri 26 32N 88 46E
105 Jamaica ■ 18 10N 77 30W
61 Jamalpur, Bangladesh 24 52N 90 2E
61 Jamalpur, India 25 18N 86 28E
64 Jambi 1 38S 103 30E
64 Jambi □ 1 30S 103 30E
60 Jambusar 22 3N 72 51E
90 James B. 53 30N 80 30W
100 James, R. 44 50N 98 0W
81 Jamestown, Australia 33 10S 138 32E
100 Jamestown, N.D. 47 0N 98 30W
96 Jamestown, N.Y. 42 5N 79 18W
62 Jamkhandi 16 30N 75 15E
62 Jammalamadugu 14 51N 78 25E
45 Jammer, B. 57 15N 9 20E
60 Jammu 32 46N 75 57E
58 Jammu and Kashmir □ 34 25N 77 0W
60 Jamnagar 22 30N 70 0E
60 Jamner 20 45N 75 45E
60 Jampur 29 39N 70 32E
61 Jamshedpur 22 44N 86 20E
44 Jämtlands □ 62 40N 13 50E
4 Jan Mayen, I. 71 0N 11 0W
58 Jand 33 30N 72 0E
31 Janda, L. de 36 15N 5 51W
81 Jandowae 26 45S 151 7E
100 Janesville 42 39N 89 1W
62 Jangaon 17 44N 79 5E
111 Januária 15 25S 44 25W
18 Janzé 47 55N 1 28W
60 Jaora 23 40N 75 10E
66 Japan ■ 36 0N 136 0E
65 Japara 6 30S 110 40E
110 Japurá, R. 3 8S 64 46W
31 Jaraicejo 39 40N 5 49E
30 Jaraiz 40 4N 5 45W
103 Jarales 34 44N 106 51W
30 Jarama, R. 40 2N 3 39W
112 Jaramillo 47 10S 67 7W
60 Jaranwala 31 15N 73 20E
33 Jardin, R. 39 12N 1 60W
105 Jardines de la Reina, Is. 20 50N 78 50W
68 Jargalant 47 2N 115 1E
19 Jargeau 47 50N 2 7E
20 Jarnac 45 40N 0 11W
19 Jarny 49 9N 5 53E
28 Jarocin 51 59N 17 29E
26 Jaroměř 50 22N 15 52E
27 Jarosław 50 2N 22 42E
77 Jarvis I. 0 15S 159 55W
40 Jaša Tomić 45 26N 20 50E
63 Jasin 2 20N 102 26E
57 Jāsk 25 38N 57 45E
27 Jasło 49 45N 21 30E
112 Jason Is, 51 0S 61 0W
92 Jasper, Canada 52 55N 118 0W
99 Jasper, U.S.A. 30 31N 82 58W
92 Jasper Nat. Park 52 53N 118 3W
92 Jasper Place 53 33N 113 25W
27 Jastrzebie Zdroj 49 57N 18 35E
27 Jászárokszállás 47 39N 20 1E
27 Jászberény 47 30N 19 55E
27 Jászladány 47 23N 20 18E
111 Jataí 17 50S 51 45W
65 Jatibarang 6 28S 108 18E
65 Jatinegara 6 13S 106 52E
33 Játiva 39 0N 0 32W
111 Jatobal 4 35S 49 33W
54 Jatt 32 24N 35 2E
109 Jaú 22 10S 48 30W
61 Jaunpur 25 46N 82 44E
65 Java, I. 7 0S 110 0E
64 Java Sea 4 35S 107 15E
64 Java Trench 10 0S 110 0E
33 Jávea 38 48N 0 10E
62 Javla 17 18N 75 9E
28 Jawor 51 4N 16 11E
27 Jaworzno 50 13N 19 22E
65 Jaya, Puncak, Mt. 4 0S 137 20E
65 Jayapura 2 28S 140 38E
65 Jayawijaya, Pegunungan 4 50S 139 0E
93 Jaydot 49 15N 110 15W
88 Jean Marie River 62 0N 121 0W
96 Jeannette 40 20N 79 36W
57 Jebāl Bārez, Kūh-e 29 0N 58 0E
72 Jebba, Morocco 35 11N 4 43W
72 Jebba, Nigeria 9 9N 4 48E
40 Jebel 40 35N 21 15E
73 Jebel, Bahr el, R. 9 40N 30 30E
14 Jedburgh 55 28N 2 33W
27 Jędrzejów 50 35N 20 15E
102 Jefferson, Mt. 38 51N 117 0W
100 Jefferson City 36 8N 83 30W
98 Jeffersonville 38 20N 85 42W
72 Jega 12 15N 4 23E
26 Jelenia Góra 50 50N 15 45E
48 Jelgava 56 41N 22 49E
65 Jember 8 11S 113 41E
16 Jemeppe 50 37N 5 30E
24 Jena 50 56N 11 33E
26 Jenbach 47 24N 11 47E
54 Jenīn 32 28N 35 18E
98 Jenkins 37 13N 82 41W
101 Jennings 30 10N 92 45W
111 Jequié 13 51S 40 5W
111 Jequitinhonha 16 30S 41 0W
72 Jerada 34 40N 2 10W
63 Jerantut 3 56N 102 22E
105 Jérémie 18 40N 74 10W
104 Jerez de Gacia Salinas 22 39N 103 0W
31 Jerez de la Frontera 36 41N 6 7W
31 Jerez de los Caballeros 38 20N 6 45W
80 Jericho, Australia 23 38S 146 6E
54 Jericho, Jordan= El Ariha 31 52N 35 27E
84 Jerilderie 35 20S 145 41E
103 Jerome 34 50N 112 0W
18 Jersey, I. 49 13N 2 7W
97 Jersey City 40 41N 74 8W
96 Jersey Shore 41 17N 77 18W
100 Jerseyville 39 5N 90 20W
54 Jerusalem 31 47N 35 10E
37 Jesenice 50 6N 13 28E
64 Jesselton=Kota Kinabalu 6 0N 116 12E
24 Jessnitz 51 42N 12 19E
61 Jessore 23 10N 89 10E
108 Jesús María 30 59S 64 5W
60 Jetpur 21 45N 70 10E
62 Jeypore 18 50N 82 38E
58 Jhal Jhao 26 20N 65 35E
60 Jhansi 25 30N 78 36E
61 Jharia 23 45N 86 18E
61 Jharsuguda 21 51N 84 1E
60 Jhelum 33 0N 73 45E
60 Jhelum, R. 31 12N 72 8E
60 Jhunjhunu 28 10N 75 20E
26 Jičín 50 25N 15 20E
56 Jiddah 21 29N 39 16E
54 Jifna 31 58N 35 13E
69 Jihchao 35 18N 119 28E
26 Jihlava 49 28N 15 35E
26 Jihočeský □ 49 8N 14 35E
27 Jihomoravsky □ 49 5N 16 30E
55 Jijiga 9 20N 42 50E
33 Jijona 38 34N 0 30W
32 Jiloca, R. 41 21N 1 39W
73 Jima 7 40N 36 55E
40 Jimbolia 45 47N 20 57E
31 Jimena de la Frontera 36 27N 5 24W
104 Jiménez 27 10N 105 0W
26 Jindřichuv Hradec 49 10N 15 2E
74 Jinja 0 25N 33 12E
68 Jinné 51 32N 121 25E
105 Jinotega 13 6N 85 59W
105 Jinotepe 11 50N 86 10W
100 Jipijapa 1 0S 80 40W
56 Jisr ash Shughur 35 49N 36 18E
83 Jitarning 32 48S 117 57E
41 Jiu, R. 43 47N 23 48E
109 Joaçaba 27 5S 51 31W
111 João Pessoa 7 10S 34 52W
109 Joaquim Távora 23 30S 49 58W
31 Jodar 37 50N 3 21W
60 Jodhpur 26 23N 73 2E
5 Joerg Plat. 75 0S 70 0W
19 Joeuf 49 12N 6 1E
91 Joggins 45 42N 64 27W
75 Johannesburg 26 10S 28 8E
14 John O'Groats 58 39N 3 3W
97 Johnson City, N.Y. 42 9N 67 0W
99 Johnson City, Tenn. 36 18N 82 21W
92 Johnson's Crossing 60 33N 133 27W
77 Johnston I. 17 10N 169 8E
63 Johore, R. 1 39N 103 57E
97 Johnstown, N.Y. 43 1N 74 20W
96 Johnstown, Pa. 40 19N 78 53W
63 Johor Baharu 1 45N 103 47E
63 Johore □ 2 5N 103 20E
19 Joigny 48 0N 3 20E
109 Joinvile 26 15S 48 55E
19 Joinville 48 27N 5 10E
46 Jokkmokk 66 35N 19 50E
98 Joliet 41 30N 88 0W
90 Joliette 46 3N 73 24W
65 Jolo, I. 6 0N 121 0E
65 Jombang 7 32S 112 12E
90 Jones, C. 54 33N 79 35W
101 Jonesboro 35 50N 90 45W
45 Jönköping 57 45N 14 10E
45 Jönköpings □ 57 30N 14 30E
45 Jonsered 57 45N 12 10E
20 Jonzac 45 27N 0 28W
101 Joplin 37 0N 94 25W
56 Jordan ■ 31 0N 36 0E
54 Jordan, R. 31 46N 35 33E
59 Jorhat 26 45N 94 20E
46 Jörn 65 5N 20 12E
72 Jos 9 53N 8 51E
109 José Batlle y Ordóñez 33 20S 55 10W
112 José de San Martín 44 4S 70 26W
82 Joseph Bonaparte, G. 14 0S 29 0E
18 Josselin 47 57N 2 33W
44 Jotunheimen, Mts. 61 30N 9 0E
56 Jounieh 33 59N 35 30E
57 Jouzjan □ 22 40N 81 10W
28 Jozefow 52 9N 21 12E
92 Juan de Fuca Str. 48 15N 124 0W
107 Juan Fernández, Arch. de 33 50S 80 0W
108 Juan Lacaze 34 26S 57 25W
108 Juárez 37 40S 59 43W
109 Juatinga, Pta. de 23 17S 44 30W
111 Juàzeiro 9 30S 40 30W
111 Juazeiro do Norte 7 10S 39 18W
73 Jûbâ 4 57N 31 35E
56 Jubaila 24 55N 46 25E
72 Juby, C. 28 0N 12 59W
32 Júcar, R. 39 40N 2 18W
104 Juchitán 16 27N 95 5W
54 Judaea=Har Yehuda, Reg. 31 35N 34 57E
26 Judenburg 47 12N 14 38E
97 Judith, Pt. 41 20N 71 30W
24 Juist, I. 53 40N 7 0E
109 Juiz de Fora 21 43S 43 19W
108 Jujuy □ 23 20S 65 40W
110 Juli 16 10S 69 25W
80 Julia Creek 20 40S 141 55E
110 Juliaca 15 25S 70 10W
110 Julianatop, Mt. 3 40N 56 30W
4 Julianehåb 60 43N 46 0W
37 Julijske Alpe, Mts. 46 15N 14 1E
60 Jullundur 31 20N 75 40E
105 Jumento Cays 23 40N 75 40E
16 Jumet 50 27N 4 25E
33 Jumilla 38 28N 1 19W
60 Junagadh 21 30N 70 30E
100 Junction City, Kans. 39 4N 96 55W
102 Junction City, Oreg. 44 20N 123 12W
80 Jundah 24 46S 143 2E
109 Jundiaí 23 10S 47 0W
92 Juneau 58 26N 134 30W
84 Junee 34 49S 147 32W
25 Jungfrau, Mt. 46 32N 7 58E
108 Junín 34 33S 60 57W
112 Junin de los Andes 39 45S 71 0W
96 Juniata, R. 40 24N 77 1W
109 Juquiá 24 19S 47 38W
14 Jura, I. 56 0N 5 50W
17 Jura, Mts. 46 45N 6 30E
21 Jura □ 46 47N 5 45E
110 Jurado 7 7N 77 46W
41 Jurilovca 44 46N 28 52W
57 Jurm 36 50N 70 45E
110 Juruá, R. 2 37S 65 44W
111 Juruti 2 9S 56 4W
19 Jussey 47 50N 5 55E
108 Justo Daract 33 52S 65 12W
24 Jüterbog 51 59N 13 6E
105 Juticalpa 14 40N 85 50W
19 Juvisy 48 43N 2 23E
67 Jyekundo 33 0N 96 50E
45 Jylland, Reg. 56 25N 9 30E
46 Jyväskylä 62 12N 25 47E

K

58 K2, Mt. 36 0N 77 0E
75 Kaap Plato 28 30S 24 0E
75 Kaapstad= Cape Town 33 55S 18 22E
65 Kabaena, I. 5 15S 122 0E
74 Kabale 9 38N 11 37W
74 Kabalo 6 0S 27 0E
74 Kabambare 4 41S 27 39E
74 Kabarega Falls 2 15S 31 38E
72 Kabba 7 57N 6 3E
74 Kabinda 6 23S 24 38E
74 Kabongo 7 22S 25 33E
80 Kabra 23 25S 150 25E
57 Kabul 34 28N 69 18E
57 Kabul □ 34 0N 68 30E
75 Kabwe 14 30S 28 29E
40 Kacanik 42 13N 21 12E
59 Kachin □ 26 0N 97 0E
55 Kachiry 53 10N 75 50E
62 Kadayanallur 9 3N 77 22E
60 Kadi 23 18N 72 23E
81 Kadina 34 0S 137 43E
49 Kadiyerka 48 35N 38 30E
72 Kaduna 10 30N 7 21E
72 Kaesŏng 37 58N 126 35E
73 Kafia Kingi 9 20N 24 25E
43 Kafirévs, Ákra 38 9N 24 8E
54 Kafr Kanna 32 45N 35 20E
54 Kafr Ra'i 32 23N 35 9E
75 Kafue, R. 15 56S 28 55E
50 Kagan 39 43N 64 33E
66 Kagawa □ 34 15N 134 0E
66 Kagoshima 31 36N 130 40E
66 Kagoshima □ 30 0N 130 0E
65 Kai, Kep. 5 35S 132 45E
85 Kaiapoi 42 24S 172 40E
69 Kaifeng 34 50N 114 27E
85 Kaikohe 35 25S 173 49E
85 Kaikoura 42 25S 173 43E
94 Kailua 21 24N 157 44W
61 Kaimganj 27 33N 79 24E
61 Kaimur Hills 24 30N 82 0E
72 Kainji Dam 10 1N 4 40E
85 Kaipara, Harbour 36 25S 174 14E
68 Kaiping 40 28N 122 10E
60 Kairana 29 33N 77 15E
72 Kairouan 35 45N 10 5E
25 Kaiserslautern 49 30N 7 43E
85 Kaitaia 35 8S 173 17E
85 Kaitangata 46 17S 169 51E
60 Kaithal 29 48N 76 26E
69 Kaiyuan 42 33N 124 4E
46 Kajaani 64 17N 27 46E
63 Kajang 2 59N 101 48E
56 Kake 34 6N 132 19E
66 Kakegawa 34 45N 138 1E
49 Kakhovka 46 46N 34 28E
62 Kakinada 16 50N 82 11E
66 Kakogawa 34 46N 134 51E
60 Kalabagh 33 0N 71 28E
65 Kalabahi 8 13S 124 31E
49 Kalach 50 22N 41 0E
59 Kaladan, R. 20 9N 92 57E
75 Kalahari, Des. 24 0S 22 0E
62 Kalahasti 13 45N 79 44E
51 Kalakan 55 15N 116 45E
42 Kalamariá 40 33N 22 55E
43 Kalamata 37 3N 22 10E
98 Kalamazoo 42 20N 85 35W
62 Kalamb 18 3N 74 48E
83 Kalamunda 32 0S 116 0E
56 Kalan 39 7N 39 32E
83 Kalannie 30 22S 117 5E
27 Kalárovo 47 54N 18 0E
60 Kalat 29 8N 66 31E
57 Kalat-i-Ghilzai 32 15N 66 58E
43 Kalávrita 38 3N 22 8E
74 Kalemie 5 55S 29 9E
59 Kalewa 22 41N 95 32E
83 Kalgoorlie 30 40S 121 22E
41 Kaliakra, C. 43 21N 28 30E
65 Kalibo 11 43N 122 22E
64 Kalimantan □ 0 0 115 0E
43 Kálimnos, I. 37 0N 27 0E
61 Kalimpong 27 4N 88 35E
48 Kalinin 56 55N 35 55E
48 Kaliningrad 54 44N 20 32E
41 Kalipetrovo 44 5N 27 14E
102 Kalispell 48 10N 114 22E
28 Kalisz 53 17N 15 55E
60 Kalka 30 56N 76 57E
62 Kallakurichi 11 44N 79 1E
45 Kållandsö, I. 58 40N 13 5E
45 Källby 58 30N 13 0E
54 Kallia 31 46N 35 30E
62 Kallidaikurichi 8 38N 77 31E
43 Kallithéa 37 55N 23 41E
43 Kallonís, Kól. 39 10N 26 10E
45 Kalmar 56 40N 16 20E

45 Kalmar □ 57 25N 16 15 E
49 Kalmyk A.S.S.R. □ 46 5N 46 1 E
50 Kalmykovo 49 0N 51 35 E
61 Kalna 23 13N 88 25 E
27 Kalocsa 46 32N 19 0 E
41 Kalofer 42 37N 24 59 E
60 Kalol 23 15N 72 33 E
75 Kalomo 17 0s 26 30 E
43 Kaloneròn 37 20N 21 38 E
61 Kalpi 26 8N 79 47 E
88 Kaltag 64 20N 158 44w
48 Kaluga 54 35N 36 10 E
62 Kalutara 6 35N 80 0 E
62 Kalyan 20 30N 74 3 E
62 Kalyani 17 53N 76 59 E
48 Kama, R. 55 45N 52 0 E
66 Kamaishi 39 20N 142 0 E
60 Kamalia 30 44N 72 42 E
55 Kamaran, I. 15 28N 42 35 E
83 Kambalda 31 10s 121 37 E
62 Kambam 9 45N 77 16 E
48 Kambarka 56 17N 54 12 E
51 Kamchatka Pol. 57 0N 160 0 E
50 Kamen 53 50N 81 30 E
49 Kamenets Podolskiy 48 40N 26 30 E
40 Kamenica 44 25N 19 40 E
37 Kamenjak, Rt. 44 46N 13 55 E
48 Kamenka 65 58N 44 0 E
41 Kameno 42 35N 27 18 E
49 Kamensk Shakhtinskiy 48 23N 40 20 E
50 Kamensk Uralskiy 56 28N 61 54 E
51 Kamenskoye 62 45N 165 30 E
41 Kamenyak 43 24N 26 57 E
24 Kamenz 51 17N 14 7 E
66 Kameoka 35 0N 135 35 E
26 Kamienna Góra 50 48N 16 2 E
74 Kamina 8 45s 25 0 E
92 Kamloops 50 40N 120 20w
26 Kamp, R. 48 35N 15 26 E
74 Kampala 0 20N 32 30 E
63 Kampar 4 18N 101 9 E
16 Kampen 52 33N 5 53 E
63 Kampong Chhnang 12 15N 104 20 E
63 Kampot 10 36N 104 10 E
60 Kamptee 21 9N 79 19 E
93 Kamsack 51 35N 101 50w
48 Kamskoye Vdkhr. 58 0N 56 0 E
49 Kamyshin 50 10N 45 30 E
69 Kan Kiang, R. 29 45N 116 10 E
103 Kanab 27 3N 112 29w
62 Kanakapura 12 33N 77 28 E
42 Kanália 39 30N 22 53 E
74 Kananga 5 55s 22 18 E
48 Kanash 55 48N 47 32 E
42 Kanastraíon, Akra 39 54N 23 40 E
66 Kanazawa 36 30N 136 38 E
63 Kanchanaburi 14 8N 99 31 E
61 Kanchenjunga, Mt. 27 50N 88 10 E
62 Kanchipuram 12 52N 79 45 E
69 Kanchow 25 51N 114 59 E
68 Kanchwan 36 29N 109 24 E
50 Kandagach 49 20N 57 15 E
57 Kandahar 31 32N 65 30 E
57 Kandahar □ 31 0N 65 0 E
48 Kandalaksha 67 9N 32 30 E
48 Kandalakshskiy Zaliv 66 0N 35 0 E
64 Kandangan 2 50s 115 20 E
85 Kandavu, I. 19 0s 178 15 E
60 Kandhla 29 18N 77 19 E
61 Kandi 23 58N 88 5 E
62 Kandukur 15 12N 79 57 E
62 Kandy 7 18N 80 43 E
96 Kane 41 39N 78 53w
86 Kane Basin 79 0N 70 0w
37 Kanfanar 45 7N 13 50 E
81 Kangaroo, I. 35 45s 137 0 E
56 Kangāvar 34 40N 48 0 E
68 Kangnŭng 37 45N 128 54 E
69 Kangshan 22 43N 120 14 E
67 Kangsu □ 38 0N 101 40 E
59 Kangto, Mt. 27 50N 92 35 E
62 Kanhangad 12 21N 74 58 E
61 Kanhar, R. 24 28N 83 9 E
62 Kanheri 19 13N 72 50 E
48 Kanin, Pol. 68 0N 45 0 E
84 Kaniva 36 22s 141 18 E
40 Kanjiža 46 3N 20 4 E
98 Kankakee 41 6N 87 50w
98 Kankakee, R. 41 23N 88 16w
72 Kankan 10 30N 9 15w
99 Kannapolis 35 32N 80 37w
61 Kannauj 27 3N 79 26 E
72 Kano 12 2N 8 30 E
66 Kanoya 31 23N 130 51 E
59 Kanpetlet 21 10N 93 59 E
61 Kanpur 26 35N 80 20 E
58 Kanrach 25 35N 65 20 E
100 Kansas, R. 39 7N 94 36w
100 Kansas □ 38 40N 98 0w
100 Kansas City, Kans. 39 0N 94 40w
100 Kansas City, Mo. 39 3N 94 30w
51 Kansk 56 20N 96 37 E
66 Kantō □ 36 0N 120 0 E
67 Kantse 31 30N 100 29 E
15 Kanturk 52 10N 8 55w
66 Kanuma 36 44N 139 42 E
75 Kanye 25 0s 25 28 E
69 Kanyu 34 53N 119 9 E
69 Kaohsiung 22 35N 120 16 E
72 Kaolack 14 5N 16 8w
68 Kaomi 36 25N 119 45 E
68 Kaoping 35 48N 112 55 E
69 Kaoyu Hu, L. 32 50N 119 25 E
60 Kapadvanj 23 5N 73 0 E
43 Kapéllo, Ákra 36 9N 23 3 E
26 Kapfenberg 47 26N 15 18 E
75 Kapiri Mposha 13 59s 28 43 E
57 Kapisa □ 34 45N 69 30 E
26 Kaplice 48 42N 14 30 E
27 Kaposvár 46 25N 17 47 E
64 Kapuas, R. 0 25s 109 24 E
81 Kapunda 34 20s 138 56 E
60 Kapurthala 31 23N 75 25 E
90 Kapuskasing 49 25N 82 30w
81 Kaputar, Mt. 30 15s 130 10 E
50 Kara 69 10N 65 25 E
50 Kara Bogaz Gol, Zaliv 41 0N 53 30 E
50 Kara Kalpak A.S.S.R. □ 43 0N 59 0 E
50 Kara Sea 75 0N 70 0 E
56 Karabük 41 12N 32 37 E
50 Karabutak 49 59N 60 14 E
60 Karachi 24 53N 67 0 E
58 Karachi □ 25 30N 67 0 E
62 Karad 17 54N 74 10 E
56 Karadeniz Boğazi 41 10N 29 5 E
56 Karadeniz Dağlari, Mts. 41 30N 35 0 E
50 Karaganda 49 50N 73 0 E
50 Karagayly 49 26N 76 0 E
62 Karaikkudi 10 0N 78 45 E
57 Karaj 35 4N 51 0 E
50 Karakas 48 20N 83 30 E
68 Karakorum, Mts. 35 20N 76 0 E
58 Karakoram P. 35 33N 77 46 E
56 Karaköse 39 44N 43 3 E
51 Karalon 57 5N 115 50 E
64 Karambu 3 53s 116 6 E
60 Karanja 20 29N 77 31 E
75 Karasburg 28 0s 18 44 E
50 Karasino 66 50N 86 50 E
46 Karasjok 69 27N 25 30 E
50 Karasuk 53 44N 78 2 E
50 Karatau 43 10N 70 28 E
50 Karatau Ra. 44 0N 69 0 E
66 Karatsu 33 30N 130 0 E
26 Karawanken, Mts. 46 30N 14 40 E
50 Karazhal 48 2N 70 49 E
56 Karbalā 32 47N 44 3 E
27 Karcag 47 19N 21 1 E
42 Kardhítsa 39 23N 21 54 E
42 Kardhítsa □ 39 15N 21 50 E
75 Kareeberge 30 50s 22 0 E
48 Karelian A.S.S.R. □ 65 30N 32 30 E
50 Kargasok 59 3N 80 53 E
50 Kargat 55 10N 80 15 E
58 Kargil 34 32N 76 12 E
48 Kargopol 61 30N 38 58 E
75 Kariba L. 16 40s 28 25 E
62 Karikal 10 59N 79 50 E
73 Karima 18 30N 21 40 E
64 Karimata, Selat, Str. 2 0s 108 20 E
62 Karimnagar 18 26N 79 10 E
66 Kariya 34 58N 137 1 E
50 Karkaralinsk 49 30N 75 10 E
49 Karkinitskiy Zaliv 45 36N 32 35 E
54 Karkur 32 29N 34 57 E
24 Karl-Marx-Stadt 50 50N 12 55 E
24 Karl-Marx-Stadt □ 50 45N 13 0 E
37 Karlovac 45 31N 15 36 E
26 Karlovy Vary 50 13N 12 51 E
45 Karlshamn 56 10N 14 51 E
44 Karlskoga 59 22N 14 33 E
45 Karlskrona 56 10N 15 35 E
25 Karlsruhe 49 3N 8 23 E
44 Karlstad 59 23N 13 30 E
88 Karluk 57 30N 155 0w
60 Karnal 29 42N 77 2 E
59 Karnaphuli Res. 22 40N 92 20 E
62 Karnataka □ 13 15N 77 0 E
26 Karnische Alpen, Mts. 46 36N 13 0 E
26 Kärnten □ 46 52N 13 30 E
74 Karonga 9 57s 33 55 E
81 Karoonda 35 1s 139 59 E
43 Kárpathos, I. 35 37N 27 10 E
48 Karpogory 63 59N 44 27 E
56 Kars 40 40N 43 5 E
50 Karsakpay 47 55N 66 40 E
50 Karshi 38 53N 65 48 E
42 Karstal Óros 41 15N 25 13 E
50 Kartaly 53 3N 60 40 E
74 Karungu 0 50s 34 10 E
62 Karur 10 59N 78 2 E
27 Karviná 49 53N 18 25 E
60 Karwan, R. 27 17N 78 5 E
61 Karwi 25 12N 80 57 E
63 Kas Kong 11 27N 102 12 E
74 Kasai, R. 3 2s 16 57 E
74 Kasama 10 16s 31 9 E
74 Kasangulu 4 15s 15 15 E
62 Kasaragod 12 30N 74 58 E
60 Kasganj 27 48N 78 42 E
57 Kāshān 34 5N 51 30 E
67 Kashgar 39 46N 75 52 E
69 Kashing 30 45N 120 41 E
60 Kashipur 29 15N 79 0 E
53 Kashmir □ 34 0N 78 0 E
48 Kasimov 54 55N 41 20 E
92 Kaslo 49 55N 117 0w
74 Kasongo 4 30s 26 33 E
43 Kásos, I. 35 20N 26 55 E
73 Kassala 15 23N 36 26 E
73 Kassalâ □ 15 20N 36 26 E
42 Kassándra, Pen. 40 0N 23 30 E
24 Kassel 51 19N 9 32 E
65 Kassue 6 58s 139 21 E
56 Kastamonu 41 25N 33 43 E
43 Kastélli 35 29N 23 38 E
42 Kastoría 40 30N 21 19 E
42 Kastoría □ 40 30N 21 15 E
42 Kástron 39 53N 25 8 E
60 Kasur 31 5N 74 25 E
51 Kata 58 46N 102 40 E
74 Katako Kombe 3 25s 24 20 E
83 Katanning 33 40s 117 33 E
42 Kateríni 40 18N 22 37 E
59 Katha 24 10N 96 30 E
82 Katherine 14 27s 132 20 E
60 Kathiawar, Reg. 22 0N 71 0 E
64 Katiet 2 21s 99 14 E
61 Katihar 25 34N 87 36 E
75 Katima Mulilo 17 28s 24 13 E
88 Katmai Mt. 58 20N 154 59w
61 Katmandu 27 45N 85 12 E
43 Kato Akhaia 38 8N 21 33 E
42 Kato Stavros 40 39N 23 43 E
60 Katol 21 17N 78 38 E
75 Katombora 18 0s 25 30 E
74 Katompi 6 2s 26 23 E
84 Katoomba 33 41s 150 19 E
27 Katowice 50 17N 19 5 E
27 Katowice □ 50 30N 19 0 E
14 Katrine, L. 56 15N 4 30 E
44 Katrineholm 59 9N 16 12 E
72 Katsina 7 10N 9 20 E
57 Kattawaz Urgan □ 32 10N 62 20 E
45 Kattegat, Str. 57 0N 11 20 E
61 Katwa 23 30N 89 25 E
16 Katwijk-aan-Zee 52 12N 4 22 E
94 Kauai, I. 19 30N 155 30w
25 Kaufbeuren 47 42N 10 37 E
46 Kaukonen 67 42N 24 58 E
48 Kaunas 54 54N 23 54 E
72 Kaura Namoda 12 37N 6 33 E
46 Kautokeino 69 0N 23 4 E
51 Kavacha 60 16N 169 51 E
40 Kavadarci 41 26N 22 3 E
62 Kavali 14 55N 80 1 E
42 Kavála 40 57N 24 28 E
42 Kavála □ 41 5N 24 30 E
42 Kavállas, Kól. 40 50N 24 25 E
41 Kavarna 43 26N 28 22 E
111 Kaw 4 30N 52 15w
66 Kawagoe 35 55N 139 29 E
66 Kawaguchi 35 52N 138 45 E
94 Kawaihae 20 5N 155 50w
74 Kawambwa 9 48s 29 3 E
66 Kawanoe 34 1N 133 34 E
60 Kawardha 22 0N 81 17 E
66 Kawasaki 35 35N 138 42 E
90 Kawene 48 45N 91 15w
85 Kawerau 38 7s 176 42 E
85 Kawhia Harbour 38 4s 174 49 E
59 Kawnro 22 48N 99 8 E
63 Kawthaung 10 5N 98 36 E
59 Kawthoolei □ 18 0N 97 30 E
59 Kayah □ 19 15N 97 15 E
62 Kayangulam 9 10N 76 33 E
103 Kayenta 36 46N 110 15 E
72 Kayes 14 25N 11 30w
81 Kayrunnera 30 40s 142 30 E
56 Kayseri 38 45N 35 30 E
64 Kayuagung 3 28s 104 46 E
51 Kazachye 70 52N 135 58 E
50 Kazakh S.S.R. □ 50 0N 58 0 E
48 Kazan 55 48N 49 3 E
41 Kazanlŭk 42 38N 25 35 E
49 Kazbek, Mt. 42 30N 44 30 E
57 Kāzerūn 29 38N 51 40 E
27 Kazincbarcika 48 17N 20 36 E
50 Kazym, R. 63 54N 65 50 E
28 Kcynia 53 0N 17 30 E
43 Kéa, I. 37 30N 24 22 E
100 Kearney 40 45N 99 3w
46 Kebnekaise, Mt. 67 48N 18 30 E
55 Kebri Dehar 6 45N 44 17w
65 Kebumen 7 42s 109 40 E
27 Kecel 46 31N 19 16 E
27 Kecskemet 46 57N 19 35 E
63 Kedah □ 5 50N 100 40 E
91 Kedgwick 47 40N 67 20w
65 Kediri 7 51s 112 1 E
27 Kedzierzyn 50 20N 18 12 E
3 Keeling Is.= Cocos Is. 12 12s 96 54 E
69 Keelung=Chilung 25 3N 121 45 E
97 Keene 42 57N 72 17w
75 Keetmanshoop 26 35s 18 8 E
93 Keewatin 47 23N 93 0w
88 Keewatin, Reg. 63 20N 94 40w
43 Kefallinía, I. 38 28N 20 30 E
65 Kefamenanu 9 28s 124 38 E
54 Kefar Gil'adi 33 14N 35 35 E
54 Kefar Sava 32 11N 34 54 E
54 Kefar Szold 33 11N 35 34 E
54 Kefar Tavor 32 42N 35 24 E
54 Kefar Vitkin 32 22N 34 53 E
54 Kefar Yona 32 20N 34 54 E
54 Kefar Zetim 32 49N 35 27 E
72 Keffi 8 55N 7 43 E
46 Keflavik 64 2N 22 35w
25 Kehl 48 34N 7 50 E
12 Keighley 53 52N 1 54w
81 Keith, Australia 36 0s 140 20 E
14 Keith, U.K. 57 33N 2 58w
88 Keith Arm, B. 65 30N 122 0w
60 Kekri 26 0N 75 10 E
51 Kël 69 30N 124 10 E
63 Kelang 3 2N 101 26 E
63 Kelantan, R. 6 11N 102 16 E
63 Kelantan □ 5 10N 102 0 E
73 Kelibia 36 50N 11 3 E
83 Kellerberrin 31 36s 117 38 E
102 Kellogg 47 30N 116 5w
15 Kells=Ceanannas Mor 53 42N 6 53w
92 Kelowna 49 50N 119 25w
92 Kelsey Bay 50 25N 126 0w
85 Kelso, N.Z. 45 54s 169 15 E
14 Kelso, U.K. 55 36N 2 27w
102 Kelso, U.S.A. 46 10N 122 57w
63 Keluang 2 3N 103 18 E
93 Kelvington 52 20N 103 30w
48 Kem 65 0N 34 38 E
48 Kem, R. 64 57N 34 41 E
50 Kemerovo 55 20N 85 50 E
46 Kemi 65 47N 24 32 E
46 Kemijärvi 66 43N 27 22 E
46 Kemijoki, R. 65 47N 24 30 E
102 Kemmerer 41 52N 110 30w
81 Kempsey 31 1s 152 50 E
25 Kempten 47 42N 10 18 E
90 Kemptville 45 0N 75 38w
61 Ken, R., India 25 46N 80 31w
14 Ken, R., U.K. 54 50N 4 4w
65 Kendal, Indonesia 6 56s 110 14 E
12 Kendal, U.K. 54 19N 2 44w
65 Kendari 3 50s 122 30 E
83 Kendenup 34 30s 117 38 E
88 Kendi 60 30N 151 0w
61 Kendrapara 20 35N 86 30 E
72 Kenema 7 50N 11 14w
59 Keng Tawng 20 45N 98 18 E
59 Keng Tung 21 0N 99 30 E
68 Kenho 50 43N 121 30 E
72 Kenitra 34 15N 6 40w
15 Kenmare 51 52N 9 35w
99 Kennedy, C.= Canaveral, C. 28 28N 80 31w
13 Kennet, R. 51 28N 0 57w
101 Kennett 36 7N 90 0w
102 Kennewick 46 11N 119 2w
88 Keno Hill 63 57N 135 25w
93 Kenora 49 50N 94 35w
98 Kenosha 42 33N 87 48w
91 Kensington 46 25N 63 34w
96 Kent 41 8N 81 20w
13 Kent □ 51 12N 0 40 E
88 Kent Pen. 68 30N 107 0w
50 Kentau 43 32N 68 36 E
98 Kenton 40 40N 83 35w
98 Kentucky, R. 38 41N 85 11w
98 Kentucky □ 37 20N 85 0w
91 Kentville 45 6N 64 29w
74 Kenya ■ 2 20N 38 0 E
74 Kenya, Mt. 0 10s 37 18 E
100 Keokuk 40 25N 91 30w
28 Kepno 51 18N 17 58 E

62 Kerala □ 11 0N 76 15E
84 Kerang 35 40S 143 55E
57 Keray 26 15N 57 30E
49 Kerch 45 20N 36 20E
54 Kerem Maharal 32 39N 34 59E
76 Kerguelan, I. 48 15S 69 10E
74 Kericho 0 22S 35 15E
64 Kerinci, Mt. 2 5S 101 0E
73 Kerkenna, Is. 34 48N 11 1E
50 Kerki 37 10N 65 0E
42 Kerkintis, L. 41 12N 23 10E
42 Kérkira 39 38N 19 50E
42 Kérkira, I. 39 35N 19 45E
16 Kerkrade 50 53N 6 4E
76 Kermadec Is. 31 8S 175 16W
57 Kermān 30 15N 57 1E
57 Kermān □ 30 0N 57 0E
56 Kermānshāh 34 23N 47 0E
56 Kermānshāh □ 34 0N 46 30E
101 Kermit 31 56N 103 3W
93 Kerrobert 52 0N 109 11W
101 Kerrville 30 1N 99 8W
15 Kerry □ 52 7N 9 35W
15 Kerry Hd. 52 26N 9 56W
68 Kerulen, R. 48 48N 117 0E
72 Kerzaz 29 29N 1 25W
46 Keski-Suomen □ 63 0N 25 0E
12 Keswick 54 35N 3 9W
27 Keszthely 46 50N 17 15W
72 Keta 5 49N 1 0E
64 Ketapang 1 55S 110 0E
92 Ketchikan 55 25N 131 40W
28 Kętrzyn 54 7N 21 22E
13 Kettering 52 24N 0 44W
102 Kettle Falls 48 41N 118 2W
100 Kewanee 41 18N 90 0W
100 Keweenaw B. 47 0N 88 0W
100 Keweenaw Pt. 47 26N 87 40W
97 Keyport 40 26N 74 12W
98 Keyser 39 26N 79 0W
51 Kezhma 59 15N 100 57E
50 Khabarovo 69 30N 60 30E
51 Khaborovsk 48 20N 135 0E
60 Khachraud 23 25N 75 20E
61 Khagaria 25 18N 86 32E
61 Khairabad 27 33N 80 47E
60 Khairpur □ 23 30N 69 8E
57 Khalij-e Fars 28 20N 51 45E
42 Khálki 39 26N 22 30E
42 Khalkidhikí □ 40 25N 23 20E
43 Khalkís 38 27N 23 42E
48 Khalmer Yu 67 58N 65 1E
48 Khalturin 58 40N 48 50E
61 Khamaria 23 10N 80 52E
60 Khambhalia 22 14N 69 41E
60 Khamgaon 20 42N 76 37E
55 Khamir 16 10N 43 45E
62 Khammam 17 11N 80 6E
67 Khan Tengri, Mt. 42 25N 80 10E
54 Khān Yūnis 31 21N 34 18E
57 Khanabad 36 45N 69 5E
56 Khānaqin 34 23N 45 25E
60 Khandwa 21 49N 76 22E
51 Khandyga 62 30N 134 50E
60 Khanewal 30 20N 71 55E
43 Khaniá 35 30N 24 4E
43 Khaniá □ 35 0N 24 0E
43 Khaníon, Kól. 35 33N 23 55E
51 Khanka, Oz. 45 0N 132 30E
60 Khanna 30 42N 76 16E
60 Khanpur 28 42N 70 35E
50 Khanty-Mansiysk 61 0N 69 0E
51 Khapcheranga 49 40N 112 0E
61 Kharagpur 22 20N 87 25E
62 Kharda 18 40N 75 40E
56 Kharfa 22 0N 46 35E
60 Khargon 21 45N 75 40E
49 Kharkov 49 58N 36 20E
41 Kharmanli 41 55N 25 55E
48 Kharovsk 59 56N 40 13E
56 Kharsaniya 27 10N 49 10E
73 Khartoum=El Khartûm 15 31N 32 35E
57 Khasab 26 14N 56 15E
57 Khāsh 28 15N 61 5E
73 Khashm el Girba 14 59N 35 58E
61 Khasi Hills 25 30N 91 30E
41 Khaskovo 41 56N 25 30E
51 Khatanga 72 0N 102 20E
73 Khatanga, R. 73 30N 109 0E
60 Khatauli 29 14N 77 43E
56 Khavari □ 37 20N 46 0E
62 Khed 18 51N 73 56E
60 Khekra 28 52N 77 20E
72 Khemis Miliana 36 11N 2 14E
72 Khenchela 35 28N 7 11E
72 Khenifra 32 58N 5 46W
49 Kherson 46 35N 32 35E
43 Khersónisos Akrotíri 35 30N 24 10E
67 Khetinsiring 32 54N 92 50E
43 Khiliomódhion 37 48N 22 51E
51 Khilok 51 30N 110 45E
43 Khíos 38 27N 26 9E
43 Khíos, I. 38 20N 26 0E
50 Khiva 41 30N 60 18E
41 Khlebarovo 43 38N 26 17E
49 Khmelnitisky 49 23N 27 0E
63 Khmer Rep.■=Cambodia ■ 12 15N 105 0E
60 Khojak P. 30 55N 66 30E
48 Kholm 57 10N 31 15E
51 Kholmsk 35 5N 139 48E
63 Khon Kaen 16 30N 102 47E
63 Khong, R. 14 7N 105 51E
51 Khonu 66 30N 143 25E
48 Khoper, R. 52 0N 43 20E
43 Khóra Sfakion 35 15N 24 9E
57 Khorasan □ 34 0N 58 0E
63 Khorat, Cao Nguyen 15 30N 102 50E
63 Khorat=Nakhon Ratchasima 14 59N 102 12E
50 Khorog 37 30N 71 36E
56 Khorramābād 33 30N 48 25E
56 Khorromshahr 30 29N 48 15E
72 Khouribga 32 58N 6 50W
57 Khugiani 31 28N 66 14E
61 Khulna 22 45N 89 34E
61 Khulna □ 22 45N 89 35E
60 Khurai 24 3N 78 23E
60 Khurja 28 15N 77 58E
60 Khushab 32 20N 72 20E
56 Khuzestan □ 31 0N 50 0E
57 Khvor 33 45N 55 0E
57 Khvormūj 28 40N 51 30E
56 Khvoy 38 35N 45 0E
57 Khyber P. 34 10N 71 8E
69 Kialing Kiang, R. 30 2N 106 18E
84 Kiama 34 40S 150 50E
84 Kiamal 34 58S 142 18E
68 Kiamusze 46 45N 130 30E
69 Kian 27 1N 114 58E
69 Kiangling 30 28N 113 16E
69 Kiangsi □ 27 45N 115 0E
69 Kiangsu □ 33 0N 119 50E
69 Kiangyin 31 51N 120 0E
68 Kiaohsien 36 20N 120 0E
43 Kiáton 38 1N 22 44E
74 Kibombo 3 57S 25 53E
74 Kibwezi 2 27S 37 57E
40 Kičevo 41 34N 20 59E
51 Kichiga 59 50N 163 5E
92 Kicking Horse P. 51 27N 116 25W
13 Kidderminster 52 24N 2 13W
24 Kiel 54 16N 10 8E
24 Kiel Canal=Nord Ostsee Kanal 54 15N 9 40E
27 Kielce 50 58N 20 42E
27 Kielce □ 50 40N 20 40E
69 Kienko 31 50N 105 30E
69 Kienow 27 0N 118 16E
67 Kienshui 23 57N 102 45E
69 Kiensi 26 58N 106 0E
69 Kienteh 29 30N 119 28E
69 Kienyang 27 30N 118 0E
49 Kiev=Kiyev 50 30N 30 28E
72 Kiffa 16 50N 11 15W
43 Kifisiá 38 4N 23 49E
43 Kifissós, R. 38 6N 23 45E
74 Kigali 1 5S 30 4E
74 Kigoma-Ujiji 5 30S 30 0E
66 Kii-Suido, Chan. 33 0N 134 50E
69 Kikiang 28 58N 106 44E
40 Kikinda 45 50N 20 30E
43 Kikládhes, Is. 37 20N 24 30E
44 Kil 59 30N 13 20E
62 Kilakarai 9 12N 78 47E
81 Kilcoy 26 59S 152 30E
15 Kildare 53 10N 6 50W
15 Kildare □ 53 10N 6 50W
74 Kilembe 0 15N 30 3E
101 Kilgore 32 22N 94 40W
74 Kilimanjaro 3 7S 37 20E
74 Kilindini 4 4S 39 40E
56 Kilis 36 50N 37 10E
15 Kilkee 52 41N 9 40W
15 Kilkenny 52 40N 7 17W
15 Kilkenny □ 52 35N 7 15W
42 Kilkís 40 58N 22 57E
15 Killala 54 13N 9 12W
15 Killaloe 52 48N 8 28W
93 Killarney, Canada 49 10N 99 40W
15 Killarney, Eire 52 2N 9 30W
15 Killary Harbour 53 38N 9 52W
14 Killiecrankie, P. of 56 44N 3 46W
14 Killin 56 27N 4 20W
43 Killíni, Mt. 37 54N 22 25E
15 Killybegs 54 38N 8 26W
84 Kilmany 38 8S 146 55E
14 Kilmarnock 55 36N 4 30W
84 Kilmore 37 25S 144 53E
74 Kilosa 6 48S 37 0E
15 Kilrush 52 39N 9 30W
74 Kilwa Kivinje 8 45S 39 25E
81 Kimba 33 8S 136 23E
100 Kimball 41 17N 103 20W
93 Kimberley, Canada 49 40N 116 10W
75 Kimberley, S. Africa 28 43S 24 46E
82 Kimberley Downs 17 24S 124 22E
102 Kimberly 42 33N 114 25W
68 Kimchaek 40 41N 129 12E
68 Kimchon 36 11N 128 4E
48 Kimry 56 55N 37 15E
64 Kinabalu, Mt. 6 0N 116 0E
93 Kincaid 49 40N 107 0W
90 Kincardine 44 10N 81 40W
93 Kindersley 51 30N 109 10W
72 Kindia 10 0N 12 52W
74 Kindu 2 55S 25 50E
48 Kineshma 57 30N 42 5E
80 King, I. 39 50S 144 0E
80 King, Mt. 25 10S 147 31E
82 King Edward, R. 14 14S 126 35E
112 King George B. 51 30S 60 30W
98 King George Is. 53 40N 80 30W
82 King Leopold, Ras. 17 20S 124 20E
82 King Sd. 16 50S 123 20E
88 King William I. 69 0N 98 0W
75 King William's Town 32 51S 27 22E
81 Kingaroy 26 32S 151 51E
67 Kingku 23 49N 100 30E
103 Kingman 35 12N 114 2W
81 Kingoonya 30 54N 135 18E
68 Kingpeng 43 30N 117 25E
103 Kings Canyon Nat. Park 37 0N 118 45W
12 Kings Lynn 52 45N 0 25E
97 Kings Park 40 53N 73 16E
13 Kingsbridge 50 14N 3 46W
15 Kingscourt 53 55N 6 48W
90 Kingston, Canada 44 20N 76 30W
105 Kingston, Jamaica 18 0N 76 50W
85 Kingston, N.Z. 45 20S 168 43E
97 Kingston, N.Y. 41 55N 74 0W
97 Kingston, Pa. 41 19N 75 58W
97 Kingston, R.I. 41 29N 71 30W
81 Kingston South East 36 52S 139 51E
105 Kingstown 13 10N 61 10W
90 Kingsville, Canada 42 3N 82 45W
101 Kingsville, U.S.A. 27 30N 97 53W
68 Kingtai 37 4N 103 59E
69 Kingtehchen 29 8N 117 21E
69 Kingtzekwan 33 25N 111 10E
14 Kingussie 47 5N 4 2W
68 Kinhsien 36 6N 107 49E
69 Kinhwa 29 5N 119 32E
93 Kinistino 52 59N 105 0W
74 Kinkala 4 18S 14 49E
66 Kinki □ 33 30N 136 0E
85 Kinleith 38 20S 175 56E
85 Kinloch 44 51S 168 20E
69 Kinmen, I. 24 25N 118 24E
45 Kinna 57 32N 12 42E
54 Kinneret 32 44N 35 34E
54 Kinneret, Yam, L. 32 49N 35 36E
14 Kinross 56 13N 3 25W
15 Kinsale 51 42N 8 31W
15 Kinsale, Old Hd. 51 37N 8 32W
67 Kinsha, R. 32 30N 98 0E
74 Kinshasa 4 20S 15 15E
69 Kinsiang 35 4N 116 25E
99 Kinston 35 18N 77 35W
14 Kintyre, Pen. 55 30N 5 35W
69 Kioshan 32 50N 114 0E
43 Kiparissía 37 15N 21 40E
43 Kiparissiakós Kól. 37 25N 21 25E
90 Kipawa Reserve Prov. Park 47 0N 78 30W
60 Kiratpur 29 32N 78 12E
25 Kirchheim 48 38N 9 20E
51 Kirensk 57 50N 107 55E
50 Kirgiz S.S.R. □ 42 0N 75 0E
56 Kirikkale 39 51N 33 32E
48 Kirillov 59 51N 38 14E
68 Kirin 43 58N 126 31E
68 Kirin □ 43 45N 125 20E
14 Kirkcaldy 56 7N 3 10W
14 Kirkcudbright 54 50N 4 3W
62 Kirkee 18 34N 73 56E
46 Kirkenes 69 40N 30 5E
14 Kirkintilloch 55 57N 4 10W
90 Kirkland Lake 48 15N 80 0W
100 Kirksville 40 8N 92 35W
56 Kirkūk 35 30N 44 21E
14 Kirkwall 58 59N 2 59W
62 Kirlampudi 17 12N 82 12E
48 Kirov 58 35N 49 40E
50 Kirovabad 40 45N 46 10E
49 Kirovakan 41 0N 44 0E
49 Kirovograd 48 35N 32 20E
48 Kirovsk 67 48N 33 50E
51 Kirovskiy 45 51N 48 11E
14 Kirriemuir 56 41N 3 0W
48 Kirsanov 52 35N 42 40E
60 Kirthar Ra. 27 0N 67 0E
46 Kiruna 67 50N 20 20E
83 Kirup 33 40S 115 50E
66 Kiryū 36 25N 139 20E
45 Kisa 57 58N 15 37E
43 Kisámou, Kól. 35 30N 23 38E
74 Kisangani 0 35N 25 15E
64 Kisaran 2 47N 99 29E
66 Kisaratzu 35 25N 139 59E
50 Kiselevsk 54 5N 86 6E
74 Kisengwa 6 0S 25 50E
61 Kishanganj 26 3N 88 14E
60 Kishangarh 27 50N 70 30E
49 Kishinev 47 0N 28 50E
66 Kishiwada 34 28N 135 22E
54 Kishon 32 33N 35 12E
61 Kishorganj 24 26N 90 40E
58 Kishtwar 33 20N 75 48E
68 Kisi 45 21N 131 0E
74 Kisii 0 40S 34 45E
88 Kiska I. 52 0N 177 30E
27 Kiskörös 46 37N 19 20E
27 Kiskundorozsma 46 16N 20 5E
27 Kiskunfélegyháza 46 42N 19 53E
27 Kiskunhalas 46 28N 19 37E
27 Kiskunmajsa 46 30N 19 48E
49 Kislovodsk 43 50N 42 45E
66 Kiso-Gawa, R. 35 2N 136 45E
27 Kispest 47 27N 19 9E
72 Kissidougou 9 5N 10 0W
62 Kistna, R.=Krishna, R. 15 43N 80 55E
27 Kisújszállzás 47 12N 20 50E
74 Kisumu 0 3S 34 45E
27 Kisvárda 48 14N 22 4E
67 Kitai 44 0N 89 27E
66 Kitaibaraki 36 50N 140 45E
66 Kitakyūshū 33 50N 130 50E
74 Kitale 1 0N 35 12E
83 Kitchener, Australia 30 55S 124 8E
96 Kitchener, Canada 43 30N 80 30W
74 Kitega 3 30S 29 58E
43 Kíthira 36 9N 23 0E
43 Kíthnos, I. 37 26N 24 27E
92 Kitimat 53 55N 129 0W
42 Kitros 40 22N 22 34E
66 Kitsuki 33 35N 131 37E
96 Kittanning 40 49N 79 30W
97 Kittatinny Mts. 41 0N 75 0W
97 Kittery 43 7N 70 42W
75 Kitwe 12 54S 28 7E
69 Kityang 23 30N 116 29E
26 Kitzbühel 47 27N 12 24E
69 Kiukiang 29 37N 116 2E
69 Kiuling Shan, Mts. 28 40N 115 0E
69 Kiungchow 19 57N 110 17E
69 Kiungchow-Haihsia, Str. 20 40N 110 0E
74 Kivu, L. 1 48S 29 0E
69 Kiyang 26 36N 111 42E
49 Kiyev 50 30N 30 28E
49 Kiyevskoye, Vdkhr. 51 0N 30 0E
48 Kizel 59 3N 57 40E
49 Kizlyar 43 51N 46 40E
50 Kizyl-Arvat 38 58N 56 15E
50 Kizyl Kiva 40 20N 72 35E
40 Kladanj 44 14N 18 42E
26 Kladno 50 10N 14 7E
26 Klagenfurt 46 38N 14 20E
48 Klaipeda 55 43N 21 10E
102 Klamath Falls 42 20N 121 50W
37 Klanjec 46 3N 15 45E
65 Klaten 7 43S 110 36E
26 Klatovy 49 23N 13 18E
92 Klawak 55 35N 133 0W
92 Kleena Kleene 52 0N 124 50W
37 Klekovača, Mt. 44 25N 16 32E
75 Klerksdorp 26 51S 26 38E
24 Kleve 51 46N 6 10E
45 Klippan 56 8N 13 10E
75 Klipplaat 33 0S 24 22E
41 Klisura 42 40N 24 28E
27 Kłobuck 50 55N 19 5E
27 Kłodzko 50 28N 16 38E
88 Klondike 64 0N 139 40W
27 Klosterneuburg 48 18N 16 19E
88 Kluane, L. 61 25N 138 50W
12 Knaresborough 54 1N 1 29W
41 Knezha 43 30N 23 56E
13 Knighton 52 21N 3 2W
37 Knin 44 1N 16 17E
26 Knittelfeld 47 13N 14 51E
40 Knjaževac 43 35N 22 18E
16 Knokke 51 20N 3 17E
100 Knoxville, Iowa 41 20N 93 5W
99 Knoxville, Tenn. 35 58N 83 57W

4 Knud Rasmussen Ld. 80 0N 55 0W
27 Knurów 50 13N 18 38E
89 Koartac 61 5N 69 36W
65 Koba 6 37S 134 37E
66 Kobe 34 45N 135 10E
45 København 55 41N 12 34E
25 Koblenz 50 21N 7 36E
28 Kobyłka 52 21N 21 10E
40 Kočane 41 53N 22 27E
40 Kočani 41 55N 22 25E
37 Kočevje 45 39N 14 50E
66 Kōchi 33 30N 133 35E
66 Kōchi □ 33 40N 133 30E
62 Kodaikanal 10 13N 77 32E
62 Koddiyar B. 8 33N 81 15E
88 Kodiak 57 48N 152 23W
88 Kodiak I. 57 30N 152 45E
60 Kodinar 20 46N 70 46E
73 Kodok 9 53N 32 7E
26 Köflach 47 4N 15 4E
72 Koforidua 6 3N 0 17W
66 Kōfu 35 40N 138 30E
45 Køge 55 27N 12 11E
45 Køge, B. 55 30N 12 20E
58 Kohat 33 40N 71 29E
59 Kohima 25 35N 94 10E
5 Kohler Ra. 77 0S 110 0W
83 Kojonup 33 48S 117 10W
50 Kokand 40 30N 70 57E
92 Kokanee Glacier Prov. Park 49 47N 117 10W
50 Kokchetav 53 20N 69 10E
54 Kokhav Mikha'el 31 37N 34 40E
67 Kokiu 23 22N 103 6E
46 Kokkola 63 50N 23 8E
63 Koko Kyunzu, Is. 14 10N 93 30E
67 Koko Nor, L. 37 0N 100 0E
98 Kokomo 40 30N 86 6W
89 Koksoak, R. 58 30N 68 10W
75 Kokstad 30 32S 29 29E
51 Kokuora 61 30N 145 0E
48 Kola 68 45N 33 8E
68 Kolan 38 43N 111 32E
62 Kolar 13 12N 78 15E
62 Kolar Gold Fields 12 58N 78 16E
41 Kolarovgrad 43 27N 26 42E
40 Kolašin 42 50N 19 31E
45 Kolding 55 30N 9 29E
65 Kolepom, I. 8 0S 138 30E
48 Kolguyev 69 20N 48 30E
62 Kolhapur 16 43N 74 15E
26 Kolín 50 2N 15 9E
62 Kollegal 12 9N 77 9E
62 Kolleru L. 16 40N 81 10E
24 Köln 50 56N 9 58E
28 Koło 52 14N 18 40E
28 Kołobrzeg 54 10N 15 35E
48 Kołomna 55 8N 38 45E
49 Kolomyya 48 31N 25 2E
59 Kolosib 24 15N 92 45E
50 Kolpashevo 58 20N 83 5E
48 Kolskiy Pol. 67 30N 38 0E
48 Kolskiy Zaliv 69 23N 34 0E
74 Kolwezi 10 40S 25 25E
51 Kolyma, R. 64 40N 153 0E
27 Komárno 47 49N 18 5E
27 Komarom 47 43N 18 7E
27 Komarom □ 47 35N 18 20E
66 Komatsu 36 25N 136 30E
48 Komi A.S.S.R. 64 0N 55 0E
27 Komló 46 15N 18 16E
66 Komoro 36 19N 138 26E
42 Komotini 41 9N 25 26E
40 Komovi, Mt. 42 40N 19 40E
63 Kompong Cham 11 54N 105 30E
63 Kompong Som 10 38N 103 30E
51 Komsomolets, Os. 80 30N 95 0E
51 Komsomolsk 50 30N 137 0E
51 Kondakovo 69 20N 151 30E
83 Kondinin 32 34S 118 8E
72 Koudougou 12 10N 2 20W
51 Kondratyevo 57 30N 98 30E
5 Kong Haakon VII Hav, Sea 65 0S 20 0E
68 Kongju 36 30N 127 0E
59 Konglu 27 13N 97 57E
69 Kongmoon 22 35N 113 1E
74 Kongolo 5 22S 27 0E
44 Kongsberg 59 39N 9 39E
48 Königsberg= Kaliningrad 54 42N 20 32E
28 Konin 52 12N 18 15E
28 Konin □ 52 15N 18 20E
40 Konjic 43 42N 17 58E
48 Konosha 61 0N 40 5E
49 Konotop 51 12N 33 7E
28 Końskie 51 15N 20 23E
28 Konstantynów Łódźki 51 45N 19 20E
25 Konstanz 47 39N 9 10E
72 Kontagora 10 23N 5 27E
56 Konya 37 52N 32 35E
83 Kookynie 29 17S 121 22E
82 Kooline 22 57S 116 20E
83 Koolyanobbing 30 48S 119 46E
81 Koonibba 31 58S 133 27E
83 Koorda 30 48S 117 35E
92 Kootenay Nat. Park 51 0N 116 0W
84 Koo-wee-rup 38 13S 145 28E
40 Kopaonik, Mts. 43 10N 21 0E
62 Kopargaon 19 51N 74 28E
47 Kopervik 59 17N 5 17E
50 Kopeysk 55 7N 61 37E
44 Köping 59 31N 16 3E
62 Koppal 15 23N 76 5E
44 Kopparbergs □ 61 20N 14 15E
37 Koprivnica 46 12N 16 45E
40 Korab, Mt. 41 44N 20 40E
24 Korbach 51 17N 8 50E
42 Korça 40 37N 20 50E
42 Korça □ 40 40N 20 50E
37 Korčula, I. 42 57N 17 0E
56 Kordestān □ 36 0N 47 0E
73 Kordofân □ 13 0N 29 0E
68 Korea B. 39 0N 124 0E
62 Koregaon 17 40N 74 10E
72 Korhogo 9 29N 5 28E
43 Korinthiakós Kól. 38 16N 22 30E
43 Korinthía □ 37 50N 22 35E
43 Kórinthos 37 26N 22 55E
66 Kōriyama 37 24N 140 23E
67 Korla 41 45N 86 4E
37 Kornat, I. 43 50N 15 20E
85 Koro Sea 17 30S 179 45W
84 Koroit 38 18S 142 24E
43 Koróni 36 48N 21 57E
28 Koronowo 53 19N 17 55E
27 Körös, R. 46 30N 142 42E
51 Korsakov 46 30N 142 42E
45 Korsør 55 20N 11 9E
28 Korsze 54 11N 21 9E
16 Kortrijk 50 50N 3 17E
84 Korumburra 38 26S 145 50E
51 Koryakskiy Khrebet, Mts. 61 0N 171 0E
43 Kos, I. 36 50N 27 15E
28 Koscierzyna 54 8N 17 59E
101 Kosciusko 33 3N 89 34W
92 Kosciusko I. 56 0N 133 40W
84 Kosciusko, Mt. 36 27S 148 16E
62 Kosgi 16 58N 77 43E
60 Kosi 27 48N 77 29E
27 Košice 48 42N 21 15E
40 Kosjerić 44 0N 19 55E
46 Koslan 63 28N 48 52E
40 Kosovska-Mitrovica 42 54N 20 52E
37 Kostajnica 45 17N 16 30E
41 Kostenets 42 15N 23 52E
73 Kôstî 13 8N 32 43E
48 Kostroma 57 50N 41 58E
28 Kostrzyn 52 24N 17 14E
28 Koszalin 54 12N 16 8E
28 Koszalin □ 54 10N 16 10E
27 Köszeg 47 23N 16 33E
60 Kot Adu 30 30N 71 0E
60 Kot Moman 32 13N 73 0E
60 Kota 25 14N 75 49E
63 Kota Baharu 6 7N 102 14E
64 Kota Kinabalu 6 0N 116 12E
63 Kota Tinggi 1 44N 103 53E
64 Kotabaru 3 20S 116 20E
64 Kotabumi 4 49S 104 46E
64 Kotawaringin 2 28S 111 27E
48 Kotelnich 58 20N 48 10E
62 Kothagudam 17 30N 80 40E
62 Kothapet 19 21N 79 28E
24 Köthen 51 44N 11 59E
47 Kotka 60 28N 26 55E
48 Kotlas 61 15N 47 0E
88 Kotlik 63 2N 163 33W
40 Kotor 42 25N 18 47E
40 Kotoriba 46 37N 16 48E
60 Kotri 25 22N 68 22E
43 Kótronas 36 38N 22 29E
26 Kotschach Mauthern 46 40N 13 0E
62 Kottayam 9 35N 76 33E
62 Kottur 10 34N 76 56E
88 Kotzebue 66 53N 162 39W
43 Koufonísi, I. 34 56N 26 8E
74 Koula-Moutou 1 15S 12 25E
80 Koumala 21 38S 149 15E
50 Kounradskiy 47 20N 75 0E
111 Kourou 5 9N 52 39W
72 Kouroussa 10 45N 9 45W
40 Kovačica 45 5N 20 38E
48 Kovdor 67 34N 30 22E
48 Kovel 51 10N 25 0E
62 Kovilpatti 9 10N 77 50E
48 Kovrov 56 25N 41 25E
62 Kovur, Andhra Pradesh 17 3N 81 39E
62 Kovur, Andhra Pradesh 14 30N 80 1E
69 Kowloon 22 20N 114 15E
69 Koyiu 23 2N 112 28E
88 Koyukuk, R. 64 56N 157 30W
42 Kozáni 40 19N 21 47E
42 Kozáni □ 40 20N 21 45E
40 Kozara, Mts. 45 0N 17 0E
40 Kozarac 44 58N 16 48E
62 Kozhikode= Calicut 11 15N 75 43E
48 Kozhva 65 10N 57 0E
28 Kozmin 51 48N 17 27E
28 Kozuchów 51 45N 15 35E
72 Kpandu 7 2N 0 18E
63 Kra, Isthmus of= Kra, Kho Khot 10 15N 99 30E
63 Kra, Kho Khot 10 15N 99 30E
63 Kra Buri 10 22N 98 46E
40 Kragujevac 44 2N 20 56E
27 Kracków 50 4N 19 57E
27 Krakow □ 50 5N 20 0E
65 Kraksaan 7 43S 113 23E
40 Kraljevo 43 44N 20 41E
26 Kralupy 50 13N 14 20E
49 Kramatorsk 48 50N 37 30E
44 Kramfors 62 55N 17 48E
37 Kranj 46 16N 14 22E
37 Krapina 46 10N 15 52E
27 Krapkowice 50 29N 17 55E
48 Krasavino 60 58N 46 26E
51 Kraskino 42 45N 130 58E
26 Kraslice 50 19N 12 31E
27 Krasnik 50 55N 22 5E
49 Krasnodar 45 5N 38 50E
48 Krasnokamsk 58 0N 56 0E
50 Krasnoselkupsk 65 20N 82 10E
50 Krasnoturinsk 59 39N 60 1E
48 Krasnoufimsk 56 30N 57 37E
50 Krasnouralsk 58 0N 60 0E
50 Krasnovodsk 40 0N 52 52E
48 Krasnovishersk 60 23N 56 59E
51 Krasnoyarsk 56 8N 93 0E
28 Krasnystaw 50 57N 23 5E
49 Krasnyy Yar 46 43N 48 23E
24 Krefeld 51 20N 6 22E
43 Kremaston, L. 38 52N 21 30E
49 Kremenchug 49 5N 33 25E
49 Kremenchugskoye, Vdkhr. 49 20N 32 30E
40 Kremenica 40 55N 21 25E
26 Krems 48 25N 15 36E
26 Kremsmünster 48 3N 14 8E
41 Krichem 46 16N 24 28E
62 Krishna, R. 15 43N 80 55E
62 Krishnagiri 12 32N 78 16E
61 Krishnanagar 23 24N 88 33E
47 Kristiansand 58 5N 7 50E
45 Kristianstad 56 5N 14 7E
45 Kristianstads □ 56 0N 14 0E
44 Kristiansund 63 10N 7 45E
44 Kristinehamn 59 18N 14 13E
46 Kristinestad 62 18N 21 25E
43 Kriti, I. 35 15N 25 0E
43 Kritsá 35 10N 25 41E
40 Kriva Palanka 42 11N 22 19E
49 Krivoy Rog 47 51N 33 20E
40 Križevci 46 3N 16 32E
37 Krk, I. 45 5N 14 56E
37 Krka, R. 45 50N 15 30E
26 Krkonoše, Mts. 50 50N 15 30E
27 Krnov 50 5N 17 40E
28 Krobia 51 47N 16 59E
26 Kročehlavy 50 8N 14 9E
27 Kroměříz 49 18N 17 21E
45 Kronobergs □ 56 45N 14 30E
48 Kronshtadt 60 5N 29 35E
75 Kroonstad 27 43S 27 19E
51 Kropotkin 58 50N 115 10E
28 Krośniewice 52 15N 19 11E
27 Krosno 49 35N 21 56E
27 Krosno □ 49 30N 21 40E
28 Krosno Odrz 52 3N 15 7E
28 Krotoszyn 51 42N 17 23E
37 Krsko 45 57N 15 30E
75 Krugersdorp 26 5S 27 46E
41 Krumovgrad 41 29N 25 38E
63 Krung Thep 13 45N 100 35E
27 Krupinica, R. 48 5N 18 53E
40 Kruševac 43 35N 21 28E
44 Krylbo 60 7N 16 15E
49 Krymskaya 44 57N 37 50E
28 Krzyz 52 52N 16 0E
72 Ksar El Boukhari 35 5N 2 52E
72 Ksar-el-Kebir 35 0N 6 0W
64 Kuala 2 46N 105 47E
63 Kuala Dungun 4 46N 103 25E
63 Kuala Kangsar 4 49N 100 57E
63 Kuala Kubu Baharu 3 35N 101 38E
63 Kuala Lipis 4 22N 102 5E
63 Kuala Lumpur 3 9N 101 41E
63 Kuala Pilah 2 45N 102 14E
63 Kuala Selangor 3 20N 101 15E
63 Kuala Terengganu 5 20N 103 8E
64 Kualakapuas 2 55S 114 20E
64 Kualakurun 1 10S 113 50E
64 Kualapembuang 3 14S 112 38E
64 Kualasimpang 4 16N 98 4E
63 Kuantan 3 49N 103 20E
49 Kuba 41 21N 48 22E
58 Kubak 27 10N 63 10E
49 Kuban, R. 45 20N 37 30E
66 Kubokawa 33 12N 133 8E
67 Kucha 41 50N 82 30E
60 Kuchaman 27 13N 74 47E
26 Kuchenspitze, Mt. 47 3N 10 14E
64 Kuching 1 33N 110 25E
66 Kuchinotsu 32 36N 130 11E
64 Kudat 7 0N 116 42E
65 Kudus 6 48N 110 51E
73 Kufra, El Wâhât et 24 17N 23 15E
26 Kufstein 47 35N 12 11E
26 Kuhnsdorf 46 37N 14 38E
57 Kūhpāyeh 32 44N 52 20E
83 Kukerin 33 13S 118 0E
42 Kukësi □ 42 15N 20 15E
40 Kula, Bulgaria 43 52N 22 36E
45 Kula, Yug. 45 37N 19 32E
61 Kula Kangri, Mt. 28 14N 90 47E
63 Kulai 1 44N 103 35E
62 Kulasekharapattanam 8 20N 78 0E
80 Kulgera 25 50S 133 18E
83 Kulin 32 40S 118 2E
83 Kulja 30 35S 117 31E
50 Kulsary 46 59N 54 1E
61 Kulti 23 43N 86 50E
50 Kulunda 52 45N 79 15E
50 Kulyab 37 55N 69 50E
67 Kum Darya, R. 41 0N 89 0E
50 Kum Tekei 43 10N 79 30E
64 Kumai 2 52S 111 45E
66 Kumamoto 32 45N 130 45E
66 Kumamoto □ 32 30N 130 40E
40 Kumanovo 42 9N 21 42E
85 Kumara 42 37S 171 12E
83 Kumari 32 45S 121 30E
72 Kumasi 6 41N 1 38E
72 Kumba 4 36N 9 24E
62 Kumbakonam 10 58N 79 25E
81 Kumbarilla 27 15S 150 55E
66 Kumagaya 36 9N 139 22E
48 Kumertau 52 46N 55 47E
44 Kumla 59 8N 15 10E
25 Kummerower See 53 49N 12 52E
72 Kumo 10 1N 11 12E
59 Kumon Bum, Mts. 26 0N 97 15E
62 Kumta 14 29N 74 32E
57 Kunar □ 35 15N 71 0E
60 Kunch 26 0N 79 10E
83 Kundip 33 42S 120 10E
60 Kundla 21 21N 71 25E
57 Kunduz 36 50N 68 50E
57 Kunduz □ 36 50N 68 50E
45 Kungälv 57 54N 12 0E
68 Kungchuling 43 31N 124 58E
67 Kungho 36 28N 100 45E
50 Kungrad 43 6N 58 54E
45 Kungsbacka 57 30N 12 7E
44 Kungsör 59 25N 16 5E
27 Kunhegyes 47 22N 20 36E
69 Kunhsien 32 30N 111 17E
65 Kuningan 6 59S 108 29E
59 Kunlong 23 20N 98 50E
52 Kunlun Shan, Mts. 36 0N 82 0E
67 Kunming 25 11N 102 37E
62 Kunnamkulam 10 38N 76 7E
68 Kunsan 35 59N 126 35E
82 Kununurra 15 40S 128 39E
80 Kunwarara 22 25S 150 7E
46 Kuopio 62 53N 27 35E
46 Kuopio □ 63 25N 27 10E
65 Kupang 10 19S 123 39E
92 Kupreanof I. 56 50N 133 30W
40 Kupres 44 1N 17 15E
49 Kura, R. 39 24N 49 24E
62 Kurandvad 16 45N 74 39E
66 Kurashiki 34 40N 133 50E
66 Kurayoshi 35 26N 133 50E
62 Kurduvadi 18 8N 75 29E
41 Kŭrdzhali 41 38N 25 21E
66 Kure 34 14N 132 32E
50 Kurgaldzhino 50 35N 70 20E
50 Kurgan 55 30N 65 0E
62 Kurichchi 11 36N 77 35E
51 Kurilskiye Os. 45 0N 150 0E
66 Kurino 31 57N 130 43E
62 Kurla 19 5N 72 52E
62 Kurnool 15 45N 78 0E
85 Kurow 44 4S 170 29E
84 Kurri Kurri 32 50S 151 28E
61 Kurseong 26 56N 88 18E
48 Kursk 51 42N 36 11E
40 Kuršumlija 43 9N 21 19E
66 Kurume 33 15N 130 30E
62 Kurunegala 7 30N 80 18E
51 Kurya 61 15N 108 10E

68 Kushan 39 58N 123 30 E
66 Kushikino 31 44N 130 16 E
66 Kushima 31 29N 131 14 E
66 Kushimoto 33 28N 135 47 E
66 Kushiro 43 0N 144 30 E
57 Kushk 34 55N 62 30 E
50 Kushka 35 20N 62 18 E
61 Kushtia 23 55N 89 5 E
88 Kuskokwim, R. 60 17N 162 27W
88 Kuskokwim B. 59 45N 162 25W
50 Kustanai 53 20N 63 45 E
56 Kutahya 39 25N 29 59 E
49 Kutaisi 42 19N 42 40 E
64 Kutaraja=Banda Aceh 5 35N 95 20 E
60 Kutch, G. of. 22 50N 69 15 E
60 Kutch, Rann of, Reg. 24 0N 70 0N
40 Kutina 45 29N 16 48 E
60 Kutiyana 21 36N 70 2 E
26 Kutná Hora 49 57N 15 16 E
28 Kutno 52 15N 19 23 E
80 Kuttabul 21 5S 148 48 E
73 Kutum 14 20N 24 10 E
56 Kuwait ■ 29 30N 47 30 E
66 Kuwana 35 0N 136 43 E
68 Kuyang 41 8N 110 1 E
48 Kuybyshev, Kuyb. Obl. 53 12N 50 9 E
48 Kuybyshev, Tatar A.S.S.R. 54 57N 49 5 E
50 Kuybyshev, Novosibirsk Obl. 55 27N 78 19 E
48 Kuybyshevskoye Vdkhr. 55 2N 49 30 E
51 Kuyumba 61 10N 97 10 E
48 Kuyto, Oz. 64 40N 31 0 E
62 Kuzhithura 8 18N 77 11 E
48 Kuznetsk 53 12N 46 40 E
48 Kuzomen 66 22N 36 50 E
37 Kvarner, G. 44 50N 14 10 E
37 Kvarneric 44 43N 14 37 E
111 Kwakoegron 5 25N 55 25W
75 Kwando, R. 16 48S 22 45 E
69 Kwangan 30 35N 106 40 E
69 Kwangchow 23 10N 113 10 E
69 Kwangchow Wan, G. 21 0N 111 0 E
68 Kwangju 35 10N 126 45 E
67 Kwangnan 24 10N 105 0 E
69 Kwangsi-Chuang Aut.Dist. □ 23 30N 108 55 E
69 Kwangtseh 27 30N 117 25 E
69 Kwangtung □ 23 35N 114 0 E
69 Kwangyuan 32 30N 105 49 E
69 Kwanhsien 30 59N 103 40 E
67 Kwantung 25 12N 101 37 E
65 Kwatisore 3 7S 139 59 E
69 Kwei Kiang, R. 23 30N 110 30 E
69 Kweichih 30 40N 117 30 E
69 Kweichow= Fengkieh 31 0N 109 33 E
69 Kweichow □ 26 40N 107 0 E
69 Kweihsien 22 59N 109 44 E
69 Kweiki 28 10N 117 8 E
69 Kweilin 25 16N 110 15 E
69 Kweiping 23 12N 110 0 E
69 Kweiting 26 0N 113 35 E
69 Kweiyang 25 30N 106 35 E
88 Kwiguk Island 62 45N 164 28W
83 Kwinana 32 15S 115 47 E
28 Kwisa, R. 51 35N 15 25 E
69 Kwo Ho, R. 33 20N 116 50 E
65 Kwoka, Mt. 0 31S 132 27 E
51 Kyakhta 50 30N 106 25 E
81 Kyancutta 33 8S 135 34 E
59 Kyaukpadaung 20 52N 95 8 E
59 Kyaukpyu 19 28N 93 30 E
59 Kyaukse 21 36N 96 10 E
75 Kyle Dam 20 14S 31 0 E
80 Kynuna 21 35S 141 55 E
74 Kyoga, L. 1 35N 33 0 E
81 Kyogle 28 40S 153 0 E
68 Kyongju 35 59N 129 26 E
59 Kyonpyaw 17 12N 95 10 E
66 Kyōto 35 0N 135 45 E
66 Kyōto □ 35 15N 135 30 E
56 Kyrínia 35 20N 33 19 E
51 Kystatyam 67 15N 123 0 E
51 Kytal Ktakh 65 30N 123 40 E
59 Kyunhla 23 25N 95 15 E
66 Kyūshū, I. 32 30N 131 0 E
66 Kyūshū □ 32 30N 131 0 E
40 Kyustendil 42 25N 22 41 E
51 Kyusyur 70 30N 127 0 E
51 Kyzyl 51 50N 94 30 E
50 Kzyl Orda 44 50N 65 10 E

L

32 La Alcarria 40 31N 2 45W
32 La Almarcha 39 41N 2 24W
32 La Almunia de Doña Godino 41 29N 1 23W
110 La Asunción 11 2N 63 53W
108 La Banda 27 45S 64 10W
30 La Bañeza 42 17N 5 54W
104 La Barca 20 20N 102 40W
19 La Bassée 50 31N 2 49 E
20 La Bastide-Puylaurent 44 35N 3 55 E
18 La Baule 47 18N 2 23 E
32 La Bisbal 41 58N 3 2 E
110 La Blanquilla, I. 11 51N 64 37W
104 La Boca 9 0N 79 30 E
19 La Bresse 48 0N 6 53 E
30 La Bureba 42 36N 3 24W
108 La Calera 32 50S 71 10W
31 La Campiña 37 45N 4 45W
19 La Capelle 49 59N 3 50 E
108 La Carlota 33 30S 63 20W
31 La Carolina 38 17N 3 38W
105 La Ceiba, Honduras 15 40N 86 50W
110 La Ceiba, Ven. 9 30N 71 0W
19 La Chapelle-d'Angillon 47 21N 2 25 E
18 La Chapelle Glain 47 38N 1 11W
20 La Charité-sur-Loire 47 10N 3 0 E
20 La Châtre 46 35N 1 59 E
25 La Chaux-de-Fonds 47 7N 6 50 E
21 La Ciotat 43 12N 5 36 E
30 La Coruña 43 20N 8 25W
30 La Coruña □ 43 10N 8 30W
100 La Crosse 43 48N 91 13W
110 La Dorada 5 30N 74 40W
30 La Estrada 42 43N 8 27W
98 La Fayette 40 22N 86 52W
19 La Fere 49 40N 3 20 E
19 La Ferté 48 57N 3 6 E
18 La Ferté-Bernard 48 10N 0 40 E
18 La Ferté-Mace 48 35N 0 21W
18 La Flèche 47 42N 0 5W
99 La Folette 36 23N 84 9W
30 La Fregeneda 40 58N 6 54W
30 La Fuente de S. Esteban 40 49N 6 15W
33 La Gineta 39 8N 2 1W
21 La Grand' Comb 44 13N 4 2 E
102 La Grande 45 15N 118 0W
21 La Grande-Motte 48 35N 1 4 E
99 La Grange 33 4N 85 0W
110 La Guaira 10 36N 66 56W
30 La Guardia 41 56N 8 52W
20 La Guerche-sur-l'Aubois 46 58N 2 56 E
105 La Mabana 23 8N 82 22W
18 La Haye du Puits 49 17N 1 33W
32 La Junquera 42 25N 2 53 E
101 La Junta 38 0N 103 30W
108 La Ligua 32 30S 71 16W
31 La Linea de la Concepción 36 15N 5 23W
93 La Loche 56 29N 109 27W
30 La Lora 42 45N 4 0W
16 La Louvière 50 27N 4 10 E
20 La Machine 46 54N 3 27 E
38 La Maddalena 41 13N 9 25 E
91 La Malbaie 47 40N 70 10W
33 La Mancha 39 10N 2 54W
30 La Mariña 43 30N 7 40W
88 La Martre, L. 63 0N 118 0W
103 La Mesa 32 48N 117 5W
32 La Muela 41 36N 1 7W
21 La Mure 44 55N 5 48 E
21 La Napoule 43 31N 6 56 E
110 La Orchila, I. 12 30N 67 0W
110 La Oroya 11 32S 75 54W
20 La Pacaudière 46 10N 3 50 E
31 La Palma 37 21N 6 38W
105 La Palma 8 15N 78 0W
72 La Palma, I. 28 40N 17 52W
108 La Pampa □ 37 0S 66 0W
110 La Paragua 6 50N 63 20W
108 La Paz, Arg. 30 50S 59 45W
110 La Paz, Bolivia 16 20S 68 10W
104 La Paz, Mexico 24 10N 110 20W
110 La Pedrera 1 18S 69 43W
66 La Perouse, Str. 45 40N 142 0 E
104 La Piedad 20 20N 102 1W
102 La Pine 40 53N 80 45W
108 La Plata 35 0S 57 55W
30 La Pola de Gordón 42 51N 5 41W
98 La Porte 41 40N 86 40W
31 La Puebla de Cazalla 37 14N 5 19W
30 La Puebla de Montalbán 39 52N 4 22W
33 La Puerta 38 22N 2 45W
108 La Quiaca 22 5S 65 35W
90 La Reine 48 50N 79 30W
20 La Réole 44 35N 0 1W
108 La Rioja, Arg. 29 20S 67 0W
32 La Rioja, Sp. 42 20N 2 20W
108 La Rioja □ 29 20S 67 0W
21 La Roche 46 4N 6 19 E
18 La Roche Bernard 47 32N 2 18W
20 La Roche-sur-Yon 46 40N 1 25W
20 La Rochefoucauld 45 44N 0 24 E
20 La Rochelle 46 10N 1 9W
33 La Roda 39 13N 2 15W
105 La Romana 18 27N 68 57W
33 La Sagra, Mt. 38 0N 2 35W
100 La Salle 41 20N 89 5W
30 La Sanabria 42 0N 6 30W
90 La Sarre 48 45N 79 15W
32 La Selva 42 0N 2 45 E
108 La Serena, Chile 29 55S 71 10W
31 La Serena, Sp. 38 45N 5 40W
21 La Seyne-sur-Mer 43 7N 5 52 E
39 La Sila, Mt. 39 15N 16 35 E
31 La Solana 38 59N 3 14W
20 La Souterraine 46 15N 1 30 E
36 La Spézia 44 8N 9 50 E
18 La Suze 47 54N 0 2 E
110 La Tagua 0 3N 74 40W
20 La Teste 44 34N 1 9W
110 La Tortuga, I. 10 56N 65 20W
21 La-Tour-du-Pin 45 34N 5 27 E
20 La Tranche 46 20N 1 26W
90 La Tuque 47 30N 72 50W
112 La Unión, Chile 40 10S 73 0W
104 La Union, Salvador 13 20N 87 50W
33 La Unión, Sp. 37 38N 0 53W
110 La Urbana 7 8N 66 56W
105 La Vega 19 20N 70 30W
110 La Vela 11 30N 69 30W
90 La Verendrye Prov. Park 47 15N 77 10W
110 La Victoria 10 14N 67 20W
72 Labé 11 24N 12 16W
63 Labis 2 22N 103 2 E
20 Labouheyre 44 13N 0 55W
108 Laboulaye 34 10S 63 30W
86 Labrador, Reg. 53 20N 61 0W
91 Labrador City 52 42N 67 0W
20 Labrède 44 41N 0 32W
65 Labuha 0 30S 127 30 E
65 Labuhan 6 26S 105 50 E
92 Lac la Biche 54 45N 111 50W
93 Lac Seul 50 28N 92 0W
20 Lacanau 44 59N 1 5W
20 Lacanau, Étang de 44 58N 1 7W
20 Lacaune, Mts. de 43 43N 2 50 E
53 Laccadive Is. 10 0N 72 30 E
90 Lachine 45 30N 73 40W
84 Lachlan, R. 34 21S 143 57 E
90 Lachute 45 39N 74 21W
96 Lackawanna 42 49N 78 50W
92 Lacombe 52 30N 113 50W
38 Laconi 39 54N 9 4 E
97 Laconia 43 32N 71 30W
20 Lacq 43 25N 0 35W
58 Ladakh Ra. 34 0N 78 0 E
43 Ládhon, R. 37 40N 21 50 E
57 Lādiz 28 55N 61 15 E
60 Ladnun 27 38N 74 25 E
48 Ladozhskoye, Oz. 61 15N 30 30 E
75 Lady Grey 30 43S 27 13 E
92 Ladysmith, Canada 49 0N 124 0W
75 Ladysmith, S. Africa 28 32S 29 46 E
76 Lae 6 40S 147 2 E
45 Laesø, I. 57 15N 10 53 E
101 Lafayette 30 18N 92 0W
72 Lafia 8 30N 8 34 E
90 Laforest 47 4N 81 12W
45 Lagan, R. 56 33N 12 56 E
30 Lage, Sp. 43 13N 9 0W
24 Lage, W. Germany 52 0N 8 47 E
44 Lågen, R. 61 8N 10 25 E
57 Laghman □ 34 20N 70 0 E
72 Laghouat 33 50N 2 59 E
31 Lagôa 37 8N 8 27W
30 Lagoaça 41 11N 6 44W
39 Lagónegro 40 8N 15 45 E
65 Lagonoy G. 13 50N 123 50 E
72 Lagos, Nigeria 6 25N 3 27 E
31 Lagos, Port. 37 5N 8 41W
104 Lagos de Moreno 21 21N 101 55W
82 Lagrange 14 13S 125 46 E
32 Laguardia 42 33N 2 35W
20 Laguépie 44 8N 1 57 E
109 Laguna 28 30S 48 50 E
103 Laguna Beach 33 31N 117 52W
68 Laha 48 9N 124 30 E
65 Lahad Datu 5 0N 118 30 E
94 Lahaina 20 52N 156 41W
64 Lahat 3 45S 103 30 E
56 Lahijan 37 12N 50 1 E
60 Lahore 31 32N 74 22 E
60 Lahore □ 31 55N 74 5 E
25 Lahr 48 20N 7 52 E
68 Laichow Wan, G. 37 30N 119 30 E
81 Laidley 27 39S 152 20 E
18 L'Aigle 48 45N 0 38 E
56 Laila 22 10N 46 40 E
69 Laipin 23 42N 109 16 E
14 Lairg 58 1N 4 24W
64 Lais 3 35S 102 0 E
68 Laiyang 36 58N 120 41 E
109 Lajes 27 48S 50 20W
40 Lajkovac 44 27N 20 14 E
27 Lajosmizse 47 3N 19 32 E
101 Lake Charles 31 10N 93 10W
99 Lake City, Fla. 30 10N 82 40W
99 Lake City, S.C. 33 51N 79 44W
97 Lake George 43 25N 73 36W
83 Lake Grace 33 7S 118 28 E
89 Lake Harbour 62 30N 69 50W
103 Lake Havasu City 34 25N 114 20W
83 Lake King 33 5S 119 45 E
103 Lake Mead Nat. Rec. Area 36 20N 114 30W
80 Lake Nash 20 57S 138 0 E
90 Lake Superior Prov. Park 47 45N 85 0W
90 Lake Traverse 45 56N 78 4W
99 Lake Worth 26 36N 80 3W
90 Lakefield 44 25N 78 16W
99 Lakeland 28 0N 82 0W
102 Lakeport 39 1N 122 56W
84 Lakes Entrance 37 50S 148 0 E
102 Lakeview 34 12N 109 59W
97 Lakewood, N.J. 40 5N 74 13W
96 Lakewood, Ohio 41 28N 81 50W
61 Lakhimpur 27 14N 94 7 E
60 Lakki 32 38N 70 50 E
43 Lakonía □ 36 55N 22 30 E
43 Lakonikós Kól. 36 40N 22 40 E
46 Lakselv 70 2N 24 56 E
61 Lakshmi Kantapur 22 5N 88 20 E
59 Lala Ghat 24 30N 92 40 E
60 Lala Musa 32 40N 73 57 E
68 Lalin 45 14N 126 52 E
20 Lalinde 44 50N 0 44 E
61 Lalitapur 27 42N 85 12 E
60 Lalitpur 24 42N 78 28 E
59 Lamaing 15 25N 97 53 E
26 Lambach 48 6N 13 51 E
18 Lamballe 48 29N 2 31W
74 Lambaréné 0 20S 10 12 E
63 Lambi Kyun, I. 10 50N 98 20 E
43 Lámbia 37 52N 21 53 E
72 Lame 10 27N 9 12 E
30 Lamego 41 5N 7 52W
81 Lameroo 35 19S 140 33 E
101 Lamesa 32 45N 101 57W
43 Lamía 38 55N 22 41 E
65 Lamitan 6 40N 122 10 E
14 Lammermuir Hills 55 50N 24 0W
65 Lamon B. 14 30N 122 20 E
63 Lampang 18 18N 99 31 E
18 Lampaul 48 28N 5 7W
73 Lampedusa, I. 35 36N 12 40 E
13 Lampeter 52 6N 4 6W
93 Lampman 49 25N 102 50W
26 Lamprechtshavsen 48 0N 12 58 E
64 Lampung □ 5 30S 105 0 E
74 Lamu 2 10S 40 55 E
14 Lanark 55 40N 3 48W
12 Lancashire □ 53 40N 2 30W
91 Lancaster, Canada 45 17N 66 10W
12 Lancaster, U.K. 54 3N 2 48W
103 Lancaster, Calif. 34 47N 118 8W
98 Lancaster, Ky. 37 40N 84 40W
96 Lancaster, N.Y. 42 53N 78 43W
97 Lancaster, Pa. 40 4N 76 19W
99 Lancaster, S.C. 34 45N 80 47W
89 Lancaster Sd. 74 0N 84 0W
69 Lanchi 29 11N 119 30 E
68 Lanchow 36 4N 103 44 E
37 Lanciano 42 15N 14 22 E
25 Landau 49 12N 8 7 E
26 Landeck 47 9N 10 34 E
102 Lander 42 50N 108 49W
18 Landerneau 48 28N 4 17W
20 Landes □ 43 57N 0 48W
20 Landes, Reg. 44 0N 1 5W
58 Landi Kotal 34 7N 71 6 E

18 Landivisiau 48 31N 4 6W
25 Landsberg 48 3N 10 52E
25 Landshut 48 31N 12 10E
45 Landskrona 56 53N 12 50E
99 Lanett 33 0N 85 15W
69 Langchung 31 31N 105 58E
20 Langeac 45 7N 3 29E
18 Langeais 47 20N 0 24E
45 Langeland, I. 54 56N 10 48E
25 Langen 53 36N 8 36E
26 Langenlois 48 29N 15 40E
24 Langeoog, I. 53 44N 7 33E
68 Langfeng 48 4N 121 10E
14 Langholm 55 9N 2 59W
63 Langkawi, Pulau 6 25N 99 45E
91 Langlade, I. 46 50N 56 20W
20 Langogne 44 43N 3 50E
20 Langon 44 33N 0 16W
19 Langres 47 52N 5 20E
19 Langres, Plat. de 47 45N 5 20E
64 Langsa 4 30N 97 57E
63 Langson 21 52N 106 42E
20 Languedoc, Reg. 43 58N 3 22E
20 Lannemezan 43 8N 0 23E
18 Lannion 48 46N 3 29W
97 Lansdale 40 14N 75 18W
90 Lansdowne House 52 5N 88 0W
91 L'Anse au Loup 51 32N 56 50W
97 Lansford 40 48N 75 55W
98 Lansing 42 47N 84 32W
108 Lanus 34 44S 58 27W
38 Lanusei 39 53N 9 31E
72 Lanzarote, I. 29 0N 13 40W
63 Lao Cai 22 30N 103 57E
65 Laoag 18 7N 120 34E
65 Laoang 12 32N 125 8E
15 Laois □ 53 0N 7 20W
19 Laon 49 33N 3 35E
63 Laos ■ 17 45N 105 0E
109 Lapa 25 46S 49 44W
20 Lapalisse 46 15N 3 44E
98 Lapeer 43 3N 83 20W
97 Laporte 41 27N 76 30W
40 Lapovo 44 10N 21 2E
46 Lappi □ 64 33N 25 10E
46 Lappland, Reg. 68 7N 24 0E
97 Laprairie 45 25N 73 30W
51 Laptev Sea 76 0N 125 0E
37 L'Aquila 42 21N 13 24E
57 Lār 27 40N 54 14E
72 Larache 35 10N 6 5W
21 Laragne-Montéglin 44 18N 5 49E
100 Laramie 41 15N 105 29W
109 Laranjeiras do Sul 25 25S 52 25W
90 Larder Lake 48 5N 79 40W
30 Laredo, Sp. 43 26N 3 28W
101 Laredo, U.S.A. 27 34N 99 29W
73 Largeau 17 58N 19 6E
21 L'Argens, R. 43 24N 6 44E
14 Largs 55 48N 4 51W
42 Lárisa 39 38N 22 28E
42 Lárisa □ 39 39N 22 24E
60 Larkana 27 32N 68 2E
56 Lárnax 35 0N 33 35E
15 Larne 54 52N 5 50W
15 Larne □ 54 55N 5 55W
82 Larrimah 15 35S 133 12E
5 Larsen Ice Shelf 67 0S 62 0W
44 Larvik 59 4N 10 0E
50 Laryak 61 15N 80 0E
20 Larzac, Causse du 44 0N 3 17E
55 Las Anod 8 26N 47 19E
33 Las Blancos 37 38N 0 49W
108 Las Breñas 27 5S 61 5W
31 Las Cabezas de San Juan 37 0N 5 58W
103 Las Cruces 32 25N 106 50W
108 Las Flores 36 0S 59 0W
112 Las Heras
108 Las Heras 32 50S 68 50W
55 Las Khoreh 11 4N 48 20E
112 Las Lajas 38 30S 70 25W
31 Las Marismas 37 5N 6 20W
72 Las Palmas 28 10N 15 28W
108 Las Piedras 34 44S 56 13W
112 Las Plumas 43 40S 67 15W
108 Las Rosas 32 30S 61 40W
108 Las Varillas 32 0S 62 50W
103 Las Vegas, Nev. 36 10N 115 5W
101 Las Vegas, N. Mex. 35 35N 105 10W
109 Lascano 33 35S 54 18W
93 Lashburn 53 10N 109 40W
59 Lashio 22 56N 97 45E
18 Lassay 48 27N 0 30W
102 Lassen Pk. 40 20N 121 0W
40 Lastovo, I. 42 46N 16 55E
37 Lastovski Kanal 42 50N 17 0E
110 Latacunga 0 50S 78 35W
90 Latchford 47 20N 79 50W
39 Laterza 40 38N 16 47E
83 Latham 29 44S 116 20E
38 Latina 41 26N 12 53E
37 Latisana 45 47N 13 1E
27 Latorica, R. 48 28N 21 50E
88 Latouche 60 0N 147 55W
80 Latrobe, Australia 41 14S 146 30E
96 Latrobe, U.S.A. 40 19N 79 21W
54 Latrun 31 50N 34 58E
62 Latur 18 25N 76 40E
48 Latvian S.S.R. □ 57 0N 25 0E
85 Lau Is. 17 0S 178 30W
24 Lauchhammer 51 35N 13 40E
24 Lauenburg 53 23N 10 33E
80 Launceston, Australia 41 24S 147 8E
13 Launceston, U.K. 50 38N 4 21W
80 Laura 33 10S 138 18E
39 Laureana di Borrello 38 28N 16 5E
101 Laurel, Miss. 31 50N 89 0W
102 Laurel, Mont. 45 46N 108 49W
14 Laurencekirk 56 50N 2 30W
99 Laurens 34 32N 82 2W
86 Laurentian Plat. 51 30N 65 0W
91 Laurentides Prov. Park 47 50N 71 50W
39 Lauria 40 3N 15 50E
99 Lauringburg 34 50N 79 25W
25 Lausanne 46 32N 6 38E
91 Lauzon 46 48N 71 4W
18 Laval 48 4N 0 48W
108 Lavapié, Pta. 37 9S 73 35W
20 Lavardac 44 12N 0 20E
20 Lavaur 43 42N 1 49E
20 Lavelanet 42 57N 1 51E
39 Lavello 41 4N 15 47E
83 Laverton 28 44S 122 29E
54 Lavi 32 47N 35 25E
109 Lavras 21 20S 45 0W
51 Lavrentiya 65 35N 171 0W
85 Lawrence, N.Z. 45 55S 169 41E
97 Lawrence, U.S.A. 42 40N 71 9W
100 Lawrence 39 0N 95 10W
99 Lawrenceburg 35 12N 87 19W
101 Lawton 34 33N 98 25W
65 Lawu, Mt. 7 40S 111 13E
44 Laxå 59 0N 14 37E
62 Laxmeshwar 15 9N 75 28E
20 Laye, R. 43 54N 5 48E
77 Laysan I. 25 30N 167 0W
40 Lazarevac 44 23N 20 17E
37 Lazio □ 42 10N 12 30E
20 Le Bacarès 42 47N 3 3E
20 Le Bouscat 44 53N 0 32E
20 Le Canourgue 44 26N 3 13E
20 Le Cap d'Agde 43 18N 3 29E
21 Le Chambon-Feugerolles 45 24N 4 18E
21 Le Creusot 46 50N 4 24E
18 Le Croisic 47 18N 2 30W
20 Le Dorat 46 14N 1 5E
105 Le François 14 38N 60 57W
18 Le Havre 49 30N 0 5E
21 Le Lavandou 43 8N 6 22E
25 Le Locle 47 3N 6 44E
38 Le Madonie, Mts. 37 50N 13 50E
112 Le Maire, Estrecho de 54 50S 65 0W
18 Le Mans 48 0N 0 10E
74 Le Marinel 10 25S 25 17E
100 Le Mars 43 0N 96 0W
105 Le Moule 16 20N 61 22W
18 Le Palais 47 21N 3 10W
18 Le Petit-Quevilly 49 26N 1 0E
20 Le Puy 45 3N 3 52E
19 Le Quesnoy 50 15N 3 38E
21 Le Teil 44 34N 4 41E
19 Le Thillot 47 52N 6 55E
19 Le Touquet-Paris-Plage 50 30N 1 36E
18 Le Tréport 50 3N 1 20E
20 Le Verdon 45 32N 1 5W
13 Lea, R. 51 30N 0 1E
100 Lead 44 20N 103 40W
93 Leader 50 50N 109 30W
14 Leadhills 55 25N 3 47W
103 Leadville 39 17N 106 23W
75 Lealui 15 10S 23 2E
90 Leamington, Canada 42 10N 82 30W
13 Leamington, U.K. 52 18N 1 32W
109 Leandro Norte Alem 27 34S 55 15W
82 Learmonth 22 40S 114 10E
93 Leask 53 5N 106 45W
100 Leavenworth 39 25N 95 0W
28 Łeba 54 45N 17 32E
98 Lebanon, Ind. 40 3N 86 55W
101 Lebanon, Mo. 37 40N 92 40W
102 Lebanon, Ore. 44 31N 122 57W
97 Lebanon, Pa. 40 20N 76 28W
99 Lebanon, Tenn. 36 15N 86 20W
56 Lebanon ■ 34 0N 36 0E
28 Lębork 54 33N 17 46E
31 Lebrija 36 53N 6 5W
108 Lebu 37 40S 73 47W
39 Lecce 40 20N 18 10E
36 Lecco 45 50N 9 27E
36 Lecco, L. di 45 51N 9 22E
32 Lécera 41 13N 0 43W
26 Lech 47 13N 10 9E
25 Lech, R. 47 19N 10 27E
26 Lechtaler Alpen, Mts. 47 15N 10 30E
20 Lectoure 43 56N 0 38E
28 Łęczyca 52 5N 19 45E
13 Ledbury 52 3N 2 25W
30 Ledesma 41 6N 5 59W
92 Leduc 53 20N 113 30W
15 Lee, R. 51 51N 9 2W
12 Leeds 53 48N 1 34W
12 Leek 53 7N 2 2W
24 Leer 53 13N 7 29E
99 Leesburg 28 47N 81 52W
16 Leeuwarden 53 15N 5 48E
83 Leeuwin, C. 34 20S 115 9E
105 Leeward Is. 16 30N 63 30W
65 Legazpi 13 10N 123 46E
28 Legionowo 52 25N 20 50E
37 Legnago 45 10N 11 19E
36 Legnano 45 35N 8 55E
28 Legnica 51 12N 16 10E
28 Legnica □ 51 20N 16 0E
58 Leh 34 15N 77 35E
97 Lehighton 40 50N 75 44W
41 Lehliu 44 29N 26 20E
24 Lehrte 52 22N 9 58E
60 Leiah 30 58N 70 58E
26 Leibnitz 46 47N 15 34E
13 Leicester 52 39N 1 9W
13 Leicester □ 52 40N 1 10W
69 Leichow Pantao, Pen. 20 40N 110 10E
16 Leiden 52 9N 4 30E
81 Leigh Creek 30 28S 138 24E
24 Leine, R. 48 54N 10 1E
15 Leinster □ 53 0N 7 10W
24 Leipzig 51 20N 12 23E
24 Leipzig □ 51 20N 12 30E
30 Leiria □ 39 46N 8 53E
31 Leiria 39 46N 8 53W
14 Leith 55 59N 3 10W
13 Leith Hill 51 10N 0 23W
27 Leitha, R. 47 54N 17 17E
15 Leitrim 54 0N 8 5W
15 Leitrim □ 54 8N 8 0W
69 Leiyang 26 24N 112 51E
43 Lekhainá 37 57N 21 16E
101 Leland 33 25N 90 52W
112 Leleque 42 15S 71 0W
25 Léman, L. 46 26N 6 30E
65 Lemery 13 58N 120 56E
56 Lemesós 34 42N 33 1E
24 Lemgo 52 2N 8 52E
45 Lemvig 56 33N 8 20E
51 Lena 72 25N 126 40E
37 Lendinara 45 4N 11 37E
24 Lengerich 52 12N 7 50E
63 Lenggong 5 6N 100 58E
108 Lengua de Vaca, Pta. 30 14S 71 38W
50 Leninabad 40 17N 69 37E
49 Leninakan 41 0N 42 50E
48 Leningrad 59 55N 30 20E
50 Leninogorsk 50 20N 83 30E
49 Leninsk 48 40N 45 15E
50 Leninsk Kuznetskiy 55 10N 86 10E
51 Leninskoye 47 56N 132 38E
49 Lenkoran 39 45N 48 50E
25 Lenne, R. 51 25N 7 30E
97 Lennoxville 45 23N 71 53E
36 Leno 45 24N 10 14E
99 Lenoir 35 55N 81 36W
99 Lenoir City 35 40N 84 20W
19 Lens 50 26N 2 50E
51 Lensk 60 48N 114 55E
39 Lentini 37 18N 15 0E
26 Leoben 47 22N 15 5E
13 Leominster, U.K. 52 15N 2 43W
97 Leominster, U.S.A. 42 30N 71 44W
104 León, Mexico 21 7N 101 30W
105 León, Nic. 12 20N 86 51W
30 León, Sp. 42 38N 5 34W
30 León □ 42 40N 5 55W
30 Léon, Mt. de 42 30N 6 18W
39 Leonforte 37 39N 14 22E
84 Leongatha 38 30S 145 58E
83 Leonora 28 49S 121 19E
74 Léopold II, L.= Mai-Ndombe, L. 2 0S 18 0E
109 Leopoldina 21 28S 42 40W
74 Léopoldville= Kinshasa 4 20S 15 15E
93 Leoville 53 39N 107 33W
31 Lepe 37 15N 7 12W
48 Lepel 54 50N 28 40E
51 Lepikha 64 45N 125 55E
30 Lequeito 43 20N 2 32W
72 Lere 9 39N 14 13E
36 Lérici 44 4N 9 48E
32 Lérida 41 37N 0 39E
32 Lérida □ 42 6N 1 0E
30 Lerma 42 0N 3 47W
43 Léros, I. 37 10N 26 50E
19 Lérouville 48 50N 5 30E
45 Lerum 57 46N 12 16E
14 Lerwick 60 10N 1 10W
21 Les Arcs 43 27N 6 29E
105 Les Cayes 18 15N 73 46W
20 Les Herbiers 46 52N 1 0W
18 Les Ponts-de-Cé 47 25N 0 30W
20 Les Sables-d'Olonne 46 30N 1 45W
21 Les Saintes-Maries 43 27N 4 25E
104 Les Tres Marías, Is. 12 20N 106 30W
39 Lésina, L. di 41 53N 15 25E
40 Leskovac 43 0N 21 58E
18 Lesneven 48 35N 4 20W
40 Lešnica 44 39N 19 20E
75 Lesotho ■ 29 40S 28 0E
51 Lesozarodsk 45 30N 133 20E
20 Lesparre-Médoc 45 18N 0 57W
18 Lessay 49 14N 1 30W
105 Lesser Antilles, Is. 12 30N 61 0W
65 Lesser Sunda Is. 7 30S 117 0E
43 Lésvos, I. 39 0N 26 20E
28 Leszno 51 50N 16 30E
28 Lezno □ 52 0N 16 30E
13 Letchworth 51 58N 0 13W
92 Lethbridge 49 45N 112 45W
110 Lethem 3 20N 59 50W
65 Leti, Kep. 8 10S 128 0E
110 Leticia 4 0S 70 0W
75 Letlhakane 24 0S 24 59E
59 Letpadan 17 45N 96 0E
59 Letpan 19 28N 93 52E
15 Letterkenny 54 57N 7 42W
41 Leu 44 10N 24 0E
20 Leucate 42 56N 3 3E
20 Leucate, Étang de 42 50N 3 0E
64 Leuser, Mt. 4 0N 96 51E
16 Leuven 50 52 4 42E
43 Levádhia 38 26N 22 54E
46 Levanger 63 45N 11 19E
21 Levant, Î. du 43 3N 6 28E
36 Lévanto 44 10N 9 37E
101 Levelland 33 38N 102 17W
14 Leven 56 12N 3 0W
14 Leven, L. 56 12N 3 22W
82 Leveque, C. 16 20S 123 0E
24 Leverkusen 51 2N 6 59E
20 Levet 46 56N 2 22E
27 Levice 48 13N 18 35E
85 Levin 40 37S 175 18E
91 Levis 46 48N 71 9W
43 Levítha, I. 37 0N 26 28E
97 Levittown 40 10N 74 51W
43 Lévka, Mt. 35 18N 24 3E
43 Levkás 38 48N 20 43E
43 Levkás, I. 38 40N 20 43E
56 Levkôsia 35 10N 33 25E
41 Levski 43 21N 25 10E
41 Levskigrad 42 38N 24 47E
13 Lewes 50 53N 0 2E
14 Lewis, I. 58 10N 6 40W
102 Lewis Ra. 20 3S 128 50E
96 Lewisburg 40 57N 76 57W
91 Lewisporte 49 15N 55 3W
102 Lewiston, Id. 45 58N 117 0W
99 Lewiston, Me. 44 6N 70 13W
102 Lewistown, Mont. 47 0N 109 25W
96 Lewistown, Pa. 40 37N 77 33W
98 Lexington, Ky. 38 6N 84 30W
100 Lexington, Mo. 39 7N 93 55W
100 Lexington, Neb. 40 48N 99 45W
99 Lexington, N.C. 35 50N 80 13W
65 Leyte, I. 11 0N 125 0E
20 Leze, R. 43 40N 5 28E
42 Lezha 41 47N 19 42E
20 Lezignan-Corbières 43 13N 2 43E
28 Lezno □ 51 40N 16 36E
20 Lezoux 45 49N 3 21E
20 l'Hospitalet 42 36N 1 47E
67 Lhasa 29 39N 91 6E
67 Lhatse Dzong 29 10N 87 45E
64 Lhokseumawe 5 20N 97 10E
69 Li Kiang, R. 18 25N 98 45E
68 Liangsiang 39 44N 116 8E
68 Liaoning □ 41 15N 122 0E
68 Liaotung, Pen. 40 0N 122 22E
68 Liaotung Wan, G. 40 30N 121 30E
68 Liaoyang 41 17N 123 11E
68 Liaoyuan 42 55N 125 10E

88 Liard, R. 61 52N 121 18W
101 Liberal 37 4N 101 0W
108 Libertador General San Martin 25 30S 64 45W
26 Liberec 50 47N 15 7E
72 Liberia ■ 6 30N 9 30W
97 Liberty 41 48N 74 45W
73 Lîbîya, Sahrâ', Des. 27 35N 25 0E
20 Libourne 44 55N 0 14W
42 Librazhdi 41 12N 20 22E
74 Libreville 0 25N 9 26E
73 Libya ■ 28 30N 17 30E
38 Licata 37 6N 13 55E
12 Lichfield 52 40N 1 50W
75 Lichinga 13 13S 35 11E
75 Lichtenburg 26 8S 26 8E
25 Lichtenfels 50 7N 11 4E
39 Licosa, Pta. 40 15N 14 53E
44 Lidingo 59 22N 18 8E
45 Lidkoping 58 31N 13 14E
38 Lido di Ostia 45 25N 12 23E
28 Lidzbark Warminski 54 7N 20 34E
82 Liebenwalde 52 51N 13 23E
26 Liechtenstein ■ 47 8N 9 35E
16 Liège 50 38N 5 35E
16 Liège □ 50 32N 5 35E
26 Lienz 46 50N 12 46E
48 Liepaja 56 30N 21 0E
16 Lier 51 7N 4 34E
41 Lieşti 45 38N 27 34E
19 Liévin 45 40N 75 40W
26 Liezen 47 34N 14 15E
15 Liffey, R. 53 21N 6 16W
15 Lifford 54 50N 7 30W
37 Lignano 45 42N 13 8E
19 Ligny-en-Barrois 48 36N 5 20E
36 Ligùria □ 44 30N 9 0E
79 Lihou Reef and Cays 17 25S 151 40E
94 Lihue 21 59N 152 24W
74 Likasi 10 55S 26 48E
67 Likiang 26 50N 100 15E
74 Likati 3 20N 24 0E
21 L'Île Rousse 42 38N 8 53E
69 Liling 27 47N 113 30E
19 Lille 50 38N 3 3E
18 Lillebonne 49 30N 0 32E
44 Lillehammer 61 8N 10 30E
45 Lillerød 55 52N 12 22E
19 Lillers 50 35N 2 28E
47 Lillesand 58 15N 8 23E
44 Lillestrøm 59 58N 11 5E
92 Lillooet 50 42N 121 56W
75 Lilongwe 14 0S 33 48E
40 Lim, R. 43 0N 19 40E
110 Lima, Peru 12 0S 77 0W
102 Lima, Mont. 44 41N 112 38W
98 Lima, Ohio 40 42N 84 5W
30 Lima, R. 41 50N 8 18W
15 Limavady □ 55 0N 6 55W
15 Limavady 55 3N 6 58W
112 Limay, R. 39 0S 68 0W
60 Limbdi 22 34N 71 51E
25 Limburg 50 22N 8 4E
16 Limburg □ 51 20N 5 55E
109 Limeira 22 35S 47 28W
15 Limerick 52 40N 8 38W
15 Limerick □ 52 30N 8 50W
45 Limfjorden 56 55N 9 0E
45 Limmared 57 34N 13 20E
43 Limni 38 43N 23 18E
42 Límnos, I. 39 50N 25 5E
111 Limoeiro do Norte 5 5S 38 0W
111 Limoera 7 52S 35 27W
20 Limoges 45 50N 1 15E
105 Limón 10 0N 83 2W
20 Limousin, Plateaux 46 0N 1 0E
20 Limousin, Reg. 46 0N 1 0E
20 Limoux 43 4N 2 12E
75 Limpopo, R. 25 15S 33 30E
74 Limuru 1 2S 36 35E
108 Linares, Chile 35 50S 71 40W
104 Linares, Mexico 24 50N 99 40W
31 Linares, Sp. 38 10N 3 40W
108 Linares □ 36 0S 71 0W
38 Línas, Mt. 39 25N 8 38E
68 Lincheng 37 26N 114 34E
12 Lincoln □ 53 14N 0 32W
108 Lincoln, Arg. 34 55N 61 30W
85 Lincoln, N.Z. 43 38S 172 30E
12 Lincoln, U.K. 53 14N 0 32W
100 Lincoln, Ill. 40 10N 89 20W
100 Lincoln, Neb. 40 50N 96 42W
4 Lincoln Sea 84 0N 55 0W
12 Lincoln Wolds 53 20N 0 5W
25 Lindau 47 33N 9 41E
45 Linderod 55 56N 13 47E
45 Linderödsåsen, Reg. 55 53N 13 53E
44 Lindesberg 59 36N 15 15E
74 Lindi 9 58S 39 38E
30 Lindoso 41 52N 8 11W
90 Lindsay, Canada 44 22N 78 43W
103 Lindsay, U.S.A. 36 14N 119 6W
68 Linfen 36 5N 111 32E
65 Lingayen 16 1N 120 14E
65 Lingayen G. 16 10N 120 15E
24 Lingen 52 32N 7 21E
64 Lingga, Kep. 0 10E 104 30E
69 Lingling 26 13N 111 37E
69 Linglo 24 20N 105 25E
69 Lingshui 18 27N 110 0E
72 Linguéré 15 25N 15 5W
63 Linh Cam 18 31N 105 31E
69 Linhai 28 51N 121 7E
68 Linho 40 50N 107 30E
69 Lini 35 5N 118 20E
69 Linkao 19 56N 109 42E
68 Linkiang 46 2N 133 56E
45 Linköping 58 28N 15 36E
68 Linkow 45 16N 130 18E
14 Linlithgow 55 58N 3 38W
14 Linnhe, L. 56 36N 5 25W
69 Linping 24 25N 114 32E
109 Lins 21 40S 49 44W
68 Linsi 43 30N 118 5E
67 Linsia 35 50N 103 0E
67 Lintan 34 59N 103 49E
98 Linton 39 0N 87 10W
68 Lintsing 36 50N 115 45W
81 Linville 26 50S 152 11E
26 Linz, Austria 48 18N 14 18E
24 Linz, Germany 50 33N 7 18E
39 Lípari, I. 38 40N 15 0E
48 Lipetsk 52 45N 39 35E
69 Liping 26 16N 109 8E
28 Lipno 52 49N 19 15E
24 Lippe, R. 51 39N 6 38E
24 Lippstadt 51 40N 8 19E
27 Liptovsky Svaty Mikuláš 49 6N 19 35E
84 Liptrap, C. 38 50S 145 55E
74 Lira 2 17N 32 57E
32 Liria 39 37N 0 35W
74 Lisala 2 12N 21 38E
31 Lisboa 38 42N 9 10W
31 Lisboa □ 39 0N 9 12W
15 Lisburn 54 30N 6 9W
15 Lisburn □ 54 30N 6 5W
88 Lisburne, C. 68 50N 166 0W
69 Lishui 28 20N 119 48W
18 Lisieux 49 10N 0 12E
20 L'Isle 43 52N 1 49E
20 L'Isle-Jourdain 43 37N 1 5E
19 l'Isle-sur-le-Doubs 47 28N 6 33E
81 Lismore, Australia 28 44S 153 21E
15 Lismore, Eire 52 8N 7 58W
90 Listowel, Canada 44 4N 80 58W
15 Listowel, Eire 52 27N 9 30W
100 Litchfield 39 10N 89 40W
84 Lithgow 33 25S 150 8E
43 Líthinon, Ákra 34 55N 24 44E
48 Lithuanian S.S.R. □ 55 30N 24 0E
37 Litija 46 3N 14 50E
97 Lititz 40 9N 76 18W
42 Litókhoron 40 8N 22 34E
26 Litoměřice 50 33N 14 10E
26 Litschav 48 58N 15 4E
105 Little Abaco I. 26 50N 77 30W
63 Little Andaman, I. 10 40N 92 15E
85 Little Barrier, I. 36 12S 175 8E
90 Little Current 45 55N 82 0W
103 Little Colorado, R. 36 11N 111 48W
100 Little Falls, Minn. 45 58N 94 19W
97 Little Falls, N.Y. 43 3N 74 50W
105 Little Inagua I. 21 40N 73 50W
90 Little Longlac 49 42N 86 58W
13 Little Ouse, R. 52 30N 0 22E
60 Little Rann 23 25N 71 25E
85 Little River 43 45S 172 49E
101 Little Rock 34 41N 92 10W
101 Littlefield 33 57N 102 17W
13 Littlehampton 50 48N 0 32W
69 Liuan 31 45N 116 30E
69 Liucheng 24 39N 109 14E
69 Liuchow 24 10N 109 10E
75 Liuwa Plain 14 20S 22 30E
101 Livermore, Mt. 30 45N 104 8W
84 Liverpool, Australia 33 55S 150 52E
91 Liverpool, Canada 44 5N 64 41W
12 Liverpool, U.K. 53 25N 3 0W
104 Livingston, Guatemala 15 50N 88 50W
102 Livingston, U.S.A. 45 40N 110 40W
74 Livingstonia 10 38S 34 5E
75 Livingstone 17 46S 25 52E
40 Livno 43 50N 17 0E
48 Livny 52 30N 37 30E
36 Livorno 43 32N 10 18E
21 Livron-sur Drôme 44 46N 4 51E
13 Lizard Pt. 49 57N 5 11W
40 Ljig 44 13N 20 18E
37 Ljubljana 46 4N 14 33E
44 Ljungan, R. 62 19N 17 23E
45 Ljungby 56 49N 13 55E
44 Ljusdal 61 46N 16 3E
44 Ljusnan, R. 61 12N 17 8E
37 Ljutomer 46 31N 16 11E
13 Llandeilo 50 54N 4 0W
13 Llandovery 51 59N 3 49W
13 Llandrindod Wells 52 15N 3 23W
12 Llandudno 53 19N 3 51W
13 Llanelli 51 41N 4 11W
30 Llanes 43 25N 4 50W
12 Llangollen 52 58N 3 10W
13 Llanidloes 52 28N 3 31W
86 Llano Estacado, Reg. 34 0N 103 0W
106 Llanos, Reg. 3 25N 71 35W
112 Llanquihue, L. 41 10S 72 50W
31 Llerena 38 17N 6 0W
32 Llobregat, R. 41 17N 2 8E
32 Lloret de Mar 41 41N 2 53E
93 Lloydminster 53 20N 110 0W
33 Lluchmayor 39 29N 2 53E
108 Llullaillaco, Mt. 24 30S 68 30W
36 Loano 44 8N 8 14E
75 Lobatse 25 12S 25 40E
24 Löbau 51 5N 14 42E
108 Lobería 38 10S 58 40W
75 Lobito 12 18S 13 35E
31 Lobón, Canal de 38 50N 6 55W
108 Lobos 35 2S 59 0W
63 Loc Ninh 11 50N 106 34E
25 Locarno 46 10N 8 47E
14 Lochaber, Reg. 56 55N 5 0W
14 Lochalsh, Kyle of 57 17N 5 43W
14 Lochboisdale 57 10N 7 20W
14 Lochgilphead 56 2N 5 37W
14 Lochmaddy 57 36N 7 10W
14 Lochnagar, Mt. 56 57N 3 14W
14 Lochy, L. 56 58N 4 55W
81 Lock 33 34S 135 46E
96 Lock Haven 41 7N 77 31W
91 Lockeport 43 47N 65 4W
14 Lockerbie 55 7N 3 21W
101 Lockhart 29 55N 97 40W
96 Lockport 43 12N 78 42W
39 Locri 38 14N 16 14E
54 Lod 31 57N 34 54E
20 Lodève 43 44N 3 19E
36 Lodi, It. 45 19N 9 30E
102 Lodi, U.S.A. 38 12N 121 16W
74 Lodja 3 30S 23 23E
32 Lodosa 42 25N 2 4W
28 Łódź 51 45N 19 27E
28 Łódź □ 51 45N 19 27E
63 Loei 17 29N 101 35E
26 Lofer 47 35N 12 41E
46 Lofoten, Is. 68 10N 13 0E
98 Logan, Ohio 39 35N 82 22W
102 Logan, Utah 41 45N 111 50W
98 Logan, W. Va. 37 51N 81 59W
88 Logan, Mt. 60 40N 140 0W
98 Logansport 31 58N 93 58W
57 Logar □ 33 50N 69 0E
32 Logrono 42 28N 2 32W
32 Logroño □ 42 28N 2 27W
31 Logrozán 39 20N 5 32W
61 Lohardaga 23 27N 84 45E
55 Loheia 15 45N 42 40E
69 Loho 33 33N 114 5E
25 Lohr 50 0N 9 35E
47 Loimaa 60 50N 23 5E
18 Loir, R. 47 33N 0 32W
18 Loir-et-Cher □ 47 40N 1 20E
21 Loire □ 45 40N 4 5E
18 Loire, R. 47 16N 2 11W
18 Loire-Atlantique □ 47 25N 1 40W
19 Loiret □ 47 58N 2 10E
110 Loja, Ecuador 3 59S 79 16W
31 Loja, Sp. 37 10N 4 10W
16 Lokeren 51 6N 3 59E
74 Lokitaung 4 12N 35 48E
46 Lokka, L. 68 0N 27 50E
45 Løkken 57 22N 9 41E
44 Lokkenverk 63 8N 9 45E
72 Lokoja 7 47N 6 45E
74 Lokolama 2 35S 19 50E
69 Lokwei 19 12N 110 30E
45 Lolland, L. 54 45N 11 30E
24 Lollar 50 39N 8 43E
41 Lom 43 48N 23 20E
74 Lomami, R. 0 46N 24 16E
108 Lomas de Zamora 34 45S 58 25W
36 Lombardia □ 45 35N 9 45E
65 Lomblen, I. 8 30S 116 20E
64 Lombok, I. 8 35S 116 20E
72 Lomé 6 9N 1 20E
74 Lomela 2 5S 23 52E
74 Lomela, R. 0 14S 20 42E
45 Lomma 55 43N 13 6E
92 Lomond 50 24N 112 36W
14 Lomond, L. 56 8N 4 38W
103 Lompoc 34 41N 120 32W
28 Łomza 53 10N 22 2E
28 Łomza □ 53 20N 22 0E
62 Lonavla 18 46N 73 29E
112 Loncoche 39 20S 72 50W
96 London, Canada 43 0N 81 15W
13 London, U.K. 51 30N 0 5W
13 London □ 51 30N 0 5W
15 Londonderry 55 0N 7 20W
15 Londonderry □ 55 0N 7 20W
82 Londonderry, C. 13 45S 126 55E
112 Londonderry, I. 55 0S 71 0W
109 Londrina 23 0S 51 10W
103 Lone Pine 36 35N 118 2W
103 Long Beach, Calif. 33 46N 118 12W
97 Long Beach, N.Y. 40 35N 73 40W
97 Long Branch 40 19N 74 0W
12 Long Eaton 52 54N 1 16W
105 Long I., Bahamas 23 20N 75 10W
90 Long I., Canada 44 23N 66 19W
97 Long I., U.S.A. 40 50N 73 20W
97 Long Island Sd. 41 10N 73 0W
91 Long Range Mts. 48 0N 58 30W
63 Long Xuyen 10 19N 105 28E
43 Longá 36 53N 21 55E
19 Longeau 47 47N 5 20E
15 Longford 53 43N 7 50W
15 Longford □ 53 42N 7 45W
64 Longiram 0 5S 115 45E
100 Longmont 40 10N 105 4W
80 Longreach 23 28S 144 14E
97 Longueuil 45 32N 73 28W
19 Longuyon 49 27N 5 35E
101 Longview, Tex. 32 30N 94 45W
102 Longview, Wash. 46 9N 122 58W
19 Longwy 49 30N 5 45W
37 Lonigo 45 23N 11 22E
24 Löningen 54 43N 7 44E
37 Lonja, R. 45 27N 16 41E
21 Lons-le-Saunier 46 40N 5 31E
46 Lønsdal 66 46N 15 26E
13 Looe 50 21N 4 26W
93 Loomis 49 15N 108 45W
93 Loon Lake 44 50N 77 15W
83 Loongana 30 52S 127 5E
15 Loop Hd. 52 34N 9 55W
67 Lop Nor, L. 40 30N 90 30E
74 Lopez, C. 0 47S 8 40E
31 Lora del Río 37 39N 5 33W
96 Lorain 41 20N 82 5W
33 Lorca 37 41N 1 42W
76 Lord Howe I. 31 33S 159 6E
103 Lordsburg 32 15N 108 45W
56 Lorestan □ 33 0N 48 30E
111 Loreto 7 5S 45 30W
18 Lorient 47 45N 3 23N
14 Lorn, Firth of 56 20N 5 40W
14 Lorne, Reg. 56 26N 5 10W
25 Lòrrach 47 36N 7 38E
19 Lorraine, Reg. 49 0N 6 0E
90 Lorrainville 47 21N 79 23W
103 Los Alamos 35 57N 106 17W
108 Los Andes 32 50S 70 40W
108 Los Angeles, Chile 37 28S 72 23W
103 Los Angeles, U.S.A. 34 0N 118 10W
103 Los Angeles Aqueduct 35 0N 118 20W
103 Los Banos 37 8N 120 56W
31 Los Barrios 36 11N 5 30W
110 Los Hermanos, Is. 11 45N 64 25W
112 Los Lagos 39 51S 72 50W
104 Los Mochis 25 45N 109 5W
32 Los Monegros 41 29N 0 3W
31 Los Palacios Villafranca 37 10N 5 55W
110 Los Roques, Is. 11 50N 66 45W
31 Los Santos de Maimona 38 37N 6 22W
110 Los Testigos, Is. 11 23N 63 6W
51 Loshkalakh 62 45N 147 20E
37 Losinj 44 35N 14 28E
14 Lossiemouth 57 43N 3 17W
20 Lot □ 44 39N 1 40E
20 Lot, R. 44 18N 0 20E
20 Lot-et-Garonne □ 44 22N 0 30E
108 Lota 37 5S 73 10W
14 Lothian □ 55 55N 3 35W
20 Lothiers 46 42N 1 33E
74 Loto 28 50S 22 28E
25 Lotschbergtunnel 46 26N 7 43E
18 Loudéac 48 11N 2 47W
20 Loudun 35 41N 84 22W
12 Loughborough 52 46N 1 11W
15 Loughrea 53 11N 8 33W

75 Louis Trichardt ... 23 0s 25 55 E
91 Louisbourg 45 55N 60 0w
90 Louiseville 46 20N 73 0w
76 Louisiade Arch. ... 11 10s 153 0 E
101 Louisiana □ 30 50N 92 0w
98 Louisville, Ky. 38 15N 85 45w
101 Louisville, Miss. ... 33 7N 89 3w
20 Loulay 46 3N 0 30w
31 Loulé 37 9N 8 0w
26 Louny .... 50 20N 13 48 E
100 Loup City .... 41 19N 98 57 E
20 Lourdes 43 6N 0 3w
75 Lourenço Marques= Maputo .... 25 58s 32 32 E
31 Lourinha 39 14N 9 17w
30 Lousã 40 7N 8 14w
81 Louth, Australia .. 30 30s 145 8 E
15 Louth, Eire 53 47N 6 33w
12 Louth, U.K. 53 23N 0 0
15 Louth □ 53 55N 6 30w
43 Loutra-Aidhipsoú . 38 54N 23 2 E
18 Louviers .... 49 12N 1 10 E
93 Love 53 29N 104 9w
41 Lovech .... 43 8N 24 43 E
100 Loveland 40 27N 105 4w
102 Lovelock 40 17N 118 25w
30 Lovios .... 41 55 E 8 4w
47 Lovisa .... 60 28N 26 12 E
26 Lovosice .... 50 30N 14 2 E
37 Lovran .... 45 18N 14 15 E
40 Lovrin .... 45 58N 20 48 E
97 Lowell 42 38N 71 19w
85 Lower Hutt .... 41 10s 174 55 E
13 Lowestoft .... 52 29N 1 44 E
28 Łowicz .... 52 6N 19 55 E
97 Lowville 43 48N 75 30w
81 Loxton .... 34 28s 140 31 E
76 Loyalty Is .... 21 0s 167 30 E
69 Loyang .... 34 41N 112 28 E
69 Loyung .... 24 25N 109 25 E
20 Lozère □ .... 44 35N 3 30 E
40 Loznica .... 44 32N 19 14 E
68 Lu-ta .... 39 0N 121 31 E
74 Lualaba, R. .... 0 26N 25 20 E
74 Luanda .... 8 58s 13 9 E
63 Luang Prabang .... 19 45N 102 10 E
75 Luangwa, R. ...... 15 40N 30 25 E
75 Luanshya .... 13 3s 28 28 E
30 Luarca 43 32N 6 32w
28 Lubań .... 51 5N 15 15 E
65 Lubang Is. .... 13 50N 120 12 E
28 Lubartów .... 51 28N 22 42 E
54 Lubban .... 32 9N 35 14 E
24 Lübben .... 51 56N 13 54 E
101 Lubbock 33 40N 102 0w
24 Lübeck .... 53 52N 10 41 E
74 Lubefu .... 4 47s 24 27 E
28 Lubin .... 51 24N 16 11 E
28 Lublin .... 51 12N 22 38 E
28 Lublin □ .... 51 5N 22 30 E
27 Lubliniec .... 50 43N 18 45 E
56 Lubnān, Mts. ..... 34 0N 36 0 E
28 Lubon .... 52 21N 16 51 E
28 Lubsko .... 51 45N 14 57 E
64 Lubuklinggau ..... 3 15s 102 55 E
64 Lubuksikaping .... 0 10N 100 15 E
75 Lubumbashi ...... 11 32s 27 28 E
74 Lubutu .... 0 45s 26 30 E
88 Lucania, Mt. 60 48N 141 25w
36 Lucca .... 43 50N 10 30 E
14 Luce B. 54 45N 4 48w
65 Lucena, Philippines 13 56N 121 37 E
31 Lucena, Sp. 37 27N 4 31w
32 Lucena del Cid 40 9N 0 17w
27 Lučenec .... 48 18N 19 42 E
39 Lucera .... 41 30N 15 20 E
33 Luchena, R. 37 44N 1 50w
24 Lüchow .... 52 58N 11 8 E
69 Luchow .... 29 2N 105 10 E
24 Luckenwalde ..... 52 5N 13 11 E
61 Lucknow .... 26 50N 81 0 E
20 Luçon 46 28N 1 10w
37 Ludbreg .... 46 15N 16 38 E
24 Lüdenscheid ...... 51 13N 7 37 E
75 Lüderitz .... 26 41s 15 8 E
60 Ludhiana .... 30 57N 75 56 E
98 Ludington 43 58N 86 27w
13 Ludlow 52 23N 2 42w
41 Ludus .... 46 29N 24 5 E
44 Ludvika .... 60 8N 15 14 E
25 Ludwigsburg ...... 48 53N 9 11 E
25 Ludwigshafen ..... 49 27N 8 27 E
24 Ludwigslust ...... 53 19N 11 28 E
101 Lufkin 31 25N 94 40w
48 Luga .... 58 40N 29 55 E
25 Lugano .... 46 0N 8 57 E
25 Lugano, L. di ..... 46 0N 9 0 E
49 Lugansk= Voroshilovgrad .. 48 35N 39 29 E
55 Lugh Ganana ..... 3 48N 42 40 E
30 Lugo, Sp. 43 2N 7 35w
37 Lugo, It. .... 44 25N 11 53 E
30 Lugo □ 43 0N 7 30w

40 Lugoj .... 45 42N 21 57 E
30 Lugones 43 26N 5 50w
50 Lugovoy .... 43 0N 72 20 E
36 Luino .... 46 0N 8 24 E
111 Luis Correia 3 0s 41 35w
108 Luján 34 45s 59 5w
69 Lukang .... 24 0N 120 19 E
61 Lukhisarai .... 27 11N 86 5 E
41 Lukovit .... 43 13N 24 11 E
28 Łuków .... 51 56N 22 23 E
75 Lukulu .... 14 35s 23 25 E
46 Luleå .... 65 35N 22 10 E
74 Lulonga, R. .... 0 43N 18 23 E
74 Lulua, R. .... 5 2s 21 7 E
74 Luluabourg= Kananga .... 5 55s 22 18 E
99 Lumberton 34 37N 78 59w
85 Lumsden .... 45 44s 168 27 E
68 Lun .... 47 55N 105 1 E
60 Lunavada .... 23 8N 73 37 E
45 Lund .... 55 41N 13 12 E
75 Lundazi .... 12 20s 33 7 E
13 Lundy, I. 51 10N 4 41w
12 Lune, R. 54 2N 2 50w
24 Lüneburg .... 53 15N 10 23 E
24 Lüneburger Heide, Reg. .... 53 0N 10 0 E
21 Lunel .... 43 39N 7 31 E
24 Lunen .... 51 36N 7 31 E
91 Lunenburg 44 22N 64 18w
19 Lunéville .... 48 36N 6 30 E
68 Lunghwa .... 41 15N 117 51 E
68 Lungkiang .... 47 22N 123 4 E
68 Lungkow .... 37 40N 120 25 E
59 Lungleh .... 22 55N 92 45 E
68 Lungsi .... 35 0N 104 35 E
60 Luni, R. .... 24 40N 71 15 E
74 Luofu .... 0 1s 29 15 E
41 Lupeni .... 45 21N 23 13 E
108 Luque 37 35N 4 16w
19 Lure .... 47 40N 6 30 E
15 Lurgan 54 28N 6 20w
75 Lusaka .... 15 28s 28 16 E
42 Lushnja .... 40 55N 19 41 E
74 Lushoto .... 4 47s 38 20 E
68 Lushun .... 38 48N 121 16 E
75 Luso .... 11 47s 19 52 E
20 Lussac-les-Châteaux .... 46 24N 0 43 E
13 Luton 51 53N 0 24w
64 Lutong .... 4 30N 114 0 E
48 Lutsk .... 50 50N 25 15 E
5 Lützow Holnbukta, B. .... 69 0s 38 0 E
16 Luxembourg ...... 49 37N 6 9 E
16 Luxembourg ■ .... 50 0N 6 0 E
16 Luxembourg □ .... 49 58N 5 30 E
19 Luxeuil-les-Bains .. 47 49N 6 24 E
73 Luxor=El Uqsur .. 25 41N 32 38 E
20 Luy, R. 43 39N 1 8w
48 Luza .... 60 39N 47 10 E
25 Luzern .... 47 3N 8 18 E
25 Luzern □ .... 47 2N 7 55 E
111 Luziania 16 20s 48 0w
65 Luzon, I. .... 16 0N 121 0 E
20 Luzy .... 46 47N 3 58 E
49 Lvov .... 49 40N 24 0 E
68 Lwanhsien .... 39 45N 118 45 E
28 Lwówek Śl .... 51 7N 15 38 E
51 Lyakhovskiye Os. . 73 40N 141 0 E
60 Lyallpur .... 31 30N 73 5 E
41 Lyaskovets .... 43 6N 25 44 E
14 Lybster 58 18N 3 16w
45 Lyckeby .... 56 12N 15 37 E
44 Lycksele .... 64 38N 18 40 E
54 Lydda=Lod ...... 31 57N 34 54 E
75 Lydenburg .... 25 10s 30 29 E
85 Lyell .... 41 48s 172 4 E
85 Lyell, Ra. .... 41 38s 172 20 E
13 Lyme Regis 50 44N 2 57w
13 Lymington 50 46N 1 32w
98 Lynchburg 37 23N 79 10w
84 Lyndhurst, N.S.W. . 33 41N 149 2 E
80 Lyndhurst, Queens. 18 56s 144 30 E
97 Lyndonville 44 32N 72 1w
97 Lynn 42 28N 70 57w
93 Lynn Lake 56 51N 101 3w
13 Lynton 51 14N 3 50w
21 Lyon .... 45 46N 4 50 E
21 Lyonnais, Reg. .... 45 45N 4 15 E
83 Lyons, R. 25 2N 115 9w
97 Lyons Falls 43 37N 75 22w
26 Lysá .... 50 11N 14 51 E
45 Lysekil .... 58 17N 11 26 E
48 Lysra .... 57 7N 57 47 E
12 Lytham St. Annes 53 45N 2 58w
85 Lyttelton .... 43 35s 172 44 E
41 Lyubimets .... 41 50N 26 5 E

M

54 Ma'ad .... 32 37N 35 36 E
69 Maanshan .... 31 40N 118 30 E
16 Maas, R. .... 51 49N 5 1 E
16 Maastricht .... 50 50N 5 40 E
12 Mablethorpe ...... 53 21N 0 14 E
109 Macaé 20 20s 41 55w
101 McAllen 26 12N 98 15w
101 McAlester 34 57N 95 40w
111 Macapá 0 5N 51 10w
80 McArthur, R. ...... 15 54s 136 40 E
111 Macau 5 0s 36 40w
69 Macau ■ .... 22 16N 113 35 E
92 McBride 53 20N 120 10w
102 McCammon 42 41N 112 11w
12 Macclesfield 53 16N 2 9w
93 McClintock 57 45N 94 15w
88 M'Clintock Chan. . 71 0N 103 0w
101 McComb 31 20N 90 30w
100 McCook 40 15N 100 35w
3 McDonald I. .... 54 0s 73 0 E
82 Macdonnell, Ras. .. 23 40s 133 0 E
81 McDouall Peak ... 29 51s 134 55 E
88 Macdougall, L. 66 20N 98 30w
14 Macduff 57 40N 2 30w
90 Mace 48 55N 80 0w
30 Maceda 42 16N 7 39w
30 Macedo de Cavaleiros 41 31N 6 57w
111 Maceió 9 40s 35 41w
72 Macenta 8 35N 9 20w
37 Macerata .... 43 19N 13 28 E
102 McGill 35 27N 114 50w
15 Macgillycuddy's Reeks, Mts. 52 2N 9 45w
108 Machagai 26 56s 60 2w
74 Machakos .... 1 30s 37 15 E
110 Machala 3 10s 79 50w
51 Machen̆a .... 61 20N 172 20 E
30 Machichaco, C. ... 43 28N 2 47w
110 Machiques 10 4N 72 34w
13 Machynlleth 52 36N 3 51w
72 Macias Nguema Biyoga, I. ...... 3 30N 8 40 E
81 Macintyre, R. ...... 28 38s 150 47 E
30 Macizo Galaico ... 42 30N 7 30w
80 Mackay, Australia . 21 36s 148 39 E
102 Mackay, U.S.A. ... 43 58N 113 37w
82 Mackay, L. .... 22 40s 128 35 E
96 McKees Rocks 40 27N 80 3w
96 McKeesport 40 21N 79 50w
92 Mackenzie 55 20N 123 5w
88 Mackenzie, Reg. .. 61 30N 144 30w
88 Mackenzie, R. 69 15N 134 8w
110 Mackenzie City ... 6 0N 58 10w
88 Mackenzie Mts. ... 64 0N 130 0w
80 McKinlay .... 21 16s 141 17 E
88 McKinley, Mt. 63 10N 151 0w
4 McKinley Sea 84 0N 10 0w
101 McKinney 33 10N 96 40w
93 Macklin 52 20N 109 56w
81 Macksville .... 30 40s 152 56 E
81 Maclean .... 29 26s 153 16 E
75 Maclear .... 31 2s 28 23 E
81 Macleay, R. ...... 30 52s 153 1 E
92 McLennan 55 42N 116 50w
83 McLeod, L. .... 24 9s 113 47 E
92 McLure 50 55N 120 20w
86 M'Clure Str. 74 40N 117 30w
102 McMinnville, Oreg. 45 16N 123 11w
99 McMinnville, Tenn. 35 43N 85 45w
93 McMurray 56 45N 111 27w
103 McNary 34 4N 109 53w
100 Macomb 40 25N 90 40w
38 Macomer .... 40 16N 8 48 E
21 Mâcon .... 46 19N 4 50 E
99 Macon 32 50N 83 37w
100 McPherson 38 25N 97 40w
76 Macquarie Is. 54 36s 158 55s
84 Macquarie, R. .... 30 7s 147 24 E
5 Mac Robertson Coast .... 68 30s 63 0 E
15 Macroom 51 54N 8 57w
56 Madā'in Sālih ..... 26 51N 37 58 E
75 Madagascar ■ .... 20 0s 47 0 E
73 Madama .... 22 0N 14 0 E
62 Madanapalle ..... 13 33N 78 34 E
76 Madane .... 5 0s 145 46 E
61 Madaripur .... 23 2N 90 15 E
59 Madauk .... 17 56N 96 52 E
96 Madawaska 45 30N 77 55w
59 Madaya .... 22 20N 96 10 E
38 Maddalena, I. ..... 41 15N 9 23 E
39 Maddaloni .... 41 4N 14 23 E
104 Madden L. 9 20N 79 37w
72 Madeira, I. 32 50N 17 0w
110 Madeira, R. 3 22s 58 45w
103 Madera 37 0N 120 1w

61 Madhupur .... 24 18N 86 37 E
60 Madhya Pradesh □ 21 50N 81 0 E
55 Madinat al Shaab .... 12 50N 45 0 E
74 Madingou .... 4 10s 13 33 E
98 Madison, Ind. 38 42N 85 20w
100 Madison, S.D. 44 0N 97 8w
100 Madison, Wis. 43 5N 89 25w
98 Madisonville 37 42N 86 30w
65 Madiun .... 7 38s 111 32 E
62 Madras, India ..... 13 8N 80 19 E
102 Madras, U.S.A. ... 44 40N 121 10w
104 Madre, Laguna 25 0N 97 30w
110 Madre de Dios, R. 10 59s 66 8w
112 Madre de Dios, I. 50 20s 75 10w
104 Madre del Sur, Sa. 17 30N 100 0w
104 Madre Occidental, Sa. 27 0N 107 0w
104 Madre Oriental, Sa. 25 0N 100 0w
30 Madrid 40 25N 3 45w
30 Madrid □ 40 30N 3 45w
31 Madridejos 39 28N 3 33w
31 Madrona, Sa. 38 27N 4 16w
31 Madroñera 39 26N 5 42w
65 Madura, I. .... 7 0N 113 20 E
65 Madura, Selat ..... 7 30s 113 20 E
83 Madura Motel .... 31 55s 127 0 E
62 Madurai .... 9 55N 78 10 E
62 Madurantakam .... 12 30N 79 50 E
66 Maebashi .... 36 23N 139 4 E
41 Măeruş .... 45 53N 25 31 E
13 Maesteg 51 36N 3 40w
105 Maestra, Sa. 20 15N 77 0w
32 Maestrazgo, Mts. de 40 30N 0 25w
75 Maevatanana ..... 16 56s 46 49 E
93 Mafeking, Canada . 52 40N 101 10w
75 Mafeking, S.Africa 25 50s 25 38 E
74 Mafia I. .... 7 45s 39 50 E
109 Mafra 36 10N 50 0w
51 Magadan .... 59 30N 151 0 E
74 Magadi .... 1 54s 36 19 E
112 Magallanes, Estrecho de, Str. 52 30s 75 0w
110 Magangue 9 14N 74 45w
91 Magdalen Is. 47 30N 61 40w
104 Magdalena, Mexico 30 50N 112 0w
103 Magdalena, U.S.A. 34 10N 107 20w
112 Magdalena, I., Chile 44 42s 73 10w
104 Magdalena, I., Mexico 24 40N 112 15w
24 Magdeburg .... 52 8N 11 36 E
24 Magdeburg □ ..... 52 20N 11 40 E
54 Magdi'el .... 32 10N 34 54 E
15 Magee, I. 54 48N 5 44w
65 Magelang .... 7 29s 110 13 E
36 Maggiorasca, Mt. .. 44 33N 9 29 E
36 Maggiore, L. ...... 46 0N 8 35 E
54 Maghar .... 32 54N 35 24 E
15 Magherafelt 54 45N 6 36w
15 Magherafelt □ 54 45N 6 36w
37 Magione .... 43 10N 12 12 E
39 Máglie .... 40 8N 18 17 E
43 Magnisía □ ...... 39 24N 22 46 E
50 Magnitogorsk .... 53 20N 59 0 E
101 Magnolia 33 18N 93 12w
91 Magog 45 18N 72 9w
92 Magrath 49 25N 112 50w
33 Magro, R. 39 11N 0 25w
111 Maguarinho, C. ... 0 15s 48 30w
59 Magwe .... 20 10N 95 0 E
56 Mahābād .... 36 50N 45 45 E
61 Mahabharat Lekh, Mts. .... 28 30N 82 0 E
62 Mahad .... 18 6N 73 29 E
55 Mahaddei Uen .... 3 0N 45 32 E
60 Mahadeo Hills .... 22 20N 78 30 E
75 Mahalapye .... 23 1s 26 51 E
57 Mahallāt .... 33 55N 50 30 E
61 Mahanadi, R. ..... 20 0N 86 25 E
61 Mahananda, R. ... 24 29N 88 18 E
97 Mahanoy City 40 48N 76 10w
60 Maharashtra □ .... 19 30N 75 30 E
62 Mahboobabad .... 17 42N 80 2 E
62 Mahbubnagar ..... 16 45N 77 59 E
73 Mahdia .... 35 28N 11 0 E
62 Mahé .... 11 42N 75 34 E
85 Maheno .... 45 10s 170 50 E
85 Mahia Pen. .... 39 9s 177 55 E
61 Mahoba .... 25 15N 79 55 E
32 Mahón .... 39 50N 4 18 E
91 Mahone Bay 44 27N 64 23w
60 Mahuva .... 25 7N 71 46 E
74 Mai-Ndombe, L. ... 2 0s 18 0 E
13 Maidenhead 51 31N 0 42w
93 Maidstone, Canada 53 5N 109 20w
13 Maidstone, U.K. .. 51 16N 0 31 E
73 Maiduguri .... 12 0N 13 20 E

61 Maijdi 22 48N 91 10E
61 Maikala Ra. 22 0N 81 0E
19 Mailly-le-Camp 48 41N 4 12E
15 Main, R. 54 43N 6 18W
25 Main, R. 50 0N 8 18E
99 Maine □ 45 20N 69 0W
18 Maine, Reg. 48 0N 0 0E
18 Maine-et-Loire □ 47 31N 0 30W
59 Maingkwan 26 15N 96 45E
14 Mainland, I., Orkney 59 0N 3 10W
14 Mainland, I., Shetland 60 15N 1 22W
60 Mainpuri 27 18N 79 4E
25 Mainz 50 0N 8 17E
108 Maipú 37 0S 58 0W
110 Maiquetía 10 36N 66 57W
59 Mairabari 26 30N 92 30E
105 Maisí, C. 20 10N 74 10W
19 Maisse 48 24N 2 21E
84 Maitland 32 44S 151 36E
66 Maizuru 35 25N 135 22E
65 Majalengka 6 55S 108 14E
54 Majd el Kurum 32 56N 35 15E
65 Majene 3 27S 118 57E
40 Majevica, Mts. 44 45N 18 50E
75 Majunga 17 0S 47 0E
61 Makalu, Mt. 27 54N 87 6E
51 Makarovo 57 40N 107 45E
40 Makarska 43 18N 17 2E
65 Makasar, Selat, Str. 1 0S 118 20E
50 Makat 47 39N 53 19E
42 Makedhonia □ 40 39N 53 19E
72 Makeni 8 55N 12 5W
49 Makeyevka 48 0N 38 0E
75 Makgadikgadi Salt Pans 20 40S 25 45E
49 Makhachkala 43 0N 47 15E
74 Makindu 2 17S 37 49E
50 Makinsk 52 37N 70 26E
56 Makkah 21 30N 39 54E
91 Makkovik 55 0N 59 10W
51 Maklakovo 58 16N 92 29E
27 Makó 46 14N 20 33E
74 Makokou 0 40N 12 50E
58 Makran Coast Ra. 25 40N 4 0E
56 Māku 39 15N 44 31E
66 Makurazaki 31 15N 130 20E
72 Makurdi 7 45N 8 32E
49 Mal Usen, R. 48 50N 49 39E
37 Mala Kapela, Mts. 44 45N 15 30E
62 Malabar Coast, Reg. 11 0N 75 0E
63 Malacca, Str. of 3 0N 101 0E
27 Malacky 48 27N 17 0E
102 Malad City 41 10N 112 20W
31 Málaga 36 43N 4 23W
31 Málaga □ 36 38N 4 58W
75 Malagasy Rep.= Madagascar ■ 19 0S 46 0E
31 Malagón 39 11N 3 52W
31 Malagón, R. 37 35N 7 29W
73 Malakâl 9 33N 31 50E
58 Malakand 34 40N 71 55E
51 Malamyzh 50 0N 136 50E
65 Malang 7 59S 112 35E
74 Malanje 9 30S 16 17E
44 Mälaren, L. 59 30N 17 10E
90 Malartic 48 9N 78 9W
56 Malatya 38 25N 38 20E
75 Malawi ■ 13 0S 34 0E
75 Malawi, L. 12 30S 34 30E
63 Malay Pen. 5 0N 102 0E
63 Malaya □ 4 0N 102 0E
56 Malayer 28 22N 56 38E
64 Malaysia ■ 5 0N 110 0E
80 Malbon 21 5S 140 17E
31 Malbooma 30 41S 134 11E
28 Malbork 54 3N 19 10E
24 Malchow 53 29N 12 25E
83 Malcolm 28 51S 121 25E
97 Malden 42 26N 71 5W
77 Malden I. 4 3S 154 59W
53 Maldive Is. 2 0N 73 0W
109 Maldonado 35 0S 55 0W
27 Malé Karpaty, Mts. 48 30N 17 20E
60 Malegaon 20 30N 74 30E
60 Malerkotla 30 32N 75 58E
19 Malesherbes 48 15N 2 24E
32 Malgrat 41 39N 2 46E
73 Malha 15 8N 26 12E
72 Mali ■ 15 0N 10 0W
40 Mali, Kanal 45 36N 19 24E
15 Malin Hd. 55 18N 7 16W
74 Malindi 3 12S 40 5E
65 Malingping 6 45S 106 2E
84 Mallacoota, Inlet 34 40S 149 40E
14 Mallaig 57 0N 5 50W
61 Mallawan 27 4N 80 12E
73 Mallawi 27 44N 30 44E
43 Mállia 35 17N 25 27E
32 Mallorca, I. 39 30N 3 0E
15 Mallow 52 8N 8 39W
46 Malmberget 67 11N 20 40E
45 Malmö 55 36N 12 59E
45 Malmöhus □ 55 45N 13 30E
41 Malnaş 46 2N 25 49E
65 Malolos 14 50N 21 2E
97 Malone 44 50N 74 19W
31 Malpartida 39 26N 6 30W
30 Malpica 43 19N 8 50W
102 Malta 48 20N 107 55W
73 Malta ■ 35 50N 14 30E
12 Malton 54 9N 0 48W
65 Maluku, Is. 3 0S 128 0E
44 Malung 60 42N 13 44E
62 Malvalli 12 28N 77 8E
62 Malvan 16 2N 73 30E
13 Malvern, U.K. 52 7N 2 19W
101 Malvern, U.S.A. 34 22N 92 50W
13 Malvern Hills 52 0N 2 19W
111 Mamanguape 6 50S 35 4W
65 Mamasa 2 55S 119 20E
18 Mamers 48 21N 0 22E
39 Mámmola 38 23N 16 13E
103 Mammoth 32 46N 110 43W
69 Mamoi 26 0N 119 25E
110 Mamoré, R. 10 23S 65 53W
72 Mamou 10 15N 12 0W
64 Mampawah 0 30N 109 5E
28 Mamry, L. 54 8N 21 42E
72 Man 7 30N 7 40W
12 Man, I. of 54 15N 4 30W
59 Man Na 23 27N 97 19E
111 Mana 5 45N 53 55W
62 Manaar, G. of 8 30N 79 0E
110 Manacapuru 3 10S 60 50W
32 Manacor 39 32N 3 12E
65 Manado 1 40N 124 45E
105 Managua 12 0N 86 20W
105 Managua, L. de 12 20N 86 30W
75 Mananjary 21 13S 48 20E
85 Manapouri, L. 45 32S 167 32E
61 Manaslu, Mt. 28 33N 84 33E
67 Manass 44 20N 86 21E
59 Manaung Kyun, I. 18 45N 93 40E
110 Manaus 3 0S 60 0W
31 Mancha Real 37 48N 3 39W
18 Manche □ 49 10N 1 20W
12 Manchester, U.K. 53 30N 2 15W
97 Manchester, Conn. 41 47N 72 30W
97 Manchester, N.H. 42 58N 71 29W
68 Manchouli 49 46N 117 24E
109 Mandaguari 23 32S 51 42W
47 Mandal 58 2N 7 25E
65 Mandala, Puncak, Mt. 4 30S 141 0E
59 Mandalay 22 0N 96 10E
68 Mandalgovi 45 40N 106 22E
56 Mandali 33 52N 45 28E
100 Mandan 46 50N 101 0W
65 Mandar, Teluk, G. 3 35S 119 4E
75 Mandimba 14 22S 35 33E
61 Mandla 22 39N 80 30E
45 Mandø, I. 55 18N 8 33E
75 Mandritsara 15 50S 48 49E
60 Mandsaur 24 3N 75 8E
83 Mandurah 32 32S 115 43E
39 Mandúria 40 25N 17 38E
60 Mandvi 22 51N 69 22E
62 Mandya 12 30N 77 0E
73 Manfalût 27 20N 30 52E
39 Manfredónia 41 40N 15 55E
39 Manfredónia, G. di 41 30N 16 10E
62 Mangalagiri 16 26N 80 36E
41 Mangalia 43 50N 28 35E
62 Mangalore 12 55N 74 47E
30 Manganeses 41 45N 5 43W
85 Mangaweka 39 48S 175 47E
64 Manggar 2 50S 108 10E
58 Mangla Dam 33 32N 73 50E
65 Mangole, I. 1 50S 125 55E
85 Mangonui 35 1S 173 32E
30 Mangualde 40 38N 7 48W
109 Mangueira, L. 33 0S 52 50W
67 Mangyai 38 6N 91 37E
50 Mangyshlak Pol. 43 40N 52 30E
100 Manhattan 39 10N 96 40W
111 Manhuaçu 20 15S 42 2W
37 Maniago 46 11N 12 40E
110 Manicoré 6 0S 61 10W
91 Manicouagan, L. 51 25N 68 15W
77 Manihiki, I. 11 0S 161 0W
65 Manila 14 40N 121 3E
65 Manila B. 14 0N 120 0E
84 Manildra 33 11S 148 41E
81 Manilla 30 45S 150 43E
59 Manipur □ 24 30N 94 0E
56 Manisa 38 38N 27 30E
98 Manistee 44 15N 86 20W
98 Manistique 45 59N 86 18W
93 Manitoba □ 55 30N 97 0W
93 Manitoba, L. 50 40N 98 30W
100 Manitou Springs 38 52N 104 55W
90 Manitoulin I. 45 40N 82 30W
98 Manitowoc 44 8N 87 40W
110 Manizales 5 5N 75 32W
62 Manjeri 11 7N 76 11E
56 Manjil 36 46N 49 30E
83 Manjimup 34 15S 116 6E
62 Manjra, R. 18 49N 77 52E
100 Mankato, Kans. 39 49N 98 11W
100 Mankato, Minn. 44 8N 93 59W
72 Mankono 8 10N 6 10W
32 Manlleu 42 2N 2 17E
84 Manly 33 48S 151 14E
81 Mannahill 32 26S 139 59E
62 Mannargudi 10 45N 79 32E
25 Mannheim 49 28N 8 29E
92 Manning 56 53N 117 39W
38 Mannu, C. 40 2N 8 24E
38 Mannu, R. 40 50N 8 23E
81 Mannum 34 57S 139 12E
65 Manokwari 0 54N 134 0E
74 Manono 7 18S 27 25E
21 Manosque 43 49N 5 47E
32 Manresa 41 48N 1 50E
60 Mansa, India 30 0N 75 27E
74 Mansa, Zambia 11 13S 28 55E
89 Mansel I. 62 0N 80 0W
84 Mansfield, Australia 37 0S 146 0E
12 Mansfield, U.K. 53 8N 1 12W
96 Mansfield, U.S.A. 40 45N 82 30W
97 Mansfield, Mt. 44 33N 72 49W
30 Mansilla de las Mules 42 30N 5 25W
20 Mansle 45 52N 0 9E
110 Manta 1 0S 80 40W
103 Manteca 37 50N 121 12W
19 Mantes-la-Jolie 49 0N 1 41E
102 Manti 39 23N 111 32W
109 Mantiqueira, Sa. da 22 0S 44 0W
36 Mántova 45 10N 10 47E
65 Manukan 8 14N 123 3E
85 Manukau 37 2S 174 54E
62 Manwath 19 19N 76 32E
49 Manych-Gudilo, Oz. 46 24N 42 38E
74 Manyoni 5 45S 34 55E
60 Manzai 32 20N 70 15E
30 Manzaneda, Cabeza de 42 12N 7 15W
105 Manzanillo, Cuba 20 20N 77 10W
104 Manzanillo, Mexico 19 0N 104 20W
105 Manzanillo, Pta. 9 30N 79 40W
73 Mao 14 4N 15 19E
93 Maple Creek 49 55N 109 27W
100 Maplewood 38 33N 90 18W
62 Mapuca 15 36N 73 46E
57 Maputo 25 58S 32 32E
56 Maqnā 28 25N 34 50E
112 Maquinchao 41 15S 68 50W
109 Mar Sa. do 25 30S 49 0W
108 Mar Chiquita, L. 30 40S 62 50W
108 Mar del Plata 38 0S 57 30W
111 Marabá 5 20S 49 5W
110 Maracaibo 10 40N 71 37W
110 Maracaibo, L. de 9 40N 71 30W
109 Maracaju 21 38S 55 9W
110 Maracay 10 15N 67 36W
73 Maradah 29 4N 19 4E
72 Maradi 13 35N 8 10E
56 Maragheh 37 30N 46 12E
111 Marajó, I. de 1 0S 49 30W
56 Marand 38 30N 45 45E
75 Marandellas 18 5S 31 42E
111 Maranguape 3 55S 38 50W
111 Maranhão=São Luís 2 39S 44 15W
111 Maranhão □ 5 0S 46 0W
37 Marano, L. di 45 42N 13 13E
110 Marañón, R. 4 50S 75 35W
56 Maraş 37 37N 36 53E
41 Mărăşeşti 45 52N 27 5E
31 Marateca 38 34N 8 40W
43 Marathókambos 37 43N 26 42E
80 Marathon 20 51S 143 32E
55 Marbat 17 0N 54 45E
31 Marbella 36 30N 4 57W
82 Marble Bar 21 9S 119 44E
97 Marblehead 42 29N 70 51W
24 Marburg 50 49N 8 44E
27 Marcal, R. 47 41N 17 32E
36 Marcaria 45 7N 10 34E
13 March 57 33N 0 5E
37 Marche □ 43 22N 13 10E
20 Marche, Reg. 46 5N 2 10E
16 Marche-en-Famenne 50 14N 5 19E
31 Marchena 37 18N 5 23W
39 Marcianise 41 3N 14 16E
19 Marck 50 57N 1 57E
108 Marcos Juárez 32 42S 62 5W
76 Marcus I. 24 0N 153 45E
97 Marcy, Mt. 44 7N 73 55W
58 Mardan 34 12N 72 2E
56 Mardin 37 20N 40 36E
14 Maree, L. 57 40N 5 30W
80 Mareeba 16 59S 145 28E
37 Maremma, Reg. 42 45N 11 15E
62 Margao 14 12N 73 58E
92 Margaret Bay 51 20N 127 20W
82 Margaret River 18 0S 126 30E
20 Margaride, Mts. de la 44 43N 3 38E
110 Margarita, Is. de 11 0N 64 0W
13 Margate 51 23N 1 24E
39 Margharita d'Savoia 41 25N 16 5E
48 Mari A.S.S.R. □ 56 30N 48 0E
85 Maria van Diemen, C. 34 29S 172 40E
45 Mariager, Fd. 56 42N 10 19E
76 Mariana Is. 17 0N 145 0E
105 Marianao 23 8N 82 24W
99 Marianna 30 45N 85 15W
75 Mariano Machado 13 2S 14 40E
26 Mariánské Lázně 49 57N 12 41E
26 Mariazell 47 47N 15 19E
55 Marib 15 25N 45 20E
45 Maribo 54 48N 11 30E
37 Maribor 46 36N 15 40E
89 Maricourt 61 36N 71 57W
105 Marie-Galante, I. 15 56N 61 16W
47 Mariehamn 60 5N 19 57E
75 Mariental 24 36S 18 0E
96 Marienville 41 27N 79 8W
45 Mariestad 58 43N 13 50E
99 Marietta, Ga. 34 0N 84 30W
98 Marietta, Ohio 39 27N 81 27W
105 Marigot 15 32N 61 18W
50 Marniisk 56 10N 87 20E
109 Marília 22 0S 50 0W
65 Marinduque, I. 13 25N 122 0E
98 Marinette 45 4N 87 40W
109 Maringá 23 35S 51 50W
101 Marion, Ill. 37 45N 88 55W
98 Marion, Ind. 40 35N 85 40W
100 Marion, Iowa 42 2N 91 36W
98 Marion, Ohio 40 38N 83 8W
99 Marion, S.C. 34 11N 79 22W
99 Marion, Va. 36 51N 81 29W
21 Maritimes, Alpes, Mts. 44 10N 7 10E
41 Maritsa 42 1N 25 50E
57 Marjan 32 5N 68 20E
62 Markapur 15 44N 79 19E
45 Markaryd 56 28N 13 35E
12 Market Drayton 52 55N 2 30W
13 Market Harborough 52 29N 0 55W
12 Market Rasen 53 24N 0 20W
5 Markham, Mt. 83 0S 164 0E
28 Marki 52 20N 21 2E
43 Markoupoulon 37 53N 23 57E
40 Markovac 44 14N 21 7E
48 Marks 51 45N 46 50E
25 Marktredwitz 50 1N 12 2E
97 Marlboro 42 19N 71 33W
80 Marlborough 22 46S 149 52E
85 Marlborough □ 41 45S 173 33E
13 Marlborough Downs 51 25N 1 55W
19 Marle 49 43N 3 47E
101 Marlin 31 25N 96 50W
62 Marmagao 15 25N 73 56E
20 Marmande 44 30N 0 10E
56 Marmara Denizi, Sea 40 45N 28 15E
37 Marmolada, Mt. 46 25N 11 55E
90 Marmora 44 28N 77 41W
19 Marne □ 49 0N 4 10E
19 Marne, R. 48 49N 2 24E
75 Maroantsetra 15 26S 49 44E
81 Maroochydore 26 35S 153 10W
27 Maros, R. 46 15N 20 13E
75 Marovoay 16 6S 46 39E
77 Marquesas Is. 9 0S 139 30W
98 Marquette 46 30N 87 21W
73 Marra, J. 7 20N 27 35E
72 Marrakech 31 40N 8 0W
80 Marrawah 40 56S 144 41E
81 Marree 29 39S 138 1E
31 Marroqui, Pta. 36 0N 5 37W
73 Marsa Brega 30 30N 19 20E
73 Marsa Susa 32 52N 21 59E
74 Marsabit 2 18N 38 0E
38 Marsala 37 48N 12 25E
37 Marsciano 42 54N 12 20E
84 Marsden 33 47N 147 32E
21 Marseille 43 18N 5 23E
100 Marshall, Minn. 44 25N 95 45W
100 Marshall, Mo. 39 8N 93 15W
101 Marshall, Tex. 32 29N 94 20W
76 Marshall Is. 9 0N 171 0E
100 Marshalltown 42 0N 93 0W
100 Marshfield 44 42N 90 10W
44 Märsta 59 37N 17 52E
59 Martaban 16 30N 97 35E
59 Martaban, G. of 15 40N 96 30E
64 Martapura, Kalimantan 3 22S 114 56E

64 Martapura, Sumatera 4 19s 104 22 E
73 Marte 12 23N 13 46 E
33 Martes, Sa. 39 20N 1 0W
81 Marthaguy Creek 30 16s 147 35 E
97 Marha's Vineyard 41 25N 70 35W
25 Martigny 46 6N 7 3 E
21 Martigues 43 24N 5 4 E
27 Martin 49 6N 18 48 E
32 Martín, R. 41 18N 0 19W
7 Martin Vaz, I. 20 30s 28 15W
39 Martina Franca 40 42N 17 20 E
105 Martinique, I. 14 40N 61 0W
105 Martinique Pass. 15 15N 61 0W
109 Martinópolis 22 11s 51 12W
96 Martins Ferry 40 5N 80 46W
26 Martinsberg 48 22N 15 9 E
98 Martinsburg 39 30N 77 57W
98 Martinsville, Ind. 39 29N 86 23W
99 Martinsville, Va. 36 41N 79 52W
85 Marton 40 4s 175 23 E
31 Martos 37 44N 3 58W
66 Marugame 34 15N 133 55 E
84 Marulan 34 43s 150 3 E
20 Marvejols 44 33N 3 19 E
60 Marwar 25 43N 73 45 E
50 Mary 37 40N 61 50 E
80 Mary Kathleen 20 35s 139 48 E
89 Mary River 70 30N 78 0W
81 Maryborough, Queens. 25 31s 152 37 E
84 Maryborough, Vic. 37 0s 143 44 E
98 Maryland □ 39 10N 76 40W
12 Maryport 54 43N 3 30W
91 Marystown 47 10N 55 10W
103 Marysvale 38 25N 112 17W
102 Marysville 39 14N 121 40W
99 Maryville 35 50N 84 0W
73 Marzūq 25 53N 14 10 E
72 Mascara 35 26N 0 6 E
57 Mashhad 36 20N 59 35 E
32 Masnou 41 28N 2 20 E
92 Masset 54 0N 132 0W
57 Masqat 23 37N 58 36 E
56 Mastura 23 7N 38 52 E
62 Masulipatnam 16 12N 81 12 E
74 Masaka 0 21s 31 45 E
65 Masamba 2 30s 120 15 E
68 Masan 35 11N 128 32 E
33 Masanasa 39 25N 0 25W
57 Masandam, Ras. 26 30N 56 30 E
74 Masasi 10 45s 38 52 E
105 Masaya 12 0N 86 7W
65 Masbate 12 20N 123 30 E
65 Masbate, I. 12 20N 123 30 E
75 Maseru 29 18s 27 30 E
90 Mashkode 47 2N 84 7W
74 Masindi 1 40N 41 43 E
56 Masjed Soleyman 31 55N 49 25 E
15 Mask, L. 53 36N 9 24W
100 Mason City 48 0N 119 0W
36 Massa 44 2N 10 7 E
36 Massa Maríttima 43 3N 10 52 E
97 Massachusetts □ 42 25N 72 0W
97 Massachusetts B. 42 30N 70 0W
39 Massafra 40 35N 17 8 E
36 Massarossa 43 53N 10 17 E
73 Massawa=Mitsiwa 15 35N 39 25 E
97 Massena 44 52N 74 55W
20 Massiac 45 15N 3 11 E
20 Massif Central Reg. 45 30N 2 21 E
96 Massillon 40 47N 81 30W
85 Masterton 40 56s 175 39 E
43 Mástikho, Ákra 38 10N 26 2 E
66 Masuda 34 40N 131 51 E
65 Mataboor 1 41s 138 3 E
31 Matachel, R. 38 50N 6 17W
90 Matachewan 47 50N 80 55W
68 Matad 47 12N 115 29 E
74 Matadi 5 52s 13 31 E
105 Matagalpa 13 10N 85 40W
90 Matagami 49 45N 77 34W
62 Matale 7 30N 80 44 E
104 Matamoros 18 2N 98 17W
91 Matane 48 50N 67 33W
88 Matanuska 61 38N 149 0W
105 Matanzas 23 0N 81 40W
62 Matara 5 58N 80 30 E
64 Mataram 8 41s 116 10 E
82 Mataranka 14 55s 133 4 E
32 Mataró 41 32N 2 29 E
32 Matarraña, R. 41 14N 0 22 E
85 Mataura 46 11s 168 51 E
104 Matehuala 23 40N 100 50W
37 Matélica 43 15N 13 0 E
39 Matera 40 40N 16 37 E
27 Mátészalka 47 58N 22 20 E
60 Mathura 27 30N 77 48 E
28 Matkinia Grn 52 42N 22 2 E
12 Matlock 53 8N 1 32W
72 Matmata 33 30N 9 59 E
111 Mato Grosso □ 14 0s 54 0W
70 Matopo 20 36s 28 20 E
30 Matosinhos 41 11N 8 42W
57 Matrah 23 37N 58 30 E
73 Matrûh 31 19N 27 9 E
69 Matsu, I. 26 9N 119 56 E
66 Matsue 35 25N 133 10 E
66 Matsumoto 36 15N 138 0 E
66 Matsusaka 34 34N 136 32 E
66 Matsuyama 33 45N 132 45 E
62 Mattancheri 9 50N 76 15 E
90 Mattawa 46 20N 78 45W
25 Matterhorn, Mt. 45 58N 7 39 E
105 Matthew Town 20 57N 73 40W
100 Mattoon 39 30N 88 20W
64 Matua 2 58s 110 52 E
110 Maturín 9 45N 63 11W
60 Mau Ranipur 25 16N 79 8 E
19 Maubeuge 50 17N 3 57 E
20 Maubourguet 43 29N 0 1 E
110 Maués 3 20s 57 45W
94 Maui, I. 20 45N 156 20 E
59 Maulamyaing 16 30N 97 40 E
108 Maule □ 36 5s 72 30W
65 Maumere 8 38s 122 13 E
75 Maun 20 0s 23 26 E
94 Mauna Loa, Mt. 19 50N 155 28 E
61 Maunath Bhanjan 25 56N 83 33 E
59 Maungmagan Is. 41 0s 97 48 E
21 Maures, Mts. 43 15N 6 15 E
21 Maurienne 45 15N 6 20 E
72 Mauritania ■ 20 50N 10 0W
71 Mauritius 20 0s 57 0 E
21 Maurienne, Reg. 45 15N 6 20 E
20 Maurs 44 43N 2 12 E
26 Mauterndorf 47 9N 13 40 E
62 Mavelikara 9 14N 76 32 E
54 Mavqi'im 31 38N 34 32 E
59 Mawkmai 20 14N 97 50 E
59 Mawlaik 23 40N 94 26 E
80 Maxwelton 39 51s 174 49 E
105 May Pen 17 58N 77 15W
32 Maya 43 12N 1 29W
104 Maya Mts. 16 30N 89 0W
105 Mayaguana I. 21 30N 72 44W
105 Mayagüez 18 12N 67 9W
83 Mayanup 33 58s 116 25 E
80 Maydena 42 45s 146 39 E
25 Mayen 50 18N 7 10 E
18 Mayenne 48 20N 0 38W
18 Mayenne □ 48 10N 0 40W
18 Mayenne, R. 47 30N 0 33W
92 Mayerthorpe 53 57N 115 15W
99 Mayfield 36 45N 88 40W
49 Maykop 44 35N 40 25 E
97 Maynard 42 30N 71 33W
90 Maynooth, Canada 45 14N 77 56W
15 Maynooth, Eire 53 22N 6 38W
88 Mayo 63 38N 135 57W
15 Mayo □ 43 47N 9 7W
30 Mayorga 42 10N 5 16W
98 Maysville 38 43N 84 16W
74 Mayumba 3 25s 10 39 E
62 Mayuram 11 3N 79 42 E
51 Mayya 61 44N 130 18 E
75 Mazabuka 15 52s 27 44 E
111 Mazagão 0 20s 51 50W
92 Mazama 49 43N 120 8W
20 Mazamet 43 30N 2 20 E
57 Mazan Deran □ 36 30N 53 30 E
38 Mazara del Vallo 37 40N 12 34 E
57 Mazar-i-Sharif 36 41N 67 0 E
112 Mazarredo 47 10s 66 50W
33 Mazarrón 37 38N 1 19W
33 Mazarrón, G. de 37 27N 1 19W
104 Mazatenango 14 35N 91 30W
104 Mazatlán 23 10N 106 30W
39 Mazzarino 37 19N 14 12 E
75 Mbabane 26 18s 31 6 E
74 M'Baiki 3 53N 18 1 E
74 Mbala 8 46s 31 17 E
74 Mbale 1 8N 34 12 E
74 Mbandaka 0 1s 18 18 E
74 Mbarara 0 35s 30 25 E
74 Mbeya 8 54s 33 29 E
74 Mbuji-Mayi 6 9s 23 40 E
74 Mbulu 3 45s 35 30 E
75 Mchinji 13 47s 32 58 E
103 Mead, L. 36 10N 114 10W
83 Meadow 26 35s 114 30 E
93 Meadow Lake 54 10N 108 10W
93 Meadow Lake Prov. Park 52 25N 109 0W
96 Meadville 41 39N 80 9W
90 Meaford 44 40N 80 36W
15 Meath □ 53 32N 6 40W
20 Meaulne 46 36N 2 28 E
19 Meaux 48 58N 2 50 E
56 Mecca=Makkah 21 30N 39 54 E
96 Mechanicsburg 40 12N 77 0W
97 Mechanicville 42 54N 73 41W
16 Mechelen 51 2N 4 29 E
24 Mecklenburger, B. 54 20N 11 40 E
82 Meda P.O. 17 20s 123 59 E
62 Medak 18 1N 78 15 E
64 Medan 3 40N 98 38 E
112 Medanosa, Pta. 48 0s 66 0W
72 Médéa 36 12N 2 50 E
110 Medellín 6 15N 75 35W
72 Médenine 33 21N 10 30 E
72 Mederdra 17 0N 15 38W
102 Medford 42 20N 122 52W
41 Medgidia 44 15N 28 19 E
41 Mediaş 46 9N 24 22 E
37 Medicina 44 29N 11 38 E
102 Medicine Bow 41 56N 106 11W
102 Medinine Bow Ra. 41 10N 106 25W
93 Medicine Hat 50 0N 110 45W
96 Medina 43 15N 78 27W
30 Medina de Rioseco 41 53N 5 3W
30 Medina del Campo 41 18N 4 55W
31 Medina-Sidonia 36 28N 5 57W
32 Medinaceli 41 12N 2 30W
34 Mediterranean Sea 35 0N 15 0 E
20 Médoc, Reg. 45 10N 0 56W
49 Medveditsa, R. 49 0N 43 58 E
51 Medvezhi Oshova 71 0N 161 0 E
48 Medvezhyegorsk 63 0N 34 25 E
13 Medway, R. 51 27N 0 44 E
83 Meeberrie 26 57s 116 0 E
83 Meekatharra 26 32s 118 29 E
24 Meerane 50 51N 12 30 E
60 Meerut 29 1N 77 50 E
74 Mega 3 57N 38 30 E
43 Megalópolis 37 25N 22 7 E
91 Mégantic 45 36N 70 56W
43 Mégara 37 58N 23 22 E
21 Mégève 45 51N 6 37 E
61 Meghalaya □ 25 50N 91 0 E
61 Meghna, R. 22 50N 90 50 E
54 Megiddo 32 36N 15 11 E
40 Mehadia 44 56N 22 23 E
60 Mehsana 23 39N 72 26 E
20 Mehun-sur-Yèvre 47 10N 2 13 E
68 Meihokow 42 37N 125 46 E
69 Meihsien 24 20N 116 0 E
59 Meiktila 21 0N 96 0 E
24 Meiningen 50 32N 10 25 E
30 Meira, Sa. de 43 15N 7 15W
25 Meiringen 46 43N 8 12 E
24 Meissen 51 10N 13 29 E
24 Meissner, Mt. 51 12N 9 50 E
20 Méjean, Causse 44 15N 3 30 E
73 Mekele 13 33N 39 30 E
72 Meknès 33 57N 5 33W
63 Mekong, R. 10 33N 105 24 E
63 Melaka 2 15N 102 15 E
63 Melaka □ 2 17N 102 18 E
64 Melalap 5 10N 116 5 E
43 Mélambes 35 8N 24 40 E
76 Melanesia, Arch. 4 0s 155 0 E
62 Melapalaiyam 8 39N 77 44 E
84 Melbourne 37 40s 145 0 E
104 Melchor Múzquiz 27 50N 101 40W
37 Méldola 44 7N 12 3 E
24 Meldorf 54 5N 9 5 E
36 Melegnano 45 21N 9 20 E
48 Melekess=Dimitrovgrad 54 25N 49 33 E
39 Melfi 41 0N 15 40 E
93 Melfort 52 50N 105 40W
30 Melgar de Fernamental 42 27N 4 17W
43 Meligalá 37 15N 21 59 E
72 Melilla 35 21N 2 57W
54 Melilot 31 22N 34 37 E
108 Melipilla 33 42s 71 15W
93 Melita 49 15N 101 5W
49 Melitopol 46 50N 35 22 E
29 Melk 48 13N 15 20 E
20 Melle 46 14N 0 10W
45 Mellerud 58 41N 12 28 E
26 Mělník 50 22N 14 23 E
109 Melo 32 20s 54 10W
14 Melrose 55 35N 2 44W
12 Melton Mowbray 52 46N 0 52W
19 Melun 48 32N 2 39 E
62 Melur 10 2N 78 23 E
93 Melville 32 2s 115 48 E
82 Melville, I., Australia 11 30s 131 0 E
86 Melville, I., Canada 75 30N 111 0W
91 Melville, L. 53 45N 59 40W
89 Melville Pen. 68 0N 84 0W
48 Memel=Klaipeda 55 43N 21 10 E
25 Memmingen 47 59N 10 12 E
101 Memphis 35 7N 90 0W
97 Memphremagog L. 45 8N 72 17W
12 Menai Str. 53 7N 4 20W
100 Menasha 44 13N 88 27W
64 Menate 0 12s 112 47 E
69 Mencheng 33 27N 116 45 E
20 Mende 44 31N 3 30 E
13 Mendip Hills 51 17N 2 40W
102 Mendocino 39 26N 123 50W
103 Mendota 36 46N 120 24W
108 Mendoza 32 50s 68 52W
108 Mendoza □ 33 0s 69 0W
110 Mene de Mauroa 10 45N 70 50W
110 Mene Grande 9 49N 70 56W
56 Menemen 38 36N 27 4 E
16 Menen 50 47N 3 7 E
38 Menfi 37 36N 12 57 E
64 Menggala 4 20s 105 15 E
31 Mengíbar 37 58N 3 48W
67 Mengtz 23 20N 103 20 E
84 Menindee 32 20N 142 25 E
100 Menominee 45 9N 87 39W
100 Menomonie 44 50N 91 54W
32 Menorca, I. 40 0N 4 0 E
64 Mentawai, Kep. 2 0s 99 0 E
21 Menton 43 50N 7 29 E
73 Menzel Temime 36 46N 11 0 E
48 Menzelinsk 55 43N 53 8 E
83 Menzies 29 40s 120 58 E
54 Me'ona 33 1N 35 15 E
16 Meppel 52 42N 6 12 E
24 Mepper 52 41N 7 20 E
32 Mequinenza 41 22N 0 17 E
43 Merabéllou, Kól. 35 10N 25 50 E
65 Merak 5 55s 106 1 E
37 Merano 46 40N 11 10 E
65 Merauke 8 29s 120 24 E
55 Merca 1 48N 44 50 E
32 Mercadal 39 59N 4 5 E
37 Mercato Saraceno 43 57N 12 11 E
103 Merced 37 25N 120 30W
108 Mercedes, Buenos Aires 34 40s 59 30W
108 Mercedes, Corrientes 29 10s 58 5W
108 Mercedes, San Luis 33 40s 65 30W
108 Mercedes, Uruguay 33 12s 58 0W
85 Mercer 37 16s 175 5 E
89 Mercy, C. 65 0N 62 30W
13 Mere 51 5N 2 16W
112 Meredith, C. 52 15s 60 40W
41 Merei 45 7N 26 43 E
19 Méréville 48 20N 2 5 E
63 Mergui 12 30N 98 35 E
63 Mergui Arch.=Myeik Kyunzu 11 30N 97 30 E
104 Mérida, Mexico 20 50N 89 40W
31 Mérida, Sp. 38 55N 6 25W
110 Mérida, Ven. 8 36N 71 8W
97 Meriden 41 33N 72 47W
102 Meridian, Id. 43 41N 116 20W
101 Meridian, Miss. 32 20N 88 42W
111 Meriruma 1 15N 54 50W
16 Merksem 51 16N 4 25 E
19 Merlebach 49 5N 6 52 E
73 Merowe 18 29N 31 46 E
83 Merredin 31 28s 118 18 E
100 Merrill 45 11N 89 41W
97 Merrimack, R. 42 49N 70 49W
92 Merritt 50 10N 120 45W
83 Merroe 27 53s 117 50 E
74 Mersa Fatma 14 57N 40 17 E
13 Mersea I. 51 48N 0 55 E
24 Merseburg 51 20N 12 0 E
12 Mersey, R. 53 25N 3 0W
12 Merseyside □ 53 25N 2 55W
56 Mersin 36 51N 34 36 E
63 Mersing 2 25N 103 50 E
13 Merthyr Tydfil 51 45N 3 23W
31 Mértola 37 40N 7 40 E
101 Mertzon 31 17N 100 48W
19 Méru 49 13N 2 8 E
74 Meru 0 3N 37 40 E
19 Méry 48 30N 3 52 E
25 Merzig 49 26N 6 37 E
103 Mesa 33 20N 111 56W
39 Mesagne 40 33N 17 49 E
43 Mesaras, Kól. 35 6N 24 47 E
57 Meshed=Mashhad 36 20N 59 35 E
103 Mesilla 32 20N 107 0W
18 Meslay-du-Maine 47 58N 0 33W
43 Mesolóngion 38 27N 21 28 E
56 Mesopotamia, Reg.=Al Jazirah, Reg. 33 30N 44 0 E
39 Messina, It. 38 10N 15 32 E
75 Messina, S.Africa 22 20s 30 12 E
39 Messina, Str. di 38 5N 15 35 E
43 Messíni 37 4N 22 1 E
43 Messinía □ 37 10N 22 0 E
43 Messiniakós Kól. 36 45N 22 5 E
37 Mestre 45 30N 12 13 E
110 Meta, R. 6 12N 67 28W
90 Metagama 47 0N 81 55W
108 Metán 25 30s 65 0W
85 Methven 43 38s 171 40 E
41 Metkovets 43 37N 23 10 E
40 Metković 43 6N 17 39 E
92 Metlakatia 55 8N 131 35W
37 Metlika 45 40N 15 20 E
101 Metropolis 37 10N 88 47W

42 Métsovon 39 48N 21 12 E
62 Mettuppalaiyam 11 18N 76 59 E
62 Mettur 11 48N 77 47 E
54 Metulla 33 17N 35 34 E
19 Metz 49 8N 6 10 E
64 Meulaboh 4 11N 96 3 E
19 Meulan 49 0N 1 52 E
64 Meureudu 5 19N 96 10 E
19 Meurthe, R. 48 47N 6 9 E
19 Meuse □ 49 8N 5 25 E
16 Meuse, R. 51 49N 5 1 E
25 Meuselwitz 51 3N 12 18 E
19 Meurthe-et-Moselle □ 48 52N 6 0 E
101 Mexia 31 38N 96 32W
111 Mexiana, I. 0 0 49 30W
104 Mexicali 32 40N 115 30W
104 Mexico, Mexico 19 20N 99 10W
100 Mexico, U.S.A. 39 10N 91 55W
104 Mexico ■ 20 0N 100 0W
104 México □ 19 20N 99 10W
24 Meyenburg 53 19N 12 15 E
20 Meymac 45 32N 2 10 E
48 Mezen, R. 66 11N 43 59 E
41 Mezdra 43 12N 23 35 E
20 Mèze 43 27N 3 36 E
48 Mezen 65 50N 44 20 E
18 Mézidon 49 5N 0 1W
20 Mézin 44 4N 0 16 E
27 Mezóberény 46 49N 21 3 E
27 Mezökövesd 47 49N 20 35 E
27 Mezötur 47 0N 20 41 E
60 Mhow 22 33N 75 50 E
104 Miahuatlán 16 21N 96 36W
31 Miajadas 39 9N 5 54W
99 Miami 25 52N 80 15W
99 Miami Beach 25 49N 80 6W
56 Miandowāb 37 0N 46 5 E
56 Mīāneh 37 30N 47 40 E
60 Mianwali 32 38N 71 28 E
69 Miaoli 24 34N 120 48 E
50 Miass 54 59N 60 6 E
41 Micăsasa 46 7N 24 7 E
27 Michalovce 48 44N 21 54 E
88 Michelson, Mt. 69 19N 144 17W
98 Michigan □ 44 40N 85 40W
98 Michigan, L. 44 0N 87 0W
98 Michigan City 41 42N 86 56W
91 Michikamau L. 54 0N 6 0W
90 Michipicoten I. 47 55N 85 45W
90 Michipicoten River 47 50N 84 58W
104 Michoacán □ 19 0N 102 0W
41 Michurin 42 9N 27 51 E
48 Michurinsk 52 58N 40 27 E
76 Micronesia, Arch. 17 0N 160 0 E
13 Mid Glamorgan □ 51 40N 3 25W
16 Middelburg, Neth. 51 30N 3 36 E
75 Middelburg, S. Africa 31 30 S 25 0 E
45 Middelfart 55 30N 9 43 E
63 Middle Andaman, I. 12 30N 92 30 E
91 Middle Brook 48 40N 54 20W
97 Middleboro 41 56N 70 52W
99 Middlesboro 36 40N 83 40W
12 Middlesbrough 54 35N 1 14W
97 Middlesex 40 36N 74 30W
97 Middletown, Conn. 41 37N 72 40W
97 Middletown, N.Y. 41 28N 74 28W
98 Middletown, Ohio 39 29N 84 25W
97 Middletown, Pa. 40 12N 76 44W
91 Middleton 44 50N 65 5W
80 Middleton P.O. 22 22 S 141 32 E
20 Midi, Canal du 43 45N 1 21 E
83 Midland, Australia 31 54 S 115 59 E
90 Midland, Canada 44 45N 79 50W
98 Midland, Mich. 43 37N 84 17W
96 Midland, Pa. 40 39N 80 27W
101 Midland, Tex. 32 0N 102 3W
61 Midnapore 22 25N 87 21 E
76 Midway Is. 28 13N 177 22W
102 Midwest 43 27N 106 11W
40 Midžor, Mt. 43 24N 22 40 E
66 Mie □ 34 20N 136 20 E
28 Międzychód 52 35N 15 53 E
28 Międzyrzec Podlaski 51 58N 22 45 E
28 Międzyrzecz 52 26N 15 35 E
27 Mielec 50 18N 21 25 E
69 Mienyang 31 18N 104 26 E
41 Miercurea Ciuc 46 21N 25 48 E
30 Mieres 43 18N 5 48W
54 Migdal 32 51N 35 30 E
54 Migdal Ha'Emeq 32 41N 35 14 E
19 Migennes 47 58N 3 31 E
37 Migliarino 44 54N 11 56 E
66 Mihara 34 25N 133 5 E
32 Mijares, R. 39 55N 0 1W
31 Mijas 36 36N 4 40W
41 Mikhaylovgrad 43 27N 23 16 E
43 Mikínai 37 43N 22 46 E
74 Mikindani 10 15 S 40 2 E
46 Mikkeli □ 61 56N 28 0 E
43 Míkonos, I. 37 30N 25 25 E
27 Mikołów 50 10N 18 50 E
42 Mikrí Prespa, L. 40 46N 21 4 E
Límni 40 46N 21 4 E
48 Mikun 62 20N 50 0 E
110 Milagro 2 0 S 79 30W
81 Milang 35 20 S 138 55 E
36 Milano 45 28N 9 10 E
39 Milazzo 38 13N 15 13 E
13 Mildenhall 52 20N 0 30 E
84 Mildura 34 13 S 142 9 E
42 Miléai 39 20N 23 9 E
81 Miles 26 37 S 150 10 E
100 Miles City 46 30N 105 50W
93 Milestone 50 0N 104 30W
96 Milford, Conn. 41 13N 73 4W
98 Milford, Del. 38 52N 75 26W
97 Milford, Mass. 42 8N 71 30W
103 Milford, Utah 38 20N 113 0W
13 Milford Haven 51 43N 5 2W
28 Milicz 51 31N 17 19 E
83 Miling 30 30 S 116 17 E
39 Militello in Val di Catania 37 16N 14 46 E
20 Millau 44 8N 3 4 E
97 Millerton 41 57N 73 32W
91 Millertown Junction 48 49N 56 28W
20 Millevaches, Plat. de 45 45N 2 0 E
81 Millicent 37 34 S 140 21 E
99 Millinocket 45 45N 68 45W
12 Millom 54 13N 3 16W
98 Millville 39 22N 74 0W
89 Milne Inlet 72 30N 80 0W
92 Milo 24 28N 103 23 E
43 Mílos, I. 36 44N 24 25 E
85 Milton, N.Z. 46 7 S 169 59 E
96 Milton, U.S.A. 41 0N 76 53W
96 Milton West 43 33N 79 53W
13 Milton Keynes 52 3N 0 42W
15 Miltown Malbay 52 51N 9 25W
96 Milverton 43 35N 80 43W
98 Milwaukee 43 9N 87 58W
102 Milwaukie 45 33N 122 39W
20 Mimizan 44 12N 1 13W
26 Mimoň 50 38N 14 45 E
56 Minā al Ahmadī 29 5N 48 10 E
56 Mina Saud 28 45N 48 20 E
57 Mīnāb 27 10N 57 1 E
66 Minamata 32 10N 130 30 E
109 Minas 34 20 S 55 15W
31 Minas de Rio Tinto 37 42N 6 22W
111 Minas Gerais □ 18 50 S 46 0W
104 Minatitlán 17 58N 94 35W
59 Minbu 20 10N 95 0 E
14 Minch, Little, Chan. 57 40N 6 50W
14 Minch, North, Chan. 58 0N 6 0W
65 Mindanao, I. 8 0N 125 0 E
65 Mindanao Sea 9 0 124 0 E
65 Mindanao Trench 8 0N 128 0 E
24 Minden 52 18N 8 54 E
101 Minden 32 40N 93 20W
65 Mindoro, I. 13 0N 121 0 E
65 Mindoro Str. 12 30N 120 30 E
13 Minehead 51 12N 3 29W
101 Mineral Wells 32 50N 98 5W
97 Minersville 40 40N 76 17W
39 Minervino Murge 41 6N 16 4 E
91 Mingan 50 20N 64 0W
49 Mingechaurskoye, Vdkhr. 40 56N 47 20 E
80 Mingela 19 52 S 146 38 E
83 Mingenew 29 12 S 115 21 E
33 Minglanilla 39 34N 1 38W
30 Mingorria 40 42N 4 40W
29 Minho Reg. 41 40N 8 30W
69 Minhow=Foochow 26 5N 119 18 E
40 Minićevo 43 42N 22 18 E
83 Minilya 23 55 S 114 0 E
69 Min Kiang, R. 26 0N 119 30 E
69 Minkiang 32 30N 114 10 E
72 Minna 9 37N 6 30 E
100 Minneapolis 44 58N 93 20W
93 Minnedosa 50 20N 99 50W
100 Minnesota □ 46 40N 94 0W
81 Minnipa 32 51 S 135 9 E
66 Mino 35 32N 136 55 E
30 Miño, R. 41 52N 8 51W
100 Minot 48 10N 101 15W
48 Minsk 53 52N 27 30 E
28 Mińsk Mazowiecki 52 10N 21 33 E
91 Minto 34 1 S 150 51 E
89 Minto, L. 48 0N 84 45W
102 Minturn 39 45N 106 25W
38 Minturno 41 15N 13 43 E
51 Minusinsk 53 50N 91 20 E
59 Minutang 28 15N 96 30 E
67 Minya Konka, Mt. 29 34N 101 53 E
91 Miquelon, I. 47 8N 56 24W
37 Mira 45 26N 12 9 E
31 Mira, R. 37 43N 8 47W
39 Mirabella Eclano 41 3N 14 59 E
62 Miraj 16 50N 74 45 E
108 Miramar 38 15 S 57 50W
21 Miramas 43 33N 4 59 E
20 Miramont 44 37N 0 21 E
111 Miranda 20 10 S 50 15W
30 Miranda de Ebro 42 41N 2 57W
30 Miranda do Corvo 40 6N 8 20W
30 Miranda do Douro 41 30N 6 16W
30 Mirandela 41 32N 98 59W
36 Mirandola 44 53N 11 2 E
109 Mirandópolis 21 9 S 51 6W
37 Mirano 45 29N 12 6 E
109 Mirassol 20 46 S 49 28W
19 Mirecourt 48 20N 6 10 E
64 Miri 4 18N 114 0 E
80 Miriam Vale 24 20 S 151 39 E
109 Mirim, L. 32 45 S 52 50W
61 Mirzapur 25 10N 82 45 E
68 Mishan 45 31N 132 2 E
98 Mishawaka 41 40N 86 8W
66 Mishima 35 10N 138 52 E
54 Mishmar Alyalon 31 52N 34 57 E
54 Mishmar Ha 'Emeq 32 37N 35 7 E
54 Mishmar Ha Negev 31 22N 34 48 E
54 Mishmar Ha Yarden 33 0N 35 56 E
38 Misilmeri 38 2N 13 25 E
109 Misiones, Arg. □ 27 0 S 54 0W
108 Misiones, Paraguay □ 27 0 S 57 0W
57 Miskīn 23 44N 56 52 E
105 Miskitos, Cayos 14 26N 82 50W
27 Miskolc 48 7N 20 50 E
65 Misool, I. 2 0 S 130 0 E
73 Misrātah 32 18N 15 3 E
101 Mission 26 15N 98 30W
92 Mission City 49 10N 122 15W
101 Mississippi □ 33 0N 90 0W
101 Mississippi, R. 29 0N 89 15W
101 Mississippi, Delta of the 29 10N 89 15W
102 Missoula 47 0N 114 0W
100 Missouri □ 38 25N 92 30W
100 Missouri, Plat. du Coteau du 46 0N 99 30W
100 Missouri, R. 38 50N 90 8W
90 Mistassini, L. 51 0N 73 40W
39 Misterbianco 37 32N 15 0 E
39 Mistretta 37 56N 14 20 E
81 Mitchell, Australia 26 29 S 147 58 E
100 Mitchell, U.S.A. 43 40N 98 0W
99 Mitchell, Mt. 35 40N 82 20W
15 Mitchelstown 52 16N 8 18W
60 Mitha Tiwana 32 13N 72 6 E
42 Míthimna 39 20N 26 12 E
43 Mitilíni 39 6N 26 35 E
104 Mitla 16 55N 96 17W
66 Mito 36 20N 140 30 E
73 Mitsiwa 15 35N 39 25 E
84 Mittagong 34 28 S 150 29 E
24 Mittelland-kanal 52 23N 7 45 E
25 Mittweida 50 59N 13 0 E
84 Mittyack 35 8 S 142 36 E
74 Mitumba, Chaîne des 10 0 S 26 20 E
66 Miyagi □ 38 15N 140 45 E
66 Miyako 39 40N 141 75 E
66 Miyakonojo 31 32N 131 5 E
66 Miyazaki 31 56N 131 30 E
66 Miyazaki 32 0N 131 30 E
54 Miyet, Bahr el 31 30N 35 30 E
66 Miyoshi 34 48N 132 32 E
68 Miyun 40 22N 116 49 E
15 Mizen Hd., Cork 51 27N 9 50W
15 Mizen Hd., Wicklow 52 52N 6 4W
41 Mizil 44 59N 26 29 E
59 Mizoram □ 23 0N 92 40 E
54 Mizpe Ramon 20 36N 34 48 E
45 Mjölby 58 20N 15 10 E
75 Mkushi 14 20 S 29 20 E
26 Mladá Boleslav 50 27N 14 53 E
40 Mladenovac 44 28N 20 44 E
28 Mława 53 9N 20 25 E
75 Mlanje, Mt. 16 2 S 35 33 E
40 Mljet, I. 42 43N 17 30 E
40 Mljetski, Kanal 42 48N 17 35 E
46 Mo 66 15N 14 8 E
65 Moa, I. 8 0 S 128 0 E
103 Moab 38 40N 109 35W
84 Moama 36 3 S 144 45 E
74 Moba 7 3 S 29 47 E
74 Mobaye 4 25N 21 5 E
100 Moberly 39 25N 92 25W
90 Mobert 48 41N 85 40W
99 Mobile 30 41N 88 3W
45 Møborg 56 24N 8 21 E
74 Mobutu Sese Seko, L. 1 30N 31 0 E
75 Moçambique 15 3 S 40 42 E
75 Moçâmedes 16 35 S 12 30 E
75 Mochudi 24 27 S 26 7 E
45 Möckeln, L. 56 40N 14 15 E
110 Mocoa 1 15N 76 45W
109 Mococa 21 28 S 47 0W
104 Moctezuma, R. 21 59N 98 34W
75 Mocuba 16 54 S 37 25 E
36 Módena 44 39N 10 55 E
103 Modesto 37 43N 121 0W
39 Módica 36 52N 14 45 E
37 Modigliana 44 9N 11 48 E
27 Mödling 48 5N 16 17 E
84 Moe 38 12 S 146 19 E
18 Moélan-sur-Mer 47 49N 3 38W
44 Moelv 60 56N 10 43 E
111 Moengo 5 45N 54 20W
74 Moero, L. 9 0 S 28 45 E
14 Moffat 55 20N 3 27W
60 Moga 30 48N 75 8 E
55 Mogadiscio 2 2N 45 25 E
55 Mogadishu= Mogadiscio 2 2N 45 25 E
72 Mogador= Essaouira 31 32N 9 42W
59 Mogaung 25 20N 97 0 E
33 Mogente 38 52N 0 45W
109 Mogi das Cruzes 23 45 S 46 20W
109 Mogi Mirim 22 20 S 47 0W
48 Mogilev 53 55N 30 18 E
49 Mogilvev Podolskiy 48 20N 27 40 E
37 Mogliano Venteto 45 33N 12 15 E
51 Mogocha 53 40N 119 50 E
103 Mogollon Mesa 43 40N 110 0W
83 Mogumber 31 2 S 116 3 E
27 Mohács 45 58N 18 41 E
97 Mohawk, R. 42 47N 73 42W
24 Möhne, R. 51 27N 7 57 E
68 Moho 53 15N 122 27 E
19 Mohon 49 45N 4 44 E
62 Moinabad 17 44N 77 16 E
50 Mointy 47 40N 73 45 E
20 Moissac 44 7N 1 5 E
31 Moita 38 38N 8 58W
33 Mojácar 37 6N 1 55W
103 Mojave 35 8N 118 8W
103 Mojave Des. 35 0N 117 30W
65 Mojokerto 7 29 S 112 25 E
61 Mokameh 25 24N 85 55 E
85 Mokau, R. 38 42 S 174 37 E
43 Mokhós 35 16N 25 27 E
69 Mokpo 34 50N 126 30 E
40 Mokra Gora 42 50N 20 30 E
16 Mol 51 11N 5 5 E
39 Mola di Bari 41 3N 17 5 E
12 Mold 53 10N 3 10W
49 Moldanan S.S.R. □ 47 0N 28 0 E
40 Moldova Nouă 44 45N 21 41 E
41 Moldoveanu, Mt. 45 36N 24 45 E
75 Molepolole 24 28 S 25 28 E
39 Molfetta 41 12N 16 35 E
32 Molina de Aragón 40 46N 1 52W
100 Moline 41 30N 90 30W
37 Molinella 44 38N 11 40 E
39 Molise □ 41 45N 14 30 E
30 Molledo 43 8N 4 6W
110 Mollendo 17 0 S 72 0W
32 Mollerusa 41 37N 0 54 E
31 Mollina 37 8N 4 38W
24 Mölln 53 37N 10 41 E
45 Mölndal 57 40N 12 3 E
94 Molokai, I. 21 8N 156 0W
84 Molong 33 5 S 148 54 E
75 Molopo, R. 28 30 S 20 13 E
43 Mólos 38 47N 22 37 E
65 Molucca Sea 4 0 S 124 0 E
65 Moluccas, Is.= Maluku, Is. 1 0 S 127 0 E
74 Mombasa 4 2 S 39 43 E
30 Mombuey 42 3N 6 20W
41 Momchilgrad 41 33N 25 23 E
62 Mominabad 18 43N 76 23W
110 Mompos 9 14N 74 26W
45 Møn, I. 54 57N 12 15 E
105 Mona, Pta. 9 37N 82 36W
105 Mona, I. 18 5N 67 54W
14 Monach Is. 57 32N 7 40W
21 Monaco ■ 43 46N 7 23 E
14 Monadhliath Mts. 57 10N 4 4W
97 Monadnock Mt. 42 52N 72 7W
15 Monaghan 54 15N 6 58W
15 Monaghan □ 54 10N 7 0W
101 Monahans 31 35N 102 50W
73 Monastir 35 50N 10 49 E
32 Moncada 39 30N 0 24W
30 Monção 42 4N 8 27W
32 Moncayo, Sa. del 41 48N 1 50W
48 Monchegorsk 67 54N 32 58 E
24 Mönchengladbach 51 12N 6 23 E
31 Monchique 37 19N 8 38W

104 Monclava 26 50N 101 30W
91 Moncton 46 7N 64 51W
30 Mondego, C. 40 11N 8 54W
30 Mondego, R. 40 9N 8 52W
37 Mondolfo 43 45N 13 8 E
30 Mondoñedo 43 25N 7 23W
36 Mondovì 44 23N 7 56 E
38 Mondragone 41 8N 13 52 E
96 Monessen 40 9N 79 50W
31 Monesterio 38 6N 6 15W
90 Monet 48 10N 75 40W
37 Monfalcone 45 49N 13 32 E
30 Monforte de Lemos 42 31N 7 33W
59 Mong Kung 21 35N 97 35 E
59 Mong Pan 20 19N 98 22 E
59 Mong Pawk 22 4N 99 16 E
59 Mong Ton 20 25N 98 45 E
59 Mong Wa 21 26N 100 27 E
59 Mong Yai 22 28N 98 3 E
83 Monger, L. 29 25S 117 5 E
61 Monghyr 25 23N 86 30 E
73 Mongo 12 14N 18 43 E
67 Mongolia ■ 47 0N 103 0 E
75 Mongu 15 16S 23 12 E
20 Monistrol 45 17N 14 11 E
93 Monk 47 7N 69 59W
80 Monkira 24 46S 140 30 E
13 Monmouth, U.K. 51 48N 2 43W
100 Monmouth, U.S.A. 40 50N 90 40W
105 Mono, Pta. del 12 0N 83 30W
39 Monópoli 40 57N 17 18 E
27 Monor 47 21N 19 27 E
33 Monóvar 38 28N 0 53W
32 Monreal del Campo 40 47N 1 20W
38 Monreale 38 6N 13 16 E
101 Monroe, La. 32 32N 92 4W
98 Monroe, Mich. 41 55N 83 26W
99 Monroe, N.C. 35 2N 80 37W
100 Monroe, Wis. 42 38N 89 40W
72 Monrovia, Liberia 6 18N 10 47W
103 Monrovia, U.S.A. 34 7N 118 1W
16 Mons 50 27N 3 58 E
37 Monsélice 43 13N 11 45 E
45 Monsterås 57 3N 16 33 E
21 Mont Cenis, Col du 45 15N 6 54 E
92 Mont Joli 48 37N 68 10W
90 Mont Laurier 46 35N 75 30W
18 Mont St. Michel 48 40N 1 30W
90 Mont Tremblant Prov. Park 46 30N 74 30W
37 Montagnana 45 13N 11 29 E
91 Montague 46 10N 62 39W
104 Montague, I. 31 40N 144 46W
20 Montaigu 46 59N 1 18W
32 Montalbán 40 50N 0 45W
39 Montalbano Iónica 40 17N 16 33 E
32 Montalbo 39 53N 2 42W
37 Montalcino 43 4N 11 30 E
30 Montalegre 41 49N 7 47W
39 Montalto Uffugo 39 25N 16 9 E
102 Montana □ 6 0S 73 0W
19 Montargis 48 0N 2 43 E
20 Montauban 44 0N 1 21 E
97 Montauk 41 3N 71 57W
97 Montauk Pt. 41 4N 71 52W
19 Montbard 47 38N 4 20 E
19 Montbéliard 47 31N 6 48 E
32 Montblanch 41 23N 1 4 E
21 Montbrison 45 36N 4 3 E
20 Montcalm, Pic de 42 40N 1 25 E
21 Montceau-les-Mines 46 40N 4 23 E
97 Montclair 40 53N 74 49W
20 Mont-de-Marsan 43 54N 0 31W
19 Montdidier 49 38N 2 35 E
111 Monte Alegre 2 0S 54 0W
111 Monte Azul 15 9S 42 53W
21 Monte Carlo 43 46N 7 23 E
108 Monte Caseros 30 10S 57 50W
30 Monte Redondo 39 53N 8 50W
36 Monte Rosa, Mt. 45 55N 7 50 E
38 Monte San Giovanni 41 38N 13 31 E
40 Monte San Guiliano 43 20N 11 42 E
39 Monte Sant 'Angelo 41 42N 15 59 E
38 Monte Santu, C. di 40 5N 9 42 E
90 Montebello 45 40N 74 55W
37 Montebelluna 45 47N 12 3 E
18 Montebourg 49 30N 1 20W
36 Montecatini 43 55N 10 48 E
110 Montecristi 1 0S 80 40W
36 Montecristo, I. 42 20N 10 20 E
37 Montefiascone 42 31N 12 2 E
105 Montego Bay 18 30N 78 0W
82 Montejinnie 16 40S 131 45 E
21 Montélimar 44 33N 4 45 E
31 Montellano 36 59N 5 36W
104 Montemorelos 25 11N 99 42W
31 Montemor-o-Novo 38 40N 8 12W
109 Montenegro □ 42 40N 19 20 E
37 Montepulciano 43 5N 11 46 E
19 Montereau 48 22N 2 57 E
103 Monterey 36 35N 121 57W
110 Montería 8 46N 75 53W
108 Monteros 27 11S 65 30W
37 Monterotondo 42 3N 12 36 E
104 Monterrey 25 40N 100 30W
111 Montes Claros 16 30S 43 50W
32 Montes de Toledo 39 35N 4 30W
102 Montesano 47 0N 123 39W
39 Montesarchio 41 5N 14 37 E
37 Montesilvano 42 30N 14 8 E
37 Montevarchi 43 30N 11 32 E
109 Montevideo 34 50S 56 11W
18 Montfort-sur Meuse 48 8N 1 58W
13 Montgomery, U.K. 52 34N 3 9W
99 Montgomery, U.S.A. 32 20N 86 20W
97 Monticello, N.Y. 41 37N 74 42W
103 Monticello, Utah 37 55N 109 27W
36 Montichiari 45 28N 10 29 E
19 Montigny-les-Metz 49 7N 6 10 E
31 Montijo 38 52N 6 39W
31 Montilla 37 36N 4 40W
100 Montivideo 44 55N 95 40W
20 Montluçon 46 22N 2 36 E
91 Montmagny 46 58N 70 43 E
19 Montmédy 49 30N 5 20 E
21 Montmélian 45 30N 6 4 E
19 Montmirail 48 51N 3 30 E
20 Montmoreau 45 23N 0 7 E
91 Montmorency 46 53N 71 11W
20 Montmorillon 46 26N 0 50 E
19 Montmort 48 55N 3 49 E
80 Monto 24 52S 151 12 E
18 Montoire 47 45N 0 52 E
31 Montoro 38 1N 4 27W
102 Montpelier, Id. 42 15N 111 29W
97 Montpelier, Vt. 44 15N 72 38W
20 Montpellier 43 37N 3 52 E
20 Montpon-Ménestrol 45 2N 0 11 E
90 Montreal 45 31N 73 34W
20 Montrejeau 43 6N 0 35 E
19 Montreuil 50 27N 1 45 E
18 Montreuil-Bellay 47 8N 0 9W
25 Montreux 46 26N 6 55 E
18 Montrichard 47 20N 1 10 E
14 Montrose, U.K. 56 43N 2 28W
103 Montrose, U.S.A. 38 30N 107 52W
32 Montsant, Sa. de 41 17N 0 1 E
32 Montsech, Sa. del 42 0N 0 45 E
32 Montseny 42 49N 1 2 E
105 Montserrat, I. 16 40N 62 10W
32 Montserrat, Mt. 41 36N 1 49 E
21 Mont-sous-Vaudrey 46 58N 5 36 E
30 Montuenga 41 3N 4 38W
32 Montuiri 39 34N 2 59 E
59 Monywa 22 7N 95 11 E
36 Monza 45 35N 9 15 E
16 Monze 16 17S 27 29 E
75 Monze, C. 24 47N 66 37 E
32 Monzón 41 52N 0 10 E
83 Mooliabeenee 31 20S 116 2 E
90 Moonbeam 49 20N 82 10W
81 Moonie 27 46S 150 20 E
81 Moonta 34 6S 137 32 E
83 Moora 30 37S 115 58 E
80 Mooraberree 25 13S 140 54 E
83 Moorarie 25 56S 117 35 E
83 Moore, L. 29 50S 117 35 E
83 Moore River 31 6S 115 32 E
14 Moorfoot Hills 55 44N 3 8W
100 Moorhead 47 0N 97 0W
25 Moosburg 48 28N 11 57 E
90 Moose, R. 43 37N 75 22W
97 Moose Creek 45 15N 74 58W
90 Moose Factory 52 20N 80 40W
93 Moose Jaw 50 30N 105 30W
100 Moose Lake 46 27N 92 48W
93 Moosomin 50 9N 101 40W
90 Moosonee 51 25N 80 51W
75 Mopeia Velha 17 30S 35 40 E
72 Mopti 14 30N 4 0W
110 Moquegua 17 15S 70 46W
27 Mór 47 25N 18 12 E
31 Móra, Sp. 40 15N 0 45W
44 Mora, Sweden 61 2N 14 38 E
32 Mora de Ebro 41 6N 0 38 E
32 Mora la Nueva 41 7N 0 39 E
60 Moradabad 28 50N 78 50 E
28 Morąg 53 55N 19 56 E
31 Moral de Calatrava 38 51N 3 33W
30 Moraleja 40 6N 6 43W
105 Morant Pt. 17 55N 76 12W
14 Morar, L. 56 57N 5 40W
33 Moratalla 38 14N 1 49W
62 Moratuwa 6 45N 79 55 E
27 Morava, R. 48 10N 16 59 E
40 Moravița 45 17N 21 14 E
83 Morawa 29 13S 116 0 E
110 Morawhanna 8 30N 59 40W
14 Moray Firth 57 50N 3 30W
36 Morbegno 46 8N 9 34 E
18 Morbihan □ 47 55N 2 50W
18 Mordelles 48 5N 1 52W
93 Morden 49 15N 98 10W
84 Mordialloc 38 1S 145 6 E
48 Mordovian A.S.S.R. □ 54 20N 44 30 E
44 Møre og Romsdal □ 63 0N 9 0 E
12 Morecambe 54 5N 2 52W
12 Morecambe B. 54 7N 3 0W
81 Moree 29 28S 149 54 E
99 Moorhead City 34 46N 76 44W
104 Morelia 19 40N 101 11W
80 Morella 23 0S 143 47 E
104 Morelos □ 18 40N 99 10W
60 Morena 26 30N 78 9 E
31 Morena, Sa. 38 20N 4 0W
103 Morenci 33 7N 109 20W
19 Moret 48 22N 2 48 E
81 Moreton, I. 27 10S 153 25 E
19 Moreuil 49 46N 2 30 E
21 Morez 46 31N 6 2 E
101 Morgan City 29 40N 91 15W
99 Morganton 35 46N 81 48W
98 Morgantown 39 39N 75 58W
18 Morgat 48 15N 4 32 E
19 Morhange 48 55N 6 38 E
92 Morinville 53 49N 113 41W
66 Morioka 39 45N 141 8 E
18 Morlaix 48 36N 3 52W
19 Mormant 48 37N 2 52 E
80 Mornington, I., Australia 16 30S 139 30 E
112 Mornington, I., Chile 49 50S 75 30W
65 Moro G. 6 30N 123 0 E
72 Morocco ■ 32 0N 5 50W
74 Morogoro 6 50S 37 40 E
104 Moroleón 20 8N 101 32W
105 Morón 22 0N 78 30W
68 Mörön, R. 47 14N 110 37 E
108 Morón 34 40S 58 40W
32 Morón de Almazán 41 29N 2 27W
31 Morón de la Frontera 37 6N 5 28W
75 Morondavo 20 17S 44 27 E
65 Morotai, I. 2 10N 128 30 E
74 Moroto 2 28N 34 42 E
12 Morpeth 55 11N 1 41W
101 Morrilton 35 10N 92 45W
111 Morrinhos 17 45S 49 10W
85 Morrinsville 37 40S 175 32 E
93 Morris 49 25N 97 30W
83 Morris, Mt. 26 9S 131 4 E
90 Morrisburg 44 55N 75 7W
97 Morristown, N.J. 40 48N 74 30W
99 Morristown, Tenn. 36 18N 83 20W
97 Morrisville 42 54N 75 39W
108 Morro, Pta. 27 6S 71 0W
103 Morro Bay 35 27N 120 54W
110 Morrosquillo, G. de 9 35N 75 40W
48 Morshansk 53 28N 41 50 E
44 Mörsil 63 19N 13 40 E
18 Mortagne, Orne 48 30N 0 32 E
20 Mortagne, Vendée 46 59N 0 57W
19 Mortagne, R. 48 33N 6 27 E
18 Mortain 48 40N 0 57W
36 Mortara 45 15N 8 43 E
108 Morteros 30 50S 62 0W
111 Mortes, R. 11 45S 50 44W
84 Mortlake 38 5S 142 50 E
84 Morundah 34 57S 146 19 E
21 Morvan, Mts. du 47 5N 4 0 E
81 Morven 26 22S 147 5 E
14 Morvern, Reg. 56 38N 5 44W
60 Morvi 22 25N 72 5 E
84 Morwell 38 10S 146 22 E
25 Mosbach 49 21N 9 9 E
59 Moscos Is. 14 0N 97 45 E
102 Moscow 46 45N 116 59W
48 Moscow=Moskva 55 45N 37 35 E
25 Mosel, R. 50 22N 7 36 E
19 Moselle □ 48 59N 6 33 E
85 Mosgiel 45 53S 170 21 E
74 Moshi 3 22S 37 18 E
46 Mosjøen 65 51N 13 12 E
48 Moskva 55 45N 27 35 E
48 Moskva, R. 55 5N 38 50 E
27 Mosonmagyaróvár 47 52N 17 18 E
110 Mosquera 2 35N 78 30W
96 Mosquito Cr. Res. 41 22N 80 45W
105 Mosquitos, G. de los 9 15N 81 0W
44 Moss 59 27N 10 40 E
84 Moss Vale 34 32S 150 25 E
93 Mossbank 50 0N 106 0W
85 Mossburn 45 41S 168 15 E
75 Mosselbaai 34 11S 22 8 E
74 Mossendjo 2 55S 12 42 E
84 Mossgiel 33 15S 144 30 E
80 Mossman 16 28S 145 23 E
111 Mossoró 5 10S 37 15W
75 Mossuril 14 58S 40 42 E
26 Most 50 31N 13 38 E
72 Mostaganem 35 54N 0 5 E
40 Mostar 43 22N 17 50 E
56 Mosul=Al Mawsil 36 20N 43 5 E
32 Mota del Cuervo 39 30N 2 52W
45 Motala 58 32N 15 1 E
14 Motherwell 55 48N 4 0W
61 Motihari 26 37N 85 1 E
32 Motilla del Palancar 39 34N 1 55W
39 Mótlola 40 38N 17 0 E
31 Motril 36 44N 3 37W
85 Motueka 41 7S 173 1 E
74 Mouila 1 50S 11 0 E
20 Moulins 46 35N 3 19¼
59 Moulmein= Maulamyaing 16 30N 97 40 E
99 Moultrie 31 11N 83 47W
73 Moundou 8 40N 16 10 E
96 Moundsville 39 53N 80 43W
99 Mount Airy 36 31N 80 37W
81 Mount Barker 34 38S 117 40 E
98 Mount Carmel, Ill. 38 20N 87 48W
97 Mount Carmel, Pa. 40 46N 76 25W
96 Mount Clemens 42 35N 82 50W
80 Mount Coolon 21 25S 147 25 E
75 Mount Darwin 16 47S 31 38 E
80 Mount Douglas 21 35S 146 50 E
85 Mount Eden 36 53S 174 46 E
92 Mount Edgecumbe 57 3N 135 21W
82 Mount Elizabeth 16 0S 125 50 E
90 Mount Forest 43 59N 80 43W
84 Mount Gambier 37 50S 140 46 E
80 Mount Garnet 17 41S 145 7 E
81 Mount Hope 34 7S 135 23 E
80 Mount Isa 20 42S 139 26 E
83 Mount Keith 27 15S 120 30 E
97 Mount Kisco 41 12N 73 44W
80 Mount Larcom 23 48S 150 59 E
83 Mount Magnet 28 2S 117 47 E
85 Mount Maunganui 37 40S 176 14 E
80 Mount Molloy 16 42S 145 20 E
80 Mount Morgan 23 40S 150 25 E
83 Mount Narryer 26 30S 115 55 E
82 Mount Newman 23 18S 119 45 E
100 Mount Pleasant, Iowa 41 0N 91 35W
98 Mount Pleasant, Mich. 43 38N 84 46W
101 Mount Pleasant, Texas 33 5N 95 0W
102 Mount Pleasant, Utah 39 40N 111 29W
102 Mount Rainier Nat. Park 46 50N 121 20W
92 Mt. Revelstoke Nat. Park 51 6N 118 0W
92 Mount Robson 52 56N 119 15W
98 Mount Sterling 38 0N 84 0W
80 Mount Surprise 18 10S 144 17 E
100 Mount Vernon, Ill. 38 19N 88 55W
97 Mount Vernon, N.Y. 40 57N 73 49W
96 Mount Vernon, Ohio 40 20N 82 30W
102 Mount Vernon, Wash. 48 27N 122 18W
81 Mount Willoughby 27 58S 134 8 E
102 Mountain Home 43 3N 115 52W
92 Mountain Park 52 50N 117 15W
103 Mountain View 37 26N 122 5W
103 Mountainair 34 35N 106 15W
15 Mountmellick 53 7N 7 20W
80 Moura, Australia 24 35S 149 58 E
110 Moura, Brazil 1 25S 61 45W
31 Moura, Port. 38 7N 7 30W
73 Mourdi, Depression du 18 10N 23 0 E
20 Mourenx 43 23N 0 36W
19 Mourmelon-le Grand 49 8N 4 22 E
15 Mourne, Mts. 54 10N 6 0W
15 Mourne, R. 54 45N 7 25W
16 Mouscron 50 45N 3 12 E
25 Moutier 47 16N 7 21 E
21 Moutiers 45 29N 6 31 E
85 Moutohora 38 27S 177 32 E
69 Mowming 21 50N 110 32 E
68 Mowping 37 25N 121 34 E
74 Moyale 3 30N 39 0 E
15 Moyle □ 55 10N 6 15W

54 Moza 31 48N 35 8 E
75 Mozambique ■ 19 0s 35 0 E
70 Mozambique Chan. 20 0s 39 0 E
48 Mozyr 52 0N 29 15 E
74 Mpanda 6 23s 31 40 E
75 Mpika 11 51s 31 25 E
28 Mrągowo 53 57N 21 18 E
73 Msaken 35 49N 10 33 E
75 Msoro 13 35s 31 50 E
74 Mtwara 10 20s 40 20 E
111 Muaná 1 25s 49 15w
63 Muang Chiang Rai 19 52N 99 50 E
63 Muang Lamphun 18 40N 98 53 E
63 Muang Phichit 16 29N 100 21 E
63 Muar=Bandar Maharani 2 3N 102 34 E
64 Muarabungo 1 40s 101 10 E
64 Muarakaman 0 2s 116 45 E
64 Muaratembesi 1 42s 103 2 E
64 Muaratewe 0 50s 115 0 E
56 Mubairik 23 22N 39 8 E
74 Mubende 0 33N 31 22 E
73 Mubi 10 18N 13 16 E
25 Mücheln 51 18N 11 49 E
14 Muck, I. 56 50N 6 15w
111 Mucuri 18 0s 40 0w
75 Mufulira 12 32s 28 15w
30 Mugardos 43 27N 8 15w
31 Muge 39 3N 8 40w
30 Mugia 43 3N 9 17w
73 Muhammad Qol 20 53N 37 9 E
25 Mühldorf 48 14N 12 23 E
24 Mühlhausen 51 12N 10 29 E
15 Muine Bheag 52 42N 6 59w
30 Muiños 41 58N 7 59w
55 Mukalla 14 33N 49 2 E
68 Mukden=Shenyang 41 48N 123 27 E
55 Mukeiras 13 59N 45 52 E
83 Mukinbudin 30 55s 118 5 E
64 Mukomuko 2 20s 101 10 E
60 Muktsar 30 30N 74 30 E
33 Mula 38 3N 1 33w
105 Mulatas, Arch. de las 6 51N 78 31w
108 Mulchén 37 45s 72 20w
24 Mulde, R. 51 10N 12 48 E
91 Mulgrave 45 38N 61 31w
31 Mulhacén, Mt. 37 4N 3 20w
24 Mülheim 51 26N 6 53w
19 Mulhouse 47 40N 7 20 E
14 Mull of Galloway, Pt. 54 40N 4 55w
14 Mull of Kintyre, Pt. 55 20N 5 45w
14 Mull, I. 56 27N 6 0w
84 Mullengudgery 31 43s 147 29 E
15 Mullet, Pen. 54 10N 10 2w
83 Mullewa 28 29s 115 30 E
15 Mullingar 53 31N 7 20w
81 Mullumbimby 28 30s 153 30 E
60 Multan □ 30 29N 72 29 E
60 Multan 30 15N 71 30 E
84 Mulwala 35 59s 146 0 E
63 Mun, R. 15 19N 105 31 E
65 Muna, I. 5 0s 122 30 E
25 Munchberg 50 11N 11 48 E
24 Muncheberg 52 30N 14 9 E
25 München 48 8N 11 33 E
98 Muncie 40 10N 85 20w
62 Mundakayam 9 30N 76 32 E
24 Münden 51 25N 9 42 E
82 Mundiwindi 23 47s 120 9 E
33 Mundo, R. 38 30N 2 15w
111 Mundo Novo 11 50s 40 29w
60 Mundra 22 54N 69 26 E
83 Mundrabilla 31 52s 127 51 E
33 Munera 39 2N 2 29w
81 Mungallala 26 25s 147 34 E
80 Mungana 17 8s 144 27 E
81 Mungindi 28 58s 149 1 E
75 Munhango 12 9s 18 36 E
25 Munich=München 48 8N 11 33 E
45 Munkedal 58 28N 11 40 E
44 Munkfars 59 50N 13 30 E
112 Muñoz Gamero, Pen. 52 30s 73 5 E
19 Munster 48 2N 7 8 E
15 Munster □ 52 20N 8 40w
24 Münster, Niedersachsen 52 59N 10 5 E
24 Münster, Nordrhein-Westfalen 51 58N 7 37 E
83 Muntadgin 31 48s 118 30 E
64 Muntok 2 5s 105 10 E
46 Muonio, R. 67 48N 23 25 E
26 Mur, R. 46 18N 16 53 E
37 Mura, R. 46 18N 16 53 E
112 Murallón, Mt. 49 55s 73 30w
74 Murangá 0 45s 37 9 E
48 Murashi 59 30N 49 0 E
20 Murat 45 7N 2 53 E
26 Murau 47 6N 14 10 E
38 Muravera 39 25N 9 35 E
30 Murça 41 24N 7 28w
84 Murchison, Australia 36 39s 145 14 E
85 Murchison, N.Z. 41 49s 172 21 E
83 Murchison, R. 26 1s 117 6 E
33 Murcia 38 2N 1 10w
33 Murcia □ 37 50N 1 30w
33 Murcia, Reg. 38 35N 1 50w
41 Mureş 46 45N 24 40 E
41 Mureşul, R. 46 15N 20 13 E
20 Muret 43 30N 1 20 E
99 Murfreesboro 35 50N 86 21w
50 Murgab 38 10N 73 59 E
81 Murgon 26 15s 151 54 E
109 Muriaé 21 8s 42 23w
24 Müritzsee 53 25N 12 40 E
48 Murmansk 68 57N 33 10 E
32 Muro 39 45N 3 3 E
48 Murom 55 35N 42 3 E
66 Muroran 42 25N 141 0 E
30 Muros 42 45N 9 5w
39 Muro Lucano 40 45N 15 30 E
101 Murphysboro 37 50N 89 20w
99 Murray, Ky. 36 40N 88 20w
102 Murray, Utah 40 41N 111 58w
81 Murray, R. 35 22s 139 22 E
81 Murray Bridge 35 6s 139 14 E
84 Murrayville 35 16s 141 11 E
58 Murree 33 56N 73 28 E
83 Murrin Murrin 28 50s 121 45 E
84 Murrumbidgee, R. 34 43s 143 12 E
84 Murrurundi 31 42s 150 51 E
61 Murshidabad 24 11N 88 19 E
60 Murtazapur 20 40N 77 25 E
84 Murtoa 36 35s 142 28 E
30 Murtosa 40 44N 8 40w
85 Murupara 38 30s 178 40 E
61 Murwara 23 46N 80 28 E
81 Murwillumbah 28 18s 153 27 E
26 Mürzzuschlag 47 36N 15 41 E
41 Musala, Mt. 41 13N 23 27 E
57 Muscat=Masqat 23 37N 58 36 E
100 Muscatine 41 25N 91 5w
74 Mushie 2 56s 17 4 E
98 Muskegon 43 15N 86 17w
98 Muskegon Heights 43 12N 86 17w
101 Muskogee 35 50N 95 25w
73 Musmar 18 6N 35 40 E
74 Musoma 1 30s 33 48 E
14 Musselburgh 55 57N 3 3w
20 Mussidan 45 2N 0 22 E
38 Mussomeli 37 35N 13 43 E
112 Musters, L. 45 20s 69 25w
84 Muswellbrook 32 16s 150 56 E
73 Mût 25 28N 28 58 E
68 Mutankiang 44 35N 129 30 E
80 Muttaburra 22 38s 144 29 E
91 Mutton Bay 50 50N 59 2w
62 Muvatupusha 9 53N 76 35 E
51 Muya 56 27N 115 39 E
58 Muzaffarabad 34 25N 73 30 E
60 Muzaffargarh 30 5N 71 14 E
60 Muzaffarnagar 29 26N 77 40 E
61 Muzaffarpur 26 7N 85 32 E
50 Muzhi 65 25N 64 40 E
18 Muzillac 47 35N 2 30w
67 Muztagh, Mt. 36 30N 87 22 E
74 Mvadhi Ousye 1 13N 13 12 E
74 Mwanza, Tanzania 2 30s 32 58 E
74 Mwanza, Zaire 7 55s 26 43 E
74 Mweka 4 50s 21 40 E
74 Mweru, L. 9 0s 28 45 E
63 My Tho 10 29N 106 23 E
59 Myanaung 18 25N 95 10 E
59 Myaungmya 16 30N 95 0 E
59 Myingyan 21 30N 95 30 E
59 Myitkyina 25 30N 97 26 E
27 Myjava 48 41N 17 37 E
61 Mymensingh=Nasirabad 24 42N 90 30 E
102 Myrtle Creek 43 0N 123 19w
102 Myrtle Point 43 0N 124 4w
28 Myślibórz 52 55N 14 50 E
27 Mystowice 50 15N 19 12 E
62 Mysore 12 17N 76 41 E
27 Myszkow 50 45N 19 22 E
46 Mývatn, L. 65 36N 17 0w
26 Mže, R. 49 46N 13 24 E

N

54 Na'an 31 53N 34 52 E
47 Naantali 60 27N 21 57 E
15 Naas 53 12N 6 40w
61 Nabadwip 23 34N 88 20 E
73 Nabenl 36 30N 10 51 E
60 Nabha 30 26N 76 14 E
54 Nabi Rubin 31 56N 34 44 E
54 Nābulus 32 14N 35 15 E
74 Nachingwea 10 49s 38 49 E
27 Náchod 50 25N 16 8 E
44 Nacka 59 17N 18 12 E
81 Nackara 32 48s 139 12 E
101 Nacogdoches 31 33N 95 30w
104 Nacozari 30 30N 109 50w
60 Nadiad 22 41N 72 56 E
57 Nadūshan 32 2N 53 35 E
48 Nadvoitsy 63 52N 34 15 E
50 Nadym 63 35N 72 42 E
45 Næstved 55 13N 11 44 E
72 Nafada 11 8N 11 20 E
65 Naga 13 38N 123 15 E
59 Nagaland □ 26 0N 95 0 E
66 Nagano 36 40N 138 10 E
66 Nagano □ 36 15N 138 0 E
66 Nagaoka 32 27N 138 51 E
62 Nagappattinam 10 46N 79 51 E
66 Nagasaki 32 47N 129 50 E
66 Nagasaki □ 32 50N 129 40 E
66 Nagato 36 15N 138 16 E
60 Nagaur 27 15N 73 45 E
62 Nagercoil 8 12N 77 33 E
60 Nagina 29 30N 78 30 E
51 Nagornyy 55 58N 124 57 E
66 Nagoya 35 10N 136 50 E
60 Nagpur 21 8N 79 10 E
27 Nagykanizsa 46 28N 17 0 E
27 Nagykörös 47 2N 19 48 E
69 Naha 26 12N 127 40 E
88 Nahannai Butte 61 5N 123 30w
54 Nahariyya 33 1N 35 5 E
56 Nahavand 34 10N 48 30 E
54 Nahf 32 56N 35 18 E
112 Nahuel Huapi, L. 41 0s 71 32w
93 Naicam 52 30N 104 30w
25 Naila 50 19N 11 43 E
91 Nain 56 34N 61 40w
18 Naintré 46 46N 0 29 E
14 Nairn 57 35N 3 54w
74 Nairobi 1 17s 36 48 E
74 Naivasha 0 40s 36 30 E
57 Najafābād 32 40N 51 15 E
56 Najd, Reg. 26 30N 42 0 E
30 Najerilla, R. 42 15N 2 45w
60 Najibabad 29 40N 78 20 E
66 Nakamura 33 0N 133 0 E
56 Nakhi Mubarak 24 10N 38 10 E
49 Nakhichevan 39 14N 45 30 E
51 Nakhodka 43 10N 132 45 E
63 Nakhon Phanom 17 23N 104 43 E
63 Nakhon Ratchasima 14 59N 102 12 E
63 Nakhon Sawan 15 35N 100 12 E
63 Nakhon Si Thammarat 8 29N 100 0 E
90 Nakina 50 10N 86 40w
60 Nakodar 31 8N 75 31 E
45 Nakskov 54 50N 11 8 E
74 Nakuru 0 15s 35 5 E
92 Nakusp 50 20N 117 45w
58 Nal, R. 26 2N 65 19 E
68 Nalayh 47 43N 107 22 E
49 Nalchik 43 30N 43 33 E
62 Nalgonda 17 6N 79 15 E
62 Nallamalai Hills 15 30N 78 50 E
30 Nalon, R. 43 32N 6 4w
73 Nālūt 31 54N 11 0 E
63 Nam Dinh 20 25N 106 5 E
63 Nam-Phan, Reg. 10 30N 106 0 E
63 Nam Tha 20 58N 101 30 E
63 Nam Tok 14 21N 99 0 E
67 Nam Tso, L. 30 40N 90 30 E
62 Namakkal 11 13N 78 13 E
75 Namaland, Reg. 29 43s 19 5 E
50 Namangan 41 30N 71 30 E
75 Namapa 13 43s 39 50 E
65 Namber 1 2s 134 57 E
81 Nambour 26 38s 152 49 E
81 Nambucca Heads 30 40s 152 48 E
67 Namcha Barwa, Mt. 29 30N 95 10 E
75 Namib Des.=Namibwoestyn 22 30s 15 0w
75 Namibia ■ 22 0s 18 9 E
75 Namibwoestyn 22 30s 15 0w
75 Namlea 3 10s 127 5 E
102 Nampa 43 40N 116 40w
75 Nampula 15 6s 39 7 E
65 Namrole 3 46s 126 46 E
46 Namsen, R. 64 27N 11 28 E
46 Namsos 64 29N 11 30 E
59 Namtu 23 5N 97 28 E
16 Namur 50 27N 4 52 E
16 Namur □ 50 17N 5 0 E
75 Namutoni 18 49s 16 55 E
75 Namwala 15 44s 26 30 E
28 Namysłów 51 6N 17 42 E
69 Namyung 25 15N 114 5 E
67 Nan Shan, Mts. 38 0N 98 0 E
92 Nanaimo 49 10N 124 0w
81 Nanango 26 40s 152 0 E
66 Nanao 37 0N 137 0 E
69 Nanchang 28 34N 115 48 E
69 Nancheng 27 30N 116 28 E
69 Nancheng=Hanchung 33 10N 107 2 E
69 Nanchung 30 47N 105 59 E
19 Nancy 48 42N 6 12 E
61 Nanda Devi, Mt. 30 30N 80 30 E
62 Nander 19 10N 77 20 E
85 Nandi 17 25s 176 50 E
62 Nandikotkur 15 52N 78 18 E
60 Nandura 20 52N 76 25 E
60 Nandurbar 21 20N 74 15 E
62 Nandyal 15 30N 78 30 E
58 Nanga Parbat, Mt. 35 10N 74 35 E
57 Nangarhar □ 34 15N 70 30 E
19 Nangis 48 33N 3 0 E
62 Nanjangud 12 6N 76 43 E
60 Nankana Sahib 31 27N 73 38 E
69 Nankang 25 42N 114 35 E
69 Nanking 32 10N 118 50 E
66 Nankoku 33 39N 133 44 E
83 Nannine 26 51s 118 18 E
69 Nanning 22 51N 108 18 E
83 Nannup 33 59s 115 45 E
61 Nanpara 27 52N 81 33 E
69 Nanping 26 45N 118 5 E
66 Nansei-Shotō, Is. 29 0N 129 0 E
83 Nanson 28 34s 114 46 E
20 Nant 44 1N 3 18 E
69 Nantan 25 0N 107 35 E
18 Nantes 47 12N 1 33w
19 Nanteuil-le-Haudouin 49 9N 2 48 E
20 Nantiat 46 1N 1 11 E
97 Nanticoke 41 12N 76 1w
92 Nanton 50 20N 113 50w
69 Nantou 23 57N 120 35 E
21 Nantua 46 10N 5 35 E
86 Nantucket I. 41 16N 70 3w
69 Nantung 32 0N 120 50 E
111 Nanuque 17 50s 40 21w
69 Nanyang 33 2N 112 35 E
68 Nanyuan 39 48N 116 23 E
74 Nanyuki 0 2N 37 4 E
33 Nao, C. de la 38 44N 0 14 E
66 Naoetsu 37 12N 138 10 E
61 Naogaon 24 52N 88 52 E
42 Náousa 40 42N 22 9 E
102 Napa 38 18N 122 17w
90 Napanee 44 15N 77 0w
85 Napier 39 30s 176 56 E
82 Napier Broome, B. 14 0s 127 0 E
82 Napier Downs 16 20s 124 30 E
110 Napo, R. 3 20s 72 40w
100 Napoleon 46 32N 99 49w
39 Nápoli 40 50N 14 5 E
66 Nara 34 40N 135 49 E
66 Nara □ 34 30N 136 0 E
60 Nara, R. 24 7N 69 7 E
84 Naracoorte 36 50s 140 44 E
62 Narasapur 16 26N 81 50 E
62 Narasaraopet 16 14N 80 4 E
63 Narathiwat 6 40N 101 55 E
61 Narayanganj 23 31N 90 33 E
62 Narayanpet 16 45N 77 30 E
20 Narbonne 43 11N 3 0 E
30 Narcea, R. 43 28N 6 6w
39 Nardo 40 10N 18 0 E
83 Narembeen 32 4s 118 24 E
83 Naretha 31 0s 124 50 E
28 Narew 52 55N 23 30 E
28 Narew, R. 52 26N 20 42 E
60 Narmada, R. 21 35N 72 35 E
60 Narnaul 28 5N 76 11 E
37 Narni 42 30N 12 30 E
38 Naro 37 18N 13 48 E
60 Narowal 32 6N 74 52 E
81 Narrabri 30 19s 149 46 E
81 Narran, R. 29 45s 147 20 E
84 Narrandera 34 42s 146 31 E
83 Narrogin 32 58s 117 14 E
84 Narromine 32 12s 148 12 E
66 Naruto 35 36N 140 25 E
46 Narvik 68 28N 17 26 E
60 Narwana 29 39N 76 6 E
51 Naryilco 28 37s 141 53 E
50 Narym 59 0N 81 58 E
50 Narymskoye 49 10N 84 15 E
50 Naryn 41 30N 76 10 E
72 Nasarawa 8 32N 7 41 E
73 Naser, Buheiret en 23 0N 32 30 E
102 Nashua, Mont. 48 10N 106 25w
97 Nashua, N.H. 42 50N 71 25w
99 Nashville 36 12N 86 46w
40 Nasice 45 32N 18 4w
60 Nasik 20 2N 73 50 E
60 Nasirabad, Bangladesh 26 15N 74 45 E
60 Nasirabad, India 26 15N 74 45 E
61 Nasirabad, Pak. 28 25N 68 25 E
105 Nassau 25 0N 77 30w
112 Nassau, B. 55 20s 68 0w
73 Nasser, L.=Naser, Buheiret en 23 0N 32 30 E

45 Nässjö 57 38N 14 45 E
90 Nastapoka Is. 57 0N 77 0W
59 Nat Kyizio 14 55N 98 0 E
110 Natagaima 3 37N 75 6W
111 Natal, Brazil 5 47S 35 13W
64 Natal, Indonesia 0 35N 99 0 E
75 Natal □ 28 30S 30 30 E
91 Natashquan 50 14N 61 46W
91 Natashquan, R. 50 6N 61 49W
101 Natchez 31 35N 91 25W
101 Natchitoches 31 47N 93 4W
60 Nathdwara 24 55N 73 50 E
97 Natick 42 16N 71 19W
84 Natimuk 36 35S 141 59 E
72 Natitingou 10 20N 1 26 E
103 National City 32 45N 117 7W
111 Natividade 11 43S 47 47W
74 Natron, L. 2 20S 36 0 E
64 Natuna Besar, Kep. 4 0N 108 0 E
64 Natuna Selatan, Kep. 3 0N 109 55 E
20 Naucelle 44 13N 2 20 E
26 Nauders 46 54N 10 30 E
24 Nauen 52 36N 12 52 E
97 Naugatuck 41 28N 73 4W
24 Naumburg 51 10N 11 48 E
76 Naurn Is. 0 25N 166 0 E
58 Naushahra 33 9N 74 15 E
30 Nava del Rey 41 22N 5 6W
31 Navahermosa 39 41N 4 28W
103 Navajo Res. 36 55N 107 30W
30 Navalcarnero 40 17N 4 5W
30 Navalmoral de la Mata 39 52N 5 16W
15 Navan = An Uaimh 53 39N 6 40W
112 Navarino, I. 55 0S 67 30W
32 Navarra □ 42 40N 1 40W
20 Navarre, Reg. 43 15N 1 20 E
105 Navassa, I. 18 30N 75 0W
30 Navia 43 24N 6 42W
30 Navia, R. 43 32N 6 43W
30 Navia de Suarna 42 58N 6 59W
50 Navoi 40 9N 65 22 E
104 Navojoa 27 0N 109 30W
48 Navolok 62 33N 39 57 E
43 Návpaktos 38 23N 21 42 E
43 Návplion 37 33N 22 50 E
60 Navsari 20 57N 72 59 E
61 Nawabganj, Bangladesh 24 35N 81 14 E
61 Nawabganj, Ut.P. 28 32N 79 40 E
61 Nawabganj, Ut.P. 26 56N 81 14 E
60 Nawabshah 26 15N 68 25 E
61 Nawada 24 50N 85 25 E
60 Nawalgarh 27 50N 75 15 E
43 Náxos, I. 37 5N 25 30 E
57 Nāy Band 27 20N 52 40 E
51 Nayakhan 62 10N 159 0 E
104 Nayarit □ 22 0N 105 0W
111 Nazaré, Brazil 13 0S 39 0W
31 Nazaré, Port. 39 36N 9 4W
54 Nazareth, Israel 32 42N 35 17 E
97 Nazareth, U.S.A. 40 44N 75 19W
59 Nazir Hat 22 35N 91 55 E
74 N'Délé 8 25N 20 36 E
74 Ndendé 2 29S 10 46 E
73 Ndjamena 12 4N 15 8 E
75 Ndola 13 0S 28 34 E
15 Neagh, L. 54 35N 6 25W
43 Neápolis, Kozan 40 20N 21 24 E
43 Neápolis, Kriti 35 15N 25 36 E
43 Neápolis, Lakonia 36 27N 23 8 E
88 Near Is. 53 0N 172 0W
13 Neath 51 39N 3 49W
80 Nebo 39 27N 90 47W
100 Nebraska □ 41 30N 100 0W
100 Nebraska City 40 40N 95 52W
25 Neckar, R. 49 31N 8 26 E
108 Necochea 38 30S 58 50W
103 Needles 34 50N 114 35W
108 Ñeembucú □ 27 0S 58 0W
60 Neemuch 24 30N 74 50 E
100 Neenah 44 10N 88 30W
93 Neepawa 50 20N 99 30W
72 Nefta 33 53N 7 58 E
49 Neftyannyye Kamni 40 20N 50 55 E
12 Nefyn 52 57N 4 31W
62 Negapatam = Nagappattinam 10 46N 79 38 E
98 Negaunee 46 30N 87 36W
63 Negeri Sembilan □ 2 50N 102 10 E
41 Negoiu, Mt. 45 48N 24 32 E
62 Negombo 7 12N 79 50 E
40 Negotin 44 16N 22 37 E
65 Negra Pt. 18 40N 120 50 E
110 Negra, Pta. 6 6S 81 10W
30 Negreira 42 54N 8 45W
112 Negro, R., Arg. 41 2S 62 47W
110 Negro, R., Brazil 3 10S 59 58W
65 Negros, I. 10 0N 123 0 E
41 Negru Vodă 43 47N 28 21 E
57 Nehbandān 31 35N 60 5 E
25 Neheim 51 27N 7 58 E
41 Nehoiaşu 45 24N 26 20 E
69 Neikiang 29 35N 105 10 E
30 Neira de Jusá 42 53N 7 14W
28 Neisse, R. 52 4N 14 47 E
110 Neiva 2 56N 75 18W
73 Nekemte 9 4N 36 30 E
30 Nelas 40 32N 7 52W
51 Nelkan 57 50N 136 15 E
62 Nellikuppam 11 46N 79 43 E
62 Nellore 14 27N 79 59 E
51 Nelma 47 30N 139 0 E
92 Nelson, Canada 49 30N 117 20W
85 Nelson, N.Z. 41 18S 173 16 E
12 Nelson, U.K. 53 50N 2 14W
85 Nelson □ 42 11S 172 15 E
112 Nelson, Estrecho 51 30S 75 0W
93 Nelson, R. 55 30N 96 50W
92 Nelson Forks 59 30N 124 0W
75 Nelspruit 25 29⅜ 30 59 E
72 Néma 16 40N 7 15W
19 Nemours 48 16N 2 40 E
66 Nemuro 43 20N 145 35 E
66 Nemuro-Kaikyō, Str. 43 30N 145 30 E
51 Nemuy 55 40N 135 55 E
15 Nenagh 52 52N 8 11W
88 Nenana 63 34N 149 7W
12 Nene, R. 52 48N 0 13 E
42 Néon Petritsi 41 16N 23 15 E
101 Neosho 35 59N 95 10W
61 Nepal ■ 28 0N 84 30 E
102 Nephi 39 43N 111 52W
97 Neptune City 40 13N 74 4W
40 Néra, R. 42 26N 12 24 E
20 Nérac 44 19N 0 20 E
51 Nerchinsk 52 0N 116 39 E
51 Nerchinskiyzavod 51 10N 119 30 E
40 Neretva, R. 43 1N 17 27 E
40 Neretvanski, Kanal 43 7N 17 10 E
31 Nerja 36 43N 3 55W
33 Nerpio 38 11N 2 16W
31 Nerva 37 42N 6 30W
54 Nes Ziyyona 31 56N 34 48W
54 Nesher 32 45N 35 3 E
44 Neslandvatn 58 57N 9 10 E
19 Nesle 49 45N 2 53 E
14 Ness, L. 57 15N 4 30W
42 Néstos, R. 41 20N 24 35 E
47 Nesttun 60 19N 5 21 E
54 Netanya 32 20N 34 51 E
16 Netherlands ■ 52 0N 5 30 E
61 Netrakona 24 53N 90 47 E
19 Nettancourt 48 51N 4 57 E
89 Nettilling L. 66 30N 71 0W
25 Neu-Isenburg 50 3N 8 42 E
25 Neu-Ulm 48 23N 10 2 E
24 Neubrandenburg 53 33N 13 17 E
24 Neubrandenburg □ 53 30N 13 20 E
25 Neuchâtel 47 0N 6 55 E
25 Neuchâtel □ 47 0N 6 55 E
25 Neuchâtel, L. de 46 53N 6 50 E
19 Neufchâteau 48 21N 5 40 E
18 Neufchâtel 49 43N 1 30 E
19 Neufchâtel -sur-Aisne 49 26N 4 0 E
18 Neuillé-Pont-Pierre 47 33N 0 33 E
25 Neumarkt 49 16N 11 28 E
24 Neumünster 54 4N 9 58 E
26 Neunkirchen, Austria 47 43N 16 4 E
25 Neunkirchen, Germany 49 23N 7 6 E
112 Neuquén 38 0S 68 0 E
108 Neuquén □ 38 0S 69 50W
24 Neuruppin 52 56N 12 48 E
27 Neusiedler See, L. 47 50N 16 47 E
24 Neuss 51 12N 6 39 E
25 Neustadt, Bayern 49 42N 12 10 E
25 Neustadt, Bayern 50 23N 11 0 E
24 Neustadt, Potsdam 52 50N 12 27 E
24 Neustadt, Rheinland-Pfalz 49 21N 8 10 E
24 Neustrelitz 53 22N 13 4 E
20 Neuvic 45 23N 2 16 E
20 Neuville 45 52N 4 51 E
19 Neuville-aux-Bois 48 4N 2 3 E
20 Neuvy-St.-Sépulchre 46 35N 1 48 E
24 Neuwied 50 26N 7 29 E
101 Nevada 37 20N 94 40W
102 Nevada □ 39 20N 117 0W
31 Nevada, Sa. 37 3N 3 15W
110 Nevada de Sta. Marta, Sa. 10 55N 73 50W
51 Nevanka 56 45N 98 55 E
20 Nevers 47 0N 3 9 E
84 Nevertire 31 50S 147 44 E
105 Nevis, I. 17 0N 62 30W
98 New Albany 38 20N 85 50W
110 New Amsterdam 6 15N 57 30W
97 New Bedford 41 40N 70 52W
99 New Bern 35 8N 77 3W
101 New Braunfels 29 43N 98 9W
85 New Brighton, N.Z. 43 29S 172 43 E
96 New Brigthton, U.S.A. 40 44N 80 19W
97 New Britain 41 41N 72 47W
76 New Britain, I. 6 0S 151 0 E
97 New Brunswick 40 30N 74 28W
91 New Brunswick □ 46 50N 66 30W
76 New Caledonia, I. 21 0S 165 0 E
98 New Castle, Ind. 39 55N 85 23W
96 New Castle, Pa. 41 0N 80 20W
97 New City 41 8N 74 0W
60 New Delhi 28 37N 77 13 E
92 New Denver 50 0N 117 25W
13 New Forest, Reg. 50 53N 1 40W
91 New Glasgow 45 35N 62 36W
76 New Guinea, I. 4 0S 146 0 E
97 New Hampshire □ 43 40N 71 40W
97 New Haven 41 20N 72 54W
101 New Iberia 30 2N 91 54W
76 New Ireland, I. 3 0S 151 30 E
98 New Jersey □ 39 50N 74 10W
96 New Kensington 40 36N 79 43W
90 New Liskeard 47 31N 79 41W
97 New London 41 23N 72 8W
103 New Mexico □ 34 30N 106 0W
83 New Norcia 30 58S 116 13 E
80 New Norfolk 42 46S 147 2 E
101 New Orleans 30 0N 90 5W
96 New Philadelphia 40 29N 81 25W
85 New Plymouth 39 4S 174 5 E
105 New Providence I. 25 0N 77 30W
13 New Radnor 52 15N 3 10W
97 New Rochelle 40 55N 73 46W
13 New Romney 50 59N 0 57 E
79 New South Wales □ 33 0S 146 0 E
100 New Ulm 44 15N 94 30W
91 New Waterford 46 13N 60 4W
92 New Westminster 49 10N 122 52W
97 New York 40 45N 74 0W
97 New York □ 42 40N 76 0W
12 Newark, U.K. 53 6N 0 48W
97 Newark, N.J. 40 41N 74 12W
96 Newark, N.Y. 43 2N 77 10W
96 Newark, Ohio 40 5N 82 30W
99 Newberry 46 20N 85 32W
97 Newburgh 41 30N 74 1W
13 Newbury 51 24N 1 19W
97 Newburyport 42 48N 70 50W
84 Newcastle, Australia 32 52S 151 49 E
91 Newcastle, Canada 47 1N 65 38W
15 Newcastle, Eire 52 27N 9 3W
75 Newcastle, S.Africa 27 45S 29 58 E
15 Newcastle, N. Ireland 54 13N 5 54W
12 Newcastle, Tyne and Tees 54 59N 1 37W
13 Newcastle Emlyn 52 2N 4 29W
80 Newcastle Waters 17 30S 133 28 E
12 Newcastle-under-Lyme 53 2N 2 15W
96 Newcomerstown 40 16N 81 36W
83 Newdegate 33 17N 118 58 E
54 Newe Etan 32 30N 35 32 E
54 Newe Sha'anan 32 47N 34 59 E
54 Newe Zohar 31 9N 35 21 E
88 Newenham, C. 58 37N 162 12W
91 Newfoundland □ 48 28N 56 0W
91 Newfoundland, I. 48 30N 56 0W
13 Newhaven 50 47N 0 4 E
82 Newman, Mt. 23 20S 119 34 E
15 Newmarket, Eire 52 13N 9 0W
13 Newmarket, U.K. 52 15N 0 23 E
97 Newmarket, U.S.A. 43 4N 70 56W
99 Newnan 33 22N 84 48W
13 Newport, Gwent 51 35N 3 0W
13 Newport, I. of Wight 50 42N 1 18W
101 Newport, Ark. 35 38N 91 15W
98 Newport, Ky. 39 5N 84 23W
97 Newport, N.H. 43 23N 72 8W
102 Newport, Oreg. 44 41N 124 2W
97 Newport, Rhode I. 41 30N 71 19W
103 Newport Beach 33 40N 117 58W
98 Newport News 37 2N 76 54W
13 Newquay 50 24N 5 6W
15 Newry 54 10N 6 20W
15 Newry & Mourne □ 54 10W 6 20W
100 Newton, Iowa 41 40N 93 3W
101 Newton, Kans. 38 2N 97 30W
97 Newton, N.J. 41 3N 74 46W
13 Newton Abbot 50 32N 3 37W
96 Newton Falls 41 11N 80 59W
14 Newton Stewart 54 57N 4 30W
14 Newtonmore 57 4N 4 7W
84 Newtown, Australia 54 37N 5 40W
13 Newtown, U.K. 52 31N 3 19W
15 Newtownabbey □ 54 40N 5 55W
15 Newtownards 54 37N 5 40W
48 Neya 58 21N 43 49 E
57 Neyshābūr 36 10N 58 20 E
62 Neyyattinkara 8 26N 77 5 E
49 Nezhin 51 5N 31 55 E
75 Ngami Depression 20 30S 22 46 E
65 Nganjuk 7 32S 111 55 E
73 Ngaoundéré 7 15N 13 35 E
85 Ngapara 44 57S 170 46 E
65 Ngawi 7 24S 111 26 E
67 Ngoring Nor, L. 34 50N 98 0 E
72 Nguru 12 56N 10 29 E
63 Nha Trang 12 16N 109 10 E
84 Nhill 36 18S 141 40 E
96 Niagara Falls, Canada 43 7N 79 5W
96 Niagara Falls, U.S.A. 43 5N 79 0W
64 Niah 3 58S 113 46 E
72 Niamey 13 27N 2 6 E
74 Niangara 3 50N 27 50 E
64 Nias, I. 1 0N 97 40 E
36 Nibbiano 44 54N 9 20 E
105 Nicaragua ■ 11 40N 85 30W
39 Nicastro 39 0N 16 18 E
21 Nice 43 42N 7 14 E
66 Nichinan 31 28N 131 26 E
82 Nicholson Ra. 27 12S 116 40 E
53 Nicobar Is. 9 0N 93 0 E
92 Nicola 50 8N 120 40W
90 Nicolet 46 17N 72 35W
56 Nicosia = Levkosia, Cyprus 35 10N 33 25 E
39 Nicosia, Italy 37 45N 14 22 E
39 Nicótera 38 33N 15 57 E
105 Nicoya, G. de 10 0N 85 0W
105 Nicoya, Pen. de 9 45N 85 40W
27 Nida, R. 50 18N 20 52 E
12 Nidd, R. 54 1N 1 12W
28 Nidzica 53 25N 20 28 E
24 Niebüll 54 45N 8 49 E
19 Niederbronn 48 57N 7 39 E
26 Niederösterreich □ 48 25N 15 40 E
24 Niedersachsen □ 52 45N 9 0 E
26 Niedere Tauern, Mts 47 18N 14 E
24 Nienburg 52 38N 9 15 E
24 Niesky 51 18N 14 48 E
111 Nieuw Amsterdam 5 53N 55 5W
111 Nieuw Nickerie 6 0N 57 10W
30 Nieves 42 7N 7 26W
19 Nièvre □ 47 10N 5 40 E
56 Niğde 37 59N 34 42 E
72 Niger ■ 13 30N 10 0 E
72 Niger, R. 5 33N 6 33 E
72 Nigeria ■ 8 30N 8 0 E
85 Nightcaps 45 57S 168 14 E
66 Niigata 37 58N 139 0 E
66 Niigata □ 37 15N 138 45 E
66 Niihama 33 55N 133 10 E
94 Niihau, I. 21 55N 160 10W
66 Niimi 34 59N 133 28 E
16 Nijkerk 52 13N 5 30 E
16 Nijmegen 51 50N 5 52 E
65 Nikiniki 9 40S 124 30 E
49 Nikolayev 46 58N 32 7 E
49 Nikolayevsk 50 10N 45 35 E
51 Nikolayevskna-Am 53 40N 140 50 E
41 Nikopol, Bulgaria 43 43N 24 54 E
49 Nikopol, U.S.S.R. 47 35N 34 25 E
40 Nikšić 42 50N 18 57 E
73 Nîl, Nahr en, R. 30 10N 31 6 E
73 Nîl el Abyad, R. 15 40N 32 30 E
73 Nîl el Azraq, R. 11 40N 32 30 E
73 Nîl el Azraq □ 12 30N 34 30 E
103 Niland 33 16N 115 30W
73 Nile, R. = Nîl, Nahren, R. 30 10N 31 6 E
96 Niles 41 8N 80 40W
62 Nilgiri Hills 11 30N 76 30 E
60 Nimbahera 24 37N 74 45 E
21 Nîmes 43 50N 4 23 E
42 Nimfaíon, Akra, G. 40 5N 24 20 E
84 Nimmitabel 36 29S 149 15 E
51 Nimneryskiy 58 0N 125 10 E
74 Nimule 3 32N 32 3 E
31 Nindigully 28 21S 148 49 E
84 Ninety Mile Beach, The 38 30S 147 10 E
56 Nineveh 36 25N 43 10 E
69 Ningming 22 10N 107 59 E
69 Ningpo 29 50N 121 30 E
68 Ningsia Hui □ 37 45N 106 0 E
69 Ningteh 26 45N 120 0 E
68 Ningwu 39 2N 112 15 E
63 Ninh Binh 20 15N 105 55 E
16 Ninove 50 51N 4 2 E
109 Nioaque 21 5S 55 50W
100 Niobrara, R. 42 45N 98 0W
72 Nioro 13 40N 15 50W
20 Niort 46 19N 0 29W
62 Nipani 16 20N 74 25 E
93 Nipawin 53 20N 104 0W
93 Nipawin Prov. Park 54 0N 104 40W
90 Nipigon 49 0N 88 17W

90 Nipigon, L. 49 40N 88 30W
111 Niquelandia 14 27S 48 27W
62 Nira, R. 17 58N 7 8E
66 Nirasaki 35 42N 138 27E
62 Nirmal 19 3N 78 20E
40 Niš 43 19N 21 58E
31 Nisa 39 30N 2 41W
55 Nisab 14 25N 46 29E
40 Nišava, R. 43 22N 21 46E
39 Niscemi 37 8N 14 21E
66 Nishinomiya 34 45N 135 20E
43 Nísiros, I. 36 35N 27 12E
45 Nissan, R. 43 22N 21 46E
45 Nissum, Fd. 56 20N 8 11E
109 Niterói 22 52S 43 0W
14 Nith, R. 55 0N 3 35W
27 Nitra 48 19N 18 4E
27 Nitra, R. 47 46N 18 10E
16 Nivelles 50 35N 4 20E
19 Nivernais, Reg. 47 0N 3 40E
62 Nizamabad 18 45N 78 7E
59 Nizamghat 28 20N 95 45E
51 Nizhne Kolymsk 68 40N 160 55E
50 Nizhne-Vartovskoye 60 56N 76 38E
51 Nizhneangarsk 56 0N 109 30E
51 Nizhneudinsk 55 0N 99 20E
50 Nizhniy Tagil 57 45N 60 0E
56 Nizip 37 1N 37 46E
27 Nizké Tatry, Mts. 48 55N 20 0E
54 Nizzanim 31 42N 34 37E
74 Njombe 9 0S 34 35E
72 Nkambe 6 35N 10 40E
72 Nkawkaw 6 36N 0 49W
74 Nkhata Bay 11 33S 34 16E
75 Nkhota Kota 12 55S 34 15E
72 Nkongsamba 4 55N 9 55E
88 Noatak 67 34N 162 59W
66 Nobeoka 32 36N 131 41E
30 Noblejas 39 58N 3 26W
39 Nocera Inferiore 40 45N 14 37E
39 Noci 40 47N 17 7E
66 Noda 47 30N 142 5E
104 Nogales, Mexico 31 36N 94 29W
103 Nogales, U.S.A. 31 33N 110 59W
66 Nōgata 33 48N 130 54E
18 Nogent-le-Rotrou 48 20N 0 50E
19 Nogent-sur-Seine 48 30N 3 30E
83 Noggerup 33 32S 116 5E
51 Noginsk 55 50N 38 25E
108 Nogoya 32 24S 59 50W
27 Nograd □ 48 0N 19 30E
30 Nogueira de Ramuin 42 21N 7 43W
32 Noguera Pallaresa, R. 42 15N 0 54E
32 Noguera Ribagorzana, R. 41 40N 0 43E
60 Nohar 29 11N 74 49E
63 Noi, R. 17 5N 105 2E
18 Noire, Mts., Finistere 48 11N 3 40W
20 Noire, Mts., Tarn 43 26N 2 12W
20 Noirétable 45 48N 3 46E
20 Noirmoutier 47 0N 2 15W
20 Noirmoutier, Î. de 46 58N 2 10W
58 Nok Kundi 28 50N 62 45E
51 Nokhhuysk 60 0N 117 45E
39 Nola 40 54N 14 29E
21 Nolay 46 58N 4 35E
36 Noli, C. di 44 12N 8 26E
88 Nome 64 30N 165 30W
18 Nonancourt 48 47N 1 11E
18 Nonant-le-Pin 48 42N 0 12E
80 Nonda 20 40S 142 28E
63 Nong Khae 14 29N 100 53E
63 Nong Khai 17 50N 102 46E
20 Nontron 45 31N 0 40E
82 Noonamah 12 38S 131 4E
81 Noondoo 28 35S 148 30E
16 Noord Beveland, I. 51 45N 3 50E
16 Noord Brabant □ 51 40N 5 0E
16 Noord Holland □ 52 30N 4 45E
16 Noordoost-Polder 52 45N 5 45E
16 Noordwijk 52 14N 4 26E
92 Nootka I. 49 40N 126 50W
44 Nora 59 32N 15 2E
90 Noranda 48 20N 79 0E
44 Norberg 60 4N 15 56E
37 Nórcia 42 50N 13 5E
19 Nord □ 50 15N 3 30E
24 Nord-Friesische, Is. 54 50N 8 20E
24 Nord-Ostsee Kanal 54 5N 9 15E
24 Nord-Süd Kanal 53 0N 10 32E
4 Nordaustlandet 79 55N 23 0E
45 Nordborg 55 5N 9 50E
24 Norddeich 53 37N 7 10E
92 Nordegg 52 29N 116 5W
24 Norden 53 35N 7 12E
24 Nordenham 53 29N 8 28E
24 Norderney 53 42N 7 9E
24 Norderney, I. 53 42N 7 15E
24 Nordhausen 51 29N 10 47E
24 Nordhorn 52 27N 7 4E
46 Nordkapp, Norway 71 11N 25 48E
4 Nordkapp, Svalbard 80 31N 20 0E
46 Nordland □ 65 40N 13 0E
25 Nördlingen 48 50N 10 30E
24 Nordrhein Westfalen □ 51 45N 7 30E
24 Nordstrand, I. 54 27N 8 50E
51 Nordvik 73 40N 110 57E
45 Nordyllands □ 57 0N 10 0E
15 Nore, R. 52 25N 6 58W
100 Norfolk, Nebr. 42 3N 97 25W
98 Norfolk, Va. 36 52N 76 15W
12 Norfolk □ 52 39N 1 0E
76 Norfolk I. 28 58S 168 3E
51 Norilsk 69 20N 88 0E
100 Normal 40 30N 89 0W
101 Norman 35 12N 97 30W
88 Norman Wells 65 40N 126 45W
18 Normandie, Reg. 48 45N 0 10E
18 Normandie, Collines de 48 55N 0 45W
90 Normandin 48 49N 72 31W
80 Normanton 17 40S 141 10E
83 Nornalup 35 0S 116 49E
112 Norquinco 41 51S 70 55W
45 Norrahammar 57 43N 14 7E
46 Norrbotten □ 66 45N 23 0E
45 Nørresundby 57 5N 9 52E
97 Norristown 40 9N 75 15W
45 Norrköping 58 37N 16 11E
44 Norrtälje 59 46N 18 42E
83 Norseman 32 8S 121 43E
45 Norsholm 58 31N 15 59E
51 Norsk 52 30N 130 0E
111 Norte, C. do 1 40N 49 55W
85 North, C. 34 23S 173 4E
85 North I. 38 0S 176 0E
97 North Adams 42 42N 73 6W
1 North America 45 0N 100 0W
63 North Andaman, I. 13 15N 92 40E
6 North Atlantic Ocean 30 0N 50 0W
93 North Battleford 52 50N 108 10W
90 North Bay 46 20N 79 30W
90 North Belcher Is. 56 30N 79 0W
92 North Bend, Canada 49 50N 121 35W
102 North Bend, Oreg. 43 28N 124 7W
96 North Bend, Pa. 41 20N 77 42W
14 North Berwick 56 4N 2 44W
99 North Carolina □ 35 30N 80 0W
14 North Channel 55 0N 5 30W
98 North Chicago 42 19N 87 50W
100 North Dakota □ 47 30N 100 0W
83 North Dandalup 32 31S 115 58E
15 North Down □ 54 40N 5 45W
13 North Downs 51 17N 0 30W
9 North European Plain 55 0N 25 0E
13 North Foreland, Pt. 51 22N 1 28E
92 North Kamloops 50 40N 120 25W
68 North Korea ■ 40 0N 127 0E
59 North Lakhimpur 27 15N 94 10E
14 North Minch 58 5N 5 55W
100 North Platte 41 10N 100 50W
4 North Pole 90 0N 0 0E
14 North Ronaldsay, I. 59 20N 2 30W
93 North Saskatchewan, R. 53 15N 105 6W
8 North Sea 56 0N 4 0E
91 North Sydney 46 12N 60 21W
97 North Syracuse 43 8N 76 8W
96 North Tonawanda 43 5N 78 50W
101 North Truchas Pk. 36 0N 105 30W
12 North Tyne, R. 54 59N 2 8W
14 North Uist, I. 57 40N 7 15W
92 North Vancouver 49 25N 123 20W
105 North Village 32 15N 64 45W
12 North Walsham 52 49N 1 22E
82 North West, C. 21 45S 114 9E
14 North West Highlands, Mts. 57 35N 5 2W
88 North West Territories □ 65 0N 100 0W
12 North York Moors 54 25N 0 50W
12 North Yorkshire □ 54 10N 1 25W
12 Northallerton 54 20N 1 26W
83 Northam 31 35S 116 42E
83 Northampton, Australia 28 21S 114 33E
13 Northampton, U.K. 52 14N 0 54W
97 Northampton, Mass. 42 22N 72 39W
97 Northampton, Pa. 40 38N 75 24W
13 Northampton □ 52 16N 0 55W
80 Northampton Downs 24 35S 145 48E
83 Northcliffe 34 36S 116 7E
24 Northeim 51 42N 10 0E
15 Northern Ireland ■ 54 45N 7 0W
78 Northern Territory □ 16 0S 133 0E
100 Northfield 44 37N 93 10W
97 Northport 45 8N 85 39W
12 Northumberland □ 55 12N 2 0W
80 Northumberland, Is. 21 45S 150 20E
91 Northumberland Str. 46 20N 64 0W
12 Northwich 53 16N 2 30W
88 Norton Sd. 64 0N 165 0W
24 Nortorf 54 14N 10 47E
97 Norwalk, Conn. 41 7N 73 27W
96 Norwalk, Ohio 41 15N 82 37W
46 Norway ■ 67 0N 11 0E
93 Norway House 53 55N 98 50W
5 Norwegian Dependency 75 0S 15 0E
4 Norwegian Sea 66 0N 1 0E
12 Norwich, U.K. 52 38N 1 17E
97 Norwich, Conn. 41 33N 72 5W
97 Norwich, N.Y. 42 32N 75 30W
97 Norwood 42 10N 71 10W
50 Nosok 70 10N 82 20E
57 Nosratabad 29 55N 60 0E
14 Noss Hd. 58 29N 3 4W
75 Nossob, R. 26 55S 20 37E
28 Noteć R. 52 44N 15 26E
43 Notios Evvoïkos, Kól. 38 20N 24 0E
92 Notikewin 57 15N 117 5W
39 Noto 36 52N 15 4E
44 Notodden, Reg. 59 35N 9 17E
91 Notre Dame B. 49 45N 55 30W
89 Notre Dame de Koartac=Koartac 60 55N 69 40W
89 Notre Dame d'Ivugivik=Ivugivik 62 20N 78 0W
96 Nottawasaga B. 44 40N 80 30W
12 Nottingham 52 57N 1 10W
12 Nottinghamshire □ 53 10N 1 0W
72 Nouadhibou 21 0N 17 0W
72 Nouakchott 18 20N 15 50W
76 Noumea 22 17S 166 30E
75 Nouport 31 10S 24 57E
90 Nouveau Comptoir 53 2N 78 55W
19 Nouzonville 49 48N 4 44E
27 Nová Bana 48 28N 18 39E
26 Nová Bystrice 49 2N 15 8E
111 Nova Cruz 6 28S 35 25W
109 Nova Esperança 23 8S 52 13W
109 Nova Friburgo 22 10S 42 30W
111 Nova Granada 20 29S 49 19W
40 Nova Gradiška 45 17N 17 28E
109 Nova Iguaçu 22 45S 43 28W
75 Nova Lisboa=Huambo 12 42S 15 54E
26 Nova Paka 50 29N 15 30E
91 Nova Scotia □ 45 10N 63 0W
75 Nova Sofola 20 7S 34 48E
111 Nova Venecia 18 45S 40 24E
41 Nova Zagora 42 32N 25 59E
41 Novaci 45 10N 23 42E
36 Novara 45 27N 8 36E
48 Novaya Ladoga 60 7N 32 16E
50 Novaya Lyalya 58 50N 60 35E
51 Novaya Sibir, Os. 75 10N 150 0E
50 Novaya Zemlya, I. 75 0N 56 0E
27 Nové Mesto 49 33N 16 7E
27 Nové Zámky 47 59N 18 11E
33 Novelda 38 24N 0 45W
36 Novellara 44 50N 10 43E
48 Novgorod 58 30N 31 25E
40 Novi Bečej 45 36N 20 10E
40 Novi Kneževac 46 4N 20 8E
41 Novi Krichim 42 22N 24 31E
36 Novi Lígure 44 45N 8 47E
41 Novi Pazar, Bulgaria 43 25N 27 15E
40 Novi Pazar, Yug. 43 12N 20 28E
40 Novi-Sad 45 18N 19 52E
37 Novi Vinodolski 45 10N 14 48E
109 Nôvo Hamburgo 29 37S 51 7W
109 Novo Horizonte 21 28S 49 13W
74 Novo Redondo 11 10S 13 48E
49 Novocherkassk 47 27N 40 5E
50 Novokazalinsk 45 40N 61 40E
48 Novokiybyshevsk 53 7N 49 58E
50 Novo-kuznetsk 54 0N 87 10E
48 Novomoskovsk 54 5N 38 15E
49 Novorossiyk 44 43N 37 52E
49 Novoshakhtinsk 47 39N 39 58E
50 Novosibirsk 55 0N 83 5E
51 Novosibirskiye Os. 75 0N 140 0E
48 Novotroitsk 51 10N 58 15E
49 Novouzensk 50 32N 48 17E
40 Novska 45 19N 17 0E
26 Novy Bydžov 50 14N 15 29E
28 Nŏvy Dwór 52 26N 20 44E
27 Nový Jičín 49 15N 18 0E
57 Now Shahr 36 40N 51 40E
84 Nowa Nowa 37 44S 148 3E
28 Nowa Sól 51 48N 15 44E
28 Nowe Warpno 53 42N 14 18E
59 Nowgong 26 20N 92 50E
28 Nowogrod 53 14N 21 53E
84 Nowra 34 53S 150 35E
27 Nowy Sącz 49 40N 20 41E
30 Noya 42 48N 8 53W
18 Noyant 47 30N 0 6E
19 Noyers 47 40N 4 0E
19 Noyon 49 34N 3 0E
18 Nozay 47 34N 1 38W
75 Nsanje 16 55S 35 12E
72 Nsawam 5 50N 0 24W
75 Nuanetsi 21 22S 30 45E
70 Nubian Des. 21 30N 33 30E
73 Nûbîya, Es Sahrâ en 21 30N 33 30E
108 Ñuble □ 37 0S 72 0W
108 Nueva Palmira 33 52S 58 20W
104 Nueva Rosita 28 0N 101 20W
108 Nueve de Julio 35 30S 60 50W
105 Nuevitas 21 30N 77 20W
112 Nuevo, G. 43 0S 64 30W
104 Nuevo Laredo 27 30N 99 40W
104 Nuevo León □ 25 0N 100 0W
85 Nuhaka 39 3S 177 45E
19 Nuits 47 10N 4 56E
21 Nuits St. Georges 47 10N 4 56E
73 Nukheila 19 1N 26 21E
50 Nukus 42 20N 59 40E
88 Nulato 64 43N 158 6W
32 Nules 39 51N 0 9W
82 Nullagine 21 53S 120 6E
83 Nullarbor 31 26S 130 55E
83 Nullarbor Plain 31 20S 128 0E
66 Numata 36 38N 139 3E
66 Numazu 35 7N 138 51E
44 Numedal 60 6N 9 6E
84 Numurkah 36 0S 145 26E
13 Nuneaton 52 32N 1 29W
88 Nunivak I. 60 0N 166 0W
68 Nunkiang 49 11N 125 12E
16 Nunspeet 52 21N 5 45E
38 Núoro 40 20N 9 20E
25 Nürnberg 49 26N 11 5E
64 Nusa Tenggara Barat 8 50S 117 30E
65 Nusa Tenggara Timur □ 9 30S 122 0E
58 Nushki 29 35N 65 59E
89 Nutak 57 30N 61 59W
62 Nuwara Eliya 6 58N 80 55E
75 Nuweveldberge 32 10S 21 45E
62 Nuzvid 16 47N 80 51E
83 Nyabing 33 30S 118 7E
97 Nyack 41 5N 73 57W
74 Nyahanga 2 20S 33 37E
73 Nyâlâ 12 2N 24 58E
75 Nyasa, L. 12 0S 34 30E
45 Nyborg 55 18N 10 47E
45 Nybro 56 44N 15 55E
50 Nyda 66 40N 73 10E
67 Nyenchen, Ra. 30 30N 95 0E
74 Nyeri 0 23S 36 56E
27 Nyirbátor 47 49N 22 9E
27 Nyíregyháza 48 0N 21 47E
46 Nykarleby 63 32N 22 31E
45 Nykøbing 54 56N 11 52E
45 Nykøbing Mors 56 49N 8 51E
45 Nyköping 58 45N 17 0E
75 Nylstroom 24 42S 28 22E
26 Nymburk 50 10N 15 1E
44 Nynäshamn 58 54N 17 57E
84 Nyngan 31 30S 147 8E
25 Nyon 46 23N 6 14E
21 Nyons 44 22N 5 10E
84 Nyora 38 20S 145 41E
27 Nysa 50 40N 17 22E
28 Nysa, R. 52 4N 14 46E
51 Nyurba 63 17N 118 20E
74 Nzega 4 10S 33 12E
72 Nzérékoré 7 49N 8 48W

O

100 Oahe Dam 44 28N 100 25W
100 Oahe Res. 45 30N 100 15W
94 Oahu, I. 21 30N 158 0W
102 Oak Creek 40 15N 106 59W
98 Oak Park 41 55N 87 45W
99 Oak Ridge 36 1N 84 5W
101 Oakdale 30 50N 92 28W
12 Oakengates 52 42N 2 29W
102 Oakesdale 47 11N 117 9W
81 Oakey 27 25S 151 43E
12 Oakham 52 40N 0 43W
103 Oakland 37 50N 122 18W
84 Oakleigh 37 54S 145 6E
96 Oakmont 40 31N 79 50W
82 Oakover, R. 20 43S 120 33E
102 Oakridge 43 47N 122 31W
93 Oakville, Man. 49 56N 97 58W

96 Oakville, Ont. 43 27N 79 41W
85 Oamaru 45 6S 170 58E
41 Oancea 45 4N 28 7E
104 Oaxaca □ 17 0N 97 0W
50 Ob, R. 62 40N 66 0E
90 Oba 49 4N 84 7W
14 Oban 56 25N 5 30W
92 Obed 53 30N 117 10W
109 Obera 27 21S 55 2W
25 Oberammergau 47 35N 11 3E
26 Oberdrauburg 46 44N 12 58E
24 Oberhausen 51 28N 6 50E
96 Oberlin 41 15N 82 10W
26 Oberösterreich □ 48 10N 14 0E
25 Oberpfälzer Wald 49 30N 12 25E
25 Oberstdorf 47 25N 10 16E
31 Obidos 1 50S 55 30W
66 Obihiro 42 55N 143 10E
24 Öbisfelde 52 27N 10 57E
51 Obluchye 49 10N 130 50E
28 Oborniki 52 39N 16 59E
37 Obrovac 44 11N 15 41E
50 Obskaya Guba 70 0N 73 0E
72 Obuasi 6 17N 1 40W
41 Obzor 42 50N 27 52E
99 Ocala 29 11N 82 5W
110 Ocaña, Col. 8 15N 73 20W
110 Ocaña, Sp. 39 55N 3 30W
110 Occidental, Cord. 5 0N 76 0W
98 Ocean City 39 18N 74 34W
92 Ocean Falls 52 25N 127 40W
76 Ocean I. 0 45S 169 50E
102 Oceanlake 45 0N 124 0W
103 Oceanside 33 13N 117 26W
14 Ochil Hills 56 14N 3 40W
44 Ockelbo 60 54N 16 45E
100 Oconto 44 52N 87 53W
104 Ocatlán 20 21N 102 42W
18 Octeville 49 38N 1 40W
110 Ocumare del Tuy 10 7N 66 46W
65 Ocussi 9 20S 124 30E
66 Ōda 5 50N 1 5W
46 Odáđahraun 65 5N 17 0W
45 Ödåkra 56 9N 12 45E
66 Odawara 35 20N 139 6E
47 Odda 60 3N 6 35E
45 Odder 55 58N 10 10E
55 Oddur 4 0N 43 35E
56 Ödemiş 38 15N 28 0E
45 Odense 55 22N 10 23E
25 Odenwald, Mts. 49 18N 9 0E
28 Oder=Odra R. 53 0N 14 12E
49 Odessa 46 30N 30 45E
101 Odessa 31 51N 102 23W
31 Odiel, R. 37 30N 6 55W
72 Odienné 9 30N 7 34W
41 Odorhei 46 21N 25 21E
28 Odra, R., Poland 53 33N 14 38E
30 Odra, R., Sp. 42 30N 4 15W
40 Odžaci 45 30N 19 17E
75 Odzi 18 58S 32 23E
111 Oeiras 7 0S 42 8W
24 Oelsnitz 50 24N 12 11E
100 Oelwein 42 39N 91 55W
82 Oenpelli 12 20S 133 4E
39 Ofanto, R. 41 8N 15 50E
72 Offa 8 13N 4 42E
15 Offaly □ 53 20N 7 30W
25 Offenbach 50 6N 8 46E
25 Offenburg 48 27N 7 56E
90 Ogahalla 50 6N 85 51W
66 Ōgaki 35 25N 136 35E
100 Ogallala 50 6N 85 51W
72 Ogbomosho 8 1N 3 29E
102 Ogden 41 13N 112 1W
97 Ogdensburg 44 40N 75 27W
36 Oglio, R. 45 15N 10 15E
80 Ogmore 22 37S 149 35E
90 Ogoki 51 35N 86 0W
74 Ogooué, R. 1 0S 10 0E
37 Ogulin 45 16N 15 16E
112 O'Higgins, L. 49 0S 72 40W
108 O'Higgins □ 34 15S 71 1W
85 Ohakune 39 24S 175 24E
101 Ohio, R. 38 0N 86 0W
98 Ohio □ 40 20N 83 0W
25 Ohre, R. 50 10N 12 30E
40 Ohrid 41 8N 20 52E
40 Ohrid, L.= Ohridsko, J. 41 8N 20 52E
40 Ohridsko, J. 41 8N 20 52E
111 Oiapoque 3 50N 51 50W
96 Oil City 41 26N 79 40W
19 Oise, R. 49 53N 3 50E
19 Oise □ 49 28N 2 30E
66 Ōita 33 15N 131 36E
108 Ojos del Salado, Cerro, Mt. 27 0S 68 40W
75 Okahandja 22 0S 16 59E
102 Okanagan 48 24N 119 24W
60 Okara 30 50N 73 25E
85 Okarito 43 15S 170 9E
75 Okavango, R. 17 40S 19 30E
75 Okavango Swamps 19 30S 23 0E
66 Okaya 36 0N 138 10E
66 Okayama 34 40N 133 54E
66 Okayama □ 35 0N 133 50E
66 Okazaki 34 36N 137 0E
99 Okeechobee, L. 21 0N 80 50W
99 Okefenokee Swamp 30 50N 82 15W
13 Okehampton 50 44N 4 1W
72 Okene 7 32N 6 11E
25 Oker, R. 52 7N 10 34E
51 Okha 53 40N 143 0E
43 Ókhi Óros 38 5N 24 25E
51 Okhotsk 59 20N 143 10E
51 Okhotsk, Sea of 55 0N 145 0E
51 Okhotskiy Perevoz 61 52N 135 35E
51 Oknotsko kolymskoy 63 0N 157 0E
66 Oki-Shotō 36 15N 133 15E
75 Okiep 29 39S 17 53E
69 Okinawa, I. 26 40N 128 0E
69 Okinawa-guntō, Is. 26 0N 127 30E
101 Oklahoma □ 35 20N 97 30W
101 Oklahoma City 35 25N 97 30W
101 Okmulgee 35 38N 96 0W
72 Okrika 4 47N 7 4E
51 Oktyabriskoy Revolyutsii Os. 79 30N 97 0E
48 Oktyabrski 53 11N 48 40E
85 Okura 43 55S 168 55E
66 Okushiri-Tō, I. 42 15N 139 30E
45 Öland, I. 56 45N 16 50E
81 Olary 32 17S 140 19E
100 Olathe 38 50N 94 50W
108 Olavarría 36 55S 60 20W
27 Oława 50 57N 17 20E
38 Ólbia 40 55N 9 30E
38 Ólbia, G. di 40 55N 9 35E
96 Olcott 43 20N 78 43W
88 Old Crow 67 35N 139 50W
90 Old Factory 52 36N 78 43W
97 Old Forge 41 22N 75 44W
99 Old Town 45 0N 68 50W
15 Oldcastle 53 46N 7 10W
24 Oldenburg 53 10N 8 10E
24 Oldenburg 54 16N 10 53E
16 Oldenzaal 52 19N 6 53E
92 Olds 51 50N 114 10W
96 Olean 42 8N 78 25W
28 Olecko 54 3N 22 30E
51 Olekminsk 60 40N 120 30E
48 Olenegorsk 68 9N 33 15E
51 Olenek 68 20N 112 30E
20 Oléron, Î. d' 45 55N 1 15W
28 Oleśnica 51 13N 17 22E
51 Olga 43 50N 135 0E
83 Olga, Mt. 25 20S 130 40E
31 Olhão 37 3N 7 48W
75 Olifants, R. 24 10S 32 40S
109 Olímpia 20 44S 48 54W
108 Olimpo □ 20 30S 58 45W
32 Olite 42 29N 1 40W
33 Oliva 38 58N 0 15W
108 Oliva 32 0S 63 38W
30 Oliva, Pta. del 43 37N 5 28W
31 Oliva de la Frontera 38 17N 6 54W
32 Olivares 39 46N 2 20W
109 Oliveira 20 50S 44 50W
30 Oliveira de Azemeis 40 49N 8 29W
31 Olivenza 38 41N 7 9W
92 Oliver 49 20N 119 30W
27 Olkusz 50 18N 19 33E
30 Olmedo 41 20N 4 43W
98 Olney 38 40N 88 0W
45 Olofström 56 17N 14 32E
27 Olomouc 49 38N 17 12E
32 Olot 42 11N 2 30E
40 Olovo 44 8N 18 35E
51 Olovyannaya 50 50N 115 10E
24 Olpe 51 2N 7 50E
28 Olsztyn 53 48N 20 29E
28 Olsztyn □ 54 0N 21 0E
41 Olt, R. 43 50N 24 40E
25 Olten 47 21N 7 53E
41 Oltenita 44 7N 26 42E
32 Oluego 41 47N 2 0W
31 Olvera 36 55N 5 18W
102 Olympia 47 0N 122 58W
102 Olympic Mts. 48 0N 124 0W
102 Olympic Nat. Park 47 35N 123 30W
102 Olympus Mt. 47 52N 123 40W
42 Olympus, Mt.= Óros Ólimbos 40 6N 22 23E
97 Olyphant 41 27N 75 36W
15 Omagh 54 36N 7 20W
15 Omagh □ 54 35N 7 20W
100 Omaha 41 15N 96 0W
102 Omak 48 25N 119 24W
55 Oman ■ 23 0N 58 0E
57 Oman, G. of 24 30N 58 30E
75 Omaruru 21 26S 16 0E
110 Omate 16 45S 71 0W
65 Ombai, Selat, Str. 8 30S 124 50E
36 Ombrone, R. 42 48N 11 15E
73 Omdurmân 15 40N 32 28E
36 Omegna 45 52N 8 23E
54 Omez 32 22N 35 0E
37 Omiš 43 28N 16 40E
66 Ōmiya 35 54N 139 38E
74 Omo, R. 8 48N 37 14E
50 Omsk 55 0N 73 38E
41 Omul, Mt. 45 27N 25 29E
28 Omulew, R. 53 5N 21 32E
66 Ōmura 33 8N 130 0E
41 Omurtag 43 8N 26 26E
66 Ōmuta 33 0N 130 26E
30 Oña 42 43N 3 25W
32 Onda 39 55N 0 17W
75 Ondangua 17 57S 16 4E
30 Ondárroa 43 19N 2 25W
72 Ondo 7 4N 4 47E
68 Ondörhaan 47 22N 110 31E
48 Onega 64 0N 38 10E
48 Onega, R. 63 0N 39 0E
85 Onehunga 36 55N 174 30E
97 Oneida 43 5N 75 40W
97 Oneida L. 43 12N 76 0W
100 O'Neill 42 30N 98 38W
97 Oneonta 42 26N 75 5W
48 Onezhskaya Guba 64 30N 37 0E
48 Onezhskoye, Oz 62 0N 35 30E
85 Ongarue 38 42S 175 19E
83 Ongerup 33 58S 118 29E
62 Ongole 15 33N 80 2E
72 Onitsha 6 6N 6 42E
66 Onoda 34 2N 131 10E
30 Ons, Is. 42 23N 8 55W
82 Onslow 21 40S 115 0E
16 Onstwedde 52 2N 7 4E
66 Ontake-San, Mt. 35 50N 137 15E
103 Ontario 34 2N 117 40W
96 Ontario, L. 43 40N 78 0W
90 Ontario □ 52 0N 88 10W
33 Onteniente 38 50N 0 35W
81 Oodnadatta 27 33S 135 30E
83 Ooldea 30 27S 131 50E
80 Oorindi 20 40S 141 1E
16 Oostende 51 15N 2 50E
16 Oosterhout 51 38N 4 51E
16 Oosterschelde, R. 51 30N 4 0E
62 Ootacamund 11 30N 76 44E
51 Opala, U.S.S.R. 52 15N 156 15E
74 Opala, Zaïre 0 37S 24 21E
37 Opatija 45 21N 14 17E
27 Opava 49 57N 17 58E
101 Opelousas 30 35N 92 0W
88 Ophir 63 10N 156 31W
28 Opoczno 51 22N 20 18E
27 Opole 50 42N 17 58E
27 Opole □ 50 40N 17 56E
85 Opotiki 38 1S 177 19E
99 Opp 31 19E 86 13W
39 Oppido Mamertina 38 16N 15 59E
44 Oppland □ 61 15N 9 30E
93 Optic Lake 54 46N 101 13W
85 Opua 35 19S 174 9E
85 Opunake 39 26S 173 52E
40 Opuzen 43 1N 17 34E
19 Or, Côtes d' 47 10N 4 50E
54 Or Yehuda 32 2N 34 50E
37 Ora 46 20N 11 19E
27 Oradea 47 2N 21 58E
46 Öraefajökull, Mt. 64 2N 16 15W
61 Orai 25 58N 79 30E
72 Oran 35 37N 0 39W
84 Orange, Australia 33 15S 149 7E
21 Orange, Fr. 44 8N 4 47E
101 Orange, U.S.A. 30 0N 93 40W
75 Orange=Oranje, R. 28 30S 18 0E
111 Orange, C. 4 20N 51 30W
75 Orange Free State □ 28 30S 27 0E
104 Orange Walk 17 15N 88 47W
99 Orangeburg 33 27N 80 53W
90 Orangeville 43 55N 80 5W
24 Oranienburg 52 45N 13 15E
75 Oranje, R. 28 41S 16 28E
75 Oranje-Vrystaat □ 28 30S 27 0E
75 Oranjemund 28 32S 16 29E
75 Orapa 24 13S 25 25E
40 Orašje 45 1N 18 42E
41 Orăştie 45 50N 23 10E
40 Oravita 45 6N 21 43E
20 Orb, R. 43 15N 3 18E
25 Orbe 46 43N 6 32E
37 Orbetello 42 26N 11 11E
84 Orbost 37 40S 148 29E
44 Örbynus 60 15N 17 43E
33 Orce 37 44N 2 28W
33 Orce, R. 37 44N 2 28W
19 Orchies 50 28N 3 14E
14 Orchy, Bridge of 56 30N 4 46W
82 Ord, Mt. 17 20S 125 34E
82 Ord, R. 15 30S 128 21E
14 Ord of Caithness 58 35N 3 37W
82 Ord River 17 23S 128 51E
30 Ordenes 43 5N 8 29W
56 Ordu 40 55N 37 53E
30 Orduña 42 58N 2 58W
31 Orduña, Mt. 37 20N 3 30W
49 Ordzhonlkidze 43 0N 44 35E
40 Orebic 43 0N 17 11E
44 Örebro 59 20N 15 18E
44 Örebro □ 59 27N 15 0E
102 Oregon □ 44 0N 120 0W
102 Oregon City 45 28N 122 35W
48 Orekhovo-Zuyevo 55 50N 38 55E
48 Orel 52 59N 36 5E
31 Orellana, Pantano de, L. 39 5N 5 10W
31 Orellana La Vieja 39 1N 5 32W
102 Orem 40 27N 111 45W
48 Orenburg 51 45N 55 6E
30 Orense 42 19N 7 55W
30 Orense □ 42 15N 7 30W
85 Orepuki 46 19S 167 46E
42 Orestiás 41 30N 26 33E
45 Øresund 55 45N 12 45E
13 Orford Ness, C. 52 6N 1 31E
21 Orgon 43 47N 5 3E
39 Ória 40 30E 17 38E
90 Orient Bay 49 20N 88 10W
110 Oriental, Cord. 5 0N 74 0W
19 Origny 49 50N 3 30E
33 Orihuela 38 7N 0 55W
90 Orillia 44 40N 79 24W
110 Orinoco, R. 8 37N 62 15W
93 Orion 49 28N 110 49W
61 Orissa □ 21 0N 85 0E
38 Oristano 39 54N 8 35E
38 Oristano, G. di 39 50N 8 22E
104 Orizaba 18 50N 97 10W
33 Orjiva 36 53N 3 24W
44 Orkanger 63 18N 9 52E
45 Orkelljunga 56 17N 13 17E
45 Örken 51 6N 6 34E
27 Orkery 47 9N 19 26E
14 Orkney □ 59 0N 3 0W
102 Orland 39 46N 120 10W
99 Orlando 28 30N 81 25W
19 Orléanais, Reg. 48 0N 2 0E
19 Orléans, Fr. 47 54N 1 52E
97 Orleans, U.S.A. 44 49N 72 10W
91 Orleans, I. d' 46 54N 70 58W
72 Orléansville=El Asnam 36 10N 1 20E
27 Orlické hory 50 15N 16 30E
51 Orlik 52 30N 99 55E
27 Orlov 49 17N 20 51E
58 Ormara 25 16N 64 33E
38 Ormea 44 9N 7 54E
65 Ormoc 11 0N 124 37E
85 Ormond 38 33S 177 56E
37 Ormož 46 25N 16 10E
12 Ormskirk 53 35N 2 54W
19 Ornans 47 7N 6 10E
18 Orne, R. 49 18N 0 14E
18 Orne □ 48 40N 0 0E
44 Örnsköldsvik 63 17N 18 40E
110 Orocué 4 48N 71 20W
30 Orol 43 34N 7 39W
91 Oromocto 45 54N 66 37W
54 Oron 30 55N 35 1E
30 Oropesa 39 57N 5 10W
111 Orós 6 15S 38 55W
42 Óros Ólimbos, Mt. 40 6N 22 23E
43 Óros Óthris, Mt. 39 4N 22 42E
38 Orosei, G. di 40 15N 9 40E
27 Orosháza 46 32N 20 42E
102 Oroville 39 40N 121 30W
81 Orroroo 32 44S 138 37E
96 Orrville 40 50N 81 46W
44 Orsa 61 7N 14 37E
48 Orsha 54 30N 30 25E
48 Orsk 51 20N 58 34E
40 Orşova 44 41N 22 25E
36 Orta, L. d' 45 48N 8 21E
39 Orta Nova 41 20N 15 40E
30 Ortegal, C. 43 43N 7 52W
20 Orthez 43 29N 0 48W
30 Ortigueira 43 40N 7 50W
36 Ortles, Mt. 46 31N 10 33E
37 Ortona 42 21N 14 24E
110 Oruro 18 0S 67 19W
18 Orvault 47 17N 1 38E
37 Orvieto 42 43N 12 8E
13 Orwell, R. 51 57N 1 17E
41 Oryakhovo 43 40N 23 57E
36 Orzinuovi 45 24N 9 55E
28 Orzyc, R. 52 47N 21 13E
28 Orzysz 53 50N 21 58E
105 Osa, Pen. de 8 0N 84 0W
100 Osage, R. 38 35N 91 57W
66 Ōsaka 34 40N 135 30E
66 Ōsaka □ 34 40N 135 30E
100 Osborne 39 30N 98 45W

45 Osby 56 23N 13 59E
101 Osceola 35 40N 90 0W
25 Oschatz 51 17N 13 8E
24 Oschersleben 52 2N 11 13E
38 Oschiri 40 43N 9 7E
40 Osečina 44 23N 19 34E
96 Oshawa 43 50N 78 45W
100 Oshkosh 44 3N 88 35W
72 Oshogbo 7 48N 4 37E
41 Osica de Jos 44 14N 24 20E
28 Osieczna 51 55N 16 40E
40 Osijek 45 34N 18 41E
37 Osimo 43 40N 13 30E
49 Osipenko= Berdyansk 46 45N 36 49E
100 Oskaloosa 41 18N 92 40W
45 Oskarshamn 57 15N 16 27E
44 Oslo 59 55N 10 45E
44 Oslofjorden 58 30N 10 0E
62 Osmanabad 18 5N 76 10E
56 Osmaniye 37 5N 36 10E
24 Osnabrück 52 16N 8 2E
109 Osorio 29 53S 50 17W
112 Osorno 40 25S 73 0W
16 Oss 51 46N 5 32E
80 Ossa, Mt. 41 80S 146 0E
33 Ossa de Montiel 38 58N 2 45W
97 Ossining 41 9N 73 50W
24 Oste, R. 53 33N 9 10E
16 Ostend=Oostende 51 15N 2 50E
24 Osterburg 52 47N 11 44E
44 Østerdalen 62 0N 10 40E
45 Östergötlands □ 58 24N 15 34E
24 Osterholz-Scharmbeck 53 14N 8 48E
44 Östersund 63 10N 14 38E
44 Østfold □ 59 25N 11 25E
24 Ostfriesische Is. 53 45N 7 15E
25 Ostfriesland, Reg. 53 20N 7 40E
44 Östhammar 60 16N 18 22E
27 Ostrava 49 51N 18 18E
28 Ostrgog 52 37N 16 33E
28 Ostróda 53 42N 19 58E
28 Ostrołeka 53 4N 21 38E
28 Ostrołeka □ 53 0N 21 30E
41 Ostrov 43 40N 24 9E
28 Ostrów Mazowiecka 52 50N 21 51E
28 Ostrów Wielkopolski 51 39N 17 49E
27 Ostrowiec-Swietokrzyski 50 57N 21 23E
40 Ostrozac 43 43N 17 49E
28 Ostrzeszów 51 25N 17 52E
39 Ostuni 40 44N 17 34E
42 Osumi, R. 40 48N 19 52E
66 Ōsumi-Kaikyō, Str. 30 55N 131 0E
66 Ōsumi-Shotō, Is. 30 30N 130 45E
31 Osuna 37 14N 5 8W
97 Oswego 43 29N 76 30W
97 Oswego, R. 43 28N 76 31W
12 Oswestry 52 52N 3 3W
27 Oświęcim 50 2N 19 11E
85 Otago □ 44 45S 169 10E
66 Ōtake 34 27N 132 25E
85 Otaki 40 45S 175 10E
66 Otaru 43 13N 141 0E
26 Otava 61 39N 27 4E
110 Otavalo 0 20N 78 20W
42 Otelec 45 36N 20 50E
30 Otero de Rey 43 6N 7 36W
102 Othello 46 53N 119 8W
85 Otira Gorge 42 53S 171 33E
75 Otjiwarongo 20 30S 16 33E
85 Otorohanga 38 11S 175 12E
39 Otranto 40 9N 18 28E
39 Otranto, C. d' 40 7N 18 30E
66 Ōtsu 42 35N 143 40E
66 Otta 61 46N 9 32E
62 Ottapalam 10 46N 76 23E
90 Ottawa, Canada 45 27N 75 42W
100 Ottawa, Ill. 41 20N 88 55W
100 Ottawa, Kans 38 40N 95 10W
89 Ottawa Is. 59 50N 80 0W
90 Ottawa, R. 45 20N 73 58W
24 Otterndorf 53 47N 8 52E
93 Otter Rapids 55 42N 104 46W
26 Ottersheim 48 21N 14 12E
45 Otterup 55 30N 10 22E
100 Ottumwa 41 0N 92 25W
72 Oturkpo 7 10N 8 15E
112 Otway, B. 53 30S 74 0W
84 Otway, C. 38 52S 143 31E
112 Otway, Seno de 53 5S 71 30W
28 Otwock 52 5N 21 20E
26 Ötz 47 13N 10 53E
26 Ötztaler Alpen, Mts. 46 58N 11 0E
72 Ouagadougou 12 25N 1 30W
72 Ouallene 24 41N 1 11E
72 Ouargla 31 59N 5 25E
72 Ouarzazate 30 55N 6 55W
74 Oubangi, R. 0 30S 17 42E
19 Ouche, R. 47 6N 5 16E
16 Oudenaarde 50 50N 3 37E
18 Oudon 47 22N 1 19W
75 Oudtshoorn 33 35S 22 14E
18 Ouessant, I. d' 48 28N 5 6W
74 Ouesso 1 37N 16 5E
72 Ouezzane 34 51N 5 42W
72 Ouidah 6 25N 2 0E
72 Oujda 34 41N 1 45W
72 Ouled Djellal 34 28N 5 2E
46 Oulu 65 1N 25 29E
46 Oulu □ 64 36N 27 20E
46 Oulujärvi, L. 64 25N 27 0E
16 Our, R. 49 53N 6 18E
111 Ouricuri 7 53S 40 5W
109 Ourinhos 23 0S 49 54W
109 Ouro Fino 22 16S 46 25W
109 Ouro Prêto 20 20S 43 30W
80 Ouse 42 25S 146 42E
13 Ouse, R., E. Sussex 50 47N 0 3E
12 Ouse, R., N. Yorks 53 42N 0 41W
18 Oust, R. 47 39N 2 6W
75 Outjo 20 5S 16 7E
93 Outlook 51 30N 107 0W
19 Outreau 50 40N 1 36E
84 Ouyen 35 1S 142 22E
36 Ovada 44 39N 8 40E
85 Ovalau, I. 17 40S 178 48E
108 Ovalle 30 33S 71 18W
75 Ovamboland, Reg. 17 20S 16 30E
30 Ovar 40 51N 8 40E
16 Over Flakkee, I. 51 45N 4 5E
16 Overijssel □ 52 25N 6 35E
16 Overpelt 51 12N 5 20E
30 Oviedo 43 25N 5 50W
30 Oviedo □ 43 20N 6 0W
44 Oviksfjällen, Mts. 63 0N 13 49E
85 Owaka 46 27S 169 40E
66 Owase 34 7N 136 5E
100 Owatonna 44 3N 93 17W
97 Owego 42 6N 76 17W
90 Owen Sound 44 35N 80 55W
74 Owendo 0 17N 9 30E
98 Owensboro 37 40N 87 5W
72 Owo 7 18N 5 30E
98 Owosso 43 0N 84 10W
45 Oxelösund 58 43N 17 15E
13 Oxford, U.K. 51 45N 1 15W
97 Oxford, Mass. 42 7N 71 52W
99 Oxford, N.C. 36 19N 78 36W
13 Oxford □ 51 45N 1 15W
93 Oxford House 54 46N 95 16W
103 Oxnard 34 10N 119 14W
66 Oyama 36 18N 139 48E
74 Oyem 1 37N 11 35E
51 Oymyakon 63 25N 143 10E
72 Oyo 7 46N 3 56E
21 Oyonnax 46 16N 5 40E
97 Oyster Bay 40 52N 73 32W
65 Ozamiz 8 15N 123 50E
99 Ozark 31 29N 85 39W
86 Ozark Plat. 37 20N 91 40W
100 Ozarks, L. of the 38 10N 93 0W
38 Ozieri 40 35N 9 0E
28 Ozorków 51 57N 19 16E
41 Ozun 45 47N 25 50E

P

63 Pa Sak, R. 14 11 100 40E
67 Paan 30 0N 99 3E
59 Pa-an 16 45N 97 40E
75 Paarl 13 45S 18 46E
28 Pabianice 51 40N 19 20E
61 Pabna 24 1N 89 18E
110 Pacaraima, Sa. 5 0N 63 0W
110 Pacasmayo 7 20S 79 35W
38 Paceco 37 59N 12 32E
60 Pachhar 24 40N 77 42E
39 Pachino 36 43N 15 4E
60 Pachora 20 38N 75 29E
104 Pachuca 20 10N 98 40W
103 Pacific Groves 37 36N 121 58W
77 Pacific Ocean 10 0N 140 0W
18 Pacy 49 2N 1 22E
65 Padalarang 7 50S 107 30E
64 Padang 1 0S 100 20E
93 Paddockwood 53 30N 105 30W
24 Paderborn 51 42N 8 44E
88 Padlei 62 10N 97 5W
89 Padloping Island 67 0N 63 0W
62 Padmanabhapuram 8 16N 77 17E
37 Pádova 45 24N 11 52E
60 Padra 22 15N 73 7E
61 Padrauna 26 54N 83 59E
13 Padstow 50 33N 4 57W
98 Paducah, Ky. 37 0N 88 40W
101 Paducah, Tes. 34 3N 100 16W
85 Paeroa 37 23S 175 41E
37 Pag, I. 44 50N 15 0E
65 Pagadian 7 55N 123 30E
71 Pagalu, I. 1 35S 3 35E
43 Pagastikós Kól. 39 15N 23 12E
103 Page 47 11N 97 37W
57 Paghman 34 36N 68 57E
37 Paglieta 42 10N 14 30E
85 Pago Pago 14 16S 170 43W
103 Pagosa Springs 37 16N 107 1W
90 Pagwa River 50 2N 85 14W
94 Pahala 20 25N 156 0W
63 Pahang, R. 3 32N 102 28E
63 Pahang □ 3 30N 103 9E
85 Pahiatua 40 27S 175 50E
68 Paicheng 45 40N 122 52E
13 Paignton 50 26N 3 33W
18 Paimboeuf 47 17N 2 0W
18 Paimpol 48 48N 3 4W
96 Painesville 41 42N 81 18W
90 Paint Hills= Nouveau Comptoir 53 2N 78 55W
103 Painted Des. 36 40N 112 0W
14 Paisley 55 51N 4 27W
110 Paita 5 5S 81 0W
68 Paiyin 36 45N 104 4E
30 Pajares 43 0N 5 48W
63 Pak Lay 18 15N 101 27E
63 Pak Sane 18 22N 103 39E
62 Pakala 13 29N 79 8E
64 Pakanbaru 0 30N 101 15E
69 Pakhoi 21 30N 109 10E
58 Pakistan ■ 30 0N 70 0E
59 Pakokku 21 30N 95 0E
69 Pakongchow 23 50N 113 0E
60 Pakpattan 30 25N 73 16E
40 Pakrac 45 17N 17 12E
27 Paks 46 38N 18 55E
63 Pakse 15 5N 105 52E
57 Paktya □ 33 0N 69 15E
32 Palafrugell 41 55N 3 10E
39 Palagonía 37 20N 14 43E
43 Palaiokastron 35 12N 26 18E
62 Palakol 16 31N 81 46E
32 Palamós 41 50N 3 10E
51 Palana 59 10N 160 10E
64 Palangkaraya 2 16S 113 56E
60 Palanpur 24 10N 72 25E
75 Palapye 22 30S 27 7E
62 Palar, R. 12 28N 80 9E
99 Palatka 29 40N 81 40W
65 Palau Is. 7 30N 134 30E
63 Palauk 13 10N 98 40E
63 Palaw 13 0N 98 50E
64 Palawan, I. 10 0N 119 0E
64 Palawan Is. 10 0N 115 0E
62 Palayancottai 8 45N 77 45E
40 Pale 43 50N 18 38E
65 Paleleh 1 10N 121 50E
64 Palembang 3 0S 104 50E
30 Palencia 42 1N 4 34W
30 Palencia □ 42 31N 4 33W
38 Palermo 38 8N 13 20E
101 Palestine 31 42N 95 35W
59 Paletwa 21 30N 92 50E
62 Palghat 10 46N 76 42E
60 Pali 25 50N 73 20E
72 Palimé 6 57N 0 37E
100 Palisade 40 35N 101 10W
60 Palitana 21 32N 71 49E
62 Palk B. 9 30N 79 30E
62 Palkonda 18 36N 83 48E
62 Palkonda Ra. 13 50N 79 20N
80 Palm, Is. 18 40S 146 35E
103 Palm Springs 33 51N 116 35W
32 Palma 39 33N 2 39E
33 Palma, B. de 39 30N 2 39E
8 Palma, I. 28 45N 17 50W
31 Palma del Rio 37 43N 5 17W
38 Palma di Montechiaro 37 12N 13 46E
105 Palma Soriano 20 15N 76 0W
111 Palmares 8 41S 35 36W
109 Palmas 26 29S 52 0W
72 Palmas, C. 4 27N 7 46W
109 Palmeira 25 25S 50 0W
111 Palmeira dos Indios 9 25S 36 30W
31 Palmela 38 32N 8 57W
88 Palmer 61 35N 149 10W
5 Palmer Ld. 73 0S 60 0W
85 Palmerston 45 29S 170 43E
85 Palmerston North 40 21S 175 39E
97 Palmerton 40 47N 75 36W
39 Palmi 38 21N 15 51E
108 Palmira, Arg. 32 59S 68 25W
110 Palmira, Col. 3 32N 76 16W
97 Palmyra 34 5N 77 18W
77 Palmyra Is. 5 52N 162 5W
62 Palni 10 30N 77 30E
62 Palni Hills 10 14N 77 33E
103 Palo Alto 37 25N 122 8W
39 Palo del Colle 41 4N 16 43E
65 Palopo 3 0S 120 16E
33 Palos, C. de 37 38N 0 40W
56 Palu 38 45N 40 0E
60 Palwal 28 8N 77 19E
65 Pamekason 7 10S 113 29E
68 Pamiencheng 43 16N 124 4E
20 Pamiers 43 7N 1 39E
99 Pamlico Sd. 35 20N 76 0W
101 Pampa 35 35N 100 58W
65 Pampanua 4 22S 120 14E
106 Pampas, Reg. 34 0S 64 0W
110 Pamplona 7 23N 72 39W
32 Pana 39 25N 89 0W
41 Panagyurishte 42 49N 24 15E
62 Panaji 15 25N 73 50E
104 Panama 9 0N 79 25W
105 Panamá ■ 8 48N 79 55W
104 Panamá, B. de 8 50N 79 20W
105 Panamá, G. de 8 4N 79 20W
104 Panama Canal 9 10N 79 56W
99 Panama City 30 10N 105 41W
65 Panarukan 7 40S 113 52E
65 Panay, I. 11 10N 122 30E
65 Panay G. 11 0N 122 30E
40 Pančevo 44 52N 20 41E
30 Pancorbo, P. 42 32N 3 5W
62 Pandharpur 17 41N 75 20E
60 Pandhurna 21 36N 78 35E
109 Pando 34 30S 56 0W
50 Panfilov 44 30N 80 0E
59 Pang-Long 23 11N 98 45E
42 Pangaíon Óros 40 50N 24 0E
74 Pangani 5 25S 38 58E
64 Pangkalanberandan 4 1N 98 20E
64 Pangkalansusu 4 2N 98 42E
89 Pangnirtung 66 8N 65 44W
103 Panguitch 37 52N 112 30W
59 Pangyang 22 10N 98 45E
60 Panipat 29 25N 77 2E
84 Panitya 35 15S 141 0E
67 Panjao 34 21N 67 0E
58 Panjgur 27 0N 64 5E
62 Panjim=Panaji 15 25N 73 50E
64 Pankalpinang 2 0S 106 0E
61 Panna 24 40N 80 15E
62 Pannuru 16 5N 80 34E
109 Panorama 21 21S 51 51W
62 Panruti 11 46N 79 35E
68 Panshih 42 55N 126 3E
38 Pantellaria, I. 36 52N 12 0E
104 Pánuco 22 0N 98 25W
62 Panvel 18 59N 73 10E
72 Panyam 9 27N 9 8E
68 Paochang 41 46N 115 30E
69 Paoki 34 25N 107 15E
39 Páola 39 21N 16 2E
67 Paoshan 25 7N 99 9E
68 Paoting 38 50N 115 30E
68 Paotow 40 35N 110 3E
69 Paoying 33 10N 119 20E
27 Papá 47 22N 17 30E
105 Papagayo, G. del 10 4N 85 50W
62 Papagni, R. 14 10N 78 30E
85 Papakura 37 45S 174 59E
104 Papantla 20 45N 97 41W
64 Papar 5 45N 116 0E
43 Papas, Ákra 38 13N 21 6E
24 Papenburg 53 7N 7 25E
76 Papua New Guinea ■ 8 0S 145 0E
37 Papuča 44 22N 15 30E
40 Papuk, Mts. 45 30N 17 30E
111 Pará=Belém 1 20S 48 30W
111 Pará □ 3 20S 52 0W
111 Paracatú 17 10S 46 50W
81 Parachilna 31 10S 138 21E
40 Paraćin 43 54N 21 27E
33 Paradas 37 18N 5 29W
61 Paradip 20 15N 86 35E
102 Paradise 47 27N 114 54W
101 Paragould 36 5N 90 30W
109 Paraguaçu Paulista 22 22S 50 35W
110 Paraguaipoa 11 21N 71 57W
110 Paraguaná, Penide 12 0N 70 0W
108 Paraguari 25 36S 57 0W
108 Paraguarí □ 26 0S 57 10W
107 Paraguay ■ 23 0S 57 0W
108 Paraguay, R. 27 18S 58 38W
111 Paraiba □ 7 0S 36 0W
109 Paraíba do Sul, R. 21 37S 41 3W
47 Parainen 60 18N 22 18E
72 Parakou 9 25N 2 40E
43 Parálion-Astrous 37 25N 22 45E
62 Paramagudi 9 31N 78 39E
111 Paramaribo 5 50N 55 10W
108 Paraná, Arg. 32 0S 60 30W
111 Paraná, Brazil 12 30S 47 40W
108 Paraná, R. 33 43S 59 15W
109 Paraná □ 24 30S 51 0W
109 Paranaguá 25 30S 48 30W
109 Paranapanema, R. 22 40S 53 9W
109 Paranavaí 23 4S 52 28W

111 Paratinga 12 40s 43 10w
81 Paratoo 32 42s 139 22 E
21 Paray-le-Monial 46 27N 4 7 E
60 Parbati, R. 25 51N 76 34 E
62 Parbhani 19 8N 76 52 E
24 Parchim 53 25N 11 50 E
28 Parczew 51 9N 22 52 E
54 Pardes Hanna 32 28N 34 57 E
26 Pardubice 50 3N 15 45 E
65 Pare 7 43s 112 12 E
30 Paredes de Nava 42 9N 4 42w
51 Paren 62 45N 163 0 E
90 Parent 47 55N 74 35w
65 Parepare 4 0s 119 40 E
75 Parfuri 22 28s 31 17 E
48 Parguba 62 58N 34 25 E
105 Paria, G. de 10 20N 62 0w
110 Pariaguan 8 51N 64 43w
64 Pariaman 0 47s 100 11 E
65 Parigi 0 50s 120 5 E
110 Parika 6 50N 58 20w
41 Paring, Mt. 45 20N 23 37 E
111 Parintins 2 40s 56 50w
90 Paris, Canada 43 20N 80 25w
19 Paris, Fr. 48 50N 2 20 E
99 Paris, Tenn. 36 20N 88 20w
101 Paris, Tex. 33 40N 95 30w
19 Parisien, Bassin 49 0N 2 30 E
102 Park City 40 42N 111 35w
102 Park Ra. 40 0N 106 30w
46 Parkano 62 5N 23 0 E
103 Parker, Ariz. 34 8N 114 16w
100 Parker, S.D. 43 25N 97 7w
98 Parkersburg 39 18N 81 31w
93 Parkerview 51 28N 103 18w
84 Parkes 33 9s 148 11 E
92 Parksville 49 20N 124 21w
62 Parlakimedi 18 45N 84 5 E
36 Parma, Italy 44 50N 10 20 E
96 Parma, Ohio 44 25N 81 41 E
102 Parma, Id. 43 49N 116 59w
111 Parnaguá 10 10s 44 10w
111 Parnaíba, Piauí 3 0s 41 40w
111 Parnaiba, São Paulo 19 34s 51 14w
111 Parnaiba, R. 3 0s 41 50w
43 Parnassós, Mt. 38 17N 21 30 E
43 Parnis, Mt. 38 14N 23 45 E
43 Párnon Óros 37 15N 22 45 E
48 Pärnu 58 12N 24 33 E
60 Parola 20 47N 75 7 E
43 Páros, I. 37 5N 25 12 E
103 Parowan 37 54N 112 56w
21 Parpaillon, Reg. 44 30N 6 40 E
108 Parral 36 10s 72 0w
84 Parramatta 33 48s 151 1 E
104 Parras 25 30N 102 20w
13 Parrett, R. 51 13N 3 1w
91 Parrsboro 45 30N 64 10w
86 Parry Is. 77 0N 110 0w
90 Parry Sd. 42 20N 80 0w
101 Parsons 37 20N 95 10w
38 Partanna 37 43N 12 51 E
20 Parthenay 46 38N 0 16w
45 Partille 57 48N 12 18 E
38 Partinico 38 3N 13 6 E
62 Parur 10 13N 76 14 E
62 Parvatipuram 18 50N 83 25 E
57 Parwan □ 35 0N 69 0 E
103 Pasadena, Calif. 34 5N 118 0w
101 Pasadena, Tex. 29 45N 95 14w
110 Pasaje 3 10s 79 40w
101 Pascagoula 30 30N 88 30w
102 Pasco 46 10N 119 0w
19 Pas-de-Calais □ 50 30N 2 30 E
24 Pasewalk 53 30N 14 0 E
63 Pasir Mas 6 2N 102 8 E
63 Pasir Puteh 5 50N 102 24 E
65 Pasirian 8 13s 113 8 E
83 Pasley, C. 33 52s 123 35 E
112 Paso de Indios 43 55s 69 0w
108 Paso de los Libres 29 44s 57 10w
108 Paso de los Toros 32 36s 56 37w
103 Paso Robles 35 40N 120 45w
91 Paspébiac 48 3N 65 17w
15 Passage West 51 52N 8 20w
97 Passaic 40 50N 74 8w
25 Passau 48 34N 13 27 E
39 Passero, C. 36 42N 15 8 E
109 Passo Fundo 28 10s 52 30w
109 Passos 20 45s 46 29w
110 Pasto 1 13N 77 17w
65 Pasuruan 7 40s 112 53 E
106 Patagonia, Reg. 45 0s 69 0w
62 Patan 17 22N 73 48 E
65 Patani 0 20N 128 50 E
68 Pataokiang 41 58N 126 30 E
97 Patchogue 40 46N 73 1w
85 Patea 39 45s 174 30 E
39 Paterno 37 34N 14 53 E
97 Paterson 40 55N 74 10w
60 Pathankot 32 18N 75 45 E
102 Pathfinder Res. 42 0N 107 0w
60 Patiala 30 23N 76 26 E
41 Pătîrlagele 45 19N 26 22 E
59 Patkai Bum, Mts. 27 0N 95 30 E
43 Patmos, I. 37 21N 26 36 E
61 Patna 25 35N 85 18 E
109 Patos, L. dos 31 20s 51 0w
111 Patos de Minas 18 35s 46 32w
43 Pátrai 38 14N 21 47 E
43 Pátraikos Kól. 38 17N 21 30 E
111 Patrocínio 18 57s 47 0w
62 Pattanapuram 9 6N 76 33 E
39 Patti 31 17N 74 54 E
60 Pattoki 31 5N 73 52 E
62 Pattukkottai 10 25N 79 20 E
105 Patuca, R. 15 50N 84 18w
104 Pátzcuaro 19 30N 101 40w
20 Pau 43 19N 0 25w
20 Pauillac 45 11N 0 46w
59 Pauk 21 55N 94 30 E
111 Paulistana 8 9s 41 9w
111 Paulo Afonso 9 21s 38 15w
101 Paul's Valley 34 40N 97 17w
61 Pauni 20 48N 79 40 E
36 Pavia 45 10N 9 10 E
41 Pavlikeni 43 14N 25 20 E
50 Pavlodar 52 33N 77 0 E
49 Pavlograd 48 30N 35 52 E
48 Pavlovo, Gorkiy 55 58N 43 5 E
51 Pavlovo, Yakut A.S.S.R. 63 5N 115 25 E
49 Pavlovsk 50 26N 40 5 E
36 Pavullo nel Frignano 44 20N 10 50 E
97 Pawtucket 41 51N 71 22w
64 Payakumbah 0 20s 100 35 E
102 Payette 44 0N 117 0w
89 Payne Bay=Bellin 60 0N 70 0w
89 Payne L. 59 30N 74 30w
83 Paynes Find 29 15s 117 42 E
108 Paysandú 32 19s 58 8w
102 Payson 40 8N 111 41w
41 Pazardzhik 42 12N 24 20 E
37 Pazin 45 14N 13 56 E
102 Pe Ell 46 30N 122 59w
97 Peabody 42 31N 70 56w
93 Peace, R. 59 30N 111 30w
92 Peace River 56 15N 117 18w
92 Peace River, Res. 55 40N 123 40w
12 Peak, The., Mt. 53 24N 1 53w
80 Peak Downs Mine 22 17s 148 11 E
84 Peak Hill 32 39s 148 11 E
81 Peake 35 25s 140 0 E
94 Pearl City 21 21N 158 0w
94 Pearl Harbor 21 20N 158 0w
110 Pebas 3 10s 71 55w
40 Peć 42 40N 20 17 E
48 Pechenga 69 30N 31 25 E
48 Pechora 65 15N 57 0 E
48 Pechora, R. 68 13N 54 10 E
48 Pechorskaya Guba 68 40N 54 0 E
101 Pecos 31 25N 103 35w
101 Pecos, R. 29 42N 101 22w
27 Pécs 46 5N 18 15 E
62 Peddapalli 18 40N 79 24 E
62 Peddapuram 17 6N 82 5 E
111 Pedra Asul 16 1s 41 16w
105 Pedregal 8 22N 82 27w
111 Pedro Afonso 9 0s 48 10w
108 Pedro de Valdivia 22 36s 69 40w
109 Pedro Juan Caballero 22 30s 55 40w
33 Pedro Muñoz 39 25N 2 56w
30 Pedrógão Grande 39 55N 8 0w
14 Peebles 55 40N 3 12w
97 Peekskill 41 18N 73 57w
12 Peel 54 14N 4 40w
88 Peel, R. 67 0N 135 0w
24 Peene, R. 54 9N 13 46 E
85 Pegasus, B. 43 20s 173 10 E
26 Peggau 47 12N 15 21 E
59 Pegu 17 20N 96 29 E
59 Pegu Yoma, Mts. 19 0N 96 0 E
69 Peh Kiang, R. 23 10N 113 10 E
68 Pehan 48 17N 120 31 E
69 Pehpei 29 44N 106 29 E
108 Pehuajó 36 0s 62 0w
24 Peine 52 19N 10 12 E
111 Peixe 12 0s 48 40w
40 Pek, R. 44 58N 21 55 E
65 Pekalongan 6 53s 109 40 E
63 Pekan 3 30N 103 25 E
100 Pekin 40 35N 89 40w
68 Peking=Beijing 39 45N 116 25 E
65 Pelabuhan Ratu, Teluk, G. 7 0s 106 32 E
65 Pelabuhanratu 7 5s 106 30 E
42 Pélagos 39 17N 24 4 E
21 Pelat, Mt. 44 16N 6 42 E
65 Peleng, I. 1 20s 123 30 E
26 Pelhřimov 49 24N 15 12 E
93 Pelican Narrows 55 12N 102 55 E
92 Pelican Portage 55 51N 113 0w
93 Pelican Rapids 52 38N 100 42 E
40 Pelješac, I. 42 58N 17 20 E
42 Pélla □ 40 52N 22 0 E
24 Pellworm, I. 54 30N 8 40 E
88 Pelly, R. 62 47N 137 19w
89 Pelly Bay 68 53N 89 51w
43 Pelopónnissos, Reg. 37 10N 22 0 E
85 Pelorus, Sd. 40 59s 173 59 E
109 Pelotas 31 42s 52 23w
109 Pelotas, R. 27 38s 51 55w
21 Pelvoux, Massif du 44 52N 6 20 E
65 Pemalang 6 53s 109 23 E
64 Pematang 0 12s 102 4 E
64 Pematangsiantar 2 57N 99 5 E
75 Pemba 16 31s 27 22 E
74 Pemba I. 5 0s 39 45 E
83 Pemberton, Australia 34 30s 116 0 E
92 Pemberton, Canada 50 25N 122 50w
90 Pembroke, Canada 45 50N 77 15w
85 Pembroke, N.Z.=Wanaka 44 33s 169 9 E
13 Pembroke, U.K. 51 41N 4 57w
32 Peña, Sa. de la 42 32N 0 45w
30 Peña de Francia, Sa. de 40 32N 6 10w
30 Penafiel 41 12N 8 17w
30 Peñafiel 41 35N 4 7w
30 Peñalara, P. 40 51N 3 57w
109 Penápolis 21 24s 50 4w
30 Peñaranda de Bracamonte 40 53N 5 13w
31 Peñarroya-Pueblonuevo 38 19N 5 16w
30 Peñas, C. de 43 42N 5 52w
112 Penas, G. de 47 0s 75 0w
72 Pendembu 8 6N 10 45w
102 Pendleton 45 35N 118 50w
111 Penedo 10 15s 36 36w
90 Penetanguishene 44 50N 79 55w
69 Penghu, I. 23 30N 119 30 E
68 Penglai 37 49N 120 47 E
69 Pengpu 33 0N 117 25 E
80 Penguin 41 8s 146 6 E
31 Peniche 39 19N 9 22w
14 Penicuik 55 50N 3 14w
32 Peñíscola 40 22N 0 24 E
68 Penki 41 20N 132 50 E
18 Penmarch 47 49N 4 21w
18 Penmarch, Pte. de 47 48N 4 22w
37 Penne 42 28N 13 56 E
62 Penner, R. 14 35N 80 11 E
12 Pennine Ra. 54 50N 2 20w
98 Pennsylvania □ 40 50N 78 0w
92 Penny 53 58N 121 1w
99 Penobscot, R. 44 30N 68 50w
84 Penola 37 25s 140 47 E
105 Penonomé 8 37N 80 25w
77 Penrhyn Is. 9 0s 150 30w
84 Penrith, Australia 33 43s 150 38 E
12 Penrith, U.K. 54 40N 2 45w
99 Pensacola 30 30N 87 10w
5 Pensacola Mts. 84 0s 40 0w
92 Penticton 49 30N 119 30w
80 Pentland 20 32s 145 25 E
14 Pentland Firth 58 43N 3 10w
14 Pentland Hills 55 48N 3 25w
62 Penukonda 14 15N 77 38 E
12 Pen-y-Ghent, Mt. 54 10N 2 15w
48 Penza 53 15N 45 5 E
13 Penzance 50 7N 5 32w
100 Peoria 40 40N 89 40w
97 Pepacton Res. 42 6N 74 54w
64 Perabumilih 3 27s 104 15 E
63 Perak, R. 3 58N 100 53 E
63 Perak □ 5 0N 101 0 E
32 Perales de Alfambra 40 38N 1 0w
43 Pérama 35 20N 24 32 E
40 Perast 42 31N 18 47 E
18 Perche, Collines du 48 30N 0 30 E
18 Perche, Reg. 48 30N 1 0 E
82 Percival Lakes 21 25s 125 0 E
80 Percy, Is. 21 39s 150 16 E
20 Perdido, Mt. 42 40N 0 50 E
110 Pereira 4 49N 75 43w
49 Perekop 46 0N 33 0 E
83 Perenjori 29 26s 116 16 E
41 Peretu 44 3N 25 6 E
49 Pereyaslav khmelnitskiy 50 3N 31 28 E
104 Pérez, I. 22 40N 89 30w
26 Perg 48 15N 14 38 E
108 Pergamino 33 52s 60 30w
37 Pergine Valsugano 46 4N 11 15 E
91 Peribonca, R. 48 45N 72 5w
20 Perigord, Reg. 45 0N 0 40 E
20 Périgueux 45 10N 0 42 E
55 Perim, I. 12 39N 43 25 E
62 Periyakulam 10 5N 77 30 E
97 Perkasie 40 22N 75 18w
24 Perleberg 53 5N 11 50 E
40 Perlez 45 11N 20 22 E
63 Perlis □ 6 30N 100 15 E
48 Perm 58 0N 57 10 E
111 Pernambuco=Recife 8 0s 35 0w
111 Pernambuco □ 8 0s 37 0w
40 Pernik 42 36N 23 2 E
83 Peron, C. 25 30s 113 30 E
20 Perpignan 42 42N 2 53 E
18 Perros-Guirec 48 49N 3 28w
100 Perry, Iowa 41 48N 94 5w
101 Perry, Okla. 36 20N 97 20w
57 Persia=Iran ■ 35 0N 50 0 E
57 Persian G. 27 0N 50 0 E
45 Perstorp 56 10N 13 25 E
83 Perth, Australia 31 57s 115 52 E
90 Perth, Canada 44 55N 76 20w
14 Perth, U.K. 56 24N 3 27w
97 Perth Amboy 40 31N 74 16w
21 Pertuis 43 42N 5 30 E
110 Peru ■ 8 0s 75 0w
100 Peru, Ill. 41 18N 89 12w
98 Peru, Ind. 40 42N 86 0w
37 Perúgia 43 6N 12 24 E
49 Pervomaysk 48 5N 30 55 E
50 Pervouralsk 56 55N 60 0 E
37 Pésaro 43 55N 12 53 E
37 Pescara 42 28N 14 13 E
37 Pescara, R. 42 28N 14 13 E
36 Péscia 43 54N 10 40 E
58 Peshawar 34 2N 71 37 E
58 Peshawar □ 35 0N 72 50 E
30 Pêso da Régua 41 40N 7 47w
111 Pesqueira 8 20s 36 42w
20 Pessac 44 48N 0 37w
27 Pest □ 47 29N 19 5 E
41 Peşteana Jiu 44 50N 23 18 E
54 Petah Tiqwa 32 6N 34 53 E
63 Petaling Jaya 3 4N 101 42 E
102 Petuluma 38 13N 122 45w
16 Petange 49 33N 5 55 E
75 Petauke 14 14s 31 12 E
90 Petawawa 45 54N 77 17w
104 Petén Itzá, L. 16 58N 89 50w
90 Peterbell 48 36N 83 21w
81 Peterborough, Australia 32 58s 138 51 E
13 Peterborough, U.K. 52 35N 1 14w
96 Peterborough, U.S.A. 42 55N 71 57w
14 Peterhead 57 30N 1 49w
12 Peterlee 54 45N 1 18w
92 Petersburg, Alas. 56 50N 133 0w
98 Petersburg, Va. 37 17N 77 26w
39 Petília Policastro 39 7N 16 48 E
91 Petit Cap 48 58N 63 58w
105 Petit Goâve 18 27N 72 51w
91 Petitcodiac 45 57N 65 11w
91 Petite Saguenay 47 59N 70 1w
60 Petlad 22 30N 72 45 E
85 Petone 41 13s 174 53 E
98 Petoskey 45 21N 84 55w
32 Petra 39 37N 3 6 E
33 Petrel 38 30N 0 46 E
21 Petreto 41 24N 8 57 E
41 Petrich 41 24N 23 13 E
41 Petrila 45 29N 23 29 E
37 Petrinja 45 28N 16 18 E
111 Petrolandia 9 5s 38 20w
90 Petrolia 52 54N 82 9w
111 Petrolina 9 24s 40 30w
50 Petropavlovsk 55 0N 69 0 E
51 Petropavlovsk-kamchatskiy 53 16N 159 0 E
109 Petrópolis 22 33s 43 9w
41 Petroşeni 45 28N 23 20 E
41 Petrosica 45 14N 25 25 E
37 Petrova Gora, Mts. 45 15N 15 45 E
40 Petrovac 42 13N 18 57 E
40 Petrovaradin 45 16N 19 55 E
48 Petrovsk 52 22N 45 19 E
51 Petrovsk-Zdbaykalskiy 51 17N 108 50 E
48 Petrozavodsk 61 41N 34 20 E
64 Peureulak 4 48N 97 45 E
51 Pevek 69 15N 171 0 E
20 Peyrehorade 43 34N 1 7 E
21 Peyruis 44 1N 5 56 E
20 Pézenas 43 28N 3 24 E
25 Pforzheim 48 53N 8 43 E
25 Pfungstadt 49 47N 8 36 E
75 Phala 23 45s 26 50 E
60 Phalodi 27 12N 72 24 E
62 Phaltan 17 59N 74 25 E
63 Phan Thiet 11 1N 108 9 E
63 Phangna 8 28N 98 30 E
63 Phanh Bho Ho Chi Minh 10 58N 106 40 E
63 Phanom Dang Raek, Ra. 14 30N 104 0 E
67 Pharo Dzong 27 45N 89 14 E

63 Phatthalung 7 39N 100 6 E
99 Phenix City 32 30N 85 0W
63 Phetchaburi 16 25N 101 8 E
63 Phichai 17 22N 100 10 E
98 Philadelphia 40 0N 75 10W
42 Philippi 41 0N 24 19 E
8 Philippine Trench= Mindanao Trench 8 0N 128 0 E
65 Philippines ■ 12 0N 123 0 E
84 Phillip, I. 38 30S 145 12 E
97 Phillipsburg 40 43N 75 12W
81 Phillott 27 53S 145 50 E
102 Philomath 44 28N 123 21W
63 Phitsanulok 16 50N 100 12 E
63 Phnom Penh 11 33N 104 55 E
103 Phoenix 33 30N 112 10W
77 Phoenix Is. 3 30S 172 0W
97 Phoenixville 40 12N 75 29W
63 Phra Nakhon Si Ayutthaya 14 25N 100 30 E
63 Phu Doan 21 40N 105 10 E
63 Phu Loi, Mt. 20 14N 103 14 E
63 Phu Ly 20 35N 105 50 E
63 Phu Quoc, I. 10 15N 104 0 E
63 Phuket 8 0N 98 28 E
60 Phul 30 19N 75 14 E
36 Piacenza 45 2N 9 42 E
81 Pialba 25 20S 152 45 E
81 Pian Creek 30 2S 148 12 E
21 Piana 42 14N 8 38 E
31 Pias 38 1N 7 29W
28 Piaseczno 52 5N 21 2 E
28 Piastów 52 12N 20 48 E
41 Piatra 43 51N 25 9 E
111 Piani □ 7 0S 43 0W
37 Piave, R. 45 32N 12 44 E
39 Piazza Armerina 37 21N 14 20 E
19 Picardie, Plaine de 50 0N 2 0 E
19 Picardie, Reg. 50 0N 2 15 E
101 Picayune 30 40N 89 40W
12 Pickering 54 15N 0 46W
90 Pickle Crow 51 30N 90 0W
8 Pico, I. 38 28N 28 20W
112 Pico Truncado 46 40S 68 10W
30 Picos Anceres, Sa. de 42 51N 6 52W
19 Picquigny 49 56N 2 10 E
84 Picton, Australia 34 12S 150 34 E
90 Picton, Canada 44 1N 77 9W
85 Picton, N.Z. 41 18S 174 3 E
91 Pictou 45 41N 62 42W
92 Picture Butte 49 55N 112 45W
112 Picún Leufú 39 30S 69 5W
62 Pidurutalagala, Mt. 7 10N 80 50 E
31 Piedrabuena 39 0N 4 10W
103 Piedras Blancas Pt. 35 45N 121 18W
104 Piedras Negras 28 35N 100 35W
36 Piermonte □ 45 0N 7 30 E
97 Piercefield 44 13N 74 35W
42 Piería □ 40 13N 22 25 E
100 Pierre 44 23N 100 20W
19 Pierrefonds 49 20N 3 0 E
27 Pieštany 48 35N 17 50 E
75 Piet Retief 27 1S 30 50 E
39 Pietraperzia 37 26N 14 8 E
75 Pietermaritzburg 29 35S 30 25 E
75 Pietersburg 23 54S 29 25 E
36 Pietrasanta 43 57N 10 12 E
90 Pigeon River 48 1N 89 42W
108 Pigüé 37 36S 62 25W
75 Piketberg 32 55S 18 40 E
98 Pikeville 37 30N 82 30W
28 Piła 53 10N 16 48 E
28 Piła □ 53 0N 17 0 E
108 Pilar 26 50S 58 10W
111 Pilar 14 30S 49 45W
28 Piława 51 58N 21 31 E
108 Pilcomayo, R. 25 21S 57 42W
61 Pilibhit 28 40N 78 50 E
28 Pilica, R. 51 52N 21 17 E
42 Pilion, Mt. 39 27N 23 7 E
60 Pilkhawa 28 43N 77 42 E
28 Pillau=Baltiisk 54 38N 19 55 E
43 Pilos 36 55N 21 42 E
103 Pima 32 54N 109 50W
81 Pimba 31 18S 136 46 E
63 Pinang □ 5 25N 100 15 E
105 Pinar del Rio 22 26N 83 40W
93 Pinawa 50 15N 95 50W
92 Pincher Creek 49 30N 113 35W
60 Pind Dadan Khan 32 55N 73 47 E
83 Pindar 28 30S 115 47 E
72 Pindiga 9 58N 10 53 E
42 Pindos Óros 40 0N 21 0 E
42 Pindus Mts.= Pindos Óros 40 0N 21 0 E
91 Pine, C. 46 37N 53 30W
101 Pine Bluff 34 10N 92 0W
82 Pine Creek 13 49S 131 49 E
93 Pine Falls 50 51N 96 11W
92 Pine Point 60 50N 114 40W
48 Pinega, R. 64 8N 41 54 E
80 Pinehill 23 38S 146 57 E
36 Pinerolo 44 47N 7 21 E
37 Pineto 42 36N 14 4 E
75 Pinetown 29 48S 30 54 E
101 Pineville 31 22N 92 30W
19 Piney 48 22N 4 21 E
63 Ping, R. 15 42N 100 9 E
83 Pingaring 32 40S 118 32 E
83 Pingelly 32 29S 116 59 E
69 Pingkiang 28 45N 113 30 E
68 Pingliang 35 32N 106 50 E
69 Pingsiang 22 2N 106 55 E
69 Pingtingshan 33 43N 113 28 E
69 Pingtung 22 38N 120 30 E
68 Pingyao 37 12N 112 10 E
109 Pinhal 22 10S 46 46W
30 Pinhel 40 18N 7 0W
68 Pinhsien 35 10N 108 10 E
83 Pinjarra 32 37S 115 52 E
84 Pinnaroo 35 13S 140 56 E
105 Pinos, I. de 21 40N 82 40W
103 Pinos, Pt. 36 50N 121 57W
31 Pinos Puente 37 15N 3 45W
65 Pinrang 3 46S 119 34 E
48 Pinsk 52 10N 26 8 E
93 Pinto Butte, Mt. 49 22N 107 25W
83 Pintumba 31 50S 132 18 E
69 Pinyang 23 12N 108 35 E
48 Pinyug 60 5N 48 0 E
103 Pioche 38 0N 114 35N
36 Piombino 42 54N 10 30 E
28 Pionki 51 29N 21 28 E
28 Piotrków Trybunalski 51 23N 19 43 E
28 Piotrków Trybunalski □ 51 20N 19 30 E
60 Pipar 26 25N 73 31 E
60 Pipariya 22 45N 78 23 E
100 Pipestone 44 0N 96 20W
91 Pipmuacan Res. 49 40N 70 25W
82 Pippingarra 20 27S 118 42 E
98 Piqua 40 10N 84 10W
109 Piracicaba 22 45S 47 30W
111 Piracuruca 3 50S 41 50W
43 Piraeus= Piraiévs 37 57N 23 42 E
43 Piraiévs 37 57N 23 42 E
43 Piraiévs □ 37 0N 23 30 E
109 Pirajui 21 59S 49 29W
37 Piran 45 31N 13 33 E
108 Pirané 25 44S 59 7W
41 Pirdop 42 40N 24 10 E
43 Pirgos, Ilia 37 40N 21 27 E
43 Pírgos, Messinia 36 50N 22 16 E
18 Piriac-sur-Mer 47 23N 2 31W
108 Piribebuy 25 29S 57 3W
111 Piripiri 4 15S 41 46W
25 Pirmasens 49 12N 7 30 E
24 Pirna 50 57N 13 57 E
61 Pirojpur 22 35N 90 1 E
40 Pirot 43 9N 22 39 E
65 Piru 3 3S 128 12 E
36 Pisa 43 43N 10 23 E
110 Pisagua 19 40S 70 15W
110 Pisco 13 50S 76 5W
41 Piscu 45 30N 27 43 E
26 Pisek 49 19N 14 10 E
39 Pisticci 40 24N 16 33 E
36 Pistóia 43 57N 10 53 E
30 Pisuerga, R. 41 33N 4 52W
28 Pisz 53 38N 21 49 E
109 Pitanga 24 46S 51 44W
77 Pitcairn I. 25 5S 130 5W
46 Pitea 65 20N 21 25 E
41 Piteşti 44 52N 24 54 E
62 Pithapuram 17 10N 82 15 E
83 Pithara 30 20S 116 35 E
42 Píthion 41 24N 26 40 E
19 Pithiviers 48 10N 2 13 E
14 Pitlochry 56 43N 3 43W
102 Pittsburg, Calif. 38 1N 121 50W
101 Pittsburg, Kans. 37 21N 94 43W
96 Pittsburgh, Pa. 40 25N 79 55W
101 Pittsburgh, Tex. 32 59N 94 58W
97 Pittsfield 42 28N 73 17W
97 Pittston 41 19N 75 50W
81 Pittsworth 27 41S 151 37 E
110 Piura 5 5S 80 45W
91 Placentia 47 20N 54 0W
102 Placerville 38 47N 120 51W
105 Placetas 22 15N 79 44W
97 Plainfield 40 37N 74 28W
101 Plainview 34 10N 101 40W
101 Plaquemine 30 20N 91 15W
30 Plasencia 40 3N 6 8W
37 Plaški 45 4N 15 22 E
91 Plaster Rock 46 53N 67 22W
108 Plata, R. de la 34 45S 57 30W
110 Plato 9 47N 74 47W
100 Platte, R. 41 4N 95 53W
100 Platteville 40 18N 104 47W
25 Plattling 48 46N 12 53 E
97 Plattsburgh 44 41N 73 30W
100 Plattsmouth 41 0N 96 0W
24 Plauen 50 29N 12 9 E
40 Plavnica 42 10N 19 20 E
98 Pleasantville 39 25N 74 30W
18 Plélan-le-Grand 48 0N 2 7W
18 Pléneuf-val-André 48 37N 2 32W
85 Plenty, B. of 37 45S 177 0 E
48 Plesetsk 62 40N 40 10 E
91 Plessisville 46 14N 71 46W
28 Pleszew 51 53N 17 47 E
41 Pleven 43 26N 24 37 E
40 Ploče 43 4N 17 26 E
28 Płock 52 32N 19 40 E
18 Ploëmeur 47 44N 3 26W
18 Ploërmel 47 55N 2 26W
41 Ploieşti 44 57N 26 5 E
24 Plön 54 8N 10 22 E
28 Płonsk 52 37N 20 21 E
28 Płoty 53 48N 15 18 E
18 Plouaret 48 37N 3 28W
26 Ploucnice 50 47N 14 13 E
18 Ploudalmézeau 48 34N 4 41W
41 Plovdiv 42 8N 24 44 E
75 Plumtree 20 27S 27 55 E
18 Pluvigner 47 46N 3 1W
105 Plymouth, Montserrat 16 42N 62 13W
13 Plymouth, U.K. 50 23N 4 9W
98 Plymouth, Ind. 41 20N 86 19W
97 Plymouth, N.H. 43 44N 71 41W
97 Plymouth, Pa. 41 17N 76 0W
26 Plzeň 49 45N 13 22 E
28 Pniewy 52 31N 16 16 E
37 Po, Foci del 44 52N 12 30 E
36 Po, R. 44 57N 12 4 E
68 Po Hai, G. 38 40N 119 0 E
51 Pobedino 49 51N 142 49 E
30 Pobladura de Valle 42 6N 5 44W
102 Pocatello 42 50N 112 25W
26 Pochlarn 48 12N 15 12 E
109 Poços de Caldas 21 50S 46 45W
26 Poděbrady 50 9N 15 8 E
51 Podkamenndya Tunguska 61 50N 90 26 E
26 Podmokly 50 48N 14 10 E
48 Podolsk 55 30N 37 30 E
48 Podporozny 60 55N 34 2 E
40 Podravska Slatina 45 42N 17 45 E
24 Poel, I. 54 0N 11 25 E
37 Poggibonsi 43 27N 11 8 E
42 Pogradeci 40 57N 20 48 E
68 Pohang 36 8N 129 23 E
37 Pohorje, Mt. 46 30N 15 7 E
40 Poiana Ruscăi Mt. 45 45N 22 25 E
90 Point Edward 43 10N 82 30W
97 Point Pleasant 38 50N 82 7W
97 Pointe Claire 45 26N 73 49W
74 Pointe-Noire 4 48S 12 0 E
105 Pointe-à-Pitre 16 10N 61 30W
19 Poissy 48 55N 2 0 E
20 Poitou, Plaines du 46 30N 0 1W
20 Poitou, Reg. 46 25N 0 15W
19 Poix 49 47N 2 0 E
19 Poix Terron 49 38N 4 38 E
28 Pojezierze Mazurski, Reg. 53 40N 21 0 E
81 Pokataroo 29 30S 148 34 E
74 Poko 3 7N 26 52 E
68 Pokotu 48 46N 121 54 E
51 Pokrovsk 61 29N 129 6 E
30 Pola de Lena 43 10N 5 49W
30 Pola de Siero 43 24N 5 39W
103 Polacca 35 52N 110 25W
28 Poland ■ 52 0N 20 0 E
5 Polar Sub-Glacial Basin 85 0S 100 0 E
13 Polden Hills 51 7N 2 50W
27 Polgar 47 54N 21 6 E
68 Poli 8 34N 12 54 E
43 Políaigos, I. 36 45N 24 38 E
39 Policastro, G. di 39 55N 15 35 E
28 Police 53 33N 14 33 E
39 Polignano a Mare 41 0N 17 12 E
21 Poligny 46 50N 5 42 E
43 Polikhnitos 39 4N 26 10 E
65 Polillo Is. 14 56N 122 0 E
39 Polístena 38 25N 16 4 E
62 Pollachi 10 35N 77 0 E
32 Pollensa 39 54N 3 2 E
50 Polnovat 63 50N 66 5 E
48 Polotsk 55 30N 28 50 E
41 Polski Trumbosh 43 20N 25 38 E
41 Polsko Kosovo 43 23N 25 38 E
102 Polson 47 45N 114 12W
49 Poltava 49 35N 34 35 E
62 Polur 12 32N 79 11 E
48 Polyarny 69 8N 33 20 E
111 Pombal, Brazil 6 55S 37 50W
30 Pombal, Port. 39 55N 8 40W
103 Pomona 34 2N 117 49W
41 Pomorie 42 26N 27 41 E
99 Pompano 26 12N 80 6W
76 Ponape, I. 6 55N 158 10 E
101 Ponca City 36 40N 97 5W
105 Ponce 18 1N 66 37W
89 Pond Inlet 72 30N 75 0W
62 Pondicherry 11 59N 79 50 E
30 Ponferrada 42 32N 6 35W
62 Ponnani 10 45N 75 59 E
59 Ponnyadaung, Mts. 22 0N 94 10 E
48 Ponoi 67 0N 41 0 E
92 Ponoka 52 35N 113 40W
65 Ponorogo 7 52S 111 29 E
20 Pons 45 35N 0 34W
18 Pont-Audemer 49 21N 0 30 E
91 Pont Lafrance 47 40N 64 58W
21 Pont St. Esprit 44 16N 4 40 E
18 Pont-l'Abbé 47 52N 4 15W
18 Pont-l'Evêque 49 18N 0 11 E
109 Ponta Grossa 25 0S 50 10W
19 Pont-à-Mousson 45 54N 6 1 E
109 Ponta Pora 22 20S 55 35W
21 Pontarlier 46 54N 6 20 E
18 Pontaubault 48 40N 1 20W
101 Pontchartrain, L. 30 12N 90 0W
18 Pontchâteau 47 26N 2 8W
31 Ponte de Sor 39 17N 7 57W
21 Ponte Leccia 42 28N 9 13 E
109 Ponte Nova 20 25S 42 54W
38 Pontecorvo 41 28N 13 40 E
36 Pontedera 43 40N 10 37 E
12 Pontefract 53 42N 1 19W
93 Ponteix 49 46N 107 29W
30 Pontevedra 42 26N 8 40W
30 Pontevedra, Ria de 42 22N 8 45W
30 Pontevedra □ 42 25N 8 39W
100 Pontiac, Ill. 40 50N 88 40W
98 Pontiac, Mich. 42 40N 83 20W
63 Pontian Kechil 1 29N 103 23 E
64 Pontianak 0 3S 109 15 E
56 Pontine Mts.= Karadeniz Dağlari, Mts. 41 30N 35 0 E
18 Pontivy 48 5N 3 0W
19 Pontoise 49 3N 2 5 E
18 Pontorson 48 34N 1 30W
36 Pontrémoli 44 22N 9 52 E
13 Pontypool 51 42N 3 1W
13 Pontypridd 51 36N 3 21S
38 Ponziane, Is. 40 55N 13 0 E
81 Poochera 32 43S 134 51 E
13 Poole 50 42N 2 2W
62 Poona=Pune 18 29N 73 57 E
62 Poonamelle 13 3N 80 10 E
110 Poopó, L. 18 30S 67 35W
83 Popanyinning 32 40S 117 2 E
110 Popayán 2 27N 76 36W
16 Poperinge 50 51N 2 42 E
51 Popigay 71 55N 110 47 E
101 Poplar Bluff 36 45N 90 22W
104 Popocatepetl, Mt. 19 10N 98 40W
37 Popovača 45 30N 16 41 E
41 Popovo 43 21N 26 18 E
27 Poprád 49 3N 20 18 E
60 Porbandar 21 44N 69 43 E
31 Porcuna 37 52N 4 11W
88 Porcupine, R. 66 35N 145 15W
37 Pordenone 45 58N 12 40 E
41 Pordim 43 23N 24 51 E
37 Poreč 45 14N 13 36 E
109 Porecatu 22 43S 51 24W
21 Poretta 42 35N 9 28 E
47 Pori 61 29N 21 48 E
46 Porjus 66 57N 19 50 E
47 Porkkala 59 59N 24 26 E
110 Porlamar 10 57N 63 51W
30 Prma, R. 42 29N 5 28W
18 Pornić 47 7N 2 5W
51 Poronaysk 49 20N 143 0 E
43 Póros 37 30N 23 30 E
21 Porquerolles, Î. de 43 0N 6 13 E
36 Porretta, P. 44 9N 10 59 E
44 Porsgrunn 59 10N 9 40 E
81 Port Adelaide 34 46S 138 30 E
92 Port Alberni 49 15N 124 50W
60 Port Albert Victor 21 0N 71 30 E
91 Port Alfred 48 18N 70 53W
92 Port Alice 50 25N 127 25W
96 Port Allegany 41 49N 78 17W
102 Port Angeles 48 0N 123 30W
90 Port Arthur, Canada= Thunder Bay 48 25N 89 10W
68 Port Arthur, China= Lushun 38 48N 121 16 E
101 Port Arthur, U.S.A. 30 0N 94 0W
Thunder Bay 48 25N 89 10W
81 Port Augusta 32 30S 137 50 E
91 Port aux Basques 47 32N 59 8W
32 Port Bou 42 25N 3 9 E
81 Port Broughton 33 37S 137 56 E
91 Port Cartier 50 10N 66 50W

85 Port Chalmers 45 49S 170 30E
97 Port Chester 41 0N 73 41W
90 Port Colborne 42 50N 79 10W
92 Port Coquitlam 49 20N 122 45W
96 Port Credit 43 34N 79 35W
78 Port Darwin 12 18S 130 55E
105 Port de Paix 19 50N 72 50W
63 Port Dickson 2 30N 101 49E
80 Port Douglas 16 30S 145 30E
92 Port Edward 54 14N 130 18W
90 Port Elgin 44 25N 81 25W
75 Port Elizabeth 33 58S 25 40E
14 Port Ellen 55 39N 6 12W
12 Port Erin 54 5N 4 45W
72 Port Étienne= Nouadhibou 21 0N 17 0W
84 Port Fairy 38 22S 142 12E
74 Port-Gentil 0 47S 8 40E
14 Port Glasgow 55 57N 4 40W
72 Port Harcourt 4 43N 7 5E
92 Port Hardy 50 41N 127 30W
89 Port Harrison= Inoucdouac 58 25N 78 15W
82 Port Hedland 20 25S 118 35E
97 Port Henry 44 0N 73 30W
91 Port Hood 46 0N 61 32W
90 Port Hope 44 0N 78 20W
96 Port Huron 43 0N 82 28W
97 Port Jervis 41 22N 74 42W
84 Port Kembla 34 29S 150 56E
63 Port Klang 3 0N 101 21E
20 Port La Nouvelle 43 1N 3 3E
15 Port Laoise 53 2N 7 20W
101 Port Lavaca 28 38N 96 38W
81 Port Lincoln 34 42S 135 52E
72 Port-Lyautey= Kenitra 34 15N 6 40W
81 Port Macquarie 31 25S 152 54E
91 Port Maitland 44 0N 66 2W
92 Port Mellon 49 32N 123 31W
91 Port Menier 49 51N 64 15W
76 Port Moresby 9 24S 147 8E
93 Port Nelson 57 5N 92 56W
75 Port Nolloth 29 17S 16 52E
89 Port Nouveau-Quebec 58 30N 65 50W
105 Port of Spain 10 40N 61 20W
102 Port Orchard 47 31N 122 47W
90 Port Perry 44 6N 78 56W
81 Port Pirie 33 10S 137 58E
88 Port Radium 66 10N 117 40W
73 Port Said= Bûr Sa'îd 31 16N 32 18E
75 Port St. Johns= Umzimvubu 31 38S 29 33E
21 Port-St.-Louis 43 23N 4 50E
91 Port St. Servain 51 21N 58 0W
75 Port Shepstone 30 44S 30 28E
92 Port Simpson 54 30N 130 20W
90 Port Stanley 42 40N 81 10W
73 Port Sudan= Bûr Sûdân 19 32N 37 9E
13 Port Talbot 51 35N 3 48W
102 Port Townsend 48 0N 122 50W
20 Port-Vendres 42 32N 3 8E
48 Port Vladimir 69 25N 33 6E
81 Port Wakefield 34 12S 138 10E
63 Port Weld 4 50N 100 38E
15 Portadown 54 27N 6 26W
100 Portage 43 31N 89 25W
93 Portage la Prairie 49 58N 98 18W
31 Portalegre 39 19N 7 25W
31 Portalégre □ 39 15N 7 40W
101 Portales 34 12N 103 25W
15 Portarlington 53 10N 7 10W
105 Port-au-Prince 18 40N 72 20W
21 Port-de-Bouc 43 24N 4 59E
18 Port-en-Bessin 49 20N 0 45W
103 Porterville 36 5N 119 0W
20 Portet 43 31N 1 25E
13 Porthcawl 51 28N 3 42W
31 Portimão 37 8N 8 32W
84 Portland, Australia 33 13S 149 59E
97 Portland, Conn. 41 34N 72 39W
99 Portland, Me. 43 40N 70 15W
102 Portland, Oreg. 45 35N 122 30W
13 Portland Bill 50 31N 2 27W
13 Portland I. 50 32N 2 25W
89 Portland Promontory 59 0N 78 0W
12 Portmadoc 52 51N 4 8W
91 Portneuf 46 43N 71 55W
21 Porto, Fr. 42 16N 8 38E
30 Porto, Port. 41 8N 8 40W
30 Porto □ 41 8N 8 20W
21 Porto, G. de 42 17N 8 34E
109 Pôrto Alegre 30 5S 51 3W
75 Porto Amélia= Pemba 12 58S 40 30E
111 Pôrto de Móz 1 41S 52 22W
38 Porto Empédocle 37 18N 13 30E
111 Porto Franco 9 45S 47 0W
111 Porto Grande 0 42N 51 24W
108 Pôrto Murtinho 21 45S 57 55W
111 Porto Nacional 10 40S 48 30W
72 Porto-Novo 6 23N 2 42E
37 Porto Recanati 43 26N 13 40E
37 Porto San Giórgio 43 11N 13 49E
111 Porto Seguro 16 20S 39 0W
37 Porto Tolle 44 57N 12 20E
38 Porto Torres 40 50N 8 23E
109 Porto União 26 10S 51 0W
21 Porto-Vecchio 41 35N 9 16E
110 Porto Velho 8 46S 63 54W
36 Portoferráio 42 50N 10 20E
37 Portogruaro 45 57N 12 50E
102 Portola 39 49N 120 28W
37 Portomaggiore 44 41N 11 47E
36 Portovénere 44 2N 9 50E
110 Portoviejo 1 0S 80 20W
14 Portpatrick 54 50N 5 7W
14 Portree 57 25N 6 11W
15 Portrush 55 13N 6 40W
13 Portsmouth, U.K. 50 48N 1 6W
97 Portsmouth, N.H. 43 5N 70 45W
98 Portsmouth, Ohio 38 45N 83 0W
97 Portsmouth, R.I. 41 35N 71 44W
98 Portsmouth, Va. 36 50N 76 50W
14 Portsoy 57 41N 2 41W
46 Porttipahta, L. 68 5N 26 40E
30 Portugalete 43 19N 3 4W
29 Portugal ■ 40 0N 7 0W
72 Portuguese Guinea ■= Guinea Bissau ■ 12 0N 15 0W
15 Portumna 53 5N 8 12W
112 Porvenir 53 10S 70 30W
47 Provoo 60 27N 25 50E
109 Posadas, Arg. 27 30S 56 0W
31 Posadas, Sp. 37 47N 5 11W
69 Poseh 23 50N 106 0E
65 Poso 1 20S 120 55E
111 Posse 14 4S 46 18W
24 Pössneck 50 42N 11 34E
90 Poste de la Baleine 55 20N 77 40W
72 Poste Maurice Cortier 22 14N 1 2E
37 Postojna 45 46N 14 12E
75 Potchefstroom 26 41S 27 7E
39 Potenza 40 40N 15 50E
37 Potenza, R. 43 25N 13 40E
37 Potenza Picena 43 22N 13 37E
30 Potes 43 15N 4 42W
75 Potgietersrus 24 10S 29 3E
49 Poti 42 10N 41 38E
72 Potiskum 11 39N 11 2E
98 Potomac, R. 38 0N 76 20W
110 Potosí 19 38S 65 50W
108 Potosí □ 20 30S 67 0W
65 Potatan 10 56N 122 38E
68 Potow 38 8N 116 31E
24 Potsdam, E. Germany 52 23N 13 4E
97 Potsdam, U.S.A. 44 40N 74 59W
24 Potsdam □ 52 40N 13 30E
97 Pottersville 42 38N 84 45W
97 Pottsdown 40 17N 75 40W
97 Pottsville 40 39N 76 12W
92 Pouce Coupe 55 40N 120 10W
97 Poughkeepsie 41 40N 73 57W
19 Pouilly 47 18N 2 57E
109 Pouso Alegre 11 55S 57 0W
85 Poverty B. 38 43S 178 0E
30 Póvoa de Varzim 41 25N 8 46W
48 Povenets 62 48N 35 0E
90 Powassan 46 5N 79 25W
100 Powder, R. 46 44N 105 26W
102 Powder River 43 5N 107 0W
102 Powell 44 45N 108 45W
103 Powell, L. 37 25N 110 45W
92 Powell River 49 48N 125 20W
13 Powys □ 52 20N 3 30W
69 Poyang 28 59N 116 40E
69 Poyang Hu, L. 29 10N 116 10E
51 Poyarkovo 49 38N 128 45E
30 Poza de la Sal 42 35N 3 31W
40 Požarevac 44 35N 21 18E
40 Požega 45 21N 17 41E
28 Poznań 52 25N 17 0E
28 Poznań □ 52 30N 18 0E
33 Pozo Alcón 37 42N 2 56W
110 Pozo Almonte 20 10S 69 50W
31 Pozoblanco 38 23N 4 51W
39 Pozzallo 36 44N 15 40E
39 Pozzuoli 40 49N 14 7E
40 Praca 43 47N 18 43E
63 Prachin Buri 14 0N 101 25E
20 Prades 42 38N 2 23E
111 Prado 17 20S 39 20W
37 Pragerska 46 27N 15 42E
26 Prague=Praha 50 5N 14 22E
26 Praha 50 5N 14 22E
20 Prahecq 46 19N 0 26W
41 Prahova, R. 44 43N 26 27E
40 Prahovo 44 18N 22 39E
41 Praid 46 32N 25 10E
111 Prainha 1 45S 53 30W
80 Prairie 20 50S 144 35E
102 Prairie City 45 27N 118 44W
100 Prairie du Chien 43 1N 91 9W
100 Prairies, Coteau des 44 0N 97 0W
64 Praja 8 39S 116 37E
111 Prata 19 25S 49 0W
37 Prato 43 53N 11 5E
37 Prátola Peligna 42 7N 13 51E
101 Pratt 37 40N 98 45W
30 Pravia 43 30N 6 12W
108 Precordillera 30 0S 69 1W
37 Predáppio 44 7N 11 58E
40 Predejane 42 51N 22 9E
93 Preeceville 52 0N 102 50W
92 Premier 56 4N 130 1W
40 Prenj, Mt. 43 33N 17 53E
24 Prenzlau 53 19N 13 51E
40 Prepansko, J. 40 45N 21 0E
63 Preparis North Chan. 15 12N 93 40E
63 Preparis South Chan. 14 36N 93 40E
27 Prerov 49 28N 17 27E
90 Prescott, Canada 44 45N 75 30W
103 Prescott, U.S.A. 34 35N 112 30W
40 Preševo 42 19N 21 39E
108 Presidencia Roque Saenz Peña 26 50S 60 30W
108 Presidente de la Plaza 27 0S 60 0W
109 Presidente Epitácio 21 46S 52 6W
108 Presidente Hayes □ 24 0S 59 0W
109 Presidente Prudente 15 45S 54 0W
41 Preslav 43 10N 26 52E
27 Prešov 49 0N 21 15E
99 Presque Isle 46 40N 68 0W
72 Prestea 5 22N 2 7W
13 Presteign 52 17N 3 0W
96 Preston, Canada 43 25N 80 20W
12 Preston, U.K. 53 46N 2 42W
14 Prestonpans 55 58N 3 0W
14 Prestwick 55 30N 4 38W
75 Pretoria 25 44S 28 12E
43 Préveza 38 57N 20 47E
88 Pribilov Is. 56 0N 170 0W
26 Příbram 49 41N 14 2E
102 Price 39 40N 110 48W
32 Priego 40 38N 2 21W
31 Priego de Córdoba 37 27N 4 12W
75 Prieska 29 40S 22 42E
27 Prievidza 48 46N 18 36E
40 Prijedor 44 58N 16 41E
49 Prikaspiyskaya Nizmennost 47 30N 50 0E
49 Prikumsk 44 30N 44 10E
40 Prilep 41 21N 21 37E
49 Priluki 50 30N 32 15E
93 Prince Albert 53 15N 105 50W
93 Prince Albert Nat. Park 54 0N 106 25W
88 Prince Albert Pen. 72 0N 116 0W
88 Prince Albert Sd. 70 25N 115 0W
89 Prince Charles I. 68 0N 76 0W
3 Prince Edward Is. 45 15S 39 0E
91 Prince Edward I. □ 44 2N 77 20W
92 Prince George 53 50N 122 50W
86 Prince of Wales, C. 53 50N 131 30W
80 Prince of Wales, I., Australia 10 35S 142 0E
88 Prince of Wales I., Canada 73 0N 99 0W
92 Prince of Wales I., U.S.A. 53 30N 131 30W
92 Prince Rupert 54 20N 130 20W
80 Princess Charlotte, B. 14 15S 144 0E
5 Princesse Astrid Kyst 71 0S 10 0E
5 Princesse Ragnhild Kyst 71 0S 30 0E
92 Princeton, Canada 49 27N 120 30W
98 Princeton, Ind. 38 20N 87 35W
98 Princeton, Ky. 37 6N 87 55W
97 Princeton, N.J. 40 18N 74 40W
98 Princeton, W.Va. 37 21N 81 8W
71 Principé, I. 1 37N 7 25E
30 Prior, C. 43 34N 8 17W
48 Priozersk 61 2N 30 4E
48 Pripyat, R. 51 20N 30 20E
40 Priština 42 40N 21 13E
99 Pritchard 30 47N 88 5W
24 Pritzwalk 53 10N 12 11E
38 Priverno 41 29N 13 10E
40 Prizren 42 13N 20 45E
38 Prizzi 37 44N 13 24E
65 Probolinggo 7 46S 113 13E
62 Proddatur 14 45N 78 30E
104 Progreso 21 20N 89 40W
42 Prokletije, Mt. 42 30N 19 45E
50 Prokopyevsk 54 0N 87 3E
40 Prokuplje 43 16N 21 36E
59 Prome 18 45N 95 30E
111 Propriá 10 13S 36 51W
21 Propriano 41 41N 8 52E
80 Proserpine 20 21S 148 36E
102 Prosser 46 11N 119 52W
27 Prostějov 49 30N 17 9E
41 Provadiya 43 12N 27 30E
21 Provence, Reg. 43 40N 5 45E
97 Providence 41 41N 71 15W
90 Providence Bay 45 41N 82 15W
105 Providencia, I. de 13 25N 81 26W
51 Provideniya 64 23N 173 18W
92 Provincial Cannery 51 33N 127 36W
19 Provins 48 33N 3 15E
102 Provo 40 16N 111 37W
93 Provost 52 25N 110 20W
40 Prozor 43 50N 17 34E
109 Prudentópolis 25 12S 50 57W
80 Prudhoe, I. 21 23S 149 45E
88 Prudhoe Bay 70 10N 148 0W
93 Prudhomme 52 22N 105 47W
27 Prudnik 50 20N 17 38E
28 Pruszez Gdańska 54 17N 19 40E
28 Pruszków 52 9N 20 49E
49 Prut, R. 45 28N 28 12E
5 Prydz B. 69 0S 74 0E
28 Przasnysz 53 2N 20 45E
27 Przemysl 49 50N 22 45E
27 Przemysl □ 50 0N 22 0E
50 Przhevalsk 42 30N 78 20E
43 Psará, I. 38 37N 25 38E
48 Pskov 57 50N 28 25E
27 Pszczyna 49 59N 18 58E
42 Ptolemaís 40 30N 21 43E
110 Pucallpa 8 25S 74 30W
69 Puchi 29 42N 113 54E
41 Pucioasia 45 4N 25 26E
62 Pudukkottai 10 28N 78 47E
104 Puebla 19 0N 98 10W
104 Puebla □ 18 30N 98 0W
31 Puebla de Guzman 37 33N 7 15W
30 Puebla de Sanabria 42 4N 6 38W
100 Pueblo 38 20N 104 40W
108 Puente Alto 33 32S 70 35W
31 Puente Genil 37 22N 4 47W
32 Puente la Reina 42 40N 1 49W
30 Puenteareas 42 10N 8 28W
30 Puentedeume 43 24N 8 10W
67 Puerh 23 11N 100 56E
105 Puerto Armuelles 8 20N 83 10W
110 Puerto Asís 0 30N 76 30W
110 Puerto Ayacucho 5 40N 67 35W
104 Puerto Barrios 15 40N 88 40W
110 Puerto Berrío 6 30N 74 30W
110 Puerto Bolívar 3 10S 79 55W
110 Puerto Cabello 10 28N 68 1W
105 Puerto Cabezas 14 0N 83 30W
110 Puerto Carreño 6 12N 67 22W
105 Puerto Cortes 15 51N 88 0W
104 Puerto Cortés 8 20N 82 20W
112 Puerto Coyle 50 54S 69 15W
110 Puerto Cumarebo 11 29N 69 21W
31 Puerto de Santa María 36 35N 6 15W
72 Puerto del Rosario 28 30N 13 52W
112 Puerto Deseado 47 45S 66 0W
110 Puerto Páez 6 13N 67 28W
110 Puerto Leguizamo 0 12S 74 46W
112 Puerto Lobos 42 0S 65 3W
33 Puerto Lumbreras 37 34N 1 48W
112 Puerto Madryn 42 48S 65 4W
33 Puerto Mazarrón 37 34N 1 15W
112 Puerto Montt 41 28S 72 57W
112 Puerto Natales 51 45S 72 25W
105 Puerto Padre 21 13N 76 35W
108 Puerto Pinasco 22 30S 57 50W
112 Puerto Pirámides 42 35S 64 20W
110 Puerto Piritu 10 5N 65 0W
105 Puerto Plata 19 40N 70 45W
65 Puerto Princesa 9 55N 118 50E
112 Puerto Quellón 43 7S 73 37W
31 Puerto Real 36 33N 6 12W
105 Puerto Rico, I. 18 15N 66 45W
112 Puerto Saavedra 38 47S 73 24W
110 Puerto Suárez 18 58S 57 52W
112 Puerto Varas 41 19S 72 59W
31 Puertollano 38 43N 4 7W
112 Pueyrredón, L. 47 20S 72 0W
48 Pugachev 52 0N 48 55E
102 Puget Sd. 47 15N 123 30W
39 Puglia □ 41 0N 16 30E
40 Pui 45 30N 23 4E
32 Puig Mayor, Mt. 39 49N 2 47E
32 Puigcerda 42 24N 1 50E
19 Puisaye, Collines de la 47 35N 3 30E
85 Pukaki, L. 44 5S 170 1E
93 Pukatawagan 55 45N 101 20W
85 Pukekohe 37 12S 174 55E
37 Pula 39 0N 9 0E
108 Pulacayo 20 25S 66 41W
68 Pulantien 39 25N 122 0E
97 Pulaski, N.Y. 43 32N 76 9W

99 Pulaski, Tenn. 35 10N 87 0W
98 Pulaski, Va. 37 4N 80 49W
28 Puławy 51 23N 21 59E
62 Pulicat L. 13 40N 80 15E
62 Puliyangudi 9 11N 77 24E
102 Pullman 46 49N 117 10W
64 Puloraja 4 55N 95 24E
28 Pułtusk 52 43N 21 6E
67 Puluntohai 47 2N 87 29E
61 Punakha 27 42N 89 52E
62 Punalur 9 0N 76 56E
58 Punch 33 48N 74 4E
58 Pune 18 29N 73 57E
60 Punjab □ 31 0N 76 0E
110 Puno 15 55S 70 3W
108 Punta Alta 38 53S 62 4W
112 Punta Arenas 53 0S 71 0W
112 Punta Delgada 42 43S 63 38W
104 Punta Gorda 16 10N 88 45W
81 Puntabie 32 12S 134 5E
105 Puntarenas 10 0N 84 50W
110 Punto Fijo 11 42N 70 13W
110 Purace, Mt. 2 21N 76 23W
13 Purbeck, I. of 50 40N 2 5W
33 Purchena Tetica 37 21N 2 21W
61 Puri 19 50N 85 58E
62 Purli 18 50N 76 35E
60 Purna, R. 21 5N 76 0E
61 Purnea 25 45N 87 31E
63 Pursat 12 34N 103 50E
61 Purulia 23 17N 86 33E
110 Purus, R. 3 42S 61 28W
41 Pŭrvomay 42 8N 25 17E
65 Purwakarta 6 35S 107 29E
65 Purwodadi, Jawa 7 7S 110 55E
65 Purwodadi, Jawa 7 51S 110 0E
65 Purwokerto 7 25S 109 14E
65 Purworedjo 7 43S 110 2E
68 Pusan 35 5N 129 0E
51 Pushchino 54 20N 158 10E
49 Pushkino 51 16N 47 9E
27 Püspökladány 47 19N 21 6E
59 Putao 27 28N 97 30E
85 Putaruru 38 3S 175 47E
68 Putehachi 48 4N 122 45E
69 Putien 22 28N 119 0E
39 Putignano 40 50N 17 5E
41 Putna, R. 45 35N 27 30E
97 Putnam 41 55N 71 55W
24 Puttgarden 54 28N 11 15E
62 Puttur 12 46N 75 12E
110 Putumayo, R. 3 7S 67 58E
20 Puy de Dôme, Mt. 45 46N 2 57E
20 Puy de Sancy, Mt. 45 32N 2 41E
20 Puy l'Evêque 44 31N 1 9E
102 Puyallup 47 10N 122 22W
20 Puy-de-Dôme □ 45 47N 3 0E
20 Puyoô 43 33N 0 56W
49 Pyatigorsk 44 2N 43 0E
59 Pyinmana 19 45N 96 20E
68 Pyŏngyang 39 0N 125 30E
17 Pyrenees, Mts. 42 45N 0 20E
20 Pyrénées-Atlantiques □ 43 15N 0 45W
20 Pyrénées-Orientales □ 42 35N 2 25E
28 Pyrzyce 53 10N 14 55E
59 Pyu 18 30N 96 35E

Q

54 Qabatiya 32 25N 35 16E
57 Qadam 32 55N 66 45E
56 Qadhima 22 20N 39 13E
60 Qadian 31 51N 74 19E
56 Qal'at al Mu'azzam 27 43N 37 27E
56 Qal'at Sālih 31 31N 47 16E
56 Qal'at Sura 26 10N 38 40E
57 Qala-i-Kirta 32 15N 63 0E
57 Qala Nau 35 0N 63 5E
54 Qalqīlya 32 12N 34 58E
73 Qâra 29 38N 26 30E
57 Qasr-e Qand 26 15N 60 45E
73 Qasr Farâfra 27 0N 28 1E
55 Qasr Hamam 21 5N 46 5E
57 Qatar ■ 25 30N 51 15E
73 Qattara, Munkhafed el 29 30N 27 30E
56 Qazvin 36 15N 50 0E
73 Qena 26 10N 32 43E
54 Qesari 32 30N 34 53E
57 Qeshm 26 55N 56 10E
57 Qeshm, I. 26 50N 56 0E
57 Qeys, Jazireh-ye 26 32N 53 56E
54 Qezi'ot 30 52N 34 28E
58 Qila Safed 29 0N 61 30E
54 Qiryat Bialik 32 50N 35 5E
54 Qiryat 'Eqron 31 52N 34 49E
54 Qiryat Gat 31 36N 35 47E
54 Qiryat Hayyim 32 49N 35 4E
54 Qiryat Mal'akhi 31 44N 34 45E
54 Qiryat Shemona 33 13N 35 35E
54 Qiryat Tiv'om 32 43N 35 8E
54 Qiryat Yam 32 51N 35 4E
55 Qîzân 16 57N 42 3E
57 Qom 34 40N 51 4E
97 Quabbin Res. 42 22N 72 18W
24 Quackenbrück 52 40N 7 59E
83 Quairading 32 0S 117 21E
97 Quakerstown 40 27N 75 20W
83 Qualeup 33 48S 116 48E
63 Quang Ngai 15 13N 108 58E
63 Quang Tri 16 45N 107 13E
63 Quang Yen 21 3N 106 52E
13 Quantock Hills 51 8N 3 10W
108 Quaraí 30 15S 56 20W
38 Quartu Sant'Elena 39 15N 9 10E
57 Qūchān 37 10N 58 27E
75 Que Que 18 58S 29 48E
84 Queanbeyan 35 17S 149 14E
91 Québec 46 52N 71 13W
91 Québec □ 50 0N 70 0W
24 Quedlinburg 51 47N 11 9E
5 Queen Alexandra Ra. 85 0S 170 0E
92 Queen Charlotte 53 28N 132 2W
92 Queen Charlotte Is. 53 10N 132 0W
92 Queen Charlotte Str. 51 0N 128 0W
86 Queen Elizabeth Is. 75 0N 95 0W
5 Queen Mary Coast 70 0S 95 0E
88 Queen Maud G. 68 15N 102 0W
5 Queen Maud Ra. 86 0S 160 0W
79 Queensland □ 15 0S 142 0E
80 Queenstown, Australia 42 4S 145 35E
85 Queenstown, N.Z. 45 1S 168 40E
75 Queenstown, S.Africa 31 52S 26 52E
111 Queimadas 11 0S 39 38W
74 Quela 9 10S 16 56E
75 Quelimane 17 53S 36 58E
69 Quemoy, I. = Kinmen, I. 24 25N 118 25E
108 Quenquén 38 30S 58 30W
104 Querétaro 20 40N 100 23W
104 Querétaro □ 20 30N 100 30W
33 Quesada 37 51N 3 4W
92 Quesnel 53 5N 122 30W
18 Questembert 47 40N 2 28W
90 Quetico 48 45N 90 55W
90 Quetico Prov. Park 48 15N 91 45W
60 Quetta 30 15N 66 55E
60 Quetta □ 30 15N 68 30E
104 Quezaltenango 14 40N 91 30W
65 Quezon City 14 38N 121 0E
63 Qui Nhon 13 40N 109 13E
110 Quibdo 5 42N 76 40W
18 Quiberon 47 29N 3 9W
108 Quiindy 25 58S 57 16W
112 Quilán, C. 43 15S 74 30W
75 Quilengues 14 12S 15 12E
20 Quillan 42 53N 2 10E
108 Quillota 32 54S 71 16W
108 Quilmes 34 50S 58 0W
62 Quilon 8 50N 76 38E
81 Quilpie 26 35S 144 11E
108 Quilpué 33 3S 71 27W
18 Quimper 48 0N 4 9W
18 Quimperlé 47 53N 3 33W
97 Quincy, Mass. 42 14N 71 0W
99 Quincy, Fla. 30 34N 84 34W
100 Quincy, Ill. 39 55N 91 20W
104 Quintana Roo □ 19 0E 88 0W
32 Quintanar de la Orden 39 36N 3 5W
33 Quintanar del Rey 39 21N 1 56W
108 Quintero 32 45S 71 30W
32 Quinto 41 25N 0 32W
30 Quiroga 42 28N 7 18W
21 Quissac 43 55N 4 0E
108 Quitilipi 26 50S 60 13W
110 Quito 0 15S 78 35W
111 Quixadá 4 55S 39 0W
54 Qumran 31 43N 35 27N
82 Quoin, I. 14 54S 129 32E
81 Quorn 32 25S 138 0E
67 Qurug-Tagh, Mts. 41 30N 90 0E
73 Qûs 25 55N 32 50E
73 Quseir 26 7N 34 16E
42 Qytet Stalin 40 47N 19 57E

R

26 Raab 47 42N 17 38E
54 Ra'anana 32 12N 34 52E
46 Raane 64 40N 24 28E
14 Raasay, I. 57 25N 6 4W
37 Rab, I. 44 45N 14 45E
27 Raba, R. 50 9N 20 30E
65 Raba 8 36S 118 55E
30 Rabaçal, R. 41 30N 7 12W
20 Rabastens 43 50N 1 43E
72 Rabat 34 2N 6 48W
76 Rabaul 4 24S 152 18E
56 Rabigh 22 50N 39 5E
27 Rabka 49 37N 19 59E
38 Racalmuto 37 25N 13 41E
40 Răcăşdia 44 59N 21 36E
91 Race, C. 46 40N 53 18W
27 Racibórz 50 7N 18 18E
98 Racine 42 41N 87 51W
26 Radbuza, R. 49 46N 13 24E
24 Radeburg 51 6N 13 45E
98 Radford 37 8N 80 32W
27 Radlin 50 3N 18 29E
28 Radom 51 23N 21 12E
28 Radom □ 51 20N 21 0E
40 Radomir 42 37N 23 4E
28 Radomka R. 51 43N 21 26E
28 Radomsko 51 5N 19 28E
37 Radovljica 46 22N 14 12E
26 Radstadt 47 24N 13 28E
13 Radstock 51 17N 2 25W
40 Raduša 42 7N 21 15E
93 Radville 49 30N 104 15W
92 Rae 62 45N 115 50W
61 Rae Bareli 26 18N 81 20E
89 Rae Isthmus 66 40N 87 30W
85 Raetihi 39 25S 175 17E
108 Rafaela 31 10S 61 30W
38 Raffadali 37 23N 13 29E
56 Rafhā 29 35N 43 35E
57 Rafsanjän 30 30N 56 5E
73 Râgâ 8 28N 25 41E
80 Raglan, Australia 23 42S 150 49E
85 Raglan, N.Z. 37 55S 174 55E
39 Ragusa 36 56N 14 42E
73 Rahad el Bardi 11 20N 23 40E
60 Rahimyar Khan 28 30N 70 25E
62 Raichur 16 10N 77 20E
61 Raiganj 25 37N 88 10E
61 Raigarh 21 56N 83 25E
60 Raikot 30 38N 75 36E
80 Railton 41 25S 146 28E
102 Rainier, Mt. 46 50N 121 50W
93 Rainy River 48 50N 94 30W
61 Raipur 21 17N 81 45E
90 Raith 48 50N 90 0W
62 Rajahmundry 17 1N 81 48E
62 Rajapalaiyam 9 25N 77 35E
60 Rajasthan □ 26 45N 73 30E
60 Rajasthan Can. 30 31N 71 0E
61 Rajbari 23 47N 89 41E
60 Rajgarh, Mad. P. 24 2N 76 45E
60 Rajgarh, Rajasthan 28 40N 75 25E
37 Rajhenburg 46 1N 15 29E
60 Rajkot 22 15N 70 56E
61 Rajmahal Hills 24 30N 87 30E
61 Rajnandgaon 21 5N 81 5E
60 Rajpipla 21 50N 73 30E
60 Rajpura 30 32N 76 32E
61 Rajshahi 24 22N 88 39E
61 Rajshahi □ 25 0N 89 0E
85 Rakaia 43 45S 172 1E
85 Rakaia, R. 43 54S 172 12E
27 Rákospalota 47 30N 19 5E
26 Rakovník 50 6N 13 42E
41 Rakovski 42 21N 24 57E
93 Raleigh, Australia 30 27S 153 2E
99 Raleigh, Canada 49 30N 92 5W
40 Ralja 44 33N 20 34E
54 Rám Alláh 31 55N 35 10E
84 Ram Head 37 47S 149 30E
54 Rama 32 56N 35 21E
39 Ramacca 37 24N 14 40E
62 Ramachandrapuram 16 50N 82 4E
62 Ramanathapuram 9 25N 78 55E
54 Ramat Gan 32 4N 34 48E
54 Ramat Ha Sharon 32 7N 34 50E
54 Ramat Ha Shofet 32 36N 35 5E
19 Rambervillers 48 20N 6 38E
19 Rambouillet 48 40N 1 48E
59 Rambre Kyun, I. 19 0N 94 0E
62 Ramdurg 15 58N 75 22E
65 Ramelau, Mt. 8 55S 126 22E
56 Râmhormoz 31 15N 49 35E
54 Ramla 31 55N 34 52E
60 Ramnaga 32 47N 75 18E
103 Ramona 33 1N 116 56W
88 Rampart 65 30N 150 10W
60 Rampur 23 25N 73 53E
60 Rampura 24 30N 75 27E
61 Rampurhat 24 10N 87 50E
90 Ramsey, Canada 47 25N 82 20W
12 Ramsey, U.K. 54 20N 4 21W
13 Ramsgate 51 20N 1 25E
61 Ranaghat 23 15N 88 35E
108 Rancagua 34 10S 70 50W
18 Rance, R. 48 31N 1 59W
109 Rancharia 22 15S 50 55W
102 Ranchester 44 57N 107 12W
61 Ranchi 23 19N 85 27E
112 Ranco, L. 40 15S 72 25W
41 Rancu 44 32N 24 15E
39 Rándazzo 37 53N 14 56E
45 Randers 56 29N 10 1E
45 Randers, Fd. 56 37N 10 20E
97 Randolph 43 55N 72 39W
44 Randsfjorden 60 25N 10 24E
46 Råneå 65 53N 22 18E
85 Rangaunu, B. 34 51S 173 15E
85 Rangitaiki, R. 37 54S 176 53E
85 Rangitata, R. 44 11S 171 30E
65 Rangkasbitung 6 22S 106 16E
59 Rangoon 16 45N 96 20E
61 Rangpur 25 42N 89 22E
62 Ranibennur 14 35N 75 30E
62 Ranipet 12 56N 79 23E
88 Rankin Inlet 62 30N 93 0W
84 Rankins Springs 33 49S 146 14E
14 Rannoch, L. 56 41N 4 20W
63 Ranong 9 56N 98 40E
64 Rantauprapat 2 15N 99 50E
65 Rantemario, Mt. 3 15S 119 57E
54 Rantis 32 4N 35 3E
98 Rantoul 40 18N 88 10W
77 Rapa Iti, Is. 27 35S 144 20W
36 Rapallo 44 21N 9 12E
65 Rapang 3 45S 119 55E
100 Rapid City 44 0N 103 0W
97 Raquette, R. 45 0N 74 42W
77 Rarotonga, I. 21 30S 160 0W
112 Rasa, Pte. 40 55S 63 20N
57 Ras al Khaima 25 50N 56 5E
73 Ra's Al-Unuf 30 25N 18 15E
57 Ra's al Tannūrah 26 40N 50 10E
73 Rashad 11 55N 31 0E
73 Rashîd 31 21N 30 22E
56 Rasht 37 20N 49 40E
62 Rasipuram 11 30N 78 25E
40 Raška 43 19N 20 39E
61 Rasra 25 50N 83 50E
25 Rastatt 48 50N 8 12E
63 Rat Buri 13 30N 99 54E
88 Rat Is. 51 50N 178 15E
60 Ratangarh 28 5N 74 35E
61 Rath 25 36N 79 37E
15 Rath Luirc 52 21N 8 40W
15 Rathdrum, Eire 52 57N 6 13W
102 Rathdrum, U.S.A 47 50N 116 58W
24 Rathenow 52 38N 12 23E
15 Rathkeale 52 32N 8 57W
15 Rathlin, I. 55 18N 6 14W
26 Ratikon, Ra. 47 3N 9 50E
60 Ratlam 23 20N 75 0E
62 Ratnagiri 16 57N 73 18E
62 Ratnapura 6 40N 80 20E
101 Raton 37 0N 104 30W
26 Ratten 47 28N 15 44E
14 Rattray Hd. 57 38N 1 50W
24 Ratzeburg 53 41N 10 46E
63 Raub 3 47N 101 52E
108 Rauch 36 45S 59 5W
85 Raukumara, Ra. 38 5S 177 55E
47 Rauma 61 10N 21 30E
61 Raurkela 22 14N 84 50E
38 Ravanusa 37 16N 13 58E
57 Rāvar 31 20N 56 51E
37 Ravenna, Italy 44 28N 12 15E
96 Ravenna, U.S.A. 41 11N 81 15W
25 Ravensburg 47 48N 9 38E
80 Ravenshoe 17 37S 145 29E
83 Ravensthorpe 33 35S 120 2E
60 Raver 21 15N 76 5E
44 Ravfoss 60 44N 10 37E
28 Rawa Mazowiecka 51 46N 20 12E
58 Rawalpindi 33 38N 73 8E
58 Rawalpindi □ 33 38N 73 8E
63 Rawang 3 19N 101 35E
90 Rawdon 46 3N 73 40W
85 Rawene 35 25S 173 32E
28 Rawicz 51 36N 16 52E
28 Rawka R. 52 9N 20 8E
83 Rawlinna 30 58S 125 28E
102 Rawlins 41 50N 107 20W
112 Rawson 43 15S 65 0W
91 Ray, C. 47 33N 59 15W
62 Rayachoti 14 4N 78 50E
62 Rayadrug 14 40N 76 50E
51 Raychikhinsk 49 46N 129 25E
92 Raymond, Canada 49 30N 112 35W
102 Raymond, U.S.A. 46 45N 123 48W
101 Raymondville 26 30N 97 50W
93 Raymore 50 25N 104 31W
101 Rayne 30 16N 92 16W
18 Raz, Pte. du 48 2N 4 47W
40 Ražana 44 6N 19 55E
40 Ražanj 43 40N 21 31E
41 Razdelna 43 13N 27 41E
41 Razelm, L. 44 50N 29 0E
41 Razgrad 43 33N 26 34E
41 Razlog 41 53N 23 28E
20 Ré, I. de 46 12N 1 30W
13 Reading, U.K. 51 27N 0 57W

97 Reading, U.S.A. 40 20N 75 53W
108 Realicó 35 0S 64 15W
20 Réalmont 43 48N 2 10E
65 Rebi 5 30S 134 7E
37 Recanati 43 24N 13 32E
40 Recas 45 46N 21 30E
60 Rechna Doab, Reg. 31 35N 73 30E
111 Recife 8 0S 35 0W
24 Recklinghausen 51 36N 7 10E
108 Reconquista 29 10S 59 45W
101 Red, R. 48 10N 97 0W
97 Red Bank 40 21N 74 4W
102 Red Bluff 40 11N 122 11W
92 Red Deer 52 20N 113 50W
93 Red Lake 51 1N 94 1W
100 Red Oak 41 0N 95 10W
100 Red Wing 44 32N 92 35W
28 Reda 54 40N 18 19E
13 Redbridge 51 35N 0 7E
12 Redcar 54 37N 1 4W
93 Redcliff 50 10N 110 50W
81 Redcliffe 27 12S 153 0E
84 Redcliffs 34 16S 142 10E
102 Redding 40 30N 122 25W
13 Redditch 52 18N 1 57W
103 Redlands 34 0N 117 0W
83 Redmond, Australia 34 55S 117 40E
102 Redmond, U.S.A. 44 19N 121 11W
18 Redon 47 40N 2 6W
105 Redonda, I. 16 58N 62 19W
30 Redondela 42 15N 8 38W
31 Redondo 38 39N 7 37W
103 Redondo Beach 33 52N 118 26W
13 Redruth 50 14N 5 14W
92 Redstone 52 8N 123 42W
93 Redvers 49 35N 101 40W
92 Redwater 53 55N 113 0W
103 Redwood City 37 30N 122 15W
15 Ree, L. 53 35N 8 0W
103 Reedley 34 40N 119 27W
102 Reedsport 43 45N 124 4W
85 Reefton 42 6S 171 51E
28 Rega, R. 53 52N 15 16E
39 Regalbuto 37 40N 14 38E
54 Regavim 32 32N 35 2E
25 Regen 48 58N 13 9E
25 Regen, R. 49 1N 12 6E
25 Regensburg 49 1N 12 7E
36 Reggio nell'Emilia 44 42N 10 38E
39 Réggio di Calábria 38 7N 15 38E
93 Regina 50 30N 104 35W
57 Registan, Reg. 30 15N 65 0E
109 Registro 24 30S 47 50W
31 Reguengos de Monsaraz 38 25N 7 32W
75 Rehoboth 17 55S 15 5E
54 Rehovot 31 54N 34 48E
24 Reichenbach 50 36N 12 19E
83 Reid 35 17S 149 8E
80 Reid River 19 40S 146 48E
99 Reidsville 36 21N 79 40W
13 Reigate 51 14N 0 11W
32 Reillo 39 54N 1 53W
19 Reims 49 15N 4 0E
54 Reina 32 43N 35 18E
112 Reina Adelaida, Arch. 52 20S 74 0W
93 Reindeer L. 57 20N 102 20W
85 Reinga, C. 34 25S 172 43E
30 Reinosa 43 2N 4 15W
30 Reinosa, P. 42 56N 4 10W
51 Rekinniki 60 38N 163 50E
111 Remanso 9 41S 42 4W
65 Rembang 6 42S 111 21E
57 Remeshk 26 55N 58 50E
19 Remiremont 48 0N 6 36E
24 Remscheid 51 11N 7 12E
97 Remsen 43 19N 75 11W
24 Rendsburg 54 18N 9 41E
51 Rene 66 2N 179 25W
90 Renfrew, Canada 45 30N 76 40W
14 Renfrew, U.K. 55 52N 4 24W
64 Rengat 0 30S 102 45E
108 Rengo 34 25S 70 52W
62 Renigunta 13 38N 79 30E
73 Renk 11 47N 32 49E
16 Renkum 51 58N 5 43E
81 Renmark 34 11S 140 43E
18 Rennes 48 7N 1 41W
18 Rennes, Bassin de 48 0N 2 0W
102 Reno 39 30N 119 0W
32 Rentería 43 19N 1 54W
102 Renton 47 30N 122 9W
61 Reotipur 25 33N 83 45E
62 Repalle 16 2N 80 45E
100 Republican, R. 39 3N 96 48W
89 Repulse Bay 66 30N 86 30W
32 Requena 39 30N 1 4W
40 Resen 41 5N 21 0E
93 Reserve 33 50N 108 54W
108 Resistencia 27 30S 59 0W
40 Reşiţa 45 18N 21 53E
89 Resolution I., Canada 61 30N 65 0W
85 Resolution, I., N.Z. 45 40S 166 40E
104 Retalhulen 14 33N 91 46W
19 Rethel 49 30N 4 20E
43 Réthímnon 35 15N 24 40E
43 Réthímnon □ 35 23N 24 28E
18 Rétiers 47 55N 1 25W
71 Réunion, Î. 22 0S 56 0E
32 Reus 41 10N 1 5E
25 Reutlingen 48 28N 9 13E
26 Reutte 47 29N 10 42E
20 Revel 43 28N 2 0E
61 Revelganj 25 50N 84 40E
92 Revelstoke 51 0N 118 0W
19 Revigny 48 50N 5 0E
77 Revilla Gigedo Is. 18 40N 112 0W
19 Revin 49 55N 4 39E
61 Rewa 24 33N 81 25E
60 Rewari 28 15N 76 40E
102 Rexburg 43 45N 111 50W
72 Rey Malabo 3 45N 8 50E
46 Reykanes, Pen. 63 48N 22 40W
46 Reykjavik 64 10N 21 57E
104 Reynosa 26 5N 98 18W
56 Reza'iyeh 37 40N 45 0E
13 Rhayader 52 19N 3 30W
16 Rheden 52 0N 6 3E
24 Rheine 52 17N 7 25E
25 Rheinland-Pfalz □ 50 50N 7 0E
24 Rheydt 51 10N 6 24E
19 Rhinau 48 19N 7 43E
100 Rhinelander 45 38N 89 29W
72 Rhir, C. 30 38N 9 54W
36 Rho 45 31N 9 2E
97 Rhode Island □ 41 38N 71 37W
75 Rhodesia=Zimbabwe 20 0S 28 30E
41 Rhodope, Mts. = Rhodopi Planina 41 40N 24 20E
41 Rhodopi Planina 41 40N 24 20E
13 Rhondda 51 39N 3 30W
21 Rhône □ 45 54N 4 35E
21 Rhône, R. 43 28N 4 42E
14 Rhum, I. 57 0N 6 20W
12 Rhyl 53 19N 3 29W
111 Riachão 7 20S 46 37W
30 Riansares, R. 39 32N 3 18W
64 Riau □ 1 0N 102 35E
64 Riau, Kep. 0 30N 104 20E
30 Riaza, R. 41 16N 3 29W
30 Ribadavia 42 17N 8 8W
30 Ribadeo 43 35N 7 5W
30 Ribadesella 43 30N 5 7W
32 Ribas 42 19N 2 15E
111 Ribas do Rio Pardo 20 27S 53 46W
29 Ribatejo, Reg. 39 15N 8 30W
12 Ribble, R. 54 13N 2 20W
45 Ribe □ 55 34N 8 30E
45 Ribe 55 19N 8 44E
19 Ribeauville 48 10N 7 20E
19 Ribécourt 49 30N 2 55E
30 Ribeira 42 36N 8 58W
109 Ribeirão Prêto 21 10S 47 50W
38 Ribera 37 30N 13 13E
24 Ribnitz-Damgarten 54 14N 12 24E
26 Říčany 50 0N 14 40E
85 Riccarton 43 32S 172 37E
37 Riccione 44 0N 12 39E
100 Rice Lake 44 10N 78 10W
75 Richards B. 28 48S 32 6E
97 Richford 45 0N 72 40W
91 Richibucto 46 42N 64 54W
102 Richland 44 49N 117 9W
80 Richmond, Australia 20 43S 143 8E
85 Richmond, N.Z. 41 4S 173 12E
75 Richmond, S. Africa 29 54S 30 8E
13 Richmond, Surrey 51 28N 0 18W
12 Richmond, Yorks. 54 24N 1 43W
102 Richmond, Calif. 38 0N 122 30W
98 Richmond, Ind. 39 50N 84 50W
98 Richmond, Ky. 37 40N 84 20W
102 Richmobd, Utah 41 55N 111 48W
98 Richmond, Va. 37 33N 77 27W
90 Richmond Gulf, L. 56 20N 75 50W
96 Richmond Hill 43 52N 79 27W
98 Richwood 38 17N 80 32W
32 Ricla 41 31N 1 24W
93 Ridgedale 53 0N 104 10W
90 Ridgetown 42 26N 81 52W
97 Ridgewood 40 59N 74 7W
96 Ridgway 41 25N 78 43W
93 Riding Mountain Nat. Park 50 55N 100 25W
26 Ried 48 14N 13 30E
37 Rienza, R. 46 49N 11 47E
24 Riesa 51 19N 13 19E
39 Riesi 37 16N 14 4E
37 Rieti 42 23N 12 50E
102 Rifle 39 40N 107 50W
48 Riga 56 53N 24 8E
91 Rigolet 54 10N 58 23W
37 Rijeka 45 20N 14 21E
40 Rijeka Crnojevica 42 24N 19 1E
16 Rijssen 52 19N 6 30E
16 Rijswijk 52 4N 4 22E
102 Riley 39 18N 96 50W
19 Rilly 49 11N 4 3E
27 Rimavaská Sobota 48 22N 20 2E
44 Rimbo 59 44N 18 21E
37 Rîmini 44 3N 12 33E
41 Rîmnicu Sărat 45 26N 27 3E
41 Rîmnicu Vîlcea 45 9N 24 21E
91 Rimouski 48 27N 68 30W
15 Rineanna 52 42N 85 7W
45 Ringe 55 13N 10 28E
44 Ringerike 60 7N 10 16E
45 Ringkøbing 56 5N 8 15E
45 Ringköbing □ 56 15N 8 30E
45 Ringsjön, L. 55 55N 13 30E
45 Ringsted 55 25N 11 46E
24 Rinteln 52 11N 9 3E
33 Rio, Pta. del 36 49N 2 24W
111 Rio Amazonas, Estuario do 1 0N 49 0W
110 Rio Branco, Brazil 9 58S 67 49W
109 Rio Branco, Uruguay 32 34S 53 25W
109 Rio Brilhante 21 48S 54 33W
105 Rio Claro 10 20N 61 25W
109 Rio Claro 22 19S 47 35W
108 Rio Cuarto 33 10S 64 25W
109 Rio de Janeiro 23 0S 43 12W
109 Rio de Janeiro □ 22 50S 43 0W
109 Rio do Sul 27 95S 49 37W
112 Rio Gallegos 51 35S 69 15W
109 Rio Grande, Arg. 53 50S 67 45W
112 Rio Grande, Brazil 32 0S 52 20W
94 Rio Grande, R. 37 47N 106 15W
111 Rio Grande do Norte □ 5 45S 36 0W
109 Rio Grande do Sul □ 30 0S 54 0W
111 Rio Largo 9 28S 35 50W
110 Rio Mulatos 19 40S 66 50W
74 Rio Muni □ 1 30N 10 0E
109 Rio Negro 26 0S 50 0W
109 Rio Pardo 15 55S 42 30W
108 Río Segundo 31 40S 63 58W
108 Río Tercero 32 10S 64 5W
30 Rio Tinto 41 11N 8 34W
111 Rio Verde, Brazil 17 43S 50 56W
104 Río Verde, Mexico 21 56N 99 59W
102 Rio Vista 38 11N 121 44W
110 Riobamba 1 50S 78 45W
20 Riom 45 54N 3 7E
110 Ríohacha 11 33N 72 55W
39 Rionero in Vulture 40 55N 15 40E
110 Ríosucio 5 30N 75 40W
110 Rioscio 7 27N 77 7W
96 Ripley 44 4N 81 32W
32 Ripoll 42 15N 2 13E
12 Ripon, U.K. 54 8N 1 31W
100 Ripon, U.S.A. 43 51N 88 50W
39 Riposto 37 44N 15 12E
40 Risan 42 32N 18 42E
20 Riscle 43 39N 0 5W
54 Rishon Le Zion 31 58N 34 48E
54 Rishpon 32 12N 34 49E
18 Risle, R. 49 26N 0 23E
41 Rîsnov 45 35N 25 27E
45 Risør 58 43N 9 13E
63 Ritchies Arch. 12 10N 93 5E
96 Rittman 40 57N 81 48W
102 Ritzville 47 10N 118 21W
36 Riva 45 53N 10 50E
18 Riva Bella-Ouistreham 49 17N 0 18W
108 Rivadavia 29 50S 70 35W
105 Rivas 11 30N 85 50W
21 Rive-de-Gier 45 32N 4 37E
109 Rivera 31 0S 55 50W
97 Riverhead 40 53N 72 40W
93 Riverhurst 50 55N 106 50W
75 Riversale 34 7S 21 15E
103 Riverside, Calif. 34 0N 117 15W
102 Riverside, Wyo. 41 12N 106 57W
81 Riverton, Australia 34 10S 138 46E
93 Riverton, Canada 51 5N 97 0W
85 Riverton, N.Z. 46 21S 168 0E
102 Riverton, U.S.A. 43 1N 108 27W
20 Rivesaltes 42 47N 2 50E
36 Riviera 44 0N 8 30E
91 Rivière Bleue 47 26N 69 2W
91 Rivière du Loup 47 50N 69 30W
91 Rivière Pentecôte 49 57N 67 1W
36 Rivoli 45 3N 7 31E
56 Riyadh = Ar Riyád 24 41N 46 42E
56 Rize 41 0N 40 30E
44 Rjukan 59 54N 8 33E
30 Roa 41 41N 3 56W
21 Roanne 46 3N 4 4E
99 Roanoke, Ala. 33 9N 85 23W
98 Roanoke, Va. 37 19N 79 55W
99 Roanoke Rapids 36 36N 77 42W
105 Roatán, I. de 16 23N 86 26W
75 Robertson 33 46S 19 50E
90 Roberval 48 32N 72 15W
77 Robinson Crusoe, I. 33 50S 78 30W
93 Roblin 51 21N 101 25W
92 Robson, Mt. 53 10N 119 10W
101 Robstown 27 47N 97 40W
31 Roca, C. da 38 40N 9 31W
111 Rocas, Is. 4 0S 34 1W
37 Roccastrada 43 0N 11 10E
109 Rocha 34 30S 54 25W
12 Rochdale 53 36N 2 10W
20 Rochefort 45 56N 0 57W
100 Rochelle 41 55N 89 5W
92 Rocher River 61 12N 114 0W
84 Rochester, Australia 36 22S 144 41E
13 Rochester, U.K. 51 22N 0 30E
100 Rochester, Minn. 44 1N 92 28W
97 Rochester, N.H. 43 19N 70 57W
96 Rochester, N.Y. 43 10N 77 40W
96 Rochester, Pa. 40 41N 80 17W
99 Rock Hill 34 55N 81 2W
100 Rock Island 41 30N 90 35W
105 Rock Sound 24 54N 76 12W
102 Rock Springs 46 55N 106 11W
8 Rockall, I. 57 37N 13 42W
5 Rockefeller Plat. 84 0S 130 0W
100 Rockford, Ill. 42 20N 89 0W
100 Rockford, Mich. 43 7N 85 33W
80 Rockhampton 23 22S 150 32E
83 Rockingham 32 15S 115 38E
97 Rockville, Conn. 41 51N 72 27W
99 Rockland, Ma. 44 6N 69 8W
98 Rockville, Md. 39 7N 77 10W
83 Rocky Gully 34 30S 117 0E
99 Rocky Mount 35 55N 77 48W
92 Rocky Mountain House 52 22N 114 55W
86 Rocky Mts. 48 0N 113 0W
96 Rocky River 41 30N 81 40W
92 Rockyford 51 13N 113 8W
44 Rødberg 60 17N 8 56E
45 Rødby 54 41N 11 23E
45 Rødbyhavn 54 39N 11 22E
91 Roddickton 50 51N 56 8W
20 Rodez 44 21N 2 33E
42 Rodhópi □ 41 10N 25 30E
43 Ródhos 36 15N 28 10E
43 Ródhos, I. 36 15N 28 10E
85 Rodney, C. 36 17S 174 50E
3 Rodriguez, I. 20 0S 65 0E
82 Roebourne 20 44S 117 9E
82 Roebuck, B. 18 5S 122 20E
82 Roebuck Plains P.O. 17 56S 122 28E
16 Roermond 51 12N 6 0E
89 Roes Welcome Sd. 65 0N 87 0W
16 Roeselare 50 57N 3 7E
47 Rogaland □ 59 12N 6 20E
37 Rogaska Slatina 46 15N 15 42E
101 Rogers 36 20N 94 0W
90 Roggan River 54 24N 78 5W
21 Rogliano 42 57N 9 30E
60 Rohtak 28 55N 76 43E
19 Roisel 49 58N 3 6E
108 Rojas 34 10S 60 45W
26 Rokycany 49 43N 13 35E
109 Rolândia 23 5S 52 0W
101 Rolla 38 0N 91 42W
80 Rollingstone 19 2S 146 24E
80 Rolleston 43 35S 172 24E
105 Rolleville 23 41N 76 0W
37 Roma, Italy 41 54N 12 30E
81 Roma, Australia 26 32S 148 49E
51 Roman 43 8N 23 54E
21 Romans 45 3N 5 3E
88 Romanzof, C. 61 49N 165 56W
37 Rome, Italy= Roma 41 54N 12 30E
99 Rome, Ga. 34 20N 85 0W
97 Rome, N.Y. 43 14N 75 29W
45 Romeleåsen, Reg. 55 34N 13 33E
19 Romilly 48 31N 3 44E
13 Romney Marsh 51 0N 1 0E
45 Rømø, I. 55 10N 8 30E
19 Romorantin-Lanthenay 47 21N 1 45E
44 Romsdal 62 25N 7 50E
14 Ronaldsay, North I. 59 23N 2 26W
14 Ronaldsay, South I. 58 47N 2 56W
111 Roncador, Sa. do 12 30S 52 30W
31 Ronda 36 46N 5 12W
31 Ronda, Sa. de 36 44N 5 3W
44 Rondane, Reg. 61 57N 9 50E
96 Rondeau Prov. Park 42 16N 81 51W
110 Rondônia □ 11 0S 63 0W
111 Rondonópolis 16 28S 54 38W
45 Rønne 55 6N 14 44E
5 Ronne Ld. 83 0S 70 0W
45 Ronneby 56 12N 15 17E
83 Ronsard, C. 24 46S 113 10E

16 Ronse 50 45N 3 35 E
75 Roodepoort-Maraisburg 26 11 S 27 54 E
60 Roorkee 29 52N 77 59 E
16 Roosendaal 51 32N 4 29 E
103 Roosevelt Res. 33 46N 111 0W
80 Roper, R. 14 43 S 135 27 E
20 Roquefort 44 2N 0 20W
32 Roquetas 40 50N 0 30 E
110 Roraima □ 2 0N 61 30W
110 Roraima, Mt. 5 10N 60 40W
44 Røros 62 35N 11 23 E
31 Rosal de la Frontera 37 59N 7 13W
108 Rosario, Arg. 33 0S 60 50W
111 Rosário, Brazil 3 0S 44 15W
104 Rosario, Mexico 23 0S 105 52W
108 Rosario, Urug. 34 20S 57 20W
108 Rosario de la Frontera 25 50S 65 0W
108 Rosario del Tala 32 20S 59 10W
109 Rosário do Sul 30 15S 54 55W
32 Rosas 42 19N 3 10 E
18 Roscoff 48 44N 4 0W
15 Roscommon 53 38N 8 11W
15 Roscommon □ 53 40N 8 15W
15 Roscrea 52 57N 7 47W
91 Rose Blanche 47 38N 58 45W
92 Rose Harbour 52 15N 131 10W
93 Rose Valley 52 19N 103 49W
105 Roseau 48 56N 96 0W
101 Rosenberg 29 30N 95 48W
102 Rosebud 31 5N 97 0W
102 Roseburg 43 10N 123 10W
84 Rosedale 38 11S 146 48 E
19 Rosendaël 51 3N 2 24 E
25 Rosenheim 47 51N 12 9 E
37 Roseto degli Abruzzi 42 40N 14 2 E
93 Rosetown 57 33N 108 0 E
73 Rosetta = Rashid 31 21N 30 22 E
102 Roseville 38 46N 121 41W
81 Rosewood 35 38S 147 52 E
54 Rosh Ha'Ayin 32 5N 34 47 E
54 Rosh Pinna 32 58N 35 32 E
45 Roshage, C. 57 7N 8 35 E
19 Rosières 48 36N 6 20 E
36 Rosignano 43 23N 10 28 E
110 Rosignol 6 15N 57 30W
45 Roskilde 55 38N 12 3 E
45 Roskilde □ 55 35N 12 5 E
45 Roskilde, Fd. 55 50N 12 2 E
48 Roslavl 53 57N 32 55 E
85 Ross, N.Z. 42 53S 170 49 E
13 Ross, U.K. 51 55N 2 34W
15 Ross □ 70 0S 170 5W
5 Ross Ice Shelf 80 0S 180 0W
5 Ross Sea 74 0S 178 0E
39 Rossano Cálabro 39 36N 16 39 E
92 Rossland 49 6N 117 50W
15 Rosslare 52 17N 6 23W
25 Rosslau 57 52N 12 15 E
72 Rosso 16 30N 15 49W
49 Rossosh 50 15N 39 20 E
93 Rosthern 52 40N 106 20W
24 Rostock 54 4N 12 9 E
24 Rostock □ 54 10N 12 30 E
49 Rostov 47 15N 39 45 E
101 Roswell 33 26N 104 32W
14 Rosyth 56 2N 3 26W
31 Rota 36 37N 6 20W
24 Rotenburg 53 6N 9 24 E
25 Rothenburg ob der Tauber 49 21N 10 11 E
13 Rother, R. 50 59N 0 40W
12 Rotherham 53 26N 1 21W
14 Rothes 57 31N 3 12W
14 Rothesay 55 50N 5 3W
65 Roti, I. 10 50S 123 0 E
84 Roto 33 0S 145 30 E
85 Rotorua 38 9S 176 16 E
85 Rotorua, L. 38 5S 176 18 E
26 Rottenmann 47 31N 14 22 E
16 Rotterdam 51 55N 4 30 E
83 Rottnest, I. 32 0S 115 27 E
25 Rottweil 48 9N 8 38 E
76 Rotuma, I. 12 25S 177 5 E
19 Roubaix 50 40N 3 10 E
26 Roudnice 50 25N 14 15 E
18 Rouen 49 27N 1 4 E
20 Rouergue, Reg. 44 20N 2 20 E
81 Round, Mt. 30 26S 152 16 E
102 Roundup 46 25N 108 35W
14 Rousay, I. 59 10N 3 2W
97 Rouses Point 44 58N 73 22W
20 Roussillon, Reg. 45 24N 4 49 E
90 Rouyn 48 20N 79 0W
46 Rovaniemi 66 29N 25 41 E
36 Rovereto 45 53N 11 3 E
37 Rovigo 45 4N 11 48 E
41 Rovinari 44 55N 23 11 E
37 Rovinj 45 18N 13 40 E
49 Rovno 50 40N 26 10 E
65 Roxas 11 36N 122 49 E
85 Roxburgh 45 33S 169 19 E
45 Roxen, L. 58 30N 15 41 E
82 Roy Hill 22 37S 119 58 E
32 Roya, Peña 40 25N 0 40W
98 Royal Oak 42 30N 83 5W
100 Royale, I. 48 0N 89 0W
20 Royan 45 37N 1 2W
19 Roye 47 40N 6 31 E
27 Rŏžnava 48 37N 20 35 E
48 Rtishchevo 52 35N 43 50 E
30 Rúa 42 24N 7 6W
85 Ruapehu, Mt. 39 18S 175 35 E
110 Rubio 7 43N 72 22W
50 Rubtsovsk 51 30N 80 50 E
88 Ruby 38 27S 145 55 E
27 Ruda Slaska 50 16N 18 50 E
81 Rudall 33 43S 136 17 E
24 Rüdersdorf 52 28N 13 48 E
45 Rudkøbing 54 56N 10 41 E
48 Rudnichny 59 38N 52 26 E
51 Rudnogorsk 57 15N 103 42 E
50 Rudnyy 52 57N 63 7 E
74 Rudolf, L. = Turkana, L. 4 10N 36 10 E
24 Rudolstädt 50 44N 11 20 E
19 Rue 50 15N 1 40 E
73 Rufa'a 14 44N 33 32 E
20 Ruffec 46 2N 0 42 E
74 Rufiji, R. 8 0S 39 20 E
108 Rufino 34 20S 62 50W
72 Rufisque 14 43N 17 17W
13 Rugby, U.K. 52 23N 1 16W
100 Rugby, U.S.A. 48 21N 100 0W
24 Rügen, I. 54 22N 13 25 E
54 Ruhâma 31 31N 34 43 E
24 Ruhla 50 53N 10 21 E
24 Ruhr, R. 51 27N 6 44 E
74 Ruki, R. 0 5N 18 17 E
74 Rukwa, L. 7 50S 32 10 E
82 Rum Jungle 13 0S 130 59 E
40 Ruma 45 8N 19 50 E
41 Rumania ■ 46 0N 25 0 E
80 Rumbalara 25 20S 134 29 E
97 Rumford 44 30N 70 30W
21 Rumilly 45 53N 5 56 E
66 Rumoi 43 56N 141 39W
97 Rumson 40 22N 74 0W
85 Runanga 42 25S 171 15 E
12 Runcorn 53 20N 2 44W
74 Rungwa 6 55S 33 32 E
60 Rupar 31 2N 76 38 E
64 Rupat, I. 1 45N 101 40 E
90 Rupert House = Fort Rupert 51 30N 78 40W
75 Rusape 18 35S 32 8 E
41 Ruse 43 48N 25 59 E
13 Rushden 52 17N 0 37W
98 Rushville 39 38N 85 22W
84 Rushworth 36 32S 145 1 E
111 Russas 4 56S 37 58W
93 Russell, Canada 50 50N 101 20W
100 Russell, Kans. 38 56N 98 55W
97 Russell, N.Y. 44 26N 75 11W
99 Russellville, Ala. 34 30N 87 44W
101 Russellville, Ark. 35 15N 93 0W
50 Russkaya Polyana 53 47N 73 53 E
75 Rustenburg 25 41S 27 14 E
101 Ruston 32 30N 92 40W
31 Rute 37 19N 4 29W
65 Ruteng 8 26S 120 30 E
102 Ruth 39 15N 115 1W
84 Rutherglen, Australia 36 5S 146 29 E
14 Rutherglen, U.K. 55 50N 4 11W
39 Rutigliano 41 1N 17 0 E
97 Rutland 43 38N 73 0W
74 Rutshuru 1 13S 29 25 E
39 Ruvo di Púglia 41 7N 16 27 E
74 Ruvuma, R. 10 29S 40 28 E
74 Ruwenzori, Mts. 0 30N 29 55 E
27 Ruzomberok 49 3N 19 17 E
74 Rwanda ■ 2 0S 30 0 E
14 Ryan, L. 55 0N 5 2W
48 Ryazan 54 38N 39 44 E
48 Ryazhsk 53 40N 40 7 E
50 Rybache 46 40N 81 20 E
48 Rybachiy Pol. 69 43N 32 0 E
48 Rybinsk = Andropov 58 3N 38 52 E
48 Rybinskoye, Vdkhr. 58 30N 38 25 E
27 Rybnik 50 6N 18 32 E
13 Ryde 50 44N 1 9W
27 Rydułtowy 50 4N 18 23 E
13 Rye 50 57N 0 46 E
12 Rye, R. 54 12N 0 53W
28 Rypin 53 3N 19 32 E
69 Ryūkyū, Is. 26 0N 128 0 E
27 Rzeszów 50 5N 21 58 E
27 Rzeszów □ 50 0N 22 0 E
28 Rzepin 52 20N 14 49 E
48 Rzhev 56 15N 34 18 E

S

54 Sa'ad 31 28N 34 33 E
57 Sa'ādatābād 30 10N 53 5 E
24 Saale, R. 51 57N 11 55 E
24 Saaler Bodden 54 20N 12 25 E
24 Saalfeld 50 39N 11 21 E
26 Saalfelden 47 26N 12 51 E
25 Saanen 46 29N 7 15 E
25 Saarbrücken 49 15N 6 58 E
25 Saarburg 49 36N 6 32 E
48 Saaremaa, I. 58 30N 22 30 E
25 Saarland □ 49 20N 0 75 E
25 Saarlouis 49 19N 6 45 E
105 Saba, I. 17 30N 63 10W
40 Šabac 44 48N 19 42 E
32 Sabadell 41 28N 2 7 E
64 Sabah □ 6 0N 117 0 E
56 Sabalan, Kuhha-ye 38 15N 47 49 E
110 Sabanalargo 10 38N 74 55W
64 Sabang 5 50N 95 15 E
111 Sabará 19 55S 43 55W
60 Sabarmati, R. 22 25N 73 20 E
54 Sabastiya 32 17N 35 12 E
38 Sabáudia 41 17N 13 2 E
73 Sabhah 27 9N 14 29 E
60 Sabi, R. 36 48N 140 4 E
33 Sabinal, Pta. del 36 43N 2 44W
104 Sabinas 27 50N 101 10W
104 Sabinas Hidalgo 26 40N 100 10W
101 Sabine, R. 30 0N 93 45W
18 Sablé 47 50N 0 21W
87 Sable, C., Canada 43 29N 65 38W
91 Sable, C., U.S.A. 25 5N 81 0W
91 Sable I. 44 0N 60 0W
20 Sables-d'Olonne, Les 46 30N 1 45W
30 Sabôr, R. 41 10N 7 7W
30 Sabugal 40 20N 7 5W
57 Sabzevār 36 15N 57 40 E
57 Sabzvāran 28 45N 57 50 E
32 Sacedón 40 29N 2 41W
97 Sackets Harbor 43 57N 76 7W
25 Säckingen 47 34N 7 56 E
99 Saco 43 29N 70 28W
102 Sacramento 38 39N 121 30 E
102 Sacramento, R. 38 3N 121 56W
103 Sacramento Mts. 32 30N 105 30W
31 Sacratif, C. 36 42N 3 28W
30 Sada 43 22N 8 15W
32 Sádaba 2 19N 1 12W
62 Sadasivpet 17 38N 77 50 E
73 Sadd el Aali 24 5N 32 54 E
66 Sado, I. 38 15N 138 30 E
31 Sado, R. 38 29N 8 55W
60 Sadri 24 28N 74 30 E
45 Sæby 57 20N 10 32 E
32 Saelices 39 55N 2 49W
56 Safaniya 28 5N 48 42 E
57 Safed Koh 34 15N 64 0 E
44 Säffle 59 8N 12 55 E
103 Safford 32 54N 109 52W
13 Saffron Walden 52 5N 0 15 E
72 Safi 32 20N 9 17W
65 Saga, Indonesia 2 40S 132 55 E
66 Saga, Japan 33 15N 130 18 E
66 Saga □ 33 15N 130 20 E
59 Sagaing 22 0N 96 0 E
60 Sagar 23 50N 78 50 E
62 Sagara 14 14N 75 6 E
67 Sagil 50 15N 91 15 E
98 Saginaw 43 26N 83 55W
98 Saginaw B. 43 50N 83 40W
89 Saglouc 62 30N 74 15W
21 Sagone 42 7N 8 42 E
21 Sagone, G. de 42 4N 8 40 E
31 Sagres 37 0N 8 58W
105 Sagua la Grande 22 50N 80 10W
103 Saguache 38 10N 106 4W
91 Saguenay, R. 48 10N 69 45W
32 Sagunto 39 42N 0 18W
30 Sahagun 42 18N 5 2W
72 Sahara 23 0N 5 0W
60 Saharanpur 29 58N 77 33 E
60 Sahaswan 28 5N 78 45 E
61 Sahibganj 25 12N 87 55 E
60 Sahiwal 30 45N 73 8 E
27 Sahy 48 4N 18 55 E
27 Saïda 34 50N 0 11 E
57 Sa'idābād 29 30N 55 45 E
62 Saidapet 13 0N 80 15 E
58 Saidu 34 50N 72 15 E
57 Saighan 35 10N 67 55 E
20 Saignes 45 20N 2 31 E
63 Saigon = Phan Bho Ho Chi Minh 10 58N 106 40 E
55 Saihut 15 12N 51 10 E
66 Saijō 34 0N 133 5 E
66 Saiki 32 35N 131 50 E
14 St. Abbs Hd. 55 55N 2 10W
26 St. Aegyd 47 52N 15 33 E
20 St. Affrique 43 57N 2 53 E
18 St. Aignan 47 16N 1 22 E
13 St. Albans, U.K. 51 46N 0 21W
97 St. Albans, U.S.A. 44 49N 73 5W
13 St. Albans Hd. 50 34N 2 3W
19 St. Amand 50 25N 3 6 E
20 St. Amand-Mont-Rond 46 43N 2 30 E
19 St. Amarin 47 54N 7 0 E
21 St. Amour 46 26N 5 21 E
26 St. Andra 46 46N 14 50 E
20 St. André-de-Cubzac 44 59N 0 26W
21 St. André-les-Alpes 43 58N 6 30 E
14 St. Andrews 56 20N 2 48W
84 St. Arnaud 36 32S 143 16 E
12 St. Asaph 53 15N 3 27W
20 St. Astier 45 8N 0 31 E
18 St. Aubin de Cormier 48 15N 1 26W
91 St. Augustin 51 19N 58 48W
99 St. Augustine 29 52N 81 20W
13 St. Austell 50 20N 4 48W
19 St. Avold 49 7N 6 40 E
105 St. Barthelémy, I. 17 50N 62 50W
12 St. Bees Hd. 54 30N 3 38 E
20 St. Benoit-du-Sault 46 26N 1 24 E
93 St. Boniface 49 50N 97 10W
21 St. Bonnet 44 40N 6 5 E
18 St. Brice en Coglès 48 25N 1 22W
13 St. Bride's B. 51 48N 5 15W
18 St. Brieuc 48 30N 2 46W
18 St. Cast 48 37N 2 18W
96 St. Catherines 43 10N 79 15W
13 St. Catherine's Pt. 50 34N 1 18W
20 St. Céré 44 51N 1 54 E
21 St. Chamond 45 28N 4 31 E
100 St. Charles 38 46N 90 30W
20 St. Chély-d'Apcher 44 48N 3 17 E
20 St. Chinian 43 25N 2 56 E
105 St. Christopher, I. 17 20N 62 40W
20 St. Ciers sur Gironde 45 17N 0 37W
97 St. Clair 40 42N 76 12W
90 St. Clair, L. 42 30N 82 45W
20 St. Claud 45 54N 0 28 E
93 St. Claude, Canada 49 40N 98 22W
21 St. Claude, Fr. 46 22N 5 52 E
100 St. Cloud 45 30N 94 11W
91 St. Cœur de Marie 48 39N 71 43W
83 St. Cricq, C. 25 17S 113 6 E
20 St. Cyprien 42 37N 3 0 E
21 St. Cyr 43 11N 5 43 E
13 St. Davids 51 54N 5 16W
13 St. David's Hd. 51 54N 5 16W
105 St. David's I. 32 22N 64 39W
19 St. Denis 48 56N 2 22 E
18 St. Denis d'Orques 48 2N 0 17W
19 St. Dié 48 17N 6 56 E
19 St. Dizier 48 40N 5 0 E
21 St.-Egrève 45 14N 5 41 E
88 St. Elias, Mt. 60 20N 141 59W
20 St. Eloy 46 10N 2 51 E
20 St. Émilion 44 53N 0 9W
21 St. Étienne 45 27N 4 22 E
21 St. Étienne de Tinée 44 16N 6 56 E
90 St. Félicien 48 40N 72 25W
91 St. Fintan's 48 10N 58 50W
21 St. Florent 42 41N 9 18 E
20 St. Florent-sur-Cher 46 59N 2 15 E
19 St. Florentin 48 0N 3 45 E
20 St. Flour 45 2N 3 6 E
21 St. Fons 45 42N 4 52 E
20 St. Foy-la Grande 44 50N 0 13 E
75 St. Francis, C. 34 14S 24 49 E
97 St. Francis, L. 45 10N 74 20W
90 St. Gabriel de Brandon 46 17N 73 24W
25 St. Gallen 47 25N 9 23 E
25 St. Gallen □ 47 10N 9 8 E
20 St. Gaudens 43 6N 0 44 E
20 St. Gaultier 46 39N 1 26 E
81 St. George, Australia 28 1S 148 41 E
105 St. George, Bermuda 32 24N 64 42W
91 St. George, Canada 45 11N 66 57W
103 St. George, U.S.A. 37 10N 113 35W
99 St. George, C. 29 36N 85 2W
84 St. George Hd. 35 11S 150 45 E
93 St. George West 50 33N 96 7W
16 St. Georges, Belgium 50 37N 4 20 E
90 St. Georges, Canada 46 42N 72 35W
111 St. George's, Fr. Guiana 4 0N 52 0W
105 St. Georges, Grenada 12 5N 61 43W
91 St. George's B. 48 20N 59 0W
11 St. George's Chan. 52 0N 6 0W

105 St. George's I. 32 22N 64 40W
19 St. Germain 48 53N 2 5E
20 St. Germain de Calberte 44 13N 3 48E
20 St. Germain-des-Fossés 46 12N 3 26E
21 St. Gervais, Haute Savoie 45 53N 6 42E
20 St. Gervais, Puy de Dôme 46 4N 2 50E
20 St. Gilles-Croix-de-Vie 46 41N 1 55W
21 St. Gilles-du-Gard 43 40N 4 26E
20 St. Girons 42 59N 1 8E
25 St. Goar 50 31N 7 43E
71 St. Helena, I. 15 55S 5 44W
75 St. Helenabaai 32 40S 18 10E
80 St. Helens, Australia 41 20S 148 15E
12 St. Helens, U.K. 53 28N 2 44W
102 St. Helens, U.S.A. 45 55N 122 50W
18 St. Helier 49 11N 2 6W
90 St. Hyacinthe 45 40N 72 58W
13 St. Ives, Cambridge 52 20N 0 5W
13 St. Ives, Cornwall 50 13N 5 29W
90 St. Jean 45 20N 73 50W
93 St. Jean Baptiste 49 15N 97 20W
20 St. Jean-d'Angély 45 57N 0 31W
20 St. Jean-de-Luz 43 23N 1 39W
21 St.-Jean-de-Maurienne 45 16N 6 28E
20 St. Jean-de-Monts 46 47N 2 4W
20 St. Jean-du-Gard 47 7N 3 52E
90 St. Jérôme 45 55N 74 0W
26 St. Johann 47 22N 13 12E
91 St. John 45 20N 66 8W
91 St. John, L. 48 40N 72 0W
105 St. John's, Antigua 17 6N 61 51W
91 St. John's, Canada 47 45N 52 40W
97 St. Johnsbury 44 25N 72 1W
97 St. Johnsville 43 0N 74 43W
98 St. Joseph, Mich. 42 6N 86 29W
100 St. Joseph, Mo. 39 46N 94 51W
90 St. Jovite 46 8N 74 38W
19 St. Julien-du-Sault 48 2N 3 18E
20 St. Junien 45 53N 0 55E
19 St. Just-en-Chaussée 49 30N 2 25E
85 St. Kilda 45 53S 170 31E
105 St. Kitts, I. 17 20N 62 40W
93 St. Laurent 50 25N 97 58W
21 St. Laurent-du-Pont 45 23N 5 45E
91 St. Lawrence 46 54N 55 23W
91 St. Lawrence, G. of 48 25N 62 0W
88 St. Lawrence, I. 63 0N 170 0W
91 St. Lawrence, R. 49 15N 67 0W
91 St. Leonard 47 12N 67 58W
20 St. Léonard-de-Noblat 45 49N 1 29E
90 St. Lin 45 44N 73 46W
18 St. Lô 49 7N 1 5W
72 St. Louis, Senegal 16 8N 16 27W
100 St. Louis, U.S.A. 38 40N 90 20W
105 St. Lucia, I. 14 0N 60 50W
75 St. Lucia, L. 28 5S 32 30E
105 St. Lucia Chan. 14 15N 61 0W
105 St. Maarten, I. 18 0N 63 5W
20 St. Maixent 46 24N 0 12W
18 St. Malo 48 39N 2 1W
18 St. Malo, G. de 48 50N 2 30W
21 St. Mandrier 43 4N 5 56E
105 St. Marc 19 10N 72 5W
21 St. Marcellin 45 9N 5 20E
102 St. Maries 47 17N 116 34W
19 St. Martin 50 42N 1 38E
105 St. Martin, I. 18 0N 63 0W
91 St. Martins 45 22N 65 38W
20 St. Martory 43 9N 0 56E
80 St. Marys, Australia 41 32S 148 11E
96 St. Marys, U.S.A. 41 30N 78 33W
13 St. Marys, I. 49 55N 6 17W
18 St. Mathieu, Pte. de. 48 20N 4 45W
88 St. Matthew I. 60 30N 172 45W
19 St. Maur 48 48N 2 30E
20 St. Médard-de-Guizières 45 1N 0 4W
13 St. Michael's Mt. 50 7N 5 30W
25 St. Moritz 46 30N 9 50E
18 St. Nazaire 47 17N 2 12W
13 St. Neots 52 14N 0 16W
19 St. Nicolas 48 38N 6 18E
16 St. Niklaas 51 10N 4 8E
19 St. Omer 50 45N 2 15E
91 St. Pacôme 47 24N 69 58W
20 St. Palais 45 40N 1 8W
91 St. Pamphile 46 58N 69 48W
91 St. Pascal 47 32N 69 48W
92 St. Paul, Canada 51 34N 57 47W
20 St. Paul, Fr. 43 44N 1 3W
100 St. Paul, U.S.A. 44 54N 93 5W
3 St. Paul, I. 30 40S 77 34E
20 St. Paul-de-Fenouillet 42 50N 2 28E
100 St. Peter 44 15N 93 57W
13 St. Peter Port 49 27N 2 31W
99 St. Petersburg 27 45N 82 40W
91 St. Pierre, Canada 46 40N 56 0W
20 St. Pierre, Fr. 45 57N 1 19W
90 St. Pierre, L. 46 10N 72 50W
18 St. Pierre-Église 49 40N 1 24W
18 St. Pierre-en-Port 49 48N 0 30E
91 St. Pierre et Miquelon □ 46 49N 56 15W
20 St. Pierre-le-Moutier 46 48N 3 7E
18 St. Pierre-sur-Dives 49 2N 0 1W
19 St. Pol 50 21N 2 20E
19 St. Pol-sur-Mer 51 1N 2 20E
26 St. Polten 48 12N 15 37E
20 St. Pons 43 30N 2 45E
20 St. Pourcain-sur-Sioule 46 18N 3 18E
19 St. Quentin 49 50N 3 16E
21 St. Rambert d'Alban 45 17N 1 35E
21 St. Raphaël 43 25N 6 46E
18 St. Servan 48 38N 2 0E
18 St. Sever Calvados 48 50N 1 3W
91 St. Siméon 47 51N 69 54W
91 St. Stephen 45 16N 67 17W
20 St. Sulpice la Pointe 43 46N 1 41E
20 St. Sulpice-Laurière 46 3N 1 29E
90 St. Thomas, Canada 42 47N 81 12W
96 St. Thomas, U.S.A. 38 23N 92 13W
105 St. Thomas, Virgin Is. 18 21N 64 56W
90 St. Tite 46 45N 72 40W
21 St. Tropez 43 17N 6 38E
16 St. Troud 50 48N 5 10E
18 St. Vaast-la-Hougue 49 35N 1 17W
26 St. Valentin 48 10N 14 32E
19 St. Valéry 50 10N 1 38E
18 St. Valéry-en-Caux 49 52N 0 43E
21 St. Vallier 43 42N 6 51E
20 St. Varent 46 53N 0 13W
26 St. Veit 46 46N 14 21E
105 St. Vincent, I. 13 10N 61 10W
20 St. Vincent-de-Tyrosse 43 39N 1 18W
105 St. Vincent Pass. 13 30N 61 0W
93 St. Walburg 53 39N 109 12W
25 St. Wendel 49 28N 7 10E
26 St. Wolfgang 47 44N 13 27E
20 St. Yrieux 45 31N 1 12E
18 Ste. Adresse 49 31N 0 5E
91 Ste. Anne de Beaupré 47 2N 70 58W
19 Ste. Benoîte 49 47N 3 30E
91 Ste. Cecile 47 56N 64 34W
20 Ste. Hermine 46 32N 1 4W
105 Ste. Marie 14 48N 61 1W
75 Ste. Marie, C. 25 36S 45 8E
19 Ste. Marie-aux-Mines 48 10N 7 12E
91 Ste. Marie de la Madeleine 46 26N 71 0W
18 Ste. Maur 47 7N 0 37E
21 Ste. Maxime 43 19N 6 39E
19 Ste. Menehould 49 5N 4 54E
18 Ste. Mère Église 49 24N 1 19W
105 Ste. Rose 16 20N 61 45W
93 Ste. Rose du lac 51 10N 99 30W
20 Saintes 45 45N 0 37W
20 Saintonge, Reg. 45 40N 0 50W
59 Sairang 23 50N 92 45E
66 Saitama □ 36 25N 137 0E
110 Sajama, Mt. 18 6S 68 54W
66 Sakai 34 30N 135 30E
66 Sakaide 34 32N 133 50E
66 Sakaiminato 35 33N 133 15E
66 Sakata 38 55N 139 56E
51 Sakhalin 51 0N 143 0E
54 Sakhnin 32 52N 35 12E
69 Sakishima-guntō, Is. 24 30N 124 0E
75 Sakrivier 30 54S 20 28E
44 Sala 59 58N 16 35E
39 Sala Consilina 40 23N 15 35E
77 Sala-y-Gomez, I. 26 28S 105 28W
108 Saladillo 35 40S 59 55W
72 Salaga 8 31N 0 31W
30 Salamanca, Sp. 40 58N 5 39W
96 Salamanca, U.S.A. 42 10N 78 42W
30 Salamanca □ 40 57N 5 40W
43 Salamis 37 56N 23 30E
30 Salas 43 25N 6 15W
30 Salas de los Infantes 42 2N 3 17W
65 Salatiga 7 19S 110 30E
48 Salavat 53 21N 55 55E
110 Salaverry 8 15S 79 0W
65 Salawati, I. 1 7S 130 54E
74 Salazar 9 18S 14 54E
19 Salbris 47 25N 2 3E
75 Saldanha 33 0S 17 58E
84 Sale, Australia 38 7S 147 0E
12 Sale, U.K. 53 26N 2 19W
72 Salé 34 3N 6 48W
50 Salekhard 66 30N 66 25E
62 Salem, India 11 40N 78 11E
97 Salem, Mass. 42 29N 70 53W
96 Salem, Ohio 40 52N 80 50W
102 Salem, Oreg. 45 0N 123 0W
98 Salem, Va. 37 19N 80 8W
97 Salem Depot 42 47N 71 12W
38 Salemi 37 49N 12 47E
21 Salernes 43 34N 6 15E
39 Salerno 40 40N 14 44E
39 Salerno, G. di 40 35N 14 45E
12 Salford 53 30N 2 17W
27 Salgótarján 48 5N 19 47E
56 Salihli 38 29N 28 9E
75 Salima 13 47S 34 26E
100 Salina 38 50N 97 40W
104 Salina Cruz 16 10N 95 10W
111 Salinas, Brazil 16 20S 42 10W
103 Salinas, U.S.A. 36 40N 121 38W
105 Salinas, B. de 11 4N 85 45W
33 Salinas, C. de 39 16N 3 4E
111 Salinópolis 0 40S 47 20W
31 Salir 47 14N 8 2W
81 Salisbury, Australia 34 46S 138 38E
13 Salisbury, U.K. 51 4N 1 48W
98 Salisbury, Md. 38 20N 75 38W
99 Salisbury, N.C. 35 42N 80 29W
13 Salisbury Plain 51 13N 2 0W
41 Sãliște 45 45N 23 56E
102 Salmon 45 12N 113 56W
102 Salmon, R. 45 51N 116 46W
97 Salmon Arm 50 40N 119 15W
97 Salmon Falls 42 55N 114 59W
83 Salmon Gums 32 59S 121 38E
102 Salmon River Mts. 45 0N 114 30W
47 Salo 60 22N 23 3E
31 Salobreña 36 44N 3 35W
21 Salon 43 39N 5 6E
32 Salou, C. 41 3N 1 10E
20 Salses 42 50N 2 55E
62 Salsette I. 19 5N 72 50E
49 Salsk 46 28N 41 30E
36 Salsomaggiore 44 48N 9 59E
102 Salt Lake City 40 45N 111 58W
60 Salt Ra. 32 30N 72 25E
108 Salta 24 47S 65 25W
108 Salta □ 24 48S 65 30W
14 Saltcoats 55 38N 4 47W
45 Saltholm, I. 55 38N 12 43E
104 Saltillo 25 30N 100 57W
108 Salto, Arg. 34 20S 60 15W
108 Salto, Uruguay 31 20S 58 10W
103 Salton Sea 33 20N 116 0W
72 Saltpond 5 15N 1 3W
44 Saltsjöbaden 59 15N 18 20E
92 Saltspring 48 54N 123 37W
73 Salum 31 31N 25 7E
62 Salur 18 27N 83 18E
36 Saluzzo 44 39N 7 29E
111 Salvador, Brazil 13 0S 38 30W
93 Salvador, Canada 52 20N 109 25W
104 Salvador ■ 13 50N 89 0W
31 Salveterra de Magos 39 1N 8 47W
30 Salvora, I. 42 30N 8 58W
59 Salween, R. 16 31N 97 37E
26 Salza, R. 47 40N 14 43E
26 Salzach, R. 48 12N 12 56E
26 Salzburg 47 48N 13 2E
26 Salzburg □ 47 25N 13 15E
24 Salzgitter 52 2N 10 22E
24 Salzwedel 52 50N 11 11E
63 Sam Neua 20 29N 104 0E
63 Sam Ngao 17 18N 99 0E
101 Sam Rayburn Res. 31 15N 94 20W
50 Sama 60 10N 60 15E
30 Sama de Langreo 43 18N 5 40W
51 Samagaltai 50 36N 95 3E
62 Samalkot 17 3N 82 13E
57 Samangan □ 36 15N 67 40E
65 Samar, I. 12 0N 125 0E
54 Samaria, Reg.= Shomron, Reg. 32 15N 35 13E
64 Samarinda 0 30S 117 9E
50 Samarkand 39 40N 67 0E
61 Sambalpur 21 28N 83 58E
60 Sambhar 26 52N 11 16E
108 Samborombón, B. 36 5S 57 20W
16 Sambre, R. 50 28N 4 52E
68 Samchŏk 37 27N 129 10E
19 Samer 50 38N 1 44E
85 Samoa Is. 14 0S 171 0W
21 Samoëns 46 5N 6 45E
41 Samokov 42 20N 23 33E
30 Samos 42 44N 7 20W
43 Sámos, I. 37 45N 26 50E
42 Samothráki, I. 40 28N 25 38E
65 Sampang 7 11S 113 13E
32 Samper de Calanda 41 11N 4 2W
64 Sampit 2 20S 113 0E
69 Samshui 23 7N 112 58E
45 Samsø, I. 55 52N 10 37E
56 Samsun 41 15N 36 15E
63 Samut Prakan 13 32N 100 40E
63 Samut Sakhon 13 31N 100 20E
63 Samut Songkhram 13 24N 100 1E
72 San 13 15N 4 45W
30 San Adrián, C. de 43 21N 8 50W
77 San Ambrosio, I. 26 21S 79 52W
105 San Andrés, I. de 12 42N 81 46W
104 San Andrés Tuxtla 18 30N 95 20W
101 San Angelo 31 30N 100 30W
108 San Antonio, Chile 33 40S 71 40W
101 San Antonio, U.S.A. 29 30N 98 30W
105 San Antonio, C. 21 50N 84 57W
33 San Antonio, C. de 38 48N 0 12E
33 San Antonio Abad 38 59N 1 19E
105 San Antonio de los Banos 22 54N 82 31W
112 San Antonio Oeste 40 40S 65 0W
39 San Bartolomeo 41 24N 15 1E
36 San Benedetto 45 2N 10 57E
101 San Benito 26 5N 97 32W
103 San Bernardino 34 7N 117 18W
65 San Bernardino Str. 12 37N 124 12E
108 San Bernardo 33 40S 70 50W
110 San Bernardo, I. de 9 45N 75 50W
105 San Blas, Cord. de 9 15N 78 30W
108 San Carlos, Arg. 33 50S 69 0W
65 San Carlos, Philippines 10 29N 123 25E
109 San Carlos, Uruguay 34 46S 54 58W
110 San Carlos, Ven. 1 55N 67 4W
110 San Carlos, Ven. 9 40N 68 36W
112 San Carlos de Bariloche 41 10S 71 25W
32 San Carlos de la Rápita 40 37N 0 35E
110 San Carlos del Zulia 9 1N 71 55W
103 San Carlos L. 33 13N 110 24W
38 San Cataldo 37 30N 13 58E
32 San Celoni 41 42N 2 30E
33 San Clemente, Sp. 39 24N 2 25W
103 San Clemente, U.S.A. 33 29N 117 45W
103 San Clemente I. 33 0N 118 30W
105 San Cristóbal, Dom. Rep. 18 25N 70 6W
110 San Cristóbal, Ven 7 46N 72 14W
104 San Cristóbal de las Casas 16 50N 92 33W
39 San Demétrio Corone 39 34N 16 22E
103 San Diego 32 50N 117 10W
112 San Diego, C. 54 40S 65 10W
37 San Dona di Piave 45 38N 12 34E
108 San Estanislao 24 39S 56 26W
30 San Esteban de Gormaz 41 34N 3 13W
36 San Felice sul Panaro 44 51N 11 9E
108 San Felipe, Chile 32 43S 70 50W
110 San Felipe, Ven. 10 20N 68 44W
32 San Felíu de Guíxals 41 45N 3 1E
107 San Felix, I. 26 30S 80 0W
108 San Fernando, Chile 34 30S 71 0W
65 San Fernando, Philippines 15 5N 120 37E
65 San Fernando, Philippines 16 40N 120 23E
31 San Fernando, Sp. 36 22N 6 17W
105 San Fernando, Trinidad 10 20N 61 30W
103 San Fernando, U.S.A. 34 15N 118 29W
110 San Fernando de Apure 7 54N 67 28W
110 San Fernando de Atabapo 4 3N 67 42W
39 San Fernando di Puglia 41 18N 16 5E
108 San Francisco, Arg. 31 30S 62 5W
103 San Francisco, U.S.A. 37 35N 122 30W
103 San Francisco, R. 32 59N 109 22W
105 San Francisco de Macoris 19 19N 70 15W
104 San Francisco del Oro 26 52N 105 50W

33 San Francisco Javier 38 40N 1 25E
39 San Fratello 38 1N 14 33E
110 San Gil 6 33N 73 8W
36 San Gimignano 43 28N 11 3E
37 San Giovanni in Persiceto 44 39N 11 12E
39 San Giovanni Rotondo 41 44N 15 42E
37 San Giovanni Valdarno 43 32N 11 30E
36 San Giuliano Terme 43 45N 10 26E
25 San Gottardo, P. del 46 33N 8 33E
109 San Gregorio 32 37S 55 40W
108 San Ignacio 26 52S 57 3W
108 San Isidro 34 29S 58 31W
109 San Javier, Arg. 27 55S 55 5W
108 San Javier, Chile 35 40S 71 45W
102 San Joaquin, R. 36 43N 121 50W
108 San Jorge 31 54S 61 50W
112 San Jorge, G. de, Arg. 46 0S 66 0W
32 San Jorge, G. de, Sp. 40 50N 0 55W
104 San José, Guatemala 14 0N 90 50W
65 San Jose, Philippines 15 45N 120 55E
65 San Jose, Philippines 10 50N 122 5E
33 San Jose, Sp. 38 55N 1 18E
103 San Jose, U.S.A. 37 20N 122 0W
112 San José, G. 42 20S 64 20W
108 San José de Mayo 34 27S 56 27W
110 San José de Ocune 4 15N 70 20W
104 San José del Cabo 23 0N 109 50W
110 San José del Guaviare 2 35N 72 38W
108 San Juan, Arg. 31 30S 68 30W
105 San Juan, Dom. Rep. 18 49N 71 12W
104 San Juan, Mexico 21 20N 102 50W
103 San Juan, R. 37 18N 110 28W
108 San Juan □ 31 9S 69 0W
108 San Juan Bautista 26 37S 57 6W
103 San Juan Capistrano 33 29N 117 46W
110 San Juan de los Morros 9 55N 67 21W
105 San Juan del Norte, B. de 11 30N 83 40W
31 San Juan del Puerto 37 20N 6 50W
103 San Juan Mts. 38 30N 108 30W
112 San Julián 49 15S 68 0W
32 San Just, Sa. de 40 45N 0 41W
108 San Justo 30 55S 60 30W
103 San Leandro 37 40N 122 6W
30 San Leonardo 41 51N 3 5W
108 San Lorenzo, Arg. 32 45S 60 45W
110 San Lorenzo, Ecuador 1 15N 78 50W
108 San Lorenzo, Paraguay 25 20S 57 32W
112 San Lorenzo, Mt. 47 40S 72 20W
32 San Lorenzo de la Parilla 39 51N 2 22W
104 San Lucas, C. de 22 50N 110 0W
39 San Lucido 39 18N 16 3E
108 San Luis 33 20S 66 20W
108 San Luis □ 34 0S 66 0W
104 San Luis de la Paz 21 18N 100 31W
103 San Luis Obispo 35 17N 120 40W
104 San Luis Potosí 22 9N 100 59W
104 San Luis Potosí □ 22 30N 100 30W
39 San Marco Argentano 39 34N 16 8E
39 San Marco in Lamis 41 43N 15 38E
104 San Marcos, Guatemala 14 59N 91 52W
101 San Marcos, U.S.A. 29 53N 98 0W
37 San Marino ■ 43 56N 12 25E
108 San Martín 33 5S 68 28W
30 San Martín de Valdeiglesias 40 21N 4 24W
36 San Martino de Calvi 45 57N 9 41E
103 San Mateo 37 32N 122 25W
112 San Matías, G. 41 30S 64 0W
104 San Miguel, Salvador 13 30N 88 12W
33 San Miguel, Sp. 39 3N 1 26E
33 San Miguel de Salinas 37 59N 0 47W
108 San Miguel de Tucumán 26 50S 65 20W
36 San Miniato 43 40N 10 50E
108 San Nicolás de los Arroyas 33 17S 60 10W
108 San Pedro, Arg. 24 12S 64 55W
108 San Pedro, Chile 21 58S 68 30W
105 San Pedro, Dom. Rep. 18 30N 69 18W
108 San Pedro □ 24 0S 57 0W
108 San Pedro, Pta. 25 30S 70 38W
31 San Pedro, Sa. de 39 18N 6 40W
108 San Pedro de Jujuy 23 12S 64 55W
104 San Pedro de las Colonias 25 50N 102 59W
33 San Pedro del Pinatar 37 50N 0 50W
104 San Pedro Sula 15 30N 88 0W
38 San Pietro, I. 39 9N 8 17E
39 San Pietro Vernotico 40 28N 18 0E
65 San Quintin 16 1N 120 56E
108 San Rafael 34 40S 68 30W
108 San Ramón de la Nueva Orán 23 10S 64 20W
36 San Remo 43 48N 7 47E
31 San Roque 28 15S 58 45W
104 San Salvador 13 40N 89 20W
105 San Salvador, I. 24 0N 74 40W
108 San Salvador de Jujuy 23 30S 65 40W
112 San Sebastián, Arg. 53 10S 68 30W
32 San Sabastián, Spain 43 17N 1 58W
37 San Severino Marche 43 13N 13 10E
39 San Severo 41 41N 15 23E
103 San Simon 32 14N 109 16W
37 San Stéfano di Cadore 46 34N 12 33E
109 San Tomé, C. de 8 58N 64 8W
112 San Valentín, Mt. 46 30S 73 30W
31 San Vicente de Alcantara 39 22N 7 8W
30 San Vicente de la Barquera 43 30N 4 29W
36 San Vincenzo 43 9N 10 32E
38 San Vito, C. 38 11N 12 41E
39 San Vito dei Normanni 40 39N 17 42E
37 San Vito di Tagliamento 45 55N 12 50E
55 Sana 15 27N 44 12E
37 Sana, R. 45 3N 16 23E
74 Sanaga, R. 3 35N 9 38E
65 Sanana 2 5S 125 50E
60 Sanand 22 59N 72 25E
56 Sanandaj 35 25N 47 7E
21 Sanary 43 7N 5 48E
20 Sancergues 47 10N 2 54E
19 Sancerre 47 20N 2 50E
19 Sancerrois, Collines du 47 25N 2 45E
20 Sancoins 46 47N 2 55E
105 Sancti Spíritus 21 52N 79 33W
90 Sand Lake 47 46N 84 31W
101 Sand Springs 36 12N 96 5W
64 Sandakan 5 53N 118 10E
63 Sandan 12 46N 106 0E
14 Sanday, I. 59 14N 2 30W
44 Sandlefjord 59 10N 10 15E
103 Sanders 35 12N 109 25W
81 Sandgate 27 20S 153 5E
56 Sandikli 38 30N 30 20E
61 Sandila 27 4N 80 31E
47 Sandnes 58 50N 5 45E
59 Sandoway 18 20N 94 30E
102 Sandpoint 48 20N 116 40W
12 Sandringham 52 50N 0 30E
83 Sandstone 28 0S 119 15E
96 Sandusky 41 25N 82 40W
45 Sandvig 55 18N 14 48E
44 Sandviken 60 38N 16 46E
59 Sandwip Chan. 22 35N 91 35E
80 Sandy, C. 24 41S 153 8E
99 Sanford, Fla. 28 45N 81 20W
97 Sanford, Me. 43 28N 70 47W
99 Sanford, N.C. 35 30N 79 10W
88 Sanford, Mt. 62 30N 143 0W
62 Sangamner 19 30N 74 15E
62 Sangareddipet 17 38N 78 4E
103 Sanger 36 47N 119 35W
24 Sangerhausen 51 28N 11 18E
64 Sanggau 0 5N 110 30E
65 Sangihe, Pulau 3 45N 125 30E
74 Sangmelina 2 57N 12 1E
33 Sangonera, R. 37 59N 1 4W
101 Sangre de Cristo Mts. 37 0N 105 0W
39 Sangro, R. 42 14N 14 32E
67 Sangsang 29 30N 86 0E
32 Sanguesa 42 37N 1 17W
21 Sanguinaires, I. 41 51N 8 36E
74 Sangwa 5 30S 26 0E
62 Sankaranayinarkovil 9 10N 77 35E
62 Sankeshwar 16 23N 74 23E
61 Sankh, R. 22 15N 84 48E
31 Sanlucar de Barrameda 36 47N 6 21W
31 Sanlúcar-la-Mayor 37 26N 6 18W
38 Sanluri 39 55N 8 55E
69 Sanmenhsia 34 46N 111 30E
39 Sannicandro Gargánico 41 50N 15 34E
27 Sanok 49 35N 22 10E
14 Sanquhar 55 21N 3 56W
72 Sansanné-Mango 10 20N 0 30E
37 Sansepolcro 43 34N 12 8E
37 Sanski Most 44 46N 16 40E
39 Sant' Agata 41 6N 14 30E
39 Sant' Ágata di Militello 38 2N 14 40E
110 Santa Ana, Ecuador 1 10S 80 20W
104 Santa Ana, Mexico 30 31N 111 8W
104 Santa Ana, Salvador 14 0N 89 40W
103 Santa Ana, U.S.A. 33 48N 117 55W
36 Sant' Ángelo 45 14N 9 25E
38 Sant' Antíoco, I. 39 2N 8 30E
37 Sant' Arcángelo di Romagna 44 4N 12 26E
104 Santa Barbara, Mexico 26 48N 105 50W
32 Santa Barbara, Sp. 40 42N 0 29E
103 Santa Bárbara, U.S.A. 34 25N 119 40W
33 Santa Barbara, Mt. 37 23N 2 50W
103 Santa Catalina, G. of 33 0N 118 0W
103 Santa Catalina I. 33 20N 118 30W
109 Santa Catarina □ 27 25S 48 30W
109 Santa Caterina, I. de 27 36S 48 30W
38 Santa Caterina Villarmo 37 37N 14 1E
109 Santa Cecilia 26 56S 50 27W
105 Santa Clara, Cuba 22 20N 80 0W
103 Santa Clara, U.S.A. 37 21N 122 0W
109 Santa Clara de Olimar 32 50S 54 54W
30 Santa Comba 43 2N 8 49W
112 Santa Cruz, Arg. 50 0S 68 50W
72 Santa Cruz, Canary Is. 28 29N 16 26W
105 Santa Cruz, Costa Rica 10 15N 85 41W
65 Santa Cruz, Philippines 14 20N 121 30E
103 Santa Cruz, Calif. 36 55N 122 10W
103 Santa Cruz, N. Mex. 35 59N 106 1W
76 Santa Cruz, I. 0 38S 90 23W
112 Santa Cruz, R. 50 10S 68 20W
31 Santa Cruz de Mudela 38 39N 3 28W
30 Santa Cruz del Retamar 40 8N 4 14W
109 Santa Cruz do Rio Pardo 22 54S 49 37W
109 Santa Cruz do Sul 29 42S 52 25W
108 Santa Elena 30 58S 59 47W
20 Santa Enimie 44 24N 3 26E
39 Sant' Eufémia, G. di 38 50N 16 10E
33 Santa Eulalia 40 34N 1 20W
108 Santa Fe, Arg. 31 35S 60 41W
31 Santa Fé, Sp. 37 11N 3 43W
103 Sante Fe, U.S.A. 35 40N 106 0W
108 Santa Fe □ 30 0S 61 0W
111 Santa Filomena 9 0S 45 50W
112 Santa Inés, I. 54 0S 73 0W
31 Santa Inés, Mt. 38 32N 5 37W
108 Santa Lucía, Arg. 31 30S 68 45W
33 Santa Lucia, Sp. 37 35N 0 58W
108 Santa Lucía, Uruguay 34 27S 56 24W
103 Santa Lucia Ra. 36 0N 121 30W
104 Santa Margarita, I. 24 30N 112 0W
36 Santa Margherita 44 20N 9 11E
109 Santa Mariá, Brazil 29 40S 53 40W
39 Santa Maria, Italy 41 3N 14 29E
32 Santa Maria, Sp. 39 39N 2 45E
103 Santa Maria, U.S.A. 34 58N 120 29W
31 Santa Maria, C. de 36 39N 7 53W
30 Santa Maria, Ria de 43 44N 7 45W
111 Santa Maria de Vitória 13 24S 44 12W
39 Santa Maria di Leuca, C. 39 48N 18 20E
110 Santa Marta 11 15N 74 13W
109 Santa Marta Grande, C. 28 43S 48 50W
103 Santa Monica 34 0N 118 30W
30 Santa Olalla 40 2N 4 25W
103 Santa Paula 34 20N 119 2W
33 Santa Pola 38 13N 0 35W
108 Santa Rosa, Arg. 36 40S 64 30W
109 Santa Rosa, Brazil 27 52S 54 29W
104 Santa Rosa, Honduras 14 40N 89 0W
102 Santa Rosa, Calif. 38 20N 122 50W
101 Santa Rosa, N. Mex. 34 58N 104 40W
103 Santa Rosa I. 34 0N 120 15W
104 Santa Rosalía 27 20N 112 30W
37 Santa Sofia 43 57N 11 55E
108 Santa Sylvina 27 50S 61 10W
109 Santa Vitória do Palmar 33 32S 53 25W
38 Santadi 39 5N 8 42E
69 Santai 31 10N 105 2E
109 Santana do Livramento 30 55S 55 30W
30 Santander 43 27N 3 51W
30 Santander □ 43 25N 4 0W
33 Santany 39 20N 3 5E
102 Santaquin 40 0N 111 51W
111 Santarem, Brazil 2 25S 54 42W
31 Santarém, Port. 39 12N 8 42W
31 Santarém □ 39 10N 8 40W
39 Santéramo in Colle 40 48N 16 45E
37 Santerno, R. 44 34N 11 58E
109 Santiago, Brazil 29 11S 54 52W
108 Santiago, Chile 33 24S 70 50W
105 Santiago, Dom. Rep. 19 30N 70 40W
105 Santiago, Panama 8 0N 81 0W
108 Santiago □ 33 30S 70 50W
30 Santiago de Compostela 42 52N 8 37W
105 Santiago de Cuba 20 0N 75 49W
108 Santiago del Estero 27 50S 64 15W
108 Santiago del Estero □ 27 50S 64 20W
31 Santiago do Cacem 38 1N 8 42W
104 Santiago Ixcuintla 21 50N 105 11W
30 Santillana del Mar 43 24N 4 6W
61 Santipur 23 17N 88 25E
31 Santisteban del Puerto 38 17N 3 15W
111 Santo Amaro 12 30S 38 50W
109 Santo Anastácio 21 58S 51 39W
109 Santo André 23 39S 46 29W
109 Santo Ângelo 28 15S 54 15W
105 Santo Domingo 18 30N 70 0W
30 Santo Domingo de la Calzada 42 26N 2 27W
39 Santo Stéfano di Camastro 38 1N 14 22E
30 Santo Tirso 41 29N 8 18W
109 Santo Tomé 28 40S 56 5W
30 Santoña 43 29N 3 20W
109 Santos 24 0S 46 20W
31 Santos, Sa. de los 38 7N 5 12W
109 Santos Dumont 22 55S 43 10W
69 Santu 25 59N 113 3E
69 Santuaho 26 36N 119 42E
54 Sanur 32 22N 35 15E
19 Sanvignes les Mines 46 40N 4 18E
69 Sanyuan 34 35N 108 54E
31 São Bartholomeu de Messines 37 15N 8 17W
109 São Borja 28 45S 56 0W
31 São Bras d'Alportel 37 8N 7 58W
109 São Carlos 22 0S 47 50W
111 São Cristóvão 11 15S 37 15W
111 São Domingos 13 25S 46 10W
111 São Francisco 16 0S 44 50W
111 São Francisco, R. 10 30S 36 24W
109 São Francisco do Sul 26 15S 48 36W
109 São Gabriel 30 10S 54 30W
109 São Gonçalo 22 48S 43 5W
109 São João da Boa Vista 21 58S 46 47W
30 São João da Pesqueira 41 8N 7 24W
109 São João del Rei 21 8S 44 15W

111 São João do Araguaia 5 23s 48 46w
111 São João do Piaui 8 10s 42 15w
109 São Leopoldo 29 50s 51 10w
109 São Lourenço 16 30s 55 5w
111 São Luís 2 39s 44 15w
109 São Luís Gonzaga 28 25s 55 0w
111 São Marcos, B. de 2 0s 44 0w
111 São Mateus 18 44s 39 50w
8 São Miguel, I. 37 33n 25 27w
109 São Paulo 23 40s 56 50w
109 São Paulo □ 22 0s 49 0w
30 São Pedro do Sul 40 46n 8 4w
111 São Roque, C. de 5 30s 35 10w
74 São Salvador do Congo 6 18s 14 16e
109 São Sebastião, I. de 23 50s 45 18w
109 São Sebastião do Paraíso 20 54s 46 59w
71 São Tomé, I. 0 10n 7 0e
109 São Vicente 23 57s 46 23w
31 São Vicente, C. de 37 0n 9 0w
21 Saône, R. 45 44n 4 50e
21 Saône-et-Loire □ 46 25n 4 50e
72 Sapele 5 50n 5 40e
110 Saposoa 6 55s 76 30w
66 Sapporo 43 0n 141 15e
39 Sapri 40 5n 15 37e
61 Sapt Kosi, R. 26 30n 86 55e
101 Sapulpa 36 0n 96 40w
56 Saqqez 36 15n 46 20e
32 Saragossa 41 39n 0 53w
40 Sarajevo 43 52n 18 26e
97 Saranac Lake 44 20n 74 10w
42 Saranda 39 59n 19 55e
109 Sarandí del Yi 33 21s 55 58w
108 Sarandí Grande 33 20s 55 50w
65 Sarangani B. 6 0n 125 13e
48 Saransk 54 10n 45 10e
48 Sarapul 56 28n 53 48e
99 Sarasota 27 10n 82 30w
97 Saratoga Springs 43 5n 73 47w
48 Saratov 51 30n 46 2e
64 Sarawak □ 2 0s 113 0e
57 Sarbāz 26 38n 61 19e
57 Sarbisheh 32 30n 59 40e
27 Sârbogârd 46 55n 18 40e
61 Sarda, R. 27 22n 81 23e
60 Sardarshahr 28 30n 74 29e
38 Sardegna, I. 39 57n 9 0e
60 Sardhana 29 9n 77 39e
38 Sardinia, I.= Sardegna, I. 39 57n 9 0e
6 Sargasso Sea 27 0n 67 0w
60 Sargodha 32 10n 72 40e
73 Sarh 9 5n 18 23e
57 Sarī 36 30n 53 11e
56 Sarikamiş 40 22n 42 35e
64 Sarikei 2 8n 111 30e
80 Sarina 21 22s 149 13e
32 Sariñena 41 47n 0 10w
68 Sariwon 38 31n 125 44e
13 Sark, I. 49 25n 2 20w
27 Sarkad 46 47n 21 17e
20 Sarlat-la-Canéda 44 54n 1 13e
112 Sarmiento 45 35s 69 5w
37 Sarnano 43 2n 13 17e
96 Sarnia 43 0n 82 30w
39 Sarno 40 48n 14 35e
48 Sarny 51 17n 26 40e
43 Saronikós Kól. 37 45n 23 45e
36 Saronno 45 38n 9 2e
27 Sárospatak 58 18n 21 33e
44 Sarpsborg 59 16n 11 12e
36 Sarracín 42 15n 3 45w
19 Sarralbe 48 55n 7 1e
19 Sarrebourg 48 43n 7 3e
19 Sarreguemines 49 1n 7 4e
30 Sarriá 42 41n 7 49w
32 Sarrión 40 9n 0 49w
21 Sartène 41 38n 9 0e
18 Sarthe □ 47 58n 0 10e
18 Sarthe, R. 47 30n 0 32w
50 Sartynya 63 30n 62 50e
57 Sarur 23 17n 58 4e
50 Sary Tash 39 45n 73 40e
50 Saryshagan 46 12n 73 48e
18 Sarzeau 47 31n 2 48w
36 Sarzana 44 7n 9 57e
55 Sasabeneh 7 59n 44 43e
61 Sasaram 24 57n 84 5e
40 Sasca Montană 44 41n 21 45e
66 Sasebo 33 15n 129 50e
93 Saskatchewan □ 53 40n 103 30w
93 Saskatchewan, R. 53 12n 99 16w
93 Saskatoon 52 10n 106 45w
51 Saskylakh 71 55n 114 1e
48 Sasovo 54 25n 41 55e
72 Sassandra 5 0n 6 8w
72 Sassandra, R. 4 58n 6 5w
38 Sássari 40 44n 8 33e
24 Sassnitz 54 29n 13 39e
36 Sassuolo 44 31n 10 47e
62 Satara 17 44n 73 58e
48 Satka 55 3n 59 1e
61 Satkhira 22 43n 89 8e
60 Satmala Hills 20 15n 74 40e
61 Satna 24 35n 80 50e
27 Sátoraljaújhely 48 25n 21 41e
60 Satpura Ra. 21 40n 75 0e
63 Sattahip 12 41n 100 54e
62 Sattenapalle 16 25n 80 6e
27 Satu Mare 47 48n 22 53e
27 Satu-Mare □ 47 45n 23 0e
47 Sauda 59 38n 6 21e
46 Sauđarkrókur 65 45n 19 40w
55 Saudi Arabia ■ 26 0n 44 0e
24 Sauerland, Mts. 51 0n 8 0e
20 Saujon 45 41n 0 55w
19 Sauldre, R. 47 16n 1 30e
19 Saulieu 47 17n 4 14e
90 Sault Ste. Marie, Canada 46 30n 84 20w
98 Saulte Ste. Marie, U.S.A. 46 27n 84 22w
18 Saumur 47 15n 0 5w
46 Saurbaer 64 24n 21 35w
40 Sava, R. 44 50n 20 26e
85 Savaii, I. 13 35s 172 25w
72 Savalou 7 57n 2 4e
100 Savanna 42 5n 90 10w
99 Savannah 32 4n 81 4w
99 Savannah, R. 32 2n 80 53w
63 Savannakhet 16 30n 104 49e
90 Savant Lake 50 20n 90 40w
62 Savantvadi 15 55n 73 54e
62 Savanur 14 59n 75 28e
60 Savda 21 9n 75 56e
72 Savé 8 2n 2 17e
20 Save, R. 43 47n 1 17e
56 Sāveh 35 2n 50 20e
72 Savelugu 9 38n 0 54w
18 Savenay 47 20n 1 55w
19 Saverne 48 39n 7 20e
36 Savigliano 44 39n 7 40e
30 Saviñao 42 35n 7 38w
21 Savoie □ 45 26n 6 35e
21 Savoie, Reg. 45 30n 5 20e
36 Savona 44 19n 8 29e
45 Sävsjö 57 20n 14 40e
45 Sävsjöström 57 1n 15 25e
65 Sawai 3 0s 129 5e
63 Sawankhalok 17 19n 99 54e
103 Sawatch Mts. 38 30n 106 30w
73 Sawknah 29 4n 15 47e
75 Sawmills 19 30s 28 2e
65 Sawu Sea 9 30s 121 50e
91 Sayabec 38 35n 67 41w
56 Sayda 33 35n 35 25e
68 Saynshand 44 55n 110 11e
97 Sayre 42 0n 76 30w
97 Sayville 40 45n 73 7w
26 Sazava 49 50n 15 0e
58 Sazin 35 35n 73 30e
12 Sca Fell, Mt 54 27n 3 14w
18 Scaër 48 2n 3 42e
36 Scandiano 44 36n 10 40e
14 Scapa Flow 58 52n 3 0w
12 Scarborough 54 17n 0 24w
25 Schaal See 53 40n 10 57e
25 Schaffhausen 47 42n 8 36e
26 Schärding 48 27n 13 27e
26 Scharnitz 47 23n 11 15e
91 Schefferville 54 50n 66 40w
26 Scheibbs 48 1n 15 9e
16 Schelde, R. 51 22n 4 15e
97 Schenectady 42 50n 73 58w
16 Scheveningen 52 6n 4 18e
16 Schiedam 51 55n 4 25e
25 Schifferstadt 49 22n 8 23e
19 Schiltigheim 48 35n 7 45e
37 Schío 45 42n 11 21e
26 Schladming 47 23n 13 41e
24 Schleswig 54 32n 9 34e
24 Schleswig-Holstein □ 54 10n 9 40e
24 Schmalkalden 50 43n 10 28e
24 Schmölin 50 54n 12 22e
24 Schneeberg 47 53n 15 55e
24 Schönebeck 52 2n 11 42e
65 Schouten, Kep. 1 0s 136 0e
25 Schramberg 48 12n 8 24e
90 Schreiber 48 45n 87 20w
26 Schruns 47 5n 9 56e
90 Schumacher 48 30n 81 16w
102 Schurz 38 59n 118 57w
97 Schuykill Haven 40 37n 76 11w
25 Schwabach 49 19n 11 3e
25 Schwäbisch Gmund 48 49n 9 48e
25 Schwabisch Hall 49 7n 9 45e
25 Schwäbische Alb, Mts. 48 30n 9 30e
68 Schwangcheng 45 27n 126 27e
68 Schwangyashan 46 35n 131 15e
26 Schwarzach R. 50 30n 11 30e
24 Schwarzenberg 50 31n 12 49e
25 Schwarzwald 48 0n 8 0e
26 Schwaz 47 20n 11 44e
25 Schweinfurt 50 3n 10 12e
25 Schwenningen 48 3n 8 32e
24 Schwerin 53 37n 11 22e
24 Schwerin □ 53 35n 11 20e
24 Schweriner See, L. 53 45n 11 26e
25 Schwetzingen 49 22n 8 35e
25 Schwyz 47 2n 8 39e
25 Schwyz □ 47 2n 8 39e
38 Sciacca 37 30n 13 3e
39 Scicli 36 48n 14 41e
55 Scillave 6 22n 44 32e
13 Scilly Is. 49 55n 6 15w
28 Scinawa 51 25n 16 26e
100 Scobey 48 47n 105 30w
84 Scone, Australia 32 0s 150 52e
14 Scone, U.K. 56 25n 3 26w
4 Scoresbysund 70 20n 23 0w
5 Scotia Sea 56 5s 56 0w
14 Scotland ■ 57 0n 4 0w
5 Scott, C. 71 30s 168 0e
100 Scott City 38 30n 100 52w
100 Scottsbluff 41 55n 103 35w
80 Scottsdale 41 9s 147 31e
97 Scranton 41 22n 75 41w
12 Scunthorpe 53 35n 0 38w
84 Sea Lake 35 28s 142 55e
90 Seaforth 43 35n 81 25w
93 Seal, R. 59 4n 94 48w
103 Searchlight 35 31n 111 57w
101 Searcy 35 15n 91 45w
102 Seattle 47 41n 122 15w
104 Sebastián Vizcaino, B. 28 0n 114 0w
102 Sebastopol 38 16n 122 56w
41 Sebeş 45 58n 23 34e
99 Sebring 27 36n 81 47w
40 Sečanj 45 25n 20 47e
19 Seclin 50 33n 3 2e
85 Secretary, I. 45 15s 166 56e
62 Secunderabad 17 28n 78 30e
100 Sedalia 38 40n 93 18w
19 Sedan 49 43n 4 57e
85 Seddon 41 40s 174 7e
85 Seddonville 41 33e 172 1e
54 Sede Ya'aqov 32 43n 35 7e
92 Sedgewick 52 48n 111 41w
54 Sedom 31 5n 35 20e
102 Sedro Woolley 48 30n 122 15w
26 Seefeld 51 53n 13 17e
75 Seeheim 26 32s 17 52e
18 Sées 48 38n 0 10e
24 Seesen 51 35n 10 10e
63 Segamat 2 30n 102 50e
32 Segorbe 39 50n 0 30w
72 Ségou 13 30n 6 10w
30 Segovia 40 57n 4 10w
30 Segovia □ 40 55n 4 10w
18 Segré 47 40n 0 52w
72 Séguéla 7 57n 6 40w
101 Seguin 29 34n 97 58w
33 Segura, R. 38 6n 0 54w
33 Segura, Sa. de 38 5n 2 45w
57 Sehkonj, Kuh-e 30 0n 57 30e
60 Sehore 23 10n 77 5e
41 Şeica Mare 46 1n 24 7e
21 Seille, R. 49 7n 6 11e
46 Seinäjoki 62 47n 22 50e
18 Seine, B. de la 49 30n 0 30w
18 Seine, R. 49 26n 0 26e
19 Seine-et-Marne □ 48 45n 3 0e
18 Seine-Maritime □ 49 40n 1 0e
72 Sekondi-Takoradi 5 2n 1 48w
63 Selangor □ 3 20n 101 30e
64 Selatan □, Kalimantan 3 0s 115 0e
65 Selatan □, Sulawesi 3 0s 120 0e
64 Selatan □, Sumatera 3 0s 105 0e
25 Selb 50 9n 12 9e
12 Selby 53 47n 1 5w
88 Seldovia 59 27n 151 43w
75 Selebi-Pikwe 22 0s 27 45e
68 Selenge 49 25n 103 59e
19 Sélestat 48 10n 7 26e
72 Sélibaby 15 20n 12 15w
93 Selkirk, Canada 50 10n 97 20w
14 Selkirk, U.K. 55 33n 2 50w
92 Selkirk Mts. 51 0n 117 10w
99 Selma, Ala. 32 30n 87 0w
103 Selma, Calif. 36 39n 119 30w
19 Seltz 48 48n 8 4w
75 Selukwe 19 40s 30 0e
65 Semarang 7 0s 110 26e
65 Semeru, Mt. 8 4s 113 3e
102 Seminoe Res. 42 0n 107 0w
101 Seminole, Okla. 35 15n 96 45w
101 Seminole, Tex. 32 41n 102 38w
50 Semiozernoye 52 35n 64 0e
50 Semipalatinsk 50 30n 80 10e
26 Semmering P. 47 41n 15 45e
57 Semnān 35 55n 53 25e
57 Semnān □ 36 0n 54 0e
65 Semporna 4 30n 118 33e
110 Sena Madureira 9 5s 68 45w
111 Senador Pompeu 5 40s 39 20w
63 Senai 1 38s 103 38e
75 Senanga 16 2s 23 14e
66 Sendai, Kagoshima 31 50n 130 20e
66 Sendai, Miyagi 38 15n 141 0e
102 Seneca 44 10n 119 2w
96 Seneca L. 42 40n 76 58w
72 Senegal ■ 14 30n 14 30w
72 Senegal, R. 16 30n 15 30w
70 Senegambia, Reg. 14 0n 14 0w
25 Senftenberg 51 30n 13 51e
111 Senhor-do Bonfim 10 30s 40 10w
37 Senigállia 43 42n 13 12e
37 Senj 45 0n 14 58e
73 Sennâr 13 30n 33 35e
90 Senneterre 48 25n 77 15w
19 Sens 48 11n 3 15e
40 Senta 45 55n 20 3e
65 Sentolo 7 55s 110 13e
32 Seo de Urgel 42 22n 1 23e
60 Seohara 29 15n 78 33e
61 Seonath, R. 21 44n 82 27e
61 Seoni 22 5n 79 30e
68 Seoul=Soul 37 20n 126 15e
91 Separation Pt. 53 40n 57 16w
63 Sepone 16 45n 106 13e
91 Sept Iles 50 13n 66 22w
41 Septemvri 42 13n 24 6e
102 Sequim 48 3n 123 9w
103 Sequoia Nat. Park 36 20n 118 30w
16 Seraing 50 35n 5 32e
65 Seram, I. 3 10s 129 0e
65 Seram Sea 3 0s 130 0e
61 Serampore 22 44n 88 30e
65 Serang 6 8s 106 10e
48 Serdobsk 52 28n 44 10e
36 Seregno 45 40n 9 12e
63 Seremban 2 43n 101 53e
75 Serenje 13 11s 30 52e
111 Sergipe □ 10 30s 37 30w
64 Seria 4 37n 114 30e
64 Serian 1 10n 110 40e
19 Sérifontaine 49 20n 1 45e
43 Sérifos, I. 37 9n 24 30e
37 Sérmide 45 0n 11 17e
50 Serov 59 40n 60 20e
75 Serowe 22 25s 26 43e
75 Serpa Pinto 14 48s 17 52e
83 Serpentine 32 22s 115 59e
38 Serpeddi, Pta. 39 19n 9 28e
33 Serpis, R. 38 45n 0 21w
48 Serpukhov 54 55n 37 28e
42 Sérrai 41 5n 23 32e
42 Sérrai □ 41 5n 23 37e
38 Serramanna 39 26n 8 56e
111 Serrinha 11 39e 39 0w
111 Sertania 8 5s 37 20w
75 Serule 21 57s 27 11e
42 Sérvia 40 9n 21 58e
31 Sesimbra 38 28n 9 20w
30 Sestao 43 18n 3 0w
36 Sesto S. Giovanni 45 32n 9 14e
36 Sestri Levante 44 17n 9 22e
20 Sète 43 25n 3 42e
111 Sete Lagôas 19 27s 44 16w
72 Sétif 36 9n 5 26e
66 Seto 35 14n 137 6e
66 Setonaikai 34 10n 133 10e
72 Settat 33 0n 7 40w
74 Setté Cama 2 32s 9 57e
36 Séttimo Tor 45 9n 7 46e
12 Settle 54 5n 2 18w
31 Setúbal 38 30n 8 58w
31 Setúbal □ 38 25n 8 35w
31 Setúbal, B. de 38 40n 8 56w
64 Seulimeum 5 27n 95 15e
49 Sevastopol 44 35n 33 30e
20 Sévérac-le-Château 44 20n 3 5e
90 Severn, R., Canada 56 2n 87 36w
13 Severn, R., U.K. 51 25n 3 0w
51 Severnaya Zemlya, I. 79 0n 100 0e
48 Severnyye Uvaly, Reg. 58 0n 48 0e
26 Severoceský □ 50 35n 14 15e
48 Severodvinsk 64 27n 39 58e
27 Severomoravsky □ 49 38n 17 40e
31 Sevilla 37 23n 6 0w
31 Sevilla □ 37 0n 6 0w
41 Sevlievo 43 1n 25 6e
18 Sèvre Nantaise, R. 47 12n 1 30w
20 Sèvre Niortaise, R. 46 20n 1 12w
88 Seward 60 0n 149 40w
88 Seward Pen. 65 0n 164 0w
108 Sewell 34 10s 70 45w
53 Seychelles, Is. 5 0s 56 0e
46 Seyđisfjörđur 65 16n 14 0w

84 Seymour, Australia 36 58S 145 10E
98 Seymour, U.S.A. 39 0N 85 50W
21 Seyssel 45 57N 5 49E
19 Sézanne 48 40N 3 40E
38 Sezze 41 30N 13 3E
73 Sfax 34 49N 10 48E
41 Sfîntu-Gheorghe 45 52N 25 48E
16 's-Gravenhage 52 7N 4 17E
75 Shabani 20 17S 30 2E
41 Shabla 43 31N 28 32E
74 Shabunda 2 40S 27 16E
50 Shadrinsk 56 5N 63 38E
13 Shaftesbury 51 0N 2 12W
62 Shahabad, Andhra Pradesh 17 10N 78 11E
60 Shahabad, Punjab 30 10N 76 55E
61 Shahabad, Ut.P. 27 36N 79 56E
57 Sháhábád, Iran 37 40N 56 50E
60 Shahada 21 33N 74 30E
62 Shahapur 15 50N 74 34E
56 Shāhbād 34 10N 46 30E
68 Shahcheng 40 18N 115 27E
57 Shahdād 30 30N 57 40E
73 Shahhat 32 40N 21 35E
57 Shāhī 36 30N 52 55E
61 Shahjahanpur 27 54N 79 57E
62 Shahpur, Karnataka 16 40N 76 48E
60 Shahpur, Mad.P. 22 12N 77 58E
56 Shāhpūr, Iran 38 12N 44 45E
57 Shahrezā 32 0N 51 55E
57 Shāhrūd 36 30N 55 0E
57 Shahsavār 36 45N 51 12E
57 Shaikhabad 34 0N 68 45E
60 Shajapur 23 20N 76 15E
96 Shaker Heights 41 29N 81 36W
49 Shakhty 47 40N 40 10E
48 Shakhunya 57 40N 47 0E
72 Shaki 8 41N 3 21E
69 Shalu 24 24N 120 26E
57 Sham, Jabal ash 23 10N 57 5E
57 Shamil 29 32N 77 18E
74 Shamo, L. 5 45N 37 30E
97 Shamokin 40 47N 76 33W
75 Shamva 17 18S 31 34E
59 Shan □ 21 30N 98 30E
68 Schanchengtze 42 2N 123 47E
72 Shanga 9 1N 5 2E
75 Shangani, R. 18 41S 27 10E
68 Shangchih 45 10N 127 59E
69 Schangchwan Shan, I. 21 35N 112 45E
69 Shanghai 31 10N 121 25E
69 Shangjao 28 25N 117 25E
69 Shangkiu 34 28N 115 42E
69 Shangshui 33 42N 115 4E
69 Shanh 47 5N 103 5E
85 Shannon 40 33S 175 25E
15 Shannon, R. 52 30N 9 53W
68 Shansi □ 37 0N 113 0E
69 Shantow 23 25N 116 40E
68 Shantung □ 37 0N 118 0E
69 Shanyang 33 39N 110 2E
69 Shaohing 30 0N 120 32E
69 Shaowu 27 25N 117 30E
69 Shaoyang 27 10N 111 30E
14 Shapinsay, I. 59 2N 2 50W
56 Shaqra 25 15N 45 16E
68 Sharin Gol 49 12N 106 27E
57 Sharjah 25 23N 55 26E
83 Shark, B. 25 15S 133 20E
96 Sharon, Pa. 41 14N 80 31W
97 Sharon, Mass. 42 5N 71 11W
48 Sharya 58 12N 45 40E
75 Shashi 21 40S 28 40E
69 Shasi 30 16N 112 20E
102 Shasta, Mt. 41 45N 122 0W
102 Shasta Res. 40 50N 122 15W
93 Shaunavon 49 35N 108 40W
97 Shawangunk Mts. 41 35N 74 30W
100 Shawano 44 45N 88 38W
90 Shawinigan 46 35N 72 50W
101 Shawnee 35 15N 97 0W
55 Shebele, Wabi 2 0N 44 0E
98 Sheboygan 43 46N 87 45W
91 Shediac 46 14N 64 32W
13 Sheerness 51 26N 0 47E
54 Shefar'am 32 48N 35 10E
12 Sheffield, U.K. 53 23N 1 28W
97 Sheffield, U.S.A. 42 6N 73 23W
60 Shegaon 20 48N 76 59E
61 Sheikhpura 25 9N 85 53E
60 Shekhupura 31 42N 73 58E
69 Shekki 22 30N 113 15E
69 Sheklung 23 5N 113 55E
91 Shelburne, Nova Scotia 43 47N 65 20W
90 Shelburne, Ont. 44 4N 80 15W
102 Shelby, Mont. 48 30N 111 59W
99 Shelby, N.C. 35 18N 81 34W
98 Shelbyville, Ind. 39 30N 85 42W
99 Shelbyville, Tenn. 35 30N 86 25W
91 Sheldrake 50 20N 64 51W
51 Shelikhova Zaliv 59 30N 157 0E
93 Shell Lake 53 19N 107 6W
93 Shellbrook 53 13N 106 24W
91 Shelter Bay 50 30N 67 20W
88 Shelton, Alaska 55 20N 105 0W
97 Shelton, Conn. 41 18N 73 7W
102 Shelton, Wash. 47 15N 123 6W
49 Shemakha 40 50N 48 28E
100 Shenandoah, Iowa 40 50N 95 25W
97 Shenandoah, Pa. 40 49N 76 13W
98 Shenandoah, R. 39 19N 77 44W
62 Shencottah 8 59N 77 18E
72 Shendam 9 10N 9 30E
73 Shendî 16 46N 33 33E
60 Shendurni 20 39N 75 36E
42 Shëngjeni 41 50N 19 35E
68 Shensi □ 35 0N 109 0E
68 Shenyang 41 35N 123 30E
84 Shepparton 36 18S 145 25E
13 Sherborne 50 56N 2 31W
72 Sherbro I. 7 30N 12 40W
91 Sherbrooke 45 24N 71 57W
102 Sheridan 44 50N 107 0W
101 Sherman 33 40N 96 35W
61 Sherpur 25 1N 90 3E
93 Sherridon 55 10N 101 5W
16 s'Hertogenbosch 51 41N 5 19E
12 Sherwood Forest 53 5N 1 5W
75 Shesheke 17 50S 24 0E
14 Shetland □ 60 30N 1 30W
62 Shevaroy Hills 11 58N 78 12E
50 Shevchenko 44 25N 51 20E
54 Shevut'Am 32 19N 34 55E
55 Shibam 16 0N 48 36E
57 Shibarghan 36 40N 65 48E
66 Shibushi 31 25N 131 0E
91 Shickshock Mts. 48 40N 66 30W
14 Shiel, L. 56 48N 5 32W
66 Shiga □ 35 20N 136 0E
67 Shigatse 29 10N 89 0E
68 Shihkiachwang 38 0N 114 32E
69 Shihpu 29 12N 121 58E
68 Shihwei 51 28N 119 59E
42 Shijaku 41 21N 19 33E
60 Shikarpur, India 28 17N 78 7E
60 Shikarpur, Pak. 27 57N 68 39E
60 Shikohabad 27 6N 78 38E
66 Shikoku, I. 33 45N 133 30E
66 Shikoku □ 33 30N 133 30E
15 Shillelagh 52 46N 6 32W
51 Shilka 52 0N 115 55E
97 Shillington 40 18N 75 58W
59 Shillong 25 30N 92 0E
66 Shimada 34 49N 138 19E
66 Shimane □ 35 0N 132 30E
51 Shimanovsk 52 15N 127 30E
66 Shimizu 35 0N 138 30E
66 Shimodate 36 20N 139 55E
62 Shimoga 13 57N 75 32E
66 Shimonoseki 33 58N 131 0E
50 Shimpek 44 50N 74 10E
14 Shin, L. 58 7N 4 30W
57 Shin Dand 33 12N 62 8E
66 Shingú 33 40N 135 33E
74 Shinyanga 3 45S 33 27E
91 Shippegan 47 45N 64 45W
66 Shirane-San, Mt. 35 40N 138 15E
57 Shíráz 29 42N 52 30E
75 Shire, R. 17 42S 35 19E
62 Shirol 16 47N 74 41E
60 Shirpur 21 21N 74 57E
69 Shiukwan 24 58N 113 3E
60 Shivpuri 25 18N 77 42E
66 Shizuoka 35 0N 138 30E
66 Shizuoka □ 35 15N 138 40E
42 Shkodra 42 6N 19 20E
42 Shkodra □ 42 5N 19 20E
42 Shkumbini, R. 41 1N 19 26E
93 Shoal Lake 50 30N 100 35W
13 Shoeburyness 51 13N 0 49E
68 Shohsien 39 30N 112 25E
63 Sholapur 17 43N 75 56E
51 Shologontsy 66 13N 114 14E
54 Shomera 33 4N 35 17E
54 Shómrón, Reg. 32 15N 35 13E
62 Shoranur 10 46N 76 19E
62 Shorapur 16 31N 76 48E
100 Shoshone 43 0N 114 27W
75 Shoshong 22 0S 26 30E
103 Show Low 34 16N 110 0W
101 Shreveport 32 30N 93 50W
12 Shrewsbury 52 42N 2 45W
62 Shrivardhan 18 10N 73 3E
13 Shropshire □ 52 36N 2 45W
69 Shucheng 31 25N 117 2E
69 Shuikiahu 32 14N 117 4E
88 Shumagin Is. 55 0N 159 0W
50 Shumikha 55 15N 63 30E
54 Shunat Nimran 31 54N 35 37E
69 Shunchang 26 52N 117 48E
88 Shungnak 66 53N 157 2W
55 Shuqra 13 22N 45 34E
57 Shúsf 31 50N 60 5E
56 Shushtar 32 0N 48 50E
54 Shuweika 32 20N 35 1E
68 Shwangliano 43 39N 123 40E
59 Shwebo 22 30N 95 45E
59 Shwegu 24 15N 96 50E
58 Shyok 34 15N 78 5E
58 Shyok, R. 35 13N 75 53E
63 Si Racha 13 20N 101 10E
58 Siahan Ra. 27 30N 64 40E
67 Siakwan 25 45N 100 10E
60 Sialkot 32 32N 74 30E
63 Siam=Thailand ■ 15 0N 100 0E
69 Sian 34 2N 109 0E
69 Sian Kiang, R. 22 30N 110 10E
69 Siangfan 32 15N 112 2E
69 Siangtan 28 0N 112 55E
69 Siangyang 32 18N 111 0E
68 Siao Hingan Ling, Mts. 49 0N 127 0E
65 Siargao, I. 9 52N 126 3E
42 Siátista 40 15N 21 33E
48 Siauhai 55 56N 23 15E
93 Sibbald 51 24N 110 10W
37 Sibenik 43 48N 15 54E
64 Siberut, I. 1 30S 99 0E
60 Sibi 29 30N 67 48E
74 Sibiti 3 38S 13 19E
41 Sibiu 45 45N 24 9E
41 Sibiu □ 45 50N 24 15E
64 Sibolga 1 50N 98 45E
59 Sibsagar 27 0N 94 36E
64 Sibu 2 19N 111 51E
65 Sibutu Pass. 4 50N 120 0E
65 Sibuyan, I. 12 25N 122 40E
65 Sibuyan Sea 12 50N 122 20E
67 Sichang 28 0N 102 10E
39 Sicilia □ 37 30N 14 30E
39 Sicilia, I. 37 30N 14 30E
38 Sicilian Chan. 37 20N 12 20E
110 Sicuani 14 10S 71 10W
40 Šid 45 6N 19 16E
62 Siddipet 18 0N 79 0E
39 Siderno Marina 38 16N 16 17E
42 Sidhirókastron 37 20N 21 46E
60 Sidhpur 23 56N 71 25E
73 Sîdi Barrâni 31 32N 25 58E
72 Sidi bel Abbès 35 13N 0 10W
72 Sidi Ifni 29 29N 10 3W
14 Sidlaw Hills 56 32N 3 10W
13 Sidmouth 50 40N 3 13W
92 Sidney, Canada 48 39N 123 24W
98 Sidney, U.S.A. 40 18N 84 6W
65 Sidoardjo 7 30S 112 46E
24 Sieburg 50 48N 7 12E
28 Siedlce 52 10N 22 20E
28 Siedlce □ 52 0N 22 0E
24 Sieg, R. 50 45N 7 5E
24 Siegen 50 52N 8 2E
63 Siem Reap 13 20N 103 52E
37 Siena 43 20N 11 20E
69 Sieyang 34 20N 108 48E
28 Sieradź 51 37N 18 41E
28 Sieradź □ 51 30N 18 40E
28 Sierpc 52 55N 19 43E
72 Sierra Leone ■ 9 0N 12 0W
102 Sierra Nevada, Mts. 40 0N 121 0W
25 Sierre 46 17N 7 31E
43 Sífnos, I. 37 0N 24 45E
20 Sigean 43 2N 2 58E
41 Sighisoara 46 12N 24 50E
64 Sigli 5 25N 96 0E
46 Siglufjördur 66 12N 18 55W
110 Sigsig 3 0S 78 50W
30 Sigüenza 41 3N 2 40W
72 Siguiri 11 31N 9 10W
103 Sigurd 38 57N 112 0W
63 Sihanoukville = Kompong Som 10 40N 103 30E
69 Sihsien 29 55N 118 23E
56 Siirt 37 57N 41 55E
69 Si Kiang, R. 22 0N 114 0E
69 Sikandarabad 28 30N 77 39E
60 Sikandra Rao 27 43N 78 24E
60 Sikar 27 39N 75 10E
72 Sikasso 11 7N 5 35W
101 Sikeston 36 52N 89 35W
51 Sikhote Alin Khrebet 46 0N 136 0E
43 Síkinos, I. 36 40N 25 8E
61 Sikkim □ 27 50N 88 50E
30 Sil, R. 42 27N 7 43W
68 Silamulun, R. 43 20N 121 0E
54 Silat adh Dhahr 32 19N 35 11E
37 Silba 44 24N 14 41E
59 Silghat 26 35N 93 0E
61 Siliguri 26 45N 88 25E
41 Silistra 44 6N 27 19E
44 Siljan, L. 60 55N 14 45E
45 Silkeborg 56 10N 9 32E
75 Silva Porto=Bié 12 22S 16 55E
103 Silver City, Panama Canal Zone 9 21N 79 53W
103 Silver City, U.S.A. 32 50N 108 18W
31 Silves 37 11N 8 26W
54 Silwan 31 59N 35 15E
26 Silz 47 16N 10 56E
64 Simanggang 1 15N 111 25E
90 Simcoe, Canada 42 50N 80 20W
90 Simcoe, L. 44 20N 79 20W
51 Simenga 62 50N 107 55E
40 Simeria 45 51N 23 1E
64 Simeulue, I. 2 45N 95 45E
49 Simferopol 44 55N 34 3E
43 Sími, I. 36 35N 27 50E
60 Simla 31 2N 77 15
93 Simmie 49 56N 108 6W
63 Simpang 4 50N 100 40E
25 Simplonpass 46 15N 8 0E
80 Simpson, Des. 25 0S 137 0E
45 Simrishamn 55 33N 14 22E
62 Sina, R. 17 23N 75 54E
73 Sinâ', Gebel el Tih Es 29 0N 33 30E
73 Sinai = Es Sinâ' 29 0N 34 0E
41 Sinaia 45 21N 25 38E
104 Sinaloa □ 25 50N 108 20W
37 Sinalunga 43 12N 11 43E
40 Sînandrei 45 52N 21 13E
110 Sincelejo 9 18N 75 24W
69 Sincheng 34 25N 113 56W
111 Sincorá, Sa. do 13 30S 41 0W
60 Sind, R. 26 26N 79 14E
65 Sindangbarang 7 27S 107 9E
60 Sindsagar Doab, Reg. 32 0N 71 30E
31 Sines 37 56N 8 51E
31 Sines, C. de 37 58N 8 53W
32 Sineu 39 39N 3 0E
69 Sinfeng 26 59N 106 55E
73 Singa 13 10N 33 57E
65 Singaparna 7 23S 108 4E
63 Singapore ■ 1 17N 103 51E
63 Singapore, Str. of 1 10N 103 40E
25 Singen 47 45N 8 50E
74 Singida 4 49S 34 48E
42 Singitikós Kól. 40 6N 24 0E
59 Singkling Hkamti 26 0N 95 45E
64 Singkawang 1 0N 109 5E
64 Singkep 0 30S 140 20E
68 Singtai 37 2N 114 30E
69 Singtze 29 30N 116 4E
69 Sinhailien 34 31N 119 0E
68 Sinhsien 38 25N 112 45E
69 Sinhwa 27 36N 111 6E
67 Sining 36 35N 101 50E
56 Sinjār 36 19N 41 52E
54 Sinjil 32 3N 35 15E
73 Sinkat 18 55N 36 49E
67 Sinkiang 35 35N 111 25E
67 Sinkiang-Uigur □ 42 0N 85 0E
68 Sinkin 39 30N 122 29E
38 Sînnai 39 18N 9 13E
111 Sinnamary 5 23N 52 57W
73 Sinnûris 29 26N 30 31E
41 Sinoe, L. 44 35N 28 50E
56 Sinop 42 1N 35 11E
69 Sinsiang 35 15N 113 55E
64 Sintang 0 5N 111 35E
31 Sintra 38 47N 9 25W
68 Sinuiju 40 5N 124 24E
69 Sinyang 32 6N 114 2E
25 Sion 46 14N 7 20E
100 Sioux City 42 32N 96 25W
100 Sioux Falls 43 35N 96 40W
90 Sioux Lookout 50 10N 91 50W
105 Siparia 10 15N 61 30W
69 Siping 33 25N 114 10E
105 Siquia, R. 12 30N 84 30W
57 Sir Bani Yas, I. 24 20N 54 0E
80 Sir Edward Pellew Group, Is. 15 40S 137 10E
88 Sir James McBrien, Mt. 62 7N 127 41W
62 Sira 13 41N 76 49E
39 Siracusa 37 4N 15 17E
61 Sirajganj 24 25N 89 47E
41 Siret, R. 47 55N 26 5E
60 Sironj 24 5N 77 45E
43 Síros, I. 37 28N 24 57E
60 Sirsa 29 33N 75 4E
62 Sirsi 14 40N 74 49E
62 Sirsilla 18 23N 78 49E
37 Sisak 45 30N 16 21E
63 Sisaket 15 8N 104 23E
33 Sisante 39 25N 2 12W
63 Sisophon 13 31N 102 59E
57 Sistan Baluchistan □ 27 0N 62 0E
30 Sistema Central 40 40N 5 55W
61 Sitamarhi 26 37N 85 30E
61 Sitapur 27 38N 80 45E
32 Sitges 41 17N 1 47E
42 Sithonia, Pen. 40 0N 23 45E
92 Sitka 57 9N 134 58W
59 Sittang Myit, R. 18 20N 96 45E
16 Sittard 51 0N 5 52E
65 Situbondo 7 45S 114 0E
62 Sivakasi 9 24N 77 47E
57 Sivand 30 5N 52 55E
56 Sivas 39 43N 36 58E
56 Siverek 37 50N 39 25E

73 Síwa 29 11N 25 31 E
60 Siwalik Ra. 28 0N 83 0 E
61 Siwan 26 13N 84 27 E
13 Sizewell 52 13N 1 38 E
45 Sjaelland, I. 55 30N 11 30 E
40 Skadarsko, J. 42 10N 19 15 E
Jezero, L. 42 10N 19 15 E
45 Skaerbaek 55 31N 9 38 E
45 Skagen 57 43N 10 35 E
47 Skagerrak, Str. 57 30N 9 0 E
92 Skagway 59 30N 135 20W
45 Skanderborg 56 2N 9 55 E
45 Skanör 55 24N 12 50 E
45 Skara 58 25N 13 30 E
45 Skaraborg □ 58 20N 13 30 E
58 Skardu 35 20N 73 35 E
44 Skarnes 50 15N 11 41 E
28 Skarzysko Kamienna 51 7N 20 52 E
92 Skenna Mts. 56 40N 128 0W
12 Skegnwss 53 9N 0 20 E
110 Skeldon 6 0N 57 20W
46 Skellefteå 64 45N 20 59 E
46 Skelleftehamn 64 41N 21 14 E
42 Skíathos, I. 39 12N 23 30 E
15 Skibbereen 51 33N 9 16W
12 Skiddaw, Mt. 54 39N 3 9W
44 Skien 59 12N 9 35 E
28 Skierniewice 51 58N 20 19 E
28 Skierniewice □ 51 50N 20 10 E
72 Skikda 36 50N 6 58 E
12 Skipton 53 57N 2 1W
43 Skíros, I. 38 55N 24 34 E
45 Skive 56 33N 9 2 E
45 Skjern 55 57N 8 30 E
44 Skoghall 59 20N 13 30 E
44 Skönsberg 62 25N 17 21 E
43 Skópelos, I. 39 9N 23 47 E
40 Skopje 42 1N 21 32 E
28 Skórcz 43 47N 18 30 E
45 Skövde 58 24N 13 50 E
51 Skovorodino 53 59N 123 55 E
99 Skowhegan 44 49N 69 40W
47 Skudeneshavn 59 10N 5 10 E
15 Skull 51 32N 9 40W
45 Skurup 55 28N 13 30 E
44 Skutskär 60 37N 17 25 E
28 Skwierzyna 52 46N 15 30 E
14 Skye, I. 57 15N 6 10W
45 Slagelse 55 23N 11 19 E
15 Slaney, R. 52 52N 6 45W
40 Slano 42 48N 17 53 E
26 Slaný 50 13N 14 6 E
41 Slatina 44 28N 24 22 E
101 Slaton 33 27N 101 38W
70 Slave Coast 6 0N 2 30 E
92 Slave Lake 55 25N 114 50W
50 Slavgorod 53 10N 78 50 E
40 Slavonska Požega 45 20N 17 41 E
40 Slavonski Brod 45 11N 18 0 E
49 Slavyansk 45 15N 38 11 E
12 Sleaford 53 0N 0 22W
14 Sleat, Sd. of 57 5N 5 47W
97 Slide Mt. 42 0N 74 23W
16 Sliedrecht 51 50N 4 45 E
15 Sligo 54 17N 8 28W
15 Sligo □ 54 10N 8 40W
63 Slim River 3 48N 101 25 E
41 Sliven 42 42N 26 19N
40 Slivnitsa 42 50N 23 0 E
37 Sljeme, Mt. 45 57N 15 58 E
97 Sloansville 42 45N 74 22W
48 Slobodskoy 58 40N 50 6 E
41 Slobozia 44 34N 27 23 E
13 Slough 51 30N 0 35W
37 Slovenija □ 45 58N 14 30 E
37 Slovenska Bistrica 46 24N 15 35 E
27 Slovenská Socialistická Rep. □ 48 40N 19 0 E
27 Slovenské Rudohorie, Mts. 50 25N 13 0 E
27 Slovensko, Reg. 48 50N 20 0 E
28 Słubice 52 50N 14 35 E
28 Słubia, R. 54 35N 16 50 E
28 Słupsk 54 28N 17 1 E
28 Słupsk □ 54 20N 17 20 E
41 Slunchev Bryag 42 40N 27 41 E
51 Slyudyanka 51 40N 103 30 E
93 Smeaton 53 30N 105 49W
40 Smederevo 44 40N 20 57 E
44 Smedjebacken 60 8N 15 25 E
92 Smith 55 10N 114 0W
88 Smith Arm, B. 66 30N 123 0W
92 Smithers 54 45N 127 10W
99 Smithfield 35 31N 78 16W
90 Smiths Falls 44 55N 76 0W
80 Smithton 40 53 S 145 6 E
31 Smoky Bay 32 22 S 133 56 E
90 Smoky Falls 50 10N 82 10W
100 Smoky Hill, R. 39 3N 96 48W
48 Smolensk 54 45N 32 0 E
42 Smolikas, Mt. 40 9N 20 58 E
41 Smolyan 41 36N 24 38 E
90 Smooth Rock Falls 49 17N 81 37W
12 Snaefell, Mt. 54 18N 4 26W
46 Snaefellsjökull.Mt. 64 50N 23 49W
102 Snake, R. 46 12N 119 2W
102 Snake River Plain 43 13N 113 0W
16 Sneek 53 2N 5 40 E
28 Sniardwy, Sezero, L. 53 46N 21 44 E
93 Snow Lake 54 53N 101 2W
12 Snowdon, Mt. 53 4N 4 8W
103 Snowflake 34 30N 110 4W
102 Snowshoe Pk. 48 13N 115 41W
31 Snowtown 33 47 S 138 13 E
84 Snowy, Mts. 36 15 S 148 20 E
101 Snyder 32 45N 100 57W
102 Soap Lake 47 29N 119 31W
111 Sobral 3 50 S 40 30W
30 Sobreira Formosa 39 46N 7 51W
28 Sochaczew 52 15N 20 13 E
67 Soche 38 24N 77 20 E
49 Sochi 43 35N 39 40 E
77 Society Is. 17 0 S 151 0W
110 Socorro, Col. 6 29N 73 16W
103 Socorro, U.S.A. 34 3N 106 58W
55 Socotra, I. 12 30N 54 0 E
33 Socúellamas 39 16N 2 47W
92 Soda Creek 52 25N 122 10W
102 Soda Springs 42 4N 111 40W
44 Söderhamn 61 18N 17 10 E
45 Söderköping 58 31N 16 35 E
44 Södermanlands □ 59 10N 16 30 E
44 Södertälje 59 12N 17 50 E
74 Sodo 7 0N 37 57 E
16 Soest, Neth. 52 9N 5 19 E
24 Soest, W. Germany 51 34N 8 7 E
42 Sofádhes 39 28N 22 4 E
75 Sofala = Beira 19 50 S 34 52 E
41 Sofiya 42 45N 23 20 E
110 Sogamoso 5 43N 72 56W
47 Sogn og Fjordane □ 61 40N 6 0 E
73 Sohâg 26 27N 31 43 E
16 Soignes 50 35N 4 5 E
19 Soissons 49 25N 3 19 E
60 Sojat 25 55N 73 38 E
56 Soke 37 48N 27 28 E
72 Sokodé 9 0N 1 11 E
48 Sokol 59 30N 40 5 E
28 Sokólka 53 25N 23 30 E
26 Sokolov 50 12N 22 7 E
27 Sokoto 13 2N 5 16 E
65 Solano 16 25N 121 15 E
30 Solares 43 23N 3 43W
28 Solec Kujawski 53 6N 18 14 E
110 Soledad, Col. 10 55N 74 46W
103 Soledad, U.S.A. 36 27N 121 16W
110 Soledad, Ven. 8 10N 63 34W
21 Solenzara 41 53N 9 23 E
19 Solesmes 50 10N 3 30 E
48 Soligalich 59 5N 42 10 E
48 Solikamsk 59 38N 56 50 E
24 Solingen 51 10N 7 4 E
44 Sollefteå 63 10N 17 20 E
44 Sollentuna 59 26N 17 56 E
32 Sóller 39 43N 2 45 E
44 Solna 59 22N 18 1 E
19 Sologne, Reg. 47 40N 2 0 E
64 Solok 0 55 S 100 40 E
104 Sololá 14 49N 91 10 E
76 Solomon Is. 8 0 S 159 0 E
25 Solothurn 47 13N 7 32 E
25 Solothrun □ 47 18N 7 40 E
37 Solta, I. 43 24N 16 15 E
57 Soltanābād 36 29N 58 5 E
56 Soltāniyeh 36 20N 48 55 E
24 Soltau 52 59N 9 50 E
97 Solvay 43 5N 76 17W
45 Sölvesborg 56 5N 14 35 E
48 Solvychegodsk 61 21N 46 52 E
75 Solwezi 12 20 S 26 26 E
14 Solway Firth 54 45N 3 38W
55 Somali Rep. ■ 7 0N 47 0 E
40 Sombor 45 46N 19 17 E
105 Somerset, Bermuda 32 20N 64 55W
97 Somerset, Mass. 41 45N 71 10W
98 Somerset, Ky. 37 5N 84 40W
13 Somerset □ 51 9N 3 0W
75 Somerset East 32 42 S 25 35 E
105 Somerset I., Bermuda 32 20N 64 55W
88 Somerset I., Canada 73 30N 93 0W
97 Somersworth 43 15N 70 51W
97 Somerville 40 34N 74 36W
39 Somma Vesuvianna 40 52N 14 23 E
19 Somme □ 40 0N 2 15 E
18 Somme, B. de la 5 22N 1 30 E
19 Somme, R. 50 11N 1 39 E
45 Sommen, L. 58 0N 15 15 E
19 Sommesous 48 44N 4 12 E
27 Somogy □ 46 19N 17 30 E
30 Somosierra, P. de 41 9N 3 35W
20 Somport, Col du 42 48N 0 31W
61 Son, R. 25 40N 84 51 E
36 Soncino 45 24N 9 52 E
45 Sønderborg 54 55N 9 49 E
25 Sondershausen 51 22N 10 50 E
45 Sonderyllands □ 55 10N 9 10 E
36 Sóndrio 46 10N 9 53 E
60 Sonepat 29 0N 77 5 E
63 Song Cau 13 20N 109 18 E
74 Songea 10 40 S 35 40 E
47 Songefjorden 61 10N 5 30 E
63 Songkhla 7 13N 100 37 E
58 Sonmiani 25 25N 66 40 E
25 Sonneberg 50 22N 11 11 E
101 Sonora 30 33N 100 37W
104 Sonora □ 37 59N 120 27W
104 Sonsonate 13 45N 89 45W
25 Sonthofen 47 31N 10 16 E
69 Soochow 31 18N 120 41 E
28 Sopot 54 27N 18 31 E
40 Sopotnica 41 23N 21 13 E
27 Sopron 47 41N 16 37 E
91 Sop's Arm 49 46N 56 56W
44 Sør Trøndelag □ 63 0N 11 0 E
38 Sora 41 45N 13 36 E
110 Sorata 15 50 S 68 50W
33 Sorbas 37 6N 2 7W
90 Sorel 46 0N 73 10W
36 Soresina 45 17N 9 51 E
21 Sorgues 44 1N 4 53 E
32 Soria 41 43N 2 32W
32 Soria □ 41 46N 2 28W
57 Sorkh, Kuh-e 35 40N 58 30 E
45 Sorø 55 26N 11 32 E
109 Sorocaba 23 31 S 47 35W
27 Soroksar 47 24N 19 9 E
60 Soron 27 55N 78 45 E
65 Sorong 0 55 S 131 15 E
74 Soroti 1 43N 33 35 E
46 Sørøya, I. 70 35N 22 45 E
31 Sorraia, R. 38 56N 8 53W
39 Sorrento 40 38N 14 23 E
46 Sorsele 65 31N 17 30 E
48 Sortavala 61 42N 30 41 E
48 Sosnogorsk 63 37N 53 51 E
51 Sosnovka 54 9N 109 35 E
27 Sosnowiec 50 20N 19 10 E
18 Sotteville 49 24N 1 5 E
74 Souanke 2 10N 14 10 E
43 Soúdas, Kól. 35 28N 24 10 E
97 Souderton 40 19N 75 19W
42 Souflíon 41 12N 26 18 E
20 Souillac 44 53N 1 29 E
68 Soul 37 33N 126 58 E
20 Soulac 45 30N 1 4W
75 Sources, Mt. aux 28 45 S 28 50 E
111 Soure, Brazil 0 35 S 48 30W
30 Soure, Port. 40 4N 8 38W
93 Souris 49 40N 100 20W
93 Souris, R. 49 39N 99 34W
111 Sousa 7 0 S 38 10W
111 Sousel 2 38 S 52 29W
73 Sousse 35 50N 10 33 E
75 South Africa ■ 30 0 S 25 0W
1 South America 10 0 S 60 0W
63 South Andaman, I. 11 50N 92 45 E
7 South Atlantic Ocean 20 0 S 20 0W
78 South Australia □ 32 0 S 139 0 E
98 South Bend, Ind. U.S.A. 41 38N 86 20W
102 South Bend, Wash. 46 44N 123 52W
99 South Boston 36 42N 78 58W
99 South Carolina □ 33 45N 81 0W
98 South Charleston 38 20N 81 40W
100 South Dakota □ 45 0N 100 0W
5 South Georgia, I. 54 30 S 37 0W
13 South Glamorgan □ 51 28N 3 26W
81 South Grafton 42 11 S 71 42W
98 South Haven 42 22N 86 20W
74 South Horr 2 12N 36 56 E
85 South Invercargill 46 26N 168 23 E
85 South Island 43 50 S 171 0 E
68 South Korea ■ 36 0N 128 0 E
5 South Magnetic Pole 66 30 S 139 30 E
98 South Milwaukee 42 50N 87 52W
5 South Orkney Is. 63 0 S 45 0W
100 South Platte, R. 41 7N 100 42W
5 South Pole 90 0 S 0 0 E
90 South Porcupine 48 30N 81 12W
90 South River 45 52N 79 21W
93 South Saskatchewan, R. 53 15N 105 5W
5 South Shetland Is. 62 0 S 59 0W
12 South Shields 54 59N 1 26W
100 South Sioux City 42 30N 96 30W
12 South Tyne, R. 54 59N 2 8W
75 South West Africa = Nambia ■ 22 0 S 18 9 E
96 South Williamsport 41 14N 77 1W
55 South Yemen ■ 15 0N 48 0 E
12 South Yorkshire □ 52 45N 1 25W
90 Southampton, Canada 44 30N 81 25W
13 Southampton, U.K. 50 54N 1 23W
97 Southampton, U.S.A. 40 54N 72 22W
89 Southampton I. 64 30N 84 0W
97 Southbridge 42 4N 72 2W
13 Southend 51 32N 0 43 E
85 Southern Alps, Mts. 43 41 S 170 11 E
83 Southern Cross 31 12 S 119 15 E
7 Southern Mid-Atlantic Ridge 30 0 S 15 0W
5 Southern Ocean 62 0 S 160 0W
14 Southern Uplands, Mts. 55 30N 4 0W
97 Southington 41 37N 72 53W
81 Southport, Australia 28 0 S 153 25 E
12 Southport, U.K. 53 38N 3 1W
13 Southwold 52 19N 1 41 E
75 Soutpansberge 22 55 S 29 30 E
20 Souvigny 46 33N 3 10 E
48 Sovetsk 57 38N 48 53 E
51 Sovetskaya Gavan 48 50N 140 0 E
29 Spain ■ 40 0N 5 0W
12 Spalding 52 47N 0 9W
91 Spaniard's Bay 47 38N 53 20W
102 Spanish Fork 40 10N 111 37W
105 Spanish Pt. 32 12N 64 45W
105 Spanish Town 18 0N 77 20W
102 Sparks 39 30N 119 45W
100 Sparta 43 55N 91 10W
99 Spartanburg 35 0N 82 0W
43 Spárti 37 5N 22 25 E
39 Spartivento, C., Italy 37 56N 16 4 E
38 Spartivento, C., Sardinia 38 52N 8 50 E
51 Spassk-Dal'niy 44 40N 132 40 E
43 Spátha, Ákra 35 42N 23 43 E
100 Spearfish 44 32N 103 52W
84 Speed 35 21 S 142 27 E
105 Speightstown 13 18N 59 30W
88 Spenard 61 0N 149 50W
88 Spence Bay 69 32N 93 31W
100 Spencer 43 5N 95 3W
81 Spencer, G. 34 30 S 137 0 E
85 Spenser, Mts. 42 15 S 172 45 E
15 Sperrin Mts. 54 50N 7 0W
25 Spessart, Mts 50 0N 9 20 E
43 Spétsai 37 16N 23 9 E
14 Spey, R. 57 40N 3 6W
25 Speyer 49 19N 8 26 E
39 Spinazzola 40 58N 16 5 E
92 Spirit River 55 45N 119 0W
27 Spišska Nová Ves 48 58N 20 34 E
26 Spittal 46 48N 13 31 E
37 Split 43 31N 16 26 E
37 Splitski Kan. 43 31N 16 20 E
25 Splugenpass 46 30N 9 20 E
102 Spokane 47 45N 117 25W
37 Spoleto 42 44N 12 44 E
97 Spotswood 40 23N 74 23W
24 Spree, R. 52 32N 13 13 E
24 Spremberg 51 33N 14 21 E
97 Spring Valley 41 7N 74 4W
75 Springbok 29 42 S 17 54 E
85 Springburn 43 40 S 171 32 E
91 Springdale, Canada 49 30N 56 6W
101 Springdale, U.S.A. 36 10N 94 5W
103 Springerville 34 10N 109 16W
85 Springfield, N.Z. 43 19 S 171 56 E
100 Springfield, Ill. 39 58N 89 40W
97 Springfield, Mass. 42 8N 72 37W
101 Springfield, Mo. 37 15N 93 20W
98 Springfield, Ohio 39 50N 83 48W
102 Springfield, Ore. 44 2N 123 0W
99 Springfield, Tenn. 36 35N 86 55W
97 Springfield, Vt. 43 20N 72 30W
75 Springfontein 30 15 S 25 40 E
91 Springhill 45 40N 64 4W
75 Springs 26 13 S 28 25 E
80 Springsure 24 8 S 148 6 E
80 Springvale, Queens. 23 33 S 140 42 E
82 Springvale, W.Australia 17 48 S 127 41 E
102 Springville 40 14N 111 35W
12 Spurn Hd. 53 34N 0 8W
40 Spuž 42 32N 19 10 E
92 Squamish 49 45N 123 10W
39 Squillace, G. di 38 43N 16 35 E
39 Squinzano 40 27N 18 1 E
65 Sragen 7 28 S 110 59 E
40 Srbobran 45 32N 19 48 E
63 Sre Umbell 11 8N 103 46 E
51 Sredinnyy Khrebet 57 0N 160 0 E
41 Sredna Gora 42 40N 25 0 E
51 Sredne Tamborskoye 50 55N 137 45 E
51 Srednekolymsk 67 20N 154 40 E
51 Srednevilyuysk 63 50N 123 5 E
41 Sredni Rodopi 41 40N 24 45 E
28 Šrem 52 6N 17 2 E
40 Sremska 44 58N 19 37 E
63 Srépok, R. 13 33N 106 16 E
51 Sretensk 52 10N 117 40 E

62 Sri Lanka ■ 7 30N 80 50 E
62 Sriharikota I. 13 40N 81 30 E
62 Srikakulam 18 14N 84 4 E
58 Srinagar 34 12N 74 50 E
62 Srinangam 10 54N 78 42 E
62 Srirangapatnam 12 26N 76 43 E
62 Srivilliputtur 9 31N 77 40 E
28 Sroda Wielkopolski. 52 15N 17 19 E
25 Stade 53 35N 9 31 E
24 Stadhagen 52 20N 9 14 E
14 Staffa, I. 56 26N 6 21W
12 Stafford 52 49N 2 9W
12 Stafford □ 52 53N 2 10W
13 Staines 51 26N 0 30W
26 Stainz 46 53N 15 17 E
40 Stalač 43 43N 21 28 E
49 Stalingrad 48 40N 44 25 E
27 Stalowa Wola 50 34N 22 3 E
12 Stalybridge 53 29N 2 2W
80 Stamford, Australia 21 15S 143 46 E
13 Stamford, U.K. 52 39N 0 29W
97 Stamford, Conn. 41 5N 73 30W
101 Stamford, Tex. 32 58N 99 50W
75 Standerton 26 55S 29 13 E
40 Stanke Dimitrov 42 27N 23 9 E
80 Stanley, Australia 40 46S 145 19 E
112 Stanley, Falkland Is. 51 40S 58 0W
102 Stanley, U.S.A. 44 10N 114 59W
70 Stanley Falls = Chutes Boyoma 0 12N 25 25 E
74 Stanleyville = Kisangani 0 41N 52 11 E
104 Stann Creek 17 0N 88 20W
51 Stanovoy Khrebet 55 0N 130 0 E
81 Stanthorpe 28 36S 151 59 E
88 Stanton 69 45N 128 52W
41 Stara Planina 43 15N 23 0 E
41 Stara Zagora 42 26N 25 39 E
28 Starachowice 51 3N 21 2 E
48 Staraya Russa 57 58N 31 10 E
77 Starbuck I. 5 37S 155 55W
28 Stargard Szczecinski 53 20N 15 0 E
101 Starkville 37 10N 104 31W
25 Starnberger See, L. 48 0N 11 0 E
28 Starogard Gd. 53 55N 18 30 E
13 Start Pt. 50 13N 3 38W
51 Staryy Keydzhan 60 0N 144 50 E
24 Stassfurt 51 51N 11 34 E
96 State College 40 47N 77 49W
97 Staten I. 54 40N 64 0W
99 Statesboro 32 26N 81 46W
99 Statesville 35 48N 80 51W
98 Staunton 38 7N 79 4W
47 Stavanger 58 57N 5 40 E
49 Stavrapol 45 2N 41 59 E
84 Stawell 36 58S 142 47 E
102 Steamboat Springs 40 30N 106 58W
96 Steelton 40 17N 76 50W
92 Steen River 59 40N 117 12W
83 Steep, Pt. 26 8S 113 8 E
74 Stefanie, L. = Chew Bahir 4 40N 30 50 E
26 Steiermark □ 47 26N 15 0 E
25 Steigerwald 49 45N 10 30 E
93 Steinbach 49 32N 96 40W
46 Steinkjer 63 59N 11 31 E
91 Stellarton 45 34N 62 40W
75 Stellenbosch 33 58S 18 50 E
36 Stelvio, P. de 46 32N 10 27 E
24 Stendal 52 36N 11 50 E
45 Stenungsund 58 6N 11 50 E
49 Stepanakert 40 0N 46 25 E
100 Stephen 48 30N 96 53W
84 Stephens Creek 31 50S 141 30 E
91 Stephenville, Canada 48 31N 58 30W
101 Stephenville, U.S.A. 32 12N 98 12W
49 Stepnoi = Elista 46 25N 44 17 E
43 Stereá Ellas □ 38 55N 22 0 E
100 Sterling, Colo. 40 40N 103 15W
100 Sterling, Ill. 41 45N 89 45W
48 Sterlitamak 53 40N 56 0 E
27 Šternberk 49 45N 17 15 E
28 Stettin = Szczecin 53 27N 14 27 E
24 Stettiner Haff 53 50N 14 25 E
92 Stettler 52 25N 112 40W
96 Steubenville 40 21N 80 39W
100 Stevens Point 44 32N 89 34W
112 Stewart, I., Chile 54 50S 71 30W
85 Stewart, I., N.Z. 46 58S 167 54 E
88 Stewart River 63 25N 139 30W
26 Steyr 48 3N 14 25 E
26 Steyr, R. 48 3N 14 25 E
92 Stikine, R. 56 40N 132 30W
43 Stilís 38 55N 22 37 E
100 Stillwater, Minn. 45 3N 92 47W
101 Stillwater, Okla. 36 5N 97 3W
102 Stillwater Mts. 39 45N 118 6W
40 Štip 41 42N 22 10 E
19 Stiring Wendel 49 12N 6 57 E
14 Stirling 56 17N 3 57W
45 Stockaryd 57 40N 14 36 E
27 Stockerau 48 24N 16 12 E
44 Stockholm 59 17N 18 3 E
44 Stockholms □ 59 40N 18 45 E
12 Stockport 53 25N 2 11W
84 Stockton, Australia 32 56S 151 47 E
12 Stockton, U.K. 54 34N 1 20W
103 Stockton, U.S.A. 38 0N 121 20W
12 Stoke-on-Trent 53 1N 2 11W
90 Stokes Bay 45 0N 81 22W
24 Stolberg 50 48N 6 13 E
51 Stolbovaya 64 50N 153 50 E
80 Stonehenge, Australia 24 22S 143 17 E
13 Stonehenge, U.K. 51 9N 1 45W
14 Stonehaven 56 58N 2 11W
93 Stonewall 50 10N 96 50W
5 Stonington Island 69 0N 67 0W
46 Storavan, L. 65 45N 18 10 E
44 Støren 63 3N 10 18 E
100 Storm Lake 42 35N 95 5W
75 Stormberg 31 16S 26 17 E
14 Stornoway 58 12N 6 23W
97 Storrs 41 48N 72 15W
44 Storsjön, L. 60 35N 16 45 E
45 Storstroms □ 49 50N 11 45 E
93 Stoughton 49 40N 103 0W
13 Stour, R., Dorset 50 43N 1 46W
13 Stour, R., Hereford and Worcester 52 20N 2 15W
13 Stour, R., Kent 51 18N 1 22 E
13 Stour, R., Suffolk 51 52N 1 16 E
13 Stourbridge 52 28N 2 8W
13 Stowmarket 52 11N 1 0 E
15 Strabane 54 50N 7 28W
15 Strabane □ 54 50N 7 28W
40 Stracin 42 13N 22 2 E
36 Stradella 45 4N 9 20 E
80 Strahan 42 8S 145 24 E
26 Strakonice 49 15N 13 53 E
41 Straldzha 42 35N 26 40 E
24 Stralsund 54 17N 13 5 E
75 Strand 34 9S 18 48 E
15 Strangford, L. 54 30N 5 37W
44 Strängnäs 59 23N 17 8 E
14 Stranraer 54 54N 5 0W
93 Strasbourg, Canada 51 10N 104 55W
19 Strasbourg, Fr. 48 35N 7 42 E
24 Strasburg 53 30N 13 44 E
84 Stratford, Australia 37 59S 147 5 E
96 Stratford, Canada 43 23N 81 0W
85 Stratford, N.Z. 39 20S 174 19 E
97 Stratford, U.S.A. 41 13N 73 8W
13 Stratford-on-Avon 52 12N 1 42W
14 Strath Spey 57 15N 3 40W
81 Strathalbyn 35 13S 138 53 E
14 Strathclyde □ 55 30N 5 0W
92 Strathmore 51 5N 113 25W
14 Strathmore, Reg. 58 23N 4 40W
90 Strathroy 42 58N 81 38W
14 Strathy, Pt. 58 35N 4 0W
97 Stratton Mt. 43 5N 72 56W
96 Strattanville 41 12N 79 20W
25 Straubing 48 53N 12 35 E
24 Strausberg 52 40N 13 52 E
81 Streaky Bay 32 51S 134 18 E
100 Streator 41 9N 88 52W
26 Stredočeský □ 49 55N 14 30 E
27 Stredoslovenský □ 48 30N 19 15 E
41 Strehaia 44 37N 23 10 E
40 Strelcha 42 30N 24 19 E
51 Strelka 58 5N 93 10 E
50 Strezhevoy 60 42N 77 34 E
42 Strimón, R. 40 47N 23 51 E
42 Strimonikós Kól. 40 33N 24 0 E
39 Strómboli, I. 38 48N 15 12 E
14 Stromeferry 57 20N 5 33W
14 Stronsay, I. 59 8N 2 38W
13 Stroud 51 44N 2 12W
97 Stroudsberg 40 59N 75 15W
45 Struer 56 30N 8 35 E
40 Struga 41 13N 20 44 E
40 Strumica 41 28N 22 41 E
96 Struthers 41 6N 80 38W
27 Strzegom 50 58N 16 20 E
28 Strzelno 52 35N 18 9 E
27 Strzyzów 49 52N 21 47 E
24 Stuben 46 58N 10 31 E
63 Stung Treng 13 26N 106 0 E
98 Sturgeon Bay 44 52N 87 20W
90 Sturgeon Falls 46 25N 79 57W
45 Sturkö, I. 56 5N 15 42 E
82 Sturt Cr. 20 8S 127 24 E
101 Stuttgart, U.S.A. 34 30N 91 33W
25 Stuttgart, W.Germany 48 46N 9 10 E
97 Stuyvesant 42 23N 73 45W
48 Styr, R. 52 7N 26 35 E
26 Styria = Steiermark 47 26N 15 0 E
73 Suakin 19 0N 37 20 E
69 Suancheng 30 58N 118 57 E
68 Suanhwa 40 35N 115 0 E
69 Suao 24 32N 121 42 E
65 Subang 7 30S 107 45 E
61 Subarnarekha, R. 21 33N 87 12 E
40 Subotica 46 6N 19 29 E
27 Sucha Beskidzka 49 44N 19 35 E
104 Suchitato 13 56N 89 0W
69 Suchow 34 10N 117 20 E
15 Suck, R. 53 16N 8 3W
110 Sucre 19 0S 65 15W
73 Sudan ■ 15 0N 30 0 E
90 Sudbury 46 30N 81 0W
73 Sûdd 8 20N 29 30 E
24 Süderbrarup 54 38N 9 47 E
27 Sudety, Reg. 50 20N 16 45 E
65 Sudirman, Pengunungan, Ra. 4 30N 137 0 E
33 Sueca 39 12N 0 21W
73 Suez = El Suweis 28 40N 33 0 E
98 Suffolk 36 47N 76 33W
98 Suffolk □ 52 16N 1 0 E
67 Sufu 39 44N 75 53 E
41 Şugag 45 47N 23 37 E
89 Sugluk = Saglouc 62 10N 75 40W
57 Suhar 24 20N 56 40 E
68 Suhbaatar 50 17N 106 10 E
24 Suhl 50 35N 10 40 E
24 Suhl □ 50 37N 10 43 E
69 Suhsien 33 28N 117 54 E
68 Suichung 40 45N 120 46 E
69 Suichwan 26 26N 114 32 E
68 Suihwa 46 40N 126 57 E
69 Suikhai 21 17N 110 19 E
69 Suiping 33 15N 114 6 E
19 Suippes 49 8N 4 30 E
15 Suir, R. 52 15N 7 0W
60 Sujangarh 27 42N 47 31 E
40 Sujica 43 52N 17 11 E
65 Sukabumi 6 56S 106 57 E
64 Sukadana 1 10S 110 0 E
63 Sukhothai 17 1N 99 49 E
49 Sukhumi 43 0N 41 0 E
60 Sukkur 27 50N 68 46 E
40 Sukovo 43 4N 22 37 E
60 Sulaiman Ra. 30 30N 69 50 E
54 Sulam Tsor 33 4N 35 6 E
65 Sulawesi, I. 2 0S 120 0 E
28 Sulechówo 52 5N 15 40 E
28 Sulejówek 52 13N 21 17 E
41 Sulina 45 10N 29 40 E
24 Sulingen 52 41N 8 47 E
46 Sulitälma 67 17N 17 28 E
46 Sulitjelma 61 7N 16 8 E
110 Sullana 5 0S 80 45W
98 Sullivan 39 5N 87 26W
37 Sulmona 42 3N 13 55 E
101 Sulphur 30 20N 93 22W
101 Sulphur Springs 33 5N 95 30W
61 Sultanpur 26 18N 82 10 E
65 Sulu Arch. 6 0N 121 0 E
65 Sulu Sea 8 0N 120 0 E
73 Suluq 31 44N 20 14 E
25 Sulzbach 49 30N 11 46 E
25 Sulzbach-Rosenberg 49 30N 11 46 E
65 Sumalata 1 0N 122 37 E
64 Sumatera □ 0 40N 100 20 E
64 Sumatera, I. 0 40N 100 20 E
102 Sumatra 46 45N 107 37W
64 Sumatra, I. = Sumatera, I. 0 40N 100 20 E
65 Sumba, Selat, Str. 9 0S 118 40 E
65 Sumba, I. 9 45S 119 35 E
65 Sumbawa, I. 8 34S 117 17 E
64 Sumbawa Besar 8 30S 117 26 E
68 Sümber 46 40N 108 50 E
65 Sumbing, Mt. 7 19S 110 3 E
65 Sumedang 6 49S 107 56 E
65 Sumenep 7 3S 113 51 E
91 Summerside 46 29N 63 41W
90 Summit 47 50N 72 20W
92 Summit Lake 54 20N 122 40W
103 Summit Pk. 37 20N 106 48W
66 Sumoto 34 21N 134 54 E
27 Sumperk 49 59N 17 0 E
99 Sumter 33 55N 80 10W
49 Sumy 50 57N 34 50 E
14 Sunart, L. 56 42N 5 35W
108 Sunchales 30 58S 61 35W
69 Sunchon 34 52N 127 31 E
64 Sunda, Selat 6 0S 105 45 E
61 Sundarbans, Reg. 22 0N 89 0 E
44 Sundbyberg 59 22N 17 58 E
12 Sunderland 54 54N 1 22W
90 Sundridge 45 45N 79 25W
44 Sundsvall 62 23N 17 17 E
64 Sungaigerung 4 58S 105 7 E
64 Sungaipakning 1 19N 102 0 E
64 Sungaipenuh 2 1S 101 20 E
64 Sungaitiram 0 45S 117 8 E
68 Sungari, R. 47 30N 132 30 E
63 Sungei Patani 5 38N 100 29 E
63 Sungei Siput 4 51N 101 6 E
65 Sungguminasa 5 17S 119 30 E
69 Sungkiang 31 0N 121 20 E
67 Sungpan 32 50N 103 20 E
69 Sungtzu Hu, L. 30 10N 111 45 E
44 Sunne 59 52N 13 12 E
102 Sunnyside 46 24N 120 2W
84 Sunshine 37 48S 144 52 E
103 Superior, Ariz. 33 19N 111 9W
100 Superior, Wis. 46 45N 92 0W
90 Superior, L. 47 40N 87 0W
63 Suphan Buri 14 30N 100 10 E
69 Supu 27 57N 110 15 E
56 Sūr, Lebanon 33 19N 35 16 E
57 Sūr, Oman 22 34N 59 32 E
48 Sura, R. 56 6N 46 0 E
65 Surabay 7 17S 112 45 E
44 Surahammar 59 42N 23 19 E
65 Surakarta 7 35S 110 48 E
60 Surat 21 12N 72 55 E
63 Surat Thani 9 3N 99 28 E
60 Surendranagar 22 45N 71 40 E
20 Surgères 46 7N 0 47W
50 Surgut 61 20N 73 28 E
61 Suri 23 50N 87 34 E
62 Suriapet 17 10N 79 40 E
54 Surif 31 40N 35 4 E
63 Surin 14 50N 103 34 E
107 Surinam ■ 4 0N 56 15W
13 Surrey □ 51 16N 0 30W
73 Surt 31 11N 16 46 E
73 Surt, Khalij
45 Surte 57 49N 12 1 E
46 Surtsey, I. 63 27N 20 15W
66 Suruga-Wan, G. 34 45N 138 30 E
66 Susaki 33 22N 133 17 E
51 Susanino 52 50N 140 14 E
102 Susanville 40 28N 120 40W
98 Susquehanna, R. 39 33N 76 5W
91 Sussex 45 45N 65 37W
51 Susuman 62 47N 148 10 E
41 Şuţeşti 45 13N 27 27 E
93 Sutherland, Canada 52 15N 106 40W
75 Sutherland, S. Africa 32 33S 20 40 E
60 Sutlej, R. 29 23N 71 2 E
12 Sutton-in-Ashfield 52 8N 1 16W
85 Suva 17 40S 178 8 E
40 Suva, Planina 43 10N 22 5 E
40 Suva Reka 42 21N 20 50 E
41 Suvarovo 13 15S 163 30W
40 Suvo Rudište, Mt. 43 17N 20 49 E
99 Suwannee, R. 29 18N 83 9W
66 Suwanose-Jima, I. 29 26N 129 30 E
77 Suwarrow Is. 13 15S 163 5W
28 Suwałki 54 8N 22 59 E
28 Suwałki □ 54 0N 22 30 E
54 Suweilih 32 2N 35 50 E
73 Suweis, Kang es 28 40N 33 0 E
69 Suwen 20 27N 110 2 E
68 Suwŏn 37 17N 127 1 E
48 Suzdal 56 29N 40 26 E
66 Suzu 37 25N 137 17 E
66 Suzuka 34 55N 136 36 E
36 Suzzara 45 0N 10 45 E
4 Svalbard, I. 66 12N 15 43W
46 Svappavaara 67 40N 21 3 E
46 Svartisen, Mt. 66 40N 14 16 E
63 Svay Rieng 11 5N 105 48 E
44 Sveg 62 2N 14 21 E
44 Svelvik 59 37N 10 24 E
45 Svendborg 55 4N 10 35 E
50 Sverdlovks 56 50N 60 30 E
86 Sverdrup Is. 79 0N 97 0W
37 Sveti Ivan Zelino 45 57N 16 16 E
40 Sveti Nikola, Mt. 41 51N 21 56 E
40 Svetozarevo 44 0N 21 15 E
41 Svilengrad 41 49N 26 12 E
41 Svishtov 43 36N 25 23 E
27 Svitavy 49 47N 16 28 E
51 Svobodnyy 51 20N 128 0 E
41 Svoge 42 59N 23 22 E
46 Svolvaer 68 15N 14 34 E
75 Swakopmund 22 37S 14 30 E
12 Swale, R. 54 6N 1 20W
84 Swan Hill 35 15S 143 31 E
92 Swan Hills 54 42N 115 49W
105 Swan Is. 17 22N 83 57W
93 Swan River 52 10N 101 25W
13 Swanage 50 36N 1 59W
84 Swansea, Australia 33 3S 151 35 E
13 Swansea, U.K. 51 37N 3 57W
28 Swarzedz 52 25N 17 4 E
69 Swatow = Shantow 23 25N 116 40 E
75 Swaziland ■ 26 30S 31 30 E
101 Sweetwater 32 30N 100 28W
75 Swellendam 34 1S 20 26 E
27 Swidnica 50 50N 16 30 E
28 Swidnik 51 13N 22 39 E
28 Swidwin 53 47N 15 49 E
27 Swiebodzice 50 51N 16 20 E
28 Swiebodzin 52 15N 15 37 E
28 Swiecie 53 25N 18 30 E
93 Swift Current 50 20N 107 45W
13 Swindon 51 33N 1 47W
28 Świndovjście 53 54N 14 16 E
25 Switzerland ■ 46 30N 8 0 E

15 Swords 53 27N 6 15W
84 Sydney, Australia 33 53S 151 10E
91 Sydney, Canada 46 7N 60 7W
91 Sydney Mines 46 18N 60 15W
4 Sydprøven 60 30N 45 35W
25 Syke 52 55N 8 50E
48 Syktyvkar 61 45N 50 40E
99 Sylacauga 33 10N 86 15W
59 Sylhet 24 43N 91 55E
24 Sylt, I. 54 50N 8 20E
92 Sylvan Lake 52 20N 114 10W
50 Sym 60 20N 87 50E
50 Syr Darya, R. 46 3N 61 0E
97 Syracuse 38 0N 101 40W
56 Syria ■ 35 0N 38 0E
51 Syul'dzhyukyor 63 25N 113 40E
48 Syzran 53 12N 48 30E
27 Szabolcs-Szatmar □ 48 2N 21 45E
27 Szarvas 46 50N 20 38E
28 Szczecin 53 27N 14 27E
28 Szczecin □ 53 27N 14 32E
28 Szczecinek 53 43N 16 41E
28 Szczythna 53 33N 21 0E
69 Szechwan □ 30 15N 103 15E
27 Szeged 46 16N 20 10E
27 Szeghalom 47 1N 21 10E
27 Székesfehérvár 47 15N 18 25E
27 Szekszárd 46 22N 18 42E
67 Szemao 22 50N 101 0E
69 Szengen 24 50N 108 0E
27 Szentendre 47 39N 19 4E
27 Szentes 46 39N 20 21E
68 Szeping 43 10N 124 18E
27 Szolnok 47 10N 20 15E
27 Szolnok □ 47 15N 20 30E
27 Szombathely 47 14N 16 38E
28 Szprotawa 51 33N 15 35E

T

68 Ta Hingan Ling, Mts. 48 0N 120 0E
67 Ta Liang Shan, Mts. 28 0N 103 0E
108 Tabacal 23 15S 64 15W
14 Tabasco □ 17 45N 93 30W
92 Taber 49 48N 111 5W
33 Tabernas 37 4N 2 26W
33 Tabernes de Valldigna 39 5N 0 13W
65 Tablas, I. 12 20N 122 10E
75 Table Mt. 34 0S 18 22E
82 Tableland 17 16S 126 51E
80 Tabletop, Mt. 23 30S 147 0E
26 Tábor 49 25N 14 39E
74 Tabora 5 2S 32 57E
72 Tabou 4 30N 7 20W
56 Tabriz 38 7N 56 20E
56 Tabuk 28 30N 36 25E
44 Täby 59 29N 18 4E
110 Tachira 8 7N 72 21W
65 Tacloban 11 1N 125 0E
110 Tacna 18 0S 70 20W
102 Tacoma 47 15N 122 30W
109 Tacuarembó 31 45S 56 0W
72 Tademait, Plateau du 28 30N 2 30E
55 Tadjoura 11 50N 44 55E
85 Tadmor, N.Z. 41 27S 172 45E
56 Tadmor, Syria 34 30N 37 55E
91 Tadoussac 48 11N 69 42W
62 Tadpatri 14 55N 78 1E
50 Tadzhik S.S.R. □ 35 30N 70 0E
68 Taegu 35 50N 128 25E
68 Taejon 35 30N 127 22E
32 Tafalla 42 30N 1 41W
75 Tafelbaai 33 35S 18 25E
13 Taff, R. 51 27N 3 9W
108 Tafi Viejo 26 43S 67 17W
57 Taftan, Kūh-e, Mt. 28 36N 61 6E
49 Taganrog 47 12N 38 50E
65 Tagbilaran 9 42N 124 3E
36 Tággia 43 52N 7 50E
37 Tagliacozzo 42 4N 13 13E
111 Taguatinga 12 26S 45 40W
85 Tahakopa 46 30S 169 23E
67 Tahcheng 46 50N 83 1E
77 Tahiti, I. 17 45S 149 30W
102 Tahoe, L. 39 6N 120 0W
72 Tahoua 14 57N 5 16E
69 Tahsien 31 12N 108 13E
73 Tahta 26 44N 31 32E
69 Tai Hu 31 10N 120 0E
69 Taichow 32 30N 119 50E
69 Taichung 24 10N 120 35E
68 Taihan Shan, Mts. 36 0N 114 0E
85 Taihape 39 41S 175 48E
69 Taiho 26 50N 114 54E
68 Taiku 37 46N 112 28E
68 Tailai 46 28N 123 18E
81 Tailem Bend 35 12S 139 29E
25 Tailfingen 48 15N 9 1E
56 Taima 27 35N 38 45E
14 Tain 57 49N 4 4W
69 Tainan 23 0N 120 15E
43 Taínaron, Ákra 36 22N 22 27E
69 Taipei 25 2N 121 30E
63 Taiping 4 50N 100 43E
112 Taitao, Pen. de 46 30S 75 0W
69 Taitung 22 43N 121 4E
69 Taiwan ■ 23 30N 121 0E
43 Taïyeto Óros, Mts. 37 0N 22 23E
54 Taiyiba, Israel 32 36N 35 27E
54 Taiyiba, Jordan 31 55N 35 17E
68 Taiyuan 38 0N 112 30E
55 Ta'izz 13 38N 44 4E
30 Tajuña, R. 40 7N 3 35W
73 Tājūra 32 51N 13 27E
63 Tak 17 0N 99 10E
66 Takachiho 32 42N 131 18E
66 Takada 37 7N 138 15E
85 Takaka 40 51S 172 50E
66 Takamatsu 34 20N 134 5E
66 Takaoka 36 40N 137 0E
85 Takapuna 36 47S 174 47E
66 Takasaki 36 20N 139 0E
66 Takatsuki 34 40N 135 37E
74 Takaungu 3 38S 39 52E
66 Takayama 36 10N 137 5E
66 Takefu 35 50N 136 10E
63 Takeo 11 3N 104 50E
57 Takhar □ 36 30N 69 30E
67 Takla Makan, Reg. 39 40N 85 0E
109 Tala 34 21S 55 46W
108 Talagante 33 40S 70 50W
110 Talara 4 30S 81 10W
65 Talaud, Kep. 4 30N 127 10E
30 Talavera de la Reina 39 55N 4 46W
108 Talca 35 20S 71 46W
108 Talca □ 35 20S 71 46W
108 Talcahuano 36 40S 73 10W
50 Taldy Kurgan 45 10N 78 45E
54 Talfit 32 5N 35 17E
69 Tali, Shensi 34 48N 109 48E
67 Tali, Yunnan 25 50N 100 0E
65 Taliabu, I. 1 45S 125 0E
68 Talien 38 53N 121 35E
62 Talikoti 16 29N 76 17E
64 Taliwang 8 50S 116 55E
88 Talkeetna 62 20N 149 50W
99 Talladega 33 28N 86 2W
99 Tallahassee 30 25N 84 15W
84 Tallangatta 36 10S 147 14E
48 Tallinn 59 29N 24 58E
101 Tallulah 32 25N 91 12W
54 Talluza 32 17N 35 18E
41 Talmaciu 45 38N 24 19E
108 Taltal 25 23S 70 40W
81 Talwood 28 27S 149 20E
72 Tamale 9 22N 0 50W
66 Tamano 34 35N 133 59E
72 Tamanrasset 22 56N 5 30E
97 Tamaqua 40 46N 75 58W
13 Tamar, R. 50 22N 4 10W
66 Tamashima 34 27N 133 18E
75 Tamatave 18 10S 49 25E
104 Tamaulipas □ 24 0N 99 0W
72 Tambacounda 13 55N 13 45W
83 Tambellup 34 4S 117 37E
80 Tambo 24 54S 146 14E
64 Tambora, I. 8 14S 117 55E
48 Tambov 52 45N 41 20E
30 Tambre, R. 42 49N 8 53W
72 Tamchaket 17 25N 10 40W
30 Tamega, R. 41 5N 8 21W
104 Tamiahua, Laguna de 21 30N 97 30W
62 Tamil Nadu □ 11 0N 77 0E
68 Taming 36 20N 115 10E
61 Tamluk 22 18N 87 58E
54 Tammun 32 18N 35 23E
99 Tampa 27 57N 82 30W
47 Tampere 61 30N 23 50E
104 Tampico 22 20N 97 50W
63 Tampin 2 28N 102 13E
55 Tamra 32 51N 35 12E
68 Tamsagbulag 47 15N 117 5E
26 Tamsweg 47 7N 13 49E
31 Tamuja, R. 39 33N 6 8W
81 Tamworth, Australia 31 0S 150 58E
13 Tamworth, U.K. 52 38N 1 2W
46 Tana 70 23N 28 13E
73 Tana, L. 12 0N 37 20E
74 Tana, R. 2 32S 40 31E
66 Tanabe 33 44N 135 22E
88 Tanacross 63 40N 143 30W
64 Tanahgrogot 1 55S 116 15E
65 Tanahmeroh 6 0S 140 7E
82 Tanami, Des. 23 15S 132 20E
88 Tanana 65 10N 152 15W
88 Tanana, R. 64 25N 145 30W
75 Tananarive = Antananarivo 18 55S 47 31E
18 Tancarville 46 50N 0 55W
60 Tanda, Ut.P. 28 57N 78 56E
61 Tanda, Ut.P. 26 33N 82 35E
41 Tandarei 44 39N 27 40E
108 Tandil 37 15S 59 6W
60 Tandlianwala 31 3N 73 9E
60 Tando Adam 25 45N 68 40E
60 Tando Mohommad Khan 25 8N 68 32E
62 Tandur 19 11N 79 30E
85 Taneatua 38 4S 177 1E
66 Tane-ga-Shima, I. 30 30N 131 0E
59 Tanen Tong Dan, Mts. 19 40N 99 0E
72 Tanezrouft 23 9N 0 11E
74 Tanga 5 5S 39 2E
61 Tangail 24 15N 90 0E
74 Tanganyika, L. 6 40S 30 0E
72 Tanger 35 50N 5 49W
65 Tangerang 6 12S 106 39E
24 Tangermünde 52 32N 11 57E
67 Tanghla Shan, Mts. 33 10N 90 0E
69 Tangshan, Anhwei 34 23N 116 34E
68 Tangshan, Hopei 39 40N 118 10E
69 Tangtu 31 37N 118 39E
69 Tangyang 30 50N 111 45E
65 Tanimbar, Kep. 7 30S 131 30E
63 Tanjong Malim 3 44N 101 27E
62 Tanjore = Thanjavur 10 48N 79 12E
64 Tanjung 2 10S 115 25E
64 Tanjungbalai 2 55N 99 44E
64 Tanjungkarang 5 25S 105 16E
64 Tanjungpandan 2 45S 107 39E
64 Tanjungredeb 2 12N 117 35E
64 Tanjungselor 2 55N 117 25E
90 Tannin 49 40N 91 0E
45 Tannis, B. 57 40N 10 10E
73 Tanta 30 45N 30 57E
62 Tanuku 16 45N 81 44E
81 Tanunda 34 30S 139 0E
62 Tanur 11 1N 75 46E
20 Tanus 44 8N 2 19E
74 Tanzania ■ 6 40S 34 0E
68 Taonan 45 30N 122 20E
69 Taoyuan 25 0N 121 4E
69 Tapa Shan, Mts. 31 45N 109 30E
104 Tapachula 14 54N 92 17W
64 Tapaktuan 3 30N 97 10E
85 Tapanui 45 56N 169 18E
30 Tapia 43 34N 6 56W
27 Tápiószele 47 45N 19 55E
60 Tapti, R. 21 5N 72 40E
85 Tapuaenuka, Mt. 41 55S 173 50E
109 Taquara 29 36S 50 46W
109 Taquaritinga 21 24S 48 30W
50 Tara 56 55N 74 30E
50 Tara, R. 56 42N 74 36E
51 Tarabagatay, Khrebet, Mts. 47 30N 84 0E
56 Tarābulus, Lebanon 34 31N 33 52E
73 Tarābulus, Libya 32 49N 13 7E
84 Tarago 35 6S 149 39E
64 Tarakan 3 20N 117 35E
85 Taranaki □ 39 5S 174 51E
30 Tarancón 40 1N 3 1W
60 Taranga Hill 24 0N 72 40E
39 Táranto 40 30N 17 11E
39 Táranto, G. di 40 0N 17 15E
110 Tarapaca 2 56S 69 46W
108 Tarapaca □ 20 45S 69 30W
110 Tarapoto 6 30S 76 20W
21 Tarare 45 55N 4 26E
20 Tarascon 42 50N 1 37E
85 Tarawera 39 2S 176 36E
85 Tarawera, L. 38 13S 176 27E
32 Tarazona 41 55N 1 43W
33 Tarazona de la Mancha 39 16N 1 55W
14 Tarbat Ness 57 52N 3 48W
58 Tarbela Dam 34 0N 72 52E
14 Tarbert 57 54N 6 49W
20 Tarbes 43 15N 0 3E
37 Tarcento 46 12N 13 12E
20 Tardets 43 7N 0 53W
84 Taree 31 50S 152 30E
21 Tarentaise, Reg. 45 30N 6 35E
31 Tarifa 36 1N 5 36W
108 Tarija 21 30S 64 40W
108 Tarija □ 21 30S 63 30W
67 Tarim, R. 41 5N 86 40E
49 Tarkhankut, Mys. 45 25N 32 30E
50 Tarko Sale 64 55N 77 50E
72 Tarkwa 5 20N 2 0W
65 Tarlac 15 30N 120 25E
80 Tarlton Downs 22 40S 136 45E
20 Tarn, R. 44 5N 1 6E
20 Tarn □ 43 50N 2 8E
27 Tarna, R. 47 31N 19 59E
45 Tarnby 55 37N 12 36E
20 Tarn-et-Garonne □ 44 8N 1 20E
27 Tarnobrzeg 50 35N 21 41E
28 Tarnobrzeg □ 50 40N 22 0E
27 Tarnów 50 3N 21 0E
27 Tarnow □ 50 0N 21 0E
27 Tarnowskie Góry 50 27N 18 54E
57 Tārom 28 11N 55 42E
37 Tarquínia 42 15N 11 45E
32 Tarragona 41 5N 1 17E
32 Tarragona □ 41 0N 1 0E
32 Tarrasa 41 26N 2 1E
32 Tárrega 41 39N 1 9E
97 Tarrytown 41 5N 73 52W
73 Tarso Emissi 21 27N 18 36E
56 Tarsus 36 58N 34 55E
108 Tartagal 22 30S 63 50W
20 Tartas 43 50N 0 48W
48 Tartu 58 25N 26 58E
56 Tartūs 34 55N 35 55E
64 Tarutung 2 0N 99 0E
37 Tarvisio 46 31N 13 35E
73 Tasāwah 26 0N 13 37E
90 Tashereau 48 40N 78 40W
62 Tasgaon 17 2N 74 39E
50 Tashauz 42 0N 59 20E
67 Tashigong 33 0N 79 30E
50 Tashkent 41 20N 69 10E
67 Tashkurgan 37 51N 74 57E
57 Tashkurghan 36 45N 67 40E
50 Tashtagol 52 47N 87 53E
65 Tasikmalaya 7 18S 108 12E
45 Tåsinge, I. 55 0N 10 36E
51 Taskan 63 5N 150 5E
85 Tasman, B. 40 59S 173 25E
85 Tasman Glacier 43 45S 170 20E
76 Tasman Sea 42 30S 168 0E
80 Tasmania, I. 49 0S 146 30E
27 Tata 47 37N 18 19E
27 Tatabánya 47 32N 18 25E
48 Tatar A.S.S.R. □ 55 30N 51 30E
50 Tatarsk 55 50N 75 20E
66 Tateyama 35 0N 139 50E
69 Tatien 25 45N 118 0E
27 Tatry, Mts. 49 20N 20 0E
67 Tatsaitan 37 55N 95 0E
109 Tatui 23 25S 48 0W
68 Tatung 40 10N 113 10E
68 Tatungkow 39 55N 124 10E
109 Taubaté 23 5S 45 30W
85 Taumarunui 38 53S 175 15E
110 Taumaturgo 9 0S 73 50W
59 Taungdwingyi 20 1N 95 40E
59 Taunggyi 20 50N 97 0E
59 Taungup Taunggya 18 20N 93 40E
13 Taunton, U.K. 51 1N 3 7W
97 Taunton, U.S.A. 41 54N 71 6W
25 Taunus, Mts. 50 15N 8 20E
85 Taupo 38 41S 176 7E
85 Taupo, L. 38 46S 175 55E
85 Tauranga 37 35S 176 11E
39 Taurianova 38 22N 16 1E
56 Taurus Mts. = Toros Daglari 37 0N 35 0E
32 Tauste 41 58N 1 18W
69 Tava Wan, G. 22 40N 114 40E
88 Tavani 62 10N 93 30W
50 Tavda 58 7N 65 8W
50 Tavda, R. 57 47N 67 16E
19 Taverny 49 2N 2 13E
74 Taveta 3 31N 37 37E
85 Taveuni, I. 16 51S 179 58W
21 Tavignano, R. 42 14N 9 20E
31 Tavira 37 8N 7 40W
13 Tavistock 50 33N 4 9W
30 Távora, R. 41 0N 7 30W
59 Tavoy 14 7N 98 18E
13 Taw, R. 51 4N 4 11W
60 Tawa, R. 22 48N 77 48E
65 Tawitawi, I. 5 2N 120 0E
14 Tay, Firth of 56 25N 3 8W
14 Tay, L. 56 30N 4 10W
14 Tay, R. 56 37N 3 58W
63 Tay Ninh 11 20N 106 5E
110 Tayabamba 8 15S 77 10E
101 Taylor 30 30N 97 30W
103 Taylor, Mt. 35 16N 107 50W
100 Taylorville 39 32N 29 20W
51 Taymyr Pol. 75 0N 100 0E
14 Tayport 56 27N 2 52W
51 Tayshet 55 58N 97 25E
14 Tayside □ 56 30N 3 35W
51 Taytay 10 45N 119 30E
69 Tayu 25 38N 114 9E
67 Tayulehsze 29 15N 98 1E
72 Taza 34 10N 4 0W
50 Tazovskiy 67 28N 78 42E
49 Tbilisi 41 50N 44 50E
73 Tchad ■ 12 30N 17 15E
73 Tchad, L. 13 30N 14 30E
74 Tchibanga 2 45S 11 12E
28 Tczew 54 8N 18 50E
85 Te Anau, L. 45 15S 167 45E
85 Te Aroha 37 32S 175 44E
85 Te Awamutu 38 1S 175 20E
85 Te Horo 40 48S 175 6E
85 Te Kuiti 38 20S 175 11E
85 Te Puke 37 46S 176 22E

39 Teano 41 15N 14 1E
31 Teba 36 59N 4 55W
72 Tébessa 35 28N 8 9E
64 Tebingtinggi 3 38S 102 1E
20 Tech, R. 42 36N 3 3E
104 Tecuala 22 24N 105 30W
41 Tecuci 45 51N 27 27E
50 Tedzhen 37 23N 60 31E
12 Tees, R. 54 34N 1 16W
12 Teesside 54 37N 1 13W
110 Tefé 3 25S 64 50W
65 Tegal 6 52S 109 8E
16 Tegelen 51 20N 6 9E
61 Teghra 25 30N 85 34E
105 Tegucigalpa 14 10N 87 0W
68 Tehchow 37 28N 116 18E
57 Tehrān 35 44N 51 30E
57 Tehrān □ 35 30N 51 0E
67 Tehtsin 28 45N 98 58E
104 Tehuacán 18 20N 97 30W
104 Tehuantepec 16 10N 95 19W
104 Tehuntepec, Istmo de 17 0N 94 30W
13 Teifi, R. 52 7N 4 42W
13 Teign, R. 50 33N 3 29W
13 Teignmouth 50 33N 3 30W
41 Teiuş 46 12N 23 40E
75 Teixeira da Silva 12 12S 15 52E
74 Teixeira de Sousa 10 42S 22 12E
31 Tejo, R. 38 40N 9 24W
85 Tekapo, L. 43 48S 170 32E
104 Tekax 20 20N 89 30W
50 Tekeli 44 50N 79 0E
56 Tekirdag 40 58N 27 30E
62 Tekkali 18 43N 84 24E
54 Tel Aviv-Yafo 32 4N 34 48E
54 Tel Mond 32 15N 34 56E
104 Tela 15 40N 87 28W
64 Telanaipura = Jambi 1 38S 103 30E
49 Telavi 42 0N 45 30E
92 Telegraph Creek 58 0N 131 10W
44 Telemark □ 59 30N 8 30E
30 Teleno 42 23N 6 22W
12 Telford 52 42N 2 29W
26 Telfs 47 19N 11 4E
68 Telisze 39 50N 112 0E
92 Telkwa 54 41N 126 56W
98 Tell City 38 0N 86 44W
62 Tellicherry 11 45N 75 30E
63 Telok Anson 4 0N 101 10E
112 Telsen 42 30S 66 50W
24 Teltow 52 24N 13 15E
64 Telukbetung 5 29S 105 17E
64 Telukbutun 4 5N 108 7E
64 Telukdalem 0 45N 97 50E
72 Tema 5 41N 0 0E
65 Temanggung 7 18S 110 10E
63 Tembeling, R. 4 4N 102 20E
31 Tembleque 39 41N 3 30W
13 Teme, R. 52 9N 2 18W
63 Temerloh 3 27N 102 25E
50 Temir 49 8N 57 6E
50 Temirtou 53 10N 87 20E
90 Temiskaming 46 44N 79 5W
84 Témora 34 30S 147 30E
103 Tempe 33 26N 111 59W
64 Tempino 1 55S 103 23E
38 Témpio Pausania 40 53N 9 6E
101 Temple 31 5N 97 28W
15 Templemore 52 48N 7 50W
24 Templin 53 8N 13 31E
112 Temuco 38 50S 72 50W
85 Temuka 44 14S 171 17E
62 Tenali 16 15N 80 35E
104 Tenancingo 18 98N 99 33W
104 Tenango 19 0N 99 40W
63 Tenasserim 12 6N 99 3E
21 Tenay 45 55N 5 30E
13 Tenby 51 40N 4 42W
21 Tenda 44 5N 7 34E
72 Tenerife, I. 28 20N 16 40W
65 Tengah□, Java 7 0S 110 0E
64 Tengah□, Kalimantan 2 20S 113 0E
67 Tengchung 24 58N 98 30E
69 Tenghsien 35 10N 117 10E
50 Tengiz, Oz. 50 30N 69 0E
62 Tenkasi 8 55N 77 20E
80 Tennant Creek 19 30S 134 0E
99 Tennessee, R. 37 0N 88 20W
99 Tennessee □ 36 0N 86 30W
66 Tenryū-Gawa, R. 34 39N 137 47E
81 Tenterfield 29 0S 152 0E
111 Teófilo Otoni 17 15S 41 30W
104 Teotihuacan 19 44N 98 50W
104 Tepic 21 30N 104 54W
26 Teplice 50 39N 13 48E
32 Ter, R. 42 1N 3 12E
30 Tera, R. 38 56N 8 3W
37 Téramo 42 40N 13 40E
84 Terang 38 3S 142 59E
8 Terceira, I. 38 43N 24 13W
62 Terdal 16 33N 75 9E
40 Teregova 45 10N 22 16E
49 Terek, R. 43 44N 46 33E
63 Terengganu □ 4 53N 103 0E
111 Teresina 5 2S 42 45W
28 Terespol 52 5N 23 36E
19 Tergnier 49 40N 3 17E
63 Teriang 3 15N 102 26E
39 Terlizzi 41 8N 16 32E
50 Termez 37 0N 67 15E
38 Términi Imerese 37 59N 13 51E
104 Términos, L. de 18 35N 91 30W
65 Ternate 0 45N 127 25E
16 Terneuzen 51 20N 3 50E
37 Terni 42 34N 12 38E
26 Ternitz 47 43N 16 2E
81 Terowie 38 10S 138 50E
92 Terrace 54 30N 128 35W
38 Terracina 41 17N 13 12E
37 Terranuova 43 38N 11 35E
20 Terrasson 45 7N 1 19E
5 Terre Adélie 67 0S 140 0E
98 Terre Haute 46 30N 75 13W
101 Terrell 32 44N 96 19W
97 Terryville 41 41N 73 1W
16 Terschelling, I. 53 25N 5 20E
32 Teruel 40 22N 1 8W
32 Teruel □ 40 48N 1 0E
41 Tervel 43 45N 27 28E
46 Tervola 66 6N 24 59E
40 Tešica 43 27N 21 45E
72 Tessalit 20 12N 1 0E
13 Test, R. 51 7N 1 30W
20 Tet, R. 42 44N 3 2E
75 Tete 16 13S 33 33E
41 Teteven 42 58N 24 17E
72 Tetouan 35 30N 5 25W
40 Tetovo 42 1N 21 2E
51 Tetyukhe = Dalnergorsk 44 40N 135 50E
93 Teulon 50 30N 97 20W
14 Teviot, R. 55 36N 2 26W
81 Tewantin 26 27S 153 3E
13 Tewkesbury 51 59N 2 8W
101 Texarkana, Ark. 33 25N 94 0W
101 Texarkana, Tex. 33 25N 94 0W
81 Texas 28 49S 151 15E
101 Texas □ 31 30N 98 30W
101 Texas City 27 20N 95 20W
16 Texel, I. 53 5N 4 50E
104 Teziutlán 19 50N 97 30W
59 Tezpur 26 40N 92 45E
75 Thabana Ntlenyana 29 30S 29 9E
75 Thabazimbi 24 40S 26 4E
63 Thailand ■ 16 0N 101 0E
63 Thakhek 17 25 104 45E
58 Thal 33 28N 70 33E
60 Thal Desert 31 0N 71 30E
81 Thallon 28 30S 148 57E
25 Thalwil 47 17N 8 35E
13 Thame, R. 51 52N 0 47W
85 Thames 37 7S 175 34E
90 Thames, R., Canada 42 19N 82 28W
13 Thames, R., U.K. 51 28N 0 43E
62 Thana 19 12N 72 59E
60 Thanesar 30 1N 76 52E
13 Thanet, I. 51 21N 1 20E
63 Thang Binh 15 50N 108 20E
82 Thangoo P.O. 18 10S 122 22E
80 Thangool 24 29S 150 35E
63 Thanh Hoa 19 35N 105 40E
62 Thanjavur 10 48N 79 12E
19 Thann 47 48N 7 5E
19 Thaon 48 15N 6 25E
81 Thargomindah 27 58S 143 46E
59 Tharrawaddy 17 30N 96 0E
42 Thásos, I. 40 40N 24 40E
103 Thatcher 32 54N 109 46W
59 Thaton 17 0N 97 39E
20 Thau, Étang de 43 23N 3 36E
59 Thaungdut 24 30N 94 30E
59 Thayetmyo 19 19N 95 11E
59 Thazi 21 0N 96 5E
105 The Bight 24 19N 75 24W
102 The Dalles 45 40N 121 11W
105 The Flatts 32 19N 64 45W
68 The Great Wall of China 37 30N 109 0E
105 The Grenadines 12 40N 61 15W
16 The Hague = s'Gravenhage 52 7N 7 14E
83 The Johnston Lakes 32 25S 120 30E
93 The Pas 53 45N 101 15W
81 Theebine 26 0S 152 30E
20 Thenon 45 9N 1 4E
80 Theodore 24 55S 150 3E
42 Thermaikós Kól. 40 15N 22 45E
102 Thermopolis 43 14N 108 10E
43 Thermopylae 38 48N 22 45E
42 Thesprotia □ 39 27N 20 22E
42 Thessalía □ 39 30N 22 0E
90 Thessalon 46 20N 83 30W
42 Thessaloníki 40 38N 23 0E
42 Thessaloníki □ 40 45N 23 0E
13 Thetford 52 25N 0 44E
91 Thetford Mines 46 8N 71 18W
81 Thevenard 32 9S 133 38E
101 Thibodaux 29 48N 90 49W
93 Thicket Portage 55 25N 97 45W
100 Thief River Falls 48 15N 96 10W
37 Thiene 45 42N 11 29E
19 Thierache, Reg. 49 51N 3 45E
20 Thiers 45 52N 3 33E
72 Thiès 14 50N 16 51W
74 Thika 1 1S 37 5E
19 Thionville 49 20N 6 10E
43 Thíra, I. 36 23N 25 27E
12 Thirsk 54 15N 1 20W
45 Thisted 56 57N 8 42E
43 Thíval 38 19N 23 19E
20 Thiviers 45 25N 0 54E
99 Thomasville, Ala. 31 55N 87 42W
99 Thomasville, Fla. 30 50N 84 0W
99 Thomasville, N.C. 35 5N 80 4W
93 Thompson 55 50N 97 34W
97 Thompsonville 42 0N 72 37W
63 Thonburi 13 50N 100 36W
21 Thonon 46 22N 6 29E
12 Thornaby on Tees 54 36N 1 19W
96 Thorold 43 8N 79 13W
20 Thouars 46 59N 0 13W
42 Thráki □ 41 9N 25 30E
42 Thrakikón Pélagos 40 30N 25 0E
102 Three Forks 45 5N 111 40W
92 Three Hills 51 43N 113 15W
97 Three Rivers 28 30N 98 10W
4 Thule 76 0N 68 0W
25 Thun 46 45N 7 38E
90 Thunder Bay 48 25N 89 10E
92 Thunder River 52 13N 119 20W
25 Thunersee 46 42N 7 42E
63 Thung Song 8 10N 99 40E
25 Thurgau □ 47 34N 9 10E
24 Thüringer Wald 50 35N 11 0E
15 Thurles 52 40N 7 53W
26 Thurn P. 47 19N 12 24E
90 Thurso, Canada 45 36N 75 15W
14 Thurso, U.K. 58 34N 3 31W
5 Thurston I. 72 0S 100 0W
45 Thy, Reg. 57 0N 8 30E
72 Tiaret 35 28N 1 21E
72 Tiassalé 5 58N 4 57W
109 Tibaji 24 19S 50 19W
37 Tiber, R. 41 44N 12 14E
54 Tiberias 32 47N 35 32E
73 Tibesti 21 0N 17 30E
67 Tibet □ 32 30N 86 0E
52 Tibet, Plateau of 35 0N 90 0E
81 Tibooburra 29 26S 142 1E
45 Tibro 58 28N 14 10E
104 Tiburón, I. 29 0N 112 30W
36 Ticino, R. 45 9N 9 14E
25 Ticino □ 46 20N 8 45E
97 Ticonderoga 43 40N 73 28E
104 Ticul 20 20N 89 50W
45 Tidaholm 58 12N 13 55E
72 Tidjikdja 18 4N 11 35W
63 Tiehling 42 25N 123 51E
16 Tiel 51 54N 5 5E
16 Tielt 51 0N 3 20E
52 Tien Shan, Mts. 42 0N 80 0E
16 Tienen 50 48N 4 57E
69 Tienshui 34 30N 105 34E
68 Tientsin 39 10N 117 0E
69 Tientung 23 47N 107 2E
31 Tierra de Barros 38 40N 6 30W
30 Tierra de Campos 42 5N 4 45W
112 Tierra del Fuego, I. 54 0S 69 0W
30 Tiétar, R. 39 55N 5 50W
109 Tietê, R. 20 40S 51 35W
98 Tiffin 41 8N 83 10W
54 Tifrah 31 19N 34 42E
99 Tifton 31 28N 83 32W
65 Tifu 3 39S 126 18E
41 Tigăneşti 44 44N 26 8E
91 Tignish 46 58N 63 57W
56 Tigris, R. = Dijlah, Nahr 31 0N 47 25E
51 Tigu 29 48N 91 38E
59 Tigyaing 23 45N 96 10E
104 Tijuana 32 30N 117 10W
104 Tikal 17 2N 89 35W
49 Tikhoretsk 45 56N 40 5E
51 Tiksi 71 50N 129 0E
16 Tilburg 51 31N 5 6E
90 Tilbury, Canada 42 17N 84 23E
13 Tilbury, U.K. 51 27N 0 24E
61 Tilhat 28 0N 79 45E
51 Tilichiki 61 0N 166 5E
90 Tillsonburg 42 53N 80 55W
43 Tílos, I. 36 27N 27 27E
81 Tilpa 30 58S 144 30E
48 Timanskiy Kryazh 65 58N 50 5E
85 Timaru 44 23S 171 14E
43 Timbákion 35 4N 24 45E
72 Timbuktu= Tombouctou 16 50N 3 0W
42 Timfi Oros, Mt. 39 59N 20 45E
43 Timfristós, Mt. 38 57N 21 50E
40 Timiş, R. 44 51N 20 39E
40 Timişoara 4543 1 21 15E
90 Timmins 48 28N 81 25W
40 Timok, R. 44 13N 22 40E
111 Timon 5 8S 42 52W
65 Timor, I. 9 0S 125 0E
82 Timor, Sea 10 0S 127 0E
72 Timris, C. 19 15N 16 30W
65 Timur□, Java 7 20S 112 0E
64 Timur□, Kalimantan 1 15N 117 0E
62 Tindivanam 12 15N 79 35E
72 Tindouf 27 50N 8 4W
45 Tinglev 54 57N 9 13E
83 Tinkurrin 33 0S 117 38E
43 Tínos, I. 37 33N 25 8E
33 Tiñoso, C. 37 32N 1 6W
69 Tinpak 21 40N 111 15E
81 Tintinara 35 48S 140 2E
31 Tinto, R. 37 12N 6 55W
63 Tioman, Pulau 2 50N 104 10E
59 Tipongpani 27 20N 95 55E
15 Tipperary 52 28N 8 10W
15 Tipperary □ 52 37N 7 55W
13 Tipton 52 32N 2 4W
62 Tiptur 13 15N 76 26E
54 Tira 32 14N 34 56E
57 Tirān 32 45N 51 0E
42 Tirana 41 18N 19 49E
42 Tirana-Durresi □ 41 35N 20 0E
36 Tirano 46 13N 10 11E
49 Tiraspol 46 55N 29 35E
54 Tirat Karmel 32 46N 34 58E
54 Tirat Tsevi 32 26N 35 51E
54 Tirat Yehuda 32 1N 34 56E
54 Tire 38 5N 27 50E
56 Tirebolu 40 58N 38 45E
14 Tiree, I. 56 31N 6 49W
41 Tîrgovişte 44 55N 25 27E
41 Tîrgu-Cârbuneşti 44 58N 23 31E
41 Tîrgu-Jiu 45 5N 23 19E
41 Tîrgu-Mureş 46 31N 24 38E
41 Tîrgu Ocna 46 15N 26 37E
41 Tîrgu Sacuesc 46 0N 26 8E
58 Tirich Mir, Mt. 36 15N 71 35E
41 Tîrnaveni 46 19N 24 13E
42 Tírnavos 39 45N 22 18E
26 Tirol □ 47 3N 10 43E
38 Tirso, L. del 40 8N 8 56E
38 Tirso, R. 39 52N 8 33E
62 Tiruchchirappalli 10 45N 78 45E
62 Tiruchendur 8 29N 78 7E
62 Tirunelveli 8 45N 77 45E
62 Tirupati 13 45N 79 30E
62 Tiruppur 11 6N 77 21E
62 Tiruppattur 12 30N 78 30E
62 Tiruturaipundi 10 32N 79 41E
62 Tiruvalla 9 23N 76 33E
62 Tiruvallur 13 9N 79 57E
62 Tiruvannamalai 12 10N 79 12E
62 Tiruvarur 10 46N 79 38E
62 Tiruvatipuram 12 39N 79 33E
62 Tiruvottiyur 13 10N 80 22E
40 Tisa, R. 45 15N 20 17E
93 Tisdale 52 50N 104 0W
27 Tisza, R. 45 15N 20 17E
27 Tiszaföldvár 76 59N 20 15E
27 Tiszafured 47 38N 20 50E
51 Tit-Ary 71 58N 127 1E
110 Titicaca, L. 15 30S 69 30W
40 Titigrad 42 30N 19 19E
40 Titov Veles 41 46N 21 47E
40 Titovo Uzice 43 55N 19 50E
74 Titule 3 15N 25 31E
96 Titusville 41 35N 79 39W
40 Tivat 42 28N 18 43E
13 Tiverton 50 54N 3 30W
37 Tívoli 41 58N 12 45E
57 Tiwī 22 45N 59 12E
72 Tizi-Ouzou 36 48N 4 2E
104 Tizimín 21 0N 88 1W
45 Tjörn, I. 58 0N 11 35E
104 Tlaxcala □ 19 30N 98 20W
104 Tlaxiaco 17 10N 97 40W
72 Tlemcen 34 52N 1 15W
28 Tłuszcz 52 25N 21 25E
60 Toba Tek Singh 31 30N 69 0E
105 Tobago, I. 11 10N 60 30W
33 Tobarra 38 35N 1 41W
65 Tobelo 1 25N 127 56E
80 Tobermorey, Australia 22 12S 138 0E
90 Tobermory, Canada 45 12N 81 40W
14 Tobermory, U.K. 56 37N 6 4W
50 Tobolsk 58 0N 68 10E
73 Tobruk = Tubruq 32 7N 23 55E
111 Tocantinopolis 6 20S 47 25W
111 Tocantins, R. 1 45S 49 10W
99 Toccoa 34 35N 83 19W
66 Tochigi 36 25N 139 45E
66 Tochigi □ 36 45N 139 45E
31 Tocina 37 37N 5 44W
44 Töckfors 59 30N 11 50E
108 Tocopilla 22 5S 70 10W

84 Tocumwal 35 45s 145 31 E
37 Todi 42 47N 12 24 E
111 Todos os Santos, B. de 12 45s 38 40w
44 Töfsingfalens, Nat. Pk. 62 15N 12 44 E
48 Togliatti 53 37N 49 18 E
72 Togo ■ 6 15N 1 35 E
66 Tōhoku □ 38 40N 142 0 E
66 Tōkamachi 37 8N 138 43 E
73 Tokar 18 27N 37 43 E
66 Tokara Kaikyō, Str. 30 0N 130 0 E
66 Tokara-Shima, I. 29 0N 129 0 E
85 Tokarahi 44 56s 170 39 E
56 Tokat 40 22N 36 35 E
76 Tokelau Is. 9 0s 172 0w
50 Tokmak 47 16N 35 42 E
66 Toku-no-Shima, I. 27 50N 129 2 E
66 Tokushima 34 0N 134 45 E
66 Tokushima □ 35 50N 134 50 E
66 Tokuyama 34 0N 131 50 E
66 Tōkyō 35 45N 139 45 E
66 Tōkyō □ 35 40N 139 30 E
85 Tolaga 38 21s 178 20 E
41 Tolbukhin 43 37N 27 49 E
30 Toledo, Sp. 39 50N 4 2w
98 Toledo, U.S.A. 41 37N 83 33w
31 Toledo, Mts. de 39 30N 4 30w
31 Toledo □ 39 40N 4 0w
37 Tolentino 43 12N 13 17 E
110 Tolima, Mt. 4 40N 75 19w
65 Tolitoli 1 5N 120 50 E
103 Tolleson 33 29N 112 10w
27 Tolna □ 46 25N 18 48 E
65 Tolo, Teluk, G. 2 20s 122 10 E
32 Tolosa 43 8N 2 5w
104 Toluca 19 20N 99 50w
68 Tolun 42 22N 116 30 E
82 Tom Price 22 50s 117 40 E
31 Tomar 39 36N 8 25w
28 Tomaszów Jubelski 50 29N 23 23 E
28 Tomaszów Mazowiecki 51 30N 19 57 E
99 Tombigbee, R. 32 0N 88 6 E
72 Tombouctou 16 50N 3 0w
103 Tombstone 31 40N 110 4w
108 Tomé 36 36s 73 6w
45 Tomelilla 55 33N 13 54 E
33 Tomellosa 39 10N 3 2w
65 Tomini, Teluk, G. 0 10s 122 0 E
14 Tomintoul 57 15N 3 22w
51 Tommot 58 50N 126 30 E
50 Tomsk 56 30N 85 12 E
45 Tomtabacken, Mt. 57 25N 14 30 E
104 Tonalá 16 8N 93 41w
110 Tonantins 2 45s 67 45w
96 Tonawanda 43 0N 78 54w
13 Tonbridge 51 12N 0 18 E
30 Tondela 40 31N 8 5w
45 Tønder 54 58N 8 50 E
85 Tonga ■ 20 0s 173 0w
85 Tongatapu, I. 20 0s 174 0w
16 Tongeren 50 47N 5 28 E
69 Tonghing 21 30N 108 0 E
63 Tongking, Reg. = Bac-Phan, Reg. 21 30N 105 0 E
14 Tongue 58 29N 4 25w
73 Tonj 7 20N 28 44 E
60 Tonk 26 6N 75 54 E
63 Tonlé Sap, L. 13 0N 104 0 E
20 Tonnay-Charente 45 56N 0 55w
20 Tonneins 44 42N 0 20 E
19 Tonnerre 47 50N 4 0 E
24 Tönning 54 18N 8 57 E
103 Tonopah 38 4N 117 12w
44 Tønsberg 59 19N 11 3 E
102 Tooele 40 30N 112 20w
81 Toompine 27 15s 144 19 E
81 Toowoomba 27 32s 151 56 E
48 Top, Oz. 65 35N 32 0 E
100 Topeka 39 3N 95 40 E
50 Topki 55 25N 85 20 E
27 Topl'a, R. 48 45N 21 45 E
92 Topley 54 32N 126 5w
108 Topocalma, Pta. 34 10s 72 2w
27 Topol'čany 48 35N 18 12 E
40 Topolvǎtu Mare 45 46N 21 41 E
102 Toppenish 46 27N 120 16w
110 Torata 17 3s 70 1w
57 Torbat-e Heydariyeh 35 15N 59 12w
91 Torbay, Canada 47 40N 52 42w
13 Torbay, U.K. 50 26N 3 31w
30 Tordesillas 41 30N 5 0w
45 Töreboda 58 41N 14 7 E
25 Torgau 51 32N 13 0 E
24 Torgelow 53 47N 14 0 E
16 Torhout 51 5N 3 7 E
30 Toriñana, C. 43 3N 9 17w
36 Torino 45 4N 7 40 E
30 Tormes, R. 41 18N 6 29w
46 Torne, R. 65 48N 24 8 E
46 Torneträsk, L. 68 20N 19 10 E
46 Tornio 65 57N 24 12 E
30 Toro 41 35N 5 24w
108 Toro, Cerro del 29 0s 69 50w
27 Törökszentmiklós 47 11N 20 27 E
42 Toronaíos Kól. 40 5N 23 30 E
96 Toronto, Canada 43 39N 79 20w
96 Toronto, U.S.A. 40 27N 80 36w
74 Tororo 0 45N 34 12 E
56 Toros Dağlari, Mts. 37 0N 35 0 E
13 Torquay 50 27N 3 31w
30 Torquemada 42 2N 4 19w
31 Torralba de Calatrava 39 1N 3 44w
39 Torre Annunziata 40 45N 14 26 E
30 Tôrre de Moncorvo 41 12N 7 8w
39 Torre del Greco 40 47N 14 22 E
31 Torre del Mar 36 44N 4 6w
33 Torre-Pacheco 37 47N 0 55w
32 Torreblanca 40 14N 0 12 E
32 Torrecilla en Cameros 42 15N 2 38w
32 Torredembarra 41 9N 1 24w
31 Torredonjimeno 37 46N 3 57w
30 Torrejoncillo 39 54N 6 28w
30 Torrelavega 43 20N 4 5w
31 Torremolinos 36 38N 4 30w
81 Torrens, L. 31 0s 137 45 E
33 Torrente 39 27N 0 28w
31 Torrenueva 38 38N 3 22w
104 Torreon 25 33N 103 25w
33 Torreperogil 38 2N 3 17w
31 Tôrres Novas 39 27N 8 33w
76 Torres Str. 10 20s 142 0 E
31 Torres Veldras 39 5N 9 15w
33 Torrevieja 37 59N 0 42w
13 Torridge, R. 51 3N 4 11w
14 Torridon, L. 57 35N 5 50w
30 Torrijos 39 59N 4 18w
97 Torrington 41 50N 73 9w
32 Torroella de Montgri 42 2N 3 8 E
31 Torrox 36 46N 3 57w
44 Torshälla 59 25N 16 28 E
45 Torsö, I. 58 44N 13 40 E
105 Tortola, I. 18 19N 65 0w
36 Tortona 44 53N 8 54 E
39 Tortorici 38 2N 14 18 E
32 Tortosa 40 49N 0 31 E
32 Tortosa, C. 40 41N 0 52 E
30 Tortosendo 40 15N 7 31w
28 Toruń 53 3N 18 39 E
28 Torun □ 53 20N 19 0 E
45 Torup 56 57N 13 5 E
66 Tosa-Wan, G. 33 15N 133 30 E
36 Toscana □ 43 30N 11 5 E
36 Toscano, Arch. 42 30N 10 30 E
32 Tossa 41 43N 2 56 E
108 Tostado 29 15s 61 50w
33 Totana 37 45N 1 30w
75 Toteng 20 22s 22 58 E
27 Tótkomlós 46 24N 20 45 E
48 Totma 60 0N 42 40 E
13 Totnes 50 26N 3 41w
111 Totness 5 53N 56 19w
104 Totonicapán 14 50N 91 20w
66 Tottori 35 30N 134 15 E
66 Tottori □ 35 30N 134 12 E
72 Toubkal, Djebel, Mt. 31 0N 8 0w
72 Touggourt 33 10N 6 0 E
72 Tougué 11 25N 11 50w
19 Toul 48 40N 5 53 E
21 Toulon 43 10N 5 55 E
20 Toulouse 43 37N 1 28 E
73 Toummo 22 45N 14 8 E
59 Toungoa 19 0N 96 30 E
18 Touques, R. 49 22N 0 6 E
18 Touraine, Reg. 47 20N 0 30 E
63 Tourane = Da Nang 16 10N 108 7 E
19 Tourcoing 50 42N 3 10 E
16 Tournai 50 35N 3 25 E
18 Tournan 48 44N 2 44 E
20 Tournay 43 13N 0 13 E
21 Tournon 45 5N 4 50 E
21 Tournus 46 35N 4 54 E
18 Tours 47 22N 0 40 E
59 Towang 27 33N 91 56 E
84 Townsend, Mt. 36 25s 148 16 E
80 Townsville 19 15s 146 45 E
98 Towson 39 26N 76 34w
13 Towyn 52 37N 4 8w
66 Toyama 36 40N 137 15 E
66 Toyama □ 36 45N 137 30 E
66 Toyama-Wan, G. 37 0N 137 30 E
66 Toyohashi 34 45N 137 25 E
66 Toyokawa 34 48N 137 27 E
66 Toyonaka 34 50N 135 35 E
66 Toyooka 35 35N 135 55 E
66 Toyota 35 5N 137 9 E
72 Tozeur 33 54N 8 4 E
30 Trabancos, R. 41 0N 5 3w
56 Trabzon 41 0N 39 45 E
103 Tracy 44 12N 95 3w
67 Tradom 30 0N 83 59 E
84 Trafalgar 38 14s 146 12 E
31 Trafalgar, C. 36 10N 6 2w
41 Traian 45 9N 27 42 E
112 Traiguón 38 12s 72 40w
92 Trail 49 5N 117 40w
15 Tralee 52 16N 9 42w
15 Tramore 52 10N 7 10w
63 Tran Ninh, Cao Nguyen 19 30N 103 10 E
45 Tranås 58 3N 14 59 E
63 Trang 7 33N 99 38 E
65 Trangan, I. 6 40s 134 20 E
39 Trani 41 17N 16 24 E
109 Tranqueras 31 8s 56 0w
93 Transcona 49 50N 97 0w
41 Transilvania, Reg. 46 38N 24 0 E
75 Transkei □ 32 15s 28 15 E
75 Transvaal □ 25 0s 29 0 E
9 Transylvanian Alps, Mts. 45 30N 25 0 E
38 Trápani 38 1N 12 30 E
84 Traralgon 38 6s 146 31 E
45 Traryd 56 35N 13 45 E
29 Tras os Montes Alto Douro, Reg. 41 30N 7 5w
37 Trasimeno, L. 43 30N 12 5 E
26 Traun 48 14N 14 15 E
26 Traunsee, L. 47 48N 13 45 E
25 Traunstein 47 52N 12 40 E
24 Travemünde 53 58N 10 52 E
98 Traverse City 44 45N 85 39w
40 Travnik 44 17N 17 39 E
83 Trayning 31 8s 117 42 E
30 Trazo 43 0N 8 30w
37 Trbovlje 46 12N 15 5 E
26 Třebíč 49 13N 15 53 E
40 Trebinje 42 44N 18 22 E
40 Trebišnica, R. 42 47N 18 8 E
27 Trebišov 48 38N 21 41 E
37 Trebnje 45 53N 15 0 E
36 Trecate 45 29N 8 42 E
13 Tredegar 51 47N 3 16w
37 Trieste 45 40N 13 46 E
13 Tregaron 52 14N 3 56w
18 Trégastel Plage 48 49N 3 30w
18 Tréguier 48 47N 3 16w
18 Trégune 47 51N 3 52w
37 Tréia 43 20N 13 20 E
109 Trenta y Tres 33 10s 54 50w
112 Trelew 43 10s 65 20w
20 Trelissac 45 13N 0 45 E
45 Trelleborg 55 20N 13 5 E
102 Tremonton 41 45N 112 10w
27 Trenčín 48 52N 18 4 E
65 Trenggalek 8 5s 111 44 E
108 Trenque Lauquen 36 0s 62 45w
12 Trent, R. 53 40N 0 40w
36 Trentino-Alto Adige □ 46 5N 11 0 E
36 Trento 46 5N 11 8 E
90 Trenton, Canada 44 10N 77 40w
97 Trenton, Mo. 40 5N 93 37w
97 Trenton, N.J. 40 15N 74 41w
91 Trepassey 46 43N 53 25w
39 Trepuzzi 40 26N 18 4 E
108 Tres Arroyos 38 20s 60 20w
109 Três Corações 21 30s 45 30s
109 Três Lagoas 20 50s 51 50w
112 Tres Montes, C. 47 0s 75 35w
109 Três Pontas 21 23s 45 29w
112 Tres Puntas, C. 47 0s 66 0w
109 Três Rios 22 20s 43 30w
30 Trespaderne 42 47N 3 24w
25 Treuenbrietzen 52 6N 12 51 E
36 Trevíglio 45 31N 9 35 E
30 Trevinca, Peña 42 15N 6 46w
37 Treviso 45 40N 12 15 E
80 Triabunna 42 28s 148 0 E
43 Triánda 36 25N 28 10 E
39 Tricase 39 56N 18 20 E
62 Trichinopoly = Tiruchchirappalli 10 45N 78 45 E
62 Trichur 10 20N 76 18 E
25 Trier 49 45N 6 37 E
37 Trieste 45 39N 13 45 E
37 Trieste, G. di 45 37N 13 40 E
39 Triggiano 41 4N 16 58 E
37 Triglav, Mt. 46 30N 13 45 E
43 Trikhonis, L. 38 34N 21 30 E
42 Tríkkala 39 34N 21 47 E
42 Tríkkala □ 39 40N 21 30 E
65 Trikora, Puncak, Mt. 4 11s 138 0 E
15 Trim 53 34N 6 48w
62 Trincomalee 8 38N 81 15 E
110 Trinidad, Bolivia 14 54s 64 50w
105 Trinidad, Cuba 21 40N 80 0w
101 Trinidad, U.S.A. 37 15N 104 30w
108 Trinidad, Uruguay 33 30s 56 50w
112 Trinidad I., Arg. 39 10s 62 0w
105 Trinidad I., Trinidad & Tobago 10 30N 61 20w
105 Trinidad & Tobago ■ 10 30N 61 20w
7 Trinidade, I. 20 20s 29 50w
101 Trinity, R. 29 47N 94 42w
88 Trinity Is. 56 33N 154 25w
73 Tripoli = Tarābulus 32 49N 13 7 E
43 Trípolis 37 31N 22 25 E
59 Tripura □ 24 0N 92 0 E
7 Tristan de Cunha, I. 37 6s 12 20w
62 Trivandrum 8 31N 77 0 E
27 Trnava 48 23N 17 35 E
37 Trogir 43 32N 16 15 E
37 Troglav, Mt. 43 56N 16 36 E
39 Tróia 41 22N 15 19 E
91 Trois Pistoles 48 5N 69 10w
90 Trois Rivières 46 25N 72 40w
50 Troitsk 54 10N 61 35 E
48 Troitsko Pechorsk 62 40N 56 10 E
45 Trollhättan 58 17N 12 20 E
46 Troms □ 69 19N 19 0 E
46 Tromsø 69 40N 19 0 E
112 Tronador, Mt. 41 53s 71 0w
44 Trondheim 63 25N 10 25 E
46 Trondheims, Fd. 63 40N 10 45 E
56 Tróodos, Mt. 34 58N 32 55 E
14 Troon 55 33N 4 40w
14 Trossachs, Reg. 56 14N 4 24w
14 Trotternish, Reg. 57 32N 6 15w
18 Trouville 49 21N 0 54 E
13 Trowbridge 51 18N 2 12w
99 Troy, Ala. 31 50N 85 58w
97 Troy, N.Y. 42 45N 73 39w
98 Troy, Ohio 40 0N 84 10w
41 Troyan 42 57N 24 43 E
19 Troyes 48 19N 4 3 E
40 Trstenik 43 36N 21 0 E
102 Truckee 39 29N 120 12w
105 Trujillo, Honduras 16 0N 86 0w
110 Trujillo, Peru 8 0s 79 0w
31 Trujillo, Sp. 39 28N 5 55w
110 Trujillo, Ven. 9 22N 70 26w
76 Truk, I. 7 25N 151 46 E
97 Trumansburg 42 33N 76 40w
63 Trung-Phan, Reg. 16 0N 108 0 E
91 Truro, Canada 45 21N 63 14w
13 Truro, U.K. 50 17N 5 2w
83 Truslove 33 20s 121 45 E
103 Truth or Consequences 33 9N 107 16w
26 Trutnov 50 37N 15 54 E
41 Tryavna 42 54N 25 25 E
27 Trzebinia-Siersza 50 11N 19 30 E
28 Trzebnica 51 20N 17 1 E
67 Tsaidam, Reg. 37 0N 95 0 E
68 Tsanghsien 38 24N 116 57 E
67 Tsangpo, R. 29 40N 89 0 E
69 Tsaochwang 35 11N 115 28 E
67 Tsaring Nor, L. 35 0N 97 0 E
75 Tsau 20 12s 22 22 E
50 Tselinograd 51 10N 71 30 E
68 Tsetserleg 47 46N 101 32 E
75 Tshabong 26 2s 22 29 E
75 Tshane 24 5s 21 54 E
75 Tshwane 22 24s 22 1N
69 Tsiaotso 35 11N 113 37 E
49 Tsimlyanskoye, Vdkhr. 47 45N 42 0 E
69 Tsin Ling Shan, Mts. 34 0N 107 30 E
68 Tsinan 34 50N 105 40 E
68 Tsincheng 35 30N 113 0 E
68 Tsinghai 38 56N 116 52 E
67 Tsinghai □ 35 10N 96 0 E
69 Tsingkiang, Kiangsi 27 50N 114 38 E
69 Tsingkiang, Kiangsu 33 30N 119 2 E
68 Tsingning 35 25N 105 50 E
69 Tsingshih 29 43N 112 13 E
68 Tsingtao 36 0N 120 25 E
69 Tsining, Inner Mongolia 40 59N 112 59 E
68 Tsining, Shantung 35 30N 116 35 E
69 Tsinyang 35 2N 112 59 E
68 Tsitsihar 47 20N 124 0 E
49 Tskhinvali 42 14N 44 1 E
48 Tsna, R. 54 32N 42 5 E
66 Tsu 34 45N 136 25 E
66 Tsuchiura 36 12N 140 15 E
66 Tsugaru-Kaikyō, Str. 41 30N 140 30 E
68 Tsuiluan 47 58N 28 27 E
75 Tsumeb 19 9s 17 44 E
69 Tsungfa 23 35N 113 35 E
69 Tsungtso 22 20N 107 25 E
69 Tsunyi 27 40N 107 0 E
66 Tsuruga 35 35N 136 0 E
69 Tsushima-Kaikyō, Str. 34 20N 130 0 E
66 Tsuyama 35 0N 134 0 E
30 Tua, R. 41 13N 7 26w
65 Tual 5 30s 132 50 E
15 Tuam 53 30N 8 50w
77 Tuamotu Arch. 17 0s 144 0w
49 Tuapse 44 5N 39 10 E
85 Tuatapere 48 7s 167 43 E
103 Tubac 31 45N 111 2w
65 Tuban 6 57s 112 4 E

109 Tubarão 28 30s 49 0w
54 Tubas 32 20N 35 22 E
56 Tubayq, Jabal at 29 40N 37 30 E
25 Tübingen 48 31N 9 4 E
73 Tubruq 32 7N 23 55 E
77 Tubuai Is. 23 20s 151 0w
110 Tucacas 10 48N 68 19w
28 Tuchola 53 33N 17 52 E
83 Tuckanarra 27 8s 118 1 E
105 Tucker's Town 32 19N 64 43w
103 Tucson 32 14N 110 59w
108 Tucumán □ 26 48s 66 2w
101 Tucumcari 35 12N 103 45w
110 Tucupita 9 4N 62 0w
111 Tucurui 3 45s 49 48w
32 Tudela 42 4N 1 39w
30 Tudela de Duero 41 37N 4 39w
65 Tuguegarao 17 35N 121 42 E
51 Tugur 53 50N 136 45 E
69 Tuhshan 25 40N 107 30 E
88 Tuktoyaktuk 69 15N 133 0w
48 Tula 54 13N 37 32 E
67 Tulan 37 24N 98 1 E
103 Tulare 36 15N 119 26w
103 Tularosa 33 4N 106 1w
75 Tulbagh 33 16s 19 6 E
110 Tulcán 0 48N 77 43w
41 Tulcea 45 13N 28 46 E
75 Tuléar 23 21s 43 40 E
75 Tuli 1 24s 122 26 E
54 Tülkarm 32 19N 35 10 E
99 Tullahoma 35 23N 86 12w
15 Tullamore 53 17N 7 30w
20 Tulle 45 16N 1 47 E
26 Tulln 48 20N 16 4 E
15 Tullow 52 48N 6 45w
80 Tully 17 30s 141 0 E
73 Tulymaythah 32 40N 20 55 E
41 Tulovo 42 33N 25 32 E
101 Tulsa 36 10N 96 0w
110 Tulua 4 6N 76 11w
51 Tulun 54 40N 100 10 E
65 Tulungagung 8 5s 111 54 E
105 Tuma, R. 13 6N 84 35w
110 Tumaco 1 50N 78 45w
110 Tumatumari 5 20N 58 55w
44 Tumba 59 12N 17 48 E
74 Tumba, L. 0 50s 18 0 E
110 Tumbes 3 30s 80 20w
81 Tumby Bay 34 21s 136 8 E
68 Tumen 42 46N 129 59 E
110 Tumeremo 7 18N 61 30w
62 Tumkur 13 18N 77 12w
14 Tummel, L. 56 43N 3 55w
58 Tump 26 7N 62 16 E
63 Tumpat 6 11N 102 10 E
111 Tumucumaque South 2 0N 55 0w
84 Tumut 35 16s 148 13 E
13 Tunbridge Wells 51 7N 0 16 E
74 Tunduru 11 0s 37 25 E
62 Tungabhadra Dam 15 21N 76 23 E
69 Tungcheng 31 0N 117 3 E
68 Tungchow 39 58N 116 50 E
69 Tungchuan 35 4N 109 2 E
69 Tungfanghsien 18 50N 108 33 E
68 Tunghwa 41 46N 126 0 E
68 Tungkiang 47 40N 132 30 E
69 Tungkwanshan 31 0N 117 45 E
68 Tungliao 43 42N 122 11 E
69 Tunglu 29 50N 119 35 E
68 Tungping 35 50N 116 20 E
69 Tungshan 29 36N 144 28 E
69 Tungshan, I. 23 40N 117 31 E
92 Tungsten 61 52N 128 1w
69 Tungtai 32 55N 120 15 E
69 Tungting Hu, L. 28 30N 112 30 E
69 Tungtze 27 59N 106 56 E
68 Tunhwa 43 27N 128 16 E
67 Tunhwang 40 5N 94 46 E
62 Tuni 17 22N 82 43 E
72 Tunis 36 50N 10 11 E
72 Tunisia ■ 33 30N 9 0 E
110 Tunja 5 40N 73 25 E
108 Tunuyán 33 55s 69 0w
51 Tuoy-khaya 62 30N 111 0w
109 Tupã 21 57s 50 28w
99 Tupelo 34 15N 88 42w
51 Tupik 54 26N 119 57 E
108 Tupiza 21 30s 65 40w
97 Tupper Lake 44 18N 74 30w
108 Tupungato, Mt. 33 15s 69 50w
110 Túquerres 1 5N 77 37w
54 Tur 31 47N 35 14 E
61 Tura 25 30N 90 16 E
56 Turayf 31 45N 38 30 E
110 Turbaco 10 20N 75 25w
40 Turbe 44 15N 17 35 E
110 Turbo 8 6N 76 43 E
41 Turda 46 35N 23 48 E
28 Turek 52 3N 18 30 E
67 Turfan 43 6N 89 24 E
67 Turfan Depression 43 0N 88 0 E
41 Tŭrgovishte 43 17N 26 38 E
11 United Kingdom ■ 55 0N 3 0w
56 Turgutlu 38 30N 27 48 E
56 Turhal 40 24N 36 19 E
32 Turia, R. 39 27N 0 19w
111 Turiaçu 1 40s 45 28w
36 Turin=Torino 45 3N 7 40 E
74 Turkana, L. 4 10N 36 10 E
50 Turkestan 43 10N 68 10 E
27 Túrkeve 47 6N 20 44 E
56 Turkey ■ 39 0N 36 0 E
82 Turkey Creek P.O. 17 2s 128 12 E
50 Turkmen S.S.R. 39 0N 59 0 E
105 Turks Is. 21 20N 71 20w
47 Turku 60 27N 22 14 E
103 Turlock 37 30N 122 55w
104 Turneffe Is. 17 20N 87 50w
16 Turnhout 51 19N 4 57w
26 Türnitz 47 55N 15 29 E
26 Turnov 50 34N 15 10 E
41 Tŭrnovo 43 5N 25 41 E
41 Turnu Măgurele 43 46N 24 56 E
40 Turnu-Severin 44 39N 22 41 E
14 Turriff 57 32N 2 58w
93 Turtle 48 52N 92 40w
93 Turtleford 53 30N 108 50w
56 Turūbah 28 20N 43 15 E
47 Turun ja Pori □ 61 0N 22 30 E
27 Turzovka 49 25N 18 41 E
99 Tuscaloosa 33 13N 87 31w
96 Tuscarora Mt. 40 10N 77 45w
99 Tuskegee 32 26N 85 42w
96 Tussey Mt. 40 25N 78 7w
62 Tuticorin 8 50N 78 12 E
111 Tutoja 2 45s 42 20w
41 Tutrakan 44 2N 26 40 E
25 Tuttlingen 47 59N 8 50 E
65 Tutuala 8 25s 127 15 E
77 Tutuila, I. 14 19s 170 50w
51 Turukhansk 65 55N 88 5 E
51 Tava, A.S.S.R. 52 0N 95 0 E
76 Tuvalu ■ 8 0s 176 0 E
56 Tuwaiq, Jabal 23 0N 46 0 E
104 Tuxpan 20 50N 97 30w
104 Tuxtla Gutiérrez 16 50N 93 10w
30 Tuy 42 3N 8 39w
63 Tuy Hoa 13 5N 109 17 E
63 Tuyen Hoa 17 55N 106 3 E
69 Tuyun 26 5N 107 20 E
56 Tuz Gölü 38 45N 33 30 E
56 Tuz Khurmātu 34 50N 44 45 E
40 Tuzla 44 34N 18 41 E
45 Tvedestrand 58 38N 8 58 E
41 Tvŭrditsa 42 42N 25 53 E
12 Tweed, R. 55 46N 2 0w
92 Tweedsmuir Prov. Park 52 55N 126 5w
102 Twin Falls 42 30N 114 30w
98 Two Rivers 44 10N 87 31w
27 Tychy 50 9N 18 59 E
101 Tyler 32 20N 95 15w
26 Týn nad Vltavou 49 13N 14 26 E
51 Tyndinskiy 55 10N 124 43 E
12 Tyne, R. 55 1N 1 26w
12 Tyne & Wear □ 54 55N 1 35w
12 Tynemouth 55 1N 1 27w
44 Tynset 62 27N 10 47 E
56 Tyre =Sur 33 19N 35 16 E
96 Tyrone 40 39N 78 10w
84 Tyrendarra 38 12s 141 50 E
44 Tyrifjorden 60 2N 10 3 E
38 Tyrrhenian Sea 40 0N 12 30 E
50 Tyumen 57 0N 65 18 E
13 Tywi, R. 51 46N 4 22w
75 Tzaneen 23 47s 30 9 E
69 Tzeki 27 40N 117 5 E
69 Tzekung 29 25N 104 30 E
69 Tzekwei 31 0N 110 46 E
68 Tzepo 36 28N 117 58 E
68 Tzeyang 32 47N 108 58 E
42 Tzoumérka, Mt. 39 30N 21 26 E

U

55 Uarsciek 2 28N 45 55 E
110 Uaupés 0 8s 67 5w
109 Ubá 21 0s 43 0w
111 Ubaitaba 14 18s 39 20w
21 Ubaye, R. 44 28N 6 18 E
66 Ube 34 6N 131 20 E
31 Ubeda 38 3N 3 23w
111 Uberaba 19 50s 48 0w
111 Uberlândia 19 0s 48 20w
63 Ubon Ratchathani 15 15N 104 50 E
31 Ubrique 36 41N 5 27w
74 Ubundu 0 22s 25 30 E
110 Ucayali, R. 4 30s 73 30w
93 Uchi Lake 51 10N 92 40w
66 Uchiura-Wan, G. 42 25N 140 40 E
92 Ucluelet 48 57N 125 32w
60 Udaipur 24 36N 73 44 E
32 Utiel 39 37N 1 11w
62 Udamalpet 10 35N 77 15 E
37 Udbina 44 31N 15 47 E
45 Uddevalla 58 21N 11 55 E
46 Uddjaur, L. 65 55N 17 50 E
62 Udgir 18 25N 77 5 E
60 Udhampur 33 0N 75 5 E
72 Udi 6 23N 7 21 E
37 Údine 46 5N 13 10 E
62 Udipi 13 25N 74 42 E
48 Udmurt A.S.S.R. □ 57 30N 52 30 E
63 Udon Thani 17 29N 102 46 E
41 Udvoy, Mts. 42 50N 26 50 E
24 Ueckermünde 53 45N 14 1 E
66 Ueda 36 30N 138 10 E
51 Uelen 66 10N 170 0w
24 Uelzen 53 0N 10 33 E
74 Uere, R. 3 42N 25 24 E
48 Ufa 54 45N 55 55 E
74 Uganda ■ 2 0N 32 0 E
88 Ugashik Lakes 57 0N 157 0w
21 Ugine 45 45N 6 25 E
51 Uglegorsk 49 10N 142 5 E
41 Ugŭrchin 43 6N 24 26 E
27 Uherské Hradiště 49 4N 17 30 E
27 Uhersky Brod 49 1N 17 40 E
26 Uhlava, R. 49 45N 13 20 E
96 Uhrichsville 40 23N 81 22w
75 Uitenhage 33 40s 25 28 E
27 Újfehértó 47 49N 21 41 E
60 Ujhani 28 0N 79 6 E
60 Ujjain 23 9N 75 43 E
27 Ujpest 47 33N 19 6 E
65 Ujung Pandang 5 10s 119 0 E
51 Uka 57 50N 162 0 E
74 Ukerewe I. 2 0s 33 0 E
59 Ukhrul 25 10N 94 25 E
48 Ukhta 63 55N 54 0 E
102 Ukiah 39 10N 123 9w
49 Ukrainian S.S.R. □ 48 0N 35 0 E
68 Ulaanbaatar 48 0N 107 0 E
68 Ulan Bator =Ulaanbaatar 48 0N 107 0 E
51 Ulan Ude 52 0N 107 30 E
68 Ulanhot 46 5N 122 1 E
40 Ulcinj 41 58N 19 10 E
62 Ulhasnagar 19 15N 73 10 E
40 Uljma 45 2N 21 10 E
30 Ulla, R. 42 39N 8 44w
84 Ulladulla 35 21s 150 29 E
14 Ullapool 57 54N 5 10w
32 Ulldecona 40 36N 0 20 E
12 Ullswater, L. 54 35N 2 52w
25 Ulm 48 23N 10 0 E
41 Ulmeni 45 4N 46 40 E
45 Ulricehamn 57 46N 13 26 E
44 Ulsberg 62 45N 10 3 E
15 Ulster □ 54 45N 6 30w
12 Ulverston 54 13N 3 7w
80 Ulverstone 41 11s 146 11 E
48 Ulyanovsk 54 25N 48 25 E
49 Uman 48 40N 30 12 E
4 Umanak 70 40N 52 0w
62 Umarkhed 19 37N 77 38 E
37 Umbertide 43 18N 12 20 E
37 Umbria □ 42 53N 12 30 E
46 Umeå 63 45N 20 20 E
57 Umm al Qaiwain 25 30N 55 35 E
54 Umm el Fahm 32 31N 35 9 E
73 Umm Keddada 13 36N 26 42 E
56 Umm Lajj 25 0N 37 23 E
57 Umm Said 25 0N 51 40 E
88 Umnak I. 53 0N 168 0w
75 Umniati, R. 17 30s 29 23 E
60 Umrer 20 51N 79 18 E
60 Umreth 22 41N 73 4 E
75 Umtali 18 58s 32 38 E
75 Umtata 31 36s 28 49 E
75 Umvuma 19 16s 30 30 E
75 Umzimvubu 31 38s 29 33 E
60 Una 20 46N 71 8 E
37 Unac, R. 44 30N 16 9 E
97 Unadilla 42 20N 75 17w
88 Unalakleet 63 53N 160 50w
88 Unalaska I. 54 0N 164 30w
103 Uncompahgre Pk. 38 5N 107 32w
84 Underbool 35 10s 141 51 E
84 Ungarie 33 38s 146 56 E
89 Ungava B. 59 30N 67 0w
89 Ungava Pen. 60 0N 75 0w
111 União 4 50s 37 50w
109 União da Vitoria 26 5s 51 0w
88 Unimak I. 54 30N 164 30w
99 Union 34 49N 81 39w
97 Union City, N.J. 40 47N 74 5w
101 Union City, Tenn. 36 35N 89 0w
102 Union Gap 46 38N 120 29w
53 Union of Soviet Socialist Republics ■ 60 0N 60 0 E
98 Uniontown 39 54N 79 45w
57 United Arab Emirates ■ 24 0N 54 30 E
94 United States of America ■ 37 0N 96 0w
93 Unity 52 30N 109 5w
60 Unjha 23 46N 72 24 E
61 Unnao 26 35N 80 30 E
14 Unst, I. 60 50N 0 55w
25 Unterwalden □ 46 50N 8 15 E
56 Ünye 41 5N 37 15 E
66 Uozu 36 48N 137 24 E
110 Upata 8 1N 62 24w
4 Upernavik 72 45N 56 0w
75 Upington 28 25s 21 15 E
60 Upleta 21 46N 70 16 E
85 Upolu, I. 13 58s 172 0w
85 Upper Hutt 41 8s 175 5 E
91 Upper Musquodoboit 45 10N 62 58w
72 Upper Volta= Burkina Faso ■ 12 0N 0 30w
44 Uppsala 59 53N 17 42 E
44 Uppsala □ 60 0N 17 30 E
56 Ur 30 55N 46 25 E
110 Uracará 2 20s 57 50w
84 Ural, Mt. 33 21s 146 12 E
48 Ural Mts. = Uralskie Gory 60 0N 59 0 E
50 Ural, R. 47 0N 51 48 E
81 Uralla 30 37s 151 29 E
50 Uralsk 51 20N 51 20 E
48 Uralskie Gory 60 0N 59 0 E
80 Urandangi 21 32s 138 14 E
93 Uranium City 59 28N 108 40w
62 Uravakonda 14 57N 77 12 E
66 Urawa 35 50N 139 40 E
50 Uray 60 5N 65 15 E
100 Urbana, Ill. 40 7N 88 12w
98 Urbana, Ohio 40 9N 83 44w
37 Urbino 43 43N 12 38 E
30 Urbión, Picos de 42 1N 2 52w
20 Urdos 42 51N 0 35w
12 Ure, R. 54 1N 1 12w
50 Urengoy 66 0N 78 0 E
56 Urfa 37 12N 38 50 E
26 Urfahr 48 19N 14 17 E
50 Urgench 41 40N 60 30 E
25 Uri □ 46 43N 8 35 E
110 Uribia 11 43N 72 16w
54 Urim 31 18N 34 32 E
41 Urlati 44 59N 26 15 E
56 Urmia, L. = Daryâcheh-ye Reza'iyeh 37 30N 45 30 E
40 Uroševac 42 23N 21 10 E
28 Ursus 52 12N 20 53
111 Uruaca 14 35s 49 16w
104 Uruapán 19 30N 102 0w
111 Uruçui 7 20s 44 28w
108 Uruguay ■ 32 30s 55 30w
108 Uruguay, R. 34 12s 58 18w
108 Uruguaiana 29 50s 57 0w
67 Urungu, R. 46 30N 88 50 E
57 Uruzgan □ 33 30N 66 0 E
41 Urziceni 44 46N 26 42 E
48 Usa, R. 65 57N 56 55 E
56 Uşak 38 43N 29 28 E
24 Usedom, I. 53 50N 13 55 E
56 Usfan 21 58N 39 27 E
50 Ush-Tobe 45 16N 78 0 E
112 Ushuaia 54 50s 68 23w
51 Ushuman 52 47N 126 32 E
13 Usk, R. 51 36N 2 58w
56 Üsküdar 41 0N 29 5 E
48 Usman 52 5N 39 48 E
51 Usolye Sibirskoye 52 40N 103 40 E
50 Uspenskiy 48 50N 72 55 E
20 Ussel 45 32N 2 18 E
51 Ussuriysk 43 40N 131 50 E
51 Ust-Ilga 55 5N 104 55 E
51 Ust-Ilimsk 58 3N 102 39 E
50 Ust Ishim 57 45N 71 10 E
51 Ust-Kamchatsk 56 10N 162 0 E
50 Ust Kamenogorsk 50 0N 82 20 E
51 Ust-Kut 56 50N 105 10 E
51 Ust Kuyga 70 1N 135 36 E
51 Ust Maya 60 30N 134 20 E
51 Ust Olenck 73 0N 120 10 E
50 Ust Post 70 0N 84 10 E
48 Ust Tsilma 65 25N 52 0 E
51 Ust-Tungir 55 25N 120 15 E
48 Ust Usa 66 0N 56 30 E
44 Ustaoset 60 30N 8 2 E
51 Ustchaun 68 47N 170 30 E
27 Ustí na Orlici 49 58N 16 38 E
26 Ustí nad Labem 50 41N 14 3 E
38 Ustica, I. 38 42N 13 10 E
51 Ustye 55 30N 97 30 E
104 Usulután 13 25N 88 28w
102 Utah □ 39 30N 111 30w
65 Utara □, Sulawesi 1 0N 120 3 E
64 Utara □, Sumatera 2 0N 99 0 E
24 Ütersen 53 40N 9 40 E
63 Uthai Thani 15 22N 100 3 E
56 Uthmaniya 25 5N 49 6 E
97 Utica 43 5N 75 18w

16 Utrecht, Neth. 52 3N 5 8E
75 Utrecht, S. Africa 27 38S 30 20E
16 Utrecht, Netherlands □ 52 6N 5 7E
31 Utrera 37 12N 5 48W
66 Utsunomiya 36 30N 139 50E
61 Uttar Pradesh □ 27 0N 80 0E
63 Uttaradit 17 36N 100 5E
12 Uttoxeter 52 53N 1 50W
47 Uudenmaa □ 60 25N 23 0E
68 Uuldza 49 8N 112 10E
47 Uusikaupunki 60 47N 21 28E
101 Uvalde 29 15N 99 48W
50 Uvat 59 5N 68 50E
74 Uvinza 5 5S 30 24E
74 Uvira 3 22S 29 3E
67 Uvs Nuur, L. 50 20N 92 30E
66 Uwajima 33 10N 132 35E
104 Uxmal 20 22N 89 46W
108 Uyuni 20 35S 66 55W
108 Uyuni, Salar de 20 10S 68 0W
50 Uzbek S.S.R. 40 5N 65 0E
20 Uzerche 45 25N 1 35E
21 Uzès 44 1N 4 26E

V

75 Vaal, R. 29 4S 23 38E
46 Vaasa 63 10N 21 35E
46 Vaasa □ 63 6N 23 0E
27 Vác 47 49N 19 10E
109 Vacaria 28 31S 50 52W
21 Vaccares, Étang de 43 32N 4 34E
60 Vadnagar 23 47N 72 40E
46 Vadsø 70 3N 29 50E
26 Vaduz 47 8N 9 31E
45 Vaggeryd 57 30N 14 10E
30 Vagos 40 33N 8 42W
27 Váh, R. 47 55N 18 0E
5 Vahsel B. 75 0S 35 0W
50 Vaigach 70 10N 59 0E
62 Vaigai, R. 9 20N 79 0E
18 Vaiges 48 2N 0 30W
60 Vaijapur 19 58N 74 45E
62 Vaikam 9 45N 76 25E
41 Vakarel 42 35N 23 40E
90 Val d'Or 48 7N 77 47W
93 Val Marie 49 15N 107 45W
30 Valadares 41 5N 8 38W
41 Valahia □ 44 35N 25 0E
25 Valais □ 46 12N 7 45E
27 Valasské Meziříčí 49 29N 17 59E
44 Valbo 60 40N 17 4E
112 Valchete 40 40S 66 20W
19 Val-d'Oise □ 49 5N 2 0E
37 Valdagno 45 38N 11 18E
48 Valdayskaya Vozvyshennost 57 0N 33 40E
31 Valdeazogues, R. 38 45N 4 55W
45 Valdemarsvik 58 14N 16 40E
31 Valdepeņas, Ciudad Real 38 43N 3 25W
31 Valdepeņas, Jaen 31 33N 3 47W
30 Valderaduey, R. 41 31N 5 42W
32 Valderrobres 40 53N 0 9E
112 Valdés, Pen 42 30S 63 45W
88 Valdez 61 14N 146 10W
112 Valdivia 39 50S 73 14W
37 Valdobbiádene 45 53N 12 0E
99 Valdosta 30 50N 83 48W
44 Valdres 61 0N 91 3E
111 Valença, Brazil 13 20S 39 5W
30 Valença, Port. 42 1N 8 34W
111 Valença da Piaui 6 20S 41 45W
21 Valence 44 57N 4 54E
20 Valence-d'Agen 44 8N 0 54E
33 Valencia, Sp. 39 27N 0 23W
110 Valencia, Ven. 10 11N 68 0W
33 Valencia, G. de 39 30N 0 20E
33 Valencia, Reg. 39 25N 0 45W
33 Valencia □ 39 20N 0 40W
31 Valencia de Alcantara 39 25N 7 14W
30 Valencia de Don Juan 42 17N 5 31W
31 Valencia del Ventoso 38 15N 6 29W
19 Valenciennes 50 20N 3 34E
41 Vălenii-de-Munte 45 12N 26 3E
15 Valentia, I. 51 54N 10 22W
100 Valentine 42 50N 100 35W
36 Valenza 45 2N 8 39E
110 Valera 9 19N 70 37W
39 Valguarnera Caropepe 37 30N 14 22E
21 Valinco, G. de 41 40N 8 52E
40 Valjevo 44 18N 19 53E
16 Valkenswaard 51 21N 5 29E
32 Vall de Uxó 40 49N 0 15W
104 Valladolid, Mexico 20 30N 88 20W
30 Valladolid, Sp. 41 38N 4 43W
30 Valladolid □ 41 38N 4 43W
36 Valle d'Aosta □ 45 45N 7 22E
110 Valle de la Pascua 9 13N 66 0W
104 Valle de Santiago 20 25N 101 15W
30 Vallecas 40 23N 3 41W
102 Vallejo 38 12N 122 15W
108 Vallenar 28 30S 70 50W
100 Valley City 46 57N 98 0W
90 Valleyfield 45 15N 74 8W
92 Valleyview 55 5N 117 25W
32 Valls 41 18N 1 15E
30 Valmaseda 43 11N 3 12W
19 Valmy 49 5N 4 45E
18 Valognes 49 30N 1 28W
108 Valparaíso 33 2S 71 40W
108 Valparaíso □ 33 2S 71 40W
75 Valsbaai 34 15S 18 40E
36 Valtellino 46 9N 10 2E
31 Valverde del Cam. 37 35N 6 47W
30 Valverde del Fresno 40 15N 6 51W
43 Vamos 35 24N 24 13E
62 Vamsadhara, R. 18 21N 84 8E
101 Van Buren, Ark. 35 28N 94 18W
91 Van Buren, Me. 47 10N 68 1W
82 Van Diemen, C. 16 30S 139 46E
82 Van Diemen, G. 12 0S 132 0E
56 Van Gölü 38 30N 43 0E
98 Van Wert 40 52N 84 31W
92 Vancouver, Canada 49 20N 123 10W
102 Vancouver, U.S.A. 45 44N 122 41W
92 Vancouver I. 49 50N 126 30W
100 Vandalia 38 57N 89 4W
45 Vandborg 56 32N 8 10E
92 Vanderhoof 54 0N 124 0W
80 Vandyke 24 8S 142 45E
45 Vänern, L. 58 47N 13 50E
45 Vänersborg 58 26N 12 27E
63 Vang Vieng 18 58N 102 32E
74 Vanga 4 35S 39 12E
62 Vaniyambadi 12 46N 78 44E
51 Vankarem 67 51N 175 50W
90 Vankleek Hill 45 32N 74 40W
46 Vännäs 63 58N 19 48E
18 Vannes 47 40N 2 47W
44 Vansbro 60 32N 14 15E
85 Vanua Levu, I. 15 45S 179 10E
76 Vanuatu Rep 15 0S 168 0E
21 Var, R. 43 39N 7 12E
21 Var □ 43 27N 6 18E
62 Varada, R. 14 56N 75 41E
18 Varades 47 25N 1 1W
61 Varanasi 25 22N 83 8E
37 Varaždin 46 20N 16 20E
36 Varazze 44 21N 8 36E
45 Varberg 57 17N 12 20E
40 Vardar, R. 40 35N 22 50E
45 Varde 55 38N 8 29E
24 Varel 53 23N 8 9E
20 Varennes-sur-Allier 49 12N 5 0E
40 Vareš 44 12N 18 23E
36 Varese 45 49N 8 50E
109 Varginha 21 33S 45 25W
44 Värmdö, I. 59 18N 18 45E
44 Värmlands □ 59 45N 13 0E
41 Varna 43 13N 27 56E
45 Värnamo 57 10N 14 3E
26 Varnsdorf 49 56N 14 38E
40 Varvarin 43 43N 21 20E
19 Varzy 47 22N 3 20E
27 Vas □ 47 10N 16 55E
31 Vascão, R. 37 31N 7 31W
32 Vascongadas, Reg. 42 50N 2 45W
43 Vasilikón 38 25N 23 40E
44 Västerås 59 37N 16 38E
46 Västerbotten □ 64 58N 18 0E
44 Västerdalälven, R. 60 33N 15 8E
44 Västernorrlands □ 63 30N 17 40E
45 Västervik 57 43N 16 43E
44 Västmanlands □ 89 5N 16 20E
37 Vasto 42 8N 14 40E
20 Vatan 47 4N 1 50E
37 Vatican City 41 54N 12 27E
39 Vaticano, C. 38 38N 15 50E
46 Vatnajökull 64 30N 16 30W
45 Vättern, L. 58 25N 14 30E
21 Vaucluse □ 44 3N 5 10E
19 Vaucouleurs 48 37N 5 40E
25 Vaud □ 46 35N 6 30E
103 Vaughan 34 37N 105 12W
21 Vauvert 43 42N 4 17E
92 Vauxhall 50 5N 112 9W
45 Växjö 56 52N 14 50E
50 Vaygach, Os. 70 0N 60 0E
24 Vechta 52 47N 8 18E
16 Vechte, R. 52 35N 6 5E
27 Vecsés 47 26N 19 19E
62 Vedaraniam 10 25N 79 50E
16 Veendam 53 5N 6 25E
16 Veenendaal 52 2N 5 34E
46 Vefsna, R. 65 50N 13 12E
30 Vegadeo 43 27N 7 4W
46 Vegafjord 65 37N 12 0E
92 Vegreville 53 30N 112 5W
31 Vejer de la Frontera 36 15N 5 59W
45 Vejle □ 55 2N 11 22E
37 Vela Luka 42 59N 16 44E
20 Velay, Mts. du 45 0N 3 40E
37 Velebit Planina, Mts. 44 50N 15 20E
37 Velebitski Kanal 44 45N 14 55E
42 Velestínon 39 23N 22 45E
110 Vélez 6 2N 73 43W
33 Velez Blanco 37 41N 2 5W
31 Vélez Málaga 36 48N 4 5W
33 Vélez Rubio 37 41N 2 5W
37 Velika Kapela, Mts. 45 10N 15 5E
40 Velika Morava, R. 44 43N 21 3E
40 Velika Plana 44 20N 21 1E
40 Veliki Backu, Kanal 45 45N 19 15E
48 Velikiy Ustyug 60 47N 46 20E
48 Velikiye Luki 56 25N 30 32E
62 Velikonda Ra. 14 45N 79 10E
41 Velingrad 42 4N 23 58E
37 Velino, Mt. 42 10N 13 20E
26 Velke Meziříci 49 21N 16 1E
38 Velletri 41 43N 12 43E
45 Vellinge 55 29N 13 0E
62 Vellore 12 57N 79 10E
16 Velsen 52 27N 4 40E
48 Velsk 61 10N 42 5E
24 Velten 52 40N 13 11E
62 Vembanad L. 9 36N 76 15E
21 Venaco 42 14N 9 10E
108 Venado Tuerto 33 50S 62 0W
21 Vence 43 43N 7 6E
31 Vendas Novas 38 39N 8 27W
20 Vendée □ 46 40N 1 20W
19 Vendeuvre 48 14N 4 27E
18 Vendôme 47 47N 1 3E
32 Vendrell 41 10N 1 30E
45 Vendsyssel, Reg. 57 22N 10 15E
37 Véneta, L. 45 19N 12 13E
37 Veneto □ 45 30N 12 0E
37 Venézia 45 27N 12 20E
110 Venezuela ■ 8 0N 65 0W
110 Venezuela, G. de 11 30N 71 0W
62 Vengurla 15 53N 73 45E
37 Venice=Venézia 45 27N 12 20E
21 Vénissieux 45 43N 4 53E
62 Venkatagiri 14 0N 79 35E
62 Venkatapuram 18 20N 80 30E
16 Venlo 51 22N 6 11E
16 Venraij 51 31N 6 0E
30 Venta de S. Rafael 40 42N 4 12W
36 Ventimiglia 43 50N 7 39E
13 Ventnor 50 35N 1 12W
21 Ventoux, Mt. 44 10N 5 17E
48 Ventspils 57 25N 21 32E
103 Ventura 34 16N 119 25W
108 Vera, Arg. 29 30S 60 20W
33 Vera, Sp. 37 15N 1 15W
104 Veracruz 19 10N 96 10W
104 Veracruz □ 19 0N 96 15W
60 Veraval 20 53N 70 27E
36 Vercelli 45 19N 8 25E
112 Verde, R. 41 56S 65 5W
24 Verden 52 56N 9 15E
21 Verdon, R. 43 43N 5 46E
19 Verdun 49 12N 5 24E
21 Verdun-sur-le-Doubs 46 54N 5 0E
75 Vereeniging 26 38S 27 57E
32 Vergara 43 9N 2 28W
42 Vergoritis, L. 40 45N 21 45E
30 Verín 41 57N 7 27W
49 Verkhniy Baskunchak 48 5N 46 50E
51 Verkhoyansk 67 50N 133 50E
51 Verkhoyanskiy Khrebet 66 0N 129 0E
19 Vermenton 47 40N 3 42E
93 Vermilion 53 20N 110 50W
93 Vermilion, R. 53 44N 110 18W
93 Vermilion Bay 49 50N 93 20W
100 Vermillion 42 50N 96 56W
97 Vermont □ 43 40N 72 50W
102 Vernal 40 28N 109 35W
90 Verner 46 25N 80 8W
18 Verneuil 48 45N 0 56E
92 Vernon, Canada 50 20N 119 15W
18 Vernon, Fr. 49 5N 1 30E
101 Vernon, U.S.A. 34 0N 99 15W
42 Véroia 40 34N 22 18E
38 Véroli 41 43N 13 24E
36 Verona 45 27N 11 0E
19 Versailles 48 48N 2 8E
72 Verte, C. 14 45N 17 30W
18 Vertou 47 10N 1 28W
19 Vertus 48 54N 4 0E
16 Verviers 50 37N 5 52E
19 Vervins 49 50N 3 53E
21 Vescovato 42 30N 9 26E
26 Veselí n Luž 49 12N 14 43E
49 Veselovskoye, Vdkhr. 47 0N 41 0E
19 Vesle, R. 49 23N 3 38E
19 Vesoul 60 40N 6 11E
47 Vest-Agde □ 58 30N 7 0E
44 Vestfold □ 59 15N 10 0E
45 Vestjællands □ 55 30N 11 20E
46 Vestmannaejar, Is. 63 27N 20 15W
4 Vestspitsbergen, I. 78 40N 17 0E
39 Vesuvio, Mt. 40 50N 14 22E
27 Veszprém 47 8N 17 57E
27 Veszprém □ 47 5N 17 55E
27 Vésztö 46 55N 21 16E
62 Vetapalem 15 47N 80 18E
45 Vetlanda 57 24N 15 3E
41 Vetovo 43 42N 26 16E
37 Vettore, Mt. 44 38N 7 5E
25 Vevey 46 28N 6 51E
20 Vézère, R. 44 53N 0 53E
110 Viacha 16 30S 68 5W
36 Viadana 44 55N 10 30E
111 Viana 3 0S 44 40W
30 Viana del Bollo 42 10N 7 10W
31 Viana do Alentejo 38 20N 8 0W
30 Viana do Castelo 41 42N 8 50W
30 Vianna do Castelo □ 41 50N 8 30W
111 Vianopolis 16 40S 48 35W
31 Viar, R. 37 36N 5 50W
36 Viaréggio 43 52N 10 13E
39 Vibo Valéntia 38 40N 16 5E
45 Viborg 56 27N 9 23E
45 Viborg □ 56 30N 9 20E
20 Vic-Fézensac 43 47N 0 19E
37 Vicenza 45 32N 11 31E
32 Vich 41 58N 2 19E
20 Vichy 46 9N 3 26E
101 Vicksburg 32 22N 90 56W
39 Vico del Gargano 41 54N 15 57E
111 Vicosa 9 28S 36 25W
20 Vic-sur-Cère 44 59N 2 38E
96 Victor 42 58N 77 24W
81 Victor Harbour 35 30S 138 37E
108 Victoria, Arg. 32 40S 60 10W
79 Victoria, Australia 21 16S 149 3E
72 Victoria, Cameroon 4 1N 9 10E
92 Victoria, Canada 48 30N 123 25W
112 Victoria, Chile 38 22S 72 29W
69 Victoria, Hong Kong 22 25N 114 15E
64 Victoria, Malaysia 5 20N 115 20E
101 Victoria, U.S.A. 28 50N 97 0W
74 Victoria, L. 1 0S 33 0E
82 Victoria, R. 15 12S 129 43E
93 Victoria Beach 50 45N 96 32W
105 Victoria de las Tunas 20 58N 76 59W
75 Victoria Falls 17 58S 25 45E
88 Victoria I. 71 0N 11 0W
15 Victoria Ld. 75 0S 160 0E
59 Victoria Taungdeik, Mt. 21 15N 93 55E
75 Victoria West 31 25S 23 4E
91 Victoriaville 46 4N 71 56W
103 Victorville 34 32N 117 18W
99 Vidalia 32 13N 82 25W
21 Vidauban 43 25N 6 27E
40 Vidin 43 59N 22 52E
30 Vidio, C. 43 35N 6 14W
112 Viedma 40 50S 63 0W
112 Viedma, L. 49 30S 72 30W
30 Vieira 41 38N 8 8W
32 Viella 42 43N 0 44E
24 Vienenburg 51 57N 10 35E
27 Vienna = Wien 48 12N 16 22E
21 Vienne 45 31N 4 53E
18 Vienne, R. 47 13N 0 5E
20 Vienne □ 45 53N 0 42E
63 Vientiane 18 7N 102 35E
24 Viersen 51 15N 6 23E
25 Vierwaldstättersee, L. 47 0N 8 30E
19 Vierzon 47 13N 2 5E
39 Vieste 41 53N 16 10E
63 Vietnam ■ 16 0N 108 0E
21 Vif 45 5N 5 41E
65 Vigan 17 35N 120 28E
36 Vigévano 45 18N 8 50E
111 Vigia 0 50S 48 5W
20 Vignemale, Pic de 42 47N 0 10W
36 Vignola 44 29N 11 0E
30 Vigo 42 12N 8 41W
30 Vigo, Ria de 42 15N 8 45W
62 Vijayadurg 16 30N 73 25E
62 Vijayawada 16 31N 80 39E
62 Vikramasingapuram 8 40N 76 47E
50 Vikulovo 56 50N 70 40E
75 Vila Cabral = Lichinga 13 13S 35 11E
31 Vila de Rei 39 41N 8 9W
30 Vila do Conde 41 21N 8 45W
31 Vila Franca de Xira 38 57N 8 59W
75 Vila Machado 19 15S 34 14E
30 Vila Nova de Foscôa 41 5N 7 9W
30 Vila Nova de Gaia 41 4N 8 40W

31 Vila Nova de Ourém 39 40N 8 35W
30 Vila Pouca de Aguiar 41 30N 7 38W
30 Vila Real 41 17N 7 48W
31 Vila Real de Sto. António 37 10N 7 28W
109 Vila Velha 20 20S 40 17W
31 Vila Viçosa 38 45N 7 27W
30 Vilaboa 42 21N 8 39W
18 Vilaine, R. 47 30N 2 27W
30 Vilar Formosa 40 38N 6 45W
30 Vilareal □ 41 36N 7 35W
51 Viliga 60 2N 156 56E
108 Villa Ana 28 28S 59 40W
108 Villa Ángela 27 34S 60 45W
108 Villa Cañás 34 0S 61 35W
72 Villa Cisneros = Dakhla 23 50N 15 53W
108 Villa Colón 31 38S 68 20W
108 Villa Constitución 33 15S 60 20W
108 Villa Dolores 31 58S 65 15W
108 Villa Guillermina 28 15S 59 29W
108 Villa Hayes 25 0S 57 20W
105 Villa Julia Molina 19 5N 69 45W
108 Villa María 32 20S 63 10W
108 Villa Ocampo 28 30S 59 20W
36 Villa Minozzo 44 21N 10 30E
108 Villa San José 32 12E 58 15W
30 Villablino 42 57N 6 19W
31 Villacañas 39 38N 3 20W
32 Villacarlos 39 53N 4 17E
30 Villacarriedo 43 14N 3 48W
33 Villacarrillo 38 7N 3 3W
30 Villacastín 40 46N 4 25W
26 Villach 46 37N 13 51E
30 Villada 42 15N 4 59W
32 Villafeliche 41 10N 1 30W
32 Villafranca 42 17N 1 46W
31 Villafranca de los Barros 38 35N 6 18W
31 Villafranca de los Caballeros 39 26N 3 21W
30 Villafranca del Bierzo 42 38N 6 50W
32 Villafranca del Panadés 41 21N 1 40E
36 Villafranca di Verona 45 20N 10 51E
30 Villagarcia de Arosa 42 34N 8 46W
108 Villaguay 32 0S 58 45W
104 Villahermosa, Mexico 17 45N 92 50W
33 Villahermosa, Sp. 38 46N 2 52W
33 Villajoyosa 38 30N 0 12W
30 Villalba 40 36N 3 59W
30 Villalba de Guardo 42 42N 4 49W
30 Villalón de Campos 42 5N 5 4W
30 Villalpando 41 51N 5 25W
30 Villaluenga 40 2N 3 54W
30 Villamañán 42 19N 5 35W
31 Villamartín 36 52N 5 38W
32 Villamayor 41 42N 0 43W
103 Villanueva 35 16N 105 31W
33 Villanueva de Castellón 39 5N 0 31W
31 Villanueva de Córdoba 38 20N 4 38W
31 Villanueva de la Serena 38 59N 5 50W
33 Villanueva del Arzobispo 38 10N 3 0W
31 Villanueva del Fresno 38 23N 7 10W
32 Villanueva y Geltrú 41 13N 1 40E
30 Villarcayo 42 56N 3 34W
39 Villaroso 37 36N 14 9E
112 Villarrica 39 15S 72 30W
33 Villarrobledo 39 18N 2 36W
32 Villarroya de la Sierra 41 27N 1 46W
31 Villarrubia de los Ojos 39 14N 3 36W
31 Villarta de San Juan 39 15N 3 25W
30 Villatobas 39 54N 3 20W
110 Villavicencio 4 9N 73 37W
108 Villazón 22 0S 65 35W
90 Ville Marie 47 20N 79 30W
101 Ville Platte 30 45N 92 17W
18 Villedieu 48 50N 1 12W
20 Villefort 44 28N 3 56E
19 Villefranche 47 19N 146 0E
20 Villefranche-de-Lauragais 43 25N 1 44E
20 Villefranche-de-Rouergue 44 21N 2 2E
21 Villefranche-sur-Saône 45 59N 4 43E
32 Villel 40 14N 1 12W
19 Villemaur 48 14N 3 40E
33 Villena 38 39N 0 52W
19 Villeneuve 48 42N 2 25E
19 Villeneuve-l'Archevèque 48 14N 3 32E
21 Villeneuve-lès-Avignon 43 57N 4 49E
20 Villeneuve-sur-Lot 44 24N 0 42E
18 Villers-Bocage 49 3N 0 40W
19 Villers-Cotterets 49 15N 3 4E
18 Villers-sur-Mer 49 21N 0 2W
19 Villerupt 49 28N 5 55E
21 Villeurbanne 45 46N 4 55E
25 Villingen 48 3N 8 29E
62 Villupuram 11 59N 79 31E
92 Vilna 54 7N 111 55W
48 Vilnius 54 38N 25 25E
26 Vils 47 33N 10 37E
16 Vilvoorde 50 56N 4 26E
51 Vilyuysk 63 40N 121 20E
36 Vimercate 45 38N 9 25E
45 Vimmerby 57 40N 15 55E
108 Viña del Mar 33 0S 71 30W
32 Vinaroz 40 30N 0 27E
98 Vincennes 38 42N 87 29W
60 Vindhya Ra. 22 50N 77 0E
63 Vinh 18 45N 105 38E
37 Vinica 45 28N 15 16E
101 Vinita 36 40N 95 12W
40 Vinkovci 45 19N 18 48E
49 Vinnitsa 49 15N 28 30E
44 Vinstra 61 37N 9 44E
41 Vinţu de Jos 46 0N 23 30E
84 Violet Town 36 19S 145 37E
37 Vipava 45 51N 13 38E
37 Vipiteno 46 55N 11 25E
65 Viqueque 8 42S 126 30E
93 Virden 49 50N 101 0W
112 Vírgenes, C. 52 19S 68 21W
105 Virgin Gorda, I. 18 45N 64 26W
105 Virgin Is., Br. 18 40N 64 30W
105 Virgin Is., U.S. 18 20N 64 50W
100 Virginia 47 30N 92 32W
98 Virginia □ 37 45N 78 0W
98 Virginia Beach 36 54N 75 58W
102 Virginia City 45 25N 111 58W
40 Virje 46 4N 16 59E
40 Virovitica 45 51N 17 21E
40 Virpazar 42 15N 19 5E
16 Virton 49 35N 5 32E
62 Virudunagar 9 30N 78 0E
37 Vis, I. 43 0N 16 10E
103 Visalia 36 25N 119 18W
65 Visayan Sea 11 30N 123 30E
45 Visby 57 37N 18 18E
86 Viscount Melville Sd. 78 0N 108 0W
16 Visé 50 44N 5 41E
40 Višegrad 43 47N 19 17E
111 Viseu, Brazil 1 10S 46 20W
30 Viseu, Port. 40 40N 7 55W
30 Viseu □ 40 40N 7 55W
62 Vishakhapatnam 17 45N 83 20E
61 Vishnupur 23 8N 87 20E
45 Vislanda 56 46N 14 30E
60 Visnagar 23 45N 72 32E
37 Višnja Gora 45 58N 14 45E
48 Vitebsk 55 10N 30 15E
37 Viterbo 42 25N 12 8E
85 Viti Levu, I. 17 30S 177 30E
51 Vitim 59 45N 112 25E
51 Vitim, R. 59 26N 112 34E
109 Vitoria, Brazil 20 20S 40 22W
32 Vitória, Sp. 42 50N 2 41W
111 Vitória da Conquista 14 51S 40 51W
111 Vitoria de Santo Antão 8 10S 37 20W
18 Vitré 48 8N 1 12W
19 Vitry-le-François 48 43N 4 33E
42 Vitsi, Mt 40 40N 21 25E
19 Vitteaux 47 24N 4 30E
39 Vittória 36 58N 14 30E
37 Vittório Véneto 45 59N 12 18E
32 Viver 39 55N 0 36W
30 Vivero 43 39N 7 38W
20 Vivonne 46 36N 0 15E
44 Vivsta 62 30N 17 18E
30 Vizcaya □ 43 15N 2 45W
62 Vizianagaram 18 6N 83 10E
21 Vizille 45 5N 5 46E
41 Viziru 45 0N 27 43E
27 Vizovice 49 12N 17 56E
39 Vizzini 37 9N 14 43E
16 Vlaardingen 51 55N 4 21E
40 Vladicin Han 42 42N 22 1E
48 Vladimir 56 0N 40 30E
40 Vladimirovac 45 1N 20 53E
51 Vladivostok 43 10N 131 53E
40 Vlasenica 44 11N 18 59E
26 Vlasim 49 40N 14 53E
16 Vlissingen 51 26N 3 34E
42 Vlóra 40 32N 19 28E
42 Vlora □ 40 12N 20 0E
26 Vltava, R. 49 35N 14 10E
36 Vobarno 45 38N 10 30E
26 Vöcklabruck 48 1N 13 39E
37 Vodnjan 44 59N 13 52E
24 Vogelsberg, Mts. 50 30N 9 15E
36 Voghera 44 59N 9 1E
75 Vohémar 13 25S 50 0E
74 Voi 3 25S 38 32E
43 Voíotía □ 38 20N 23 0E
21 Voiron 45 22N 5 35E
26 Voitsberg 47 3N 15 9E
42 Voiviis, L. 39 30N 22 45E
45 Vojens 55 16N 9 18E
76 Volcano Is. 25 0N 141 0E
49 Volga, R. 45 55N 47 52E
49 Volga Heights, Mts. 51 0N 46 0E
49 Volgograd= Stalingrad 48 40N 44 25E
49 Volgogradskoye, Vdkhr. 50 0N 45 20E
26 Völkermarkt 46 34N 14 39E
25 Völkingen 49 15N 6 50E
16 Vollenhove 52 40N 5 58E
51 Volochanka 71 0N 94 28E
48 Vologda 59 25N 40 0E
42 Vólos 39 24N 22 59E
48 Volsk 52 5N 47 28E
72 Volta, L. 7 30N 0 15E
72 Volta Noire, R. 8 41N 1 33W
109 Volta Redonda 22 31S 44 5W
36 Volterra 43 24N 10 50E
36 Voltri 44 25N 8 43E
38 Volturno, R. 41 1N 13 55E
42 Vólvi, L. 40 40N 23 34E
49 Volzhskiy 48 56N 44 46E
16 Voorburg 52 5N 4 24E
26 Voralberg □ 47 20N 10 0E
42 Vóras Oros, Mt. 40 57N 21 45E
45 Vordingborg 55 0N 11 54E
43 Voríai Sporádhes, Is. 39 15N 23 30E
42 Vóras Evvoïkos Kól. 38 45N 23 15E
48 Vorkuta 67 48N 64 20E
48 Voronezh 51 40N 39 10E
49 Voroshilovgrad 48 38N 39 15E
19 Vosges, Mts. 48 20N 7 10E
19 Vosges □ 48 12N 6 20E
47 Voss 60 38N 6 26E
51 Vostochnyy Sayan 54 0N 96 0E
77 Vostok, I. 10 5S 152 23W
48 Votkinsk 57 0N 53 55E
48 Votkinskoye, Vdkhr. 57 30N 55 0E
30 Vouga, R. 40 41N 8 40W
30 Vouzela 40 43N 8 7W
19 Vouziers 49 22N 4 40E
48 Vozhe, Oz. 60 45N 39 0E
51 Voznesenka 46 51N 35 26E
49 Voznesensk 47 35N 31 15E
48 Voznesenye 61 0N 35 45E
41 Vrancei, Mt. 46 0N 26 30E
51 Vrangelya, Os. 71 0N 180 0E
40 Vranica, Mt. 43 59N 18 0E
40 Vranje 42 34N 21 54E
27 Vranov 48 53N 21 40E
37 Vransko 46 17N 14 58E
41 Vratsa 43 13N 23 30E
40 Vrbas 45 0N 17 27E
40 Vrbas, R. 45 6N 17 31E
37 Vrbnik 45 4N 14 32E
37 Vrbovsko 45 24N 15 5E
26 Vrchlabí 49 38N 15 37E
75 Vredenburg 32 51S 18 0E
62 Vriddhachalam 11 30N 79 10E
60 Vrindaban 27 37N 77 40E
43 Vrondádhes 38 25N 26 7E
40 Vrpolje 43 42N 16 1E
40 Vršac 45 8N 21 18E
40 Vrsacki, Kanal 45 15N 21 0E
75 Vryburg 26 55S 24 45E
75 Vryheid 27 54S 30 47E
27 Vsetín 49 20N 18 0E
16 Vught 51 38N 5 20E
40 Vukovar 45 21N 18 59E
92 Vulcan, Canada 50 25N 113 15W
41 Vulcan, Rumania 45 23N 23 17E
37 Vulci 42 23N 11 37E
62 Vuyyuru 16 28N 80 50E
60 Vyara 21 8N 73 28E
51 Vyatskiye 56 5N 51 0E
48 Vyazma 55 10N 34 15E
48 Vyborg 60 42N 28 45E
27 Vyehodné Beskydy, Mts. 49 30N 22 0E
26 Vychodočeský □ 50 20N 15 45E
27 Východoslovenský □ 48 50N 21 0E
48 Vyg, Oz. 63 30N 34 0E
12 Vyrnwy, L. 52 48N 3 30W
27 Vyškov 49 17N 17 0E
26 Vyšší Brod 48 36N 14 20E
48 Vytegra 61 15N 36 40E

W

72 Wa 10 7N 2 25W
16 Waal, R. 51 55N 4 30E
91 Wabana 47 40N 53 0W
98 Wabash 40 48N 85 46W
98 Wabash, R. 37 46N 88 2W
93 Wabowden 54 55N 98 35W
28 Wabrzeźno 53 16N 18 57E
91 Wabush City 52 40N 67 0W
101 Waco 31 33N 97 5W
73 Wad Banda 13 10N 27 50E
73 Wad Hamid 16 20N 32 45E
73 Wâd Medanî 14 28N 33 30E
66 Wadayama 35 19N 134 52E
16 Waddeniladen, Is. 53 30N 5 30E
16 Waddenzee 53 15N 5 15E
83 Wadderin Hill 32 0S 118 25E
97 Waddington 44 51N 75 12W
92 Waddington, Mt. 51 10N 125 20W
31 Waddy, Pt. 24 58S 153 21E
93 Wadena, Canada 52 0N 103 50W
100 Wadena, U.S.A. 46 25N 95 2W
25 Wadenswil 47 14N 8 30E
73 Wadi Halfa 21 53N 31 19E
27 Wadowice 49 52N 19 30E
96 Wadsworth 39 44N 119 22W
16 Wageningen 51 58N 5 40E
89 Wager Bay 66 0N 91 0W
84 Wagga Wagga 35 7S 147 24E
83 Wagin 33 17S 117 25E
28 Wagrowiec 52 48N 17 19E
65 Wahai 2 48S 129 35E
100 Wahpeton 46 20N 96 35W
62 Wai 17 56N 73 57E
85 Waiau 42 39S 173 5E
85 Waiau, R. 42 46S 173 23E
26 Waidhofen, Austria 48 49N 15 17E
26 Waidhofen, Austria 47 57N 14 46E
65 Waigeo, I. 0 20S 130 40E
85 Waihi 37 23S 175 52E
85 Waihou, R. 37 10S 175 32E
85 Waikaremoana, L. 38 49S 177 9E
85 Waikari 42 58S 172 41E
85 Waikato, R. 37 23S 174 43E
85 Waikerie 34 9S 140 0E
85 Waikokopu 39 3S 177 52E
85 Waikouaiti 45 36S 170 41E
85 Waimakariri, R. 43 24S 172 42E
85 Waimarino 40 40S 175 20E
85 Waimate 44 53S 171 3E
65 Waingapu 9 35S 120 11E
93 Wainwright 52 50N 110 50W
85 Waiouru 39 29S 175 40E
85 Waipara 43 3N 172 46E
85 Waipawa 39 56S 176 38E
85 Waipiro 38 2S 176 22E
85 Waipu 35 59S 174 29E
85 Waipukurau 40 1S 176 33E
85 Wairakei 38 37S 176 6E
85 Wairau, R. 41 32S 174 7E
85 Wairoa 39 3S 177 25E
85 Waitaki, R. 44 56S 171 7E
85 Waitara 38 59S 174 15E
85 Waiuku 37 15S 174 45E
69 Waiyeung 23 12N 114 32E
66 Wajima 37 30N 137 0E
74 Wajir 1 42N 40 20E
66 Wakasa 35 20N 134 24E
66 Wakasa-Wan 34 45N 135 30E
85 Wakatipu, L. 45 6S 168 30E
93 Wakaw 52 39N 105 44W
66 Wakayama 34 15N 135 15E
66 Wakayama □ 34 50N 135 30E
76 Wake, I. 19 18N 166 36E
12 Wakefield, U.K. 53 41N 1 31W
85 Wakefield, N.Z. 41 24S 173 5E
97 Wakefield 42 30N 71 3W
89 Wakeham Bay = Maricourt 61 36N 71 57W
66 Wakkanai 45 28N 141 35E
65 Wakre 0 30S 131 5E
41 Walachia = Valahia □ 44 40N 25 0E
27 Walbrzych 50 45N 16 18E
28 Walbrzych □ 50 50N 16 30E
13 Walbury Hill 51 22N 1 28W
81 Walcha 30 55S 151 31E
16 Walcheren, I. 51 30N 3 35E
28 Wałcz 53 17N 16 28E
24 Waldbröl 50 52N 7 36E
102 Walden 40 47N 106 20W
99 Waldron 50 53N 102 35W
83 Walebing 30 40S 116 15E
11 Wales ■ 52 30N 3 30W
84 Walgett 30 0S 148 5E
83 Walkaway 28 59S 114 48W
90 Walkerton 44 10N 81 10W
102 Walla Walla 46 3N 118 25W
102 Wallace 47 30N 116 0W
90 Wallaceburg 42 40N 82 30W

81 Wallal 26 32S 146 7E
82 Wallal Downs 19 47S 120 40E
81 Wallaroo 33 56S 137 39E
12 Wallasey 3 26S 3 2W
84 Wallerawang 33 25S 150 4E
80 Wallahallow 17 50S 135 50E
97 Wallingford 43 27N 72 58W
76 Wallis Arch. 13 20S 176 20E
102 Wallowa 45 40N 117 35W
12 Wallsend 54 59N 1 30W
81 Wallumbilla 26 33S 149 9E
12 Walney, I 54 5N 3 15W
84 Walpeup 35 10S 142 2E
13 Walsall 52 36N 1 59W
101 Walsenburg 37 42N 104 45W
24 Walsrode 52 51N 9 37E
62 Waltair 17 44N 83 23E
24 Waltershausen 50 53N 10 33E
90 Waltham, Canada 45 57N 76 57W
97 Waltham, U.S.A. 42 22N 71 12W
75 Walvisbaai 23 0S 14 28E
75 Walvis Bay = Walvisbaai 23 0S 14 28E
74 Wamba 2 10N 27 57E
31 Wanaaring 29 38S 144 0E
85 Wanaka, L. 44 33S 169 7E
65 Wanapiri 4 30S 135 50E
97 Wanaque 41 3N 74 17W
81 Wanbi 34 46S 140 17E
62 Wandiwash 12 30N 79 30E
81 Wandoan 26 5S 149 55E
85 Wanganui 39 35S 175 3E
84 Wangaratta 36 21S 146 19E
81 Wangary 34 33S 135 29E
68 Wangtu 38 42N 115 4E
69 Wanhsien 30 45N 108 20E
75 Wankie 18 18S 26 30E
93 Wanless 54 11N 101 21W
69 Wanning 18 45N 110 28E
69 Wantsai 28 1N 114 5E
69 Wanyang Shan, Mts. 26 30N 113 30E
69 Wanyuan 32 3N 108 16E
102 Wapato 46 30N 120 25W
55 Warandab 7 20N 44 2E
62 Warangal 17 58N 79 45E
85 Ward 41 49S 174 11E
57 Wardak □ 34 15N 68 0E
60 Wardha 20 45N 78 39E
97 Ware 42 16N 72 15W
24 Waren 53 30N 12 41E
24 Warendorf 51 57N 8 0E
81 Warialda 29 29S 150 33E
65 Warkopi 1 12S 134 9E
85 Warkworth 36 24S 174 41E
13 Warley 52 30N 2 0W
93 Warman 52 25N 106 30W
75 Warmbad, S.W. Africa 28 25S 18 42E
75 Warmbad, S.W. Africa 19 14S 13 51E
84 Warncoort 38 30S 143 45E
102 Warner Ra. 41 30S 120 20W
99 Warner Robins 32 41N 83 36W
24 Warnermünde 54 9N 12 5E
83 Waroona 32 50S 115 55E
60 Warora 20 14N 79 1E
84 Warracknabeal 36 9S 142 26E
84 Warragul 38 10S 145 58E
81 Warrego, R. 30 24S 145 21E
84 Warren, Australia 31 42S 147 51E
96 Warren, Ohio 41 18N 80 52W
96 Warren, Pa. 41 52N 79 10W
101 Warren 33 35N 92 3W
15 Warrenpoint 54 7N 6 15W
100 Warrensburg 38 45N 93 45W
75 Warrenton, S. Africa 28 9S 24 47E
102 Warrenton, U.S.A. 46 11N 123 59W
72 Warri 5 30N 5 41E
12 Warrington, U.K. 53 25N 2 38W
99 Warrington, U.S.A. 30 22N 87 16W
84 Warrnambool 38 25S 142 30E
58 Warsak Dam 34 10N 71 25E
98 Warsaw 41 14N 85 50W
28 Warszawa 52 13N 21 0E
28 Warszawa □ 52 35N 21 0E
28 Warta, R. 52 35N 14 39E
13 Warwick □ 52 20N 1 30W
81 Warwick, Australia 28 10S 152 1E
13 Warwick, U.K. 52 17N 1 36W
97 Warwick, U.S.A. 41 43N 71 25W
92 Wasa 49 45N 115 50W
86 Wasatch Mts. 40 30N 111 15W
103 Wasco, Calif. 35 37N 119 16W
102 Wasco, Oreg. 45 45N 120 46W
100 Waseca 44 3N 93 31W
12 Wash, The 52 58N 0 20W
96 Washago 44 46N 79 21W
102 Washington □ 47 45N 120 30W
98 Washington, D.C. 38 52N 77 0W
98 Washington, Ind. 38 40N 87 8W
100 Washington, Iowa 41 20N 91 45W
100 Washington, Mo. 38 33N 91 1W
97 Washington, N.J. 40 45N 74 59W
99 Washington, N.C. 35 35N 77 1W
98 Washington, Ohio 39 34N 83 26W
96 Washington, Pa. 40 10N 80 20W
77 Washington I. 4 43N 160 24W
97 Washington, Mt. 44 15N 71 18W
16 Wassenaar 52 8N 4 24E
24 Wasserkuppe, Mt. 50 30N 9 56E
90 Waswanipi 49 30N 77 0W
65 Watangpone 4 29S 120 25E
97 Waterbury 41 32N 73 0W
15 Waterford 52 16N 7 8W
15 Waterford □ 51 10N 7 40W
16 Waterloo, Belgium 50 43N 4 25E
100 Waterloo, Iowa 42 27N 92 20W
96 Waterloo, N.Y. 42 54N 76 53W
97 Watertown, N.Y. 43 58N 75 57W
100 Watertown, S.D. 44 57N 97 5W
100 Watertown, Wis. 43 15N 88 45W
99 Waterville 44 35N 69 40W
97 Watervliet 42 46N 73 43W
65 Wates 7 53S 110 6E
13 Watford 51 38N 0 23W
83 Watheroo 30 15S 116 0W
105 Watling, I. 24 0N 74 30W
93 Watrous 51 40N 105 25W
74 Watsa 3 4N 29 30E
83 Watson 30 19S 131 41E
92 Watson Lake 60 12N 129 0W
103 Watsonville 37 58N 121 49W
25 Wattwil 47 18N 9 6E
84 Waubra 37 21S 143 39E
84 Wauchope 31 28S 152 45E
93 Waugh 49 40N 95 20W
98 Waukegan 42 22N 87 54W
100 Waukesha 43 0N 88 15W
100 Waupun 43 38N 88 44W
100 Wausau 44 57N 89 40W
98 Wauwatosa 43 6N 87 59W
82 Wave Hill 17 32N 131 0E
13 Waveney, R. 52 28N 1 45E
85 Waverley 39 46S 174 37E
100 Waverly 42 40N 92 30W
16 Wavre 50 43N 4 38E
73 Wâw 7 45N 28 1E
101 Waxahachie 32 22N 96 53W
80 Wayatinah 42 19S 146 27E
99 Waycross 31 12N 82 25W
98 Waynesboro, Pa. 39 46N 77 32W
98 Waynesboro, Va. 38 4N 78 57W
99 Waynesville 35 31N 83 0W
57 Wazirabad, Afghanistan 36 44N 66 47E
60 Wazirabad, Pak. 32 30N 74 8E
13 Weald, The 51 7N 0 9E
12 Wear, R. 54 55N 1 22W
101 Weatherford 32 45N 97 48W
97 Webster 42 4N 71 54W
100 Webster City 42 30N 93 50W
100 Webster Green 38 38N 90 20W
65 Weda 0 30N 127 50E
112 Weddell I. 51 50S 61 0W
5 Weddell Sea 72 30S 40 0W
84 Wedderburn 36 20S 143 33E
91 Wedgeport 43 44N 65 59W
81 Wee Waa 30 11S 149 26E
102 Weed 41 29N 122 22W
16 Weert 51 15N 5 43E
28 Wegliniec 51 18N 15 10E
69 Wei Ho, R. 35 45N 114 30E
24 Weida 50 47N 12 3E
68 Weifang 36 47N 119 10E
68 Weihai 37 30N 122 10E
25 Weilheim 47 50N 11 9E
24 Weimar 51 0N 11 20E
69 Weinan 34 30N 109 35E
25 Weingarten 47 49N 9 39E
25 Weinheim 47 50N 11 9E
80 Weipa 12 24S 141 50E
93 Weir River 57 0N 94 10W
96 Weirton 40 22N 80 35W
102 Weiser 44 10N 117 0W
25 Weissenburg 49 2N 10 58E
24 Weissenfels 51 11N 11 58E
24 Weisswasser 51 30N 14 36E
26 Wêitra 48 41N 14 54E
26 Weiz 47 13N 15 39E
28 Wejherow 54 35N 18 12E
93 Wekusko 54 45N 99 45W
31 Welbourn Hill 27 21S 134 6E
98 Welch 37 29N 81 36W
25 Welden 48 27N 10 40E
75 Welkom 28 0S 26 50E
96 Welland 43 0N 79 10W
12 Welland, R. 52 53N 0 2E
80 Wellesley, Is. 17 20S 139 30E
13 Wellingborough 52 18N 0 41W
84 Wellington, Australia 32 30S 149 0E
90 Wellington, Canada 43 57N 77 20W
85 Wellington, N.Z. 41 19S 174 46E
12 Wellington, U.K. 52 42N 2 31W
101 Wellington, U.S.A. 37 15N 97 25W
85 Wellington □ 40 8S 175 36E
112 Wellington, I. 49 30S 75 0W
12 Wells, Norfolk 52 57N 0 51E
13 Wells, Somerset 51 12N 2 39W
102 Wells, U.S.A. 41 8N 115 0W
83 Wells, L. 26 44S 123 15W
97 Wells River 44 9N 72 4W
96 Wellsburg 40 15N 80 36W
28 Wełna, R. 42 9N 77 53W
26 Wels 48 9N 14 1E
84 Welshpool, Australia 38 42S 146 26E
13 Welshpool, U.K. 52 40N 3 9W
12 Wem 52 52N 2 45W
102 Wenatchee 47 30N 120 17W
69 Wenchang 19 38N 110 42E
72 Wenchi 7 46N 2 8W
69 Wenchow 28 0N 120 35E
102 Wendell 42 50N 114 51W
69 Wensiang 34 35N 110 40E
12 Wensleydale 54 20N 2 0W
67 Wensu 41 15N 80 14E
68 Wenteng 25 15S 23 16E
84 Wentworth 34 2S 141 54E
75 Wepener 29 42S 27 3E
75 Werda 25 15S 23 16E
24 Werdau 50 45N 12 20E
24 Werder 52 23N 12 56E
24 Werdohl 51 15N 7 47E
25 Werne 51 38N 7 38E
24 Wernigerode 51 49N 0 45E
84 Werribee 37 54S 144 40E
84 Werris Creek 31 8S 150 38E
25 Wertheim 49 44N 9 32E
24 Wesel 51 39N 6 34E
24 Weser, R. 53 32N 8 34E
91 Wesleyville 49 8N 53 36W
80 Wessel, Is. 11 10S 136 45E
98 West Bend 43 25N 88 10W
61 West Bengal □ 25 0N 90 0E
13 West Bromwich 52 32N 2 1W
100 West Des Moines 41 30N 93 45W
112 West Falkland, I. 51 30S 60 0W
100 West Frankfort 37 56N 89 0W
24 West Germany ■ 51 0N 9 0E
13 West Glamorgan □ 51 40N 3 55W
97 West Hartford 41 45N 72 45W
97 West Haven 41 18N 72 57W
101 West Helena 34 30N 90 40W
101 West Memphis 35 5N 90 3W
13 West Midlands □ 52 30N 2 0W
101 West Monroe 32 32N 92 7W
99 West Palm Beach 26 44N 80 3W
97 West Pittston 41 19N 75 49W
105 West Pt. 18 14N 78 30W
101 West Point, Miss. 33 36N 88 38W
98 West Point, Va. 37 35N 76 47W
13 West Sussex □ 50 55N 0 30W
98 West Virginia □ 39 0N 18 0W
84 West Wyalong 33 56S 147 10E
12 West Yorkshire □ 53 45N 1 40W
99 Westbrook 43 41N 70 21W
80 Westbury 41 30S 146 51E
24 Westerland 54 51N 8 20E
78 Western Australia □ 25 0S 118 0E
62 Western Ghats, Mts. 15 30N 74 30E
14 Western Isles □ 57 30N 7 10W
63 Western Malaysia □ 4 0N 10 2E
85 Western Samoa ■ 14 0S 172 0W
16 Westerschelde, R. 51 25N 4 0E
24 Westerstede 51 15N 7 55E
24 Westerwald, Mts. 50 39N 8 0E
97 Westfield 42 9N 72 49W
85 Westland □ 43 33S 169 59E
92 Westlock 54 20N 113 55W
15 Westmeath □ 53 30N 7 30W
98 Westminster 39 34S 77 1W
103 Westmorland 33 2N 115 42W
64 Weston, Malaysia 5 10N 115 35E
98 Weston, U.S.A. 39 3N 80 29W
13 Weston-super-Mare 51 20N 2 59W
15 Westport, Eire 53 44N 9 31W
85 Westport, N.Z. 41 46S 171 37E
14 Westray, I. 59 18N 3 0W
92 Westview 49 50N 124 31W
102 Westwood 40 26N 121 0W
65 Wetar, I. 7 30S 126 30E
92 Wetaskiwin 52 55N 113 24W
97 Wethersfield 41 43N 72 40W
16 Wetteren 51 0N 3 53E
24 Wetzlar 50 33N 8 30E
101 Wewaka 35 10N 96 35W
15 Wexford 52 20N 6 28W
15 Wexford □ 52 20N 6 40W
93 Weyburn 49 40N 103 50W
26 Weyer 47 51N 14 40E
13 Weymouth, U.K. 50 36N 2 28W
97 Weymouth, U.S.A. 42 13N 70 53W
85 Whakatane 37 57S 177 1E
89 Whale, R. 57 40N 67 0W
93 Whale Cove 62 10N 93 0W
14 Whalsay, I. 60 22N 1 0W
85 Whangamomona 39 8S 174 44E
85 Whangarei 35 43S 174 21E
85 Whangaroa, Harbour 35 4S 173 46E
12 Wharfe, R. 53 51N 1 7W
100 Wheatland 42 4N 105 58W
103 Wheeler Pk. 38 57N 114 15W
96 Wheeling 40 2N 80 41W
12 Whernside, Mt. 54 14N 2 24W
96 Whitby, Canada 43 50N 78 50W
12 Whitby, U.K. 54 29N 0 37W
98 White, R., Ind. 38 25N 87 44W
101 White, R., Ark. 33 53N 91 3W
81 White Cliffs 30 50S 143 10E
13 White Horse, Vale of 51 37N 1 30W
97 White Mts. 44 15N 71 15W
73 White Nile, R. = Nîl el Abyad 9 30N 31 40E
97 White Plains 41 2N 73 44E
90 White River 48 35N 85 20W
97 White River Junc. 43 28N 72 20W
48 White Sea= Beloye More 66 30N 38 0E
102 White Sulphur Springs 46 35N 111 0W
85 Whitecliffs 43 26S 171 55E
97 Whitefield 44 23N 71 37W
102 Whitefish 48 25N 114 22W
97 Whitehall, N.Y. 43 32N 73 28W
102 Whitehall, Wis. 44 20N 91 19W
12 Whitehaven 54 33N 3 35W
92 Whitehorse 60 45N 135 10W
93 Whiteshell Prov. Park 50 0N 95 25W
80 Whitewood 21 28S 143 30E
93 Whitewood 50 20N 102 20W
14 Whithorn 54 55N 4 25W
85 Whitianga 36 47S 175 41E
97 Whitman 42 4N 70 55W
103 Whitney, Mt. 36 35N 118 14W
97 Whitney Point 42 19N 75 59W
13 Whitstable 51 21N 1 2E
80 Whitsunday, I. 20 15S 149 4E
88 Whittier 60 46N 148 48W
91 Whittle, C. 50 11N 60 8W
81 Whyalla 33 2S 137 30E
90 Wiarton 44 50N 81 10W
101 Wichita 37 40N 97 29W
101 Wichita Falls 33 57N 98 30W
14 Wick 58 26N 3 5W
103 Wickenburg 33 58N 112 45W
83 Wickepin 32 50S 117 30E
96 Wickliffe 41 46N 81 29W
15 Wicklow 53 0N 6 2W
15 Wicklow □ 52 59N 6 25W
15 Wicklow Mts. 53 0N 6 30W
83 Widgiemooltha 31 30S 121 34E
12 Widnes 53 22N 2 44W
28 Wiecbork 53 22N 17 30E
25 Wiedenbrück 51 50N 8 18E
28 Wielbark 53 24N 20 55E
28 Wieluń 51 15N 18 40E
27 Wien 48 12N 16 22E
27 Wiener Neustadt 47 49N 16 16E
28 Wieprz, R. 51 34N 21 49E
16 Wierden 52 22N 6 35E
25 Wiesbaden 50 7N 8 17E
12 Wigan 53 33N 2 38W
14 Wigtown 54 52N 4 27W
14 Wigtown B. 54 46N 4 15W
84 Wilcannia 31 30S 143 26E
24 Wildeshausen 52 54N 8 25E
26 Wildon 46 52N 15 31E
98 Wildwood 39 5N 74 46W
26 Wilhelmsburg, Austria 48 6N 15 36E
24 Wilhelmsburg, W. Germany 53 28N 10 1E
24 Wilhelmshaven 53 30N 8 9E
97 Wilkes-Barre 41 15N 75 52W
15 Wilkes Ld. 69 0S 120 0E
5 Wilkes Sub-Glacial Basin 68 0S 140 0E
93 Wilkie 52 27N 108 42W
96 Wilkinsburg 40 26N 79 50W
96 Willard 41 3N 82 44W
103 Willcox 32 13N 109 53W
105 Willemstad 12 5N 69 0W
82 Willeroo 15 14S 131 37E
81 William Creek 28 58S 136 22E
83 Williams, Australia 33 0S 117 0E
103 Williams, U.S.A. 35 16N 112 11W
92 Williams Lake 52 20N 122 10W
98 Williamsburg 37 17N 76 44W
98 Williamson 37 46N 82 17W
96 Williamsport 41 18N 77 1W
84 Williamstown, Australia 37 46S 144 58E
97 Williamstown, U.S.A. 42 41N 73 12W
97 Willimantic 41 45N 72 12W

100 Williston 48 10N 103 35W
102 Willits 39 28N 123 17W
100 Willmar 45 5N 95 0W
96 Willoughby 41 38N 81 26W
84 Willow Tree 31 40S 150 45E
75 Willowmore 33 15S 23 30E
80 Willows, Australia 23 45S 147 25E
102 Willows, U.S.A. 39 30N 122 10W
98 Wilmette 42 6N 87 44W
98 Wilmington, Del. 39 45N 75 32W
99 Wilmington, N.C. 34 14N 77 54W
98 Wilmington, Ohio 39 29N 83 46W
99 Wilson 35 44N 77 54W
103 Wilson, Mt. 37 55N 105 3W
84 Wilson's Promontory 39 5S 146 28E
13 Wilton 51 5N 1 52W
13 Wiltshire □ 51 20N 2 0W
83 Wiluna 26 40S 120 25E
19 Wimereux 50 45N 1 37E
13 Winchester, U.K. 51 4N 1 19W
97 Winchester, Conn. 41 53N 73 9W
98 Winchester, Ind. 40 10N 84 56W
98 Winchester, Ky. 38 0N 84 8W
98 Winchester, Va. 39 14N 78 8W
12 Windermere, L. 54 20N 2 57W
75 Windhoek 22 35S 17 4E
26 Windischgarsten 47 42N 14 21E
80 Windorah 25 24S 142 36E
13 Windrush, R. 51 42N 1 25W
84 Windsor, Australia 33 34S 150 44E
91 Windsor, Nova Scotia 44 59N 64 5W
90 Windsor, Ont. 42 25N 83 0W
13 Windsor, U.K. 51 28N 0 36W
105 Windward Is. 13 0N 63 0W
92 Winfield, Canada 52 58N 114 26W
101 Winfield, U.S.A. 37 15N 97 0W
84 Wingen 31 50S 150 58E
90 Wingham 43 55N 81 25W
90 Winisk, R. 55 17N 85 5W
93 Winkler 49 15N 98 0W
26 Winklern 46 52N 12 53E
72 Winneba 5 25N 0 36W
102 Winnemucca 41 0N 117 45W
93 Winnepegosis, L. 52 40N 100 0W
98 Winnetka 42 8N 87 46W
101 Winnfield 31 57N 92 38W
82 Winning 23 9S 114 32E
93 Winnipeg 49 50N 97 15W
93 Winnipeg, L. 52 30N 98 0W
93 Winnipegosis 52 40N 100 0W
97 Winnipesaukee, L. 43 35N 71 20W
100 Winona 44 2N 91 45W
97 Winooski 44 31N 73 11W
97 Winooski, R. 44 30N 73 15W
16 Winschoten 53 9N 7 3E
103 Winslow 35 2N 110 41W
97 Winsted 41 55N 73 4W
99 Winston-Salem 36 7N 80 15W
99 Winter Haven 28 0N 81 42W
99 Winter Park 28 34N 81 19W
25 Winterthur 47 30N 8 44E
80 Winton 22 21S 143 0E
85 Winton 46 8S 168 20E
19 Wintzenheim 48 4N 7 17E
81 Wirrulla 32 24S 134 31E
12 Wisbech 52 39N 0 10E
100 Wisconsin □ 44 30N 90 0W
100 Wisconsin Rapids 44 25N 89 50W
14 Wishaw 55 46N 3 55W
28 Wisła, R. 54 22N 18 55E
27 Wisłoka, R. 50 27N 21 23E
24 Wismar 53 53N 11 23E
19 Wissant 50 52N 1 40E
19 Wissembourg 49 2N 7 57E
75 Witbank 25 51S 29 14E
12 Witham, R. 52 56N 0 4E
12 Withernsea 53 43N 0 2W
13 Witney 51 47N 1 29W
75 Witsand 34 24S 20 50E
24 Witten 51 26N 7 19E
24 Wittenberg 51 51N 12 39E
24 Wittenberge 53 0N 11 44E
24 Wittenburg 53 30N 11 4E
82 Wittenoom 22 15S 118 20E
24 Wittengen 52 43N 10 43E
24 Wittow, I. 54 37N 13 21E
24 Wittstock 53 10N 12 30E
25 Witzenhausen 51 20N 9 50E
28 Wkra R. 52 27N 20 44E
65 Wlingi 8 5S 112 25E
28 Włocławek 52 39 19 2E
28 Wrocław 51 10N 17 0E
97 Woburn 42 31N 71 7W
84 Wodonga 36 5S 146 50E
27 Wodzisław Śl. 50 1N 18 26E
65 Wokam, I. 5 45S 134 28E
90 Wolfe I. 44 7N 76 27E
24 Wolfenbüttel 52 10N 10 33E
26 Wolfsberg 46 50N 14 52E
24 Wolfsburg 52 27N 10 49E
24 Wolgast 54 3N 13 46E
112 Wollaston, Is. 55 40S 67 30W
93 Wollaston L. 58 20N 103 30W
88 Wollaston Pen. 69 30N 113 0W
84 Wollongong 34 25S 150 54E
28 Wołomin 51 21N 16 39E
93 Wolseley 50 25N 103 15W
86 Wolstenholme, C. 62 50N 78 0W
13 Wolverhampton 52 35N 2 6W
80 Wonarah P.O. 19 55S 136 20E
81 Wondai 26 20S 151 49E
83 Wongan Hills 30 53S 116 42E
68 Wŏnju 37 30N 127 59E
68 Wŏnsan 39 20N 127 25E
84 Wonthaggi 38 29S 145 31E
92 Wood Buffalo Nat. Park 59 30N 113 0W
83 Woodanilling 33 31S 117 24E
84 Woodend 37 20N 144 33E
102 Woodland 38 40N 121 50W
93 Woodridge 49 20N 96 20W
83 Woodroffe, Mt. 26 20S 131 45E
93 Woods, L. of the 49 30N 94 30W
80 Woodstock, Australia 19 22S 142 45E
91 Woodstock, N.B. 46 11N 67 37W
90 Woodstock, Ont 43 10N 80 45W
13 Woodstock, U.K. 51 51N 1 20W
96 Woodstock, Vt. 43 37N 72 31W
100 Woodstock, Ill. 42 17N 88 30W
97 Woodsville 44 10N 72 0W
85 Woodville 40 20S 175 53E
101 Woodward 36 24N 99 28W
83 Woolgangie 31 12S 120 35E
81 Woolgoolga 30 7S 153 12E
81 Woombye 26 40S 152 55E
84 Woomelang 35 37S 142 40E
81 Woomera 31 9S 136 56E
84 Woonona 34 32S 150 49E
97 Woonsocket 42 0N 71 30W
100 Woonsockett 44 5N 98 15W
83 Wooramel 25 45S 114 40E
83 Wooramel, R. 25 47S 114 10E
83 Wooroloo 31 45S 116 25E
96 Wooster 40 38N 81 55W
75 Worcester, S. Africa 33 39S 19 27E
13 Worcester, U.K. 52 12N 2 12W
97 Worcester, U.S.A. 42 14N 71 49W
26 Wörgl 47 29N 12 3E
12 Workington 54 39N 3 34W
12 Worksop 53 19N 1 9W
102 Worland 44 0N 107 59W
25 Worms 49 37N 8 21E
83 Worsley 33 15S 116 2E
26 Wörther See, L. 46 37N 14 19E
13 Worthing 50 49N 0 21W
100 Worthington 43 35N 95 30W
65 Wosi 0 15S 128 0E
92 Wrangell 56 30N 132 25W
88 Wrangell Mts. 61 40N 143 30W
14 Wrath, C. 58 38N 5 0W
12 Wrekin, The, Mt. 52 41N 2 35W
12 Wrexham 53 5N 3 0W
92 Wright, Canada 51 45N 121 30W
65 Wright, Philippines 11 42N 125 2E
88 Wrigley 63 0N 123 30W
28 Wrocław 51 5N 17 5E
28 Wrocław □ 51 0N 17 0E
28 Września 52 21N 17 36E
83 Wubin 30 8S 116 30E
68 Wuchang, Heilungkiang 44 51N 127 10E
69 Wuchang, Hupei 30 34N 114 25E
69 Wuchow 23 26N 111 19E
68 Wuchung 38 4N 106 12E
69 Wuhan 30 32N 114 22E
69 Wuhu 31 21N 118 30E
72 Wukari 7 57N 9 42E
59 Wuntho 23 55N 95 45E
24 Wuppertal 51 15N 7 8E
83 Wurarga 28 15S 116 12E
25 Würzburg 49 46N 9 55E
24 Wurzen 51 21N 12 45E
69 Wusih 31 30N 120 30E
67 Wusu 44 10N 84 55E
68 Wutai Shan 39 4N 113 35E
67 Wutunghliao 29 25N 104 0E
67 Wuwei 38 0N 102 30E
69 Wuyi Shan, Mts. 26 40N 116 30E
68 Wuying 48 10N 129 20E
68 Wuyuan 41 45N 108 30E
83 Wyalkatchem 31 8S 117 22E
98 Wyandotte 42 14N 83 13W
81 Wyandra 27 12S 145 56E
84 Wycheproot 36 0N 143 17E
13 Wye, R. 51 37N 2 39W
13 Wymondham 52 34N 1 7E
82 Wyndham 15 33S 128 3E
81 Wynnum 27 29S 152 58E
81 Wynyard, Australia 40 59S 145 45E
93 Wynyard, Canada 51 45N 104 10W
Canada 51 45N 104 10W
102 Wyoming □ 42 48N 109 0W
84 Wyong 33 14S 151 24E
28 Wyrzysk 53 10N 17 17E
28 Wyszków 52 36N 21 25E
98 Wytheville 37 0N 81 3W

X

42 Xánthi 41 10N 24 58E
42 Xánthi □ 41 10N 24 58E
98 Xenia 39 42N 83 57W
63 Xieng Khouang 19 17N 103 25E
43 Xilókastron 38 4N 22 43E
75 Xinavane 25 2S 32 47E
111 Xingu, R. 1 30S 51 53W
43 Xiniás, L. 39 2N 22 12E
111 Xique-Xique 10 40S 42 40W

Y

80 Yaamba 23 8S 150 22E
67 Yaan 30 0N 102 59E
41 Yablanitsa 43 2N 24 5E
51 Yablonovy Khrebet 53 0N 114 0E
54 Ya'Bud 32 27N 35 10E
108 Yacuiba 22 0S 63 25W
62 Yadgir 16 45N 77 5E
54 Yagur 32 45N 35 4E
69 Yaicheng 18 14N 109 7E
102 Yakima 46 42N 120 30W
68 Yakoshih 49 13N 120 35E
66 Yaku-Shima, I. 30 20N 130 30E
51 Yakut A.S.S.R. □ 66 0N 125 0E
88 Yakutat 59 50N 139 44W
51 Yakutsk 62 5N 129 40E
80 Yalboroo 20 50S 148 30E
83 Yalgoo 23 16S 116 39E
104 Yalkubul, Pta. 21 32N 88 37W
84 Yallourn 38 10S 146 18E
49 Yalta 44 30N 34 10E
68 Yalu, R. 47 30N 123 30E
67 Yalung Kiang, R. 32 0N 100 0E
50 Yalutorovsk 56 30N 65 40E
66 Yamagata 37 55N 140 20E
66 Yamagata □ 38 30N 140 0E
66 Yamaguchi 34 10N 131 32E
66 Yamaguchi □ 34 20N 131 40E
50 Yamal Pol. 71 0N 70 0E
56 Yamama 24 5N 47 30E
66 Yamanashi □ 35 40N 138 40E
84 Yamba 29 30S 153 22E
41 Yambol 42 30N 26 36E
65 Yamdena, I. 7 45S 131 20E
59 Yamethin 20 26N 96 9E
82 Yampi, Sd. 15 15S 123 30E
69 Yamhsien 21 45N 108 31E
41 Yamrukchal, Mt. 42 44N 24 52E
54 Yamun 32 29N 35 14E
61 Yamuna, R. 27 0N 78 30E
66 Yanai 33 58N 132 7E
62 Yanam 16 47N 82 15E
48 Yanaul 56 25N 55 0E
83 Yandanooka 29 18S 115 29E
59 Yandoon 17 2N 95 39E
74 Yangambi 0 47N 24 20E
69 Yangchow 32 25N 119 25E
68 Yangchuan 38 0N 113 29E
50 Yangi-Yer 40 17N 68 48E
69 Yangtze Kiang, R. 31 40N 122 0E
100 Yankton 42 55N 97 25W
81 Yanna 26 58S 146 0E
69 Yanping 22 25N 112 0E
41 Yantra, R. 43 35N 25 37E
69 Yao Shan, Mts. 24 0N 110 0E
74 Yaoundé 3 50N 1 35E
65 Yap Is. 9 30N 138 10E
65 Yapen, I. 1 50S 136 0E
65 Yapen, Teluk, G. 1 30S 136 0E
80 Yaraka 24 53S 144 3E
48 Yaransk 57 13N 47 56E
13 Yare, R. 52 40N 1 45E
48 Yarensk 61 10N 49 8E
67 Yarkand= Soche 38 24N 77 20E
58 Yarkhun, R. 36 30N 72 45E
91 Yarmouth 43 53N 65 45W
48 Yaroslavl 57 35N 39 55E
83 Yarra Yarra Lakes 29 12S 115 45E
82 Yarraloola 21 34S 115 52E
81 Yarraman 26 46S 152 1E
50 Yar-Sale 66 50N 70 50E
51 Yartsevo 60 20N 90 0E
110 Yarumal 6 58N 75 24W
85 Yasawa Is. 17 0S 177 23E
63 Yasothon 15 50N 104 10E
84 Yass 34 50S 149 0E
54 Yas'ur 32 54N 35 10E
88 Yathkyed, L. 63 0N 98 0W
66 Yatsushiro 32 30N 130 40E
54 Yattah 31 27N 35 6E
60 Yaval 21 10N 75 42E
54 Yavne 31 52N 34 45E
66 Yawatehama 33 27N 132 24E
57 Yazd 31 55N 54 27E
57 Yazdan 33 30N 60 50E
101 Yazoo City 32 48N 90 28W
26 Ybbs 48 12N 15 4E
59 Ye 15 15N 97 51E
83 Yealering 32 35S 117 30E
59 Yebyu 14 15N 98 13E
33 Yecla 38 35N 1 5W
68 Yehsien 37 12N 119 58E
51 Yelanskoye 61 25N 128 0E
81 Yelarbon 28 33S 150 49E
48 Yelets 52 40N 38 30E
14 Yell, I. 46 42N 2 20W
62 Yellamanchilli 38 0N 117 20E
62 Yellandu 17 36N 80 20E
83 Yellowdine 31 18S 119 39E
92 Yellowhead P. 53 0N 118 30W
92 Yellowknife 62 30N 114 10W
88 Yellowknife, R. 63 30N 113 30W
102 Yellowstone Nat. Park 44 35N 110 0W
102 Yellowtail Res. 45 6N 108 8W
80 Yelvertoft 20 13S 138 53E
55 Yemen ■ 15 0N 44 0E
59 Yenangyaung 20 30N 95 0E
69 Yencheng 36 44N 110 2E
51 Yeniseysk 58 39N 92 4E
50 Yenisey, R. 68 0N 86 30E
50 Yeniseyskiy Zaliv 72 20N 81 0E
68 Yenki 43 12N 129 30E
68 Yentai 37 30N 121 22E
51 Yenyuka 58 20N 121 30E
13 Yeo, R. 51 1N 2 46W
60 Yeola 20 0N 74 30E
60 Yeotmal 20 20N 78 15E
13 Yeovil 50 57N 2 38W
80 Yeppoon 23 5S 150 47E
49 Yerevan 40 10N 44 20E
51 Yermakovo 52 35N 126 20E
51 Yerofey Pavlovich 54 0N 122 0E
54 Yeroham 30 59N 34 55E
49 Yershov 51 15N 48 27E
13 Yes Tor 50 41N 3 59E
20 Yeu, Î.d' 46 42N 2 20W
69 Yeungchun 22 15N 111 40E
69 Yeungkong 21 55N 112 0E
49 Yeysk Stavo 46 40N 38 12E
108 Yhatí 25 45S 56 35W
109 Yhú 25 0S 56 0W
42 Yiannitsa 40 46N 22 24E
57 Yibal 22 10N 56 8E
69 Yilan 24 47N 121 44E
68 Yin Shan, Mts. 41 0N 111 0E
68 Yinchwan 38 30N 106 20E
69 Yingcheng 31 0N 113 44E
68 Yingkow 40 38N 122 30E
69 Yingtan 28 12N 117 0E
42 Yioura, I. 39 23N 24 10E
74 Yirga Alem 6 34N 38 29E
43 Yíthion 36 46N 22 34E
68 Yitu 36 40N 118 24E
69 Yiyang 28 45N 112 16E
54 Yizre'el 32 34N 35 19E
46 Ylivieska 64 4N 24 28E
101 Yoakum 29 20N 97 10W
65 Yogyakarta 7 49S 110 22E
66 Yokkaichi 35 0N 136 30E
66 Yokohama 35 30N 139 32E
66 Yokosuka 35 20N 139 40E
66 Yonago 35 25N 133 19E
68 Yŏngchŏn 35 55N 138 55E
97 Yonkers 40 57N 73 51W
19 Yonne □ 47 50N 3 40E
19 Yonne, R. 48 23N 2 58E
54 Yoqne'am 32 39N 35 7E
83 York, Australia 31 52S 116 47E
12 York, U.K. 53 38N 1 7W
100 York, Nebr. 40 55N 97 35W
98 York, Pa. 39 57N 76 43W
80 York, C. 75 55N 66 25W
82 York, Sd. 14 30S 125 0E
93 York Factory 57 0N 92 30W
12 York Wolds 54 0N 0 30W
81 Yorke, Pen. 34 40S 137 35E
93 Yorkton 51 11N 102 28W
83 Yornup 34 2S 116 10E
103 Yosemite Nat. Park 31 50N 119 30W
48 Yoshkar Ola 56 49N 47 10E
69 Yŏsu 34 47N 127 45E
54 Yotvata 29 53N 35 2E
15 Youghal 51 58N 7 51W
84 Young 34 19S 148 18E
108 Young 32 44S 57 36W
81 Younghusband, Pen. 34 45S 139 15E
96 Youngstown 43 16N 79 2W
83 Yoweragabbie 28 10S 117 30E

69 Yoyang 29 27N 113 10 E
98 Ypsilanti 42 18N 83 40W
102 Yreka 41 44N 122 40W
21 Yssingeaux 45 9N 4 8 E
45 Ystad 55 26N 13 50 E
14 Ythan, R. 57 26N 1 12W
51 Ytyk-kel 62 20N 133 28 E
69 Yu Shan, Mt. 23 30N 121 0 E
69 Yuan Kiang, R. 28 40N 110 30 E
69 Yuanling 28 30N 110 5 E
67 Yuanyang 23 10N 102 58 E
102 Yuba City 39 12N 121 45W
104 Yucatán □ 21 30N 86 30W
105 Yucatán, Canal de 22 0N 86 30W
103 Yucca 34 56N 114 6W
50 Yudino 55 10N 67 55 E
82 Yuendumu 22 16S 131 49 E
40 Yugoslavia ■ 44 0N 20 0 E
69 Yukikow 31 29N 118 17 E
88 Yukon Territory □ 63 0N 135 0W
88 Yukon, R. 65 30N 150 0W
51 Yukti 63 20N 105 0 E
69 Yülin, Hainan 18 10N 109 31 E
69 Yülin Kwangsi-Chuang 22 30N 110 50 E
103 Yuma, Ariz. 32 45N 114 45W
100 Yuma, Colo. 40 10N 102 43W
67 Yumen 41 13N 96 55 E
83 Yuna 28 20S 115 0 E
83 Yunndaga 29 45S 121 0 E
69 Yungan 25 50N 117 25 E
69 Yungchun 25 20N 118 15 E
69 Yungfu 24 59N 109 59 E
69 Yungshun 29 3N 109 50 E
69 Yungtsi 34 50N 110 25 E
69 Yunlin 23 45N 120 30 E
67 Yunnan □ 25 0N 102 30 E
69 Yunsiao 24 0N 117 20 E
81 Yunta 32 35S 139 33 E
50 Yurga 55 42N 84 51 E
50 Yuribei 71 20N 76 30 E
110 Yurimaguas 5 55S 76 0W
69 Yütu 5 0N 115 24 E
68 Yutze 37 45N 112 45 E
69 Yuyang 28 44N 108 46 E
69 Yuyao 30 0N 121 20 E
51 Yuzhno-Sakhalinsk 47 5N 142 5 E
19 Yvelines □ 48 40N 1 45 E
25 Yverdon 46 47N 6 39 E
18 Yvetot 49 37N 0 44 E

Z

16 Zaandam 52 26N 4 49 E
40 Žabalj 45 21N 20 5 E
51 Zabaykalskiy 49 40N 117 10 E
55 Zabid 14 10N 43 17 E
27 Zabkowice Slaskie 50 22N 19 17 E
57 Zabol 31 0N 61 25 E
57 Zaboli 27 10N 61 35 E
27 Zabrzé 50 24N 18 50 E
57 Zabul □ 32 0N 67 15 E
104 Zacapa 14 59N 89 31W
104 Zacatecas 22 49N 102 34W
104 Zacatecas □ 23 30N 103 0W
104 Zacatecoluca 13 29N 88 51W
37 Zadar 44 8N 15 8 E
63 Zadetkyi Kyun, I. 10 0N 98 25 E
31 Zafra 38 26N 6 30W
28 Zagań 51 39N 15 22 E
73 Zagazig 30 40N 31 12 E
42 Zagorá 39 27N 23 6 E
37 Zagreb 45 50N 16 0 E
56 Zagros, Kudhā-ye 33 45N 47 0 E
27 Zagyva, R. 47 10N 20 13 E
54 Zahala 32 8N 34 49 E
57 Zāhedān 29 30N 60 50 E
62 Zahirabad 17 43N 77 37 E
56 Zahlah 33 52N 35 50 E
74 Zaïre ■ 3 0S 23 0 E
74 Zaïre, R. 6 4S 12 24 E
40 Zaječar 43 53N 22 18 E
51 Zakamensk 50 23N 103 17 E
49 Zakavkazye 42 0N 44 0 E
56 Zākhū 37 10N 42 50 E
43 Zákinthos 37 47N 20 54 E
43 Zákinthos, I. 37 45N 27 45 E
27 Zakopane 49 18N 19 57 E
27 Zala □ 46 42N 16 50 E
27 Zalaegerszeg 46 53N 16 47 E
31 Zalamea de la Serena 38 40N 5 38W
37 Žalec 46 16N 15 10 E
73 Zalingei 13 5N 23 10 E
75 Zambeze, R. 18 46S 36 16 E
75 Zambia ■ 15 0S 28 0W
65 Zamboanga 6 59N 122 3 E
28 Zambrów 53 0N 22 15 E
104 Zamora, Mexico 20 0N 102 21W
30 Zamora, Sp. 41 30N 5 45W
30 Zamora □ 41 30N 5 46W
28 Zamość 50 50N 23 22 E
28 Zamość □ 50 40N 23 0 E
33 Záncara, R. 39 18N 3 18W
16 Zandvoort 52 22N 4 32 E
96 Zanesville 39 56N 82 2W
56 Zanjan 36 40N 48 35 E
83 Zanthus 30 55S 123 29 E
74 Zanzibar 6 12S 39 12 E
74 Zanzibar, I. 6 12S 39 12 E
72 Zaouiet Reggane 26 32N 0 3 E
40 Zapadna Morava, R. 43 50N 20 15 E
27 Západné Beskydy, Mts. 49 30N 19 0 E
51 Zapadnyy Sayan 53 0N 94 0 E
26 Západočeský □ 49 35N 13 0 E
27 Západoslovenský □ 48 30N 17 30 E
112 Zapala 39 0S 70 5W
48 Zapolyarnyy 69 26N 30 48 E
49 Zaporozhye 47 50N 35 10 E
32 Zaragoza 41 39N 0 53W
32 Zaragoza □ 41 35N 1 0W
57 Zarand 30 46N 56 34 E
108 Zárate 34 5S 59 2W
110 Zaraza 9 21N 65 19W
72 Zaria 11 0N 7 40W
27 Zarów 50 56N 16 29 E
110 Zaruma 3 40S 79 30W
28 Žary 51 37N 15 10 E
31 Zarza de Alange 38 49N 6 13W
30 Zarza de Granadilla 40 14N 6 3W
73 Zarzis 33 31N 11 2 E
51 Zashiversk 67 25N 142 40 E
58 Zaskar Mts. 33 15N 77 30 E
26 Žatec 50 20N 13 32 E
40 Zavala 42 50N 17 59 E
57 Zavareh 33 35N 52 28 E
40 Zavidocići 44 27N 18 13 E
51 Zavitinsk 50 10N 129 20 E
27 Zawiercie 50 30N 19 13 E
51 Zayarsk 56 20N 102 55 E
50 Zaysan, Oz. 48 0N 83 0 E
40 Ždrelo 44 16N 21 28 E
28 Zduńska Wola 51 37N 18 59 E
92 Zeballos 49 49N 126 50W
16 Zeebrugge 51 19N 3 12 E
80 Zeehan 41 52S 145 25 E
16 Zeeland □ 51 30N 3 50 E
54 Zefat 32 58N 35 29 E
24 Zehdenick 52 59N 13 20 E
55 Zeila 11 15N 43 30 E
16 Zeist 52 5N 5 15 E
54 Zeita 32 23N 35 2 E
24 Zeitz 51 3N 12 9 E
40 Zelenika 42 27N 18 37 E
40 Zeleznik 44 43N 20 23 E
26 Zell am See 47 19N 12 47 E
24 Zella-Mehlis 50 40N 10 41 E
40 Zemun 44 51N 20 23 E
40 Zenica 44 10N 17 57 E
24 Zerbst 51 59N 12 8 E
25 Zermatt 46 2N 7 46 E
51 Zeya 54 2N 127 20 E
30 Zêzere, R. 40 0N 7 55W
28 Zgierz 51 45N 19 27 E
28 Zgorzelec 51 10N 15 0 E
50 Zhanatas 43 11N 81 18 E
49 Zhdanov 47 5N 37 31 E
51 Zheleznogorsk-Ilimskiy 56 34N 104 8 E
51 Zhigansk 66 35N 124 10 E
49 Zhitomir 50 20N 28 40 E
48 Zhlobin 52 55N 30 0 E
51 Zhupanovo 51 59N 15 9 E
28 Zielona Góra 51 57N 15 31 E
28 Zielona Góra □ 51 57N 15 30 E
72 Ziguinchor 12 25N 16 20W
54 Zikhron Ya'aqov 32 34N 34 56 E
56 Zile 40 15N 36 0 E
27 Žilina 49 12N 18 42 E
73 Zillah 28 40N 17 41 E
26 Zillertaler Alpen, Mts. 47 6N 11 45 E
67 Zilling Tso, L. 31 40N 89 0 E
51 Zima 54 0N 102 5 E
75 Zimbabwe ■ 20 0S 28 30 E
41 Zimnicea 43 39N 25 21 E
72 Zinder 13 48N 9 0 E
55 Zinjibar 13 5N 46 0 E
103 Zion Nat. Park 37 25N 112 50W
110 Zipaquira 5 0N 74 0W
54 Zippori 32 64N 35 16 E
57 Zirko, I. 25 0N 53 30 E
26 Zirl 47 17N 11 14 E
104 Zitácuaro 19 20N 100 30W
27 Zitava, R. 48 14N 18 21 E
24 Zittau 50 54N 14 47 E
40 Živinice 44 27N 18 36 E
41 Zlatitsa 42 41N 24 7 E
48 Zlatoust 55 10N 59 30 E
27 Zlin=Gottwaldov 49 13N 17 41 E
73 Zlitan 32 25N 14 35 E
28 Złotoryja 51 8N 15 55 E
28 Złotów 53 22N 17 2 E
28 Żmigród 51 28N 16 53 E
28 Żnin 52 51N 17 44 E
26 Znojmo 48 50N 16 2 E
54 Zohar 31 36N 34 42 E
75 Zomba 15 30S 35 19 E
56 Zonguldak 41 28N 31 50 E
41 Zorleni 46 14N 27 44 E
110 Zorritos 3 50S 80 40W
25 Zossen 52 13N 13 28 E
72 Zouérabe 22 35N 12 30W
40 Zrenjanin 45 22N 20 23 E
32 Zuera 41 51N 0 49W
73 Zuetina 30 58N 20 7 E
55 Zufar, Reg. 17 40N 54 0 E
25 Zug 47 10N 8 31 E
25 Zuger-see, L. 47 7N 8 35 E
25 Zugspitze, Mt. 47 25N 10 59 E
16 Zuid Holland □ 52 0N 4 35 E
33 Zújar, R. 37 34N 2 50W
31 Zújar, R. 38 30N 5 30 E
31 Zújar, Pantano del 38 55N 5 35W
74 Zula 15 17N 39 40 E
32 Zumaya 43 19N 2 15W
75 Zumbo 15 35S 30 26 E
40 Županja 45 4N 18 43 E
25 Zürich □ 47 26N 8 40 E
25 Zürich 47 22N 8 32 E
25 Zürich-see 47 18N 8 40 E
16 Zutphen 52 9N 6 12 E
73 Zuwarah 32 58N 12 1 E
50 Zverinogolovskoye 55 0N 62 30 E
27 Zvolen 48 33N 19 10 E
40 Zvonce 42 57N 22 34 E
40 Zvornik 44 26N 19 7 E
25 Zweibrücken 49 15N 7 20 E
24 Zwenkau 51 13N 12 19 E
26 Zwettl 48 35N 15 9 E
24 Zwickau 50 43N 12 30 E
24 Zwischenahn 53 12N 8 1 E
16 Zwolle 52 31N 6 6 E
51 Zyryanka 65 45N 150 51 E
50 Zyryanovsk 49 43N 84 20 E
28 Żyrardów 52 3N 20 35 E
27 Zywiec 49 41N 19 12 E